Cross-Cultural Management
Volume II

The International Library of Critical Writings on Business and Management

1. Cross-Cultural Management
   Gordon Redding and Bruce W. Stening

Future titles will include:

Negotiation, Decision Making and Conflict Management
Max H. Bazerman

Human Resource Management
Paul R. Sparrow

Strategic Management
Julian Birkinshaw

The Management of Innovation
John Storey

Wherever possible, the articles in these volumes have been reproduced as originally published using facsimile reproduction, inclusive of footnotes and pagination to facilitate ease of reference.

For a list of all Edward Elgar published titles visit our site on the World Wide Web at
http://www.e-elgar.co.uk

Cross-Cultural Management Volume II

Managing Cultural Differences

Edited by

Gordon Redding

Senior Affiliate Professor of Asian Business
and Director, Euro-Asian Centre
INSEAD, France

and

Bruce W. Stening

Professor of Management
National Graduate School of Management
Australian National University, Australia

THE INTERNATIONAL LIBRARY OF CRITICAL WRITINGS ON BUSINESS AND MANAGEMENT

An Elgar Reference Collection
Cheltenham, UK • Northampton, MA, USA

Published by
Edward Elgar Publishing Limited
Glensanda House
Montpellier Parade
Cheltenham
Glos GL50 1UA
UK

Edward Elgar Publishing, Inc.
136 West Street
Suite 202
Northampton
Massachusetts 01060
USA

A catalogue record for this book is available from the British Library.

Library of Congress Cataloguing in Publication Data

Cross-cultural management / edited by Gordon Redding and Bruce W. Stening.
p. cm. — (International library of critical writings on business and management ; 1)
(Elgar reference collection)
Includes index.
Contents: 1. The theory of culture — 2. Managing cultural differences.
1. Industrial management—Social aspects. 2. Industrial management—Cross-cultural studies. 3. Intercultural communication. 4. Culture. I. Redding, S. G. II. Stening, Bruce W. (Bruce William), 1949– III. Series. IV. Series: Elgar reference collection

HD30.19.C76 2003
306—dc21

2002044678

ISBN 1 84064 460 5 (2 volume set)

Printed and bound in Great Britain by MPG Books Ltd, Bodmin, Cornwall

Contents

Acknowledgements

The editors and publishers wish to thank the authors and the following publishers who have kindly given permission for the use of copyright material.

Academy of Management and Copyright Clearance Center for articles: J. Stewart Black and Mark Mendenhall (1990), 'Cross-Cultural Training Effectiveness: A Review and a Theoretical Framework for Future Research', *Academy of Management Review*, **15** (1), January, 113–36; Taylor H. Cox and Stacy Blake (1991), 'Managing Cultural Diversity: Implications for Organizational Competitiveness', *Academy of Management Executive*, **5** (3), August, 45–56; Geert Hofstede (1993), 'Cultural Constraints in Management Theories', *Academy of Management Executive*, **7** (1), February, 81–94; Shaker A. Zahra and Hugh M. O'Neill (1998), 'Charting the Landscape of Global Competition: Reflections on Emerging Organizational Challenges and their Implications for Senior Executives', *Academy of Management Executive*, **12** (4), November, 13–21; Rosabeth Moss Kanter and Thomas D. Dretler (1998), '"Global Strategy" and its Impact on Local Operations: Lessons from Gillette Singapore', *Academy of Management Executive*, **12** (4), November, 60–68; Andrew C. Inkpen (1998), 'Learning and Knowledge Acquisition through International Strategic Alliances', *Academy of Management Executive*, **12** (4), November, 69–80; Karl Moore and Julian Birkinshaw (1998), 'Managing Knowledge in Global Service Firms: Centers of Excellence', *Academy of Management Executive*, **12** (4), November, 81–92; Karen Roberts, Ellen Ernst Kossek and Cynthia Ozeki (1998), 'Managing the Global Workforce: Challenges and Strategies', *Academy of Management Executive*, **12** (4), November, 93–106; Marie-Claude Boudreau, Karen D. Loch, Daniel Robey and Detmar Straub (1998), 'Going Global: Using Information Technology to Advance Competitiveness of the Virtual Transnational Organization', *Academy of Management Executive*, **12** (4), November, 120–28; Steven X. Si and Garry D. Bruton (1999), 'Knowledge Transfer in International Joint Ventures in Transitional Economies: The China Experience', *Academy of Management Executive*, **13** (1), February, 83–90.

Blackwell Publishing Ltd for excerpt: Nancy J. Adler (1994), 'Competitive Frontiers: Women Managing Across Borders', in Nancy J. Adler and Dafna N. Izraeli (eds), *Competitive Frontiers: Women Managers in a Global Economy*, Chapter 2, 22–40.

Braybrooke Press Ltd for article: T.K. Das and Bing-Sheng Teng (1997), 'Sustaining Strategic Alliances: Options and Guidelines', *Journal of General Management*, **22** (4), Summer, 49–64.

Elsevier Science for articles and excerpts: Sidney Gray (1995), 'Cultural Perspectives on the Measurement of Corporate Success', *European Management Journal*, **13** (3), September, 269–75; Myrtle P. Bell and David A. Harrison (1996), 'Using Intra-National Diversity for International Assignments: A Model of Bicultural Competence and Expatriate Adjustment', *Human Resource*

Management Review, **6** (1), 47–74; Denice Welch and Lawrence Welch (1997), 'Being Flexible and Accommodating Diversity: The Challenge for Multinational Management', *European Management Journal*, **15** (6), December, 677–85; Rosalie L. Tung (1998), 'A Contingency Framework of Selection and Training of Expatriates Revisited', *Human Resource Management Review*, **8** (1), 23–37; David C. Thomas (1998), 'The Expatriate Experience: A Critical Review and Synthesis', in Joseph L.C. Cheng and Richard B. Peterson (eds), *Advances in International Comparative Management*, Volume 12, 237–73; Arvind Parkhe (1998), 'Building Trust in International Alliances', *Journal of World Business*, **33** (4), 417–37; Ben L. Kedia and Ananda Mukherji (1999), 'Global Managers: Developing a Mindset for Global Competitiveness', *Journal of World Business*, **34** (3), 230–51; Paul F. Buller and Glenn M. McEvoy (1999), 'Creating and Sustaining Ethical Capability in the Multi-National Corporation', *Journal of World Business*, **34** (4), 326–43; Timothy Kayworth and Dorothy Leidner (2000), 'The Global Virtual Manager: A Prescription for Success', *European Management Journal*, **18** (2), April, 183–94; Joseph J. DiStefano and Martha L. Maznevski (2000), 'Creating Value with Diverse Teams in Global Management', *Organizational Dynamics*, **29** (1), Summer, 45–63; Roger L.M. Dunbar and Suresh Kotha (2000), 'Managing Institutional and Cultural Contrasts: The Case of Sanyo Electric in the United States', in Joseph L.C. Cheng and Richard B. Peterson (eds), *Advances in International Comparative Management*, Volume 13, 149–73; Hartmut H. Holzmüller and Barbara Stöttinger (2001), 'International Marketing Managers' Cultural Sensitivity: Relevance, Training Requirements and a Pragmatic Training Concept', *International Business Review*, **10**, 597–614.

Harvard Business Review and Harvard Business School Publishing Corporation for article: Thomas Donaldson (1996), 'Values in Tension: Ethics Away From Home', *Harvard Business Review*, **74** (5), 48–9, 52–6, 58, 60, 62.

Geert Hofstede for: Table 2.5, Table 2.6, Table 2.7 and Table 2.8 in Lisa Hoecklin (1995), 'Culture: What It Is, What It Is Not and How It Directs Organizational Behaviour', in *Managing Cultural Differences: Strategies for Competitive Advantage*, Chapter 2, 36, 38.

Human Resource Planning Society for articles: Michael Harvey (1996), 'Addressing the Dual-Career Expatriation Dilemma', *Human Resource Planning*, **19** (4), 18–39; Vladimir Pucik and Tania Saba (1998), 'Selecting and Developing the Global Versus the Expatriate Manager: A Review of the State-of-the-Art', *Human Resource Planning*, **21** (4), 40–54.

Journal of International Business Studies for articles: Allan G. Thompson (1996), 'Compliance with Agreements in Cross-Cultural Transactions: Some Analytical Issues', *Journal of International Business Studies*, **27** (2), 375–90; Aimin Yan and Ming Zeng (1999), 'International Joint Venture Instability: A Critique of Previous Research, A Reconceptualization, and Directions for Future Research', *Journal of International Business Studies*, **30** (2), 397–414.

Kluwer Academic Publishers B.V. for articles: William A. Wines and Nancy K. Napier (1992), 'Toward an Understanding of Cross-Cultural Ethics: A Tentative Model', *Journal of Business Ethics*, **11** (11), November, 831–41; Daniel W. Skubik (1995), 'Ethics and Australian International Business: Which Way to Asia?', *Journal of Business Ethics*, **14** (8),

August, 643–52; David J. Fritzsche, Y. Paul Huo, Sakae Sugai, Stephen Dun-Hou Tsai, Cheong Seok Kim and Helmut Becker (1995), 'Exploring the Ethical Behavior of Managers: A Comparative Study of Four Countries', *Asia Pacific Journal of Management*, **12** (2), October, 37–61.

Los Angeles Times Syndicate International for articles: J. Stewart Black and Hal B. Gregersen (1992), 'Serving Two Masters: Managing the Dual Allegiance of Expatriate Employees', *Sloan Management Review*, **33** (4), Summer, 61–71; Sumantra Ghoshal and Nitin Nohria (1993), 'Horses for Courses: Organizational Forms for Multinational Corporations', *Sloan Management Review*, **34** (2), Winter, 23–35; Stephen E. Weiss (1994), 'Negotiating with "Romans" – Part 1', *Sloan Management Review*, **35** (2), Winter, 51–61; Stephen E. Weiss (1994), 'Negotiating with "Romans" – Part 2', *Sloan Management Review*, **35** (3), Spring, 85–99; James K. Sebenius (1998), 'Case Study: Negotiating Cross-Border Acquisitions', *Sloan Management Review*, **39** (2), Winter, 27–41; Hal B. Gregersen, Allen J. Morrison and J. Stewart Black (1998), 'Developing Leaders for the Global Frontier', *Sloan Management Review*, **40** (1), Fall, 21–32.

McGraw-Hill Companies, Inc. for excerpt: Paul W. Beamish (2000), 'The Design and Management of International Joint Ventures', in Paul W. Beamish, Allen J. Morrison, Philip M. Rosenzweig and Andrew C. Inkpen (eds), *International Management: Text and Cases*, Fourth Edition, Chapter 7, 113–31.

Pearson Education Limited for excerpt: Lisa Hoecklin (1995), 'Culture: What It Is, What It Is Not and How It Directs Organizational Behaviour', in *Managing Cultural Differences: Strategies for Competitive Advantage*, Chapter 2, 23–49.

Philosophy Documentation Center for article: John Hendry (1999), 'Universalizability and Reciprocity in International Business Ethics', *Business Ethics Quarterly*, **9** (3), July, 405–20.

Taylor and Francis Ltd (http://www.tandf.co.uk/journals) for articles: Aminu Mamman (1995), 'Employee Intercultural Effectiveness in a Multicultural Workplace: Theoretical Propositions, Strategies and Direction for Future Research', *International Journal of Human Resource Management*, **6** (3), September, 528–52; Michael Harvey, Cheri Speier and Milorad M. Novicevic (1999), 'The Role of Inpatriation in Global Staffing', *International Journal of Human Resource Management*, **10** (3), June, 459–76; Hilary Harris and Chris Brewster (1999), 'The Coffee-Machine System: How International Selection Really Works', *International Journal of Human Resource Management*, **10** (3), June, 488–500.

Every effort has been made to trace all the copyright holders but if any have been inadvertently overlooked the publishers will be pleased to make the necessary arrangement at the first opportunity.

In addition the publishers wish to thank the Marshall Library of Economics, Cambridge University, the Library of the University of Warwick and the Library of Indiana University at Bloomington, USA for their assistance in obtaining these articles.

Introduction

Gordon Redding and Bruce W. Stening

Volume II of this collection of articles on cross-cultural management builds on the framework of culture provided in the first volume and addresses matters of practical concern confronting managers working in cross-cultural environments. As we will explore, while that typically means managers working across national boundaries, those are not the only circumstances in which cultural differences must be dealt with.

There is a tendency for many of us to dive immediately into exploring day-to-day concerns and regard theory or conceptual frameworks as either unnecessary or hard work. As we often learn to our significant cost later, such short cuts are extremely unwise. In order to solve such practical issues as how best to manage an overseas subsidiary or the most effective manner to negotiate with people from a specific, dissimilar culture, it is essential that one first understands the broader context within which such issues reside. In the case of our subject matter this implies the need for a thorough understanding of what culture is and how it impacts upon organizations and individuals. Only then can one be confident that the most critical variables in any specific situation have been identified and that when any managerial action is instigated the most important variables are being addressed in order to achieve the outcomes desired. In an oft-quoted aphorism of Kurt Lewin (1951), there is nothing more practical than a good theory. For that reason readers are strongly encouraged first to delve into the conceptual dimensions of culture set out in Volume I before embarking on a consideration of the matters dealt with in this volume.

The environment in which international business is undertaken today is fundamentally different to that which confronted organizations even a decade or so ago. While the term 'globalization' may be one that has become hackneyed, the phenomenon itself is real. With the exception of a handful of 'rogue' states, we are all part of a much more tightly connected and competitive world in which traditional political boundaries are of decreasing importance. The consequences for almost all organizations, wherever they are located and whether or not they define themselves as being engaged directly in international business, are profound, requiring them to be much more flexible, entrepreneurial, dynamic, innovative, collaborative, networked and risk-taking – among other things! The consequences for the managers of those organizations are correspondingly significant, not least in dealing with the far greater demands of managing the increased number of cross-cultural interactions.

This volume provides perspectives on the challenges of managing in such a context under seven main headings. In Part I, consideration is given to just what globalization is and what is implied in being a global manager. Some interesting comparisons are made of the attributes that made managers successful in earlier eras and what characteristics are likely to be essential in the new environment. Logically, this discussion progresses to the matter of how global organizations can be managed effectively. In Part II, attention is given to different structures for global organizations, knowledge and information technology (IT) management, creation of global workforces, the cultural dimensions of corporate 'success' and other such concerns. The question of how to manage cultural diversity, both domestically and internationally is the subject of several chapters in Part III. Part IV provides advice on how to negotiate across cultures. This provides an important basis for the discussion in Part V of the creation and management of international joint ventures and strategic alliances. Given that the task of managing global organizations still often falls to persons sent abroad for finite periods, it was essential that a number of articles be provided which identify various dimensions of selecting, training and managing expatriates – these comprise Part VI. Finally, in Part VII several perspectives are canvassed on the importance of ethics and social responsibility in international business.

The central criterion for choosing the 44 chapters for this volume was that they provide an interesting and useful perspective on an important issue confronting organizations and managers operating in a cross-cultural context. The pool from which these articles were selected contains literally thousands of both conceptual and empirical works. The problem encountered by the editors was not in finding articles to include but, rather, in deciding which to leave out. Merely by flicking through this volume it will quickly be evident that one of the decisions made by the editors was to exclude articles that contained a lot of 'numbers'. This deserves an explanation, which is not that either editor has a serious aversion to numbers per se. Rather, we felt strongly that the focus of this book should be on deriving general lessons relevant to cross-cultural management. Though culture-specific examples are provided throughout the chapters included here, and while many chapters draw heavily on empirical 'numbers-oriented' articles, many fine research articles were excluded because they were considered *too* narrowly focused and therefore of limited generalizability. That is not to say that mulitivariate statistical analysis cannot be helpful in identifying important relationships between variables or that culture-specific material is not important. However, we felt it more important here to present articles that synthesized much of that material and let readers make their decisions about what matters to explore in greater detail later through a careful scrutiny of the footnotes and references.

Globalization and the Global Manager

The chapters in Part I of Volume II address the issue of the nature of globalization and the characteristics required of those who will be managers in this new world. In Chapter 1, Hal Gregersen, Allen Morrison and Stewart Black report on an empirical study which explored the views of senior managers about the necessary attributes of global managers and the means by which such leaders could be developed. A survey of Fortune 500 firms which constituted a part of the study showed that the need for competent global leaders outranked all other challenges in creating a globally successful company. Despite that, they report that most firms do not have comprehensive systems for developing such persons. An interesting feature of this chapter is the profiles of several managers who clearly are global leaders.

Chapter 2 by Ben Kedia and Ananda Mukherji specifically addresses the issue of the type of mindset required to be an effective global manager, arguing that essentially it is that of someone who can integrate three forces, namely, global business, regional/country pressures and worldwide functions. Adopting a classification scheme similar to Miles and Snow's

(1978) defenders, prospectors, analysers and reactors typology of strategic responses by organizations, they compare the globally oriented integrator with, in order, the domestically oriented defender, the explorer and the controller mindsets. While, as they point out, specific knowledge and skills are required, they are meaningless unless the manager has been able to develop a global mindset. The transition from defender to integrator is one through which individuals proceed at varying speeds; moreover, it should be said, not everyone makes it through.

Zahra and O'Neill (Chapter 3) present the results of a Delphi study carried out among the authors of articles at a conference on global competitiveness. Nine of those articles constitute a special issue of the *Academy of Management Executive* containing the Zahra and O'Neill article. As Zahra and O'Neill point out, the two issues ranked as most critical and important by the panel of experts – who are the competitors, and what global leadership strategies create above average returns – 'serve as an illustration of how little we do know about global competition'. They argue that we know too little about the environments in which global competition is conducted but posit that if the rate of change in those environments is as revolutionary and discontinuous as many people believe, there is a critical need for organizations to develop their systems of learning in order that they can transform and adapt themselves quickly and effectively.

One of the most widely discussed topics in recent literature has been the difference between traditional international managers, in particular expatriates, and global (or transnational) managers. Reviewing a very large number of studies, Pucik and Saba (Chapter 4) not only profile the difference between the two types and the characteristics of successful managers in each category but, more importantly, pinpoint human resource practices that can effectively select and develop each. In that latter respect, their article is important in underlining that such phenomena as global mindsets do not just happen, they must be developed and nurtured.

No writer has been more cited in the cross-cultural management literature than Geert Hofstede. While most attention has been paid to his empirical work, his article entitled 'Cultural Constraints in Management Theories' (Chapter 5) is a useful link between the two volumes of this book demonstrating that it behoves us to seek solutions to management problems that are culturally sensitive. He provides a number of examples of how theories emanating from one culture may be of very limited value in another. His chapter is useful in encouraging us to think about the limitations, for example, of using theories that stress market processes and the individual and put the focus on managers rather than workers outside the culture in which most of such theories were developed – the United States.

The chapter from Lisa Hoecklin's book (Chapter 6 in this volume) is also helpful in providing a bridge between the two volumes in that, besides summarizing a number of concepts of culture and discussing more concretely the impact of culture on organizational behaviour, it adds a useful description of the work of Trompenaars. The five dimensions employed in the latter work are universalism versus particularism (societal versus personal obligations); individualism versus collectivism (personal versus group goals); neutral versus affective relationships (emotional orientation in relationships); specific versus diffuse relationships (degree of involvement in relationships); and achievement versus ascription (legitimation of power and status).

Managing the Global Organization

Managing an organization in the global economy is a non-trivial problem, requiring attention to a multitude of matters. Among them are setting a strategic direction for the organization, deciding how best to structure it, putting in place the human resources to run it and deciding the criteria by which its success will judged. To deal with these matters comprehensively would require a full volume rather than a part of one. The articles selected for inclusion here address some of the most important matters and give a flavour for the broader challenges awaiting the cross-cultural manager.

Chapter 7 by Ghoshal and Nohria restates the well-known fact from organization theory that an organization's structure must 'fit' (among other things) its environment and discusses the sorts of features of international environments that will shape any multinational corporation's structure. Though there are many issues pertaining to structure that are not canvassed in this chapter, it provides a very lucid discussion of some of the most important considerations.

As organizations become increasingly global in their scale of operations and their perspective, the task of managing their workforce becomes ever more complex. In Chapter 8, Roberts and her co-authors focus on three key issues: first, deployment, getting the appropriate human resources to where they are required in the organization, irrespective of geographic location; second, knowledge and innovation dissemination, spreading essential knowledge and practices throughout the organization, irrespective of where they originated; and, third, identifying and developing talent on a global basis. They provide specific advice on how strategies can be developed to ensure that those aims are realized.

For a very long time, organizations operating internationally underutilized a key human resource – women. They did so on the basis of a number of largely unfounded assumptions such as women not being interested in (international) careers and 'foreigners' being unwilling to work with women managers. Nancy Adler has given considerable attention to this topic and in this extract (Chapter 9) from one of her books once again nails several of these myths. Notably, she points out that simply because local women are discriminated against in some of the places to which female expatriates might be assigned does not mean that those expatriates will themselves be discriminated against. As she succinctly puts it, 'Local managers see women expatriates as foreigners who happen to be women, not as women who happen to be foreigners' and treat them accordingly. Though it might be hoped that these messages are getting through to organizations, there remains much evidence that they are not.

Chapter 10 by Kanter and Dretler also sets out to dispel various myths, in this case that integration across global operations implies that the individual entities will lose their local (country) identity. In their study of Gillette Singapore they demonstrate that successful companies recognize the need to acknowledge country differences and to respect local norms. The lesson is that globalization does not imply the need for uniformity, quite the opposite in fact. They point out that being successful in the global economy 'means becoming knowledgeable about local needs, skillful at managing local changes and expert at forging cross-boundary relationships'.

In Chapter 11, Dunbar and Kotha show how for a Japanese firm to adapt successfully to the United States attention must be given to both cultural and competitive dynamics. An attempt to impose Japanese ways of doing things was ultimately resisted at the very time that market pressures required high levels of loyalty and commitment of local employees. The case is a fascinating insight into the complexities of operating an enterprise in an unfamiliar cultural and business environment.

Gray (Chapter 12) provides a short but interesting insight into national cultural differences in how the success of an enterprise is assessed and the disclosure of success-related information. He points out that profit may not be the universal or sole criterion for corporate success that some people suppose and that it should be accepted that there can be a set of diverse criteria by which performance is judged.

Most advanced economies are now based more on the provision of services than upon the production of goods. Correspondingly, the majority of firms are in the services industry. In Chapter 13, Moore and Birkinshaw consider how the knowledge that underpins the operations of such firms can best be assimilated, built and disseminated around the organization. They argue that informal, ad hoc and word-of-mouth approaches are inadequate means of achieving those objectives and that a more effective method is to create centres of excellence which are given the specific responsibility of leveraging and making knowledge available throughout the organization. They provide a number of examples of how these centres work in practice.

'Marketing' covers a multitude of different activities undertaken in organizations from product development to sales force management, advertising, pricing and channel management, to name a few. Chapter 14 by Holzmüller and Stöttinger considers the demands on those with the responsibility for decisions in this area by first addressing again the broader question of what 'culture' is and how it impacts upon management. Indeed, the strength of this chapter is that it is not a checklist of rules to be slavishly applied; instead, the authors emphasize the need for managers involved in international marketing to understand fundamental issues related to culture before focusing on the particular matters before them.

Chapter 15 by Boudreau and her co-authors confronts managers with the phenomenal changes that are altering their lives and transforming their organizations as a result of new information and communications technologies. They argue that many organizations will become virtual, the characteristics of which they say are dependence on a federation of alliances and partnerships with other organizations, relative spatial and temporal independence and a high degree of flexibility. There are a number of examples of business organizations that are already a long way down this path; some of us would argue that universities are headed firmly in that same direction.

The virtual organization is a theme taken up in Chapter 16 by Kayworth and Leidner. They argue that while there are many reasons why virtual teams are becoming very common, they face significant challenges in respect of effective communication, their ability to handle cultural differences, ability to use the new information technologies and the capacity of the leaders of the teams to manage the projects on which they were engaged.

Managing Cultural Diversity

One of the consequences of globalization has been the necessity that people work with others of quite different cultural backgrounds in teams, often separated by geography as well. In Chapter 17, DiStefano and Maznevski argue that culturally heterogeneous teams fall into two categories of performance, doing either significantly better or significantly worse than homogeneous teams. The difference, they suggest, is in how each is managed. In their view, those that outperform homogeneous teams are not only good at identifying cultural differences (an exercise in *mapping*), but also at *bridging* those differences (communicating in ways that take the differences into account) and *integrating* them (undertaking activities to create team-level ideas by monitoring participation patterns, resolving disagreements and creating new perspectives). A number of useful examples are provided of how these so-called MBI principles can successfully be put into practice.

The Cox and Taylor article (Chapter 18) is an important one for several reasons: it highlights the fact that cultural diversity is just as much a domestic phenomenon for some countries (the United States, Canada, Australia and a number of other places) as an international one; it sets out a number of arguments (cost, resource acquisition, marketing, creativity, problem solving and system flexibility) for the competitive advantage provided by cultural diversity; it references numerous studies which have examined the conditions under which such advantage can be achieved; and it provides specific recommendations for how to transform traditional organizations into multicultural ones.

Chapter 19 by Mamman also provides a comprehensive review of the literature in this field, reinforcing the standpoint of the earlier articles that there is a multitude of factors that impinge on effectiveness and that managing cultural diversity is a complex matter.

There has been much discussion in the past ten years or so of the importance of corporate cultures and how they might be managed. Taking a contrary viewpoint to that adopted by many, Welch and Welch (Chapter 20) argue that, even if they can be created, very strong corporate cultures might, in multinational corporations anyway, militate against the need for flexibility, responsiveness and innovativeness. They suggest that multinationals have much to gain by 'encouraging and sponsoring critique and diversity'. Their chapter is useful in encouraging us to think again about prescriptive solutions to organizational problems, especially in an international environment.

Negotiating across Cultures

Negotiating is central to what managers, and especially global managers, do. Be it agreeing on a contract, forming a joint venture relationship, or persuading a multitude of potential stakeholders as to the merits of one's case, studies of managerial behaviour consistently reinforce this as one of the most frequent, difficult and poorly performed of managerial tasks. The global manager is charged with the responsibility of negotiating the best possible terms for their organization while taking care not to ride roughshod over the cultural sensitivities of the persons with whom they are negotiating and bearing in mind the need to take a long-term view. As much as any other in this book, this area of cross-cultural management is a minefield littered with the bodies of those who have tried but failed. The chapters in this section provide both some useful frameworks and advice on how to manoeuvre one's self through this potentially hazardous course.

Weiss's two-part article (Chapters 21 and 22) sets out eight culturally responsive strategies that can be adopted, contingent upon on each negotiating party's familiarity with the other's culture. The framework is elucidated by numerous examples of how and why specific negotiations were either successful or not. As in many other areas, the key is not only in understanding what strategy is best in what circumstances but, equally importantly, in developing the skills to implement it to best effect, especially learning how to operate in what is inherently a highly dynamic and multidimensional situation.

Negotiating a deal is only part of the process. Ensuring that the other party complies with what was agreed is another matter altogether, as countless businesspersons have found to their great cost. Chapter 23 by Thompson is very useful in pointing out to those who approach the problem from a legalistic perspective that in many cultures legal remedies are frequently arduous, lengthy, complicated, expensive and ultimately unfruitful. He points out that when one assesses the risk of non-compliance it is essential that a much deeper understanding is sought of whether and under what circumstances someone is likely to comply with what was apparently agreed. Besides the legal process, compliance, he points out, can be achieved through mechanisms associated with reputational processes, social control and psychological or emotional factors. A number of examples are provided of how these mechanisms operate differently across societies.

Chapter 24 focuses specifically on negotiations surrounding acquisitions, providing a case study of an Italian company that has overcome many seemingly insurmountable obstacles on many different occasions and over a long period of time in its acquisition of foreign companies. The issues confronted by the company that are discussed by Sebenius are not just narrowly cultural but involve differences in such things as political systems and corporate governance arrangements. From this example of best practice, the author distills a number of general principles of effective negotiation.

International Joint Ventures and Strategic Alliances

International business is conducted through a variety of means such as: exporting, selling through agents, establishing licensing arrangements, setting up wholly owned subsidiaries, creating joint ventures or entering into strategic alliances, each implying different levels of commitment. The types of cross-cultural management challenges encountered in each are different and none are without their difficulties. However, the problems encountered in joint ventures are often particularly thorny. Of all the modes of international business, this is the one that most closely parallels a marriage: a formal, tightly integrated, complex and multifaceted arrangement in which the two (or more – like marriages in some cultures, international joint ventures (IJVs) can be polygamous) parties agree to come together on a long-term basis to achieve some common objectives. Like marriages, IJVs should not be entered into lightly and require on-going attention. Sadly, like marriages in many cultures, IJVs often fail. Part V comprises seven articles that examine the nature of IJVs and other forms of strategic alliance, what makes them work and why they sometimes fail.

Chapter 25 by Paul Beamish, probably the most prolific and influential writer on this subject, maps the territory, as it were, providing a crisp explication of what IJVs are and how they can best be managed.

Yan and Zeng's contribution (Chapter 26) sets about defining instability and failure in IJVs and isolating the factors which contribute to such problems. It is a helpful article (like some others, but not all) in seeking complex, multivariate explanations for outcomes. Though cultural differences are frequently significant contributors to instability, they are not the sole factor; the specific form of organizational structure, the nature of the external environment and a number of other influences must be taken into account as well. This is an important point and one too often overlooked by those who would ascribe all problems to 'culture', poorly defined as that often is by such persons.

A vital question in the operation of IJVs is how information and knowledge is disseminated. Given the complexity of the environments in which IJVs usually function, the means by which learning is achieved is very important. Indeed, one of the main reasons that an IJV is formed may be to obtain information that could not otherwise be accessed. Si and Bruton address this matter in Chapter 27 by examining how foreign companies operating in China have gone about it. The chapter provides yet another perspective on the most effective means by which to manage in the complexity of a cross-cultural environment.

Chapter 28 by Inkpen furthers this discussion of how the complementarity of international partners can provide invaluable opportunities for each in learning from the other. Inkpen points out that tacit knowledge is just as important as explicit knowledge but, by its nature, is both more difficult to identify and describe and harder to acquire. This is a message that must be understood at all levels in cross-cultural management: that which is least visible, most amorphous and often highly ambiguous is usually the most critical to come to grips with.

Trust is a critical ingredient in all aspects of successful international business. It, too, however, is a complex concept, the meaning of which varies from culture to culture. Chapter 29 by Parkhe is the second of two articles; in the first part (Parkhe, 1998) he defined the concept while in this second part he examines the mechanisms by which it can be developed. Trust, like so many other things in international business partnerships, is difficult to achieve and to maintain. Without it, the relationship will not be soundly based and in all likelihood will quickly degrade.

Chapter 30 by Das and Teng summarizes the practical implications of much of the literature in this field and sets out a seven-stage process for the management of all forms of international business alliances.

Expatriation and Repatriation: Issues of Cultural Adaptation

It is fair to say that no topic has received more attention in the literature on cross-cultural management than that of expatriates. Matters of expatriate selection and training, cultural adaptation, repatriation to one's culture of origin and so forth have been thoroughly explored both conceptually and empirically in hundreds if not thousands of articles and books. The reasons for this attention are fairly obvious: sizeable numbers of people have been sent abroad on assignment for their organizations (not just corporations but governmental agencies, religious bodies and the like), particularly since World War II; the costs of such assignments are often significant (a rule of thumb frequently used is three times the person's salary package in their own country); failure (typically measured by early return) is not uncommon; and the costs of failure may be considerable, both to their organization in financial terms and to the individual expatriate and his or her family in emotional and other respects. Though it is true (as several authors in this volume have pointed out – see, for example, Pucik and Saba in Chapter 4) that global managers are different in character to traditional expatriates and that over time the former will assume more importance than the latter in many fields, the topic of expatriate adaptation still looms large for organizations.

David Thomas (Chapter 31) provides a comprehensive overview of the subject area and an insightful review of studies which have sought explanations for expatriate success and failure. As he and earlier reviewers have concluded, there are no simple explanations. A multitude of factors including those associated with the individual (personality, demographics, previous experience, nationality and gender), the organization and the specific job involved, and the general environment in which the expatriate experience is undertaken must be considered. As in most matters associated with human behaviour, there are often paradoxes such as that, on the one hand, married expatriates frequently adjust better than single persons but, on the other, one of the principal reasons for expatriate failure (in some cultural groups anyway) is the inability of the spouse to adjust.

One of the pressures faced by expatriates is that in order to do their job effectively and to enjoy their assignment they must to one degree or another accommodate themselves to the environment in which they find themselves, adopting a modus operandi different to that which they used at home. There are many role pressures on the expatriate, too, from local stakeholders that might be at variance with the expectations held of them by people back at headquarters who might regard them as having 'gone native'. This often stressful situation is discussed by Black and Gregersen in Chapter 32. They provide suggestions as to how this conflict between allegiance to the parent firm and allegiance to the local operation can be alleviated.

There was a time (not that long ago) when expatriates were almost exclusively male and where the spouse was, thus, female. As some earlier chapters in this volume (most notably, Adler's) pointed out, increasingly females are being engaged in senior roles as expatriate or global managers. Be that manager male or female, another change that has occurred is that nowadays spouses are frequently seeking employment themselves. This implies an added dimension to the expatriate management 'problem', that of finding jobs for two persons, not just one. Harvey (Chapter 33) examines this issue in the context of such theoretical constructs as career and family life-cycles and provides a model by which corporations can resolve international dual-career relocation decisions.

Though there was a time when many organizations sent people abroad with little or no training, these days substantial resources are typically expended to try to ensure that the high investments involved in setting up expatriates and their families are not lost because of the inability of those persons to adapt to their new working and social environment. Chapter 34 by Black and Mendenhall reviews the literature in this field, assessing what training works and what does not. While subsequent studies (including their own) have examined this subject further, this chapter provides the most thorough framework mapping the key variables.

The literature on expatriation has typically concentrated on the issues faced by large (usually American) multinational companies sending home-country managers to their overseas subsidiaries. Harvey, Speier and Novicevic (Chapter 35) highlight once more and in a complementary manner the changed context of international business in pointing out that in global organizations, sending host-country and third-country nationals to headquarters might bring significant benefits. Such inpatriates will, by their diverse backgrounds, bring different and useful perspectives to problems. Ultimately, in the truly global organization, one will not talk of either expatriates or inpatriates but rather of transpatriates.

In Chapter 36, Harris and Brewster challenge the view that expatriate selection is a rational business. Their article is included here because it reinforces the reality that formal rationality in organizations is rare and that decision making is typically a messy, non-linear process affected by organizational politics and a host of other influences. Mirroring the garbage-can model of organizational decision making propounded by such writers as March and Olsen (1976), in which decisions are often the result of a coincidence of problems, solutions and participants in some time and place, they argue that the decision about whom to send on an expatriate assignment is just as likely to be made during a chance coffee-machine encounter as by any rational process of selection.

In Chapter 37, Rosalie Tung assesses whether the contingency paradigm of selection and training that she put forward in a 1981 article still holds. In the original article she had hypothesized that the criteria for selection should be different depending on the nature of the overseas assignment and that training was especially important for assignments to countries where the cultural distance was large and where extensive and intensive contacts with the host society were required. She concluded that, while the paradigm still held, the selection criteria and training programmes need to be more complex, reflecting important changes in the broad environmental and organizational context since the original study. Besides that finding, the article is helpful in fleshing out the changes that emerged in international human resource management over a 20-year period.

Further exploring the nature of expatriate effectiveness, Bell and Harrison (Chapter 38) examine how the particular characteristics of bicultural individuals might be used to the advantage of global organizations. For example, they examine the contribution of dual language fluency and a broad role repertoire. A model is presented of bicultural competencies that recognizes the complex interaction of effects in determining any outcomes such as effectiveness, which is a useful antidote to the many bivariate models which are posited.

Ethics and Corporate Social Responsibility in Cross-Cultural Context

The topic of ethics is a difficult one at the best of times. In a cross-cultural setting it is especially so. There are innumerable examples of organizations and managers who have found themselves in an awful mess and, in the case of individuals, sometimes in jail as a consequence of their lack of appreciation of the different ethical frameworks that guide behaviour in different cultural contexts. What is right and proper in one place may be completely unacceptable in another. Recognizing what is or is not acceptable conduct is only one half of the problem; the other is knowing what to do when confronted with the choice between one's own standards and those of another. An old adage is 'when in Rome, do as the Romans do'. Sensible though this might seem at first-glance, the clear implication of this culturally relativistic philosophy is that no set of standards is better or worse than any other, a proposition that many people would find unacceptable. The chapters in this section have been selected in the first place to provide a broader frame of reference within which to consider ethical issues and to throw some light on the nature of ethical dilemmas and, more broadly, what it means to act 'responsibly'. Additionally, several of the chapters provide some decision-making tools to assist managers in resolving ethical problems that they may encounter.

One of the most prolific contributors to this literature is Thomas Donaldson. The article included here (Chapter 39) is directed at practitioners and is designed to ease such people into the more weighty and subtle philosophical dimensions of the topic. It is useful in making clear just how easily an action that might seem somewhat innocuous can spell the beginning of a rapid slide down a very slippery ethical slope.

Hendry's contribution (Chapter 40) is a critique of Donaldson's theory of ethical universalism and has been included because it discusses a number of interesting and contrasting perspectives by some of the leading writers on international business ethics. One of the great difficulties that all who practice cross-cultural management face is shedding their ethnocentricities. Hendry argues that while Donaldson's theory professes to be universalistic it, too, exhibits various ethnocentric biases.

There is no ideal path for making one's way through the maze of international business ethics to a position which is ethically defensible. Rather, there are a variety of routes that might be taken. It is instructive, though, to be guided through the key considerations that will be confronted along the way and with some alternative suggestions on the way through. The model proposed by Wines and Napier (Chapter 41) is one such road map. Daniel Skubik (Chapter 42) provides another. In both cases the authors provide concrete examples of problems and decision-making frameworks that are both logical and practical to assist managers in their day-to-day problem solving.

The concrete differences in the ethics of managers cross-culturally are illustrated in Chapter 43 by Fritzsche and his colleagues in which comparisons are provided among American, Japanese, Korean and Taiwanese managers. Though there were differences in indicated behaviour between all four groups across the issues examined, there was also an apparent clustering of the East Asian samples compared to the American group. The authors discerned that the rationale behind the two cluster's choices of action was somewhat different, for which they provide a cultural and social explanation. The chapter is useful, then, in underlining the impact of culture on all aspects of international managerial behaviour.

The final chapter by Buller and McEvoy (Chapter 44) argues that being willing and able to think through ethical dilemmas can provide a significant competitive advantage to corporations operating internationally. The authors posit that achieving this capability is a function of various things, most importantly leadership that commits to following ethical principles, an organizational culture in which learning about how to behave ethically can be achieved and the implementation of human resource management practices (such as selection, training, performance appraisal and rewards systems) that make it more likely that ethical principles will be followed.

Acknowledgements

Gordon Redding gratefully acknowledges the assistance of the Euro Asia Centre at INSEAD, and its library staff in particular.

Bruce Stening would like to acknowledge the diligent research assistance provided by Nilouki Kurian. He is also very grateful for the additional time that was made available to him by virtue of his colleague, Mark Dodgson, assuming the considerable burdens of directorship of the National Graduate School of Management during the duration of this project.

References

Lewin, Kurt (1951), *Field Theory in Social Science*, New York: Harper, p. 20.
March, J.G. and J.P. Olsen (1976), *Ambiguity and Choice in Organizations*, Bergen, Norway: Universitetsforlaget.
Miles, R.E. and C.C. Snow (1978), *Organizational Strategy, Structure and Process*, New York: McGraw-Hill.
Parkhe, A. (1998), 'Understanding trust in international alliances', *Journal of World Business*, **33** (3), 219–40.
Tung, R.L. (1981), 'Selection and training of personnel for overseas assignments', *Columbia Journal of World Business*, Spring, **16** (1), 68–78.

Part I
Globalization and the Global Manager

[1]
Developing Leaders for the Global Frontier

Hal B. Gregersen ▪ Allen J. Morrison ▪ J. Stewart Black

Hal B. Gregersen is an associate professor of international strategy and leadership, Marriott School of Management, Brigham Young University. Allen J. Morrison is an associate professor of multinational marketing at the Richard Ivey School of Business, University of Western Ontario. J. Stewart Black is managing director and principal, Center for Global Assignments, and visiting professor, University of California, Irvine.

Imagine the experiences of explorers such as Magellan or Cook as they scanned the horizon of the great Pacific Ocean for days; they had no reliable charts, an unfamiliar hemisphere of stars, shark-infested waters, a crew losing confidence with each passing day, storm clouds gathering in the distance, waves crashing over the ship's bow, and wind howling. In many ways, the new business world is just as dangerous, filled with brutal storms of competitors, endless seas of change, seemingly strange cultures, confusing marketing channels, and unknown frontiers of technology.

The great difference, however, is that only a few great and courageous explorers were needed in the days of Magellan. Once the seas and their islands were charted, the coordinates didn't change. In contrast, the islands, mountains, rivers, and valleys of today's global business world are not static; they change. Markets, suppliers, competitors, technology, and customers are constantly shifting. Consequently, global business now requires all leaders to be explorers, guided by only the faintest glimmer of unfamiliar stars and excited by the opportunity and uncertainty of untapped markets.

At current growth rates, trade *between* nations will exceed total commerce *with-*

Figure 1
Quantity and Quality of Global Leaders*

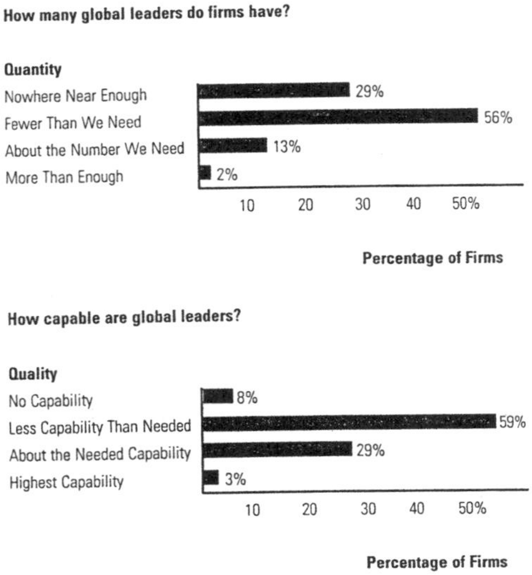

* Based on survey of U.S. *Fortune* 500 firms in 1997.

in nations by 2015.[1] In industries such as semiconductors, automobiles, commercial aircraft, telecommunications, computers, and consumer electronics, it is impossible to survive and not scan the world for competitors, customers, human resources, suppliers, and technology.

These forces of change help explain why leadership models of the past will not work in a global future. Provincial Japanese models of leadership have worked in Japan because Japanese leaders largely interacted with other Japanese. The same has been true for American, German, or French leadership models. In the future, a new breed of leader will be needed. Recently, Jack Welch, CEO of General Electric, commented:

"The Jack Welch of the future cannot be like me. I spent my entire career in the United States. The next head of General Electric will be somebody who spent time in Bombay, in Hong Kong, in Buenos Aires. We have to send our best and brightest overseas and make sure they have the training that will allow them to be the global leaders who will make GE flourish in the future."[2]

Most companies lack an adequate number of globally competent executives. Based on the results of a three-year study, we found that almost all companies claim that they need more global leaders, and most want future global leaders of higher caliber and quality *(see the sidebar for details on the study).*

Of the U.S. *Fortune* 500 firms we surveyed, 85 percent do not think they have an adequate number of global leaders *(see Figure 1)*; 67 percent of the firms think that their existing leaders need additional skills and knowledge before they meet or exceed needed capabilities. Jack Riechert, recently retired CEO of Brunswick Corporation, reflects the sentiments of many senior executives we interviewed: "Financial resources are not the problem. We have the money, products, and position to be a dominant global player. What we lack are the human resources. We just don't have enough people with the needed global leadership capabilities."

Another aspect of our survey is the high rating of global leadership compared to other factors in a company's global business success *(see Table 1).*

Characteristics of Global Leaders

As multinational firms compete in the unpredictable

Description of Research

We conducted our research from 1994 through 1997 in two separate efforts:

First, we interviewed 130 executives in fifty firms across Europe (fifteen firms), North America (twenty-five firms), and Asia (ten firms). Of these interviews, ninety were with senior executives. We asked the executives to identify someone in their company who is "an exemplar of future global leadership — whom senior management saw as clearly being given global leadership responsibilities and who would serve as a role model of global leadership to others in the future." We conducted interviews with forty such leaders. In all 130 interviews, we asked two questions: (1) What are the key characteristics of effective global leaders? (2) What are the key means of developing these characteristics?

Second, we sent a survey to human resource managers responsible for executive development in U.S. *Fortune* 500 firms in 1997. We received usable surveys from 108 firms. The survey asked about (1) the importance of global leadership compared to other resources (e.g., financial), (2) the quantity and quality of their global leaders, (3) the importance of global leadership characteristics (identified in the interviews described above), and (4) their current and future development efforts.

Table 1
Importance of Global Leadership Compared to Other Needs*

Dimension	Average Rating
Competent Global Leaders	6.1
Adequate Financial Resources	5.9
Improved International Communication Technology	5.1
Higher Quality Local National Workforce	5.0
Greater Political Stability in Developing Countries	4.7
Greater National Government Support of Trade	4.5
Lower Tariff/Trade Restrictions in Other Countries	4.4

1 = Not at all important; 7 = Extremely important

* Based on survey of U.S. *Fortune* 500 firms in 1997.

business frontier, they must confront two persistent, perplexing questions:

1. What are the characteristics of leaders who can guide organizations that span diverse countries, cultures, and customers?
2. How can companies effectively develop these leaders?

Our research revealed that every global leader needs a set of context-specific abilities and must have a core of certain characteristics. Roughly one-third of global business leaders' success depends on the knowledge and skills for specific contexts. For example, corporate cultures, industry dynamics, and "country of origin" management practices can permeate a company's worldwide operations and require unique knowledge and skills for successful leadership. About two-thirds of the characteristics apply generically to leaders, regardless of their managerial position, corporate culture, industry norms, or country-of-origin management practices. These general global leadership characteristics include exhibiting character, embracing duality, and demonstrating savvy. Most important, the leaders in our study saw inquisitiveness as the force underlying these characteristics.

Unbridled Inquisitiveness

While all leaders have substantial intelligence, all are not necessarily inquisitive. Constantly crossing cultural, language, political, social, and economic borders makes global business complex and uncertain. As a consequence, constant learning is required for success. Global business is physically taxing on managers. Travel, jet lag, and working in different languages and across different cultures can be tiring. For unsuccessful leaders, these aspects are just too overwhelming. Successful leaders are invigorated by the differences around them. They are driven by a sense of adventure and a desire to see and experience new things.

When studying individuals on international assignments, researchers have found this same characteristic to be important in cross-cultural adjustment and job performance.[3] They have called it adventuresomeness, curiosity, or open-mindedness. While international assignment responsibilities are not the same as global leadership, it does seem that whether a manager is crossing one country border or many, inquisitiveness is key to success *(see the sidebar on Mikell Rigg McGuire).*

Global leaders stated repeatedly that inquisitiveness is the fuel for increasing their global savvy, enhancing their ability to understand people and maintain integrity, and augmenting their capacity for dealing

Inquisitiveness: Mikell Rigg McGuire

In one of the fastest growing divisions of Franklin-Covey (the result of a merger of Franklin Quest and the Covey Leadership Center), Mikell Rigg McGuire, age thirty-five, vice president of international, deals with operations in more than sixty countries. Although she is constantly traveling with her team, rather than being stressed by the travel, she is invigorated. Before going overseas, McGuire watches international news networks and reads international magazines; she collects books and articles on the specific place she is to visit. She talks to friends who might know people in the country and calls them up to ask if they can help her understand the country. They might send her a book on art, for example, which "reflects what is important to them about the country," she commented. She continues to learn as she travels to "get that feel for the place."

On a recent assignment, her team committed to spending at least one evening out on each leg of the trip to explore the culture. They wanted to "take in a piece or flavor of that country to experience it." Sometimes they stayed in traditional local hotels, instead of generic American ones. McGuire's approach to building inquisitiveness into Franklin-Covey rests on this assumption:

"It is pretty tough to create open-mindedness. It almost starts from infancy and increases from all your experiences. Instead, I prefer building a team of people who show a nugget of inquisitiveness and open-mindedness. Then, you mentor them. It is an ongoing process to build these capabilities, not something that happens overnight."

with uncertainty and managing tensions. Inquisitiveness enables global leaders to not only develop the characteristics of character, duality, and savvy, but also build a complex understanding of how all three work together.

Personal Character

From our interviews, we determined that personal character involves two components: emotionally connecting with people from various backgrounds and exhibiting uncompromising integrity.

Emotional Connection. A genuine emotional connection with people throughout the company's worldwide operations is a function of a three-step process: (1) a sincere interest in and concern for others, (2) an effort to really listen to people, and (3) an understanding of different viewpoints. Leaders in the survey pointed out that understanding different viewpoints is *not* the same as embracing them but does lead to respecting them.[4] This process is particularly challenging when cultural and language differences confound communication. Ample opportunity exists for misunderstanding and taking and giving offense. Without the ability to connect with individuals, cultural diversity becomes a huge obstacle to effective leadership.

In the literature on expatriates, we have found similar concepts. For example, willingness to communicate with host country nationals has been found to facilitate the cross-cultural adjustment of expatriates.[5] Ethnocentricity and sociability also relate to making connections across cultures and have been discussed extensively in the literature.[6]

Fundamentally, emotional connection is important because it leads to goodwill. In turn, employees give leaders the benefit of the doubt on difficult matters, put forth their best efforts, and make sacrifices. In global organizations with webs of interrelated units that must cooperate and coordinate to meet customer needs, goodwill — rather than clear lines of command and control — is what leaders need to achieve global initiatives *(see the sidebar on Jon Huntsman)*.

Integrity. Executives described integrity in terms of ethical behavior and loyalty to the company's agreed-on values and strategy. Both personal and company standards are substantially more prone to compromise overseas.[7] When far removed from corporate oversight, managers are often tempted to change themselves and their organizations to appeal to local values and demands. Yet despite the opportunities for short-term advantage, the global leaders we studied were most effective when they consistently maintained the highest ethical standards in personal and company matters. Successful global leaders indicated that integrity significantly increased the overall levels of trust throughout the organization. They pointed out that when crossing cultural, national, functional, and business unit lines, trust is an essential, irreplaceable ingredient for effec-

Connection: Jon Huntsman, Jr.

Jon Huntsman, Jr., thirty-nine, is vice chairman of Huntsman Corporation, a firm started by his father in 1970. Huntsman is the largest privately held chemical manufacturing company in the United States, with annual worldwide sales approaching $6 billion and 7,000 employees in twenty-one countries.

Despite huge responsibilities, Huntsman works hard to stay connected to his employees. In his interview, he pointed out that his company was built on acquisitions that resulted from the failures of such giants as Shell, Texaco, Monsanto, Eastman Chemical, and Hoechst Celanese. According to Huntsman, these failures occurred in part because their leaders failed to connect with employees and inspire commitment. To stay connected to employees, Huntsman and a team of senior executives visit each of the company's facilities every December and meet every employee in its plants worldwide. Huntsman commented:

"In December, we are gone every single day before Christmas. We visit every Huntsman factory, every facility around the world. We shake everyone's hand. We talk to every spouse and child and learn about what they are doing. Where are you going to school? What do you like doing? Is your family happy? What can we do for you? We also give them each a holiday gift. Maybe it's a television, or a stereo, or a cruise. We want them to know how much we appreciate them. We want to make our employees feel they are the most important people in the universe. We honestly believe this.

"Making these visits is never easy. We are gone the entire month. But I love the visits. We all derive incredible energy from them. We love the people."

Huntsman's ability to connect emotionally with employees stems from his sincere interest in them. His curiosity about their culture and their personal circumstances allows him to truly understand their capabilities, motivation, and values. This connection brings huge rewards to the company and creates goodwill where insights and ideas percolate up from the factory floor. He remarked:

"Making these visits lets us connect with our people personally. We believe that the best ideas come from the factory floor. When people have met me, shaken my hand, and talked to me, they feel they know me. I challenge them by saying, 'Here is my number. If you have a good idea, a way to work more efficiently, call me.' And they do!"

tive execution. They were quick to add that quite often the difference between winners and losers in global competition is great execution, not great strategy, and added that for great execution, you need employees' trust and commitment.

They felt that their high level of inquisitiveness actually facilitated their ability to maintain ethical integrity. All acknowledged that definitions of allowable ethical behavior varied from country to country. However, their inquisitiveness led them to probe below the surface, deep into people's ethical values. For example, one manager made the following observation: "It's true that practices differ from one country to another. 'Gifts' might be more or less accepted from one country to another. However, around the world, employees and customers alike trust managers who conduct business above board and on the basis of business merit" *(see the sidebar on Lane Cook)*.

Duality

Global leaders embrace duality by managing uncertainty, essentially knowing when to act and when to gather more information, and balancing tensions, understanding what needs to change and what needs to stay the same from country to country and region to region.

Capacity for Managing Uncertainty. At the heart of any multinational, uncertainty reigns supreme, and successful leaders have a capacity for managing in changing conditions. In the global business arena, they confront a dearth of quality data and a staggering number of questions; for example: What is a country's real market potential? Is this country a good platform for global operations? How secure is the local currency? How long will it take to train local managers? While purely domestic executives face some of these same questions, the degree of uncertainty that global managers face is exponentially higher. The recent Asian financial and currency crisis underscores this point.

Once again in the literature on expatriates, we find an interesting parallel in terms of this characteristic for managing uncertainty. Researchers discuss the characteristic less in terms of management and more in terms of tolerance. In fact, most studies referred to tolerance for ambiguity. Research on expatriates has found that crossing from one's home culture into a foreign one creates significant uncertainty and that those who have a reasonably high tolerance for ambiguity tend to cope and adjust better.[8]

In the global arena where uncertainty can come from not just one country but a dozen or more at a time,

---

Integrity: Lane Cook

In 1994, DSL, a $200 million California-based international shipping company, hired Lane Cook to work in its new Mexico City office. DSL has facilities throughout the United States as well as Hong Kong, Taiwan, Korea, China, and Singapore. It focuses on consolidated shipments for the retail industry and considers major retailers like Wal-Mart, Sears, Target, and J.C. Penney its main customers.

DSL de Mexico had been through tough times, including the dramatic devaluation of the peso against the U.S. dollar and the loss of a major U.S. customer that decided to build its own distribution and warehouse facility in Mexico, only 1.5 miles from DSL's building. With so much unused capacity and costs already cut to the bone, Cook was under enormous pressure to raise revenues. He believed that the key to growth was developing local business.

In 1996, Cook had nearly completed negotiations on an agreement with a medium-sized, Mexico City-based general merchandise retailer, SuperMart (a disguised name). SuperMart was to take possession of the goods in Asia and contract with DSL to ship them to Mexico via the United States. Normally, DSL would have selected the transportation company to bring the freight from the U.S. border to Mexico City, but, in this case, the negotiator for SuperMart, Jose Hernandez (a disguised name) would sign the agreement only if he could select the Mexican transportation company. According to Cook:

"I thought this was a little peculiar. I was even more concerned when I later heard a rumor that Hernandez had a bank account here in Mexico City as well as a bank account in Laredo, Texas, and that the trucking company he selected had promised to make a payment to his U.S. bank account whenever a shipment was made. The Laredo bank would then wire the money to Hernandez's Mexico City account.

"I had a choice. On the one hand, I could just ignore the rumors and sign the deal. We needed the business, but if the rumors were true, we weren't paying these kickbacks. Or I could investigate and ask Hernandez about the whole thing.

"As I checked into it, it seemed okay, but I approached Hernandez anyway. When I did, he denied the rumor categorically. Yes, he had a bank account in Laredo, but so did many wealthier Mexicans who worried about the stability of the peso. Quite frankly, I think he was a little offended that I raised the issue, but we were able to work it out."

Cook was guided in his decision making by his commitment to three principles: first, that he was morally obligated to ensure that customers were not being cheated; second, that he not engage in any activities that reflected negatively on his company, either in Mexico or elsewhere; and third, that his peers and superiors would approve his actions. DSL de Mexico is now highly favored by sophisticated local and international retailers wanting a shipper that provides high-quality, ethical service worldwide.

While global leaders allow time for research, they do not allow the search for clarity to jeopardize first-mover advantages.

many managers may be tempted to do more research, which they believe will reduce the risk of poor decisions.[9] Yet, in many parts of the world and for many products, collecting accurate data sometimes takes so long that the data are useless by the time they are available. Furthermore, in today's hypercompetitive business environment, waiting for clarity works only if everyone else also waits. While global leaders allow time for research, they do not allow the search for clarity to jeopardize first-mover advantages. They quickly separate the "figure from background" and do not wait for the entire picture to come into focus before moving ahead. They know that speed and a capacity for uncertainty are tightly intertwined *(see the sidebar on Gary Griffiths).*

Unique Ability to Balance Tensions. In addition to uncertainty, managers must balance various tensions as they confront the pressures for both global integration and local responsiveness. Successful leaders indicated that it is generally a mistake to either globalize or localize *all* activities.[10] Rather, some activities like R&D may be most appropriately carried out worldwide, while other activities such as advertising and promotion may be best carried out locally or regionally. These leaders stressed that the perspective should not be one of just tolerating tensions but of embracing their inherent duality. A global executive with an engineering background commented:

"If you design a bridge to be completely rigid, it will collapse. If you let it swing freely, no one will be able to use it. Oscillation within a range is good and necessary for the bridge to function. The same is true for global organizations and leaders. That is why effective global leaders embrace duality and tensions."

These tensions include product standardization versus local adaptation, headquarters' management style versus the subsidiary's approach, corporate labor relations policies versus host country norms, and global brand image versus local consumer preferences. Embracing duality requires leaders to view tensions as necessary *and* good *(see the sidebar on Stephen Burke).*

Savvy

Because globalization increases both the opportunities for business and the challenges in getting things done, leaders need to be more savvy, much like a high-hurdle runner needs the ability to jump higher than a low-hurdle runner. In our research, we found two dimensions: business savvy and organizational savvy.

Business Savvy. Global business savvy enables managers to recognize worldwide market opportunities. They either locate new markets for the company's

---

Managing Uncertainty: Gary Griffiths

Marriott Corporation assigned Gary Griffiths to the position of director of finance when it opened its first hotel in Poland — the Warsaw Marriott. From the outset, Griffiths faced an endless stream of significant challenges everyday. One was setting up a bank account in Poland. After calling the local bank that planned to open a branch in the hotel complex, Griffith discussed the account with the bank's vice president, who answered, "I understand what you need, but we do not have room in our system for your accounts until we open our new branch in six months. I'm sorry, but we can't help you." Then the bank vice president continued, "I can't open a business account for your company, but let me open a personal account for you." Griffiths called the treasurer of Marriott in the United States to announce that he was ready for the first transfer of cash to the hotel, $200,000. The treasurer answered, "Terrific! Give me the name on the account." Griffiths hesitantly responded, "Gary Griffiths." There was a long pause on the other end of the line.

The funds were ultimately transferred to Griffiths' personal bank account, but they were declared "missing" in the bank's system for fifty-six days, and the Warsaw Marriott still had no operating cash. Griffiths drove to Austria and picked up U.S. $25,000 cash at the Vienna Marriott and brought it back to Poland. Reentering Poland alone with the money, Griffiths was extremely nervous, because he had to declare to a border guard with a machine gun that he was transporting $25,000, more than fifty years of wages for the guard. Griffiths made it through safely, returned to the hotel, and deposited the money, directly into his personal account.

After living through this and other experiences filled with endless uncertainty, Griffiths concluded:

"Things are not the same when you get out there in the world. You have to be willing to understand new environments and figure out how to deal with them. You have to learn to improvise. You must be ready to change how you do business. You must relish the uncertainty of it all."

---

goods and services or gain more efficient access to the company's existing markets. To recognize new market opportunities, to arbitrage opportunities involving cost and quality differences across company affiliates, and to maximize efficiencies by reducing redundancies, global leaders must understand competitive conditions.[11] Leaders know the sources and location of comparative advantage, country-specific conditions, countries' political and financial stability, and so on. They also understand international disciplines such as finance, accounting, marketing, operations, human resource management, and strategy. They comprehend issues that domestic-oriented leaders just don't have to face — such as how real movements in exchange rates can create opportunities to (1) lower prices and increase market share while keeping profit margins stable, or (2) keep prices and market share constant and reap additional profits *(see the sidebar on Steve Holliday)*.[12]

Global leaders have intimate knowledge of their firms' capabilities *and* their ability to mobilize resources to capture market opportunities.

Organizational Savvy. Global leaders have intimate knowledge of their firms' capabilities *and* their ability to mobilize resources to capture market opportunities. They know the strengths and weaknesses of the organization, are familiar with the company's subsidiaries and competitive positions, and know key overseas managers.[13] Due to changes in cultures, languages, government regulations, increased physical distances, and shifting time zones, as well as unclear lines of authority, the depth and breadth of

Balancing Tensions: Stephen Burke

Stephen Burke, age thirty-nine, was president of broadcasting for ABC, part of Disney's recent ABC/Capital Cities acquisition. In 1992, Michael Eisner, CEO of the Walt Disney Company, asked Burke to take the position of vice president in charge of park operations and marketing at EuroDisneyland.

EuroDisneyland, a (quasi) joint venture between Disney and the French government, opened in April 1992 amid a storm of bad publicity. From the beginning, the project was beset with problems:

- Attendance was off 10 percent from projections.
- Per-person spending in the park was less than half that in Japan.
- Hotel occupancy rates were 37 percent versus 92 percent in Disney's U.S. properties.
- Labor costs were significantly higher than those in the United States because of the inability to dramatically increase and decrease staff during peak and off seasons.
- Negative publicity and headlines abounded, like "Disney Is Cultural Chernobyl."
- Protests from French farmers continued because of the French government's appropriation of farm land for the Disney theme park.
- Some workers resisted the Disney management style and dress code.
- Construction cost overruns were nearly $2 billion.
- Operating losses were approaching $1 billion.

Burke and the local management team faced the task of devising and implementing strategic changes that would ensure growth and financial health. The first significant change was renaming the park. "Euro" seemed more like a chemical mix of unnatural ingredients than a place. Yet the name "Disneyland" was magical. Burke remarked: "With Disneyland, you get a magical place, and everybody loves Paris. By including 'Paris' in the name, the French would be more receptive. Also, by definition, we can tie the park to the city in our marketing and advertising campaigns."

After changing the park's name to Disneyland Paris, Burke continued to struggle with a central challenge: How to make the park profitable and strike a balance between Disney tradition and local culture? In the end, to retain the Disney image, Burke:

- Improved hiring to focus on outgoing, friendly Disney cast members.
- Increased training to emphasize and teach friendly service and cleanliness.
- Introduced seasonal pricing for entry to the park.
- Used traditional Disney characters throughout the park.

To adapt Disney to French culture, Burke:

- Removed the ban on alcohol in the theme parks.
- Lowered customary Disney premium prices by 20 percent to 30 percent on admission, merchandise, hotels, and food.
- Relaxed Disney's normal hierarchical managerial style and encouraged more individual initiative.
- Cut managerial staff by almost 1,000.

These and other changes had a positive impact on the park's financial results. Attendance figures rose about 17 percent. Hotel occupancy rates went up, and the hotels were fully booked during peak times. People spent more money in the park. In the third quarter of the 1995 fiscal year, the park posted its first operating profits. By the time Burke left in 1997, the press had mostly positive things to say about the park.

Burke balanced various tensions between global corporate imperatives and local market conditions. He not only managed well in the high uncertainty between headquarters in Burbank and executives in Paris, but between Disney management and local employees and among banks, creditors, the parent company, and the park's own interests. According to Burke, "Balancing tensions is both the art and fun of global leadership."

organizational savvy required to execute effectively is far greater for global leaders *(see the sidebar on Ta-Tung Wang)*.

Developing Global Leaders

Organizations seeking to globalize need look no further than their own leaders to determine if their efforts will succeed or fail. Does the organization have enough global leaders? If not, it must ask if its leaders are born or made. Based on our interviews, the consensus was that global leaders are born and *then* made.

Assessing Talent

Global leaders, like great musicians or athletes, need superior talent, abundant opportunity, and excellent education and training to succeed. Not everyone has the ability to become one, so companies should not give opportunity and education to just anyone. Companies need to assess whether they are hiring enough young managers with the required baseline level of leadership talent to ensure that, even with normal turnover, they will have future global leaders.

Colgate-Palmolive, a company with decades of international business experience, often hires entry-level marketing candidates who have already demonstrated such characteristics and capabilities. It intentionally hires newly minted undergraduates or MBAs who have lived or worked abroad, speak more than one language, or can demonstrate their preexisting aptitude for global business. Still, even individuals with potential need outstanding developmental opportunities. In our research, firms with comprehensive development systems performed better financially than firms without such systems. However, most firms do not have comprehensive systems for developing global leaders *(see Figure 2)*.

Figure 2
Systems for Developing Global Leaders*

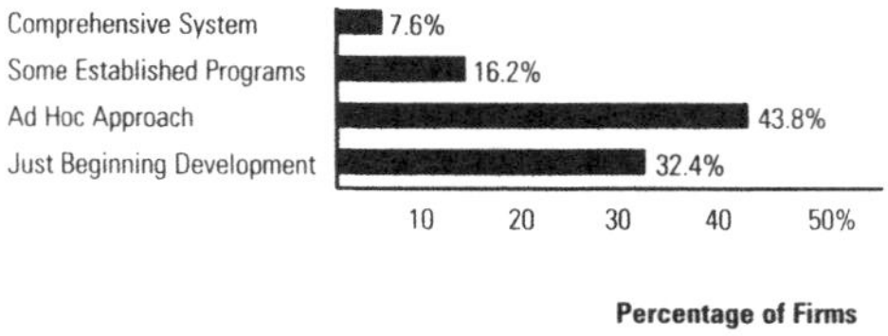

* Based on survey of U.S. *Fortune* 500 firms in 1997.

The Development Process

How are global leaders made? The basic mental process for development is to understand the whole world, not just one country. For most of us, that requires both some rearranging and stretching of our mind-sets. However, it usually takes a pretty hard blow to the head and some real tugging before we rearrange and stretch our minds enough to encompass the whole earth.[10] Direct confrontations with new terrain can create a sharp contrast between what we know and what lies before us.

We might consider the example of one American's seemingly simple trip to a traditional Japanese restaurant. As this very tall businessman walked in,

Business Savvy: Steve Holliday

Steve Holliday, age forty, is managing director of British-Borneo Oil & Gas Ltd., a medium-sized British oil and gas exploration and production company with international operations that range from Southeast Asia to the Gulf of Mexico. Holliday knows that recognizing global market opportunities is far more than "playing global chess" with competitors. Simply watching where competitors move and then defending against those moves is not enough. He commented:

"In the early 1990s, Hong Kong-based China Light & Power (CL&P) was supplying about two-thirds of Hong Kong's electric power. We saw an almost insatiable, unmet demand for electricity in southern China. So we formed a joint venture with CL&P to build a $3.5 billion coal-powered plant at Black Point in Hong Kong's New Territories. We agreed to provide 60 percent of the capital; the rest was to come from CL&P. CL&P's expertise was in coal-fired plants, and the intention was for them to serve as plant operator.

"As the negotiations proceeded, ARCO China came into the picture. It had just discovered a major gas field in the South China Sea and wanted to find a market for its gas. In the end, Exxon had a huge power plant that would rely on a competitor's gas. Some would argue that the deal just didn't make sense. But since the plant began operations in early 1996, it has proven to be a great, highly profitable investment for Exxon."

It is this ability to think beyond the borders in a borderless world and to recognize business opportunities through the fog of time zones, cultures, and past experiences that separates global leaders from the rest.

he hit his head on the wooden beam over the entry with such force that it shook and rattled the doors and windows and caused the other patrons to fear an impending earthquake. The American did the same thing the very next day. Finally, on his third trip to the restaurant, he remembered to duck when entering.

Most of us are like this person. It takes getting hit in the head — hard and probably more than once — before we are ready to change our mind-sets. And we need to expand our minds to recognize global opportunities and to marshal worldwide organizational resources. We need to emotionally connect with people who are different from ourselves and engender their good will. We need to understand people of different ethics and demonstrate integrity in a way that inspires trust. We need to embrace the constant dualities and tensions of global and local business demands. One reason that inquisitiveness differentiates between successful global leaders and those who struggle with worldwide responsibilities is that it ignites and fuels the motivation to go through this mind-altering process.

Strategies for Developing Global Leaders

In our research across Europe, North America, and Asia, we found four strategies that, when properly used, are effective at developing global leaders: travel, teams, training, and transfers.

Travel

Foreign travel, the first strategy, must put potential global leaders in the middle of the country, its culture, economy, political system, market, and so on, uninsulated by the common corporate cocoon of a western luxury hotel, car and driver, dutiful staffers, and choreographed itinerary. When Procter & Gamble CEO John Pepper travels, he visits several families' homes in each country to see firsthand how they use products, before he goes to his hotel or office. His approach helped him see that the French prefer front-load washers and would not easily change to top-load washers. This, in turn, helped Pepper better manage the introduction of a new cold-water detergent brand globally and, at the same time, find a way to meet the local need for distributing the detergent evenly throughout the clothes in front-load washers. This led to the invention of an innovative plastic ball into which a customer pours the detergent; it evenly distributes the detergent through little holes.

The successful global leaders in our survey consistently described two ways to enhance the developmental potential of international travel: First, take detours. Often the greatest contrasts and opportunities for stretching and rearranging minds are found off the beaten path. Second, get wet. Dive into the

Organizational Savvy: Ta-Tung Wang

Ta-Tung Wang was born in the Peoples' Republic of China in 1944. After completing an undergraduate degree in Taiwan, Wang moved to the United States for graduate work. After graduation, he worked for Kentucky Fried Chicken. In 1986, he was made vice president of KFC Southeast Asia with headquarters in Singapore.

Wang saw that KFC had a competitive edge over any other major U.S. fast-food chain in developing the Chinese market; the Chinese preferred chicken to beef. Initially, Wang found a required local partner with access to a consistent supply of KFC-approved chickens by tapping into resources at KFC's parent company (R.J. Reynolds, at the time), resulting in contacts at the Ministry of Light Industry in Beijing. These contacts led Wang to the Beijing Corporation Animal Production (BCAP), a secure supplier of KFC's most important ingredient, chicken.

After countless visits to Beijing to find a site for the restaurant, Wang learned that a three-story building across the street from Tiananmen Square was available. As lease negotiations proceeded, the city agency that controlled the lease asked Wang for ten years rent up front, a total of U.S. $1 million in cash. Wang remarked:

"I asked the local negotiators how they came up with the $1 million figure. They said they needed that much to finish the building. My local Chinese partners said, 'That's crazy! Don't sign.' Of course I didn't have signing authority for $1 million from KFC, but I said to the negotiators on the spot, 'Let's do it.'"

Wang knew who to call at KFC and what to say. The money arrived in Beijing a few days later. The results of this risk? According to Wang, "It was a fantastic success. KFC got all its money back in less than a year."

How did KFC achieve such returns when it could not exchange China profits into hard currency and was stuck with soft local currency RMB? Wang tapped the parent company's world-class countertrade financial skills. By this time, KFC had been sold to PepsiCo, which also owned Taco Bell and Pizza Hut. Between KFC and these other chains, there was a huge, on-going need for employee uniforms. Wang met this need by funneling most of KFC's soft currency RMB profits in China into buying uniforms for export to the United States and other countries, thus exporting the profits from China to the United States.

Without Wang's organizational savvy, KFC would never have moved so quickly and so profitably into China or found such capable partners.

shops, markets, schools, homes, and so forth to find out what local life is really like.

Teams

The second strategy is to establish teams in which individuals with diverse backgrounds and perspectives work together closely.[15] Contrasting views and values can force members to think globally. Managed well, a culturally diverse team can also produce better business decisions.

Recently, Black & Decker implemented a 360 degree performance appraisal and feedback system, using a team from the United States and several Asian countries, including Singapore and Malaysia. Tracy Billbrough, president of Black & Decker Eastern Hemisphere, felt that the global team experience helped him better understand how to connect emotionally with people from different cultural backgrounds and appreciate why those connections aided in successful implementation.

Working in a foreign locale every day makes it possible to have mind-altering, head-cracking experiences.

Multicultural teams can be quite problematic, however, if not managed well. To help make teams more effective in developing global leaders:

- People should become team members before becoming team leaders.
- In general, people should be members or leaders of single-function, multicultural teams before becoming members or leaders of multiple-function, multicultural teams.
- Companies should give team members adequate training in topics such as cross-cultural communication, conflict resolution, and multicultural team dynamics.

Training

The third strategy, training, can supply all the contrast and confrontation of teams with a structured learning environment. For example, Sunkyong, one of the five largest industrial organizations in Korea, has a global leader program that involves both classroom and action learning projects for participants from the company's worldwide businesses. One project examined liquid natural gas opportunities in China. Its outcome helped Sunkyong avoid some costly mistakes; the training program teams discovered partners who were much more capable and competent than those the Chinese government had been promoting. Y.C. Kim, director of human resources, felt that exposure to various people through the company-provided training program enhanced his organizational savvy, and he met people who could help him in the future.

To enhance global leadership development, effective training programs should have these characteristics:

- Participants should come from the company's worldwide operations.
- Programs should include topics on international strategy and vision, worldwide organizational structure and design, change management, cross-cultural communication, international business ethics, multicultural team leadership, new market entry, dynamics of developing countries and markets, and managing in uncertainty.
- To ensure that the training encourages people to rearrange and stretch their minds, programs should include action learning components such as a field-based business project.

Transfers

The fourth, most powerful strategy is to provide overseas assignments.[16] We asked leaders: "What has been the most powerful experience in your life for developing global leadership capabilities?" Eighty percent identified living and working in a foreign country as the single most influential experience in their lives. Given the respondents' diverse nationalities, functional experiences, company affiliations, and so on, this finding is significant. More than any of the other three strategies, working in a foreign locale every day makes it possible to have mind-altering, head-cracking experiences.

Not everyone is open to the potential of an international assignment. People usually have one of four basic responses:

Broken heads. People with no global leadership potential have such thick heads they do not even realize when they have hit them and hence learn nothing from the assignment.
Bruised heads. Those with little potential realize that they have hit their heads, but they go back to being just as they were before the mishap and learn almost nothing.

Bright heads. People with a moderate amount of potential learn to duck after they first hit their heads; that is, they learn country-specific lessons.
Brilliant heads. When unexpectedly hit in the head, people with significant talent do not ignore it, do not try to simply reconstruct their original mind-sets, and do not create unique mental maps for each new situation and country. Instead, they continually monitor little bumps and major cracks and then update contingent, general mental maps that transcend country boundaries.

For example, NORTEL (Northern Telecom) maximizes the learning impact of international transfers by carefully managing each phase. NORTEL establishes candidate pools for international assignments, encourages informed self-selection, provides predeparture training, establishes support mechanisms, plans for repatriation, debriefs employees and families on return, and uses repatriates' international skills and knowledge throughout the organization. NORTEL's strategic and systematic approach to international transfers produces increased market reach, quick innovation transfers, sound strategic alliances, and better global leaders.

How can firms enhance the power and effectiveness of international assignments?

Select the person carefully. Begin by thinking about how the person and the company will use the international experience in the future.
Consider the person's family. Ensure that family members are well suited for the assignment. Their difficulties could cause the global leader to lose the development potential of the assignment.
Provide training. Training helps people adjust quickly, be resilient, and better capture the potential of an assignment.
Facilitate repatriation. Companies need to retain people to leverage their international development. Unfortunately, approximately 25 percent of U.S. expatriates who successfully complete an international assignment leave their company within a year. Companies such as Monsanto, however, employ certain strategies to retain and better utilize potential global leaders after international assignments: They provide a sponsor to help with placement and reentry and plan for repatriation three to six months in advance. They help employees locate a suitable position before their return. They allow some "down time" for employees to put things in place at home. They provide repatriation training and facilitate the family's readjustment. They provide the opportunity to use international experience and allow for reasonable autonomy in the first job following repatriation.

Conclusion

Like explorers of old, today's global leaders face uncharted seas. While the characteristics these leaders must possess could clearly benefit domestic leaders, the difference is that global leaders cannot succeed without them. Our research suggests that most companies clearly lack the quantity or quality of global leaders they need — today or in the future. In the near term, this may create a valuable "free agent market" for those with proven capabilities until more leaders can be developed.

References

This research was funded in part by the David M. Kennedy Center for International Studies and the Center for International Business Education and Research at Brigham Young University. The authors' book, *Global Explorers: The Next Generation of Leaders*, will be published by Routledge in March 1999.

■ 1. R. Daft, *Management* (New York: Dryden, 1997).
■ 2. J. Welch, speech at General Electric, Spring 1997.
■ 3. For a complete review of characteristics related to international assignment success, see:
J.S. Black, H.B. Gregersen, M.E. Mendenhall, and L. Stroh, *Globalizing People through International Assignments* (Reading, Massachusetts, Addison-Wesley, 1998); and
J.S. Black and H.B. Gregersen, *So You're Going Overseas: A Handbook for Personal and Professional Success* (San Diego, California: Global Business Publishers, 1998).
■ 4. For a discussion of the relationship between global effectiveness and understanding culture, see:
S. Weiss, "Negotiating with 'Romans' — Part 1," *Sloan Management Review*, volume 35, Winter 1994, pp. 51-61; and
L. Hoecklin, *Managing Cultural Differences: Strategies for Competitive Advantage* (Wokingham, England: The Economist Intelligence Unit and Addison-Wesley, 1995).
■ 5. For the first major review of this concept, see:
M.E. Mendenhall and G. Oddou, "The Dimensions of Expatriate Acculturation: A Review," *Academy of Management Review*, volume 10, number 1, 1985, pp. 39-47.
■ 6. For example, see:
J.S. Black, "Personal Dimensions and Work Role Transitions: A Study of Japanese Expatriate Managers in America," *Management International Review*, volume 30, number 2, 1990, pp. 119-134.
■ 7. M. Nyaw and I. Ng, "A Comparative Analysis of Ethical Beliefs: A Four Country Study," *Journal of Business Ethics*, volume 13, number 7, 1994, pp. 543-555; and
M. Philips, "Bribery," *Ethics*, July 1984, pp. 621-636.
■ 8. For a review, see:
Black et al. (1998), chapter three.
■ 9. The trade-offs between gathering too much data and too little are discussed in:
G. Stalk, "Time — The Next Source of Competitive Advantage," *Harvard Business Review*, volume 66, July-August 1988, pp. 41-51.
■ 10. For an academic perspective, see:
A. Morrison and K. Roth, "A Taxonomy of Business-Level Strategies in Global Industries," *Strategic Management Journal*, volume 13, number 6, 1992, pp. 399-417;
M. Porter, "Changing Patterns of International

Competition," *California Management Review*, volume 28, Winter 1986, pp. 9-40; and
S. Ghoshal, "Global Strategy: An Organizing Framework," *Strategic Management Journal*, volume 8, number 6, 1987, pp. 425-440.
■ 11. For a more complete discussion of arbitrage advantages that come through globalization, see:
G. Ragazzi, "Theories of the Determinants of Direct Foreign Investment," *IMF Staff Papers*, July 1973, pp. 471-498.
For a discussion of the advantages of global integration, see:
C.K. Prahalad and Y. Doz, *The Multinational Mission* (New York: Free Press, 1987).
■ 12. For a discussion of the impact of exchange rates on global competition, see:
R. Aliber, "The MNE in a Multiple-Currency World," in J. Dunning, ed., *The Multinational Enterprise* (London: Allen & Unwin, 1971); and
D. Lessard, "Transfer Prices, Taxes, and Financial Markets: Implications of International Financial Transfers within the Multinational Corporation," D. Lessard, ed., *International Financial Management: Theory and Application*, second edition (New York: Wiley, 1985).
■ 13. H. Crookell and A. Morrison, "Subsidiary Strategy in a Free Trade Environment," *Business Quarterly*, volume 55, Autumn 1990, pp. 33-39; and
K. Roth and A. Morrison, "Implementing Global Strategy: Global Subsidiary Mandates," *Journal of International Business Studies*, volume 23, number 4, 1992, pp. 715-735.
■ 14. For an excellent discussion of the challenges of learning in a global context, see:
D. Leonard-Barton, *Wellsprings of Knowledge: Building and Sustaining the Sources of Innovation* (Boston: Harvard Business School Press, 1995); and
Y. Doz, K. Asakawa, J. Santos, and P. Williamson, "The Metanational Corporation" (Banff, Canada: Academy of International Business Annual Meeting, paper, 26-29 September 1997).
■ 15. R. Belbin, *Management Teams: Why They Succeed or Fail* (London: Heinemann, 1991);
P. Evans, E. Lank, and A. Farquar, "Managing Human Resources in the International Firm: Lessons from Practice," in P. Evans, Y. Doz, and A. Laurent, eds., *Human Resource Management in International Firms: Change, Globalization, Innovation* (London: Macmillan, 1989).
■ 16. Black et al. (1992);
"The Fast Track Leads Overseas," *Business Week*, 1 November 1993, pp. 64-68; and
L. Ioannou, "Cultivating the New Expatriate Executive," *International Business*, July 1994, pp. 40-50.

Reprint 4012

[2]

Global Managers: Developing A Mindset For Global Competitiveness

Ben L. Kedia **Ananda Mukherji**

There is increasing evidence that large scale globalization is rendering traditional ways of doing business largely irrelevant. There is a growing need for managers to become global managers with a global perspective. We suggest that a global perspective consists of a global mindset supported by appropriate skills and knowledge. Managers have a number of mindsets that range from the domestically-oriented defender, *and continuing on to the* explorer, *the* controller, *and the globally-oriented* integrator. *For global managers to be effective, they need to develop the global mindset of an* integrator. *A global mindset allows meaningful global strategizing that requires managers to effectively integrate the three global forces of (1) global business, (2) regional/country pressures, and (3) worldwide functions. A global mindset and a holistic global strategy should create conditions to build the worldwide organization characterized by specialization, interdependency, and coordination. A global outlook is a process of moving an organization's structure, process, people, and culture from a set of highly autonomous business units to one that becomes an integrated and effective global network.*

As the focus of business shifts from the domestic environment to the global, business leaders and managers will have to increasingly look for ways to redefine their strategies and realign their organizations to the new and more complex global realities. This, essentially, is the challenge for global managers—to articulate a viable global strategy, facilitate and develop supportive processes by which globalization can be managed, and create appropriate conditions by which the overall strategy, process, culture, and structure can be meaningfully aligned to achieve organizational effectiveness. The challenges of global competition, corporate downsizing, industrial renaissance, and economic dislocation are the new watchwords of American business (Jusela, 1994). The challenges, however, are not restricted to meeting changes in the global competitive environment, but also to look at ways to improving organizational performance and increasing

Ben L. Kedia, The Robert Wang Center for International Business, 220 Fogelman Executive Center, The University of Memphis, Memphis, TN 38152 . Ananda Mukherji, Department of Management and Marketing, Texas A&M International University, 5201 University Boulevard, Laredo, TX 78041.

individual development simultaneously (Porras & Silvers, 1991).

In a world where communication and transportation technology have reduced barriers considerably, an additional challenge is to develop a mindset that is global to increase organizational effectiveness, and yet maintain efficient business operations. The question really is, what are firms to do to enhance their competitive abilities in the face of increased pressures of global competition, and yet maintain their long term viability as effective business entities? There is considerable evidence that large scale changes are taking place in the global arena. Although economic growth rates for developed countries have slowed down and stabilized between 2 and 4%, the growth rates of newly industrialized countries are burgeoning between 5 and 11% (*Fortune*, 1995). In an earlier report, the World Bank has forecasted that by the year 2020, the five largest economies, based on purchasing power parity, would be China, the US, Japan, India, and Indonesia (World Bank, 1992), displacing Germany and France from the ranks of the top five. The emerging economic reality with its new players implies that existing concepts may have to be seriously reviewed and reconsidered. For any business, the conventional model will no longer have the same validity, and the greatest opportunities and challenges would be from the global market and its attendant challenges to operate differently (Rhinesmith, 1993).

According to Yip (1992), the globalization phenomenon is taking place on account of four globalization drivers, and managers need to be cognizant of these drivers. These are market drivers, cost drivers, competitive drivers, and government drivers. (1) *Market Drivers*—Although more salient in industrialized nations, per capita income has been increasing worldwide. This has resulted in greater purchasing power and an increased demand for goods worldwide. There has also been a convergence in lifestyles, tastes, aspirations, and expectations of consumers. Increased global travel has also created a new class of global consumers. (2) *Cost Drivers*—Another set of factors impacting globalization is lowered manufacturing and production costs. Consequently, economies of scale, availability of low labor costs, accelerated technological innovation, and improved transportation have been a part of cost drivers. (3) *Competitive Drivers*—Competitive drivers affecting globalization are new global competitors, increased formation of global strategic alliances, and more countries becoming competitive battlegrounds. (4) *Government Drivers*—Globalization is also impacted by government drivers. These include factors like the emergence of trading blocks, large scale privatization, and reduction in trade barriers.

Companies are now confronted by the rapid globalization of markets and competition, the increasing importance of speed and flexibility as key sources of competitive advantage, and the growing proliferation of partnership relations with suppliers, customers, and competitors (Ghoshal, Arnzen, & Brownfield, 1992). The prevailing conditions in the global environment make it necessary for companies to respond with radically different management approaches to succeed. Over the last few years there have been a number of writers who have helped define, develop, and better understand the mindset for global managers (see Jusela, 1994; Kefalas & Neuland, 1997; Rhinesmith, 1993; and Tichy, 1992). Similarly, there have been a number of articles on the strategic demands and challenges today's managers face in the global environment (Bartlett & Ghoshal, 1992; Murtha, Lenway & Bagozzi, 1998; and Prahalad & Lieberthal, 1998). Based on an extensive review of the literature, we propose to do two things. One, is to develop the essentials of the global mindset based on available literature and suggestions made by various scholars in the field. In this process, we propose to examine those mindsets that we feel are less useful in today's highly competitive and turbulent global environment. Two, is to briefly outline the forces facing managers in today's highly competitive global environment, and how our proposed global mindset may be useful in balancing and integrating the various forces and multiple challenges emanating from global business, regional/country pressures, and worldwide functions. The issues we specifically address in this paper are:

- changing orientation of managers
- developing a global perspective
- role, qualities, and requirements of global leadership
- evolution of managerial mindsets
- strategizing and integrating globally

Globalization can be conceptualized as a situation where political borders become increasingly more irrelevant, economic interdependencies are heightened, and national differences due to dissimilarities in societal cultures are central issues of business. The world, on account of these complex and dynamic forces, becomes a "global marketplace" (Lane, DiStefano & Maznevski, 1997). This requires global managers to possess a global perspective. A global manager is one who has reorganized his or her way of thinking and has an altered mindset. Lane et al., (1997) suggest that thinking globally means extending concepts and models from one-to-one relationships to holding multiple realities and relationships in mind simultaneously, and then acting skillfully on this more complex reality. Thus, to be globally competitive, global managers need to have openness that allows a global mindset to form, evolve, and develop.

Changing Orientation of Managers

Over the last decade or so, with notable changes taking place in the global competitive environment, the orientation of managers has changed considerably. This change has taken place both in terms of levels, and in terms of priorities. From a level perspective, most traditional training focused on the individual executive with the objective of broadening the perspective of managers with the hope that individuals will somehow find ways to influence choices and actions within their corporations (Ghoshal et al., 1992). The focus has shifted from the level of the individual manager to that of teams and groups,

Figure 1

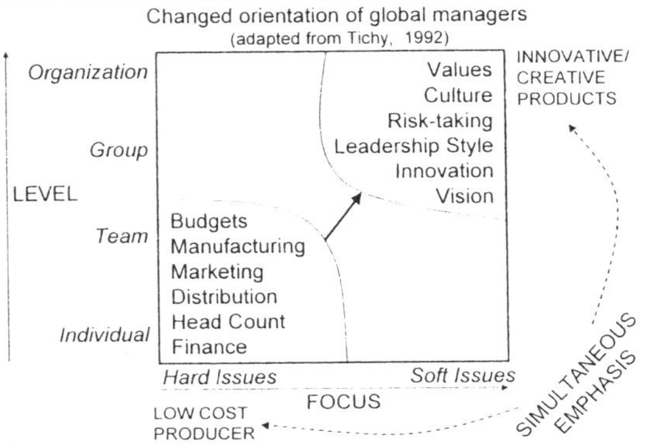

and indeed the target now is the entire organization that needs to be trained and reoriented to face the emerging global challenges (Tichy, 1992).

Other than level of training, managers were traditionally trained in what may be defined as "hard" as opposed to "soft" issues (Tichy, 1992: p. 210). The focus in "hard" issues training was to become the low cost producer. Consequently, the "hard" issues were oriented toward drivers of the bottom line, and the emphasis was on budgets, manufacturing, marketing, distribution, head count, and finances. However, in the face of reduced market power and increased global competition, the focus is now shared with "soft" issues that emphasize the need to be creative and to deliver innovative products simultaneously. The orientation, consequently, has shifted toward drivers of the top line and the emphasis is on values, culture, vision, leadership style, innovative behavior, and risk-taking. The framework given in Figure 1, adapted from Tichy (1992), illustrates this changed orientation of levels and of priorities. The challenge for global managers is the ability to focus on hard and soft issues simultaneously.

Earlier theoretical contributions suggested that the fundamental international problem facing managers was to reconcile the conflicting pressures of adapting to a standardized technology and product, or to respond to local market needs and requirements (Murtha et al., 1998). These conflicting pressures were considered to be mutually exclusive and existed linearly in terms of zero-sum trade-offs, that Fayerweather (1982: p. 211) termed as "unification" or "fragmentation" strategies.

However, technological and theoretical developments have indicated that international business strategy can be conceptualized along multiple dimensions. Rather than conceive strategy along one dimension, researchers (Doz & Prahalad, 1991; Prahalad & Doz, 1981, 1987) have suggested that strategy consists of balancing the twin pressures of global integration and local responsiveness concurrently. Consequently, paying simultaneous attention to various dimensions of strategy (Murtha et al., 1998) is considered to be an appropriate way to balance these forces. Organizational capabilities to exploit the full strategic potential of these complex pressures of integration, responsiveness, and coordination (Murtha et al., 1998) require global mindsets that equilibrate these forces rather than predispose decisions in favor of one dimension at the expense of the others (Prahalad & Doz, 1987). Bartlett and Ghoshal's (1989) definition of a transnational mentality implies the ability to balance these complex forces in pursuit of a unique strategy that blends them. It is worth mentioning that the organizational context, in terms of culture, corporate policies, and motivation, must be geared toward forming and sustaining a holistic global outlook. In other words, a transnational mentality or a global mindset is a completely different way of looking at the world and synthesizing the many complex forces.

Like much of strategy research on cognitive issues (Prahalad & Bettis, 1986; Grant, 1988), we focus on the mindset of the global manager whose impact is felt at the organizational level. We take the liberty of shifting our level of analysis from the manager to the organization in the belief that organizational actions, in terms of strategies and postures, are an aggregation of the mindset of the key and dominant decision makers. Like Prahalad & Bettis (1986), who used the manager's dominant logic to establish a linkage between the pattern of diversification and performance, we propose to use the mindset of global managers to explain actions and strategies of organizations taken in international business.

Framework to Develop a Global Perspective

For managers to orient themselves and their priorities to the changed international realities, we suggest that a triad consisting of a global mindset, knowledge, and skills, is needed by managers to be globally competitive. Although a global mindset is a state of being essentially characterized by openness, and an ability to recognize complex interconnections, global managers need a certain set of supportive knowledge and skills to sustain the mindset. Knowledge and skills are needed to meet the changing, emerging, and increasingly complex conditions associated with globalization (Rhinesmith, 1993). Figure 2 provides an illustration of how global mindset, knowledge, and skills are interrelated.

Global Mindset

A global mindset, according to Rhinesmith (1993: p. 24), "is a way of being rather than a set of skills. It is an orientation of the world that allows one to see certain things that others do not. A global mindset means the ability to scan the world from a broad perspective, always looking for unexpected trends and opportunities that may constitute a threat or an opportunity to achieve personal, professional or organizational objectives." A global mindset is for each manager to realize his or her firm's interdependence on the global

Figure 2

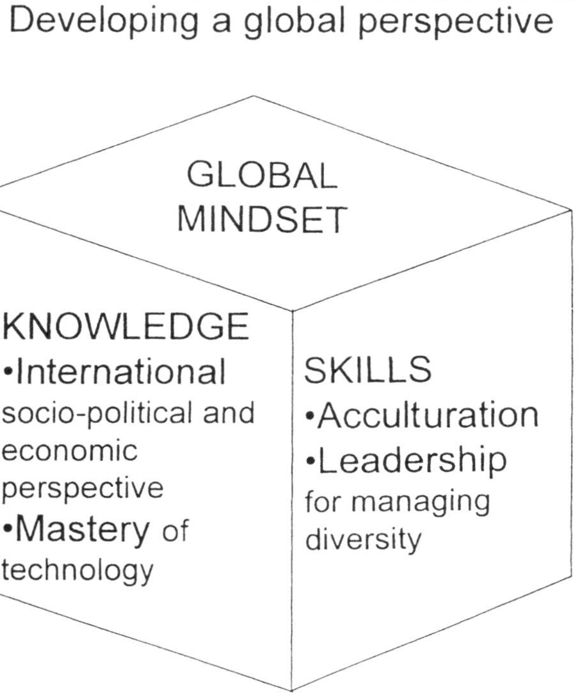

economy even when the firm's activities are seemingly confined to the domestic environment. However, to sustain and develop a global mindset, a manager also needs knowledge and skills.

We conceptualize a global mindset for global managers to be a necessary condition to effectively handle global competition, however, it is not a sufficient condition. The sufficient conditions that enhance and sustain a global mindset are knowledge and skills. A manager needs to have knowledge of different aspects of the interdependent world. Skills, on the other hand, are certain human and behavioral abilities that managers have that help them to do their work more effectively in the global context. It is this unique combination of global mindset, knowledge, and skills that is necessary and sufficient for the making of global managers.

Given the changed level of training and the new priorities for global managers, coupled with knowledge and skills required for a global mindset, global managers have to play a leadership role. To do this, global managers have to define their role, and develop certain qualities that make them true global managers (Kets de Vries & Mead, 1992). The primary role of the global manager, according to Kets de Vries and Mead, is to act as a catalyst within the organization. Here the global manager has to be sensitive to cultural diversity, and to manage cultural diversity. An effective global manager is one who values diversity and is able to leverage differences in a meaningful way. Apart from a catalytic role, global managers need to develop and possess certain important traits. One, is the capacity for envisioning and being able to give meaning to the vision. Two, is to be able to understand increasingly complex environments, and the ability to recognize complex patterns in the environment. Three, is to be able to instill values and to inspire others. Finally, an effective global manager should be able to build and maintain organizational networks at the global level.

In a general way, many requirements of global management may not differ from those of the non-global management mindset. At an abstract level, effective management, whether in the global or domestic environment, requires traits like creating vision and instilling values. However, apart from a common set of traits, global management requires a set of specialized skills, capabilities, and competencies that are not part of the traditional education system and managerial experience. Our focus is on this emerging set of capabilities that is increasingly assuming salience. A global mindset, to distinguish it from a non-global mindset, is one that is characterized by unique time and space perspectives, and a general predisposition (Kefalas & Neuland, 1997). A unique time perspective is one of taking a long-term view when dealing with international business activities. Similarly, a unique space perspective is one where managers with a global mindset will extend their personal space well beyond their immediate surroundings, both in terms of geography as well as in real and potential relationships with other people. Also, managers with a global mindset will exhibit a general predisposition by being more tolerant of other peoples and cultures, consider cultural diversity an asset, thrive on ambiguity, balance contradictory forces, and rethink boundaries (Kefalas & Neuland, 1997; Rhinesmith, 1993).

In addition, other characteristics of a global mindset include emotional connection, capacity for managing uncertainty, ability to balance tensions, and savvy (Gregerson, Morrison, & Black, 1998). The first of these is a genuine emotional connection with people throughout the organization's worldwide operations. The second is to have the capacity to manage under conditions that are constantly changing and inherently complex. The third is to confront and balance the various tensions of global integration and local responsiveness (Prahalad & Doz, 1987). Finally, to exhibit business savvy and organizational savvy (Gregerson et al., 1998), where business savvy enables a manager to recognize worldwide market opportunities, and organization savvy implies intimate knowledge of the firm's capabilities, and the ability to mobilize worldwide resources to capture market opportunities.

Knowledge for a Global Mindset

Knowledge is more attuned toward factual information rather than cognitive and behavioral skills. Knowledge is appreciation of the existence of differences, and it is the appropriate use of knowledge that requires skills. In this particular case, knowledge is to do with a number of factors that make a global manager's work more effective. One critical area of knowledge is mastery over technology, and the ability to use technology, information systems, and telecommunications effectively in an organization's global activities. Another important knowledge-based issue is to know about socio-political factors of different countries, and how these socio-political factors impact business operations. A third area of knowledge is that of culture and cross-cultural issues that impact management.

Thus, apart from the socio-political, economic, and cultural dimensions of the global environment and other countries, global managers need to be aware of the technical dimensions of knowledge. This does not only include the technologies associated with communication, information, and computers, but also the impact of technology on the global operations of the firm. The fact that technology drives business in subtle and powerful ways is something a global manager has to be aware of. Technology impacts the firm's production processes such as new and improved computer numeric control machines that drastically improve quality, to flexible manufacturing systems that make scale economies and long deliveries irrelevant. However, it is the power of technology to make certain products, processes, or services obsolete much faster today than it was a few years ago that is of critical importance. Moreover, with decreased product life cycle and increased and more expensive product development cycles, global managers are faced with a challenge of understanding technology, and assessing its impact on the global operations of the firm.

Increased global competition has impacted a number of areas, most notably manufacturing and communications. The role and function of manufacturing in the global environment have increasingly become a competitive weapon. Some of the more prevalent practices include total quality management (TQM), just-in-time (JIT), factory automation, employee involvement, and outsourcing (Fatehi, 1996). Communication and information technology are critical factors in the operations and successful performance of MNCs. Crossing national borders, MNCs are particularly vulnerable to multiple political, cultural, and economic systems within which they operate, and an effective management information system is crucial for the success of MNCs (Fatehi, 1996).

Knowledge requirements for global managers are the basic building blocks toward a global perspective, and a global mindset. Constantly striving for a bigger, better picture will expand one's knowledge (Rhinesmith, 1993), and that a global manager's technical, business, and industry knowledge is the most fundamental quality that allows him or her to successfully manage the competitive process, both domestic and foreign. This knowledge must be broad as well as deep, and must include a well developed international dimension that includes constant scanning of information, and competitive and market conditions on a global basis. Another important area is country-specific knowledge that implies some understanding of social, political, and economic development and policies of the concerned countries (Lane et al., 1997). This suggests that the relationship between trade, export, industrial, and agricultural development policies are important, as is information on taxation, banking, exchange rules, currency repatriation, and so forth.

As mentioned earlier, country-related information has to be complemented by cross-cultural knowledge as well. This is a true challenge for global managers in that they not only learn about the world and application of business principles, technology, and competitiveness to the international arena, but ultimately a challenge that becomes deeply personal in accepting and adjusting to other values, experiences, and lifestyles (Rhinesmith, 1993). One key to being a successful manager in a global organization is to understand cultural differences that exist among different nations and societies. Only an awareness of the complex phenomenon of culture will allow managers to become open-minded enough to move to the next level that allows an understanding the different dimensions of culture, and how behaviors are affected.

Skills for a Global Mindset

Skills are the ability to put knowledge into action. Managers may be knowledgeable, say for example about culture, but may not possess the complex skills to use that knowledge effectively. The skill in this case is to know how behavior is affected, and what the dimensions of culture are. Knowledge and understanding should be the basis to take action (Lane et al., 1997), as intellectual action may not transfer directly and automatically into a high degree of skill unless considerable practice is involved. Putting knowledge into practice is the essential way to develop skills. One important skill for the global manager is the need for acculturation of other cultures. Another important skill is the ability to lead and indeed leverage diversity to the advantage of the company.

The human factor may ultimately come to represent the new competitive edge for the global corporation, more than physical and other resources (Baird, Briscoe, Tuden, & Rosansky, 1994). The presumed strength of US firms in the quality of their management and their leadership training may in fact be their disguised weakness (Rhinesmith, 1993). A major shift affecting corporate America is from vertical values, such as individualism and autonomy, to horizontal values, such as interdependence and networking. It is a transformation from a predominantly masculine value system to an androgynous one. The new value set calls for each person to have both masculine and feminine characteristics. The nurturing style of expressing power, along with the sharing perspective of empowerment, seems to encourage productivity in high-performing organizations. In reinforcing the process perspective, Ribbens (1996) found in an empirical study that the most effective managers were those who changed their behavior or explained their actions. Managers who tried to influence the expectation of others or who avoided conflicting expectations were regarded as less effective.

The challenges for global managers is one of acculturation, followed by developing skills to lead and motivate a diverse workforce. In today's dynamic international environment, there is great need to be flexible and responsive. The world that managers face is one that is filled with complexity and contradictions. The earlier model of efficiency, hierarchy, control, and centralization is being replaced by a model of responsiveness, decentralization, partnership, and teamwork. To be globally competitive, organizations have to become increasingly more organic in structure, and more fluid in their responses. Structures in organizations have become more and more fuzzy, with ill-defined boundaries. To be globally competitive and responsive in this organic manner, strong process mechanisms need to be developed to support these needs along with a well developed global mindset.

The challenge for global managers is to understand what culture means, and look for creative ways to leverage diversity at the workplace towards greater organizational effectiveness, and higher levels of performance. American attributes of individualism, and goal- and achievement-orientation, along with being competitive and aggressive have to be accommodated with priorities of other cultures that stress shared goals and a communitarian outlook. Culture is a deep-rooted characteristic of persons and groups, and rather than think of changing other people's cultures, global managers should consider how best to use the different cultures of others to meet organizational objectives. Because culture and language are so closely connected, global managers could improve their skills by learning one or more languages. This is likely to increase their effectiveness when using a language that is understood by the people the global manager is managing.

Globalization will obviously require strategic thinking that involves identifying different ways for people to meet their goals and determine which actions will get them where they want to be (Stumpf, 1989). Given the increased complexity that a highly competitive global environment creates, Stumpf suggests that strategic thinking involves a number of key process-oriented factors. These involve a manager's ability, given the changed global circumstances, to know the business and markets, manage subunit rivalry, find and overcome threats, stay on strategy, be an entrepreneurial force, and to accommodate diversity. Awareness and understanding of culture and being able to use diversity of people effectively is essentially a form of strategic thinking.

For global managers to be acculturated requires that they develop greater sensitivity to foster greater levels of understanding. There are considerable benefits that are likely to accrue when managers are sensitive to culture, and have the skills to use this knowledge to benefit both the organization as well as the individual. In short, a combination of knowledge and skills will go a long way in increasing managerial effectiveness in international operations, developing cosmopolitan organizational representatives, improving cross-cultural skills of employees in general, and enhancing job effectiveness. Given the dynamics of today's complex world, a global manager has to have a global mindset based on knowledge and skills so that organizations can survive and grow.

Developing a Global Mindset

"Constantly crossing cultural, language, political, social, and economic borders makes global business complex and uncertain, . . . and constant learning is required for success" (Gregerson et al., 1998, p. 23). Other than constant learning, these authors suggest global managers require adventuresomeness, curiosity, and open-mindedness, among other characteristics. However, the key question is how to develop and sustain the characteristics required for successful global managers? There are a number of strategies for developing successful global leaders (Gregerson et al., 1998), and include:

- *Foreign travel* to put potential leaders in the middle of a country so as to absorb its culture, economy, political system, market, and other crucial details.
- Establish *teams* in which individuals with diverse backgrounds and perspectives work closely together.
- Purposeful *training* developed around an effective and structured learning environment
- *Transfers* to foreign locations to live, work, and learn from the experience of overseas assignments.

The Changing Mindset of Managers

The terms globalization and global outlook have been increasingly used in business literature. As Rhinesmith (1993: p. 2) observes, "Globalization has arrived in the world but not in most of the world's organizations." He goes on to state that there is little doubt that to be viable during the next century, all organizations, whether international or domestic, will need to be more global in their outlook if not in their operations. There is increasing appreciation of the fact that more emphasis has to be placed in developing the human mind and, consequently, business organizations to remain competitive in the face of globalization.

The important question is, in what ways has managerial outlook evolved in the context of thinking globally? Among managers in western nations, there is one fundamental characteristic in the evolution of the global mindset. European managers, for historical, cultural, and political reasons, are generally exposed to a multitude of cultures, regions, languages, and customs. In short, they have far greater environmental heterogeneity to contend with. American managers, on the other hand,

Table 1
The Changing Managerial Perspectives

Mindset	Outlook	Strategy
Ethnocentrism: Home-country perspective	Centralized/Controlled	International
Polycentrism/Regiocentrism: Host-country perspective	Decentralized/Autonomous	Multinational
Geocentrism: Global perspective	Networked/Interdependent	Transnational

are usually exposed to a relatively more homogeneous environment. American managers, generally, are faced with lesser variety in terms of language and culture. One may use Chakravarthy and Perlmutter's (1985) framework of *ethnocentrism, polycentrism, regiocentrism,* and *geocentrism* to explain managerial mindsets (see Table 1).

The initial mindset of managers, especially those from a more homogeneous environment, when thinking globally is one of *ethnocentrism*. In this mindset, managers use a home-country standard as a reference point in managing international activities. The outlook is one of centralized decision-making and high control over operations. Managers with such a mindset may follow an international strategy of maintaining control from the home-country, and replicating home-country systems and procedures abroad. The next level of evolution is one of *polycentrism* or *regiocentrism*, and here, as international investment and involvement increase, the host-country culture and practices assume salience. This may be extended to include a number of similar countries in the region, and host-country standards are used as a reference point in managing company operations. The strategies typically followed are likely to be multinational strategies that emphasize decentralized and autonomous global operations. For the evolutionary process to reach the level of a global mindset, a *geocentric* mindset has to be reached. Here the managerial outlook is one of creating a global network and a preference for following a transnational strategy that is integrative and interdependent.

Managerial Mindsets

There has been a great deal of evolution and change in the perspectives of business managers. Here we will outline some typical mindsets that managers have and can be used to explain how these unique mindsets impact analysis of the environment and drive business decisions. The mindsets that have been conceptualized and developed here, and explained in the sections that follow have been adapted and modified from Baird (1994). The intent is not so much to chart a historical path but to provide an insight into different kinds of mindsets that currently exist, and how much work is involved in moving from one mindset to another. As competition, culture, and nation-states are closely bounded together, this exposition of four mindsets we provide will make clear that some mindsets are less effective in today's world of heightened global competition and increased economic interdependencies. The four mindsets are also closely associated with a firm's strategy that may range from the least global to the most global mindset, and are also indicative of the level of development of a global perspective consisting of a global mindset, knowledge, and skills. The four mindsets we classify and explain in some detail are: (1) Defender; (2) Explorer; (3) Controller; and (4) Integrator.

The Defender

The *defender* is a traditional mindset that is internally focused, and is essentially oriented to the domestic market and its needs (Baird, 1994). The *defender* is basically uninterested in other markets and cultures, and assumes any foreign element in the domestic market to be an unwanted and a temporary aberration. If the activities of foreigners become significant or threatening to any degree, the *defender* looks to the government and other collective representations to protect itself and its markets. It is not uncommon for the *defender* to ask for trade barriers, quotas, duties, laws, and special agreements to obtain protection, and all this is done with the hope of discouraging foreigners from sharing the domestic market. The *defender* is satisfied with its domestic operations, and is generally uninterested in making foreign forays.

The attitudes and beliefs of the *defender* follows the theme that what is different, in terms of culture and people, is dangerous. The *defender* acknowledges that others exist, but is uninterested in their existence. Faced with limited foreign advertising, production, or distribution, the *defender* makes no conscious effort to cultivate or understand foreign clients, competitors, or markets. The *defender* is unaware that there exists a connection, in many cases a strong one, between the activities of foreign competitors and the future of the domestic market. When faced with increased competition, the *defender* prefers to retreat within the protective custody of the domestic legal and political system rather than aggressively confront the foreign competition. There is almost no international element in the business strategies that the *defender* formulates and implements.

A classic example of the *defender* mindset is the reaction of the American steel industry that was faced with a steep decline between the 1960s and the 1980s. Mueller (1985: p. 214) states that "The mid-1960s also marked the start of a political response by the large American steel producers to the increasing presence of foreign competition in their home markets. For this purpose, US producers arranged a truce with their traditional adversary, the United Steel Workers union (USW), and enlisted its support in vigorous publicity and lobbying campaigns against imported steel. These and subsequent efforts had considerable success in obtaining government intervention in the quantities and prices of steel brought into the United States. . . . . " Another example of a *defender* reaction is the attempt by the US footwear industry to obtain import protection (that was denied by President Reagan) in the mid-1980s to combat severe competition from foreign producers. The attempts by the U.S. textile and machine tools industries to seek government relief and intervention in the mid-1970s when faced with stiff foreign competition indicates the working of a *defender* mindset.

The Explorer

The *explorer*, although largely inward-looking like the *defender*, is aware that business opportunities may exist in foreign markets. The *explorer* is aware that there are differences across nationalities and cultures around the world, but does not necessarily consider foreign cultures to be dangerous or to be avoided. To the *explorer*, foreign markets, notwithstanding the different cultures, present opportunities for increasing sales and expanding distribution of products (Baird, 1994). The *explorer*, however, treats its international forays with a lot of caution while moving into foreign markets to find new customers for its products and services. The *explorer* also focuses on closely studying the foreign environment to help increase its own business. However, the international forays of the *explorer* are relatively small when compared to the size of its domestic business.

As long as the mindset is that of the *explorer*, the domestic market will always predominate. The foreign or international business of the *explorer*, whether it be manufacturing, distributing, or selling, is controlled from the head office located in the home country. The foreign forays the *explorer* undertake serve to provide intelligence to the head office to estimate foreign competitive threats, assess political changes, and monitor competitors. The foreign operations of the *explorer* are centrally managed from head office usually with highly centralized decision-making and operational control to oversee the communication and distribution lines established abroad. The *explorer* prefers to follow strategies like exporting and franchising, and has limited investment commitments overseas.

Attempts made some years ago by Lotus Corporation to go international indicate an *explorer* mindset. Although Lotus officials assumed from the start that business productivity software had a natural global market (Yoffe, 1990), nothing substantial materialized until the hiring of Digate as CEO. Although Lotus had considered international issues, its initial international ventures were basically a gigantic mess. Lotus took some lighthearted forays into international markets and its first attempt at an international plan "was bizarre, and needless to say it went nowhere" (Yoffe, 1990: p. 39). Similarly Seiko, the Japanese electronics giant, exhibited an *explorer* mindset in its initial international forays. Seiko's management made a number of trips to the United States and Europe to study production methods used in these locations (Yoffe, 1990). Seiko, however, was quick to learn and developed a more aggressive mindset from that of an *explorer* to one that was interested in developing long-range global plans and a dominant market share.

The Controller

The *controller* is more externally oriented than the *explorer*. The *controller* wishes to dominate the overseas markets through well developed systems and procedures that have worked very well at home. Unlike the *explorer*, the *controller* is willing to make a larger investment commitment internationally, and the proportion of foreign sales to domestic sales is considerable. The *controller*, however, follows an ethnocentric mindset (Chakravarthy & Perlmutter, 1985). Ethnocentrism implies that strategic decisions are guided by the values and interests of the parent company in its international activities. The *controller* establishes full-scale development, production, and distribution facilities abroad (Baird, 1994). Because of a multitude of interactions in different foreign markets on account of the need to produce and sell abroad, the *controller* is forced to understand the nature of culture, and how it impacts business. The *controller* would, however, like to impose the home culture and practices on its foreign operations wherever possible. The foreign cultures and markets must be used to the extent that it furthers the interests of the parent company.

The *controller* may follow some variations of its unique mindset to further its own ends. One such variation is a polycentric mindset which implies that strategic decisions are tailored to suit the cultures of the various countries in which the *controller* operates, or a regiocentric mindset where decisions are blended between the interests of the *controller* and its subsidiaries on a limited regional basis (Chakravarthy & Perlmutter, 1985). The culture of the *controller*, however, is the dominant one in business operations and strategic decision making. The *controller*, while allowing for a certain degree of independence in the activities of its many dispersed units, maintains financial and strategic control. Most often it is in the form of payment to the parent company, or in the parent company making important transfer pricing decisions, distribution of corporate overhead charges, and allocation of resources. Most importantly, the *controller's* head office spends much time and resources on mechanisms for controlling, and to lesser extent coordinating, diverse units and geographic distribution. The approach is that the parent company is supreme, and all important decisions must have the approval and sanction of the head office.

Some industries, dictated by the nature of their products and unique business operations, take on a *controller* like mindset. Typically industries that have a high proportion of franchising in the food industry are likely to exhibit a *controller* mindset. For example, Coke, McDonald's, and Pizza Hut are firms from the fast food industry that, perhaps, exemplify managing and strategizing with a *controller* mindset. A *controller* mindset could also be associated with the traditional multinational corporations where foreign offices and investments were made to replicate home country cultures, systems, and procedures. For instance, McDonald's closing down of its India operations, and Pizza Hut shutting down its Moscow property may indicate shortcomings associated with a *controller* mindset. Recently, Coke overestimated the strength of its brand name among India's consumers as it based its advertising strategy on its worldwide image, only to find the advantage slip to Pepsi that had customized its campaign and specifically tailored it for the Indian market (Prahalad & Lieberthal, 1998). To cite a Coke executive, "We're so successful in international business that we applied a tried and true formula . . . and it was the wrong formula to apply in India" (quoted from Prahalad & Lieberthal, 1998, p. 72).

The Integrator

The *integrator*, we argue, is the manager with a global perspective with a real global mindset based on heightened awareness (knowledge), and enhanced abilities (skills). The *integrator* holds a multiple cultural perspective and creates a worldwide web of relationships with suppliers, developers, designers, distributors, competitors, and customers (Baird, 1994). The *integrator* also weaves together a complex web of partnerships, alliances, and relationships that shift and reconfigure over time as new threats and opportunities appear. The *integrator* is able to use his or her knowledge skillfully in actions leading toward organizational effectiveness. The *integrator* is typified as one who is aware, who understands, and who is competent. The *integrator* creates a global perspective or global mindset by obtaining information about the world, using the information experientially, and develops abilities and skills by being totally immersed in the dynamics of the complex environment. The *integrator* has the ability to first understand the external world with its unique differences and opportunities. The *integrator* is also able to bridge differences in a meaningful way, and finally is able to manage the differences between people, values, and cultures.

The *integrator* is able to leverage differences and synergistically integrate the many disparate elements in his or her complex world. The *integrator* knows not only how to deal with a second party, but is also aware how the second party deals with the third, and how the third party deals with the second (Baird, 1994). *Integrators* coordinate more than they control, and spend a lot of their time and resources improving coordination and cooperation among the different elements of the worldwide system. The *integrator* sees his or her role as that of creating effective and embedded networks, which in turn allows appropriate linking and leveraging. The key to network building is active management of cross-company and cross-cultural issues (Hagel, 1996). A critical function for managers is to develop and sustain mechanisms for knowledge flow and transfer from one part of the global system to another. *Integrators*, in a sense, create information networks to manage mutual interdependencies and to increase the payoff from diversity. *Integrators* understand that competitive success comes from a win-win strategy (Brandenburger & Nalebuff, 1993), and not from the old win-lose (zero sum game) that may be a part of the mindset of *defenders*, *explorers*, and *controllers*. The *integrator* is more interested in leveraging than restraining, integrating than empire building, coordinating than controlling, and managing change than creating stability.

Attempts by Toyota of Japan may be examples of an *integrator* mindset. Toyota is not merely a company but a confederation of firms more properly called the Toyota Group (Yoffe, 1990). It is part of a *keiretsu* whose distinguishing trait is the links among member firms that may be described as a thick and complex web of relationships not matched elsewhere. As Yoffe (1990) mentions, Toyota is at the apex of a hierarchy of firms worldwide that consist of primary, secondary, and tertiary suppliers and subcontractors. Toyota, along with Nissan, Hitachi, Mitsubishi, and other large Japanese firms, represents an *integrator* mindset in its outlook and strategy which is one of leveraging, sharing, and developing complementarities. However, Toyota, while following more of an *integrator's* mindset in some of its domestic operations, still retains a *controller's* mindset when operating overseas[2] in attempting to impose its culture and practices on its foreign operations.

Some of the illustrations provided here have been discussed in articles by Prahalad and Lieberthal (1998) when they suggest that organizations need to discard their imperial mindset regarding international business. The actions of Fiat of Italy is a classic attempt at evolving into and practicing with an integrator's mindset. Ford recently introduced its Escort model in India and priced it around $21,000, putting it straightaway into the luxury car market, and far away from the real market and competition offered by the dominant and popular Maruti–Suzuki priced at $10,000. Fiat, with its experience in Brazil, another big emerging market like India, had already designed a car, the Palio, for the demanding Brazilian market. Fiat is now on the verge of transferring its knowledge and experience to India to compete with Maruti–Suzuki rather than Ford. Similarly, Philips Electronics introduced a two-in-one video-CD player in China that has sold over 15 million units. This product and its marketing is likely to be successful in other emerging Asian economies. Yet the same product has no market in the developed world. In contrast, both Revlon and Kellogg have found it difficult to succeed in China and India because these companies did not approach their markets in a holistic manner. As Prahalad and Lieberthal (1998, p. 72) state, "Tailoring products to the big emerging markets is not a trivial task. Minor cultural adaptations or marginal cost reductions will not do the job. Instead, to overcome an implicit imperialism, companies must undergo a fundamental rethinking of every element of their business model."

From an evolutionary or developmental perspective, the *defender* has little or no global orientation, and also has limited skills and knowledge to effectively operate in a globally competitive environment. The *explorer* has knowledge about the international environment, and a restricted set of skills to operate in the global environment in a limited manner. Because of its many limitations and inadequacies, the *explorer* is able to pursue only a very limited range of international business

Table 2
The Four Mindsets and Global Perspectives

Mindsets →	Defender	Explorer	Controller	Integrator
LEVEL OF GLOBAL PERSPECTIVE	None	Surface level	Intermediate level	Deep level
GLOBAL IDENTITY SELF	Maintain self sufficiency	Define differences	Redefine self	Integrate
OTHERS	Acknowledge	Explore	Control	Leverage diversity

Notes: Adapted from Baird, 1994.

activities on account of its surface level global perspective. The *controller* has more knowledge of the global environment as well as considerably more skills about the international marketplace. The *controller*, however, has a limited global mindset, and consequently it has an ethnocentric-efficiency orientation in its international operations. The *controller* has an intermediate level global perspective. The *integrator*, we suggest, has a well developed and a deep level global perspective. The *integrator* has a true global mindset with the appropriate level of knowledge and skills.

In facing global competitiveness, the *explorer* is the least effective, the *controller* is somewhat more effective, and the *integrator* is the most effective. We suggest that a given mindset is associated with a particular world view and perspective, and with a specific type of strategy. For mindsets and strategies to change, appropriate training efforts have to be made to move it from one mindset to another. Table 2 provides an overview of the four mindsets within a global perspective.

Readers may be concerned over our advocacy of the *integrator* mindset as being appropriate and relevant in today's complex global reality. With competition likely to take place in the big emerging markets of Brazil, China, and India, MNCs will no longer be able to consider these as new markets for existing products. In short, MNCs will have to discard their "imperialist mindset" (Prahalad & Lieberthal, 1998, p. 69), so as to adapt, design, manufacture, and market products that suit the unique requirements of these markets. The mindsets of *defenders, explorers,* and *controllers* will simply not be able to assess, understand, and react to the new global realities. It is only the *integrators* who have developed the mindset, skills, and knowledge to be dynamic and effective players in the global arena. Our argument is that the global mindset is an evolutionary process. Some managers and organizations remain at an early stage of the evolution, and progress to the level of a *defender, explorer,* or *controller.* Other managers and organizations evolve quickly through the various stages, or move effortlessly to mindset of *integrators.* We contend that *integrators* have the required mindset, capability, and flexibility to adapt and manage in today's complex global environment. Having any of the other three mindsets implies both limitations

Figure 3

Integrating and strategizing globally
(adapted from Bartlett & Ghoshal, 1992)

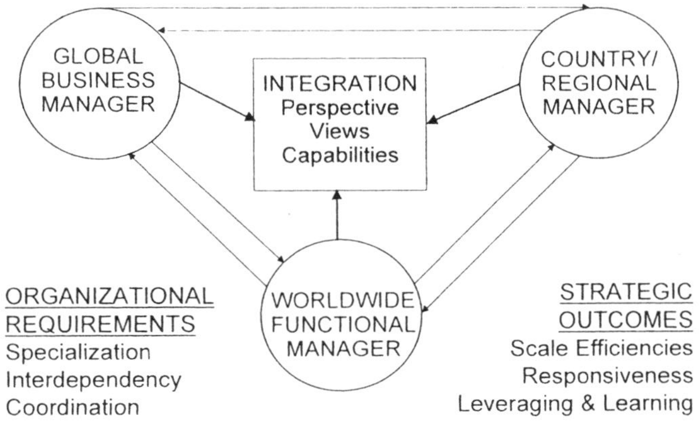

and a lack of capabilities in effectively managing today's complexities.

Strategizing and Integrating Globally

The important issue in having a true global mindset is not to be able to do all things, rather it is to be able to understand the complexities of managing an interdependent and complex global network, and in playing the required part within the network to ensure high degrees of coordinating, leveraging, and integrating. Bartlett and Ghoshal (1992) have suggested that the key functions in a global environment are a combination of specialization and integration. The ability of a manager to integrate comes from having a global mindset that is based on requisite knowledge and skills needed to operate effectively in the global context. Researchers argue that key aspects of international strategic capabilities derive from managers' cognitive processes that balance competing business, country, and functional concerns (Perlmutter, 1969; Prahalad & Doz, 1987; Kogut, 1985; Bartlett & Ghoshal, 1989, and Hedlund, 1993).

This view is supported by Bartlett & Ghoshal (1992) who suggest that there are three fundamental dynamics of global operations (see Figure 3). One, is global scale efficiency and competitiveness, and this is the responsibility of the global business manager. The global business manager's role is to be a strategist, architect, and coordinator. Two, is national level responsiveness and flexibility, and this is the responsibility of the country or regional manager. The country or regional manager's role is one of being a sensor, builder, and contributor. Three, is worldwide leveraging and learning capability, and this is the responsibility of the worldwide functional manager. The worldwide functional manager's role is that of scanner, cross-pollinator and champion. These three dynamics correspond to the business, country, and functional concerns mentioned earlier, and are, according to Bartlett & Ghoshal (1992), the triad on which global strategies can be built. The critical part is the meshing of these forces which entails integrating different perspectives, view balancing, resource leveraging and sharing, and capabilities building (Bartlett & Ghoshal, 1992). The higher the degree of integration, the more global and effective the strategy. Traditionally, there would be a high degree of coordination between two of these three forces, resulting in less than optimal global strategies. With managers developing a global mindset, we suggest that all three forces of strategizing globally can be meaningfully integrated resulting in true and effective global strategies. All three roles require a global mindset, but there is also the need to integrate the multiple pressures and challenges of business, function, and region, and here the manager with a global mindset, irrespective of the level or position within the company, plays a crucial role. In short, a global mindset is required not only at the business, regional, and functional levels, but also at the crucial corporate requirement to integrate all three forces. In addition, managers with a global mindset will need to balance and integrate the forces consisting of scale economies, responsiveness and flexibility, and resource leveraging and capability building.

Conclusion and Discussion

Based on the dynamic changes taking place, there is a need to have global managers with a global perspective. This global perspective consists of a mindset, knowledge, and skills. A global mindset, in its simplest form will allow a manager from one part of the world to be comfortable in another on account of knowledge and skills that are based on understanding and awareness. A global mindset, in other words, will make a manager more competent and effective. A global manager must be able to lead and motivate diverse work teams, and this skill comes from knowing and using knowledge of cultural differences. Global managers have to coach teams as well as to lead. Global managers must seek out and acquire knowledge. Not only must he or she know how to use high technology in managerial activities, but also to understand and assess the impact of technology on the global activities of the firm.

We suggest that globalization has preceded, in many cases, the abilities of managers to grasp with the new and complex realities. As we have stated, there are still many managerial mindsets that are completely out of tune with the requirements of today's global business requirements. The challenge is to identify which mindsets managers belong to, and to understand how their mindsets are inhibiting them from being effective. The next challenge is to create an appropriate environment to move managers from a relatively dysfunctional mindset to one that creates a global perspective.

Notes

1. A version of this paper was presented at the NIBS International Seminar, Rennes International School of Business, France in March, 1997.
2. We are grateful to one of our anonymous reviewers for pointing out why corporations like Toyota may simultaneously pursue different mindsets.

References

Baird, L. (1994). *Meeting global challenges: The executive perspective*. Unpublished working paper. University of Boston, Boston, MA.

Baird, L., Briscoe, J., Tuden, L., & Rosansky, L. M. H. (1994). World class executive development. *Human Resource Planning*, *17*(1): 1–10.

Bartlett, C. K. & Ghoshal, S. (1989). *Managing across borders: The transnational solution*. Boston, MA, The Harvard Business School Press.

Bartlett, C. K. & Ghoshal, S. (1992). What is a global manager. *Harvard Business Review*, Sep-Oct, *70*(5): 124–132.

Berry, J. K. (1990). Linking management development to business strategies. *Journal of Training & Development Journal*, *44*(8): 20–22.

Brandenburger, A. M. & Nalebuff, B. J. (1993). The right game: Use game theory to shape strategy. *Harvard Business Review*, Jul-Aug: 57–71.

Chakravarthy, B. & Perlmutter, H. V. (1985). Strategic planning for a global economy. *Columbia Journal of World Business*, Summer: 3–10.

Doz, Y. L. & Prahalad, C. K. (1991). Managing DMNCs: A search for a new paradigm. *Strategic Management Journal*, Special Issue, *12*: 145–164.

Fatehi, K. (1996). *International management: A cross-cultural and functional perspective*. Upper River Saddle, NJ: Prentice-Hall.

Fayerweather, J. (1982). *International business strategy and administration*. New York, NY: Ballinger.

Fortune. (1995). *March, 20*: 109.

Ghoshal, S., Arnzen, B., & Brownfield, S. (1992). A learning alliance between business and business schools: Executive education as a platform for partnership. *California Management Review*, *35*(1): 50–67.

Global Economic Prospects. (1992). Washington, D. C.: The World Bank.

Gregerson, H. B., Morrison, A. J., & J. S. Black. (1998). Developing leaders for the global frontier. *Sloan Management Review*, *1*(40): 21–39.

Hagel, J. (1996). Spider versus spider. *McKinsey Quarterly*, *1*: 4–18.

Hedlund, G. (1993). Assumptions of hierarchy and heterarchy with application to the management of the multinational corporation. In S. Ghoshal and D. E. Westney (Eds.), *Organization theory and the multinational corporation* (pp. 211–236). New York, NY: St. Martin's Press.

Jusela, G. E. (1994). Meeting the global competitive challenge: Building systems that learn on a large scale. In W. L. French, C. H. Bell, & R. A. Zawacki (Eds.) *Organization development and transformation: Managing effective change*, (pp. 369–397). Boston, MA: Irwin.

Kefalas, A. G. S. & Neuland, E. W. (1997). Global mindsets: An exploratory study. A paper presented at the Academy of International Business Conference in Monterrey, Mexico.

Kets de Vries, M. F. R., & Mead, C. (1992). The development of the global leader within the multinational corporation. In V. Pucik, N. M. Tichy, & C. K. Bartlett (Eds.), *Globalizing management: Creating and leading the competitive organization* (pp. 187–205). New York, NY: John Wiley & Sons, Inc.

Kogut, B. (1985). Designing global strategies: Profiting from operational flexibility. *Sloan Management Review*, *26*(4): 27–38.

Lane, H. W., DiStefano, J. J. & Maznevski, M. L. (1997). *International management behavior*, 3rd Edition. Cambridge, MA, Blackwell Publishers, Inc.

Mueller, H. (1985). The changing U.S. position in the international market: Output, trade and performance. In M. Hochmuth and W. Davidson (Eds.), *Revitalizing American industry: Lessons from our competitors* (pp. 213–262). Cambridge, MA: Ballinger Publishing Company.

Murtha, T. P., Lenway, S. A. & Bagozzi, R. P. (1998). Global Mind-sets and cognitive shift in a complex multinational corporation. *Strategic Management Journal, 19*(2): 97–114.

Perlmutter, H. V. (1969). The tortuous evolution of the multinational corporation. *Columbia Journal of World Business*. Jan-Feb: 9–18.

Porras, J. I. & Silvers, R. C. (1991). Organization development and transformation. *Annual Review of Psychology, 42*: 51–78.

Prahalad, C. K. & Doz, Y. L. (1981). An approach to strategic control in MNCs. *Sloan Management Review, 22*: 5–13.

Prahalad, C. K. & Doz, Y. L. (1987). *The multinational mission: Balancing local demands and global vision*. New York, The Free Press.

Prahalad, C. K. & Lieberthal, K. (1998). The end of corporate imperialism. *Harvard Business Review*, July-August: 69–79.

Ribbens, B. A. (1996). Torn between expectations? *Academy of Management Executive, 10*(2): 65–66.

Rhinesmith, S. H. (1993). *A manager's guide to globalization: Six keys to success in a changing world*. New York, Irwin.

Stumpf, S. A. (1989). Work experiences that stretch the managers' capacity for strategic thinking. *Journal of Management Development, 8*(5): 31–39.

Tichy, N. M. (1992). Global development. In V. Pucik, N. M. Tichy, & C. K. Bartlett (Eds.), *Globalizing management: Creating and leading the competitive organization* (pp. 206–224) New York: John Wiley & Sons, Inc.

Yip, G. S. (1992). *Total global strategy: Managing for worldwide competitive advantage*. Englewood Cliffs, NJ, Prentice Hall.

Yoffe, D. B. (1990). *International trade and competition: Cases and notes in strategy and management*. New York, NY, McGraw Hill.

[3]

© Academy of Management Executive, 1998, Vol. 12, No. 4

Charting the landscape of global competition: Reflections on emerging organizational challenges and their implications for senior executives

Shaker A. Zahra and Hugh M. O'Neill

Executive Overview

In November 1998, authors of papers in the special issue met to discuss their papers, receive feedback, and integrate themes. After the presentations, the authors devoted a morning to discussion of common themes in the papers, and the identification of opportunities for further integration and research. This article presents a synthesis of those discussions.

Issues of global competitiveness currently dominate the professional business press. Daily, almost hourly, reports about problems and opportunities in different countries and industries prompt thought and analysis. This public visibility, though, does not guarantee depth of insight or lead to substantive change. Indeed, Adler and Bartholomew (1992) note "strategy is internationalizing faster . . . than the managers and the executives themselves." Slow learning managers and firms risk becoming extinct, selected out by an increasingly demanding and unforgiving competitive environment.

Environmental determinism, though, is an expensive form of education. We hope individuals, and organizations, can learn to proactively adapt. That learning is dependent, in part, on the store of scholarly research available to inform the learning. And, some researchers can be just as slow as managers in adapting. Some would say, slower. Consequently, the rate of research about global competitiveness may not match the rate of change in the business environment. In an attempt to facilitate the development of research on global competitiveness, we issued a call for papers for a special AME issue, and held a conference to explore emerging research into these efforts.

In this article, we present a summary analysis of some of the key ideas that emerged from the conference. In presenting this analysis, one of our goals is to document the obvious—there is a considerable learning opportunity in this field. Managers and firms need to learn more about the changing patterns of global competitiveness, the driving forces behind these changes, and the implications of these changes for companies' operations—and, indeed, survival. Managers looking to the scholarly literature for guidance quickly realize that our reservoir of knowledge is modest.

Our second goal in writing this article is more aggressive. We present a summary model, as a way to guide future research in this exciting, emerging field of inquiry. The world is changing, and as a consequence, our way of thinking about that world may have to change in significant ways.

The article is based on two forms of analysis. First, we synthesized the ideas presented at the conference on global competitiveness. The varied papers were textually analyzed and thematically summarized. The themes were then presented to a panel of experts (conference authors), who did a form of a Delphi analysis on the themes, to identify the most important questions that might be investigated in the field. Second, we then used inductive means to categorize the themes presented, to develop a model that represented what we believe to be the most important implications of the conference and its papers.

Issues—what do we need to know?

Table 1 lists the issues, which were first identified in a review of the series of papers, and then ranked by participants in the start of a Delphi process. Participants were asked to rank the themes as very critical and important, important but not critical, or interesting but not critical/important. The table presents the themes grouped within these categories.

Table 1
Issues as Ranked by Expert Authors

CRITICAL AND IMPORTANT
Who are the competitors?
What global leadership approaches will cause above average returns?
Organization as community
Acquisition of knowledge
Choosing the alliance to maximize learning
How do managers in the firm become global?
The it requirements of a global organization
IT—source of distinctive competence or minimum floor for entry
Purpose—how does it integrate the competing values (financial, hr, market, etc)?
What are the requirements for strategic thinking?
CRITICAL
Activism by institutional investors
Defining purpose
The it requirements of a transnational organization
Is reputation more or less important in global (versus domestic) competition?
Cooperation as a response to institutional investors
What forces break the inertia of domestic orientation? What cause shift to global id?
How executives design a global human resource strategy
The structure of the alliance as a predictor of learning
How does reputation cross borders?
Short term and long term pressures
What are "clusters" in international competition?
Sense-making/cognition of leader
Alliance as a means to learning versus other forms of learning
Reputation—what does the exec do to manage reputation?
INTERESTING
How competitors view each other, and transmute to global firms
Convergence across changing cognitive structures
How is the strategy related to the hr design
Flows versus stocks, or the dynamics in capability
What are the short term vs long term issues that are common in rep management?
How does a reputation turn bad?
How does a reputation turn good?
The virtual organization—unique or ubiquitous?

In this article, we focus discussion on those questions identified as the most important issues. The first two issues—who are the competitors, and what global leadership strategies create above average returns—serve as an illustration of how little we do know about global competition. The reasons for their prominent placement on this list goes far beyond their role as symbols of our knowledge shortfalls, however. For example, in their paper on strategic groups, Thomas, Pollack and Gorman (1998) suggest that the strategic group (i.e., who the competitors are) is an important linking point between environments and managers. They write that "the structure of the industry both determines and is determined by the managerial perceptions of the environment." More importantly, they note that the industry is made up of a collection of strategic groups. In turn, then, the thinking and action of managers in the firm is strongly influenced by their perception and definition of their strategic group.

Given the importance of the strategic group as a shaper of perceptions and/or interpretations, the question of "who is the competitor" takes on great importance in predicting the pattern and outcomes in global competition. The characteristics of the strategic group, as well as the relationship between an initial global competitor and the strategic group, will influence the unfolding patterns of competition.

The characteristics of the strategic group, as well as the relationship between an initial global competitor and the strategic group, will influence the unfolding patterns of competition.

Take, for example, the presence of a homogeneous strategic grouping focused domestically and the entry of a competitor (or perhaps series of competitors) from a distant point on the globe. The intertwined perceptions of the homogenous strategic group may lead to an exaggerated focus on differences between the new entrant and the established companies, because the focus on differences maintains the integrity of the initial grouping. In turn, the focus on differences may lead to a mutual discounting of the value of those differences and simultaneous enhancement of the value of the common characteristics of the homogenous group. In a sense, then, the homogeneity of the initial strategic group can lead to a form of strategic blindness that obscures managers' realization that the very concept of their industry is undergoing fundamental changes. The incumbent group doesn't react, or reacts too slowly, to an entrant and competition intensifies. Such ineffective, indeed wrong, responses to industry shifts can have devastating consequences for firms and their shareholders.

This hypothesis about the impact of homogeneity on competitive entrance and response captures the history of the American automobile industry, with respect to Japanese entry to the American market, reasonably well. Perhaps more importantly, history may be repeating itself. In their paper, Ireland and Hitt (1998) describe Samsung Group's ambitious plan to enter the automotive market in 1998, and to rank among the top ten by 2010. Industry incumbents (a homogenous group?) are dumbfounded. Hitt and Ireland quote one observer: "There's no *logical* opening in the marketplace where Samsung can step in (emphasis added). . ."

What determines this logic? In large part, if Thomas and his colleagues are right, the observer's experience in an established strategic group influences any notion of what is "logical." Logic may differ for newer competitors. Unencumbered by undepreciated fixed assets or outdated cognitive maps of the industry, a new competitor can redefine the rules. Unencumbered by a previous set of supplier or customer commitments, a new competitor can redefine the value chain. Unencumbered by notions about the dominant value of profits, an entrant can define a longer time frame to wait for returns. The point is, the competitor brings a new logic to the industry that often defies that industry's recipe, one unlikely to be discerned by an observer who defines the entry as "illogical."

Just as this industry observer may bring a set of reference-group induced blinders to the issues of global competition, researchers engaged in the study of competition wear paradigm-induced blinders. The study of business as the study of competition may be a reflection of the historically unique American experience. American firms typically compete with each other for the purpose of maximizing shareholder wealth. Globally, some non-American firms may cooperate with each other for the purpose of increasing domestic employment. Their rules, and consequently, their game, may be different. As a result, the research questions become more complex. "Who is the competition" may not mean what companies, but what national systems. The question may then become is competition or cooperation better (e.g., Moore, 1996). The "logic" that assumes a given system of industrial organization is better, therefore, may be faulty. At minimum, this logic should be subjected to more serious cross-national investigations. Strategic groups are important, and American researchers (as members of a group) may be blinded to the limits of their thinking. Other national systems of industrial organizations have successfully proven themselves where it counts the most: in the global market arena. They have shown that countries can achieve excellence and do this while employing different strategies.

Like the first two issues, the issue of the organization as community illustrates the profound influence that trends in global competition hold for the way we do and should think about organizations. Ireland and Hitt (1998) describe the organizational community wherein "sharing among inspired and committed citizens facilitates the emergence of the collective magic that creates intellectual capital and knowledge." Sharing? Citizen? Magic? This is a long way from the opportunistic world of agency theory.

A key component in the Ireland and Hitt organizational community is the concept of the great group, where members of the group equally share responsibility for the outcomes of group work. They describe relationships of mutual influence, where "every member of the great group serves, at different times, as a leader, peer or subordinate." Ireland and Hitt strongly imply that top management teams—the CEO's team—should be a great group.

Don Hambrick, in a talk about his study of CEO's, repeated a story told during one of his interviews. "Every CEO has four to six direct reports, two or three of whom would stab the CEO to get his or her job."

Every CEO has four to six direct reports, two or three of whom would stab the CEO to get his or her job.

We'll call this the ignoble group. Which is more common in practice? Ireland and Hitt's great group or Hambrick's ignoble group? We suspect a poll of most observers of organizational life in the last years of the twentieth century would say they'd seen few ignoble groups, but even fewer great groups, in practice.

Ireland and Hitt quote Drucker (1997) who writes that the future "has already happened." Has anything happened that might portend great groups and organizational communities? One strong trend in recent years has been the escalation of CEO salaries, with a consequent increase of the separation between the CEO and all members of the firm, financially and socially. This separation makes it difficult, if not impossible, to develop a sense of responsible stewardship that leads to the development of a great group. A second recent trend has been the move to contingent workers. As Hitt, Keats and DeMarie note, globalization requires flexibility, and contingent workers provide some flexibility because they are easier to let go. How frequently does a country let go of its citizens? Can contingency workers and salary escalation co-exist with organizational community and great groups?

Not easily. But, as Einstein once observed, the thinking that caused our problems in the first place is likely to be incapable of resolving them. As Roberts, Kossek, and Ozek (1998) cleverly illustrate in their paper, problems in global firms require a different mindset. Tradition won't work; the past doesn't always reveal the solutions to new problems.

Recent efforts to extend ownership to large numbers of professional workers may be the future that's already happened, the key to organizational communities and great groups. Firms like Microsoft and Cisco offer stock options to all their professional workers. While there is still a gap between the CEO and ordinary citizens, some citizens can make fortunes. These highly educated and well paid citizens demonstrate the will to reinvest in their own training and education, should technological or global conditions render them redundant. These wealth enhancing payment systems serve the same function as lifetime employment once did for Japan's companies (and may still do for some members and some companies).

Is employee ownership the path to the "magic" that Ireland and Hitt describe? Is this form of binding the interests of owners and professionals superior to the Japanese system of lifetime employment? We don't know. Chances are, though, the winning options for organizational design can be uncovered through better theory and improved research.

Quite logically, given the complex issues suggested to this point, an important issue identified by the experts was that of the acquisition of knowledge. Do firms learn? How?

Based on the material presented to this point, we can develop some interesting propositions about learning. Thomas and his colleagues suggest a link between characteristics of the strategic group and learning. So, for example, homogeneity and stability in groups should foster less learning. Heterogeneity and instability (perhaps up to some threshold point) should lead to more learning. Similarly, organizations designed as communities and organizations dominated by great groups should be more creative than their traditional counterparts.

Hitt, Keats, and DeMarie (1998) note that "in periods of dynamic change that produce strategic discontinuities, learning must be nonlinear. . ." If the change from nonglobal to global competition is a dynamic change, then organizational learning must be nonlinear. The implications of nonlinear learning for organizations (and individuals) are important even if the incidence of dynamic change or strategic discontinuities is limited.

The requirements for non-linear learning are somewhat paradoxical. For example, Hitt, Keats and DeMarie note that firms attempt to develop strategic flexibility by preserving and developing human capital in areas of the firm's core competence. But core competencies don't necessarily transfer across discontinuous environments. One resolution to this difficulty is to adopt a second order definition of core competence, by suggesting that in a dynamic environment a firm's core competence is the ability to abandon traditional core competencies and replace them with new ones. Unfortunately, empirical evidence about firm experience in adapting to competency destroying change does not lead to sanguine conclusions about an organization's abilities to do this. Lei, Hitt and Bettis (1996) aptly describe conditions that can enhance the evolution of dynamic core competencies.

A second resolution of this difficulty is to identify the conditions under which core competencies are likely to survive the conditions of discontinuous environmental change. Prahalad and Hamel (1990) identify one set of conditions in their initial specification of the concept, when they suggest that the core competency should have value across several types of products and industries. The diversification across industries can offer some protection against discontinuous change in any single industry.

		Environment	
		Continuous	Discontinuous
Resource-Based	Established	+	+/−
Core Competence	Emerging	(−)?	−→+

A third resolution of this difficulty rests on the Ireland and Hitt's description of the collective magic of the organizational community. Markets exhibit remarkable resiliency in the long term, as customers appear and disappear and producers band and disband over time. Organizational communities, if formed, may be able to achieve similar survival properties.

Alternately, a fourth resolution of the paradoxes around discontinuous change may lie in promoting options that lessen the friction in market changes. Perhaps, some organizations should be abandoned, rather than maintained, if they can't learn. Managers should recognize the upper limits of organizational evolutions; sometimes the best way to maximize shareholders' wealth is to disband the organization and let shareholders invest their money elsewhere. Learning when and how to dissolve organizations is a skill, not a sign of organizational defect.

One form of learning, and an issue given the same ranking by the conference participants as the acquisition of knowledge, is the use of alliances to maximize learning. Once again, the material presented previously provides a foundation for interesting issues about alliances. Alliances within a competitive group, especially a homogenous competitive group, will lead to less new learning. Ireland and Hitt's organizational communities may foster the conditions that favor learning, by increasing the firm's absorptive capacity. Alliances in organizational communities, especially those that increase heterogeneity within the firm's reference group, can foster more learning, especially the acquisition of radically new insights and knowledge.

Inkpen's work enriches these propositions. He notes that the acquisition of knowledge is a three part process—acquiring, transferring and integrating. The propositions about a partner's position in the firm's reference group apply more to the first stage in the process, rather than either the second or the third stage. In applying the construct of homogeneity to the transference and integration of knowledge, we'd suggest that high levels of homogeneity increase the opportunity for knowledge transference and integration. In contrast, high levels of heterogeneity would decrease the opportunity for transference and integration. Inkpen provides support for this proposition, in describing a partner's comment about an alliance: "what the joint venture does would never work in our company." Put differently, since it's not similar to what we've done before (i.e., not homogeneous), it won't work here.

Hence, once again, we have a paradox. The knowledge that is most likely to transfer across an alliance is the knowledge most similar to the firm's existing knowledge base.
Nonlinear learning, that type of learning that Hitt, Keats and DeMarie assert may be required in shifts to global competition, doesn't transfer well or integrate well. Inkpen notes that unrelated knowledge is difficult to acquire (or transfer or integrate), and tacit knowledge is difficult to acquire (or transfer or integrate). Unrelated knowledge or tacit knowledge is nonlinear.

The knowledge that is most likely to transfer across an alliance is the knowledge most similar to the firm's existing knowledge base.

The solution to the paradox requires research. Apparently, firms do need some investment in learning to learn. Inkpen's thesis suggests that individual tolerance for ambiguity is one of the barriers to learning. He writes: "With ambiguity comes misunderstanding and reluctance to dig deeper into the value of knowledge." One way to invest in learning to learn, then, may be to increase individual tolerance for ambiguity in the firm. As noted earlier, one way to increase individual will to respond to ambiguity may be to provide opportunities for financial rewards. This tolerance for ambiguity flourishes primarily in environments where organizational cultures value and welcome discontinuous change. Ireland and Hitt's organizational communities would cherish and maintain such cultures.

Petrick, Scherer, Brodzinski, Quinn, and Ainina suggest that global leaders demonstrate behavioral complexity: "excellent global leaders are able to understand complex issues from different managerial perspectives and act out a cognitively complex strategy by playing multiple roles in a highly integrated and complementary way." Hart and Quinn (1993) provided evidence showing a positive relationship between high levels of CEO behavioral complexity and firm performance. We might expect that behavioral complexity increases tolerance for ambiguity, and increases receptivity to learning unrelated knowledge or tacit knowledge.

These notions of tolerance for ambiguity, behavioral complexity, and capacity for learning are directly related to the next issue identified as most important by our group of experts. How do managers become global?

Interestingly, the presumption that managers do become global may, in itself, extend a past paradigm beyond its use. We can imagine this urbane, multi-lingual world traveler who moves smoothly from one continent to the next, from one culture to the next, from one century to the next. As of yet, though, the global chameleon doesn't exist in great numbers. And is very expensive. Roberts, Kossek and Ozeki make both these points, in observing that aspatial careers are rare, and that expatriates usually cost three times the expense of local nationals.

Given the rare nature and the high expense of global managers, an important issue then is how the problems of global competition become manageable. Roberts and colleagues provide a set of solutions, combining flexibility in task assignments with astute use of information technology for deployment decisions and communication technology for teaming. Through the interface of people and technology, rather than one manager becoming global, several managers can coordinate their activity to act globally. The task of enabling seamless coordination is distinctly different, and perhaps more complex, than the task of making individual managers global.

One tool for the creation of these global teams is the use of information technology, an issue that ranked as very important in our experts' opinion.

Boudreau, Loch, Robey, and Straub describe relationships between information technologies and forms of global strategies, specifically, Bartlett and Ghoshal's transnational strategy. Information and communication technology make globalization accessible. For example, groupware provides a key means for managers to communicate easily with minimal disruption due to space and time. Similarly, language translation software can facilitate communication across languages.

These technologies are so new, though, that we know little about what they can do, and perhaps even less about new problems they may cause. Given the needs for coordination in a global enterprise, the computer's ability to speed transaction processing is vital. In a dynamic environment, though, relationships are also important. Electronically facilitated relationships may not provide the enduring bonds necessary for actors to resolve conflict or manage ambiguity. Therefore, the issue of balance between tech touch and personal touch is important, and an issue that is not well understood. The demands for transactional and relational relationships may differ across strategies, in ways we've yet to understand.

We've also yet to understand the problems that computer-facilitated communication may cause. Just as exposure to homogenous competitor groups can limit the range of thinking within an organization, common exposure to standard data might induce a form of rigidity in organizations.

One important issue about information technology (IT) is its ability to offer firms sustainable advantage. The technologies described by Boudreau and her colleagues are generic—any organization can use them. There is some evidence that technological innovations diffuse quickly through organization populations, and sometime are oversold or overpurchased. Under conditions of fast diffusion, information technologies may not provide distinct advantage to their adopters. If this is the case, then the organization's ability to create its own unique uses for technology increases in importance.

The final two issues our experts identified as most important are purpose and strategic thinking—two of the perennial topics of discussion and debate in the literature.

Hitt, Keats, and DeMarie describe the importance of developing a strategic vision, which we interpret as similar to purpose. While the theme of developing and communicating common vision or purpose is almost dogma in current thought about strategy, the shift to global competition should foster renewed thinking about the characteristics and impact of vision.

The most frequently cited characteristic of vision is its singularity, that is, the entire firm shares one vision. However, it is not clear that singularity of vision is either possible or desirable in a global organization.

Hitt, Keats, and DeMarie provide two hints at why singular visions may not be a characteristic of global organizations. First, they describe the need for a dynamic core in the global organization. If cores are dynamic, visions should be dynamic as well. Second, they note the need for contingent employees in the global organization. The vision, at least implicitly, will differ for contingent employees.

Most, if not all, discussions of vision describe the construct at the firm level, and describe the content of the vision in positive terms. As Thomas and his colleagues aptly noted, the unit of analysis most relevant for discussing firm behavior may be the strategic group. In switching to this level, we can theorize that firms in the same strategic group have similar (or perhaps the same) vision. A relevant strategic grouping of firms might be based on the firm's country of origin. To the extent that firms from the same country share similar visions, those visions might represent nationalistic aspirations. Is Pepsi-Cola a global firm, or an American firm with global distribution? Is Honda a global firm, or a Japanese firm with global distribution? It's unlikely that either Pepsi-Cola or Honda would explicitly verbalize their nationalistic intentions. It is easy to imagine, though, that some nation states see more than clever color schemes behind Pepsi's red, white, and blue advertising theme.

The final issue identified by the experts as most important is the issue of strategic thinking. The ability to think beyond the limited field view provided by existing strategic groups, the will to overcome potential learning biases in alliances, the skill to think in non-linear manners, all are aspects of strategic thinking that we've discussed to this point.

Roberts, Kossek and Ozeki describe a situation that illustrates a form of bounded rationality (irrationality) caused by cultural differences. Here is their story:

> Norwegian work-family values differ from those in the U.S., and it is common for men who are senior in their organizations to leave work at 3 P.M. to pick up their children after school. While U.S. norms are beginning to tilt somewhat more toward family in the work-family balance, leaving at 3:00 in the afternoon still signals a lack of commitment to the job in most U.S. workplace. . .it was very difficult for U.S. managers to trust that their Norwegian employees would get the job done in a crisis

It is unclear if the US managers understood the source of their distrust in this environment. It is unclear if the Norwegians perceived the mistrust, and acted in kind. Our guess is that the US managers did not fully understand either the cause or the consequences of their mistrust, and the Norwegians did feel and respond to this mistrust.

The story illustrates how subconscious syllogism can undermine relationships in a firm building a global strategy. Strategic thinking requires an understanding of the subtle blinders imposed by culture and strategy, and the links between thought, action and reaction

Strategic thinking requires an understanding of the subtle blinders imposed by culture and strategy, and the links between thought, action and reaction.

We have commented on the issues identified as most important by participants at the conference. The differences in ranking are slight. To this point, we've tried to demonstrate how those issues labeled as most important are inter-related, and we could echo that theme throughout all the items.

For the sake of suggesting research themes, we grouped the items based on their similarity.

An organizing model

Figure 1 presents our summary model of the themes identified in this special conference on global competitiveness.

The dependent variable in the model is global competition. While the level of interest in global competition is quite high, it is not apparent that global competition is an accomplished fact in all industries. Some industries have been global for decades. Other industries are fast approaching global status. Still other industries have strong cross-national competition, while some remain predominantly national in orientation. The level of global competition, then, is a dependent variable in our model.

There are at least four characteristics of global competition that might be predicted: the overall level of rivalry among in the globalized industry, the level of globalization, the rate of movement to globalization, and nature of the change driving globalization.

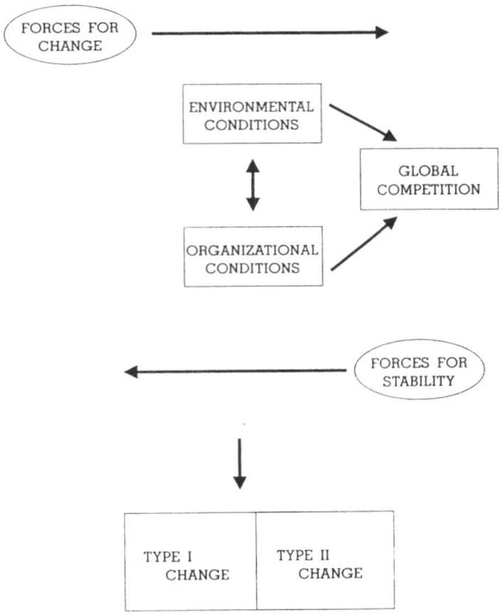

FIGURE 1
Summary Model

The model is a force-field model, in that there are forces for stability and forces for change toward global competition. These forces lead to creative tensions that propel managers to act; to redraw their industries' boundaries; to adopt new ideas.

There are two classes of independent variables in the model (the environment and the organization) and an interaction effect that reflects the joint forces of the environmental and organizational variables.

Finally, we believe there are two types of adaptation to a global state in the model.

Throughout the papers presented in the conference and appearing in this special issue, the environment is viewed as an influential force in determining the rate and type of change toward global competition. Specific aspects of the environment include the competitors, the relationships between the competitors, the clusters among the competitors, and the activism by investors (or other powerful external stakeholders). Any or all these variables can profoundly influence patterns in global competition.

Organizational factors also influence the rate of organizational response to global competition. For example, organizational reputation may or may not transfer across borders. Organization managers vary in their cognitive responses to global competition, both because managers differ to what they actually see, and differ in response when seeing the same thing. Organizations vary widely in their ability to respond to different types of change.

Factors in the external environment and the organization interact, challenging managers to respond creatively and act in innovative ways. For example, a competitive group will have members high and low in reputation. Actions by members on different ends of the reputation scale may be perceived differently, and may result in different rates of movement toward global competition. Similarly, entrants may be perceived as low or high in reputation, and therefore trigger responses that will differ among low and high reputation producers. In tomorrow's global marketplace, organizational reputation and identity will play more significant roles in shaping competitive rivalries, within and across strategic groups or nations.

There are two different types of adaptation to global competition.

Type I is best described as classic adaptation pattern. The rate of change in the environment is evolutionary, and a central executive formulates plans for globalizing the firm, and implements those plans. The environment and the organization go through predictable phases or stages in the change process.

Type II is best described as an emergent adaptation pattern. Here, the rate of change in the environment is revolutionary, and a number of actors engage in a series of disjointed steps in an attempt to keep up with the frequently unanticipated changes.

Given this general model, several points might be made about the papers presented in the conference.

First, global competition is generally accepted as a given, and variance in either the rate or type of global competition is rarely mentioned. We conclude, therefore, that it would be useful to learn more about patterns of global competition.

Second, only a few of the papers specifically address the influence of the environment as it relates to patterns in global competition. This is understandable, as there has been limited time to understand how to define variation in types or levels of global environments. Fortunately, the paper by Hitt et al. offers an interesting portrayal of tomorrow's global landscape.

Third, given the lack of attention to the environment, we know little about the interactions between the environment and the organization. We believe that these interactions between environments and organizations provide the best opportunities for explaining variance in future global competition.

Fourth, most of the papers give only limited recognition to the Type II form of adaptation. Of course, we need first to know the proportion of changes to global competition that require Type II adaptation. If the proportion is anything like we imagine, then we need to know more about the art or science of Type II adaptation.

The authors represented in this special issue, and the speakers at our conference, have provided a great service, and given us grand ideas. These ideas provide a foundation for better practice and better research. It's up to us, as executives and researchers alike, to build on that foundation. Let the building continue!

About the Authors

Shaker A. Zahra is Professor of Strategic Management at the J. Mack Robinson College of Business Administration at Georgia State University in Atlanta, Georgia. His research interests include global strategy, entrepreneurship in established and young companies, and global aspects of technology management in emerging industries. He is the author or coauthor of five books. His research has appeared in several journals that include the *Academy of Management Journal, Strategic Management Journal, Journal of Management, Journal of Management Studies, Decision Sciences,* Journal of *Business Venturing, Academy of Management Executive,* among others. He has served on the editorial boards of 10 journals and served as guest co-editor of special issues of the *Academy of Management Review* and *Entrepreneurship: Theory* *and Practice*. The recipient of several research and teaching awards, Professor Zahra has been as a guest lecturer at several universities outside the U.S.

Hugh M. O'Neill is an associate professor and chair of the management area at the Kenan-Flagler Business School, the University of North Carolina at Chapel Hill. A graduate of Syracuse University (BA), Polytechnic Institute of New York (MS), and the University of Massachusetts (PhD), he is the outgoing editor of the *Academy of Management Executive* and is a former member of the executive board of the Academy of Management's business policy and strategy division. O'Neill's research interests are in downsizing, entrepreneurship, management, new business information, strategic management, and strategic management planning and implementation. He has been published in the *Academy of Management Review*, the *Journal of International Management*, *Strategic Management Journal*, and the *Academy of Management Executive*.

[4]

Selecting and Developing the Global Versus the Expatriate Manager: A Review of the State-of-the-Art

Vladimir Pucik, Professor, IMD, Lausanne, Switzerland; Tania Saba, Assistant Professor, School of Industrial Relations, University of Montreal

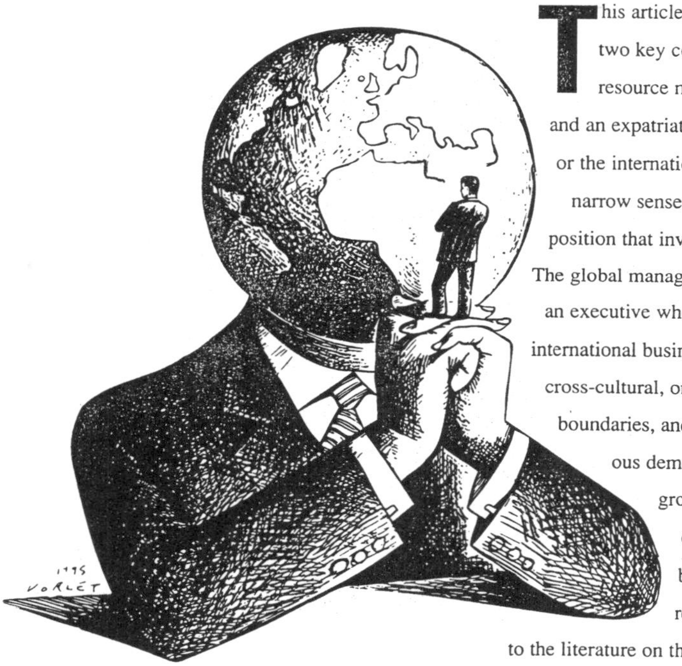

This article presents a working definition of two key concepts in international human resource management: a global manager and an expatriate manager. The expatriate manager or the international manager is defined, in a narrow sense, as an executive in a leadership position that involves international assignments. The global manager is defined, in a broad sense, as an executive who has a hands-on understanding of international business, has an ability to work across cross-cultural, organizational, and functional boundaries, and is able to balance the simultaneous demands of short-term profitability and growth. The article's objectives are to clarify the main differences between the two concepts, to review the principal contributions to the literature on this subject, and to identify the organizational processes and human resource management tools that can influence both the success of the expatriate assignments and the development of global competencies.

"The thing that wakes me up in the middle of the night is not what might happen to the economy or what our competitors might do next. What does wake me up is worrying about whether or not we have the leadership capability and the talent to implement the new and more complex global strategies."
–Dave Whitman, CEO, Whirlpool Corporation

Defining the Expatriate vs. the Global Manager

It is widely agreed that the critical factor for companies to succeed in global competition is effective development of global managers and executives (Pucik, 1985; Bartlett & Ghoshal, 1989; Evans, 1992; Tichy & Sherman, 1993; Gates, 1994). However, in management development literature, there seems to be a great deal of confusion about the meaning of various terms defining expatriate/international/global managers. In an effort to clarify the differences between the expatriate and the global manager, this article explores the definitions of the two concepts, and explains the differences in behaviors, competencies, and characteristics of the two types of managers. The article also identifies and compares the human resource practices necessary for an effective development of the expatriate and global managers.

Building and sustaining organizational capabilities for global operations is a critical challenge for most globalizing firms. Meeting this challenge requires changes in cognitive processes through which managers frame business problems.

Building and sustaining organizational capabilities for global operations is a critical challenge for most globalizing firms (Nohria & Ghoshal, 1997). Meeting this challenge requires changes in cognitive processes through which managers frame business problems (Murtha, Lenway & Bagozzi, 1998). Global thinking places high value on sharing information, knowledge, and experience across national, functional, and business boundaries and on balancing competing country, business, and functional priorities that emerge in the globalization process. This set of attitudes is often described as global mindset.

The emphasis on the mindset helps to differentiate between expatriate (international) and global managers. The definition of an expatriate/international manager is linked to the location of the assignment whereas the global manager is defined by his or her frame of mind. The term "expatriate (or international) manager" defines an executive who is able to assume a leadership position fulfilling international assignments across countries and cultures. In this review, the terms expatriate manager and "international manager" are used as equivalents, as these terms are interchangeable in most of the literature. The term "global manager" (or "transnational manager" as it is sometimes called in the literature) usually refers to an executive assigned to a position with a cross-border responsibility, who has a flexible and open mind, with a well-rounded understanding of international business and an ability to work across cross-cultural and cross-functional boundaries, who perceives global competition as an opportunity, and who is able to balance the simultaneous demands of global integration and national responsiveness (Pucik, 1991; Bartlett & Ghoshal, 1989; 1992). Some global managers may be expatriates; many, if not most, have been expatriates at some point in their career, but probably only few expatriates are global managers.

A literature review[1] shows that although a great number of studies deal with the international or the expatriate manager, there seem to be fewer studies (most of them conceptual, not empirical) about global managers. Within the abundant research on expatriate managers, most of the work has been focused on the issue of selecting managers for international assignments resulting in lists of criteria, competencies, and characteristics that the international manager should possess, as well as on the identification of personality and psychometric tests that could be used to measure such personal qualifications. At the same time, researchers have analyzed the causes of failure in overseas assignments and have introduced HR practices that would help organizations select, develop, and retain competent expatriate managers (Tung, 1981; Mendenhall & Oddou, 1985; Dülfer, 1990; Ronen, 1990; Oddou, 1991; Arthur & Bennett, 1995).

EXHIBIT I

The 21st-Century Expatriate Manager Profile (adapted from Howard, 1992)

Skills	Managerial Implications
	Core Skills
Multidimensional Perspective	Extensive multi-product, multi-industry, multi-functional, multi-company, multi-country, and multi-environment experience
Proficiency in Line Management	Track record in successfully operating a strategic business unit(s) and/or a series of major overseas projects
Prudent Decision-Making Skills	Competence and proven track record in making the right strategic decisions
Resourcefulness	Skillful in getting himself or herself known and accepted in the host country's political hierarchy
Ability as a Team Builder	Adept in bringing a culturally diverse working group together to accomplish the major mission and objective of the organization
	Augmented Skills
Computer Literacy	Comfortable exchanging strategic information electronically
Prudent Negotiating Skills	Proven track record in conducting successful strategic business negotiations in multicultural environment
Ability as a Change Agent	Proven track record in successfully initiating and implementing strategic organizational changes
Visionary Skills	Quick to recognize and respond to strategic business opportunities and potential political and economic upheavals in the host country
Effective Delegatory Skills	Proven track record in participative management style and ability to delegate

In contrast, research on global managers is relatively scarce. Besides defining what the global manager's competencies and behavior should be and how they differ from that of the expatriate manager, studies revealing the global manager's profile, the determinants of the successful global manager, and the effective HR practices to develop the global manager are still mainly at a conceptual stage (Kupfer, 1988; Pucik, 1992; Adler & Bartholomew, 1992; Evans, 1992; Kets de Vries & Mead, 1992; Tichy, 1992; Bartlett & Ghoshal, 1992; Yeung & Ready, 1995, Werther, Wachtel & Veal, 1995).

BEHAVIORS AND COMPETENCIES

Expatriates' Behaviors and Competencies. In one of the earliest articles on this subject, Hays (1974) categorizes expatriate managers into four types. The structure reproducer is responsible for reproducing in the foreign subsidiary a structure similar to that of another part of the company. The technical troubleshooter is sent to analyze and solve a technical problem. The operational expatriate is the individual who carries out a well-defined position in an ongoing business, and the chief executive officer oversees and directs the entire foreign operation. Similarly, Derr and Oddou (1991) identify two types of expatriates: those who are assigned abroad to "fix" a problem, including those assigned to line management and specialized functional positions, and those who go abroad as "high-potentials" to broaden their development before moving up to senior management. In this context, Pucik (1992) differentiates between "demand-driven" and "learning-driven" international assignments.

A number of researchers focused on competencies of effective international managers. According to Dülfer (1990), international managers must have clear managerial qualifications, in addition to purely technical and professional skills and competencies. They should be able to perform tasks as members of a team, reflect on complex problems in an appropriate way, improvise and find new solutions in the face of unexpected changes, impart confidence in their own ability to solve problems in difficult situations, and most of all, motivate all members of the organization to cooperate. McCall (1992) has

proposed (as an outcome of a research project aimed at developing an assessment instrument to identify leadership potential in future international executives) that individuals who are bound to be successful in international assignments are those who show ability to learn from experience. International managers should show curiosity about how things work, have a sense of adventure, demonstrate readiness/hardiness about learning, be biased toward action, accept responsibility for learning and change, respect differences among people, seek and use feedback, and have shown consistent growth over time.

Focusing on one key competency expected of expatriate managers, the "international knowledge," Rothwell (1992) explored its three principal components: general knowledge about the world and global economy; national information about conditions in a specific country; and business understanding of strategy, process, and leadership style. Looking toward the future, Howard (1992) has summarized the skills required of the 21st-century expatriate manager (see Exhibit 1).

Global Managers' Behaviors and Competencies. According to Bartlett and Ghoshal (1989; 1992), global managers are individuals that have been selected for, developed by, and co-opted into the broader transnational organization. Their principal characteristic is the ability to resolve complex and potentially contradictory issues embedded in the global environment. Bartlett and Ghoshal refer to these sets of behaviors and competencies as the building of a global matrix in the mind of the global manager, but they add that there is no such thing as a universal global manager. Rather, there are three groups of global specialists — business managers, country managers, and functional managers — that should together lead the organization to achieve global-scale efficiency and integration, national-level responsiveness and flexibility, and cross-market capacity to leverage learning on a worldwide basis (see Exhibit 2).

A number of recent contributions to the discussion of globalization of management focused on identification of key competencies of global managers with references to the traditional leadership literature. Tichy (1992) refers to global managers/leaders as "globalists," characterized as individuals who have a global mindset — i.e., those who can conceptualize complex geopolitical and cultural forces as they impact business, and possesses a well-honed set of global leadership skills and behaviors, such as an ability to build effective cross-cultural teams; the energy, skills, and talents to be global networkers; and skills as global "change agents." Kets de Vries and Mead (1992) identify global leaders as individuals with the capacity of envisioning (indicating future direction in an increasingly complex

EXHIBIT 2

The Three Groups of Global Specialists (adapted from Bartlett & Ghoshal, 1992)

Groups of Global Specialists	Skills and Competencies
Business Manager	■ Recognize opportunities and risks across national and functional boundaries ■ Coordinate activities and link capabilities across those barriers ■ Capture full benefit of integrated worldwide operations
Roles:	*Strategist, Architect, and Coordinator*
Country Manager	■ Meet local customers' needs ■ Satisfy the host government's requirements ■ Defend the company's market position against local and external competitors
Roles:	*Sensor, Builder, and Contributor*
Functional Manager	■ Build an organization that can use learning to create and spread innovations ■ Scan for specialized information leading-edge knowledge and best practices worldwide ■ Champion innovations that may offer transnational opportunities and applications
Roles:	*Scanner, Cross-Pollinator, and Champion*

EXHIBIT 3

Differences Between the Expatriate and the Global Manager

(Adler & Bartholomew, 1992)

	Expatriate Manager	Transnational Manager
Global Perspective	■ Focuses on a single foreign country and on managing relationships between headquarters and that country	■ Understands worldwide business environment from a global perspective
Local Responsiveness	■ Becomes an expert on one culture	■ Must learn about many foreign cultures' perspectives, tastes, trends, technologies, and approaches to conducting business
Synergistic Learning	■ Works with and coaches people in each foreign culture separately or sequentially ■ Integrates foreigners into the headquarters' national organizational culture	■ Works with and learn from people from many cultures simultaneously ■ Creates a culturally synergistic organizational environment
Transition and Adaptation	■ Adapts to living in a foreign culture	■ Adapts to living in many foreign cultures
Cross-cultural Interaction	■ Uses cross-cultural interaction skills primarily on foreign assignments	■ Uses cross-cultural skills on a daily basis throughout his or her career
Collaboration	■ Interacts with colleagues from within clearly defined hierarchies of structural and cultural dominance and subordination	■ Interacts with foreign colleagues as equals
Foreign Experience	■ Expatriation or inpatriation primarily to get the job done	■ Transpatriation for career and organization development

environment), the ability to instill values and inspire others and build and maintain organizational networks, the capacity for "pattern recognition" (sorting out relevant from irrelevant information), and the ability to cope with stress.

Research conducted by the Ashridge Management Research Group led to differentiation within two sides of the global managers' competencies (Barham & Antal, 1994). The first set of competencies is linked to the active roles that the global manager should play in order to manage across a number of countries and cultures simultaneously. The "doing" competencies, as Barham calls them, consist of championing international strategy, operating as cross-border coach and coordinator, acting as intercultural mediator and change agent, and managing personal effectiveness for international business. (The other set of global competencies, or what Barham refers to as the "being" competencies, are presented later in the section on the attributes of successful global managers.) Finally, in a recent study of managers in major global companies, Yeung and Ready (1995) identify six leadership capabilities that corporations value in global managers. These capabilities are as follows: to be a catalyst/manager of strategic change; to be a catalyst/manager of cultural change; to articulate a tangible vision, values, and strategies; to exhibit a strong customer orientation; to empower others to do their best; and to get results, or manage strategy to action.

Several studies concentrated on global managers' way of thinking, or "global mindset." In an 1993 article, Rhinesmith defined the global manager as an executive with a global mindset, able to scan the world from a broad perspective, always looking for unexpected trends and opportunities to achieve his or her personal, professional, or organizational objectives. Rhinesmith (1993; 1995) defines the mindset as "a predisposition to see the world in a particular way that sets boundaries and provides explanations for why things are the way they are, while at the same time establishing guidance for ways in which we should behave." In this respect, individuals with a global mindset should be able to drive for the bigger, broader picture, balance paradoxes, trust process over structure, value differences, manage change, and seek lifelong learning.

Is global mindset a measurable construct? Recently, Murtha, Lenway, and Bagozzi (1998) discussed the application of a survey instrument designed to evaluate individual and organizational progress toward creating a global mindset operationalized as an ability to balance the con-

tradictory pressures of global integration, responsiveness, and coordination. They have created a scale to assess the degree to which managers develop global mindsets, the impact of policy variables on organizational and individual differences concerning globalization, and most important, individual and organizational progress in becoming global and factors that account for variations in the speed of globalization across and within organizations. An interesting question that can be addressed using the global mindset scale is whether one can acquire a global mindset (to become a global manager) without ever leaving his or her home country as an expatriate.

Comparing the Two Sets of Behaviors and Competencies. Reviewing the behaviors and competencies required of expatriate and transnational managers, Adler and Bartholomew (1992) summarize the main differences between the two concepts (see Exhibit 3). The differences in skill characteristics are seen as driven primarily by the degree of cultural and organizational complexity facing managers during their careers.

FACTORS ASSOCIATED WITH EXPATRIATE AND GLOBAL MANAGERS' FAILURE

Much of the normative literature on the expatriate process is based on the argument that the expatriate failure rate is high (Baker & Ivancevich, 1971; Misa & Fabricatore, 1979; Tung, 1981; Black, Gregersen & Mendenhall, 1992). The study of predictors of expatriate failure now has a long history in management literature. In contrast, we are not aware of any study that focuses on predictors of failure of global managers.

Findings by Dowling (1990), Scullion (1994), and Weeks (1992) suggest that shortages of experienced and capable expatriate managers have become more acute over the past five years. They are caused on the demand side by the ever-increasing pace of internationalization, while on the supply size, the organizational capability to develop effective expatriate executives is hindered by the inadequate management of the expatriation process, from selection and and handling of the initial culture shock to repatriation (Howard, 1980, 1992; Mendenhall, Dunbar & Katcher 1990; Dülfer, 1990; Hogan & Goodson, 1990; Feldman & Tompson, 1992; Weeks, 1992; Gregersen, 1995).

Recently, however, Harzing (1995) reviewed the literature on expatriate failure measured as a premature reentry and concluded that this argument is not fully substantiated by empirical evidence. She adds that measuring the failure rate as the percentage of expatriate managers returning home before the expiration of their assignment contract is inadequate for two reasons: (1) it is far more damaging for a company if an expatriate who fails to perform adequately stays until the completion of the overseas assignment; and (2) a completion of the overseas assignment does not mean that the expatriate failure has been avoided. Nevertheless, Harzing concludes that HR executives should continue to examine expatriate failure, but more attention should be paid to the reasons behind the failure (defined as premature return, the lack of cross-cultural adjustment, and poor performance during international assignment), which may include a variety of individual as well as organizational factors.

INDIVIDUAL FACTORS

First, the expatriate inability to manage and cope effectively can be caused by personal issues. Personality attributes such as the inability to deal with stressful situations, lack of the right attitudes and skills to communicate with people from different cultures, and the inadaptability of the family to the new environment are frequently cited as reasons that cause an expatriate manager to return prematurely from the international assignment (Mendenhall, Dunbar & Oddou, 1987; Hogan & Goodson, 1990; Black, Gregersen & Mendenhall, 1992; Scullion, 1992; 1994). Some of these personality characteristics will be examined in more detail later while reviewing the literature on the attributes of successful expatriate managers.

Aside from the personality attributes that may cause the failure of the expatriate assignments, the literature has focused on three additional individual-level issues:

A) Willingness to Relocate. Brett and Stroh (1995) studied empirically the willingness of American managers to relocate internationally. The focus of the study was to provide an intentional measure of that willingness. The results showed that American managers' decision to relocate were definitely influenced by their spouse's feelings about international relocation and by their own attitude toward moving in general. It was also influenced by the number of children at home and employer's policies (Harvey, 1996). In recent research on international mobility, Forster (1992) focused on four key dimensions (related to job mobility) to explain the attitudes toward accepting assignments abroad: 1) the performance of employees abroad and the causes of expatriate failures (Tung, 1982; Pucik, 1988; Black & Mendenhall, 1992); 2) the personality profiles and psychological attributes of successful international managers (Phatak, 1974; Tung, 1981; Black & Mendenhall, 1990); 3) the effect of language and cultural training on expatriates (Gertsen, 1990; Black, 1990); and 4) and the effects of national cultural differences on the outcomes of international assignments (Gould & Penley, 1985; Gertsen, 1990; Smith, 1992).

B) Family Issues. The inability of the spouse to adjust to the new country was cited in many empirical studies as a reason for expatriate failure (Tung, 1981; Black & Stephens, 1989; Dowling, 1990; Swaak, 1995). Dual-career couples are also more likely to turn down international assignments because of the expected negative effects of a career interruption (Stephens & Black, 1991). It is clear that future research should include investigations of the effects of dual-earner families. Companies should implement practices such as job-search assistance and pooling available positions in a geographically based consortium of companies (Catalyst, 1981).

C) Expatriate Commitment. Black and Gregersen (1992) and Gregersen (1992) have explained expatriate failure by taking a closer look at the forms of allegiance developed by the expatriate toward both the local operation and the parent company. They have identified four types of expatriate commitment: the "freer agents" with low level of commitment to both the parent and the local operation; those who "leave their heart at home"; those who "go native"; and those who become "dual citizens" — expatriates with high allegiance to both the parent and local affiliate. In their study, developing a high dual allegiance seems to be the best way to prevent failure after an international assignment and has proven to have positive personal and organizational consequences.

ORGANIZATIONAL FACTORS

The ineptitude of the organizations in providing effective expatriate selection, training, and preparation programs and support policies during and after the completion of the international assignment is regarded as a very important reason in determining the failure of overseas appointments. In the same vein, many authors have described the difficulty of managing dual-career marriages, the lack of career planning, the poor orientation programs, the ineffective cross-cultural training, and the unattractive compensation packages as common organizational factors that would imminently lead to overseas failure (Mendenhall, Dunbar & Oddou, 1987; Blocklyn, 1989; Hogan & Goodson, 1990; Dunbar & Katcher, 1990; Derr & Oddou, 1991; Rothwell, 1992; Forster, 1992; Howard, 1992; Wederspahn & Stahl, 1992; Harrison, 1994). Criticizing what they believe is "the most common American approach" to expatriate selection, Black, Gregersen, and Mendenhall (1992) add that the global assignment is destined to fail if it is based only on a superficial selection of candidates on the presumable technical and managerial competence to put "the foreign fire out." Others argue that the typical selection process often fails to take into consideration the candidates' cross-cultural ability or the family disposition to live abroad (Stone, 1991).

DETERMINANTS OF EXPATRIATE AND GLOBAL MANAGERS' SUCCESS

The research on determinants of expatriate success is also much more developed than research on global managers, with an emphasis on expatriate selection and the expatriation process. The dominant theme of the literature reflects the opinion that expatriate selection and development is still mainly focused on technical competence as the key determinant of an expatriate manager's success, but that stronger efforts should be deployed by organizations to assess other, "softer" factors, such as relational, cross-cultural, and interpersonal abilities as well as adaptability potential of the spouse and other family members (Tung, 1981; Bennett, 1989; Cope, 1992; Scullion, 1994).

In one of the earliest studies of the expatriation process, Tung (1981) identified four groups of variables that contribute to expatriate success: technical competence on the job; personality traits or relational abilities; environmental variables; and the family situation. Tung (1981) adds that the importance of these selection criteria varies according to the category of tasks the international manager is expected to perform: chief executive officer; functional head; troubleshooter; and international operative.

Mendenhall and Oddou (1985) identified four key dimensions in the expatriate adjustment

because they believe that expatriate acculturation is a multidimensional process. The self-oriented dimension is composed of three sub-factors: reinforcement substitution; stress reduction; and technical competence. This dimension measures the expatriate's ability of adjustment. The others-oriented dimension measures the expatriate's ability to interact effectively with host-country nationals and consists of two sub-factors: relationship development and willingness to communicate. The perceptual dimension refers to the ability to understand why foreigners behave the way they do. Expatriate managers should be non-judgmental and non-evaluative in interpreting the behavior of host-country nationals. The cultural-toughness dimension refers to the understanding of differences between countries.

Ronen (1990) incorporates the dimensions of expatriate success identified by Tung (1981) and Mendenhall and Oddou (1985) and identifies five categories of attributes of success: job factors; relational dimensions; motivational state; family situation; and language skills. Oddou (1991) states that there are never any guarantees in identifying what constitutes the "right" person for the international assignment. However, a few indicators might be helpful to identify the potential expatriate. The candidate's capacity to adapt to change (new structures, new rules and new faces), his or her open-mindness, sociability, self-confidence, whether or not he or she has a supportive family, and the candidate's capacity to deal with stress are essential elements that enhance a firm's chances of employing a successful expatriate.

With respect to global managers, the scope of the literature is much more sparse. Kets de Vries and Mead (1992) identified five principal categories of factors contributing to the development of global leaders: management development; adaptability factors; leadership factors; personal development; and training and education. These five categories are broadly comparable to those identified by Tung (1981), Mendenhall and Oddou (1985), and Ronen (1990), and together can be grouped as professional and technical competence, relational abilities, leadership factors, family situation, and cultural awareness (see Exhibit 4).

From a psychological perspective, according to Wills and Barham (1992), core competencies of international managers may be described as cognitive complexity, emotional energy, and psychological maturity. The cognitive complexity refers to the ability to see multiple dimensions in a situation, and to identify the relationships between those different dimensions. The emotional energy is the ability to deal with stressful situations. The psychological maturity refers to three additional attributes of global managers: their strong curiosity that drives them to learn; their willingness to apply a great deal of psychological energy to unravel the complexity of a situation; and their strong personal morality (Barham & Antal, 1994).

Developing International and Global Managers

Not surprisingly, the majority of conceptual and empirical studies in this area have thus far focused mainly on HR practices related to expatriates. Research on global managers is substantially less developed, and still basically in a conceptual stage. The primary emphasis of the empirical studies is on the expatriation process, selection, and training; not much work has been done on performance management and compensation of globalization. Most of the studies are descriptive, although a sophistication of the analysis continues to increase. The key challenge is the operationalization of the outcome variables that are seldom linked to objective measures of individual or organizational performance.

HR MANAGEMENT PRACTICES SUPPORTING EFFECTIVE DEPLOYMENT OF EXPATRIATES

We have reviewed the recent literature on HR management practices related to expatriate managers in order to identify examples of effective HR techniques that may support effective deployment of expatriate managers (see Exhibit 5). The HR practices are categorized into five major activities: staffing; training and career development; performance appraisals and compensation; expatriation process; and repatriation. Reflecting the nature of the field, information on HR practices is mostly drawn from North American firms and European data; data on non-Western firms appear only infrequently. The list of citations is meant to be illustrative, not exhaustive, but whenever appropriate, examples of companies that have implemented the practice (as cited in the literature) are included. We have also noted the type of research methodology used in the article reviewed.

A number of key themes emerge from our review. In the area of staffing and selection, the thrust of HR activities in leading global firms — consistent with recommendations based on past research — is on enlarging the pool of potential candidates for international assignments, as well as on making sure that the international track attracts those with the best potential to succeed in the firm. Assessment for international assignment is becoming increasingly rigorous and often involves the candidate's spouse. The structure of assignments is becoming more flexible.

From the management development perspective, international assignments are increasingly viewed as an intrinsic part of career progression, providing opportunities for both a transfer of

EXHIBIT 4

Characteristics of the Successful Expatriate and Global Manager

	Expatriate Manager			Global Manager
	Tung (1981)	**Mendenhall and Oddou (1985)**	**Ronen (1990)**	**Kets de Vries and Mead (1992)**
Professional and Technical Competence (1)	Technical Competence on the Job ■ Experience in company ■ Technical knowledge of business ■ Previous overseas experience ■ Managerial talent ■ Overall experience and education	Self-Oriented Dimension ■ Technical competence	Job Factors ■ Technical skills ■ Acquaintance with host-country and headquarters operations ■ Managerial skills ■ Administrative competence	Management Development ■ Early responsibility ■ Variety of tasks ■ Early international experience ■ Corporate values
Relational Abilities (2)	Personality Traits and Relational Abilities ■ Communicative ability ■ Maturity and emotional stability ■ Respect for culture of host country ■ Adaptability and flexibility in new environment	■ Reinforcement substitution ■ Stress reduction Perceptual Dimension ■ Nonjudgmentalism ■ Nonevaluative in interpreting the behavior of host-country nationals	Relational Dimensions ■ Tolerance for ambiguity ■ Behavioral flexibility ■ Nonjudgmentalism ■ Cultural empathy and low ethnocentrism ■ Interpersonal skills	Adaptability Factors ■ Narcissistic development ■ Cultural diversity in family ■ Early international experience ■ Bilingualism ■ Multiple roots
Leadership Factors (3)		Others-Oriented Dimension (expatriate ability to interact effectively with host-country nationals) ■ Relationship development ■ Willingness to communicate	Motivational State ■ Belief in the mission ■ Congruence with career path ■ Interest in overseas experience ■ Interest in the specific host-country culture ■ Willingness to acquire new patterns of behaviour and attitudes	Leadership Factors ■ Self-confidence ■ Responsibility ■ Curiosity ■ Imagination ■ Hardiness ■ Decision-making skills ■ Envisioning ■ Communication skills ■ "Core values" ■ Career goals and expectations
Family Situation (4)	Family Situation ■ Stability of marital relationship ■ Spouse's and family's adaptability		Family Situation ■ Willingness of spouse to live abroad ■ Adaptive and supportive spouse ■ Stable marriage	Personal Development ■ Supportive spouse ■ Adaptable spouse ■ "Movable children" ■ Variety of interest
Cultural Awareness (5)	Environmental Factors ■ Flexibility in other cultures	Cultural-Toughness Dimension refers to the understanding of differences between countries	Language Skills ■ Host-country language ■ Non-verbal communication	Training and Education ■ Analytical skills ■ Professional skills ■ Study in another culture ■ Study in international languages

knowledge as well as learning of new competencies by the international manager. Leading global firms invest heavily in the training of their international managers. However, not only is training provided in the pre-departure stage, but it is targeted to help the expatriates continue learning about the host culture and improve their international skills during the assignment.

Managing the cost of compensating expatriate managers often shows in surveys as an item of major concern for international HR executives (McKay, 1994; Reynolds, 1995). However, this concern is not yet reflected in the academic literature. Most of the discussion and recommendations are focused on the effectiveness of various financial incentives. In a number of articles, there seems to be an implicit yearning for a better model of expatriate compensation (e.g., delivering the same or more positive outcomes — performance and retention — for less money), but the alternative designs are still not yet well-articulated or tested. Similarly, the area of expatriate performance management (e.g., criteria, process, outcomes) is also substantially unexplored.

An important component of effective expatriate management policies is geared toward the expatriation process, before and throughout the duration of an assignment. There is a strong consensus in the literature about the need to invest in thorough training and orientation programs not only for the expatriate, but also for his or her family. After posting, the quality of the support network inside the host country, as well as linkage with the home office, may influence how expatriates perform. In addition, family well-being is seen as an increasingly important prerequisite of expatriate effectiveness.

Finally, the repatriation stage of the international assignment is receiving growing attention in order to reduce the perceived high turnover of returning executives. Visible successful returns can also have a positive impact on willingness of others to accept an international assignment. While an international assignment cannot be a shelter against organizational upheavals, much more can be done to improve the odds of success, at relatively low cost. The best practices focus on advance planning in order to provide meaningful opportunities upon return that create value for the employee as well as for the company, and on emotional and logistical support during the transition.

HR PRACTICES THAT SUPPORT DEVELOPMENT OF GLOBAL MANAGERS

Based on the observations in the literature, we have categorized various normative statements and prescriptions regarding the impact of HR practices on development of global leaders into five areas: selection; career development and training; performance management and compensation; organizational design; and global communication. In particular, our objective was to capture those HR practices that can support effective development of global managers and are already in the process of being implemented at leading North American and European firms (Adler & Batholomew, 1992; Kets de Vries & Mead, 1992; Pucik, 1992; Tichy, 1992; Yeung & Ready, 1995).

A number of "global" HR practices stand out. Staffing sheds its ethnocentric image; global managers can come from anywhere in the world. International assignments start early and flexibility is the key; they can take various forms linked to the developmental needs. Global mindset and global leadership become an integral part of performance management criteria. Tasks of global managers are structured to cross intra-organizational boundaries, often through membership in transnational teams. Emphasis is on the quality of the management process, open communication, and creation of global competitive culture.

In comparison with the earlier discussion of HR practices supporting development of international managers, the focus on global managers may require a qualitative leap in aligning HR with the requirements of globalization, as all key HR activities are intimately linked to the effectiveness of the management development process. However, as in the case of international managers, international assignments are the essential development tool, although they may happen much earlier in an executive career as "global learning" becomes the primary objective. Therefore, an effective execution of international transfers will continue to demand attention.

Conclusions and Implications

To be successful in global competition, companies need both expatriate/international and global managers. We have defined the former, in a narrow sense, as an executive in a leadership position that involves international assignments. The global manager is defined, in a broad sense, as an executive who has a hands-on understand-

EXHIBIT 5

Human Resource Practices that Can Effectively Select and Develop Successful Expatriate Managers

HR Activity	(References)	Cited Examples
Staffing	(1,2,3,4,5,7,13,18,20,22,24,25)	
Consider external recruitment to fill management positions abroad		
Use third-country nationals for international assignments		3M
Invest in promoting international opportunities to students		Colgate-Palmolive
Recruit students who have lived or were educated abroad		Colgate-Palmolive, Citibank
Recruit women for international assignments		
Provide short-term assignments to increase the pool of employees with international experience		
Base the selection of international managers on long-term human resource forecasts		Avon, Coca-Cola Foods
Give new international assignees realistic career and job previews		Ciba-Geigy
Interview the spouse of the manager as part of the selection process		Dow Chemicals
Make international assignment planning a part of a career development process		3M, Matsui & Co. USA
Communicate the value of international assignments to the company's global mission		
Make international assignments a condition for advancement to senior management		Whirlpool, Dow Chemicals, Westinghouse Electric, 3M, Arthur Andersen
Training and Career Development	(3,5,6,8,9,11,12,13,16,17,18,21,24)	
Provide expatriate managers with technical training to enhance their international background		Bechtel, Nordson
Provide language training, cultural and business orientation		Ciba-Geigy
For high-potentials, provide a challenging international assignment within three to five years after entry		3M, UBS (E)
Provide opportunities to learn about international finance, marketing and other international functional areas		Colgate-Palmolive
Encourage international managers to manage a multicultural workforce		
Use international assignment as a leadership top management development tool		ABB, Monsanto, Nordson, Bechtel, Motorola
Performance Appraisals and Compensation	(10,11,12,15,20,24)	
Modify the performance evaluation system to incorporate the distinctive conditions of local countries		
Ensure timely performance review		
Provide financial counselling for international managers		KPMG-Peat Marwick
Provide a relocation allowance and a reentry bonus		
Provide an equitable international compensation package		
Expatriation Activities	(3,4,5,7,8,12,13,18,19,20,21,22)	
Provide the international manager with an orientation program before the assignment		Dow Chemicals, Ciba-Geigy, Intel, Chevron Overseas Petroleum
Send the expatriate for a visit to the host country (provide a period of orientation abroad)		Colgate-Palmolive
Involve the family in the orientation program		Intel, Ciba-Geigy, Gillette
Establish mentor relationships between expatriates and executives from home location for general career advice to reduce the "out of sight out of mind" dilemma		Colgate-Palmolive, 3M, Ciba-Geigy, Dow Chemicals, Honeywell, Northern Telecom
Develop a network of contacts to keep the expatriate up-to-date on day-to-day activities of home-country operations for social support and information exchange		Colgate-Palmolive, Intel, Bechtel, Honeywell, Northern Telecom
Organize social activities at the foreign site in order to facilitate exchange of information and problem solving in an informal setting		
Assist the expatriate's spouse in finding a job		Gillette, Intel
Assist expatriate in finding schools for children		
Repatriation Activities	(3,5,7,8,12,13,18,19,21,22,24	
Plan a specific assignment for the returning expatriate		ABB, Dow Chemicals
Provide opportunities for the returning manager to use knowledge and skills learned internationally		3M, Monsanto, UBS, Honeywell
Monitor career paths of international managers so that they are not relegated to the "slow track" because of their international assignments		3M
Get the high-performing international managers recognized/promoted upon return home		ABB
Assign the repatriated employee and family to a welcome group composed of other families who have lived abroad		Intel, Dow Chemicals

Key to References: 1. Bennett, 1989 - Interviews; **2.** Black et al., 1992 - C*; **3.** Blocklyn, 1989 - CS** (3 US MNCs); **4.** Copeland, 1995 - Interviews; **5.** Derr & Oddou, 1991 - S*** (135 Expats US MNCs); **6.** Dunbar & Katcher, 1990 - Interviews; **7.** Feldman et al., 1992 - S (459 US graduate students); **8.** Gates, 1994 - S (158 US HR Managers); **9.** Harrison, 1994 - C; **10.** Howard, 1980 - S (81 Expats 27 US MNCs); **11.** Klaus, 1995 - C; **12.** Oddou, 1991 - S (165 Expats/US MNCs); **13.** Oddou & Mendenhall, 1991 - S (135 Expats/US MNCs); **14.** Pucik, 1984 - C; **15.** Reynolds, 1995 - C; **16.** Rothwell, 1992 - C; **17.** Scullion, 1992 - S (45 British MNCs); **18.** Seibert et al., 1995 - C S (2 US MNCs); **19.** Shilling, 1993 - Interviews; **20.** Solomon, 1995a - Interviews; **21.** Solomon, 1994b - Interviews; **22.** Solomon, 1994c - Interviews; **23.** Stephens & Black, 1991 - S (67 US Expats in Japan); **24.** Weeks, 1992 - S (130 US MNCs); **25.** Werther et al, 1995 - CS (3 US MNCs)
***C: conceptual; **C: Case Study; ***S: Survey**

ing of international business, has an ability to work across cross-cultural, organizational, and functional boundaries, and is able to balance the simultaneous demands of short-term profitability and growth. In short, global managers are defined by their state of mind, in contrast to expatriate/international managers who are identified by location as executives in leadership positions that involve cross-border assignments (Pucik, 1997).

In spite of this major conceptual difference, the review of research seems to indicate that at least some of the attributes of successful expatriate and global managers may be identical. They are related to five fundamental factors: professional and technical competence; relational abilities; leadership factors; family situation; and cultural awareness. However, because of the differences between expatriate managers and global managers in their current and future roles in the organization, there are naturally also significant differences in expectations regarding the full set of desired competencies, role behaviors, and way of thinking. The requirements put on global managers are substantially more complex and dynamic, reflecting the ever-changing nature of the global competitive environment.

The emerging emphasis on cultivating the manager's mind, versus the traditional emphasis on competencies in the job, may require rethinking the traditional HR approaches to global leadership development. First, truly global leadership development should focus on providing a broad spectrum of high-potential employees worldwide

EXHIBIT 6

Human Resource Practices that Support the Development of Global Managers

Staffing

Recruiting worldwide for positions anywhere in the world

Selection criteria do not favor any particular culture

The point of entry does not limit future opportunities

Staffing decisions support fast transfer of knowledge across boundaries

Implementing global job posting system

Involving top management in the global staffing process

Career Development & Training

Training delivered by transnational faculty to multicultural teams

Early international experience encouraged

International assignments can take on many forms, linked to a manager's development needs

International assignments integrated into the career-planning process

International assignments encourage global learning

Training stimulating a sense of cultural empathy and adaptability

Emphasis on socialization aspects of management development

Performance Management & Compensation

Performance incentives and rewards reflect global contributions

Performance appraisals focus on global mindset and behaviors

Flexible international compensation system to encourage "low cost" mobility

Career opportunities equitable across the world

Emphasizing rewarding careers rather than short-term outcomes only

Organizational Design

Designing jobs across boundaries to increase global learning

Focus on process, not on structure and procedures

Removing HR barriers to organizational flexibility

HR systems aligned with needs of transnational teams

Global Communication

Building informal communications across boundaries

Promoting a global competitive culture

Cited authors: Adler & Bartholomew, 1992; Bartlett & Ghoshal, 1992; Evans, 1989; 1992; Kets de Vries, 1992; Pucik, 1985; 1991; 1992; Rhinesmith, 1995; Snow, Davison, Snell & Hambrick, 1996; Tichy, 1992; Werther, Wachtel & Veale, 1995 with opportunities to acquire and enhance their global leadership skills and capabilities (Pucik, 1997). Second, the purpose of international assignments shifts considerably; learning from the experience becomes one of the key objectives. Finally, such a process starts with a very careful selection of future global managers and continues throughout a manager's career, touching all traditional HR activities.

Obviously, the HR function therefore plays an indispensable role in the development of future global leaders. In fact, taking the lead in developing global leaders provides HR executives with an excellent opportunity to become an integral player in implementing global business strategy and influencing organizations' competitiveness (Galbraith, 1992; Keller & Campbell, 1992; Kesler, 1995; Yeung & Ready, 1995; Lawson & Limbrick, 1996). The integrating capability of the HR function in leveraging key global talent and its capacity to play the role of global catalyst can undoubtedly determine its ability to become a value-adding function in the organization.

The emerging emphasis on cultivating the manager's mind, versus the traditional emphasis on competencies in the job, may require rethinking the traditional HR approaches to global leadership development.

Focusing on the operational responsibilities of the HR function, efforts should be aimed to ensure successful international assignments and other developmental experiences that help managers and executives worldwide to enhance their global perspective. This implies evaluating and aligning the key staffing, development, and performance management processes so they are consistent with what we know already accounts for the critical factors in developing global managers. Another value-adding opportunity for the HR function is to support global integration, coordination, and learning by creating favorable conditions for the diffusion of global knowledge and perspective throughout the firm, thus creating a favorable environment where global mindsets can flourish.

From a strategic perspective, Eichinger and Ulrich (1995) recently reviewed the future trends facing HR professionals. They suggested that in a number of areas, the traditional HR competencies need to be enhanced, or new competencies developed. Many of the new requirements listed reflect the challenges of globalization, the critical one being the need to fill the global leadership bench (i.e., the development of global managers). The first step in developing global leaders is to create a truly global HR function, as the ability to develop managers with global mindset inside the HR organization is one of the critical prerequisites influencing the ability of the organization to globalize. The HR function could and should serve as a role model of globalization; therefore, the HR leadership needs to have a well-rounded knowledge of global HR and business issues, including a deep understanding of the new global competitive environment and the impact it has on the management of people worldwide.

Footnote

[1] This review is based on major European and North American journals. Contributions from Asia are covered only to the degree they appear in Western publications.

Biographical Sketches

Vladimir Pucik *is professor at the International Institute for Management Development (IMD) in Lausanne, Switzerland. Previously, he was Associate Professor and Academic Director of International Programs at the Center for Advanced Human Resource Studies at the ILR School, Cornell University. His research interests include management practices in global firms, transnational human resource policies, international alliance strategies, and comparative management, with a particular emphasis on the Far East and Europe. He has published extensively in academic and professional journals. Dr. Pucik's most recent major work is* Globalizing Management: Creating and Leading the Competitive Organization. *He has consulted and conducted workshops for major corporations worldwide. Dr. Pucik also teaches regularly in a number of international executive programs.*

Tania Saba *is an assistant professor in the School of Industrial Relations at the University of Montreal. She was a visiting fellow at Cornell University for the academic year 1995-1996, conducting research in the area of international human resource management. Her research interests include older workers' management,*

career management, and human resource management in international firms. She has published in academic and professional journals on various issues in career management.

References

Adler, N.J. and Bartholomew, S. 1992. "Managing Globally Competent People." *Academy of Management Executive*, 6(3): 52-65.

Arthur W. and Bennett W. 1995. "The International Assignee: The Relative Importance of Factors Perceived to Contribute to Success." *Personnel Psychology*, 48: 99-115.

Baker, J.C. and Ivancevich, J. 1971. "The Assignment of American Executive Abroad: Systematic, Haphazard, or Chaotic?" *California Management Review*, 13: 39-44.

Barham, K. and Aantala, B. 1994. "Competences for the Pan-European Manager." In P.S. Kirkbride (Eds.) *Human Resource Management in Europe: Perspectives for the 1990s*, London: Routledge.

Bartlett, C.A. and Ghoshal, S. 1992 "What is a Global Manager?" *Harvard Business Review*, September/October: 124-132.

Bartlett, C.A. and Ghoshal, S. 1989. *Managing Across Borders: The Transnational Solution*. Massachusetts: Harvard Business School Press.

Bennett, A. 1989. "The Chief Executives in Year 2000 Will Be Experienced Abroad." *The Wall Street Journal*, 27 February: A1.

Black, J.S. 1990. "The Relationship of Personal Characteristics with the Adjustment of Japanese Expatriate Managers." *Management International Review*, 30: 119-134.

Black, J.S. and Gregersen, H.B. 1992. "Serving Two Masters: Managing the Dual Allegiance of Expatriate Employees." *Sloan Management Review*, Summer: 61-71.

Black, J.S., Gregersen, H.B., and Mendenhall, M.E. 1992. *Global Assignments: Successfully Expatriating and Repatriating International Managers*. San Francisco: Jossey-Bass.

Black, J.S. and Mendenhall, M.E. 1990. "Cross-cultural Effectiveness: A Review and a Theoretical Framework." *Academy of Management Review*, 15 (1): 113-136.

Black, J.S. and Stephens, G.K. 1989. "The Influence of the Spouse on American Expatriate Adjustment and Intent to Stay in Pacific Rim Overseas Assignments." *Journal of Management*, 15(4): 529-544.

Blocklyn, P. 1989. "Developing the International Executive." *Personnel*, March: 44-47.

Brett, J.M. and Stroh, L.K. 1995. "Willingness to Relocate Internationally." *Human Resource Management*, 34(3): 405-424.

Calof, J.L. and Beamish, P.W. 1994. "The Right Attitude for International Success." *Business Quarterly*, Autumn:105-110.

Catalyst. 1991. *Corporations and Two Career Families*. New York: Catalyst.

Cope, N. 1992. "In Search of Euroman." *Management Today*, June: 50-53.

Copeland, A.P. 1995. "Helping Foreign Nationals Adapt to the US." *Personnel Journal*, February: 85- 87.

Derr, B.C. and Oddou, G.R. 1991. "Are US Multinationals Adequately Preparing Future American Leaders For Global Competition?" *International Journal Of Human Resource Management*, 2(2): 227-244.

Dowling, P. 1989. "Hot Issues Overseas." *Personnel Administrator*, January: 66-72.

Dowling, PJ. and Schuler, R.S. 1990. *International Dimensions of HRM*, PWS-Kent.

Dülfer, E. 1990. "Human Resource Management in Multinational and Internationally Operating Companies." In R. Pieper (Ed.) *HRM: An International Comparison*, Berlin: Walter De Gruyter.

Dunbar, E. and Katcher, A. 1990. "Preparing Managers for Foreign Assignments." *Training and Development Journal*, September: 45-47.

Eichinger, B. and Ulrich, D. 1995. "Are you Future Agile?" *Human Resource Planning*, 18(4): 30-43.

Evans, P.A.L. 1992. "Developing Leaders and Managing Development." *European Management Journal*, 10(1): 1-9.

Feldman, D.C. and Tompson, H.B. 1992. "Entry Shock, Culture Shock: Socializing the New Breed of Global Managers." *Human Resource Management*, 31(4): 345-362.

Forster, N. 1992. "International Managers and Mobile Families: The Professional and Personal Dynamics of Trans-national Career Pathing and Job Mobility in the 1990s." *International Journal of Human Resource Management*, Vol. 3, (3): 605-623.

Galbraith, J. 1992. "Positioning Human Resource as a Value-Adding Function: The Case of Rockwell International." *Human Resource Management*, 31(4): 287-300.

Gates, S. 1994. "The Changing Global Role of the Human Resource Function." The Conference Board, Report Number 1062-94-RR, New York.

Gertsen, M. 1990. "Intercultural Competence and Expatriates." *International Journal of Human Resource Management*, 1(3): 341-362.

Gould, S. and Penley, L.E. 1985. "A Study of the Correlates of the Willingness to Relocate." *Academy of Management Journal*, 28(2): 472-478.

Gregersen, H.B. 1995. "Keeping High Performers After International Assignments: A Key to Global Executive Development." *Journal of International Management*, 1(1): 3-31.

Gregersen, H.B. 1992. "Commitments to a Parent Company and a Local Work Unit During Repatriation." *Personnel Psychology*, 45: 29-54.

Harrison, K.K. 1994. "Developing Successful Expatriate Managers: A Framework for the Structural Design and Strategic Alignment of Cross-Cultural Training Programs." *Human Resource Planning*, 17(3): 17-35.

Harvey, M. 1996. "Addressing the Dual-Career Dilemma." *Human Resource Planning*, 19(4):18-39.

Harzing, A.W. 1995. "The Persistent Myth of High Expatriate Failure Rates." *International Journal of Human Resource Management*, 6(2): 457-474.

Hays, R. 1974. "Expatriate Selection: Insuring Success and Avoiding Failure." *Journal of International Business Studies*, 5(1): 25-37.

Hogan, G.W. and Goodson, J.R. 1990. "The Key to Expatriate Success." *Training and Development Journal*, January: 50-52.

Howard, C.G. 1980. "The Expatriate Manager and the Role of the MNC." *Personnel Journal*, October: 838-844.

Howard, C.G. 1992. "Profile of the 21st Century Expatriate Manager." *HRMagazine*, June: 93-100.

Keller, D.A. and Campbell, J.F. 1992. "Building Human Resource Capability." *Human Resource Management*, Spring/Summer, 31(1 & 2): 109-126.

Kesler, G.C. 1995. "A Model and Process for Redesigning the HRM Role, Competencies, and Work in a Major Multi-National Corporation." *Human Resource Management*, 34 (2): 229-252.

Kets de Vries, M.F.R. and Mead, C. 1992. "The Development of the Global Leader Within the Multinational Corporation." In V. Pucik, N. Tichy, and C. Barnett (Eds.), *Globalizing Management: Creating and Leading the Competitive Organization*, New York: John Wiley and Sons.

Klaus, K.J. 1995. "How to Establish an Effective Expatriate Program — Best Practices in International Assignments Administration." *Employee Relations Today*, Spring: 59-69.

Kupfer, A. 1988. "How to be a Global Manager." *Fortune*, March 14: 52-58.

Lawson, T.E. and Limbrick, V. 1996. "Critical Competencies and Developmental Experiences for Top HR Executives." *Human Resource Management*, 35: 67-85.

McCall, M.W. Jr. 1992. "Identifying Leadership Potential in Future International Executives: Developing a Concept." Massachusetts: ICEDR Working Paper 92-01.

McKay, J. 1994. "International Benefits Policy: A U.S. Multinationals Perspective." *Employee Benefits Journal*, December: 22-25.

Mendenhall, M.E., Dunbar, E., and Oddou, G.R. 1987. "Expatriate

Selection, Training and Career-Pathing: A Review and Critique." *Human Resource Management*, 26(3): 331-345.

Mendenhall, M.E. and Oddou, G.R. 1985. "The Dimensions of Expatriate Acculturation: A Review." *Academy of Management Review*, 10: 39-47

Misa, K.F and Fabricatore, J. 1979. "Return on Investment of Overseas Personnel." *Financial Executive*, vol. 47: 42-46.

Moynihan, M. 1993. *The Economist Intelligence Unit Global Manager: Recruiting, Developing, and Keeping World Class Executives*. New York: McGraw-Hill.

Murtha, T.P., Lenway, S.A., and Bagozzi, R.P. 1998. "Global Mindsets and Cognitive Shirt in a Complex Multinational Corporation." *Strategic Management Journal*, 19: 97-114.

Nohria, N. and Ghoshal, S. 1997. The Differentiated Network: Organizing Multinational Corporations for Value Creation. San Francisco: Jossey-Bass Publishers.

Oddou, G.R. 1991. "Managing Your Expatriates: What the Successful Firms Do?" *Human Resource Planning*, 14(4): 301-306.

Oddou, G.R. and Mendenhall, M.E. 1991. "Succession Planning for the 21st Century: How Well are we Grooming Our Future Business Leaders?" *Business Horizons*, January-February: 26-34.

Pucik, V. 1984. "The International Management of Human Resources." In C.J. Fombrun, N.M. Tichy, and M.A. Devana (Eds.), *Strategic HRM*. New York: John Wiley and Sons.

Pucik, V. 1985. "Strategic Human Resource Management in a Multinational Firm." In V. Pucik, *Strategic Management of Multinational Corporations*, New York: John Wiley and Sons

Pucik, V. 1991. "The Executive of the Future: Learning to Compete." Executive Development for Global Competitiveness, 1991 Annual Conference of the University Consortium for Executive Education.

Pucik, V. 1992. "Globalization and Human Resource Management." In V. Pucik, N. Tichy, and C. Barnett (Eds.), *Globalizing Management: Creating and Leading the Competitive Organization*, New York: John Wiley and Sons.

Pucik, V., Tichy, N., and Barnett, C. (Eds.). 1992. *Globalizing Management: Creating and Leading the Competitive Organization*, New York: John Wiley and Sons.

Pucik, V. 1997. "Human Resource in the Future: An Obstacle or a Champion of Globalization?" *Human Resource Management*, Spring, 36(1): 163-167.

Reynolds, C. 1995. *Compensating Globally Mobile Employees: Approaches to Developing Expatriate Pay Strategies for the Evolving International Corporation*. American Compensation Association.

Rhinesmith, S.H. 1993. *A Manager's Guide to Globalization: Six Keys to Success in a Changing World*. American Society for Training and Development.

Rhinesmith, S.H. 1995. "Open the Door to a Global Mindset." *Training and Development*, May: 35-43.

Ronen, S. 1990. "Training the International Assignee." *Training and Career Development*, San Francisco: Jossey Bass.

Rothwell, S. 1992. "The Development of the International Manager." *Personnel Management*, January, 24(1): 33-35.

Scullion, H. 1992. "Attracting Management Globetrotters." *Personnel Management*, 24(1): 28-32.

Scullion, H. 1994. "Staffing Policies and Strategic Control in British Multinationals." *International Studies of Management and Organizations*, 24(3): 86-104.

Seibert, K.W., Hall, D.T, and Kram, K.E. 1995. "Strengthening the Weak Link in Strategic Executive Development: Integrating Individual Development and Global Business Strategy." *Human Resource Management*, 34(4): 549-567.

Shilling, M. 1993. "How to Win at Repatriation." *Personnel Journal*, September: 40-46.

Smith, P. 1992. "Organizational Behaviour and National Cultures." *British Journal of Management*, 3: 39-51.

Snow, C.C., Davison, S.C., Snell, S.A., and Hambrick, D.C. 1996. "Use Transnational Teams to Globalize your Company." *Organizational Dynamics*, Spring: 50-67.

Solomon, C.M. 1994a. "Staff Selection Impacts Global Success." *Personnel Journal*, January: 88-101.

Solomon, C.M. 1994b. "Learning to Manage Host-Country Nationals." *Personnel Journal*, March: 60- 67.

Solomon, C.M. 1994c. "Global Operations Demand that HR Rethink Diversity." *Personnel Journal*, July: 41-50.

Solomon, C.M. 1994d. "Success Abroad Depends on More Than Job Skills." *Personnel Journal*, April: 51-60.

Solomon, C.M. 1995. "Repatriation: Up, Down or Out?" *Personnel Journal*, January: 28-37.

Stephens, G.K. and Black, J.S. 1991. "The Impact of Spouse's Career Orientation on Managers during International Transfers." *Journal of Management Studies*, 28(4): 417-428.

Stevens, T. 1995. "Managing Across Boundaries." *Industry Week*, 244(5): 24-30.

Stone, R.M. 1991. "Expatriate Selection and Failure." *Human Resource Planning*, 14(1): 9-18.

Swaak, R.M. 1995. "Today's Expatriate Family: Dual Careers and Other Obstacles." *Compensation and Benefits Review*, May/June: 21-26.

Tichy, N. 1992. "Global Development" in V. Pucik, N. Tichy, and C. Barnett (Eds.), *Globalizing Management: Creating and Leading the Competitive Organization*, New York: John Wiley and Sons.

Tichy, N. and Sherman, S. 1993. *Control Your Destiny or Someone Else Will*. New York: Currency Doubleday.

Tung, R.L. 1981. "Selection and Training of Personnel Overseas Assignments." *Columbia Journal of World Business*, 16(1): 68-78.

Tung, R.L. 1982. "Selection and Training Procedures of US, European and Japanese Multinationals." *California Management Review*, 25: 57-71.

Wederspahn, G.M. and Stahl, M. 1992. "Costing Failures in Expatriate Human Resources Management." *Human Resource Planning*, 15(3): 27-35.

Weeks, D.A. 1992. "Recruiting and Selecting International Managers." The Conference Board, Report Number 998, New York.

Werther, W.B, Wachtel, J.M., and Veale, D.J. 1995. "Global Deployment of Executive Talent." *Human Resource Planning*, 18: 20-29.

Wills, S. and Barham, K. 1994. "Being an International Manager." *European Management Journal*, 12(1): 49-58.

Yeung, A.K. and Ready, D.A. 1995. "Developing Leadership Capabilities of Global Corporations: A Comparative Study in Eight Nations." *Human Resource Management*, 34(4): 529-547.

[5]

© Academy of Management Executive, 1993 Vol. 7 No. 1

Cultural constraints in management theories

Geert Hofstede, University of Limburg, Maastricht, the Netherlands

Executive Overview

Management as the word is presently used is an American invention. In other parts of the world not only the practices but the entire concept of management may differ, and the theories needed to understand it, may deviate considerably from what is considered normal and desirable in the USA. The reader is invited on a trip around the world, and both local management practices and theories are explained from the different contexts and histories of the places visited: Germany, Japan, France, Holland, the countries of the overseas Chinese, South-East Asia, Africa, Russia, and finally mainland China.

A model in which worldwide differences in national cultures are categorized according to five independent dimensions helps in explaining the differences in management found; although the situation in each country or region has unique characteristics that no model can account for. One practical application of the model is in demonstrating the relative position of the U.S. versus other parts of the world. In a global perspective, U.S. management theories contain a number of idiosyncracies not necessarily shared by management elsewhere. Three such idiosyncracies are mentioned: a stress on market processes, a stress on the individual, and a focus on managers rather than on workers. A plea is made for an internationalization not only of business, but also of management theories, as a way of enriching theories at the national level.

In My View

Lewis Carroll's *Alice in Wonderland* contains the famous story of Alice's croquet game with the Queen of Hearts.

Alice thought she had never seen such a curious croquet-ground in all her life; it was all ridges and furrows; the balls were live hedgehogs, the mallets live flamingoes, and the soldiers had to double themselves up and to stand on their hands and feet, to make the arches.

You probably know how the story goes: Alice's flamingo mallet turns its head whenever she wants to strike with it; her hedgehog ball runs away; and the doubled-up soldier arches walk around all the time. The only rule seems to be that the Queen of Hearts always wins.

Alice's croquet playing problems are good analogies to attempts to build culture-free theories of management. Concepts available for this purpose are themselves alive with culture, having been developed within a particular cultural context. They have a tendency to guide our thinking toward our desired conclusion.

As the same reasoning may also be applied to the arguments in this article, I better tell you my conclusion before I continue—so that the rules of my game are understood. In this article we take a trip around the world to demonstrate that there are no such things as universal management theories.

Diversity in management *practices* as we go around the world has been recognized in U.S. management literature for more than thirty years. The term "comparative management" has been used since the 1960s. However, it has taken much longer for the U.S. academic community to accept that not only practices but also the validity of *theories* may stop at national borders, and I wonder whether even today everybody would agree with this statement.

An article I published in *Organizational Dynamics* in 1980 entitled "Do American Theories Apply Abroad?" created more controversy than I expected. The article argued, with empirical support, that generally accepted U.S. theories like those of Maslow, Herzberg, McClelland, Vroom, McGregor, Likert, Blake and Mouton may not or only very partly apply outside the borders of their country of origin—assuming they do apply within those borders. Among the requests for reprints, a larger number were from Canada than from the United States.

Management Theorists are Human

Employees and managers are human. Employees as humans was "discovered" in the 1930s, with the Human Relations school. Managers as humans, was introduced in the late 40s by Herbert Simon's "bounded rationality" and elaborated in Richard Cyert and James March's *Behavioral Theory of the Firm* (1963, and recently re-published in a second edition). My argument is that management scientists, theorists, and writers are human too: they grew up in a particular society in a particular period, and their ideas cannot help but reflect the constraints of their environment.

The idea that the validity of a theory is constrained by national borders is more obvious in Europe, with all its borders, than in a huge borderless country like the U.S. Already in the sixteenth century Michel de Montaigne, a Frenchman, wrote a statement which was made famous by Blaise Pascal about a century later: *"Vérite en-deça des Pyrenées, erreur au-delà"*—There are truths on this side of the Pyrenées which are falsehoods on the other.

From Don Armado's Love to Taylor's Science

According to the comprehensive ten-volume Oxford English Dictionary (1971), the words "manage," "management," and "manager" appeared in the English language in the 16th century. The oldest recorded use of the word "manager" is in Shakespeare's "Love's Labour's Lost," dating from 1588, in which Don Adriano de Armado, "a fantastical Spaniard," exclaims (Act I, scene ii, 188):

"Adieu, valour! rust, rapier! be still, drum! for your manager is in love; yea, he loveth".

The linguistic origin of the word is from Latin *manus*, hand, via the Italian *maneggiare*, which is the training of horses in the *manege;* subsequently its meaning was extended to skillful handling in general, like of arms and musical instruments, as Don Armado illustrates. However, the word also became associated with the French *menage*, household, as an equivalent of "husbandry" in its sense of the art of running a household. The theatre of present-day management contains elements of both *manege* and *menage* and different managers and cultures may use different accents.

The founder of the science of economics, the Scot Adam Smith, in his 1776 book *The Wealth of Nations*, used "manage," "management" (even "bad management") and "manager" when dealing with the process and the persons involved in operating joint stock companies (Smith, V.i.e.). British economist John Stuart Mill (1806-1873) followed Smith in this use and clearly expressed his distrust of such hired people who were not driven by ownership. Since the 1880s the word "management" appeared occasionally in writings by American engineers, until it was canonized as a modern science by Frederick W. Taylor in *Shop Management* in 1903 and in *The Principles of Scientific Management* in 1911.

While Smith and Mill used "management" to describe a process and "managers" for the persons involved, "management" in the American sense—which has since been taken back by the British—refers not only to the process but also to the managers as a class of people. This class (1) does not own a business but sells its skills to act on behalf of the owners and (2) does not produce personally but is indispensable for making others produce, through motivation. Members of this class carry a high status and many American boys and girls aspire to the role. In the U.S., the manager is a cultural hero.

Let us now turn to other parts of the world. We will look at management in its context in other successful modern economies: Germany, Japan, France, Holland, and among the Overseas Chinese. Then we will examine management in the much larger part of the world that is still poor, especially South-East Asia and Africa, and in the new political configurations of Eastern Europe, and Russia in particular. We will then return to the U.S. via mainland China.

Germany

The manager is not a cultural hero in Germany. If anybody, it is the engineer who fills the hero role. Frederick Taylor's *Scientific Management* was conceived in a society of immigrants—where large number of workers with diverse backgrounds and skills had to work together. In Germany this heterogeneity never existed.

Elements of the mediaeval guild system have survived in historical continuity in Germany until the present day. In particular, a very effective apprenticeship system exists both on the shop floor and in the office, which alternates practical work and classroom courses. At the end of the apprenticeship the worker receives a certificate, the *Facharbeiterbrief*, which is recognized throughout the country. About two thirds of the German worker population holds such a certificate and a corresponding occupational pride. In fact, quite a few German company presidents have worked their way up from the ranks through an apprenticeship. In comparison, two thirds of the worker population in Britain have no occupational qualification at all.

The highly skilled and responsible German workers do not necessarily need a manager, American-style, to "motivate" them. They expect their boss or *Meister* to assign their tasks and to be the expert in resolving technical problems. Comparisons of similar German, British, and French organizations show the Germans as having the highest rate of personnel in productive roles and the lowest both in leadership and staff roles.

Business schools are virtually unknown in Germany. Native German management theories concentrate on formal systems. The inapplicability of American concepts of management was quite apparent in 1973 when the U.S. consulting firm of Booz, Allen and Hamilton, commissioned by the German Ministry of Economic Affairs, wrote a study of German management from an American view point. The report is highly critical and writes among other things that "Germans simply do not have a very strong concept of management." Since 1973, from my personal experience, the situation has not changed much. However, during this period the German economy has performed in a superior fashion to the U.S. in virtually all respects, so a strong concept of management might have been a liability rather than an asset.

Japan

The American type of manager is also missing in Japan. In the United States, the core of the enterprise is the managerial class. The core of the Japanese enterprise is the permanent worker group; workers who for all practical purposes are tenured and who aspire at life-long employment. They are distinct from the non-permanent employees—most women and subcontracted teams led by gang bosses, to be laid off in slack periods. University graduates in Japan first join the permanent worker group and subsequently fill various positions, moving from line to staff as the need occurs while paid according to seniority rather than position. They take part in Japanese-style group consultation sessions for important decisions, which extend the decision-making period but guarantee fast implementation afterwards. Japanese are to a large extent controlled by their peer group rather than by their manager.

Japanese are to a large extent controlled by their peer group rather than by their manager.

Three researchers from the East-West Center of the University of Hawaii, Joseph Tobin, David Wu, and Dana Danielson, did an observation study of typical preschools in three countries: China, Japan, and the United States. Their results have been published both as a book and as a video. In the Japanese preschool, one teacher handled twenty-eight four-year olds. The video shows one particularly obnoxious boy, Hiroki, who fights with other children and throws teaching materials down from the balcony. When a little girl tries to alarm the teacher, the latter answers "what are you calling me for? Do something about it!" In the U.S. preschool, there is one adult for every nine children. This class has its problem child too, Glen, who refuses to clear away his toys. One of the teachers has a long talk with him and isolates him in a corner, until he changes his mind. It doesn't take much imagination to realize that managing Hiroki thirty years later will be a different process from managing Glen.

American theories of leadership are ill-suited for the Japanese group-controlled situation. During the past two decades, the Japanese have developed their own "PM" theory of leadership, in which P stands for performance and M for maintenance. The latter is less a concern for individual employees than for maintaining social stability. In view of the amazing success of the Japanese economy in the past thirty years, many Americans have sought for the secrets of Japanese management hoping to copy them.

There are no secrets of Japanese management, however; it is even doubtful whether there is such a thing as management, in the American sense, in Japan at all. The secret is in Japanese society; and if any group in society should be singled out as carriers of the secret, it is the workers, not the managers.

France

The manager, U.S. style, does not exist in France either. In a very enlightening book, unfortunately not yet translated into English, the French researcher Philippe d'Iribarne (1989) describes the results of in-depth observation and interview studies of management methods in three subsidiary plants of the same French multinational: in France, the United States, and Holland. He relates what he finds to information about the three societies in general. Where necessary, he goes back in history to trace the roots of the strikingly different behaviors in the completion of the same tasks. He identifies three kinds of basic principles (*logiques*) of management. In the USA, the principle is the *fair contract* between employer and employee, which gives the manager considerable prerogatives, but within its limits. This is really a labor *market* in which the worker sells his or her labor for a price. In France, the principle is the *honor* of each class in a society which has always been and remains extremely stratified, in which superiors behave as superior beings and subordinates accept and expect this, conscious of their own lower level in the national hierarchy but also of the honor of their own class. The French do not think in terms of managers versus nonmanagers but in terms of *cadres* versus *non-cadres;* one becomes cadre by attending the proper schools and one remains it forever; regardless of their actual task, cadres have the privileges of a higher social class, and it is very rare for a non-cadre to cross the ranks.

The conflict between French and American theories of management became apparent in the beginning of the twentieth century, in a criticism by the great French management pioneer Henri Fayol (1841-1925) on his U.S. colleague and contemporary Frederick W. Taylor (1856-1915). The difference in career paths of the two men is striking. Fayol was a French engineer whose career as a *cadre supérieur* culminated in the position of Président-Directeur-Général of a mining company. After his retirement he formulated his experiences in a pathbreaking text on organization: *Administration industrielle et générale*, in which he focussed on the sources of authority. Taylor was an American engineer who started his career in industry as a worker and attained his academic qualifications through evening studies. From chief engineer in a steel company he became one of the first management consultants. Taylor was not really concerned with the issue of authority at all; his focus was on efficiency. He proposed to split the task of the first-line boss into eight specialisms, each exercised by a different person; an idea which eventually led to the idea of a matrix organization.

Taylor's work appeared in a French translation in 1913, and Fayol read it and showed himself generally impressed but shocked by Taylor's "denial of the principle of the Unity of Command" in the case of the eight-boss-system.

Seventy years later André Laurent, another of Fayol's compatriots, found that French managers in a survey reacted very strongly against a suggestion that one employee could report to two different bosses, while U.S. managers in the same survey showed fewer misgivings. Matrix organization has never become popular in France as it has in the United States.

Holland

In my own country, Holland or as it is officially called, the Netherlands, the study by Philippe d'Iribarne found the management principle to be a need for *consensus* among all parties, neither predetermined by a contractual relationship nor by class distinctions, but based on an open-ended exchange of views and a balancing of interests. In terms of the different origins of the word "manager," the organization in Holland is more *menage* (household) while in the United States it is more *manege* (horse drill).

At my university, the University of Limburg at Maastricht, every semester we receive a class of American business students who take a program in European Studies. We asked both the Americans and a matched group of Dutch students to describe their ideal job after graduation, using a list of twenty-two job characteristics. The Americans attached significantly more importance than the Dutch to earnings, advancement, benefits, a good working relationship with their boss, and security of employment. The Dutch attached more importance to freedom to adopt their own approach to the job, being consulted by their boss in his or her decisions, training opportunities, contributing to the success of their organization, fully using their skills and abilities, and helping others. This list confirms d'Iribarne's findings of a contractual employment relationship in the United States, based on earnings and career opportunities, against a consensual relationship in Holland. The latter has centuries-old roots; the Netherlands were the first republic in Western Europe (1609-1810), and a model for the American republic. The country has been and still is governed by a careful balancing of interests in a multi-party system.

In terms of management theories, both motivation and leadership in Holland are different from what they are in the United States. Leadership in Holland presupposes modesty, as opposed to assertiveness in the United States. No U.S. leadership theory has room for that. Working in Holland is not a constant feast, however. There is a built-in premium on mediocrity and jealousy, as well as time-consuming ritual consultations to maintain the apparence of consensus and the pretense of modesty. There is unfortunately another side to every coin.

The overseas Chinese
Among the champions of economic development in the past thirty years we find three countries mainly populated by Chinese living outside the Chinese mainland: Taiwan, Hong Kong and Singapore. Moreover, overseas Chinese play a very important role in the economies of Indonesia, Malaysia, the Philippines and Thailand, where they form an ethnic minority. If anything, the little dragons—Taiwan, Hong Kong and Singapore—have been more economically successful than Japan, moving from rags to riches and now counted among the world's wealthy industrial countries. Yet very little attention has been paid to the way in which their enterprises have been managed. *The Spirit of Chinese Capitalism* by Gordon Redding (1990), the British dean of the Hong Kong Business School, is an excellent book about Chinese business. He bases his insights on personal acquaintance and in-depth discussions with a large number of overseas Chinese businesspeople.

Overseas Chinese American enterprises lack almost all characteristics of modern management. They tend to be small, cooperating for essential functions with other small organizations through networks based on personal relations. They are family-owned, without the separation between ownership and management typical in the West, or even in Japan and Korea. They normally focus on one product or market, with growth by opportunistic diversification; in this, they are extremely flexible. Decision making is centralized in the hands of one dominant family member, but other family members may be given new ventures to try their skills on. They are low-profile and extremely cost-conscious, applying Confucian virtues of thrift and persistence. Their size is kept small by the assumed lack of loyalty of non-family employees, who, if they are any good, will just wait and save until they can start their own family business.

If nothing else, the general lack of success in economic development of other countries should be sufficient argument to doubt the validity of Western management theories in non-Western environments.

Overseas Chinese prefer economic activities in which great gains can be made with little manpower, like commodity trading and real estate. They employ few professional managers, except their sons and sometimes daughters who have been sent to prestigious business schools abroad, but who upon return continue to run the family business the Chinese way.

The origin of this system, or—in the Western view—this lack of system, is found in the history of Chinese society, in which there were no formal laws, only formal networks of powerful people guided by general principles of Confucian virtue. The favors of the authorities could change daily, so nobody could be trusted except one's kinfolk—of whom, fortunately, there used to be many, in an extended family structure. The overseas Chinese way of doing business is also very well adapted to their position in the countries in which they form ethnic minorities, often envied and threatened by ethnic violence.

Overseas Chinese businesses following this unprofessional approach command a collective gross national product of some 200 to 300 billion US dollars, exceeding the GNP of Australia. There is no denying that it works.

Management Transfer to Poor Countries
Four-fifths of the world population live in countries that are not rich but poor. After World War II and decolonization, the stated purpose of the United Nations and the World Bank has been to promote the development of all the world's countries in a war on poverty. After forty years it looks very much like we are losing this war. If one thing has become clear, it is that the export of Western—mostly American—management practices *and* theories to poor countries has contributed little to nothing to their development. There has been no lack of effort and money spent for this purpose: students from poor countries have been trained in this country, and teachers and Peace Corps workers have been sent to the poor countries. If nothing else, the general lack of success in economic development of other

countries should be sufficient argument to doubt the validity of Western management theories in non-Western environments.

Assuming that with so-called modern management techniques and theories outsiders can develop a country has proven a deplorable arrogance.

If we examine different parts of the world, the development picture is not equally bleak, and history is often a better predictor than economic factors for what happens today. There is a broad regional pecking order with East Asia leading. The little dragons have passed into the camp of the wealthy; then follow South-East Asia (with its overseas Chinese minorities), Latin America (in spite of the debt crisis), South Asia, and Africa always trails behind. Several African countries have only become poorer since decolonization.

Regions of the world with a history of large-scale political integration and civilization generally have done better than regions in which no large-scale political and cultural infrastructure existed, even if the old civilations had decayed or been suppressed by colonizers. It has become painfully clear that development cannot be pressure-cooked; it presumes a cultural infrastructure that takes time to grow. Local management is part of this infrastructure; it cannot be imported in package form. Assuming that with so-called modern management techniques and theories outsiders can develop a country has proven a deplorable arrogance. At best, one can hope for a dialogue between equals with the locals, in which the Western partner acts as the expert in Western technology and the local partner as the expert in local culture, habits, and feelings.

Russia and China

The crumbling of the former Eastern bloc has left us with a scattering of states and would-be states of which the political and economic future is extremely uncertain. The best predictions are those based on a knowledge of history, because historical trends have taken revenge on the arrogance of the Soviet rulers who believed they could turn them around by brute power. One obvious fact is that the former bloc is extremely heterogeneous, including countries traditionally closely linked with the West by trade and travel, like Czechia, Hungary, Slovenia, and the Baltic states, as well as others with a Byzantine or Turkish past; some having been prosperous, others always extremely poor.

The industrialized Western world and the World Bank seem committed to helping the ex-Eastern bloc countries develop, but with the same technocratic neglect for local cultural factors that proved so unsuccessful in the development assistance to other poor countries. Free market capitalism, introduced by Western-style management, is supposed to be the answer from Albania to Russia.

Let me limit myself to the Russian republic, a huge territory with some 140 million inhabitants, mainly Russians. We know quite a bit about the Russians as their country was a world power for several hundreds of year before communism, and in the nineteenth century it has produced some of the greatest writers in world literature. If I want to understand the Russians—including how they could so long support the Soviet regime—I tend to re-read Lev Nikolayevich Tolstoy. In his most famous novel *Anna Karenina* (1876) one of the main characters is a landowner, Levin, whom Tolstoy uses to express his own views and convictions about his people. Russian peasants used to be serfs; serfdom had been abolished in 1861, but the peasants, now tenants, remained as passive as before. Levin wanted to break this passivity by dividing the land among his peasants in exchange for a share of the crops; but the peasants only let the land deteriorate further. Here follows a quote:

"(Levin) read political economy and socialistic works . . . but, as he had expected, found nothing in them related to his undertaking. In the political economy

books—in (John Stuart) Mill, for instance, whom he studied first and with great ardour, hoping every minute to find an answer to the questions that were engrossing him—he found only certain laws deduced from the state of agriculture in Europe; but he could not for the life of him see why these laws, which did not apply to Russia, should be considered universal. . . . Political economy told him that the laws by which Europe had developed and was developing her wealth were universal and absolute. Socialist teaching told him that development along those lines leads to ruin. And neither of them offered the smallest enlightenment as to what he, Levin, and all the Russian peasants and landowners were to do with their millions of hands and millions of acres, to make them as productive as possible for the common good."

In the summer of 1991, the Russian lands yielded a record harvest, but a large share of it rotted in the fields because no people were to be found for harvesting. The passivity is still there, and not only among the peasants. And the heirs of John Stuart Mill (whom we met before as one of the early analysts of "management") again present their universal recipes which simply do not apply.

Citing Tolstoy, I implicitly suggest that management theorists cannot neglect the great literature of the countries they want their ideas to apply to. The greatest novel in the Chinese literature is considered Cao Xueqin's *The Story of the Stone*, also known as *The Dream of the Red Chamber* which appeared around 1760. It describes the rise and fall of two branches of an aristocratic family in Beijing, who live in adjacent plots in the capital. Their plots are joined by a magnificent garden with several pavillions in it, and the young, mostly female members of both families are allowed to live in them. One day the management of the garden is taken over by a young woman, Tan-Chun, who states:

"I think we ought to pick out a few experienced trust-worthy old women from among the ones who work in the Garden—women who know something about gardening already—and put the upkeep of the Garden into their hands. We needn't ask them to pay us rent; all we need ask them for is an annual share of the produce. There would be four advantages in this arrangement. In the first place, if we have people whose sole occupation is to look after trees and flowers and so on, the condition of the Garden will improve gradually year after year and there will be no more of those long periods of neglect followed by bursts of feverish activity when things have been allowed to get out of hand. Secondly there won't be the spoiling and wastage we get at present. Thirdly the women themselves will gain a little extra to add to their incomes which will compensate them for the hard work they put in throughout the year. And fourthly, there's no reason why we shouldn't use the money we should otherwise have spent on nurserymen, rockery specialists, horticultural cleaners and so on for other purposes."

As the story goes on, the capitalist privatization—because that is what it is—of the Garden is carried through, and it works. When in the 1980s Deng Xiaoping allowed privatization in the Chinese villages, it also worked. It worked so well that its effects started to be felt in politics and threatened the existing political order; hence the knockdown at Tienanmen Square of June 1989. But it seems that the forces of privatization are getting the upper hand again in China. If we remember what Chinese entrepreneurs are able to do once they have become Overseas Chinese, we shouldn't be too surprised. But what works in China—and worked two centuries ago—does not have to work in Russia, not in Tolstoy's days and not today. I am not offering a solution; I only protest against a naive universalism that knows only one recipe for development, the one supposed to have worked in the United States.

A Theory of Culture in Management

Our trip around the world is over and we are back in the United States. What have we learned? There is something in all countries called "management," but its meaning differs to a larger or smaller extent from one country to the other, and it takes considerable historical and cultural insight into local conditions to understand its processes, philosophies, and problems. If already the word may mean so many different things, how can we expect one country's theories of management to apply abroad? One should be extremely careful in making this assumption, and test it before considering it proven. Management is not a phenomenon that can be isolated from other processes taking place in a society. During our trip around the world we saw that it interacts with what happens in the family, at school, in politics, and government. It is obviously also related to religion and to beliefs about science. Theories of management always had to be interdisciplinary, but if we cross national borders they should become more interdisciplinary than ever.

Cultural differences between nations can be, to some extent, described using first four, and now five, bipolar *dimensions*. The position of a country on these dimensions allows us to make some predictions on the way their society operates, including their management processes and the kind of theories applicable to their management.

As the word culture plays such an important role in my theory, let me give you my definition, which differs from some other very respectable definitions. Culture to me is *the collective programming of the mind which distinguishes one group or category of people from another*. In the part of my work I am referring to now, the category of people is the nation.

Culture is a *construct*, that means it is "not directly accessible to observation but inferable from verbal statements and other behaviors and useful in predicting still other observable and measurable verbal and nonverbal behavior." It should not be reified; it is an auxiliary concept that should be used as long it proves useful but bypassed where we can predict behaviors without it.

The same applies to the *dimensions* I introduced. They are constructs too that should not be reified. They do not "exist"; they are tools for analysis which may or may not clarify a situation. In my statistical analysis of empirical data the first four dimensions together explain forty-nine percent of the variance in the data. The other fifty-one percent remain specific to individual countries.

The first four dimensions were initially detected through a comparison of the values of similar people (employees and managers) in sixty-four national subsidiaries of the IBM Corporation. People working for the same multinational, but in different countries, represent very well-matched samples from the populations of their countries, similar in all respects except nationality.

The first dimension is labelled *Power Distance*, and it can be defined as the degree of inequality among people which the population of a country considers as normal: from relatively equal (that is, small power distance) to extremely unequal (large power distance). All societies are unequal, but some are more unequal than others.

The second dimension is labelled *Individualism*, and it is the degree to which people in a country prefer to act as individuals rather than as members of groups. The opposite of individualism can be called *Collectivism*, so collectivism is low individualism. The way I use the word it has no political connotations. In collectivist societies a child learns to respect the group to which it belongs, usually the family, and to differentiate between in-group members and out-group members (that is, all other people). When children grow up they remain members of their group, and they expect the group to protect them when they are in trouble. In return, they have to remain loyal to their group throughout life. In individualist societies, a child learns very early to think of itself as "I" instead of as part of "we". It expects one day to have to stand on its own feet and not to get protection from its group any more; and therefore it also does not feel a need for strong loyalty.

The third dimension is called *Masculinity* and its opposite pole *Femininity*. It is the degree to which tough values like assertiveness, performance, success and competition, which in nearly all societies are associated with the role of men, prevail over tender values like the quality of life, maintaining warm personal relationships, service, care for the weak, and solidarity, which in nearly all societies are more associated with women's roles. Women's roles differ from men's roles in all countries; but in tough societies, the differences are larger than in tender ones.

The fourth dimension is labelled *Uncertainty Avoidance*, and it can be defined as the degree to which people in a country prefer structured over unstructured situations. Structured situations are those in which there are clear rules as to how one should behave. These rules can be written down, but they can also be unwritten and imposed by tradition. In countries which score high on uncertainty avoidance, people tend to show more nervous energy, while in countries which score low, people are more easy-going. A (national) society with strong uncertainty avoidance can be called rigid; one with weak uncertainty avoidance, flexible. In countries where uncertainty avoidance is strong a feeling prevails of "what is different, is dangerous." In weak uncertainty avoidance societies, the feeling would rather be "what is different, is curious."

The fifth dimension was added on the basis of a study of the values of students in twenty-three countries carried out by Michael Harris Bond, a Canadian working in Hong Kong. He and I had cooperated in another study of students' values which had yielded the same four dimensions as the IBM data. However, we wondered to what extent our common findings in two studies could be the effect of a Western bias introduced by the common Western background of the researchers: remember Alice's croquet game. Michael Bond resolved this dilemma by deliberately introducing an Eastern bias. He used a questionnaire prepared at his request by his Chinese colleagues, the *Chinese Value Survey* (CVS), which was translated from Chinese into different languages and answered by fifty male and fifty female students in each of twenty-three countries in all five continents. Analysis of the CVS data produced three dimensions significantly correlated with the three IBM dimensions of power distance, individualism, and masculinity. There was also a fourth dimension, but it did not resemble uncertainty avoidance. It was composed, both on the positive and on the negative side, from items that had not been included in the IBM studies but were present in the Chinese Value Survey because they were rooted in the teachings of Confucius. I labelled this dimension: *Long-term* versus *Short-term Orientation*. On the long-term side one finds values oriented towards the future, like thrift (saving) and persistence. On the short-term side one finds values rather oriented towards the past and present, like respect for tradition and fulfilling social obligations.

Table 1 lists the scores on all five dimensions for the United States and for the other countries we just discussed. The table shows that each country has its own configuration on the four dimensions. Some of the values in the table have been estimated based on imperfect replications or personal impressions. The different dimension scores do not "explain" all the differences in management I described earlier. To understand management in a country, one should have both knowledge of and empathy with the entire local scene. However, the scores should make us aware that people in other countries may think, feel, and act very differently from us when confronted with basic problems of society.

Table 1
Culture Dimension Scores for Ten Countries
PD = Power Distance; ID = Individualism; MA = Masculinity; UA = Uncertainty Avoidance; LT = Long Term Orientation)
H = top third, M = medium third, L = bottom third (among 53 countries and regions for the first four dimensions; among 23 countries for the fifth)

	PD	ID	MA	UA	LT
USA	40 L	91 H	62 H	46 L	29 L
Germany	35 L	67 H	66 H	65 M	31 M
Japan	54 M	46 M	95 H	92 H	80 H
France	68 H	71 H	43 M	86 H	30*L
Netherlands	38 L	80 H	14 L	53 M	44 M
Hong Kong	68 H	25 L	57 H	29 L	96 H
Indonesia	78 H	14 L	46 M	48 L	25*L
West Africa	77 H	20 L	46 M	54 M	16 L
Russia	95*H	50*M	40*L	90*H	10*L
China	80*H	20*L	50*M	60*M	118 H

* estimated

Idiosyncracies of American Management Theories

In comparison to other countries, the U.S. culture profile presents itself as below average on power distance and uncertainty avoidance, highly individualistic, fairly masculine, and short-term oriented. The Germans show a stronger uncertainty avoidance and less extreme individualism; the Japanese are different on all dimensions, least on power distance; the French show larger power distance and uncertainty avoidance, but are less individualistic and somewhat feminine; the Dutch resemble the Americans on the first three dimensions, but score extremely feminine and relatively long-term oriented; Hong Kong Chinese combine large power distance with weak uncertainty avoidance, collectivism, and are very long-term oriented; and so on.

The ideal principle of control in organizations in the market philosophy is competition between individuals.

The American culture profile is reflected in American management theories. I will just mention three elements not necessarily present in other countries: the stress on market processes, the stress on the individual, and the focus on managers rather than on workers.

The Stress on Market Processes

During the 1970s and 80s it has become fashionable in the United States to look at organizations from a "transaction costs" viewpoint. Economist Oliver Williamson has opposed "hierarchies" to "markets." The reasoning is that human social life consists of economic transactions between individuals. We found the same in d'Iribarne's description of the U.S. principle of the contract between employer and employee, the labor market in which the worker sells his or her labor for a price. These individuals will form hierarchical organizations when the cost of the economic transactions (such as getting information, finding out whom to trust etc.) is lower in a hierarchy than when all transactions would take place on a free market.

From a cultural perspective the important point is that *the "market" is the point of departure or base model*, and the organization is explained from market failure. A culture that produces such a theory is likely to prefer organizations that internally resemble markets to organizations that internally resemble more structured models, like those in Germany of France. The ideal principle of control in organizations in the market philosophy is *competition* between individuals. This philosophy fits a society that combines a not-too-large power distance with a not-too-strong uncertainty avoidance and individualism; besides the USA, it will fit all other Anglo countries.

The Stress on the Individual
I find this constantly in the design of research projects and hypotheses; also in the fact that in the U.S. psychology is clearly a more respectable discipline in management circles than sociology. Culture however is a collective phenomenon. Although we may get our information about culture from individuals, we have to interpret it at the level of collectivities. There are snags here known as the "ecological fallacy" and the "reverse ecological fallacy." None of the U.S. college textbooks on methodology I know deals sufficiently with the problem of multilevel analysis.

Culture can be compared to a forest, while individuals are tree. A forest is not just a bunch of trees: it is a symbiosis of different trees, bushes, plants, insects, animals and micro-organisms, and we miss the essence of the forest if we only describe its most typical trees. In the same way, a culture cannot be satisfactorily described in terms of the characteristics of a typical individual. There is a tendency in the U.S. management literature to overlook the forest for the trees and to ascribe cultural differences to interactions among individuals.

A striking example is found in the otherwise excellent book *Organizational Culture and Leadership* by Edgar H. Schein (1985). On the basis of his consulting experience he compares two large companies, nicknamed "Action" and "Multi." He explains the differences in culture between these companies by the group dynamics in their respective boardrooms. Nowhere in the book are any conclusions drawn from the fact that the first company is an American-based computer firm, and the second a Swiss-based pharmaceutics firm. This information is not even mentioned. A stress on interactions among individuals obviously fits a culture identified as the most individualistic in the world, but it will not be so well understood by the four-fifths of the world population for whom the group prevails over the individual.

One of the conclusions of my own multilevel research has been that culture at the national level and culture at the organizational level—corporate culture—are two very different phenomena and that the use of a common term for both is confusing. If we do use the common term, we should also pay attention to the occupational and the gender level of culture. National cultures differ primarily in the fundamental, invisible values held by a majority of their members, acquired in early childhood, whereas organizational cultures are a much more superficial phenomenon residing mainly in the visible practices of the organization, acquired by socialization of the new members who join as young adults. National cultures change only very slowly if at all; organizational cultures may be consciously changed, although this isn't necessarily easy. This difference between the two types of culture is the secret of the existence of multinational corporations that employ, as I showed in the IBM case, employees with extremely different national cultural values. What keeps them together is a corporate culture based on common practices.

Managers are much more involved in maintaining networks; if anything, it is the rank-and-file worker who can really make decisions on his or her own, albeit on a relatively simple level.

The Stress on Managers Rather than Workers
The core element of a work organization around the world is the people who do the work. All the rest is superstructure, and I hope to have demonstrated to you that it may take many different shapes. In the U.S. literature on work organization, however, the core element, if not explicitly then implicitly, is considered the manager. This may well be the result of the combination of extreme individualism with fairly strong masculinity, which has turned the manager into a culture hero of almost mythical proportions. For example, he—not really she—is supposed to make decisions all the time. Those of you who are or have been managers must know that this is a fable. Very few management decisions are just "made" as the

myth suggests it. Managers are much more involved in maintaining networks; if anything, it is the rank-and-file worker who can really make decisions on his or her own, albeit on a relatively simple level.

An amusing effect of the U.S. focus on managers is that in at least ten American books and articles on management I have been misquoted as having studied IBM *managers* in my research, whereas the book clearly describes that the answers were from IBM *employees*. My observation may be biased, but I get the impression that compared to twenty or thirty years ago less research in this country is done among employees and more on managers. But managers derive their *raison d'être* from the people managed: culturally, they are the followers of the people they lead, and their effectiveness depends on the latter. In other parts of the world, this exclusive focus on the manager is less strong, with Japan as the supreme example.

Conclusion

This article started with *Alice in Wonderland*. In fact, the management theorist who ventures outside his or her own country into other parts of the world is like Alice in Wonderland. He or she will meet strange beings, customs, ways of organizing or disorganizing and theories that are clearly stupid, oldfashioned or even immoral—yet they may work, or at least they may not fail more frequently than corresponding theories do at home. Then, after the first culture shock, the traveller to Wonderland will feel enlightened, and may be able to take his or her experiences home and use them advantageously. All great ideas in science, politics and management have travelled from one country to another, and been enriched by foreign influences. The roots of American management theories are mainly in Europe: with Adam Smith, John Stuart Mill, Lev Tolstoy, Max Weber, Henri Fayol, Sigmund Freud, Kurt Lewin and many others. These theories were re-planted here and they developed and bore fruit. The same may happen again. The last thing we need is a Monroe doctrine for management ideas.

The issues explored here were presented by Dr. Hofstede, the Foundation for Administrative Research Distinguished International Scholar, at the 1992 Annual Meeting of the Academy of Management, Las Vegas, Nevada, August 11, 1992.

About the Author

Geert Hofstede is a professor of organizational anthropology and international management at the University of Limburg at Maastricht, the Netherlands. He holds a M.Sc. degree in Mechanical Engineering from Delft Technical University, and a Ph.D. in Social Psychology from Groningen University, both in his native Netherlands.

He worked in Dutch as well as international business companies in roles varying from production worker to director of Human Resources. From 1965-1971, he founded and managed the Personnel Research department of IBM Europe. Since then, he has been teaching and researching at various international management institutes in four different European countries. In 1991 he held a Visiting Research Fellowship at the East-West Center, Honolulu, while simultaneously teaching at the College of Business Administration, University of Hawaii. He is a honorary professor of the University of Hong Kong.

Geert Hofstede is the founder and first director of the Institute for Research on Intercultural Cooperation (IRIC) at the University of Limburg, and an internationally recognized expert in the field of national and organizational culture research and theory. He has been a consultant to national and international business and government organizations. He wrote a pathbreaking book *Culture's Consequences* (Sage, 1980). A more popular book *Cultures and Organizations: Software of the Mind* appeared in 1991; translations have appeared or are under way into ten other languages. His articles—more than a hundred—have been published in the journals and readers of different countries of Europe, Asia, and North America.

[6]

Culture: what it is, what it is not and how it directs organizational behaviour

Most people who have visited or worked in another country would readily agree that cultural differences exist. They might point to such things as different styles of dress, language, food or mannerisms as examples of how cultures differ. It is much more difficult to go beyond such relevant, yet superficial differences in talking about culture. If you are fluent in another language, some of the more 'hidden' differences become more apparent, such as how and when people use humour, how formally or informally they behave towards others in different contexts, and the different meanings and use of silence, power, influence, gender, position, and so on. But these are most often noticed in a particular situation, labelled as 'strange' or different and then disregarded because we have no way of classifying these peculiarities into a 'language of culture'. Because culture is about pervasive, deeply held and implicit beliefs and values, it is indeed difficult to find a language with which to discuss it or to explore its consequences.

> 'It is helpful... to think of culture as analogous to music: (a) If another person hasn't heard a particular piece of music, it is impossible to describe. (b) Before the days of written scores, people had to learn informally by imitation. (c) People were able to exploit the potential of music only when they started writing musical scores.' (Hall, 1973)

The difficulty of finding terms with which to explore differences in culture does not seem to stop people from talking about culture as if it were a 'thing', hovering over a society and influencing behaviour in a direct and uniform way. At the end of 1990 when Renault of France lost out on the Skoda deal to Volkswagen of Germany, the international press reported that Renault blamed its failure on culture (*International Herald Tribune*, 1990). They seemed to think that Germany had a culture closer to the Czech culture than did France. The validity of the claim is not the issue here. The point is that the perception of culture as the determinant of such an important outcome is so readily offered (and, it could be added, accepted) as an explanation when most people would have a difficult time being specific about *what that might really mean* except in terms of the superficial examples given above. Culture is not a 'thing' which can be experienced directly through the senses, just as 'needs', 'social systems', 'evil' and 'peace' are not directly tangible or visible. They are ideas constructed from within a society. 'Culture' does not exist in a simple and easily defined form for a specifiable number of people in a bounded area. And, obviously, a society does not consist of individuals with entirely uniform mental characteristics or personalities.

What culture is

(1) *A shared system of meanings.* Culture dictates what groups of people pay attention to. It guides how the world is perceived, how the self is experienced and how life itself is organized. Individuals of a group share patterns that enable them to see the same things in the same way and this holds them together. Each person carries within them learned ways of finding meaning in their experiences. In order for effective, stable and meaningful interaction to occur, people must have a shared system of meaning. There must be some common ways of understanding events and behaviour, and ways of anticipating how other people in your social group are likely to behave. For example, waving a hand or planting a kiss has no clear meaning without the context being understood. Furthermore, the intended meaning of a gesture need not coincide with the perceived meaning except where cultural identities match. It is only when the meanings *do* coincide that effective communication can happen.

(2) *Relative.* There is no cultural absolute. People in different cultures perceive the world differently and have different ways of doing things, and there is no set standard for considering one group as intrinsically superior or inferior to any other. Each national culture is relative to other cultures' ways of perceiving the world and doing things.

(3) *Learned.* Culture is derived from your social environment, not from your genetic make-up.
(4) *About groups.* Culture is a collective phenomenon that is about shared values and meanings.

The noted business author and scholar Geert Hofstede describes culture as the 'collective programming of the mind' and explains that it lies between human nature on one side and individual personality on the other (Hofstede, 1991). Figure 2.1 shows his model of three levels of uniqueness in human mental programming.

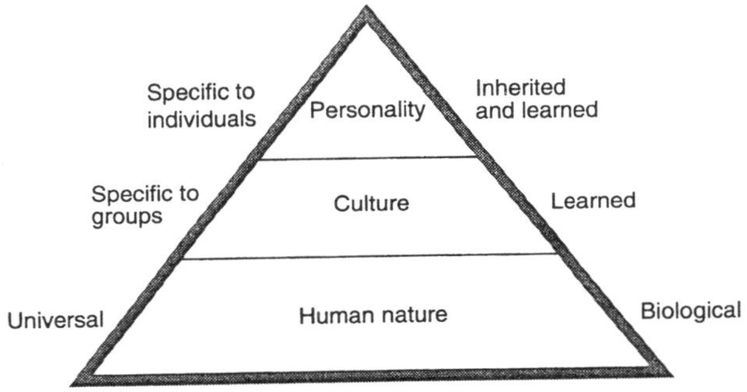

Figure 2.1 Three levels of human mental programming. (*Source*: Adapted from Hofstede, 1991)

What culture is not

(1) *Right or wrong.*
(2) *Inherited.*
(3) *About individual behaviour.* There are wide variations in individual values and behaviour within each national culture.

Different layers of culture

Each person carries around several layers of cultural 'programming'. It starts when a child learns basic values: what is right and wrong, good and bad, logical and illogical, beautiful and ugly. Culture is about your fundamental assumptions of what it is to be a person and how you should

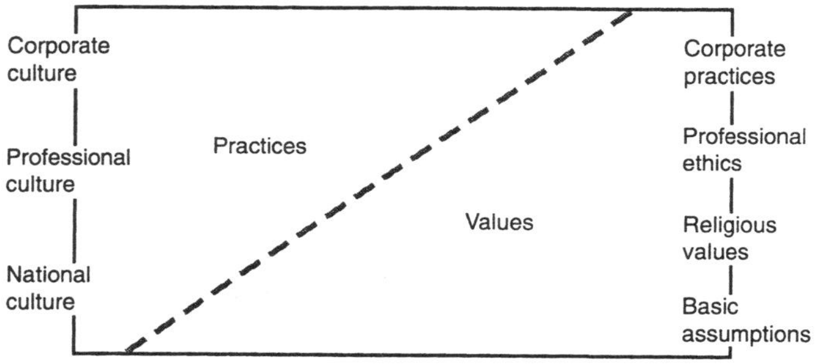

Figure 2.2 Layers of cultural 'programming'. (*Source*: Adapted from Hofstede, 1991)

interact with other persons within your own group (which again is a boundary culturally drawn) and with outsiders. This 'first level' of culture is the deepest, the most difficult to change and will vary according to the culture in which we grow up.

Other layers of culture are learned or 'programmed' in the course of education, through professional or craft training and in organizational life. Some of the aspects of culture learned later have to do with conventions and ethics in your profession (that is, what it means to be a lawyer, accountant or doctor; the way a particular organization functions, how people get promoted or how office politics are played, and so on). These layers are more ways of doing things, or *practices*, as opposed to fundamental assumptions about how things are (see Figure 2.2).

Because of the timing and sequence of learning these values and ways of doing things, their capacity for change is also different. André Laurent uses the diagram shown in Figure 2.3 to illustrate change capability (Laurent, 1989). Individuals and societies have a lower capability for change than do organizations.

Cultural values taken for granted

Cultural values are very difficult to talk about because they are taken for granted. They become like a problem solved regularly in the same way: it ceases to be a problem. Rather, it ceases to be a conscious act and becomes just another assumption. It is only when a person's assumptions are challenged that they realize that these assumptions even exist.

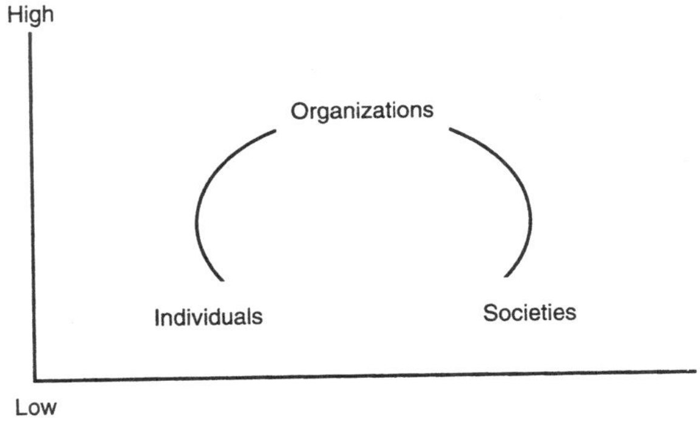

Figure 2.3 Change capability. (*Source*: Evans, Doz, and Laurent, eds., 1989)

Definitions of culture

There are many descriptions and definitions of culture (see Box 2.1).

Attempts to classify national cultures in terms of the importance attached to different values

The most widely known research in the attempt to compare national cultures in terms of broad value differences is the pioneering work of Geert Hofstede. From his research with a very large sample of employees from 50 countries and three regions within a single organization, IBM, Hofstede identified four dimensions of work-related value differences. These are power distance, uncertainty avoidance, individualism/collectivism and masculinity/femininity. Values, according to Hofstede's definition, are 'a broad tendency to prefer certain states of affairs over others'. These differences in preferences, or values, have important implications for managers and organizations operating across cultural borders. He describes the dimensions as follows (Hofstede, 1991). (Box 2.2 gives some of the most useful questions and responses in defining the meanings of each of these dimensions.)

Box 2.1 Concepts of culture by some of the gurus

Tylor E. (1871). That complex whole which includes knowledge, beliefs, art, morals, laws, customs and any other capabilities and habits acquired by man as a member of society.

Herskovits M.J. (1948). The man-made part of the human environment.

Kroeber A.L. and Kluckhohn C. (1952). Transmitted patterns of values, ideas and other symbolic systems that shape behaviour.

Becker and Geer (1970). Set of common understandings expressed in language.

van Maanen J. and Schein E.H. (1979). Values, beliefs and expectations that members come to share.

Schwartz M.C. and Jordon D.K. (1980). Pattern of beliefs and expectations shared by members that produce norms shaping behaviour.

Hofstede G.H. (1980). The collective programming of the mind which distinguishes the members of one human group from another.

Louis M.R. (1983). Three aspects: (1) some content (meaning and interpretation) (2) peculiar to (3) a group.

Hall E.T. and Hall M.R. (1987). Primarily a system for creating, sending, storing and processing information.

Harris P.R. and Moran R.T. (1987). A distinctly human capacity for adapting to circumstances and transmitting this coping skill and knowledge to subsequent generations.

Power distance

Power distance is the extent to which inequality (a pecking order or hierarchy) is seen as an irreducible fact of life. It would condition the extent to which employees accept that their boss has more power than they have and the extent to which they accept that their boss's opinions and decisions are right *because* he or she is the boss. A low power distance organizational setting is one where employees accept that their boss has more power and is right only when he or she knows the best way to do something and knows the correct answers. A report in a British newspaper described some of the different conceptions of power distance when British Petroleum attempted to mix 40 workers from 13 nations in a modern European finance office (*The Independent*, 1991).

Box 2.2 Hofstede's four dimensions of culture-related values

Value	*Questionnaire item*	*Response*
Power distance	How frequently, in your experience, does the following problem occur: employees being afraid to express their disagreement with their managers?	Frequently
Uncertainty avoidance	Company rules should not be broken, even if the employee thinks it is in the company's best interest.	Strongly agree
	How long do you think you will continue working for this company?	Until I retire
Individualism	How important is it to you to have a job which leaves you sufficient time for your personal or family life?	Very
	How important is it to you to have considerable freedom to adapt your own approach to the job?	Very
Femininity	How important is it to you to have a good working relationship with your manager?	Very
	How important is it to you to work with people who cooperate well with one another?	Very
Masculinity	How important is it to you to have an opportunity for high earnings?	Very
	How important is it to you to get the recognition you deserve when you do a good job?	Very

(*Source*: Smith P.B. and Bond M.H. *Social Psychology Across Cultures: Analysis and Perspectives*, p.39. London: Harvester Wheatsheaf)

The article reported that: 'Germans felt more comfortable in formal hierarchies, while Dutch members had a relaxed approach to authority. UK, Scandinavian and Dutch managers all expected their decision-making to be challenged, while French managers thought that authority to make decisions came as a right of office.'

In the larger power distance cultures superiors and subordinates consider each other as unequal; the hierarchical system is felt to be based on some existential inequality. Indigenous organizations centralize power more and subordinates are expected to be told what to do. Superiors are believed to be entitled to privileges in a high power distance culture. There are more visible signs of status, and contacts between superiors and subordinates are supposed to be initiated only by superiors.

In smaller power distance situations subordinates and superiors consider each other as more equal; the hierarchical system is just an inequality of roles, established for convenience and which may change depending on the circumstances. Organizations have a tendency to become decentralized, with flatter hierarchies and a limited number of supervisory personnel. Privileges for the top ranks are essentially undesirable, and superiors are expected to be accessible to subordinates. Organizations more often have in place ways of dealing with employee complaints about alleged power abuse (Adler, 1986).

Table 2.1 Power distance (PD) scores.

Score rank	*Country or region*	*PD score*	*Score rank*	*Country or region*	*PD score*
1	Malaysia	104	27/28	South Korea	60
2/3	Guatemala	95	29/30	Iran	58
2/3	Panama	95	29/30	Taiwan	58
4	Philippines	94	31	Spain	57
5/6	Mexico	81	32	Pakistan	55
5/6	Venezuela	81	33	Japan	54
7	Arab countries	80	34	Italy	50
8/9	Equador	78	35/36	Argentina	49
8/9	Indonesia	78	35/36	South Africa	49
10/11	India	77	37	Jamaica	45
10/11	West Africa	77	38	USA	40
12	Yugoslavia	76	39	Canada	39
13	Singapore	74	40	Netherlands	38
14	Brazil	69	41	Australia	36
15/16	France	68	42/44	Costa Rica	35
15/16	Hong Kong	68	42/44	West Germany	35
17	Colombia	67	42/44	UK	35
18/19	Salvador	66	45	Switzerland	34
18/19	Turkey	66	46	Finland	33
20	Belgium	65	47/48	Norway	31
21/23	East Africa	64	47/48	Sweden	31
21/23	Peru	64	49	Ireland (Republic of)	28
21/23	Thailand	64			
24/25	Chile	63	50	New Zealand	22
24/25	Portugal	63	51	Denmark	18
26	Uruguay	61	52	Israel	13
27/28	Greece	60	53	Austria	11

Table 2.2 Business areas affected by power distance.

Low power distance	*High power distance*
Less centralization	Greater centralization
Flatter organization pyramids	Steep organization pyramids
Managers seen as making decisions after consulting with subordinates	Managers seen as making decisions autocratically and paternalistically
Close supervision negatively evaluated by subordinates	Close supervision positively evaluated by subordinates
Managers like to see themselves as practical and systematic; they admit a need for support	Managers like to see themselves as benevolent decision-makers
Higher-educated employees hold much less authoritarian values than lower-educated ones	Higher- and lower-educated employees hold similar values about authority

Source: Adapted from Hofstede G. (1984). *Culture's Consequences: International Differences in Work-Related Values*, abridged edn. Thousand Oaks, CA: Sage Publications Inc. Reproduced with permission of McGraw-Hill.

Uncertainty avoidance

Uncertainty avoidance is the lack of tolerance for ambiguity and the need for formal rules. This dimension measures the extent to which people in a society feel threatened by and try to avoid ambiguous situations. They may do this by establishing more formal rules, rejecting deviant ideas and behaviour, and accepting the possibility of absolute truths and the attainment of unchallengeable expertise.

Lifetime employment is more common in high uncertainty avoidance countries such as Japan, Portugal and Greece, whereas high job mobility more commonly occurs in low uncertainty avoidance countries such as Singapore, Hong Kong, Denmark and the USA (Adler, 1986).

Management implications of power distance and uncertainty avoidance

These two dimensions, power distance and uncertainty avoidance, affect our thinking about organizations. In addition to the affected business areas listed in Tables 2.2 and 2.4, taking these two dimensions together reveals differences in the implicit model people from different cultures may have about organizational structure and functioning. Organizing demands answers to two important questions:

(1) Who has the power to decide what?
(2) What rules or procedures will be followed to attain the desired ends?

Table 2.3 Uncertainty avoidance (UA) scores.

Score rank	*Country or region*	*UA score*	*Score rank*	*Country or region*	*UA score*
1	Greece	112	28	Equador	67
2	Portugal	104	29	West Germany	65
3	Guatemala	101	30	Thailand	64
4	Uruguay	100	31/32	Iran	59
5/6	Belgium	94	31/32	Finland	59
5/6	Salvador	94	33	Switzerland	58
7	Japan	92	34	West Africa	54
8	Yugoslavia	88	35	Netherlands	53
9	Peru	87	36	East Africa	52
10/15	France	86	37	Australia	51
10/15	Chile	86	38	Norway	50
10/15	Spain	86	39/40	South Africa	49
10/15	Costa Rica	86	39/40	New Zealand	49
10/15	Panama	86	41/42	Indonesia	48
10/15	Argentina	86	41/42	Canada	48
16/17	Turkey	85	43	USA	46
16/17	South Korea	85	44	Philippines	44
18	Mexico	82	45	India	40
19	Israel	81	46	Malaysia	36
20	Colombia	80	47/48	UK	35
21/22	Venezuela	76	47/48	Ireland (Republic of)	35
21/22	Brazil	76			
23	Italy	75	49/50	Hong Kong	29
24/25	Pakistan	70	49/50	Sweden	29
24/25	Austria	70	51	Denmark	23
26	Taiwan	69	52	Jamaica	13
27	Arab countries	68	53	Singapore	8

Table 2.4 Business areas affected by uncertainty avoidance.

Low uncertainty avoidance	*High uncertainty avoidance*
Greater readiness to live by the day	More worry about the future
Less emotional resistance to change	More emotional resistance to change
Less hesitation to change employers	Tendency to stay with same employer
Loyalty to employer is not seen as a virtue	Loyalty to employer is seen as a virtue
Managers should be selected on other criteria than seniority	Managers should be selected on the basis of seniority
More risk-taking	Less risk-taking
Hope of success	Fear of failure
A manager need not be an expert in the field he or she manages	A manager must be an expert in the field he or she manages
Conflict in organizations is natural	Conflict in organizations is undesirable
Delegation to subordinates can be complete	Initiative of subordinates should be kept under control
Employee optimism about the motives behind company activities	Employee pessimism about the motives behind company activities
Rules may be broken for pragmatic reasons	Rules should not be broken

Source: Adapted from Hofstede G. (1984). *Culture's Consequences: International Differences in Work-Related Values*, abridged edn. Thousand Oaks, CA: Sage Publications Inc. Reproduced with permission of McGraw-Hill.

The answer to the first question is influenced by indigenous cultural norms of power distance; the answer to the second question by the cultural norms about uncertainty avoidance. Taken together these two dimensions reveal a remarkable contrast in a society's acceptance and conception of an organization and the mechanisms that are employed in controlling and coordinating activities within it (Hofstede, 1991).

Some researchers have tried to measure the link between the 'implicit' models of organization and objectively assessable characteristics of organizational structure. In the 1970s, Owen James Stevens, an American professor at INSEAD business school in France, presented his students with a case study exam which dealt with a conflict between two department heads within a company (Hofstede, 1991). His students consisted primarily of French, German and British students. In Figure 2.4 their countries are located in the lower right, lower left and upper left quadrants respectively. Stevens had noticed a difference in the way 200 students of different nationalities had handled the case in previous exams. The students had been required individually to come up with both their diagnosis of the problem and their suggested solution. Stevens sorted these exams by the nationality of the author and then compared the answers. The results were striking. The majority of French diagnosed the case as negligence by the general manager to whom the two department heads reported. The solution they preferred was for the opponents in the conflict to take the issue to their common boss, who would issue orders for settling such dilemmas in the future. Stevens interpreted the implicit organization model of the French as a 'pyramid of people': the general manager at the top of the pyramid, and each successive level at its proper place below.

The majority of the Germans diagnosed the case as a lack of structure. They tended to think that the competence of the two conflicting department heads had not been clearly specified. The solution they preferred was to establish specific procedures which could include calling in a consultant, nominating a task force, or asking the common boss. According to Stevens, the Germans saw the organization as a 'well-oiled machine' in which intervention by management should be limited because the rules should settle day-to-day problems.

The majority of the British diagnosed the case as a human relationships problem. They saw the two department heads as poor negotiators who would benefit from attending, preferably together, a management course to improve their skills. Stevens thought their implicit model of a 'village market' led them to look at the problem in terms of the demands of the situation determining what will happen, rather than hierarchy or rules.

A society's position on these two dimensions does seem to influence the implicit model of the organization in that society, and the kinds of coordination mechanisms that people in that culture would tend to rely upon.

Employees in high power distance and low uncertainty avoidance countries such as Singapore, Hong Kong and Indonesia tend to think of their organizations as traditional families. The patriarch, or head of the

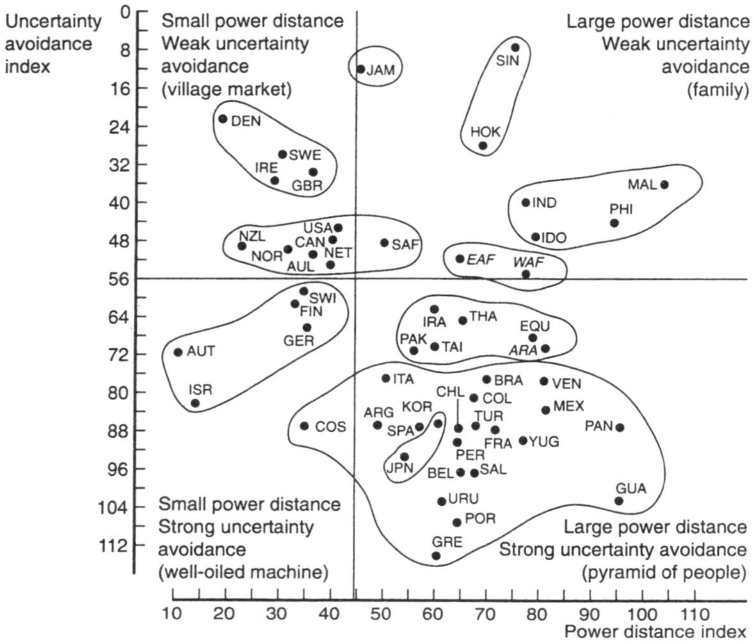

Key

ARA Arab-speaking countries (Egypt, Lebanon, Lybia, Kuwait, Iraq, Saudi Arabia, United Arab Emirates)
ARG Argentina
AUL Australia
AUT Austria
BEL Belgium
BRA Brazil
CAN Canada
CHL Chile
COL Columbia
COS Costa Rica
DEN Denmark
EAF East Africa (Kenya, Ethiopia, Tanzania, Zambia)
EQA Equador
FIN Finland
FRA France
GBR Great Britain
GER West Germany (formerly)
GRE Greece
GUA Guatemala
HOK Hong Kong
IDO Indonesia
IND India
IRA Iran
IRE Ireland (Republic of)
ISR Israel
ITA Italy
JAM Jamaica
JPN Japan
KOR South Korea
MAL Malaysia
MEX Mexico
NET Netherlands
NOR Norway
NZL New Zealand
PAK Pakistan
PAN Panama
PER Peru
PHI Philippines
POR Portugal
SAF South Africa
SAL Salvador
SIN Singapore
SPA Spain
SWE Sweden
TAI Taiwan
THA Thailand
TUR Turkey
URU Uruguay
USA United States
VEN Venezuela
WAF West Africa (Nigeria, Ghana, Sierra Leone)
YUG Yugoslavia (formerly)

Figure 2.4 Power distance and uncertainty avoidance scores.

family, is expected to protect family members physically and economically in exchange for unwavering loyalty from its members. The most likely coordination and control mechanism for the family is a standardization of work processes by specifying the contents of work – who does the chores.

Employees in countries such as France, Brazil, Portugal and Mexico that are high on both dimensions tend to view organizations as pyramids of people rather than as families. Everyone knows who reports to whom, and formal and activating lines of communication run vertically through the organization. Management reduces uncertainty and provides coordination and control by emphasizing who has authority over whom and in what way this authority can be exercised.

Where high uncertainty avoidance and low power distance are combined, in such countries as Israel, Austria, Germany and Switzerland, organizations are perceived as well-oiled machines; they are highly predictable without the imposition of a strong hierarchy. Uncertainty is reduced by clearly defining roles and procedures. Coordination and control are achieved primarily through standardization and certification of skills, specifying the training required to perform the work.

In cultures where there is low uncertainty avoidance and low power distance, the relevant organizational model is a 'village market'. Countries such as Denmark, Ireland, Norway, the UK and the USA are representative of this model. People will feel less comfortable with strict and formal rules or with what would be perceived as unnecessary layers of hierarchy. Control and coordination tends to take place through mutual adjustment of people through informal communication, and by specifying the desired results.

Individualism/collectivism

Individualism is a concern for yourself as an individual as opposed to concern for the priorities and rules of the group to which you belong. The majority of the people in the world live in societies where the interests of the group take precedence over the interests of the individual. In these societies, the group to which you belong is the major source of your identity and the unit to which you owe lifelong loyalty. For only a minority of the world's population do individual interests prevail over group interests. People in these cultures tend to think of themselves as 'I' and as distinct from other people's 'I's (Hofstede, 1984). People tend to classify themselves and each other by individual characteristics, rather than by group membership. Healthy people in individualistic societies are thought to be independent of others and able to 'stand on their own two feet'.

36 Culture: what it is, what it is not and how it directs organizational behaviour

Table 2.5 Individualism (IDV) scores.

Score rank	*Country or region*	*IDV score*	*Score rank*	*Country or region*	*IDV score*
1	USA	91	26/27	Arab countries	38
2	Australia	90	28	Turkey	37
3	UK	89	29	Uruguay	36
4/5	Canada	80	30	Greece	35
4/5	Netherlands	80	31	Philippines	32
6	New Zealand	79	32	Mexico	30
7	Italy	76	33/35	East Africa	27
8	Belgium	75	33/35	Yugoslavia	27
9	Denmark	74	33/35	Portugal	27
10/11	Sweden	71	36	Malaysia	26
10/11	France	71	37	Hong Kong	25
12	Ireland	70	38	Chile	23
	(Republic of)		39/41	West Africa	20
13	Norway	69	39/41	Singapore	20
14	Switzerland	68	39/41	Thailand	20
15	West Germany	67	42	Salvador	19
16	South Africa	65	43	South Korea	18
17	Finland	63	44	Taiwan	17
18	Austria	55	45	Peru	16
19	Israel	54	46	Costa Rica	15
20	Spain	51	47/48	Pakistan	14
21	India	48	47/48	Indonesia	14
22/23	Japan	46	49	Colombia	13
22/23	Argentina	46	50	Venezuela	12
24	Iran	41	51	Panama	11
25	Jamaica	39	52	Equador	8
26/27	Brazil	38	53	Guatemala	6

Table 2.6 Business areas affected by individualism.

Low individualism	*High individualism*
Involvement of individuals with organizations primarily moral	Involvement of individuals with organizations primarily calculative
Employees expect organizations to look after them like family – and can become very alienated if organization dissatisfies them	Organizations are not expected to look after employees from the cradle to the grave
Organization has great influence on members' well-being	Organization has moderate influence on members' well-being
Employees expect organization to defend their interests	Employees are expected to defend their own interests
Promotion from inside and based on seniority	Promotion from inside and outside, and based on market value
Less concern with fashion in management ideas	Managers try to be up-to-date and endorse modern management ideas
Policies and practices vary according to relations	Policies and practices apply to all
Belief in group decisions	Belief in individual decisions
Emphasis on belonging to organization; membership ideal	Emphasis on individual initiative and achievement; leadership ideal
Private life is invaded by organizations and clans to which you belong; opinions are predetermined	Everyone has a right to a private life and their opinion

Source: Adapted from Hofstede G. (1984). *Culture's Consequences: International Differences in Work-Related Values*, abridged edn. Thousand Oaks, CA: Sage Publications Inc. Reproduced with permission of McGraw-Hill.

Box 2.3 Difference in work ethos between an individualist and a collectivist society

Christopher Earley, an American management researcher, gave 48 management trainees from southern China and a matched group of 48 management trainees from the USA an 'in-basket task' consisting of 40 separate items requiring between two and five minutes each (Earley, 1989). The tasks involved such activities as writing memos, evaluating plans and rating job candidates' application forms. Half of the participants from each country were given an individual goal of 20 items; the other half were given a group goal of 200 items to be completed in one hour by 10 people. In addition, half of the participants from either country, both from the group and from the individual goal subsets, were asked to mark each item with their name; the other half turned them in anonymously.

The Chinese, collectivist, participants performed best when operating with a group goal *and* anonymously. They performed worst when operating individually and with their name marked on their work. The individualist American participants performed best when operating individually and with their work attributed to them personally, and performed very poorly when operating as a group and anonymously.

Masculinity/femininity

These values concern the extent of emphasis on work goals (earnings, advancement) and assertiveness, as opposed to personal goals (friendly atmosphere, getting along with the boss and others) and nurturance. The first set of values is thought to be associated with males and the second more with females. According to Hofstede's definitions, masculine societies define gender roles more rigidly than feminine societies. For example, more masculine societies would happily have occupations restricted to men or to women only, whereas in feminine societies women may drive trucks or be surgeons while men may more easily be nurses or house husbands. Of the countries covered by Hofstede's research, Scandinavian countries are the most feminine, the USA slightly masculine, and Japan and Austria the most highly masculine. In both of these latter countries, women are generally expected to stay at home and care for the children without working outside the home, especially in their middle years. In Sweden women are expected to work and both parents are offered leave to care for newborn children. Women both on Volvo's assembly line and as top executives have been accepted as unexceptional for decades.

Table 2.7 Masculinity (MAS) scores.

Score rank	*Country or region*	*MAS score*	*Score rank*	*Country or region*	*MAS score*
1	Japan	95	27	Brazil	49
2	Austria	79	28	Singapore	48
3	Venezuela	73	29	Israel	47
4/5	Italy	70	30/31	Indonesia	46
4/5	Switzerland	70	30/31	West Africa	46
6	Mexico	69	32/33	Turkey	45
7/8	Ireland	68	32/33	Taiwan	45
	(Republic of)		34	Panama	44
7/8	Jamaica	68	35/36	Iran	43
9/10	UK	66	35/36	France	43
9/10	West Germany	66	37/38	Spain	42
11/12	Philippines	64	37/38	Peru	42
11/12	Colombia	64	39	East Africa	41
13/14	South Africa	63	40	Salvador	40
13/14	Equador	63	41	South Korea	39
15	USA	62	42	Uruguay	38
16	Australia	61	43	Guatemala	37
17	New Zealand	58	44	Thailand	34
18/19	Greece	57	45	Portugal	31
18/19	Hong Kong	57	46	Chile	28
20/21	Argentina	56	47	Finland	26
20/21	India	56	48/49	Yugoslavia	21
22	Belgium	54	48/49	Costa Rica	21
23	Arab countries	53	50	Denmark	16
24	Canada	52	51	Netherlands	14
25/26	Malaysia	50	52	Norway	8
25/26	Pakistan	50	53	Sweden	5

Table 2.8 Business areas affected by masculinity.

Low masculinity	*High masculinity*
Less occupational segregation by gender	Some occupations are typically male, others female
Greater belief in equality of the sexes	Belief in inequality of the sexes
Some young men and women want careers, others do not	Young men expect to make a career; those who do not see themselves as failures
Organizations should not interfere with people's private lives	Organizational interests are a legitimate reason for interfering with people's private lives
More women in more qualified and better-paid jobs	Fewer women in more qualified and better-paid jobs
Lower job stress	Higher job stress
Less industrial conflict	More industrial conflict
Appeal of job restructuring permitting group integration	Appeal of job restructuring permitting individual achievement

Source: Adapted from Hofstede G. (1984). *Culture's Consequences: International Differences in Work-Related Values*, abridged edn. Thousand Oaks, CA: Sage Publications Inc. Reproduced with permission of McGraw-Hill.

Hofstede's work was based upon the analysis of over 100,000 responses to a questionnaire issued by IBM in its heydays during the 1970s. Hofstede did not invent these dimensions, but through deep analysis of the relationships between the answers to this questionnaire, he found they explained many of the differences that were evident between the widespread offices of what was essentially a very unifying global culture. IBM at the time was the most successful company in the world. These dimensions and Hofstede's tables of country positions in them are now recognized by all those who have any professional exposure to multicultural affairs. But there are still those who can profit from examining their implications in greater depth. One factor Hofstede continues to emphasize is that you cannot value values. From any one national's position, other nationals can seem strange. If they are seen because of this difference to be worse, then this strange difference will never become better understood.

Later work by the group of researchers in Hong Kong calling itself the Chinese Culture Connection found that by asking questions about work culture which Chinese might choose to ask instead of those used by IBM, three of Hofstede's dimensions were again revealed, but that uncertainty avoidance disappeared, and was replaced by an altogether different dimension, originally called Confucian dynamism. This dimension featured such factors as long-term versus short-term, thrift versus conspicuous expenditure and truth as an absolute versus truth as dependent upon who speaks. This latter case anticipates universalism versus particularism which we will explore next.

Hofstede's work provides an important framework in which to consider the effects of cultural differences on managing cultural differences; especially in terms of understanding people's conceptions of an organization, the mechanisms that are considered appropriate in controlling and coordinating the activities within it, and the roles and relations of its members. Another compelling description of how cultures differ has been developed by a Dutch economist and consultant, Fons Trompenaars. Encouraged by Hofstede, and building primarily from the work of Kluckhohn and Strodtbeck on value orientations (Kluckhorn and Stodtbeck, 1961), Charles Hampden-Turner's dilemma theory (Hampden-Turner, 1983), and Talcott Parsons's work in the 1950s, Trompenaars's research revealed seven dimensions of culture. Five of Trompenaars's dimensions will be discussed in this book because of their relevance to issues considered here. They provide another useful way for managers to consider how cultural differences affect organizations and management practices.

Fons Trompenaars's research

Over a 10-year period, Trompenaars administered research questionnaires to over 15,000 managers from 28 countries. The relative positions of each country for each of the dimensions that he defined are based on the responses of at least 500 managers. Responses of 23 countries are included in this report. The country abbreviations are given below.

Box 2.4 Trompenaars's country abbreviations

Abbreviation	Country	Abbreviation	Country
ARG	Argentina	IDO	Indonesia
AUS	Austria	ITA	Italy
BEL	Belgium	JPN	Japan
BRZ	Brazil	MEX	Mexico
CHI	China	NL	Netherlands
CIS	Former Soviet Union	SIN	Singapore
		SPA	Spain
CZH	Czechoslovakia	SWE	Sweden
FRA	France	SWI	Switzerland
GER	Germany (excluding former GDR)	THA	Thailand
		UK	United Kingdom
		USA	United States
HK	Hong Kong	VEN	Venezuela

The five dimensions that are most relevant to the business areas discussed in this book are as follows.

(1) Universalism versus particularism: societal versus personal obligation.
(2) Individualism versus collectivism: personal versus group goals.
(3) Neutral versus affective relationships: emotional orientation in relationships.
(4) Specific versus diffuse relationships: degree of involvement in relationships.
(5) Achievement versus ascription: legitimation of power and status.

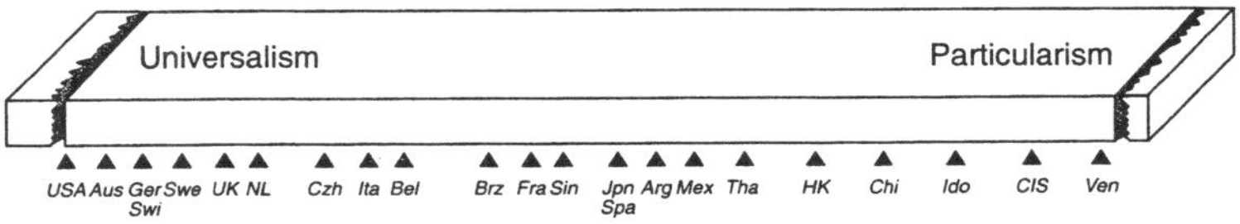

Figure 2.5 Universalism versus particularism. (*Source*: Adapted from Trompenaars, 1993)

Universalism versus particularism

Universalism applies where people believe that what is true and good can be discovered, defined and 'applied' everywhere. Particularism is said to prevail where the unique circumstances and relationships are more important considerations in determining what is right and good than abstract rules.

A clear example of this dimension in business is the role of the contract in different cultures. While weighty contracts tend to be a way of life in universalist cultures, more particularist cultures tend to rely on relationships with people they hold in high regard for enforcement of a deal. Encounters between universalist and particularist business people may result in both sides being sceptical of each other's trustworthiness. The universalist business person might think, 'How can you trust them [a particularist], they will always help their friends!' A particularist might think of a universalist, 'You cannot trust them, they would not even help a friend!'

The distribution of scores across the countries from which this scale was drawn shows a separation between East and West, and between North and South, notoriously the two divides that show up most in any global political or organizational issue (see Figure 2.5).

Table 2.9 Business areas affected by universalism/particularism.

Universalism	*Particularism*
Focus is more on rules than on relationships	Focus is more on relationships than on rules
Legal contracts are readily drawn up	Legal contracts are readily modified
A trustworthy person is the one who honours their 'word' or contract	A trustworthy person is the one who honours changing circumstances
There is only one truth or reality, that which has been agreed to	There are several perspectives on reality relative to each participant
A deal is a deal	Relationships evolve

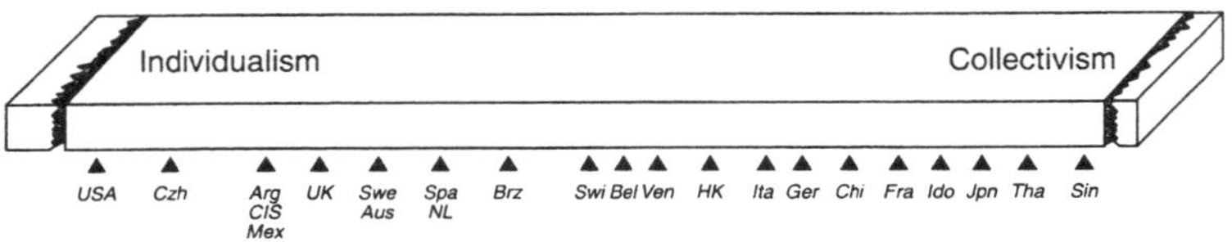

Figure 2.6 Individualism versus collectivism. (*Source*: Adapted from Trompenaars, 1993)

Individualism versus collectivism

This is familiar from Hofstede's work described previously. Essentially it concerns how groups have resolved the problem: does a person regard himself or herself primarily as an individual or primarily as part of a group? Furthermore, should society focus on individuals so that they can contribute to society as and if they wish, or is it more important to consider the collectivity first since it is shared by many individuals?

Within more collectivist societies, the particular group with which individuals choose to identify varies a great deal. It could be their trade union, their family, their nation, their corporation, their religion, their profession or the state apparatus. For example, the French tend to identify with *La France*, *La Famille*, *Le Cadre*; the Japanese with Japan and with the corporation; members of the former Eastern bloc with the Communist Party; and the Irish with the Roman Catholic Church.

International management is seriously affected by individualist or collectivist preferences within various countries. Negotiations, decision-making and motivation are the most critical areas. Practices such as promotion for recognized achievements and pay-for-performance, for example, assume that individuals seek to be distinguished within the group and that their colleagues approve of this happening. They also rest on the assumption that the contribution of any one member to a common task is easily distinguishable and that no problems arise from singling them out for praise. None of this may be true in more collectivist cultures.

Table 2.10 Business areas affected by individualism/collectivism.

Individualism	*Collectivism*
More frequent use of 'I' and 'me'	More frequent use of 'we'
In negotiations, decisions typically made on the spot by a representative	Decisions typically referred back by delegate to the organization
People ideally achieve alone and assume personal responsibility	People ideally achieve in groups which assume joint responsibility
Holidays taken in pairs, or even alone	Holidays taken in organized groups or with extended family

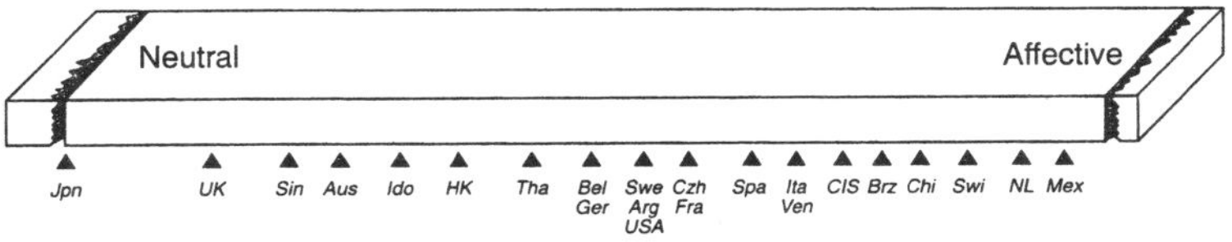

Figure 2.7 Neutral versus affective relationships. (*Source*: Adapted from Trompenaars, 1993)

Neutral versus affective relationships

All human beings have emotions, but this dimension concerns the different contexts and ways that cultures choose to *express* emotions. In affective cultures, expressing emotions openly is more 'natural', whereas in more neutral cultures people believe that emotions should be held in check so as not to cloud issues or give the appearance of being out of control.

There is a tendency for neutral cultures to consider anger, delight or intensity in the workplace as 'unprofessional'. Conversely, affective cultures would probably regard their neutral colleagues as emotionally dead, or as hiding their true feelings behind a mask of deceit. This dimension determines two fundamental questions:

(1) Should emotion be *exhibited* in business relations?
(2) Is emotion a corrupting influence on objectivity and reason?

Americans tend to exhibit emotion yet separate it from 'objective' and 'rational' decisions. Italians and southern European nations in general tend to exhibit and *not* to separate. Dutch and Swedes tend *not* to exhibit and to separate. Once again, there is nothing 'good' or 'bad' about these differences. You could argue that emotions held in check will twist judgements despite all efforts to be 'rational'. Or you could argue that emotions make it harder for anyone present to think straight. But as discussed in Chapter 1, the whole notion of rationality as a category of thought separate from other kinds of thought and emotion is a particular cultural preference. It is clear that even apparently scientific 'objectivity' cannot be separated from the particular cultural context in which it is embedded.

In Hofstede's model, the willingness to express emotion is seen as part of uncertainty avoidance. In his view, one reason for the need to manage uncertainty is a greater indigenous anxiety, a more prevalent fear of the unknown; this implies greater emotional volatility and therefore expressiveness. Since it is only one component, however, relative comparisons of scores are not easy to make.

Table 2.11 Business areas affected by neutral/affective relationships.

Affective	*Neutral*
Show immediate reactions either verbally or non-verbally	Opaque emotional state
Expressive face and body signals	Do not readily express what they think or feel
At ease with physical contact	Embarrassed or awkward at public displays of emotion
	Discomfort with physical contact outside 'private' circle
Raise voice readily	Subtle in verbal and non-verbal expressions

Specific versus diffuse relationships

This dimension deals with the degree of involvement individuals are comfortable with in dealing with other people. Every individual has various levels to their personality, from a more public level to the inner, more private level. However, there can be cultural differences in the relative size of people's public and private 'spaces' and also in the degree to which they feel comfortable sharing those parts of their personality with other people. In more specific cultures, Trompenaars says people tend to have a larger public area and a smaller private area. They prefer to keep their private life separate, guarding it very closely. In more diffuse cultures, the private 'space' is usually larger while the public area is smaller and somewhat more carefully guarded. While diffuse cultures may come across as cool initially, once in the more closely guarded public space, the private space is more accessible than in specific cultures. In other words, the whole individual tends to be involved in relationships in diffuse cultures.

For example, the circle diagrams in Figure 2.9 compare the more specific North Americans with the more diffuse Germans. North Americans are characterized by a small, intimate private layer that is well separated from the more public outer layers. In Germany, on the other hand, personality structures are characterized by a large private area

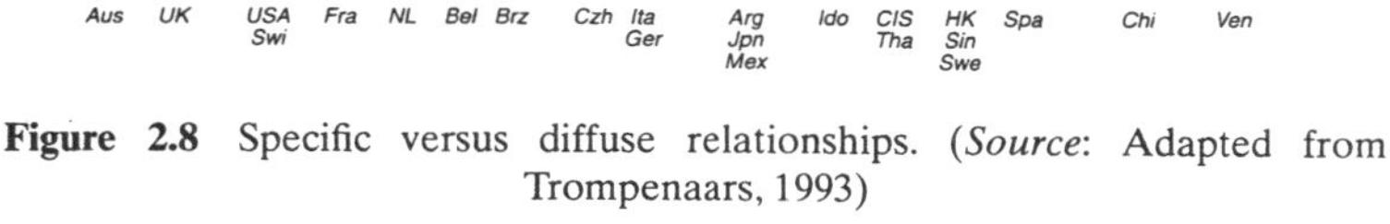

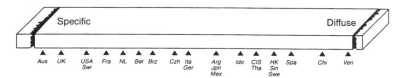

Figure 2.8 Specific versus diffuse relationships. (*Source*: Adapted from Trompenaars, 1993)

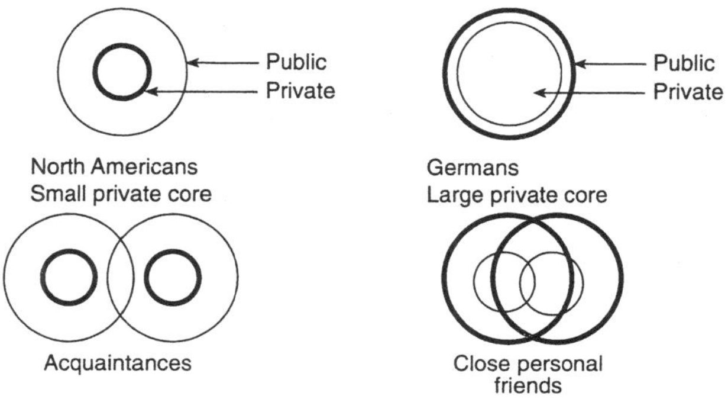

Figure 2.9 Privacy. (*Source*: Adapted from Trompenaars, 1993)

separated from a relatively small public layer. This means, for example, that it is not uncommon for German business colleagues to interact for years on a formal name basis while in the USA the norm is to be on a first-name basis immediately. To Americans, Germans seem reserved and difficult to get to know, while Germans may consider Americans intrusive and disrespectful.

Doing business with a culture more diffuse than your own appears very time consuming. In specific cultures, business can be done in a mental subdivision called 'commerce' or 'work', which is kept apart from the rest of life. In diffuse cultures, everything is connected to everything else. Your business partner may wish to know where you went to school, who your friends are, what you think of life, politics, art, literature and music. This is not 'a waste of time' because such preferences reveal character and form friendships. They also make deception near to impossible. The initial investment in building relationships is as important, if not more so, than the *deal* in some cultures.

Table 2.12 Business areas affected by specific/diffuse relationships.

Specific	*Diffuse*
More 'open' public space, more 'closed' private space	More 'closed' public space, but, once in, more 'open' private space
Appears direct, open and extrovert	Appears indirect, closed and introvert
'To the point' and often appears abrasive	Often evades issues and 'beats about the bush'
Highly mobile	Low mobility
Separates work and private life	Work and private life are closely linked
Varies approach to fit circumstances, especially with use of titles (for example, Herr Doktor Müller at work is Hans in social environments or in certain business meetings)	Consistent in approach, especially with use of titles (for example, Herr Doktor Müller is Herr Doktor Müller in any setting)

Achievement versus ascription

The last of the five Trompenaars cultural dimensions relevant to organizations deals with how status and power in a society are determined. Each society is presented both with characteristics assumed by a person as a birthright and with those that are left to be filled in through competition, personal effort or luck. Status can be based either on what someone does, or on what someone is. Cultures differ in the ways they have solved this dilemma.

In achievement-oriented countries, business people are evaluated by how well they perform an allocated function. Relationships are functionally specific. I relate to a colleague as, say, a sales manager. The justification of my role lies in the sales records. Another person in that role must be expected to be compared with me and I with that person. Success is universally defined as increased sales. My relationship to manufacturing, R&D, planning and so on is *instrumental*. I either sell what they have developed, manufactured and planned, or I do not. I *am* my functional role.

In ascriptive cultures, status is attributed to those who 'naturally' evoke admiration from others, that is older people, males, highly qualified people and/or people skilled in a particular technology or project deemed to be of national importance. To show respect for status is to assist the people so distinguished to fulfil the expectations society has of them. The status is generally independent of a task or specific function. The individual is particular and not easily compared with others. His (or her) performance is partly determined by the loyalty and affection shown him by subordinates and which he, in turn, displays. He (and in ascriptive cultures it is generally males who are in the positions of power) *is* the organization in the sense of personifying it and wielding its power.

While achievement-oriented organizations justify their hierarchies by claiming that senior people 'achieve more' for the organization because their authority, justified by skill and knowledge, benefits the organization, ascription-oriented organizations justify their hierarchies

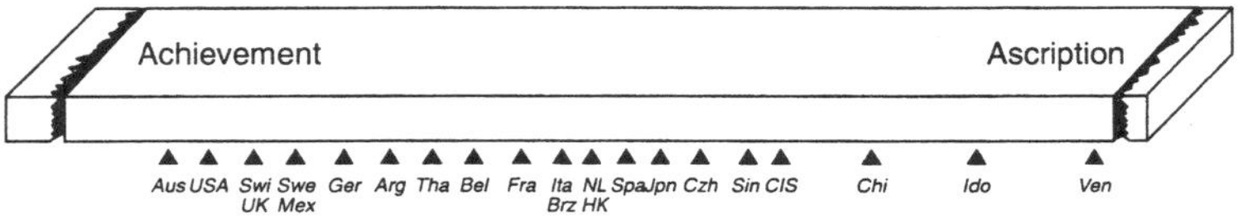

Figure 2.10 Achievement versus ascription. (*Source*: Adapted from Trompenaars, 1993)

as central to creating the power to get things done. This may consist of power *over* people and be coercive, or it may consist of power *through* people and be participative. There is great variation within ascriptive cultures in the form that power takes. Whatever form power takes, the ascription of status to people is intended to be exercized as power and that power is supposed to enhance the effectiveness of the organization.

Achievement versus ascription has no direct match in Hofstede's terms. High power distance environments would be more likely to contain the ascriptive assumption. Those oriented towards the masculine would be places where the achievement orientation should flourish. But again there is no direct linkage between the two.

Culture and Dutchmen

It should not escape your notice that the two most prominent presenters of models of national culture in the past generation have both been Dutch and have both used bipolar dimensions as a means of communicating their models, each based upon a questionnaire response.

Trompenaars started with dimensions, mostly taken from Talcott Parsons, and produced questions based upon short value-laden dilemmas to produce the spread of national responses. Hofstede took existing data, and arrived at his four original dimensions through regression, then named the dimensions which arose using existing expressions.

For the novice intercultural enquirer, the two could have offered a more conveniently integratable model, but each gives something different to the experienced. The major dimensions which distinguish nations wishing to work closer together without abandoning or de-emphasizing their differences would seem to be:

- Power distance: how convinced are people that differences in power are given and accepted?
- Uncertainty avoidance: how much are people prepared to deal with the unexpected?
- Collectivism/individualism: which carries most weight – the individual or the group?
- Universalism/particularism: which has the greatest impact – the rule of law or the rule of the person who makes it?

These four dimensions should help managers most to identify how to create global competitiveness from diversity.

48 Culture: what it is, what it is not and how it directs organizational behaviour

Summary

Culture is difficult to measure and to discuss because it involves shared ways of perceiving the world that members of a group take for granted. Culture is learned, and can be considered only relative to other cultures. There is no absolute right or wrong in cultural preferences.

Although there are different levels of cultural programming, national culture gives people their basic assumptions and values, that is, their ways of viewing the world. Other levels of programming are more about practices or ways of doing things. Because these are learned at such an early age and remain unquestioned, however, often throughout life, national cultural values are more difficult to change than other levels of culture.

In order to grasp better the impact of culture on international business, a few researchers have come up with ways of describing categories of differences in national cultures. Two Dutchmen, Hofstede and Trompenaars, have promoted the most expressive and popular of these. Their dimensions, which are presented in this chapter, do help to clarify some of the most important ways in which cultures differ and how those differences affect organizations generally. They provide a useful framework for managers to understand some of the differences they encounter in doing business and managing across cultures.

What becomes clear in the following chapters is that managers can more successfully manage differences in culture if they:

(1) Understand their own cultural biases and assumptions.
(2) Consider the reasons why different cultures' ways of doing things make sense in the light of their cultural assumptions.
(3) View cultural assumptions and ways of doing things not as irreconcilable differences, but rather as different starting points that can be integrated to develop uniquely competitive solutions.

References

Adler N.J. (1986). *International Dimensions of Organizational Behavior.* Belmont, California: PWS-Kent Publishing Company

Earley C.P. (1989). Social Loafing and Collectivism: A Comparison of the United States and the People's Republic of China, *Administrative Science Quarterly*, **34**, 565–581

Hall E.T. (1973). *The Silent Language.* New York: Doubleday

Hampden-Turner C. (1983). Is there a new paradigm? A tale of two concepts. *Personnel Management Review*, **56**

Hofstede G. (1984). *Culture's Consequences: International Differences in Work-Related Values*. Beverly Hills, California: Sage Publications

Hofstede G. (1991). *Cultures and Organizations: Software of the Mind*. London: McGraw-Hill

The Independent (1991). 31 December, p. 3

International Herald Tribune (1990). 11 December, p. 11

Kluckhohn F. and Strodtbeck F.L. (1961). *Variations in Value-Orientations*. Connecticut: Greenwood Press

Laurent A. (1989). A cultural view of organizational change. In *Human Resource Management in International Firms: Change, Globalization, Innovation* (Evans P., Doz Y. and Laurent A., eds.) London: Macmillan, pp. 83-94

Trompenaars F. (1993). *Riding the Waves of Culture*. London: The Economist Books

Part II
Managing the Global Organization

[7]

Horses for Courses: Organizational Forms for Multinational Corporations

Sumantra Ghoshal • Nitin Nohria

ONE OF THE MOST ENDURING IDEAS OF ORGANIZATION THEORY IS THAT AN ORGANIZATION'S STRUCTURE AND MANAGEMENT PROCESS MUST "FIT" ITS ENVIRONMENT, in the same way that a particular horse might be more suited to one course than another. Ghoshal and Nohria show the continued relevance of this classic insight for the organization of multinational corporations. They offer a simple scheme to classify the environment and structure of MNCs. Then, based on data on forty-one large MNCs, they show how some combinations of environment and structure fit better than others. What drives fit is the principle of requisite complexity — the complexity of a firm's structure must match the complexity of its environment. Though developed for MNCs, their argument can also apply to multidivisional firms that operate in different markets or business segments.

Sumantra Ghoshal is associate professor of business policy, INSEAD. Nitin Nohria is assistant professor at the Harvard Business School.

About two decades ago, business academics told managers that when it came to organization design, one size did not fit all. Different companies, facing different business demands, needed different kinds of organizations. More complex and turbulent environments called for more complex organizational approaches, and the nature and extent of organizational complexity had to match the firm's strategic complexity. In its initial formulation, before the hedge that "it all depends" made it too complicated to mean anything at all, this contingency theory of organizations provided managers with some simple guidelines to help them decide on the kind of organization they should adopt.[1]

For multinational corporations (MNCs), such guidelines were available in the "stages model" proposed by Stopford and Wells[2] (see Figure 1). This model defined the strategic complexity faced by an MNC in terms of two dimensions: the number of products sold internationally ("foreign product diversity," shown on the figure's vertical axis) and the importance of international sales to the company ("foreign sales as a percentage of total sales," shown on the horizontal axis). Stopford and Wells suggested that at the early stage of foreign expansion, when both foreign sales and the diversity of products sold abroad were limited, worldwide companies typically managed their international operations through an international division. Subsequently, some companies expanded their sales abroad without significantly increasing foreign product diversity; they typically adopted an area structure. Companies facing substantial increases in foreign product diversity tended to adopt the worldwide product division structure. Finally, when both foreign sales and foreign product diversity were high, companies resorted to the global matrix.

Over the two decades since Stopford and Wells presented this simple, descriptive model, academic research on MNCs has developed a far more elaborate understanding of MNC organizations. It is increasingly clear, for example, that the formal macrostructure described in the stages model is only a partial representation of a worldwide organization. To use a biological metaphor suggested by Christopher Bartlett, organizations have an anatomy (formal structure), but they also have a physiology (core management processes) and a psychology (the mind-sets of their managers). To analyze the organizational capabilities a company needs, one must look not only to the anatomy but also to the physiology and psychology.[3]

Further, the prescription of matching organizational characteristics to environmental and strategic demands is also under challenge. Environments do not stand still for organizations to catch up, and organizations themselves, as organic entities, are in a continuous state of flux. Instead of a mechanistic and static view of fit, one needs to recognize the fluid, multidimensional, and changing nature of both environments and organizations. What is needed is not just fit but fit and flexibility.[4]

Figure 1 The Stopford and Wells Model of MNC Organizations

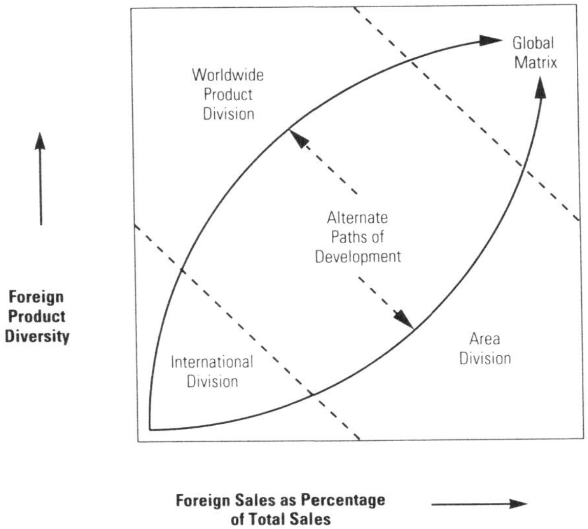

Unfortunately, academic research and conclusions are inevitably simplified and stripped of nuances. Just as the earlier stages model was converted into a set of simplistic prescriptions, so has this new research been recast as an orgy of complexity. Bartlett and Ghoshal, for example, have repeatedly argued that companies must simplify wherever possible to protect clarity of responsibility and initiative and that the more complex or "transnational" integrated network organization should be used only for MNCs operating in highly complex environments.[5] Yet their findings have often been interpreted as an all-or-nothing call for this "transnational" structure in all companies.[6]

In this article we wish to make the following two points. First, although the Stopford and Wells model has its deficiencies, it does not follow that MNCs are too organizationally complex for any meaningful yet simple classification. Managers need simple organizational models and classification schemes as a starting point for thinking about the core attributes of their organizational needs. Similarly, academics need them in order to build theory and develop analytical and testable propositions. Therefore, we will propose here a useful classification scheme for MNC organizations, one that is not defined in terms of traditional structural forms (e.g., area, product, matrix, etc.), but that is based on the company's internal pattern of headquarters-subsidiary relations. Any organizational model or classification scheme is built on simplifications and, therefore, suffers from some deficiencies. Our scheme is no exception. However, in this paper we will demonstrate its usefulness for both managers and academics.

Second, although flexibility is important, so is fit. Organizational complexity is costly and difficult to manage, and simplicity, wherever possible, is a virtue. Just as a company can suffer from too simple an organization if it is operating in a complex and turbulent environment, so can it also pay an efficiency penalty for adopting an organization too complex for its environmental demands. Although insensitive to the reality of constant flux in both environments and organizations and, therefore, somewhat unfashionable in current organization research, the concept of fit remains one of the relatively few simple and robust findings in organization theory.[7] We will demonstrate here the continued validity of this concept of environment-organization fit and of the positive relationship of such fit with firm performance.

The Empirical Database

Our empirical analysis is based primarily on a database that has been described fully elsewhere.[8] This database consists of information on all wholly-owned subsidiaries of sixty-six large MNCs in ten prespecified countries. It was obtained from a mailed questionnaire survey completed by one correspondent from each firm, typically a senior headquarters manager with responsibility for the firm's international operations. These managers assigned values, on a scale of one (low) to five (high), to a number of variables indicative of the local context (competitive intensity in the local market, technological dynamism of the local environment, extent of local government regulations, and local resources available to the subsidiary) and the structure of the headquarters-subsidiary relation (extent to which its governance is based on centralization, formalization, and normative integration). Although each variable was measured through a single indicator, the reliability and validity of the measures were tested through a multiple-indicator, multiple-respondent survey administered at the headquarters and subsidiary levels in three large MNCs.[9] In the following analysis, we rely wholly on this database to measure structural attributes of MNCs.

We obtained additional measures, following the framework proposed by Prahalad and Doz, to classify MNC environments in terms of the twin demands of global integration and national responsiveness.[10] To measure global integration, we use Kobrin's "index of integration," which we consider a theoretically well-grounded and empirically precise measure of this complex construct.[11] To measure national responsiveness, we use two indicators. The first, extent of government regulations, comes from our questionnaire data. The second, advertising intensity, is computed from the industry averages published in *Advertising Age*.

Finally, we use three different economic indicators — average annual return on net assets, average revenue growth, and average annual growth in return on net assets to measure company performance. Specifically, we compute average values of these three variables for the period 1982 to 1986 as they appear in the relevant annual reports (the company survey was conducted in 1986). Corporate performance can be measured in different ways corresponding to the firms' different goals, but we employ these three economic measures because our purpose is to explore performance difference across a broad sample of firms and because these measures are recognized as both fairly comprehensive and highly important to the companies themselves.[12]

We have complete data (including Kobrin's index) for only forty-one of the sixty-six companies in the database. Accordingly, data on only these forty-one companies are

Table 1 The Companies Surveyed and Their Principal Businesses

Name of Company	Home Country	Principal Industry
1. Air Products and Chemicals	United States	Industrial chemicals
2. Alcan	Canada	Nonferrous metals
3. Baker International	United States	Machinery
4. Bertelsmann	Germany	Printing and publishing
5. Blue Bell	United States	Textiles
6. British-American Tobacco (BAT)	United Kingdom	Tobacco
7. BSN Groupe	France	Food
8. Caterpillar	United States	Construction and mining machinery
9. Colgate-Palmolive	United States	Drugs and pharmaceuticals
10. Continental Group	United States	Metals
11. Cummins	United States	Engines
12. Deere & Co.	United States	Construction and mining machinery
13. Digital Equipment Corp.	United States	Computers
14. DuPont	United States	Chemicals
15. Electrolux	Sweden	Household appliances
16. Emhart Corporation	United States	Machinery
17. Firestone	United States	Rubber
18. Freuhauf Corporation	United States	Automobiles
19. Friedrich Krupp	Germany	Metals
20. General Foods	United States	Food
21. General Motors	United States	Automobiles
22. Glaxo	United Kingdom	Drugs and pharmaceuticals
23. Hoechst AG	Germany	Chemicals
24. Honeywell	United States	Scientific measuring instruments
25. ICI	United Kingdom	Chemicals
26. Jacobs Suchard	Switzerland	Food
27. Kodak	United States	Photographic equipment
28. Mannesmann	Germany	Metals
29. Norsk Hydro	Norway	Chemicals
30. Norton	United States	Machinery
31. R.J. Reynolds	United States	Tobacco
32. Reckitt & Colman	United Kingdom	Drugs and pharmaceuticals
33. Rio Tinto-Zinc	United Kingdom	Metals
34. Schneider	France	Machinery
35. Seagram	Canada	Beverages
36. Siemens	Germany	Machinery
37. Solvay & Cie	Belgium	Chemicals
38. Swedish Match	Sweden	Paper and forestry
39. Timken	United States	Machinery
40. United Biscuits	United Kingdom	Food
41. Volvo	Sweden	Automobiles

used in the empirical analysis reported in this paper. Table 1 lists these companies and their principal businesses.

The paper is organized as follows. First, we draw on the existing literature to classify the environments of the forty-one companies into four categories. These categories reflect firms' varying needs to respond to distinct local conditions and to integrate across national boundaries. Second, we use Lawrence and Lorsch's dimensions of structural differentiation and integration to classify the forty-one companies into four structural categories. Finally, we hypothesize a one-to-one fit between the environmental and structural categories and test this hypothesis against the information in our database.

Classifying the Environments of MNCs

Each MNC subsidiary operates in a different national environment. In each country, the local subsidiary must be responsive to local customers, governments, and regulatory agencies for its ongoing institutional legitimacy and economic success. To some extent, then, the MNC must respond to the different contingencies presented by the multiple environments in which it operates. Such contingencies have been categorized in the multinational management literature as "forces for national responsiveness."[13]

These different local environments may also be linked to each other — because there are common customer preferences across countries; because economies of scale, scope, and national comparative advantage create incentives for specialization and interdependence; because knowledge developed in one environment is transferable or adaptable in another; or because key players in the MNC's environment are transnational, such as its multinational clients, suppliers, competitors, and even regulatory agencies (such as the EEC). These linkages across national boundaries pressure the subsidiaries to coordinate their activities; they have been described as "forces for global integration."[14]

These two forces — for national responsiveness and for global integration — are not opposite ends of a spectrum. Although they are related, we can consider them as separate dimensions. Thus, a company with a weak force for national responsiveness does not automatically have a strong force for global integration and vice versa. For instance, businesses such as pharmaceuticals, telecommunications, and computers may simultaneously face strong demands for both global integration and local responsiveness. In computers, the growing commoditization of hardware combined with high capital intensity and scale economics constitute powerful forces for global integration. At the same time, the increasing market demands for integration of hardware from diverse sources with software and services to provide "solutions" to customer problems create equally strong needs for local responsiveness.

The weak-weak combination is also possible. The business of producing and marketing cement is an example. Cement products are highly standardized, and marketing and distribution systems are similar across countries. Thus demands for local responsiveness are weak. However, the trade-offs between the economics of cement production and transport costs are such that global integration is not attractive.

Of course, weak-strong combinations of both sorts are possible as well. Semiconductors and airplane engines confront strong forces for global integration, given their high capital intensities and significant scale economies, but relatively weak forces for national responsiveness because product standardization is relatively high and customer demands are relatively uniform in different geographic markets. In contrast, businesses such as legal services or nonbranded foods are likely to face weak forces for global integration and strong demands for national responsiveness.

Four Types of MNC Environments

The environmental contingencies faced by the MNC as a whole can, therefore, be conceived in terms of the extent to which it must respond to strong and unique national environments and the extent to which it must respond to the linkages across these national environments. Adopting the terms used by Bartlett and Ghoshal, we broadly distinguish among four environmental conditions faced by MNCs: (1) a *global environment* in which the forces for global integration are strong and for local responsiveness weak, (2) a *multinational environment* in which the forces for national responsiveness are strong and for global integration weak, (3) a *transnational environment* in which both contingencies are strong, and (4) a placid *international environment* in which both contingencies are weak (see Figure 2).[15]

We adopted the following procedure to classify the environment of each of the forty-one MNCs in our sample as one of these four types. Kobrin's index of integration, which we use to measure the forces of global integration in different business environments, is the ratio of the total intrafirm trade (the sum of affiliate-to-affiliate, affiliate-to-parent, and parent-to-affiliate sales) to the total international sales (sum of total sales of parent and of all affiliates) of all the MNCs in an industry. As

Figure 2 The Environment of MNCs: Classification of Businesses

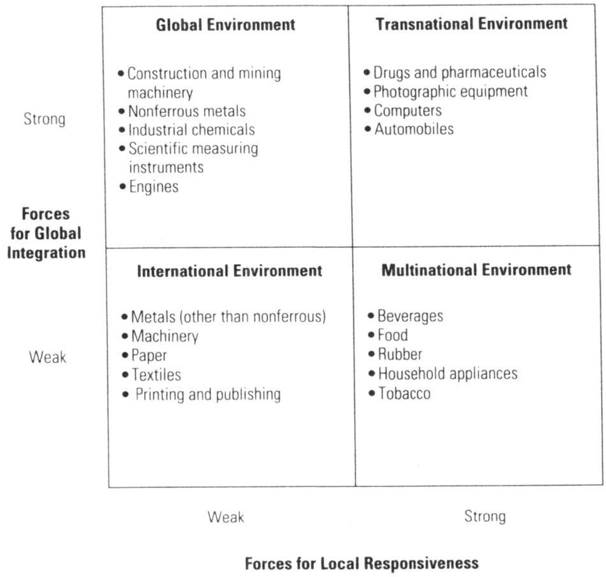

Global Environment
• Construction and mining machinery
• Nonferrous metals
• Industrial chemicals
• Scientific measuring instruments
• Engines
Transnational Environment
• Drugs and pharmaceuticals
• Photographic equipment
• Computers
• Automobiles
International Environment
• Metals (other than nonferrous)
• Machinery
• Paper
• Textiles
• Printing and publishing
Multinational Environment
• Beverages
• Food
• Rubber
• Household appliances
• Tobacco
Strong
Forces for Global Integration
Weak
Weak
Strong
Forces for Local Responsiveness

Kobrin argues, global integration cannot be measured simply on the basis of bilateral flows. One must consider the overall system of interdependencies: "Transnational integration implies more than interdependence in the sense that events in one business environment significantly influence those in another; it implies dependence of subsidiaries on the multinational system." According to Kobrin, cross flows of products within the total MNC system, aggregated to all MNCs in the industry, is one of the most effective ways to measure the forces of global integration. It allows for a systematic and data-driven specification of global industries and avoids the pitfalls of anecdotal and descriptive evidence. Also, the actual measures correlate highly with industry research and development (R&D) intensity — another widely used proxy for the forces of global integration — and are "certainly in accord with an intuitive, case-study-based concept of global integration." Kobrin's index is a continuous variable and, as he notes, any particular cutoff point to delineate "high" and "low" categories is bound to be somewhat arbitrary. We use 20 percent (intrafirm trade as a percentage of total sales) as our cutoff point; we classify businesses such as automobiles (44 percent), computers (38 percent), photographic equipment (32 percent), engines (30 percent), scientific measuring instruments (29 percent), industrial chemicals (26 percent), nonferrous metals (23 percent), pharmaceuticals (21 percent), and construction and mining machinery (21 percent) as confronting strong forces of global integration. The remaining businesses confront weak forces for global integration.

We use two indicators to distinguish between businesses facing strong and those facing weak forces of national responsiveness. The first is the advertising-to-sales ratio of the industry, as published in *Advertising Age*. The second is an average of the values we received on our questionnaire for the extent of local regulation, by industry (for example, we averaged the ratings given by computer companies on the extent of local regulations to come up with the computer industry average). The two measures are only weakly correlated (rank correlation 0.32, Ø = 0.11). Given that both regulations and customer preferences can act as powerful forces for local responsiveness, we categorize any business that falls above the sample mean on either of these two indicators as facing strong forces of national responsiveness and one that falls below on either indicator as facing relatively weak forces of national responsiveness.

Figure 2 shows how juxtaposition of these two indicators leads to the categorization of the different business environments into international, multinational, global, and transnational.

Structure Classifications

The main criticism of models that define MNC structure in terms of function, geography, product division, or as a matrix has been that the formal organization chart is a poor representation of how an organization really functions. Organizations represent a set of relationships among individuals, groups, and units, and very different relationship patterns can flourish within the same formal structure. To understand, describe, or categorize organizations, therefore, one must focus on the pattern of these relationships. Accordingly, we suggest that an MNC's structure may be conceived more fruitfully as a nexus of the relationships between its different national subsidiaries and its headquarters.

The nature of each headquarters-subsidiary relationship is the basic unit in this conceptualization. These relationships can be described in terms of the three basic governance mechanisms that underlie them. The first of these is *centralization*, which concerns the role of formal authority and hierarchical mechanisms in the company's decision-making processes. The second is *formalization*, which represents decision-making through bureaucratic mechanisms such as formal systems, established rules, and prescribed procedures. The third is *normative integration*, which relies neither on direct headquarters involvement nor on impersonal rules but on the socialization of managers into a set of shared goals, values, and beliefs that then shape their perspectives and behavior. We believe that centralization, formalization, and normative integration, collectively, constitute a fairly comprehensive characterization of the mechanisms by which corporate-division relations may be governed in multiunit organizations such as MNCs.[16]

Analyses of MNC organizations have often assumed that headquarters-subsidiary relationships are identical for all subsidiaries throughout the company. There is growing evidence, however, that each headquarters-subsidiary relation can be governed by a different combination of the above-mentioned three mechanisms.[17] Therefore, we conceptualize the MNC's overall structure in terms of the pattern of variation in its different headquarters-subsidiary relationships.

Four Structural Patterns

Using Lawrence and Lorsch's dimensions of differentiation and integration, we envision MNC structures in terms of four patterns. In the first structure — *structural uniformity* — there is little variance in how the different subsidiaries are managed, and a common "company way" is adopted for the governance of all headquarters-subsidiary relationships. The emphasis may be on one of the three governance types or a combination. Of central importance is a strong and uniform governance mechanism for the whole company; overall integration is high, and there is little attention to differentiation.

A second structure — *differentiated fit* — represents companies that adopt different governance modes to fit each subsidiary's local context. The local context can vary in a number of ways. Two of the most important ways are environmental complexity (the level of technological dynamism and competitive intensity) and the amount of local resources available to the subsidiary.[18] When a company recognizes these differences, it can explicitly differentiate its headquarters-subsidiary relationships to ensure that the management processes fit each local context. We have previously developed a scheme that matches structures to subsidiary contexts.[19] Briefly, this scheme is as follows:

1. Low environment complexity and low levels of local resources dictate a high level of centralization and low levels of formalization and normative integration;
2. Low environment complexity and high levels of resources dictate a low level of centralization and high levels of formalization and normative integration;
3. High environment complexity and low resource levels indicate a moderate level of centralization, a low level of formalization, and a high level of normative integration; and
4. High environment complexity and high resource levels indicate a low level of centralization, a moderate level of formalization, and a high level of normative integration.

Based on the theoretical justification and empirical support provided for this scheme in our earlier paper, we use this logic to describe and identify companies adopting the differentiated fit structure. Note that differentiation is the dominant characteristic of this structure and that it lacks a strong firmwide integrative mechanism.

A third structural pattern is when a firm adopts the logic of differentiated fit but overlays the distinctly structured relationships with a dominant overall integrative mechanism — whether through strong centralization, formalization, or normative integration. We call such structures *integrated variety*.

Finally, a fourth pattern is one in which there is neither a dominant integrative mechanism nor an explicit pattern of differentiation to match local contexts. We call this pattern *ad hoc variation*.

We adopted the following procedure to classify each of the forty-one companies into these four structural categories. We aggregated the measures of centralization, formalization, and normative integration for all of a company's subsidiaries to arrive at a firmwide average of these measures. These averages were used as indicators of the strength of the firm's integrative mechanisms. When a firm's average measure for any of these three structural variables exceeded the median value across all the firms in the sample, the company was considered to have a strong integrative mechanism along that dimension; otherwise it was considered to have a weak integrative mechanism along that dimension (see Figure 3).

Figure 3 Companies with Strong Integrative Mechanisms

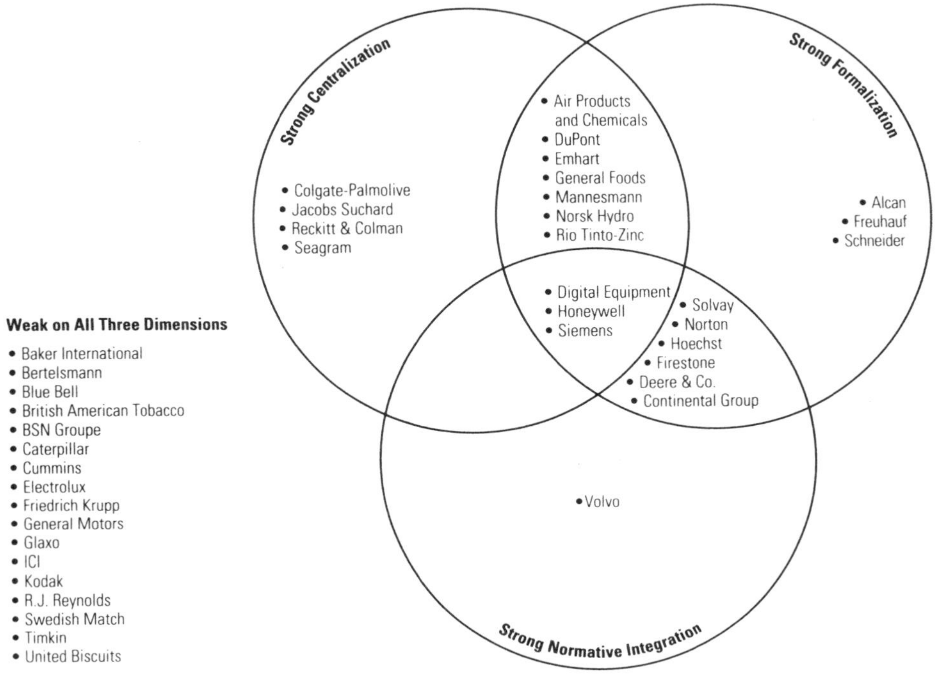

Some of the companies appear to have strong integration mechanisms along a single dimension.[20] For example, Seagram, Jacobs Suchard, Reckitt & Colman, and Colgate-Palmolive appear to have a high level of centralization; Alcan, Freuhauf, and Schneider demonstrate a high level of formalization; whereas Volvo appears to have strong normative integration throughout the company. We do not have detailed case studies on all of the companies to cross-check these survey findings, but the results are consistent with some widely known management systems in these firms. Seagram, for example, is well known for its extremely strong and highly centralized financial control system; all sales proceeds deposited in its subsidiaries' bank accounts are transferred daily to a central account managed by corporate headquarters while the central account remits to each local bank account the amounts required to cover specific operating expenses. Alcan's worldwide planning systems are well known, as are Volvo's decade-long efforts to pioneer a new work style and corporate culture that have often been hailed as unique among Western automobile companies.

Other firms appear to have strong integrative mechanisms along multiple dimensions. DuPont, Air Products and Chemicals, Mannesmann, General Foods, Emhart, Norsk Hydro, and Rio Tinto-Zinc appear to have strong levels of both centralization and formalization; Deere & Co., Firestone, Continental Group, Hoechst, Norton, and Solvay & Cie appear to combine formalization with strong firmwide normative integration. Others like Digital Equipment Corporation, Siemens, and Honeywell appear to have high levels of all three mechanisms. Again, the findings are consistent with what little we know about some of these companies. Digital, for example, has long had highly centralized engineering, product development, and base product marketing functions; has built elaborate formal rules and systems for revenue and profit planning, pricing and discounts, and manufacturing; and has enjoyed a strong set of shared values concerning management of people,

Figure 4 Mapping Integration and Differentiation

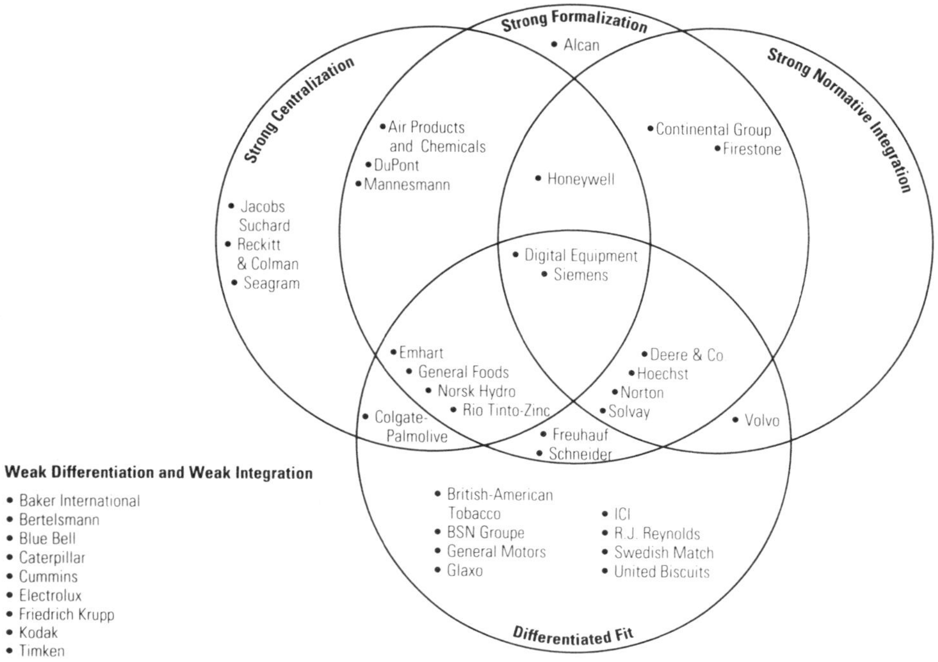

commitment to individual initiatives, and working through consensus.

The remaining companies in the sample appear to lack strong, firmwide integration along any of the three dimensions. They do not have uniform, centralized control over their worldwide activities to any significant extent. They appear to lack institutionalized rules and procedures as well as the glue of any strongly shared norms, values, and culture.

We measured the extent of structural differentiation by comparing the fit between each subsidiary's local context and the type of relationship it had with headquarters. For each company, each subsidiary was classified as high or low on the measures of environmental complexity and local resources. Each subsidiary was then classified as high, moderate, or low on the levels of centralization, formalization, and socialization that characterized its relationship with headquarters. If the headquarters-subsidiary relationship was suited to the subsidiary context (as described above), we considered the subsidiary to represent appropriate differentiation and counted the case as a "fit." If not, we counted the case as a "misfit." For each company, the extent of differentiation was measured as the ratio of the number of its "fit" to its "misfit" subsidiaries. When this ratio for a company exceeded the median value for the sample, it was classified as strongly differentiated in its structure; otherwise, the company was classified as weakly differentiated.

Figure 4 shows the results of this analysis, superimposed on the preceding analysis of integrative mechanisms. Some of the companies in the sample, such as Caterpillar, Cummins, Baker International, Bertelsmann, Blue Bell, Friedrich Krupp, Kodak, Timken, and Electrolux appear to lack systematic differentiation and, at the same time, do not have any strong integrative mechanism. These, then, correspond to the overall category we have characterized as *ad hoc variation.* Others, such as General Motors, Glaxo, BSN Groupe, British-American Tobacco, ICI, R.J. Reynolds, Swedish Match, and United Biscuits appear to have strong and systematic internal differentiation but lack strong firmwide integration; these correspond to our *differentiated fit* category. Firms such as Digital, Siemens, General Foods, Emhart, Norsk Hydro, Rio Tinto-Zinc, Colgate-Palmolive, Freuhauf, Schneider, Deere & Co., Hoechst, Norton, and Solvay have strong differentiation as well as strong integration (through one or more of the three integration mechanisms); these we place in the *integrated variety* category. Finally, the remaining companies demonstrate high integration through one mechanism or a combination of the three mechanisms but are not systematically differentiated internally. These firms belong to the category we have described as *structural uniformity*.

Figure 5 summarizes these findings, showing how the forty-one companies distribute among the four structural categories we have proposed.

Figure 5 The Structure of MNCs: Classification of Companies

Structural Integration	Structural Differentiation: Low	Structural Differentiation: High
High	**Structural Uniformity** • Air Products and Chemicals • Alcan • Continental Group • DuPont • Firestone • Honeywell • Jacobs Suchard • Mannesmann • Reckitt & Colman • Seagram	**Integrated Variety** • Colgate-Palmolive • Deere & Co. • Digital Equipment • Emhart • Freuhauf • General Foods • Hoechst • Norsk Hydro • Norton • Rio Tinto-Zinc • Schneider • Siemens • Solvay • Volvo
Low	**Ad Hoc Variation** • Baker International • Bertelsmann • Blue Bell • Caterpillar • Cummins • Electrolux • Friedrich Krupp • Kodak • Timken	**Differentiated Fit** • British-American Tobacco • BSN Groupe • General Motors • Glaxo • ICI • R.J. Reynolds • Swedish Match • United Biscuits

Organization-Environment Fit

Our basic argument is that for effective performance, the MNC's organizational structure should fit its overall environmental contingencies. We hypothesize that structural uniformity is best suited to global environmental conditions, differentiated fit to multinational environments, integrated variety to transnational environments, and ad hoc variety to international environments.

The logic underlying these hypotheses is straightforward. In global environments, the cross-national linkages create forces for firmwide coordination that predominate over the local environmental forces. Having a common integrative structure in these situations not only enables the MNC to respond to these linkages across these environments, it also economizes on the administrative burden that managing a highly differentiated system imposes.

In multinational environments, in contrast, the MNC must respond to the local environments to be competitive. The most effective structures are likely to be those that are differentiated to respond to the local environments' needs. Here, the administrative burden of a complex differentiated system is almost a cost of doing business, but the MNC must avoid the additional administrative complexity of a strong overlying integrative mechanism.

In transnational environments, it is important for the MNC to be responsive not only to local contingencies but also to cross-national linkages. As such it needs a structure of requisite differentiation overlaid with a strong companywide integrative mechanism. Here the administrative costs of such a complex system are both necessary and justified.

In contrast, placid international environments have neither strong forces of differentiation nor strong forces of integration, and a company in such a situation might derive little benefit from systematic organizational design. Such a firm can probably avoid the costs of both differentiation and integration.

It is important to note that it is the competing costs and benefits of differentiation and integration that underlie these issues of fit. In principle, if there were no administrative cost associated with organizational complexity, one might always recommend a structure of integrated variety, because such a structure would be best able to respond to minor variations in environments as well as to a great variety of linkages. But the costs associated with administrative complexity are significant and thus lead us to the idea of requisite complexity.

To test these hypotheses, we juxtaposed the environmental (Figure 2) and structural (Figure 5) classifications of the forty-one companies, as shown in Figure 6. Each cell in this figure represents a particular environment-structure combination. Cell 1, for example, identifies those companies that, during the study period, confronted an environment of relatively weak forces of both global integration and local responsiveness and whose organizations were neither strongly differentiated internally nor strongly integrated through firmwide mechanisms. Such a combination — an international environment and an ad-hoc variation organization — represents a good fit and, according to our theory, should on average outperform firms in Cells 2, 3, and 4, which operate with the same relatively simple organizational approach but face the more complex multinational, global, or transnational environments. Similarly, the firms in Cell 1 should also outperform, on average, firms in Cells 5, 9, and 13 because these companies adopt the more complex organizational approaches, thereby expending effort and resources on organizational integration and differentiation that are not necessary for responding to the demands of their relatively simple international environment.

Following this logic, it becomes clear that the seventeen companies in the four diagonal cells (1, 6, 11, and 16) — all of which represent good environment-structure fits — should, on average, outperform the twenty-four companies in the other twelve cells, all of which represent misfits. As shown in Table 2, actual performances of these forty-one companies conform to our prediction. On all three dimensions of performance — average return on net assets, growth in these returns,

Figure 6 Mapping of Environment and Structure

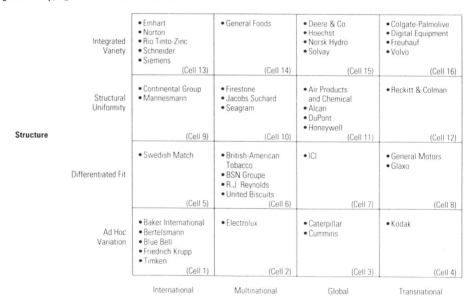

Structure	International	Multinational	Global	Transnational
Integrated Variety	• Emhart • Norton • Rio Tinto-Zinc • Schneider • Siemens (Cell 13)	• General Foods (Cell 14)	• Deere & Co. • Hoechst • Norsk Hydro • Solvay (Cell 15)	• Colgate-Palmolive • Digital Equipment • Freuhauf • Volvo (Cell 16)
Structural Uniformity	• Continental Group • Mannesmann (Cell 9)	• Firestone • Jacobs Suchard • Seagram (Cell 10)	• Air Products and Chemical • Alcan • DuPont • Honeywell (Cell 11)	• Reckitt & Colman (Cell 12)
Differentiated Fit	• Swedish Match (Cell 5)	• British-American Tobacco • BSN Groupe • R.J. Reynolds • United Biscuits (Cell 6)	• ICI (Cell 7)	• General Motors • Glaxo (Cell 8)
Ad Hoc Variation	• Baker International • Bertelsmann • Blue Bell • Friedrich Krupp • Timken (Cell 1)	• Electrolux (Cell 2)	• Caterpillar • Cummins (Cell 3)	• Kodak (Cell 4)

Environment

Table 2 Performance of Companies with Environment-Structure Fit and Misfit

Performance Measures	Companies in Cells 1, 6, 11, & 16 (diagonal = fit)	Companies in Cells 2, 3, 4, 5, 7, 8, 9, 10, 12, 13, 14, & 15 (others = misfit)	p-Value Difference
1. Average RONA (1982–1986)	5.72	3.69	<0.001
2. RONA Growth (1982–1986)	6.41	2.32	<0.001
3. Revenue Growth (1982–1986)	7.19	4.98	<0.001

and revenue growth — the seventeen companies representing good environment-structure fit outperform by statistically significant margins the twenty-four companies that lack such fit.

Conclusion

Empirical results from a correlational analysis do not provide proof of a causal argument. In this case, our ability to draw any conclusive inferences from the findings is additionally constrained because of the small and nonrandom sample of companies we have considered and because of our relatively simple and coarse-grained measurement procedure. Despite these limitations, we do believe that we have provided some preliminary evidence for our proposition that the appropriate level of organizational complexity leads to effective performance in multiunit organizations like MNCs. In this process, we have also suggested a useful way to classify the environment and structure of MNCs. Our findings, we believe, provide some justification for the approach we have advocated.

In the recent past, MNC managers have been at the receiving end of a diverse and often conflicting set of organizational prescriptions. On the one hand, influential academics and consultants have been urging them to abandon simplistic structures and processes and instead to build multidimensional network organizations with distributed management roles and tasks, overlapping responsibilities and relationships, and built-in ambiguity and redundancy.[21] On the other hand, equally strong voices have been arguing that the performance problems faced by many large MNCs are often attributable to the complexities of their organizations and that managers must have the courage to reestablish organizational simplicity by reverting to direct decision making and unambiguous accountability.[22] Admittedly, these prescriptions are more complex than we are painting them. Nevertheless, the intense advocacy accompanying these arguments has made it difficult for managers to get a perspective on such diverse prescriptions.

We believe that the issues we have raised in this paper will be useful to these managers, if only to structure internal debate and discussions on organizational choices. To reiterate, managers need a detailed understanding of their companies' environmental demands to evaluate the kind of organizational capabilities they need to build. Unnecessary organizational complexity in a relatively simple business environment can be just as unproductive as unresponsive simplicity in a complex business environment. To return to the title of this paper, companies require different organizational horses to manage superior performance in different environmental courses. What we have proposed here is a method for analyzing these environmental courses and for selecting the appropriate organizational horses.

We need to point out that the part of our study reported in this paper took a static picture of these companies. In reality, environmental demands evolve over time and managers need to adopt a dynamic view about organizational capabilities. Even though we have not carried out detailed case research on how the different industries covered in this study have been evolving, the limited information we have suggests that the environmental demands in at least some of them may be becoming more complex. In the food and beverages businesses, for example, the forces of global integration appear to be getting stronger, driven, among other factors, by the growing proliferation of regional and global brands. In the scientific measuring instrument business, on the other hand, the need for local responsiveness is increasing as stand-alone products are giving way to integrated systems consisting of packages of hardware, software, and related services. As a result, these and many other businesses may be evolving to the more complex transnational category, and companies competing in these businesses may need to build the kind of organizational form we have described as "integrated variety." Managers need to be sensitive to such changes in environmental demands — indeed, they should drive such changes when appropriate — and must develop the ability to differentiate and integrate their organizations to lead or respond to such evolving business conditions.

We focused here on the MNC. Our argument can easily be extended, however, to any multidivisional firm.

Consider, for instance, the case of a firm in which each division operates in a different market or business segment. Once again, the overall environmental contingencies faced by such a firm can be characterized in terms of the extent to which each of its business segments have unique and strong forces for local responsiveness and the extent to which these businesses are linked. In a sense, this is similar to identifying the nature of the firm's diversification, whether it is in related or unrelated business segments. Similarly the firm's overall structure can be conceived in terms of the pattern of variation in the governance of the different corporate-division relationships. Again the same four structural patterns may be identified, and we would expect the environment-structure fit to follow the logic of requisite complexity. In this situation, then, all we have done is change the source of environmental variation from geography, in the case of MNCs, to different business segments, in the case of the multiproduct firm. Of course, in some situations, the source of environmental variation in the firm's different units may well be driven by both geography and product markets. Though operationally more complex, this situation can just as easily be accommodated under the same general theoretical rubric.

> Companies require different organizational horses to manage superior performance in different environmental courses.

Finally, let us emphasize once again that in reiterating the two-decade-old notion of environment-organization fit, we do not wish to detract from the much more sophisticated analysis of organization-environment interactions that is the focus of current research on the topic. The perspectives in these studies add richness to our understanding of the underlying processes of influence and adaptation and of the limits of those processes. However, in focusing on those processes and in highlighting the second-order benefits from characteristics such as deliberate misfit and organizational ambiguity, what we often tend to overlook are the first-order benefits of fit and organizational simplicity. We take them for granted, perhaps, but an occasional reminder of these taken-for-granted aspects of organizational analysis may help in placing the rest in proper perspective. ◆

References

1. This contingency theory had two separate roots. Lawrence and Lorsch stated it as a set of environment-organization contingencies, as did Thompson. See:
P.R. Lawrence and J.W. Lorsch, *Organization and Environment* (Boston: Graduate School of Business Administration, Harvard University, 1967); and
J.D. Thompson, *Organizations in Action* (New York: McGraw-Hill, 1967).
Alfred Chandler, on the other hand, suggested the need for a match between strategy and organization as he described the rationale for and process of evolution of the multidivisional organization in corporate America. See:
A. Chandler, *Strategy and Structure: Chapters in the History of the American Industrial Enterprise* (Cambridge, Massachusetts: MIT Press, 1962). The subsequent literature on contingency theory adopted one or both sets of views, building in this process a model of environment-strategy-organization linkages.
2. See J. Stopford and L.T. Wells, Jr., *Managing the Multinational Enterprise* (New York: Basic Books, 1972). This research followed the work of Chandler, focusing on strategy-organization contingencies.
3. See C.A. Bartlett, "Building and Managing the Transnational: The New Organizational Challenge," *Competition in Global Industries*, ed. M.E. Porter (Boston: Harvard Business School Press, 1986).
4. See Bartlett (1986); and:
C.A. Bartlett and S. Ghoshal, *Managing across Borders: The Transnational Solution* (Boston: Harvard Business School Press, 1989).
5. See Bartlett and Ghoshal (1989).
6. This interpretation is manifest, for example, in:
W.G. Egelhoff, "Exploring the Limits of Transnationalism" (Paper presented at the annual meeting, Academy of International Business, Toronto, 11-14 October 1990).
7. For a comprehensive review and a spirited defense of the concept of fit and the contingency perspective that underlies it, see:
L. Donaldson, *In Defense of Organization Theory* (Cambridge: Cambridge University Press, 1985).
8. This database was developed in the course of the first author's doctoral dissertation work and is fully described in his unpublished thesis: "The Innovative Multinational: A Differentiated Network of Roles and Relationships" (Boston: Harvard Business School, 1986).
Parts of the database relevant to the analysis presented in this paper have also been described in:
S. Ghoshal and N. Nohria, "Internal Differentiation within Multinational Corporations," *Strategic Management Journal* 10 (1989): 323-337.
9. The 438 companies in the database are those that responded to the questionnaire we sent to the 438 North American and European MNCs listed in:
J. Stopford, *World Directory of Multinational Enterprises* (Detroit, New Jersey: Galo Research Company, 1983).
While we are not aware of any specific bias in the sample that would *a priori* invalidate any of our findings, the generalizability of our conclusions remains constrained because of the small size and potential non-representativeness of the sample. For a detailed description of the sample and of the reliability and validity of our measures, see:
Ghoshal and Nohria (1989).
10. See C.K. Prahalad and Y.L. Doz, *The Multinational Mission: Balancing Local Demands and Global Vision* (New York: The Free Press, 1987).

11. See S.J. Kobrin, "An Empirical Analysis of the Determinants of Global Integration," Special Issue, *Strategic Management Journal* 12 (1991): 17-31.
12. Steers describes some of the different performance measures and their relevance and implications. See:
R.M. Steers, "Problems in the Measurement of Organizational Effectiveness," *Administrative Science Quarterly* 20 (1975): 546-558.
Venkatraman argues for the appropriateness of the measures we adopt. See:
N. Venkatraman, "A Concept of Fit in Strategy Research: Toward Verbal and Statistical Correspondence," *Academy of Management Review* 14 (1989): 423-444.
13. See Prahalad and Doz (1987).
14. For one of the earliest descriptions of MNC environments in these terms, see:
J. Fayerweather, *International Business Strategy and Administration* (Cambridge, Massachusetts: Ballinger Press, 1978).
For one of the most recent and comprehensive elaborations, see:
Prahalad and Doz (1987).
For a discussion of the factors that drive the needs for global integration and national responsiveness, see:
G.S. Yip, "Global Strategy. . . In a World of Nations?" *Sloan Management Review*, Fall 1989, pp. 29-41.
15. Our characterization and terminology need some clarifications. Bartlett and Ghoshal (1989) considered three sets of environmental forces: those of global integration, national responsiveness, and worldwide learning. Strong demands along each of these dimensions were characterized as "global," "multinational," and "international" industries, respectively, whereas "transnational" industries were defined as those facing strong demands simultaneously along all three dimensions. In this paper, we use the relatively simpler two dimensional conceptualization proposed by Prahalad and Doz (1987). In our framework, global and multinational industries are defined the same way as in Bartlett and Ghoshal (1989), but international and transnational industries are defined as those facing weak-weak and strong-strong combinations of the forces of global integration and national responsiveness. This characterization is consistent with the use of the terminology in Bartlett (1986), except that he did not define the "international" industry environment explicitly in that paper.
16. There is well-established support for these mechanisms in organization theory. Since the landmark studies of the Aston Group, centralization and formalization have been central constructs in analyzing the structure of complex organizations. See:
D.S. Pugh, D.J. Hickson, C.R. Hinings, and C. Turner, "The Dimensions of Organization Structure," *Administrative Science Quarterly* 13 (1968): 65-105.
Van Maanen and Schein have since argued that normative integration should be considered as another primary element in the structure of organizational relations. See:
J. Van Maanen and E.H. Schein, "Toward a Theory of Organizational Socialization" in *Research in Organizational Behavior*, ed. B.M. Staw (Greenwich, Connecticut: JAI Press, 1979).
17. For a recent review of the evidence and arguments for internal differentiation in headquarters-subsidiary relationships, see:
A.K. Gupta and V. Govindarajan, "Knowledge Flows and the Structure of Control within Multinational Corporations," *Academy of Management Review* 16 (1991): 768-792.
18. See Ghoshal and Nohria (1989).
For alternative conceptualizations of subsidiary context, see:
T.A. Poynter and A.M. Rugman, "World Product Mandates: How Will Multinationals Respond?" *Business Quarterly* 47 (1982): 54-61; and:
Gupta and Govindarajan (1991).
19. See Ghoshal and Nohria (1989).
20. It is interesting to observe that there is one null set in this analysis: none of the companies combines high levels of centralization and socialization while lacking formalized systems. Perhaps this is merely an artifact of the sample or a reflection of measurement error. Or perhaps this combination is administratively infeasible. At this stage we can only speculate on this issue, but it may be a starting point for an interesting future study.
21. For the most provocative and articulate statement of this view, see:
G. Hedlund, "The Hypermodern MNC: A Helterarchy?" *Human Resource Management* 25 (1986): 9-35.
22. See N. Tichy and R. Charan, "Speed, Simplicity, and Self-Confidence: An Interview with Jack Welch," *Harvard Business Review*, September-October 1989, pp. 112-120.

Reprint 3422

[8]

© Academy of Management Executive, 1998, Vol. 12, No. 4

Managing the global workforce: Challenges and strategies

Karen Roberts, Ellen Ernst Kossek, and Cynthia Ozeki

Executive Overview

The globalization of the workplace has become a fact of life for a substantial segment of U.S. companies, bringing a dramatic expansion of the scope of workforce management and a whole host of new organizational challenges. Using data collected from interviews with international human resource managers in eight large companies, this paper identifies three practical challenges to managing the global workforce and four strategies for meeting those challenges. The three challenges are: deployment, knowledge and innovation dissemination, and talent identification and development. The four strategies are: aspatial careers, awareness-building assignments, SWAT teams, and virtual solutions. A diagnostic framework for each challenge is provided that indicates when to use which strategy and basic implementation points are presented.

The line went dead. Steve Prestwick slowly hung up the telephone, wondering what he could possibly say to the executive committee monitoring the Singapore R&D center project. Shortly after being assigned to help staff the facility, he had attended a committee meeting that left him excited about tapping into the potential of the company's large global work force. "Get the best people from everywhere," said one executive. "Don't just rely on information from headquarters. Try to find out what the people in Europe or Japan might know," chimed in another. And from the CEO, "Let's use this as an opportunity to develop a global mindset in some of our more promising people." The vision sounded great, and Steve's role seemed simple: put together a team with all the experts needed to get the new facility up and running smoothly in its first two years.

Right away Steve began having trouble finding out who had the right skills, and even where the choices seemed obvious, he wasn't getting anywhere. The engineer who refused the assignment over the telephone was the best the company had in her field. She told him that spending two years in Singapore wouldn't really help her career. Plus, it would be hard on her children and impossible for her husband, a veterinarian with a growing practice. Not only did he need a top engineering manager, but Steve also had to find a highly competent corps of technical researchers who knew about the company and its approach to R&D. He also needed technicians who could set up the facility. He thought he would bring in people from the U.S. to select and set up equipment, then lead a research team of local engineers that the U.S. engineers would train in company practices and technologies. To his chagrin, most of the U.S. technical people he had talked to weren't interested in such an assignment. A European perspective might be useful, but he didn't even have records on possible candidates from the other overseas offices. Steve was on his own, and he had less than a week to come up with a plan.

What Can Steve Do?

Although Steve is fictional, he is facing a composite of real problems for global HR managers. The need to develop a global perspective on human resource management has been part of the managerial landscape for well over a decade, but there is no consensus about what tools to use. Adler and Bartholomew noted that organizational "strategy (the what) . . . is internationalizing faster than implementation (the how) and much faster than the managers and executives themselves (the who)."[1] Steve has been given an assignment that reflects his organization's commitment to manage globally but little guidance about how to meet his goals.

The challenges, strategic approaches, and diagnostic framework we present are based on interviews with senior managers in large corporations with reputations for excellence in international operations. We chose the firms in this study using three criteria. First, we wanted firms experienced in operating internationally that could comment on the evolution of transnational HR management. Second, we wanted variation across industries to assure that we were not uncovering information idiosyncratic to certain types of industries. Third, we selected firms whose recruitment policies indicated a commitment to the strategic use of HRM in global management.

We sent the most senior international HR professional in each firm a letter describing our study and requesting an interview. We asked that they identify any other HR professionals in their organization whom we might also interview. Based on this process, we interviewed 24 professionals at eight firms.[2] The letter listed four questions that we wanted to cover during the interview:

1. What are the key global pressures affecting human resource management practices in your firm currently and for the projected future?
2. What is the level and substance of knowledge about human resource issues that human resource professionals should possess?
3. What are examples of leading edge international human resource practices in your organization?
4. To what extent is international knowledge needed by entry level professionals in human resource management at your organization?

The questions were deliberately broad, reflecting our exploratory approach. Each interview lasted 1½ to 2 hours. During the interviews, we asked for any additional materials the HR managers thought would be valuable to our study. Once we had begun to analyze our interview information, we used follow-up phone calls both to those we interviewed as well as to other professional contacts to supplement or clarify the data from the interviews.

The information from these interviews was distilled into a two-dimensional framework. One dimension was the set of challenges these executives saw confronting global managers. The second was a set of four prototypical strategies to address these challenges.

The Challenges

In the course of each interview, we asked these executives to describe their vision of the ideal global internal labor market. Three broad features emerged from their responses:

(1) Deployment: easily getting the right skills to where they are needed in the organization regardless of geographical location;
(2) Knowledge and innovation dissemination: spreading state of the art knowledge and practices throughout the organization regardless of where they originate; and,
(3) Identifying and developing talent on a global basis: identifying who has the ability to function effectively in a global organization and developing those abilities.

Although skill deployment, information dissemination, and talent identification have long been basic HR challenges, in the global environment, these issues are overlaid with the complexities of distance, language, and cultural differences. Part of the challenge to global management is to reinterpret successful past practices in terms of these complexities.

Deployment

All the organizations had a history of operating internationally, but had relied on a headquarters-subsidiary structure and the traditional expatriate model of human resource staffing where U.S. nationals held most positions of authority. This arrangement was adequate in yesterday's international organization because leadership, decision-making authority, and organizational power flowed from the parent site to the foreign subsidiaries. Today, however, new technologies, new markets, innovation, and new talent no longer solely emanate from headquarters but are found cross-nationally, making the expatriate model obsolete.[3] Further, the cost of deploying an expatriate has become excessive. One Merck and Co., Inc., executive estimated that it was three times more expensive to have an expatriate than a local national in any given job.

All of the organizations were developing alternative ways to get the right people to where the work is on an as-needed basis. The key innovation is that organizations are making distinctions between when it is necessary to physically move a person to a particular location and when the person's skills can be delivered through other means. Permanent transfers are no longer seen as the only method for delivering certain services to parts of the organization, giving way to short-term assignments and virtual deployment. Getting managers to stop relying on physical transfers and to think globally about resources is not easy.

Getting managers to stop relying on physical transfers and to think globally about resources is not easy.

Managers will use company-wide job postings when there is a formal job opening, but will not think outside their units, let alone countries, when it comes to finding the expertise to solve a specific problem, such as poor market response to a new consumer product or dysfunctional work relationships that are due to cross-cultural ignorance.

Knowledge dissemination/Innovation transfer

The HR executives cited two global information flow blockages: disseminating knowledge from one location to another and spreading innovation. Under earlier expatriate structures, information flowed from the center out. Current global organizations need structures where all units concurrently receive and provide information. Valuable market and production technology information are being produced outside the parent location. One example of the perils of not using local expertise in collecting market information is Marks & Spencer, Britain's largest retailer. The company failed routinely overseas until it found its niche by selling M&S branded clothes in Hong Kong, a former British colony.[4]

The executives at both Dow Chemical Co. and Merck saw this challenge as being one of cross-functional communication, where the greatest opportunities for growth and innovation are at hand-off points between functions. These executives saw hand-off opportunities as easily lost in a global environment, primarily because of the difficulties of establishing cross-cultural trust. As one manager noted:

> As long as diversity is not valued, trust of people from different backgrounds is not developed. There is a tendency to duplicate functions so one does not have to rely on people one does not trust. As a result, rather than having a single global enterprise, many international companies are operating more like a collection of lots of smaller companies.

All of the executives we interviewed noted that language compounded the trust problem. Although English was the business language in all of these organizations, halting speech, misused words, strange grammar, and mispronounced words can subtly undermine the perception that the speaker is competent.

Talent Identification and Development

One executive at General Motors Corp. began his interview with us by noting that:

> ... the key global issue [for GM] is how to transform the organization internally to become globally competitive. Even for employees who may never go overseas, it is necessary to constantly sensitize everyone to the fact that they are in a global business.

All the executives reiterated this theme in one way or another. But, eventually, each interview came to the reality that not everyone in the organization is going to thrive and prevail in a global environment. Therefore, one of the larger challenges of managing the global labor force is identifying who is most likely to grasp the complexities of the transnational operations and function well in that sort of environment. As one Merck executive described it:

> In the 1940s, transactions were the basis for determining the types of skills managers needed. The [new] challenge to [global human resource management] is to learn to talk in terms of "stories." Organizations need people who understand the business and who are able to see where the business is going globally and the cultures that need to be bridged, people able to manage conflict and change.

One aspect of this challenge is that the scope of the transnational organization is so large that just collecting information about employees is difficult. Also, all of the executives we interviewed acknowledged that there were cultural biases in the selection process that probably caused talented people to be overlooked. One Amoco Corp. executive gave the example of their operations in Norway. Norwegian work-family values differ from those in the U.S., and it is common for men who are senior in their organizations to leave work at 3 p.m. to pick up their children after school. While U.S. norms are beginning to tilt somewhat more toward family in the work-family balance, leaving early still signals a lack of commitment to the job in most U.S. workplaces.[5] The Amoco executive noted that it was very difficult for U.S. managers to trust that their Norwegian employees would get the job done in a crisis and thus had trouble seeing them as potential global managers. Duplicative staffing was sometimes the result.

A final component of this challenge was motivating employees to want to spend time overseas. Most of the executives considered overseas experience a *sine qua non* for promotion to top jobs in their organizations. But, for a variety of reasons, many talented employees do not want to move overseas. One executive noted that, "talent marries other talent," and that spousal careers are increasingly an obstacle to overseas assignments.[6] Another point, made by both Merck and Amoco, was that the expected growth in their industries was in locations that were not viewed as desirable by employees from developed countries. An Amoco executive noted that in some West African countries where Amoco had operations, 30 to 35 percent of the population was thought to be HIV positive, dramatically undermining the appeal of those countries to potential expatriates.

Four Strategies for Managing the Global Workforce

The managers we interviewed described how their organizations had moved away from the traditional expatriate assignment and the new arrangements they were using to meet the three challenges above. Tables 1 through 4 summarize the key points of each of the strategies.

Aspatial Careers

Aspatial careerists have borderless careers, typically working in multiple countries over the course of their work lives. The chief difference between the aspatial career and the expatriate assignment is that these careers exist in an environment where authority and expertise are no longer thought to reside exclusively at the parent company. Aspatial careerists can come from any part of the globe.

Aspatial careers can take several forms. An employee may live and work overseas with frequent moves; others may have a geographically stationary home base but are required to travel and to have the ability to think about the organization in ways that are spatially neutral. If they relocate, their families go with them.

The aspatial careers model does not overcome the high costs associated with the traditional expatriate model. As a result, only a small percent of most organizations' employees follow aspatial career paths. GM estimates that there are only about 900 of its employees pursue aspatial careers. Merck has approximately 250 employees on this path out of a workforce of 37,000.[7]

Aspatial careerists are usually managers, not technicians. Over the course of their several moves, they accumulate rich contextual knowledge, also known as tacit or implicit knowledge. Successful aspatial careerists develop an in-depth understanding of global organizations because they have managed across cultures and know how culture affects work.

They have also developed extensive global networks that help them identify and draw on exper-

Table 1
Aspatial Careers

Who	What	
Globally oriented, highly mobile people, with proven ability and company loyalty	Corps of experts with borderless careers on long-term overseas assignment	
How		
Deployment	**Knowledge Dissemination**	**Talent ID & Development**
Geographically relocate employees with high level skills and rich cross-cultural perspective	Employees with in-depth global experiences & networks in leadership positions across sites	Rotation as development
Implementation Points		
• Encourage company over country culture • Assign within culturally homogenous regions • Use pan-region selection meetings • Evolve selection criteria that are shared across countries • Provide cross-cultural training for families • Recognize family life-cycle realities		

tise throughout their organizations. These managers' global insights tend to filter through the organization rather than be distributed by means of explicit training or the introduction of new technology. One exception is when companies use aspatial careers to develop technical personnel below the top management level. A plant manager at Dow described cross-national rotation of engineers as part of a strategy for cross-training and to assure comparability of engineering skill level across Dow plants in all countries.

Successful aspatial careerists develop an in-depth understanding of global organizations because they have managed across cultures and know how culture affects work.

Through long rotations with in-depth experience, aspatial careerists acquire globally applicable skills. One company had a manager who had begun his career as a health care expert in France. He then spent four years in London, three in Tokyo, and three in Switzerland, at each point deepening his health care expertise and expanding his network. He had become a repository of cross-cultural health care information as well as a someone who knew the players across these different sites. His gradually accumulated information made him an insightful manager and valuable to the company.

The talent identification potential of aspatial careers is not yet fully realized. Several companies noted that they are beginning to explicitly view their aspatial careerists as a recruiting pool for the highest level of corporate management. The underlying logic is that those who have rotated across different countries have the global perspective needed at the top of the organization. However, none of the companies we interviewed had fully committed to reliance on aspatial career experience as an indicator of top management potential. Rather, several admitted that their companies still had difficulties with recognizing the value-added of overseas experience when reintegrating those who have been overseas into home country operations.

Awareness-Building Assignments

The primary purpose of awareness-building assignments is to develop cross-country sensitivity in high-potential employees in a short time. These assignments last anywhere from 3 months to one year. Families are not expected to relocate, so that depending on assignment length, regular home visits might be part of this strategy. Usually this assignment is made early in one's career and typically an employee will only have one such assignment.[8]

At the end of an awareness-building assignment, a high potential employee is expected to have a broadened cultural perspective and an appreciation of the diversity in the organization. One of the Dow executives summarized the purpose of these assignments:

> Overseas assignments are no longer used just to get the "overseas stamp" . . . We may transfer them to acquire knowledge available only overseas, or perhaps as way to export a leading-edge practice to an overseas location. Often, though, an overseas assignment is not specifically a technical transfer—we

Table 2
Awareness Building Assignments

Who		What
High potential employees early in their careers		3 to 12 month assignments
	How	
Deployment	**Knowledge Dissemination**	**Talent ID & Development**
Technically competent, high potential employees	Cross-cultural immersion to produce global perspective	• Screening for ability to function out of own culture • Develop globally aware future performers
	Implementation Points	
• Use to bridge geofunctional disconnects • Rotate employees with demonstrable competence • Manage the adjustment cycle • Use to develop local nationals		

are going more for [developing an employee with an] 'open mind'.

GM also incorporates a training component in the form of short-term cross-function transfers and/or cross-plant training. This can be a mechanism for innovation dissemination. GM has found that rotated employees must demonstrate technical competence to be accepted at the overseas site. As one GM executive described it:

> If the need is to cultivate openness and develop cross-cultural awareness, it has to be done early in one's career. However, the reality is that those who go overseas first have to demonstrate technical competence to be accepted in a different location, and this is more necessary than cultural awareness.

Several firms use these assignments to aculturate local nationals who after the rotation will spend most of their careers in their home countries. These assignments serve as screens for global awareness potential. Awareness-building assignments are not long enough to develop in-depth cultural knowledge. However, an employee who can shed provincialism and learn that value can be added from any location in the company is one who is likely to function effectively in the global organization.

SWAT Teams

SWAT teams are highly mobile teams of experts, deployed on a short-term basis, to troubleshoot, solve a very specific problem, or complete a clearly defined project. (The name derives from the special weapons and tactics units used by many police departments.) SWAT teams play a role like that of the technical troubleshooter, an individual sent to a foreign location to analyze and solve a particular operational problem.[9]

SWAT teams comprise nomadic experts who are identified internationally and deployed as internal consultants on an as-needed basis. As a Dow executive described the objective of this approach, the company does not "expect to move people across areas but does want to leverage resources across our different businesses." At GM, the SWAT team takes the form of an expert network, internal consultants deployed throughout the organization. The actual amount of time spent overseas varies with the purpose or project but in general is under three months.

The primary strength of this approach is that it permits the organization to cultivate highly specialized knowledge and expertise on a limited basis, and to apply that expertise wherever it is needed within the organization. One difference between SWAT teams and awareness-building assignments is that there is no explicit developmental component to the SWAT team model other than to complete whatever project is defined. Development of cross-cultural awareness on the part of SWAT team members may be a by-product of the job but it is not its intention.

Once a SWAT team has been assembled, it can be redeployed each time a situation requiring its skillset emerges. Frequent opportunities to apply their skills in different settings can add significantly to the existing skill accumulation of team members, providing the developmental component to the SWAT team strategy.

Table 3
SWAT Teams

Who		What
Technical specialists		Short-term, project-length assignments
	How	
Deployment	**Knowledge Dissemination**	**Talent ID & Development**
Specialized skills on an as-needed basis	Transfer of technical processes & systems	Specialized skills honed through varied & frequent applications
	Implementation Points	
• Best SWAT team member has single contributor mindset • Use to spread acultural innovation • Good at smaller locations or at start-up • Recognize clear limitations		

Table 4
Virtual Solutions

Who		What
Non-rotating employees who need overseas connections		Electronic communications
How		
Deployment	**Knowledge Dissemination**	**Talent ID & Development**
Videoconferencing & E-mail allow virtual deployment	Web pages, bulletin boards, intranets, distance learning & interactive training disperse information across locations	GHRIS, electronic job posting, video & virtual interviews ID and screen for assignments
Implementation Points		
• Encourage virtual friendships • Couple with cross-culture awareness training • GHRIS works best with standardized information • GHRIS trade-off between standardized information & universal access • Global job posting for clearly defined jobs • Don't expect instant results		

Virtual Solutions

Virtual solutions are a collection of practices that exploit the rapidly evolving electronic communication technologies. These include use of all forms of the Internet and intranets, videoconferencing, electronic expert systems, and electronic databases coupled with user-friendly front-end systems. The chief advantages to this strategy are the low cost of communication and the uncoupling of real time from virtual time. Awareness-building and virtual solutions are the strategies with which most of the firms we interviewed had had the least experience, but also were the approaches they saw as having the most potential for managing and developing the global workforce.

Internet and intranets, including E-mail, are the most democratic form of overseas deployment, allowing communication among employees regardless of organizational level. Videoconferencing has a similar advantage; however, videoconferencing facilities are a scarce resource compared with E-mail in most organizations. Both Dow and Merck managers said that their videoconferencing rooms were in constant use.

Virtual international teams design software at IBM Corp. Communication through intranets allows for 24-hour product development. One team includes software developers from the U.S., several former Soviet Union states, and India. The work is usually initiated in the U.S. At the end of the day, the U.S. team transmits its files via the intranet to the Soviet team, which works on the project until the end of the work day. The Soviet team then sends its work on to the Indian team whose work day ends at the start of business for the U.S. team, which picks up the files and continues the production cycle.

A more sophisticated virtual deployment tool is the use of virtual reality. NASA uses virtual reality to train international teams of astronauts.[10] These teams need to perform complex tasks requiring lengthy training. Actually convening these teams of astronauts from different countries at a single geographical location for months at a time is prohibitively expensive and disrupts family life. A virtual simulation of a repair of the Hubble telescope was constructed for training purposes and allowed team members to simulate the repair as though in the same room. One Russian and one U.S. member virtually shook hands at the end of the repair exercise. However, this simulation took months to develop. While virtual reality is almost as good as being there, it is also almost as expensive.

All the companies have web pages on the Internet with company background and product information, as well as public information about new developments. E-mail is in common use and electronic bulletin boards to solve technical problems were becoming more common. At the time of our interviews, comparable intranet systems with proprietary information were in development. This sort of communication is one mechanism to break down some of the barriers to information flow erected by technical chauvinism. Reiterating the theme of cross-cultural distrust, one GM executive noted that "technically skilled people in one country feel their training and skills are superior [to those of employees from other countries] and they have little to learn from their international counterparts." He noted this was a substantial problem in motivating technical employees to rotate overseas and that use of E-mail and electronic bulletin boards is expected to ameliorate this problem as technical solutions are offered cross-nationally and recognized as valid.

One solution not yet widely implemented is distance learning. Ford Motor Co. uses this commonly to continuously update the skills of its engineers, videotaping classes that employees can play individually or as a group. The students can then hold discussion groups and interact with the instructor who holds electronic office hours at predetermined time. Another version is a highly interactive broadcast class where students can interact with the instructor across networks that permit student questions and discussion, even pop quizzes. However, distance learning is still in its infancy and was not cited as a commonly used tool.

All the firms had Global Human Resource Information Systems (GHRIS), which allowed for global job posting. The companies stressed that talent identification below the highest level on a global basis was key to the success of the company. Amoco Corp., Dow, and Merck used their GHRIS to store career data about their employees useful for selection and, on a more limited basis, for job posting. Amoco has implemented a worldwide job posting system that allows all employees to use electronic systems to learn about and apply for jobs.[11]

Diagnosing the Challenges

We developed a diagnostic framework for evaluating each of the challenges and deciding among the four strategies.

Diagnosing the Deployment Challenge

The challenge of global deployment is getting the needed skills from one part of the organization to another inexpensively. Not all of the tools associated with each of the strategic solutions were equally effective in all situations. There are two components to deciding among the deployment strategies: contact time required and extent to which the skills can be applied out of cultural context.

If the need is for on-going on-site leadership, in-depth cultural understanding, and/or skills that can only be successfully applied if culturally embedded, use aspatial careers. To provide short-term training or skills application that requires cultural sensitivity, use awareness-building assignments. SWAT teams offer on-site technical skills, knowledge of production process, operations, and/or systems that need to be implemented, with little cultural content. Virtual solutions provide frequent, brief iterative interactions, with only a little cultural component to the interaction, or a wide sweep of the organization to search for or communicate technical details or information.

Diagnosing the Knowledge and Innovation Dissemination Challenge

The information organizations need to stay competitive ranges from highly technical to informally communicated background information. The effectiveness of each of the four strategies depends on the type of knowledge or innovation being disseminated. Choosing among the four strategies depends on the technical complexity of the information that is to be shared and the extent to which it must be culturally embedded. If the knowledge or innovations to be disseminated can be successfully shared only when communicated in a cultural context, use aspatial careers. Awareness-building assignments succeed when the knowledge is primarily cultural awareness and cross-cultural sensitivity training. If the knowledge is defined technology or practices with minimal cultural content, use SWAT teams. If the knowledge requires on-going and frequent information exchanges among dispersed employees, use virtual solutions.

Diagnosing Talent Identification and Development Challenges

Development of a global mindset is essential to operating globally. Executives are looking for a similar set of characteristics among their global managers.[12] Merck looks for people who have a broad perspective and can intelligently apply practical leadership skills to guide change in the organization. Baxter International looks for "patience, flexibility, communication skills, intellectual curiosity about the rest of the world." GM looks for a skillset that includes, "communication skills, the ability to value diversity, and the ability to be objective."

Cultural training notwithstanding, a manager from Merck noted the difficulty of finding people with this skillset:

> Merck uses two-thirds selection and one-third development ... [We rely more on selection than development in our selection criteria because] it is difficult to impart needed skills,

and people don't get that much out of classroom training—they are more likely to remember what they had for dinner than what went on in the training session... We are looking for people with curiosity and a mix of skills.

This suggests that organizations should select well, then develop. Companies that need to identify and develop leaders with in-depth cultural knowledge and proven cross-cultural abilities and are willing to spend time and money to have those people, should use aspatial careers. To identify and develop high potential performers with an understanding that they are functioning in a global organization and an appreciation of cultural diversity, companies should use awareness-building assignments. SWAT teams provide mobile and technically competent specialists whose skills tend to be needed on a short-term basis. Virtual solutions identify employees using shared selection criteria to fill vacancies with well-understood job requirements.

Implementing the Strategies

Following are examples of how companies implemented each of the strategies, including some of the obstacles they have encountered.

Implementing the Aspatial Career Strategy

All the companies encourage the development of a culture of company over country. Baxter has deployed leadership throughout the organization regardless of national origin: the VP for the European region is of U.S. origin located in Germany; the VP for the Diagnostics division is an Italian located in Switzerland; the VP of Cardiovascular is Irish and located in France; the Hospital group is lead by French person in Belgium. This is not just a happy accident but the result of an explicit strategy on Baxter's part to develop a company-over-country identity, where the managers focus on the competitive strategies of the entire company, not only for the region in which they reside. Baxter has eliminated country-based organization and reorganized by product group or business function. Also, the position of country general manager has been eliminated to encourage a business-over-country orientation.

These geographically fluid careers are more successful if rotations occur within culturally homogeneous regions. Both Baxter and GM have divide their global operations into regions, and Baxter is deliberate about rotating employees within rather than across regions as much as possible. This policy is consistent with results from a study of Singaporean managers showing that the cultural similarity between origin and destination locations positively affected employee and spouse willingness to relocate.[13] GM also uses a regional basis for determining benefit plans, distinguishing between intracontinental (policies reflecting continent-wide norms) and intercontinental policies (policies applied at GM sites world-wide). This distinction simplifies within-region rotations.

Schlumberger uses a "borderlands career track" version of aspatial careers in which rotating employees move often across adjoining borders. The cultural homogeneity of border areas allows the company to move people quickly with minimal adjustment."[14]

One identification mechanism used by several companies is the pan-regional meeting. This meeting takes place regularly, three to four times a year, where higher- (but not just the highest-) level managers and sometimes technical people within a geographical region meet to exchange information and network. The meetings last several days to a week and are used to showcase potential aspatial careerists. HR people are included and charged with identifying potential talent for global reassignment. Dow holds four annual meetings, one in each region, where managers are asked to recommend, review, and present the top 1.5 percent of the employees in terms of high management potential. Because it is important for managers to present very talented people, these annual meetings are high pressure events. These meetings are used also to identify candidates for awareness-building assignments.

An informal outcome from Dow's meetings is the evolution of a shared understanding of what is meant by global competencies. This evolves out of formal identification and presentation of high potential talent at the pan-regional meetings. Each meeting serves as an iteration in the development of global selection criteria. This evolving understanding of the managerial traits required by the global organization is used to identify candidates for both aspatial careers and awareness-building assignments.

A key component to motivating talented employees to go overseas, even for a short time, is their belief that the organization values overseas experience. This will be especially true for aspatial careerists, but also true to a lesser extent for awareness-building assignments and SWAT team employees. Most organizations send a mixed message to employees about the value of overseas experience.[15]

There is often a sharp decline in authority, responsibility, and autonomy for the employee returning to the parent company. Most aspatial careerists are at or near the top of the overseas organization and in many cases behave like CEOs. Their jobs at

Most organizations send a mixed message to employees about the value of overseas experience.

the parent site are of necessity of lower status. The more hierarchical an organization, the more difficult this problem will be. Structuring jobs of returning aspatial employees to allow sufficient autonomy and identifying explicit ways to fully utilize their overseas expertise is important. GM does this by using returned overseas employees in the first round selection process for aspatial careers and awareness-building assignment candidates.

The firms varied in how they valued overseas experience. At one firm it was impossible to receive more than 1000 Hay points (from the Hay Group's method of evaluating jobs based on technical skills, problem-solving, and accountability) without an international experience, so employees were willing to relocate to avoid that career ceiling. At another extreme, one executive candidly described his organization as a having a top management that stressed overseas experience; below top management, however, was a headquarter-centered culture, where overseas experience was viewed as inferior.

GM sets up home-based mentor relationships between each overseas employee and what they call a repatriation facilitator. This provides a support system for the overseas employee but also helps home-based employees value what the overseas employee can contribute upon return. GM also uses home leave where rotated employees present their overseas projects and show how they will contribute to home operations. GM has found that repatriated employees are more successful when brought back into a unit where the manager has had some overseas experience.

Recognizing family needs is key to successful aspatial career deployment. According to numerous studies, family circumstances are the leading cause of overseas assignment failures.[16] Spousal careers and child care are important family considerations and cited in one survey as the top family reasons to refuse an overseas assignment.[17] Cultural awareness training for family members was just beginning at several of the companies we studied and held promise for smoothing family transitions. GM uses relocation facilitators and assigns mentor families to aspatial career families early in their assignments. Job seeking assistance and/or partial remuneration for loss of job income for spouses were provided by most of the companies we studied, but these were considered feasible only if the family was staying overseas at least two years.

It is also important to recognize that all aspatial careerists may not stay aspatial forever. Although some individuals will spend their entire careers outside of their native countries, most eventually return to the parent site. One driver of this decision is family life-cycle change, which pushes an employee to move the family back home. For example, executives wanting their children to go to U.S. high schools so they can get into U.S. colleges was a factor noted by GM.

Implementing the Awareness-Building Assignment Strategy

The missed opportunities at hand-off points described earlier by a Merck executive are often the result of geofunctional disconnects. These are points where functional and geographical boundaries are coterminous, compounding cross-functional cooperation problems. Awareness-building assignments can effectively bridge these gaps when they are used to collect consumer market information. Amoco uses awareness-building assignments to develop product preference sensitivity in employees who design products used or sold overseas. Two examples of the need to develop intimate knowledge of local markets are Proctor & Gamble's faulty start selling all-temperature detergents to Japanese housewives who wash clothes only in cold water and GM's attempt to sell two-door trucks to Chinese with a strong preference for four-door vehicles.[18] Baxter learned this lesson after medical equipment intended for Japan was designed and sized using U.S. patients as the standard. The firm now has a cross-cultural training program, often in the form of awareness-building assignments, for engineers who design products for global markets.

Awareness-building assignments blur the traditional distinction between learning and contributing jobs. Most of the executives we interviewed noted that these assignments should be used judiciously. The awareness-building benefit will be lost if the rotated employee is perceived as having nothing to offer the overseas site. The challenge is to select people early enough in their careers that the assignments serve as screens for future potential but not so early that they have few skills to offer.

Merck gives awareness-building assignments to more mature employees, believing that generating a global mindset is more a selection than a developmental issue, and that mature workers can develop a global awareness if the predisposition is there. Both Merck and Baxter note, however, that language ability limits the candidate pool. At Merck, this has meant that more overseas employees are rotated for awareness-building assignments in the U.S. than the other way around.

Awareness-building assignments must avoid the negative effects of what is termed the "intercultural adjustment cycle."[19] A Dow executive described a cycle on long-term overseas assignments. During the first three months, employees are euphoric about the new country, soak up the culture, and enjoy the superficial differences between the overseas post and the home country. Because most rotated employees are top performers in their home country, however, by the third month they become discouraged by the drop in their productivity and by their lack of linguistic or cultural fluency. During the next three to six months, relocated employees and their families begin to miss their home countries and find fault with the overseas sites. At about nine months, the employees regain the confidence they had before being sent overseas and function as competent members of the overseas society.

Most aspatial careerists will pass through the cycle to regain their sense of competence, but an awareness-building assignment may not last through the entire adjustment cycle. An assignment that ends during the euphoric period will leave the employee with a superficial understanding of the overseas location. An assignment ending during the trough of the cycle may leave the employee soured about overseas experiences and negative about the global scope of the organization. Rather than trying to avoid the adjustment cycle, organizations should use training to prepare employees for it. The virtue of the adjustment cycle is that its low point prompts individuals to reconceptualize their mental frames and begin to develop in-depth understanding of the new cultures.

Since a solution to the problem of motivating aspatials to go to unattractive locations is to develop indigenous talent. Amoco, Baxter, and Merck give awareness-building assignments to local nationals. Rotations to headquarters familiarize them with the company mission and culture, while rotations to various world-wide production locations familiarize them with operations. Local nationals must be given challenging assignments in the U.S. or the rotation may be demotivating.

Implementing the SWAT Team Strategy

Two factors seemed to help optimize the staffing of SWAT teams. First, despite the likelihood that work will be done on a team basis, individual contributor-type employees with a technical orientation are the best candidates. Second, because technical challenges are what motivates them, mechanisms such as outside training are needed to keep SWAT team members on the leading edge.

SWAT teams are best used to export clearly defined technologies or practices. While some training may have to take place at the overseas site to allow those employees to become users, knowledge or innovations conveyed by a SWAT team do not usually have a developmental or cross-cultural component. The SWAT team approach is most easily applied in a manufacturing setting where production processes are less dependent on cultural idiosyncracies. For example, GM uses what they refer to as internal consulting teams to collect information about best manufacturing processes and to disseminate them to other plants world-wide.

In some cases, SWAT assignments are used at sites that are too small to have a sustained need for certain skills, especially in developing countries. In Pakistan, for example, where the human resource/industrial relations function is a part-time job, a traveling unit of negotiators travels from site to site at contract negotiation time, completes the negotiations, secures a contract, and leaves. Both GM and Merck use teams of internal experts and external consultants to do global benefit planning. These teams immerse themselves in local government regulations and set up the benefit plan for each site.

SWAT team assignments can be useful in setting up new operations where start-up skills are needed for a brief period. Amoco uses SWAT teams when it is deciding whether or not to permanently locate in a country. Because location usually depends on finding oil and securing drilling rights, Amoco may be in a country for a relatively long time before withdrawing.[20] Using SWAT teams during start-ups also requires more cultural-awareness training than the conventional SWAT team assignment.

SWAT teams have their very clear limitations, tending to draw on the manufacturing model to conceptualize deployment and information dissemination challenges, and applying that model to nonproduction situations. The pure SWAT team approach will be effective only when interpersonal relationships and cultural understanding are of minimal importance to the transfer of knowledge or innovation. The development of interpersonal relationships and cultural awareness is time consuming and the benefits are often intangible, but in many cases these are necessary prerequisites for information exchange and effective working relationships. If these are needed, the SWAT team strategy will fail.

Implementing the Virtual Solutions Strategy

The virtual solutions model allows cross-national relationships to form below the level of top management. Virtual communications that are not necessarily task-oriented but that foster interpersonal exchanges enable task information to flow more smoothly. In addition, opportunities for innovation can occur at electronic hand-off points if information about production methods, problems, and solutions is shared informally.

In most cases, electronic communication is not yet a perfect substitute for direct contact. Small misunderstandings can become full-blown E-mail wars because of the absence of such communication cues as tone of voice and facial expression.

Small misunderstandings can become full-blown E-mail wars because of the absence of such communication cues as tone of voice and facial expression.

Cultural differences and differing abilities in the language of the exchange increase the likelihood of misunderstanding. Thus, virtual deployment is best used in conjunction with some other form of cultural awareness building. Recognizing this, one Dow executive encourages modest expectations for E-mail initially—to develop in employees "a different mentality, to get them to agree that there are more than one way to skin a cat."[21]

Both Dow and Baxter use employee questionnaires designed by international teams to collect information about operations, practices, and values across the firm to build cross-cultural data bases. These data bases can be retrieved by employees throughout the organization and can supplement other cultural training for virtual solution users. The Baxter survey is customized to fit local conditions and uses local terminology appropriate to each culture. The Dow instrument measures climate as well as management practices.

All of the companies had a Human Resource Information System (HRIS) in place, but varied in the degree to which it could be characterized as a global system. Merck has developed templates that vary with the employee's level in the organization. Employees lower in the organization are less likely to be relocated globally and thus fewer data are required about them for the GHRIS. Approximately one hundred pieces of data are entered into the GHRIS for lower level employees, compared with approximately four hundred entries for higher level employees.

Storing benefit information continues to be a GHRIS challenge. Dow has developed regional benefit models and determined that approximately 80 percent of the data needed for any given employee is standard across nations. The remaining nonstandard 20 percent is country-specific. However, some of this nonstandard information can be collapsed into a smaller number of models, each with its own data template. One example, cited by Dow, is that while there is no world-wide set of educational certifications, most countries' educational systems can be classified into one of a few models. Decisions about which information can be standardized globally and which need to reflect local custom were made after a series of global stakeholder meetings.

One Dow executive commented that to be truly valuable, a GHRIS must be a dynamic tool, evolving over time. He also said that this is easy to say, but something of a headache to implement. One significant gap between the ideal and the reality of a GHRIS is the ability to combine universal access with standardized information. Amoco uses a kiosk system to allow employees to enter information about themselves but has found that not all employees have the ability to do this. Dow has faced the same challenge and has decided to sacrifice universal access for completeness of standardized information.

Global job posting works best for those jobs with relatively well-understood skill requirements. The more subtle or idiosyncratic the skill requirements, the more difficult the job description is to translate globally. As noted earlier, employees below a certain level are not likely to rotate internationally, so clarity about skill requirements also helps screen out certain types of postings for which the company reasonably wants to recruit only locally.

There are technological hurdles to implementing the virtual solutions model, and one should not expect instant results. Even when using established technologies like video broadcasting, learning will take on new forms and periods of adjustment will be required.

What can Steve do?

There is no instant solution to Steve's problem. The people he wants with the skills he needs are not going to convene in Singapore to work together for two years. But, by employing a combination of strategies, Steve can accomplish his goal. He can:

- Select a SWAT team to come in and set up the equipment, a clearly defined task that can be accomplished in a short time with minimal interpersonal contact. Technical people from Tokyo, just a few hours away by plane, could fly in three or four times to set up the equipment and conduct inspections once the facility is running.
- Virtually connect the talented engineer with the Singapore team using E-mail, the phone, and video conferencing, combining this with a short-term awareness-building assignment to foster personal relationships with the technical team and build cross-cultural understanding.
- Ask European, Asian, and South American regional heads to set up regular regional talent ID meetings to nominate potential people for both aspatial career and awareness-building assignments at their next regional conference. The list can be used to select people to conduct initial training sessions and handle early troubleshooting in Singapore as well as a few who may be suited for a longer-term assignment to the new facility.
- Post jobs on an internal bulletin board or intranet web site with full details about the skills required, so that interested and qualified people can also volunteer for Singapore assignments.
- Set up a web page for the site and E-mail technically capable people throughout the organization to stay tuned for brainstorming sessions during the R&D process. Good ideas will win prizes.
- Start scouting for a local national to head up the R&D center, then begin the development with an awareness assignment to headquarters to teach about company culture.

This version of using the four strategies to manage a cross-national workforce differs from the traditional staffing mindset with which Steve initially approached the problem. These strategies allow firms operating on a global basis to make the best use of their widely dispersed internal resources and find innovative solutions to their HR problems.

Endnotes

[1] Adler, N. and Bartholomew, S. 1992. "Managing Globally Competent People," *Academy of Management Executive*, 6(3), 52.

[2] The companies included: Amoco, Baxter, Dow (interviews at both U.S. and Canadian locations), General Motors, IBM, Merck, and Wyeth-Ayerst. Some information about distance learning as an knowledge dissemination/innovation transfer tool was also collected from Ford Motor Co.

[3] See Taylor, S., Beechler, S., and Napier, N. 1996. "Toward an Integrative Model of Strategic International Human Resource Management," *Academy of Management Review*, 21(4), 959–985 for a description of the information flows in a globally integrated organization.

[4] *Fortune*. 1995. "Retailers Go Global." February 20, 102–108.

[5] *Fortune*. 1997. "Is Your Family Wrecking Your Career (And Vice Versa)?" March 3, 70–90.

[6] This is consistent with the findings of a study by Brett, Stroh & Reilly of *Fortune* 500 company managers who were willing to relocate. They found that spouse willingness to move was the most significant factor in an employee's willingness to move. See Brett, J., Stroh, L., and Reilly, A. 1993. "Pulling Up Roots in the 1990s: Who's Willing to Relocate?" *Journal of Organizational Behavior*, 14(1), p. 49–60.

[7] This total workforce number excludes employees of recent acquisitions by Merck.

[8] Use of these assignments as a tool is still evolving and this aspect could easily change.

[9] Schuler, R., Fulkerson, J., and Dowling, P. 1991. "Strategic Performance Measurement and Management in Multinational Corporations," *Human Resource Management*, 30(3), 365–392.

[10] Loftin, R. B. 1996. "Hands Across the Atlantic," *Virtual Reality Special Report*, 3(2), 39–41.

[11] See Kossek, E. E. 1993. "Globalization: What Every Human Resource Professional Should Know—Examples from Amoco Production Company," presented at the National Research Symposium of the Human Resource Planning Society, June.

[12] Their list corresponds closely to that described in Tung, R. 1993. "Managing National and Intranational Diversity," *Human Resource Management*, 32(4), 461–477.

[13] Ayree, S., Chay, Y. W., and Chew, J. 1996. "An Investigation of the Willingness of Managerial Employees to Accept an Expatriate Assignment," *Journal of Organizational Behavior*, 17(3), 267–283.

[14] This strategy may not be for every organization, at least as it is implemented by Schlumberger. These paths require a move every three years. At the time of the move, employees are only permitted to move up to 2000 pounds of personal effects and are expected to take the next plane out once a new assignment has been made. As one employee commented, "they treat their people like cattle." See Kossek, E. E., cited above.

[15] See Oddou, G. and Mendenhall, M. 1991. "Succession Planning for the 21st Century," *Business Horizons*, 34(1), 26–34 for a brief description of this problem.

[16] See Arthur, W. and Bennett, W. 1995. "The International Assignee: The Relative Importance of Factors Perceived to Contribute to Success," *Personnel Psychology*, 48, 99–115, and Tung, R. 1981. "Selection and Training of Personnel for Overseas Assignments," *Columbia Journal of World Business*, Spring, 68–78.

[17] Greenfield, C. 1996. *Work/Family Game*. Boston: Towers Perin.

[18] An alternative way of expressing this is that companies producing overseas to sell overseas need to identify sources of customer value. See Bartness, A. and Cerny, K. 1991. "Building Competitive Advantage through a Global Network of Capabil-

ities," *California Management Review*, 35(2), 78–103, for a full discussion of the identification process.

[19] Grove, C. L. and Torbiorn, I. 1985. "A New Conceptualization of Intercultural Adjustment and the Goals of Training," *International Journal of Intercultural Relations*, 9(16), 205–233.

[20] See Kossek, E. E. cited above.

[21] After saying this, he noted that "more than one way to skin a cat" was precisely the type of phrase that needed to be eliminated from international communications.

About the Authors

Karen Roberts is an associate professor in the School of Labor and Industrial Relations at Michigan State University. She received her PhD from the Department of Urban Studies at M.I.T. She worked as an economist at the Workers' Compensation Research Institute in Cambridge, MA, and as senior economist at DRI/McGraw Hill. Her research interests include the international labor markets, workers' compensation, contingent workers in the labor force, and disability in the workplace. Her work has appeared in journals such as *Journal of Human Resources, Industrial Relations, Journal of Risk and Insurance, Human Resource Management Journal, Journal of Labor Research, Human Resource Management Review*, and *Economic Development Quarterly*. She has recently completed a study of the relationship between the use of contingent workers and international trade and published a book on NAFTA.

Ellen Ernst Kossek is an associate professor of Human Resource Management and Organizational Behavior at Michigan State University's Graduate School of Labor and Industrial Relations. She holds a PhD in organizational behavior from Yale University, an MBA from the University of Michigan, and an AB in psychology (cum laude) from Mount Holyoke. Her articles have appeared in *Journal of Applied Psychology, Personnel Psychology, Journal of Organizational Behavior, Journal of Applied Behavioral Science, Human Relations, Academy of Management Executive, Organizational Dynamics, Human Resource Planning, Human Resource Management, American Psychological Association, Journal of Community, Work, and Family, Center for Creative Leadership* publications and elsewhere. Her published books include *Child Care Challenges for Employers* (LRP Publications, 1991), *The Acceptance of Human Resource Innovation: Lessons for Managers* (Quorum, 1989) and *Managing Diversity: Human Resource Strategies for Transforming the Workplace* (with Sharon Lobel-Blackwell, 1996). Prior to becoming a professor, she worked in human resources for Hitachi, IBM, GTE, and John Deere & Co. in Japan, Geneva, Switzerland, and the U.S.

Cynthia Ozeki is a third-year doctoral student in Labor and Industrial Relations at Michigan State University. After graduating from Brigham Young University in 1986, she lived and worked in Japan for several years before returning to the U.S. to continue her education. Her research interests include international HRM, work and family issues, and comparative labor relations. She has published in *Journal of Applied Psychology*.

[9]

Competitive Frontiers: Women Managing Across Borders

Nancy J. Adler

> It doesn't make any difference if you are blue, green, purple, or a frog, if you have the best product at the best price, they'll buy.
>
> American woman manager based in Hong Kong

About the single most uncontroversial, incontrovertible statement to make about women in international management is that there are very few of them. The evidence is both subjective and objective (17). As an executive in a global firm, would you hire a woman for an international management position? Would you send her abroad as an expatriate manager? Would she succeed? Would hiring her increase or decrease your firm's competitiveness?

Global Competition

Business today increasingly competes on a worldwide basis. Few firms have the luxury of competing primarily within their own domestic market. Whereas some firms use country-specific multidomestic strategies, and thus compete in independent domestic markets, a much greater number have embraced globally integrated strategies structured around worldwide lines of business (11). As global competition continues to intensify, firms are evolving transnational strategies. Such strategies simultaneously require the local responsiveness demanded by multidomestic strategies, the worldwide integration demanded by global strategies, along with an increased emphasis on organizational learning and innovation (14). These business dynamics lead to:

> transnational networks of firms and divisions within firms, including an increasingly complex web of strategic alliances. Transnational firms . . . are less hierarchically structured than firms operating in the previous phases. Power is no longer centered in a single headquarters that is . . . dominated by any one national culture. As a consequence, both structural and cultural dominance are minimized, with cross-cultural interaction no longer following any predefined "passport hierarchy" (10).

These organizational changes are affecting the numbers and roles of women managers.

Women and Transnational Corporations

Given the increasing importance of transnational corporations, it is encouraging that their impact on women in management, to date, has been primarily positive. Transnational corporations include women in ways that domestic, multidomestic, and multinational firms do not. First, the extremely competitive business environment forces transnational firms to select the very best people available. The opportunity cost of prejudice – of rejecting women and limiting selection to men – is much higher than in previous economic environments. As *Fortune* succinctly stated, "The best reason for believing that more women will be in charge before long is that in a ferociously competitive global economy, no company can afford to waste valuable brainpower simply because it's wearing a skirt" (18:56). This competitive advantage is heightened by a growing worldwide education differential favoring women.

Second, whereas domestic and multidomestic companies hire primarily local nationals and, therefore, must closely adhere to local norms on hiring – or not hiring – women managers, transnational corporations are not similarly limited. Because the corporate culture of transnational firms is not coincident with the local culture of any particular country, transnationals have greater flexibility in defining selection and promotion criteria that best fit the firm's needs rather than those that most closely mimic the historical patterns of a particular country. Said simply, transnationals can and do hire local women managers even in countries in which the local companies rarely do so.

U.S.-based transnational corporations, for example, have often hired local women managers when local firms would not. This dynamic has been particularly pronounced in Japan, where foreign corporations have had difficulty attracting top-ranked male applicants (25;35). American firms have led the way in hiring well-qualified Japanese women, while Japanese firms are still extremely reluctant to hire them (36). Interestingly, while still hiring fewer women than most American firms, Japanese multinationals operating in the United States hire more women managers in their American affiliates than they do in their home country operations (33).

By hiring women, transnationals act as role models for firms in many countries that have not seriously considered promoting significant numbers of women into managerial positions. The greater the number of expatriates involved in foreign affiliates, the less likely they are to follow local human resource practices – including being less likely to restrict the number of women managers (33). The firm's transnational character allows it organizational freedoms and imposes competitive demands not present in domestic or multidomestic environments.

Third, transnational corporations have begun to send women abroad as expatriate managers (4). Because transnationals use expatriates and local managers, they can benefit from the greater flexibility that many cultures afford foreign women. As will be described, most countries do not hold foreign women to the same professionally limiting roles that restrict local women (6;23). The outstanding success of these women expatriate managers in all geographical areas – Africa, the Americas, Asia, Europe, and the Middle East – is encouraging firms both to continue sending women abroad (6;30) and to begin to promote more local women into management (23).

Fourth, whereas domestic, multidomestic, and multinational firms have been characterized by structural hierarchies, transnationals are increasingly characterized by networks of equals. Recent research suggests that women work particularly well in such networks:

> women . . . are countering the values of the hierarchy with those of the web. . . . when describing their roles in their organizations, women usually refer . . . to themselves as being in the middle of things. . . . Inseparable from their sense of themselves as being in the middle . . . [is] women's notion of being connected to those around them (22:52,45–46).

Not surprisingly, transnational firms see women managers as bringing needed collaborative and participative skills to the workplace (31).

Fifth, leading management scholars have identified innovation as a key factor in global competitiveness (14;21;32). An inherent source of innovation is well-managed diversity, including gender diversity (8). Women bring diversity to transnational corporations that have heretofore been primarily male dominated.

Transnational corporations thus include more women than their predecessors could (or would) and benefit organizationally from their professional contributions in new ways. They benefit both from women's increased representation at all levels of the organization as well as from their unique ways of contributing to the organization that complement those of men.

Fundamental Assumptions: Different Approaches

Given the current scarcity of women in the managerial ranks, transnational firms can use two approaches to unleash the potential of women managers: they can increase the number of women managers and executives, and they can encourage their unique contribution. Unfortunately, many of their predecessors – domestic, multidomestic, and multinational firms – adopted neither approach or limited themselves by focusing on only one of the two approaches.

As shown in Table 2.1, firms have traditionally made one of two fundamentally different assumptions about the ideal role of women in management. Although generally implicit, the first reflects an equity approach based on assumed similarity, while the second defines a complementary contribution approach based on assumed difference. The first focuses on increasing the representation of women managers; the second, on increasing their utilization at all levels of the organization.

The first, the equity approach, based on assumed similarity, has been used most pervasively in the United States. In this approach, firms assume that women are identical, as professionals, to men, and therefore equally capable of contributing in ways similar to those of men. From this equity perspective, the primary question is one of entry into and representation within management. Is the firm hiring and

Table 2.1 Two approaches to women in management

Assumptions	*Equity approach*	*Complementary contribution approach*
Fundamental assumptions	Similarity	Difference
Women's and men's contributions	Identical	Complementary
Fairness based on	Equity	Valuing difference
Strategic goal	Equal access	Recognizing and valuing difference
Assessment	Quantitative	Qualitative
Measured by	Statistical proportion of women at each hierarchial level	Assessing women's contribution to organization's goals
Process	Counting women	Assessing women's contribution
Measurement of effectiveness		
Women's contribution	Identical to men's	Complementary to men's
Norms	Identical for men and women	Unique to men and women
Based on	Historical "male" norms	Women's own contribution
Referent	Men	Women
Acculturation process	Assimilation	Synergy
Expected behavior	Standardized	Differentiated
Based on	Male norms	Female norms
Essence	"Dress for success" business suit	Elegant, feminine attire
Example	United States: "The melting pot"	France: "Vive la différence!"

Source: Nancy J. Adler (1986-7)"Women in Management Worldwide," *International Studies of Management and Organization* 16(3-4):3-32.

promoting sufficient numbers of women managers? Primary change strategies include affirmative action programs, equal rights legislation, and structural changes designed to avoid tokenism and to train women in managerial skills traditionally neglected during their formal education and informal socialization.

Given the equity approach's emphasis on equal entry into and equal representation within the male-dominated world of management, the equity approach's implicit goal for women managers is assimilation. Firms expected women to think, dress, and act like the men who had traditionally held the aspired-to management positions. Understandably, firms measured effectiveness against male norms: could she do what he had been doing as well as he had been doing it? Or, according to *Fortune* (31:58), "If you can't join 'em, beat 'em . . . the way to overcome [discrimination] is to . . . start outdoing men at their own game." The potential for women to make unique, but equally valuable, contributions to organizations remained outside the logic of the equity approach and therefore largely unrealized.

In contrast, the second approach, the complementary contribution approach, is based on the assumption of difference, not similarity. Originally used to describe Swedish managers (34), it has been pervasive throughout Europe and Japan and is evident in most other areas of the world. In the complementary contribution approach, firms assume women and men differ and therefore are capable of making different, but equally valuable, contributions to the organization (13;16;19;20;24; 26;27;28). Unlike in the equity approach, the goal is not assumed to be equal statistical representation but, rather, equivalent recognition of and benefit from women's and men's differing patterns and styles of contribution at all levels of the organization.

From this second perspective, change strategies focus first on identifying the unique contributions of women and men managers; second, on creating enabling conditions to encourage and reward both types of contribution; and third, on creating synergy – on combining women's and men's contributions to form more innovative and powerful organizational solutions to business challenges. Under this second set of assumptions, firms expect women managers to think, dress, and act like women. Women managers' thinking and behavior, though similar in many ways to that of their male colleagues, is seen to differ in important respects.

Progress, as measured by the equity approach, is quantitative – a statistical accounting of the proportion of women managers in the organization by rank, salary, and status. As measured by the complementary contribution approach, progress is qualitative – an assessment of the organization's track record in encouraging and rewarding women and men for making unique contributions and for building organizationally effective combinations of those contributions; that is, for increasing innovation and organizational learning.

Interestingly, each approach has tended to be labeled as heresy when viewed through the eyes of the other. From the perspective of the equity approach, viewing women (or any other distinct group) as different was seen as tantamount to judging them as inferior (16). Recognizing differences among women and men managers was implicitly equated with prejudice (8). From this point of view, only one best way to manage exists, and equity demands that women be given equal access to that one way. By contrast, the complementary contribution approach posits that there are many equally valid, yet different, ways to manage. The best approach, based on recognizing, valuing, and combining differences, is synergistic. From this second perspective, not to see a woman manager's uniqueness is to negate her identity and, consequently, to negate the potential for her unique contribution to the organization.

To predict what women's roles in management will be in the late 1990s and the twenty-first century, we must understand the underlying assumptions that firms make in each country about the role of women in management (15). To what extent is difference viewed as heresy as opposed to a potential resource? To what extent is uniqueness seen as a constraint rather than as a valuable asset? Unlike their predecessors, transnational firms view woman managers' increased representation and potentially unique contribution as complementary sources of competitive advantage rather than as either–or solutions, or, even more limiting, as societal constraints.

Unexpected Success: Women Managing Across Borders

Cross-border business is fundamental to transnational firms. Unlike their predecessors, such firms define managerial roles transnationally, with expatriate assignments forming a central component. Given the historical scarcity of local women managers in most countries, firms have questioned if women can function successfully in cross-border managerial assignments. They have believed that the relative absence of local women managers formed a basis for accurately predicting the potential for success, or lack thereof, of expatriate women.

Given the importance of these questions to future business success, a multipart study was conducted on the role of women as expatriate managers. The research revealed the story of a noun, *woman*, that appears to have gotten mixed up with an adjective, *foreign*, when predicting expatriate managers' success. It revealed a set of assumptions that managers and executives make about how foreigners would treat expatriate women, based on their beliefs about how foreign firms treat their own local women. The problem with the story is that the assumptions proved to be false. Moreover, because the assumptions fail to accurately reflect reality, they are inadvertently causing executives to make decisions that are neither effective nor equitable.

The first part of the study sought to determine the proportion of women that companies select for expatriate positions. It surveyed 686 major North American multinational firms. The firms reported sending over thirteen thousand (13,338) expatriate managers abroad, of whom 402, or 3 percent, were women. Thus, North American firms send 32 times as many male as female expatriate managers abroad (1;4). In comparison with this 3 percent in international management, women held 37 percent of domestic U.S. management positions, twelve times as many as they held abroad (38).

Although the 3 percent represents significantly fewer women working as expatriate managers than the proportion holding domestic management positions, this should not be viewed strictly as a poor showing but rather as the beginning of a new trend. The vast majority of women who have ever held expatriate management positions were sent so recently that they are currently still working abroad.

Given transnationals' needs for the best-qualified managers – whether women or men – the second, third, and fourth parts of the study sought to explain why so few women hold international management positions. Each part addressed one of the three most commonly held *myths* about women in international management:

Myth 1: Women do not want to be international managers.
Myth 2: Companies refuse to send women abroad.
Myth 3: Foreigners' prejudice against women renders them ineffective, even when they are interested in international assignments and are successful in being sent.

These beliefs were labeled "*myths*" because, although widely held by both women and men, their accuracy had never been tested.

Myth 1: Women do not want to be international managers

Is the problem that women are less interested than men in pursuing international careers? The study tested this myth by surveying more than a thousand graduating MBAs from seven top management schools in the United States, Canada, and Europe (3;5). The results revealed an overwhelming case of no significant difference: female and male MBAs display equal interest, or lack of interest, in pursuing international careers. More than four out of five MBAs – both women and men – want an international assignment at some time during their careers. Both female and male MBAs, however, agree that firms offer fewer opportunities to women than to men, and significantly fewer opportunities to women pursuing international careers than to those pursuing domestic careers.

Although there may have been a difference in the past, women and men today are equally interested in international management, including expatriate assignments. The first myth – that women do not want to be international managers – is, in fact, truly a myth.

Myth 2: Companies refuse to send women abroad

If the problem is not women's lack of interest, is it that companies refuse to select women for international assignments? To test if the myth of corporate resistance was true, human resource vice presidents and managers from 60 of the largest North American multinationals were surveyed (2). Over half of the companies reported that they hesitate to send women abroad. Almost four times as many reported being reluctant to select women for international assignments than for domestic management positions. When asked why they hesitate, almost three-quarters reported believing that foreigners were so prejudiced against women that the women managers could not succeed even if sent. Similarly, 70 percent believed that dual-career issues were insurmountable. In addition, some human resource executives expressed concern about the women's physical safety, the hazards involved in traveling in underdeveloped countries, and, especially in the case of single women, the isolation and loneliness.

Many of the women who succeeded in being sent abroad as expatriate managers report having confronted some form of corporate resistance before being sent abroad. For example:

> *Malaysia*: "Management assumed that women didn't have the physical stamina to survive in the tropics. They claimed I couldn't hack it [in Malaysia]."

> *Thailand*: "My company didn't want to send a woman to that 'horrible part of the world.' They think Bangkok is an excellent place to send single men, but not a woman. They said they would have trouble getting a work permit for me, which wasn't true."

> *Japan and Korea*: "Everyone was more or less curious if it would work. My American boss tried to advise me, 'Don't be upset if it's difficult in Japan and Korea.' The American male manager in Tokyo was also hesitant. Finally the Chinese boss in Hong Kong said, 'We have to try!' Then they sent me."

A few women experienced severe resistance from their companies to sending any women managers abroad. Their firms seemed to offer them an expatriate position only after all potential male candidates had turned it down. For example:

> *Thailand*: "Every advance in responsibility is because the Americans had no choice. I've never been chosen over someone else."

> *Japan*: "They never would have considered me. But then the financial manager in Tokyo had a heart attack, and they had to send someone. So they sent me, on a month's notice, as a temporary until they could find a man to fill the permanent position. It worked out, and I stayed."

Although most of the women are sent in the same capacity as their male expatriate colleagues, some companies demonstrate their hesitation by offering temporary or travel assignments rather than regular expatriate positions. For instance:

> *Hong Kong*: "After offering me the job, they hesitated: 'Could a woman work with the Chinese?' So my job was defined as temporary, a one-year position to train a Chinese man to replace me. I succeeded and became permanent."

These sentiments concur with those of 100 top-line managers in *Fortune 500* firms, the majority of whom believe that women face overwhelming resistance when seeking managerial positions in international divisions of U.S. firms (37). Similarly, 80 percent of U.S. firms report believing that women would face disadvantages if sent abroad (30). Thus, the second myth is in fact true: firms are hesitant, if not outright resistant, to sending women managers abroad.

Myth 3: Foreigners' "prejudice" against women expatriate managers

Is it true that foreigners are so prejudiced against women that women could not succeed as international managers? Would sending a woman manager abroad be neither fair to the woman nor effective for the company? Is the treatment of local women the best predictor of expatriate women's potential to succeed? The fundamental question was, and remains, the following: is the historical discrimination against local women worldwide a valid basis for predicting expatriate women's success as international managers?

To investigate the myth that foreigners' prejudice against women renders them ineffective as international managers, a survey was taken of over a hundred women managers from major North American firms who were on expatriate assignments around the world. Fifty-two were interviewed while in Asia or after having returned from Asia to North America (6;23). Since most of the women held regional responsibility, their experience represents multiple countries rather than just their country of foreign residence.

Who are the women expatriate managers? The women were very well educated and internationally experienced. Almost all held graduate degrees, the MBA being the most common. Over three-quarters had had extensive international interests and experience prior to their present company sending them abroad. On average, the women spoke two or three languages, with some speaking as many as six fluently. In addition, they had excellent social skills. Nearly two-thirds were single and only three (6 percent) had children.

Firms using transnational strategies sent more women than did those using other strategies, with financial institutions leading all other industries. On average, their international assignments lasted 2.5 years, with a range from six months to six years. The women supervised from zero to 25 subordinates, with the average falling just below five. Their titles and levels within their firms varied. Some held very junior positions – for example, assistant account manager – others held senior positions, including one regional vice president. In no firm did a woman expatriate hold her company's number one position in the region or in any country.

The women were considerably younger than the typical male expatriate. Their ages ranged from 23 to 41 years, with the average age being just under 30. This reflects the relatively high proportion of women sent by financial institutions – an industry that sends fairly junior managers on international assignments – and the relatively low proportion sent by manufacturing firms, which select fairly senior managers for expatriate positions (such as a country or regional director).

The decision to go For most firms, the women expatriates were "firsts." Only 10 percent followed another woman into her international position. Of the 90 percent who were "firsts," almost one-quarter represented the first woman manager the firm had ever sent abroad. Others were the first women sent to the region, the first sent to the particular country, or the first to fill the specific expatriate position. Clearly, neither the women nor the companies had the luxury of role models or of following previously established patterns. Except for several major financial institutions, both the women and the companies found themselves experimenting, in the hope of success.

Most women described themselves as needing to encourage their companies to consider the possibility of assigning international positions to women in general and to themselves in particular. In more than four out of five cases, the woman initially suggested the idea of an international assignment to her boss and company. For only six women did the company first suggest the assignment.

Since most firms had never considered sending a woman manager abroad, the women used a number of strategies to introduce the idea and to position their careers internationally. Many explored the possibility of an international assignment during their original job interview and eliminated companies from consideration that were totally against the idea. In other cases, the woman informally introduced the idea to her boss and continued to mention it at appropriate moments until the company ultimately decided to offer her an expatriate position. A few women formally applied for a number of international assignments prior to actually being selected and sent.

Many women attempted to be in the right place at the right time. For example, one woman who predicted that Hong Kong would be her firm's next major business center arranged to assume responsibility for the Hong Kong desk in New York, leaving the rest of Asia to a male colleague. The strategy paid off; within a year, the company elevated their Hong Kong operations to a regional center and sent her to Asia as their first woman expatriate manager.

Most women claimed that their companies had failed to recognize the possibility of selecting women for international assignments, rather than having thoroughly considered the idea and then having rejected it. For the majority of the women, the obstacle appeared to be the companies' naiveté, not malice. For many women, the most difficult hurdle in their international careers involved getting sent abroad in the first place, not – as most had anticipated – gaining the respect of foreigners and succeeding once sent.

Did it work? The impact of being a woman Almost all of the women expatriate managers (97 percent) reported that their international assignments were successful. This success rate is considerably higher than that reported for North American male expatriates. Although the women's assessments are subjective, objective indicators support the contention that most of the assignments, in fact, had succeeded. For example, the majority of the firms (after experimenting with their first woman expatriate manager) decided to send more women abroad. In addition, most companies promoted the women on the basis of their foreign performance or offered them other international assignments following completion of the first one.

Advantages Given the third myth, women would be expected to experience a series of difficulties caused by their being female and, perhaps, to create a corresponding set of solutions designed to overcome each difficulty. This was not the case. Almost half of the women expatriates (42 percent) reported that being female served as more of an advantage than a disadvantage; 16 percent found it to be both positive and negative; 22 percent saw it as being either irrelevant or neutral; and only 20 percent found it to be primarily negative.

The women reported numerous professional advantages to being female. Most frequently, they described the advantage of being highly visible. Foreign clients were curious about them, wanted to meet them, and remembered them after the first encounter. The women therefore found it easier than their male colleagues to gain access to foreign clients' time and attention. The women gave examples of this high visibility, accessibility, and memorability:

> *Japan*: "It's the visibility as an expat, and even more as a woman. I stick in their minds. I know I've gotten more business than my two male colleagues. . . . [My clients] are extra interested in me."

> *Thailand*: "Being a woman is never a detriment. They remembered me better. Fantastic for a marketing position. It's better working with Asians than with the Dutch, British, or Americans."

India and Pakistan: "In India and Pakistan, being a woman helps in marketing and client contact. I got in to see customers because they had never seen a female banker before. . . . Having a female banker adds value to the client."

Again contrary to the third myth, the women managers discovered a number of advantages based on their interpersonal skills, including that the local men could talk more easily about a wider range of topics with them than with their male counterparts. For example:

Japan: "Women are better at putting people at ease. It's easier for a woman to convince a man. . . . The traditional woman's role . . . inspires confidence and trust, less suspicion, not threatening."

Indonesia: "I often take advantage of being a woman. I'm more supportive than my male colleagues. . . . [Clients] relax and talk more. And 50 percent of my effectiveness is based on volunteered information."

Korea: "Women are better at treating men sensitively, and they just like you. One of my Korean clients told me, 'I really enjoyed . . . working with you.' "

Many women also described the high social status accorded local women and found that such status was not denied them as foreign women. The women often received special treatment that their male counterparts did not receive. Clearly, it was always salient that they were women, but being a woman was not antithetical to succeeding as a manager.

Hong Kong: "Single female expats travel easier and are treated better. Never hassled. No safety issues. Local offices take better care of you. They meet you, take you through customs. . . . It's the combination of treating you like a lady and a professional."

Japan: "It's an advantage that attracts attention. They are interested in meeting a *gaijin*, a foreign woman. Women attract more clients. On calls to clients, they elevate me, give me more rank. If anything, the problem, for men and women, is youth, not gender."

In addition, most of the women described benefiting from a "halo effect." The majority of the women's foreign colleagues and clients had never met or previously worked with a woman expatriate manager. Similarly, the local community was highly aware of how unusual it was for North American multinationals to send women managers abroad. Hence, the local managers assumed that the women would not have been sent unless they were "the best," and therefore expected them to be "very, very good."

Indonesia: "It's easier being a woman here than in any place in the world, including New York City. . . . I never get the comments I got in New York, like 'What is a nice woman like you doing in this job?' "

Japan: "They assumed I must be good if I was sent. They became friends."

Some women found being female to have no impact whatsoever on their professional lives. Many of these women worked primarily with the overseas Chinese:

> *Hong Kong*: "There are many expat and foreign women in top positions here. If you are good at what you do, they accept you. One Chinese woman told me, 'Americans are always watching you. One mistake and you are done. Chinese take a while to accept you and then stop testing you.'"

> *Asia*: "There's no difference. They respect professionalism . . . including in Japan. There is no problem in Asia."

Disadvantages The women also experienced a number of disadvantages in being female expatriate managers. Interestingly enough, the majority of the disadvantages involved the women's relationship with their home companies, not with their foreign colleagues and clients. As noted earlier, a major problem involved the women's difficulty in obtaining an international position in the first place.

Another problem involved home companies initially limiting the duration of the women's assignments to six months or a year, rather than offering the more standard two to three years. While temporary assignments may appear to offer companies a logically cautious strategy, in reality they create an unfortunate self-fulfilling prophecy. When the home company is not convinced that a woman can succeed (and therefore offers her a temporary rather than a permanent position), it communicates the company's lack of confidence to foreign colleagues and clients as a lack of commitment. The foreigners then mirror the home company's behavior by also failing to take the woman manager seriously. Assignments become very difficult or can fail altogether when companies demonstrate a lack of initial confidence and commitment. As one expatriate woman working in Indonesia stated, "It is very important to clients that I am permanent. It increases trust, and that's critical."

A subsequent problem involved the home company limiting the woman's professional opportunities and job scope once she was abroad. More than half of the women expatriates experienced difficulties in persuading their home companies to give them latitude equivalent to that given to their male counterparts, especially initially. For example, some companies, out of supposed concern for the woman's safety, limited her travel (and thus the regional scope of her responsibility), thereby excluding very remote, rural, and underdeveloped areas. Other companies, as mentioned previously, initially limited the duration of the woman's assignment to six months or a year, rather than the more standard two to three years. For example:

> *Japan*: "My problem is overwhelmingly with Americans. They identify it as a male market . . . geisha girls. . . ."

> *Thailand (petroleum company)*: "The Americans wouldn't let me on the drilling rigs, because they said there were no accommodations for a woman. Everyone blames it on something else. They gave me different work. They had me on the sidelines, not planning and communicating with drilling people. It's the expat Americans, not the Thais, who'll go to someone else before they come to me."

A few companies limited the women to working only internally with company employees, rather than externally with clients. These companies often implicitly assumed that their own employees were somehow less prejudiced than were outsiders. In reality, the women often found the opposite to be true. They faced more problems from home country nationals within their own organizations than externally from local clients and colleagues. As one woman described it:

> *Hong Kong*: "It was somewhat difficult internally. They feel threatened, hesitant to do what I say, resentful. They assume I don't have the credibility a man would have. Perhaps it's harder internally than externally, because client relationships are one-on-one and internally it's more of a group; or perhaps it's harder because they have to live with it longer internally; or perhaps it's because they fear that I'm setting a precedent or because they fear criticism from their peers."

Managing foreign clients' and colleagues' initial expectations was one area that proved difficult for many women. Some found initial meetings to be "tricky," especially when a male colleague from their own company was present. Since most local managers had never previously met a North American expatriate woman who held a managerial position, there was considerable ambiguity as to who she was, her status, her level of expertise, authority, and responsibility, and therefore the appropriate form of address and demeanor toward her.

> *People's Republic of China*: "I speak Chinese, which is a plus. But they'd talk to the men, not to me. They'd assume that I, as a woman, had no authority. The Chinese want to deal with top, top, top level people, and there is always a man at a higher level."

> *Asia*: "It took extra time to establish credibility with the Japanese and Chinese. One Japanese manager said to me, 'When I first met you, I thought you would not be any good because you were a woman.'"

Since most of the North American women whom local managers had ever met previously were expatriates' wives or secretaries, they naturally assumed that the new woman was not a manager. Hence, they often directed initial conversations to male colleagues, not to the newly arrived woman manager. Senior male colleagues, particularly those from the head office, became very important in redirecting the focus of early discussions back toward the woman. When this was done, old patterns were quickly broken and smooth ongoing work relationships were established. When the pattern was ignored or poorly managed, the challenges to credibility, authority, and responsibility became chronic and undermined the women's effectiveness.

As mentioned earlier, many women described the most difficult aspect of the international assignment as getting sent abroad in the first place. Overcoming resistance from the North American home company frequently proved more challenging than gaining local clients' and colleagues' respect and acceptance. In most cases, assumptions about foreigners' prejudice against women expatriate managers appear to have been exaggerated. The anticipated prejudice and the reality did not match. It appears that foreigners are not as prejudiced as many North American managers had assumed.

The *Gaijin* Syndrome

One pattern is particularly clear: first and foremost, foreigners are seen as foreigners. Like their male colleagues, female expatriates are seen as foreigners, not as local people. A woman who is a foreigner (a *gaijin)* is not expected to act like the local women. Therefore, the societal and cultural rules governing the behavior of local women that limit their access to managerial positions and responsibility do not apply to foreign women. Although women are considered the "culture bearers" in all societies, foreign women are not expected to assume the cultural roles that societies have traditionally reserved for their own women. As one woman expatriate in Japan stated, "The Japanese are very smart: they can tell that I am not Japanese, and they do not expect me to act as a Japanese woman. They will allow and condone behavior in foreign women that would be absolutely unacceptable in their own women." Similarly a Tokyo-based personnel vice president for a major international bank explained that "Being a foreigner is so weird to the Japanese that the marginal impact of being a woman is nothing. If I were a Japanese woman, I couldn't be doing what I'm doing here. But they know perfectly well that I'm not" (29:1,27).

Many of the women expatriates related similar examples of their unique status as "foreign women" rather than as "women" per se:

> *Japan and Korea*: "Japan and Korea are the hardest, but they know that I'm an American woman, and they don't expect me to be like a Japanese or Korean woman. It's possible to be effective even in Japan and Korea if you send a senior woman with at least three or four years of experience, especially if she's fluent in Japanese."

> *Asia*: "It's the novelty, especially in Japan, Korea, and Pakistan. All of the general managers met with me. . . . It was much easier for me, especially in Osaka. They were charming. They didn't want me to feel bad. They thought I would come back if they gave me business. You see, they could separate me from the local women."

> *Pakistan*: "Will I have problems? No! There is a double standard between expats and local women. The Pakistanis test you, but you enter as a respected person."

> *Japan*: "I don't think the Japanese could work for a Japanese woman . . . but they just block it out for foreigners."

> *Hong Kong*: "Hong Kong is very cosmopolitan. I'm seen as an expat, not as an Asian, even though I am an Asian American."

Conclusion

It seems that we have confused the adjective *foreign* with the noun *woman* in predicting foreigners' reactions to expatriate women. We expected the most salient characteristic of a woman expatriate manager to be that she is a *woman* and predicted her success based on the success of the local women in each country. In fact, the most salient characteristic is that expatriates are *foreign*, and the best predictor of their success is the success of other foreigners (in this case, other North Americans) in the particular country. *Local managers see women expatriates as foreigners who happen to be women, not as women who happen to be foreigners*. The difference is crucial. Given the uncertainty involved in sending women managers to all areas of the world, our assumptions about the greater salience of gender (female/male) over nationality (foreign/local) have caused us to make false predictions concerning women's potential to succeed as international executives and managers.

The third myth – that foreigners' prejudice precludes women's effectiveness as international managers – is, in fact, definitely a myth. Of the three myths, only the second myth proved to be true. The first myth proved false: women *are* interested in working internationally. The third myth proved false: women *do* succeed internationally, once sent. However, the second myth proved to be true: companies are hesitant, if not completely unwilling, to send women managers abroad. Given that the problem is caused primarily by the home companies' assumptions and decisions, the solutions are also largely within their control.

Recommendations

In considering women managers for international assignments, both the companies and the women need to approach the decision and the assignment in a number of new ways.

Recommendations to companies

Do not assume that it will not work. Do not assume that foreigners will treat expatriate women managers the same way they treat their own local women. Our assumptions about the salience of gender over nationality have led to totally inaccurate predictions. Therefore, do not confuse adjectives with nouns; do not use the success or failure of local women to predict that of foreign women managers.

Do not confuse the role of a spouse with that of a manager. Although the single most common reason for male expatriates' failure and early return from international assignments is the dissatisfaction of their wives, this does not mean that women cannot cope in a foreign environment. The role of the spouse (whether male or female) is much more ambiguous and, consequently, the cross-cultural adjustment is much more demanding for the spouse than for the employee (8). Wives have had trouble adjusting, but their situation is not analogous to that of women managers and therefore is not predictive.

Do not assume that a woman will not want to go abroad. Ask her. Although both single and married women need to balance private and professional life considerations, many are very interested in taking international assignments. Moreover, the proportion of women interested in working abroad is identical to that of men and can be predicted to increase over the coming decade.

Offer flexible benefits packages. Given that most expatriate benefits packages have been designed to meet the needs of traditional families (employed husband, nonemployed wife, and children), companies should be prepared to modify their benefits packages to meet the needs of managers who are single (women and men) and dual-career couples. Such modifications might include increased lead time in announcing assignments, executive search services for the partner in dual-career couples, and payment for "staying connected" (including telephone and airfare expenses) for couples who choose some form of commuting rather than both simultaneously relocating abroad.

Give women every opportunity to succeed. Accord her full status at the outset – not that of a temporary or experimental expatriate – with the appropriate title to communicate the home office's commitment to her. Do not be surprised if local colleagues and clients initially direct their comments to male managers rather than to the new woman expatriate during their first meeting with her. However, do not accept such behavior; redirect discussion, where appropriate, to the woman. Such behavior from foreign colleagues should not be interpreted as prejudice but rather as a reaction to a new, ambiguous, and unexpected situation.

Recommendations to women expatriate managers

The women expatriates had a number of suggestions for the women managers who will follow in their footsteps.

Assume naiveté, not malice. Realize that sending women abroad is new, perceived as risky, and still fairly poorly understood. In most cases, companies and foreign managers are operating on the basis of untested assumptions, many of which are faulty, not on the basis of prejudice. The most successful approach is to be gently persistent in "educating" the company to be open to the possibility of sending a woman abroad and granting her the status and support usually accorded to male peers in similar situations.

Be outstanding. Given that expatriating women is perceived as risky, no woman will be sent abroad if she is not seen as technically and professionally well qualified. In addition, beyond being extremely well qualified, arrange to be in the right place at the right time.

Address private life issues directly. For single women the issue of loneliness and for married women the issue of managing a dual-career relationship must be addressed. Contact with other expatriate women has proven helpful in both situations. For dual-career couples, most women consider it critical to have discussed the possibility of an international assignment with their husbands long before it became a reality and to have developed options that would work for them as a couple. For most couples, this means creating alternatives that have never, or rarely, been tried in the particular company.

Realize that expatriate status inadvertently helps to solve some of the role overload problems experienced by women who are managers, wives, and mothers.

Since most expatriate managers can afford household help while on an expatriate assignment, but not in their home countries, they are able to reduce substantially the demands on their time. As one American expatriate manager in Hong Kong stated, "It would be impossible for me to do what I'm doing here if I was still in the United States. There just wouldn't be enough time!"

Global competition is, and will continue to be, intense in the 1990s. Transnational corporations, faced with the most intense global competition, may well continue to lead in hiring and promoting women into significant international management positions. Can they risk not choosing the best person just because her gender does not fit the traditional managerial profile? Needs for competitive advantage, not an all-consuming social conscience, may answer the question, if not in fact define it. Successful companies will select both women and men to manage their international operations. The option of limiting international management to one gender has become an archaic "luxury" that no company can afford. The only remaining question is how quickly and effectively each company will increase the number and use of women in their worldwide managerial workforce.

Notes

I would like to thank the Social Sciences and Humanities Research Council of Canada for its generous support of the research reported here. I owe special thanks to Dr. Homa Mahmoudi for her creativity and professional insight in helping to conduct the Asian interviews. This article is based on Dr. Adler's recent work on transnationals (Adler, 1993; Adler and Bartholomew, 1992) and her research on women expatriate managers (Adler, 1979; 1984*a*; 1984*b*; 1984*c*; 1986; 1987; Jelinek and Adler, 1988). The equity and complementary contribution approaches were originally presented in Adler (1986–87) and Adler and Izraeli's first book, *Women in Management Worldwide* (1988).

References

All quotes by the women expatriates are taken from Dr. Adler's research interviews. While the names of the women cannot be released, each of them was working in the country listed at the time of the interview.

(1) Adler, Nancy J. (1979) "Women as Androgynous Managers: A Conceptualization of the Potential for American Women in International Management," *International Journal of Intercultural Relations* 3(4):407–435.

(2) Adler, Nancy J. (1984*a*) "Expecting International Success: Female Managers Overseas," *Columbia Journal of World Business* 19(3):79–85

(3) Adler, Nancy J. (1984*b*) "Women Do Not Want International Careers: And Other Myths About International Management," *Organizational Dynamics* 13(2):66–79.

(4) Adler, Nancy J. (1984*c*) "Women in International Management: Where Are They?" *California Management Review* 26(4):78–89.

(5) Adler, Nancy J. (1986) "Do MBAs Want International Careers?" *International Journal of Intercultural Relations* 10(3):277–300.

(6) Adler, Nancy J. (1987) "Pacific Basin Managers: A Gaijin, Not a Woman," *Human Resource Management* 26(2):169–191.

(7) Adler, Nancy J. (1986–87) "Women in Management Worldwide," *International Studies of Management and Organization* 16(3–4):3–32.
(8) Adler, Nancy J. (1991) *International Dimensions of Organizational Behavior*, 2nd edn. Boston: PWS-KENT Publishing.
(9) Adler, Nancy J. (1993) "Competitive Frontiers: Women Managers in the Triad," *International Studies of Management and Organization*, in press.
(10) Adler, Nancy J., and Bartholomew, Susan (1992) "Managing Globally Competent People," *Academy of Management Executive* 6(3):52–65.
(11) Adler, Nancy J., and Ghadar, Fariborz (1990) "Strategic Human Resource Management: A Global Perspective," in Rudiger Pieper (ed.), *Human Resource Management in International Comparison*, pp. 235–260. Berlin: de Gruyter.
(12) Adler, Nancy J., and Izraeli, Dafna N. (eds.) (1988) *Women in Management Worldwide*. Armonk, N.Y.: M. E. Sharpe.
(13) Aptheker, B. (1989) *Tapestries of Life: Women's Work, Women's Consciousness, and the Meaning of Daily Experience*. Amherst: University of Massachusetts Press.
(14) Bartlett, Christopher A., and Ghoshal, Sumantra (1989) *Managing across Borders: The Transnational Solution*. Boston: Harvard Business School Press.
(15) Berthoin Antal, Ariane, and Izraeli, Dafna N. (1993) "A Global Comparison of Women in Management: Women Managers in Their Homelands and as Expatriates," in Ellen Fagenson (ed.), *Women in Management: Trends, Issues and Challenges in Managerial Diversity, Women and Work*, Vol. 4. Newbury Park, Calif.: Sage.
(16) Calvert, Linda McGee, and Ramsey, V. Jean (1992) "Bringing Women's Voice to Research on Women in Management: A Feminist Perspective," *Journal of Management Inquiry* 1(1):79–88.
(17) Caulkin, S. (1977) "Women in Management," *Management Today* (September):58–63.
(18) Fisher, Anne B. (1992) "When Will Women Get to the Top?" *Fortune*, September 21, pp. 44–56.
(19) Fossan, J. (1989) "Women in Organization," *Implementing Strategies and Achieving Change*. Seminar Research Report. Berlin: Aspen Institute.
(20) Gilligan, Carol (1982) *In a Different Voice*. Cambridge, Mass.: Harvard University Press.
(21) Hammond, Valerie, and Holton, Viki (1994) "The Scenario for Women Managers in Britain in the 1990s," in Nancy J. Adler and Dafna N. Izraeli (eds.), *Competitive Frontiers: Women Managers in a Global Economy*, pp. 224–242. Cambridge (USA)/ Oxford (England): Blackwell Publishers.
(22) Helgesen, S. (1990) *The Female Advantage: Women's Ways of Leadership*. New York: Doubleday.
(23) Jelinek, Mariann, and Adler, Nancy J. (1988) "Women: World-Class Managers for Global Competition," *Academy of Management Executive* 2(1):11–19.
(24) Korabik, Karen (1988) "Is the Ideal Manager Masculine? The Contribution of Femininity to Managerial Effectiveness." Paper presented at the annual meetings of the Academy of Management, Anaheim, Calif.
(25) Lansing, P., and Ready, K. (1988) "Hiring Women Managers in Japan: An Alternative for Foreign Employers," *California Management Review* 30(3):112–127.
(26) Loden, M. (1987) *Feminine Leadership or How to Succeed in Business without Being One of the Boys*. New York: Times Books.
(27) Miller, Jean Baker (1976) *Toward a New Psychology of Women*. Boston: Beacon.
(28) Miller, Jean Baker (1982) "Women and Power," Working Paper. Wellesley, Mass.: Wellesley College, Stone Center for Development Services and Studies.

(29) Morganthaler, E. (1978) "Women of the World: More U.S. Firms Put Females in Key Posts in Foreign Countries," *Wall Street Journal*, March 16:1,27.
(30) Moran, Stahl, and Boyer, Inc. (1988) *Status of American Female Expatriate Employees: Survey Results*. Boulder, Colo.: International Division.
(31) Perry, Nancy J. (1992) "If You Can't Join 'em, Beat 'em," *Fortune*, September 21, pp. 58–59.
(32) Porter, Michael (1990) *The Competitive Advantage of Nations*. New York: The Free Press.
(33) Rosenzweig, Philip M., and Nohria, Nitin (1992) "Human Resource Management in MNC Affiliates: Internal Consistency or Local Isomorphism," Working Paper. Boston: Harvard Business School.
(34) Steen, Gunilla Masreliez (1987) "Male and Female Culture: A View From Sweden." Working paper originally presented at the International Federation of Training and Development Organizations conference.
(35) Steinhoff, Patricia G., and Tanaka, Kazuko (1988) "Women Managers in Japan," in Nancy J. Adler and Dafna N. Izraeli (eds.), *Women in Management Worldwide*, pp. 103–121. Armonk, N.Y.: M. E. Sharpe.
(36) Steinhoff, Patricia G., and Tanaka, Kazuko (1994) "Women Managers in Japan," in Nancy J. Adler and Dafna N. Izraeli (eds.), *Competitive Frontiers: Women Managers in a Global Economy*, pp. 79–100. Cambridge (USA)/Oxford (England): Blackwell Publishers.
(37) Thal, N., and Cateora, P. (1979) "Opportunities for Women in International Business," *Business Horizons* 22(6):21–27.
(38) *Yearbook of Labor Statistics* (1986) (1987) (1991) Geneva: International Labor Office.

[10]

© Academy of Management Executive, 1998, Vol. 12, No. 4

"Global strategy" and its impact on local operations: Lessons from Gillette Singapore

Rosabeth Moss Kanter and Thomas D. Dretler

Executive Overview

Among the myths about global strategy is the assumption that it means integration across international operations that causes a loss of country identity and dissociation of product lines from their local context, as they report to global product managers. This article advances a different view, in which global strategy is synonymous with holistic approaches—not necessarily international ones—that can tighten local integration in the interest of global goals. The experience of Gillette after the acquisition of Parker Pen shows that mergers and acquisitions by global companies can involve local integration across divisions in order to create within-country synergies. It also shows that tapping the power of global brands often requires acknowledging country differences and respecting local norms—thus strengthening, rather than weakening, the local country unit and enhancing relationships across functions and divisions within it.

"Global" is among the most overused and least understood words in business today. The phrase "going global" is used to refer to everything from opening a firm's first international sales office to taking a trip outside the United States. Scott McNealy, CEO of Sun Microsystems, received almost full page coverage in the New York Times a few years ago just because he traveled personally to Southeast Asia. And the uses of "global" are often imprecise. One company with operations in Mexico and Brazil calls itself "global" when it is really "hemispheric." An Asian consumer products company has been pursuing what it calls "globalization" by moving from its Philippine and Hong Kong bases into Indonesia, Singapore, and Malaysia, a strategy that was at best regional. An increasingly global economy is clearly important to businesses today, and understanding of global strategy is a critical element in any leader's repertoire. Information technology and trade that link the world have made export markets a vital part of the sales growth plan for manufacturing and, increasingly, service companies of all sizes. Even companies with a low percentage of international sales have international suppliers, compete with international companies in their home markets, and must meet world class quality standards in order to hold their local business.[1]

Myths and Misunderstandings

What does global strategy really mean? Examination of the use of the words global and globalization by business executives and by the media indicate the prevalence of six major myths or misunderstandings. Uncritical acceptance of these myths prevents companies from taking full advantage of global opportunities.

Myth #1: That global is synonymous with international, meaning simply having a presence in other countries whether or not there is any connection among activities across countries. Having a sales office, a factory, or a representative in other countries does not by itself make a company global, especially if country operations run independently, with few ties between them, and all power and influence resides at U.S. headquarters. Nortel's Turkish subsidiary, Netas, won Nortel's international quality award a few years ago; but few, if any, American and Canadian managers subsequently traveled to Turkey to learn best practices from Netas. Quaker Oats had a gem in its European pet food operations but sold the pet food division because of aspirations to be a beverage giant in the U.S.—and then later worried about insufficient international reach. Failing to include international outposts as key company resources prevents companies from crafting effective global strategies.

Failing to include international outposts as key company resources prevents companies from crafting effective global strategies.

The second misunderstanding is the flip side of the first. If global implies something more than international activities, then it involves homogenization. Thus, ***myth #2: That global strategy means doing everything the same way everywhere.*** Coca-Cola is one of the world's great universal global brands, made with virtually a world formula and with a logo and brand identity known even in remote villages of underdeveloped countries. But the global product is handled very differently in each market. Local variations include different local bottling and distribution partners (such as the Coca-Cola-Schweppes joint venture in the U.K. or the San Miguel partnership in the Philippines), different container sizes, different names ("Coca-Cola Light" instead of "Diet Coke" in Europe), and different product forms (fewer dispensing machines outside the U.S. means less demand for just the syrup).

The third confusion is about the identity of so-called global companies, as contained in ***myth #3: That globalizing means becoming a stateless corporation with no national or community ties.*** This myth is increasingly refuted by the rise of corporate citizenship. Indeed, one could argue that the more global the scope of business operations, the greater the need to make local connections in order to gain good will from customers, employees, and politicians who care about their local roots.[2] Companies must become insiders in all their markets in order to be globally effective—which is why Percy Barnevik, CEO of Asea Brown Boveri, prefers to call ABB a multilocal rather than a global company. At Kanter's suggestion, Novartis, the pharmaceutical giant created by the merger of Sandoz and Ciba, announced its new global identity with a day of local community service throughout the world. Becoming great local citizens can pay off within domestic as well as foreign markets. When entire blocks of businesses were burned and looted during 1992 riots in Los Angeles, residents protected McDonald's stores because of community service projects such as the Ronald McDonald House for sick children.

A corollary is ***myth #4: That globalization requires abandoning country images and values.*** On the contrary, global products sometimes derive identity from their place of origin, like the famous Marlboro man, who once sold American culture as part of the cigarette. Indeed, country images can be so strong that some companies borrow ones that aren't even theirs to create an international brand, like Haagen-Daz ice cream, an American brand that suggests Scandinavia, or Au Bon Pain, an American chain of French bakery-style cafes that is exporting frozen French-style bread dough to Latin America from its Boston factory.

The process of globalization is also misunderstood by some companies. ***Myth #5: That globalizing means tacking on acquisitions or alliances in other countries, without much integration or change.*** Just because a company has a partner or even a subsidiary outside its home country doesn't make it global, unless there is some value-added in every market because of the international ties. Pharmacia & Upjohn, the troubled drugmaker, reportedly stumbled because it never melded its Swedish and American operations and cultures—nor those of the Italian company that Pharmacia had purchased before the merger. Without synergies, there is no global strategy. Similarly, it remains to be seen whether international airline agreements such as the Lufthansa/United Airlines alliance (now expanding to encompass SAS and Thai Air) confer more benefits than smooth transfers among flights. If all United does is help travelers book a Lufthansa flight at its ticket counters and share lounges and frequent flyer points, United is no more global than it was before the alliance.

Finally, there is a common assumption that global strategy involves activities outside the home country, as in ***myth #6: that to qualify as global, a strategy must involve sales or operations in another country.*** Union Pacific Resources of Fort Worth, Texas, grew aggressively by pursuing what it calls a "home alone" strategy—concentrating on oil and gas exploration in the western United States while its competitors roam the world. But unlike myopic, parochial, domestic companies of the past, UPR scanned the world for opportunities, noted where its competition was strong, and considered all the areas in which it could best deploy new technology.[3] In short, global thinking is what's important for companies, not just counting international sales. That thought process, in turn, will expand opportunities in any market the company pursues.

If global strategy doesn't necessarily equate with international, universal, and unconnected to country identity, what does it mean? This is the question we sought to explore in our work with Gillette, especially in the Asia-Pacific region.

Global connotes holistic, integrated activity. Global strategy involves thinking in an integrated way about all aspects of a business—its suppliers, production sites, markets, and competition. It involves assessing every product or service from the perspective of both domestic and international market standards. It means embedding international perspectives in product formulations at the point of design, not as afterthoughts. It means meeting world standards even before seeking world markets and being world class even in local markets. It means deepening the company's understanding of local and cultural differences in order to become truly global.

Global success rests on the ability to listen and learn in locations far from the home base. Searching internationally for concepts as well as customers and suppliers can stimulate innovation and ease eventual entry into new markets. Consider how one Japanese auto company used an alliance with a car-leasing company in China to learn about use and repair of cars in that emerging market long before it considered manufacturing in China or even exporting its own cars there. International contacts suggest new ideas to bring to strategic discussions.

Global success rests on the ability to listen and learn in locations far from the home base.

Global strategy involves focusing on areas of excellence against a backdrop of worldwide possibilities, determining the synergies that exist across markets and alliance partners as well as the differences that must be taken into account in various locations. What we discovered in the case of Gillette was that effective globalization required strong local integration across functions and divisions in every place the company operated.

The Gillette Company and Its International Organization

The Gillette Company is the world leader in male grooming products. Founded in 1901, the company has consistently led a category that includes blades and razors, shaving preparations, and electric shavers. Gillette also holds the number one position worldwide in various female grooming products such as wet shavers and hair epilation devices. The company is the world's top seller of writing instruments, correction products, toothbrushes and oral care appliances. Gillette's leadership in over 200 countries and territories is fueled by 50 manufacturing facilities in 24 nations.

Gillette has long demonstrated a commitment to international markets. Between 1905 and 1909, the company established manufacturing facilities in Canada, England, France, and Germany. By 1919, branch offices or companies were started in Copenhagen, Madrid, Milan, Istanbul, Calcutta, Sydney, Brussels, Geneva, Buenos Aires, Singapore, and Shanghai. Gillette's traditional multinational strategy was to market and distribute its latest and most technologically advanced products in only the world's most developed regions. Emerging markets were valued and deemed important to the company's continued growth, but the products available there may have been launched five, 10, or 15 years earlier in countries like the United States. This "Stone Age theory" according to Gillette CEO Alfred Zeien, survived until the late 1980s, when Gillette discovered that the forces of change had made such an approach obsolete. Beginning with the worldwide launch of Sensor in 1990, Gillette became one of the first truly global companies. Today, the latest and most technologically advanced Gillette products and manufacturing systems can be found almost anywhere in the world.[4]

To support Gillette's increasingly global focus, the company went through a restructuring in 1988, creating three principal divisions. The North Atlantic Group manufactures and markets the company's traditional shaving and personal care products in North America and Western Europe. The Diversified Group comprises the Stationery division's North Atlantic arm; as well as the Braun, Oral-B, and Jafra companies, each organized on a worldwide product line basis. The International Group produces and sells the company's Shaving, Personal Care, and Stationery products in all markets except North America and Western Europe.

The International Group is divided into three regions: Latin America; Africa, Middle East, and Eastern Europe (AMEE); and Asia-Pacific. Each area has a Group Vice President that oversees Gillette's sales of Shaving, Personal Care, and Stationery products in that region. The Asia-Pacific group markets are Japan, Hong Kong, China, Australia, Singapore, Korea, Indonesia, Thailand, Taiwan, Malaysia, the Philippines, New Zealand, South Pacific, South Korea, and Indochina.

Gillette's global strategy includes a clear understanding of local differences—that each market presents unique challenges, requirements, and opportunities. In the rapid growth Asia-Pacific region, for example, Gillette has used merger integration as a vehicle for developing a wholly integrated approach to individual markets. In Singapore, the acquisition of Parker Pen in 1993 triggered the establishment of a new organizational structure that has allowed Gillette to show one face to the customer and act as a single, integrated entity to suppliers in the region. While the integration reflects a global strategy, the ability to pull it off required a local sensitivity and orientation. Indeed, the story of Gillette Singapore's merger with Parker Pen illuminates the link between global strategy and local mastery. It demonstrates how managing local integration is key to unleashing the power of global brands.

Gillette Singapore and the Search for Global Integration in the Asia-Pacific Region

In the 1960s, Gillette established an Asia-Pacific manufacturing presence with a blades, toiletries, and liquid paper facility in Australia. In 1970, it added a small, old-style, double-edged blade plant in Malaysia. Over time, the company began constructing larger factories in areas such as the Philippines, Indonesia, and Thailand. By the early 1980s, Gillette had gradually put together Asian sales forces and an infrastructure in the region.

In June 1984, Gillette announced the $188.5 million purchase of Oral-B Laboratories, the leading marketer of toothbrushes in the United States. A profitable and well-managed company, Oral-B manufactured top-quality products that were distributed through many of the same channels that already existed within the Gillette network. As Gillette's technological expertise was in metals and other shaving-related raw materials, it saw no reason to disrupt the Palo Alto-based Oral-B operation with a heavy-handed management takeover. On the contrary, the value of the Oral-B acquisition was in benefiting from distribution channel synergies. Keeping Oral-B managers focused on a product-line basis was key to making the acquisition a success.

While the Oral-B management and reporting structure remained intact, managers at established Gillette operations in developing regions like Asia-Pacific were tapped to assist with sales and share with Oral-B such back-room services as finance and operations. This concept was a difficult one for many Gillette employees to accept. The Gillette Company culture was one where performance reigned supreme. Managers were pushed to set and consistently meet aggressive growth numbers in all of their markets. Gillette managers viewed the first Oral-B employees to arrive in Malaysia as nuisances and threats to their livelihoods. Gillette sales people were paid and evaluated relative to how much product they sold. As far as they were concerned, any time spent on Oral-B was time lost on a Gillette-managed product. The company incentive structure was such that sales people had nothing to gain and everything to lose by helping Oral-B.

To remedy this situation, Corporate Controller Chuck Cramb introduced the concept of notional accounting. This double counting procedure allowed both Oral-B and Gillette managers to take credit for the same sales. Still, implementation of this concept was not easy. According to Norman Roberts, former Asia-Pacific Group VP and a champion of local integration, "Managers had to learn how to cooperate with people that they had no direct authority over."

The Gillette Company culture was one where performance reigned supreme. Managers were pushed to set and consistently meet aggressive growth numbers in all of their markets.

Over the next several years, employees throughout Asia-Pacific became introduced to the notional accounting concept and the prospect of shared services. While each market was different, an initial display of resistance and turf-guarding was the norm. One issue that proved particularly disruptive in the company's effort to build cohesion was Gillette's strong shaving affiliation. In a company identified the world over for its shaving dominance, Oral-B managers couldn't help but feel like second class citizens. At the same time, managers on the shaving side were wary of spending their time on Oral-B for fear of losing ground on the core business. For headquarters, the challenge was to convince employees that Gillette was more than a shaving company. This was easier said than done. Still, despite the difficulties, Roberts felt strongly that a collaborative environment was necessary to take advantage of Gillette's established infrastructure in developing markets.

As Group VP, Roberts had the latitude to organize Asia-Pacific operations in a way that he felt would best maximize current and future performance. In 1992, he drafted and distributed to general managers in all AP markets a simple, one-page document called the Campus Charter. In it he wrote, "the campus concept is simply that in Asia-Pacific it is more efficient for the various divisions of the Gillette Company (Shaving, Stationery, Oral Care, Braun) to operate under the same roof sharing common services."

Essentially, the Campus Charter asked business unit managers to maintain their reporting autonomy while sharing support services such as finance, information technology, human resources, and, in some instances, sales. The new structure was designed to not only exploit synergies and avoid duplication but also to advance Gillette's global integration strategy by showing one face to the customer and allowing the company to act as a single entity to suppliers in developing markets.

In May 1993, Gillette acquired Parker Pen Holdings Limited of the U.K. for 285 million British pounds (equivalent to $460 million U.S. dollars on the date of purchase). Originally a division of a Wisconsin-based firm, Parker was sold to U.K. investors as part of $100 million management buyout in 1985. As a British company, it battled aggressively with Waterman, located just across the English Channel. When Gillette bought the French company in 1987, it was buoyed by Gillette's deep pockets and strong distribution network. Through Waterman, Gillette enjoyed a 21 percent shaie of the luxury segment of the world pen market. With the 1993 addition of Parker to the company's Paper Mate and Waterman brands, Gillette would own 40 percent of that market and become the clear worldwide leader in writing instruments.

Despite its strong market position, Parker maintained a close-knit and familial corporate culture. Perhaps because of its origins as a family-owned company, Parker had a flat organizational structure and prospered in an informal environment. It had a single-brand, high-end product line of which members of the company were extremely proud.

With the Parker Pen integration on the immediate horizon, Norman Roberts decided that now was the time for Asia-Pacific markets to embrace a full-fledged campus approach. Although already operating within a system of shared services and notional accounting, the prospect of physical relocation presented the opportunity for an organizational restructuring in the region.

The Four Lessons of Gillette Singapore

At the urging of Norman Roberts, Gillette Singapore would be the first Asia-Pacific market to fully integrate Parker Pen and establish formal campus operations. Gillette Singapore is the marketing and distribution arm for the Gillette Company in the 633-square mile, Southeast Asian nation-state of Singapore. Originally established in 1919, Gillette's modern-day Singapore operation came into being during the mid-1970s. Consistently the most profitable market (on a per capita basis) in the Asia-Pacific region, Gillette Singapore's 1993 sales were nearly $9 million in an area containing only three million people. Gillette-managed businesses (Shaving, Oral Care, and Personal Care) accounted for 57 percent, 31 percent and less than 1 percent of profits respectively. Non-Gillette-managed Stationery was responsible for 12 percent of earnings. Braun (another non-Gillette managed business) did not do business out of Gillette Singapore at the time.

The new organizational structure called for the current GM of Shaving and Personal Care in Singapore to assume the additional role of campus dean. In this capacity he would be responsible for overseeing all integration activities.

At the new Gillette Singapore campus, Shaving and Personal Care would be a division of nearly 20 people, including a 10-person sales force reporting directly to the GM. Also depending on this sales team would be the Oral Care division, which would have a staff of only four, along with a business manager. The Gillette Stationery division, naturally, would experience a complete shake-up. Formally a seven-person group that relied heavily on the Shaving sales force, this department would expand to over 20, in part because Parker's Singapore office housed its regional general management, as well. As a result, the Singapore Campus would contain a regional GM for Stationery in addition to a person in charge of the local operation. Under these people, would be Marketing and Promotion departments, as well as an exclusive eight-person Singapore sales team. If the Stationery division was to be dominated by Parker people, the support functions would split right down the middle. The financial controllers of each office would be teamed up to head Finance. Under them would be clerks and various support staff numbering close to 20. Also greatly expanded would be the Materials Management office, whose five-person staff would triple and handle warehouse and other operations-related activities for the entire Campus. Initially there would be no Information Technology (IT) or Human Resources (HR) function but, once established, all four support areas (Finance, Materials Management, IT, and HR) would report directly to the campus dean.

The integration of Parker Pen and establishment of Campus operations in Singapore was both a tremendous challenge and an unqualified success. For Gillette headquarters in Boston, local integration of International Group operations was key to implementing its global corporate strategy. For those on the ground in Singapore, the experience provided several practical lessons that could be useful to other global players.

The Need for Integration Across Functions and Divisions

Tapping the power of global brands and the economies of global production requires greater integration across functions and divisions at the local level—and thus, strong local management. Even though Gillette was organized around worldwide or superregional product groups and functional groups, managers on the ground in various countries did not report to international bosses outside of their local territory, thus losing connection with their local base. The campus concept was born from the vision of showing one face to the customer. Without coordinated activities, the total effectiveness of Gillette's operations in Singapore would have been nothing more than the sum of its parts. Instead, the global synergies that Gillette sought were manifested through local relationships.

In Singapore, Personal care, Oral care—and eventually, the newest acquisition, Duracell—all benefited from Shaving's relationships and clout with local distribution channels. The new Stationery sales force—responsible for both Parker and Waterman stocks—also has considerably enhanced leverage. Indeed, when operational synergies are the motivation for an acquisition, the need for links between the combining organizations is high.[5] Housing all business units under one roof allows the relevant stakeholders—customers, suppliers, employees, and community members—to view Gillette Singapore as one company with one vision and one way of operating. Employees are better able to understand, exchange ideas with, and transfer into other divisions. The strong operational integration required by the campus creates a new and universally-accepted culture—one that can be consistently displayed to those outside the organization.[6] Besides the obvious benefits of costcutting, the Campus approach delivers bottom-line value by strengthening Gillette's brand identity in Singapore. Individual product lines are more easily associated with the Gillette name—thus elevating their perceived value in the marketplace. Like other successful integrators, Gillette understands that well conceived acquisitions ensure that valuable customers win too.[7] The emphasis on local integration in international markets is one reason the Gillette Company has developed such powerful global brands. Indeed, as the actual amount of resource sharing between two firms increases, and the years since the merger increase, so do performance benefits from the merger.[8]

The Need to Manage Change

Managing globalization means managing change, and handling a variety of human issues connected with local settings. Defining global strategy is a high-level corporate function that can be done for the whole corporation with a single plan. But operationalizing it means managing multiple changes in multiple places. Creating the Gillette Singapore Campus and integrating Parker Pen was identified by Singapore managers as the most difficult change management challenge in recent memory. For all its strategic importance and global significance, successful integration was about dealing with people and managing resistance to change—and the nitty-gritty basics mattered.

For example, when the word got out that a new office location for the campus would have to be found, ex-Parker employees (who had been working at Parker headquarters on the east side of the island) threatened to quit if a new location was chosen in the west. Long-time Gillette employees, on the other hand, had grown accustomed to the west and were reluctant to commute the ten to twenty extra miles east. This posed a significant dilemma—especially since high-turnover at a target company has proved to be negatively correlated with successful integration.[9] Eventually, the Gillette Singapore GM plotted on a map the homes of every campus employee, then chose a new site on the side of the island inhabited by the greatest number of employees. When a new space in the east finally was found, employees and managers from all business units jockeyed for position regarding office space and transition responsibilities. While Gillette headquarters did have some standard guidelines regarding the size and type of office for various management levels, senior Asia-Pacific executives from different divisions lobbied the Gillette Singapore GM for extra space to house and support their particular business unit activities.

Furthermore, while the new structure was still

being shaped, several managers tried to position themselves for greater power and authority in the new regime. Managers who weren't involved in the initial integration planning were particularly demanding and more likely to view the merger as a threat.[10] At Gillette, where the razor-and-blade division had long been dominant, the people not assigned to Shaving had power issues, and either wanted to change divisions or get some assurance (usually financial) that their contributions were valued. For those that weren't as vocal, it was by no means a sign of contentment. Individuals on both the Gillette and Parker sides were nervous about the proposed integration. For better or worse, they had established a routine in their old jobs; they knew what to expect and they knew what was expected of them. In the new environment, there would be new opportunities, challenges, and conditions. There also would be new rivalries and jealousies. Bringing together different units under one roof meant bringing together people with different wage scales and benefits packages. It didn't matter to an ex-Parker finance person in Singapore that his counterpart in Taiwan or Brussels or the United States was making the same money. He wanted to be paid on an equitable basis with the person sitting next to him. Indeed, the issue of pay-equity is critical—and successful acquirers will craft a new compensation system that fosters cooperation and the creation of a merged corporate culture.[11] That Gillette had historically paid higher salaries than Parker was no longer relevant. Parker had become part of Gillette—and Parker people wanted be paid the same money as their coworkers doing the same job.

The Need to Respect Local Cultures

Global processes must be tailored to local cultures. Many M&A experts in the U.S. have cited speed as a key element of successful integration. Two such experts write that "fast track integration ensures that anticipated gains are realized as soon as possible. Shaving one month off the integration timetable can generate millions of dollars for the bottom line of the combined organization."[12] Despite this widely held belief, Gillette wisely gave Singapore time to handle relationships and action steps in a way that was respectful of the norms and customs of the area.

Soon after the acquisition was announced in May 1993, the Gillette Singapore GM (a Singaporean in his mid thirties) paid a visit to the GM of Parker, a Chinese gentleman in his early sixties. As is customary in Asia, the two men discussed the merger in a pleasant, courteous manner. Although soon to be campus dean, and in many ways senior to his Parker counterpart, the younger GM was careful to lay out transition steps that would be amenable to the Parker side—and to defer to his elder in many subtle ways that would communicate the proper respect. Of course, the Parker GM and his employees had many questions about how the new organization would be shaped. In this part of the world, time was needed to feel out a new relationship. Various meetings and get-acquainted sessions were organized between Parker and Gillette over the next several months. Of course, time was important—but the Gillette Singapore GM knew that rushing things could have disastrous results. A December 1, 1993, joint reporting deadline was pushed back to March 1, 1994. Gillette could have demanded that Singapore move faster, but imposing one-size-fits-all policies without reevaluating for cultural appropriateness can be a costly mistake.[13] Even the Singapore Campus' eventual move-in date had cultural significance. In Chinese society, it is very important to choose an auspicious day for such a significant event. Both Gillette and Parker employees helped select a date in late February that they all felt was worthy of commemorating this organizational marriage. Recognizing that different cultures require different rules of conduct and administrative procedures, Gillette is able to solidify its presence around the globe.[14] Its sensitivity to local considerations improves the chances for global success.

Recognizing that different cultures require different rules of conduct and administrative procedures, Gillette is able to solidify its presence around the globe.

The Need to Understand a Corporation's Culture

In global companies, business cultures can be even stronger than country cultures. During the Parker integration, Gillette Singapore's campus dean, a native of the area, was promoted and replaced by an American expatriot. The move was seen as positive by many, and the new GM was a powerful force in helping to bridge the cultural gap between the two organizations. Why was an American effective in this role? Because the integration issues had less to do with country culture and race than they did standard business practices and philosophies. Parker and Gillette were very different types of companies. Gillette was performance-driven, relatively centralized and formal, and promoted mass-market products throughout the world. Parker, on the other hand, was familial, informal, and identified itself as producer of a prestigious pen. Research has shown that some cultural problems associated with combining organizations are more amplified in domestic, rather than cross-national settings.[15]

Indeed, the challenge in melding Parker and Gillette's operations in Singapore was not about country origin—in fact, the majority of employees on both sides were from Asia—but about corporate culture. For ex-Parker people, the Gillette Singapore campus was located not two miles from where they had previously worked. Former Parker employees even outnumbered Gillette staff in the new organization. The biggest adjustment was in combating the feelings of lost autonomy. Regardless of the circumstances, most cases show that people at the acquired company are likely to have higher anxiety levels than those at the buying firm.[16]

Despite Gillette's obvious sensitivities, several Parker employees likened their experiences to a new form of colonization—an imperialistic takeover that left no ambiguity between conqueror and conqueree. For Parker employees, the Gillette acquisition meant that they could no longer operate in the congenial atmosphere that many of them felt made the company unique. According to one particularly reluctant Gillette Singapore employee, "At the old Parker, coming to work was enjoyable and fun. After the move, I would wake up and say, 'Oh no, another day.' " Does this reaction suggest a heavy-handed takeover by Gillette? Probably not. What it does reflect, however, is the difficulty many people have adjusting to new business environments. The absorption of an organization characterized by very different value systems, expectations, and world views will tend to be associated with massive value destruction by acquired employees.[17] In fact, the Parker veteran said he spent several years working for the firm in Europe and enjoyed the experience just as much as he did in his home country of Singapore. For him and many others, stress and uneasiness about globalization comes not from entering new markets, but from integrating with other corporate cultures at home.

The Real Meaning of Global Strategy

We initially began our exploration of Gillette's Asia-Pacific operations with an eye toward understanding how global strategy redefined country operations, reducing the power of countries as activities fell under international groups that managed them uniformly across wide geographic territories and attempted to wipe out local differences. In short, we too had been influenced by the prevalent myths and misunderstandings about globalization.

What we found instead when we examined global strategy in one of the world's most global companies was that local integration and local relationships became even more important as Gillette sought to gain the power of global brands. We saw that global strategy required a great deal of local coordination, across divisions and products as well as across functions. This local coordination, in turn, left room for incorporating local differences and variations into global thinking—including variations in consumer preferences, infrastructure, and employee expectations.

This case study reinforces our conclusion that the best definition of "global" is "integrated," not "international." Companies with international activities have greater need for multiple forms of integration, but they do not always build the linkages across countries or products or functions that allow them to think about all of their resources simultaneously and therefore to tap the power of the whole. The key to success in the global economy is for companies to behave in a more integrated fashion—to tap the collaborative advantage that comes from being able to use all their resources and being able to work across boundaries.[18] That means becoming knowledgable about local needs, skillful at managing local changes, and expert at forging cross-boundary relationships—and doing this in many places at the same time with a global, or holistic, strategy in mind.

Endnotes

[1] Kanter, R. M. 1995. *World Class: Thriving Locally in the Global Economy*. New York, NY: Simon and Schuster.

[2] Kanter, R. M. 1997. *Rosabeth Moss Kanter on the Frontiers of Management*. Boston: HBS Press, Chapter 1.

[3] Barnevik, P. and Kanter, R. M. 1994. *Global Strategies*. Boston, MA: HBS Press.

[4] Kanter, R. M. 1995. *World Class: Thriving Locally in the Global Economy*. New York, NY: Simon and Schuster.

[5] Pablo, A. 1994. Determinants of Acquisition Integration Level: A Decision-Making Perspective. *Academy of Management Journal*, August 803–836.

[6] Olie, R. 1994. Shades of Culture and Institutions in International Mergers. *Organization Studies*, 381–405.

[7] Smith, K. and Quella, J. 1995. Seizing the Moment to Capture Value in a Strategic Deal. *Mergers & Acquisitions*, January/February 25–30.

[8] Very, P., et al. 1996. A Cross-National Assessment of Acculturative Stress in Recent European Mergers. *International Studies of Management and Organization*, Spring 59–86.

[9] Begley, T., and Yount, B. 1994. Enlisting Personnel of the Target to Combat Resentment. *Mergers & Acquisitions*, September/October 27–32.

[10] Reece, R. 1996. Easing the Transition During a Merger or Acquisition. *Bank Marketing*, August 38–42.

[11] *The Wall Street Journal*. 1997, February 14. Merged Firms Often Face Culture Clash; Businesses Offer Advice on Ways to Avoid Minefields. Feb. 14, 9A.

[12] Galpin, T. and Robinson, D. 1997. Merger Integration: The Ultimate Change Management Challenge. *Mergers & Acquisitions*, January/February 24–28.

[13] *The Wall Street Journal*. 1997. Side Effects: Cross-Border Merger Results in Headaches for a Drug Company; Pharmacia and Upjohn Faces Culture Clash; Europeans Chafe Under U.S. Rules; Even Logo is Troublesome. Feb. 4, 1A.

[14] Very, P., et al. 1996. A Cross-National Assessment of Acculturative Stress in Recent European Mergers. *International Studies of Management and Organization*, Spring, 59–86.

[15] Hakanson, L. 1995. Learning through Acquisitions: Management and Integration of Foreign R&D Laboratories. *International Studies of Management and Organization*, Spring/Summer 121–157.

[16] Harrington, L. 1997. Making the Most of a Merger. *Transportation and Distribution*, January 36–40.

[17] Hakanson, L. 1995. Learning through Acquisitions: Management and Integration of Foreign R&D Laboratories. *International Studies of Management and Organization*, Spring/Summer 121–157.

[18] Kanter, R. M. 1997. *Rosabeth Moss Kanter on the Frontiers of Management*. Boston: HBS Press, Chapter 20.

About the Authors

Rosabeth Moss Kanter holds the Class of 1960 Chair as professor of business administration at the Harvard Business School. Her new book, *Rosabeth Moss Kanter on the Frontiers of Management*, published by the Harvard Business School Press (1997), brings together for the first time many of the landmark articles she published in the *Harvard Business Review* and links them with new commentary and overviews designed to help managers understand their roles in organizations undergoing massive change and to provide a comprehensive look at the challenges of leadership and innovation still to be met. Kanter has published 12 books and over 150 articles. "Best article" awards include a McKinsey Award from the *Harvard Business Review*. She taught previously at Brandeis, Harvard, and Yale Universities (1977–1986). She cofounded and is board chair of Goodmeasure, Inc., a consulting firm, whose *A Tale of "O": On Being Different*, is a best-selling video on workplace diversity. Kanter has received numerous national honors, including a Guggenheim Fellowship, 18 honorary doctoral degrees, and several Woman of the Year awards. She has been a consultant to major corporations all over the world, including Bell Atlantic, Quaker Oats, and BankBoston in the U. S., Novartis, Volvo, and Inmarsat in Europe, and San Miguel in Asia.

Thomas D. Dretler is chief operating officer of EduVentures, LLC, a Boston investment services firm specializing in education companies. He was previously director of Goodmeasure, Inc., a management consulting firm chaired by Professor Rosabeth Moss Kanter. Dretler also managed a Harvard Business School program on business investment in public education, welfare to work, and urban investment. A Phi Beta Kappa graduate of the Johns Hopkins University and a Harvard Business School MBA, Dretler also served as a consultant to former President Jimmy Carter's Atlanta Project and developed public-private partnerships with the Atlanta Committee for the Olympic Games.

[11]

MANAGING INSTITUTIONAL AND CULTURAL CONTRASTS

THE CASE OF SANYO ELECTRIC IN THE UNITED STATES

Roger L. M. Dunbar and Suresh Kotha

ABSTRACT

This paper considers some of the issues that a Japanese firm deals with in establishing and then managing a presence in the United States. It highlights how adaptation to the United States involves understanding and responding to both cultural and competitive dynamics. Specifically, the Sanyo case suggests how these conditions co-evolved, interacted, and changed over time. The case also illustrates how foreign firms competing in the United States should not underestimate the importance of cultural and competitive dynamics and how these can co-evolve over time in unmanaged ways. These dynamics, generally not apparent at entry, can and do play an important role as a firm adapts in a foreign setting.

More generally we argue that cross-cultural research needs to explore "phenomenon in the making" in order to understand how adaptation to a foreign setting occurs. A more qualitative approach enables researchers to emphasize the impact of the foreign setting and the process by which a firm constructs a view of itself in an evolving

Advances in International Comparative Management, Volume 13, pages 149-173.

ISBN: 0-7623-0589-4

world. The paper concludes by discussing possible implications for future research and practice on foreign firms seeking to establish a presence in the United States.

INTRODUCTION

Important differences in social structures and cultural beliefs distinguish Japan and the United States. Their respective governments manage their economies in different ways (Fallows, 1994; Lodge, 1987). Underlying norms and managerial values (Abegglen & Stalk, 1985; Lincoln, Hanada, & Olson, 1981; Ouchi, 1981) differ. As a result, managers rely on contrasting approaches to structure firm work and have different expectations about the management processes (Aoki, 1990; Kotha, Dunbar, & Bird, 1995; Lincoln, Hanada, & McBride, 1986). These differences can lead to contrasts in how business is approached and in how operations are managed (Kagono et al., 1985).

As managers assess financial opportunities in other countries, the potential disruptions that may stem from cultural and management differences can be downplayed or even ignored. Yet such differences can be very important. For example, they may make it difficult for firm managers operating in another country to recognize when, how, and where they should change their approach to maintain success (Murtha & Lenway, 1994). Yet if a firm continues to rely on home country practices not accepted abroad, its managers may inadvertently become involved in unanticipated conflicts and losses (Kogut, 1991).

This paper focuses on Sanyo Electric's efforts to establish a corporate presence in the United States. The study describes how Sanyo entered the United States and established its television and microwave manufacturing facility in Arkansas and then examines various issues that emerged for Sanyo over a decade. It concludes by discussing implications for Japanese managers establishing a corporate presence in the United States.

BACKGROUND LITERATURE

A growing body of research has considered how Japanese firms become established in the United States. The evidence suggests that generally Japanese firms have preferred to establish greenfield subsidiaries rather than acquire established facilities (Hennart & Park, 1994). They may prefer greenfield startups because this choice means they do not have to take over or rely on unknown "foreign" management (Kogut & Singh, 1988). Further, since Japanese managers are in control from the start, the Japanese perceive the venture as less risky (Li, 1995). Cole and Deskins (1988) studied Japanese greenfield automobile startups to identify factors impacting plant location. They concluded that, "Japanese plant sitings [in the auto industry] reflected a pattern in which avoidance of blacks is *one* factor in their site location decision" (p. 17, italics in the original), with the NUMMI plant being an important exception.

Japanese electronic firms entering the United States have usually focused exclusively on core businesses where they have an established competitive advantage (Chang, 1995). This is typical of many MNCs that have manufacturing operations overseas and provide their overseas affiliates with technical know-how and firm-specific organizing capabilities (Buckley & Casson, 1976; Caves, 1982). The subsidiary imports the parent's technologies along with experienced firm managers; these managers then implement practices that have proven effective in the home country (Zaheer, 1995).

Other studies have considered how Japanese manufacturing firms manage in the United States after successfully establishing a subsidiary (Cole & Deskins, 1988). Adler (1993), for example, examined the impact of work practices introduced at NUMMI, a joint venture between General Motors and Toyota Corporation. He highlighted how managers were able to develop a social context emphasizing commitment to continuous improvement and an intense focus on standardization. Introducing this new set of cultural beliefs helped NUMMI become highly efficient and learn over time (Brown & Reich, 1989).

In contrast, Milkman (1991) examined the work practices of Japanese manufacturers not involved in the automobile industry. She found that these plants usually employed a few hundred employees to do simple fabricating and assembly work. She noted that so-called "Japanese" organization practices such as emphasis on teamwork, job rotation, cross training, quality circles, and so on were almost nonexistent in these plants. Most did not employ any of the "lean" manufacturing systems such as just-in-time inventory systems used at NUMMI. Instead, the work organization in these plants strongly resembled that of nonunion American firms. She also noted that within these plants, most labor-related decisions were assigned to American human resource executives who advocated policies designed to avoid unionization (see also Beechler & Yang, 1994).

We add to these studies of Japanese adaptation patterns in the United States by examining Sanyo Manufacturing Company. Our purpose is to explore how a Japanese firm adapts to the U.S. environment and works toward overcoming its "liability of foreignness" (Hymer, 1976). Of specific interest is what happens after the Japanese firm has successfully entered the U.S. market and has implemented the parent firm's organizing practices. *How may these operating practices brought from Japan evolve as they are implemented by a U.S. workforce with different beliefs and work expectations*?

MNCs must also find ways to support and maintain the firm-specific competitive advantages and capabilities located in their overseas affiliates (Buckley & Casson, 1976; Caves, 1982; Zaheer, 1995). This becomes an important issue over time since the competitive dynamics of global industries inevitably erode firm-specific advantages. The parent must introduce new capabilities and advantages into the local subsidiary, or the local firm must develop new technical capacities and advantages to replace the aging ones that served it well in facilitating market entry. This leads to the additional question: *How may changes in competitive global dynamics impact the relationship between Japanese parent firms and their U.S. subsidiaries?*

METHODOLOGY

Our broad purpose is to explore how cultural and competitive dynamics may impact Japanese firms operating in the United States and how these effects evolve over time. To do this, we must rely on case material (Yin, 1994). The present research involves a longitudinal case study of Sanyo Electric, a Japanese firm that started U.S. manufacturing operations in 1977. To understand the context, we describe Sanyo's history before it established itself in the United States and then outline the specific issues Sanyo encountered as it attempted to cope with both U.S. cultural contexts and globally changing competitive conditions.

The processes Sanyo used to establish itself in the United States are necessarily unique, and this raises questions about the extent it is possible to generalize from them. While the specific events are unique to Sanyo, the underlying processes, priorities, and values used to manage them are not, and it is these that provide a basis for generalization (Tsoukas, 1989). The analytical task is to identify these underlying processes, priorities, and values that may have affected how Sanyo adapted, for they may have implications for other firms. The approach should enable us to tease out the multiplicity of factors that may have exerted influence, delineate linkages, and draw implications. A case study approach is well suited for this type of work (Kotha, 1998; Yin, 1994).

We chose Sanyo because it is an example of a firm based in a high-technology industry that had the support of many favorable conditions when it first entered the United States. The Japanese government had supported consumer electronics firms that, like Sanyo, had developed export capabilities to compete against U.S. manufacturers. Sanyo had also built up a mutually beneficial distribution relationship with Sears Corporation. When a government-managed marketing agreement limited television imports but placed no limits on Japanese firms manufacturing televisions in the United States, Sears helped Sanyo establish a manufacturing facility in the United States.

Despite these initially favorable conditions, questions linger about how long sources of competitive advantage will last in a globally competitive market. In the 1980s this became a concern for Sanyo and other industry participants as they faced severe competition that made it necessary to find new ways to compete. These later developments provided an opportunity for us to examine how Sanyo handled adversity. While flexibility is most often needed in times of adversity, differences in cultural values and management beliefs tend to reduce flexibility.

We were interested in how issues reflecting such differences might have arisen for Sanyo.

Data Collection

Following Campbell's (1975) dictum that multiple sources of inference about a phenomenon are analogous to degrees of freedom in statistics, we focused on multiple sources of data, including industry reports, business publications, and interviews. For data on Sanyo's operations in the United States, we identified approximately 40 newspaper and magazine articles in the Nexus/Lexus database that focused on the firm.[1] We drew on case studies of the firm (Hayes & Clark, 1981) and the TV industry (Choate, 1991; Dertouzos, Lester, & Solow, 1989; Porter, 1983). We also drew on a case describing the competitive situation faced by the Consumer Electronics Group of General Electric (Collis, 1988).

By phone, we interviewed Benny Goolsby of the International Union of Electrical Workers in Memphis, who briefed us about the union's relationship with Sanyo and provided material on his union's position in the various disputes. We also interviewed a reporter from the *Daily Times-Herald*, the newspaper in Forrest City, Arkansas that had covered Sanyo's TV manufacturing facility. He provided us with insights into why he thought Sanyo made certain decisions. Data from these different sources gave us a sense for what had happened at the Sanyo plant and the sorts of issues that had arisen. Together, these sources served as the basis for our case study of Sanyo's U.S. operations.

SANYO ELECTRIC CORPORATION

Sanyo Electric is a Japanese electronics firm headquartered in Osaka, Japan. Until the 1970s the firm had no manufacturing facilities in the United States. During the 1960s, however, it exported large numbers of TVs to the United States, to Sears, Roebuck & Co (Sears) in particular. At that time, Sears had a joint television production venture with Warwick Electronics, a subsidiary of the Whirlpool Corporation. It employed as many as 2,500 people in the venture's production facility located in Forrest City, Arkansas. The venture was 25 percent owned by Sears and served as a captive supplier of color TVs.

The Warwick facility found it difficult to meet the new quality and technology standards and the much more competitive prices when Japanese competition arrived in the mid-1960s. As customer returns increased, Sears became dissatisfied with Warwick and turned to Japanese producers to obtain TV sets. Four of the five assembly lines at the Warwick plant had been closed by the early-1970s, and employment had been cut to less than 400 people (Hayes & Clark 1981). Losses mounted to over $9 million in 1975 on sales of $71 million as demand ebbed and employee morale fell. An employee described the Warwick situation as follows (quoted in Hayes & Clark, 1981):

> This was really a desolate place.... People were continually being laid off, and the handwriting was on the wall for every one to see. There was no money, so we were letting equipment run down. We were having terrible quality problems and spending nights and weekends reworking sets so that we could keep up with our delivery schedules. The management group was working as hard as it could, and yet things kept getting worse. It was really demoralizing.

The TV Industry

In the 1950s U.S. television technology was state-of-the-art and U.S. manufacturers dominated world output. At the time, U.S. firms were buying cheap TV parts from Japanese partner firms and actively supported these firms in efforts to improve their ability to manufacture TV components (Dertouzos et al., 1989, p. 223). To increase the components the Japanese firms could make, the U.S. firms transferred their monochrome technology to these firms in the 1950s, and then their color technology in the 1960s. They did so because they anticipated that with these increased technology transfers, the range of components their partners could manufacture at low cost would increase still further. The goal from the standpoint of the U.S. manufacturers was to decrease costs (Porter, 1983).

In 1956 the fledgling Japanese television manufacturers formed the Home Electronic Appliance Market Stabilization Council. The council promoted Japanese TV producer growth and set minimum price levels for televisions designated for domestic sale. These minimum price levels guaranteed profit margins for televisions sold in Japan, while tariff and nontariff barriers effectively blocked foreign firms from entering this protected market. The Japanese firms used the resulting profits to invest in and improve the television-design knowledge transferred to them by U.S. firms.

In the early 1960s MITI decided to target the Japanese consumer electronics industry with governmental support to help it sell overseas. Supported by MITI, the Japanese firms worked to establish a product presence in the U.S. TV market. To coordinate their export efforts, they organized the Television Export Council in 1963. Their sources of competitive advantage at the time included superior technology, superior manufacturing processes, and high-quality products (Porter, 1983). They offered these superior TVs to importers like Sears and other retailers at prices well below those of U.S. producers.[2] By the late 1960s Japanese TVs were flooding into the United States and they quickly gained a dominant share of the U.S. market (Porter, 1983).

In 1968 the U.S. manufacturers requested protection from the U.S. government, alleging Japanese TV sets were being dumped in the United States.[3] Three years later the Treasury Department responded to these complaints and charged Japanese firms with dumping TVs.[4] By 1975 a minefield of proceedings and investigations faced Japanese firms (e.g., Hitachi, Mitsubishi, Sanyo, Sharp, and

Table 1. US Color TV Production by Japanese Firms

	1973	1974	1975	1976	1977	1978	1979
Sony	130	250	275	370	400	450	475
Matsushita	-	-	300	400	460	600	700
Sanyo	-	-	-	-	300	600	680
Toshiba	-	-	-	-	-	60	175
Mitsubishi	-	-	-	-	-	60	120
Hitachi	-	-	-	-	-	-	20
Sharp	-	-	-	-	-	-	100
	130	250	575	770	1160	1770	2270

Source: Porter, M. E. 1983. The U.S. Television Set Market, 1970-1979.

Toshiba). To represent them in resolving these cases, the Japanese firms hired Harald Malmgren, who had been the deputy special-trade representative for the Nixon and Ford administrations. In three months he worked out a compromise that became known as the Orderly Marketing Agreement (OMA). The Japanese would limit their television exports from Japan to the United States to 1.5 million units annually for three years. They would be permitted to use whatever manufacturing facilities they established in the United States to fill any demand that exceeded this quota. Many Japanese television makers quickly responded by establishing manufacturing facilities in the United States (see Table 1).

Sanyo Enters the United States

Sanyo had manufactured many of the TVs imported by Sears. Sears discussed with Sanyo the idea of providing technical help to its failing Warwick facility. Both were aware of the new import restrictions and Sanyo's consequent need for U.S. manufacturing facilities (Krisher, 1981). The discussions soon moved to the possibility that Sanyo might buy out Whirlpool's share of the Warwick venture. Sears arranged a buyout for $10.3 million and provided Sanyo with a loan arrangement to underwrite the purchase. A Sanyo Electric subsidiary, the Sanyo Manufacturing Company (SMC), was established on January 1, 1977 at Forrest City.

Forrest City is located in Northeast Arkansas, west of Memphis in the Mississippi cotton delta.[5] The city population is stable at 15,000 residents with around 50 percent white and 50 percent black. Around a third of the city population are illiterate, 30 percent are on welfare, incomes are generally low, and unemployment has hovered for many years around 20 percent.[6]

Sanyo was welcomed to Forrest City. People were afraid that the town's main employer, Warwick, would disappear, as had in fact been gradually happening. To manage the facility, SMC sent 26 managers and technicians from Japan. They were instructed to live throughout the city and to do, eat, play, and go to school just as the Americans did. It appears that all of these men knew the technology and business practices of Sanyo Electric, their parent corporation, very well. It is not clear whether they had considered or even knew much about what it might be like to live in a cultural and social environment like Forrest City.

Mr. Satoshi Iue from Osaka was SMC's president. He managed relations between the SMC subsidiary and Sanyo's Headquarters in Osaka. Mr. Tanemichi Sohma, a Japanese national, was appointed Vice President for Administration and Personnel and put in charge of day-to-day plant operations. He had attended the University of Southern California in the 1950s, and his English language ability was better than most of his colleagues. He managed the relations between the Japanese managers and local employees and between the plant and the local community. Five of the new top SMC executives, including Sohma, came from Japan. The other four SMC executives were Americans inherited from Warwick's previous management group. The Japanese managers and technicians supervised operations at different levels and throughout the plant.

Establishing Control and Commitment

Sohma wanted to build a cooperative relationship between plant workers and management, and he launched many initiatives within SMC to make good relations a reality. The new management also sought to win the trust and confidence of Forrest City's citizens. To announce their arrival, Sanyo invited everyone in Forrest City to a welcome party. They quickly cleaned, painted, and renovated the run-down plant. When they needed new hires, they specifically sought to rehire workers who had previously worked for Warwick and had been laid off.

Quality Emphasis

SMC imported many of its transistor components from Japan to Forrest City where the workers assembled them into TVs. Within the plant, SMC's new management consistently emphasized that their primary concern was improved product quality. According to a worker at the factory (Hayes & Clark, 1981, p. 3):

> The first thing Sanyo did when they took over [was that] they retained essentially all employees and managers who were there.... They did move some people around, though. For example, they took the former manager of Quality Control—who really had been taking a lot of heat from everybody during the previous two years, because of the quality problems we were having—and made him the plant manager. That, by the way, was just one of the signals they gave that the number-one priority for the plant was improving quality. All they talked about was quality.

In pursuing quality, many of the Japanese managers and technicians spent their time standing very close to the employees, watching what they did, correcting them, and providing training. The managers thought this was necessary. Some workers reported that at times they thought this behavior was amusing, and most found the Japanese to be very fussy always wanting everything done exactly the particular way that they thought was right. The workers were well aware of how the Japanese had installed quality checks everywhere. They admitted, however, that the Japanese approach had vastly improved product quality.

Building a Happy Family

More than 60 percent of the workers at the SMC plant were black, and the International Union of Electrical Workers (IUE) organized these hourly workers. Sohma met with the union and explained that the company wanted to build a partnership with them. He emphasized Sanyo's intent to improve quality. To help achieve this goal, he asked the union to discuss production policies, methods, and goals with management, and to join management in implementing a start-to-finish quality program that would guarantee no defective TV would ever leave the plant. Initially, the union was pleasantly shocked at this approach but also somewhat at a loss to know how to respond. They had difficulty because they recalled how Warwick's management had always insisted production policies were management's prerogative. Workers had learned to close their eyes carefully to the many defective TVs leaving the plant. They saw the new approach as a big and positive change.

The work style that developed at SMC was noisy, busy, and casual. Believing little things counted, Sohma and his managers tried to notice and respond to anything and everything that could cause employees discomfort. Whenever they could, they remedied the matter immediately. In turn, they expected the workers to correct anything they noticed was wrong on the assembly line and also to do this immediately. Managers tried to be sensitive to both manufacturing requirements and workers' needs. When equipment was lacking, it was immediately purchased. When workers made mistakes, they were immediately counseled rather than discharged. In the first year, "Sanyo set out to create a 'big happy family' atmosphere to enhance morale" (Reid, 1977).

Firm loyalty was also very important to Sohma, the Japanese managers, and SMC. Sohma recognized how some of Warwick's established labor practices destroyed rather than encouraged loyalty. It had been Warwick's custom, for example, to let people go immediately after the Christmas production season. Sohma pledged to the union that Sanyo would seek to smooth production to phase out the need for repeated layoffs and recalls. Local employees were impressed by this commitment. They saw it as demonstrating a cooperative attitude toward workers and a willingness to use power and authority to change things in ways that benefited everyone.

Yet while Sohma consistently preached mutuality and shared responsibility for the production process, he did not give up the hierarchical power or the privileges that he and the other SMC executives enjoyed.[7] The authority accorded Japanese managers and technicians always distinguished them from the rest of the plant workforce. Sanyo also made little effort to modify other labor practices inherited from Warwick. For example, practices associated with Japanese firms such as lifetime employment or seniority-based pay systems were not introduced.

Operating Management

To facilitate sharing the management process, a management supervisory committee was appointed, including three managers from the United States and three from Japan. Decision making within this committee turned out to be slow and difficult. The U.S. managers thought the Japanese managers alluded to or implied what they wanted rather than giving explicit instructions. Not sensitive to the subtle cues offered by the Japanese managers, they would wait for instructions not realizing that these had already been given. This frustrated all sides. The difficulties were never resolved, and the committee was eventually abandoned. There were similar difficulties with attempts to introduce quality circles and other teamwork practices, and Sanyo managers eventually abandoned these efforts.

Building Control and Commitment

The 1979 Strike

Though Sohma seemed to be the person in charge at Forrest City, many decisions had to be referred back to headquarters in Japan for approval. This requirement could cause delays and misunderstandings, in part because many Japanese executives at Sanyo Electric's headquarters were not familiar with business life in the United States.

This became an issue in 1979 when a union strike lasting eight weeks was called. The strike was concerned with cost-of-living increases that had been promised but never implemented by the previous Warwick management. The union considered these increases a commitment that had been won and hence kept. SMC's local management thought that given the many contributions they had made to improve the workers lot in Forrest City, the union should not be holding Sanyo responsible for agreements made with Warwick. Both sides needed a clearer understanding of the expectations each had for the other. As the strike entered its third week, headquarters management in Osaka became worried, suspecting something was terribly wrong in Forrest City.[8] Reasoning based on their Japanese experience that such a long strike must mean Sohma had gravely offended the workers, they directed him to call his workforce together, humble himself before them, and apologize for the terrible things he had done. In touch with the realities of the local situation, Sohma refused. His Osaka bosses did not understand these realities, and they rebuked Sohma, believing he had become too Americanized and was proving untrustworthy. Eventually, Sohma was able to resolve the issues amicably. SMC also entered into a new five-year contract with Sears commencing in 1980.[9]

Sanyo imported the major components for its U.S. models, allowing Osaka to leverage its home-country scale advantages. The managers' job at Forrest City was to persuade workers to increase their production rate so this facility could also achieve the cost advantages associated with high volume. The Japanese managers were well aware, for example, that Sanyo's plants back in Osaka achieved the same quality as Forrest City but were 25 percent more efficient. Forrest City needed to achieve these standards for Osaka to effectively implement its global strategy based on volume and low costs.

This meant continuing pressures to reduce costs. It also meant that SMC management could not always keep the well-intentioned promises it had made to workers. According to Mr. Nakai, a Japanese manager for SMC (Krisher, 1981):

> Given different American conditions, we haven't been totally able to transplant the Japanese way to America. There are good periods and also slow periods, with heavy sales focused on November and December for the Christmas season. We've naturally had to adjust our production schedule and lay off some workers, as do other American manufacturers.

In discussing the emerging differences between Japanese managers and U.S. workers, Mr. Nakai said (Krisher, 1981):

> American workers maintain a much looser relationship toward their company compared with the Japanese.... However, we learned some lessons from that [1979 strike] and are now trying to improve the situation. In Japan, the union lives with the company and never pulls the trigger unless it finds itself in an extremely serious situation. It tries as much as possible to work with us on the same ground, because its members' future and prosperity are directly linked to ours. The important question for us right now is how to instill this concept in our American workers.

For their part, the U.S. workers had seen the vast improvements in quality, efficiency, and volume achieved at the plant since the takeover by Sanyo. The continual pressure for production improvements was gradually generating doubts about whether the Japanese managers would ever be satisfied.

As production rates were increased as much as tenfold and workforce numbers were increased only threefold, Sanyo increased its commitment to the facility. One step was to add microwave ovens to the product mix. By 1981 the plant employed 1,750 workers making televisions, 350 working in a furniture shop, and 250 making microwave ovens. Sanyo invested in total around $60 million in the Forest City plant.

As well as increasing its commitment by working with local suppliers, Sanyo worked with local political leaders to attract additional Japanese investment to the area. In 1981, for example, Sanyo helped orchestrate a Far East tour by Arkansas Governor White to persuade Asian firms to establish plants in the area. Responding to Sanyo's recommendations, several Japanese and Far East firms located manufacturing and servicing facilities around Memphis and in the North East Arkansas area. In 1982 the union contract was successfully renegotiated without further incident.

Losing Control and Commitment

Competition Intensifies

In 1984 production capacity in the United States was 13.1 million TV sets while actual production was 11.5 million sets, around 89 percent of capacity. But TV

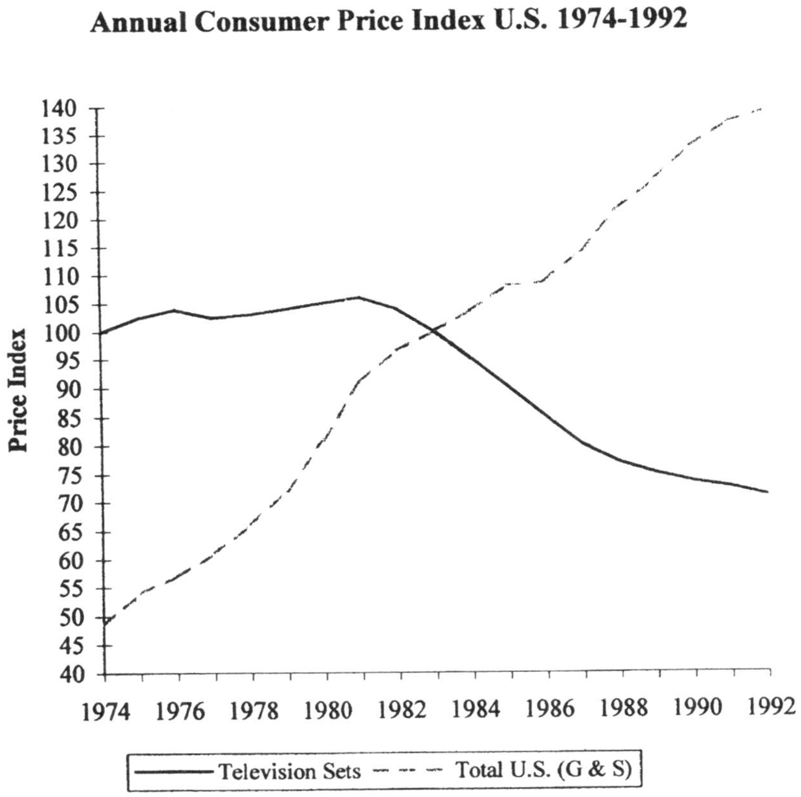

Source: Based on figures provided in The U.S. Consumer Electronics Industry in Review—1993 edition.

Figure 1. Television Set Prices versus Total Sales of All Goods and Services 1974-1992

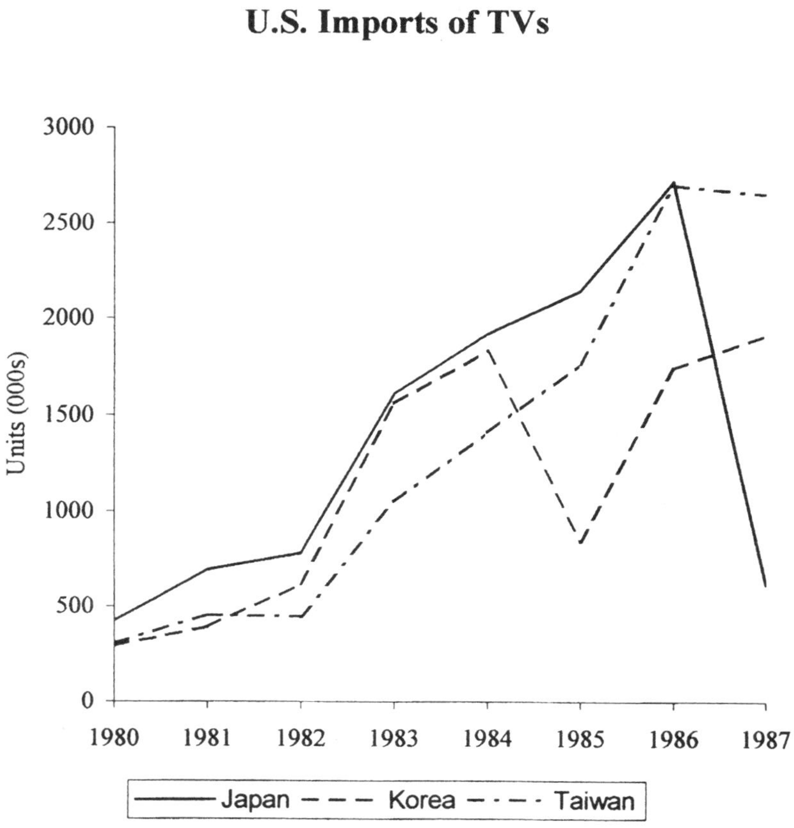

Source: Based on figures provided in Collis (1988).

Figure 2. Imported Television sets: Japan versus Korea and Taiwan 1980-1987

manufacturers from South Korea and other Asian countries were about to enter the U.S. market. They offered products of comparable quality to the Japanese televisions, but lower price. The timing of their entry also coincided with efforts by Japanese firms to expand their production capacity. At the time, however, demand for televisions was actually leveling off. With slowing demand and growing over capacity, firms started to employ price-cutting strategies to increase market share. SMC found itself less protected and facing more market challenges than it had ever experienced since coming to the United States. Forced to lower prices, managers now felt greatly increased pressure to improve their efficiency. Like most industry participants at the time, Sanyo had moved from a position where it had been making profits to a new position where it was forced to sustain losses.

Two years later U.S. industry production capacity had grown by 50 percent and was more than 17 million TV sets. This reflected the large capacity expansions undertaken by Japanese firms producing in the United States and new entrants coming from Korea and Taiwan. In contrast, actual television production had dropped to 11.2 million sets or just 66 percent of the expanded capacity. A shake out was about to occur among the 20 or so firms producing televisions in the United States (Porter, 1983) (see Figures 1 and 2).[10]

The 1985 Strike

Observing these changing competitive conditions, SMC had to renegotiate with its labor union in 1985. Knowing the competitive pressures it faced, Sanyo pressed the union to relax its rules relating to seniority rights and worker flexibility. They also proposed reductions in medical benefits and insurance costs. But the union resisted. Wilford W. Banks Jr., president of local 1106 of the IUE, was convinced that Sanyo just wanted more production and didn't want to have to pay for the extra effort. The atmosphere became bitter and for a short time, it was also violent (Byrne, 1988):

> The demands [of Japanese management] sparked a 21-day strike. Pickets carried signs that read: "Japs go home" and "Remember Pearl Harbor." Windows were broken, guns were fired, a car was overturned, and at one point the plant was nearly overrun by strikers.

Police arrested the picketers, and they hit the strikers. Eventually, a new 42-month contract ended the strike, but the union and the firm felt the strike had left a bitter legacy.

By 1986 SMC employed 1,700 people who produced 1.2 million TV sets and 500,000 microwave ovens. SMC was the largest Japanese TV producer in the United States with annual sales of $40 million. Yet due to increased competition reflecting industry overcapacity and price competition, the firm also lost $14 million. SMC asked the union to accept a 20 percent wage cut as a sign of solidarity and loyalty to the firm. In response the union agreed to forgo a 3 percent wage increase along with cost-of-living increases and to allow SMC some flexibility in reassigning employees.[11] After most of its requests had been rejected, SMC began examining other ways to achieve cost reductions and reestablish cost competitiveness. With continuing industry overcapacity, intense competition, and sinking prices, Sanyo headquarters in Osaka considered whether it should keep the Forrest City facility open. Given competitive pressures and the union's intransigence, it seemed imperative to relocate production to where it would be possible to reduce costs to compete successfully. According to Darrell Carter, VP for operations (Risen, 1988):

> All the Japanese consumer electronics companies [with plants in the United States] are being faced with difficult decisions on job security.... They can't compete with imports from Korea and Taiwan, and so they are setting up feeder plants in Mexico, building parts and products they used to make in the U.S.

Sanyo decided to scale back its operations in Forrest City drastically and shift its labor-intensive production to a Maquiladora in Tijuana, Mexico where the labor costs were about an eighth of those in Arkansas. According to Annette Bradley, a worker at SMC (Risen, 1988):

> I don't know if it was bad management, or bad parts, but I know one thing was they could get cheaper labor in Mexico.... I feel bad. They're taking jobs from the U.S. to Mexico because of cheaper labor, and it hurts the States and it hurts the people. I know they're human, they're out to make a dollar just like the rest of us are, but it's just that it would have been better if they would have just tried to work a little bit more with us, instead of just ship everything out.

Employment dropped from 1,200 in 1986 to 650 in 1988 including just 190 hourly workers. Sanyo may well have intended to withdraw from Arkansas completely, but Governor Bill Clinton made a successful appeal to Sanyo Electric's chairman in Osaka (*Economist*, 1993).[12]

Locally, Sanyo Japanese management had become increasingly frustrated with the "way of thinking" of American workers. Sanyo had faced fierce competition for years and had attempted to work with the union, improve product quality, and build workforce loyalty and commitment. The Sanyo managers were therefore frustrated that at a time of obvious firm need, there was no corresponding readiness on workers' part to make any sacrifice whatsoever on behalf of SMC.

DISCUSSION AND IMPLICATIONS

The way Sanyo entered the United States, the actions it took to establish good relations with its workforce, and the processes that then led to labor-management conflict at a critical juncture are worthy of discussion. The case illustrates how Sanyo's initial competitive advantage drawn from its parent and its trading relationships was eroded as its superior organizing principles and technological capabilities diffused to competitors in the United States and other parts of the world. It also illustrates how cultural and competitive dynamics interact and co-evolve to create new and unanticipated issues for a Japanese firm adapting to the U.S. environment.

Cultural Dynamics

Sanyo's Entry Process

Sanyo's impetus for establishing U.S. facilities can be traced to the Orderly Marketing Agreement of 1976 that effectively limited Japanese television exports. The agreement meant that if Japanese firms were to maintain their sales they had to produce their televisions in the United States. Sanyo implemented its entry into the United States strongly influenced by its established relationship with Sears.

Sears' actions reflect U.S. and not Japanese institutional and cultural norms. From Sears' point of view, its agreements with Sanyo reflected efforts to secure control and power over a committed and reliable supplier of a critical good (Porter, 1983). The Orderly Marketing Agreement threatened this relationship, and Sears wished to ensure a steady supply of high-quality TVs for its stores. Therefore, it encouraged Whirlpool to relinquish control of the Warwick facility to Sanyo and then guaranteed to buy a significant portion of Sanyo's television output from the Forrest City plant. These generous terms encouraged Sanyo to export its organizing methods and technologies directly from Osaka to Forrest City. It did this following the location and sales path presented to it by Sears.

Sears may be an unusual partner for Sanyo to follow because many of Sears' behaviors are in stark contrast to the institutional norms and culturally sanctioned behaviors Sanyo would expect from Japanese firms. A joint venture partnership (with Whirlpool) would certainly not have been thrown aside so easily in Japan. If a Japanese industry were threatened by foreign competition, government agencies would have held discussions with firms to assess how the consumer benefits of higher quality and cheaper TVs, for example, should be weighed against the national cost of losing an entire manufacturing industry. The fact that the basic technology had been created and developed by the firms now being forced to leave the industry would also have been discussed, and it would have been argued that this contribution justified a case for special consideration and support. Japanese post-World War economic history suggests a consistent preference for decisions that preserve industries as opposed to those that protect and favor consumer benefits (Fallows, 1994).

How Did Sanyo Establish Control and Commitment at the Warwick Facility?

The changes undertaken by Sanyo after its entry into the United States suggest that it sought to upgrade its Forrest City facility by directly transferring and imposing the parent company's technology and organizing practices on to its new subsidiary. Initially Sanyo focused on changing plant conditions and worker behaviors to improve TV quality and reliability. To staff the plant, Sanyo did not hesitate to employ members of the unionized workforce of the previous owner. In fact, they even went further, rehiring workers the previous owner had laid off. This policy is consistent with Brannen's (1995) observations that many Japanese top managers have great faith in plant workers. They believe that if these people are shown appropriate respect, they willingly work hard, cooperate, and produce. This new attitude was also in strong contrast to the Whirlpool approach that had shown little respect for workers while emphasizing volume and ignoring quality. The workers in Forrest City liked the contrasting approach introduced by Sanyo.

The Japanese changes were intended to institutionalize a different approach to work. While the initial focus placed an emphasis on quality, this was to be just the beginning. The approach was expected to extend to an emphasis on quantity and culminate in processes directed toward continuous improvement. Sohma was the interface between the Japanese managers, the American workers, and the union, and so his role in the change effort was critical. Through his efforts, Sanyo effectively communicated its changed approach and won support from the labor force. It is likely that the historic unemployment in Forrest City and the low employee morale associated with Warwick's final days gave Sanyo management more power and also made the union more cooperative to management's initial requests (Beechler & Yang, 1994).

How Did Sanyo Lose Control and Commitment of Its Workforce?

As their initial concerns about their jobs faded and the improved output quality became accepted as normal, workers became more aware of how relentlessly the Japanese managers pursued increased efficiency. In work areas the managers were never satisfied and always wanted improvements. U.S. workers noted that while the Japanese de-emphasized status distinctions to improve work performance, they claimed special privileges in other areas. Yet they also expected the same organizational loyalty and sacrifice from workers as well as managers. The union felt that the Japanese did not appreciate how the combination of unrelenting pressures for work improvements, obvious privileges reserved for supervisors, and demands that everyone should be equally loyal to Sanyo were perceived as inconsistent conditions.

This state of affairs seems similar to the "bicultural alienation" discussed by Brannen and Sanyal (1993). The items in their "bicultural alienation scale" examine apparently positive aspects of supervisory behavior. These include the following assessments: supervisors seeking input from workers, workers feeling like valued group members, suggestions being valued, Japanese and Americans placing a similar value on hard work, and workers' participation and contributions at group meetings being valued. Yet Brannen and Sanyal (1993) found that as Japanese managers exert pressures for continual improvement and also emphasize their own privileged status, U.S. workers associate the scale behaviors with exploitation and new tricks to get more for less out of workers.

Such perceptions may be particularly likely in the United States where, unlike in Japan, the legal environment sanctions a competitive relationship between management and unions. In addition, people with individualistic values like U.S. workers may not respond well to organizational pressures for additional improvement unless they are provided with incentives that assure them additional individual (mostly financial) rewards. Given the increasingly competitive situation that

Sanyo's managers found themselves in and their expectations of employee loyalty, however, they did not consider offering further financial incentives. In fact, they asked for wage cuts. They reasoned that if the Forrest City workers were loyal to Sanyo, as the Japanese managers believed they should be, they would make needed extra efforts without need of further reward. But as Brannen and Sanyal (1993) note, if U.S. workers perceive themselves to be subject to continual and unfair pressure, they can become alienated rather than loyal.

When this culminated in a strike, many of Sanyo's Japanese managers were no longer optimistic about their ability to motivate U.S. workers. They reverted to negative stereotypes. As summarized by Brannen (1995), these stereotypes include beliefs that Americans "only think of themselves," and "only do things for money." The result can become a mutually negative cycle involving negative stereotyping on the one hand, and alienation and noncooperation on the other. This seems to be what eventually led to an embittered relationship between the union and SMC management after the second strike. Subject to direct market pressures and confronted with striking workers expressing no firm loyalty, Sanyo's managers became more self-centered and abandoned the idea and their ideal of "family" and community building.

Competitive Dynamics

Another area of interest is the way the competitive dynamics of the global television industry evolved and how this affected Warwick facility's competitive advantage. In 1977 Japanese electronic manufacturers had competitive advantages over U.S. firms based on their superior technology, superior manufacturing processes, higher-quality products, and prices that were significantly lower than those of U.S. manufacturers (Porter, 1983). But so far as Sanyo was concerned, industry competitive dynamics were not particularly significant at the time it entered the United States. With its superior product technology and demand guaranteed by Sears, SMC was initially buffered from the competitive dynamics of the U.S. industry.

This protection did not last, however. As the 1980s moved forward, the competitive pressures that plagued television manufacturers in particular, and electronic goods manufacturers in general, led to important changes. Increasingly, industry attention focused on financial returns enhanced by identifying those components that "added value" and could be priced to generate profits. The industry, including Sanyo, organized itself increasingly around component production. Components that required high skill and added high value were built most often in developed countries like Japan. Simpler, more standardized, or assembly line tasks were done in locations where labor costs were low such as Mexico and low-cost Asian countries. From a financial standpoint, these developments raised questions about the desirability of maintaining the SMC assembly plant in Arkansas.

Given this new competitive situation with new suppliers ready to offer the same quality but at lower prices than Sanyo (*Economist*, 1993), Sears was ready to abandon SMC in the same way it had abandoned its U.S. suppliers two decades earlier. This was a significant threat to SMC since Sears took 70 percent of its total output. With industry competition growing and price cuts the norm, Sears was no longer a reliable or a patient partner. Forced to lower prices, Sanyo managers felt enormous pressure to secure cost reductions and improve efficiency. They passed on this pressure directly to the workforce, but the U.S. workforce did not have the loyalty that Sanyo might have been able to count on from its Japanese employees in times of organizational need. The U.S. workers would not tolerate any increased managerial pressure, and in Forrest City, most didn't care about global competitive dynamics.

Building Competitive Advantage

Facing new competitive pressures, Sanyo needed to find new sources of competitive advantage. Taylor, Beechler, and Napier (1996) argue that a firm can use three generic orientations to build competitive advantage in a foreign country. When it entered the United States, Sanyo adopted an "exporting" approach, establishing the firm's competitive advantage through parent technology and organizing practices. A theoretical alternative is an "adaptive" approach where a firm imitates the local practices. This didn't make sense for Sanyo in 1977 because its technology and manufacturing practices were superior to those of U.S. firms. The third alternative is an "integrative" approach where a firm identifies the best ideas in its separate locations and then develops and builds its own unique integrative approach. This third approach was ultimately needed in Forrest City if SMC was to develop U.S.-based sources of competitive advantage.

Our analysis of Sanyo indicates that the three alternatives may not always be clear to managers, and in practice, the appropriate choice probably changes in response to competitive conditions (Beechler & Yang, 1994). In Sanyo's case, its exporting approach initially made sense. Later, however, Sanyo's increasing difficulties in implementing its Osaka practices in Forrest City and the mounting competitive pressures signaled that the firm's initial sources of competitive advantage might be eroding. Some form of integration accommodating the different values and priorities of the Japanese and U.S. workforces probably needed to be considered. Yet Sanyo management does not seem to have recognized the context-specific nature of some of the practices it attempted to transfer and did not take steps to explore the implications when they failed to transfer. Instead, Sanyo management simply abandoned elements that didn't transfer and sought no replacement for the functions performed by these abandoned elements. As the original sources of competitive advantage Sanyo brought to Forrest City eroded over time, the firm became increasingly vulnerable. The resource that Sanyo seems to have assumed it could rely on was employee loyalty. But when firm managers called for firm loyalty, none was there.

A comparison of Sanyo with NUMMI may be useful. Both firms took over an established U.S. plant and workforce and worked with American unions. Adler (1993) notes that success at NUMMI was due to two important factors. One aspect is the emphasis on standardized practices; both Sanyo and NUMMI plants shared this characteristic. Additionally, Adler (1993) reports that NUMMI established a social context committed to continuous improvement. Sanyo wanted this too, but failed to implement it. Perhaps the status differences and privileges that remained in Forrest City but were eliminated at NUMMI were symbolically important enough in an American context to sabotage implementing a continuous improvement culture. In addition, training programs explaining the continual improvement programs were reportedly extensive at NUMMI, while they were absent at Sanyo.

Implications

The Sanyo case highlights issues that come up when a Japanese firm enters the United States. Adaptation in a foreign setting involves understanding and responding to both cultural and competitive dynamics. The Sanyo case suggests how these conditions co-evolve, interact, and change over time. More generally, cross-cultural research needs to explore "phenomenon in the making" to understand how adaptation in a foreign setting evolves. A more qualitative approach enables researchers to emphasize the impact of the foreign setting and the process by which a firm socially constructs its evolving world in this context.

Our analysis suggests that partner relationships are sensitive to and change in response to competitive pressures. U.S. partner commitments may be focused on the short term and what is currently convenient. Also, the U.S. personnel who originally negotiated such deals are less likely to be with their firm when times change. Japanese partners are, in addition to short-term commitments, concerned about loyalty and longer-term issues. These contrasting perspectives can lead to misunderstandings at times of growing competitive pressure when worker sacrifices and loyalty might help a firm survive, but these expectations are simply not part of a short-term view. Therefore the success of foreign alliances with U.S. firms is affected by changing competitive dynamics (i.e., the speed at which foreign superior practices and technology diffuse in the United States) and other societal-level factors (cf. Cheng, 1994). This suggests the following proposition:

Proposition 1. The success of alliances is affected by how the respective parties interpret the short-term and long-term consequences of changing competitive and social dynamics.

Our analysis of Sanyo's U.S. operations indicates that U.S. workers welcome worker participation in the production process. They may perceive unfairness, however, if there are continual pressures for improvement and management receives obvious privileges the workforce does not enjoy. Such inconsistencies may sabotage efforts to establish a continuous improvement culture. In addition since a continuous improvement culture is not the norm in U.S. unionized firms, implementing it may require support from an extensive training program. Learning from the experiences of other ventures such as NUMMI can help Japanese managers put in place mechanisms to make continuous improvements efforts successful (Adler, 1993).

Proposition 2. Japanese firms that adopt work practices accounting for both plant- and societal-level factors are more likely to succeed in sustaining the commitment of their U.S. workforce.

More generally, managers going abroad make decisions that balance a reliance on what they know from their home country with what they learn, and must adapt to, in the new country. This is an area of cross-cultural research which seems critical to practitioners (cf. Taylor, 1991). We suspect that firms from different countries use different approaches reflecting their cultural origins in successfully transferring home country practices to a foreign setting. We also suspect they differ in the extent to which they adapt the home country practices to the local environment. The parameters that influence these decisions are an important area for future research.

We also found that the changing nature of competitive dynamics affects firm competitive advantages. The Sanyo case indicates that while parent-based competitive advantage was needed to enter the U.S. market, it eroded over time. If a firm is in a foreign country for some time, it will probably need to develop a more integrated base of competitive advantage that draws in ideas from both the local facility and the parent. In other words, successful adaptation in a foreign setting involves understanding and responding to both the cultural *and* competitive dynamics.

Proposition 3. Foreign firms that explicitly develop an integrated base of competitive advantage drawing on local conditions are likely to be more successful than firms that only emphasize transferring parent-based competitive advantage.

We suspect that firms from different countries use different approaches reflecting their cultural origins in deciding the extent to which to invest efforts in developing an integrated base of competitive advantage. These bases will include a combination of social and technical factors and are likely to vary across industry. While initially, Sanyo's human resources practices were appealing to its U.S.

workforce, later events uncovered difficulties in adaptation that probably made an integrated base of competitive advantage impossible to achieve for this firm. As Sanyo's experience is limited to the consumer electronics industry, it is hard to generalize to other industries. Other firm case studies will probably be necessary to identify how an integrated base of competitive advantage can be developed in other industries.

CONCLUSIONS

Sanyo is an example of a Japanese firm that imposed Japanese ways of doing things when it established its facilities in the United States and then assessed the ongoing developments based on Japanese values. Though the Sanyo managers had great confidence in their methods and values and succeeded in bringing about many important improvements supported by their U.S. workforce, eventually these efforts reached an upper bound. The Japanese managers had difficulty accepting this state of affairs, for their corporate strategy was based on expansion and the lowering of production costs. But Sanyo's continual push for improvement led to worker alienation, strikes, and rejection right at the time that continued strategic success for Sanyo required worker loyalty, commitment, and sacrifice. The Sanyo case illustrates that foreign firms competing in the United States should not underestimate the importance of cultural and competitive dynamics and how these co-evolve over time in unmanaged ways. These dynamics, generally not apparent at entry, can and do play an important role as a firm adapts in a foreign setting.

ACKNOWLEDGMENTS

Authors are listed alphabetically. We thank Allan Bird, Anil Nair, Myles Shaver, and D. Eleanor Westney for their helpful comments on the earlier versions of this paper.

NOTES

1. We also contacted Mr. Naoki Nakamura, president of Sanyo's operations in the United States. He responded to our request in a gracious manner but noted, "because of some past incidents that have occurred it would be in our best interests that you choose another Japanese company." We informed him that while we were disappointed in his unwillingness to partake in the study, we intended to continue with our focus on Sanyo Electric's U.S. operations.

2. The Japanese firms not only offered TVs to importers at prices U.S. manufacturers believed were below cost, in addition, they offered rebates of up to $40 per set and additional payments for "market research." While these Japanese tactics appalled U.S. manufacturers, U.S. importers liked them and willingly agreed to import Japanese TVs.

3. In 1951 there were over 90 U.S.-owned firms that manufactured TVs. By 1968, 28 firms manufactured TVs. By 1976 only six U.S.-owned firms remained. As a result of the Japanese imports, U.S.

employment in television production dropped 50 percent between 1966 and 1970, another 30 percent between 1971 and 1975, and a further 25 percent between 1977 and 1981.

4. This finding meant that anti-dumping levies could be collected from firms to offset the advantage they had gained. The calculation of such levies required accurate information from the Japanese firms, however, and they would not provide this data. Although it was possible to impute the figures, to do so would have invited retaliation and a trade war.

5. General Nathan Bedford Forrest, a flamboyant hero of the confederate cavalry, founded Forrest City in 1866. General Forrest is remembered for several reasons. During the Civil War he is reputed to have had approximately 20 horses shot out from under him. After the war, he settled in Forrest City, where he became the first grand wizard of the Ku Klux Klan (KKK). He later resigned as the KKK became too violent for him.

6. The media has periodically highlighted the racial tensions that have historically pervaded Forrest City and the surrounding county. Court-ordered school integration directly impacted the area in 1965. In 1969, for example, students at a black high school rioted after a favorite teacher was fired for "insubordination." A private school, Forrest City Academy, was founded in the 1970s for whites only. Its closure in the 1980s reflected the greater tolerance characteristic of more recent times. In 1988 the Forrest City High School held its first integrated prom. The media watching closely not only reported no incidents but pronounced it an outstanding success.

7. As an example, Sohma explained to the union that Japanese managers found it repulsive when workers smoked on the production line. With union cooperation he phased out smoking among line workers. Some Japanese executives reasoned that because they were not workers on the line, this agreement did not apply to them and they continued to smoke in the plant. They also claimed special parking privileges and other perks. In this way Sohma supported distinctions and privileges accorded to Japanese managers but not to workers.

8. Strikes in Japan are usually symbolic expressions of a breakdown in relations between management and workers. Having effectively signaled their concerns by wearing armbands and working even harder than usual, for example, workers most often then call off their strike.

9. Under the terms of the contract, Sears "agreed to purchase at least 70% of its annual requirements of color televisions receivers for sale in the United States from SMC.... During 1980 about 82% of the company's production went to Sears; the remainder was sold through SMC's parent company" (Hayes & Clark, 1981, p. 3).

10. Most of the firms producing in the United States were foreign-owned. Many were Japanese subsidiaries but several were more recently established subsidiaries of Korean and Taiwanese multinationals. The Korean and Taiwanese firms were prepared to compete just as fiercely on quality and price criteria as the Japanese had done two decades earlier.

11. The union had asked its auditor to check SMC's books and assess whether a request to cut wages by 20 percent was justified. The auditor's perspective was in terms of Sanyo's relative labor costs and not in terms of Osaka's need to establish a strategic advantage through cost competitiveness. When he reported Sanyo's problems were not located in its relative labor costs, the union rejected SMC's request.

12. The *Economist* noted (1993, p. A29): "Some say that Sanyo did not pull out altogether only because Mr. Clinton, on a trip to Japan, appealed to Sanyo's chairman in person to save the plant. He intervened again when Sears cut back on its Sanyo orders, arranging a new retailing deal with Wal-Mart chain (which is based in Arkansas)."

REFERENCES

Abegglen, J. C., & Stalk, G. (1985). *Kaisha.* Basic Books, New York.

Adler, P. S. (1993, January-February). Time and motion regained. *Harvard Business Review*, 97-109.

Aoki, M. (1990). Towards an economic model of the Japanese firm. *Journal of Economic Literature, 28*, 1-27.

Beechler, S., & Yang, J. Z. (1994). The transfer of Japanese-style management to American subsidiaries: Contingencies, constraints and competencies. *Journal of International Business Studies, 25* (3), 467-79.

Brannen, M. Y. (1995). Does culture matter? Negotiating a complementary culture to support technological innovation. In J. K. Liker, J. E. Ettlie, & J. C. Campbell (Eds.), *Engineered in Japan.* New York: Oxford University Press.

Brannen, M. Y., & Sanyal, A. (1993). Bicultural alienation in Japanese-Owned companies: A preliminary study in scale development. Paper presented at the *Academy of International Management Meetings*, October 20-24, Maui, Hawaii.

Brown, C., & Reich, M. (1989, Summer). When does union Management cooperation Work? A look at NUMMI and GM-Van Nuys. *California Management Review*, 26-41.

Buckley, P. J., & Casson, M.C. (1976). *The future of the multinational enterprise.* London: MacMillan.

Byrne, J. A. (1988, July 14). At Sanyo's Arkansas plant the magic isn't working. *Business Week.*

Campbell, D. (1975). "Degrees of freedom" and the case study. *Comparative Political Studies, 8* (2), 178-193.

Caves, R. (1982). *Multinational enterprise and economic analysis.* New York: Cambridge University Press.

Chang, S. J. (1995). International expansion strategy of Japanese firms: Capability building through sequential entry. *Academy of Management Journal, 38* (2). 383-407.

Cheng, J. L. C. (1994). On the concept of universal knowledge in organizational science: Implications for cross-national research. *Management Science, 40* (1), 162-168.

Choate, P. (1991, September 30). Japan and the big squeeze. *The Washington Post*, p. D1.

Cole, R. E., & Deskins, D. R., Jr. (1988, Fall). Racial factors in site location and employment patterns, *California Management Review.*

Collis, D. J. (1988). General Electric—Consumer electronics group. *Harvard Business School case # 389-048.* Boston, MA: Harvard Business School Press.

Dertouzos, M. L., Lester, R. K., & Solow, R. M. (1989). *Made in America: Regaining the Productive Edge.* Cambridge, MA: MIT Press.

Economist (1993, March 6). The limits of success: East Arkansas: American survey, A29+.

Fallows, J. (1994). *Looking at the sun: The rise of the new East Asian economic and political system.* New York: Pantheon.

Hayes, R., & Clark, K. (1981). Sanyo Manufacturing Corporation—Forrest City, Arkansas. *Harvard Business School Case # 9-682-045.* Boston, MA: Harvard Business School Press.

Hennart, J. F., & Park, Y. (1994). Location, governance, and strategic determinants of Japanese manufacturing investment in the United States. *Strategic Management Journal, 15*, 419-436.

Hymer, S. H. (1976). *The international operations of national firms: A study of direct investment.* Cambridge, MA: MIT Press.

Kagono, T., Sakakibara, K., Nonaka, I., & Okumura, A. (1985). *Strategic Vs. Evolutionary Management: A U.S.-Japan Comparison of Strategy and Organization.* Amsterdam: North-Holland.

Kogut, B. (1991). Country capabilities and the permeability of borders. *Strategic Management Journal, 12*, 33-47.

Kogut, B., & Singh, H. (1988). The effect of national culture on the choice of entry mode. *Journal of International Business Studies, 19*, 411-432.

Kotha, S. (1998). Competing on the Internet: How Amazon.com is rewriting the rules of competition. *Advances in Strategic Management, 15*, 239-265.

Kotha, S., Dunbar R. L. M., & Bird, A. (1995). Strategic action generation: A comparison of emphasis placed on generic competitive methods by U.S. and Japanese managers. *Strategic Management Journal, 16*, 195-220.

Krisher, B. (1981, June 15). How the Japanese Manage in the U.S. *Fortune*, pp. 97-99.

Li, J. (1995). Foreign entry and survival: effects of strategic choices on performance in international markets. *Strategic Management Journal, 12*, 33-47.

Lincoln, J. R., Hanada, M., & Olson, J. (1981). Cultural orientations and individual reactions to organizations: a study of employees of Japanese-owned firms. *Administrative Science Quarterly, 26*, 93-115.

Lincoln, J. R., Hanada, M., & McBride, K., (1986). Organizational structures in Japanese and US manufacturing. *Administrative Science Quarterly, 31* (3), 338-364.

Lodge, G. C. (1987). Introduction: Ideology and country analysis. In G. C. Lodge & E. F. Vogel (Eds.), *Ideology and national competitiveness: An analysis of nine countries* (pp. 1-28). Boston: Harvard Business School.

Milkman, R. (1991). *Labor relations and economic globalization.* LA: UCLA Institute of Industrial Relations.

Murtha, T. P., & Lenway, S. A. (1994). Country capabilities and the strategic state: How national political institutions affect multinational corporations' strategies. *Strategic Management Journal*, Special Summer Issue, *15*, 113-129.

Ouchi, W. (1981). *Theory Z: How American business can meet the japanese challenge.* Addison-Wesley, Reading, MA.

Porter, M. E. (1983). The U.S. television set market, prewar to 1970 (pp. 449-481). and the U.S. television set market, 1970-1979 (pp. 482-511). *Cases in Competitive Strategy*. New-York: Free Press.

Reid, T. R. (1977, September 2). A curious marriage. *The Washington Post*, p. A1+.

Risen, J. (1988, August 16). Disillusionment grows at Japanese-owned plants in U.S. *The Los Angeles Times*, C1+.

Taylor, W. (1991, March-April). The logic of global business:An interview with ABB's Percy Barnevik. *Harvard Business Review*, 91-105.

Taylor, S, Beechler, S., & Napier, N. (1996). Towards an integrative model of strategic international human resource management. *Academy of Management Review, 21* (4), 959-985.

Tsoukas, H. (1989). The epistemological status of idiographic research in the comparative study of organizations: A realist perspective. *Academy of Management Review, 14* (4), 551-561.

Yin, R. K. (1994). *Case study research: Design and methods* (2nd ed.). Thousand Oaks, CA: Sage Publications.

Zaheer, S. (1995). Overcoming the liability of newness. *Academy of Management Journal, 38* (2), 341-363.

[12]

Pergamon

0263-2373(95)00017-8

European Management Journal Vol. 13, No. 3, pp. 269–275, 1995

0263-2373/95 $9.50+0.00

Cultural Perspectives on the Measurement of Corporate Success

SIDNEY GRAY, *FME Professor of International Business, University of Warwick Business School*

This paper discusses some insights that an understanding of national cultural differences might provide into problems relating to the measurement of corporate success and the disclosure of success-related information in an increasingly international business context.

Arguments and evidence are presented which suggest that the measures of profits and information disclosed by companies around the world are significantly influenced by national cultural characteristics. Profits reported by UK and US companies are, for example, prepared on a much more optimistic basis and have a more short-term orientation compared to those by German and Japanese companies. International performance comparisons and evaluations of relative strategic success based on published data must, therefore, be viewed with extreme caution and necessarily require further interpretation.

The purpose of this article is to examine the extent to which national culture is an important influence on the measurement of corporate success and the disclosure of success-related information to stakeholders, competitors and the public at large in an increasingly global business context.

In deciding to focus on the issue of corporate success or performance, a cultural bias is immediately introduced in that an achievement orientated society is assumed thus creating a need for relevant measures. As McClelland (1961) has shown, there are wide differences in achievement motivation around the world with the US and UK very strongly motivated in this regard compared to France, Sweden and Japan. Indeed, as Hofstede (1991) points out, even the word 'achievement' is difficult to translate into other languages.

However, given that our interest here is to measure the comparative success of large corporations competing in the global economy and given the widespread interest of international investors, economists and the media in such measures it seems reasonable to explore this issue further. The next problem concerns the criteria for success. Naturally much depends on corporate objectives which would seem to be influenced in turn by the cultural and business context of the home country of the corporation concerned. There is considerable evidence that the balance of corporate objectives varies substantially across countries — from an emphasis on financial measures, such as profit, return on investment, and shareholder value in the US and UK to an emphasis on non-financial measures such as market share and sales growth in Japan (see Shields, et al., 1991). Of course, financial viability is a prerequisite to survival so to that extent all companies are interested in satisfactory profits and cash flows to sustain operations.

Given the emphasis on financial performance measures evident in many Western countries and especially those where stock markets are a major influence, there is an interesting question concerning the extent to which reliable comparisons can be made. While some diversity of measurement and reporting practices is evident from prior research, the significance of national culture as an influential factor is only now beginning to be appreciated.

In this paper, first, the nature of culture and its relevance to measurement and disclosure practices will be explored. Then, research findings relevant to the influence of national culture on both performance measurement and disclosure behaviour will be evaluated. Finally, the discussion will review the implications of the findings for further research and decision-makers at all levels.

Cultural Influences on Corporate Performance and Public Reporting in an International Context

First, what do we mean by culture, and how is it likely to impact on the measurement and reporting of corporate performance? Culture is an intangible asset: it is part of our human software. It is a social and behavioural phenomenon which is largely invisible and unconscious. As with all intangibles, culture is difficult to recognise and to measure. While there are many definitions of culture, Geert Hofstede (1980; 1991) suggests that it is useful to think of culture as 'the collective programming of the mind which distinguishes one category of people from another'. Culture manifests itself at the levels of symbols, heroes, rituals and values. Furthermore, culture has many layers: from national culture, to organisational or corporate culture, to occupational culture. In the context of values, which reflect deep-seated tendencies, national culture refers to the values of most members of a country or society. Organisational culture refers to the sub-culture of values shared by most members of an organisation. Occupational culture refers to the sub-culture of values shared by those with a distinct occupation.

The origins of national values can be found in a complex web of environmental factors and historical circumstances. Such values tend to change only slowly and usually in response to external factors such as international trade and investment, technological change and the upheavals of war and colonisation. Hofstede (1980) attempted to identify and quantify national values from a study of a multinational corporation's operations in more than 50 countries. The values identified were: power distance, uncertainty avoidance, individualism and masculinity. As regards organizational functioning and work practices, the dimensions of power distance and uncertainty avoidance were reckoned to be most relevant in that the basic problems of management were perceived to be concerned with the distribution of power and the avoidance or reduction of unwanted uncertainties.

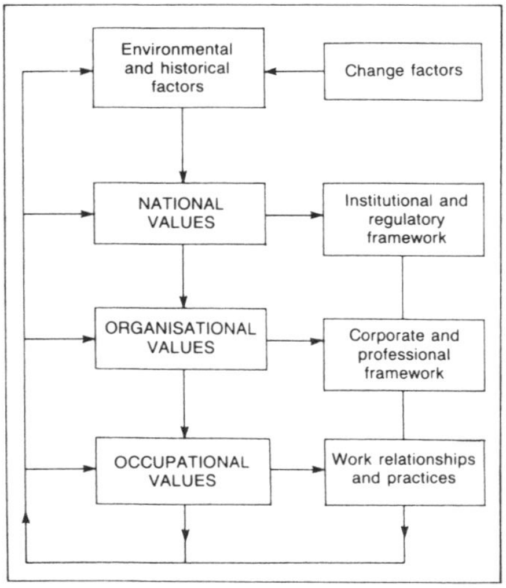

Figure 1 Culture and Accounting (1)

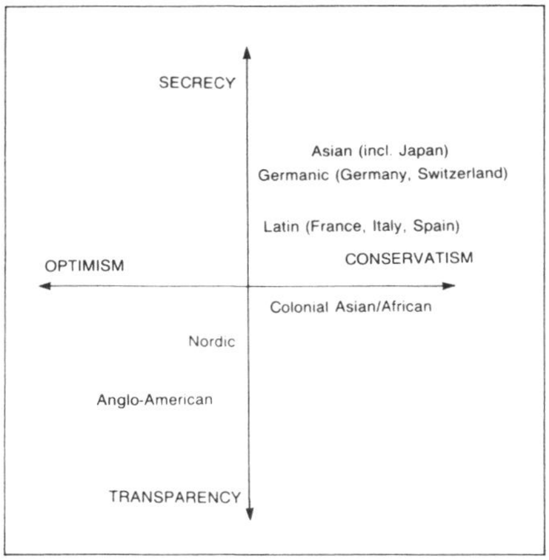

Figure 2 Culture and Accounting (2)

Given that culture or values identified at national level may be reflected to some extent in organisational and occupational sub-cultures, subject to refinements, additions and variations as the case may be, it may be expected that such values impact on accountants and accounting systems and practices (Gray, 1985; 1988). In Figure 1 a model of this process is hypothesised which suggests that national values influence the institutional and regulatory framework of accounting, organisational values influence the corporate and professional framework of accounting, and occupational values influence the behaviour of accountants in their work relationships and practices. As accounting practice is very much based on conventions rather than scientific laws of nature, it seems likely that national values will be relatively influential. Accordingly, it may be possible to identify a set of accounting values, labelled as professionalism, uniformity, conservatism and secrecy, which may be related to national values and which impact on financial reporting practices (Gray,1988). Figure 2 shows a pattern of hypothesised relationships in respect of conservatism and secrecy which are linked to measurement and disclosure practices respectively.

Differences in measurement and reporting systems and practices internationally may thus tend to reflect cultural differences. Similarly, patterns of behaviour identified with certain groups of countries will also tend to be consistent with cultural groupings.

Culture has the potential, therefore, to provide us with a very interesting and important insight into the development of financial reporting internationally. In order, however, to explore the extent to which culture may be a significant influence it is also necessary to learn more about the nature of international differences in financial reporting practices. We will then be in a better position to evaluate the likely relevance of the relationship between culture and accounting.

In essence, financial reporting practices are concerned, first, with the measurement of income and financial position and, second, with the disclosure of both financial and non-financial information relevant to an assessment of corporate performance, prospects and risks. Both the measurement and disclosure dimensions relate to the investment decision-making and stewardship purposes of using accounting information. But what is the nature and extent of international financial reporting differences in practice and what is the likely impact of such differences on comparative assessments of corporate performance and success?

International Differences in Performance Measurement Behaviour

While there is a growing awareness of the diversity of measurement practices internationally, and action by the International Accounting Standards Committee (IASC) to reduce this, there is much less known about the overall impact of accounting differences on income and shareholders equity and key indicators derived from them e.g. earnings per share. After all, differences in respect of various aspects of measurement may well compensate for each other to the extent that their overall impact may not be significant. The important question is whether accounting differences impact systematically on measures of income. In other words, do these differences really matter?

In order to compare the impact of accounting differences between countries it is necessary to have some agreed yardstick for comparison and then to measure the extent of the adjustment required to bring income into line with it. One way to do this is to construct an index using, for example, US GAAP as the yardstick. Such an index, termed by Gray (1980) as the 'conservatism' index to reflect an important accounting value (and one which appears to be linked to national cultural values), may be constructed as follows: $1-(RA-RD/RA)$ where RA = adjusted return or profit and RD = disclosed return or profit. An index value greater than 1 means that reported earnings are higher, or less conservative, than a US GAAP measure of income would have been. On the other hand, an index value of less than 1 means that reported earnings are lower, or more conservative. In this way, the relative impact and quantitative significance of accounting differences can be assessed.

Using this approach, research by Weetman and Gray (1990), based on an analysis of 37 UK companies providing reconciliations to US GAAP on Form 20-F, found systematic differences between UK and US GAAP for the period 1985–87. UK measures of income were between 9 per cent and 25 per cent higher, on average, than US measures of income as a result of differences in accounting principles. An earlier study by Gray (1980) of 15 French, 28 German and 29 UK companies, using an index based on the 'European Method' of financial analysis, also found systematic differences between UK companies on the one hand and French and German companies on the other. French and German measures of income were significantly lower than UK measures of income. More recent research by Weetman and Gray (1991), based on a US GAAP yardstick, showed that Swedish measures of income tended to be lower than US measures while Dutch measures tended to be higher than US measures though not as high as the UK.

In addition to studies based on actual company practices, which must surely be the ideal approach if we are to really understand the dynamics of financial reporting behaviour internationally, there have been some attempts to simulate the impact of accounting differences on income and shareholders equity. A recent simulation exercise by Simmonds and Azieres (1989), based on a simplified version of the acccounts of a multinational group, provided some insight into the range of income and asset measures possible in Europe despite the harmonisation efforts of the EC. The highest measures of income and return on net assets occurred in the case of the UK in contrast to the lowest in the case of Spain, closely followed by Belgium and Germany.

> *The impact on income and shareholders' equity of country accounting differences can be measured by a 'conservatism' index*

Outside Europe and the US, research by Aron (1990) into Japanese measures of earnings indicated that they were significantly lower than US GAAP measures of earnings. In fact, they were estimated to be as much as 40 per cent lower, on average, using judgementally based market-wide adjustments for the effect of tax deductible reserves, consolidation practices, and depreciation.

The research to date provides us with the beginnings of a global perspective on financial reporting behaviour so far as the measurement of profits is concerned. From Figure 3 it can be seen, taking the US as the yardstick for comparison with an index number of 100, that US accounting principles tend to result in significantly lower, or more 'conservative', measures of earnings than the UK but significantly higher, or less 'conservative', measures than Japan. The UK would thus seem to be at one extreme i.e. the most optimistic or 'creative', with Japan at the other i.e. the most cautious. The continental European countries, on the other hand, are to a large extent bunched together in a more 'conservative' grouping compared to the US. This scenario provides, of course, very much a judgemental impression based on the limited evidence available to date.

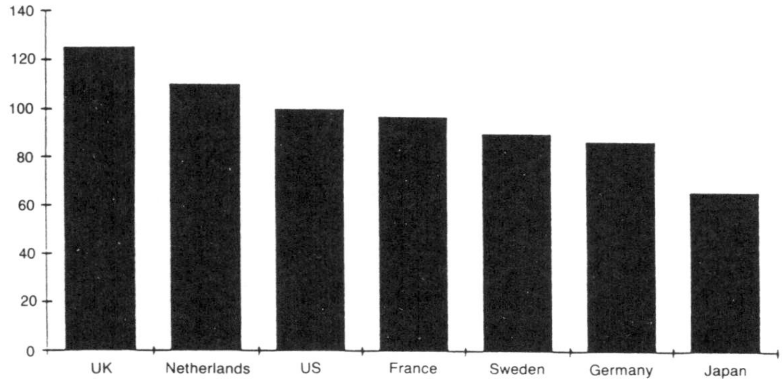

Figure 3 International Accounting Differences: Earnings Index Based on US GAAP

At the same time, the evidence on earnings differences does appear to be consistent with a cultural perspective which would suggest a continuum of 'conservatism' to reflect the impact of national cultural values on attitudes to accounting measurement. The pattern of reporting behaviour also appears to be associated with the *a priori* relationships hypothesised earlier from an analysis of national values i.e. we would expect the UK and US to be less 'conservative' relative to Germany and Japan (Gray, 1988).

In this regard, it is somewhat ironic that the observed pattern of behaviour impacts on reported profits in a way which has tended to be completely the opposite to indicators of national economic growth in recent years. Thus US and UK companies are likely to have been deluding themselves in their assessments of relative success when making financial performance comparisons with their German or Japanese competitors.

International Differences in Information Disclosure Behaviour

While there is an awareness of the diversity of information disclosure practices internationally, similar to the situation in respect of income measurement, there appears to be much less concern by the IASC, for example, to deal with disclosure issues except in the context of policy disclosures relating to measurement methods. There is also a lack of comprehensive data about the nature and extent of information disclosure internationally and whether or not differences between countries are significant. Information disclosure in practice includes both financial and non-financial information, both quantitative and narrative, and extends to issues related to, for example, corporate strategy, employee relations, social responsibility and the environment. An important question then concerns whether or not overall differences in disclosure levels are reflected at the disaggregated level e.g. segmental information, foreign currency information, research and development information, social responsibility information and so on. It may be that a lack of disclosure in one area is compensated by additional disclosure in another. Similar disclosure levels may thus mask significant differences in content while different disclosure levels may be the result of different types of disclosures. In other words, are there significant disclosure differences between countries in terms of overall disclosure and in relation to the disclosure of specific items of information?

While we can look at individual items of disclosure across countries, one way to build up a picture of disclosure behaviour internationally is to construct disclosure indices both at the overall and disaggregated level using disclosure data extracted on a company by company basis. Ideally, any index created by this process should be shown as a proportion i.e. the actual score awarded to a company compared to the maximum potential score applicable to that company. Thus the disclosure index for each company becomes D/M, the number of disclosures (D) as a proportion of the maximum score (M). Gray, et al. (1992), for example, have used this type of index approach in a recent comparative study of voluntary disclosures by UK and US multinationals which found both a country effect and a multi-listing, or internationalisation, effect.

While there have been a number of international surveys of disclosure practices (e.g. Tonkin, 1990), there have been relatively few empirical studies which comprehensively focus on comparative international disclosure behaviour (see Choi, 1973; Barrett, 1977; Meek and Gray, 1989; and Gray and Vint, 1992).

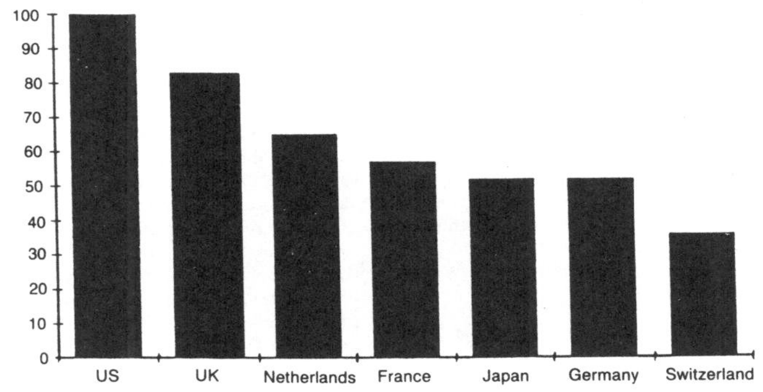

Figure 4 International Disclosure Differences

In a recent study of corporate disclosure practices, using a data base of 30 countries (Gray, et al., 1984), disclosures were ranked from 0 to 6 according to the extent of disclosure (Gray and Vint, 1992). It was found here that there was a wide range of disclosure practices internationally. The most extensive disclosures were by US and UK companies with an overall average of 3.1 and 2.8 respectively. Not so far behind was Japan in 5th place. However, Switzerland , by way of contrast, was ranked 24th with an average score of 1.7, almost half that of the US.

Another perspective on disclosure has been contributed by an attempt to provide a comparative international analysis of disclosure levels across the world's major stock exchanges (Biddle and Saudagaran, 1989). This research attempted to rank countries on a judgmental basis initially but subsequent research (Biddle and Saudagaran, 1992) relied on a questionnaire survey of the views of international capital market participants. Consistent with surveys of corporate disclosure practices, the US, Canada and the UK were perceived to have the highest disclosure levels whereas Switzerland had the lowest. In between were The Netherlands, France, Japan and Germany in that order.

While further research into the quantitative impact of disclosure differences is desirable, a global pattern of overall disclosure behaviour is beginning to emerge as shown in Figure 4 which endeavours to bring together some of the findings to date. From this it would seem that significantly higher disclosure levels are found in the US. At the next level are Canada and the UK who are significantly above the Continental European grouping. While disclosure levels in Japan appear to be very similar to Germany, Switzerland represents a significantly lower level of disclosure behaviour compared to all other countries with major capital markets. The relationships depicted are, of course, very much judgemental at this stage.

At the same time, the evidence does suggest a range of disclosure behaviour consistent with a cultural perspective suggesting a continuum of 'secrecy' or 'transparency' to reflect national value characteristics. The pattern of reporting behaviour also appears to be associated with the *a priori* relationships hypothesised earlier from an analysis of national cultural values i.e. the US and UK are likely to be much more open and transparent compared to Japan, Germany and Switzerland (Gray, 1988). While a more open approach may seem desirable from a capital market perspective, consistent with an emphasis in the US and UK on broad share ownership and highly developed stock markets, there could well be significant implications in terms of competitive disadvantage i.e. there is a danger that the information disclosed may benefit competitors from countries with different attitudes to the public disclosure of information.

Prospects for Further Research: Possibilities and Problems

So far as comparative international measures of corporate success are concerned, the recognition of the significant influence of national culture provides us with some valuable insights into how we might better understand and use such measures internationally.

While the evidence available to date is limited it is encouraging in that it suggests an association between national cultural values and measurement and disclosure practices. Thus there is substantial scope for further work to more rigorously assess the significance of cultural influences on measurement attitudes and their impact in terms of contributing to the international diversity of performance measures.

One of the most fundamental problems is to gather more comprehensive and reliable information about the impact of accounting differences on the measurement of earnings and assets and on information disclosure practices. What we have at present only provide some partial glimpses and insights into a complex reality. The empirical evidence available covers only a limited number of companies in a limited number of countries. To go beyond this will require cross-national collaborative projects of significant proportions involving substantial resources. This is essential, however, if we are to gather evidence which will fully reveal the impact and significance of international differences. It is also important if we are to know the extent to which national practices are responding to various change factors including efforts by agencies concerned to promote international harmonisation.

The extent of corporate financial disclosure in any country seems to have a strong cultural determinant

Even more difficult, though, is how to rigorously explain the significant differences, or systematic diversity, in international measurement and disclosure practices which exist? More specifically, how can we determine empirically the extent to which culture is a significant explanatory variable? This is, of course, extremely difficult to do given that culture is largely invisible and unconscious and that national values are woven into the fabric of a society's institutions, business and professional organizations, and work practices. Culture should perhaps be viewed as an underlying variable embedded in a society and its values and practices. As such it does not lend itself easily to measurement. However, to the extent that culture is reflected in attitudes then cross-national questionnaire survey and interview techniques may be useful. It could be though that the kind of global analysis that we are pursuing here is an impossible task and that a deeper micro-level country analysis is more appropriate. Certainly, more in-depth country analyses are desirable in any event. But to the extent that countries may be ranked or grouped by cultural characteristics it should be possible to evaluate the significance of hypothesised relationships between culture and measurement practices. Furthermore, other variables of interest could be incorporated into the analysis in the context of a modelling approach. Such work at the macro-level of analysis would provide support for more detailed work at the micro-level to better understand the evolution and impact of national cultural influences on corporate behaviour.

Some Policy Implications

Performance measures related to profits are not reliable indicators of the comparative success of large corporations in an international context. Such measures are strongly influenced by national cultural differences and can only be correctly interpreted within their own cultural and business context.

To the extent that comparative international indicators are considered useful how can sensible progress be made? Given the variety of corporate objectives and differences in priorities across countries it would seem desirable to adopt a more holistic approach to the measurement of corporate success incorporating both financial and non-financial indicators. In contrast, current endeavours to harmonise measurement practices are likely to be little more than artificial exercises lacking cultural commitment. Of course, we also have the choice of judging others by our own criteria (with consequent potential for lack of understanding and communication) but to do this will require an awareness of the impact of culture on measurement practices in other countries so that adjustments can be made, to the extent feasible, to the profit measures involved.

Given that a more holistic approach is judged desirable then what kinds of indicators might seem appropriate assuming that we can overcome different attitudes to the public disclosure of information about performance? From an economic perspective, a range of growth and value indicators would seem relevant. Sales volume information could be reported, together with operating margins, on a market segment basis as well as at the corporate level. In addition, measures of value which are growth or output orientated could be included. Shareholder value as measured in a stock market context would not be suitable as its significance is contextually biased. However, value added, being defined as the value of outputs less the cost of externally purchased inputs, is a measure which significantly limits the impact of culturally influenced measurement practices compared to profit. This is because it is a measure of gross output i.e. before taking account of employee and other internal costs. Value added is a measure of interest to all stakeholders in contrast to profit with its focus on returns to investors. This should be distinguished from a net surplus approach which takes account of all costs including the cost of capital to arrive at so-called economic 'added value' (Kay, 1993). The economic added value approach is unsuitable for the purposes of international comparison because it is even more contextually biased than measures of profit in that capital costs continue to be strongly influenced by local factors despite the increasing internationalisation of financial markets.

Another indicator, besides value added, which is also relatively independent of cultural influence is that of cash flow which could be assessed in the context of operating, investment and financing activities. This would seem to be an important indicator of financial viability as well as future potential.

As regards non-financial indicators, information about market performance and relations with customers would seem relevant e.g. market share, pricing strategy, product quality, product innovation. In addition, a holistic approach would suggest indicators concerning relationships with other stakeholders such as employees e.g. health, safety, compensation and benefits, employment, and also the public at large e.g. product safety, impact on the environment, pollution control.

In conclusion, perceptions and measures of corporate success in an international context are culturally influenced and diverse; thus moves towards making global comparisons should be matched by the selection of a set of success indicators which reflect that diversity and also communicate in areas of common concern. It is not possible nor is it desirable to focus primarily on measures related to profits as international indicators of corporate success.

References

Aron, P.H. Japanese P/E Multiples in an Era of Increasing Uncertainty. *Report No. 41, Daiwa Securities America* (August 1990).

Barrett, M.E. The Extent of Disclosure in Annual Reports of Large Companies in Seven Countries. *International Journal of Accounting* (Spring 1977).

Biddle, G. and Saudagaran, S. The Effects of Financial Disclosure Levels on Firms' Choices among Alternative Foreign Stock Exchanges. *Journal of International Financial Management and Accounting* (Spring 1989).

Biddle, G. and Saudagaran, S. Financial Disclosure Levels and Foreign Stock Exchange Listings. *Journal of International Financial Management and Accounting* (Summer 1992)

Choi, F.D.S. Financial Disclosure and Entry to the European Capital Markets. *Journal of Accounting Research* (Autumn 1973).

Gray, S.J. The impact of International Accounting Differences from a Security Analysis Perspective: Some European Evidence. *Journal of Accounting Research* (Spring 1980).

Gray, S. J. Cultural Influences and the International Classification of Accounting Systems. *EIASM Workshop on Accounting and Culture* (Amsterdam, 1985)

Gray, S.J. Towards a theory of Cultural Influence on the Development of Accounting Systems Internationally. *Abacus* (March 1988).

Gray, S.J., Campbell, L. G. and Shaw, J.C. *International Financial Reporting* (Macmillan, 1984).

Gray, S.J., Meek, G.K. and Roberts, C.B. International Capital Market Pressures and Voluntary Disclosure Decisions by US and UK Multinationals. *Paper presented at the AAA Annual Meeting, Washington* (1992).

Gray, S.J. and Vint, H.M. The impact of Culture on Accounting Disclosures: some International Evidence. *University of Glasgow Working Paper* (1992).

Hofstede, G. *Culture's Consequences: International Differences in Work-Related Values* (Sage 1980)

Hofstede, G. The Cultural Context of Accounting. In Cushing, B.(Ed) *Accounting and Culture* (AAA, 1987)

Hofstede, G. *Cultures and Organisations* (McGraw-Hill, 1991)

Kay, J. *Foundations of Corporate Success* (Oxford University Press, 1993).

McClelland, D. *The Achieving Society* (Van Nostrand, 1961)

Meek, G.K. and Gray, S.J. Globalization of Stock Markets and Foreign Listing Requirements: Voluntary Disclosures by Continental European Companies Listed on the London Stock Exchange. *Journal of International Business Studies* (Summer 1989).

Shields, M. D., Chow, C. W., Kato, Y. and Nakagawa, Y. Management Accounting Practices in the US and Japan: Comparative Survey Findings and Research Implications. *Journal of International Financial Management and Accounting* (Spring 1991).

Simmonds, A. and Azieres, O. *Accounting for Europe. Success by 2000 AD?* (Touche Ross Europe, 1989).

Tonkin, D. (Ed) *World Survey of Published Accounts* (Lafferty, 1990).

Weetman, P and Gray, S.J. International Financial Analysis and Comparative Corporate Performance: the Impact of UK versus US Accounting Principles. *Journal of International Financial Management and Accounting* (Summer/Autumn 1990).

Weetman, P and Gray, S.J. A Comparative International Analysis of the Impact of Accounting Principles on Profits: The USA versus the UK, Sweden and the Netherlands. *Accounting and Business Research* (Autumn 1991).

SIDNEY GRAY,
Warwick Business School, University of Warwick, Coventry CV4 7AL

Sidney J. Gray is the Foundation for Management Education Professor of International Business at Warwick Business School, University of Warwick. He is co-author with Lee Radebaugh of International Accounting and Multinational Enterprises *and has published widely on international accounting issues. He is an Associate Editor of the* Journal of International Financial Management and Accounting *and is an Editorial Board Member of the* Journal of International Business Studies *and* Management International Review. *He is a former Secretary General of the International Association for Accounting Education and Research.*

[13]

© Academy of Management Executive, 1998, Vol. 12, No. 4

Managing knowledge in global service firms: Centers of excellence

Karl Moore and Julian Birkinshaw

Executive Overview

Service firms that are global players benefit primarily from their ability to manage their proprietary knowledge—assimilating new knowledge from around the world, building new knowledge through the interaction of professional employees, and disseminating knowledge effectively throughout the firm. Centers of excellence represent the best practice of managing knowledge. Formally charged with the responsibility of leveraging and/or making knowledge available throughout the firm, the center of excellence provides a focal point for knowledge development and dissemination and replaces an old-fashioned reliance on informal, word-of-mouth mechanisms. However, a center also raises substantial organizational and motivational challenges.

Building Global Competitiveness in Service Firms

Electra Services Europe[1] undertook a major reorganization in 1994, replacing its old country-focused operations with Europe-wide business units. For John Skelton, the new head of corporate marketing in Brussels, the change was an opportunity to seek out and leverage the pockets of expertise that he knew existed in Electra Europe. Using his extensive personal network, Skelton put together a list of best-practices in core marketing activities: the key account management guru was based in Stockholm; the London unit had leading-edge groups in business intelligence and customer loyalty measurement; database marketing was done best in Paris, and so on. These and others were designated as centers of excellence, on whose leading-edge expertise in core marketing areas other units throughout Europe could draw.

Three years later, Electra's Center of Excellence model was only a partial success. Some centers are funded by the local country, so their priorities tend to be towards helping local colleagues; some have attempted to charge for their services, but have found that administering the billing system takes half their time; and a few are funded through Brussels, but there is great reluctance at a top management level to increase the size of the headquarters group. Visibility is also a problem: while the centers of excellence are well-known in their local markets and in a few business units, the large majority of Electra's European operations are still ignorant of them, and of the expertise they offer.

Electra's story illustrates challenges facing many global service firms. Unlike manufacturing firms that can rely on patented technologies or unique products, service firms gain their competitive advantage primarily through their ability to make use of their proprietary knowledge on a global scale. Electra, like many other firms, has adopted the center of excellence model as a way of more effectively exploiting its geographically-dispersed expertise. While the advantages of the approach are many, the management problems it presents are substantial.

We conducted interviews in eighteen global service firms (Table 1) in the consulting, engineering, financial services, and transportation sectors. We define a center of excellence[2] as a small group of individuals recognized for their leading-edge, strategically-valuable knowledge, and mandated to leverage and/or make that knowledge available throughout the global firm.

Table 1
The Firms Studied

Company	Home Country	Industry Sector	Types of Centers identified	Number of interviews
Andersen	USA	Consulting	Focused Virtual Charismatic	8
Bovis	UK	Construction	Focused	3
Bull	France	Consulting/IT	Focused	3
Citibank	USA	Banking	Virtual	3
DHL	Netherlands	Express Delivery	Focused	2
Electra	USA	Marketing services	Focused Charismatic	5
Ernst & Young	USA	Accounting	Focused	1
KPMG	USA	Consulting	Virtual	1
IBM	USA	Consulting/IT	Virtual Charismatic	7
McKinsey & Company	USA	Consulting	Focused Virtual	2
Monitor	USA	Consulting	Focused Virtual	2
Oxford Univ. Press	UK	Publishing	Focused	2
P&O	UK	Shipping	Focused	4
Royal & Sun Alliance	UK	Insurance	Focused	3
Skandia	Sweden	Insurance	Focused	3
Unisys	USA	Consulting/IT	Focused Virtual Physical Location	4

Knowledge Production in the Global Service Firm

The advantages of global reach to manufacturing companies are self-apparent. Materials can be sourced from the lowest-cost location; manufacturing plants can be built to serve multiple national markets; R&D costs can be amortized over a much broader customer base than before. For service firms,[3] however, the benefits of globalization are more equivocal. If we think in terms of a value chain of activities, global service firms typically replicate the entire value chain in each country of operation, rather than centralizing certain parts in the lowest-cost country.[4] Competitive advantage is gained not through the sharing of activities but through the transfer of intangible assets from country to country. These intangible assets include

Competitive advantage is gained not through the sharing of activities but through the transfer of intangible assets from country to country.

the corporate name, image and reputation, proprietary services, operating procedures, and know-how about key customer bases. Increasingly, the source of these intangible assets is not the headquarters of the firm, but the various affiliate companies around the world. Top management's task is to develop, leverage, and disseminate knowledge on a worldwide basis, and to foster an environment in which intercountry learning can occur.[5]

For a global service firm, new knowledge comes primarily from interactions with clients, and interactions between team members around the world.[6] Client interactions represent a two-way flow of knowledge, in which the service firm uses its expertise to address a client's needs, enhancing and sharpening that expertise through usage. To the extent that market needs continue to evolve, this form of interaction is central to the knowledge creation process. As one respondent explained:

> Things pop out of the woodwork in our organization because of something at a client's site, which are then socialized through the community over time . . . . At some stage someone says, this is a significant amount of work being done, we are responding well to it, and making money; what we now need to do is formalize the competence ... A lot of the best stuff gets created in the client's environment. It's usually a response to a real problem.

This market understanding is perhaps even more valuable in a global firm where there exists a greater range of opportunities to learn from a more diverse set of customer needs. Few headquarters organizations can keep up with the rapid changes in their global market.. Firm headquarters were once urged to tap into the learning of their foreign affiliates' interactions with customers around the world.[7] The experience of top firms, however, suggests that merely tapping into the affiliates is no longer sufficient. Service firms need to move to the next stage of global development in which the knowledge and ideas emanating from affiliate companies are leveraged and utilized *in situ* rather than simply being brought back to headquarters.

The other key source of innovations is the interaction of internal teams as they fulfill client needs. Team members combine and build on prior experiences to create new techniques or ideas. But these creative solutions are often not shared with other teams in their own country, let alone globally. Even the individual team members tend to lose the knowledge over time unless it is somehow institutionalized into the system.

To harness these two powerful sources of innovation and learning, global service firms have adopted a number of approaches—enriching the airline industry by flying employees around the world for meetings, pouring millions into groupware such as Lotus Notes, staging video conferences, and mailing client proposals and reports to numerous recipients. Though these solutions have contributed something, centers of excellence have emerged as an organizational innovation that brings greater focus to the effort to harness worldwide learning.

Figure 1 illustrates the concept of a center of excellence. Traditionally, many global service firms adopted one of two basic organizational models. One was a center-driven approach in which the foreign affiliates were seen as adapting centrally-created services to their local clients' needs. The other was a country-focused approach in which the various foreign units shared a corporate name, but undertook their work with little or no interaction with their affiliates around the world.[8] As firms moved toward a more global organizational model, an informal network typically emerged in which individuals developed contacts through their work in international teams and their attendance at group-wide events. Such networks were invaluable as a means of spreading ideas, but the spread was restricted to existing relationships. Thus, when John in London won a telecom-

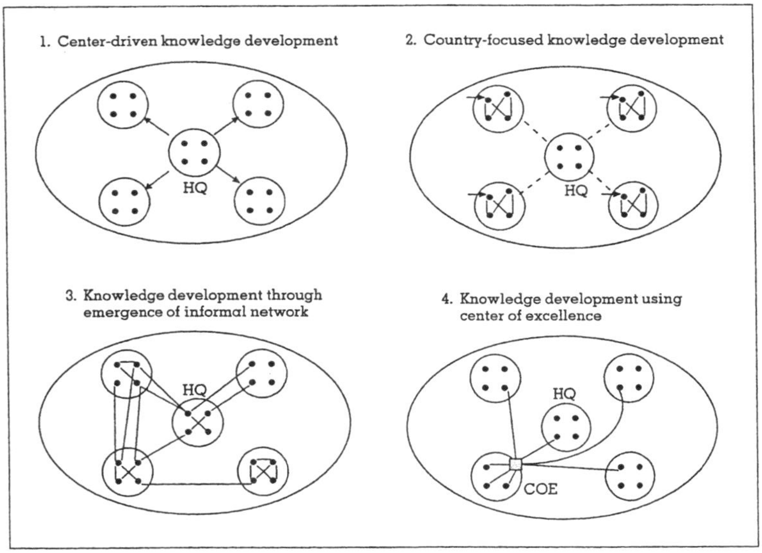

FIGURE 1
Models of organization in global service firms

munications contract, he would call his old acquaintance, Deborah, in New York to find out about her experiences with similar jobs. But his counterparts in Stockholm or Tokyo might have had far more relevant and valuable expertise in that area. Most service firms have recognized that relying on informal networks is not sufficient and that more formalized approaches to knowledge management can enhance both the quantity and quality of the knowledge flows throughout the firm.

What is a Center of Excellence?

A good example of a center of excellence is a major engineering company's center for airport construction. This small unit, based in London, comprises the firm's leading experts in airport construction and the records of all previous airport projects undertaken around the world. The unit has no formal authority over the activities of other affiliates, but it is frequently called on to help with new projects, such as the new airport in Hong Kong. As a senior manager explained:

> When there are markets that require quite a high degree of specialized knowledge, to access clients, to bring presentational skills or technology know-how in, then we create centers of excellence.

We identified three distinct types of centers of excellence in our research, but all shared a number of common themes. First, centers were established only in areas that top management felt to be of strategic importance to the firm. Second, the heart of each center of excellence was the leading-edge knowledge of a small number of individuals (between one and ten) responsible for the continual maintenance and upgrading of the knowledge in question. Third, the centers of excellence all had an implicit dual role—to leverage and/or transfer their current leading-edge capabilities, and to continually fine-tune and enhance those capabilities so that they remained state-of-the-art. Clearly the balancing act that stems from managing these two rather different activities is far from easy, but it is probably more difficult still to separate them.

Finally, many centers of excellence were not—despite their name—fixed in a single geographic location. Some consisted of a small number of individuals living in multiple locations but regularly meeting on projects and at conferences. Others consisted of a larger number of individuals connected primarily through their firms' groupware or Intranet. While there are clear drawbacks to such configurations, the firms in our study saw the geographical dispersion of their centers of excellence as a great strength, because it allowed them to exploit their global reach. Group members, it was argued, can learn from one another, tap into opportunities in multiple markets, and quickly combine their resources in ways that less globally-minded firms cannot.

But the centers of excellence we studied were also rather different from one another on a number of dimensions. Each firm had to some degree adopted its own approach, but we were able to discern three generic types of centers of excellence (Table 2) that we have labelled Charismatic, Focused and Virtual.

Charismatic Centers of Excellence

Charismatic centers of excellence are simply individuals who are internationally recognized for their knowledge or expertise in a certain area. These individuals can be brought in from outside or they can emerge as experts in the course of their careers with the firm. In two consulting firms we studied, senior professors had been hired from academic positions to provide visionary concepts and greater legitimacy to the practice area in question. By contrast, two investment banks preferred to identify their stars internally, and assign them as centers of excellence. At Chase Manhattan Bank, for example, the approach was described as follows:

Charismatic centers of excellence are simply individuals who are internationally recognized for their knowledge or expertise in a certain area.

> One concept we're pushing is centers of excellence. We're breaking down the various technologies into categories. Within each group will be what we call top guns. These are the individuals who are recognized leaders in their discipline, who can be called on to answer questions or provide advice in their area of expertise . . . A top gun would then evaluate a new product, and share the results of the analysis within the bank's technical community.[9]

The objective of the charismatic center is to leverage the expertise of the key individual as effectively as possible. He or she typically travels a great deal, performing advisory roles in a rela-

Table 2
Characteristics of Four Types of Centers

	Charismatic Center	Focused Center	Virtual Center
Nature of knowledge/capability	One "guru," internationally recognized for his/her knowledge	Leading edge practice developed by small team in a single location	Leading edge practice held by a larger group in several locations
Manifestation of center	One person plus administrative support. Based in one place, but travels frequently	Small group (3–10) people plus support. Based in one place, but travel frequently	Large group of people in multiple locations. Access to common database, and proprietary tools.
Primary purpose of center	Leverage the individual's expertise on a global basis	Identify emerging practises and make them available globally	Build and leverage leading edge practice through a formalized system
How is center formed?	Individual specially designated or hired for leading expertise	Emerges from project work	Designated by top management, often as a result of project work
How is center utilized?	Individual is called upon to advise on projects and disseminate his/her knowledge	Individuals in center transfer their practice to others	Knowledge is codified and routinized; people draw from collectively held body of knowledge

tively large number of projects, but not getting involved in the details of any. For example, we observed that it is common at McKinsey to have consulting directors attached to projects who act as expert advisors to the project team. Charismatic centers will have support staff at their home office location but usually no professional staff other than the key individual.

Charismatic centers have another objective, namely the transfer of the star individual's knowledge to other professional employees. Especially when an individual has been brought in from outside, the objective is clearly to build a capability in the firm that had been lacking. Rather than a codification process,[10] however, the transfer is much more likely to be achieved through the key individual's working with colleagues on projects, almost in a master-apprentice relationship.

Focused Centers of Excellence

Focused centers of excellence, the most common type, are typically based around a single area of knowledge, also called a capability or best practice. The objective, broadly stated, is to identify and build on emerging knowledge and make it available globally. Andersen Consulting, for example, has a multimedia center of excellence in Windsor, UK, consisting of a small group of consultants who are responsible for building the firm's capability in multimedia technology. Electra, as mentioned earlier, has focused centers in London, Paris, Stockholm, and Milan for various corporate marketing services. These centers have a clearly identifiable physical location, but it is understood that the individuals that are part of the center will travel frequently, to ensure that their expertise is made available to other affiliates around the world. It is also possible that focused centers will attract individuals who do not actually live in the home base for the center, though such cases typically end up becoming more like virtual centers (see below).

Focused centers of excellence typically emerge through project or client work. In one insurance firm we studied, the South African operation had developed a center of excellence in direct marketing through its efforts to get around the country's weak infrastructure. In McKinsey, the Business to Business marketing center of excellence grew out of a set of techniques that were developed over a series of client projects.[11] It appears that the process in the early stages is usually somewhat haphazard, but at a critical juncture the decision is made to recognize the center, and to put some additional resources behind it.

Once established, focused centers appear to be used in two distinct ways. One approach is to leverage the core individuals' expertise by bringing them onto related projects around the world as advisors. As one respondent explained:

> We encourage people throughout the organization to go to (the key people in the center of excellence) to seek their advice on a client, on how to put a proposal together, on pricing, on technical jargon, on other firms with whom to collaborate. They will try to be leveraging their skills through people in the other parts of the company.

The other approach is for individuals in the center to disseminate their capability to others in the firm through the development of materials and training courses. This approach appears to work better when the capability can be routinized. However the two approaches are also somewhat complementary, and in most cases the center of excellence managers we spoke to appeared to be leveraging their capability and disseminating it at the same time.

Virtual Centers of Excellence

In Virtual centers of excellence,[12] the core individuals live and work in different cities, and while they all know one another and meet intermittently, their principle means of interaction is through electronic media. Of necessity, virtual centers rely to a large degree on the codification of their knowledge base. Unlike focused centers, in which the core individuals work together to build a mutually held but tacit body of knowledge, virtual centers can function effectively only if knowledge is shared through computer databases and certain proprietary tools.[13]

What does a virtual center look like? The most obvious manifestation is actually the codified element: the systems, tools and methods that the virtual center has developed over its lifetime. At the same time, it should be clear that a computer system is not a virtual center, unless the system in question is maintained, renewed and owned by the individuals who have the leading edge knowledge. In other words, it is not the system *per se* that is the virtual center, it is the individuals' collective knowledge coupled with the codified part of their knowledge in the system that constitutes the virtual center.

Virtual centers offer two important advantages over focused centers. The first is that they represent a system through which key individuals living in different parts of the world can keep in touch and share their knowledge. From the interviews we conducted, it seems this function works only once the individuals in question know one another. As one respondent observed:

> It is possible to work electronically with someone you have never met, but once you have got to know the other person you can be far more effective. The quality of the interaction improves by an order of magnitude.

The second advantage of virtual centers is that they bring in more individuals than could possibly work together as a single team, and eventually institutionalize some of the knowledge developed in the virtual center. Taken to its natural conclusion, in fact, some elements of knowledge become so widely known and well understood that they become common knowledge—part of the firm's standard operating procedures, or routines.[14] Andersen Consulting, for example, talks about the shift from competence to capability, where competence refers to a group of 15–20 people with a certain skill, and capability to a group of 300–500.

Andersen Consulting, for example, talks about the shift from competence to capability, where competence refers to a group of 15–20 people with a certain skill, and capability to a group of 300–500.

Not all virtual centers follow this evolutionary path towards a firm-wide institutionalization of knowledge. Some types of knowledge are, by their nature, hard to codify and thus remain the natural proclivity of a few experts. But other types of knowledge, such as the tools and systems developed by consulting companies, are well-suited to this cycle of discovery, development, fine-tuning, formalization, and institutionalization, and thus lend themselves very nicely to the evolutionary model described here. The virtual center of excellence has a very special role in such cases, because it has to develop a body of knowledge, gradually include more and more individuals in the fine-tuning and formalization of that knowledge, and then be prepared to let go once its usage has been institutionalized in the firm.

Comparing the Three Types of Centers of Excellence

We can compare the three types of centers in terms of the characteristics of their knowledge bases. Figure 2 maps them according to, (a) how codifiable their knowledge is, i.e. the degree to which the knowledge can be written down in procedures, manuals and models, and (b) the specificity of the knowledge to the firm, i.e. the extent to which the knowledge is proprietary and specific rather than general and widely held.

Both focused and virtual centers represent extremely firm-specific knowledge. Their knowledge bases typically emerge through client interactions and they are therefore embedded in a firm's particular way of doing business. The difference between the two, as we have already noted, is that

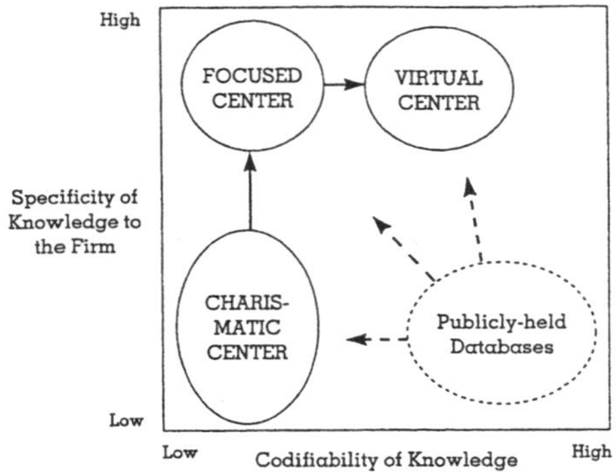

FIGURE 2

Comparison of four types according to knowledge characteristics

NB: Arrow indicates possible evolutionary trajectory. E.g., focused centers could evolve into virtual centers

virtual centers involve more people and are more geographically dispersed, which leads to a greater degree of codification of the underlying knowledge. In our experience, virtual centers tend to evolve out of focused centers along the evolutionary lines discussed earlier, but one could also see them evolving from charismatic centers as well.

Charismatic centers have a very low level of codifiability and, typically, a low level of firm specificity. A clear indicator of a low level of firm specificity is to ask: could this individual be as valuable to a competitor as he/she is to us? In cases where independent consultants or professors are brought in to head up a new center in a firm, the answer would certainly be yes. In cases where the individual is internationally recognized and well connected to the firm's internal network, the answer is only partially yes. Thus, we can envisage some breadth to the positioning of charismatic centers on figure 2. In terms of evolution, one would expect a charismatic center's knowledge to become more firm-specific over time, but probably not codified. However, the expectation in many firms was that charismatic centers should use their expertise to inform and build focused centers, for example by transferring some of their knowledge to a number of other key individuals.

What sort of center lies in the lower-right quadrant of figure 2? These are essentially public-source databases, such as those that can be found on the Internet or on CD-ROMs. These databases are not firm-specific, but the knowledge they contain is highly codified. Of course, such knowledge bases can be extremely valuable to the maintenance of charismatic, focused, and virtual centers. At the same time, they are clearly not centers of excellence because they are not proprietary to the firm.

When should a firm use a particular type of center? As the above analysis indicates, the three types of centers represent different but complementary approaches to managing knowledge. Focused centers represent an effective way of leveraging existing knowledge bases by raising the profile of specific groups of individuals and making their knowledge available worldwide. Charismatic centers are very effective when a firm wants to leverage the unique capabilities of its star performers; they can also be used as a means of raising the profile of a practice area by bringing in a well-known outsider. Virtual centers represent an effective way of bringing together the knowledge of a group of dispersed individuals, integrating it into a coherent whole, and disseminating it throughout the firm. More broadly, we suggest that firms need to think in terms of their entire knowledge profile—what they have, what is needed, how codifiable it is, how firm-specific, and so on. As with most of the firms in our study, some combination of different types of centers is usually needed to cover the breadth of knowledge demands firms are dealing with.

Other Manifestations of Centers of Excellence

Before finishing this section, we have to acknowledge one other common manifestation of centers of excellence, namely physical centers with an important knowledge-development role. For example, the Swedish Insurance firm Skandia built a Future Center just outside Stockholm with company exhibits, future concepts in insurance services, and facilities for planning meetings and development courses. The Future Center is used internally, as a place where new ideas are developed and tried out, and externally, as a place where potential customers can see Skandia's vision of the future. Other companies have established various learning centers. One consulting firm we spoke to had created a Thought Leadership Center in California. The Bank of Montreal built a Learning Center just outside Toronto.

Such examples, however, do not fit our definition of centers of excellence. While many leading-edge ideas are developed at these centers, it is the groups that did the developing, not the building in which they were developed. Physical entities like Skandia's Future Center may provide the stimulus for the emergence of virtual centers of excellence, but they cannot be considered centers in their own right.

Physical centers do offer one important insight into the center of excellence phenomenon. A central feature of such centers is that they are created through a top-down decision to build new knowledge, rather than the more bottom-up process of identifying and recognizing existing bodies of knowledge that is typical in focused and virtual centers. If physical centers do indeed inspire the emergence of genuine centers of excellence, they can perhaps be seen as strategic investments in the future, perhaps as a means of building knowledge areas that senior management have judged to be lacking. When thinking in terms of the firms' entire knowledge profile, then, physical centers provide a useful complement to charismatic centers of excellence as a means of stimulating the development of new knowledge.

The Center of Excellence Life-Cycle

For most of the firms we talked to, centers of excellence were seen as living organisms that emerged to fill a specific need and that would one day evolve or die out. In the words of one manager, "there was no intention to create a permanent something, because this is where the skills are . . . (Rather) we see it as a transitory four to five year phenomenon." Our study found cases of birth, death, and evolution, and a number of important suggestions about how the cycle should be managed.

Establishing New Centers of Excellence

Most firms have gone through a process of developing informal networks with de facto centers that lead the knowledge accumulation and dissemination process. The question here is really whether and when a more formalized center of excellence model be adopted. As we see it, a center of excellence requires both recognition and resources for it to move beyond an informal system. Recognition means communicating to staff worldwide that the center in question has an important strategic role. Resources means building the appropriate support systems and gaining access to the necessary staff to make the center viable.

Centers of excellence, we suggest, should be established on the basis of strategic importance. Firms need to focus their resources where they are most valued. As one manager explained: "If the market place says infrastructure projects are big now, we will develop a center of excellence for infrastructure projects. If nobody is doing theme parks, then that goes to go to the bottom of the list." Particularly in cases where the level of resources committed to a center is high (e.g., making several professional employees full time center employees) the strategic payoff has to be substantial. Furthermore, there is a question of focus. Centers of excellence need to be visible if they are to be effective, and visibility will obviously be compromised if they are fighting for space in the firm's newsletter or there appear to be several centers doing similar things. One way of circumventing this problem, of course, is through powerful information systems that help employees to target the knowledge they need.

Centers of excellence need to be visible if they are to be effective, and visibility will obviously be compromised if they are fighting for space in the firm's newsletter or there appear to be several centers doing similar things.

Centers of excellence are formed through two different processes. The more common is a bottom-up emergent process, in which top management formally recognize the importance of an existing knowledge base. Such cases rely on the entrepreneurial spirit of the core individuals, and the mentorship of a senior manager, to get noticed, rather than any sort of central-planning system. This process is most often seen in focused centers, and to a lesser degree in charismatic centers.

The alternative process is top-down, in that it is driven by senior management's recognition that certain knowledge areas need to be actively developed within the firm. Some charismatic centers emerge in this way, in that they are industry experts hired by the firm for their specific knowledge. Virtual centers also exhibit a top-down process to a large degree, because it takes a conscious and sustained effort to make them work. The more advanced process of knowledge institutionalization is, in particular, one that is likely to occur only through top management sponsorship.

Building and Maintaining the Center of Excellence

The center's primary role is to leverage or make available its distinctive knowledge base throughout the firm. It also has the less visible but equally important role of continuously sharpening its knowledge to ensure that it stays on the leading edge. Unfortunately, the former role tends to drive out the latter, simply because most center of excellence managers are very busy. It is much easier to put off a conference or a planning retreat than the demands of colleagues from around the world. Building the center of excellence thus becomes a frequently neglected duty.

In all three types of centers, the key individuals kept their knowledge sharp through project and client interaction. In many cases they also attended international conferences, read the relevant journals, and built up networks of outsiders to ensure that they were on top of the latest trends. Virtual centers, in addition, were maintained through the continuous updating of their common database, and through the enhancement of the existing set of tools and concepts.

How much time should be spent on exploiting the existing knowledge base and how much on exploring new ones? In charismatic and focused centers the emphasis should clearly be on exploiting, given that a certain amount of exploration will happen naturally in the course of project work. In virtual centers, however, the level of exploration should be much higher, because the objective of such centers is to bring together and integrate knowledge. Even in virtual centers, however, people we spoke to were happy if they could devote even one quarter of their time to the more forward-looking part of their job.

The End of the Life-Cycle: Renewal or Closure?

The third stage of the life-cycle has not yet received much attention, even in cutting edge service firms that have used centers of excellence for a few years. As is the case in any organizational form, it is perhaps harder to end something then start it. Empires are built, resources are committed and a sense of identity develops around the center. But over time, the value of the center is likely to diminish. In some cases, the knowledge in question may have been disseminated throughout the firm, in which case the center will have worked itself out of a job. One engineering firm explained its philosophy on the center of excellence life-cycle thus:

> How long do they last? About 40 years. There are one or two that basically have just died out. Tall buildings was one . . . its not that we don't do any tall buildings, its just that we have enough experience globally that we don't need it as a center of excellence. Because what made it a specialist is now common knowledge, it's widely dispersed.

In this case, the tall building center of excellence ceased to exist, and the staff transferred its attention to other projects. In other cases, focused and charismatic centers evolved into virtual centers. Interestingly, we saw no cases of virtual centers' dying out, despite the earlier logic that they could lose their reason for being if their knowledge base became widely disseminated. Perhaps no examples had existed for long enough for us to see the process run its course.

The other reason for centers to die out is when their knowledge base is eclipsed by others or becomes less relevant in a new competitive environment. Where centers are set up according to industries or technologies, it is to be expected that demand for services in the various industries and technologies will vary over time. New centers are therefore established to meet emerging client demands, and old centers are allowed to die out.

Managing the closure of a center of excellence is actually far easier than it sounds, simply because the center is typically a small number of professionals, most of whom have adaptable skills that can be transferred to other areas of the business.

Managing the closure of a center of excellence is actually far easier than it sounds, simply because the center is typically a small number of professionals, most of whom have adaptable skills that can be transferred to other areas of the business.

Moreover, rather than thinking in terms of closure, the preferred model we identified can best be termed renewal. Here, the individuals in the center were actively looking ahead, and seeking out new areas into which the existing center could evolve. The comments of one consulting company respondent exemplify this issue very effectively:

> Each of the competencies and market units (i.e. centers) are responsible for constantly re-energizing their capability. There is a constant pressure to look for new areas of practice and to look for and create an investment program for taking them from initial ideas into substantial capabilities around the world.

In the firms we studied, little attention had been given to the center of excellence life-cycle, presumably because most were still in the very early stages of using the concept. But clearly this will have to change. For most firms, the best approach is probably to actively manage the life-cycle, to target new areas of knowledge that need to be developed or disseminated, and to identify those that are no longer a strategic priority. The alternative is to let the birth and death of centers of excellence take care of itself, almost through a competitive process of natural selection. We have seen this work in a couple of firms, but it is risky because it can engender the development of a secretive, noncooperative culture.

Motivations and Incentives

A consistent and recurring problem in managing centers of excellence appears to be one of motivation. Most of the individuals we talked to had an existing responsibility that was measured, for example, in terms of billable hours, and a center of excellence responsibility on top that was not formally measured. These individuals obviously knew that their center of excellence was important, but if the compensation and reward system favored their existing responsibilities, it was very clear which part of their work would get neglected when time was short.

A consistent and recurring problem in managing centers of excellence appears to be one of motivation.

How can firms get around this motivational problem? We heard conflicting stories during the research. Some respondents saw the center of excellence model working as it is, with no changes to incentive systems. They argued that the motivation comes from within:

> They get a little bit in the newspaper, they don't get paid any more ... They are thought of as having superior knowledge or experience in that particular area, and people want to talk to them.

The more usual view, however, was that systems need to be created to build individual motivation. One approach, in theory, is to manipulate the hard systems, such as reporting structures, appraisal systems, and bonus packages. However, we saw no evidence for this occurring, presumably because firms are worried that such structures would detract from the primary responsibilities of professional employees. The only structural change we observed was where one individual was given full-time responsibility for managing a center—for example, McKinsey's industry specialists. This was attempted only in cases where the center in question was broad enough in scope that it could withstand the cost of full-time professional staff. In most cases, centers were deliberately kept lean.

Most firms, instead, preferred to work on the soft systems, those relating to the social community of which the employees are part. As explained by one respondent:

> ... We need to understand what creates the behavior of knowledge sharing ... This is the socialization of people actually knowing each other. Because I am more likely to respond to a request (from a colleague) if I know him, if he's a good guy. I am going to respond because I know he'd do the same for me, but if I've never heard of him, maybe I'll get to it tomorrow ...

Such an approach may not be entirely satisfactory either, but in essence it is the direction most firms seem to be going. Firms are making small concessions to the hard elements of the organization, such as formal acknowledgment of centers of excellence elements on annual appraisals, but working primarily on the softer elements. These firms had developed organizational cultures in which many professionals appeared to be willing to contribute with virtually no formal recognition. What seemed to be encouraging them was a sense that they needed to put something back in the system because they had taken a considerable amount out. There was also an intangible desire to be recognized by their peers around the world.

The extent to which there were motivation problems varied between the types of centers. Individuals in virtual centers appeared to have the hardest jobs, both because they had a substantial exploration-oriented component to their work and because their support groups were dispersed around the world. Individuals in focused centers suffered from motivational problems but to a lesser degree than those in virtual centers, perhaps because their identity with the center was more concrete. And charismatic centers suffered very little from motivational problems; their center of excellence role was usually closely aligned with their day-to-day work, and the high profile nature of their work resulted in a lot of peer recognition.

The Role of Senior Management

While we have focused on the centers of excellence themselves, because we believe they are an important but under-recognized model for helping service firms to manage their worldwide knowledge assets, there are also a number of important implications for how global services should be run in their entirety. Although senior managers in service firms typically play a much less intrusive role in the day-to-day activities of their employees than their counterparts in the manufacturing sector, they nonetheless have an important part to play in shaping the overall direction of the firm and building an organization in which knowledge is created and disseminated effectively. Below we identify the three key issues for senior managers to consider if they are currently using the center of excellence model, or thinking of doing in the near future.

Managing the Firm's Knowledge Portfolio

Focused centers capture emergent capabilities; virtual centers represent more codified capabilities; charismatic centers often represent capability gaps that the firm is trying to fill. Senior management's responsibility, is to make the strategic decisions about what sorts of centers to build, and the specific knowledge areas or capabilities that the centers are expected to manage. Most centers emerge over time through a rather haphazard process that is shaped by senior management only in its latter stages. But there is an opportunity for senior managers to become more involved in the earlier stages of center evolution, and even to begin to set priorities on what sorts of knowledge areas should be developed in the first place.

Senior managers also have to think about the where of centers of excellence. When establishing centers, most firms have a natural bias towards identifying excellence in the home country or in the largest market. A thorough investigation, however, might well reveal hitherto-unknown expertise in distant parts of the organization. Such latent centers are a valuable source of expertise, and send the important signal that all parts of the firm have an important role to play in knowledge development.

Managing the Center of Excellence Life-Cycle

One of the primary risks in using centers of excellence is that the life-cycle is not managed, and the firm ends up with too many centers, some of which are strategic but most of which are not.

Some centers of excellence will die out naturally, perhaps because they were not well-resourced in the first place, or perhaps because internal competition pushes the individuals behind them into other areas. But in other cases, particularly when there are dedicated resources attached to a center, the center of excellence will likely endure for longer than it is needed, unless decisive action is taken by senior managers. The process, then, involves an ongoing assessment of what role the centers of excellence serve, and whether that role can be better fulfilled through other means.

Motivating Employees to Build and Use the Centers of Excellence

Incentive and motivation issues are central to making the center of excellence model effective. Structural changes are probably not appropriate unless the center has a broad-based knowledge development role (e.g., a learning center). Resourcing centers with full-time individuals is effective for managing the centers of excellence, but it creates unwanted overhead. Soft management tools, such as building a cooperative culture, create strong social networks, and enhance the overall levels of communication in the firm. Related to the development of social networks is the need to build strong internal information networks such as Lotus Notes. Because many firms we spoke to were still struggling to build up-to-date and reliable computer infrastructure, they were severely hampered in their ability to manage their centers of excellence effectively. Managers should ensure that the proposed center of excellence solution is backed up by the appropriate technology before it is introduced.

Conclusion

The center of excellence model is attractive because it provides the focal points for knowledge development and dissemination, rather than relying on old-fashioned, informal, word-of-mouth mechanisms. However, we should acknowledge the emergence of Internet/Intranet systems as one possible way that the center of excellence model could be eclipsed. The Intranet offers a low-cost forum for worldwide information exchange. Centers that emerge there need not rely on top management to identify and broadcast their abilities. But Intranets are unlikely to ever be the whole solution to the problem of management of tacit knowledge, which by definition needs human interaction to be transferred. And on a practical level, Intranet usage in large firms is still patchy, and the software is of variable quality.[15] But it seems likely that an increasing amount of intrafirm communication will take place over the Intranet, which will in turn lead to changes in structural approaches to knowledge management like centers of excellence.

We should stress that many firms function quite effectively without centers of excellence. Centers of excellence are most appropriate: (a) when the key source of competitive advantage for the firm is tacit knowledge (rather than knowledge embodied in technology or physical assets); and (b) when the activities of the firm are so large or so dispersed that professional staff members cannot possibly know all their colleagues. These conditions hold for global service firms, and they probably hold for the service side of a great many multinational manufacturers as well. But we are wary about generalizing too far. If either of these conditions is absent, the center of excellence model may add relatively little value, and indeed be very costly to administer. In which case a firm can function better without it.

Endnotes

[1] Electra is a disguised name.

[2] While we use the term center of excellence exclusively in this article, it should be clear that the firms in our study used a plethora of names to describe the same phenomenon. These included: center of competence, community of practice, best practice, capability center, and future center.

[3] We define service firms as those whose primary value-added to customers is in the form of an intangible service, rather than in the transformation of inputs into a physical product. In terms of service firms studied in this research, our focus is on the consulting, insurance, banking, shipping, engineering, publishing, and information technology industries.

[4] Though there are certainly opportunities even within service firms to benefit from cost differences between countries. Back-office activities are frequently located in low-cost countries, and even in professional activities there are benefits to be gained from tapping into well-educated but relatively low-salary countries such as Ireland.

[5] Knowledge management is currently receiving a lot of research attention. See I. Nonaka and H. Takeuchi, *The Knowledge Creating Company*, 1995, Oxford University Press; G. Hedlund, A Model of Knowledge Management and the N-Form Corporation, *Strategic Management Journal*, Vol. 15, 1995.

[6] Knowledge can also be gained through external non-client relationships and through conferences and journals, but much of this knowledge is essentially a public good, so it offers no potential for competitive advantage unless it can somehow be transformed by the firm.

[7] See C. A. Bartlett and S. Ghoshal, 1986, Tap your subsidiaries for global reach, *Harvard Business Review*.

[8] These two models parallel the ethnocentric and polycentric models described in: Perlmutter, H. 1969. The Tortuous Evolution of the Multinational Corporation. *Columbia Journal of World Business*, 4: 9–18. The next two are variants of his geocentric model.

[9] *ABA Banking Journal*. 1992. An interview with Craig Goldman of Chase Manhattan. March 1992: 62.

[10] Codification is a process through which tacit knowledge, that which is personal, context-specific and hard to formalize, becomes explicit, i.e. transmittable in formal, systematic language.

[11] Bartlett, C.A. 1996. McKinsey and Company. Harvard Business School Publishing, Case study 396-357.

[12] It is interesting to compare virtual centers to communities of practice, which are emergent bodies of professionals drawn together by common interests and experiences. In many ways the two are quite similar, but they differ in two important ways: (a) virtual centers have a clear deliverable, while communities of practice do not; and (b) communities of practice are by definition unformalized learning groups, whereas virtual centers are an attempt to structure interaction between people. See: Stewart, T. 1997. *Intellectual Capital*. Nicholas Brealey: London.

[13] In this regard, virtual centers could perhaps be better called spheres or webs of excellence, in the sense that they are interconnected, flexible, and quickly adopted to new demands.

[14] Nelson, R. and Winter, S. 1982. *An evolutionary theory of economic change*. Cambridge, MA: Harvard University Press.

[15] One consulting company we studied, for example, had an impressive project database, but when anyone tried to use it their search typically resulted in a deluge of mostly useless material, or none at all. Quality control in such databases is still very hard to achieve.

About the Authors

Karl J. Moore is on the faculty of Templeton College, Oxford University, where he teaches international business strategy, primarily to executives. He has also taught at McGill University, Dartmouth, and the London Business School. The author of more than 50 books, chapters, articles, and papers, his research focuses on global competitive advantage and emerging issues in high tech industries. His book, the *U.K. Venture Capital Market*, was published by Wiley & Sons in 1997.

Julian M. Birkinshaw is an assistant professor at the Institute of International Business, Stockholm School of Economics. His research is centered around issues of strategy and organization in large multinational firms, and in particular on how firms can effectively manage their geographically dispersed resources. His research has been published in *Strategic Management Journal*, *Journal of International Business Studies*, *Sloan Management Review* and a number of other journals.

Pergamon

International Business Review 10 (2001) 597–614

INTERNATIONAL BUSINESS REVIEW

www.elsevier.com/locate/ibusrev

International marketing managers' cultural sensitivity: relevance, training requirements and a pragmatic training concept

Hartmut H. Holzmüller [a,1], Barbara Stöttinger [b,*]

[a] *Department of Marketing, University of Dortmund, 44221 Dortmund, Germany*

[b] *Department of International Marketing and Management, Vienna University of Economics and Business Administration, Augasse 2-6, 1090 Vienna, Austria*

Received 22 December 2000; revised 2 April 2001; accepted 13 May 2001

Abstract

With the shift from national to international and global business, new challenges have emerged for managers engaged in transnational business activities. The complexity of the tasks involved in international marketing requires an approach that demonstrates cultural sensitivity. As a consequence, the question arises as to whether international marketing managers are well-prepared to deal effectively with culturally overlapping situations.

While it is widely accepted that culture is substantially affecting international marketing decisions, pragmatic concepts of how to achieve cultural sensitivity in international marketing are lacking. This paper aims to narrow this gap. The importance of cultural sensitivity in international marketing is highlighted, training requirements are identified, and a recently introduced concept of culture is assessed for its usefulness and applicability in an international marketing context. © 2001 Elsevier Science Ltd. All rights reserved.

Keywords: Cultural standards; International management training; Cultural sensitivity

* Corresponding author. Tel.: +43-1-313-36/5104; fax: +43-1-313-36/793.

E-mail addresses: h.holzmueller@wiso.wiso.uni-dortmund.de (H. H. Holzmüller); barbara.stoettinger@wu-wien.ac.at (B. Stöttinger).

[1] Tel.: +49-231-755-3270; fax: +49-231-755-3231.

PII: S0969-5931(01)00034-8

1. Introduction

Looking at the development of business activities over the last few decades, one trend is clearly discernible: the shift from local or national toward international or global business. Targeting markets beyond the home market implies that marketing activities become considerably more heterogeneous and complex than those carried out in the domestic market. This is due to differences in government policies, rates of economic development and growth, the socio-cultural environment, or consumer attitudes and behaviour (Czinkota & Ronkainen, 1996; Douglas & Craig, 1995).

As a result, most international marketing tasks are non-routine tasks that require a multi-faceted range of actions, as they are often worked out in co-operation with or tailored to people with a different cultural background. For example, advertising depends on culture-specific influences, such as differences in communication styles, communication objectives, information processing, cultural attitudes or linguistic characteristics. These specific conditions determine the nature of advertising practices in different markets. In addition, advertising may also be used to stimulate changes in social behaviour. However, walking this tightrope requires not only knowledge of different advertising techniques but also emotional sensitivity to assess the techniques' appropriateness in a different cultural environment (De Mooij, 1998; Usunier, 1996). This example is representative of many international marketing situations that call for not only cognitive marketing skills but also, at the same time and equally importantly, non-cognitive, emotional abilities with respect to handling foreign cultures.

How should international marketing managers prepare themselves for these culturally overlapping situations, where they may be confronted with stereotypes such as "it is the manager's instinct or character which determines success or failure in these situations", or, in order to understand cultural differences and to avoid "culture-caused" errors, be led to believe that reading travel guides, international marketing textbooks and complying with general rules of manners is sufficient (Jandt, 1995; Samovar & Porter, 1997)? Many firms still demand cognitive skills such as a certain professional background or the command of a foreign language as key prerequisites for international marketing assignments (Deresky, 2000; Mendenhall, Punnett, & Ricks, 1995; Thomas, 1991b). As outlined exemplarily in the case of advertising, "knowing" about the differences between markets is no longer sufficient. International marketing activities require "soft" skills such as understanding the way people think, the way they relate their wishes and desires to actions and how they combine them with feelings. In a theoretical context, the development of this cultural sensitivity has been discussed extensively. Most approaches, however, still lack practical application (Adler, 1997; Mendenhall et al., 1995; Usunier, 1996).

The objective of this paper is threefold: (a) draw the attention of scholars to the fact that—despite the undisputed impact of culture on international marketing decision making—no operational concepts are at hand of how to develop cultural sensitivity among international marketing managers; (b) assess the usefulness of well-established cultural concepts for their applicability in cultural sensitivity training; and (c) report on a recently introduced, robust and parsimonious cultural concept and demonstrate its practical scope and limitations for international marketing training purposes. Consequently, the paper first discusses the relevance of cultural sensitivity in the context of international marketing management. Based on these insights, typical training requirements are identified and existing cultural concepts are assessed with respect to their applicability for culture sensitivity training. In the core part, the concept of cultural standards initially developed in psychology by Thomas and co-workers (1991b, 1996) will be transferred to the international marketing context. The new concept is outlined in detail and evaluated for its benefits and limitations in international marketing use. The paper concludes with suggestions for future research in this area.

2. Cultural sensitivity—a key determinant of cultural competence

Extensive research across disciplines has investigated the question of how to create culturally competent managers (e.g. Chen & Starosta, 1996; Hinckley & Perl, 1996; Post, 1997; Shanahan, 1996; Spitzberg & Cupach, 1989). From the numerous definitions of competence, one subsumes the ongoing discussion quite well: competence may be described as (work-related) knowledge, skills and aptitudes, which serve productive purposes in firms. It distinguishes outstanding from average performers (Dalton, 1997; Kochanski, 1997; Nordhaug 1993, 1998).

When operationalising cultural competence, previous research has focused mostly on one of the following dimensions: the affective (motivation), the cognitive (knowledge) or the conative (skills) dimension. However, as results have shown, this emphasis on just one dimension falls short of depicting this complex construct. Therefore, more recent attempts to measure cultural competence integrate all three dimensions. Among these holistic approaches, the so-called "Third Culture Approach" by Gudykunst, Wiseman, and Hammer (1977) has found a particularly widespread reception in the field. Under the "Third-Culture" approach, a manager displays cultural competence, when he/she interprets and judges culturally overlapping situations neither from an ethnocentric perspective nor from an idealised host culture perspective, but assumes a neutral position. To achieve this neutral position, Gudykunst et al. (1977) stress the importance of the affective component of cultural competence, which may be called cultural sensitivity. In their model, cultural sensitivity is a prerequisite which instils the acquisition of knowledge (cognitive dimension) and skills (conative dimension). Gudykunst et al. (1977) see cultural sensitivity as the psychological link between home and host culture. This notion clearly contradicts the current business practice mentioned earlier, where language or professional knowledge and skills are deemed key prerequisites for successful foreign assignments.

This Third-Culture Approach lends itself well to understanding the Concept of Cultural Standards which we can apply to the discipline as a suitable tool to train cultural competence. As will be described later in more detail, the concept of Cultural Standards places a strong emphasis on the affective components of cultural competence, but at the same time provides the trainee with knowledge and skills needed to successfully handle culturally overlapping situations.

3. Defining culture-sensitive marketing activities

The driving forces of globalisation, such as converging market needs, advances in international transportation networks or the dramatic improvement in communication technology spur the dynamic changes in today's international business. Moreover, the pace of these developments is more than likely to accelerate and makes it possible to envision that the future of international business is vastly different from today. No longer will international managers be able to succeed solely on their domestic cultural understanding skills alone, but they will have to change and adapt quickly to cultural differences and environmental changes (e.g. Keegan & Schlegelmilch, 2001; Mendenhall et al., 1995; Parhizgar, 1999).

As Mendenhall et al. (1995) put it, international managers are not the only people to deal with a complex and uncertain environment; the nature of international business in itself is already highly complex and unstable. In analogy, we attribute this complexity and instability to international marketing managers' professional activities at least to the same extent. They not only have to deal with internal stakeholders, such as the home and the host country organisation, but are involved in multiple interactions with external contingencies such as the host country's consumers, distribution partners, market research institutions or advertising agencies. Several fields of marketing where culture and culture-sensitive actions matter are outlined in Fig. 1. In the following section, some of the typical international marketing tasks that require cultural sensitivity will be discussed in more detail.

Three key areas of international marketing activities in Fig. 1 are singled out to depict how critical cultural sensitivity is appropriate for their success. This selection is made for demonstration purposes. It should not be interpreted as a value judgement

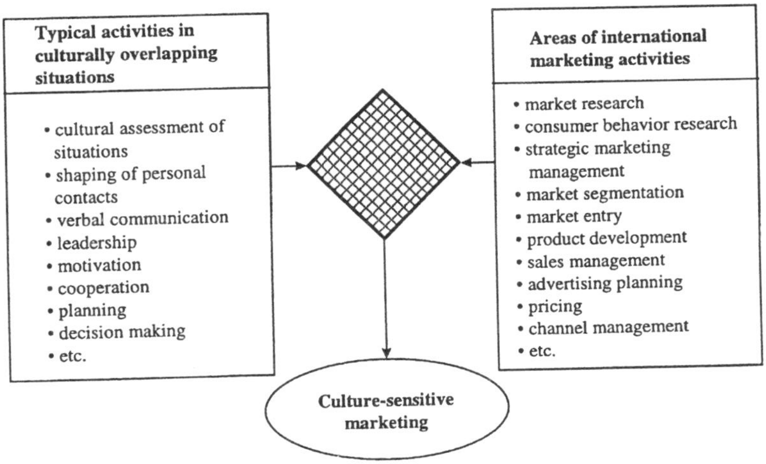

Fig. 1. Areas of culture-sensitive marketing.

indicating which international marketing activities may require more cultural sensitivity than others.

In international market research, the main difficulties lie in establishing cross-national equivalence at various stages in the research process (Cavusgil & Das, 1997). While in the home market the researcher can usually rely on personal experience to avoid failure, cultural sensitivity is vital for getting meaningful and high quality results in an international research setting. The host country's different cultural environment calls for culture-sensitive activities when assessing potential research problems, carrying out field activities and interpreting the findings derived (Craig & Douglas, 2000). Without the appropriate knowledge and the relevant cultural sensitivity, misinterpretations are the rule, as numerous examples show. One of the most well-known international marketing research failures was produced in a Reader's Digest study of pasta consumption in Europe. It detected that French and German consumers eat significantly higher amounts of pasta than Italians. This false assumption was based on an ill-defined phrasing in the questionnaire. Ignoring the idiosyncrasies of Italian cuisine, in which fresh and therefore unpackaged pasta is much more frequently used, respondents were asked the questions with regard to packaged and branded pasta (Cundiff & Hilger, 1988).

Strategic planning in international marketing is another area that has to focus on cultural aspects (Terpstra & Sarathy, 1997). Meaningful industry analysis and environmental scanning, a prerequisite for strategy formulation, has to take into consideration the behaviour of competitors, typical trade terms or managerial attitudes (Terpstra & David, 1991). To deal with foreign environments, not only culture-related know-how is the key to success. In order to properly understand and eventually anticipate, for instance, competitive reactions, cultural sensitivity is crucial.

Finally, in international sales management, international negotiations are highly culture-sensitive situations. Following the model of work-related values by Hofstede (1991, 1997), cultures with high uncertainty avoidance spend considerable time investigating the culture with which they will negotiate. They also require a great deal of information before they are willing to make a decision (Samovar & Porter, 1997). This, however, is only a very rough insight into a complicated field of action. Most likely, direct negotiations are much more influenced by individual patterns of behaviour which are embedded in the local culture (Ghauri & Usunier, 1996). To overcome these barriers in culturally overlapping situations, especially in relationship-prone societies, it is important to train personnel not only in certain models of culture but also in developing cultural awareness, empathy and emotional acceptance.

Given these examples of international marketing activities, the need for cultural sensitivity seems undisputed. However, the question arises as to how these demands can be translated into adequate training tools. This is addressed next.

4. A cultural sensitivity training outline

When developing cultural sensitivity in the context of international business, a major focus lies in preparing managers confronted with culturally overlapping situations with respect to two goals: (1) identifying features of the host country's cultural orientation systems which have an effect on activities and actions; and (2) incorporating these features in their spectrum of actions to accomplish specific marketing tasks under foreign cultural frameworks and in interaction with partners shaped by these frameworks. As will be explained later on in more detail, cultural orientation systems are developed through socialisation within a specific cultural environment. They influence perception, thought, values and behaviour of society members and, in their way, establish membership of this society.

Despite the high failure rates of international assignments due to a lack of international managers' cultural sensitivity and the unsuccessful integration of family members into the host culture (e.g. Bird & Dunbar, 1991; Black, 1988; Black & Gregersen, 1991; Harvey, 1985), participants in such training most commonly do not expect major difficulties regarding their competence in culturally overlapping situations. They have hardly any idea about which effects cultural differences can have on private and business matters (Bittner, 1996; Bittner & Reisch, 1994). Taking these circumstances into account, an exemplary sequence of training issues in intercultural preparatory programmes is outlined below.

4.1. Create a learning need

The first step in a "culture training" is to create awareness among the participants that a confrontation of different cultural orientation systems is bound to lead to problems in interaction. Participants need to realise that misunderstandings are not a result of personality or character but are due to the unreflected transfer of home-country cultural patterns. In this phase, it is also necessary to encourage reflection on one's own culture and personality. This facilitates learning success and prevents the establishment of learning barriers (e.g. Bittner, 1996; Goodman, 1994).

4.2. Put received judgements into perspective

This training step aims at understanding and accepting different cultural standards which represent the operationalisation of a country's cultural orientation system. This training phase focuses on the fact that the mere knowledge of a different cultural framework does not necessarily lead to a willingness to accept and to adjust to these conditions. This training step addresses the problem of different cultures' significance and superiority, which often results in highly visible ethnocentric arrogance (Hentze & Kammel, 1994). The learning effect consists of questioning internalised values, which are often accepted without reflection and are therefore seen as superior to others.

4.3. Partially adopt local judgements

This training step demonstrates to trainees why the majority of interaction partners in the target country appreciate their own culture as it is. This appears necessary in order to partially adopt cultural values. Mentally, it imposes entirely different behaviour on the trainees than merely accepting the fact that some aspects of one's own cultural orientation system are (unfortunately so far) not common in the target culture (e.g. Bittner, 1996; Landis & Bhagat, 1996).

4.4. Weighting the personal influence

Here, the training intention can be subsumed under the label of "training humbleness". Due to the intensive analysis of intercultural matters, the trainees realise that opportunities to influence a local culture are far less than expected before the training. Bittner (1996) calls it the path from a manager's self-understanding as a "high-carat manager" towards a "mediator between cultural worlds". This changed perspective can produce massive insecurity which needs to be dealt with adequately. For a final integration of single training steps, it seems desirable to give a robust orientation framework (Bhawuk & Triandis, 1996).

This leads to the fundamental question of which concept of culture represents the theoretical foundation for such a training. For the purpose of developing cultural sensitivity, the concept of culture selected should provide extensive coverage of the complex phenomenon "culture" and, for applicability purposes, be action-relevant rather than merely abstract. In the following section, key concepts of culture are presented and evaluated for their practical relevance to cultural sensitivity training.

5. In the "jungle" of cultural concepts

Literature abounds on the notion and concept of "culture". Even attempts to systematise the findings presented there into different "schools" only yield highly complex and sophisticated categorisations (Allaire & Firsirotu, 1984). According to Ajiferuke and Boddewyn (1970), this is mainly because culture is a universal term that has as many meanings as people use it.

From an international marketing research perspective, the different notions of culture can be assessed with respect to their pragmatic qualities, such as manageable complexity, reasonable cost of data collection and their applicability and relevance to everyday marketing activities. A way to take these demands into account is to systematise the various concepts of culture along two dimensions: first, the concept's methodological focus, and second, the scope of variables that depict "culture" (Fig. 2). A categorisation in line with the methodological focus of a concept opens up two opposing directions: first, a body of research based on a positivistic approach, which captures the phenomenon of culture exclusively through collecting relevant data by means of questionnaires (Hofstede, 1997), and second, research work comprising highly interpretative approaches, such as "objective hermeneutics" (Oevermann, Allert, Konau, & Krambeck, 1979). The second dimension, which relates to the scope of variables that depict culture, is based on how many cultural aspects are considered within the research design. Even within this dimension, two approaches may be differentiated. The universal approach focuses on only a few aspects or cultural dimensions which are characteristic of many different cultures

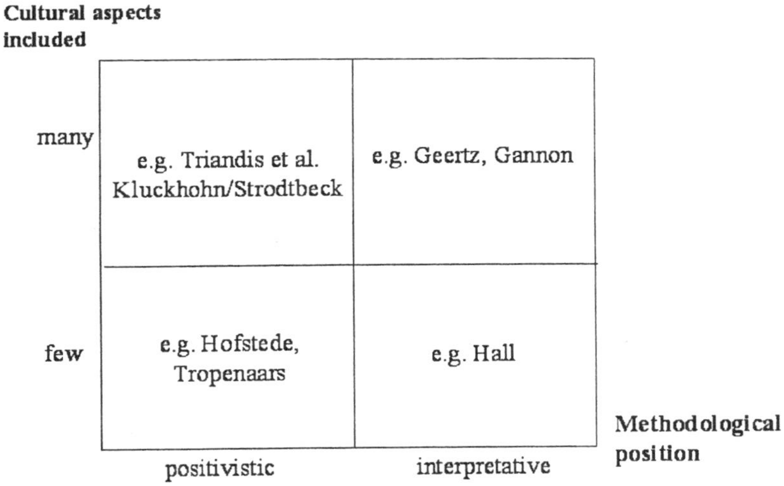

Fig. 2. Typology of culture concepts.

and are selected particularly with regard to their stability across cultures. In contrast, the culture-relativistic approach is based on the notion of culture as a context made up of a large number of single cultural aspects. This set of variables serves as a framework for analysis through which significance and meaning is added to individual actions only. The typology (see Fig. 2) depicts all the above-mentioned culture concepts and can be considered as a first, but by no means exhaustive, approach towards systematisation.

Although this typology does not entirely do justice to concept specifics, it can be used to position and assess the approaches mentioned above in view of their applicability. The works of Hofstede (1991, 1997), which are grounded on a value-based concept of culture, or of Trompenaars (1993) are typical examples of some positivistic orientation which includes only a few cultural dimensions (lower left quadrant in Fig. 2). In contrast, Hall's (1990) widely used concept of culture is characteristic of an interpretative approach, which focuses on three cultural aspects, namely, the context of verbal communication and the way people deal with space and with time. Geertz's (1993) concept of culture is a context-related and culture-relativistic one. It can be considered as a typical example of an interpretative approach which includes a large number of cultural aspects. Finally, the concept of "subjective" culture by Triandis, Vassiliou, Vassiliou, Tanaka, and Shanmugam (1972) or the work of Kluckhohn and Strodtbeck (1961) represents a positivistic and context-related approach.

In order to assess the practical applicability of different types of cultural concepts from a marketing perspective, the following criteria were used: (a) relevance for culturally overlapping marketing situations; (b) coverage of the phenomenon of "culture"; (c) cross-cultural explanatory power; and (d) economy of data collection. Culture concepts are particularly well suited for analysing cross-cultural activities, if they allow for specific behavioural measures to be deduced. Furthermore, their applicability will increase the more a broad-based coverage of experienceable cultural similarities and differences is obtained. Considering the geographic scope, culture concepts that may be applied more universally are considered preferable due to the increasing globalisation of markets. Finally, the economy of data collection and interpretation also plays an important role in its assessment with regard to practical relevance.

Based on these arguments, none of the concepts outlined above—as reflected in the typology in Fig. 2—is ideally suited to be applied in international marketing (see Table 1). While a multi-faceted concept of culture results in a more extensive coverage of "culture" and leads to more precise behavioural instructions for marketing activities in culturally overlapping situations, its universal applicability and economy in collecting data is low. A similar trade-off prevails in an assessment along the methodological dimension. The more interpretative the approach, the higher its managerial relevance and coverage of cultural phenomena is. In contrast, these approaches, however, lack cross-cultural explanatory power and economy in data collection.

None of the extreme positions in Fig. 2 is appropriate when it comes to developing cross-cultural sensitivity training to carry out international marketing activities effectively. On the contrary, concepts of culture offering a limited range of cultural variables are more suited to conceptualising sensitivity training. A mid-range complexity facilitates the collection and processing of information among trainees. With respect to the methodological dimension, a mix between positivistic and interpretative approaches seems particularly favourable, as it prevents an overemphasis on "objective" cultural aspects and establishes a balance between universality and economy.

Table 1
Assessment of the practicability of cultural concepts in international marketing management

Criteria	Concepts of culture			
	Few aspects		Many aspects	
	Positivistic	Interpretative	Positivistic	Interpretative
Coverage of the phenomenon "culture"	− −	−	+	+ +
Relevance for culturally overlapping situations	− −	−	+	+ +
Cross-cultural explanatory power	+ +	−	+	− −
Economy of data collection	+ +	+	−	− −

One culture concept that represents these middle positions and meets sensitivity training demands in a cross-cultural context is the concept of cultural standards developed by Thomas et al. (1991b, 1996).

6. The concept of cultural standards

The concept of cultural standards, whose cornerstones are outlined in the following section, has its origins in various disciplines: cross-cultural psychology and communications research as well as in international exchange research and socio-psychological attribution research.

6.1. Notion and definition of "culture" in the concept of cultural standards

Based on the assumption that a person's capacity to act requires sufficient orientation in his/her home environment, Thomas et al. (e.g. 1989, 1991b, 1995, 1996) argue that this prerequisite is not always met in culturally overlapping situations. In general, people enter intercultural interactions and activities relying on information and experiences that are shaped by their own cultural background. Consequently, conflict-ridden and straining incidents occur due to the clash of the contrary cultural orientation systems of the people involved.

Cultural orientation systems are developed through a process of individual socialisation within a specific cultural environment. According to Thomas et al. (1991b, 1996), they are universal for society members but specific to each society, organisation or group. The cultural orientation systems are formed in a society and passed on from generation to generation. They influence perception, thought, values and behaviour of society members and, in their way, establish membership of this society. Consequently, culture may, if it is considered as an orientation system, provide a framework that helps society members to structure their behavioural field and enables them to find independent ways of coping with their environment.

As cultural orientation systems are specific to a society, the modes of behaviour of people from foreign countries with different sets of cultural rules can only be vaguely anticipated. As a result, inappropriate actions and reactions, misunderstandings, misleading situations, a feeling of uncertainty and, at worst, an inability to react or interact may occur (Thomas, 1991b; Thomas & Hagemann, 1996).

6.2. Cultural standards

Cultural orientation systems are operationalised by means of so-called cultural standards. These standards comprise all ways of perception, thought, judgement and actions which are considered normal, generally accepted by, typical of and binding on a certain culture. The cultural standards also serve as benchmarks for the assessment of one's own behaviour, the behaviour of others and for behavioural adjustment (Müller & Thomas, 1991; Thomas, 1996). Major importance is attached to those cultural standards which apply to a large number of situations and cover a wide range of behavioural aspects. Standards that meet these requirements are, for example, those which are relevant to human interactions, as they determine perception, assessment and activities.

Cultural standards display themselves at different levels of abstraction. On the highest aggregate level, cultural standards are expressed as general norms and values. On a more specific level, they appear as behavioural guidelines. If deviations beyond certain limits of tolerance occur, disapproval will be generated and sanctions will follow. The range of validity of different cultural standards varies cross-culturally: while some standards show an equivalent meaning in two or more cultures, others change their meaning in part or entirely or are not observed at all in another cultural environment. Cultural standards can also change their significance or their limits of tolerance across cultures (Thomas & Hagemann, 1996; Thomas, 1991b). Within a cultural framework, standards are not explicitly perceived by society members. It is only through contact with foreign cultures that their existence and their effects become manifest.

6.3. Determination of cultural standards

Cultural standards are empirically derived by researching culturally overlapping situations in two cultures of interest. Interacting partners with different cultural backgrounds automatically generate "critical" incidents due to their own cultural orientation systems. Incidents of this kind are perceived as unpleasant, annoying and depressing to the persons involved. They are difficult to cope with and can preoccupy the persons involved for a long period of time. To empirically capture these situations, interviews are used to investigate cross-cultural incidents which the interviewees experienced (Critical Incident Analysis; Flanagan, 1954).

After consolidating the individual results, the differences triggering critical incidents between cultural orientation systems are elaborated. For that purpose, research groups for both cultures involved are installed to identify specific behavioural patterns and provide explanations for these patterns. Each judge is familiar with his/her home country's cultural orientation system and its cultural standards and holds assumptions about their effectiveness in the host culture. For example, to explain behaviour in a Chinese–German culturally overlapping situation, Chinese judges would use Chinese culture standards, whereas Germans would use assumptions of what they perceive to be a Chinese cultural standard. These judgements are contrasted in pairs and synthesised in a way that cultural standards emerge. Supported by findings from other disciplines such as philosophy, religious sciences and linguistics, core cultural standards are consolidated and their vertical and horizontal interrelations are elucidated (Thomas, 1991a,b).

Looking at the typology of culture concepts (see Fig. 2), Thomas's concept of cultural standards holds a position in the matrix's centre combining interpretative and positivistic methodological approaches. On the one hand, the concept relies on an interpretative approach by using qualitative interviews. On the other hand, it also draws on positivistic methods, as the data are consolidated by means of quantitative analysis. For validation purposes, the consolidated data are, in turn, subjected to interpretative analysis. As to the number of cultural variables included, Thomas's concept also holds a middle position.

6.4. Examples of cultural standards

In the past few years, intensive research was done at the Department of Psychology, University of Regensburg, to identify similarities and differences between German and US, Chinese and South Korean cultural standards. One set of cultural standards in the US and Germany is particularly well documented, namely that of "interpersonal distance regulation", as it is very likely to produce considerable misunderstandings in culturally overlapping situations (Markowski & Thomas, 1995; Müller & Thomas, 1991). It is reported that Germans assess US-Americans as friendly, open and amenable, but superficial and unreliable. In contrast, US-Americans who had contact with Germans describe them as reserved, shy and stubborn (Thomas, 1991b). These examples point out that culturally overlapping situations bear a high potential for misunderstandings, insult and emotional stress, which might, for example, put the success of business relations at risk.

Contrary cultural standards on how to overcome psychological personal distance to other people may serve to explain these deviating attributions. American cultural standards demand minimising this distance. Consequently, it is considered an obligation to react and to establish contact with every person in the field of vision. In general, openness in peripheral personal matters (e.g. general personal information, helpfulness and hospitality) is extensive, whereas central personal affairs (e.g. personal problems, emotions and attitudes) are dealt with far less frankly. From a German perspective, peripheral personal matters are hardly enlarged on during first social contacts (typical norm: "do not be obtrusive!"). The distance appears only after a prolonged period of getting acquainted and results in a comparatively high sincerity with regard to central personal affairs (Markowski & Thomas, 1995; Müller & Thomas, 1991). In the following (see Table 2), central cultural standards in the US and Germany are outlined, which were empirically derived.

Table 2
Central cultural standards in the US and Germany

In the US	In Germany
Individualism	Formalism
Egalitarian orientation	Power orientation
Action orientation	Performance of one's duty
Achievement/competition orientation	Family orientation
Interpersonal distance regulation	Interpersonal distance regulation
Social acceptance	Physical distance regulation
Calmness/"easy-going"	Frankness/outspokenness
Patriotism	Personal property
Relation between sexes	Traditional role expectations
Future orientation	

Source: Markowski & Thomas (1995) and Müller & Thomas (1991).

An analysis of central cultural standards in China and South Korea served to confirm a well-known norm in interpersonal relations—i.e. face-saving, the importance and explanatory power of which were elucidated for everyday situations. From a European perspective, this cultural standard is difficult to understand in its variety and consequences. It is a typically Chinese culture-specific phenomenon that also exists in Germany, but plays only an inferior and less differentiated role. Its main focus is put on saving a person's status in interpersonal relations. If this status is damaged or ill-respected through personal or other people's misbehaviour, this will imply shame and disgrace (Brück & Thomas, 1995).

Typical behavioural patterns that comply with this cultural standard include avoiding or retreating quickly from potentially "dangerous" social situations, ending the interaction and keeping self-control, avoiding public criticism and confrontation as well as striving for harmony (Thomas, 1989). This has led Thomas (1996) to propound the following findings for German–Chinese interactions: while in the Germans' view their task-orientation prepares the ground for interpersonal relations, the Chinese take the exact opposite approach: only after establishing a positive personal relationship will business contacts promise success.

These examples of cultural standards indicate that knowledge of one's own and the target country's cultural orientation system makes the emotional handling of cross-cultural differences significantly smoother. It also allows managers engaged in culturally overlapping situations to adapt better to the specific demands of these situations. As a result, training material for cultural orientation trainings has been developed which is based on the concept of cultural standards.

6.5. Application of the concept of cultural standards in education and training programmes

The data which are collected during the interviews contain a large number of exemplary situational descriptions (i.e. of critical incidents). Therefore, they can be drawn on as a starting point for the development of relevant training programmes. The so-called cultural assimilator programmes are based on the idea that interaction partners understand and react more efficiently in interactive processes if these processes make sense to them. The acting individuals show better understanding when they discover why interaction partners pursue certain goals and why certain incidents and behavioural patterns occur in a certain cultural environment the way they do (Thomas & Hagemann, 1996; Triandis et al., 1972). Assimilators can either be culture-specific ones, which are designed and used to prepare individuals from one cultural group for interaction with another cultural group, or culture-general ones, which prepare individuals for experiences regardless of particular cultural backgrounds (Cushner & Landis, 1996).

In the German-speaking area, some assimilator programmes that are based on the concept of cultural standards are already available. Thomas (1989) reports on the development of a programme for interacting with Chinese people in a business context. Similar programmes are available for German trainees in the US (Müller & Thomas, 1991). Furthermore, culture assimilator programmes for US expatriates in

Germany (Markowski & Thomas, 1995) as well as in China and South Korea (Brück & Thomas, 1995) are at hand. These training programmes are based on the descriptions of intercultural, interactive situations which can only be solved "culturally correctly" by applying the underlying cultural standards. After each description of an exemplary situation, the programme offers various possible solutions of which only one corresponds to the actual target culture's orientation system. Each alternative proposed is accompanied by explanatory comments of why the solution chosen is right or wrong. By means of representative and illustrative examples and built-in learning loops, the trainees get an opportunity to acquire knowledge of cultural standards and their implications for everyday life in culturally overlapping situations.

In line with the holistic view of cultural competence, the training materials allow for not only a cognitive but also an emotional analysis of a target culture. During the process of establishing cultural standards, it encompasses the conative (skills) dimension by drawing on particular skills which worked well or failed in a critical incident. Knowledge (cognitive dimension) is created as the training draws on interactive situations (such as negotiations, marketing activities, everyday situations, etc.) which are rehearsable and familiar to the individuals being trained. In this way they may learn about cultural universalities and specifics between the home and the target culture. Finally and foremost, the concept of cultural standards places a strong emphasis on the affective dimension. As the differences between "culturally competent" and "incompetent" reactions to training situations are too subtle to be solved through knowledge alone, the right reaction requires a high degree of cultural sensitivity. This may eventually even lead to positive attitudes towards foreign culture, increased acceptance of local norms and a reduction in emotional barriers (Lange, 1994).

7. Limitations and outlook for future research

These remarks are by no means supposed to give the impression that the concept of cultural standards is the only approach that can be applied in the development of culture-sensitive marketing. Thomas's concept of cultural standards is but one approach and constitutes a comparatively new form of dealing with cultural problems in international marketing management. As it has not yet been subject to extensive research, weaknesses in the concept have to be put into perspective.

Despite its inherent practicability and its imminent applicability to international marketing training, this concept has weaknesses. Due to its degree of novelty it is not strongly rooted in culture-theoretic basic research (Demorgon & Molz, 1996; Krewer, 1996). Although it was developed out of practical experiences in intercultural communications research, it may not be considered atheoretic due to its scientific background in social psychology and communication sciences. However, from an anthropological and culture-sociological perspective, the highly extensive concept of culture falls short of theoretical foundation. Moreover, it should be noted that the concept takes on a more traditionalistic notion of culture, which reflects only a few constructivist and systemic aspects (Allaire & Firsirotu, 1984).

Cultural standards are candid shots and therefore meet the dynamic character of culture to a limited extent only. Besides, it still remains unclear what kinds of interrelationships between cultural standards exist and how they are weighted and hierarchically structured. This implies that, at present, no definitive findings as to the singular importance, the extent of overlapping and the central significance of single cultural standards have been established. However, the concept's basic outline suggests that future research efforts will result in considerable improvements in its dynamic as well as its relational aspects.

Another issue which requires further consideration are the variances within a culture which may have an impact on the stability of cultural standards. Variables such as age or gender may interfere with uniform cultural standards within a national context. Some countries are also culturally more heterogeneous (e.g. the US) than others (e.g. Japan). The influence of these variations has not yet been investigated and is thus not reflected in the training material.

In a business context, limits regarding the concept of cultural standards also come to the fore due to its bicultural focus. As national cultural standards can only be determined by comparing one's home culture to a target culture, generalisation is limited and results in the development of country- and culture-related material. As data are only gathered in a specific context, such as in a business environment, an additional limitation to their application prevails. So far there has been no evidence of whether cultural standards identified in a specific context are applicable across different social environments. In other words, it still remains unclear whether findings obtained in a student exchange programme, among managers or development aid workers are equally relevant or valid.

The time dimension and its potential influence on the concept of cultural standards is another aspect which has not been dealt with so far. The concept of cultural standards lends itself well to examining initial interactions between individuals. However, to what extent individual perspectives change, as interactions take place over time and relationships develop, still remains to be clarified.

Notwithstanding the above limitations, the research avenues which are provided are likely to overcome the deficits due to the inherent potential of this concept. Based on our own experiences with the training material and the reactions of trainees who have worked with it, we believe that the concept of cultural standards is superior to other theoretical concepts and especially suitable for the development of culture-sensitive marketing.

References

Adler, N. J. (1997). *International dimensions of organizational behavior* (3rd ed.). Cincinnati: South-Western College Publ.

Ajiferuke, M., & Boddewyn, J. (1970). Culture and other explanatory variables in comparative management studies. *Academy of Management Journal*, 453–458.

Allaire, Y., & Firsirotu, M. (1984). Theories of organizational culture. *Organization Studies*, *3*, 193–226.

Bhawuk, D. P. S., & Triandis, H. C. (1996). The role of culture theory in the study of culture and intercultural training. In D. Landis, & R. S. Bhagat (Eds.), *Handbook of intercultural training* (pp. 17–34). Thousand Oaks: Sage Publications.

Bird, A., & Dunbar, R. (1991). Getting the job done over there: improving expatriate productivity. *National Productivity Review, Spring*, 145–156.

Bittner, A. (1996). Psychologische Aspekte der Vorbereitung und des Trainings von Fach- und Führungskräften auf einen Auslandseinsatz. In A. Thomas (Ed.), *Psychologie interkulturellen Handelns* (pp. 317–339). Göttingen: Hogrefe—Verlag für Psychologie.

Bittner, A., & Reisch, B. (1994). *Interkulturelles Personalmanagement. Internationale Personalentwicklung, Auslandsentsendungen, interkulturelles Training*. Wiesbaden: Gabler.

Black, J. S. (1988). Work role transitions: a study of American expatriate managers in Japan. *Journal of International Business Studies, 19*(3), 227–294.

Black, J. S., & Gregersen, H. (1991). The other half of the picture: antecedents of spouse cross-cultural adjustments. *Journal of International Business Studies, 22*(3), 461–478.

Brück, A., & Thomas, A. (1995). *Interkulturelles Orientierungstraining für Südkorea*. Heidelberg: Springer.

Cavusgil, S. T., & Das, A. (1997). Methodological issues in empirical cross-cultural research: a survey of the management literature and a framework. *Management International Review, 37*(1), 71–96.

Chen, G. M., & Starosta, W. J. (1996). Intercultural communication competence. A synthesis. In *Communication yearbook* (pp. 353–383).

Craig, S. C., & Douglas, S. P. (2000). *International marketing research* (2nd ed.). Chichester: John Wiley & Sons.

Cundiff, E. W., & Hilger, M. T. (1988). *Marketing in the international environment* (2nd ed.). Englewood Cliffs: Prentice-Hall.

Cushner, K., & Landis, D. (1996). The intercultural sensitizer. In D. Landis, & R. S. Bhagat (Eds.), *Handbook of intercultural training* (pp. 198–202). London: Sage Publishers.

Czinkota, M. R., & Ronkainen, I. (1996). *Global marketing*. New York: The Dryden Press.

Dalton, M. (1997). Are competency models a waste? *Training and Development, October*, 46–49.

De Mooij, M. (1998). *Global marketing and advertising. understanding cultural paradoxes*. London: Sage Publications.

Demorgon, J., & Molz, M. (1996). Bedingungen und Auswirkungen der Analyse von Kultur(en) und interkulturellen Interaktionen. In A. Thomas (Ed.), *Psychologie interkulturellen Handelns* (pp. 43–85). Göttingen: Hogrefe—Verlag für Psychologie.

Deresky, H. (2000). *International management* (3rd ed.). Reading: Addison-Wesley.

Douglas, S. P., & Craig, C. S. (1995). *Global marketing strategy*. New York: McGraw-Hill.

Flanagan, J. C. (1954). The critical incident technique. *Psychological Bulletin, 51*, 327–358.

Geertz, C. (1993). *Local knowledge*. London: Fontana Press.

Ghauri, P., & Usunier, J. -C. (1996). *International business negotiations*. Oxford: Pergamon.

Goodman, N. R. (1994). Cross-cultural training for the global executive. In Brislin, R. W., & Yoshida, T. (Eds.). *Improving intercultural interactions* (Vol. 3), (pp. 34–54) Thousand Oaks: Sage Publications.

Gudykunst, W. B., Wiseman, R. L., & Hammer, M. R. (1977). Determinants of a sojourner's attitudinal satisfaction. A path model. In B. Ruben (Ed.), *Communication yearbook I* (pp. 415–425). New Brunswick.

Hall, E. T. (1990). *The hidden dimension* (13th ed.). New York: Doubleday.

Harvey, M. G. (1985). The executive family: an overlooked variable in international assignments. *Columbia Journal of World Business, Spring*, 84–92.

Hentze, J., & Kammel, A. (1994). Erfolgsfaktoren im internationalen Management: Zur Bedeutung der interkulturellen Personalführung in der multinationalen Unternehmung. *Die Unternehmung, 48*(4), 265–275.

Hinckley, S., & Perl, V. (1996). The competence of the global manager. *Global Management, 1*, 138–148.

Hofstede, G. (1991). *Cultures and organizations. Software of the mind*. London: Harper Collins Business.

Hofstede, G. (1997). *Cultures and organizations: software of the mind*. New York: McGraw-Hill.

Jandt, F. E. (1995). *Intercultural communication—an introduction*. London: Sage Publications.

Keegan, W. J., & Schlegelmilch, B. B. (2001). *Global marketing management*. London: Prentice Hall.

Kluckhohn, F., & Strodtbeck, F. L. (1961). *Variations in value orientations*. Westport, CT: Greenwood Press.

Kochanski, J. (1997). Competency-based management. *Training and Development, October*, 41–44.

Krewer, B. (1996). Kulturstandards als Mittel der Selbst- und Fremdreflexion in interkulturellen Begegnungen. In A. Thomas (Ed.), *Psychologie interkulturellen Handelns* (pp. 147–163). Göttingen: Hogrefe—Verlag für Psychologie.

Landis, D., & Bhagat, R. S. (1996). A model of intercultural behavior and training. In D. Landis, & R. S. Bhagat (Eds.), *Handbook of intercultural training* (pp. 1–16). Thousand Oaks: Sage Publishers.

Lange, C. (1994). *Interkulturelle Orientierung am Beispiel der Trainingsmethode "Cultural Assimilator"*. Göttingen.

Markowski, R., & Thomas, A. (1995). *Interkulturelles Orientierungstraining für Deutschland. Übungsmaterial zur Vorbereitung amerikanischer Studenten, Praktikanten und Schüler auf das Studium in Deutschland*. Heidelberg.

Mendenhall, M., Punnett, B. J., & Ricks, D. (1995). *Global management*. Cambridge: Blackwell.

Müller, A., & Thomas, A. (1991). *Interkulturelles Orientierungstraining für die USA*. Saarbrücken: Verlag Breitenbach.

Nordhaug, O. (1993). *Human capital in organisations competence, training and learning*. Oslo: Scandinavian University Press.

Nordhaug, O. (1998). Competence specificities in organisations. *International Studies of Management and Organisation*, *28*(1), 8–29.

Oevermann, U., Allert, T., Konau, E., & Krambeck, J. (1979). Die Methodologie einer "objektiven Hermeneutik" und ihre allgemeine forschungslogische Bedeutung in den Sozialwissenschaften. In H.-G. Soeffner (Ed.), *Interpretative Verfahren in den Sozial- und Textwissenschaften*. Stuttgart: Metzler.

Parhizgar, K. D. (1999). Globalization of multicultural management. In K. Becker (Ed.), *Culture and international business* (pp. 1–24). Binghampton: International Business Press.

Post, H. A. (1997). Building a strategy on competencies. *Long Range Planning*, *30*(5), 733–740.

Samovar, L. A., & Porter, R. E. (1997). *Intercultural communication—a reader* (8th ed.). London: Wadsworth Publishing Company.

Shanahan, D. (1996). From language learner to multicultural manager. *European Management Journal*, *14*(3), 315–320.

Spitzberg, B. H., & Cupach, W. R. (1989). *Handbook of interpersonal competence research*. New York.

Terpstra, V., & David, K. (1991). *The cultural environment of international business* (3rd ed.). Cincinnati: South Western Publishing Company.

Terpstra, V., & Sarathy, R. (1997). *International marketing* (7th ed.). Fort Worth: The Dryden Press.

Thomas, A. (1989). Interkulturelles Handlungstraining in der Managerausbildung. *WiSt—Wirtschaftswissenschaftliches Studium*, *6*, 281–287.

Thomas, A. (1995). Die Vorbereitung von Mitarbeitern für den Auslandseinsatz: Wissenschaftliche Grundlagen. In T. M. Kühlmann (Ed.), *Mitarbeiterentsendung ins Ausland* (pp. 85–117). Göttingen: Verlag für angewandte Psychologie.

Thomas, A. (1996). Analyse der Handlungswirksamkeit von Kulturstandards. In A. Thomas (Ed.), *Psychologie interkulturellen Handelns* (pp. 107–135). Göttingen: Hogrefe—Verlag für Psychologie.

Thomas, A. (1991a). Intercultural Orientation for Managers, 30. In *International Congress of the International Institution of Sociology*, Kobe, Japan.

Thomas, A. (1991b). Psychologische Wirksamkeit von Kulturstandards im interkulturellen Handeln. In A. Thomas (Ed.), *Kulturstandards in der internationalen Begegnung* (pp. 55–70). Saarbrücken: Verlag Breitenbach.

Thomas, A., & Hagemann, K. (1996). Training interkultureller Kompetenz. In N. Bergemann, & A. L. J. Sourisseaux (Eds.), *Interkulturelles Management* (pp. 173–199). Heidelberg: Physica.

Triandis, H. C., Vassiliou, V., Vassiliou, G., Tanaka, Y., & Shanmugam, A. V. (1972). *The analysis of subjective culture*. New York, NY: Wiley.

Trompenaars, F. (1993). *Riding the waves of culture. Understanding cultural diversity in business*. London: Nicholas Brealey.

Usunier, J. -C. (1996). *Marketing across cultures* (2nd ed.). New York: Prentice Hall.

Hartmut H. Holzmüller holds the Chair of Marketing at Universität Dortmund, Germany. Most of his academic work has been published in German. Some of his work has been included in major international conference proceedings and published in international journals such as *Journal of International Marketing, Advances* *in International Marketing*, and *Management International Review*. His main research interests are in cross-cultural marketing, with specific reference to consumer behaviour, and export decision making. He is affiliated with universities in Austria, France, Germany, Ukraine, and the USA.

Barbara Stöttinger is Assistant Professor at the Department of International Marketing and Management at the Wirtschaftsuniversität Wien. Her work has been published in leading journals such as *Journal of International Marketing*, *Advances in International Marketing*, and *International Marketing Review* and included in major international conference proceedings. Her main research interests are in global marketing, with particular focus on the internationalisation process of small- and medium-sized industries, export performance and success factor research.

[15]

© Academy of Management Executive, 1998, Vol. 12, No. 4

Going Global: Using information technology to advance the competitiveness of the virtual transnational organization

Marie-Claude Boudreau, Karen D. Loch, Daniel Robey, and Detmar Straub

Executive Overview

It has become almost axiomatic that business success depends on expanding the global reach of an organization. Moreover, the adoption of the transnational organizational model for a multinational enterprise is widely acknowledged as the preferred means of going global. Designing effective transnational organizations depends on the effective deployment of advanced information technologies. Because globalization requires employees and business partners to be geographically and temporally distant from one another, deploying information technologies within a virtual organization is an obvious choice for overcoming spatial and temporal boundaries.

There is little doubt that the competitive landscape has changed dramatically over the past dozen years. Throughout most of the 1980s and 1990s, radical reorientation in customer demands, industry regulations, and technological innovations produced a challenging new environment in which world businesses now compete. Organizations have extended their activities around the world, as indicated by the tremendous growth in the number of multinational organizations.[1] According to a recent survey conducted by the American Management Association, survival in the global business arena has become a major concern of three out of four senior executives.[2] Managing interdependencies between nations is inherently more complex than managing activities within a single nation, and many globalization efforts have been crushed under the weight of unmet coordination needs. Therefore, it is critically important to design organizations that can compete effectively in the global business environment.

While the mandate for global enterprises is widely acknowledged, the preferred organizational form is unclear. In order to structure their global enterprises, executives need to understand forms such as virtual organizations, networked organizations, learning organizations, temporary organizations, T-form organizations, and many other exotic alternatives. Typically, advanced information technologies play a central role in such structures because technology permits new organizational designs to overcome the spatial and temporal dispersion that accompanies increased global reach. Confronted with choices among a wide array of structural alternatives and their enabling technologies, executives need guidance based on criteria that they understand and trust.

Criteria for Successful Transnational Organizations

Michael Porter defines global industries as those "in which a firm's competitive position in one country is significantly influenced by its position in other countries."[3] For Porter, competition in global industries requires the integration of activities on a worldwide basis rather than splitting the world into isolated markets or sites for operations. Global industries, therefore, impose daunting coordination requirements upon firms that seek to compete successfully. These requirements are best met by what Bartlett and Ghoshal describe as transnational companies.[4] Transnational enterprises may be contrasted with companies using global, multinational, or international strategies. Each of these four enterprise strategies faces different competitive issues, but the transnational enterprise must respond to a multiplicity of competitive challenges, as summarized in Table 1.

The global strategy is used when an enterprise locates its headquarters in one country while its operations are performed in one or more other countries.[5] Many domestic organizations adopted this approach in order to broaden their markets by exporting their products. Under this approach, an organization operates in a centralized manner. Efficiency, obtained through economies of scale, is the key criterion of effectiveness sought by the global company. Many Japanese firms, such as Honda and Nissan, have used this approach to expand their markets within United States.

In a multinational strategy, national or regional operations are relatively autonomous and decentralized in order to increase sensitivity to differences among the individual countries in which it operates. The key competitive issue is responsiveness to local markets. Alcoa, Honeywell, and General Foods are among the best-known examples of companies that have developed regional subsidiaries by means of this strategy.

Under an international strategy, enterprises compete on a worldwide basis against other international companies. The international approach calls for a more horizontal structure and establishes strategic linkages between countries in which a firm operates. Because the key to success in this approach lies in an enterprise's ability to transfer knowledge to overseas units, learning constitutes its key issue. General Electric, Procter & Gamble, and L. M. Ericsson are organizations that have adopted this approach.

According to Bartlett and Ghoshal, organizations will be most competitive if they simultaneously meet the challenges of global efficiency, local responsiveness, and learning. Meeting these challenges requires firms to adopt a transnational strategy in which each organizational activity is performed in a location where it can be best accomplished. For example, Verifone, Inc., a subsidiary of Hewlett-Packard that produces low-cost terminals for credit card and check authorization, has pursued a strategy of responsiveness to emerging markets around the globe. The company locates its manufacturing activities near defined centers of excellence to take advantage of already established economies of scale and to provide access to the best intellectual or capital resources. VeriFone's employees are dispersed all over the world with less than seven percent of them located at the nominal corporate headquarters in California. Yet all employees are linked electronically and can share knowledge relevant to major decisions. Verifone's transnational strategy simultaneously promotes efficiency, responsiveness, and learning.

Clearly, the transnational enterprise strategy poses the greatest challenges for organizations seeking to increase their global competitiveness. The primary difficulty is to design an organizational form that is capable of being efficient and responsive, and that enables the transfer of knowledge across locations.

The primary difficulty is to design an organizational form that is capable of being efficient and responsive, and that enables the transfer of knowledge across locations.

For many firms, the answer to the problem of going global is to adopt a virtual organizational design.

Table 1
Enterprise Strategies and their Key Competitive Issues

Types of Enterprise Strategies	Key Competitive Issues
Global	Efficiency
Multinational	Responsiveness
International	Learning
Transnational	Efficiency Responsiveness Learning

The Virtues of Going Virtual

Virtual organizations have been widely discussed during the past decade.[6] Unfortunately, the virtues of going virtual are often asserted without an exact definition of the meaning of a virtual organization. Here, we define three characteristics of the virtual organization and demonstrate how each characteristic enhances global competitiveness. Table 2 summarizes these arguments.

The central feature of virtual organizations is their dependence on a federation of alliances and partnerships with other organizations. A virtual organization operates as a federated collection of enterprises tied together through contractual and other means, such as partial ownership arrange-

Table 2
Characteristics of Virtual Organizations and their Effects on Global Competitiveness

Characteristics	Effects on Competitiveness	Examples
Dependence on a federation of alliances and partnerships with other organizations	Corporate functions can be easily integrated with functions provided by allied partners to enhance and extend corporate reach worldwide.	Sun Microsystems Nike Reebok
Relative spatial and temporal independence	Geographical boundaries can be easily transcended, providing competitive presence in global markets and improving access to natural and human resources	Eastman Kodak Tandem Services
Flexibility	Resources can be easily reassigned to respond to shifting opportunities in global markets	Allergan Pharmaceuticals Intel

ments. Specific arrangements include joint ventures, strategic alliances, minority investments, consortia, coalitions, outsourcing, and franchises. The practice of permeating organizational boundaries through partnerships and alliances has enabled virtual enterprises to realize tremendous advantages. For example, the development of the B-1 bomber required teams from as many as 2,000 separate corporations to work together. They formed a virtual organization to accomplish the design and manufacture this product, an effort that required several years to complete. The virtual organization's goal is to extract the maximum value from its partners while making the minimum investment in permanent staff, fixed assets, and working capital. This is typically accomplished by assigning to its partners as many functions as possible—except for the core strategic functions that are difficult for competitors to replicate. Core strategic competencies are retained because they provide the company with sustainable competitive advantage.

Although traditional organizations may also use partnerships and alliances, virtual organizations use the federation concept as their primary principle of organizing. Consequently, the major challenge in designing a virtual organization is to create seamless integration among a variety of federated organizations. When this is accomplished, customers are unaware that separate organizations are servicing their needs. This creates an essential advantage for the transnational company by allowing, for example, local production and services to be seamlessly integrated with worldwide customer support.

The high tech and sports footwear industries provide good examples of federated arrangements. In the high tech arena, for example, Sun Microsystems views itself as an intellectual holding company that designs computers.[7] All other functions, including product ordering, manufacturing, distribution, marketing, and customer service are handled through contractual arrangements with partners located throughout the world. In the volatile sports footwear industry, neither Nike nor Reebok own many production facilities. Rather, they outsource nearly all footwear production to firms based in Taiwan, South Korea, and other Asian countries. Many other industries are finding that the distribution of value-adding tasks across a federation of firms helps to provide effective worldwide sales and service.

A second characteristic of a virtual organization is its relative spatial and temporal independence. No organization operates completely independent of space or time, but virtual organizations are able to overcome vast spatial and temporal barriers by linking together geographically remote resources. This characteristic is extremely important to the transnational firm, which operates more effectively if it can transcend geographical boundaries. Virtual organizations often allow individual employees to perform their work in a variety of locations: home, car, office, or on airplanes.

Virtual organizations often allow individual employees to perform their work in a variety of locations: home, car, office, or on airplanes.

Moreover, employees performing services need not be located close to their customers if customer contact can be mediated by other means, notably advanced communication technologies. The characteristic of spatial independence acknowledges that the physical location of work can be decided by more relevant criteria than the need that workers contributing to a common task work in the same place.

Global markets require sensitivity to local product and service needs, and spatial and temporal dispersion allow the virtual organization to be locally responsive yet centrally coordinated. For example, a virtual team was used recently by Eastman Kodak to develop a single-use camera for the European market.[8] While the camera's functional features were similar to those marketed worldwide, Kodak wanted to adapt the product's appearance and supporting features so that it would appeal to European buyers. Two German engineers worked with the design team, first in Rochester, N. Y., and later through telecommunications links from Germany. By creating a virtual team that could function independently of time and space, Kodak was able to respond rapidly to a local market opportunity.

Tandem Services Company, the systems integration unit of Tandem Computers, provides a second example of spatial and temporal independence. In the mid-1980s, Tandem Services employed a virtual office design for an urgent project involving information systems developers from London, Tokyo, and several U.S. cities.[9] A plan for passing work from one time zone to the next was devised, so that program code was written by developers in London, tested in the United States, and debugged in Tokyo. By the time the London developers came to work the next day, another cycle was ready to begin. This approach allowed the project to receive attention around the clock. Quite literally, the sun never set on Tandem Services' global virtual team.

A third characteristic of a virtual organization is its flexibility. Parts of virtual organizations may be formed, disbanded, and reformed to respond rapidly to changing business needs. Flexibility is an important asset for transnational companies because opportunities in global markets are constantly shifting. The geographically dispersed work force of the virtual organization may be molded into temporary teams to seize new business opportunities when they arise. In more conventionally organized competitors, reaction time is slowed by rigid organizational structures. The most competitive companies have the dexterity to shift resources to capitalize on new opportunities, while less nimble competitors may be stuck with underutilized resources.

Intel for example, has used virtual teams for a medley of projects: formulating and delivering sales strategies for specific products, developing new products, and manufacturing microprocessor elements. Comprising members from company locations in Ireland, Israel, England, France, and Asia, the teams came together quickly, did their work, then disbanded and regrouped with a variety of other teams. Allergan Pharmaceuticals also uses temporary global teams throughout its organization, improving time-to-market for new products and creating effective marketing strategies for its customers around the world. Allergan's teams potentially draw resources from the corporation's entire employee base.[10]

When applied to the design of transnational organizations, these three characteristics of the virtual organization potentially contribute to enhanced global competitiveness. Virtual organizations react to customers' needs more quickly, bring new products to market faster, and change their contours more rapidly than other organizations. However, to achieve this potential, the virtual organization must respond to its most serious challenge, coordination. Virtual organizations incur higher coordination costs because of the numerous external and internal relationships that must be managed across time and space. Because of the federated and dispersed nature of virtual organizations, traditional coordination and control mechanisms are ineffective. While designing any organization requires careful attention to the technologies by which work is performed, virtual organizations would simply not exist without the advanced information technologies that link their parts together.

Matching Information Technology to Transnational Business Requirements

Information technology facilitates the coordination among loosely federated components, overcomes the spatial and temporal barriers that characterize conventional organizational structures, and promotes flexibility. Indeed, information technology has the capability to enable dramatic organizational transformation and to make traditional forms obsolete. But which information technologies and applications specifically enable virtual transnational organizations to be competitive?

In Table 3, we propose a representative group of information technologies and applications that match the need of the transnational business for efficiency, local responsiveness, and learning capability. Executives may draw on these enabling technologies to respond to the needs of the transnational enterprise. Where a technology or application is well suited to a business need, we have placed an asterisk in the appropriate cell of the table. Blank cells indicate a less obvious match, but it is still conceivable that applications could contribute to meeting the need. For example, EDI systems are shown contributing to efficiency and responsiveness, as explained below. However, EDI systems could also contribute to learning, if, for example, electronic transaction histories were ar-

Table 3
Technologies and Applications for Meeting the Needs of the Transnational Enterprise

Representative Information Technologies and Applications	Efficiency	Responsiveness	Learning
Electronic Data Interchange (EDI)	•	•	
Interorganizational Systems (IOS)	•	•	
Electronic Commerce using Internet	•	•	•
Language Translation Software		•	
Mass Customization Technology		•	
Extranet		•	•
Groupware	•		•
Intranet	•		•
Organizational Memory Systems (OMS)		•	•

chived and analyzed for market trends and tendencies. Since most EDI systems are not designed with this feature in mind, we do not consider EDI to be an obvious match with needs for learning.

Electronic Data Interchange

Electronic data interchange (EDI) facilitates both efficiency and responsiveness, linking the computer systems of buyers and sellers to allow the transmission of structured data in a machine-readable format using a standard communication protocol. EDI is becoming the norm in many intercompany transactions, particularly in ordering, distribution, and payables and receivables. In the retailing industry, EDI systems have enabled firms to reduce their logistics cycle for ordering and stocking to a few days. The competitive advantage accruing to the leaders in the EDI movement is so pronounced that many experts expect that fully half of today's retailers will be out of business by 2001.[11] Similar payoff is found in the fabric industry where the average EDI-equipped firm takes only ten days to process orders, compared with an average of 125 days for other firms. The Port of Rotterdam's EDI system clears cargo in an average of 15 minutes and has substantially reduced the errors and returns of export order documents. Each of these examples illustrates the efficiency gains that can result from EDI and the greater responsiveness of firms to their customers.

Interorganizational Systems

Interorganizational systems (IOS) are types of information systems that permit the coupling of transactions between organizations, making them more efficient and responsive. Interorganizational systems are different from internal systems in that they include more provisions for reliability, data security, user privacy, and system integrity. The classic example of an IOS was American Hospital Supply's Analytical Systems Automatic Purchasing System (ASAP), which provided the capability of customers to order, track, and manage the status of purchases for over 100,000 health-care products.[12] Insurance carriers also use IOS links with independent agents. Contemporary IOSs may even cross industry boundaries. For example, Singapore's TradeNet system couples trade agents, government agencies, port authorities, freight forwarders, shipping companies, banks, and insurance companies with customers and immigration officials. The efficiency and responsiveness gains are impressive. Clearing the port, which formerly required two to four days, may now take as little as ten minutes. As a result of this IOS, Singapore remains a port of choice in the Far East, where competition is growing.[13]

Electronic Commerce using Internet

Electronic commerce provides the capability of buying and selling products and information via telephone lines, computer networks, and other electronic means. The Internet, the largest network of computer networks, is the medium usually favored for electronic commerce because it allows an organization to cut service costs while increasing the speed of service delivery. Electronic commerce is considered a primary means by which organizations may expand rapidly into high growth emerging markets of the world. As transnational companies become skilled in their use of the Internet, they will be able to pursue global electronic commerce more efficiently, saving important advertising, communication, and administrative costs. Moreover, the Internet can increase responsiveness by notifying individual customers when new products in their areas of interest become available and by creating customized products and services. Finally, transnational companies using the

Internet can increase their knowledge about consumer habits, be able to define trends, and turn consumer statistics into long-term customer relationships.

The banking industry is currently being reshaped by electronic commerce. Bank customers are now able to conduct most of their personal financial, investment and, in some cases, insurance transactions through their personal computer terminals. Through electronic commerce, banks and other companies can develop new products and services and penetrate new markets, all without regard to geographical location and often cutting costs in the process. For example, it has been estimated that a bank's cost of processing an electronic transaction originating anywhere in the world is six times lower than the cost of processing a local customer's check.[14]

Language Translation Software

Among the primary skills for managers of transnational organizations is the awareness of other cultures through the learning of the appropriate foreign languages.

Among the primary skills for managers of transnational organizations is the awareness of other cultures through the learning of the appropriate foreign languages.

Language translation software allows the translation from one language to another, and therefore may be used to increase the speed and local responsiveness of an enterprise. While allowing a foreign written or verbal communication to be translated into the language of the recipient, such software also reduces cultural gaps between countries. An enterprise that can capture knowledge at a plant in Sweden and quickly transfer that knowledge to another location in Brazil without language barriers can gain advantage over local and other international enterprises.[15]

Mass Customization Technology

Mass customization technology allows businesses to modify products and services to suit local needs, while retaining the advantages of large-scale production of those products and services. The key to mass customization is the ability of information technologies to control the introduction of customized features into the production process. Systems that allow firms to produce products on assembly lines to suit individual preferences are commonly exploited in the automobile industry.[16] Made-to-order cars can be delivered to individuals within a relatively short period because of the ability of computer systems to control the assembly of custom components at the precise moment needed in the factory process. While mass customization was originally associated with manufacturing, successful examples now occur in telecommunications, mass media, and software development. Mass customization in media software, for instance, gives news broadcasters the ability to deliver local news to its particular market as well as to a national audience.

Extranets

An extranet is an application of Internet technology that provides specific external parties with limited access to corporate information. Most commonly, an organization's customers and partners can use extranets to acquire account information and coordinate shipments of supplies. The package delivery industry, which serves worldwide markets, makes extensive use of extranets and promotes responsiveness by giving customers access to the firm's internal tracking system. In addition, by automatically tracing customers' inquiries on an extranet, a firm can acquire new knowledge about its customers' needs. One of the best examples of this type of system is the Federal Express package tracking system that allows customers to trace the status of packages in transit.[17] In many ways, these systems are the ultimate in responding to local needs and can make a transnational more competitive than local companies that lack such systems.

Groupware

Global teams are becoming more common. Nearly three-fifths of the companies in a recent survey report moderate or extensive experience with global teams.[18] The major challenge to effective global teamwork is to dissolve distance and time so that people from diverse cultures can work together profitably. Groupware technology can be part of the solution. Groupware is more than just an electronic messaging system. It typically integrates electronic messaging with screen sharing, group scheduling, meeting support, group writing and other applications. These features support team leadership, facilitate group processes, and extend the team's technical and managerial competence. A leading example of a groupware product that supports these processes is IBM's Lotus Notes.

As a tool, groupware is a primary enabler of dispersed work teams because it facilitates efficient and accurate sharing of ideas, streamlines processes, and makes parallel task execution possible. These features render a global team more time and cost efficient. Groupware also helps group members to learn from each other's expertise. Because teams are composed of experts in different specialties, the sharing of knowledge through groupware increases the overall level of knowledge of team members. For example, CIGNA International recognized that the knowledge spread across 55 international units could be shared from country to country, thus increasing learning.

Intranet

Learning can be enhanced with intranets, which are Web-based, firewall-protected networks that connect all employees through common, hyperlinked interfaces to documents, messaging, and multimedia information sources. Despite their internal orientation, intranets promote communication and information sharing across global boundaries. Intranets typically give employees access to newsletters, human resources information, calendars, product inventories, and recruiting data. Electronic mail is frequently included within intranets to guard messages against outside surveillance. The rapid access to crucial internal information that intranets allow can increase learning by transnational firms because intranets may be connected to from anywhere in the world.

The experience of DHL Systems illustrates how both efficiency and learning can be enhanced by intranets. By placing an enterprise software license on an intranet, DHL was able to save enormous time and effort in contrast to its former practice of distributing the license to over 220 countries via conventional electronic media. Moreover, DHL's 15 formal intranet sites supported learning by facilitating communication among 20,000 employees about corporate activities, including global programs and services, competition, internal job postings, and meeting calendars and minutes.[19]

Organizational Memory Systems

Until recently, information systems and information technologies were not expressly targeted to support organizational learning and memory. This has changed since the introduction of organizational memory systems (OMS), which consist of electronic systems for storing both structured and unstructured documents.[20] A mnemonic subsystem of the OMS integrates, supports, and automates the acquisition, retention, maintenance, search, and retrieval of information. Such systems provide a means by which knowledge from prior experience can be shared widely and applied to current problems.

An example of an OMS is the system developed and used for complex software development projects.[21] This OMS captured the detailed rationale behind decisions made in system requirements engineering. By tracking group processes and decisions, the system became an important part of organizational memory for the software development group using it. It allowed system developers to enhance their learning about requirement specification, as well as to increase their responsiveness to requests about the origin and evolution of those requirements.

The information technologies discussed are often acquired and implemented without much thought to their role in supporting corporate strategy. By making an explicit connection between these technologies and the needs of the transnational organization, we hope to guide managers in their efforts to become more globally competitive. By supporting the virtual organizational form, these technologies enable greater efficiency, responsiveness, and learning in the transnational firm.

Guidelines for Managers

Managers can prepare for the transformation of their global business organizations by following some basic guidelines.

First, managers wishing to commit to the transnational strategy as a means of achieving greater global competitiveness should:

- Insist on commitment to the transnational strategy at the highest organizational levels. Individual units cannot accomplish transnational strategies on their own because all worldwide business units are affected. All top executives must be on board.

Individual units cannot accomplish transnational strategies on their own because all worldwide business units are affected. All top executives must be on board.

- Educate top executives in the underlying strategy of transnational organizations. Make them understand that geographical boundaries should no longer be viewed as limitations on business practice.

- Train all employees in the tactics that support the transnational strategy. This requires an organization-wide commitment to using new tools to coordinate the far-flung components of the virtual organization. More importantly, it requires a healthy spirit of cooperation among partners to make alliances work.

Second, executives need to:

- Encourage initiatives that rely on information technology to create economies of scale in both manufacturing and services. Specifically, deploy EDI, IOS, and Electronic Commerce technologies to create seamless flows of information among suppliers, customers, clients, vendors, intermediaries, and consumers.
- Develop systems that permit the firm to respond quickly to local market conditions and to local cultural characteristics. Specifically, adopt language translation software, extranet, and mass customization technologies that allow firms to tailor their products and services to the local market while benefiting from the mass production of the base commodity.
- Design and implement systems that transfer knowledge and spread expertise throughout the firm. Specifically, implement groupware, intranets, and OMS to capture, disseminate, and preserve knowledge to enhance competitiveness.

We do not consider the virtual organization to be a passing fad. Because the feasibility of virtual organizational designs, and their application to the transnational company, depend upon information technologies that continue to evolve, we are confident that the principles of virtual organizational design will endure well into the 21st century. Technologies are becoming more powerful, and business is becoming more dependent upon them. There is little to be gained from a nostalgic return to old-fashioned designs. Managers in the 21st century must be able to compete effectively in global markets.

No one can predict with certainty the precise configuration of 21st century organizations or how they will function. Whatever their specific form, however, organizations will be thoroughly infused with information technology. Advantages offered by the technologies described in this article can greatly enhance corporate global competitiveness. Firms that leverage virtual organizational forms can potentially unleash electronic engines of unprecedented power, changing their industries in a fashion comparable to the changes of the industrial revolution.[22]

Three caveats are in order, however. First, the selection of an appropriate organizational form is only one aspect of the transnational corporate strategy. Indeed, an understanding of the consequences of a transnational strategy for managerial systems, coordination mechanisms, and control processes are other aspects that need to be considered when going global. It is folly to imagine successful global competition without providing employees the proper orientation, training, and cultural exposure. Second, the virtual organizational form is not the only design for an organization that can work for the transnational organization. Other, more traditional structures can be employed if adequate care is given to communication requirements and coordination needs among the parts of a traditional structure. We believe that coordination is more easily attained by using appropriate information technologies within the virtual form, but it is clear that other options exist. Third, information technology should not be considered as a simple determinant of the virtual organization. Information technology cannot transform an organization on its own. Rather, information technology enables the realization of managerial intentions, but managers need to demonstrate sensitivity to the unanticipated consequences of information technologies in organizations.

In addition, adoption of the virtual organization and its supporting technologies raises issues about the identity and culture of an organization. Temporary federations of disparate operations, all linked through electronic networks, do not inspire the same images of corporate solidarity or cultural identity that many managers desire. While acknowledging the positive benefits of traditional structures, we do not feel that global competitiveness depends on cultural unity as much as it depends upon the willingness and capability to respond to business opportunities anywhere in the world. Indeed, a unified corporate culture may reduce a company's appetite for global business by reducing sensitivity to cultural diversity.

Executives with a good grasp of the requirements for the transnational virtual enterprise will pay particular attention to information technology. Depending on the firm's current capabilities to support the strategic goals of efficiency, responsiveness, and learning, managers will want to focus on those technologies that address areas of deficiency. If the firm were wholly lacking in systems that support learning, for example, then investments in intranets and organizational memory systems would be appropriate. Fitting the correct technologies to the firm's specific needs will effectively advance the cause of greater global competitiveness.

Endnotes

[1] Emmott, B. 1993 Survey of Multinationals: Creatures of Imperfection. *The Economist*, March 27, 53–57.

[2] Global Distinction, *Journal of Business Strategy*, September/October 1996, 9.

[3] Porter, M. E. 1986. Changing Patterns of International Competition. *California Management Review* (28) 2.

[4] Bartlett, C. A. and Ghoshal, S. 1987 Managing Across Borders: New Strategic Requirements. *Sloan Management Review*, 7–17.

[5] A useful analysis of the types of enterprise strategies described here may be found in Hordes, M. W., Clancy, J. A. and Baddaley, J. 1995. A Primer for Global Start-Ups. *Academy of Management Executive* (9) 2, 7–11.

[6] See, for example, Davidow, W. H. and Malone, M. S. 1992. *The Virtual Corporation: Structuring and Revitalizing the Corporation for the 21st Century*. New York: Harper Business. Lucas, Jr., H. C. Jr., 1996. *The T-Form Organization*. San Francisco: Jossey-Bass. and Quinn, J. B. 1992. *Intelligent Enterprise*. New York; Free Press Inc.

[7] Drtina, R. E. 1994. The Outsourcing Decision. *Management Accounting* (75) 9, 56–62.

[8] Geber, B. 1995. Virtual Teams. *Training* (32) 4, 36–40.

[9] Caldwell, B. 1996. The Virtual Office Gets Real, *Information Week*, n563, 32.

[10] Solomon, C. M. 1995. Global Teams: The Ultimate Collaboration. *Personnel Journal* (74) 9, 49–58.

[11] Keen, P. G. W. 1995. *Every Manager's Guide to Information Technology*, Boston: Harvard Business School Press.

[12] Luftman, J. N. "Applying the Strategic Alignment Model," in Luftman, J. N. 1996. *Competing in the Information Age* New York: Oxford University Press, 43–69.

[13] Konsynski, B. "Electronic Commerce and the Extended Enterprise," in Luftman, *op. cit.*, 216–241.

[14] Kalakota R. and Whinston, A. B. 1996. *Frontiers of Electronic Commerce*. Reading, MA: Addison-Wesley.

[15] Hordes et al., *op. cit.*

[16] Pine, B. J., Victor, B., and Boynton, A. C. 1993. Making Mass Customization Work, *Harvard Business Review* (71) 5, 108–111.

[17] Nash, K. S. 1996. Extranet: Best of Both 'nets, *Computerworld* (30) 33, 1, 107.

[18] Axel, H. 1996. Company Experiences with Global Teams. *HR Executive Review* (4) 2, 3–18.

[19] O'Keefe, S. 1997. Bridging the Distances, *Financial Executive* (13) 4, 35–36.

[20] Stein, E. W. and Zwass, V. 1995. Actualizing Organizational Memory with Information Systems, *Information Systems Research* (6) 2, 85–117.

[21] Ramesh B. and Dhar V. 1992. Supporting Systems Development by Capturing Deliberations during Requirement Engineering, *IEEE Transactions on Software Engineering*, 18, 498–510.

[22] Mowshowitz, A. 1994. Virtual Organization: A Vision of Management in The Information Age, *Information Society*, 10, 267–288.

About the Authors

Marie-Claude Boudreau is a doctoral student in the Computer Information Systems Department at Georgia State University. She received her master of business administration in management information systems from l'Université Laval in Canada in 1995. She also earned a Diplôme d'Enseignement Supérieur Spécialisé (DESS) from l'École Supérieure des Affaires de Grenoble in France in 1994, and a bachelor of business administration (with distinction) from l'Université Laval in 1993. She has published articles in *Information Systems Research* and *Information Technology & People*.

Karen D. Loch is an associate professor of decision sciences at Georgia State University. Her current research interests span international IT studies, security and ethical concerns, and knowledge management. She has published in journals such as *Communications of the ACM, MIS Quarterly, Information Systems Journal, Journal of Global Information Management*, and one book on international IT education. She serves as associate editor for the *Journal of Global Information Technology Management* and as review board member for *Information Resources Management Journal* and *The Journal of Global Information Management*.

Daniel Robey holds a joint appointment as professor in the Departments of Computer Information Systems and Management at Georgia State University. His current research investigates the consequences of information systems in organizations and the processes of system development and implementation. He is associate editor for *Accounting, Management and Information Technologies* and serves on editorial boards for *Information Systems Research, Organization Science, Canadian Journal of Administrative Sciences, Information Technology & People*, and *Journal of Information Technology Management*. He has published articles in such journals as *Academy of Management Journal, Academy of Management Review, Information Systems Research, Management Science*, and *Organization Science*.

Detmar W. Straub is a professor of computer information systems at Georgia State University. He has published research in the areas of computer security, technological innovation, and international IT studies. He holds a DBA in MIS from Indiana University and a PhD in English from Penn State. He has published articles in such journals as *Sloan Management Review, Management Science, Information Systems Research, MIS Quarterly, Communications of the ACM, Journal of MIS, Computers & Security*, and *Information & Management*. He is currently an associate editor for *Information Systems Research*.

[16]

Pergamon

European Management Journal Vol. 18, No. 2, pp. 183–194, 2000

Printed in Great Britain
0263-2373/00 $20.00

PII: S0263-2373(99)00090-0

The Global Virtual Manager: A Prescription for Success

TIMOTHY KAYWORTH, *Baylor University, Texas*
DOROTHY LEIDNER, *INSEAD, France*

Global virtual teams have emerged in response to the growing demands placed upon organizations to rapidly coordinate individuals located in geographically dispersed locations. Virtual teams promise to improve cycle time, reduce travel costs, and reduce redundancies across organizational units. Moreover, the use of global virtual teams provides an opportunity to coordinate complex business tasks across a potentially far-flung confederation of organizations. However, virtual teams are beset with a range of challenges inherent to their dispersed, and often impersonal, nature. While all teamwork involves challenges to be managed, the tools at the disposal of virtual teams limits the options they have for addressing the difficulties of coordination. This field-based research study was undertaken to assess the core issues and challenges faced by a group of twelve culturally diverse global virtual teams with members from Europe, Mexico, and the United States. Our findings suggest that global virtual teams face significant challenges in four areas: communication, culture, technology, and project management (leadership). Drawing from the members' assessments of their virtual team experiences, each area of challenge is discussed in detail. This is followed by a set of managerial prescriptions that outline specific critical success factors useful for the implementation of virtual teams. © 2000 Elsevier Science Ltd. All rights reserved

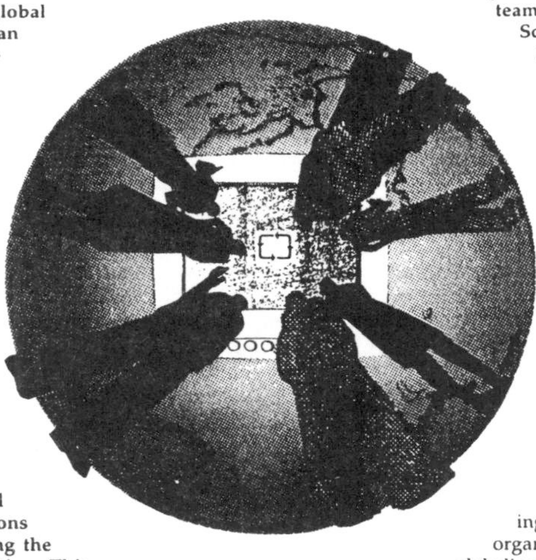

Introduction

As firms stand poised for conducting business in the 21st century, they face a host of challenges brought on by a changing business environment. The growing popularity of inter-organizational alliances combined with a growing tendency to flatter organizational structures and globalization has accelerated the need for firms to coordinate activities that span geographical as well as organizational boundaries (Townsend *et al.*, 1998). In addition, the shift from production to service related businesses has spawned a new generation of knowledge worker not bound to physical work locations. Taken together, these factors suggest that firms are faced with increased challenges to coordinate tasks across time zones, physical boundaries, and cultures, as well as organizational contexts.

Driven by these demands, traditional face-to-face teams face pressure to operate in a virtual environment and to coordinate activities among team members in physically dispersed locations. Consequently, the global virtual team has emerged as a new form of organizational structure, supported by enabling information and communication technologies, able to meet the challenges of this new work context. Townsend *et al.* (1998) describe this emergent structure:

'Virtual teams are composed of coworkers geographically and organizationally linked through telecommunications and information technologies attempting to achieve an organizational task' (p. 17).

Given a global business context, the deployment of virtual teams is an attractive management strategy for a variety of reasons. First, it allows dispersed organizations to maximize their expertise without having to physically relocate individuals. The required expertise for a given task or project may be dispersed at multiple locations throughout the organization, however, a virtual team may facilitate the 'pooling' of this talent to provide focused attention to a particular problem without having to physically relocate individuals. In addition, virtual teams may allow organizations to unify the varying perspectives of different cultures and business customs to avoid counterproductive ethno-centric biases (Solomon, 1995). Other benefits include cost reduction, cycle-time reduction, integration of distant members, and improved decision-making and problem solving skills (Lipnack and Stamps, 1997; Townsend *et al.*, 1998)

Perhaps the growing importance of virtual teams can best be summarized by Hargrove (1998) who states: 'in the future, the source of human achievement will not be extraordinary individuals, but extraordinary combinations of people.' As firms face the challenges of business in the 21st century, the use of global virtual teams will provide a significant opportunity to coordinate complex business tasks across a potentially far-flung confederation of organizations.

However, as companies seek to leverage the potential benefits of virtual teams, they must also face the numerous complexities inherent to this new type of work group. First, communication among virtual teams may be extremely difficult to manage and less effective than more traditional settings (McGrath and Hollingshead, 1994; Warkentin *et al.*, 1997; Hightower and Sayeed, 1995, 1996). Given the separation across time and space, firms will need to adopt innovative technologies to provide rich channels of communication to facilitate task coordination among globally dispersed team members. These communications problems may also be magnified by different time zones, disparity among technology infrastructures, as well as differences in technology proficiency among team members. Finally, when cultural differences are added to this mix of potential issues, the management of virtual teams may become exceedingly complex. Regarding culture, Solomon (1995) states:

'The fundamentals of global team success aren't very different from the practices that work for domestic work teams. But there are more variables. Overlay cultural behavior and expectations on the roles of communication, team leadership and group dynamics, and you immediately understand. Moreover, there are logistics to overcome: challenges inherent in working in different time zones, lots of travel, and busy conflicting schedules' (p. 50).

Given this milieu of cultural, technical, communication, and logistical issues, a fundamental assumption of this paper is that the problem space faced by managers in the implementation of virtual teams may be much more varied and complex than that of traditional team settings. To investigate this relatively new phenomenon, initial research should focus on uncovering emerging issues and challenges inherent to virtual team settings. Such exploratory research will help to inform practice of potential management strategies and to frame questions for subsequent academic research.

This paper discusses the results of an exploratory global virtual team project undertaken with members from Mexico, Europe, and the United States. The goal of this work is (1) to identify specific issues and challenges faced by virtual teams, (2) to identify critical success factors, and (3) to stimulate compelling ideas for future research. To accomplish these goals, we first present the research methodology used to undertake this study. This section includes discussion related to sample selection, group task assignments, and data collection methods. Next, we present research findings that describe the numerous types of challenges faced by the virtual team participants in this study. Throughout this section, respondent anecdotes are provided to richly illustrate the type of challenges faced by global virtual team members. The third section provides a set of guidelines (critical success factors) useful for managers in the implementation of virtual teams. The paper concludes with a discussion of limitations and directions for future research.

Research Methodology

Given the complexity of this phenomenon as well as the lack of empirical research to date, we adopted a field-based quasi-experiment that would allow us to observe the dynamics of global virtual teams as they unfolded over time. This strategy permitted us to identify key issues, critical success factors, as well as additional research questions through observing the interaction among a culturally diverse group of physically dispersed team members. Field-based experiments are useful for a number of reasons. First, they allow researchers to observe specific phenomena without loss of valuable contextual information. Second, they provide a means for investigating specific processes or dynamics that occur longitudinally over time. Finally, they are appropriate for studying emerging areas of interest where key constructs and their relationships may be poorly defined. Use of such an intrusive methodology permits us to evaluate the nature and role of virtual teams without losing valuable contextual information (Eisenhardt, 1989; Yin, 1989).

Sample Selection

To study global virtual teams, we created twelve virtual teams, each composed of 5–7 members from three universities located in Europe, Mexico, and the United States. The participating European students were selected from an executive MBA program at a leading business school. The Mexican participants were graduate students from a variety of technical and business backgrounds while the US students were composed of upper level business undergraduates attending a cross-disciplinary introductory course to MIS. Each virtual team contained one team leader from the European chosen school and at least two students from each of the two remaining schools. High levels of prior work experience among team leaders help to ensure a more realistic setting for the study. The teams were designed to emulate a matrix organizational structure, whereby team leaders reported to their professor, in terms of receiving performance assessment, and team members reported to their professors. Hence, the team leaders had to motivate the team members to achieve the requisite quality necessary for them to obtain a high performance rating from their professor. However, the team leaders could not motivate the team members through threats, since the members reported neither to the team leader nor to the team leader's 'boss' for their performance assessment.

Our strategy was to create highly diverse virtual teams of reasonable size to provide a realistic setting to study global virtual team dynamics. Since multiple nationalities were represented on each team, we could expect a requisite degree of diversity in terms of language, customs, and perceptual differentiation. In addition, there was a wide range of technical competence among students as well as infrastructure capability among member educational institutions. All these factors helped to ensure a realistic setting for a virtual team not unlike those used by major organizations.

Task Assignment

Each team was assigned a mandatory task to complete a research project on a given topic. Each project addressed a specific aspect of information technology and team leaders were asked to produce a written report that specifically addressed the theme of the topic (see Appendix A for list of topics). Each team was allotted six weeks to complete the project and team leaders were given the following instructions:

> 'You are not to research the content or write the report. Rather, you are to guide the team, give helpful comments on content, structure, organization, writing, and to point the members to appropriate places to find information and resolve any difficulties.'

Although virtual team members were given basic guidelines regarding project task and deliverables, no further advice was given to teams regarding how they were to accomplish the task. This was the responsibility of the project team leader. The US students received the following instructions:

> 'Guidance on this project will come from your project leader in Europe. Your main objective will be to segment the work among yourselves and to complete the project as specified by the project leader. The exact details on how your group will communicate (e.g. frequency, what technology, time of day) will all be handled by your group.'

Consequently, these guidelines helped to ensure that project team leaders would not do all the work and that high levels of communication among team members and their respective team leaders would be necessary to complete the task. Apart from these guidelines, individual teams were given complete autonomy to assign priorities, set schedules, meeting times, and to decide on which telecommunications technologies to interact with. Although certain computer mediated communication systems (CMCS) were recommended (e.g. TCBWorks, PowWow), none were required.

Team members and leaders were evaluated on the overall quality of the final research paper and assigned an individual grade that was a substantial part of the overall grade for the class in which he or she was a participant. In addition, team leaders were asked to evaluate individual performances of their respective team members and individual members were asked to rate the team leader's effectiveness.

Data Collection

Upon completion of the project, the team members were administered a series of open-ended questions (Appendix B) to assess their perceptions of the virtual team project. Since one set of responses was received per team, each set represents a composite of individual team member perceptions of the virtual team project. For qualitative studies involving multiple cases, both Yin (1989) and Eisenhardt (1989) suggest that data analysis should first focus on identification of unique insights relative to specific cases. As each case (e.g. virtual team) is analyzed individually, certain themes or patterns may begin to emerge and to catch the researcher's attention. This within-case analysis reduces the danger of attempting to generalize patterns across teams prematurely before the within-case analysis has been completed. Eisenhardt (1989) states:

'The overall idea is to become intimately familiar with each site as a single case. This allows unique patterns to occur before investigators attempt to generalize patterns across cases' (540).

The data analysis was completed according to these 'pattern analysis' techniques described above.

Research Findings

Upon analysis of our data, we were able to identify four basic classes of issues faced by virtual team groups: communications, culture, technology, and project management. The following pages discuss these types of challenges in detail.

Communication

Regardless of the environment (e.g. traditional vs. virtual teams), effective communication is essential to group functioning (Trevino *et al.*, 1990). However virtual teams potentially face a much greater strain on communications as team members attempt to interact, share meaning, and reach consensus in the absence of rich face-to-face interaction. Given these constraints on communications, virtual team members must seek a variety of means to transmit information, meaning, and symbols over time and space through one or more electronic channels.

In the absence of face-to-face interaction, all 12 virtual teams relied heavily on a variety of information technologies to communicate among themselves (Appendix C). Of the 12 teams, nine chose to rely solely on e-mail for information exchange while the remaining three groups used a combination of e-mail and web-based collaboration technologies. Two of these three groups built team web pages to facilitate information exchange and project management.

Member comments suggests that the three groups utilizing a wider range of communication technologies were much more satisfied with their ability to communicate and with their project outcomes. Specific examples of this occurred for those teams that supplemented e-mail with web-based communications tools (e.g. mIRC, PowWow) and group web pages. In contrast to e-mail, these technologies afforded team members much richer mediums for interaction and management of information. One group noted:

'Our team used PowWow for our 'face-to-face' communication. Our most effective planning and project implementation arose during our conversations. The direct communication allowed for team brainstorming and input in a timely manner. This process could have been done via e-mail, but it would have taken days to reach the results that we were able to reach.'

Other comments suggest that these rich computer mediated communication systems (CMCS) greatly facilitated teams' abilities to plan, to exchange ideas, and to reach consensus on a variety of issues:

'Once we learned how to access the program [PowWow], we were immediately in business. We were greatly appreciative that everyone's comments could be seen simultaneously, even though we were all in different locations.'

While the web communication tools facilitated synchronous group interaction, team web pages allowed groups to maintain essential project information for team members to access on an 'as needed' basis:

'Our web page was the home base of our operations. Our page was responsible for displaying our progress. Our team leader posted links to other sites that would offer beneficial information for our project. Each member's progress was posted. The agenda for each team meeting was posted along with an outline for the context of the report.

Candy [leader] set up a web page for our team, which provided general information on our project. This web page included an outline, deadlines, and the e-mail addresses of our team members. We referred to this web-page when formulating our rough draft of ideas.'

This evidence suggests that those groups most effective at communication were able to draw from a variety of technologies (e.g. e-mail, web collaboration, WebPages) each offering specific benefits contingent upon the given needs (e.g. collaboration, volume of information, need for immediate feedback) of the group.

In contrast, those groups who relied almost exclusively upon one type of CMCS (e.g. e-mail) experienced much higher levels of difficulty with communication than their counterparts. These e-mail communication problems could be attributed in part to the seven-hour time zone differences between the European project leaders and North American team members. Moreover, since e-mail communication is asynchronous in nature, team members experienced significant time delays in sending and receiving e-mails and were unable to interact in the same rich way afforded by web-based collaboration tools. These inherent weaknesses often resulted in lost meanings and untimely decision-making. Group 2 commented on these problems:

'Obviously, e-mail presented some difficult time constraints due to time zones and work/school schedules.'

Regarding the use of e-mail, other groups noted:

'Time zones were a major team hurdle. The team leader is seven hours ahead of the other groups. He would usually e-mail at 2:00 pm his time. The message would get to us at 7:00 am in the morning, and we would e-mail our leader in the afternoon. If we e-mailed the message at 2:00 pm our time, the message would get to the leader at 9:00 pm. Information took a day to send and receive.

Our whole project paper was put together through a series of e-mails. To me, this was a tedious and strenuous ordeal. Because our communication process only involved the use of e-mails, our ideas and problems weren't addressed by the necessary deadlines. In our experiences, our e-mail responses weren't replied to in a timely manner. This was a result of the differences in time zones.'

Our findings support the notion that information technology has limits and may not be able to transfer the same rich social, emotional, and non-verbal information present in traditional face-to-face settings (Walther and Burgoon, 1992; Townsend *et al.*, 1998). For example, information rich non-verbal cues such as facial expressions, voice inflections, and gestures, normally present in traditional settings, may be lost or distorted through computer mediated communication systems (Kiesler and Sproull, 1992; Warkentin *et al.*, 1997). Group 2 noted these types of problems:

'Talking to someone face-to-face is always better than over the phone or by e-mail. It gives you an opportunity to see facial and body expressions, hear voice emphasis and inflection, and sense such things as approval or misunderstanding.'

Consequently, even those virtual team groups utilizing rich web-based collaboration technologies suffered from the lack of face-to-face contact. The severity of this information loss was determined to a large extent by the richness of the technology being used. Thus, teams relying solely on e-mail tended to experience a greater degree of information loss and distortion than the three teams utilizing richer forms of communication channels.

Communications effectiveness among virtual teams was also impacted by a variety of cultural, technical, and human factors. The sections below discuss each of these influences.

Culture

Culture has been defined by Hofstede (1980) as 'the collective programming of the mind which distinguishes the members of one group from another.' Thus, culture is learned and may be manifested in different ways according to nationality, ethnicity, or even organizational settings. In virtual team settings, culture may have a profound impact on how individuals perceive information, act upon it, and relate to other individuals. As team members communicate, they will tend to filter information through their cultural 'lenses', thereby giving rise to a potentially broad range of misinterpretations or distortions (Solomon, 1995). Thus, a Mexican team member may view the same issue in a totally different way than a member from a European project manager does. Although cultural differences may bring a greater variety of perspectives to bear on a problem domain, they may also create additional communication challenges for team members. Our findings suggest that cultural differences among virtual team members acted to intensify some of the communications problems noted above.

Over half of the virtual teams observed that cultural differences significantly affected their ability to communicate ideas and to coordinate the project. By far, the most common cultural issue was the language barrier between Mexican students and their US counterparts. These linguistic differences accounted for a great deal of information loss and distortion as individual members attempted to decipher communication through their own cultural perspective. The following comments by team members help to illustrate these problems:

'First and foremost, a language barrier between our group and the Mexican students proved quite challenging. The Mexican students often could not interpret our e-mail messages accurately. Also, even though the Mexican students provided excellent research material, we had to spend extra time editing and rewording material in order to make it presentable.

The Mexican students sent e-mails in broken English. This made most of their messages difficult to decipher.

The language barrier was another communication problem — we received part of the paper in Spanish! Once when we received the English version, it was very apparent that their grammar and vocabulary [English] were underdeveloped.

The main problems our group encountered dealt with being able to understand our team leader and communicate with him. These problems occurred due to cultural differences and differences in time zones.'

In addition to language differences, some cultures may vary in their sense of urgency or timing to complete projects and to meet deadlines. Hofstede (1980) has defined this dimension of culture in terms of the relative degree to which a particular culture is formal versus informal. More formal cultures will tend to a greater sense of urgency to set specific timetables and to diligently keep to deadlines. In contrast, informal cultures may place less emphasis on setting and meeting deadlines. Given the potentially diverse composition of virtual teams, groups may consist of individuals from both formal and informal cultures. As a result, team members may have conflicting perspectives on certain attitudes related to project schedules, planning, and punctuality with deadlines. This dynamic was evident through the comments of Group 10:

'The team leader needs to remember that there are cultures

that are more relaxed than others and may need more prompting to provide information on a timely basis.'

This indirect reference by American students to their foreign counterparts suggests that virtual team members need to be aware of these differences and identify project management strategies to overcome these cultural barriers.

Cultural differences may also be attributed to factors other than nationality or ethnicity. For example, different organizations may have diverse work cultures as manifested by deeply held core beliefs and assumptions. Consequently, although individuals may have similar national or ethnic backgrounds, they may still exhibit radically different cultural assumptions as engendered by the organization for whom they work. This differentiation in work culture was observed by Group 11 who commented on their project leader's management style:

'Another issue which arose, was cultural differences. With the project leader, he wrote good English but approached the project in a very business like manner, which required the team members to adjust accordingly.'

Technology

Virtual team groups experienced varying levels of difficulty in using information technology. The most common problem encountered was the inability to send and receive e-mail messages:

'Technical problems which hindered our team's performance included the Mexican internet server rejecting our e-mails and the French server accepting our e-mails, but not delivering them to our project manager.

Working on a virtual team required the use of innovative technology. Our group encountered a roadblock when the server went down before one of our group meetings. We had no way of alerting our team leader that we would not be able to attend our PowWow session.'

While all three locations experienced difficulties with technology, the problems were more acute with the Mexican team members:

'Our group was constantly having problems with e-mails from Mexico. The messages were either too large or the contents were not transmitted properly. Perhaps if we had set up a web-page, we could have eliminated some of our problems.

The majority of time we sent them [Mexican students] mail, it was returned. Another problem we encountered was scrambled mail.'

Groups using web-based collaborative tools were not immune to technology problems. One group using PowWow as a collaborative tool experienced technical 'glitches' that inexplicably kicked chat participants out of the session. In addition, network limitations resulted in delays for incoming message traffic:

'We decided to conduct virtual team meetings using the mIRC chat program. On the three occasions when we met, we often encountered problems in accessing the chat room. Sometimes it took as much as 30 minutes to access the room. There was a 10 to 15 second delay in the program, so our messages were not instant. Also, the mIRC program 'killed' users or knocked them out of the room.'

In spite of the advantages of such synchronous collaborative tools, these types of problems made it very difficult for the particular group to maintain any type of structure or theme throughout the meeting. Given time delays as well as the inherent limitations of the technology (e.g. inability to transfer contextual and non-verbal information), their conversations lacked focus:

'During our initial meeting, we did not accomplish much related to the work assignment, because everyone was trying to 'talk' at the same time, without any structure.'

Although this team became more proficient at managing the structure of the meeting, they still encountered language barriers during these sessions:

'During our second meeting, we were more structured, but encountered communication barriers.'

In addition to these technological barriers, there was some evidence that variance among individual's level of skill or familiarity with information technology may have played a significant role in team success in utilizing rich CMCS. One group noted:

'When we began this project, our technical knowledge was limited. When our team leader suggested the use of PowWow for 'face to face' meetings, we were not sure how to access this service.'

These comments suggest that level of technical expertise may play a pivotal role in virtual teams ability to adopt and successfully use innovative information technologies.

Project Management

Given the multi-faceted challenges associated with virtual teams, it was not surprising that virtual team members perceived project management to be an important element of success. Four of the 12 teams perceived virtual team leaders to be extremely effective and four, adequate, while the remaining four felt that their virtual team leader's performance hindered project success:

'Unfortunately, I cannot say that our group leader was key to our success. I had a hard time getting any direction from him. I also encountered difficulties on the different levels we conversed on. He had difficulty bringing things down to our level, and I often had to go to someone else for clarification.'

From our analysis of virtual team member comments, we identified several challenges related to effective project management. First, effective project managers were able to articulate project goals and to assign responsibilities with specific schedules and work deadlines. In contrast, those virtual team leaders unable to effectively articulate goals and plans for achieving them were perceived to be much less effective by team members. The following comments illustrate both positive and negative examples of this:

'He was an extremely effective team leader in our virtual team project. He provided us with a clean and precise outline of goals.

She was extremely effective in her role in managing our virtual team. She provided appropriate deadlines, while remaining flexible to the fact that we have other responsibilities in school. Lastly, she specified exactly what she expected from us and when she expected it, giving us the guidance we needed.

He gave us deadlines without asking us how much time we needed, or whether it was even plausible. Then, he wouldn't care about the deadlines — indirectly creating an attitude that timing was not important. Carlos also did not adequately explain his idea/view of the project. We had to get clarifications from others, because when we did ask him for clarity, he did not do a good job of it.'

Another challenge of project management was related to the degree to which project managers were able to provide continuous feedback throughout the life of the project. The ability to provide suggestions and advise and to solicit team member's opinions was considered highly desirable, while the absence of this type of continual feedback had adverse effects on several groups:

'The incompetence of our leader hindered our success. She never acknowledged our suggestions concerning the use of web technology despite our repeated efforts to encourage the use of such techniques. She failed to give us direction, and never encouraged our group to explore any technologies. Not once did she collaborate with the Mexicans in our group, and she gave unreasonable deadlines.'

In contrast, it was evident that effective project managers put a high priority on regular communication; providing valuable advice while at the same time soliciting feedback from individual team members:

'Our project leader was very effective in directing our team's activities. She contacted us promptly with her ideas concerning the electronic commerce project. She seemed eager to take the leadership role while still inquiring into other's ideas and suggestions. She responded quickly to questions and comments that the team members had.

Our team leader was quite effective in offering ideas and suggestions without telling us what to do. He was also willing and anxious to hear our opinions and ideas on the topic. After hearing our suggestions, he would direct and advise us.'

Third, effective project managers were perceived to be highly flexible, whereas ineffective leaders tended to be less yielding to the needs of respective team members. Given the multiple challenges of global virtual team settings, flexibility seemed to be the 'order of the day'. Therefore, team members placed a high premium on the leader's ability to remain flexible to accommodate a variety of possible situations:

'The project manager's flexibility contributed to our success. Our virtual team leader, established a fair schedule of deadlines for our group. She was more than willing to work with us and our schedules. For example, she offered to conduct a virtual team meeting at 2 am in the morning to accommodate us.

In order to deal with the time differences, he was very flexible with his personal schedule, allowing us to have team meetings at odd hours of the day for him.

At first our project leader proposed an extensive paper on our topic, however, he was very reasonable and eager to compromise when we approached him about the length of our assignment.'

In addition, virtual team leaders judged to be more empathetic about their team members were considered to be much more effective than those who were less caring. The following comments illustrate both positive and negative examples of this:

'If we were ever unclear about a topic or meaning, he would research with us to find the answer. This care and concern contributed to his effectiveness.

He never attempted to persuade the Mexican students to get involved and do their fair share of the project, and he certainly never attempted to help us out with the added work load. Many of our pleas for advice and direction went unanswered as well. This led to resentment of our project manager as well as the Mexican students.

He did a great job of delegating responsibilities to each group member. He was faithful in communicating suggestions to help improve our work. He was very patient with the deadlines he projects, and gave us a clear picture of what he wanted each of us to accomplish.'

Since virtual team environments provide a radically different social context, the ability to develop relational links among team members may be hindered. The inability to develop these relationships within a social context may negatively impact such outcomes as creativity, morale, decision-making quality, and process loss (Walther and Burgoon, 1992). Furthermore, the lack of a social context may alter or hinder the process through which team members develop trust (Jarvenpaa *et al.*, 1998). Consequently, these arguments suggest that one role of team leaders should be to provide a setting for group socialization processes to occur:

'An important part of working with a team is trusting and getting to know one's teammates. By allowing this important step, team morale is built and members are more receptive to one another's contributions.

Trust was the big issue — we needed to learn to trust that team members would do their best possible job. This is all you can really ask of anyone.'

Evidence of the use of rich communication channels to facilitate socialization was apparent from our study. In at least two groups, team leaders played a pivotal role in helping to engender a sense of trust and cohesion among team members:

'He [the leader] allowed us to get to know each other on PowWow. We joked with each other and established a high level of trust among the members of the group. This trust fostered a unique working relationship, which proved to be very successful.

One method that the leader would use to help us through the times was humor. He sent us jokes and tried to lighten the mood. I think that was an excellent idea. Humor works well in tough situations.'

Critical Success Factors

Although this study was limited to the 12 virtual teams studied, a number of implications useful for management practice can be drawn from our findings. Table 1 summarizes these critical success factors for each of the four areas of challenge described above.

Communication

The complexities of virtual team environments (e.g. time, distance, culture) may place a significant strain on the ability of team members to frame issues, achieve mutual levels of understanding, and to reach consensus on key decisions. Consequently, the ability to achieve effective communication patterns is essential to the success of virtual team functioning. Regarding the importance of communication, one team noted:

'Communication! Communication! Communication! Without frequent and effective communication, a virtual team cannot exist; much less accomplish an often difficult task. Communication must be clear and decisive, but not commanding or overbearing.'

Our analysis of team comments identifies several strategies useful for facilitating effective communications in virtual team environments. First, virtual teams need to engage in continuous communications over a wide range of computer mediated computer systems (CMCS). Given the lack of rich face-to-face interaction inherent to virtual team settings, groups must strive to communicate in a frequent, ongoing manner with constant feedback from team leaders. This can be accomplished through setting specific guidelines regarding meeting times, frequency, and specific agendas for discussion. Furthermore, team leaders should seek to establish specific rules of engagement that govern exactly how and when team members should communicate with each other. For example, a simple rule of engagement may state: 'all meeting times will be scheduled according to London Standard Time.' Such policies, normally taken for granted in face-to-face settings, may be extremely important in the virtual environment.

A third suggestion is that virtual team members conduct periodic face-to-face meetings either through videoconferencing or in actual face-to-face settings. Research suggests that rich face-to-face interaction can facilitate communication through building team trust (Jarvenpaa *et al.*, 1998) and enabling team members to exchange valuable social, emotional, and contextual information (Kiesler and Sproull, 1992; Warkentin *et al.*, 1997; Dubrovsky *et al.*, 1991).

Finally, the importance of getting to know one's vir-

Table 1 Critical Success Factors for Global Virtual Teams

Virtual team challenge	Critical success factors for effective global virtual teams
Communication	• Emphasize continuous communication
	• Set meeting schedules and rules of engagement
	• Conduct periodic face-to-face meetings
	• Engage in team building activities at onset of virtual team creation
Culture	• Instil a sense of cultural awareness
	• Create teams from complementary cultures
Technology	• Utilize multiple computer mediated communications system (CMCS)
	• Train team members in the use of various CMCS
	• Ensure infrastructure compatibility among geographic locations
	• Assess political and economic barriers to international telecommunications
Project management (leadership)	• Set clear team goals and provide continuous performance feedback
	• Build team cohesiveness
	• Express flexibility and empathy towards virtual team members
	• Exhibit cultural awareness

tual team peers is vitally important to subsequent team member communication effectiveness. The rationale for this is that team trust and cohesiveness can create a sense of unity, which can breed communication effectiveness among team members (Jarvenpaa *et al.*, 1998). This rationale is evident from numerous comments received from virtual team members:

'Get to know your team members. The more you know about your partners, the more comfortable you will feel in working with them. This comfort will aid in productivity and communication.

I would recommend that the team as a whole meet online and have a 'chat' session to learn about each other's personalities, cultural backgrounds, and work habits. This should help facilitate better communication over the life of the project and prevent miscommunications and unintended insults.'

These comments suggest that a very useful strategy might be to engage in team building activities as a virtual team is initially created to engender a sense of trust, cohesiveness, and awareness of each other's differences. The importance of this strategy is noted by Townsend *et al.* (1998) who comment:

'Developing virtual teams goes well beyond the technical problem of linking them together. As workers increasingly interact in a virtual mode, it is imperative that they rebuild the interpersonal interaction necessary for organizational effectiveness.'

Culture

Earlier comments suggests that cultural differences among team members may lead to various instances of miscommunication since different cultures may tend to certain biases, assumptions, or views of the world. These cultural differences may not necessarily be a reflection of such factors as ethnicity, language, nationality, or religion. Rather, cultural differences may also be a reflection of the distinct organizational cultures to which teams belong. Regardless of the source, the fact remains that the 'cultural factor' may lead to information distortion and various instances of miscommunication. To offset these problems, it is vitally important to undertake a strategy to build awareness of cultural distinctions among team members. This could be accomplished through various team-building exercises as discussed earlier as well as through more formal training methods.

Organizations should also seek where possible to assemble virtual teams with members from complementary cultures. Although culture is difficult to measure, research by Hofstede (1980) suggests that culture clusters depend upon the relative positions of four primary dimensions (collectivism, uncertainty avoidance, masculinity vs femininity, and power distribution). Team member cultural differences could be assessed based upon where they lie along each of these four dimensions. Presumably, multicultural teams could then be assembled based upon the 'degree of fit' across these dimensions. Alternatively, and more realistically, firms should train virtual team members in the communication styles of various cultures to increase their intercultural awareness.

Technology

Several teams in this study adopted multiple computer mediated communication systems to accommodate a variety of communication needs. A contingency perspective would suggest that different types of CMCS might be appropriate depending upon the specific communication needs. For example, group discussion of a critical design issue on a software project may require a more rich communication channel due to the need for high group interaction, immediacy of feedback, as well as the need to view others' comments in a synchronous manner. These types of communication needs would be best served by a web-based collaboration or GSS tool able to provide immediate feedback to team members. In contrast, simple e-mail may be effectively used for communication needs requiring less interaction and less immediate feedback. An example of this might be the need to distribute a weekly status report among team members. These arguments suggest two management strategies in the design of virtual teams. First, managers should seek to provide a broad portfolio of information technologies (CMCS) to accommodate the varying communications needs of team members. Some of these technologies might include desktop video conferencing systems (DVCS), group support systems (GSS), collaborative software systems (e.g. LotusNotes), as well as the internet and intranets (Townsend *et al.*, 1998). Second, management should place a high emphasis on training virtual team members across a wide variety of technologies. Team members familiar with multiple technologies such as those described above will be much more likely to adopt and use these technologies in an effective manner. Regarding the importance of training, Townsend *et al.* (1998) note:

'What is different about the virtual team is the amount of technical training that is required to empower the team member to function in the virtual environment. Learning to use all of the traditional team skills in an environment where most interactions take place through a telecommunications medium is a critical challenge.'

As evidenced from this study, differences in IT infrastructure capabilities among geographic regions led to problems in transmitting information in a timely and effective manner. Therefore, virtual team designers should also consider the relative strengths and weaknesses of the infrastructures represented by the various geographic regions of virtual team members.

Additionally, team designers should assess the various political (e.g. transborder data flow regulations) and economic (e.g. transmission costs) ramifications of communicating across national boundaries. Overall, managers should follow a strategy that seeks to maintain low telecommunications costs while at the same time maintaining high quality transmission capabilities across team member countries.

Project Management

Given the inherently complex nature of virtual team environments, the quality of project management (e.g. team leadership) becomes a vital issue (Hooijberg *et al.*, 1997). Numerous remarks by virtual team members suggest that the project leader's ability to manage these teams had a significant impact on the perceived success of virtual team performance. Based on our analysis of these comments, several themes emerged that identify certain qualities of effective project management as demonstrated by virtual team leaders. First, effective team leaders were able to set clear goals for individual team members and to provide constant feedback regarding performance relative to these goals. Second, effective team leaders were able to engage in activities to build cohesiveness among team members. As noted earlier, some team leaders incorporated their sense of humor or were able to share personal aspects of their lives in order to get to know their team members better. A third dimension of effective project management was demonstrated by the leader's degree of flexibility and empathy expressed towards other team members. This need for leader concern and understanding towards virtual team members was a consistent theme throughout the project. Finally, virtual team designers should seek virtual team leaders with high degrees of awareness towards other cultures. Team leaders with a variety of work and personal experience in other cultures will potentially have a greater degree of awareness regarding the potential for cultural biases that may lead to information distortion and miscommunications. As these 'culturally aware' individuals manage virtual teams, they will be much more likely to recognize and deal with culturally based team issues in a more consistent and effective fashion. These arguments are supported by Odenwald (1993) who states:

> 'Leaders must be flexible, willing to support the team process, have a desire to help the team work together, understand team cultural factors, be able to listen and communicate, and be able to understand other members behaviors' (p. 50).

Conclusions

Although the small sample size precludes vast generalization, the study provides rich insights into some of the types of challenges faced by culturally diverse global virtual teams. Through these insights, we have been able to articulate a set of critical success factors believed to be important in the successful design and deployment of virtual teams. While some of the success factors for virtual teams are no different from success factors for face-to-face teams, and certainly three of the major domains — communication, culture, and project management — are equally important in face-to-face environments, some of the challenges within these domains are unique to the virtual environment. For example, such problems as delayed communication, misunderstandings arising from lack of response, lack of a shared context within which to interpret messages, and inability to monitor team members, are more pronounced in the virtual environment. More significantly though, the solutions at the disposal of team leaders to address the problems of teamwork are quite different in the virtual environment from the face-to-face. In face-to-face environments, increased monitoring can be employed as can frequent one-on-one discussions with various members. In the virtual environment, much of the control and reward capabilities of the leader are reduced so that the leader must create inventive solutions to address team problems.

Several issues for future research emerge from this study. The 12 virtual teams in this project were given the freedom to select whatever CMCS seemed to be most appropriate for the assigned task. Interestingly, there was a significant variance among teams in their adoption and use of various technologies (see Appendix C). While some teams adopted e-mail alone, others adopted e-mail, internet collaborative tools, as well web pages. Anecdotal evidence suggests that team member experience with technology may have had a significant role in their adoption of technology, however, this is not clear. Future research is needed to identify those factors that lead to the adoption and diffusion of technology in virtual team environments.

A second research issue has to do with the effect of culture on virtual team communication patterns and effectiveness. Although culture is widely assumed to have a crucial role in communication effectiveness, how much of a role does it really play? Additional research is needed to investigate how technology use might vary across cultures.

Another issue has to do with team member performance evaluation. Under most conditions, virtual team leaders will be in a position to evaluate other virtual team members even though in a matrix structure they might not have reward power. In traditional face to face settings, subordinates may engage in certain behaviors designed to favorably influence the perceptions of their supervisor (e.g. showing up to work early and leaving late). However, how might team members attempt to shape the perceptions of their supervisor given the inherent lack of face-to-face interaction in virtual team settings. Research needs to assess the types and nature of communication utilized by employees in their attempts to favorably shape supervisor perceptions.

References

Denison, D.R., Hooijberg, R. and Quinn, R.E. (1995) Paradox and performance: toward a theory of behavioral complexity in managerial leadership. *Organization Science* **6**(5), 524–540.

Dubrovsky, V., Kiesler, S. and Sethna, B. (1991) The equalization phenomenon: status effects in computer-mediated and face-to-face decision making groups. *Human – Computer Interaction* **6**(1), 119–146.

Eisenhardt, K.M. (1989) Building theories from case study research. *Academy of Management Review* **14**(4), 532–550.

Hightower, R.T. and Sayeed, L. (1995) The impact of computer mediated communication systems on biased group discussion. *Computers in Human Behavior* **11**(1), 33–44.

Hightower, R.T. and Sayeed, L. (1996) Effects of communication mode and prediscussion information distribution characteristics on information exchange in groups. *Information Systems Research* **7**(4), 451–465.

Hofstede, G. (1980) Motivation, leadership, and organization. do American theories apply abroad? *Organizational Dynamics* **Summer**, 42–63.

Hooijberg, R., Hunt, J.G. and Dodge, G.E. (1997) Leadership complexity and development of the leaderplex model. *Journal of Management* **23**(3), 375–408.

Kiesler, S. and Sproull, L. (1992) Group decision-making and communication technology. *Organizational Behavior and Human Decision Processes* **52**(1), 96–123.

Jarvenpaa, S.L., Knoll, K. and Leidner, D.E. (1998) Is anybody out there? Antecedents of trust in global virtual teams. *Journal of Management Information Systems* **14**(4), 29–64.

Lipnack, J. and Stamps, J. (1997) *Virtual Teams: Reaching Across Space, Time and Organizations with Technology*. John Wiley and Sons, New York.

McGrath, J.E. and Hollingshead, A.B. (1994) *Groups Interacting with Technology: Ideas, Evidence, Issues, and An Agenda*. Sage, London.

Odenwald, S. (1993) A guide for global training. *Training and Development* **47**(7), 22–31.

Solomon, C.M. (1995) Global teams: the ultimate collaboration. *Personnel Journal* **74**(9).

Townsend, A.M., deMarie S.M. and Hendrickson, A.R. (1998) Virtual teams and the workplace of the future. *Academy of Management Executive* **August**.

Trevino, L.K., Daft, R.L. and Lengel, R.H. (1990) Understanding manager's media choices: a symbolic interactionist perspective. In *Organizations and Communication Technology*, eds Fulk and Steinfeld. Sage Publications, Newbury Park, CA.

Walther, J.B. and Burgoon, J.K. (1992) Relational communication in computer mediated interaction. *Human Communication Research* **19**(1), 50–889.

Warkentin, M., Sayeed, L. and Hightower, R. (1997) Virtual teams vs face-to-face teams: an exploratory study of web-based conference systems. *Decision Sciences* **28**(4).

Yin, R.K. (1989) *Case Study Research: Design and Methods*. Sage Publications, Newbury Park, CA.

Appendix A

Virtual Team Topics

Team 1: 'Strategic use of Internet'

Team 2: 'The Strategic Impact of the Internet in the Textile Sector'

Team 3: 'Quality-Based IS Development'

Team 4: 'Use of EIS in the Management of Universities'

Team 5: 'Strength and Weaknesses of Virtual Teams'

Team 6: 'Integration of DSS, EIS and ES/KBS'

Team 7: 'Potential of Electronic Commerce '

Team 8: 'Use of Expert Systems in the Financial Sector '

Team 9: 'Relevance of DSS and EIS in Decision-Making'

Team 10: 'Requirements Specification of a DSS/EIS'

Team 11: 'Role of Intranets in the organizations'

Team 12: 'Strategic Planning of IS/IT in the government sector'

Appendix B

Open-ended Questions

1. As a group, how successful do you feel your virtual team was in accomplishing the task given to you by the project manager?
2. What factors contributed to your success? What factors hindered you in your efforts to complete this project? (Note: e.g. technical issues, culture, group dynamics, project leadership)
3. To what extent did you use various technologies to communicate with team members (e.g. e-mail, web communication tools)? How effective were these technologies?
4. What were some of the novel and unique problems/issues/challenges associated with working with groups in a virtual team environment? (e.g. group dynamics)
5. How effective was your project manager in directing your team's activities? What made him/her effective or ineffective?
6. After completing this project, you have been asked by a consulting firm to make recommendations on how to run a successful international (e.g. cross-cultural) virtual team. How would you answer this question (e.g. what are the critical dos and don'ts)?

Appendix C

Team use of computer mediated communication systems

Team number	Technology used	Comments
1	E-mail	Didn't use web technology because of lack of technology in Mexico
2	E-mail	E-mail was ineffective with long delays in sending and receiving e-mails
3	E-mail	Group tried to use collaborative CMCS, however project manager did not express support of this move
4	E-mail, Virtual Chat (mIRC)	Used e-mail for individual communication and Virtual Chat for group interaction
5	E-mail, PowWow, WebPages	Used e-mail for daily messages, PowWow for group conferencing, and WebPage to store research information
6	E-mail	E-mail used to communicate effectively across time zones
7	E-mail	E-mail was effectively used to share ideas, suggestions, and questions
8	E-mail	Group suggested use of collaborative tool, however, project manager didn't feel it was necessary
9	E-mail, PowWow, WebPages	E-mail used to communicate meeting schedules and individual progress. WebPage used as 'home base' of operation display agendas and project progress. PowWow used as a collaborative tool to facilitate group planning and implementation
10	E-mail	E-mail was not effective
11	E-mail	E-mail was effective due to low number of team members
12	E-mail	Tried to use PowWow, but were unsuccessful

TIMOTHY KAYWORTH, *Hankames School of Business, Baylor University, Waco, Texas 76798, USA. E-mail: kayworth@baylor.edu*

Timothy Kayworth is Assistant Professor of MIS at Baylor University. Previous experience is with Coopers and Lybrand. His current research centers on the management of IT in organizations and the impacts of IT infrastructure and its development within organizations.

DOROTHY LEIDNER, *INSEAD, Boulevard de Constance, 77305, Fontainebleau, Cedex, France.*

Dorothy Leidner is Associate Professor of Information Systems at INSEAD, France. Her current research interests include knowledge management systems, the rôle of IT in transforming organizational culture, internet-based education, and electronic commerce strategies.

Part III
Managing Cultural Diversity

[17]

Organizational Dynamics, Vol. 29, No. 1, pp. 45–63, 2000

ISSN 0090-2616/00/$–see frontmatter
PII S0090-2616(00)00012-7

Creating Value with Diverse Teams in Global Management

JOSEPH J. DISTEFANO   MARTHA L. MAZNEVSKI

INTRODUCTION

Today's economy increasingly requires people to collaborate in teams that cross cultural and geographic boundaries. Sometimes team members are all located in the same physical setting. More and more frequently, they are scattered across a city, a country, or the globe. In theory, these teams should create significant competitive advantage by bringing together different ideas, pools of knowledge, and approaches to work. However, in practice global teams do not often create the value expected. Instead, members clash, and the teams are either paralyzed into inaction or worse. With today's workforce demographics, the existence of culturally diverse teams is inevitable; and with today's competitive environment, firms cannot afford to forego their value.

A few years ago we began a systematic study of multicultural teams. The literature told us that diverse teams have a lot of potential. Compared to homogeneous teams they can be more creative, generate more and better alternatives to problems, and generate more and better criteria for evaluating alternatives. However, in no research did diverse teams outperform homogeneous ones on overall solution quality, and in only one study did they equal the homogeneous teams. But a couple of studies and a wealth of anecdotal evidence suggested a slightly different story. Diverse teams tend to perform either better or worse than homogeneous ones, with more performing worse than better (see Fig. 1). We set out to determine what distinguished the poor performers from the high performers, and to develop ways of helping culturally diverse teams at the bottom of the performance graph leapfrog the homogeneous teams and create value.

Why Focus on Multicultural Teams?

Members of global teams differ from each other in many important ways: gender, thinking style, function or profession, and so

Our research was augmented by consulting relationships, executive education sessions, and case-writing experiences in many companies. To illustrate the principles described here, we have drawn from these experiences; however, because of the sensitive nature of some of the examples, we have not named the specific teams or organizations as we recount their stories here. All names given are pseudonyms, but the industries have been maintained. The organizations we have worked with include: Arthur Andersen, Caltex, Canadian Imperial Bank of Commerce, Ciba–Geigy, Citibank, Commercial Union Assurance Company, Deloitte Touche, Dow Chemical, Ernst & Young, Exxon, Fairfax County Board of Education, First Brands, General Electric, Hong Kong Civil Service Training and Development Center, Hong Kong Productivity Council, Human Factors AS, Husky Oil, IBM, Kodak, London Life, Manulife, Millipore, Polysar, Royal Bank, Salvatore Ferragamo, Schneider Electric, Shell, Sony, Sun Life Insurance Company, the World Bank, and many universities.

Joseph J. DiStefano, is professor of organizational behavior and international management at the International Institute for Management Development (IMD) in Lausanne. He has been actively teaching, researching and consulting in the North America, Europe and the Asia-Pacific region for over thirty years. Until recently, he was on the faculty of the Richard Ivey School of Business, including three years as the Shirley Chan Memorial Professor of International Business and executive director of Ivey's Cheng Yu Tung Management Institute in Hong Kong. DiStefano earned a B.S. in mathematics at Rensselaer Polytechnic Institute, an MBA at Harvard Business School, and an MA and PhD in social psychology at Cornell University. He is the recipient of The University of Western Ontario's Pleva Award for Excellence in Teaching and serves on both private sector and voluntary boards of directors in the U.S. and Canada.

DiStefano's research interests include cross-cultural management, organizational effectiveness and human resource management. He has written over 100 cases and numerous articles and has (co)authored several books and monographs, including *International Management Behavior*, 4th ed. (in English and Chinese), *Human Resource Development & Management* (in English and Chinese) and *Effective Managerial Action*.

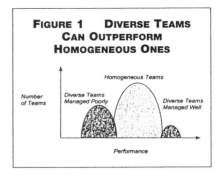

FIGURE 1 DIVERSE TEAMS CAN OUTPERFORM HOMOGENEOUS ONES

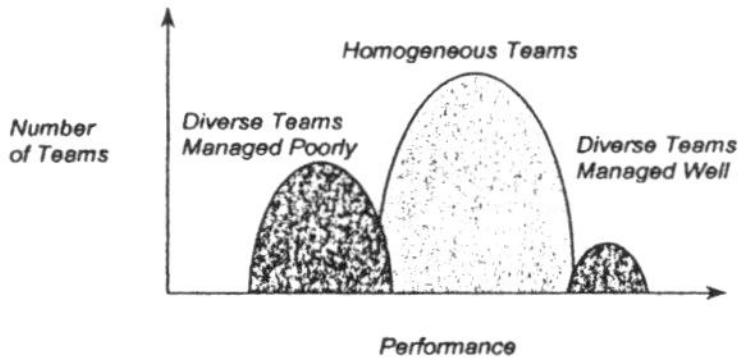

on. Why do we focus our attention on the multicultural nature of these teams? Cultural differences are especially important to global teams for two main reasons. First, cultural differences provide the greatest potential to hinder effective interaction within teams. Culture is a society's or defined group's assumptions and norms for how people interact with each other and approach what they do. Each society develops a different set of assumptions and norms under which to operate, and different professions, functions, and even genders within a society or organization can have different cultures themselves. Team members from different cultures therefore come to the group setting with very different predefined notions about how a group should proceed. Furthermore, cultural values and norms are deeply held, and almost always implicit and taken for granted. Their deepest effects on behavior and interaction are usually hidden, and extremely difficult to identify and address. Cultural differences inevitably hinder smooth interaction.

On the other hand, because of the nature of culture, cultural differences also provide the greatest potential for creating value. Culture affects what we notice, how we interpret it, what we decide to do about it, and how we execute our ideas. Multicultural teams, then, have an enormous wealth of material with which to create innovative approaches to complex organizational challenges, and a broad range of operating modes with which to develop new ways of implementing solutions. Today's business cannot flourish without the creative value afforded by high-performing global teams.

With this acknowledgment of culture and its impact, we launched our study of the multicultural dynamics in teams.

Global Teams Come in Three Models

The first thing we noticed was that global teams fell into one of three clear performance categories, not just into the two we expected. We called these patterns destroying, equalizing, and creating.

The destroyers

Some multicultural teams were unmitigated disasters. Their members mistrusted each other, guarded information jealously, and took every opportunity to attack other members. One European member explained his team's poor performance to us forcefully: "Those Brits on our team are too serious, the Germans are so stuck up about engineering they don't think anyone else has a brain, and the French couldn't care less about production quotas." In these cases, the energy that could have been channeled into effective work was drained into negative stereotyping. "Team" decisions were made by the manager or formal leader without genuine discussion among members. The "team" destroyed value rather than creating it.

The equalizers

The second pattern was the most puzzling; it was also the one we saw most frequently. If a diverse team had been working together for a while, members typically told us with pride, "We handle our differences well! They don't affect our performance—we moved beyond that long ago. We have great meetings. Everyone gives their input; we resolve things pretty quickly and move on. Frankly, all this diversity hype is blown way out of proportion." These teams' senior managers, though, usually told a slightly different story. One executive told us, "I guess they are getting

Martha L. Maznevski, is assistant professor of organizational behavior and international management at the McIntire School of Commerce, University of Virginia. She earned a BEd from the University of Toronto, and a BA in anthropology and PhD in business administration, focusing on international organizational behavior, from the University of Western Ontario. She researches, teaches, and consults in the areas of strategic human resources, multicultural team performance, international management, and global leadership, with recent activities in North America, Europe and Asia. She has presented and published numerous articles on these subjects, and is a co-author of the textbook *International Management Behavior*. Her current research focuses on the on-going dynamics of high-performing teams and networks in multinational organizations.

things accomplished. But they assembled the best minds in the company, then produced a compromise that didn't even approach the expected cost savings. We might get the benefits we hoped for eventually, but I'm more than a little disappointed!"

In a word: mediocrity. The teams helped their companies stay in the game. But by not allowing the differences to surface in any way, the teams suffered because they couldn't leverage them for innovation or performance advantages. We began to call this pattern "equalizing": suppressing differences to smooth processes, and in turn suppressing differences in ideas and perspectives. We suspect most culturally diverse teams that think of themselves as "doing well" are really equalizers.

The creators

Some multicultural teams, of course, do perform at high levels, with results exceeding even their own expectations. These teams go far beyond the buzzwords "value diversity." Differences are explicitly recognized and accepted, even nurtured, and their implications are incorporated into every facet of the group's processes. Watching these teams is like watching a top-performing jazz ensemble. The players all recognize the mastery of the others, and understand the potential for synergy arising from their combinations. They develop a constantly shifting dynamic that incorporates innovation into cooperative structures. We've seen these unique teams create value by bringing highly successful products to market in record time, achieving quantum leaps in cost savings in a price-competitive industry, inventing new types of alliances with global suppliers and clients, and moving successfully into territory that others have been unable to conquer.

How did these high performing teams achieve such success? We found that the key was not in the membership—on average, their members weren't any better in their individual areas than those on destroying or equalizing teams. The key to unlocking creative synergy was in the team's interaction processes—how they understood, incorporated, and leveraged their differences.

THREE STEPS TO CREATING VALUE: MAP, BRIDGE, INTEGRATE

Creator teams interacted according to the three principles of mapping, bridging, and integrating (MBI). To **map**, they described the differences among members and the impact of those differences in objective, measurable ways. To **bridge**, they communicated in ways that explicitly took the differences into account. **Integrating** directed them to create team-level ideas by carefully monitoring participation patterns, resolving disagreements, and creating new perspectives. We have since introduced these principles, summarized in Fig. 2, to many destroying and equalizing teams and observed dramatic turnarounds in their performance. By applying these principles in a dedicated and committed way, any global team can become a creator.

Mapping to Understand Differences

The principle of mapping requires a commitment to understand the underlying characteristics affecting each member's approach to the team. In a multinational team it may seem obvious that members will have different perspectives, but deliberately mapping these differences develops an appreciation of how they affect teamwork. There are three steps to the mapping principle: selecting which characteristics to map, describing members' characteristics, and identifying their impact.

Define the territory

This is usually a simple, although not trivial, matter. At some level we are all different, but acknowledging this is not terribly helpful. The idea here is to identify which differences will make a difference. Which ones will most likely raise barriers to interaction? Which dif-

FIGURE 2 CREATING VALUE IN DIVERSE TEAMS: THE MBI APPROACH

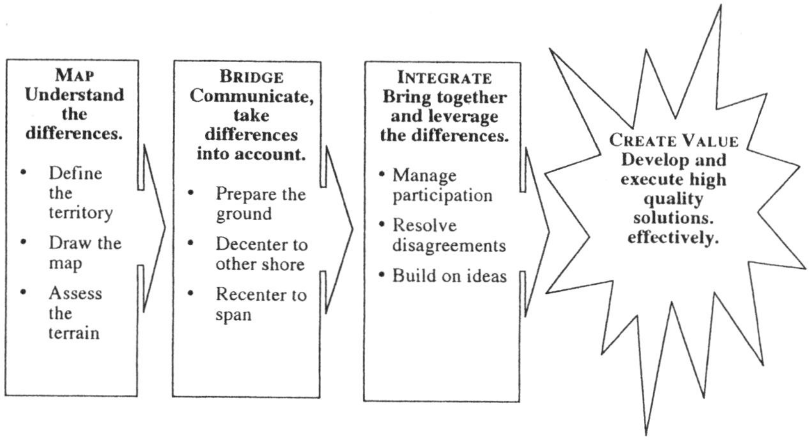
MAP
Understand the differences.
• Define the territory
• Draw the map
• Assess the terrain
BRIDGE
Communicate, take differences into account.
• Prepare the ground
• Decenter to other shore
• Recenter to span
INTEGRATE
Bring together and leverage the differences.
• Manage participation
• Resolve disagreements
• Build on ideas
CREATE VALUE
Develop and execute high quality solutions. effectively.

ferences can be most leveraged to help the team achieve its objectives? In almost any multinational team, cultural differences will influence how the team works together—as well as offer enormous potential for innovation—so mapping culture is critical. But differences associated with personality, thinking or learning style, gender or profession may also affect the team's dynamics in important ways. Members must fully understand these differences to prevent their negative effects and realize their positive potential.

Draw the map

In this step, teams assess each member's characteristics on the selected dimensions. Teams can map their difference profiles on their own, for example as guided by the Appendix, or tap the expertise of their human resource departments. In situations where success and failure represent high stakes, investing in survey instruments to map differences is wise. When trying to understand the type and extent of differences among team members, there is nothing as compelling as having your own data with a numerical comparison to others. Members who assume they are "pretty similar" are often shocked to find out how different their scores are on cultural values or thinking style. This surprise itself often leads to an insightful exploration of the implications for performance.

Assess the terrain

To assess the terrain, the team uses the map of members' dimensions to help understand past, current, and future potential dynamics. Ideally, the team maps its characteristics early and anticipates both problems and potential, incorporating mechanisms to alleviate the former and leverage the latter into their ongoing processes. Sometimes mapping comes after interaction has already happened, and can help explain past incidents. Most global teams do not take the time to map cultural differences up front; they just rely on broad generalizations (stereotypes) they have heard. But by not mapping, these teams cannot address the differences objectively, and the problems caused by the differences cannot be resolved. These teams turn to mapping culture after becoming frustrated with a lack of performance. They use the mapping to understand the problems that have already occurred, and set the stage for future expectations.

Develop cartographers

In practice, mapping is not as simple as it sounds. In fact, good mapping is often the most difficult stage for multicultural teams, because it requires a great amount of energy seemingly outside the team's official mandate. It is easy to start with good intentions, but then slip into negative stereotyping—assuming that people who see things differently or present them in different ways are not valuable. This is what destroying teams do, and this is the fatal step that begins their destruction. A Uruguayan was on a team of petroleum executives that also included two Americans and single members from Britain, Japan and Belgium. The team was engaged in a critical discussion of an acquisition opportunity. Three times the Uruguayan tried to raise issues of who would compose the top executive team. He was overruled each time by the dominance of the American and British managers, who dismissed his concerns about people as much less important than the financial analysis and because, "he's always bringing up the soft issues. How were we supposed to know that this time it was related to hard stuff?"

It is also deceptively appealing to ignore differences and focus on similarities. This is what equalizing teams do. The differences don't get in the way and things go smoothly, but the differences also never get used to help the team. A bank operations group in Toronto, made up of a rich diversity of Asians, South Americans, Caribbeans, Central Europeans and French–Canadians, was preparing to work as a self-managed team. They were performing fine, but improvements had been leveling off, and they found themselves vaguely disappointed in their inability to improve productivity. They mapped their cultural differences, and then sat down to watch a videotape of their most recent meeting. All members were surprised when they saw their own behavior. A Thai woman spoke for them all when she exclaimed, "That's not me; that's me acting like our old boss!" They realized that they had been suppressing their normal behavior. In the absence of their former supervisor (an Anglo–Canadian) they had been trying to behave just like him. Dampening their preferred modes, of course, had also interfered with their ability to use their differences. They used this insight to adapt to their new responsibilities; over time, they improved both their functioning as a team and their work output.

Creator teams assume differences and use the map as a starting point to frame the differences and talk about them. They use their differences to explain problems when things don't go as expected. They are committed to continued mapping, adding more detail to their descriptions as their experiences working together continue. In a large California research and development (R&D) operation of a French-owned global electrical manufacturer, the American senior manager was experiencing difficulties with two of his research teams. Looking more carefully at their makeup, he realized the team leaders of the groups were from Poland and Belgium, and that their groups were extremely diverse in their cultural makeup. The Polish leader had 14 different nationalities in his team of 16 and the Belgian's team of 12 people contained eight different nationalities. The senior manager had each team map their cultural differences, share the information within the team, and then work to learn as much as possible about the cultures of the other members and how the differences related to their interactions within the team. It was both the mapping and the incorporating of that knowledge into their work that made them effective.

This team, as did all the other creator teams we observed, realized quickly that mapping by itself is not enough to generate value in a diverse team. Even if the mapping principle is fully realized, high performance doesn't automatically follow. Creator teams were also committed to the next principle and skilled at its implementation.

Bridging to Communicate Across Differences

Bridging, or communicating effectively across the differences to bring people and ideas together, is the next important principle in the MBI approach. Effective communication is "sending and receiving meaning *as it was intended.*" We are all too familiar with miscommunication, especially in situations marked by diversity. Those stories can be humorous, but they tend to have unfortunate endings. The key to bridging is to prevent miscommunication. There are three steps to building a strong bridge in a diverse team: Prepare, Decenter, and Recenter.

Prepare the ground

Preparing well sets the foundation for building a good bridge. Team members must encourage and reinforce two important attitudes: *motivation* to communicate and integrate effectively, and *confidence* to overcome any difficulties. We always want others to understand us, but we are often much less anxious to understand others. Even after mapping to understand important differences, team members may not be motivated to use these differences to improve performance. Confidence is sometimes even more elusive. In fact, team members are generally more confident before mapping than they are immediately afterward. The complexity surprises and discourages them. However, once teams take the initial efforts to bridge and integrate well, good results and more refined skills follow quickly, with improved confidence.

Each team becomes motivated and gains confidence differently, but motivation and confidence should *always* be related to the team's task. In a financial services firm, global cross-functional client teams looked at examples of other teams and how much they had increased business. In one case the multiple was 100-fold, with a significant starting base. Then each team estimated its client's potential business, and worked with related data. After seeing how much potential business there was, the teams engaged with strong commitment towards those goals. They were prepared to bridge. In a large multinational, senior managers put together cross-national, cross-functional teams to achieve extraordinary cost cutting in strategic areas of the company. To prepare the teams, these senior managers attended the teams' first meetings, reinforcing the task's importance and magnitude as well as top management's confidence in the team members.

A diverse team can't always count on senior managers to prepare the ground. The bank managers overseeing the operations team described earlier couldn't provide quantitative measures for the team's improvement, and frankly were skeptical that this team could become truly self-managed. But the team members themselves were proud of the progress they had already made in moving towards self-management. They had a history of taking each new problem, addressing it systematically, and then resolving it. When they ran into some difficulties posed by their differences—starting with an argument about hosting a senior manager from another part of the organization—they became anxious. Rather than give in to destroying or equalizing, they attacked this new issue with enthusiasm and discipline. Their motivation and confidence were internal: they wanted to improve performance, and to prove to senior management that they could do this. Rather than ignore their differences, they were prepared to bridge them.

Decenter: Build to the other shore

Decentering is the second step to building a bridge in a diverse team. To decenter, members of the team take what they know about each other's differences from mapping and apply it to adapt their own behavior and thinking. They change their conversation style and adapt their interaction behaviors according to the culture of the people they're working with. Decentering is not quite the same as empathy. Empathy is getting inside another person's skin, thinking as the other person thinks and feeling what the other person feels. But decentering goes beyond identifying with the other and *uses* the understanding gained by mapping in both listening to others and responding to them. Decentering is empathy in practice, with the map as a translation key.

The other important element in decentering is *suspending judgment*. We have a nearly universal tendency to react instinctively to differences as bad. "They" are different from "us." "We" are right and good; therefore "they" are wrong and bad. Even when people are conscious about cultural or other differences, the evaluative instinct kicks in quickly. This tends to be even more common when the differences are subtle rather than overt, or when time is tight. But effective communication requires seeing any difference as a function of us *and* them: difference just "is," it is not inherently good or bad.

A very open, almost aggressive, consulting audit partner in a financial services client team was confused by the behavior of her audit subordinate, a newly minted C.A./C.P.A. who had recently emigrated from Hong Kong. He initially appeared to agree with an approach the partner suggested, but then she learned from a third party that he was "refusing" to follow through. The partner confronted the auditor with the inconsistency, and was pleased when he reconfirmed his cooperation during the meeting. The project was started as planned. However, soon rumors circulated that the auditor had balked again.

This time, rather than storming in and confronting her teammate right away, the partner stopped and tried to see things from his point of view. She knew that he was very highly respected for his auditing skills and his work with clients—it was easy to forget that, with all the strife of the past couple of weeks—but the team wasn't benefiting. What was going on? She finally realized that very different modes of communicating were operating here. Her map of American versus Hong Kong Chinese culture reminded her that Americans expect open discussion, even with difficult topics. Consistent with this, she was being open with her subordinate. On the other hand, the Chinese culture tends to deal with negative communication in an indirect manner to retain the face of everyone involved. The Hong Kong manager felt insulted and threatened by what the American thought was "straight talk." He removed himself from the offensive situation by saying he agreed to do something he had no intention of doing. In his own culture, he wouldn't be expected to keep his word because it was obtained only by what he experienced as coercion. Instead, he expressed his real intentions only in highly indirect ways—which would have been clear to anyone in his own culture.

Trying to salvage the team, the partner invited the manager to a meeting. She planned it off-site and during lunch to remove the formality of the work setting, and to save face for her Chinese subordinate. After about half an hour of what the partner defined as "small talk," but which she understood was important in Chinese cultures for building and reinforcing the relationship, she apologized for not listening to him and for forcing her own solutions on the group. She described her understanding of the communication problem, being careful not to blame either one of them, but simply to explain it as an unfortunate situation arising from their different backgrounds—a situation she thought they should try to resolve for the good of the team and the firm. He had been blaming himself for the problem, and he was frustrated with his inability to say things in a way she could understand. In this setting, and with both people prepared to bridge their differences, they were able to decenter and suspend judgment. The partner asked the auditor to describe what he saw as the pitfalls in the project. She was amply rewarded for her efforts: he brought up several important issues that would have caused enormous problems later if they weren't addressed now.

Decentering is a skill, not just something people either can or can't do. Everyone can learn to see things from others' perspectives, particularly with the help of good maps, and can learn to suspend judgment. Team members can increase decentering in the team by questioning, paraphrasing, and openly testing themselves during interactions with other team members. When a team first works together, or first starts using its differences productively, decentering is time-consuming. But the time spent more than returns its investment as the team's work progresses. And the time needed to decenter shrinks as the team improves its skills at bridging.

Recenter: Span the bridge

Recentering, the third step to building a good bridge, is finding or developing shared ground upon which to build a new basis of interacting. This process, too, depends on having a good working knowledge of the team's internal differences. First you decenter—get out of your own mode of operating and into other people's modes—then you reconnect, with a very different way of communicating than before. Teams need shared ground around two things for good bridging: defining the situation itself, and interacting with each other.

For example, what is a meeting for? The definition differs widely, depending on whom you talk to. In the United States, a team meeting is held to make decisions. Members bring information and input to the meeting, and come prepared to compare and analyze alternatives in a constructive way. In Japan, a team meeting is held to publicly confirm decisions that were discussed among members in smaller groups as they developed their analyses. This intensive discussion among members explores issues just as thoroughly as the American model does, but saves face by ensuring that conflict is private rather than public. In Mexico, a meeting is a time to build relationships and trust with each other. Once you trust someone, then decisions can be made easily in other ways. In the Netherlands, a meeting may be a time to identify all the weaknesses and criticisms of a particular approach or plan: "Why bother talking about what's good? Those things don't need to be changed." Think about how much we take for granted that everyone has the same assumptions about what meetings are for. If there's this much variation in how to define a meeting, think about how to define the team's task! Recentering provides this common ground.

Members of a global team should explicitly agree on some common definitions of their own situation and the team's purpose. What kind of a team is this? Can we question the company's strategy, or should we take it as given? Should we evaluate projects based purely on potential net income, or do we have a budget restriction or other constraints to take into account? How soon do we need to see a return? What makes a proposal acceptable? What makes a presentation to senior management good? When a team is homogeneous, it's fairly safe to assume after a few brief exchanges that everyone's on the same footing. But the more diverse the team is, the more important it is to keep revisiting these issues.

Teammates should also agree on how to interact with each other. This is another place where diverse teams often begin to fall apart. Destroyer teams tend to dismiss or ridicule each other's norms, and then members on the receiving end withdraw from the interaction. Equalizer teams manage to agree on a set of norms for everyone without much anguish: they just use the norms of the majority or dominant group. But the best creator teams find a way to agree out loud that different members can operate under different norms. Recall the financial services team, where the Hong Kong Chinese auditor and American partner had difficulty communicating with each other. Understanding their differences helped the situation but didn't prevent the problem from happening again. Recognizing the importance of their communication to the team, they finished their long lunch meeting by discussing how to keep the lines open with each other. The partner agreed to check in with the auditor privately on a regular basis, and to try to listen for those indirect signals of disagreement and follow up on them tactfully. "I can't say I'll catch everything," she told him, "but I'll try to get better at it." The auditor agreed to try to speak up when he disagreed during a meeting, or at least to write it down and get it to the partner right away. He also told the partner that when he disagreed with her, his senior, he probably broke eye contact or switched topics, warning her that these were classic avoidance strategies to follow up on. And—critical to their ability to work together—both agreed not to interpret the other's actions as trying to undermine the team or other team members.

Integrating to Leverage Differences

Although good bridging is critical, understanding each others' perspectives doesn't guarantee that the group can bring everything together and come up with good decisions. For that, the team needs to integrate, our third principle of managing diversity well. Integrating is where understanding (from mapping) and communicating (from bridging) get converted into productive results. There are three important steps to integrating: managing participation, resolving disagreements, and building on ideas. All three require good mapping and bridging.

Manage participation for basic leverage

Any team needs to have high quality raw material—ideas from team members—from which to build great performance. You can't get good ideas from team members if they don't participate in some active way in the team's ongoing dialogue and discussion. Unfortunately, this is much more difficult than it sounds. People with different cultural values tend to subscribe to vastly different norms for participating. It may seem unreasonable to suggest, as we did above, that the group encourage different norms for participation from different people. It can take more time, and certainly takes more energy. But consider the consequences of enforcing similarity on participation modes.

Losing the assets. A very culturally diverse team of top managers from the downtown offices of a national bank were reviewing their decision-making. One of the managers spoke up and said, "Actually, I think we've been very good. We listen to everyone, we always make sure we ask if anyone disagrees with where we're going. And we're doing better than our competitors are here, so we must be doing something right!"

Another concurred, saying "I think you're right. There's obviously always room for improvement, but all things considered, we get all the right ideas out from everyone, right gang?" The rest of the group nodded, and several others gave supporting examples. After a few minutes of self-congratulation, the team was ready to move on to something else when one woman, originally from Korea, cleared her throat nervously and raised her hand tentatively. She was sitting at the back corner of the large square table, where she was easily overlooked by those leaning forward into the discussion. "Oh—Judy. Did you want to add something before we go on to other things?"

Judy took a deep breath and said: "Not one of you understands how hard it is for me to talk in meetings with you. I have to rehearse everything I'm going to say fifteen times in my mind. My throat gets tight, and I feel like I have to yell. I have to keep telling myself that no matter how wrong it seems, you don't think I'm being rude. Half the time by the time I say my piece, you think you've gone beyond the point, and my information doesn't get considered, and I don't absorb anything for the next minute after I've spoken. I've learned to cope so you really don't know I'm going through this, and my feelings aren't the point here. But do you think I can *think* properly under all that? What frustrates me most is that *the team really isn't getting my best ideas*, the ones that could make a difference!"

About 20 seconds into the shocked and awkward silence after Judy's statement, one of the men—who had not taken part in the previous conversation—stated quietly that as an Indonesian he also had difficulty speaking up in the group. He often had observations that the group didn't come around to until later, but he just hadn't found a way to speak up enough to get others to listen to him. By adjusting their team norms on participation to include Judy and others, the team could generate a wider scope of ideas to draw from.

In contrast, in much of both North and South America it is not only acceptable to speak openly aloud, it is expected that people will interrupt whenever they feel it is important, and that there will be little or no silence. We have watched members of these cultures try hard not to keep talking or interrupting during a meeting, to no avail. Even after watching themselves on videotape and expressing astonishment at how much they dominated the dialogue, when "caught in the moment" of a good discussion they simply could not hold back. They were extremely uncomfortable with silence, feeling a need to fill it. In their attempts to try to conform to other norms, they became as frustrated and uncomfortable as the East Asian managers in the example above, with the same results.

Tools and techniques. There are many ways of managing participation well. A global chemical R&D team, recognizing the strong cultural differences among members, assigned one member the role of "process leader." This person was given explicit license and *obligation* to curb the dominance of any individual, interrupt those talking freely on behalf of more reserved members hesitant to interrupt, and invite participation from members who were more silent. Team members also agreed to make a special effort never to interrupt certain individuals, but agreed that it was still okay to interrupt others. The process leader became especially helpful in managing meetings held over conference call, where visual cues for conversation norms are absent. The team's meetings became much more productive. Eventually, the process leader role was rotated through the group. Although the group needed the process leader's interventions less and less frequently, the very fact that they knew someone was monitoring the processes helped them interact more comfortably.

A second solution is to vary the modes of meeting and sharing information. This allows everyone to contribute in the way in which he or she is most comfortable, and ends up leveraging everyone's strengths. For example, the new president of a U.S. multinational's Asia–Pacific subsidiary found it difficult to get his diverse team of country managers to participate in U.S.-style meetings. He began to solicit detailed e-mails about the topic before the meeting. "What are your ideas?" he would ask. To his surprise, he received very thoughtful responses from those who had been most quiet during the past meetings. He tried to deliberately bump into team members in the hall or cafeteria, and chat with them about the issues. He also encouraged them to do the same with each other, and to share the outcomes of their discussions with him. He kept in frequent contact with the team members over the phone, and again encouraged them to do the same with each other. He also began to vary modes of participating when the whole group met together. He encouraged members to talk to each other "on the side" briefly, then asked one to summarize their discussion for the rest of the group. This was particularly effective when he paired people who both spoke the same non-English language, but one spoke stronger English than the other. He began to find that he was able to get insights from those not fluent in speaking English that he would never have received otherwise. He held frequent breaks, but requested that everyone stick around and chat with each other during at least some of those breaks. Even though it seemed to take more time on a day to day basis, he found that meetings went more quickly and were more productive, more than making up for the lost time. Of course, he got better ideas. But more than that, he found that broadening the scope of the team's interaction was beneficial to everyone, not just to those who were uncomfortable with the dominant modes. Greater trust was developed, better ideas started flowing, and the team was more committed to the solutions they generated together.

Each team must develop its own techniques for managing participation. Having a process leader and varying the modes of gathering information and meeting are particularly strong techniques because they allow flexibility and adaptation. Almost all creator teams we have seen incorporate both of these ideas.

Resolve disagreements to increase leverage

Once ideas are out, disagreements about them inevitably follow. To use the ideas, or to develop even better ones, it's necessary to resolve conflict. In teams where members are similar, people use their common set of rules regarding how to express, detect and resolve conflict. In diverse teams, as you might expect, the processes are a lot more complicated. Resolving the conflict becomes much more difficult when there is disagreement about how to resolve conflict in the first place.

Teams that become adept at mapping, bridging and participating find that their worst conflicts—the personal ones—diminish and become manageable. Mapping helps members anticipate and detect conflict in its early stages, before it becomes destructive. It also helps members understand the source of the conflict when it arises. Bridging well ensures that disagreements don't arise because of miscommunication, and generates high levels of trust and comfort among team members. When disagreements *do* arise, decentering provides a way to talk about the problems without blaming one another, and in a more objective way using each other's preferred modes of interacting. When participation is managed well, information is introduced when it is needed, rather than after conflict has already arisen. What is left is truly substantive, and can be resolved constructively. This is where having a process leader, whether it's the team's senior decision-maker or someone else on the team, really helps.

Wait! Some conflicts are hidden! In the earlier section about mapping, we cited an example of a team of petroleum executives from the U.S., U.K., Uruguay, Japan, and Belgium who were working on an acquisition. In that case, their disagreement about the relative priority to be given to financials versus staffing the top team was open and explicit. But later in their deliberations, the British member stood up, went to the flip chart and wrote in bold letters, DO NOTHING! "In my view," he said, "this academic 'straw man' is finally worth following. We are far from ready to do a deal. The financials are all wrong, and they aren't ready to compromise. We should move on and look for another potential acquisition."

He paused for a reaction. No one spoke and he was about to resume his argument when the Japanese executive, who had remained silent throughout the first 45 minutes of the discussion, cleared his throat and said, "Wait." He, too, was greeted with silence. Expecting elaboration from his Japanese colleague, the British manager waited with his pen poised. But after a brief moment the Japanese manager failed to add anything further and the U.K. manager stroked boldly through his earlier phrase and rewrote under it, WAIT. And he proceeded to explore other potential targets for acquisition.

Later that evening one of the two Americans on the team, nicknamed Tex, asked his Japanese counterpart over dinner why he had said, "Wait." Tex noted, "I expected you to continue and provide a counterargument, or elaborate in some way. Did you really mean, 'Do nothing,' as Ian seemed to conclude?"

"Not at all," replied Yoshi-san, "I meant that we should continue to collect more information about the company, check on the reasons for their executives being so rigid about the valuation, and wait a bit longer to see if the circumstances might change their bargaining position."

"But why didn't you say so?" asked Tex with a slight edge of frustration. "You didn't ask," replied Yoshi-san simply.

Here we have the most difficult of conflicts, one in which at least one of the parties assumed agreement, whereas the other chose not to raise the differences any more openly than he had. In the absence of a good map to indicate that perhaps "Wait" was not the equivalent of "Do Nothing," Ian assumed similarity. Neither did any of the other members of the team understand that Yoshi-san, with a greater sensitivity to hierarchy, had deferred to the more senior Ian and Tex, waiting for them to invite him to elaborate.

In this case, Tex had picked up a subtle clue that the pause after Yoshi-san's "Wait" didn't quite seem to equate to agreement. And he learned that one of the most important parts of multicultural effectiveness is knowing what you don't know. In this case, it was the need to pay attention to differences in language and hierarchy, rooted in cultural values that are part of an easy-to-use framework. It was a lesson not missed by Tex, for in a later discussion about the acquisition he made a direct inquiry of Yoshi-san regarding his experience with a similar deal in Tokyo years before. Although he had not volunteered his knowledge until asked, once Tex invited his participation, Yoshi-san gave a 10 minute "core dump" of his memory about the deal, making a significant contribution to the group's decision about how to proceed.

Tools and techniques. There are several techniques a team can use to resolve conflicts in a way that both helps the company and reinforces relationships among team members. In the example above, the team shifted the focus from the conflict itself to questions that might contribute to or resolve the conflict. In other situations, the team may re-center again on broader or higher level objectives, or clarify the relationship among the various perspectives. Many disagreements arise because of uncertainty or equivocal information, and in these cases a productive technique is to identify a set of questions whose answers would help distinguish between possible solutions, and a list of further information needed. The team can then discuss how to answer the questions or obtain the information, and proceed to clarify the issues. Often, once the new information is brought to the discussion, the disagreement is resolved much more easily.

A multinational merger implementation team combined several of these techniques when they had strong disagreements about how to consolidate the head offices and subsidiaries. Upon exploring the reasons for their conflict, they realized they had different assumptions about people's reactions, abilities to work together, and subsequent consequences. They had previously reviewed these differences in the early stages of the team's development, but in the heat of the discussions had forgotten their previous mapping. Once they resurfaced these differences, the team designed a decision tree with a set of contingency plans based on the probability of different events occurring, and agreed which path would be taken under which circumstances. Although this process took some time, the team was able to respond quickly and effectively to changes and reactions when they unrolled the implementation, and the process went much more smoothly than people in the two companies had anticipated.

There is no magic formula to make conflict disappear, and what we know about teams would suggest that cognitive conflict, or task-based conflict, is actually very helpful. For a diverse team, the important thing is to keep the task in mind and avoid personal conflict, and to find ways to bring all the perspectives out and discuss them. Perseverance becomes critical.

Build on ideas for optimal leverage

The final step to integrating is building on ideas. This should be familiar to anyone who has taken team building training. But as with other aspects of working in diverse teams, when dealing with differences—especially those hidden from our awareness—it is easier said than done. As in the case of the Latin American who tried to raise the issue of how to staff a merged company, it is easier to reject others' ideas when we misunderstand them or miss their intent. Both these errors are more likely in situations where differences get in the way.

One helpful thing to do is to see individual ideas as only the starting point for discussion. Everyone needs to be able to let go of idea ownership, and grasp onto idea generation on behalf of the team. At the end of a good meeting, it is often impossible to remember who initiated which idea. The petroleum merger meetings described above ended with this outcome, after Tex had incorporated Yoshi-san and the Uruguayan into the discussion. Another way to avoid premature closure on ideas is to set up a stage of activity where divergent thinking is encouraged *before* ideas are screened out. Team-building veterans will recognize variants of this in brainstorming, Delphi technique, and nominal group technique (NGT).

A good rule of thumb to follow is to resist the temptation to compromise. We are often tempted to "split the difference," or to say, "I'll give in this time, but you owe me one," especially when under time pressures. Neither is effective in producing synergistic ideas. Understanding differences and trying to bridge them encourages more productive means of engagement. If I try to understand your ideas and ways of thinking and behaving, my own repertoire of ideas and behaviors will be expanded. And by entertaining your approaches with fuller understanding, I am more likely to see new possibilities emerge from our interaction.

A financial-services global client team deliberately built on ideas as they developed account strategies. Encouraged by their improved understanding of each other's differences, they generated powerful ideas that helped the clients and the team. One new idea they surfaced was using the map of differences developed within their team to understand the key decision-maker *inside the client's organization*. They then framed their approach (decentering) with his preferences as a guide. Using the MBI principles to help facilitate relations between the team and others works with internal customers, too. The global resource team charged with cutting costs knew they had to start the rollout of their new processes inside the Japanese subsidiary. So, they brought in a colleague who had worked with the head of the Tokyo office to help them build an effective cultural map and plan their implementation.

Evolving to Keep Performance High

MBI is a set of principles for developing a unique team's own best way to perform well. It does not prescribe one best way for every team. That may have worked in yesterday's homogeneous workforce, but it doesn't translate to sustained performance today, and especially not globally. Every team is different, and every team needs to operate differently to capture the potential offered by its members. The appropriate map, communication norms, and integration styles will be unique to each team. Finding or developing them lifts a diverse team from destroying, carries it over the equalizers, and places it squarely among the creators.

To sustain this level of performance, teams need to examine their processes regularly and adapt to new members, new situations, and the general development of the team. In short, the team must *evolve*. For example, the management team of a global supplier-customer alliance met in person only once every three months. Between these meetings they interacted over e-mail, phone, and conference call. They thought the process issues were important enough, though, that they set aside at least one hour of every face-to-face conference agenda to address, "How are we managing ourselves? What could we be doing better to facilitate the team?" During this time they candidly reviewed the past months' communications, resolved miscommunications, and identified ways they could improve things in the future. This alliance was the best performing of many alliances engaged in by both companies, and the managers transferred the best practices learned here into other projects.

An excellent way to assess processes is to videotape the group during an important decision-making meeting. As uncomfortable as many people are with this at the beginning of taping, they soon forget the camera's rolling. The insights are always tremendous, and debriefing discussions immediately result in improved processes among team members. As one American remarked, "I couldn't believe how even my physical movements dominated the table, while Ron [a Filipino American], without us even noticing, actually worked his way off-camera within the first five minutes, and we never saw or heard from him again. But we know he's had the most experience with this type of decision!" This manager took on "learning not to dominate but to facilitate" as a personal learning goal for the rest of the project, and was a key to unlocking the team's final success.

When time is short or the team members are already well versed with the MBI principles, simply taking a few minutes to debrief a meeting—using MBI to frame the discussion—can bring up the most relevant points. It also gets the team into the important habit of thinking consciously about processes.

With this attention to processes, even as the team's mandate, membership, or environment changes, the team can adapt and develop new modes of operating. The team can evolve, changing how teammates work together and creating value for the company.

BUT ISN'T THIS JUST "COMMON SENSE" FOR ALL GROUPS?

The short answer is, "Yes." The more accurate answer is, "Yes, but. . . " Our research and research conducted by others shows that both culturally diverse and homogeneous groups can improve their constructive behaviors over time, achieving increases in performance. But the difficulties are greater the more diverse the group is, and the negative impact of ineffective behaviors on performance is much greater for diverse groups. Most important, the different perspectives on a diverse team offer more potential for becoming a creating team, so diverse teams stand to benefit much more from these processes. Because cultural differences usually present the most difficult case for teams, they also offer the greatest opportunities for value.

The second "but" is that these processes take time and effort to learn. Finding and using a good map, for example, is often difficult for team members to do on their own. Learning to decenter and recenter are difficult when you can't step out of the context and watch yourself objectively. Negotiating new norms and then abiding by them can be tiring. For some teams, and even for diverse teams doing some more straightforward or structured tasks, all this effort simply may not be worth it.

But for diverse teams working on high stakes projects or on those requiring unique, innovative solutions to complex dilemmas, the MBI processes pay off well. Like the creator team described in Appendix A, these teams can avoid destroying or equalizing, and can create that elusive synergy by understanding their differences, communicating across their differences, and managing their differences. Diverse teams are a reality of today's global workforce. Companies should begin to go beyond struggling with diversity's barriers to performance and use these opportunities to create value.

APPENDIX A
MAPPING CULTURE

According to the Cultural Orientations Framework, based on anthropological theories developed in the 1950s and 1960s, every society must address a limited set of issues concerning interaction among people and with the environment. There is a limited set of typical responses to each issue, and every individual prefers one or sometimes two responses over the others for each issue. Most people who grew up in the same society tend to have the same set of preferences, but not always. For example, most Americans prefer individualism over collectivism over hierarchy for relationships, but many Americans are more collective than individualistic. *No one response is better than the others in all situations.* The best solutions to a company's most complex problems will inevitably incorporate a variety of these perspectives.

The five most important issues and their corresponding typical responses are listed in the table here. More information can be obtained from the resources listed in the selected bibliography.

Mapping Your Own Cultural Orientations

For each of the main issues, decide which response best fits with your perspectives and priorities, which fits second best, and which least fits how you approach the issue. For example, for "activity," if in most circumstances you like to take action quickly and work to achieve tangible goals, you are usually impatient with long, drawn-out decision-making, but become outright frustrated with spontaneous and "gut-level" decision-making, you would rank your activity choices as "doing" over "thinking" over "being." Of course, no one prefers the same response across all situations. But almost everyone does have a stable ranking of responses they tend to rely on, and most cultures also have a clear ranking of responses.

Mapping the Team's Cultural Diversity

Have everyone in the team map his or her own culture, and then compare your maps. Use your similarities and differences to understand how you've worked together in the past. Try to think of a meeting in which some people thought their ideas were being dismissed, or some people wanted to incorporate things that didn't make sense to others, or some people dominated or stayed quiet while others thought this wasn't appropriate. How can these situations be understood better given the cultural information you now have? What did you miss then, that would have helped your interactions? How could you have used the different perspectives to help you perform better in the past?

Then, as you move forward and engage in other meetings, try to bring out cultural explanations for your differences in approach whenever you can. Incorporate what you know about your cultural differences (mapping) into bridging and integrating processes. After a while, you'll find yourself anticipating some of these differences, and even encouraging the different perspectives so you can incorporate them into your team's decision making and processes.

APPENDIX B
CREATOR TEAM IN ACTION

We recently witnessed a consulting services team in Hong Kong that has evolved to use their cultural diversity to full advantage. They had completed a cultural mapping of their differences and knew that the mix of American, Italian, Anglo-Australian, Korean-Chinese-Australian, Cantonese, and Singaporean members meant a rich potential for synergy as well as for misunderstanding.

Recently, Franco, the Italian leader of the team, requested that Sheila, the Anglo-Australian marketing manager, and Tan Swee Ling, the Singaporean accounting manager, follow up with a major supplier over the Cantonese vendor's shortfalls in the two critical areas of marketing and accounting. Several days after the Cantonese contact assured Sheila and Swee Ling that the problems would be quickly resolved, major difficulties in both areas interfered with the consulting firm's customer relations.

Tan Swee Ling had made multiple requests for corrections on the errors, but the vendor had not responded. Frustrated by this inattention, Franco decided to write an e-mail directly to C.K., the Cantonese manager of the vendor. Knowing that he needed to modify his normally intense style of confrontation, he started his letter of complaint with thanks for the earlier discussions with Sheila and Swee Ling. He then continued with a carefully worded statement describing customers' complaints about the vendor's services. He took special care to preserve face for C.K., while still indicating the areas needing to be corrected.

APPENDIX A

The Cultural Orientations Framework

Issue 1: Relationships among People.
What basic relationships among people are most natural and/or most effective? Who is everybody responsible for, who must be taken care of, and who must everyone obey and be accountable to?

Response 1: Collective	Response 2: Hierarchical	Response 3: Individualistic
Oneís major responsibility is to and for a larger group such as extended family or peer group. In effective teams and organizations, individual contributions are not identified, and roles and responsibilities are highly fluid.	Interaction is most effective when there is unequal distribution of power and responsibility. Those higher in the hierarchy have power over and responsibility for those lower.	Oneís major responsibility is to and for oneís self and immediate family. In effective teams and organizations, individual contributions are identified and each person has a specific role and set of responsibilities.

Issue 2: Relationship to Environment.
What kind of relationship do we have with the world around us? How do we see ourselves in relation to the world around us? What is our role with respect to the world around us?

Response 1: Harmony	Response 2: Mastery	Response 3: Subjugation
We are not separate from our environment, but are part of it. Organizational problems are best resolved by adjusting elements in a large system to achieve and maintain balance over the big picture and long term.	We can and should control our environment. Organizational problems are best resolved by identifying which elements to change, and then changing them. If you control the environment, you will have fewer problems.	There is a large element of our environment that we cannot and should not control. We should not jump to make changes before we see if the problem can work itself out, or before waiting to see how the problem fits into a larger plan outside of our control.

Issue 3: Mode of Activity.
What mode of activity best suits interdependence and interaction in our society? How should we engage in activity, and how should we count on others to act?

Response 1: Being	Response 2: Doing	Response 3: Thinking
Teams and organizations function best if we do everything in its own time. We should identify broad goals and adapt them as circumstances arise, and should conduct work and move towards goals as seems appropriate at a given time. It is important to enjoy the process.	Teams and organizations function best if we set agendas with specific goals, constantly strive to achieve those goals, and continually engage in productive work.	Teams and organizations function best if we approach everything we do with great deliberation and rational thought, and with a great deal of attention to detail We should not act until we are certain we are doing the best thing.

Issue 4: Human Nature.
What is the basic, underlying nature of humans? Is human nature (a) essentially good or evil; and (b) basically changeable or not?

Response A1: Good	Response A2: Evil	Response B1: Changeable	Response B2: Unchangeable
Assumption that humans are essentially good; if they do bad things, it is an anomaly or because of forces in the environment. People should be trusted at first.	Assumption that humans are essential evil; if they do good things it is because they are consciously trying to overcome their nature. People should not be trusted until they have earned the trust.	A personís basic nature can change. If a person is essentially good now, he or she can change to become essentially evil, and vice versa.	A personís basic nature cannot change. A person who is good now will always stay good, and vice versa.

Issue 5: Time.
How do we think about time? What role does it play in our decision-making and day-to-day life?

Response 1: Past	Response 2: Present	Response 3: Future
We should have a strong respect for tradition and our past. In making decisions, we should rely strongly on what has worked in the past.	We should be interested in our past only as it helps us understand today. Todayís needs are most important, and the short-term future should also be considered.	We should be interested in the past and present only in how they have potential to affect the long-term future. We should easily sacrifice things today to benefit the long-term future.

Because both Sheila and Swee Ling had been involved in the issues, he saved the e-mail into a file and gave a copy to each of them, requesting that they review it "for accuracy and tone." A few minutes later Sheila came back to him waving the piece of paper.

"Well! She will hardly know you are concerned, with this wording!" she exclaimed.

Franco replied, "I'm actually pleased with your reaction. I wanted it to be calmer than I feel. I'm sure that she will get the message, but I tried to be more subtle than my usual bluntness, given the cultures of the people involved."

After waiting for two hours, Franco approached Swee Ling's desk. "I really wanted to send that e-mail out to C.K. before we leave. Have you had a chance to look at it, Swee Ling?" he asked.

Swee Ling was surprised, "Oh, since it was an e-mail, I thought you had already sent it," she replied.

Franco said, "No, that's why I asked for your input. What did you think?" Swee Ling gave a look that suggested disapproval, but she also showed her usual hesitation. "Come on, come on," Franco urged, "Spit it out. What do you think?"

"Don't send it!" she finally admitted. "Just don't send it."

Franco fell apart laughing and called Sheila over to Swee Ling's desk. "How typical of you two!" and he went on to explain the sharp differences in their interpretations. Inviting them into his office, Franco said, "OK, Swee Ling, Sheila thought the e-mail was too understated and you are telling me not to send it. What's going on?"

Swee Ling replied with her usual indirect answer. She indicated that it was better for C.K. to respond to the company's concerns because she wanted to, rather than because she had to. Franco replied with his usual impatience, noting that he had softened his approach so much that Sheila had objected that C.K. would miss the point of his dissatisfaction. He noted that he had deliberately omitted sending a copy to C.K.'s boss, whom he knew well, wanting to save face for her. After more discussion Swee

Ling continued to strongly advise that Franco not send the memo. But she didn't suggest any alternatives. Finally, Franco asked her if it would make sense for him to send the e-mail directly to Swee Ling and ask *her*—Swee Ling—to follow up.

"Perfect! That's O.K. to do," came the quick answer from Swee Ling.

An hour after rewording the memo so it was appropriate for its new recipient, he emailed it to Swee Ling. To his utter amazement, in another hour a startling e-mail appeared on his own screen from C.K. It was directed to several members of her company involved in the issues of concern and was copied to her boss, Franco, Sheila, and Swee Ling. It was extremely blunt and told her staff on no uncertain terms that she had received a fax from Franco complaining about items that must be corrected immediately.

Now Franco was really confused. He hadn't sent a fax to her at all, and the tone of the email from C.K. to her staff was highly authoritarian and harsh. What was going on? He sought out Swee Ling, who had just read her copy of the e-mail and was smiling broadly.

"Well, *that* certainly worked out as we wanted it to!" she chuckled.

"Yes, but *how*???" Franco laughed. "What happened? I didn't send a fax, and my message was to you, not to her. What's going on?" he repeated.

Swee Ling explained. "I called her and told her that you had sent me a note with concerns and had asked me to follow up. We talked some about the issues, and she asked me to send her a fax of your note. After she got it, we talked some more, and she said not to worry and that she would resolve it. Her copying her boss and indicating that your letter was stronger than it really was, enabled her to show her own strength in solving the problems for you. And she did it her way!"

Here is a team that used its cultural diversity to full advantage. They had a good understanding of their own differences *(mapping)* and of the need to consider the different approaches of the vendor *(decentering)*. Franco involved his own team members *(building participation)* initially in checking his wording *(decentering)* and later *in recognizing and resolving the conflict* between his approach and Swee Ling's advice. The reworded and redirected documents are examples of both *building on others' ideas* and *recentering*. The outcome not only accomplished what Franco wanted and needed, but raised Swee Ling's status in the group and provoked a discussion that caused the team to learn even more. The performance turned out to be higher in both the outcome with the vendor and the development of the team. What more could one want?!

SELECTED BIBLIOGRAPHY

Our research was strongly influenced by studies on diverse teams, as reviewed well by S.E. Jackson, "Team Composition in Organizational Settings: Issues in Managing an Increasingly Diverse Workforce," in S. Worchel, W. Wood, and J.A. Simpson (Eds.), *Group Process and Productivity* (Newbury Park: Sage, 1991): 138–173; F.J. Milliken and L.L. Martins, "Searching for Common Threads: Understanding the Multiple Effects of Diversity in Organizational Groups," *Academy of Management Review* 21 (1996): 402–433; and S. G. Cohen and D.E. Bailey, "What Makes Teams Work: Group Effectiveness Research from the Shop Floor to the Executive Suite," *Journal of Management* 23 (1997): 239–290. Two publications on culturally diverse teams that highly complement the material here are S.C. Snow, S. Canney Davison, S.A. Snell, and D.C. Hambrick, "Use Transnational Teams to Globalize your Company," *Organizational Dynamics* 24, no. 4 (1996): 50–67; and S. Canney Davison and K. Ward, *Leading International Teams* (Berkshire, UK: McGraw–Hill International, 2000).

The principles of bridging were adapted from work conducted by Norwegian psychologist Rolv M. Blakar and presented in English in his book *Communication: A Social Perspective on Clinical Issues* (Oslo: Universitetsforlaget, 1984); and the article "Towards a Theory of Communication in Terms of Preconditions: A Conceptual Framework and Some Empirical Explorations," in H. Giles and R.N. St. Clair (Eds.), *Recent Advances in Language, Communication, and Social Psychology* (London: Lawrence Erlbaum Associates, 1985).

More on mapping culture and applying the MBI approach in multicultural settings can be found in the book *International Management Behavior*, 4th ed., by H.W. Lane, J.J. DiStefano and M.L. Maznevski (Cambridge, MA: Blackwell, 2000). Some good resources for cultural mapping include N.J. Adler, *International Dimensions of Organizational Behavior*, 3rd ed., (Cincinnati, OH: South-Western College Publishing, 1997); G.H. Hofstede, *Cultures and Organizations: Software of the Mind*, (New York: McGraw–Hill, 1997); and F. Trompenaars, *Riding the Waves of Culture: Understanding Cultural Diversity in Business* (Avon: The Bath Press, 1993).

[18]

© Academy of Management Executive, 1991 Vol. 5 No. 3

Managing cultural diversity: implications for organizational competitiveness

Taylor H. Cox, University of Michigan
Stacy Blake, University of Michigan

Executive Overview

The recent business trends of globalization and increasing ethnic and gender diversity are turning managers' attention to the management of cultural differences. The management literature has suggested that organizations should value diversity to enhance organizational effectiveness. However, the specific link between managing diversity and organizational competitiveness is rarely made explicit and no article has reviewed actual research data supporting such a link.

This article reviews arguments and research data on how managing diversity can create a competitive advantage. We address cost, attraction of human resources, marketing success, creativity and innovation, problem-solving quality, and organizational flexibility as six dimensions of business performance directly impacted by the management of cultural diversity. We then offer suggestions for improving organizational capability to manage this diversity.

Article

Workforce demographics for the United States and many other nations of the world indicate that managing diversity will be on the agendas of organizational leaders throughout the 90s. For example, a recent report on the workforces of 21 nations shows that nearly all of the growth in the labor force between now and 2000 will occur in nations with predominately non-Caucasian populations. Behind these statistics are vastly different age and fertility rates for people of different racioethnic groups. In the United States for example, the average white female is 33 years old and has (or will have) 1.7 children. Corresponding figures for blacks are 28 and 2.4, and for Mexican-Americans, 26 and 2.9.[1]

Leading consultants, academics and business leaders have advocated that organizations respond to these trends with a "valuing diversity" approach. They point out that a well managed, diverse workforce holds potential competitive advantages for organizations.[2] However, the logic of the valuing diversity argument is rarely made explicit, and we are aware of no article that reviews actual data supporting the linkage of managing diversity and organizational competitiveness. This article reviews the arguments and research data on this link, and offers suggestions on improving organizational capability for managing cultural diversity. As shown in Exhibit 1, the term managing diversity refers to a variety of management issues and activities related to hiring and effective utilization of personnel from different cultural backgrounds.

Diversity as a Competitive Advantage

Social responsibility goals of organizations is only one area that benefits from the management of diversity. We will focus on six other areas where sound management can create a competitive advantage: (1) cost, (2) resource acquisition, (3) marketing, (4) creativity, (5) problem-solving, (6) organizational flexibility.[3] Exhibit 2 briefly explains their relationship to diversity management.

The first two items of the exhibit, the cost and resource acquisition arguments, are what we call the "inevitability-of-diversity" issues. Competitiveness is affected by

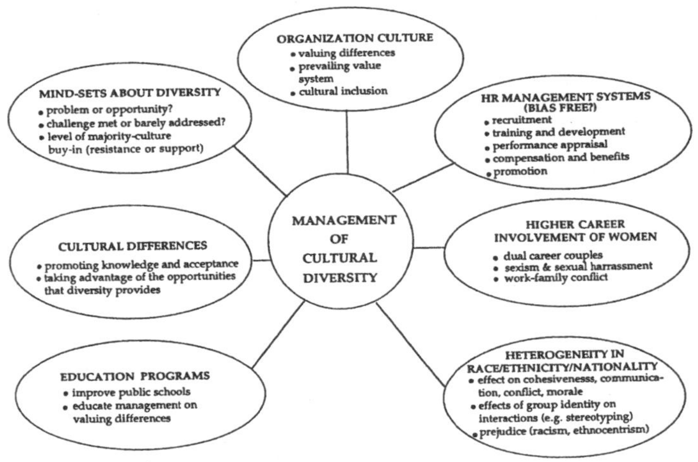

Exhibit 1. Spheres of Activity in the Management of Cultural Diversity

the *need* (because of national and cross-national workforce demographic trends) to hire more women, minorities, and foreign nationals. The marketing, creativity, problem-solving, and system flexibility argument, are derived from what we call the "value-in-diversity hypothesis"—that diversity brings net-added value to organization processes.

Cost

Organizations have not been as successful in managing women and racioethnic minorities (racially and/or ethnically different from the white/Anglo majority) as white males. Date shows that turnover and absenteeism are often higher among women and racioethnic minorities than for white males. For example, one study reported that the overall turnover rate for blacks in the United States workforce is forty percent higher than for whites. Also, Corning Glass recently reported that between 1980-87, turnover among women in professional jobs was double that of men, and the rates for blacks were 2.5 times those of whites. A two-to-one ratio for women/men turnover was also cited by Felice Schwartz in her article on multiple career tracks for women in management.[4]

Organizations have not been as successful in managing women and racioethnic minorities (racially and/or ethnically different from the white/Anglo majority) as white males.

Job satisfaction levels are also often lower for minorities. A recent study that measured job satisfaction among black and white MBAs revealed that blacks were significantly less satisfied with their overall careers and advancement than whites.[5]

Frustration over career growth and cultural conflict with the dominant, white-male culture may be the major factor behind the different satisfaction levels. Two recent surveys of male and female managers in large American companies found that although women expressed a much higher probability of leaving their current employer than men, and had higher actual turnover rates, their primary reasons for quitting were lack of career growth opportunity or dissatisfaction with rates of progress. One of the surveys also discovered that women have higher actual turnover rates at all ages, and not just during the child-bearing and child-rearing years.[6]

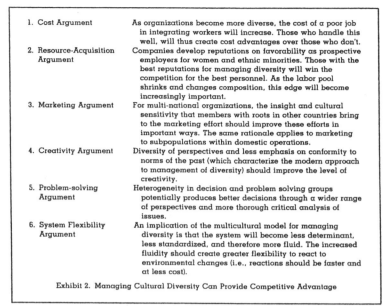

1. Cost Argument	As organizations become more diverse, the cost of a poor job in integrating workers will increase. Those who handle this well, will thus create cost advantages over those who don't.
2. Resource-Acquisition Argument	Companies develop reputations on favorability as prospective employers for women and ethnic minorities. Those with the best reputations for managing diversity will win the competition for the best personnel. As the labor pool shrinks and changes composition, this edge will become increasingly important.
3. Marketing Argument	For multi-national organizations, the insight and cultural sensitivity that members with roots in other countries bring to the marketing effort should improve these efforts in important ways. The same rationale applies to marketing to subpopulations within domestic operations.
4. Creativity Argument	Diversity of perspectives and less emphasis on conformity to norms of the past (which characterize the modern approach to management of diversity) should improve the level of creativity.
5. Problem-solving Argument	Heterogeneity in decision and problem solving groups potentially produces better decisions through a wider range of perspectives and more thorough critical analysis of issues.
6. System Flexibility Argument	An implication of the multicultural model for managing diversity is that the system will become less determinant, less standardized, and therefore more fluid. The increased fluidity should create greater flexibility to react to environmental changes (i.e., reactions should be faster and at less cost).

Exhibit 2. Managing Cultural Diversity Can Provide Competitive Advantage

Organizations' failure to manage women and racioethnic minorities as successfully as white males translates into unnecessary costs. Since eighty-five percent of net additions to the workforce during the decade of the 90's are expected to be women and radioethnic minorities, these costs will escalate in the coming years.

Organizations that fail to make appropriate changes to more successfully use and keep employees from different backgrounds can expect to suffer a significant competitive disadvantage compared to those that do. Alternatively, organizations quick to create an environment where all personnel can thrive should gain a competitive cost advantage over nonresponsive or slowly responding companies.

Cost implications in managing diversity also occur in benefits and work schedules. In one study, companies were assigned an "accommodation score" based on the adoption of four benefit-liberalization changes associated with pregnant workers. Analysis revealed that the higher a company's accommodation score, the lower the number of sick days taken by pregnant workers and the more willing they were to work overtime during pregnancy.[7]

Two other studies investigated the effect of company investment in day care on human resource cost variables. In one study, turnover and absenteeism rates for working mothers using a company-sponsored child development center were compared to those who either had no children or had no company assistance. Absenteeism for the day-care users versus the other groups was thirty-eight percent lower and the turnover rate was less than two percent compared to more than six percent for the nonbenefit groups. The second study showed that in a company that initiated an in-house child care facility, worker attitudes improved on six measures including organizational commitment and job satisfaction. In addition, turnover declined by sixty-three percent.[8]

Greater use of flextime work scheduling is another type of organizational accommodation to diversity. A recent field experiment assessing the impact of flextime use on absenteeism and worker performance found that both short- and long-term absence declined significantly. Three out of four worker efficiency measures also increased significantly.[9]

Cost savings of organizational changes must be judged against the investment. Nevertheless, the data strongly suggests that managing diversity efforts have reduced absenteeism and turnover costs, as cited earlier.

A recent field experiment assessing the impact of flextime use on absenteeism and worker performance found that both short- and long-term absence declined significantly.

Research evidence relevant to cost implications of managing diversity on some dimensions other than benefit and work-schedule changes comes from a UCLA study of the productivity of culturally heterogeneous and culturally homogeneous work teams. Among the heterogeneous teams, some were more and some were less productive than the homogeneous teams.[10] This research suggests that if work teams "manage" the diversity well, they can make diversity an asset to performance. For example, all members should have ample opportunity to contribute and potential communications, group cohesiveness, and interpersonal conflict issues need to be successfully addressed. Alternatively, if diversity is ignored or mishandled, it may detract from performance.

Actual cost savings from improving the management of diversity are difficult to determine. It is, however, possible to estimate those related to turnover. For example, let us assume an organization has 10,000 employees in which 35 percent of personnel are either women or racioethnic minorities. Let us also assume a white male turnover rate of ten percent. Using the previous data on differential turnover rates for women and racioethnic minorities of roughly double the rate for white males, we can estimate a loss of 350 additional employees from the former groups. If we further assume that half of the turnover rate difference can be eliminated with better management, and that total turnover cost averages $20,000 per employee, the potential annual cost savings is $3.5 million. This example only addresses turnover, and additional savings may be realized from other changes such as higher productivity levels.

Although accurate dollar cost savings figures from managing diversity initiatives of specific companies are rarely published, Ortho Pharmaceuticals has calculated its savings to date at $500,000, mainly from lower turnover among women and ethnic minorities.[11]

Resource Acquisition

Attracting and retaining excellent employees from different demographic groups is the second "inevitability"-related competitiveness issue. As women and racioethnic minorities increase in proportional representation in the labor pool, organizations must compete to hire and retain workers from these groups. Recently published accounts of the "best companies" for women and for blacks have made public and highlighted organizations which are leaders in organizational change efforts to effectively manage diversity.[12] In addition to listing the best companies, the publications also discuss why certain companies were excluded from the list.

The impact of these publications on recruitment of quality personnel has already begun to surface. Merck, Xerox, Syntex, Hoffman-La Roche, and Hewlett-Packard have been aggressively using favorable publicity to recruit women and racioethnic minorities. According to company representatives, the recognitions are, in fact, boosting recruiting efforts. For example, Merck cites its identification as one of the ten best companies for working mothers as instrumental in recent increases in applications.[13]

Although accurate dollar cost savings figures from managing diversity initiatives of specific companies are rarely published, Ortho Pharmaceuticals has calculated its savings to date at $500,000, mainly from lower turnover among women and ethnic minorities.[11]

As these reputations grow, and the supply of white males in the labor market shrinks, the significance of the resource acquisition issue for organizational competitiveness will be magnified.

Marketing

Markets are becoming as diverse as the workforce. Selling goods and services is facilitated by a representational workforce in several ways. First, companies with good reputations have correspondingly favorable public relations. Just as people, especially women and racioethnic minorities, may prefer to work for an employer who values diversity, they may also prefer to buy from such organizations.

Second, there is evidence that culture has a significant effect on consumer behavior. For example, in the Chinese culture, values such as a tradition of thrift, and teenagers' deference to their parent's wishes in making purchases, have been identified as affecting consumer behavior.[14] While much of the research on cross-cultural differences in consumer behavior has focused on cross-national comparisons, this research is also relevant to intra-country ethnic group differences.

Immigration from Latin America and Asia will continue to be high in the 90's. This represents a large influx of first-generation Americans having strong ties to their root cultures. Acculturation patterns among Asian and Hispanic Americans indicates that substantial identity with the root cultures remain even after three or more generations of United States citizenship. This implies that firms may gain competitive advantage by using employee insight to understand culture effects on buying decisions and map strategies to respond to them.

USA Today provides a good example. Nancy Woodhull, president of Gannett News Media, maintains that the newspaper's marketing success is largely attributable to the presence of people from a wide variety of cultural backgrounds in daily news meetings. Group diversity was planned and led to a representation of different viewpoints because people of different genders and racioethnic backgrounds have different experiences shaped by group identities.

Just as people, especially women and racioethnic minorities, may prefer to work for an employer who values diversity, they may also prefer to buy from such organizations.

Avon Corporation used cultural diversity to turn around low profitability in its inner-city markets. Avon made personnel changes to give Black and Hispanic managers substantial authority over these markets. These formerly unprofitable sectors improved to the point where they are now among Avon's most productive U.S. markets. Avon President Jim Preston commented that members of a given cultural group are uniquely qualified to understand certain aspects of the world view of persons from that group.

In some cases, people from a minority culture are more likely to give patronage to a representative of their own group. For at least some products and services, a multicultural salesforce may facilitate sales to members of minority culture groups.

Cultural diversification of markets is not limited to U.S. companies. Globalization is forcing major companies from many nations to address cultural difference effects among consumers. The fact that the U.S. contains one of the most culturally heterogeneous populations in the world represents a possible advantage in "national" competitiveness. Just having diversity, however, is not sufficient to produce benefits. We must also manage it.

Creativity
Advocates of the value-in diversity hypothesis suggest that work team heterogeneity promotes creativity and innovation (see endnote 1). Research tends to support this relationship. Kanter's study of innovation in organizations revealed that the most innovative companies deliberately establish heterogeneous teams to "create a marketplace of ideas, recognizing that a multiplicity of points of view need to be brought to bear on a problem" (p. 167). Kanter also specifically noted that companies high on innovation had done a better job than most on eradicating racism, sexism, and classism and, tended to employ more women and racioethnic minorities than less innovative companies.[15]

If people from different gender, nationality, and racioethnic groups hold different attitudes and perspectives on issues, then cultural diversity should increase team creativity and innovation.

Research by Charlene Nemeth found that minority views can stimulate consideration of non-obvious alternatives in task groups. In a series of experiments, participants were asked to form as many words as possible from a string of 10 letters. Individual approaches to the task were determined and then groups formed that were either majority (all members subscribed to the strategy for forming letters advocated by the majority of participants) and minority (non-majority individuals were present in the groups). Nemeth found that the "minority" groups adopted multiple strategies and identified more solutions than the "majority" groups. She concluded that the groups exposed to minority views were more creative than the more homogeneous, majority groups. She further concluded that persistent exposure to minority viewpoints stimulates creative thought processes.

Another experiment compared the creativity of teams that were homogeneous on a series of attitude measures against teams with heterogeneous attitudes. Problem solution creativity was judged on originality and practicality. Results indicated that as long as the team members had similar ability levels, the heterogeneous teams were more creative than the homogeneous ones.[16] If people from different gender, nationality, and racioethnic groups hold different attitudes and perspectives on issues, then cultural diversity should increase team creativity and innovation.

Attitudes, cognitive functioning, and beliefs are not randomly distributed in the population but tend to vary systematically with demographic variables such as age, race, and gender.[17] Thus, an expected consequence of increased cultural diversity in organizations is the presence of different perspectives for problem solving, decision making and creative tasks.

Specific steps must be taken however, to realize this benefit. The research shows that in order to obtain the performance benefits, it was necessary for heterogeneous team members to have awareness of the attitudinal differences of other members. Similarly, diversity needs to be managed in part, by informing work-group members of their cultural differences. In recognition of this, cultural awareness training has become a standard element of organization change projects focusing on managing diversity.

Problem Solving
Diverse groups have a broader and richer base of experience from which to approach a problem. Thus, managing diversity also has the potential to improve problem solving and decision making.

In the 1960s, several University of Michigan studies discovered that heterogeneous groups produced better quality solutions to assigned problems than homogeneous groups. Dimensions of group diversity included personality measures and gender. In one study, sixty-five percent of heterogeneous groups produced high quality solutions (solutions that provided either new, modified, or integrative approaches to the problem) compared to only twenty-one percent of the homogeneous groups. This difference was statistically significant. The researchers noted that "mixing sexes and personalities appears to have freed these groups from the restraints of the solutions given in the problem."[18]

Decision quality is best when neither excessive diversity nor excessive homogeneity are present.

Later studies also confirmed the effects of heterogeneity on group decision quality. The same conclusion is indirectly indicated by research on the "groupthink" phenomenon—the absence of critical thinking in groups caused partly by excessive preoccupation with maintaining cohesiveness. Most of the examples of groupthink cited in the literature, such as the decision of the Kennedy administration to invade Cuba in 1961, portray decision processes as producing disastrous results. Because group cohesiveness is directly related to degrees of homogeneity, and groupthink only occurs in highly cohesive groups, the presence of cultural diversity in groups should reduce its probability.[19]

Decision quality is best when neither excessive diversity nor excessive homogeneity are present. This point has been well summarized by Sheppard: "Similarity is an aid to developing cohesion; cohesion in turn, is related to the success of a group. Homogeneity, however, can be detrimental if it results in the absence of stimulation. If all members are alike, they may have little to talk about, they may compete with each other, or they may all commit the same mistake. Variety is the spice of life in a group, so long as there is a basic core of similarity."[20]

A core of similarity among group members is desirable. This theme is similar to the "core value" concept advocated in the organization culture literature.[21] Our interpretation is that all members must share some common values and norms to promote coherent actions on organizational goals. The need for heterogeneity, to promote problem solving and innovation, must be balanced with the need for organizational coherence and unity of action.

Additional support for the superior problem solving of diverse workgroups comes from the work of Nemeth cited earlier. In a series of studies, she found that the level of critical analysis of decision issues and alternatives was higher in groups subjected to minority views than in those which were not. The presence of minority views improved the quality of the decision process regardless of whether or not the minority view ultimately prevailed. A larger number of alternatives were considered and there was a more thorough examination of assumptions and implications of alternative scenarios.[22]

The presence of minority views improved the quality of the decision process regardless of whether or not the minority view ultimately prevailed.

In sum, culturally diverse workforces create competitive advantage through better decisions. A variety of perspectives brought to the issue, higher levels of critical analysis of alternatives through minority-influence effects, and lower probability of groupthink all contribute.

System Flexibility

Managing diversity enhances organizational flexibility. There are two primary bases for this assertion. First, there is some evidence that women and racioethnic minorities tend to have especially flexible cognitive structures. For example, research has shown that women tend to have a higher tolerance for ambiguity than men. Tolerance for ambiguity, in turn, has been linked to a number of factors related to flexibility such as cognitive complexity, and the ability to excel in performing ambiguous tasks.[23]

Studies on bilingual versus monolingual sub-populations from several nations show that compared to monolinguals, bilinguals have higher levels of divergent thinking and of cognitive flexibility.[24] Since the incidence of bilingualism is much greater among minority culture groups (especially Hispanics and Asians) than the majority-white Anglo group, this research strongly supports the notion that cognitive flexibility is enhanced by the inclusion of these groups in predominantly Anglo workforces.

The second way that managing cultural diversity may enhance organizational flexibility is that as policies and procedures are broadened and operating methods become less standardized, the organization becomes more fluid and adaptable. The tolerance for different cultural viewpoints should lead to greater openness to new ideas in general. Most important of all, if organizations are successful in overcoming resistance to change in the difficult area of accepting diversity, it should be well positioned to handle resistance to other types of change.

Suggestions for Organization Change

We have reviewed six ways in which the presence of cultural diversity and its effective management can yield a competitive advantage. Organizations wishing to maximize the benefits and minimize the drawbacks of diversity, in terms of workgroup cohesiveness, interpersonal conflict, turnover, and coherent action on major organizational goals, must creat "multicultural" organizations. The typical organization of the past has been either monolithic (homogeneous membership with a culture dominated by one cultural group) or plural (obstensively diverse membership but still culturally monolithic and without valuing and using differences to benefit the organization). By contrast, the multicultural organization is one where members of nontraditional backgrounds can contribute and achieve to their fullest potential.

The multicultural organization's specific features are as follows: (1) Pluralism: reciprocal acculturation where all cultural groups respect, value, and learn from one another; (2) full structural integration of all cultural groups so that they are well represented at all levels of the organization; (3) full integration of minority culture-group members in the informal networks of the organization; (4) an absence of prejudice and discrimination; (5) equal identification of minority- and majority-group members with the goals of the organization, and with opportunity for alignment of organizational and personal career goal achievement; (6) a minimum of inter-group conflict which is based on race, gender, nationality, and other identity groups of organization members.[25]

Five key components are needed to transform traditional organizations into multicultural ones.

1. Leadership
2. Training
3. Research
4. Analysis and change of culture and human resource management systems
5. Follow up

Each of these are briefly discussed.

Leadership

Top management's support and genuine commitment to cultural diversity is crucial. Champions for diversity are needed—people who will take strong personal stands on the need for change, role model the behaviors required for change, and assist with the work of moving the organization forward. Commitment must go beyond sloganism. For example, are human, financial, and technical resources being provided? Is this item prominently featured in the corporate strategy and consistently made a part of senior level staff meetings? Is there a willingness to change human resource management systems such as performance appraisal and executive bonuses? Is there a willingness to keep mental energy and financial support focused on this for a period of years, not months or weeks? If the answer to all of these questions is yes, the organization has genuine commitment, if not, then a potential problem with leadership is indicated.

Top management commitment is crucial but not sufficient. Champions are also needed at lower organizational levels, especially key line managers. Many organizations are addressing the leadership requirement by the formation of task forces or advisory committees on diversity, often headed by a senior manager. Some companies also have a designated manager for diversity who oversees the work company-wide (examples include Corning Inc. and Allstate Insurance). We advise using the manager of diversity in addition to, rather than as a substitute for, a broader involvement team such as a diversity task force. This is especially important in the early stages of the work.

Training
Managing and valuing diversity (MVD) training is the most prevalent starting point for managing diversity. Two types of training are popular: awareness training and skill-building training. Awareness training focuses on creating an understanding of the need for, and meaning of managing and valuing diversity. It is also meant to increase participants' self awareness on diversity related issues such as stereotyping and cross-cultural insensitivity. Skill-building training educates employees on specific cultural differences and how to respond to differences in the workplace. Often the two types are combined. Avon, Ortho Pharmaceuticals, Procter and Gamble, and Hewlett-Packard are examples of companies with extensive experience with training programs.

Training is a crucial first step. However, it has limitations as an organization change tool and should not be used in isolation. It is also important to treat training as an on-going education process rather than a one-shot seminar.

Research
Collection of information about diversity related-issues is the third key component. Many types of data are needed including traditional equal-opportunity profile data, analysis of attitudes and perceptions of employees, and data which highlights the career experiences of different cultural groups (e.g., are mentors equally accessible to all members).

Research has several important uses. First, it is often helpful for identifying issues to be addressed in the education process. For example, data indicating differences of opinion about the value in diversity based on culture group can be used as a launching point for mixed-culture discussion groups in training sessions. Second, research helps identify areas where changes are needed and provides clues about how to make them. Third, research is necessary to evaluate the change effort. Baseline data on key indicators of the valuing diversity environment needs to be gathered and periodically updated to assess progress.

Culture and Management Systems Audit
A comprehensive analysis of the organization culture and human resource systems such as recruitment, performance appraisal, potential assessment and promotion, and compensation should be undertaken. The primary objectives of this audit are: (1) to uncover sources of potential bias unfavorable to members of certain cultural groups, and (2) to identify ways that corporate culture may inadvertently put some members at a disadvantage.

It is important to look beyond surface data in auditing systems. For example, research that we reviewed or conducted indicates that even when average performance ratings for majority versus minority culture members are essentially the same, there may be differences in the relative priority placed on individual performance criteria, the distribution of the highest ratings, or the relationship between performance ratings and promotion.[26] The audit must be an in-depth analysis, and the assistance of an external cultural diversity expert is strongly advised.

To identify ways that corporate culture may put some members at a disadvantage, consider a scenario where a prominent value in the organization culture is "aggressiveness." Such a value may place certain groups at a disadvantage if the norms of their secondary or alternative culture discouraged this behavior. This is indeed the case for many Asians and for women in many countries including the United States. While it is conceivable that the preservation of this value may be central to organizational effectiveness (in which case the solution may be to acknowledge the differential burden of conformity that some members must bear and to give assistance to them in learning the required behaviors), it may also be that the organizational values need to change so that other styles of accomplishing work are acceptable and perhaps even preferred. The point is that the prevailing values and norms must be identified and then examined critically in light of the diversity of the workforce.

The results of the audit must be translated into an agenda for specific changes in the organization culture and systems which management must then work to implement.

Follow-up

The final component, follow-up, consists of monitoring change, evaluating the results, and ultimately institutionalizing the changes as part of the organization's regular on-going processes. Like other management efforts, there is a need for accountability and control for work on diversity. Accountability for overseeing the change process might initially be assigned to the diversity task force, or if available, manager of diversity. Ultimately, however, accountability for preserving the changes must be established with every manager. Changes in the performance appraisal and reward processes are often needed to accomplish this.

The results of the audit must be translated into an agenda for specific changes in the organization culture and systems which management must then work to implement.

Follow-up activities should include additional training, repetition of the systems audit, and use of focus groups for on-going discussions about diversity issues.[27]

Conclusion

Organizations' ability to attract, retain, and motivate people from diverse cultural backgrounds, may lead to competitive advantages in cost structures and through maintaining the highest quality human resources. Further capitalizing on the potential benefits of cultural diversity in work groups, organizations may gain a competitive advantage in creativity, problem solving, and flexible adaptation to change. We have identified steps that organizations can take toward accomplishing this.

While this article has reviewed a significant amount of relevant research, additional work clearly needs to be done, especially on the "value-in-diversity" issues. Nevertheless, the arguments, data, and suggestions presented here should be useful to organizations to build commitment and promote action for managing diversity efforts in the 1990s and beyond.

Endnotes

[1] See William B. Johnston, Global Work Force 2000, *Harvard Business Review*, March-April, 1991 and "Middle-age at 26," Wall Street Journal, April 10, 1990.

[2] For examples of the competitive advantage argument, see R. Roosevelt Thomas Jr., "From Affirmative Action to Affirming Diversity," *Harvard Business Review*, 2, March/April 1990, 107-117; Lennie Copeland, "Learning to Manage a Multicultural Workforce," *Training*, May 1988, 48-56; Barbara Mandrell and Susan Kohler-Gray, "Management Development that Values Diversity," *Personnel*, 67, March 1990, 41-47; Katherine Etsy, "Diversity is Good for Business," *Executive Excellence*, 5, 1988, 5-6; and A.G. Sodano and S.G.Baler, "Accommodation to Contrast: Being Different in the Organization," *New Directions in Mental Health*, 20, 1983, 25-36.

[3] This focus is not intended to undermine the importance of social, moral, and legal reasons for attention to diversity. We have chosen to address its relevance for other types of goals,such as worker productivity and quality of decision making, because the impact of diversity in these areas has received relatively little attention in the past compared to the equal-opportunity related goals.

[4] See the following sources for details on the turnover data: B.R. Bergmann and W.R. Krause, "Evaluating and Forecasting Progress in Racial Integration of Employment," *Industrial and Labor Relations Review*, 1968, 399-409; Carol Hymowitz, "One Firm's Bid to Keep Blacks, Women," *Wall Street Journal*, February 16, 1989, Sec. B, 1; Felice Schwartz, "Management Women and the New Facts of Life," *Harvard Business Review*, January/February 1989, 65-76.

[5] Taylor Cox, Jr. and Stella Nkomo, "A Race and Gender Group Analysis of the Early Career Experience of MBA's," *Work and Occupations*, forthcoming in 1991.

[6] These surveys were reviewed by Cathy Trost, "Women Managers Quit not for Family but to Advance their Corporate Climb," *Wall Street Journal*, May 2, 1990. For additional evidence on this point, including discussions of the cultural-conflict issue, see Schwartz, Endnote 3; A.M. Morrison, R.P. White and E. Van Velsor, "Executive Women: Substance Plus Style," *Psychology Today*, August 1987, 18-25; and Gail DeGeorge, "Corporate Women: They're about to Break Through to the Top," *Business Week*, June 22, 1987, 72-77.

[7] "Helping Pregnant Workers Pays Off," *USA Today*, December 2, 1987.

[8] Stewart A. Youngblood and Kimberly Chambers-Cook, "Child Care Assistance Can Improve Employee Attitudes and Behavior," *Personnel Administrator*, February 1984, 93-95+.

[9] Jay S. Kim and Anthony F. Campagna, "Effects of Flextime on Employee Attendance and Performance: A Field Experiment," *Academy of Management Journal*, December 14, 1981, 729-741.

[10] Reported in Nancy Adler, *International Dimensions of Organizational Behavior* (Boston: Kent Publishing Co., 1986), 111.

[11] The figure of $20,000 is based on computations of Michael Mercer for turnover costs of a computer programmer. Readers may wish to consult one of the following sources for turnover cost formulas and then use their own job structure to determine cost factors for the actual turnover costs: Michael Mercer, "Turnover: Reducing the Costs," *Personnel*, Vol. 5, 1988, 36-42; Rene Darmon, "Identifying Sources of Turnover Costs, *Journal of Marketing*, 1990, Vol. 54, 46-56. The data on Ortho is provided in Juliane Bailey, "How to be Different but Equal," *Savvy Woman*, November, 1989, 47+.

[12] Examples of these publications include Baila Zeitz and Lorraine Dusky, *Best Companies for Women* (New York: Simon and Schuster, 1988); and "The 50 Best Places for Blacks to Work," *Black Enterprise*, February 1989, 73-91.

[13] Selwyn Feinstein, "Being the Best on Somebody's List Does Attract Talent," *Wall Street Journal*, October 10, 1989. For other examples supporting the resource acquisition argument, see Joel Dreyfuss, "Get Ready for the New Work Force," *Fortune*, April 23, 1990, 165-181.

[14] S.G. Redding, "Cultural Effects on the Marketing Process in Southeast Asia," *Journal of Market Research Society*, Vol. 24, 19, 98-114.

[15] Rosabeth Moss-Kanter, *The Change Masters*, (New York: Simon and Schuster, 1983).

[16] For details on the research in this section, readers should see: Charlan Jeanne Nemeth, "Differential Contributions of Majority and Minority Influence," *Psychological Review*, 93, 1986, 23-32 and H.C. Triandis, E.R. Hall, and R.B. Ewen, "Member Homogeneity and Dyadic Creativity," *Human Relations*, 18, 1965, 33-54.

[17] Susan E. Jackson, "Team Composition in Organizational Settings: Issues in Managing a Diverse Workforce," in *Group Process & Productivity*, J. Simpson, S. Warchel and W. Wood (eds), Beverly Hills, CA: Sage Publications, 1989).

[18] L. Richard Hoffman and Norman R.F. Maier, "Quality and Acceptance of Problem Solving by Members of Homogeneous and Heterogeneous Groups," *Journal of Abnormal and Social Psychology*, 62, 1961, 401-407. The quote in the text is from page 404.

[19] For reviews of research on the effect of group heterogeneity on problem solving, see M.E. Shaw, *Group Dynamics: The Psychology of Small Group Behavior*, (New York: McGraw Hill, 1981); J.E. McGrath, *Groups: Interaction and Performance*, (Englewood Cliffs, N.J.: Prentice Hall, 1984); and Irving Janis, *Victims of Groupthink*, (Boston: Houghton Mifflin Co., 1972).

[20] C.R. Shepard, *Small Groups*, (San Francisco: Chandler Publishing Co., 1964), 118.

[21] See Ed Schein, "Organizational Socialization and the Profession of Management," in D.A. Kolb, I.M. Rubin, and J.M. McIntyre (Eds.), *Organizational Psychology*, Englewood Cliffs: Prentice-Hall, 1984, 7-21; and Y. Weiner, "Forms of Value Systems: A Focus on Organizational Effectiveness and Cultural

Change and Maintenance," *Academy of Management Review*, 13, 1988, 534-545.

[22] See Charlan Jeanne Nemeth, "Dissent, Group Process, and Creativity," *Advances in Group Processes*, 2, 1985, 57-75; and Charlan Jeanne Nemeth and Joel Wachter, "Creative Problem Solving as a Result of Majority versus Minority Influence," *European Journal of Social Psychology*, 13, 1983, 45-55.

[23] See Naomi G. Rotter and Agnes N. O'Connell, "The Relationships Among Sex-Role Orientation, Cognitive Complexity, and Tolerance for Ambiguity," *Sex Roles*, 8 (12), 1982, 1209-1220; and David R. Shaffer et al., "Interactive Effects of Ambiguity Tolerance and Task Effort on Dissouance Reduction," *Journal of Personality*, 41(2), June, 1973, 224-233.

[24] These research studies are reviewed by Wallace Lambert, "The Effects of Bilingualism on the Individual: Cognitive and Sociocultural Consequences," in Peter A. Hurnbey (Ed.), *Bilingualism: Psychological, Social, and Educational Implications*, New York: Academic Press, 1977, 15-27.

[25] This discussion of traditional versus multicultural organizations is based on Taylor Cox's article, "The Multicultural Organization" which appeared in the May, 1991 issue of *The Executive*.

[26] For a specific example of race differences in priorities of performance rating criteria, see Taylor Cox and Stella Nkomo, "Differential Performance Appraisal Criteria," *Group and Organization Studies*, 11, 1986, 101-119. For an example of subtle bias in performance rating distributions see Asya Pazy's article: "The Persistence of Pro-Male Bias," *Organization Behavior and Human Decision Processes*, 38, 1986, 366-377.

[27] For additional discussion of organization change processes to manage diversity including specific examples of what pioneering companies are doing in this area, please see Taylor Cox's article "The Multicultural Organization" (endnote 24).

About the Authors

Taylor Cox, Jr. is assistant professor of Organizational Behavior at The University of Michigan where he frequently teaches executive courses on career issues of women, non-whites and older workers. He has published many articles on race, gender, and age as factors in organization behavior and careers, and is a consultant to several Fortune 1000 companies on managing and valuing cultural diversity.

Stacy Blake is a graduate student in the doctoral program in Organizational Psychology at the University of Michigan. She received her B.S. from the University of Maryland College Park and is presently a National Science Foundation Research Fellow. Her current research examines the impact of mentoring and internships in the effort to recruit and retain people of color in the corporate setting. She is also interested in multicultural organizational development.

[19]

The International Journal of Human Resource Management 6:3 September 1995

Employee intercultural effectiveness in a multicultural workplace: theoretical propositions, strategies and direction for future research

Aminu Mamman

Abstract This paper attempts to identify some of the key factors that can impinge on employee intercultural effectiveness in a multicultural workplace. Behavioural, attitudinal, cognitive and personality factors have been recognized as the main psychological factors that can impinge on intercultural effectiveness. Because intercultural effectiveness can be influenced by employee's sociobiological background, employee's ethnicity, age, country of origin, educational/professional attainment and religion are noted as among the factors that can impinge on intercultural effectiveness as well. In addition to these factors, employees' intercultural effectiveness is argued to be influenced by prior experience and organizational factors such as structure, systems, policies. Given the significance of sociobiological background, strategies for managing this background have been presented. Finally, the paper offers direction for future research.

Keywords Intercultural effectiveness, diversity, managing identity

Introduction

Speculation about the implications of the complexity and diversity of the workforce is now a popular theme in the human resource management literature. As a result, many organizations are considering these issues seriously. This is for two main reasons. First, organizations have to deal increasingly with the growing heterogeneity of the workforce. Second, a diverse workforce holds potential competitive advantages for organizations in the years ahead (Copeland, 1988a; Cox, 1991; Cox and Blake, 1991; Etsy, 1988; Laudicina, 1993; Thomas, 1990). Appreciation of the potential benefits of workforce diversity has ushered in a considerable amount of research and theorizing (e.g. Copeland, 1988a, 1988b; Cox, 1991; Cox and Blake, 1991; Jackson *et al.*, 1992; Motwani *et al.* 1993; Stephenson and Krebs, 1993; Thomas, R.R., 1990; Thomas, D.A., 1993; Tsui *et al.*, 1992; Tung, 1993). Although these researches have led to increasing understanding of the topic, the current effort seems to concentrate on how organizations can take advantage of workforce diversity (e.g. Cox, 1991; Cox and Blake, 1991; Jackson *et al.*, 1992) or how the dominant group in the workplace can adapt to the changes affecting their work setting (Sauers, 1993; Tung, 1993). Despite evidence which indicates that some minority groups in the workplace are handicapped by their inability to manage issues pertaining to their biological backgrounds (Dickens and Dickens, 1982), limited attention has been paid to how 'minority' employees can adapt to the diversity of the work setting. Indeed, Waters (1992) expresses the view that traditional management courses do little to help the business student or practitioner deal with race-based interpersonal

0985-5192

conflicts, and management textbooks tend to avoid the topic of race and its organizational implications. Similarly, some commentators express concern for the inadequacy of literature on interracial encounters in the workplace (Asante and Davis, 1989). The main theme of this paper is the issue of how minority employees can adjust effectively in a multicultural workplace.

Objectives

The objectives of this paper are threefold: first, to underscore the relevance of employee's psychological and sociobiological backgrounds in a multicultural work setting. Implicitly, this objective will attempt to answer questions such as, what factors impinge on or determine employee intercultural effectiveness in a multicultural workplace? How do these factors operate to influence intercultural effectiveness? Second, with the aid of relevant literature on interpersonal interaction, organizational socialization, cross-cultural interaction and expatriate adjustment, the paper will put forward strategies for managing sociobiological background in a multicultural workplace. Finally, issues for future research direction will be highlighted.

Methodology

Given that experts from many disciplines (e.g. social psychology, sociology) have addressed issues related to intercultural interaction, a multidisciplinary review of literature would seem central to the achievement of the objectives set above. Indeed, such an approach is essential because interpretation of the dynamics of workplace interaction can only be adequately explained by a multidisciplinary approach. The choice of literature will be governed by its potential to contribute to the objectives set above. For example, the use of literature on expatriate management and cross-cultural interaction should help in identifying factors critical to intercultural effectiveness in a multicultural workplace. Similarly, contact and uncertainty reduction theories should help in developing strategies for managing sociobiological backgrounds. In the first part of the article, the dominant approach for explaining intercultural effectiveness will be presented. In the second part, the relevance of sociobiological background and its implications for employee intercultural effectiveness will be discussed. The final part presents the conclusion and direction for future research. Before proceeding to the main theme of the paper, it would seem appropriate to define some of the key terms that will be used throughout.

Definitions

Multicultural workplace A multicultural workplace is a work setting which is heterogeneous in terms of race, ethnicity, beliefs, culture, gender, age, country of origin, and physical ability. The degree of heterogeneity (multiculturalness) will vary from one organization to the other. To qualify as a genuine multicultural organization, workforce diversity should be reflected in the formal structure, systems and policies of the organization (Jackson *et al.*, 1992). The adoption of this broad definition is necessary given that 'identity' which is central to multicultural interaction transcends cultural backgrounds (Collier and Thomas, 1988).

Indeed, experts argue that almost all variables influencing *intracultural* interaction are relevant in analysing *intercultural* interaction (Collier, 1989; Collier and Thomas, 1988; Dinges, 1983; Gudykunst and Kim, 1984; Gudykunst, 1988; Hammer, 1989).

Dominant group The term 'dominant group' will be used to refer to members of the dominant 'culture' in a multicultural workplace.

Employee The term 'employee' will be used to refer to members of a minority 'culture' in a multicultural work setting.

Employee intercultural effectiveness Adopting Brislins *et al.*'s (1986) definition of intercultural effectiveness, in this paper an interculturally effective employee is viewed as someone who feels good about interacting with other groups (minority and majority), where tasks requiring interaction are completed effectively with neither of the party suffering from any invisible stress-related symptoms. It is important to note that an employee can adjust to a multicultural workplace without interacting with the dominant group, but he/she cannot be interculturally effective without interacting with them. In other words, adjustment and effectiveness are not synonymous.

Sociobiological and psychological backgrounds Employee's sociobiological background encompasses his/her culture, ethnicity, country of origin, age, gender, religion, educational attainment and linguistic ability. His/her psychological background relates to his/her cognition, behaviour, attitudes and personality.

Intercultural effectiveness in a multicultural workplace: the dominant approach

Analytically, an employee will need two things to ensure intercultural effectiveness in a multicultural workplace. First, the employee would need to develop ways to address his/her *psychological* predispositions in order to understand and appreciate other people's culture. Second, an employee would need to address other people's attitudes and behaviours towards his/her *sociobiological* background. This section concentrates on the psychological predisposition and how it can affect intercultural effectiveness. In the next section, employee sociobiological background will be discussed.

Arguing for the concept of 'culture toughness' or 'culture gap' experts contend that adjustment in a 'foreign' setting is very much influenced by the cultural novelty of the setting (Black *et al.*, 1991; Gullahorn and Gullahorn, 1963; Torbiorn, 1982; Dinges, 1983). According to Black *et al.* (1991), the greater the difference between the two cultures (the host's and the stranger's) the more difficult it would be for the stranger to adjust, and empirical evidence confirms this view (Babiker *et al.*, 1980; Gudykunst, 1985). For example, Gudykunst (1985) found that culturally similar people display high attributional confidence and shared network which in turn reduces uncertainty and anxiety. Similarly, Bobad and Wallbott (1986) report that there is a higher degree of anxiety associated with interactions with people who are unfamiliar than with people who are familiar with each other. There is also research evidence to suggest that cultural similarity generates reciprocal feelings: people who are similar culturally tend to like each other (Brewer and Campbell, 1976). Various dimensions of the dominant group's culture can have varying significance for employee intercultural effectiveness. Prominent among these dimensions of culture are power distance, uncertainty avoidance, masculinity–femininity, individualism–collectivism, concept of time, use of language (verbal and body), perception and use of space, orientation to nature and activity. The implications of these factors for attitudes and behaviours in the workplace have been widely reported (see Adler, 1991; Hofstede, 1980, 1991; Triandis *et al.*, 1988).

How to achieve intercultural effectiveness

To appreciate how intercultural effectiveness can be achieved in a multicultural work setting it is necessary to take into account employees' 'psychological predispositions'. The literature on expatriate adjustment is full of useful information relevant to employee adjustment and effectiveness in a multicultural workplace (Black *et al.*, 1991; Tung, 1993). In this section the dominant view regarding intercultural effectiveness will be presented and implications for employees' intercultural effectiveness in a multicultural workplace will be discussed.

Cognitive dimension It is widely agreed that when in a foreign setting, the cognitive disposition of a stranger is a key determinant of his/her intercultural effectiveness (Detweiler, 1980; Gudykunst 1988; Mendenhall and Oddou, 1986; Singer, 1987; Triandis, 1976, 1977). This relates to how a stranger acquires and uses knowledge in his/her daily interactions. It has been argued that people process information through categorization which is, to a certain degree, culturally determined (Gertsen, 1990; Gudykunst and Kim, 1984; Oddou and Mendenhall, 1984; Singer, 1987; Triandis, 1976). Therefore, experts argue, when strangers acquire knowledge of different cultures, the influence of their cultural background on the way they process and use information will be less (Detweiler, 1975). In other words, acquisition of knowledge of different cultures can improve intercultural effectiveness. Research evidence suggests the utility of this proposition (Detweiler, 1978, 1980). As part of a minority in a multicultural workplace an employee should be aware of the cultural differences between and within groups in the organization. Indeed, even within the same culture there are cognitive differences between men and women and between old and young (Gudykunst and Kim, 1984; Kim, 1977; Segall *et al.*, 1990; Triandis *et al.*, 1993). Appreciation of these differences is necessary for effective functioning in a multicultural workplace.

Behavioural dimension Rules governing social behaviour vary across societies and groups. Therefore experts underscore the significance of demonstrating culturally appropriate behaviours in a foreign setting (Brien and David, 1971; Hammer *et al.*, 1978; Mendenhall and Oddou, 1986; Ruben, 1976). The argument for a behavioural approach is made against the background that there is a world of difference between knowing and doing. Some of the behavioural dimensions of intercultural effectiveness that have been identified by researchers (e.g. Gudykunst and Hammer, 1984; Hammer, 1987; Hammer *et al.*, 1978) include: (a) the ability to establish interpersonal relationships. This consists of the ability to develop and maintain satisfying interpersonal relationships with strangers, accurately understand their feelings, work with them effectively, empathize and deal effectively with their different social customs; (b) the ability to communicate effectively. This includes the ability to enter into meaningful dialogue, initiate interaction and deal with misunderstandings and interpersonal conflict and different communication styles. In a multicultural workplace an employee will need to develop appropriate social skills to deal with members of the dominant group. Not only are these skills vital for successful socialization at work, but they are essential for getting the job done. Given the diversity of the workforce, what will be considered as appropriate behaviour can vary with background (e.g. cultural background, ethnicity, gender, age, group/professional/occupational norms). Effective interaction therefore will require developing a range of social skills to deal with the heterogeneity of the workforce.

Attitudes and personality dimensions It has been argued that the acquisition and demonstration of culturally appropriate social skills should be complemented with the right attitude and personality (Brislin, 1981; Ruben, 1976). This is because strangers may face situations which will demand unique attitudes and traits. Among the personality and attitudinal factors are flexibility, self-confidence, self-efficacy, openness, motivation, orientation to knowledge, cultural empathy, openness to information and optimism. Developing appropriate attitudes as described above can be essential in a multicultural work setting. For example, as a minority, self-confidence and self-efficacy will be extremely vital for managing sociobiological background. This is because, without self-confidence for example, the employee is likely to confirm the stereotype others may hold about him/her. Also, an employee will need cultural empathy to appreciate the dominant group's attitudes and behaviours. Without cultural empathy, the employee is likely to misinterpret others' attitudes and behaviours. This can result in interpersonal conflict and stress leading to low productivity, absenteeism and turnover.

Experience dimension Experts in expatriate management maintain that people who have had prior experience with foreign assignments are more likely to find it easier to adjust to a foreign setting than those who have not (e.g. Black *et al.*, 1991). In the same vein, it seems reasonable to expect employees who have had prior working experience with a diverse workforce to be more effective interculturally than those who have not. Similarly, it can be argued that the longer an employee stays in a multi-cultural workplace the more likely he/she will acquire the knowledge relevant for reducing uncertainty during intercultural interaction. Indeed, research on expatriate management indicates that sometimes intercultural effectiveness increases with the duration of the assignment (Adler, 1975; Dodd, 1982; Kim, 1977; Torbiorn, 1982). This is because the longer the expatriate stays or is expected to stay in a foreign setting the more likely it will be that the expatriate will put an extra effort in learning to adjust to the environment.

Organizational factor Given that predeparture training has been found to improve expatriate intercultural effectiveness (Black and Mendenhall, 1990), it would seem reasonable to argue that employee intercultural effectiveness in a multicultural workplace will be influenced by the level of organizational support of workforce diversity. The more the organization is committed to valuing diversity the more likely it is that its policies, systems and structures will enhance employee intercultural effectiveness (Jackson *et al.*, 1992). For example, some organizations provide training programmes to enable their employees to adjust to the growing diversity of the workplace (Cox, 1991; Jackson *et al.*, 1992; Tung, 1993). Equal opportunity and affirmative action law is another factor that can indirectly influence employee intercultural effectiveness in a multicultural workplace. If the organization is genuinely committed to equal opportunity in the workplace its policies and programmes should enhance employees' intercultural effectiveness.

Intercultural effectiveness: the sociobiological dimension

In the previous section, experts underscore the need for changing or moderating 'psychological disposition' in order to function effectively in a multicultural workplace. However, given that some sociobiological characteristics can impinge on intercultural effectiveness, rather than concentrating exclusively on changing psychological background, the employee will need to develop strategies for managing those aspects of his background which cannot be easily changed. This section highlights some of the key sociobiological factors that can affect employees' intercultural effectiveness. It will be followed by strategies for managing sociobiological factors.

Ethnicity According to Fishman (1977), ethnicity is an aspect of group self-recognition and its recognition in the eyes of outsiders. It includes both the 'inherited' and the 'acquired' attributes. The former refers to biological origin and is, therefore, hereditary or descent-related, the latter relates to how members of ethnic groups behave and what their members do in order to express their membership. This refers to things such as language or mode of dressing. In sum, ethnicity can take the form of physical appearance, material culture, customs, beliefs, attitudes and behaviours. It is widely agreed however that the 'meaning' of ethnicity in the eyes of many people can change with time (Arens, 1975; Fishman, 1977; Patterson, 1975; Smith, 1975) and the way it is conceived can be conflicting (Isajiw, 1974). Nevertheless, its relevance to intercultural interaction cannot be ignored.

That ethnicity can affect interpersonal interaction has already been acknowledged (e.g Brigham, 1971; Buriel and Vasquez, 1982; Casas *et al.*, 1987; Cauthen *et al.*, 1971; Collier and Thomas, 1988; Davies and Turner, 1984; Oliver and Vaughan, 1991; Wilson and Lavelle, 1990). For example, research evidence suggests that, in social behaviours which are quite intimate, some people are more likely to reject others on the basis of race (Triandis and Davis, 1965). Thus, some ethnic groups can be perceived by some more favourably (Haarmann, 1984; Punetha *et al.*, 1988; Segall *et al.*, 1990; Wallace and Wimalatissa, 1992). Indeed empirical evidence indicates that people from different ethnic backgrounds tend to vary in their level of adjustment and experience in a given cultural setting (Graham, 1983; Punetha *et al.*, 1988; Rubin and Smith, 1990; Szalay and Inn, 1988; Tanaka *et al.*, 1994). It is probably true to say that the 'ethnicity factor' does not play a role in all intercultural interactions. This begs the question: 'In what situation does the ethnic background of the employee become relevant?' According to the distinctive theory of selective perception

(McGuire and Padawer-Singer, 1976), we notice any aspect of ourselves, or of another, to the extent to which that characteristic is unique in that social setting. For example, research evidence has shown that when a person is overtly or symbolically confronted with members of other ethnic groups, the encounter will arouse his own ethnic role and the individual is also likely to regard these 'strangers' primarily in terms of their ethnic affiliation (Bochner and Perks, 1971; Bochner and Ohsako, 1977).

Although ethnicity is a key element in interpersonal interaction, what matters is not the actual ethnicity but the meaning people attach to it. As one commentator puts it:

> What matters is not just actual difference in skin colour, but the way these are related to, invested with meaning and importance through interaction. What is significant are the patterns of relations that are established, the lines along which they are drawn, and the myths and assumptions that go along with and inform this.
>
> (Figueroa, 1984: 19).

Thus, the meaning people attach to their own ethnicity and how others perceive them can significantly influence intercultural interaction. This is because ethnicity is used as a means of social stratification between strangers (Figueroa, 1984; Meadows, 1967; Postiglione, 1988; Triandis and Triandis, 1960). Therefore, central to the understanding of the role of ethnicity in intercultural interaction are the perceptions of the those interacting, which are largely influenced by stereotype, prejudice and ethnocentricism (Stening, 1979).

Country of origin The relevance of employee's country of origin during interpersonal interaction has since been acknowledged (Collier, 1989; Stening, 1979; Triandis and Triandis, 1960). Collier (1989) observed that the outcome of intercultural interaction can be influenced by the country of origin of the 'actors'. Research evidence has shown that country of origin is a significant cue in predicting the behaviours of foreigners (Bochner and Ohsako, 1977). It has also been noted that strangers' intercultural experiences can vary with their country of origin (Barker *et al.*, 1991; Cui and Berg, 1991; Dean and Popp, 1990). The reason why country of origin is relevant to employee's intercultural effectiveness can be found in the meaning attached to being an immigrant from Cambodia, Vietnam, Ghana, Libya, England, Germany, Russia, etc. Country of origin connotes status, competence, friendship or enmity, level of civilization, etc. The meaning attached to country of origin partly influences attitudes and behaviour of parties to intercultural interaction. Like ethnicity, perception of a stranger's country of origin is influenced by stereotype, prejudice and ethnocentricism.

Research evidence indicates that attitudes towards strangers are sometimes influenced by the level of modernity (Brewer and Campbell, 1976). The stereotypical image the dominant group holds of the employee's country of origin can be influenced by prior experience with people from similar background, international relations and colonial/imperial history. For example, it has been noted that people from developing countries have a positive stereotype of the 'competencies' of people from developed countries (Adler, 1991; Ferrari, 1972; Kidder, 1977), whereas people from developed countries tend to hold a negative stereotype of the 'competencies' of people from developing countries (Adler, 1991;

Marin and Salazar, 1988; Segall *et al.*, 1990). According to Brewer and Campbell (1976), people who are perceived as backward are less likely to be attractive than people who are not. However, Brewer and Campbell (1976) argue that progress can be a source of resentment especially if the two groups differ culturally. Some commentators maintain that people who share something in common by virtue of familiarity are more likely to hold accurate and positive stereotypes of one another (Lindgren and Marrash, 1970). Thus, irrespective of the relative backwardness of the employee's country of origin, if he/she shares something in common with the dominant group, he/she might experience favourable attitudes from them.

The relationship that exists or existed between their respective countries can affect the perceptions of the members of the countries of one another (Marin and Salazar, 1988; Reigrotski and Anderson, 1959; Salazar, 1982). Using the concept of the 'parallelism stereotype', some commentators argue that, when two groups are in a state of conflict, each tends to hold a view of the other that contrasts markedly with the view each holds of itself (Brofenbrenner, 1961). Similarly, when two countries are on good terms, respective members of the countries tend to have positive attitudes towards each other (Ogunlade, 1971). In a cross-national study of American countries, Marin and Salazar (1988) found that people whose respective countries are in conflict tend to have negative perceptions of each other. Indeed, intergroup theory and research evidence indicate that the process and outcomes of social intercourse can be influenced by prior knowledge and experience between the groups (Brewer and Campbell, 1976; Pittam *et al.*, 1990; Stephen and Stephen, 1989).

Religion It has been observed that religion can influence stranger's adaptation in a foreign setting (Hoffman, 1990; Mahmoudi, 1992). However, religion as an element of culture has not been well articulated in the adjustment literature. This is because the current approach does not take into account the fact that people may significantly share the same culture (i.e. in their daily repertoire) and yet vary significantly on religious practices and beliefs. Similarly, a stranger might share the same religion with the host but vary in his/her cultural upbringing. Such variations can have a significant influence on social interaction. However, as will be demonstrated shortly, the significance of religion for intercultural effectiveness will depend on the type of religion, the religiosity of the participants and the stereotype of religions that they hold. To appreciate the influence of religion on a stranger's intercultural effectiveness it is necessary to understand the 'meaning' of religion across cultures. For example, in the predominantly 'Christian West', religion is a private matter. In the course of social interaction one's creed does not significantly influence the process and outcome of the interaction. Social intercourse is usually narrowly focused on a specific issue. And, more often than not, people do not openly express their emotional attachment to their religion (Christianity). Thus, in the West, religion may not significantly affect intercultural effectiveness.

Unlike Christianity, Islam is considered by its followers as a culture in its own right (a way of life). For people who adhere to the teaching of Islam, their daily interaction with the stranger will be governed by the teaching and practice of Prophet Muhammad. According to this teaching, all strangers should be respected and treated well. But, more, a stranger who is a Muslim should be regarded as a brother or sister and be treated accordingly. Thus, the employee might find his/her chances of building and maintaining relationships enhanced by the mere fact that he/she shares the same religion with some co-workers. In fact, citing Rokeach and Mezzei (1966), Liebowitz and Lombardo (1980) make the point that most people would accept a stranger of another race who holds beliefs similar to their own. That religion can affect attitudes and behaviours during social interaction has already been recognized. For example, religious beliefs have been found to influence how people perceive and react to each other. In a study of Muslims, Buddhists and Catholics, Bochner (1976) found that those whose religion is more salient and less differentiated from other societal structures tend to look doubtfully at members of other faiths.

Gender According to Segall *et al.* (1990), gender refers to the meanings attached to being male or female, as reflected in social status, roles and attitudes regarding the sexes. And gender role refers to division of labour between the sexes which varies across and within cultures (Figueroa, 1984). Research evidence indicates that gender role equality is higher in individualistic cultures than in collectivistic cultures (Best and Williams, 1984; Chi-Ching, 1992; Dowling and Schuler, 1990; Hofstede, 1980; Salamon, 1977; Tomeh and Gallant, 1984). Indeed, the celebrated cross-cultural study by Hofstede (1980) revealed that some cultures tend to have high differentiation in gender role (high in Masculinity), whereas others tend to have low differentiation in gender role (high in Femininity). Hence, to many, the varying gender role is essential in predicting the likelihood of female adjustment in a foreign work setting (Brislin *et al.*, 1986; Collier, 1989; Gudykunst and Kim, 1984; Kim, 1977; Torbiorn, 1982). In fact, research evidence has confirmed that there are some unique cultural difficulties which female expatriates may experience in collectivistic cultures (Brivins and Beck, 1992; Westwood and Leung, 1992).

Even within the same culture, attitudes and behaviours between men and women do vary (Ayers-Nachamkin *et al.*, 1982; Hall, 1984; Segall *et al.*, 1990). For example, research evidence indicates that women are less competitive than their male counterparts. They prefer to collaborate and resolve conflict in a consensual way (Tannen, 1990). These variations in attitudes and behaviour between sexes can be a subject of misinterpretation which can lead to stereotype and prejudice. Indeed, anti-discrimination and affirmative action law emanated from the failure of some organizations to address the issue of sexual stereotyping and other kinds of attitudes and behaviour.

Age It has been observed that age is an important factor in subsequent adaptation to a foreign setting. The older one becomes the more difficult it is to adapt to a new cultural system (Gudykunst and Kim, 1984; Guthrie, 1975; Kim, 1977). In other words, younger people are more flexible in adapting to a new environment. Having said that, in some societies age has status connotations. In such societies, the older the person the more likely he/she will be respected. Also, some societies believe that the older one gets, the wiser one becomes (Harris and Moran, 1991). According to Harris and Moran, 'if an American is considerably younger than the African, the latter will have little confidence in the American'. It follows, therefore, that older employees can also have advantages over younger employees in a society that puts a high premium on age.

Educational/professional attainment It has been reported that, due to its ability to expand the capacity to learn new things and challenges of life, education enables people to adjust much more easily to unfamiliar situations (Case *et al.*, 1989; Dodd, 1982; Kim, 1977; Yum, 1982). In some societies, educational qualifications are highly valued and can be a significant determinant of social status. Therefore, other things being equal, employees perceived to have high levels of education by the dominant group would command respect and hence improve their chances of receiving favourable responses during interaction (Harris and Moran, 1991). Indeed, research indicates that educational attainment is likely to influence social acceptance (Schwarzwald and Hoffman, 1993). Having said that, high educational attainment can attract jealousy and resentment from some members of the organization, especially if educational attainment is viewed as a source of power and/or career advancement. Thus, managing this aspect of demographic background is essential for successful interaction in a workplace.

Linguistic factor Experts underscore the relevance of linguistic ability to a stranger's intercultural effectiveness. It is assumed that if a stranger understands and speaks the host language he/she will be interculturally effective (Dowling and Schuler, 1990; Stening, 1979). While this assumption is, in many cases valid, there are other dimensions of linguistic ability that need to be taken into account. For example, language and the style in which it is used can be construed to mean competence (Chebat *et al.*, 1989; Rubin and Smith, 1990), friendliness or aggressiveness (Page and Balloun, 1978) or a measure of social status (Scotton, 1977). In an extensive review of literature on the effect of voice characteristics, Gelinas-Chebat and Chebat (1992) note numerous studies which confirm the relationship between voice characteristics and perception of speaker's emotion, personality, attitudes, influence, competence and expertise.

A study by Rubin *et al.* (1991) revealed that managers who have certain intonations in their speech were rated highly. Another study indicates that reaction to some Asian tutors' teaching by a sample of students in the USA was influenced by the intonation of the tutors as well as their actual abilities (Rubin and Smith, 1990). Although speaking the dominant group's language can be useful way of breaking down the cultural barrier and enhancing intercultural effectiveness, given that some employees might speak with a 'unique' intonation, their linguistic ability will not always be appreciated by the majority. According to Norton (1983: 99), communicator style is 'the way one verbally and paraverbally interacts to signal how literal meaning should be taken, interpreted, filtered, or understood'. What is perceived to be an acceptable communication style is culturally determined (Porter, 1972; Norton, 1983). In an intercultural encounter the dominant group might expect to hear standard 'appropriate' language and, when faced with linguistic variability, may react negatively (Inglis, 1993). Thus, a major challenge for the employee is to develop skills for managing linguistic ability. Attitudes towards employees' linguistic ability are generally influenced by the dominant group's level of ethnocentricism. The higher the level of ethnocentricism the more likely that linguistic ability will be a significant factor during intercultural interaction.

How sociobiological background affects intercultural effectiveness

Having demonstrated in the previous sections that various aspects of an employee's sociobiological background *can* affect his/her intercultural effectiveness in a multicultural work setting, this section is concerned with *how* aspects of an employee's sociobiological background influence his/her intercultural effectiveness. Basically, this can be summarized under three main headings, namely stereotype, ethnocentricism and prejudice.

Stereotype This is a social process in which people are assigned attributes solely on the basis of their group identity (Tajfel, 1969; Wiseman *et al.*, 1989). Unlike prejudice, which is normally a negative perception, stereotypes can take the form of positive as well as negative attributes, or both. For example, a study of the mutual perceptions of Arabs and Jews indicates that both groups agree that Jews excel intellectually rather than socially, while the opposite holds true for the Arabs; and Jews emphasize their intellectual advantage while the Arabs emphasize their social superiority (Bizman and Amir, 1982). This stereotype (regardless of its accuracy) significantly influences the meaning Jews and Arabs attribute to themselves and each other. Similar studies on inter-ethnic perception have been reported elsewhere (Marjoribanks and Jordan, 1986; Oliver and Vaughan, 1991). Because most people always try to justify the stereotype they hold about others, even to the extent of 'inventing differences' (Summer, 1906) and 'projecting similarity' (Adler, 1991), the stereotypical image of members of the minority group held by the dominant group influences attitudes and behaviours during interaction.

Ethnocentricism There are two dimensions of ethnocentricism considered in this paper, and each has different consequences for employees' intercultural effectiveness. According to Summer (1906), ethnocentricism relates to positive feelings towards one's own group and negative feelings towards others. Research evidence supports this view. For example, studies revealed that people generally like their own groups best and perceive them in most positive light and perceive 'out-groups' less favourably (Brewer and Campbell, 1976; Marjoribanks and Jordan, 1986). Those who concur with Summer's definition view ethnocentricism as an attitude inspired by negative feelings (Mayer, 1984). Others, such as Adler (1991) and Gudykunst and Kim (1984), view ethnocentricism as a tendency to identify one's 'in-group' behaviour and to evaluate 'out-group' (others) according to that standard. In this approach, the emphasis is on conformity as opposed to just negative feelings towards others. Thus, in an ethnocentric work setting, employees will be required to conform to the dominant group's standards of behaviour.

It should be noted that an employee's reactions to the dominant group's perception of his/her sociobiological identity can be significantly influenced by his/her perception of his/her own identity *vis-à-vis* others. Research evidence indicates that reactions to negative perception of ethnicity can vary with cultural background. A study revealed that Indians react in a hostile manner to negative perceptions (Coelho, 1958) whereas Japanese respond passively (Bennett *et al.*, 1958). Generally, conflict arises when there is incongruence in the 'actors'' perceptions of each others' sociobiological status.

Prejudice According to Allport (1958: 10), prejudice is 'an antipathy based upon a faulty and inflexible generalisation. . . .The net effect of prejudice is to place the object of prejudice at some disadvantage not merited by his own misconduct.' Similarly, Adler (1991) noted that people can have stereotypes which can be extremely difficult to modify. Because of the false and inflexible assumptions about other people's identity, prejudice has a greater consequence on 'stranger's' intercultural effectiveness than ordinary stereotype and ethnocentrism. When an employee is interacting with a member of the dominant group who has a false and inflexible view of his/her sociobiological identity which is hard to modify or eliminate, the intercultural effectiveness of the employee will be circumscribed. To be effective under this situation will require a persistent effort on the part of the employee to modify or even to reduce the prejudice (Cox, 1991). In general, perception of sociobiological background can be categorized into stereotype, ethnocentricism and prejudice. Each of these attitudes can have different level of impact on employee intercultural effectiveness (see Figure 1).

Low		High →
Stereotype (caused by misinformation)	Ethnocentricism (caused by isolation)	Prejudice (caused by isolation and stereotype)

Figure 1 *Varying level of impact of dominant group's attitudes on employee's intercultural effectiveness*

Strategies for ***managing*** perception of sociobiological background

This section is an attempt to develop strategies for managing stereotype, prejudice and ethnocentricism as described in Figure 1 above. The strategies will be based on uncertainty reduction theory, contact theory and organizational socialization literature. The theoretical background will be presented followed by the proposed strategies.

A review of some literature

(a) Uncertainty reduction theory Reducing uncertainty has been found to be central to intercultural effectiveness (Bobad and Wallbott, 1986; Gudykunst, 1985, 1988; Witte, 1993). According to Gudykunst (1988), uncertainty reduction is a cognitive construct that relates to the capacity of individuals to foresee and explain their own behaviour and that of others during interaction. This ability is essential at the initial stage of the interaction, at various stages of the interaction and during several interactions (Berger, 1979; Gudykunst *et al.*, 1987). Uncertainty reduction also relates to the idea that perception of each other becomes more accurate the more we know each other (Hunt, 1986). According to Berger (1979), individuals use three strategies to reduce uncertainty about others. First, people use *passive* strategy (secondary source of information) to reduce uncertainty. This includes reading books, watching movies and television, and observation in order to gain knowledge of the 'object' of uncertainty. As Berger points out, this strategy has the danger of reinforcing stereotypes held about others, since people will not be able to confirm their perception through direct contact. Second, people use *active* strategy to reduce uncertainty. According to Berger (1979), this strategy has the potential of changing attitude and/or increasing the accuracy of stereotype. Hamilton and Bishop (1976) have confirmed this. The strategy relies on asking others about the 'object' of uncertainty. Third, people use *interactive* strategy. This is when information about the 'object' is obtained through direct interaction using methods such as interrogation and self-disclosure. To Gudykunst (1988) reducing uncertainty includes the following: correcting stereotype, developing networks and favourable contacts, understanding and appreciating one's culture and that of others (Gudykunst, 1988).

(b) Contact theory This theory is similar to uncertainty reduction theory. It centres on the premise that negative attitudes towards strangers are mainly caused by misunderstanding and/or misinformation as a result of isolation. The more people get in contact with each other, the more they understand each other; then this leads to gradual acceptance of differences between people. Hence, frequent contact has been argued to reduce negative perception and increase social acceptability (Amir, 1969; Dodd, 1982; Lindgren and Marrash, 1970; Zajonic, 1968). Research evidence lends support to this proposition (Kealey, 1989; Zajonic, 1968). In fact, experts have advised organizations to redesign jobs to facilitate racial interaction by encouraging common goals and intergroup interdependence (Amir, 1969; Pettigrew and Martin, 1987), and research evidence suggests that this approach can produce positive outcomes (Aronson *et al.*, 1978).

It is important to note that contact does not always produce positive attitudes among the participants unless certain conditions are met. According to Amir (1969), contact will produce positive outcome when:

> (a) the contact is between members of a majority group and higher status members of minority: (b) there is equal status contact between members of the groups; (c) an 'authority' and/or the social climate is in favour of and promotes the contact; (d) the contact is of intimate rather than casual nature; (e) the intergroup contact is pleasant and rewarding; (f) members of both groups interact in functionally important activities or develop common goals or superordinate goals that are higher in ranking and in importance than the individual goals of the groups.
>
> (Amir, 1969: 338)

Relative to other interactions, workplace interaction is more likely to satisfy the conditions mentioned above. Thus, contact between groups, if properly managed, should produce positive outcomes. For example, the organization can promote intercultural contact through valuing diversity programmes; status can be 'equalized' if the minority occupies a high position. Therefore, in line with contact theory, increase in contact at workplace should reduce misunderstanding and create an atmosphere of favourable and effective interaction. However, because contact will not always guarantee positive attitudes (O'Driscoll *et al.*, 1983; Ray, 1983), the employee should be tactful and avoid putting the dominant group on the defensive during workplace interaction.

(c) Organizational socialization tactics Literature on organizational socialization indicates that to be successful in adapting to the new environment an employee should 'change' either him/herself or the situation (Dawis and Lofquist, 1984). In other words, he/she should either change others' attitudes and/or behaviour or prepare to accommodate them. In the same vein, Nicholson (1984) proposed that organizational socialization tactics can take the form of (a) changing neither oneself or the situation (*replication*); (b) changing self not the situation (*absorption*); (c) changing the situation not self (*determination*); (d) changing self and the situation (*exploration*). Similarly, Schein (1978) maintains that employees respond to organizational socialization by (a) rebelling against all values and norms, (b) accepting only some of the norms and values (*creative individualism*) or (c) accepting all values and norms (*conformity*).

Writing on the coping strategies of gays and lesbians in the workplace, Lucas and Kaplan (1994) note three strategies: first, the *staying in the closet strategy* in which 'closeted employees feel that they have no choice but to avoid talking about their personal life at workplace for fear of giving themselves away'; Lucas and Kaplan (1994) suggest that such people often lie to protect themselves and often face ethical dilemmas which result in psychological stress. Second, there is the *coming out strategy* employees who adopt this strategy often reveal their sexuality in the same way that others (heterosexuals) do. According to Lucas and Kaplan, people who use this strategy feel empowered, honest, valued and connected. However, as the authors admit, this strategy is not without risk. This is because people 'may be jeopardizing whatever credibility and influence they've built at work. No matter how competent and skilled they are, they fear they may be devalued by their managers and co-workers once their sexual orientation is known' (Lucas and Kaplan, 1994: 36). The third strategy is the *avoiding the issue strategy* employees who use this strategy avoid dealing with the issue. They tend to become vague, distant professionals who isolate themselves from close relationships with co-workers, team members and mentors. 'Such people tend to be aloof at work, they steer clear of situations in which they might reveal the everyday information people typically share with co-workers. If they do participate in informal discussions, they try to redirect attention away from themselves' (Lucas and Kaplan, 1994: 37). In an empirical study of racial dynamics between African-Americans and White Americans, Thomas (1993) found that the groups used two strategies for interaction: (a) *denial and suppression* and (b) *direct engagement*. In the former, the parties pretend that racial differences do not exist, while in the latter the parties openly discuss their racial differences. Thomas maintains that the effectiveness of the strategy will vary with the situation. In other words, both strategies can be appropriate when used contextually.

Proposed strategies

On the basis of the literature reviewed, it is proposed that managing sociobiological background should be based on taking a proactive stance when interacting with the dominant group. Proactive interaction refers to taking the initiative to understand others with the aim of reducing misunderstanding and correcting misconception. Indeed, research evidence confirms that the ability and motivation of the stranger to understand an unfamiliar situation can enhance intercultural effectiveness (Kealey, 1989; Stephen and Stephen, 1985; Ward and Searle, 1991). Advising intercultural interactants, Dodd (1982) suggests that strangers should force themselves to go out of their way to meet others. By doing that they gradually gain personal confidence and ultimately learn a lot more about others. If possible, an employee should not *suppress* his/her identity but should tactically *express* it by educating the dominant group and correcting any misconception and misinformation. In an article titled 'Managing Cross-National and Intra-National Diversity', Tung (1993) also advocates open discussion of matters pertaining to ethnicity and gender. Similarly, Fitzsimmons and Eyring (1993: 2404–7) argue that another way to value diversity is to talk about it openly and positively. Workers should be encouraged to view their diversity as a strength which may be of great value in specific work situations. The strategies for managing sociobiological background are presented in detail in the following sections.

(a) Passive strategy This strategy can be referred to as 'do-nothing' or 'avoidance' strategy. It is based on the assumption that there are situations when the employee cannot correct the perceptions of the dominant group, for example when he/she does not interact frequently with them; or they are not willing to 'entertain' him/her; or they hold inflexible attitudes that seem unlikely to change or modify. Indeed, research evidence indicates that 'suppression' of sociobiological identity during interracial interaction is one of the strategies used by employees at the workplace (Lucas and Kaplan, 1994; Thomas, 1993). It has been argued that at an early stage of adjustment in an organization (i.e. sense-making/settling-in stage) employees take time to assess the extent to which their experience vary with their expectations (Louis, 1980). It therefore follows that the passive strategy can be appropriate during the early stage of joining the organization or work group.

(b) Reactive strategy This strategy refers to reacting or/and responding to any question or inquiry regarding employee's sociobiological background. Rather than avoiding the question or suppressing it, an employee should be willing to entertain questions. Indeed, self-disclosure has been argued to be a prerequisite for personal growth and development (Hellriegel *et al.*, 1989). By answering questions and queries the employee is helping to reduce uncertainty on the part of the dominant group. Given that stereotypes are usually influenced by ignorance, an employee should take advantage of responding to questions to correct any negative perception of his/her identity by educating the dominant group through provision of information concerning his/her actual rather than perceived identity. This strategy can be appropriate if the employee is at an early stage of entry into the organization; if he/she occupies a lower position, has infrequent interaction with the dominant group, and the dominant group exhibits an inflexible attitude.

(c) **Proactive strategy** This strategy goes beyond responding to questions or inquiries. Here, the employee is expected to initiate interaction in order to know more about the dominant group's attitudes and to encourage the dominant group to know more about his/her background. An employee should take advantage of this interaction to correct any misconception, misinformation and negative stereotyping by educating the other party through provision of accurate information. Because perception of sociobiological background sometimes has implications for an employee's ability and competence, demonstration of culturally 'appropriate' behaviour, professionalism and competence on the job should contribute to correcting negative perceptions. The stranger's motivation to interact with others has been argued to be a significant determinant of reduction of anxiety (i.e. fear of negative consequences of ineffectiveness) (Gudykunst, 1988; Witte, 1993). Therefore, employee willingness and ability to initiate interaction with the dominant group should improve the chance of reducing anxiety. The outcome of this strategy could depend on factors such as the frequency of interaction, the position of the employee (Asante and Davies, 1989; Kahn *et al.*, 1964), level of intimacy, stage of entry into the organization or work group (Dodd, 1982), willingness of the dominant group to discuss issues pertaining to sociobiological identity (Thomas, 1993). Table 1 illustrates how one of the factors (frequency of interaction) can influence the choice of strategy.

Table 1 *Choice of strategy based on frequency of interaction and type of attitude*

Frequency of interaction	*Stereotype*	*Ethnocentricism*	*Prejudice*
Infrequent	Reactive strategy	Reactive strategy	Passive strategy
Frequent	Proactive strategy	Proactive strategy	Reactive strategy
Very Frequent	Proactive strategy	Proactive strategy	Proactive strategy

Central to managing the interaction is the idea of 'self-monitoring'. This refers to the ability of the employee to adjust his/her behaviours to 'fit' the reaction of the other party (DeVito, 1988). Through 'self-monitoring' the employee can switch from one strategy to the other. Indeed, for the above strategies to succeed, the employee should be willing and able to switch from one strategy to the other. When using these strategies, the employee should avoid putting the other party on the defensive. In a longitudinal study stretching up to eight years, Gibb (1960) discovered that a defensive-reduction strategy is characterized by spontaneity in communication, description as opposed to evaluation, empathy as opposed to neutrality, equality as opposed to superiority (DeVito, 1988; Gibb, 1978).

Future research direction

This paper set out to highlight the key factors that can influence employees' intercultural effectiveness in a multicultural workplace. Also, the paper aimed to develop strategies for managing sociobiological background in a multicultural workplace. Psychological, sociobiological and organizational factors have been identified as the key elements that can impinge on employee intercultural effectiveness. The strategies proposed for managing employees' sociobiological backgrounds were centred on changing or moderating psychological background and managing or adapting to sociobiological background.

Given that much of what we know about employees' attitudes and behaviour in a workplace is based on studies carried out in a homogenous workforce, more studies are needed to explore the dynamics of employees' interaction in a multicultural workplące. Such investigation could be central to effective management of employees in a multicultural workplace. In light of this observation, this section presents a series of research questions and observations that can guide future research on this important topic.

The first issue concerns the proposed strategies for managing sociobiological background. The strategies proposed in this paper might need further refining to ensure their effectiveness. For example, an interaction strategy that works for one person might not work for another. Similarly, what proves successful in a particular interaction might not be in another. Future research should investigate questions such as: What factors impinge on the effectiveness of the proposed strategies? What are the potential effects of profession/occupation, position, role, competence and performance on the effectiveness of the proposed strategies?

Second, the effect of sociobiological variables on intercultural effectiveness could vary with time. For instance, the effect of country of origin could decrease or increase with the state of international relations between countries. Similarly, given that the meaning attached to ethnicity changes with time, its impact on intercultural effectiveness could vary accordingly. In the same vein, the impact of some variables on intercultural effectiveness could vary with the stage of entry into the organization. Therefore, future research is needed to explore questions such as: Does length of service in the organization moderate the impact of employee's sociobiological background on his/her intercultural effectiveness? To what extent, if at all, does employee's country of origin affect his intercultural effectiveness during an international crisis? How can managers and trainers tackle the issue of changing attitudes and perceptions in their 'diversity training programmes'?

Third, other things being equal, employee intercultural effectiveness could vary with the intensity of attitude. As a related research issue, researchers may investigate how varying levels of attitudes affect intercultural effectiveness. For example, we need to know whether a 'hostile' working environment requires aggressive diversity programmes, or whether a subtle approach will be the most appropriate.

Fourth, the impact of an employee's sociobiological background could transcend formal interactions. For example, based on sociobiological background, an employee might be perceived as incompetent but 'socially attractive'; or he/she might be viewed as competent but 'socially unattractive'. Moreover, on the basis of his/her sociobiological background, the employee might be perceived as incompetent and 'socially unattractive'. Thus, the wider the *breadth* of perception of employee's sociobiological background the more likely that his/her intercultural effectiveness in a work setting will be affected. Again, research is needed to verify the concept of *breadth* and its potential impact on employee intercultural effectiveness. For example, questions such as: Does employee's ability to make friends at work affect their performance or vice versa? How does employee's experience with the dominant group affect their performance on the job? Answers to these questions would help in understanding the dynamics of workplace intercultural interaction and its implication for productivity.

Fifth, it can be argued that the more frequently a particular attitude is experienced the greater will be its impact on intercultural effectiveness. This suggests that an employee's intercultural effectiveness could vary with the frequency of his/her experience (positive or negative). Researchers may investigate how the frequency with which an employee experiences a particular attitude affects intercultural effectiveness and productivity.

Sixth, it is plausible that, when two or more variables operate at the same time (e.g. ethnicity and gender), the effect of the sociobiological factor on intercultural effectiveness is likely to be greater than if one variable (e.g. gender) were to operate. Therefore, researchers may investigate which 'combination' of employee backgrounds is likely to enhance or diminish intercultural effectiveness. Similarly, it would be useful to know which aspect of an employee's sociobiological background(s) is likely to have a *neutralizing effect*. For example, does profession and/or position neutralize the potential effect of ethnicity or gender in an intercultural interaction.

Seventh, perhaps one of the major tasks for researchers today is to identify appropriate models for human resource management practices which will suit a multicultural organization. For example, need to find answers to questions such as: Which structure and job design is most appropriate for a multicultural organization? Which reward system is most likely to be effective in a multicultural worksetting? We also need to ponder on the issue of performance management and career within the context of valuing diversity.

Finally, it is hoped that this paper has contributed to the field by identifying the key factors that are critical to employee intercultural effectiveness in a multicultural workplace. It is hoped that the proposed interaction strategies will prove useful to employees, managers and trainers in their 'diversity efforts'. Finally, it is hoped that the directions for future research will stimulate more research on this important topic.

Aminu Mamman
Faculty of Business
Northern Territory University
Australia

Acknowledgements

The author wishes to thank two anonymous reviewers for their constructive criticisms and Dr Ram Vemuri for useful comments and editorial assistance.

References

Adler, N.J. (1991). *International Dimensions of Organizational Behaviour*. Boston, MA: PSW-Kent.

Adler, P.S (1975) 'The Transactional Experience: An Alternative View of Culture Shock', *Journal of Humanistic Psychology*, 15(4): 13–23.

Alderfer, C (1990) 'Reflections on Race Relations and Organizations', *Journal of Organizational Behaviour*, 11: 493–5.

Allport, G. W. (1958) *The Nature of Prejudice*. New York: Doubleday Anchor.

Amir, Y. (1969) 'Contact Hypotheses in Ethnic Relations', *Psychological Bulletin*, 71: 319–41

Arens, W. (1975) 'The Social History of an Ethnic Group', *Africa*, 45: 426–37.

Aronson, E., Stephan, C., Sikes, J., Blaney, N. and Snapp, M. (1978) *The Jigsaw Classroom*. Beverly Hills, CA: Sage.

Asante, M.K. and Davies, A. (1989) 'Encounters in the Interracial Workplace'. In Asante, M.K. and Gudykunst, W.B. (ed.) *Handbook of International and Intercultural Communication*. Newbury Park, CA: Sage, p. 375.

Ayers-Nachamkin, B., Cann, C.H., Reed, R. and Horne, A. (1982) 'Sex and Ethnic Differences in the Use of Power', *Journal of Applied Psychology*, 67(4): 464–71.

Babiker, I., Cox, J. and Miller, P. (1980) 'The Measurement of Culture Distance and its Relationship to Medical Consultations, Symptomatology and Examinations Performance of Overseas Students at Edinburgh University', *Social Psychiatry*, 15: 109–16.

Barker, M., Child, C., Gallois, C., Jones, E. and Callan, V.J. (1991) 'Differences in Overseas Students in Social and Academic Situations', *Australian Journal of Psychology*, 43(2): 79–84.

Bennett, J.W., Passin, H. and McKnight, R.K. (1958) *In Search of Identity: The Japanese Overseas Scholar in America and Japan*. Minneapolis: University of Minnesota Press.

Berger, C.R. (1979) 'Beyond Initial Interactions'. In Giles, H. and St. Clair, R. (eds) *Language and Social Psychology*. London: Edward Arnold, pp. 122–44.

Best, D. and Williams, J. (1984) 'A Cross-Cultural Examination of Self and Ideal Self Description using Transactional Analysis Ego States'. In Lagunes, I. and Poortinga, Y. (eds) *From a Different Perspective: Studies of Behaviour across Cultures*. Lisse, The Netherlands: Swets & Zeitlinger.

Bizman, A. and Amir, Y. (1982) 'Mutual Perceptions of Arabs and Jews in Israel', *Journal of Cross-cultural Psychology*, 13(4): 461–9.

Black, J.S. and Mendenhall, M. (1990) 'Cross-Cultural Training Effectiveness: A Review and a Theoretical Framework for Future Research', *Academy of Management Review*, 15(1): 113–36.

Black, J.S., Mendenhall, M. and Oddou, G. (1991) 'Toward a Comprehensive Model of International Adjustment: An Integration of Multiple Theoretical Perspective', *The Academy of Management Review*, 16(2): 291–317.

Bobad, E. and Wallbott, H. (1986) 'The Effects of Social Factors on Emotional Reactions'. In Sherer, K., Wallbott, H. and Summerfield, A. (eds) *Experiencing Emotions: A Cross-Cultural Study*. Cambridge: Cambridge University Press.

Bochner, S. (1976) 'Religious Role Differentiation as an Aspect of Subjective Culture', *Journal of Cross-cultural Psychology*, 7: 3–19.

Bochner, S. and Ohsako, T. (1977) 'Ethnic Role Salience in Racially Homogenous and Heterogenous Societies'. *Journal of Cross-Cultural Psychology*, 8(4): 477–92.

Bochner, S. and Perks, R.W. (1971) 'National Role Evocation as a Function of Cross-National Interaction', *Journal of Cross-cultural Psychology*, 2: 157–64.

Brewer, M.B. and Campbell, D.T. (1976) *Ethnocentricism and Intergroup Attitudes*. New York: Wiley.

Brien, M. and David, K. (1971) 'Intercultural Communications and the Adjustment of the Sojourner', *Psychological Bulletin*, 76: 215–30.

Brigham, J.C. (1971) 'Ethnic Stereotypes', *Psychological Bulletin*, 76: 15–38.

Brislin, R. (1981) *Cross-Cultural Encounters: Face-to-Face Interaction*. New York: Pergamon Press.

Brislin, R., Cushner, K., Cherrie, C. and Yong, M. (1986) *Intercultural Interactions: A Practical Guide*. Beverly Hills, CA: Sage.

Brivins, A. and Beck, J.E. (1992) 'The Expatriates: A Study of Female Expatriates in Hong Kong (Preliminary Findings)', *Proceedings of First International Conference on Expatriates Management*, Hong Kong, 23–25 November 1992: 179–84.

Bronfenbrenner, U. (1961) 'The Mirror Image in Soviet–American Relations: A Social Psychological Report', *Journal of Social Issues*, 17: 45–56.

Buriel, R. and Vasquez, R. (1982) 'Stereotypes of Mexican Descent Persons', *Journal of Cross-cultural Psychology*, 13(1): 59–70.

Casas, J.M., Ponterotto, J.G. and Sweeney, M. (1987) 'Stereotyping and Stereotyper', *Journal of Cross-cultural Psychology*, 18(1): 45–57.

Case, C.E., Greeley, A.M. and Fuchs, S. (1989) 'Social Determinants of Racial Prejudice', *Sociological Perspective*, 32(4): 469–83.

Cauthen, N.R., Robinson, E.A. and Krauss, H.H. (1971) 'Stereotypes: A Review of Literature: 1926 to 68', *Journal of Social Psychology*, 84: 103–25.

Chebat, J.C., Filiatrault, P. and Perrien, J. (1989) 'Limits of Credibility: The Case of Political Persuasion', *Journal of Social Psychology*, 130: 157–69.

Chi-Ching, E.Y. (1992) 'Perceptions of External Barriers and the Careers Success of Female Managers in Singapore', *The Journal of Social Psychology*, 132(5): 661–74.

Coelho, G.V. (1958) *Changing Images of America: A Study of Indian Students' Perceptions*. Glencoe, Ill.: Free Press.

Collier, M.J. (1989) 'Cultural and Intercultural Communication Competence: Current Approaches and Directions for Future Research', *International Journal of Intercultural Relations*, 13: 287–302.

Collier, M.J. and Thomas, M. (1988) 'Cultural Identity: An Interpretive Perspective.' In Kim, Y.Y. and Gudykunst, W.B. (eds) *Theories in Intercultural Communication*. Newbury Park, CA: Sage, pp. 99–120.

Copeland, L. (1988a) 'Learning to Manage a Multicultural Workforce', *Training*, May: 48–56.

Copeland, L. (1988b) 'Valuing Workforce Diversity', *Personnel Administrator*, November.

Cox, T. (1991) 'The Multicultural Organization', *Academy of Management Executive*, 5(2): 34–47.

Cox, T. and Blake, S. (1991) 'Managing Cultural Diversity: Implications for Organizational Competitiveness', *Academy of Management Executive*, 5(3): 45–56.

Cui, G. and Berg, S.V. (1991) 'Testing the Construct Validity of Intercultural Effectiveness', *International Journal of Intercultural Relations*, 15: 227–41.

Davies, J. and Turner, I.F. (1984) 'Frendship Choices in an Integrated Primary School in Northern Ireland', *British Journal of Social Psychology*, 23: 185–6.

Dawis, R.V. and Lofquist, L.H. (1984) *A Psychological Theory of Work Adjustment*. Minneapolis: University of Minnesota Press.

Dean, O. and Popp, G.E. (1990) 'Intercultural Communication Effectiveness as Perceived by American Managers in Saudi Arabia and Managers in the USA', *International Journal of Intercultural Relations*, 14: 405–24.

Detweiler, R. (1975) 'On Inferring the Intentions of a Person from Another Culture', *Journal of Personality*, 43: 591–611.

Detweiler, R. (1978) 'Culture, Category-Width, and Attribution: A Model-Building Approach to the Reasons for Culture Effects', *Journal of Cross-Cultural Psychology*, 9(3): 259–84.

Detweiler, R. (1980) 'Intercultural Interaction and the Categorisation Process: A Conceptual Analysis and Behaviour Outcome', *International Journal of Intercultural Relations*, 4: 275–93.

DeVito, J.A. (1988) *Human Communication*, 4th edition. New York: Harper & Row.

Dickens, F. and Dickens, L. (1982) *The Black Manager*. AMACOM Publishing.

Dinges, N. (1983) 'Intercultural Competence'. In Landis, D. and Brislin, R.W. (eds) *Handbook of Intercultural Training*, Vol. 1. New York: Pergamon Press.

Dodd, C.H. (1982) *Dynamics of Intercultural Communication*. William C. Brown.

Dowling, P.J. and Schuler, R.S. (1990) *International Dimensions of Human Resource Management*. Boston, MA: PWS-Kent.

Etsy, K. (1988) 'Diversity is Good for Business', *Executive Excellence*, 5: 5–6.

Ferrari, S. (1972) 'Human Behaviour in International Groups', *Management International Review*, 12(6): 31–5.

Figueroa, P.M. (1984) 'Race Relations and Cultural Differences: Some Ideas on a Racial Frame of Reference'. In Verma, G.K. and Bagley, C. (eds) *Race Relations and Cultural Differences*. London: Croom Helm.

Fishman, J.A. (1977) 'Language and Ethnicity'. In Giles, H. (ed.) *Language, Ethnicity, and Intergroup Relations*. London: Academic Press, pp. 15–57.

Fitzsimmons, D.S. and Eyring, A.R. (1993) 'Valuing and Managing Cultural Diversity in the Workplace', *American Journal of Hospital Pharmacists*, 50: 2404–7.

Gelinas-Chebat, C. and Chebat, J.C. (1992) 'Effects of Two Voice Characteristics on the Attitudes towards Advertising Messages', *The Journal of Social Psychology*, 132(4): 447–59.
Gertsen, M.C. (1990) 'Intercultural Competence and Expatriates', *The International Journal of Human Resource Management*, 1(3): 341–62.
Gibb, J.R. (1960) 'Sociophysiological Process of Work Instruction'. In Henry, N.B. (ed.) *Dynamics of Instructional Groups*. 59th Yearbook of the National Society for the Study of Education (part 2).
Gibb, J.R. (1978) 'Defensive Communication'. In Ebing, A. (ed.) *Behavioural Decisions in Organization*, 2nd edition. Glenview, Ill.: Scott, Foresman, pp. 277–82.
Graham, M.A. (1983) 'Acculturative Stress among Polynesian, Asian, and American Students on the Brigham Young University Hawaii Campus', *International Journal of Intercultural Relations*, 7: 79–100.
Gudykunst, W.B. (1977) 'Intercultural Contact and Attitude Change: A Review of Literature and Suggestions in Future Research', *International and Intercultural Communication Annual*, 4: 1–16.
Gudykunst, W.B. (1985) 'The Influence of Cultural Similarity, Type of Relationships, and Self-Monitoring on Uncertainty Reduction Processes', *Communication Monographs*, 52: 203–17.
Gudykunst, W.B. (1988) 'Uncertainty and Anxiety'. In Kim, Y.Y. and Gudykunst, W.B. (eds) *Theories in Intercultural Communication*. Newbury Park, CA: Sage, pp. 123–56.
Gudykunst, W.B. and Hammer, M.R. (1984) 'Dimensions of Intercultural Effectiveness: Culture Specific or Culture General', *International Journal of Intercultural Relations*, 8: 1–10.
Gudykunst, W.B. and Hammer, M.R. (1988) 'Host and Strangers: An Uncertainty Reduction Based Theory of Intercultural Adaptation'. In Kim, Y.Y. and Gudykunst, W.B. (eds) *Cross-cultural Adaptation: Current Approaches*. Newbury Park, CA: Sage, pp. 106–37.
Gudykunst, W.B. and Kim, Y.Y. (1984) *Communicating with Strangers. An Approach to Intercultural Communication*. New York: Random House.
Gudykunst, W.B., Nishida, T. and Chua, E. (1987) 'Perceptions of Social Penetration in Japanese–North American Dyads', *International Journal of Intercultural Relations*, 11: 171–89.
Gullahorn, J. and Gullahorn, J. (1963) 'An Extension of U Curve Hypothesis', *Journal of Social Issues*, 19: 33–47.
Gunn, A. (1979) 'National Health Problems in Students Care', *Journal of the American College Health Association*, 27: 322–3.
Guthrie, G. (1975) 'A Behavioural Analysis of Culture Learning'. In Brislin, R.W., Bochner, S. and Lonner, W.J. (eds) *Cross-Cultural Perspective on Learning*. New York: Wiley.
Haarmann, H. (1984) 'The Role of Ethnocultural Stereotypes and Foreign Languages in Japanese Commercials', *International Journal of the Sociology of Language*, 50: 101–21.
Hall, J. (1984) *Nonverbal Sex Differences*. Baltimore: Johns Hopkins University Press.
Hamilton, D.L. and Bishop, G.D. (1976) 'Attitudinal and Behavioural Effects of Initial Integration of White Suburban Neighbourhoods', *Journal of Social Issues*, 32: 47–67.
Hammer, M.R. (1987) 'Behavioural Dimensions of Intercultural Effectiveness: A Replication and Extension', *International Journal of Intercultural Relations*, 11: 65–88.
Hammer, M.R. (1989) 'Intercultural Communication Competence'. In Asante, M.K. and Gudykunst, W.B. (eds) *Handbook of International and Intercultural Communication*. Newbury Park, CA: Sage, pp. 247–60.
Hammer, M.R., Gudykunst, W.B. and Wiseman, R.L. (1978) 'Dimensions of Intercultural Effectiveness: An Exploratory Study', *International Journal of Intercultural Relations*, 2: 282–393.
Harris, P.R. and Moran, R.T. (1991). *Managing Cultural Differences*. Houston, Tex.: Gulf Publishing.

Hawes, F. and Kealey, D.J. (1981) 'An Empirical Study of Canadian Technical Assistance', *International Journal of Intercultural Relations*, 5: 239–58.

Hellriegel, D., Slocum, J.W., and Woodman, R.W. (1989) *Organizational Behaviour*, 5th edition. New York: West Publishing.

Hoffman, D.M. (1990) 'Beyond Conflict: Culture, Self, and Intercultural Learning among Iranians in the US', *International Journal of Intercultural Relations*, 14: 275–99.

Hofstede, G. (1980) *Culture's Consequences: International Differences in Work-related Values*. Beverly Hills, CA: Sage.

Hofstede, G. (1991) *Cultures and Organizations: Software of the Mind*. New York: McGraw-Hill.

Hunt, J.W. (1986) *Managing People at Work*, 2nd edition. New York: McGraw-Hill.

Inglis, M. (1993) 'The Communicator Style Measure Applied to Non-native Speaking Teaching Assistants', *International Journal of Intercultural Relations*, 17: 89–105.

Isajiw, W.W. (1974) 'Definitions of Ethnicity', *Ethnicity*, 1: 111–24.

Jackson, B.W., LaFasto, F., Schultz, H.G. and Kelley, D. (1992) 'Diversity', *Human Resource Management*, 31(1 & 2): 21–34.

Kahn, R.L., Wolfe, D.M., Quinn, R.P. and Shock, J.D. (1964) *Organizational Stress*, New York: Wiley.

Kealey, D.J. (1989) 'A Study of Cross-Cultural Effectiveness: Theoretical issues, Practical Applications', *International Journal of Intercultural Relations*, 13: 387–428.

Kidder, L. (1977) 'The Inadvertent Creation of a Neocolonial Culture: A Study of Western Sojourners in India', *International Journal of Intercultural Relations*, 1: 48–60.

Kim, Y.Y. (1977) 'Communication Patterns of Foreign Immigrants in the Process of Acculturation', *Human Communication Research*, 4: 66–77.

Laudicina, E.V. (1993) 'Diversity and Productivity: Lessons from the Corporate Sector', *Public Productivity and Management Review*, 16(1): 457–63.

Liebowitz, S.J. and Lombardo, J.P. (1980) 'Effects of Race, Beliefs, and Level of Prejudice on Responses to Black and White Strangers', *The Journal of Social Psychology*, 110: 293–4.

Lindgren, H.C. and Marrash, J. (1970) 'A Comparative Study of Inter-Cultural Insight and Empathy', *Journal of Social Psychology*, 80: 135–41.

Louis, M.R. (1980) 'Surprise and Sense Making: What Newcomers Experience in Entering Unfamiliar Organizational Settings', *Administrative Science Quarterly*, 25: 226–51.

Lucas, J.H. and Kaplan, M.G. (1994) 'Unlocking the Corporate Closet', *Training and Development*, January: 35–8.

McGuire, W.J. and Padawer-Singer, A. (1976) 'Trait Salience in the Spontaneous Self-Concept', *Journal of Personality and Social Psychology*, 33: 743–54.

Mahmoudi, K.M. (1992) 'Refugee Cross-Cultural Adjustment: Tibetans in India', *International Journal of Intercultural Relations*, 16(1): 17–32.

Marin, G. and Salazar, J.M. (1988) 'Determinants of Hetero and Autostereotype', *Journal of Cross-cultural Psychology*, 16(4): 403–22.

Marjoribanks, K. and Jordan, D.F. (1986) 'Stereotyping among Aboriginal and Anglo-Australians: The Uniformity, Intensity, Direction, and Quality of Auto and Hetero Stereotypes', *Journal of Cross-Cultural Psychology*, 17(1): 17–28.

Mayer, J.C. (1984) 'Towards an Explanation of Ethnocentricism versus Ethnorelativism Based upon Reference Group Orientation'. In Verma, G.K. and Bagley, C. (eds) *Race Relations and Cultural Differences*. London: Croom Helm.

Meadows, P. (1967) 'Insiders and Outsiders: Toward a Theory of Overseas Cultural Groups', *Social Forces*, 46: 61–71.

Mendenhall, M. and Oddou, G. (1986) 'Acculturation Profiles of Expatriate Managers: Implications for Cross-Cultural Training Programs', *Columbia Journal of World Business*, Winter: 73–9.

Motwani, J., Harper, E., Subramanian, R. and Douglas, C. (1993) 'Managing the Diverse Workplace: Current Efforts and Future Directions', *SAM Advance Management Journal*, Summer: 16–21.

Nicholson, N. (1984) 'A Theory of Work Role Transitions', *Administrative Science Quarterly*, 29: 172–91.

Norton, R.W. (1983) *Communicator Style – Theory, Application and Measures*, Beverly Hills, CA: Sage.

Oddou, G. and Mendenhall, M. (1984) 'Person Perception in Cross-Cultural Setting: A Review of Cross-cultural and Related Cognitive Literature', *International Journal of Intercultural Relations*, 8: 77–96.

O'Driscoll, M., Haque, A. and Oshako, T. (1983) 'Effects of Contact and Perceived Attitude Differences on Social Distance among Australian, Japanese and Pakistani Students', *Journal of Social Psychology*, 120: 163–8.

Ogunlade, J.A. (1971) 'National Stereotype of University Students in Western Nigeria', *Journal of Cross-Cultural Psychology*, 2: 173–80.

Oliver, P. and Vaughan, G. (1991) 'How We See One Another: Interethnic Perceptions of New Zealand Teenagers', *Journal of Intercultural Studies*, 12(1): 17–38.

Page, R.A. and Balloun, J.L. (1978) 'The Effect of Voice Volume on the Perception of Personality', *The Journal of Social Psychology*, 105: 65–72.

Parker, W.S. (1976) 'Black–White Differences in Leadership Behaviour Related to Subordinates Reactions', *Journal of Applied Psychology*, 61: 140–7.

Patterson, O. (1975) 'Context and Choice in Ethnic Allegiance: A Theoretical Framework and Caribbean Case Study'. In Glazer, N. and Moynihan, D.P. (eds) *Ethnicity: Theory and Experience*. Cambridge, MA: Harvard Univesity Press, pp. 305–49.

Pettigrew, T.F. and Martin, J. (1987) 'Shaping the Organizational Context for Black American Inclusion', *Journal of Social Issues*, 43(1): 41–78.

Pinder, C.C. and Schroeder, K.G. (1987) 'Time to Proficiency Following Transfers', *Academy of Management Journal*, 30: 336–53.

Pittam, J., Kashima, Y. and Iwawaki, S. (1990) 'Dimensionality and National Function in Australian and Japanese Ethnic Stereotypes', *Australian Journal of Psychology*, 42(3): 297–308.

Porter, R.E. (1972) 'An Overview of Intercultural Communication'. In Movar, L.A. sa and Porter, R.E. (eds) *Intercultural Communication: A Reader*. Belmont, CA: Wadsworth.

Postiglione, G.A. (1988) 'The Structuring of Ethnicity in Hong Kong', *International Journal of Intercultural Relations*, 12: 247–67.

Punetha, D., Giles, H. and Young, L. (1988) 'Interethnic Perceptions and Relative Deprivation'. In Kim, Y.Y. and Gudykunst, W.B. (eds) *Cross-cultural Adaptation: Current Approaches*, Newbury Park, CA: Sage, pp. 252–66.

Ray, J.J. (1983) 'Racial Attitudes and the Contact Hypothesis', *Journal of Social Psychology*, 119: 3–10.

Reigrotski, E. and Anderson, N. (1959) 'National Stereotype and Foreign Contacts', *Public Opinion Quarterly*, 23: 515–28.

Rokeach, M. and Mezzei, L. (1966) 'Race and Beliefs as Factors in Social Choice', *Science*, 151: 167–72.

Ruben, B.D. (1976) 'Assessing Communication Competency for Intercultural Adaptation', *Group and Organizational Studies*, 1: 334–54.

Rubin, D.L. and Smith, K.A. (1990) 'Effects of Accent, Ethnicity, and Lecture Topic on Undergraduates' Perceptions of Non-Native English-Speaking Teaching Assistants', *International Journal of Intercultural Relations*. 14: 337–53.

Rubin, D., Dettart, J. and Heintzman, M. (1991) 'Effects of Accented Speech and Culture Typical Compliance-Gaining Style on Subordinates' Impressions of Managers', *International Journal of Intercultural Relations*. 15: 267–83.

Salamon, S. (1977) 'Family Bonds and Friendship Bonds: Japan and West Germany', *Journal of Marriage and Family*, 39: 807–20.

Salazar, J.M. (1982) 'Research on Nationalism in Venezuela: An Example of an Approach to Applying Social Psychology', *Spanish Language Psychology*, 2: 185–92.

Sauers, D. (1993) 'Managing Workforce Diversity: A Challenge for New Zealand Business in the 1990s', *Asia Pacific Journal of Human Resource*, 31(3): 44–51.
Schein, E. (1978) 'Organizational Socialization and the Profession of Management'. In Elbing, A. (ed.) *Behavioural Decisions in Organizations*, 2nd edition. Glenview, Ill: Scott, Foresman, pp. 308–21.
Schwarzwald, J. and Hoffman, M.A. (1993) 'Academic Status and Ethnicity as a Determinant of Social Acceptance', *Journal of Cross-cultural Psychology*, 24(1): 71–80.
Scotton, C.M. (1977) 'Linguistic Performance as a Socioeconomic Indicator', *The Journal of Social Psychology*, 102: 35–45.
Segall, M.H., Dasen, P.R., Berry, J.W. and Poortinga, Y.H. (1990) *Human Behaviour in Global Perspective*. New York, Oxford, Sydney: Pergamon Press.
Singer, M.R. (1987) *Intercultural Communication: A Perceptual Approach*, Englewood Cliffs, NJ: Prentice-Hall.
Smith, W.R. (1975) 'Beyond the Plural Society: Economics and Ethnicity in Middle American Towns', *Ethnology*, 14: 225–44.
Stening, B.W. (1979) 'Problems in Cross-Cultural Contact: A Literature Review', *Internal Journal of Intercultural Relations*, 3: 269–313.
Stephen, W.G. and Stephen, C.W. (1985) 'Intergroup Anxiety', *Journal of Social Issues*, 41: 157–76.
Stephen, W.G. and Stephen, C.W. (1989) 'Antecedents of Intergroup Anxiety in Asian-Americans and Hispanic-Americans', *International Journal of Intercultural Relations*, 13(2): 203–19.
Stephenson, K. and Krebs, V. (1993) 'A More Accurate Way to Measure Diversity', *Personnel Journal*, October: 66–74.
Summer, W.G. (1906) *Folkways*. Boston, MA: Ginn.
Szalay, L. and Inn, a. (1988) 'Cross-Cultural Adaptation and Diversity: Hispanic Americans'. In Kim, Y.Y. and Gudykunst, W.B. (eds) *Cross-Cultural Adaptation: Current Approaches*. Newbury Park, CA: Sage.
Tajfel, H. (1969) 'Cognitive Aspects of Prejudice', *Journal of Social Issues*, 25: 79–97.
Tanaka, T., Takai, J., Kohyama, T. and Fujihara, T. (1994) 'Adjustment Patterns of International Students in Japan', *International Journal of Intercultural Relations*, 18(1): 55–75.
Tannen, D. (1990) *You Just Don't Understand: Men and Women in Conversation*. New York: Ballantine Books.
Thomas, D.A. (1993) 'Racial Dynamics in Cross-Race Developmental Relationships', *Administrative Science Quarterly*, 38: 169–94.
Thomas, R.R. (1990) 'From Affirmative Action to Affirmative Diversity', *Harvard Business Review*, 2: 107–17.
Tomeh, A. and Gallant, C. (1984) 'Familial Sex Role Attitudes: A French Sample', *Journal of Comparative Family Studies*, 15: 389–405.
Torbiorn, I. (1982) *Living Abroad: Personal Adjustment and Personnel Policy in the Overseas Setting*. New York: Wiley.
Triandis, H. (1976) *Interpersonal Behaviour*, Monterey, CA: Brooks/ Cole.
Triandis, H. (1977) 'Subjective Culture and Interpersonal Relations across Cultures'. In Loeb-Adler, L. (ed.) *Issues in Cross-cultural Research. Annals of the New York Academy of Sciences*, 285: 418–34.
Triandis, H.C. and Davis, E.E. (1965) 'Race and Beliefs as Determinants of Behavioural Intentions', *Journal of Personality and Social Psychology*, 2: 715–25.
Triandis, H.C. and Triandis, L.M. (1960) 'Race, Social Class, Religion, and Nationality as Determinants of Social Distance', *Journal of Abnormal and Social Psychology*, 61: 110–18.
Triandis, H.C., Brislin, R. and Hui, C.H. (1988) 'Cross-Cultural Training across the Individualism-Collectivism Divide', *International Journal of Intercultural Relations*, 12: 269–89.

Triandis, H.C., Kurowski, A.T. and Chan, D.K.S. (1993) 'Extracting the Emics of Diversity', *International Journal of Intercultural Relations*, 17: 217–34.

Tsui, A.S., Egan, T.D. and O'Reilly, C.A. (1992) 'Being Different: Relational Demography and Organizational Attachment', *Administrative Science Quarterly*, 37: 549–79.

Tung, R.L. (1993) 'Managing Cross-National and Intra-National Diversity', *Human Resource Management*, 32(4): 461–77.

Wallace, J. and Wimalatissa, W. (1992) 'Mapping Mutual Perceptions of Managerial Behaviour in Multicultural Settings'. Paper presented at the Australia New Zealand Academy of Management Conference, University of Western Sydney, Nepean, 6–9 December.

Ward, C. and Searle, W. (1991) 'The Impact of Value Discrepancies and Cultural Identity on Psychological and Sociocultural Adjustment of Sojourners', *International Journal of Intercultural Relations*, 15: 209–55.

Waters, H. (1992) 'Race, Culture and Interpersonal Conflict', *International Journal of Intercultural Relations*, 16: 437–54.

Westwood, R.I. and Leung, S.M. (1992) 'Expatriate Female Managers In Hong Kong: A *Gweipo*, Not a Woman', *Proceedings of the First International Conference on Expatriate Management*, Hong Kong, 23–25 November: 157–68.

Wilson, D. and Lavelle, S. (1990) 'Interracial Frendship in a Zimbabwean Primary School', *The Journal of Social Psychology*, 130(1): 111–13.

Wiseman, R.L., Hammer, M.R. and Nishida, H. (1989) 'Predictors of Intercultural Communication Competence', *International Journal of Intercultural Relations*, 13: 349–70.

Witte, K. (1993) 'A Theory of Cognition and Negative Affect: Extending Gudykunst and Hammer's Theory of Uncertainty and Anxiety Reduction', *International Journal of Intercultural Relations*, 17: 197–215.

Yum, J.O. (1982) 'Communication Diversity and Information Acquisition among Korean Immigrants in Hawaii', *Human Communication Research*, 8: 154–69.

Zajonic, R.B. (1968) 'Attitudinal Effects of Mere Exposure', *Journal of Personality and Social Psychology*, 9(2): 1–27.

[20]

Pergamon

European Management Journal Vol. 15, No. 6, pp. 677–685, 1997

0263-2373/97 $17.00 + 0.00

PII: S0263-2373(97)00051-0

Being Flexible and Accommodating Diversity: The Challenge for Multinational Management

DENICE WELCH and LAWRENCE WELCH, *Norwegian School of Management, Oslo*

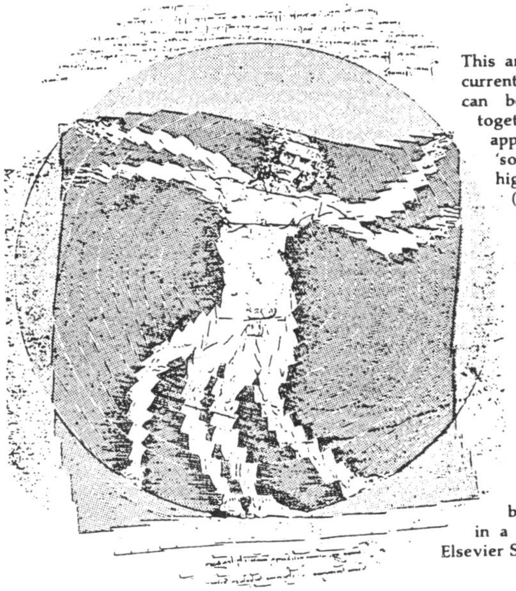

This article presents an opposing view to the current populist position that corporate culture can be utilised to bind the multinational together. It critically examines the appropriateness of corporate culture as a 'soft' control mechanism, concluding that highly committed, inculcated managers (believers) may actually be a barrier to the goals of flexibility, responsiveness and innovativeness in the face of rapidly changing, diverse global operations. However, the calculatively compliant manager is not proferred as an alternative. Rather, we argue that the quest for conformity to a given corporate culture may be counter-productive. The real challenge for multinationals is to develop mechanisms that encourage mixed voices and messages, and support a diversity of perspectives. It is suggested that multinationals might even look at the university model, in which it has long been recognised that knowledge advances in a climate of critique and dissent. © 1997 Elsevier Science Ltd

Managing a large multinational in the 1990s presents a paradox: simultaneously thinking globally while acting locally, in a way that encourages corporate learning and competitiveness. As a way of coping with this paradox, various writers advocate that multinational corporations should be restructured: removing layers of hierarchy and bureaucracy; delegating so that subsidiary employees are more autonomous in local matters; thus de-emphasising the role of headquarters as the central hub. Through these measures, it is generally argued that the large, dispersed multinational should become more flexible – at times resembling a federation of smaller companies that effectively compete in various markets through swift local responses combined with the benefits of size (see, for example, Bartlett and Ghoshal, 1989; Ghoshal and Bartlett, 1990, 1995a, 1995b; Ghoshal and Nohria, 1993; Hamel and Prahalad, 1994; Hedlund, 1994). The challenge remains, though, of how to manage such an entity. A major concern has been that too much autonomy at the subsidiary level would reduce the power of the centre to control and coordinate global operations. For example, lack of central control may result in negative consequences such as unacceptable levels of duplication, dysfunctional inter-unit rivalry, and even 'rogue' or illegal behaviour (for example, Daiwa Bank: Baker, 1996). Besides, the centre will always find it difficult to abdicate its power to monitor and control subsidiary behaviour.

To offset the potential disadvantages of greater subsidiary autonomy, multinational management has been exhorted to foster horizontal communication through cross-functional and cross-border teamwork, accompanied by informal, personal relationships, and to build a strong corporate culture that would provide the 'glue' to keep the transnational unified behind a common purpose (Ghoshal and Bartlett, 1990). Ghoshal and Nohria (1993: 28) use the term normative integration wherein corporate culture becomes a governance mechanism:

which relies neither on direct headquarters involvement nor on impersonal rules but on the socialization of managers into a set of shared goals, values, and beliefs that then shape their perspectives and behavior.

The logic of these writers' arguments is both persuasive and seemingly simple. By strengthening a company-wide 'sense of belongingness', it should be possible to create an environment wherein employees consistently act in a way that benefits the good of the company as a whole – alleviating the need for direct supervision and rigid rules. As a senior executive of the Swedish multinational Electrolux is quoted as saying:

We increasingly control the organization through the mindset ... If people's mindsets are aligned, they will come up with the same conclusions as you (Lester, 1994: 40).

This line of reasoning builds on the growing interest in the potential use of corporate culture as a 'soft' control mechanism (Alvesson and Berg, 1992; Baliga and Jaeger, 1985; Edstrom and Galbraith, 1977; Hofstede, 1992). While such use might seem attractive from a company perspective, and there has been a growing body of normative literature that advocates cultural control as a management tool (for example, Deal and Kennedy, 1982; Ghoshal and Bartlett, 1995a and 1995b; Kilmann *et al.*, 1985; Peters and Waterman, 1982), many questions remain regarding the use of corporate culture as a control mechanism. Willmott (1993: 517) for example, points out:

Considering the volume and influence of books and articles that celebrate corporate culturism in its various guises, there is a remarkable dearth of serious, critical analysis of this phenomenon.

Therefore, in this article, we critically examine cultural control with particular reference to multinational management. In this context, we do not review the extensive literature on corporate culture, but rather critically examine its feasibility as a multinational control mechanism. We further pose the question: could highly committed, inculcated managers actually be a barrier to flexible multinational management?

Corporate Culture as a Control Mechanism

For the purposes of this article, the term 'corporate culture' is used in its broadest sense, following Fenwick *et al.* (1993: 8): 'it is holistic, historically determined, related to ritual and symbols, socially constructed, "soft" and difficult to change'. Despite the inherent difficulties, there is a widely expressed belief in the ability of management to determine the corporate culture. For instance, Flamholtz (1996) considers that organisational culture is a variable, subject to design, and can be the product of management decision. Further, the perspective of corporate culture as a manageable variable has led to its advocacy as a useful, social control mechanism. To illustrate, Deal and Kennedy (1982: 15) argue:

We think people are a company's greatest resource, and the way to manage them is not directly by computer reports, but by the subtle cues of culture. A strong culture is a powerful lever for guiding behavior; it helps employees do their jobs a little better.

The underlying motive of cultural control, then, is to ensure that employees assume appropriate work behaviours, in such a way as to enable the removal of direct supervision in diverse locations. Employees who adopt appropriate behaviours that are enshrined in corporate norms and values can be trusted to act in the interest of corporate performance. Delegation and decentralisation are therefore considered more feasible options. Thus, corporate culturism expects and requires employees to internalise management driven values; to adopt and cherish them as their own (Willmott, 1993).

Bartlett and Ghoshal (1995: 16) are two authors who take the idea of internalisation to its logical conclusion when they offer the concept of self-discipline:

In a culture based on discipline rather than compliance, individual behaviour tends to be embedded – built from the bottom up rather than imposed or driven from the top down.

The emphasis is on voluntary adherence to corporate norms and expectations that becomes a way of life (Ghoshal and Bartlett, 1994: 97). This may be likened to the concept of 'high commitment management' aimed at producing behaviour which is 'primarily self-regulated rather than controlled by sanctions and pressures external to the individual' (Wood 1996: 41). Clearly, this emphasis has considerable appeal for a multinational in its attempt to develop a unified global entity, with a sense of belongingness, despite its diversity. To realise this goal, however, an MNC's top management has to devise effective means of articulating and disseminating the company's value system (Welch *et al.*, 1994). In fact, the enormity of this task for the CEO of a major multinational is illustrated by Ghoshal and Bartlett (1994: 86) in recounting the experience of ABB:

Barnevik [ABB's CEO] and his top management team have had to redefine key organizational relationships and basic management behaviors, a task that has taken several years to accomplish.

This involved Barnevik and his top managers in much travel (often for more than 200 days a year) and many meetings, as they visited the various ABB operations, demonstrating the managerial time and resources that may be tied up in the effort to transmit corporate values.

To assist in disseminating the desired value system, proponents of corporate culture as a control mechanism advocate the use of a 'cascading' process, where top management articulate the key elements of the corporate value system to senior managers, who then return to their units and repeat the message to their managers, and so on, down the line. However, transmitting top management expectations is only part of the process of cultural control. It also depends on people in key positions being able to convince those below them that the espoused corporate values are worthy of acceptance, so that the real objective – adoption of consistent, appropriate work behaviours – is achieved throughout the global operations. A variety of organizational programmes are often introduced to support the inculcation agenda: promotion and reward systems, company training programmes, company videos and meetings, internal newsletters and other forms of communication, and artifacts (logos, slogans, etc.). The aim is a consistent, aligned programme to reinforce the value system driven by top management.

Apart from the time and resources required to implement, building mutual confidence or trust between managers and employees, essential for effective coordinated action (McAllister, 1995), is not without its problems, particularly as management has to be willing to relinquish some of its direct control. These challenges perhaps can be best illustrated through a brief discussion of two recent workplace trends: empowerment and restructuring. Conformity to corporate norms and values would appear to underpin the concept of empowerment. Indeed, it could be argued that empowerment is a logical outcome of inculcation: if employees are imbued with the precepts of corporate norms and values, then the need for direct supervision will diminish, because devolution of responsibility and autonomy down the line is possible as inculcated employees can be trusted to adopt desired work behaviours.

However, removal of direct supervision does not mean the removal of managerial control. In fact, in the effort to maintain control, some managerial actions may run counter to the principles of empowerment even when top management is seeking to enshrine it into the corporate ideology (Hendry, 1995). For example, in their study of middle managers in a downsizing company, O'Neill and Lenn (1995: 25) found that, while recognising the importance of empowerment, the managers interviewed concluded that the company fell short of that objective. One interviewee is quoted as saying:

We talk about empowerment, but we've still got shackles on people. We have to go to senior managers for permission, and they don't want to approve anything.

The reluctance of middle and upper-level management to relinquish their power can become a strong source of resistance to change (Donkin, 1994; Marschan *et al.*, 1996), indicating also the strength of a prevailing culture, and the difficulty of engineering cultural change.

That managerial control remains an important issue, even when employee involvement in activities and decision-making is espoused, is further illustrated in the way in which companies have sought to impart a 'quality' ethos throughout their operations. According to Beardwell and Holden (1994: 584):

The compulsory nature of TQM [total quality management] with its top-down overtones suggests a system whereby worker empowerment is restricted very much within the boundaries set by management.

Whether it is empowerment, TQM, or any other system or programme, if it is seen as important to company performance, management will want to control the process, and thus display a high level of reluctance in relying on soft control measures. In fact, what we tend to see in the company examples proferred in the literature is the 'soft' operating (almost incongruously) alongside the 'hard'. Even in the much-vaunted ABB case, Ghoshal and Bartlett (1995a: 95) offer an example of this 'doublespeak'. A member of ABB's top-level executive committee explains his handling of a problem of overlapping facilities in Europe. Rather than directing the process:

he turned the problem over to the managers, told them which options were unacceptable, and gave them a tight deadline to find a solution. When he realized that some managers were not fully committed to the kind of collaboration he was urging on his team, he replaced them.

Such mixed signals may interfere with the required level of trust that underscores the use of 'soft' control measures. That is, management actions may, in fact, signal 'we do not trust' (McAllister, 1995; Wood, 1996), producing an increase in cynicism, even parody, among employees about the corporate value system.[1]

As important, the trend towards reliance on adherence to corporate values as a soft control mechanism has been developing at a time of widespread organisational restructuring that has resulted in large-scale 'downsizing' and its associated job-shedding, as companies seek to become less hierarchical, and more competitive through disposal of non-core activities. According to emerging research evidence on the employment consequences of industry restructuring, the traditional psychological contract between organisations and their employees has been changing dramatically with a substantial drop in job security and permanence (Hiltrop, 1995; O'Neil and Lenn, 1995; Holbeche, 1994). An effect may well be wider questioning of fundamental corporate values and strategies, making it difficult for individual managers to internalise the value system, whatever they might publicly espouse. Fear of unemployment or 'survivor's guilt' may produce the ostensible required behaviours but employees who perceive large-scale redundancies as a severing of trust are likely to find it difficult to give unquestioning loyalty to the company. In general, there appears to be a developing contradiction between managerial espousal and action that is likely to have consequences for the ability of companies to use corporate culture as a means of 'soft' control (Holden, 1996; Willmott, 1993).

Commitment to the Corporate Value System?

Even if one accepts the validity, legitimacy, and ethics, of cultural control, a central issue – that of the degree (or level) of internalisation – remains. The issue of the degree of commitment to 'shared values' has received little consideration, especially in the literature on corporate culture as an inimitible, sustainable competitive advantage (e.g. Barney, 1986), and corporate culture as the MNC's unifying glue (e.g. Ghoshal and Bartlett, 1990; Ghoshal and Nohria, 1993; Hedlund, 1986). Perhaps this omission is partly due to the fact that MNCs would be hard pressed to define what is the desired degree of internalisation of corporate values, and partly because it would be difficult to accurately gauge the extent of inculcation within a large, dispersed multinational. Essentially, is it possible, even desirable, to achieve the same level of commitment to corporate values throughout a large multinational to the extent that every employee has fully internalised the corporate value system, regardless of nationality, age, gender, educational background, skill level, and status with the MNC? A related question is the degree of commitment required by those in positions of influence: that is, to what extent should those entrusted with transmitting values have to first internalise them in order to achieve the desired outcomes in terms of appropriate work behaviour?

The remainder of this article, then, focuses on the above questions regarding the degree of commitment to corporate values. To this end, we draw an analogy between corporate culture and religious faith, given the emphasis in the cultural control literature on the role of internalisation of corporate values (quasi-belief system) in driving the actions of employees (see, for example, Willmott, 1993; and Bartlett and Ghoshal, 1995, on self-discipline). The analogy is strengthened when one looks at the synonyms for commitment; duty, obligation, faithfulness, devotion, pledge, resolution, even imprisonment.

In reality, despite what overt behavioural displays and verbal utterances might indicate, people are bound to differ in the extent to which they internalise the company's values and are thereby committed to upholding them. As with religious faith, there is a wide range of possible degrees of commitment to corporate values. Figure 1 demonstrates this variation. It is presented as a way of illustrating the different degrees of commitment that may be encountered, and as a basis for discussion. This range is shown as a continuum from zealot to heretic. Taking the extremes, a *zealot* strongly believes in the company's values and, therefore, is highly committed to upholding them. Such a person has not only internalised corporate values but exhibits almost missionary zeal in seeking to convert others by whatever means available, including coercion. Conversely, the *heretic* does not believe in the company's value system and is highly uncommitted, to an extent that (s)he is prepared to openly challenge the appropriateness of the

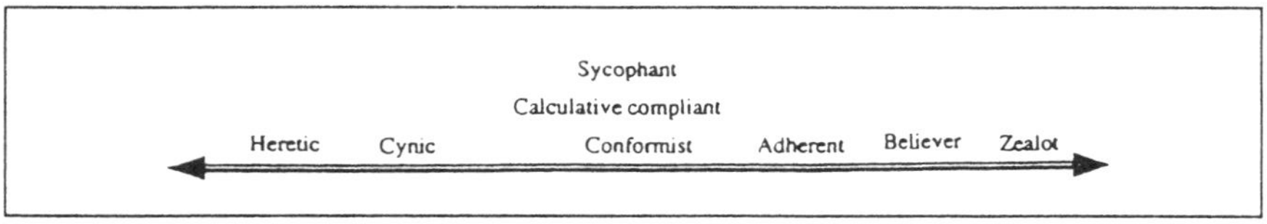

Figure 1 Commitment to Corporate Value System

corporate culture (or at least key elements of it) and confront others with an alternative view.

It should be expected that many, if not most, employees, including upper level managers, are likely to fall between the two extremes, although exhibiting different behavioural responses reflecting the varying degrees of commitment to the company value system, as shown in Figure 1. Some individuals could be classified as *believers*: those who internalise corporate values, are committed to them, but do not seek to inculcate others in the same way as the highly committed zealot. *Adherents* may have a relatively 'lukewarm' belief in the corporate value system but are readily able to rationalise their commitment to the espoused values. These two groups lie to the right of centre on the continuum.

The mere fact that senior management articulates and actively promotes a certain set of corporate values, reinforced through actions, particularly those relating to promotion and reward, will almost automatically ensure that the majority of personnel will at least overtly espouse adoption, and even engage in appropriate behaviours. In other words, we suggest that most tend to be clustered in the middle of the continuum. There are a number of variants within this broad compliant group. As Willmott (1993: 537) argues: 'Instead of a deep identification with corporate values there can be selective, calculative compliance'. Individuals who are *calculatively compliant* are neither believers nor disbelievers, but simply recognise where their best interests lie. They will espouse shared values and engage in appropriate behaviours in order to protect their jobs, enhance their careers, obtain rewards, etc. For example, Rousseau (1996: 51) quotes a Xerox executive who explains his behavioural change during that company's major re-orientation:

> *I never paid much attention the first time through, since I thought this thing would be gone by now, I thought it was another ice cream flavor. But I got scared when I saw that [the new CEO] had picked it up with vigor. So we know we can't hide in the weeds anymore.*

Other individuals could be termed *conformists*. They tend to give little forethought: they 'know the score' and simply deliver. Bordering on these groups are *sycophants* who 'model themselves on the boss in order to enhance their promotion chances' (Glaister and Thwaites, 1993: 27).

To the left of centre on our continuum are the *cynics*. This group may exhibit similar behavioural patterns to the compliant bulk but hold contrary views and thus are not committed to the corporate value system. Such persons will often express concerns about the prevailing wisdom in situations where they feel secure from retribution. In particular situations, they may mock the value system, hold it up to ridicule, or make it the butt of humour. It is even feasible that a strong underground counter-culture emerges, as was apparent in the former socialist economies of Eastern Europe. Improved personal electronic communication systems within MNCs have facilitated the international transfer of various forms of parody and counter-cultures.[2] In this respect, such people are acting to negate the impact that the mandated value system may have within the organisation. At the extreme, they may act as 'value saboteurs'. The difference between the cynic and the heretic is the extent of disbelief and lack of commitment, combined with the preparedness to be open and vocal.

The idea of a consistent set of internalised corporate values among staff would appear to be an unattainable goal

It could be expected that there is considerable movement along the continuum by different individuals over time, depending on their experience within the company, such as positive or negative reinforcement of the desired or undesired behaviours. For example, a heretic faced with possible dismissal from the company for openly challenging the prevailing wisdom may quickly move underground, becoming a 'value subversive' or 'saboteur'. There may also be those who begin as cynics but gradually find that a new value emphasis (such as customer service) produces positive results on the job. This may in turn increase the level of work satisfaction, so that these persons begin to internalise the corporate value system to the point of becoming 'adherents'.

Other employees may find that their ready commitment and support, even belief, is tested by experiences where they have tried to adopt and adhere to the dictates of the corporate value system but find that they are 'punished' for so doing. For example, in applying the 'quality value system', a department manager may reject substandard components, thereby causing delays in delivery to customers. Instead of being praised for this action, the manager is sanctioned, and may conclude that the values which are stressed by the company 'are a joke', a sentiment that may be covertly expressed to avoid further 'punishment'. As discussed earlier, the pressure for reoganisation forced by market changes may be felt at the individual level, causing adjustment in the degree of personal commitment to the corporate value system. Preliminary studies of the consequences of downsizing have shown a redrawing of the psychological contract, and a shift in loyalty away from the company (Holbeche, 1994; Hiltrop, 1995). In the terms of Figure 1, a 'believer' may shift towards 'calculative compliant' behaviour, or an even more extreme position towards the left of the continuum. Other factors may also come into play: such as, the individual's age, tenure and position in the company, financial circumstances, experience in other firms, and professional affiliation.

Compounding Elements for the MNC

Given the many different responses and positions that individuals may assume, the idea of a consistent set of internalized corporate values among staff would appear to be an unattainable goal. Apart from the individual and organisational factors discussed above, and the role played by top management in shaping and transferring corporate culture, external elements intervene to affect the degree of commitment to corporate culture. National culture is one such element. The growing body of research on subsidiary inculcation indicates the difficulties that multinationals face in attempting to impose parent company values on their diverse foreign affiliates (see for example, Evans, 1986; Forsgren and Pahlberg, 1991; Hofstede, 1980; Rosenzweig and Singh, 1991; Trompenaars 1993). Even though the transfer of expatriates may be used to assist in normative control, there is no guarantee that this will produce the degree of commitment to a shared corporate culture to the extent considered appropriate for corporate culture control purposes. Ferner and Edwards (1995: 243) exemplify this in relating the control experiences of British MNEs, quoting one Italian manager:

My former boss, an American, suddenly decided to cut costs. He issued the instructions and expected them to be followed but it did not happen because the culture was not there. We just put the letters away in a drawer. He was surprised at this outcome, and no savings were made.

The variety of possible foreign operation modes adds a further element of complexity to the issue of shared corporate values. The literature on international joint ventures is replete with examples of clashes of corporate and national cultures within the joint venture, and their negative impact on joint venture operations (see for example Harrigan 1996). Building a cohesive value system becomes even more problematic when the parent company has minority or no equity interest through modes such as licensing, management contracts, and some forms of franchising. In the broader literature on corporate values as a 'soft' control mechanism in MNCs, the impact of such alternative modes has been virtually ignored.

Implications for Multinational Management

The corporate environment faced by MNCs is characterised by factors such as diversity, changeability, and global competitiveness, demanding a high level of flexibility in multinational operations. The problem for MNCs though is that responses to environmental changes may require alterations in the company's value profile. Adjustments could be minor – such as a strengthening of the emphasis on customer satisfaction – through to radical changes: for example, when an organic organisation becomes more mechanistic, moving from informal to tight, formal control. Such radical changes are often evidenced in situations where there is a change in Chief Executive Officer; or in mergers and acquisitions, where employees are faced with the reconstruction, and even sometimes the repudiation, of past, enshrined value systems (Nahavandi and Malekzadeh, 1988). For cultural change to be effectively enacted throughout the multinational, managers in a wide variety of locations, operating in diverse cultures, need to be able to communicate and implement the changes decided upon at the global level. To do so, managers have to be able to take new approaches, follow new strategies, and redirect staff objectives; that is, the flexible multinational would seem to require flexible managers.

At a broader level, it is recognised within the literature that it is very difficult to change corporate culture (Alvesson, 1989), and as Weick (1985: 385) points out, while culture may be valued because it provides coherence and meaning, it can also be a liability: 'A coherent statement of who we are makes it harder for us to become something else'. Indeed, the more committed the person, the more resistant he or she will be to changes made to the corporate value system. In terms of Figure 1, when flexibility is demanded, the 'believer' can become a hindrance. An individual manager may have been profoundly influenced by the past corporate inculcation process and achieved status through his adoption, personal adherence, and evangelism of the prevailing value system. If the manager believes that (s)he is now being asked to compromise heretofore strongly-held personal beliefs, he may well resist the change, perhaps openly, or may instead seek to sabotage the new initiatives, or resign. There could well seem to be a loss of face on the part of such managers in front of subordinates as a result of the company's change in direction. As Green (1988: 124) has argued:

How can people who are reared within a particular value and belief system and who are judged according to their adherence to the rules, then turn round and overthrow the system that in nurturing them has also enchained them?

In terms of the corporate value system, the calculatively compliant person would seem to fit the bill as this type of individual is able to exhibit the new, appropriate behaviours when it becomes evident the self-interest requires these changes. Such a response could be described as 'commitment-for-hire'. Some of the best examples of this type of flexibility are professional football and basketball players who frequently switch teams and have little difficulty in quickly shifting loyalties. Indeed, using the 'free agent' analogy, Hirsch (1987) suggests that managers might likewise regard themselves as primarily members of a profession and, in the light of changes in employment conditions, the company connection might well take second place.

Similarly, it could be argued that the mutlinational is better served by having managers who are able to 'up anchor and reanchor' in a new value system, and do so without incurring psychological discomfort. As a consequence, such a person is able to easily communicate the 'value shift' to subordinates. While this may appear calculative in the extreme, in fact such a manager is being totally consistent in his allegiance to the company: if the company wants X today and Z tomorrow, then the company will be fully supported in this without the manager experiencing cognitive dissonance as a result of the inevitable sudden shifts in the 'value' wind. In this sense, the person is not merely being pragmatic or calculative, but is acting consistently. From the perspective of MNC top management, 'flexible loyalty' may be preferred, rather than strong commitment to espoused values. In fact, one could argue that the 'zealots' and 'believers' in Figure 1 are the most dangerous for company health because of the inherent difficulty these persons may encounter in adapting to alterations in the corporate value system, and a range of associated changes.

Conclusion

Over the centuries, various organisations and regimes have attempted to control mindsets without success. The collapse of the former Soviet Union is a recent example of this. Companies, management consultants and some researchers would do well to remember the lessons of history in this regard. It is somewhat paradoxical that attempts at control of people's mindsets are offered as a modern multinational management solution without more rigorous investigation of its associated psychological, behavioural and ethical implications, and without reference to broader organizational and societal considerations. This paper represents an attempt to draw attention to the need for debate on this issue.

When one critically examines the idea of shared corporate values as an MNC control mechanism, it would appear that little has changed over the years. Like its precursors, the modern multinational seeks to control the behaviour of its employees in order to achieve its goals. Bartlett and Ghoshal (1995: 16) illustrate this through their example from Corning:

To build self-discipline, Houghton (new CEO) would simply walk out on presentations when managers were unable to define exactly how they would meet their targets, and he refused to consider bonuses for promotions for those who did not deliver on promised performance.

Stripped to its basics, the concept of 'self-discipline', as presented, appears to be little more than a reclothing of *The Organisation Man* (Whyte, 1956).

In fact, companies might be disturbed by the results of their cultural inculcation programmes should they achieve their goal: a workforce of 'believers'. As argued above, in the multinational world of diversity, change and shifting value emphases, 'believers' could become a barrier to necessary change within the organisation. In such circumstances, the MNC needs people who are able to be flexible and readily adapt to the changing corporate climate and requirements of its external environment. The calculatively compliant manager might therefore be regarded as more appropriate to the multinational's need for flexibility rather than a 'believer'. However, while this type of individual – the ultimate flexible manager – may assist in the quest for responsiveness and control, the dangers of conformity and lack of innovativeness may even be enhanced.

The focus of this article has been to explore the feasibility of corporate culture as a soft control mechanism for multinationals. Based on the analysis presented herein, we question the current populist position that corporate culture can be utilised, particularly by multinationals, to bind the organisation together, and be part of a company's sustainable competitive advantage. There is considerable debate in the corporate culture literature about whether corporate culture can be managed. For example, Green (1988: 121, 124) states:

You do not control culture, at best you shape it ... If culture could be levered into shape then, by now, someone would have discovered the method. The metaphors of fine-tuning and fit which abound in much of the (structural static) literature on culture and strategy are altogether inappropriate for something as complex as human social systems.

We would go further, though, and suggest that the real issue is *not* the use of corporate culture as a 'soft' control mechanism but, rather, how can a multinational achieve the desired extent of flexibility, responsiveness and innovativeness. The relentless pursuit of shared values may well be a distraction in which MNCs can ill afford to indulge. Instead, multinationals need to be as serious about encouraging and sponsoring critique and diversity as they appear to have been about their corporate value systems. In cybernetics, the Law of Requisite Variety, stresses the importance of internal variety if an organism is to successfully adapt to its external environment, as change ensues (Crainer, 1996: 17). Toleration of a certain level of conflict and deviant behaviour might assist in overcoming undue conformity but, companies may need to go much further: to welcome and learn from independent and challenging perspectives within the organisation so that they can function more effectively and responsively in diverse environments. We suggest that concentration on the development of processes and practices that encourage the airing of, and response to, mixed voices and messages arising from the various parts of the multinational would be more beneficial to competitive positioning than the current fixation on consistent, shared, corporate values.

Within its widespread network, the multinational is in a unique position to experiment with different approaches, for example, in far-flung subsidiaries, while at the same time maintaining a relatively consistent overall position.

In this respect, one might urge a somewhat revolutionary approach: that multinationals look at the ultimate knowledge institutions – universities – where constant challenge to prevailing paradigms is the essence of their knowledge activities, through the accommodation of dissent, alternative views, and different theories. There is, in universities, and perhaps should be in multinationals, a recognition that knowledge will not advance without challenge. Accommodating challenge, though, is a difficult issue for upper level managers and chief executive officers in modern multinationals. One might even argue that the positions have now been reversed: it is top management, shielded from questioning voices within the organisation, who now reside in the 'ivory tower', not the university professor.

Notes

1. One could suggest here that the seemingly universal appeal of the cartoon strip 'Dilbert', created by Adams (1996), reflects a readiness to embrace the parody of such mixed messages sent by management in their attempts to manage the corporate value system as a soft control mechanism.
2. In his book, *The Dilbert Principle*, Scott Adams (1996) cites examples people have sent to him via electronic mail.

References

Adams, S. (1996) *The Dilbert Principle*. HarperBusiness, New York.

Alvesson, M. (1989) The culture perspective on organizations: instrumental values and basic features of culture. *Scandinavian Journal of Management* **5**(2), 123–136.

Alvesson, M. and Berg, P.O. (1992) *Corporate Culture and Organizational Symbolism*. Walter de Gruyter, Berlin.

Baliga, A. and Jaeger, B.R. (1985) Control systems and strategic adaptation: lessons from the Japanese experience. *Strategic Management Journal* **6**(2), 115–134.

Barney, J.B. (1986) Organizational culture: can it be a source of sustained competitive advantage? *Academy of Management Review* **11**(3), 656–665.

Bartlett, C. and Ghoshal, S. (1989) *Managing Across Borders: The Transnational Solution*. Harvard Business School Press, Boston.

Bartlett, C. and Ghoshal, S. (1995) Rebuilding behavioral context: turn process reengineering into people rejuvenation. *Sloan Management Review* **37**(1), 11–23.

Baker, G. (1996) Sumitomo buys Daiwa's US assets for $60m. *Financial Times* January 30, 1.

Beardwell, I. and Holden, L. (1994) *Human Resource Management: A Contemporary Perspective*. Pitman, London.

Crainer, S. (1996) *Key Management Ideas*. Pitman, London.

Deal, T. and Kennedy, A.A. (1982) *Corporate Cultures. The Rites and Rituals of Corporate Life*. Addison-Wesley, Reading, MA.

Donkin, R. (1994) Empowerment in virgin territory. *Financial Times* May, 27.

Edstrom, A. and Galbraith, J.R. (1977) Transfers of managers as a coordination and control strategy in multinational organizations. *Administrative Science Quarterly* **22**(2), 248–263.

Evans, P. (1986) The strategic outcomes of human resource management. *Human Resource Management* **25**(1), 149–167.

Fenwick, M., Welch, D. and De Cieri, H. (1993) Organizational control through staff transfers: a concept revisited. Paper presented at the 19th European International Business Association Annual Meeting, Lisbon, 12–14 December.

Ferner, A. and Edwards, P. (1995) Power and the diffusion of organizational change within multinational enterprises. *European Journal of Industrial Relations* **1**(2), 229–257.

Flamholtz, E. (1996) Effective organizational control: a framework, applications, and implications. *European Management Journal*, **14**(6), 596–611.

Forsgren, M. and Pahlberg, C. (1991) Managing international networks. Paper presented at the 7th I.M.P. Conference on International Business Networks: Evolution, Structure and Management, Uppsala, Sweden, 6–8 September.

Ghoshal, S. and Bartlett, C.A. (1990) The multinational corporation as an interorganizational network. *Academy of Management Review* **15**(4), 603–625.

Ghoshal, S. and Bartlett, C.A. (1994) Linking organizational context and managerial action: the dimensions of quality of management. *Strategic Management Journal* **15**, 91–112.

Ghoshal, S. and Bartlett, C.A. (1995a) Changing the role of top management: beyond structure to processes. *Harvard Business Review* January–February, 86–96.

Ghoshal, S. and Bartlett, C.A. (1995b) Building the entrepreneurial corporation: new organizational processes, new managerial tasks. *European Management Journal* **13**(2), 139–155.

Ghoshal, S. and Nohria, N. (1993) Horses for courses: organizational forms for multinational corporations. *Sloan Management Review* Winter, 23–35.

Glaister, K. and Thwaites, D. (1993) Managerial perception and organizational strategy. *Journal of General Management* **18**(4), 15–33.

Green, S. (1988) Strategy, organizational culture and symbolism. *Long Range Planning* **21**(4), 121–129.

Hamel, G. and Prahalad, C.K. (1994) *Competing for the Future*. Harvard Business School Press, Boston.

Harrigan, K.R. (1996) *Managing for Joint Venture Success*. Lexington, Boston.

Hedlund, G. (1986) The hypermodern MNC – a heterarchy? *Human Resource Management* **25**(1), 9–35.

Hedlund, G. (1994) A model of knowledge management and the N-form corporation. *Strategic Management Journal* **15**, 73–90.

Hendry, J. (1995) Process reengineering and the dynamic balance of the organisation. *European Management Journal* **13**(1), 52–57.

Hiltrop, J- M. (1995) The changing psychological contract: the human resource challenge of the 1990s. *European Management Journal* **13**(3), 286–294.

Hirsch, P. (1987) *Pack Your Own Parachute*. Addison-Wesley, Reading, MA.

Hofstede, G. (1980) *Culture's Consequences*. Sage, Beverly Hills, CA.

Hofstede, G. (1992) *Cultures and Organizations: Software of the Mind*. McGraw-Hill, London.

Holbeche, L. (1994) *Career Development in Flatter Structures*, Research Report. Roffey Park Management Institute, Horsham, West Sussex.

Holden, L. (1996) HRM and employment involvement in Britain and Sweden: a comparative study. *International Journal of Human Resource Management* **7**(1), 59–81.

Kilmann, R., Saxton, M.L., Serpa, R. and Associates. (1985) *Gaining Control of the Corporate Culture*. Jossey-Bass, San Francisco.

Lester, T. (1994) Close the personnel department? *International Management* April, 40–41.

McAllister, D.J. (1995) Affect- and cognition-based trust as foundations for interpersonal cooperation in organizations. *Acadmy of Management Journal* **38**(1), 24–69.

Marschan, R., Welch, D. and Welch, L. (1996) Control in less-hierarchical multinationals: the role of personal networks and informal communication. *International Business Review* **5**(2), 137–150.

Nahavandi, A. and Malekzadeh, A.R. (1988) Acculturation in mergers and acquisition. *Academy of Management Review* **13**(1), 79–90.

O'Neill, H.M., and Lenn, D.J. (1995) Voices of survivors: words that downsizing CEOs should hear. *Academy of Management Executive* **9**(4), 23–33.

Peters, T. and Waterman, R. (1982) *In Search of Excellence*. Harper and Row, New York.

Rosenzweig, P.M. and Singh, I. V. (1991) Organizational environments and the multinational enterprise. *Academy of Management Review* **16**(2), 340–361.

Rousseau, D.M. (1996) Changing the deal while keeping the people. *Academy of Management Executive* **10**(1), 50–58.

Trompenaars, F. (1993) *Riding the Waves of Culture: Understanding Cultural Diversity in Business*. Nicholas Brealey, London.

Welch, D., Fenwick, M. and De Cieri, H. (1994) Staff transfers as a control strategy: an exploratory study of two Australian organizations. *International Journal of Human Resource Management* **5**(2), 473–489.

Weick, K.E. (1985) The significance of corporate culture. In *Organizational Culture* P.J. Frost *et al*. Sage Publications, Newbury Park.

Whyte, W.H. (1956) *The Organisation Man*. Simon and Schuster, New York.

Willmott, H. (1993) Strength is ignorance; slavery is freedom: managing culture in modern organisations. *Journal of Management Studies* **30**(4), 515–551.

Wood, S. (1996) High commitment management and unionization in the UK. *International Journal of Human Resource Management* **5**(2), 51–68.

DENICE E. WELCH,
Department of Management and Organisation, Norwegian School of Management, P.O. Box 580, N-1301, Sandvika, Norway.

Denice Welch is currently Associate Professor of International Management, Norwegian School of Management in Oslo. Her research interests and publications cover international human resource management, multinational management, and international strategy. She has taught on international business graduate programmes in Australia, Finland and Norway.

LAWRENCE S. WELCH,
Department of Marketing and Logistics, Norwegian School of Management, P.O. Box 580, N-1301, Sandvika, Norway.

Lawrence Welch is Professor of International Marketing, Norwegian School of Management, Oslo. He has published widely on internationalisation issues since the late 1970s, including work with Nordic scholars. Recent research interests include de-internationalisation, export groups, networks, the role of language in multinational management and pre-expatriation issues.

Part IV
Negotiating across Cultures

[21]

Negotiating with "Romans" – Part 1

Stephen E. Weiss

In a global economy, managers constantly negotiate with people from other cultures, whether the issue is coordinating operations within a multinational firm, arranging a joint venture, or convincing a foreign government to approve construction of a plant. Yet managers have had to rely on simplistic formulas — following lists of "dos and don'ts" — or very demanding ones — "doing as the Romans do" — to deal with the cultural aspects of these negotiations. Actually, a number of strategies are available. The author presents these strategies in a framework based on the parties' level of familiarity with each other's cultures and the extent to which they can explicitly coordinate their strategies. These factors determine the subset of strategies that are realistically feasible for an individual manager. Part 2 of this article, which will describe a methodology for choosing among these strategies, will appear in the Spring 1994 issue.

Stephen E. Weiss is associate professor of policy and international business at York University, Faculty of Administrative Studies (Toronto).

"Smith," an American, arrived at the French attorney's Paris office for their first meeting. Their phone conversations had been in French, and Smith, whose experience with the language included ten years of education in the United States, a year of residence in France with a French family, and annual trips to Paris for the previous seven years, expected to use French at this meeting. "Dupont," the Frenchman, introduced himself in French. His demeanor was poised and dignified; his language, deliberate and precise. Smith followed Dupont's lead, and they went on to talk about a mutual acquaintance. After ten minutes, Dupont shifted the topic by inquiring about Smith's previous work in international negotiations. One of Dupont's words — "opérations" — surprised Smith, and he hesitated to respond. In a split second, Dupont, in fluent English, asked: "Would you like to speak in English?"[1]

Smith used the approach to cross-cultural interaction most widely advocated in the West, with a history dating back to St. Augustine: "When in Rome, do as the Romans do." It had seemed to be a reasonable way to convey cooperativeness, sensitivity to French culture, and respect for Dupont as an individual. But Smith overlooked important considerations, as have many other people who continue to recommend or follow this approach.[2]

The need for guidance for cross-cultural negotiators is clear. Every negotiator belongs to a group or society with its own system of knowledge about social interaction — its own "script" for behavior.[3] Whether the boundaries of the group are ethnic, organizational, ideological, or national, its culture influences members' negotiations — through their conceptualizations of the process, the ends they target, the means they use, and the expectations they hold of counterparts' behavior. There is ample evidence that such negotiation rules and practices vary across cultures.[4] Thus cross-cultural negotiators bring into contact unfamiliar and potentially conflicting sets of categories, rules, plans, and behaviors.

Doing as "Romans" do has not usually resolved this conflict effectively. (Throughout this article, the terms "Romans" and "non-Romans" are used as shorthand for "other-culture negotiators" and "own-culture negotiators," respectively.) "Fitting in" requires capabilities that relatively few non-Romans possess; most cultures involve much more than greeting protocols.[5] The approach takes for granted that Romans accept a non-Roman's behaving like a Roman when, actually, many Romans believe in at least some limits for outsiders.[6] Also, the approach presumes, misleadingly, that a Roman will always act Roman with a non-Roman in Rome.

Today's challenges should motivate a cross-cultural

negotiator to search for additional approaches or strategies. An American negotiator may meet on Tuesday with a group of Japanese who speak through an interpreter and meet on Thursday one-on-one with a Japanese who is fluent in English and a long-time personal friend. In addition, geographical referents are blurring: just off of Paris's Boulevard St. Germain, an American can go to a Japanese restaurant in search of Japanese food and customs, yet find there Chinese waiters who speak Chinese to each other and French to their customers. Indeed, Americans negotiate with Japanese not only in Tokyo and Los Angeles but at third sites such as London. They may forgo face-to-face meetings to communicate by fax, E-mail, telephone, or video conference. Some of these negotiators have one day to finalize a sale; others have fourteen months to formulate a joint venture agreement. This variety of people and circumstances calls for more than one strategic approach.

What are the options for conducting negotiations in culturally sensitive ways? What should non-Roman negotiators do, especially when they lack the time and skills available to long-time expatriates?[7] How should the non-Roman businessperson prepare to use a culturally responsive strategy for negotiation with a particular Roman individual or group in a particular set of circumstances?

This article presents a range of eight culturally responsive strategies for Americans and other groups involved in cross-cultural negotiations at home and abroad. The corresponding framework takes into account the varying capabilities of different negotiators across different circumstances and thus provides options for *every* cross-cultural negotiator. Among other benefits, it enables a negotiator to move beyond the popular, one-size-fits-all lists of "dos and don'ts" for negotiating in a particular culture to see that what is appropriate really depends on the negotiating strategy. In short, this article offers the manager a broadened, realistic view of strategies for effective cross-cultural negotiation.

Eight Culturally Responsive Strategies

Stories of cross-cultural conflict — faux pas and "blunders" — abound.[8] They highlight feelings of anxiety, disorientation, misunderstanding, and frustration, and they tempt negotiators to try to minimize apparent behavioral differences by "matching" or "imitating" their counterparts' ways. But there are more fundamental goals for a cross-cultural negotiator.

Consider what often happens when Americans negotiate with Japanese. Viewing negotiation as a process of exchange involving several proposal-counterproposal iterations, Americans inflate their demands in initial proposals and expect later to give and receive concessions. Their Japanese counterparts often do not promptly reciprocate with a counterproposal. Thus the Americans offer concessions, hoping that they will kick the exchange model — "the negotiations" — into gear. The Japanese, however, ask many questions. By the end of the talks, the Americans feel frustrated with the extent of their concessions and conclude that Japanese do not negotiate. Although the Americans may believe that the Japanese are shrewdly trying to determine how much their American counterparts will concede, it is quite likely that these Japanese are operating from a different model of negotiation: negotiation as a process of gathering information, which, when consistent and complete, will reveal a "correct, proper, and reasonable" solution.[9]

Research on communication suggests that the minimal, fundamental goal for non-Romans is to ensure that both sides perceive that the pattern of interaction makes sense.[10] For negotiation to occur, non-Romans must at least recognize those ideas and behaviors that Romans intentionally put forward as part of the negotiation process (and Romans must do the same for non-Romans). Parties must also be able to interpret these behaviors well enough to distinguish common from conflicting positions, to detect movement from positions, and to respond in ways that maintain communication. Yet a non-Roman's own script for negotiation rarely entails the knowledge or skills to make such interpretations and responses.

Figure 1 shows the range of negotiation characteristics that may vary across cultures. The basic concept of the process, for instance, may be one of distributive bargaining, joint problem solving, debate, contingency bargaining, or nondirective discussion. Groups and organizations may select their negotiators for their knowledge, experience, personal attributes, or status. Protocol may range from informal to formal; the desired outcome may range from a contract to an implicit understanding.

A culturally responsive strategy, therefore, should be designed to align the parties' negotiating scripts or otherwise bring about a mutually coherent form of negotiator interaction. This definition does *not* assume that the course of action is entirely premeditated; it can emerge over time. But a culturally responsive strategy does involve a clear goal and does consist of means by which to attain it. Effectively implemented, such a strategy enables the negotiators to convey their respective concerns and to respond to each other's concerns as they attempt to reach agreement.

By contrast, strategies that do not consider cultural factors are naive or misconceived. They may sometimes be successful for non-Romans, but they are hardly a reliable course of action. One such strategy is to deliberately ignore ethnic or other group-based differences and operate as if "business is business anywhere in the world." A "business is business" approach does not avoid culture; it actually represents a culture, one usually associated with U.S. businesspeople or a cosmopolitan elite. Negotiators cannot blithely assume the predominance of this particular business culture amid the multiple cultures represented in their negotiations.

The framework shown in Figure 2 organizes eight culturally responsive strategies according to the negotiator's level of familiarity with the counterpart's culture; the counterpart's familiarity with the negotiator's culture; and the possibility for explicit coordination of approaches.[11] For the sake of clarity, it focuses on negotiations between two parties, each belonging to one predominant culture.

"Familiarity" is a gauge of a party's current knowledge of a culture (in particular, its negotiation scripts) *and* ability to use that knowledge competently in social interactions.[12] Operationally, high familiarity denotes fluency in a predominant Roman language, extensive prior exposure to the culture, and a good track record in previous social interactions with Romans (which includes making correct attributions of their behavior).[13] This is no mean accomplishment; it takes some twenty-four to thirty-six months of gradual adaptation and learning for expatriates to "master" how to behave appropriately.[14] Note that negotiators can consider using the strategies feasible at their level of familiarity and *any* strategies corresponding to lower levels of familiarity.

The strategies in brackets in the figure are those that require coordination between parties. Although all negotiators must ultimately coordinate their approaches with counterparts during the talks, if only tacitly, sometimes parties can explicitly address coordination and coherence issues.

Figure 1 Cultural Characteristics of Negotiation

General Model

1. Basic Concept of Process
   Distributive bargaining / Joint problem-solving / Debate / Contingency bargaining / Nondirective discussion
2. Most Significant Type of Issue
   Substantive / Relationship-based / Procedural / Personal-internal

Role of the Individual

3. Selection of Negotiators
   Knowledge / Negotiating experience / Personal attributes / Status
4. Individuals' Aspirations
   Individual ←→ Community
5. Decision Making in Groups
   Authoritative ←→ Consensual

Interaction: Dispositions

6. Orientation toward Time
   Monochronic ←→ Polychronic
7. Risk-Taking Propensity
   High ←→ Low
8. Bases of Trust
   External sanctions / Other's reputation / Intuition / Shared experiences

Interaction: Process

9. Concern with Protocol
   Informal ←→ Formal
10. Communication Complexity
    Low ←→ High
11. Nature of Persuasion
    Direct experience / Logic / Tradition / Dogma / Emotion / Intuition

Outcome

12. Form of Agreement
    Contractual ←→ Implicit

Source: Adapted from S.E. Weiss with W. Stripp, *Negotiating with Foreign Business Persons* (New York: New York University Graduate School of Business Administration, Working Paper #85-6, 1985), p.10.

Low Familiarity with Counterpart's Culture

The negotiator who has had little experience with a counterpart's culture has a choice of two culturally responsive strategies and, depending on the counterpart's familiarity with the negotiator's culture, a possible third. If the counterpart's familiarity level is low, neither party is well equipped cross-culturally; their interaction can be facilitated by changing the people involved.[15] That is, the negotiator can employ an agent or adviser or involve a mediator. If the counterpart's familiarity level is high, a third strategy becomes feasible: inducing the Roman to follow the negotiating script of one's own cultural group.

• **Employ Agent or Adviser.** To augment his or her own capabilities, a business negotiator can employ cultural experts, translators, outside attorneys, financial advisers, or technical experts who have at least moderate and preferably high familiarity with both the counterpart's and the negotiator's cultures. These experts serve two distinguishable roles, as "agents" who replace the negotiator at the negotiating table or as "advisers" who provide information and recommend courses of action to the negotiator.

In 1986, a U.S. chemical company that had bartered chemicals for tobacco from Zimbabwe hired an American commodities trader in London to negotiate the sale of the tobacco and some chemicals to Egyptian officials and executives. The Egyptians were offering payment in commodities; the U.S. company sought $20 million cash. As an agent, the American trader engaged in lengthy meetings, rounds of thick coffee, and late-night talks with the Egyptians and succeeded in arranging cash sales of the Egyptian commodities to the United Kingdom, Bangladesh, and other countries.[16]

The value of this strategy depends on the agent's attributes. Skilled, reputable agents can interact very effectively with a negotiator's counterpart. However, their employment may give rise to issues of increased structural complexity, trust, and ownership of the process, not to mention possible cultural tensions between principal and agent.[17] Clearly decipherable by a counterpart, this strategy works well when the counterpart accepts it and the particular agent involved.

Employing an adviser involves other actions and effects.

Between 1983 and 1986, IBM prepared proposals for a personal computer plant for approval by Mexico's National Commission on Foreign Investment. The company hired Mexican attorneys, consulted local experts such as the American Chamber of Commerce and U.S. embassy staff, and met with high-level Mexican government officials. These advisers provided information about political and social cultures and the foreign investment review process, access to influential individuals, and assessments of the leanings of key decision makers on the commission.[18]

A negotiator can select this strategy unilaterally and completely control its implementation. Of all eight strategies, this one is the least decipherable, sometimes even undetectable, by the counterpart. It is also uniquely incomplete in that it does not directly provide a script for negotiating. The negotiator must go on to select, with or without the adviser's assistance, a complementary strategy.

• **Involve a Mediator.** The use of go-betweens, middlemen, brokers, and other intermediaries is a common practice within many cultures and represents a potentially effective approach to cross-cultural negotiation as well. It is a joint strategy; both negotiator and counterpart rely on a mutually acceptable third party to facilitate their interaction. In its most obvious form, the strategy involves contacting a mediator prior to negotiations and deliberately bringing him or her into the talks. A mediator may also emerge, as happens when the "introducer" (*shokaisha* in Japanese[19]) who first brought the negotiator to the counterpart continues to play a role or, in team-on-team negotiations, when an individual involved in the talks who does not initially have authority as a mediator, such as an interpreter, becomes a de facto mediator in the

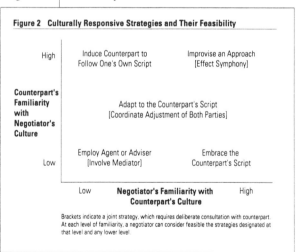

Figure 2 Culturally Responsive Strategies and Their Feasibility

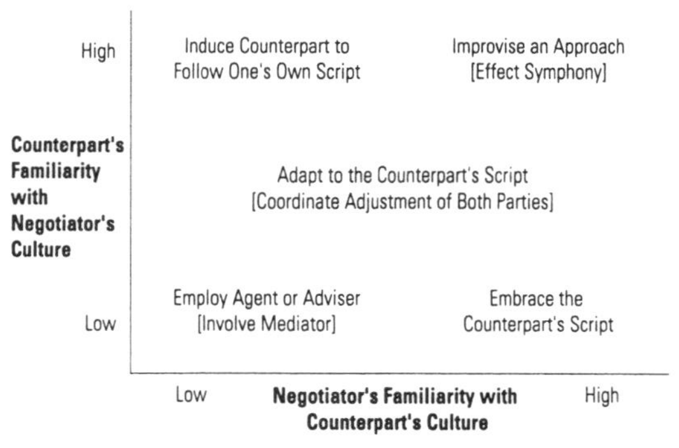

Brackets indicate a joint strategy, which requires deliberate consultation with counterpart. At each level of familiarity, a negotiator can consider feasible the strategies designated at that level and any lower level.

course of the negotiation. Such cross-cultural mediators should be at least moderately and preferably highly familiar with the cultures of both parties.

In the 1950s, an American truck manufacturer negotiated a deal to sell trucks to a Saudi contractor because of the intermediation of Adnan Khashoggi. Khashoggi, the son of the personal physician of the founder of Saudi Arabia, had met the manufacturer while in college in the United States and learned about the contractor's needs upon returning to Saudi Arabia. This was his first "deal," long before his involvement with Lockheed and Northrop. By the 1970s, each of his private jets reportedly contained two wardrobes: "one of three-piece suits, shirts, and ties; . . . the other of white cotton thobes [and] headdresses, . . . the full traditional Arabian regalia."[20]

With this strategy, a negotiator faces some uncertainty about the negotiation process: Will the mediator use one side's negotiation script at the expense of the other's? If the mediator is from a third culture, will he or she use that culture's ways — or introduce something else?[21] In relying on a mediator, the negotiator relinquishes some control of the negotiation. Then again, the mediator can educate the negotiator about the counterpart's culture and bring out ideas and behavior from each side that make the interaction coherent. It is important to find an individual who is not only appropriately skilled but who will also maintain the respect and trust of both parties.[22]

• **Induce the Counterpart to Follow One's Own Script.** Deliberately inducing the counterpart to negotiate according to the model common in one's own culture is feasible when the counterpart is highly familiar with one's culture. Possibilities for inducement range from verbal persuasion to simply acting as if the counterpart will "come along" — as happens when Americans speak English to non-American counterparts known to speak English as a second language.

When U.S.-based ITT and CGE of France conducted merger talks in the mid-1980s, negotiators used "an American business — American M&A [merger and acquisition]" approach, according to French participants. The French went along with it (despite their unfavorable impressions that it consisted of a "vague" general concept of the deal, emphasis on speed, and formulation of long contracts), because only U.S. law and investment firms had the capacity to carry out this highly complex negotiation. Although their motivations are not exactly known, ITT lawyers have stated that their chief negotiator followed their own methodical style, one developed within ITT.[23]

The pros and cons of this strategy hinge on the counterpart's perception of the negotiator's motivations for pursuing it. The counterpart may conclude that the negotiator is naive or deliberately ignorant of cultural differences; arrogant; culturally proud but not antagonistic; or merely using an expedient strategy.[24] It is reported that IBM's Thomas Watson, Sr., once said: "It's easier to teach IBM to a Netherlander than to teach Holland to an American."[25] Using one's own ways could also be the result of mistakenly concluding that the two parties share one culture (e.g., Americans and English-speaking Canadians).

For this strategy to work most effectively, the negotiator should convey that it is not based on a lack of respect for the counterpart or for the counterpart's culture. It is the counterpart, after all, who is being called on to make an extra effort; even with a high level of familiarity with the negotiator's culture, a counterpart usually feels more skilled and at ease with his or her own ways. (Were the counterpart to *offer* to follow the negotiator's script, we would be talking about an embrace strategy by the counterpart, which is described below.)

Moderate Familiarity with Counterpart's Culture

The negotiator who already has had some successful experience with a counterpart's culture gains two more strategic options, provided that the counterpart is at least moderately familiar with the negotiator's culture. The unilateral strategy is to adapt one's usual approach to the counterpart's. The joint version is to coordinate adjustment between the two cultures.

• **Adapt to the Counterpart's Script.** Negotiators often modify their customary behavior by not expressing it to its usual degree, omitting some actions altogether, and following some of the counterpart's ways. The adapt strategy refers to more than this behavior, however; it refers to a broad course of action usually prompted by a deliberate decision to make these modifications.[26]

In the early 1980s, American negotiators in the Toyota-Ford and GM-Toyota talks over car assembly joint ventures prepared by reading books such as James Clavell's Shogun *and Edwin Reischauer's* The Japanese, *watching classic Japanese films (e.g., "Kagemusha"), and frequenting Japanese restaurants. Then they modified their usual negotiating behavior by: (1) paying extra attention to comportment and protocol, (2) reducing their expectations about substantive progress in the first few meetings, (3) providing Japanese counterparts with extensive, upfront information about their company and the U.S. business environment, and (4) trying "not to change positions too much once they had been voiced."*[27]

A major challenge for the negotiator considering this strategy is to decide which aspects of his or her customary negotiating script to alter or set aside. The aspects most seriously in conflict with the counterpart's may not be easily changed or even readily apparent, and those most obviously in conflict or easily changed may not, once changed, markedly enhance the interaction. Marketing specialists have distinguished between customs to which non-Romans must conform, those to which non-Romans may but need not conform, and those from which non-Romans are excluded.[28] Although a marketing specialist has a fixed, one-sided target in seeking entry into the counterpart's arena, these distinctions may also guide some of the cross-cultural negotiator's deliberations.

A counterpart usually notices at least some evidence of a negotiator's use of the adapt strategy. Deciphering all of the modifications is difficult. It may also be difficult for a counterpart to distinguish an adapt strategy from a badly implemented embrace strategy (described below). Further, if both the negotiator and the counterpart pursue this strategy on their own initiative, their modifications may confuse rather than smooth the interaction. Still, a negotiator can independently make the choice to adapt and usually finds at least some areas within his or her capacity to do so.

• **Coordinate Adjustment of Both Parties.** The parties may develop, subtly or overtly, a joint approach for their discussions; they may negotiate the process of negotiation. The jointly developed script is usually a blend of elements from the two parties' cultures; it is not totally distinct from them yet not wholly of one or the other. It may take various forms.

At the outset of a 1988 meeting to discuss the telecommunications policies of France's Ministry of Industry and Tourism, the minister's chief of staff and his American visitor each voiced concern about speaking in the other's native language. They expressed confidence in their listening capabilities and lacked immediate access to an interpreter, so they agreed to proceed by each speaking in his own language. Their discussion went on for an hour that way, the American speaking in English to the Frenchman, and the Frenchman speaking in French to the American.

In a special case of this strategy, the parties "bypass" their respective home cultures' practices to follow the negotiating script of an already existing, third culture with which both have at least moderate familiarity. The parties know enough about the other's culture to recognize the limits of their capabilities in it and the desirability of additional guidance for their interaction.

Negotiations over MCA's acquisition by Matsushita Electric Industrial Company in 1990 were conducted largely via interpreters. At one dinner, MCA's senior American investment banker and Matsushita's Japanese head of international affairs were stymied in their effort to communicate with each other until they discovered their fluency in the same second language. They conversed in French for the rest of the evening.[29]

Professional societies, trade groups, educational programs and institutions, and various other associations can similarly provide members with third scripts for conduct. This phenomenon is dramatically illustrated, within and between teams, when people who do not share a language play volleyball or soccer socially. The sport provides a script for behavior.

Overall, this strategy has the benefits of the adapt strategy while minimizing the likelihood of incompatible "adjustments." For some Roman counterparts (e.g., Arabs and Chinese), verbally explicit implementation of this strategy for interaction will be awkward — even unacceptable.[30] Other groups' members will appreciate its decipherability and the shared burden of effort that it implies. Since both parties must go along with it, the negotiator's opportunity to "veto" also preserves some control over its implementation.

High Familiarity with Counterpart's Culture

Finally, the negotiator highly familiar with a counterpart's culture can realistically contemplate, not only the five aforementioned strategies, but at least one and possibly two more. If the counterpart is not familiar with the negotiator's culture, the negotiator can unilaterally embrace the other's negotiating script (i.e., "do as the Romans do"). If both parties are highly familiar with each other's cultures, they can jointly or unilaterally search for or formulate a negotiating script that focuses more on the individuals and circumstances involved than on the broader cultures. Such strategies may radically change the process.

• **Embrace the Counterpart's Script.** The embrace strategy calls for the negotiator to use the negotiation approach typical of the counterpart's culture.

In the 1970s, Coca-Cola undertook negotiations with a state-run, foreign trade organization in the People's Republic of China in order to produce and sell cola drinks there. The company sent one of its research chemists, a China-born man with no business background, to Cambridge University to study Chinese language and culture studies for a full year. Later acclaimed to be highly knowledgeable about China, this chemist was the most active negotiator for Coca-Cola in what became a ten-year endeavor.[31]

Relatively few individuals should attempt this strategy. It demands a great deal of the negotiator, especially when the cultures involved differ greatly. In general, it requires bilingual, bicultural individuals — those who have generally enjoyed long-term overseas residence.

When implemented well, especially when very different cultures are involved, this strategy is clearly decipherable by a counterpart. (When it is not, a counterpart may confuse it with an adapt strategy.) Furthermore, the embrace strategy can make the interaction relatively easy and comfortable for the counterpart. The strategy requires considerable effort by the negotiator, and its implementation remains largely — but not completely — within the negotiator's control.

• **Improvise an Approach.** To improvise is to create a negotiation script as one negotiates, focusing foremost on the counterpart's particular attributes and capabilities and on the circumstances. Although all negotiators should pay some attention to the Roman counterpart as an individual, not all can or should improvise. The term is used here as it is used in music, not in the colloquial sense of "winging it" or of anyone being able to do it. Musical improvisation requires some preconception or point of departure and a model (e.g., a melody, basic chord structure) that sets the scope for performance. Similarly, the negotiator who improvises knows the parties' home cultures and is fully prepared for their influence but can put them in the background or highlight them as negotiation proceeds.

In the early 1990s, Northern Telecom, a Canadian-owned telecommunications equipment supplier with many Americans in its executive ranks and headquarters in both Mississauga, Ontario, and McLean, Virginia, maintained a "dual identity." Its personnel dealt with each other on either an American or a Canadian basis. On the outside, the company played up its Canadian identity with some governments (those unenthusiastic about big American firms, or perhaps not highly familiar with American ways), and played up its American identity with others.[32]

This strategy is feasible only when both parties are highly familiar with the other's culture. Without that level of familiarity, the negotiator would not know what the counterpart is accustomed to or how he or she is affected, and would not be able to invoke or create ways to relate to the counterpart effectively; nor would the counterpart recognize or respond to these efforts appropriately. At the same time, since the counterpart is highly skilled in at least two cultures and may introduce practices from both or either one of them, it is extremely important to consider the counterpart as an individual, not just as a member of a culture. High familiarity enables the negotiator to do just that, because he or she does not need to devote as much effort to learning about the counterpart's culture as other negotiators do.

During the Camp David "peace" talks between Egypt, Israel, and the United States in the late 1970s, then President Jimmy Carter set up a one-on-one meeting with Prime Minister Menachem Begin to try to break an impasse. Carter took along photos of Begin's eight grandchildren, on the backs of which he had handwritten their names. Showing these photos to Begin led the two leaders into talking about their families and personal expectations and revitalized the intergovernmental negotiations.[33]

This strategy is often used at high levels, especially at critical junctures, but it need not be limited to that. It can counteract the treatment of a counterpart as an abstraction (e.g., stereotype) and can facilitate the development of empathy. It also seems particularly efficacious with counterparts from cultures that emphasize affective, relationship factors over task accomplishment and creativity or presence over convention.

On the down side, the cultural responsiveness of the improvise strategy is not always decipherable by the counterpart. When a top-level negotiator is involved, the counterpart may assume that the negotiator's strategy is to appeal to status or authority rather than to recognize cultural issues. If the strategy overly "personalizes" negotiation, its implementation can lead to the kinds of problems once pointed out in former U.S. Secretary of State Henry Kissinger's "personal diplomacy": becoming too emotionally involved, failing to delegate,

Table 1 Recommended Behavior for Americans Negotiating with the Japanese* (by type of culturally responsive strategy)

Employ

- Use "introducer" for initial contacts (e.g., general trading company).
- Employ an agent the counterpart knows and respects.
- Ensure that the agent/adviser speaks fluent Japanese.

Induce

- Be open to social interaction and communicate directly.
- Make an extreme initial proposal, expecting to make concessions later.
- Work efficiently to "get the job done."

Adapt

- Follow some Japanese protocol (reserved behavior, name cards, gifts).
- Provide a lot of information (by American standards) up front to influence the counterpart's decision making early.
- Slow down your usual timetable.
- Make informed interpretations (e.g., the meaning of "it is difficult").
- Present positions later in the process, more firmly and more consistently.

Embrace

- Proceed according to an information-gathering, *nemawashi* (not exchange) model.
- "Know your stuff" cold.
- Assemble a team (group) for formal negotiations.
- Speak in Japanese.
- Develop personal relationships; respond to obligations within them.

Improvise

- Do homework on the individual counterpart(s) and circumstances.
- Be attentive and nimble (improvising entails different behaviors for different Japanese).
- Invite the counterpart to participate in mutually enjoyed activities or interests. (e.g., golf).

*These are examples, not a complete listing, of attitudes and behaviors implied by a negotiator's use of each strategy.

undercutting the status of other possible representatives, and ignoring those one does not meet or know.[34] The strategy may not be appropriate for all cultures and may be difficult to orchestrate by a team of negotiators. It also offers fewer concrete prescriptions for action and greater uncertainty than the four other unilateral strategies. Nevertheless, its malleability should continue to be regarded as a major attribute.

• **Effect Symphony.** This strategy represents an effort by the negotiator to get both parties to transcend exclusive use of either home culture by exploiting their high familiarity capabilities. They may improvise an approach, create and use a new script, or follow some other approach not typical of their home cultures. One form of coordination feasible at this level of familiarity draws on both home cultures.

For their negotiations over construction of the tunnel under the English Channel, British and French representatives agreed to partition talks and alternate the site between Paris and London. At each site, the negotiators were to use established, local ways, including the language. The two approaches were thus clearly punctuated by time and space. Although each side was able to use its customary approach some of the time, it used the script of the other culture the rest of the time.[35]

Effecting symphony differs from coordinating adjustment, which implies some modification of a culture's script, in that both cultures' scripts may be used in their entirety. It is also one resolution of a situation where both parties start out independently pursuing induce or embrace strategies. Perhaps the most common form of effecting symphony is using a third culture, such as a negotiator subculture.

Many United Nations ambassadors, who tend to be multilingual and world-traveled, interact more comfortably with each other than with their compatriots.[36] *Similarly, a distinct culture can be observed in the café and recreation area at INSEAD, the European Institute of Business Administration, which attracts students from thirty countries for ten intensive months.*

Overall, the effect symphony strategy allows parties to draw on special capabilities that may be accessible only by going outside the full-time use of their home cultures' conventions. Venturing into these uncharted areas introduces some risk. Furthermore, this strategy, like other joint strategies, requires the counterpart's cooperation; it cannot be unilaterally effected. But then, as former U.S. Ambassador to Japan Edwin Reischauer suggested about diplomatic protocol, a jointly established culture — the "score" of a symphony — makes behavior predictable.[37] It can also make it comprehensible and coherent.

Table 2 Recommended Behavior for Americans Negotiating with the French*
(by type of culturally responsive strategy)

Employ

- Employ an agent well-connected in business and government circles.
- Ensure that the agent/adviser speaks fluent French.

Induce

- Be open to social interaction and communicate directly.
- Make an extreme initial proposal, expecting to make concessions later.
- Work efficiently to "get the job done."

Adapt

- Follow some French protocol (greetings and leave-takings, formal speech).
- Demonstrate an awareness of French culture and business environment.
- Be consistent between actual and stated goals and between attitudes and behavior.
- Defend views vigorously.

Embrace

- Approach negotiation as a debate involving reasoned argument.
- Know the subject of negotiation *and* broad environmental issues (economic, political, social).
- Make intellectually elegant, persuasive yet creative presentations (logically sound, verbally precise).
- Speak in French.
- Show interest in the counterpart as an individual but remain aware of the strictures of social and organizational hierarchies.

Improvise

- Do homework on the individual counterpart(s) and circumstances.
- Be attentive and nimble (improvising entails different behaviors for different French individuals).
- Invite counterpart to participate in mutually enjoyed activities or interests (e.g., dining out, tennis).

*These are examples, not a complete listing, of attitudes and behaviors implied by a negotiator's use of each strategy.

Implications

A cross-cultural negotiator is thus not limited to doing as the Romans do or even doing it "our way" or "their way." There are eight culturally responsive strategies. They differ in their degree of reliance on existing scripts and conventions, in the amount of extra effort required of each party, and in their decipherability by the counterpart. As a range of options, these strategies offer the negotiator flexibility and a greater opportunity to act effectively.

Because the strategies entail different scripts and approaches, they also allow the negotiator to move beyond the simplistic lists of behavioral tips favored to date in American writings. For example, an American working with Japanese counterparts is usually advised to behave in a reserved manner, learn some Japanese words, and exercise patience.[38] Such behavior applies primarily to an adapt strategy, however, and different strategies call for different concepts and behaviors. Table 1 gives some examples of how an American might behave with Japanese counterparts, depending on the unilateral strategy employed.

Similarly, for his meeting with Dupont in Paris, Smith could have considered strategies other than "embrace" and its associated script. An adapt strategy may not have necessitated speaking exclusively in French. Table 2 suggests some ways he might have behaved, given each unilateral strategy. Smith might also have contemplated using strategies in combination (e.g., "adapt," then "embrace"), especially if meetings had been scheduled to take place over a number of months.

At the same time, only the negotiator highly familiar with the counterpart's culture can realistically consider using all eight strategies. The value of high familiarity, as a current capability or as an aspiration to achieve, should be clear. The value of the cultural focus should also be clear, notwithstanding the importance of also focusing on the individual counterpart (Part 2 of this article will expand on this point). Culture provides a broad context for understanding the ideas and behavior of new counterparts as well as established acquaintances. It also enables the negotiator to notice commonalities in the expectations and behavior of individual members of a team of counterparts, to appreciate how the team works as a whole, and to anticipate what representatives and constituents will do when they meet away from the cross-cultural negotiation. As long as the negotiator intends to go on negotiating with other Romans, it behooves him or her to pay attention to commonalities across negotiation experiences with individual Romans — to focus on cultural aspects — in order to draw lessons that enhance effectiveness in future negotiations.

As presented here, the eight culturally responsive negotiation strategies reflect one perspective: feasibility in light of the negotiator's and counterpart's familiarity with each other's cultures. That is a major basis for selecting a strategy, but it is not sufficient. This framework maps what is doable; it should not be interpreted as recommending that the best strategies for every negotiation are those at the highest levels of familiarity — that improvising is always better than employing advisers. The best strategy depends on additional factors that will be discussed in Part 2. In its own right, the framework represents a marked shift from prevailing wisdom and a good point of departure for today's cross-cultural negotiators. ◆

References

I carried out the early stages of this work during my visits at the Euro-Asia Centre at INSEAD and Dartmouth College's Tuck School of Business. For comments on earlier drafts, I thank Ellen Auster, J. Stewart Black, Tamara Johnson, Andre Laurent, Tom Murtha, David Saunders, Susan Schneider, Jim Tiessen, William Weiss, Sloan Management Review *editors, and anonymous reviewers. Portions of this material were presented at the Academy of International Business annual meeting (1991), the Pacific Rim Forum of the David Lam Centre for International Communication at Simon Fraser University (1992), the Academy of Management annual conference (1992), the Negotiation Workshop at York University (1993), and the Joint Centre for Asia-Pacific Studies at the University of Toronto (1993).*

1. All examples that are not referenced come from personal communication or the author's experiences.

2. Contemporary academic advocates of this approach for negotiators include:

S.T. Cavusgil and P.N. Ghauri, *Doing Business in Developing Countries* (London: Routledge, 1990), pp. 123-124;

J.L. Graham and R.A. Herberger, Jr., "Negotiators Abroad — Don't Shoot from the Hip," *Harvard Business Review*, July-August 1983, p. 166; and

F. Posses, *The Art of International Negotiation* (London: Business Books, 1978), p. 27.

3. The concept of a script has been applied by:

W.B. Gudykunst and S. Ting-Toomey, *Culture and Interpersonal Communication* (Newbury Park, California: Sage, 1988), p. 30.

4. See, for example, N.C.G. Campbell et al., "Marketing Negotiations in France, Germany, the United Kingdom, and the United States," *Journal of Marketing* 52 (1988): 49-62; and

J.L. Graham et al., "Buyer-Seller Negotiations around the Pacific Rim: Differences in Fundamental Exchange Processes," *Journal of Consumer Research* 15 (1988): 48-54.

For evidence from diplomacy, see:

R. Cohen, *Negotiating across Cultures* (Washington, D.C.: U.S. Institute of Peace Press, 1991); and

G. Fisher, *International Negotiation: A Cross-Cultural Perspective* (Yarmouth, Maine: Intercultural Press, 1980).

5. See J.L. Graham and N.J. Adler, "Cross-Cultural Interaction: The International Comparison Fallacy," *Journal of International Business Studies* 20 (1989): 515-537. The authors conclude that their subjects adapted to some extent, but a lack of adaptability could also be convincingly argued from their data.

6. For an experimental study showing that moderate adaptation by Asians in the United States was more effective than substantial adaptation, see:

J.N.P. Francis, "When in Rome? The Effects of Cultural Adaptation on Intercultural Business Negotiations," *Journal of International Business Studies* 22 (1991): 403-428.

7. The majority of leaders of North American firms still lack any expatriate experience and foreign language ability, according to:

N.J. Adler and S. Bartholomew, "Managing Globally Competent People," *The Executive* 6 (1992): 58.

8. See, for example, D. Ricks and V. Mahajan, "Blunders in International Marketing: Fact or Fiction?" *Long Range Planning* 17 (1984): 78-83. Note that the impact of faux pas may vary in magnitude across cultures. In some cultures, inappropriate behavior constitutes an unforgivable transgression, not a "slip-up."

9. M. Blaker, *Japanese International Negotiating Style* (New York: Columbia University Press, 1977), p. 50.

10. See V.E. Cronen and R. Shuter, "Forming Intercultural Bonds," *Intercultural Communication Theory: Current Perspectives*, ed. W.B. Gudykunst (Beverly Hills, California: Sage, 1983), p. 99. Their concept of "coherence" neither presumes that the interactants make the same sense of the interaction nor depends always on mutual understanding.

11. Although similar in form, this plot differs in theme from the "model of conflict-handling responses" developed by:

K.W. Thomas and R.H. Kilmann, *Thomas-Kilmann Conflict Mode Instrument* (Tuxedo, New York: Xicom, Inc., 1974).

It also differs in key variables from the "Dual Concerns" model of:

D.G. Pruitt and J.Z. Rubin, *Social Conflict: Escalation, Stalemate, and Settlement* (New York: Random House, 1986), p. 35ff.

Moreover, neither of these models appears to have yet been applied cross-culturally.

12. This notion of familiarity draws on Dell Hymes's concept of communicative competence. See:

R.E. Cooley and D.A. Roach, "A Conceptual Framework," *Competence in Communication*, ed. R.N. Bostrom (Beverly Hills, California: Sage, 1984), pp. 11-32.

13. See, for example, R.W. Brislin et al., *Intercultural Interactions* (Beverly Hills, California: Sage, 1986);

A.T. Church, "Sojourner Adjustment," *Psychological Bulletin* 91 (1982): 545-549;

P.C. Earley, "Intercultural Training for Managers," *Academy of Management Review* 30 (1987): 685-698; and

J.S. Black and M. Mendenhall, "Cross-cultural Training Effectiveness: A Review and Theoretical Framework for Future Research," *Academy of Management Review* 15 (1990): 113-136.

14. J.S. Black and M. Mendenhall, "The U-Curve Adjustment Hypothesis Revisited: A Review and Theoretical Framework," *Journal of International Business Studies* 22 (1991): 225-247.
15. Changing the parties involved is commonly mentioned in dispute resolution literature. See, for example:
R. Fisher and W. Ury, *Getting to Yes* (Boston: Houghton Mifflin, 1981), pp. 71-72.
16. S. Lohr, "Barter Is His Stock in Trade," *New York Times Business World*, 25 September 1988, pp. 32-36.
17. For empirical research on negotiating representatives and their boundary role, constituents, and accountability within a culture, see:
D.G. Pruitt, *Negotiation Behavior* (New York: Academic Press, 1981), pp. 41-44, 195-197.
With respect to agents, see:
J.Z. Rubin and F.E.A. Sander, "When Should We Use Agents? Direct vs. Representative Negotiation," *Negotiation Journal*, October 1988, pp. 395-401.
18. S.E. Weiss, "The Long Path to the IBM-Mexico Agreement: An Analysis of the Microcomputer Investment Negotiations, 1983-1986," *Journal of International Business Studies* 21 (1990): 565-596.
19. J.L. Graham and Y. Sano, *Smart Bargaining: Doing Business with the Japanese* (New York: Ballinger, 1989), p. 30.
20. R. Lacey, *The Kingdom: Arabia and the House of Sa'ud* (New York: Avon Books, 1981), pp. 464-466. See also:
P.E. Tyler, "Double Exposure: Saudi Arabia's Middleman in Washington," *The New York Times Magazine*, 7 June 1992, pp. 34ff.
21. For additional ideas about what a mediator may do, see:
P.J.D. Carnevale, "Strategic Choice in Mediation," *Negotiation Journal* 2 (1986): 41-56.
22. See J.Z. Rubin, "Introduction," *Dynamics of Third Party Intervention*, ed. J.Z. Rubin (New York: Praeger, 1981), pp. 3-43; and
S. Touval and I.W. Zartman, "Mediation in International Conflicts" *Mediation Research*, eds. K. Kressel and D.G. Pruitt (San Francisco: Jossey-Bass, 1989), pp. 115-137.
23. S.E. Weiss, "Negotiating the CGE-ITT Telecommunications Merger, 1985-1986: A Framework-then-Details Process," paper presented at the Academy of International Business annual meeting, November 1991.
24. Such positions have been associated with people in nations with long-established cultures, such as China, France, and India. For instance, some Mexican high officials who speak English fluently have insisted on speaking Spanish in their meetings with Americans. While this position could be influenced by the historical antipathy in the U.S.-Mexico relationship and the officials' concern for the status of their office, it also evinces cultural pride.
25. "IBM World Trade Corporation," Harvard Business School, reprinted in S.M. Davis, *Managing and Organizing Multinational Corporations* (New York: Pergamon Press, 1979), p. 53.
26. Adapting has been widely discussed in the literature. See, for example:
S. Bochner, "The Social Psychology of Cross-Cultural Relations," *Cultures in Contact*, ed. S. Bochner (Oxford: Pergamon, 1982), pp. 5-44.
27. S.E. Weiss, "Creating the GM-Toyota Joint Venture: A Case in Complex Negotiation," *Columbia Journal of World Business*, Summer 1987, pp. 23-37; and
S.E. Weiss, "One Impasse, One Agreement: Explaining the Outcomes of Toyota's Negotiations with Ford and GM," paper presented at the Academy of International Business annual meeting, 1988.
28. P.R. Cateora and J.M. Hess, *International Marketing* (Homewood, Illinois: Irwin, 1971), p. 407.
29. C. Bruck, "Leap of Faith," *The New Yorker*, 9 September 1991, pp. 38-74.
30. See C. Thubron, *Behind the Wall* (London: Penguin, 1987), pp. 158, 186-187.
31. L. Sloane, "Lee, Coke's Man in China," *The New York Times*, 5 February 1979, p. D2.
32. W.C. Symonds et al., "High-Tech Star," *Business Week*, 27 July 1992, pp. 55-56.
33. Found among the exhibits at the Carter Center Library and Museum, Atlanta, Georgia.
34. R. Fisher, "Playing the Wrong Game?" *Dynamics of Third Party Intervention*, ed. J.Z. Rubin (New York: Praeger, 1981), pp. 98-99, 105-106.
On the additional problem of losing touch with constituencies, see the 1989-1991 Bush-Gorbachev talks described in:
M.R. Beschloss and S. Talbott, *At the Highest Levels* (Boston: Little, Brown, 1993).
35. See C. Dupont, "The Channel Tunnel Negotiations, 1984-1986: Some Aspects of the Process and Its Outcome," *Negotiation Journal* 6 (1990): 71-80.
36. See, for example, C.F. Alger, "United Nations Participation as a Learning Experience," *Public Opinion Quarterly*, Summer 1983, pp. 411-426.
37. E.O. Reischauer, *My Life between Japan and America* (New York: Harper and Row, 1986), p. 183.
38. N.B. Thayer and S.E. Weiss, "Japan: The Changing Logic of a Former Minor Power," *National Negotiating Styles*, ed. H. Binnendijk (Washington, D.C.: Foreign Service Institute, U.S. Department of State, 1987), pp. 69-72.

Reprint 3524

[22]

Negotiating with "Romans" – Part 2

Stephen E. Weiss

CHOOSING THE RIGHT STRATEGY FOR NEGOTIATIONS WITH SOMEONE FROM ANOTHER CULTURE IS A DIFFICULT TASK FOR WHICH MANAGERS HAVE FEW established guidelines. Implementing that strategy well can often be even more challenging. Whether you know a little or a lot about your counterpart's culture — whether you are a novice or an experienced negotiator — you will find useful advice in this article on effectively choosing and implementing a culturally responsive strategy. Part 1, published in the Winter 1994 issue, presented eight culturally responsive strategies in a framework based on their feasibility.

Stephen E. Weiss is associate professor of policy and international business at York University, Faculty of Administrative Studies (Toronto).

Managers are increasingly called on to negotiate with people from other cultures. Cross-cultural negotiation need not be as frustrating nor as costly as it is often made out to be; it can be a productive and satisfying experience. Which of these outcomes a manager achieves depends in part on the negotiation strategies taken in response to — or better, in anticipation of — the counterpart's plans and behavior. There are eight culturally responsive strategies for a manager to consider (see Figure 1).[1] Clearly, the quality of a negotiation outcome and a manager's satisfaction with it also depend on how well he or she chooses and implements one of these approaches.

This article presents five steps for selecting a culturally responsive strategy and then offers various tips for implementation, such as making the first move, monitoring feedback, and modifying the approach. These guidelines reflect four basic, ongoing considerations for a strategy: its *feasibility* for the manager, its fit with the counterpart's likely approach and therefore its capacity to lead to *coherent interaction,* its *appropriateness* to the relationship and circumstances at hand, and its *acceptability* in light of the manager's values. There are challenges involved in all of these efforts, and they are pointed out below rather than ignored or belittled, as happens in much cross-cultural negotiation literature. Thus, from this article, managers stand to gain both an operational plan and the heightened awareness necessary to use a culturally responsive negotiation strategy effectively.

The cross-cultural negotiator cannot take common knowledge and practices for granted and thereby simply concentrate on the individual.

Selecting a Strategy

Every negotiator is advised to "know yourself, the counterpart, and the situation."[2] This advice is useful but incomplete, for it omits the relationship — the connection — between the negotiator and the counterpart.[3] (For clarity, the negotiator from the "other" culture will be called the "counterpart" in this article.) Different types of relationships with counterparts and even different phases of a relationship with a particular counterpart call for different strategies.

For the cross-cultural negotiator, the very presence of more than one culture complicates the process of understanding the relationship and "knowing" the counterpart. In contrast to the "within-culture" negotiator, the cross-cultural negotiator cannot take common knowledge and practices for granted and thereby simply concentrate on the individual. It becomes important to actively consider the counterpart in two respects: as a member of a group and as an individual.

The right balance in these considerations is not easily struck. An exclusive emphasis on the group's culture will probably lead the negotiator off the mark because individuals often differ from the group average. Members of the same group may even differ very widely on certain dimensions. At the same time, the degree of variation tolerated between group members is itself an aspect of culture. For example, Americans have traditionally upheld the expression, "He's his own man," while Japanese believed that "the protruding nail is hammered down." The cross-cultural negotiator should thus consider both the counterpart's cultural background and individual attributes, perhaps weighting them differently according to the culture involved, but mindful always that every negotiation involves developing a relationship with a particular individual or team.[4]

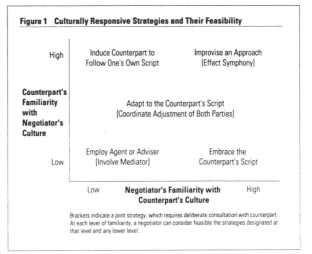

Figure 1 Culturally Responsive Strategies and Their Feasibility

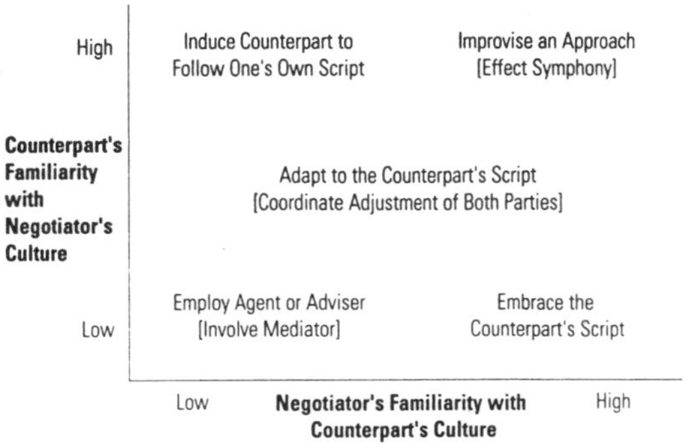

Brackets indicate a joint strategy, which requires deliberate consultation with counterpart. At each level of familiarity, a negotiator can consider feasible the strategies designated at that level and any lower level.

For years, Japanese managers have come to one of my classes each term to negotiate with graduate students so the students can experience negotiating first-hand and test the often stereotypical descriptions they have read about Japanese negotiating behavior. I deliberately invite many Japanese, not just one or two. The students invariably express surprise when the Japanese teams "deviate" from the Japanese negotiating script, as the students understand it, and when differences appear in the behavior of various Japanese teams.

The five steps for selecting a culturally responsive negotiation strategy take into account these complexities:

1. Reflect on your culture's negotiation script.
2. Learn the negotiation script of the counterpart's culture.
3. Consider the relationship and circumstances.
4. Predict or influence the counterpart's approach.
5. Choose your strategy.

These steps take minutes or months, depending on the parties and circumstances involved. Each step will probably not require the same amount of time or effort. Furthermore, the sequencing of the steps is intended to have an intuitive, pragmatic appeal for an American negotiator, but it should not be treated rigidly. Some steps will be more effective if they are coupled or treated iteratively. Nor should these efforts start at the negotiation table when time, energy, resources, and introspection tend to be severely limited. Every one of these steps merits *some* attention by every cross-cultural negotiator before the first round of negotiation.

It is important to remember that the procedure represented by these five steps is itself culturally embedded, influenced by the author's cultural background and by that of the intended audience (American negotiators).[5] Not all counterparts will find the pragmatic logic herein equally compelling. As two Chinese professionals have observed, "In the West, you are used to speaking out your problems. . . . But that is not our tradition," and "In our country, there are so many taboos. We're not used to analytic thinking in your Western way. We don't dissect ourselves and our relationships."[6] Even with this procedure, culture continues to influence what we do and how we do it.

One way to deal with this inescapable cultural bias is to acknowledge it and remain aware of the continual challenges of effectively choosing and implementing a strategy. Often these challenges do not stand out — books on international negotiation have not addressed them — yet they can hamper, even ruin, a negotiator's best efforts. Each step below thus includes a list of cautions for cross-cultural negotiating.

1. Reflect on Your Culture's Negotiation Script

Among members of our "home" group, we behave almost automatically.[7] We usually have no impetus to consider the culture of the group because we repeatedly engage in activities with each other without incident or question. It is easy to use these "natural," taken-for-granted ways in a cross-cultural situation — too easy.

> *A book on international negotiation published by the U.S. State Department displays the flags of six nations on its front cover. On initial copies of the book, the French flag appeared in three bands of red, white, and blue. The actual French flag is blue, white, and red.*[8]

A cross-cultural negotiator should construct a thoughtful, systematic profile of his or her culture's negotiation practices, using personal knowledge and other resources. Let's say you want to develop an "American negotiator profile." There is a vast amount of research and popular literature on negotiation in the United States.[9] For insights about American culture more broadly, consider both Americans' self-examinations and outsiders' observations.[10] Then organize this information into the profile represented in Figure 2.[11] The profile consists of four topic areas: the general model of the negotiation process, the individual's role, aspects of interaction, and the form of a satisfactory agreement. The left side of the ranges in Figure 2 generally fit the American negotiator profile (e.g., the basic concept is distributive bargaining, the most significant issues are substantive ones, negotiators are chosen for their knowledge, individual aspirations predominate over community needs, and so forth).

Figure 2 Negotiator Profile

General Model

1. Basic Concept of Process

   Distributive bargaining / Joint problem-solving / Debate / Contingency bargaining / Nondirective discussion

2. Most Significant Type of Issue

   Substantive / Relationship-based / Procedural / Personal-internal

Role of the Individual

3. Selection of Negotiators

   Knowledge / Negotiating experience / Personal attributes / Status

4. Individuals' Aspirations

   Individual ◄——► Community

5. Decision Making in Groups

   Authoritative ◄——► Consensual

Interaction: Dispositions

6. Orientation Toward Time

   Monochronic ◄——► Polychronic

7. Risk-Taking Propensity

   High ◄——► Low

8. Bases of Trust

   External sanctions / Other's reputation / Intuition / Shared experiences

Interaction: Process

9. Concern with Protocol

   Informal ◄——► Formal

10. Communication Complexity

    Low ◄——► High

11. Nature of Persuasion

    Direct experience / Logic / Tradition / Dogma / Emotion / Intuition

Outcome

12. Form of Agreement

    Contractual ◄——► Implicit

Source: Adapted from S.E. Weiss with W. Stripp, *Negotiating with Foreign Business Persons* (New York: New York University Graduate School of Business Administration, Working Paper #85-6, 1985), p.10.

This profile should also uncover the values that support these tendencies. For instance, distributive bargaining implies certain attitudes toward conflict and its handling (direct), toward business relationships (competitive), and toward the purpose of negotiation (to maximize individual gains). Since some of your group's tendencies and values may not align with your own, develop a personal profile as well. Doing so does not require probing deeply into your unconscious. Simply ask yourself, "What do I usually do at times like this? Why? What do I gain from doing it this way?" These kinds of questions resemble those used in basic negotiation training to distinguish an underlying interest from a bargaining position, namely, "What does this bargaining position do for me? Why?"

> *In the mid-1980s, a white American banker planned to include an African-American analyst on his team for a forthcoming visit to white clients in South Africa. When they learned about this, the clients intimated their preference that she not attend. While*

Table 1 Cautions: Understanding Your Own Culture's Script

- Beware of psychological and group biases, such as denial and "groupthink."
- Probe for assumptions and values; they are seldom identified explicitly in day-to-day life.
- Don't become rigidly wedded to your own ways.
- Take time during negotiations to step out of the action and reflect on your behavior.

the banker wanted to serve his clients, he also had strong feelings about including the analyst and about basing qualifications on merit. She was the best analyst on his staff. The banker's values swayed his decision: he told his clients that he would not make the trip without this analyst on his team.[12]

Developing cultural and personal profiles is an ongoing task. Instead of writing them up once and moving on, return to them and refine them as you gain experience and understanding. The value of such a process is considerable. It increases your self-awareness; it helps you explain your expectations and behavior to a counterpart; it prepares you to make decisions under pressure; it allows you to compare your culture to another on a holistic rather than fragmented basis; it helps you determine a counterpart's level of familiarity with your culture; its products — profiles — can be used in future negotiations with other cultural groups; it motivates interest in other cultures; and it enables you to act consistently and conscientiously.

This process demands a good deal of effort, especially at the outset (note the cautions in Table 1). But as a negotiator, you will find such reflection to be a good basis for developing a cross-cultural negotiation strategy.

2. Learn the Negotiation Script of the Counterpart's Culture

This step applies to both the negotiator highly familiar with a counterpart's culture and the one who knows next to nothing about it.[13] The highly familiar negotiator should review what he or she knows and gather additional information to stay current. The uninitiated negotiator should begin to construct a negotiator profile from the ground up. Ideally, this process involves learning in the active sense: developing the ability to use the counterpart's cultural and personal negotiation scripts, as well as "knowing" the scripts and related values.

Learning these scripts enhances the negotiator's ability to anticipate and interpret the counterpart's behavior. Even a negotiator with low familiarity who is likely to employ an agent needs some information in order to interact effectively with the agent and to assess the agent's performance. Although few negotiators learn everything about a counterpart before negotiation, advance work allows for assimilation and practice, provides a general degree of confidence that helps the negotiator to cope with the unexpected, and frees up time and attention during the negotiation to learn finer points.

Again, the negotiator profile framework is a good place to start. Try especially to glean and appreciate the basic concept of negotiation because it anchors and connects the other dimensions. Without it, a negotiator, as an outsider, cannot comprehend a counterpart's actions; they appear bizarre or whimsical. Moreover, if you focus merely on tactics or simple "do and don't"-type tips and reach a point in a transaction for which you have no tip, you have no base — no sense of the "spirit of the interaction" — to guide you through this juncture. For instance, the "spirit" of French management has been described like this:

French managers see their work as an intellectual challenge requiring the remorseless application of individual brainpower. They do not share the Anglo-Saxon view of management as an interpersonally demanding exercise, where plans have to be constantly "sold" upward and downward using personal skills. The bias is for intellect rather than for action.[14]

Continuing with this example, let's say you are preparing to negotiate with a French counterpart. You may find information about French negotiation concepts and practices in studies by French and American researchers and in natives' and outsiders' popular writings.[15] In addition to general nonfiction works on French culture, novels and films can convey an extraordinary sense of interactions among individuals and groups.[16] Other sources include intensive culture briefings by experts and interviews with French acquaintances, colleagues, and compatriots familiar with French culture, and, in some cases, even the counterpart.

Here, as in reflections on your own culture, make sure to consider core beliefs and values of the culture. Keep an eye on the degree of adherence to them as well as their substantive content.

A Frenchman involved in the mid-1980s negotiations between AT&T and CGE over a cross-marketing deal revealed his own culture's concern for consistency in thought and behavior as he discussed AT&T's con-

duct. He described the AT&T representatives' style as "very strange" because they made assurances about "fair" implementation while pushing a very "tough" contract.

Moving from information gathering to assimilation and greater familiarity with a culture usually requires intensive training on site or in seminars.[17] Some Japanese managers, for example, have been sent overseas by their companies for three to five years to absorb a country's culture before initiating any business ventures. When the time comes, familiarity may be assessed through tests of language fluency, responses to "critical incidents" in "cultural assimilator" exercises, and performance in social interactions in the field.[18]

Whether or not you have prior experience working with a particular counterpart or other inside information, try to explore the counterpart's own negotiation concepts, practices, and values. They can be mapped in a negotiator profile just as you mapped your own values.

This entire undertaking poses challenges for every negotiator, regardless of the strategy ultimately chosen. One of the highest hurdles may be the overall nature of the learning itself. Learning about another culture's concepts, ways, and values seems to hinge on the similarity between that culture and one's own. Learning is inhibited when one is isolated from members of that culture (even if one is living in their country) and "may fail to occur when attitudes to be learned contradict deep-seated personality orientations (e.g., authoritarianism), when defensive stereotypes exist, or at points where home and host cultures differ widely in values or in conceptual frame of reference."[19] Other significant challenges can be seen in Table 2. Remember that, ultimately, you have access to different strategies for whatever amount of learning and level of familiarity you attain.

3. Consider the Relationship and Circumstances

Negotiators and counterparts tend to behave differently in different relationships and contexts.[20] One does not, for instance, act the same way as a seller as one does as a buyer. So a negotiator should not count on the same strategy to work equally well with every counterpart from a given cultural group (even if the counterparts have the same level of familiarity with the negotiator's culture) or, for that matter, with the same counterpart all the time. The peaks and valleys that most relationships traverse require different strategies and approaches. In the same vein, circumstances suggest varying constraints and opportunities.

To continue your preparations for a negotiation, consider particular facets of your relationship with the counterpart and the circumstances. The most important facets on which to base strategic choices have not yet been identified in research and may actually depend on the cultures involved. Furthermore, laying out a complete list of possibilities goes beyond the scope of this article.[21] But the following considerations (four for relationships, four for circumstances) seem significant.

• **Life of the Relationship.** The existence and nature of a prior relationship with the counterpart will influence the negotiation and should figure into a negotiator's deliberations. With no prior contact, one faces a not-yet personal situation; general information and expectations based on cultural scripts will have to do until talks are under way. Parties who have had previous contact, however, have experienced some form of interaction. Their expectations concerning the future of the relationship will also tend to influence negotiation behavior.[22] In sum, the negotiator should acknowledge any already established form of interaction, assess its attributes (e.g., coherence) and the parties' expectations of the future, and decide whether to continue, modify, or break from the established form. These decisions will indicate different culturally responsive strategies.

Table 2 Cautions: Learning about the Counterpart's Culture

- Don't be too quick to identify the counterpart's home culture. Common cues (name, physical appearance, language, accent, and location) may be unreliable. The counterpart probably belongs to more than one culture.
- Beware of the Western bias toward "doing." In Arab, Asian, and Latin groups, ways of being (e.g., comportment, smell), feeling, thinking, and talking can more powerfully shape relationships than doing.
- Try to counteract the tendency to formulate simple, consistent, stable images. Not many cultures are simple, consistent, or stable.
- Don't assume that all aspects of the culture are equally significant. In Japan, consulting all relevant parties to a decision (*nemawashi*) is more important than presenting a gift (*omiyage*).
- Recognize that norms for interactions involving outsiders may differ from those for interactions between compatriots.
- Don't overestimate your familiarity with your counterpart's culture. An American studying Japanese wrote New Year's wishes to Japanese contacts in basic Japanese characters but omitted one character. As a result, the message became "Dead man, congratulations."

Table 3 Cautions: Considering the Relationship and Circumstances

- Pay attention to the similarities *and* differences, in kind and in magnitude, between your negotiator profiles and those of the counterpart.
- Be careful about judging certain relationship aspects as major (big picture issues) and minor (fine details). This dichotomy, let alone the particular contents of the two categories, is not used in all cultures.
- Consider the relationship from the counterpart's perspective.
- Identify the relationship factors and circumstances most significant to you *and* the counterpart.
- Beware of the use and abuse of power.
- Discover the "wild cards" either party may have.
- Remember that the relationship will not remain static during negotiation.

• **Fit of Respective Scripts.** Having completed steps 1 and 2, you can easily compare your negotiator profiles, both cultural and individual, with those of the counterpart. Some culture comparisons based on the negotiator profile in Figure 2 have already been published.[23] Noting similarities as well as differences will enable you to identify those aspects of your usual behavior that do not need to change (similarities) and those aspects that do (major differences) if you choose a strategy that involves elements of both your negotiation script and the counterpart's (e.g., the adapt strategy). The number and kinds of differences will also suggest how difficult it would be to increase your level of familiarity with the counterpart's culture or to use certain combinations of strategies.

Do not allow such a comparison to mislead you. Some people overemphasize differences. Others, focusing on superficial features, overestimate similarities and their understanding of another culture (e.g., when Americans compare American and Canadian cultures). The cautions in Table 3 can help you stay on track.

Of course, a negotiator highly familiar with the counterpart's culture who plans to adopt an embrace strategy, operating wholly within that culture, has less need for these comparisons.

• **Balance of Power.** It may seem that power would have a lot to do with the choice of strategy. A more powerful party could induce the other to follow his or her cultural script. A less powerful party would have to embrace the other's script. A balance of power might suggest an adapt or improvise strategy.

But the issue is not so simple. The tilt of the "balance" is not easily or clearly determined; parties often measure power using different scales.[24] Indeed, forms of power, their significance, and appropriate responses are all culturally embedded phenomena.[25] Furthermore, it makes little sense to rely on power and disregard a counterpart's familiarity with one's culture when one's goal is coherent interaction. This is not to say that one could not benefit from an imbalance of power *after* choosing a culturally responsive strategy or in other areas of negotiation. Still, since power is culturally based and Americans have a general reputation for using it insensitively, American negotiators should be extremely careful about basing the strategy decision on power.

• **Gender.** Consider the possible gender combinations in one-on-one cross-cultural relationships: female negotiator with female counterpart, male negotiator with male counterpart, male negotiator with female counterpart, and female negotiator with male counterpart. Within most cultures, same-gender and mixed relationships entail different negotiating scripts. There are few books on negotiation designated for American women, but communication research has shown that men tend to use talk to negotiate status, women tend to use it to maintain intimacy, and they are often at cross-purposes when they talk to each other.[26] The debates over how American women should act in male-dominated workplaces further substantiate the existence of different scripts. In a sense, gender groups have their own cultures, and mixed interaction within a national culture is already cross-cultural.

Mixed interaction across national and other cultures holds even greater challenges. One of the primary determinations for a woman should be whether a male counterpart sees her first as a foreigner and second as a woman, or vice versa. According to some survey research, Asian counterparts see North American businesswomen as foreigners first.[27] The opposite may be true in parts of France. Edith Cresson, former French prime minister, once said, "Anglo-Saxons are not interested in women as women. For a [French] woman arriving in an Anglo-Saxon country, it is astonishing. She says to herself, 'What is the matter?'"[28] Thus, although current information about negotiating scripts for other countries tends to be based on male-male interactions, complete culturally-based negotiator profiles should include gender-based scripts.

Whether your negotiation involves mixed or same-gender interaction, try to anticipate the counterpart's perception of the gender issue and review your core beliefs. Gender-based roles in France, for instance, may appear so antithetical (or laudable) that you will not entertain (or will favor) the embrace strategy.

With regard to circumstances, the second part of step 3, there are at least four relevant considerations.

• **Opportunity for Advance Coordination.** Do you have — or can you create — an opportunity beforehand to coordinate strategy with your counterpart? If so, consider the joint strategies. If not, concentrate at the outset on feasible, unilateral strategies.

• **Time Schedule.** Time may also shape a negotiator's choice in that different strategies require different levels of effort and time. For the negotiator with moderate familiarity of the counterpart's culture but an inside track on a good agent, employing an agent may take less time than adapting to the counterpart's script. The time required to implement a strategy also depends on the counterpart's culture (e.g., negotiations based on the French script generally take longer than the American script). And time constrains the learning one can do to increase familiarity. Imagine the possibilities that open up for a diligent negotiator when discussions are scheduled as a series of weekly meetings over a twelve-month period instead of as one two-hour session.

• **Audiences.** Consider whether you or the counterpart will be accompanied by other parties, such as interpreters, advisers, constituents, and mass media. Their presence or absence can affect the viability and effectiveness of a strategy. If no one else will attend the meeting, for instance, you have no one to defer to or involve as a mediator at critical junctures.

During the early months of the ITT-CGE telecommunications negotiations in 1985 and 1986, fewer than ten individuals were aware of the talks. That permitted the parties to conduct discussions in ways not possible later, when over a hundred attorneys, not to mention other personnel, became involved. At the same time, that choice may have ruled out the initial use of some culturally responsive strategies.

• **Wild Cards.** Finally, you should assess your own and the counterpart's capacities to alter some relationship factors and circumstances. Parties may have extra-cultural capabilities such as financial resources, professional knowledge, or technical skills that expand their set of feasible options, bases for choice, or means of implementation.

During the GM-Toyota joint venture negotiations in the early 1980s, Toyota could afford to and did hire three U.S. law firms simultaneously for a trial period in order to compare their advice and assess their compatibility with the company. After three months, the company retained one of the firms for the duration of the negotiations.

4. Predict or Influence the Counterpart's Approach. The last step before choosing a strategy is to attempt to determine the counterpart's approach to the negotiation, either by predicting it or by influencing its selection. For the effectiveness of a culturally responsive strategy in bringing about coherent interaction depends not only on the negotiator's ability to implement it but also on its complementarity with the counterpart's strategy. Embracing the counterpart's script makes little sense if the counterpart is embracing your script. Further, reliable prediction and successful influence narrow the scope of a negotiator's deliberations and reduce uncertainty. And the sooner the prediction, the greater the time available for preparation. While these concerns relate to the parties' relationship (step 3), they have a direct impact on interaction that merits a separate step.

Assuming that your counterpart will not ignore cultural backgrounds and that each of you would adopt only a unilateral strategy, you can use Figure 3 to preview all possible intersections of these strategies.[29] They fall into three categories: complementary, potentially but not inherently complementary, and conflicting. Thus the figure shows the coherence of each strategy pair.

Among these pairs, adapt-adapt and improvise-improvise might seem inherently complementary. The catch is that parties can adapt or improvise in conflicting ways. Of all the potentially complementary cells, the improvise-improvise interaction may, however, be the most likely to become coherent, given the nature of the improvise strategy and the capabilities it entails.

Not all of the strategies in Figure 3 will be available to you in every situation. Remember that in addition to potential coherence, your choice will be based on your familiarity with the counterpart's culture, the counterpart's familiarity with yours, appropriateness, and acceptability.

• **Prediction.** Sometimes a counterpart will make this step easy by explicitly notifying you of his or her strategy in advance of your talks. If the counterpart does not do that, there may be telling clues in the counterpart's prenegotiation behavior, or other insiders (associates or subordinates) may disclose information.

Without direct and reliable information, you are left to predict the counterpart's strategy choice on the basis of his or her traits and motivations. Some counterparts will have a rational, task-directed orientation. Strategy research based on this perspective shows that counterparts seeking to coordinate their actions with a negotia-

Figure 3 The Inherent Coherence of Parties' Culturally Responsive Strategies

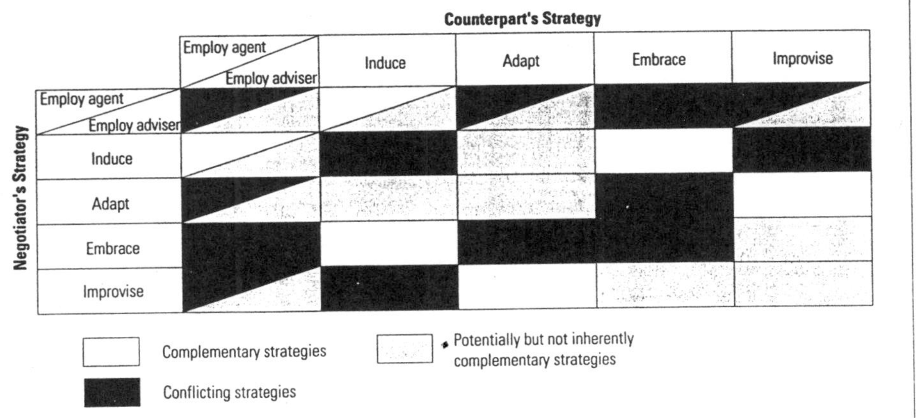

tor often select the course of action most prominent or salient to both parties (e.g., choosing a river as a property boundary).[30] Other counterparts will focus on what is socially proper. Indeed, whether a counterpart even responds to the cross-cultural nature of the interaction may vary with his or her cosmopolitanism. A cosmopolitan counterpart may lean toward adapt and improvise strategies, whereas a counterpart having little experience with other cultures may be motivated primarily by internal, cultural norms. In the latter case, the counterpart's negotiator profile may be used to predict some behavior. For example, the internally focused individual from a culture with high communication complexity (reliance on nonverbal and other contextual cues for meaning), which often correlates with low risk-taking propensity, would be more likely to involve a mediator than to coordinate adjustment (which is too explicit) or to embrace or improvise (which are too uncertain).[31]

• **Influence.** Whether or not you can predict a counterpart's strategy choice, why not try to influence it? If you predict a strategy favorable to you, perhaps you can reinforce it; if unfavorable, change it; and if predicted without certainty, ensure it. Even if prediction proves elusive, it behooves you to try to influence the counterpart.

The first task in this process is to determine your own preferred strategy based on the criteria in step 5. This may appear to be jumping ahead, but choosing and influencing go hand in hand. They will go on throughout negotiation, for new information will come to light and necessitate reassessments.

Once you have chosen a strategy, use the matrix in Figure 3 to locate interaction targets. Your prime targets should be the coherent (complementary) combinations, followed by the potentially coherent ones. For example, if you intend to employ an agent, influence the counterpart to use the induce strategy.

Some negotiators may also contemplate targeting conflicting strategies. In this line of thinking, a conflict could bring out the parties' differences so dramatically as to provide valuable lessons and "working" material for both the negotiator and counterpart. Influencing the counterpart to pursue a strategy that conflicts with one's own (or selecting one by oneself if the counterpart has already set a strategy) might establish that one is not a negotiator who can be exploited. However, these effects lie outside of our main purposes of demonstrating responsiveness to cultural factors and establishing a coherent form of interaction. Furthermore, such conflict often confuses, causes delays, and provokes resentment. (Note also the other cautions in Table 4.)

With respect to means of influence, Americans sometimes preemptively take action, such as using English in conversation without inquiring about a non-American counterpart's wishes or capabilities, but there are other, often more mutually satisfactory, ways to influence a counterpart. They range from direct means, such as explicitly requesting a counterpart to choose a particular strategy, to tacit means, such as disclosing one's level of familiarity with the counterpart's culture, revealing one's own strategy choice, or designating a meeting site likely to elicit certain types of conduct. For example, in 1989, then U.S. Secretary of State James Baker hosted his Soviet counterpart Eduard Shevardnadze in Jackson Hole, Wyoming, instead of Washington, D.C. Prenegotiation communications may also be carried out by advance staff or through back channels. As you evaluate these options, bear in mind that their effectiveness will probably differ according to the counterpart's culture and personal attraction to you.[32]

Table 4 Cautions: Predicting or Influencing the Counterpart's Approach

- Try to discern whether the counterpart's culture categorically favors or disfavors certain strategies.
- Don't fixate on "what's typical" for someone from the counterpart's cultural group.
- Recognize the difficulty in accurately assessing the counterpart's familiarity with your culture's negotiating script.
- Heed the line, however fuzzy, between influencing and "meddling" — a U.S. diplomat was detained in Singapore in 1988 for interfering in internal affairs.*
- Track changes in the counterpart's strategic choices over time.
- Don't focus so obsessively on parties' strategies that you ignore the richness of the relationship or the context.

* F. Deyo, *Dependent Development and Industrial Order* (New York: Praeger, 1981), p. 89.

5. Choose Your Strategy

When you have completed the previous steps, it is time to choose a strategy or a combination of strategies. Four selection criteria emerge from these steps. The strategy must be feasible given the counterpart and cultures involved; able to produce a coherent pattern of interaction, given the counterpart's likely approach; appropriate to the relationship and circumstances; and acceptable, ideally but not necessarily, to both parties. These criteria apply to the prenegotiation choice of strategy, but you may also use them to assess your strategy during negotiation.

A possible fifth criterion would be your degree of comfort with a strategy. Even negotiators highly familiar with two cultures' scripts favor one script over another in certain circumstances. So if the four criteria above do not direct you to only one right strategy, consider, at the end, which of the remaining strategies you would be most comfortable implementing.

Apply the four criteria in order, for their sequence is deliberate and designed for negotiators with a pragmatic orientation (e.g., Americans). Feasibility, after all, appears first. Acceptability appears later because the value judgment it involves impedes deliberation in cross-cultural situations when used too early.[33] (Note that counterparts from other cultural groups may prefer to use a list that begins with appropriateness or acceptability.)

Each criterion deserves attention. Feasibility and coherence considerations may narrow your choices down to one unilateral strategy, yet you should still check that choice for its appropriateness, given the relationship and circumstances, and its consonance with core beliefs and values. For a negotiation scheduled to take place over many years, for example, the negotiator might look at a strategy that is potentially but not inherently complementary to the counterpart's (see Figure 3) or at combinations or progressions of strategies. For a negotiation where the negotiator cannot narrow strategy options by reliably predicting the counterpart's strategy, the negotiator may actually have to rely on the last two criteria. And when a negotiator wishes to consider joint strategies, relationship factors and circumstances are essential to consult. In sum, the support of all four criteria for a particular strategy choice should give you confidence in it.

Occasionally, criteria may conflict. Feasibility and coherence point to an embrace strategy for a counterpart's induce strategy, but the negotiator may find aspects of the counterpart culture's script unacceptable (e.g., *fatwa*, Iran's death threat.) Or the embrace-induce strategy pairing may have worked well in a cross-cultural relationship for years, but now you expect your counterpart to be at least moderately familiar with your culture. The resolution of such conflicts begs for further research. In the meantime, you may want to defer to your core beliefs and values. Values define the very existence of your home group and your membership in it; by ignoring or violating them you risk forfeiting your membership.[34]

As an example of strategy selection based on all four criteria, consider an American, Smith, who is preparing for a confidential, one-on-one meeting with a Frenchman he has never met before, Dupont.

Smith once lived in France and, as the meeting is being held in Dupont's Paris office, his gut feeling is to speak in French and behave according to Dupont's culture — that is, to use an embrace strategy. However, he takes the time to evaluate his options. Smith realizes that he is no longer familiar enough with French language and culture to use an embrace strategy, and the short lead time prevents him from increasing his familiarity. With a moderate level of familiarity, he has five feasible strategies: employ an agent or adviser, involve a mediator, induce Dupont

Table 5 Cautions: Choosing a Strategy

- Don't assume the counterpart will use the same criteria or order you do (e.g., efficiency is not a universal concern).
- Watch out for parties' miscalculations and conflicting impressions (e.g., the counterpart's assessments of your respective levels of cultural familiarity may differ from yours).
- Proceed carefully when criteria conflict; further research may help.
- Don't treat an embrace strategy, by mere definition, as costly or a concession.

to follow his script, adapt to Dupont's script, or coordinate adjustment by both parties. Smith does some research and learns that Dupont has only a moderate level of familiarity with American negotiation practices. That rules out the induce strategy. The relationship and circumstances make an agent or mediator inappropriate. An adapt strategy would be hit-or-miss because Smith has no cues from previous face-to-face interaction and only one meeting is planned. Overall, the best strategy choice is to coordinate adjustment.

A complicated situation will require more complex considerations. (See also the cautions on choosing a strategy in Table 5.) But the five steps above — reflect, learn, consider, predict, and choose — constitute a sound and useful guide for strategy selection.

Implementing Your Strategy

The full value of the most carefully selected strategy rests on effective implementation, a formidable task in the general fluidity of negotiations and especially in the multifaceted process of most cross-cultural negotiations. It is here, in a negotiation's twists and turns, that a negotiator deals head on with distinctions between the counterpart's attributes as an individual and as a member of a cultural group. Simply adhering to one's own plan of action is difficult — and may become undesirable. For the negotiator must ensure that the strategy complements the counterpart's approach and enables the two of them to establish and maintain a coherent form of interaction.

Whatever the chosen culturally responsive strategy, a negotiator may enhance the effectiveness of first moves and ongoing efforts by generally respecting the counterpart and his or her group's culture and by demonstrating empathy (both of which may take different forms for different cultures). These qualities, among others, have been recommended in the literature on cross-cultural competence and are consistent with cultural responsiveness.[35] They do not necessitate lowering one's substantive negotiation goals.[36]

First Moves

The strategies of employ agent, embrace, and induce entail complete, existing scripts for negotiation. Pursuing one of these strategies essentially involves following the script associated with it. The adapt strategy involves modifications of your own script, at least some of which should be determined beforehand. With the improvise strategy, you ought to give some advance thought to a basic structure even if much of the path will emerge as you travel on it. Thus you have a starting point for each of the five unilateral strategies.

These strategies assume that when a counterpart recognizes your strategy, he or she will gravitate toward its corresponding script.[37] The counterpart wants to understand you and to be understood; that is what occurs in *coherent* interaction. If you have accurately assessed the counterpart's level of familiarity with your culture and ability to use a particular script, and if the counterpart recognizes the strategy you are using, you stand a better chance of achieving coherence.

Should you make the first strategic move or wait until the counterpart does? This decision affects the transition from preliminary "warm-up" discussions to negotiation of business matters. It depends, in part, on whether you need to gather more information about the counterpart's strategic intentions and abilities. This would matter when both parties have at least moderate familiarity with each other's cultures and have more than one unilateral strategy they can realistically choose, and when you have chosen a strategy (e.g., adapt, improvise) that relies on cues from the counterpart. The decision over timing also depends on whether you need to make the strategy you have chosen distinguishable from another one (e.g., improvise from adapt) and want to clearly establish this strategy at the outset. (Note that if a negotiator has chosen to employ an agent or has successfully influenced the counterpart, then timing should not be an issue.) In sum, to decide on timing, you should weigh the benefits of additional information against the costs of losing an opportunity to take leadership and set the tone of the interaction, a loss that includes being limited in your strategy options by the counterpart's strategy choice.

The three joint strategies are explicit and coordinated by definition. Once parties have decided to use a joint strategy, first moves consist of fleshing out particulars. Which mediator? What kinds of adjustments? What basic structure will underlie improvisation? These discussions may require the intermediate use of one of the five unilateral strategies.

Parties coordinating adjustment might consider trading off their respective priorities among the twelve cultural aspects in the negotiator profiles. If your counterpart values certain interpersonal conduct (protocol) more than the form of the agreement, for example, and you value the latter more than the former, the two of you could agree to adhere to a certain protocol and, on agreement, to draw up a comprehensive legal document. This pragmatic approach will probably appeal more to Western counterparts than to Asian ones, however, particularly if the Asian counterparts have only low or moderate cultural familiarity. So take this approach with caution rather than presuming that it will always work.

Whichever joint strategy you adopt, pursue it visibly in your first moves. Especially in first-time encounters, a counterpart reads these moves as indications of one's integrity ("sincerity," in Japan) and commitment to coordination.

Ongoing Efforts

A cross-cultural negotiator has myriad concerns and tasks, including vigilant attention to the cautions in the tables presented thus far. Still, as negotiation proceeds, one's most important task is concentrating on interaction with the counterpart. Parties' actions and reactions evidence adherence to and departures from a given negotiation script, fill out the incomplete scripts associated with some strategies (i.e., adapt, improvise, effect symphony), and determine the ultimate effectiveness of every one of the eight culturally responsive strategies. These interactions occur so quickly that analyzing them makes them seem fragmented and in "slow motion." Nevertheless, some analysis can have tremendous value.

As you negotiate, shift most of your attention from the counterpart's culture to the counterpart as an individual. Specifically, monitor feedback from him or her, be prepared to modify, shift, or change your strategy, and develop *this* relationship.

• **Monitor Counterpart's Feedback.** A counterpart's reactions to your ideas and conduct provide critical information about the counterpart personally and about the effectiveness of your chosen strategy with this particular individual. As you use that information to make continual adjustments and to evaluate your strategy, you may want to return to the four criteria of feasibility, coherence, appropriateness, and acceptability.

Some verbal and nonverbal cues transcend cultures in signaling positive or negative reception to a negotiator's use of a certain script. They range from a counterpart's statements ("Things are going well," "We don't do things that way") to a tightening of the corner of the mouth and cocked head, which convey contempt.[38]

In one film of the "Going International" series, an American manager urges his Saudi counterpart to expedite delivery of supplies from the docks to the hospital building site. He points out that the supplies have already sat at the dock for a week just because of paperwork, he personally is "in a crisis," "nobody works here" on Thursday and Friday (it is now Tuesday), and during the upcoming Ramadan observance "things really slow down." At various points during these remarks, the Saudi does not respond at all to a direct question, perfunctorily sets aside a written schedule he receives, and looks disparagingly at the American's shoes. In the end, the Saudi states, "Mr. Wilson, my people have been living for many years without a hospital. We can wait two more weeks."[39]

Admittedly, a counterpart's statements can be more or less honest or truthful, and the gradations are often fuzzy to an outsider. A number of cultures distinguish between saying what is socially acceptable (*tatemae* in Japanese) and saying what is truly on one's mind (*honne*). Other standards may also differ across cultures.

Many cues (e.g., silence) do not carry consistent meaning from culture to culture. Generally, individuals learn the culturally specific meanings as they become familiar with a culture. Negotiator profiles include some cues and imply others under dimensions such as "communication complexity" and "nature of persuasion." A negotiator can use these cues when he or she embraces the counterpart's culture.

Then again, some singularly powerful cues are very subtle. (See other cautions for strategy implementation in Table 6.)

In the 1950s, an American couple — the lone foreigners — at a Japanese wedding banquet in Tokyo were socializing and dining like everyone else. All of a sudden, everyone else finished eating and left the reception. Residents of Japan for many years, the Americans concluded later that a signal had been sent at some point, and they had not even detected it.

In cross-cultural interactions that do not involve embracing or inducing, or when a negotiator cannot clear-

Table 6 Cautions: Implementing Your Strategy

- Remember that cross-cultural interaction can be creative and satisfying, not always taxing.
- Stay motivated.
- Separate your observations of the counterpart's behavior from your interpretations and conclusions about his or her intentions.
- Notice the changes as well as the constants in the counterpart's behavior over time.
- Try to pick up even the subtle cues.
- Give some thought to whether the counterpart might be feigning low familiarity with your culture and language.
- Don't get in too deep; don't unwittingly lead the counterpart to think your familiarity with his or her culture is higher than it actually is.
- Accept some of the limitations that the counterpart's culture may impose on outsiders; not all limitations can be surmounted no matter how well or long you try.
- Balance your responsiveness to cultural factors with your other aspirations and needs as a negotiator.

ly decipher the counterpart's strategy, nonuniversal cues are disconcertingly difficult to detect and interpret correctly. You can handle ambiguous cues (e.g., the hesitation of a counterpart who has so far been loquacious) by keeping them in mind until additional cues and information convey and reinforce one message. Other ambiguous cues may be decoded only by asking the counterpart; alternatively, they remain unclear. Dealing with these cues is a very real and ongoing challenge.

• **Be Prepared to Modify, Shift, or Change.** Even the well-prepared negotiator faces some surprises and some negative feedback in a negotiation. You want to be nimble enough to respond effectively. "Modifying" refers to refining implementation of a strategy without abandoning it; "shifting" refers to moving from one strategy to another within a previously planned combination of strategies; and "changing" refers to abandoning the strategy for another, unplanned one.

Making alterations is relatively easy with some counterparts.

> *For the first round of the 1980-1981 Ford-Toyota talks, Ford negotiators employed a bilingual Japanese staffer from their Japan office. The Toyota team, apparently confident in their English language abilities, suggested that Ford not bring the interpreter to subsequent meetings, so that the negotiators could "talk directly." Ford negotiators obliged and changed their approach.*

On other occasions, one may have to explain modifications, shifts, and changes before they are made in order to minimize the odds of being perceived as unpredictable or deliberately disruptive. One may also deflect criticism by directly or indirectly associating these actions with changes in circumstances, the subject on the agenda, phase of the discussion, or, when negotiating as part of a team, personnel. For ideas about specific modifications to make, other than those prompted by your counterpart, review the counterpart's negotiator profile. Changes in strategy should be shaped by both a negotiator's culturally relevant capabilities and the strategy being abandoned. You may go relatively smoothly from an adapt to a coordinate adjustment strategy, for example, but not from inducing to embracing or from involving a mediator to employing an agent.

Over time, some movement between strategies may occur naturally (e.g., adapt to coordinate adjustment), but a *shift* as defined here involves a preconceived combination, or sequence, of strategies (e.g., coordinate adjustment, then effect symphony). A negotiator could plot a shift in strategies for certain types of counterpart feedback, variation in circumstances or relationship factors, or, especially during a long negotiation, for a jump in his or her level of cultural familiarity.

• **Develop *This* Relationship.** Pragmatic Americans may view the cultivation of a relationship with the counterpart primarily as an instrument for strategy implementation. Concentrating on coherent interaction and a satisfactory relationship usually does enhance a culturally responsive strategy's effectiveness. But the strategy should also — even primarily — be seen as serving the relationship.

> *Riding describes the views of Mexican negotiators when they returned home from Washington after the negotiations over Mexico's insolvency in 1982: " 'We flew home relieved but strangely ungrateful,' one Mexican official recalled later. 'Washington had saved us from chaos, yet it did so in an uncharitable manner.' Even at such a critical moment, the substance and style of the relationship seemed inseparable."*[40]

Many of your non-American counterparts will be accustomed to an emphasis on relationships. Indeed, greater attention to relationship quality may be the most common distinction between negotiators from American and non-American cultures.

Developing a relationship with a particular counterpart requires an attentiveness to its life and rhythms. The form of your interaction can evolve across different scripts and approaches, especially after many encounters. There is also the potential for culturally driven conflict, which you should be willing to try to resolve.

Clearly, such a relationship should be treated dynamically, whether time is measured in minutes or in months. In that light, you can continuously learn about the counterpart and the counterpart's culture *and* educate the counterpart about you and your culture. Over a long period, you may experiment with a counterpart's ways in noncritical areas (at low risk) to develop skills within and across culturally responsive strategies. In this way, you can expand the number of feasible strategies, giving both you and the counterpart more flexibility in the ways you relate to each other.

Toward Cross-Cultural Negotiating Expertise

A friend of mine, a third-generation American in Japan who was bilingual in Japanese and English, used to keep a file of items that one must know . . . to function in Japan. . . . [He] never stopped discovering new things; he added to the file almost every day.[41]

Over the years, many cross-cultural negotiators have essentially asked, "What happens when you're in Rome, but you're not Roman?" The most common advice available today was first offered 1,600 years ago: "Do as the Romans do." Yet these days, a non-Roman in Rome meets non-Romans as well as Romans and encounters Romans outside of Rome. The more we explore the variety of parties' capabilities and circumstances and the more we question the feasibility, coherence, appropriateness, and acceptability of "doing as Romans do," the more apparent the need becomes for additional culturally responsive strategies.

The range of strategies presented here provides every negotiator, including one relatively unfamiliar with a counterpart's culture, with at least two feasible options. Combinations of strategies further broaden the options.

If there is "something for everyone" here, the value of developing and sustaining cross-cultural expertise should still be clear. That includes high familiarity with a "Roman" culture — knowing the cognitive and behavioral elements of a Roman negotiating script and being able to use the script competently. The negotiator at the high familiarity level enjoys the broadest possible strategic flexibility for negotiations with Romans and the highest probability that, for a particular negotiation, one strategy will solidly meet all four selection criteria.

A negotiator can also gain a great deal from learning about more than one other culture. For lack of space I have concentrated on negotiations between two individuals, each belonging to one cultural group, but most cross-cultural negotiations involve more than two cultures: most individuals belong to more than one group; negotiations often occur between teams that have their own team cultures in addition to the members' ethnic, national, and organizational backgrounds; and multiparty, multicultural negotiations occur as well. In short, the non-Roman highly familiar with culture A still encounters cultures B, C, and D. Even though a negotiator may need to focus only on the one culture that a counterpart deems predominant at any one point in time, there are several to explore and manage across time, occasions, and people.[42]

As soon as he was assigned to GM's Zurich headquarters in the mid-1980s, Lou Hughes, one of GM's main representatives in the GM-Toyota negotiations of the early 1980s, began taking German lessons because GM's main European plant was located in Germany. Now president of GM Europe, Hughes' effectiveness as an executive has been attributed in part to his cultural sensitivity and learning.[43]

In the process of exploring other cultures, one may discover an idea or practice useful for all of one's negotiations.

Another American negotiator in the GM-Toyota talks was so impressed with the Toyota negotiators' template for comparing parties' proposals that he adopted it and has relied on it since for his negotiations with others.

It is in this spirit of continuous learning that this article has presented culturally responsive strategies, selection criteria, key steps in the choice process, and implementation ideas. If negotiators with a moderate amount of cross-cultural experience have the most to gain from these tools, first-time negotiators have before them a better sense of what lies ahead, and highly experienced negotiators can find some explanation for the previously unexplained and gain deeper understanding. In addition, the culture-individual considerations and ongoing challenges highlighted throughout the article will serve all cross-cultural negotiators. Perhaps we can all travel these paths more knowingly, exploring and building them as we go. ◆

References

1. S.E. Weiss, "Negotiating with 'Romans' — Part 1," *Sloan Management Review*, Winter 1994, pp. 51-61. All examples that are not referenced come from personal communication or the author's experiences.
2. See J.K. Murnighan, *Bargaining Games: A New Approach to Strategic Thinking in Negotiations* (New York: William Morrow and Co., 1992), p. 22.
3. G.T. Savage, J.D. Blair, and R.L. Sorenson, "Consider Both Relationships and Substance When Negotiating Strategically," *The Executive* 3 (1989): 37-47; and
S.E. Weiss, "Analysis of Complex Negotiations in International Business: The RBC Perspective," *Organization Science* 4 (1993): 269-300.
4. Attending to both culture and the individual has also been supported by:
S.H. Kale and J.W Barnes, "Understanding the Domain of Cross-National Buyer-Seller Interactions," *Journal of International Business Studies* 23 (1992): 101-132.
5. To speak of an "American culture" is not to deny the existence of cultures within it that are based on ethnic, geographic, and other boundaries. In fact, the strategies described in Part 1 of this article and the five steps described here can be applied to these cross-cultural negotiations as well. These ideas deserve the attention of those, for example, who are concerned about diversity in the workplace.
6. C. Thubron, *Behind the Wall* (London: Penguin, 1987), pp. 158, 186-187.
7. See R. Keesing as quoted in:
W.B. Gudykunst and S. Ting-Toomey, *Culture and Interpersonal Communication* (Newbury Park, California: Sage, 1988), p. 29.
8. H. Binnendijk, ed., *National Negotiating Styles* (Washington, D.C.: Foreign Service Institute, U.S. Department of State, 1987).
9. For a review of popular books, see:
S. Weiss-Wik, "Enhancing Negotiator's Successfulness: Self-Help Books and Related Empirical Research," *Journal of Conflict Resolution* 27 (1983): 706-739. For a recent research review, see:
P.J.D. Carnevale and D.G. Pruitt, "Negotiation and Mediation," *Annual Review of Psychology* 43 (1992): 531-582.
10. For self-examinations, see:
G. Althen, *American Ways: A Guide for Foreigners in the United States* (Yarmouth, Maine: Intercultural Press, 1988);
E.T. Hall and M.R. Hall, *Understanding Cultural Differences* (Yarmouth, Maine: Intercultural Press, 1990); and
E.C. Stewart and M.J. Bennett, *American Cultural Patterns* (Yarmouth, Maine: Intercultural Press, 1991).
The views of outsiders include:
A. de Tocqueville, *Democracy in America, 1805-1859* (New York: Knopf, 1980);
L. Barzini, *The Europeans* (Middlesex, England: Penguin, 1983), pp. 219-253; and
Y. Losoto, "Observing Capitalists at Close Range," *World Press Review*, April 1990, pp. 38-42.
11. The original framework appeared in:
S.E. Weiss with W. Stripp, "Negotiating with Foreign Business Persons: An Introduction for Americans with Propositions on Six Cultures" (New York: New York University Graduate School of Business Administration, Working Paper No. 85-6, 1985).
12. Although I am not certain, my recollection is that the clients relented, and the bank team made the trip to South Africa. The point, however, is that the banker took a stand on an issue that struck values dear to him. Other examples include whether or not to make "questionable payments" and how to handle social settings in France and in Japan when one is allergic to alcohol or cigarette smoke.
On payments, see:
T.N. Gladwin and I. Walter, *Multinationals under Fire* (New York: John Wiley & Sons, 1980), p. 306.
On smoking, see:
W.E. Schmidt, "Smoking Permitted: Americans in Europe Have Scant Protection," *New York Times*, 8 September 1991, p. 31.
On the other hand, some customs, while different, may not be abhorrent or worth contesting. An American male unaccustomed to greeting other men with "kisses" (the translation itself projects a bias) might simply go along with an Arab counterpart who has initiated such a greeting.
13. Murnighan (1992), p. 28; and
Kale and Barnes (1992), p. 122.
14. J.L. Barsoux and P. Lawrence, "The Making of a French Manager," *Harvard Business Review*, July-August 1991, p. 60.
15. For example, for each of the four categories respectively, see:
D. Chalvin, *L'entreprise négociatrice* (Paris: Dunod, 1984) and
C. Dupont, *La négociation: conduite, théorie, applications*, 3rd ed. (Paris: Dalloz, 1990);
N.C.G. Campbell et al., "Marketing Negotiations in France, Germany, the United Kingdom, and the United States," *Journal of Marketing* 52 (1988): 49-62 and
G. Fisher, *International Negotiation: A Cross-Cultural Perspective* (Yarmouth, Maine: Intercultural Press, 1980);
L. Bellenger, *La négociation* (Paris: Presses Universitaires de France, 1984) and
A. Jolibert and M. Tixier, *La négociation commerciale* (Paris: Les éditions ESF, 1988); and
Hall and Hall (1990).
16. Nonfiction writings include:
J. Ardagh, *France Today* (London: Penguin, 1987);
L. Barzini, (1983);
S. Miller, *Painted in Blood: Understanding Europeans* (New York: Atheneum, 1987); and
T. Zeldin, *The French* (New York: Vintage, 1983).
Fictional works include the classics by Jean-Paul Sartre and Andre Malraux and, more recently, A. Jardin, *Le Zèbre* (Paris: Gallimard, 1988).
17. I will leave to others the debate over the effectiveness of training focused on "skills" versus other types of training. Somewhat surprisingly, some research on individuals' perceived need to adjust suggests that "interpersonal" and documentary training have comparable effects. See:
P.C. Earley, "Intercultural Training for Managers," *Academy of Management Review* 30 (1987): 685-698.
Note also that a number of negotiation seminars offered overseas do not directly increase familiarity with negotiation customs in those countries. These seminars import and rely on essentially American concepts and practices.
18. On cultural assimilator exercises, see:
R.W. Brislin et al., *Intercultural Interactions: A Practical Guide* (Beverly Hills, California: Sage, 1986).
19. J. Watson and R. Lippitt, *Learning across Cultures* (Ann Arbor, Michigan: University of Michigan Press, 1955), as quoted in:
A.T. Church, "Sojourner Adjustment," *Psychological Bulletin* 91 (1982): 544.

20. See Savage, Blair, and Sorenson (1989), p. 40.
The following all include relationship factors (e.g., interest interdependence, relationship quality, concern for relationship) in their grids for strategic selection:
R. Blake and J.S. Mouton, *The Managerial Grid* (Houston, Texas: Gulf, 1964);
Gladwin and Walter (1980); and
K.W. Thomas and R.H. Kilmann, *Thomas-Kilmann Conflict Mode Instrument* (Tuxedo, New York: Xicom, Inc., 1974).
21. For more extensive lists, see:
Weiss (1993).
22. D.G. Pruitt and J.Z. Rubin, *Social Conflict: Escalation, Stalemate, and Settlement* (New York: Random House, 1986), pp. 33-34.
23. Weiss with Stripp (1985);
F. Gauthey et al., *Leaders sans frontières* (Paris: McGraw-Hill, 1988), p. 149-156, 158; and
R. Moran and W. Stripp, *Dynamics of Successful International Business Negotiations* (Houston, Texas: Gulf, 1991).
24. P.H. Gulliver, *Disputes and Negotiations* (New York: Academic, 1979), pp. 186-190, 200-207.
25. G. Hofstede, *Culture's Consequences* (Beverly Hills: Sage, 1984).
26. The literature on women and negotiation includes:
M. Gibb-Clark, "A Look at Gender and Negotiations," *The Globe and Mail*, 24 May 1993, p. B7;
J. Ilich and B.S. Jones, *Successful Negotiating Skills for Women* (New York: Playboy Paperbacks, 1981); and
C. Watson and B. Kasten, "Separate Strengths? How Men and Women Negotiate" (New Brunswick, New Jersey: Rutgers University, Center for Negotiation and Conflict Resolution, Working Paper).
On gender-based communication, see:
D. Tannen, *You Just Don't Understand* (New York: William Morrow and Co., 1990).
27. N.J. Adler, "Pacific Basin Managers: Gaijin, Not a Woman," *Human Resource Management* 26 (1987): 169-191.
This corresponds with the observation that "the different groups a person belongs to are not all equally important at a given moment." See:
K. Lewin, *Resolving Social Conflicts* (New York: Harper & Row, 1948), p. 46, according to:
Gudykunst and Ting-Toomey (1988), p. 201.
28. A. Riding, "Not Virile? The British Are Stung," *New York Times*, 20 June 1991, p. A3.
See the disguises used by a female American reporter in:
S. Mackey, *The Saudis: Inside the Desert Kingdom* (New York: Meridian, 1987).
On the other hand, the all-woman New York City-based firm of Kamsky and Associates has been widely recognized for their business deals in the People's Republic of China. See also:
C. Sims, "Mazda's Hard-driving Saleswoman," *New York Times*, 29 August 1993, Section 3, p. 6; and
M.L. Rossman, *The International Business Woman* (New York: Praeger, 1987).
29. This interaction format draws on a game theoretic perspective and borrows more directly from:
T.A. Warschaw, *Winning by Negotiation* (New York: McGraw-Hill, 1980), p. 79.
30. T.C. Schelling, *The Strategy of Conflict* (New York: Oxford University Press, 1960), p. 53-58. The prominence of many courses of action would seem, however, to rest on assumptions that are culturally based and thus restricted rather than universal.
31. On risk-taking propensity, see:
Gudykunst and Ting-Toomey (1988), pp. 153-160.
32. For discussions of similarity-attraction theory and research, see:
K.R. Evans and R.F. Beltramini, "A Theoretical Model of Consumer Negotiated Pricing: An Orientation Perspective," *Journal of Marketing* 51 (1987): 58-73;
J.N.P. Francis, "When in Rome? The Effects of Cultural Adaptation on Intercultural Business Negotiations," *Journal of International Business Studies* 22 (1991): 403-428; and
J.L. Graham and N.J. Adler, "Cross-Cultural Interaction: The International Comparison Fallacy," *Journal of International Business Studies* 20 (1989): 515-537.
33. N. Dinges, "Intercultural Competence," in *Handbook of Intercultural Training*, vol 1., D. Landis and R.W. Brislin, eds. (New York: Pergamon, 1983), pp. 176-202.
34. Individual members do instigate change and may, over time, cause a group to change some of its values. Still, at any given point, a group holds to certain values and beliefs.
35. See Dinges (1983), pp. 184-185, 197; and
D.J. Kealey, *Cross-Cultural Effectiveness: A Study of Canadian Technical Advisors Overseas* (Hull, Quebec: Canadian International Development Agency, 1990), p. 53-54.
At the same time, Church cautiously concluded in his extensive review of empirical research that effects of personality, interest, and value on performance in a foreign culture had not yet demonstrated strong relationships. See:
Church (1982), p. 557.
36. This advice parallels the now widely supported solution for the classic negotiator's dilemma of needing to stand firm to achieve one's goals and needing to make concessions to sustain movement toward an agreement: namely, "be firm but conciliatory," firm with respect to goals, but conciliatory with respect to means. See:
Pruitt and Rubin (1986), p. 153.
37. Sometimes counterparts do not actually desire an agreement but some side effect. Thus their behavior may differ from that described here. See:
F.C. Ikle, *How Nations Negotiate* (Millwood, New York: Kraus Reprint, 1976), pp. 43-58.
38. See "Universal Look of Contempt," *New York Times*, 22 December 1986, p. C3.
39. "Going International" film series, Copeland Griggs Productions, San Francisco.
40. A. Riding, *Distant Neighbors: A Portrait of Mexicans* (New York: Vintage Books, 1984), p. 487.
41. E.T. Hall, *Beyond Culture* (Garden City, New York: Anchor Press, 1977), p. 109.
42. The assertion concerning the predominance of one culture at a time was made by:
Lewin (1948).
43. A. Taylor, "Why GM Leads the Pack in Europe," *Fortune*, 17 May 1993, p. 84.

Reprint 3537

[23]

COMPLIANCE WITH AGREEMENTS IN CROSS-CULTURAL TRANSACTIONS: SOME ANALYTICAL ISSUES

Allan G. Thompson*
The University of Melbourne

Abstract: Assessing whether the other party is likely to fulfil all obligations can be arduous when a transaction is international. The mechanisms that underpin compliance with agreements, and the functional detail of these mechanisms, may vary in relative importance between countries, perplexing the foreign operative. Additionally, a foreigner may suffer from informational constraints, communication distortions, and difficulty in achieving full acceptance in the local business culture.

INTRODUCTION

Parkhe [1993a] lists the dynamic evolution of cooperative relationships as one of the three major areas requiring theoretic development in international business studies. Cooperative relationships may encompass connections with partners, licensees, agents, distributors, subcontractors, major customers, and suppliers. The number of relevant empirical studies is also limited, although the available studies clearly show the significance of the issues. Thus dissatisfaction with many international joint ventures is well documented [Beamish 1988]. The theoretic and empirical limitations are of course related, since sensible empirical investigation must be built upon a sound analytical framework. Current theory does not provide an adequate framework. This paper considers aspects of theories of cooperative relationships in an international context, using experience from Australian-Southeast Asian transactions for illustrative purposes.

Two major bodies of current literature are relevant to the issues. The first is the extensive economics literature on so-called transaction cost analysis, including the determinants of compliance with commercial agreements [Buckley and Casson 1988; Casson 1991, 1993; Milgrom and Roberts 1992; Sako 1992; Simon 1993; Alter and Hage 1993]. The principal focus of this paper is to suggest modifications or extensions to those theories that may be required for international studies.

The second major body of literature examines the role of trust in commercial relationships [Madhok 1995; Hill 1990; Beamish 1988; Shapiro 1987; Ring and

*Dr. Allan G. Thompson (Dip.Ed., M.Com., Ph.D.) is currently an Associate in the Department of Business Development and Corporate History at the University of Melbourne. He is the former Director of the Asian Business Centre and Coordinator of the Asian Business Research Progam at that University.

Van de Ven 1992; Zajac and Olsen 1993]. That seems especially relevant to Asia because of the importance which has been attached to trust and personal relations in Asian business [Hamilton 1991; Lim and Gosling 1983; Hamzah-Sendut, Datuk, Madsen, and Tin Sin 1989]. The trust literature is a rich source of ideas, but for the purposes of this paper there are three difficulties. The first is that despite important insights into the causes and consequences of trust in business relationships, too much of the focus in the literature is on the presence or absence of trust. In transactions between two firms, trust or distrust are seldom absolute, and action is often based upon the degree of trust or confidence in the other party. Firms have available a range of actions from which they can choose, according to whether they perceive that the risk of cheating by the other party is extreme, high, moderate, low, or negligible. The firm can vary deposit or collateral requirements, require a guarantor or insurance, vary the rate of interest and so on. The assessment of the degree of risk needs to be drawn as finely as possible in a competitive environment. The cost of underestimating risk may be default. Overestimating risk may result in forfeiting a profitable deal, or in offering uncompetitive terms, causing the other party to turn to alternative suppliers or partners. Accurate judgment of the degree of risk of default is therefore crucial to competitive transactional judgments. To consider only the presence or absence of trust is not sufficient to provide a basis for examining those judgments.

That aspect of the trust literature does not entirely negate its value, but a second problem is that there are the irreconcilable definitional inconsistencies, what Shapiro [1987] calls a "confusing potpourri of definitions," in the trust literature. To some writers trust is shared expectations about behaviour [Zucker 1986]. To others, personal integrity is central to the issue of trust [Casson 1991]. However, integrity or honesty is irrelevant to other usages. Gosling [1983] identifies societies that, he argues, rely on 'personal trust', but in which cheating and suspicion is common, not only in the community at large, but even within small 'trust' groupings. The economist Dasgupta [1988] defines trust simply in terms of confidence in the ability to predict behaviour – even to the point where an habitual liar can be 'trusted' in the sense that promises indicate unfailingly what he/she will not do. (For other definitions of trust in economic relationships, see Buckley and Casson [1988]; Sako [1992]; Lever-Tracy [1992].) Other writers distinguish between 'system' trust and 'personal' trust [Wong 1991], or 'structural' trust and 'social' trust [Madhok 1995]. To construct an analytical framework based upon such diverse approaches seems to invite confusion. There is also a danger that in choosing between these disparate definitions, we may forego the insights of writers who have used approaches that are inconsistent with the chosen definition.

Perhaps the most important limitation of the trust approach is that, although 'trust' undoubtedly influences assessments of commercial risk, under most definitions other factors must be considered as well. That can only be avoided by a very broad definition, such as that of Dasgupta [1988]. Then the concept becomes analytically imprecise because it is multi-causal: "You trust him because, knowing what you know of his disposition, his available options, his ability and so forth, you expect that he will choose to do it" [Dasgupta 1988, p. 50]. When defined less broadly, factors other than trust, such as the legal system, influence cooperative relationships. Consequently, this paper considers the theory of cross-cultural commercial transactions from a compliance perspective, introducing concepts from the rich trust literature where appropriate.

COMPLIANCE IN COMMERCIAL TRANSACTIONS

Compliance is achieved when both parties to a commercial transaction honour the agreement between them. That is achieved when both parties carry out formal (written) and informal (verbal) promises [Buckley and Casson 1988], competently perform agreed tasks [Sako 1992], and deal with unforseen contingencies in a way which is fair and consistent with the spirit of the agreement [Kreps 1990]. 'Competently perform' and 'fair' are judged by reference to community standards or expectations (see Zucker [1986] for discussion about the role of expectations).

Except for simultaneous exchanges of products whose qualities can be determined by inspection, all commercial transactions entail the risk that one party will fail to fulfil the expectations of the other, in whole or in part. Conceptually, all complex transactions require assessment of that risk, even though in practice many, if not most, transactions are underpinned by previous assessments of the other party's compliance behaviour, and the assumption that they will continue to act as before.

To assess the probability of noncompliance (risk), a firm must attempt to judge whether the other party perceives their maximum commercial advantage opportunistically, or from a longer run, more enduring perspective. Perceived maximum advantage is determined by a matrix of circumstances, of which the repercussions of default, or more accurately the anticipated repercussions of default, are of special importance. A firm must not only try to assess how the other party perceives the consequences of default, but how it is likely to react to that perception.

It should be noted that although we suggest that estimates of the probability of default are vital to business decisions, we are not suggesting that specifying particular levels of risk allow a prediction of a firm's responses. A firm may refuse a high risk deal if it already has a full order book, but may accept a deal with the same level of risk if business is slow. It may impose different conditions on similar deals according to the availability and cost of finance, any prior experience with that firm, whether it is likely to lead to long-term orders, and other considerations that may vary from business to business and over time. However, we would argue that estimates of the probability of noncompliance will always be a major constituent of decisions about transactions other than simple simultaneous exchanges.

INTERNATIONAL COMMERCIAL COMPLIANCE

The fundamental theses of this paper are that the operation of compliance mechanisms can be distorted by being international, and that judgments about the probability of compliance are made more difficult by being cross-cultural. Three specific hypotheses are:

- that the four identified mechanisms that encourage conformity may vary in relative importance between societies, causing difficulties of adjustment and understanding;
- that the operating detail of compliance mechanisms may vary between societies, requiring different organizational responses;
- that compliance mechanisms may be distorted and modified in important ways when transactions are cross-cultural.

We begin by specifying the nature of the compliance mechanisms that underlie analysis of these hypotheses.

THE NATURE OF COMPLIANCE MECHANISMS

Four mechanisms encourage complying behaviour or punish noncomplying behaviour.

- Legal process has traditionally occupied centre stage as a compliance mechanism in modern trading systems. A standard argument is that strong legal processes are necessary to develop the impersonal trading relationships that are indispensable for large modern economic systems to function effectively (for a review, see Wong [1991]).
- Reputation processes have been the subject of intense study by game theorists and transaction cost analysts and these theories are used increasingly by business writers [Casson 1991; Milgrom and Roberts 1992; Sako 1992; Parkhe 1993b]. However, economists' definitions of rewards for complying with agreements use the concept of 'utility', which is too all-embracing and imprecise for our purposes. In this paper, we limit the meaning of the reputation mechanism to the pecuniary repercussions from failing to comply with an agreement, which in practice is the primary focus of most game theory analysis.
- Anthropologists and sociologists emphasize social mechanisms for ensuring compliance with agreements (e.g., Granovetter [1985]). Social mechanisms may function simply by the two parties acting in consonance with common social expectations about appropriate behaviour

[Zucker 1986]. If that process fails, punishments for dishonest behaviour may include such actions as social ostracism, expelling the person from a group (or refusing an application for membership), or excluding the person from marks of prestige, such as membership of a group of 'elders'. There also may be indirect mechanisms through close associates such as members of professional and trade associations and members of a family or clan [Zucker 1986].

Social and reputation mechanisms may act in tandem and reinforce one another. Social groupings may be active in the operation of the reputation mechanism, since social contacts may provide information, expert advice and leverage [Simon 1993; Milgrom and Roberts 1992].

- Casson [1991] has recently analyzed the economic role of personal integrity as a psychological element in the compliance process. The underlying principle is that people can derive psychological or emotional returns as well as material returns from dealing honestly.[1] Honest dealing bestows self-esteem, or avoids feelings of guilt that may be caused by cheating.

  Although Casson [1991] incorporates the emotional return into reputation analysis by defining it as a 'utility', it is separated here because the processes differ. The integrity or conscience of the individual drives the emotional return. The reputation mechanism, as defined in this paper, does not depend upon personal integrity.

Which of the four mechanisms is predominant? Authors, and disciplines, tend to emphasize one or another. It is argued here that in practice most firms will be conscious of each of the four mechanisms at some time. Firms must be capable of assembling information relevant to all four mechanisms, for three reasons:

- The key mechanism may differ in different transactions. Personal integrity may be the key issue in a partnership with a sole trader. Some simple transactions may rely entirely upon legal enforcement, but more complex agreements may be only partly legally enforceable.[2]
- Availability of information relevant to each of the mechanisms may vary in different situations. The information issue will be discussed in detail below.
- Circumstance may determine the relevance of mechanisms. For instance, the literature emphasizes the importance of prior experience, or what game theory economists call 'repeat encounters' in the reputation mechanism. While there can be no doubt about the importance of repeat encounters:
  - Although the majority of transactions may be repeat encounters, an

expanding company may do a significant amount of business without the guidance of previous encounters between the two parties. If so, risk assessments must be based on what can be learned about the experience of others in dealing with the firm [Kreps 1990; Milgrom and Roberts 1992]. However the capacity to share experiences can be influenced by such factors as the geographic dispersal and the mobility of customers [Hill 1990] and, as we shall see, by the way in which networks operate.

- Even repeat encounters may not be an infallible guide if circumstances alter. A firm may alter its behaviour after a take-over that subjects it to a new board of directors, if it has a new CEO, or a new marketing or finance director. This suggests that reputation is a complex amalgam of institutional and individual factors. Reputation and the behaviour of the firm cannot be entirely separated from the individuals operating within it. Institutional culture is capable of change as key individuals within it change, although a degree of continuity in behaviour may be expected. Moreover, diversification, vertical integration, changes in the firm's technological status in the industry, its financial structure, or changes in government policy may affect a firm's behaviour.

Such variations explain why a firm may require an information system capable of gathering data that are germane to all mechanisms. Indeed, in a single complex transaction, a firm may seek information relevant to all four mechanisms when estimating the risk of noncompliance. It may seek advice about what part of the transaction can be protected by the law, it may attempt to gather information about the past performance of the other party in similar transactions, it may attempt to monitor changes in the internal and external circumstances which might alter the other party's behaviour, it may investigate the characteristics of the affiliates and associates of the other party, and it may attempt to assess the integrity of key decisionmakers in the firm. For simpler transactions the relative weight placed on each of the indicators may vary with circumstances.

DIFFERENCES IN THE RELATIVE IMPORTANCE OF COMPLIANCE MECHANISMS

Notwithstanding the observation that the four mechanisms may vary in importance with time and circumstance, it seems probable that there are systematic differences between societies in their dependence upon the four mechanisms. It is emphasised that if there are differences, they are differences of degree, or in the relative importance of the four mechanisms.[3]

- There is little doubt that there are variations in the efficacy of legal compliance mechanisms because of varying degrees of legal sophistication. For example, it is widely agreed that the law does not offer the same level of commercial protection in many Southeast Asian countries as in most Western countries. Legal problems occur in protecting technology and intellectual property and in administration of the law by 'due process' [Simson 1986; Thompson 1981a, 1981b, 1982].

- There is a long history, especially in anthropology, of identifying networking as a special feature of some Asian societies. It is widely discussed as an element in Japanese business, both by academics and experienced business practitioners [Zimmerman 1985: Morgan and Jeffrey 1991; Dore 1991]. It is also widely argued that 'trust', personalized relationships and handshake deals are more pervasive in many Southeast Asian societies than in some 'Western' countries (various articles in Hamilton [1991]; and Lim and Gosling [1983]). Networking has been associated especially with the Chinese minority groups in those societies [Barton 1983]. Networking is relevant to the operation of both the reputation and social mechanisms.
- There are some general indications that social influences are stronger in many Asian societies than in the West. In many Asian countries, expectations about behaviour often emphasize communal or group responsibilities rather than individual rights compared to most Western countries.[4] There is also widespread belief that in many Asian societies shame has more importance than guilt in comparison with many European societies. 'Oriental face' is part of the shame syndrome. Shame operates as a social process whereas guilt is an emotional process.
- Variations in behavior between one society and another as a result of the emotional returns to honesty is explicit in Casson's [1991] thesis. He argues that the psychological returns to honest dealing can vary according to the prevailing moral code in a particular community and the moral element can be altered or manipulated by leaders. The proportion of transactions with psychological dimensions will vary according to the strength of the moral code, and to the proportion of the population that comes under the influence of the strong moral code.

  Whether higher [or lower] levels of integrity are to be found in Asian societies is an open question. Certainly many foreigners report ethical problems in dealing with Asians [Armstrong et al. 1990]. However, those observations may not be so much a reflection of problems of integrity, but of some communication difficulties of foreigners, which will be discussed further below.

The above suggests that there is a prima facie case for the following hypothesis: there are systematic differences in the balance, or the importance, of the legal, pecuniary, social, and emotional compliance mechanisms between Asian and some Western countries.

We now suggest some secondary hypotheses about the commercial implications.

- It may be difficult for a person from a society that emphasizes one compliance mechanism to accept that equal rates of compliance will be achievable in a society that emphasizes another. An Australian working in Indonesia may be uncomfortable with handshake deals and may not believe that reputation (or social sanctions, or personal integrity) is an adequate substitute for an effective legal system. By contrast, it is claimed that Asians may resent being obliged to sign a contract because it implies that they are not to be trusted [Kao 1991]; and an emphasis on contract may indicate that the other party is not committed to developing the level of personal trust necessary to create an effective working relationship.
- Established procedures for assessing risk in particular classes of contract at home may not work as well when transplanted to another culture. The firm will need to develop alternative procedures for assessing and handling risk for that class of contract in the foreign environment.
- In countries where legal processes are weak, but reputation or social processes are important, firms may avoid licensing arrangements, preferring JVs or other modes of entry that are less dependent upon legal enforcement.[5]

VARIABLE OPERATING DETAIL OF COMPLIANCE PROCESSES

There are reasons for suspecting not only that compliance mechanisms may vary in relative importance, but also that the operation of some compliance processes may vary from society to society. If there are differences of process, efficient cross-cultural business will require that they be understood.

- Networks may be used for a different range of functions in different societies. For instance most networks in Australia seem to be principally for lobbying purposes, whereas the networks of Southeast Asia seem to include systematic exchange of significant commercial information. They are used to exchange information on creditworthiness and reliability of business people, and to access the influence and the contacts of other members. Networks may also act as a form of insurance, by enforcing compliance with business standards, as has been noted elsewhere [Greif 1993].

  These differences may require different organizational responses. Business people appear to work assiduously at networking in Southeast Asia, through a high degree of socializing in voluntary associations, secret societies, clubs and charitable institutions [Barton 1983]. Foreign managers may be unwilling to devote sufficient time if they do not recognize the importance of social occasions for commercial networking.

Some functions of networking may be difficult for foreigners to appreciate and adjust to, for instance the idea that the rate of interest at which money can be borrowed, or even whether it can be borrowed at all, depends more upon personal contacts than upon the official balance sheet of the company [Thompson 1983].

- There may be 'functional substitutes' in different societies.[6] In the reputation mechanism, firms will seek information about the financial health of a client firm, and therefore its capacity to pay. In a country such as Australia, the information may be sought from formal sources such as professional credit rating agencies. In some Southeast Asian countries, however, credit rating agencies are rarely used because the ratings are based on publicly available company reports that are themselves regarded as unreliable. Credit rating information can be more reliably obtained through informal sources such as personal contacts, but the foreigner may simply assume the information is not obtainable.

Hypothesis: The operating detail of compliance processes may vary between societies, requiring different organizational responses.

MODIFICATIONS TO COMPLIANCE MECHANISMS IN CROSS-CULTURAL BUSINESS

We suggest a number of subhypotheses about the ways in which compliance mechanisms may be distorted when they are cross-cultural. Distortion here means that the mechanisms operate differently for foreigners than for locals, or that foreigners may be disadvantaged when inserting themselves into local compliance mechanisms, and in gathering the required information.

- Anecdotal evidence suggests that foreigners believe themselves to be discriminated against in legal processes in Southeast Asian countries. That may reflect xenophobia, or it may be that the foreigner does not, or cannot, become an insider in a system in which personal contacts, social standing, or bribery influence the administration of the law (see Simson [1986]). Although the supporting evidence is very limited, the commercial importance of the issue suggests that further investigation is warranted.

- Gaining access to local knowledge has been shown to be an important determinant of international success [Beamish 1988]. The information requirements of the reputation mechanism may be especially arduous for foreigners. Casson [1991] argues that a great deal of information is required before incentives to comply can be analysed in conventional game theory, information that he argues will seldom be available in the real world. Nevertheless he argues that "reputation works well in small, compact and isolated social groups." We will examine the latter judgment to tease out our understanding of the information issue.

- The first major determinant of the reputation effect is how many other relevant businesses learn about dishonest acts. There may be two ways by which information may be spread. First, a party to a business negotiation may investigate the past behaviour of the other party in order to judge the probability of default. Probability here has its usual statistical meaning and so the reliability of estimating the probability of default depends inter alia upon the number of observations collected in relation to the whole population of actions. The smaller the whole population, the lower the cost of collecting observations that are representative of the behaviour of the other party. A second way in which information might be spread is if an injured party to a transaction attempts to punish the defaulting party by informing third parties of the default. How effectively the defaulting party will be punished depends upon the proportion of its clients and potential clients that can be informed. Other things being equal, the smaller the client base the easier it will be to inform a significant proportion of clients (see Hill [1990]).

  This analysis suggests a general point: that the cost of dishonesty through the reputation mechanism is related to what might be called the 'network reach' of a negotiating party, i.e., the proportion of clients and potential clients of a defaulting party whom the negotiating party can access. It is important to note that the actions of a dishonest trader in a particular deal will be influenced by what that trader believes to be the 'network reach' of the other party to the deal. If the dishonest trader believes that the other party will be incapable of informing the dishonest trader's other clients and potential clients about an act of dishonesty, he/she will be more likely to cheat because it is judged that the reputation impact will be minimal.

  The 'network reach' of a foreigner is likely to be less than that of a local business person or may be perceived to be less. That may be so because the foreigner's main networks are in the home country; and some networks may be based on kinship, language or other ascribed criteria from which the foreigner is excluded. These difficulties are additional to the problems of understanding the nuances of networking in a foreign environment.

- A second major factor determining the flow of information about a default is the extent to which the parties are prepared to share information. We have noted that the functions normally performed by network groups may vary, and that includes information sharing. We further suggest that a firm is more likely to provide information to others if by doing so it improves its access to reciprocal information, and if it is confident that the information will be used with discretion.

Preparedness to share also varies because individual firms may have unequal acceptance within a network.

Providing information has immediate and potential costs. There will be direct costs of responding to an information request. Moreover, admitting that one's firm has been cheated may also harm the stature of the firm's management. Further, the information may be going to a potential competitor, strengthening its position. Alternatively, a firm may wish to continue trading with a charlatan firm if it can devise appropriate safeguards against further cheating. However, providing information to a third party about a default may further damage the trading relationship.

The costs of providing information need to be offset by a potential benefit, such as whether the other party will provide information in return. Reciprocity, or more precisely, confidence in reciprocity, may determine whether information is made available. Confidence in reciprocity is more likely in small groups, which may be an important reason why reputation mechanisms may work better in small groups, though reciprocity is not precluded in larger groups.

Confidence in the discretion of an inquiring firm may also determine willingness to disclose information. Some types of information are sensitive, especially where noncompliance is of a form that is difficult to prove legally, such as reactions to unforseen contingencies. In such cases, even when a firm is convinced that the other party has acted in bad faith, it may be cautious about declaring that judgment to third parties.

Finally, within a given network group, access to information may differ for individual members according to how well they are perceived to be integrated into the network. While all newcomers will take time to be accepted as integrated network members, it may be even more difficult for foreigners to be perceived as fully cooperative insiders. That is particularly likely if control and final decisionmaking are perceived to remain with a foreign 'head office'. Further, if networking is personalised, the habit of transnationals of rotating senior staff between home and a foreign post may threaten the perception of integration.

- Foreigners may be disadvantaged in social mechanisms. Zucker [1986] argues that trust will be breached if two parties do not hold common expectations about acceptable behaviour. Clearly the social mechanism of common expectations is less likely in cross-cultural transactions. Moreover social anthropology clearly shows that there are distinctions in the moral standards applied to different groups: "every man in society lives in the middle of a series of concentric circles of trust . . . those nearest to him . . . are always his allies. Those beyond the furthest circle are those who do not belong to his moral community, so that when he comes in conflict with them, he need have no consideration about what is right and what is wrong" [Bailey 1971]. This reasoning suggests that social standing in the community may not be influenced by actions towards someone outside that community. In effect the society may ignore the cheating of foreigners.

- Communication difficulties may disturb compliance cross-culturally:
  - For a firm to rely upon the emotional mechanism, it must assess the personal integrity of the other party. Casson [1991] argues that assessing integrity is both relatively easy and less costly than assessing reputation. The judgment that integrity is easy to assess is contentious. Internationally, this judgment is even more questionable. What is popularly called the 'inscrutability of Orientals' has some basis, since it has been shown that reading the emotions and reactions of people from a different culture can be deceiving [McCall and Warrington 1989].
  - Differences in the nature of honesty may be among the important differences in behavioural expectations of the two parties in cross-cultural transactions. Two societies may have the same degree of honesty (in Casson's terminology, the same crime rate) but may nevertheless define differently the components of honest or of cheating behaviour. Debates about comparative corruption (see Van Roy [1970–71]; Heidenheimer [1970]), indicate how definitions of honest and dishonest behaviour may vary between societies. It is increasingly accepted that corruption needs to be defined according to the moral codes of particular societies. There is also a growing literature on the problems created by different ethical outlooks in international business (see Armstrong et al. [1990] and references cited therein).

    Differences in the definition of honesty may mean that people from one society may believe that they are being cheated when the other party is behaving honestly by their code of conduct. This distinction may distort the perception of compliance, which of course is fundamental to the relationship between the two parties.
  - The importance of perceptions may have an even wider application because simple miscommunication between members of different societies can be common, as is shown in the extensive literature on international negotiation (see Adler and Graham [1989]). Miscommunication, from whatever cause, may disturb each of the compliance mechanisms.

In this section we have touched upon various aspects of information and communication. Clearly a major aspect of any investigation of compliance in cross-cultural commerce must examine sources of information and any difficulties of a transnational firm in tapping local information sources, together with the strategies that may best allow it to access those sources. Investigation of strategies should include the possible use of intermediaries, such as local partners or agents, in overcoming the problems of achieving insider status in a foreign country.

Hypothesis: Compliance mechanisms may be distorted and modified in important ways when transactions are cross-cultural.

SUMMARY AND CONCLUSIONS

Space does not permit the formal specification of all working hypotheses that derive from the above analysis, so we are limited to enunciating some principles upon which hypotheses will be based.

It is assumed that a firm making judgments about the likelihood of compliance by potential trading partners will attempt to construct an information system that provides data relevant to all four processes identified in this paper. It does so because informational constraints and changes in circumstances may result in variations in the efficacy of each of the four processes between industries and firms, over time, and for different classes of contract.

Although that implies variability in compliance processes for different types of transaction, it is assumed that there can be systematic differences in the balance or importance of the four mechanisms from one society to another. The study of compliance in cross-cultural trade needs to consider problems that may arise from variations in the importance of the four processes. It also needs to consider whether the functional detail of each compliance mechanism varies between countries.

A final principle that needs to be incorporated into the study of compliance cross-culturally is that there may be elements of compliance processes that may be distorted or modified by being cross-cultural. A particularly important aspect of distortion may be unequal access to information.

The theoretic framework could explain why a high compliance, 'high trust' society might nevertheless be one in which foreigners suffer significantly from cheating, or believe that they do. It may be possible to overcome diminished levels of compliance, but surely only if foreign firms understand the reasons why they are not matching local compliance levels.

NOTES

1. For similar analysis using the concept of altruism, see Simon [1993].
2. The theoretic economic literature is increasingly emphasising the limitations of legal mechanisms, especially the difficulties of defining and assigning property rights and of

interpreting and enforcing an agreement by a third party, particularly for service contracts, or for types of contracts where quality is difficult to determine by inspection [Dasgupta 1988; Casson 1991, 1993; Milgrom and Roberts 1992].

3. The relative importance of different mechanisms may also vary over time in the same society. Using a different taxonomy, Zucker [1986] demonstrates this point in the USA.

4. Casson [1993] distinguishes between 'organic' morality which favours social obligation and conformity, and 'atomistic' morality which stresses individual rights.

5. I am indebted to an anonymous *JIBS* reviewer for this point.

6. For functional substitutes in social mechanisms see Zucker [1986].

REFERENCES

Adler, Nancy & John L. Graham. 1989. Cross-cultural interaction: The international comparison fallacy? *Journal of International Business Studies*, 20(3): 515–37.

Alter, Catherine & Jerald Hage. 1993. *Organizations working together*. Newbury Park, Calif.: Sage.

Armstrong, Robert W., Bruce W. Stening, John K. Ryans, Larry Marks & Michael Mayo. 1990. International marketing ethics: Problems encountered by Australian firms. *Asia Pacific International Journal of Marketing*, 2(2): 5–18.

Bailey, Frederick G., editor. 1971. *Gifts and poison: The politics of reputation*. Oxford, U.K.: Blackwell.

Barton, Clifton. 1983. Trust and credit: Some observations regarding business strategies of overseas Chinese traders in South Vietnam. In L. Y. C. Lim & L. A. P. Gosling, editors, *The Chinese in Southeast Asia*, Vol. 1 (Ethnicity and economic activity). Singapore: Maruzen Asia.

Beamish, Paul W. 1988. *Multinational joint ventures in developing countries*. London & New York: Routledge.

Buckley, Peter & Mark Casson. 1988. A theory of cooperation in international business. In F. J. Contractor & P. Lorange, editors, *Cooperative strategies in international business*. Lexington, Mass: D.C. Heath.

Casson, Mark. 1991. *The economics of business culture: Game theory, transaction costs, and economic performance*. Oxford, U.K.: Clarendon Press.

——. 1993. Cultural determinants of economic performance. *Journal of Comparative Economics*, 17 (June): 418–42.

Dasgupta, Parta. 1988. Trust as a commodity. In D. Gambetta, editor, *Trust: Making and breaking co-operative relationships*. New York: Blackwell.

Dore, Ronald. 1991. *International markets and national traditions: Japanese capitalism in the 21st century*. Hong Kong: University of Hong Kong, Department of Sociology.

Gosling, L.A. Peter. 1983. Chinese crop dealers in Malaysia and Thailand: The myth of the merciless monopsonistic middleman. In L. Y. C. Lim & L. A. P. Gosling, editors, *The Chinese in Southeast Asia*, Vol. 1 (Ethnicity and economic activity). Singapore: Maruzen Asia.

Granovetter, Mark. 1985. Economic action and social structure: The problem of embeddedness. *American Journal of Sociology*, 91(3): 481–510.

Greif, Avner. 1993. Contract enforceability and economic institutions in early trade: The Maghribi coalition. *American Economic Review*, 83 (June): 525–48.

Hamilton, Gary, editor. 1991. *Business networks and economic development in East and Southeast Asia*. Hong Kong: University of Hong Kong, Centre of Asian Studies.

Hamzah-Sendut, Tan Sri Datuk, John Madsen & Gregory Thong Tin Sin. 1989. *Managing in a plural society*. Singapore: Longman.

Heidenheimer, Arnold J., editor. 1970. *Political corruption: Readings in comparative analysis*. New York: Holt, Rinehart and Winston.

Hill, Charles W. L. 1990. Cooperation, opportunism, and the invisible hand: Implications for transaction cost theory. *Academy of Management Review*, 15(3): 500–13.

Kao, Cheng-shu. 1991. 'Personal trust' in the large businesses in Taiwan: A traditional foundation for contemporary economic activities. In G. Hamilton, editor, *Business networks and economic development in East and Southeast Asia*. Hong Kong: University of Hong Kong, Centre of Asian Studies.

Kreps, David M. 1990. Corporate culture and economic theory. In J. E. Alt & K. A. Shepsle, editors, *Perspectives on positive political economy*. Cambridge & New York: Cambridge University Press.

Lever-Tracy, Constance. 1992. Interpersonal trust in ethnic business – Traditional, modern or postmodern? *Policy Organisation and Society*, Special Trust Issue 5 (Winter): 50–63.

Lim, Linda Y. C. & L. A. Peter Gosling, editors, 1983. *The Chinese in Southeast Asia*, Vol. 1 (Ethnicity and economic activity). Singapore: Maruzen Asia.

Madhok, Anoop. 1995. Revisiting multinational firms' tolerance for joint ventures: A trust-based approach. *Journal of International Business Studies*, 26(1): 117–37.

McCall, J. B. & M. B. Warrington. 1989 (second edition). *Marketing by agreement: A cross-cultural approach to business negotiation*. Chichester, U.K.: John Wiley.

Milgrom, Paul & John Roberts. 1992. *Economics, organization and management*. Englewood Cliffs, N.J.: Prentice-Hall.

Morgan, James C. & J. Jeffrey. 1991. *Cracking the Japanese market*. New York: Free Press.

Parkhe, Arvind. 1993a. Messy research, methodological predispositions, and theory development in international joint ventures. *Academy of Management Review*, 18(2): 227–68.

——. 1993b. Strategic alliance structuring: A game theoretic and transaction cost examination of interfirm cooperation. *Academy of Management Journal*, 36(4): 794–829.

Ring, Peter Smith & Andrew H. Van de Ven. 1992. Structuring cooperative relationships between organizations. *Strategic Management Journal*, 13: 483–98.

Sako, Mari. 1992. *Prices, quality and trust: Interfirm relations in Britain and Japan*. Cambridge, U.K.: Cambridge University Press.

Shapiro, Susan. 1987. The social control of impersonal trust. *American Journal of Sociology*, 93 (November): 623–58.

Simon, Herbert A. 1993. Altruism and economics. *American Economic Review*, 83 (May): 156–61.

Simson, Stuart. 1986. Suharto family in milk factory deal. *Business Review Weekly*, 8 (May): 24–32.

Thompson, Allan G. 1981a. *Australian companies in Indonesia: Establishment and operating experience*. Melbourne: University of Melbourne.

——. 1981b. *Australian companies in Thailand: Establishment and operating experience*. Melbourne: University of Melbourne.

——. 1982. *Australian companies in Malaysia: Establishment and operating experience*. Melbourne: University of Melbourne.

——. 1983. *Australian companies in the Philippines: Establishment and operating experience*. Melbourne: University of Melbourne.

Van Roy, Edward. 1970–71. On the theory of corruption. *Economic Development and Cultural Change*, 19: 86–110.

Wong, Siu-lun. 1991. Chinese entrepreneurs and business trust. In G. Hamilton, editor, *Business networks and economic development in East and Southeast Asia*. Hong Kong: University of Hong Kong, Centre of Asian Studies.

Zajac, Edward J. & Cyrus P. Olsen. 1993. From transaction cost to transaction value analysis: Implications for the study of interorganizational strategies. *Journal of Management Studies*, 30: 131–45.

Zimmerman, Mark. 1985. *How to do business with the Japanese*. New York: Random House.

Zucker, Lynne G. 1986. Production of trust: Institutional sources of economic structure, 1840–1920. In B. M. Staw & L. L. Cummings, editors, *Research in oganizational behaviour*, Vol. 8. Greenwich, Conn.: JAI Press.

[24]

Case Study
Negotiating Cross-Border Acquisitions

James K. Sebenius

James K. Sebenius is the Gordon Donaldson Professor of Business Administration at the Harvard Business School.

Driven by competitive pressures for globalization and facilitated by the liberalization of markets worldwide, cross-border mergers and acquisitions grew explosively during the 1980s, paused in the early 1990s, and are again increasing. Particularly in Europe, the number of cross-border deals soared from around 400 in 1986 to almost 2,000 in 1991 — representing almost 60 percent of all deals in Europe — and are now around 1,500 annually. The value of such deals has grown proportionately more than their impressive raw numbers;[1] indeed, on a single remarkable day — "Mad Monday," 13 October 1997 — more than $120 billion in cross-border European mergers and acquisitions were announced. While analysts have dissected many economic and financial aspects of this powerful trend, they have paid relatively little attention to the negotiating processes involved in these transactions. In this case study, I explore a sequence of acquisition negotiations by one Italian firm, Societa Metallurgica Italiana SpA (SMI), that consistently overcame seemingly insurmountable obstacles. From SMI's skillful approach, I distill broad lessons for effectively negotiating cross-border deals.

Many companies negotiate cross-border transactions routinely, using familiar scripts for effective deal making: "map" or enumerate and characterize the parties, assess their interests and their no-deal alternatives, envision potential agreements and the bargaining range, craft processes for both creating value and claiming it, pay attention to the sustainability of agreements, and so on.[2]

Yet, when financial negotiations cross borders, this general advice needs elaboration to fit the context, especially for inherently challenging transactions. Another country's politics, culture, and corporate governance policies can erect nearly insurmountable obstacles. In "fortress" Germany, for example — in which one of SMI's most successful deals was consummated — only three hostile takeovers have been completed since 1945, despite numerous attempts. Even friendly mergers occur far less frequently in Germany than in the United Kingdom or the United States.[3]

Italian tire manufacturer Pirelli's abortive effort to acquire German competitor Continental Gummiwerke exemplifies the efforts of many outsiders to make acquisitions in Germany. In 1990, Pirelli — with full financing and the apparent support from a majority of Continental's shareholders, including Deutsche Bank — tried to negotiate a merger with Continental. The process triggered a widely publicized, acrimonious confrontation, and Pirelli failed to secure a sufficient voting stake in its German competitor, suffering a humiliating rebuff from Continental management and a loss of more than $430 million.

The German "fortress" can prevent even its own firms from mounting hostile acquisitions of domestic competitors. In March 1997, German steel manufacturer Fried. Krupp AG Hoesch-Krupp launched a hostile takeover bid for compatriot rival Thyssen AG, a publicly traded company in the unusual position of having 80 percent of its shares widely disbursed among German investors. The bid — which, if successful, would have eliminated thousands of jobs — triggered fierce retaliation from Germany's steelworking unions and strong opposition from political leaders. Steelworkers staged massive strikes to protest the takeover plan, and approximately 30,000 union members demonstrated at the headquarters of Deutsche Bank and Dresdner Bank, the two German institutions financing Krupp Hoesch's bid. Within days, Krupp Hoesch rescinded its bid and was cowed into establishing a friendly joint steel manufacturing venture with Thyssen.

Like Pirelli, Assurances Generales de France (AGF), the second-largest French insurer, was repulsed by the German "fortress" when it attempted to forge an equity-linked strategic alliance with German insurance giant Aachener and Munchener Beteiligung in 1990. Three years after AGF's overtures were blocked, Michele Albert, chairman of the French insurer until 1994, commented:

"[The] takeover bid . . . is virtually unknown in Japan, Switzerland, and Germany. Approximately a third of German companies issue registered shares which may not be sold or transferred without the express authorization of the company. What is more, the board of directors (in its capacity as legal representative of the firm) may in some cases withhold its reasons for turning down a share-transfer request. This prerogative is a highly effective delaying tactic: you have no vote and no right to join in an increase in capital as long as the share transfer has not been approved by the company in question."[4]

Of course, takeover bids, especially hostile ones, typically stimulate aggressive negotiations, but Albert underscores the potential influences of differences in corporate governance and political economy on negotiating strategy for cross-border deals. The Italian firm I examine here has quietly shown a mastery of such difficult negotiations and completed major deals in its home country and in France, Spain, and Germany. Its success is all the more remarkable given that Italian firms are generally underrepresented acquirers in Europe (accounting for only 3 percent to 6 percent of cross-border purchases from 1991 to 1994, despite its 15.5 percent share of EU GDP). Furthermore, its most significant acquisition — a German firm that propelled the combined group to European dominance — occurred in what Albert and others have described as the world's most forbidding setting for would-be acquirers.

As a student of negotiations, I was intrigued by SMI's history of acquisitions. SMI, the holding company that owns KM Europa Metal, belongs to the Orlando group, headed by Luigi Orlando. (For SMI's organizational structure, *see Figure 1.*) SMI is in the copper transformation business, purchasing refined copper and its alloys and converting them to rolled form, tubes, laminates, and brass bars. In 1965, as one of many small and medium-sized Italian competitors, SMI had four plants and 3,800 employees, and produced 63,000 tons of copper products annually. At a

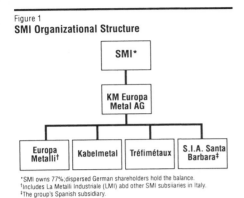

Figure 1
SMI Organizational Structure

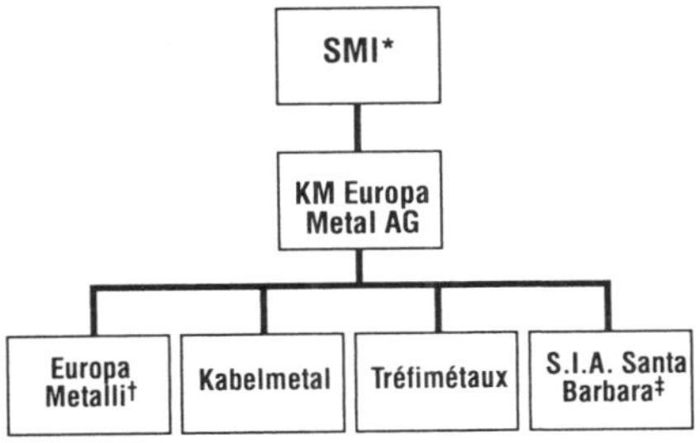

*SMI owns 77%;dispersed German shareholders hold the balance.
†Includes La Metalli Industriale (LMI) abd other SMI subsiiaries in Italy.
‡The group's Spanish subsidiary.

time when privatization was anathema in Italy, SMI nevertheless acquired and effectively privatized the copper division of the state-owned Finmeccanica, its primary Italian competitor, significantly rationalizing the Italian market and strengthening its position.

In 1986, in a second round of negotiations, SMI acquired its major French competitor, Tréfimétaux, a subsidiary of Pechiney, the vast French aluminum concern. SMI skillfully acquired the company over the staunch objections of most Tréfimétaux managers and with the unlikely but necessary blessing of the French government, which had nationalized the parent, Pechiney, only four years earlier. This was, again, an unlikely outcome: a *private Italian firm* acquiring a *state-owned French firm* that opposed the deal.

In 1990, SMI set its sights on Kabelmetal AG, a German competitor producing nearly 14 percent of Europe's semifinished copper. To many, Kabelmetal was a more audacious acquisition target than Tréfimétaux. The scale of this prospective transaction was daunting, but even more formidable were the traditionally high barriers to cross-border acquisitions in Germany. This was, after all, only several months after Pirelli's ill-fated attempt to merge with Continental. Yet SMI, with a carefully orchestrated negotiating strategy played out among multiple layers of shareholders and managers at its German target, prevailed, successfully acquiring Kabelmetal toward the end of the year.

On 5 October and 21 December 1995, I interviewed Sergio Ceccuzzi, Vorstand (management board) member of KM Europa Metal AG (responsible for strategy, financial policy, and management control) and chairman of Europa Metalli SpA, a KM Europa Metal subsidiary in his office, part of the Palazzo della Gherardesca. This ornate fifteenth-century Medici palace has served as the Florence headquarters of SMI since 1939. Our discussion centered on his firm's approach to negotiating a relentless series of acquisitions, mostly across national borders, that led SMI from its roots as a minor Italian player in the copper transformation business to its current industry-leading incarnation as KM Europa Metal AG. Viewed narrowly, this is but the parochial story of a minor Italian firm in a series of consolidating industry transactions. To cogniscenti of negotiation, however, this is like classifying Machiavelli as an adviser to sixteenth-century art collectors. Following this shortened, edited version of our conversation, I summarize some lessons from SMI's experiences. In the *sidebar*, I recount SMI's growth and performance.

James Sebenius: *Could you please tell me about SMI's main thrusts and approach to acquisitions?*

Sergio Ceccuzzi: SMI's business mainly involves the purchase and transformation of refined copper and scrap, not mining, raw material, or refining. Obviously, this business is very capital intensive. The Italian industry in the 1960s was composed of numerous small and medium-sized enterprises, quite unlike Kennecott or Anaconda in the United States, which were vertically integrated, often from mining through finished products. In formulating a fundamental strategy for growth, we at SMI made two basic decisions. First, we had to continue investing heavily in existing operations to ensure that we had the latest technologies and processes. Second, we had to grow through acquisition. We were *not* interested in growth by acquiring unrelated businesses in order to diversify; rather, we sought to acquire only firms that amplified our line of business.

We felt that no one knew our business better than we did — from our technology to our markets to our competitors. So we decided to employ advisers in our transactions only *after* we had directly approached the people on the other side — whom we typically knew well — and had negotiated a positive conclusion, at least in principle. Afterward, of course, the bankers and lawyers could craft an appropriate financial and legal structure to support the business arrangement we had already worked out. Often they added a great deal to the process, but we did not want to cede control of the negotiations to the merchant bankers. We wanted to call the shots until it was appropriate, nearer the end, for them to help.

The "Delta" Acquisition

Could you take me back to the late 1960s, when SMI was but one competitor among many in the Italian market?

At that time, we faced a major competitor in the copper-transformation business — Finmeccanica, a nationalized conglomerate. It was losing its entire share capital each year — some 3 billion lira on sales of about 50 billion lira — and every year, it was replenished by the government. Finmeccanica's production volume and pricing policies were causing "storms" in the market. Yet, to mention privatization at that time in Italy was to go against all major political and ideological currents.

So how did you proceed?

The Finmeccanica chief executive naturally did not enjoy the continual losses from what, for the conglomerate, was a noncore business. Likewise, the Italian Treasury did not look kindly on continual losses that it had to replenish annually. So we decided to provisionally acquire Delta, Finmeccanica's copper transformation operation for a modest sum, invest heavily in it, and after three years, if it had reached break-even, we would acquire it for a previously agreed-on price.

For Finmeccanica, then, the worst outcome would have been that it reacquired a firm in which substantial investments had been made?

Yes, and the government would have been spared ongoing losses.

That makes sense, but a similar argument could have been made about virtually any money-losing, publicly owned enterprise at the time. Why was this argument persuasive in your case?

For more than five years before the agreement, SMI had publicly called attention to Finmeccanica's losses and the costs to Italian citizens of replenishing its share capital. Thus, even though Delta was not a quoted company, its dismal results were well known.

"Our investment proposals enabled us to overcome the resistance of Delta's trade unions, which had been ideologically opposed to any privatization."

Further, this was a noncore part of an industrial group; we proposed making investments in Delta that its parent company had not been making or was making ineffectually. Our investment proposals enabled us to overcome the resistance of Delta's trade unions, which, in the past, had been ideologically opposed to any privatization. Overall, our plan would bring improvements for both workers and management, not to mention the government's fiscal situation. In effect, these players eventually functioned as our allies.

SMI had a relatively apolitical image. Except for a very small defense business, the government was not one of our major customers — unlike the automobile, construction, or electronics businesses, which sold to the public sector and often were quite active politically. Our technical image and lack of political involvement sometimes hurt us here in Italy when it came to winning certain contracts, but in this case, our Delta proposal was seen as the right thing to do, both technically and managerially. And our big bet on Delta, embodied in the three-year formula, was by no means a sure thing.

The TLM Acquisition

Where did your acquisition strategy lead after the Delta transaction?

We turned our attention to our other major Italian competitor, Trafilerie e Laminatoli di Metalli SpA (TLM). Before World War II, an Italian family had owned it. After the war, it became part of Tréfimétaux, the French company that was part of the Ugine Kuhlmann group owned by Pechiney, the huge French company with a dominant presence in aluminum.

How did you approach TLM?

Initially, instead of contacting TLM's parent corporations in France (Tréfimétaux and Pechiney), we approached TLM directly, proposing to the company's Italian/French management a merger of our firms, thus allowing both SMI and TLM to become more competitive in the Italian market. We had ideas for a strong restructuring that would lead to a more competitive combined entity. Of course, we knew the managers personally and felt that they understood both the market and the logic of the proposal. However, when we quietly raised the possibility, they were sharply divided. For one thing, we had been their competitors for decades, and naturally, they had seen us as the enemy. For another, an acquisition would almost certainly have led to the replacement of several of their senior managers.

So where did you go from there?

We approached Pechiney, not Tréfimétaux management, which would have opposed the idea strongly. Pechiney senior managers were interested, so we began discussions.

TLM was the Italian subsidiary of Tréfimétaux, which, in turn, was the French copper subsidiary of Pechiney?

SMI's Performance Record

In making its acquisitions, SMI succeeded not only at negotiations, but also in folding acquired companies into its industrial group. Typically, SMI's major acquisitions have been followed by a gestation period during which SMI incurs short-term declines in profitability while absorbing and streamlining a newly consolidated competitor, after which the SMI group emerges larger and more profitable. When SMI acquired Tréfimétaux, the French company was suffering extensive losses. SMI invested heavily in the company and thoroughly restructured it. As a result, within three years. Tréfimétaux was producing significantly more semifinished copper with far fewer workers and had become the most profitable company in the SMI group, achieving a return on equity in excess of 15 percent in 1989.

The acquisition of Kabelmetal again evinced the long-term effectiveness at SMI's acquisition and rationalization strategy in 1989, the year before the Kabelmetal acquisition, the SMI group as a whole achieved a return on equity of approximately 5 percent. With the acquisition. employment swelled from slightly more than 5,500 to over 11,000. The costs of absorbing such a large competition were high, and the impact was exacerbated by widespread recession in Europe during the early 1990s. Nonetheless, SMI methodically adhered to its strategy, streamlining the combined operations, eliminating redundant assets and employees, and riding out short-term surges in costs to achieve long-term growth in profitability.

Between 1991 and 1995, SMI reduced groupwide employment from 11,290 to 8,700 workers while increasing annual output from 700,000 to 750,000 metric tons (*see the figures*). At the same time, the company achieved a near fivefold improvement in groupwide return on equity, which rose from less than 2 percent to more than 9 percent.

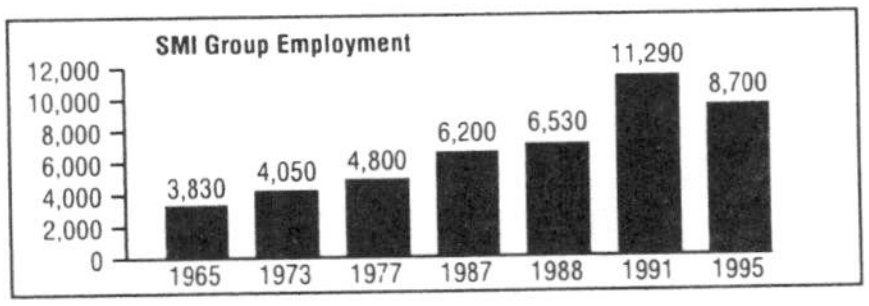

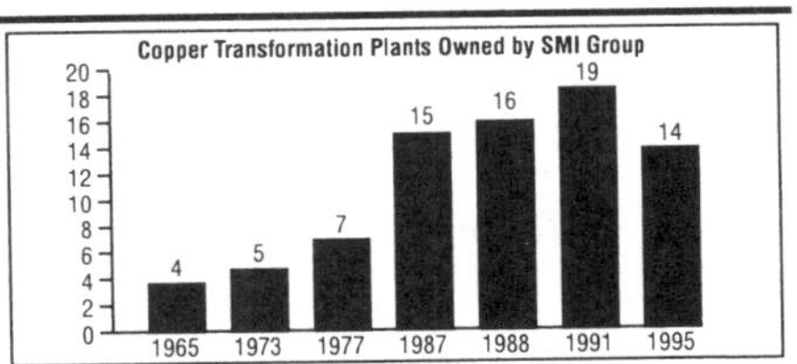

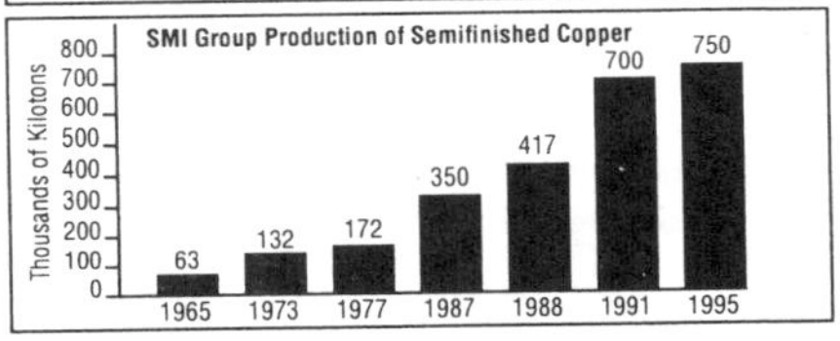

SMI is continuing its consolidation strategy with a mixture of Italian. German. and French management. In 1993, still top-heavy after acquiring Kabelmetal, the SMI group lost US $80 million but implemented major restructuring. The streamlined group, which SMI folded into the new intermediate holding company, KM Europa Metal AG, became Europe's main producer of semifinished copper and copper alloy products, accounting for more than 30 percent of European output, double that of nearest rivals, Outokumpu of Finland and Wieland Werke of Germany. Operating fourteen plants across Europe in 1995, the SMI group earned net income of $13.3 million on sales of slightly more than US $3 billion see table), and in mid-1996, the positive trend continued.

KM Europa Metal AG: Financial, Production, and Employment Statistics (1995)

	Sales (Millions of US$)	Percentage of Group Sales	Percentage of European Output by Weight†	Number of Employees
Europa Metalli*	$749	24%	NA	1,976
Kabelmetal	$1,425	46%	NA	4,556
Tréfimétaux	$789	26%	NA	2,132
S.I.A. Santa Barbara	$128	4%	NA	38
KM Europa Metal AG	$3,092	100%	29.3%‡	8,702

*Europa Metalli includes La Metalli Industriale (LMI) and other SMI subsidiaries in Italy. Restructuring the group was effected in June 1995. Results for Europa Metalli in its subsidiary role during 1995 exist only for 1 July 1995 through 31 December 1995. Data in the table reflect an extrapolation of these results to cover the entire year.
†Production of semifinished copper and copper alloy products (excluding copper conductor).
‡15.0% of world output.

Yes, TLM was an Italian company, controlled by Pechiney and traded on the Milan Stock Exchange. At the time, Pechiney was a private company, not yet nationalized.

How did you talk about structuring the deal with Pechiney?

First, because TLM was also in aluminum, we began with the presumption that TLM's aluminum operations would remain with Pechiney as part of its core business. In this way, Pechiney could remain focused on its major concern, aluminum, while still participating in a copper-oriented business with SMI.

Second, we proposed creating a new entity, a holding company called Europa Metalli SpA, to which SMI would contribute its overall operations and TLM would contribute its copper operations. Pechiney would be a passive participant with 16 percent ownership, while SMI would control 84 percent of the new company. Essentially, we completed the TLM deal on this basis.

The Tréfimétaux Deal

But your longer-term objective must have been to merge with Tréfimétaux, a major copper transformer in France, not merely their Italian subsidiary (TLM)?

Yes, all along we had contemplated a merger with Tréfimétaux, but discussions went nowhere for two years. Then Pechiney, Tréfimétaux's parent, was nationalized in 1982 during the first Mitterrand administration.

We had to wait ten years for an opportunity to advance this agenda. During this period, Pechiney tried to force the sale of its 16 percent stake in Europa Metalli to SMI on terms that we felt were unfair and certainly unattractive. Arbitration eventually went against Pechiney, but, as you can imagine, relationships were soured in the process.

Ultimately, a series of unforeseen events resulted in an opportunity. First, new management was installed at Pechiney. Second, Tréfimétaux began losing a great deal of money — about US $65 million between 1985 and 1986 — causing a financial drain and a management diversion for Pechiney. Third, in 1986, Prime Minister Jacques Chirac's government came into power with a more favorable view of privatization. Of course, this was hardly a mandate for privatizing French firms by selling them to Italians!

Luigi Orlando, chairman and CEO of SMI, personally asked the new head of Pechiney about his plans for Tréfimétaux, especially given its mounting losses and Pechiney's new strategic plan. Two months later, Orlando received an answer as part of a newly clarified strategic framework for Pechiney: "On the one hand, Tréfimétaux represents 10 percent of our turnover, and we do not consider it to be of strategic value. On the other hand, if we simply divested ourselves of this activity, we would face much difficulty in obtaining political consent. Therefore, we will entertain proposals only for participation rather than for 'brutal' acquisitions. These proposals will also be evaluated by the government, whose consent will be fundamental. And Pechiney will have to play a role in the new incarnation of Tréfimétaux."

The proposal we had already prepared was compatible with his response. It provided for some Pechiney participation as long as SMI had a relative voting majority, allowing us to exercise indirect control over Tréfimétaux.

But, if I understand correctly, Tréfimétaux management was completely against any acquisition. And wouldn't the French government have reacted negatively to any transaction that appeared to be privatization, let alone an acquisition by a private Italian firm?

Yes, there seemed to be no point in trying to negotiate with Tréfimétaux management. And with the realities of French corporate governance, which generally give the parent company virtually absolute control over the subsidiary, it made sense to negotiate directly with the parent. So we worked very hard with Pechiney both on the deal itself and on constructing a serious industrial plan to rationalize the fragmented copper transformation industry in France and Italy. We also closely negotiated issues of management structure with Pechiney, which absorbed the employees we did not want in the new entity.

Naturally, the French government worried about the potential closure of major French operations, given likely opposition by workers and the attendant political consequences. So, following an exhaustive study, we agreed not to close certain large-scale facilities in France for three years.

Before Pechiney would even embark on such a process, you must have had a basic price negotiation.

Of course. We had reached agreement in principle on the basic elements of the deal, which we discussed extensively until it was obvious to everyone that the combination made eminent industrial sense.

In any new joint enterprise, we had to move beyond the general rationale of the deal to specifically value the component parts. SMI was easy to value, given its positive performance and trend, but the net worth of Tréfimétaux was another story, since it was losing money. We simply proposed valuing it at zero, having Pechiney recapitalize it to cover the losses and make a long-term, low-interest loan. Naturally, Pechiney argued vigorously in favor of a higher price, citing goodwill and the like. This was the only aspect of the deal on which we were unyielding.

What gave you confidence that playing hardball on your pricing position would not blow the deal?

You say "hardball." We did hold to our valuation, but our manner was extremely gentle, not strident or threatening. Having convinced Pechiney that we were the logical partner, having ascertained that it had no good alternatives but noting the difficult state of the market and worsening prospects for a stand-alone Tréfimétaux, we treated our valuation principle as a deal breaker, and Pechiney unenthusiastically concurred. But we counterbalanced this "imposition" with strong willingness to be flexible on all other dimensions of the deal.

"The complex *deal* structure was driven by more fundamental *business* decisions."

How did the transaction work financially?

There were many technicalities. In essence, Pechiney would contribute Tréfimétaux to Europa Metalli following a significant restructuring. Remember, Europa Metalli was jointly owned by SMI and Pechiney. In return, Pechiney would receive a more valuable ownership position in the new larger entity along with certain control prerogatives.

Pechiney agreed to cover Tréfimétaux's losses through 1986 by means of a recapitalization to which it would be the major subscriber. In effect, it would reduce Tréfimétaux's share capital by the amount of its losses, contribute enough capital to boost the capital value of the shares up to par, and then contribute those shares to the new entity. It was a kind of "share recapitalization."

Then we constructed a formula for Europa Metalli that revalued its shares upward. In return for Pechiney's in-kind contribution (the recapitalized Tréfimétaux shares plus loan), it received more valuable shares in the new entity. Pechiney ended up with a 22 percent ownership stake in the restructured and larger Europa Metalli (EM), although its share was later reduced to 16 percent.

How else did you propose to structure the transaction so it would be more acceptable in France, especially to the government?

It was important to present the transaction as a restructuring of our industrial activities in Italy and France, an objective that was well served by the carefully drawn industrial plan and other features. The somewhat involved transaction structure I described should (and was) considered to be a *consequence* of a sensible business restructuring initiative in the French and Italian markets. In short, the complex *deal* structure was driven by more fundamental *business* decisions.

Moreover, Pechiney could accurately describe the transaction as a new joint activity since it would contribute Tréfimétaux's operations to an enhanced EM and boost the value of its holdings in the rationalized and much larger entity.

In the new EM, Pechiney would get three board seats and a place on the executive committee, which made decisions on any significant issues. These arrangements would last for five years and were renewable for two-year terms. If, at any time, Pechiney decided to sell or dispose of its EM stock, we would have the right of first refusal.

Operationally, how was this plan negotiated? How did it come to be accepted, in particular, by the French government?

In effect, SMI had to reach agreement with the French government. Yet, in line with our apolitical

"Once we agreed in principle and to the one tough issue — price — we operated in an atmosphere of increasing trust and collaboration."

stance in Italy, we decided to undertake explicit negotiations only with Pechiney senior management, which itself negotiated with the French Ministries of Industry and the Treasury. Now Pechiney carefully apprised the two ministries of the state of the SMI-Pechiney negotiations and no doubt helped Pechiney and us understand all pertinent governmental requirements. In a very loose sense, Pechiney played a mediating role between SMI and the French government.

Formally, however, Pechiney alone presented and negotiated the plan with the French Ministries of Industry and the Treasury. SMI scrupulously stayed out of the process and steered clear of the politics. Obviously, Pechiney had an advantage in such French negotiations. Of course, the French government officials had to satisfy themselves that the industrial plan over which we had labored was indeed workable. And they paid enormous attention to the plan's operational and other details before saying *oui*.

Could you tell more about the negotiations involved in working out these arrangements?

After we had reached a meeting of the minds on the general nature of the transaction, two main working groups — one business and one financial — negotiated the specifics. We prepared a general draft outlining the main areas for negotiation. We divided it into six sections with a logically interdependent structure; another section related the pieces to the whole. Different people worked on different parts of the deal. Each team consisted of a senior executive, a financial executive, and a lawyer. In a sense, after initial discussions, we wrote the theme, and the two sides jointly wrote the screenplay.

We met several times, alternating between France and Italy. By fax, we exchanged innumerable versions of the evolving document, which was written in English. Lawyers played a tightly circumscribed role, formulating the appropriate legal language for the developing agreement, but they were wholly subordinate to the business people. At times, such as when a complex arbitral mechanism had to be invented, they were especially useful. And financial advisers and auditors helped us with specialized expertise. But once we agreed in principle and to the one tough issue — price — we operated in an atmosphere of increasing trust and collaboration.

How did you deal with the former Tréfimétaux management?

When we earlier acquired TLM — which, like SMI, was an Italian firm — SMI executives moved into the upper-level management positions; however, our view of acquisitions abroad was entirely different. In France, we were committed to using local management. Both SMI and Tréfimétaux had been founded almost a century before the transaction; each company had a long, independent tradition, and each had been the other's competitor. So we needed to evaluate both the potential loyalty of Tréfimétaux managers to the combined entity and their technical and managerial suitability. As it happened, we did not accept the existing general manager but ended up promoting a divisional manager from within Tréfimétaux. Under his direction, coordinated with our Italian activities, we executed the industrial plan. By the way, Pechiney hired the managers with whom we did not wish to work.

When all was said and done, Pechiney remained a relatively passive, but significant participant in a restructured EM, having contributed a fair amount of capital by way of the share recapitalization?

Yes, but for Pechiney, this was a great deal less expensive than continuing to cover the large, apparently increasing losses of Tréfimétaux. So Pechiney did well relative to the alternative of no deal at all. And not only did it have a financial stake, but it was our partner in discussing and developing a broader European strategy. This new arrangement was for them a valuable window on a larger strategic process.

And how did the French government fare?

The French government maintained major operations in France, at least for a while. It cut off a significant financial hemorrhage. It could accurately describe its actions as a competitive restructuring and much-needed rationalization of Pechiney's copper activities across the French and Italian markets. French executives secured substantial representation on the board and the executive committee, together with the right to participate in strategic decisions for EM. No wholesale disposition or sell-off of a major French asset, in particular to a private Italian firm, had occurred. And EM's holding company, SMI, did not hold an outright majority, so control could not technically be said to have been ceded upstream either.

And how about SMI?

Through Europa Metalli, SMI could now coordinate and control both the French and Italian activities in the copper transformation and fabrication markets. In return for this substantial increase in control — with its high potential for restructuring and market rationalization — SMI accepted the very large risk that Tréfimétaux, even in this new setting, would continue to suffer huge losses. This risk was magnified by the agreement to maintain key French operations. All told, this was a major bet for SMI.

"We spent much time finding ways to integrate the entities psychologically, while signaling to the French that we genuinely valued them."

Thinking back to the Tréfimétaux managers, whose objections were overridden in the process, what steps did you take afterward to make them effective, committed managers in the new Italian-French enterprise?

During the negotiations, the Tréfimétaux managers' behavior was Pechiney's problem. And, as you recall, we did remove some managers at the completion of the acquisition for business reasons, though we acted very quickly to complete any bloodletting. We did not drag out the process. Then we had a *French* company that had to coordinate an industrial plan with its Italian shareholder. We introduced Italian managers into the process, although this was mainly at the board level rather than the operating level. Indeed, the managing director of Europa Metalli was responsible for essential cooperation and coordination of these two different companies with different managements.

We spent much time finding ways to integrate the entities psychologically, while signaling to the French that we genuinely valued them. For example, we combined some crucial advanced R&D activities and put them fully in French hands. And we staged events at which managers from the two companies were able to get to know each other better. For example, we had a strategic management consultant conduct an interactive seminar — on the logic of *our* joint Italian-French strategy — so the two sides could get to know each other personally. In 1993, however, we changed the management structure dramatically so we were no longer *coordinating* activities but actively *managing* them.

How were you doing that?

In late 1992, when I assumed responsibility for the group's industrial activities, Europe was in a recession. Early the following year, to enable EM to cope better with the recession and to strengthen SMI's hand in running the company, we created an informal management structure. A main feature was an executive board, which I currently chair. The board is made up of one French and two Italian members. Each is directly or vertically responsible for an international division (tubes, rods, or bars). We also internationalized various staff functions (MIS, financial systems, administrative systems, procurement, and so on) and assigned responsibility for these horizontal functions to board members.

While this informal structure confers no legal authority on board members — I cannot even sign a binding letter in my capacity as chairman — it has the advantage of being well-recognized and accepted within the French and Italian entities, while allowing each to maintain its formal identity as a distinct, local firm. But de facto authority and responsibility are assigned carefully to those board members whose skills match critical needs. And the structure has worked very well, going far beyond coordination to active management. By virtually any measure, the combined and restructured Italian-French operations have exceeded expectations in the five years following the transaction by overcoming, with remarkable resilience, the difficulties imposed by the recession of the early 1990s.

Lessons from the Tréfimétaux Deal

If I were drawing lessons from this negotiating experience, I would first note how long the process took from conception to realization. It was preceded by absolute clarity about SMI's strategic objectives, which endured over time. The industrial logic of the ultimate combination — rationalized French and Italian copper transformation activities — was powerful and can be seen as the engine behind the various moves

Yes, so far so good. But logic was not enough. Almost ten years elapsed before a combination of circumstances — a privatized Pechiney, new management, large Tréfimétaux losses — seemed to ripen the situation for new initiatives. And "ripeness" was hardly sufficient; conceptualizing and structuring the deal took considerable effort to overcome the barriers.

Second, it appears that after SMI executives conceptualized the plan, and events became more promising, there were at least three hurdles: Pechiney management, the French government, and Tréfimétaux management. Under the right terms, Pechiney could rid itself of a problem division that the French company had acquired almost incidentally, that was separate from the company's core strategy, and that was losing money. Any proposed deal, whatever its merits, could be blocked by either or both the French government and Tréfimétaux management.

The essence of SMI's negotiating strategy involved a sequential approach, by which SMI sought first to build a deal-favoring coalition in a series of deliberate, incremental steps and then to draw in, or ultimately subdue, any parties that might obstruct an agreement. You perceived that the possibility of a natural coalition between senior Pechiney management and SMI executives arose, given the right price; this would be the deal-driving coalition.

You orchestrated a carefully planned sequence of coalition-building events: first, SMI deal with Pechiney to cement an alliance; next, Pechiney worked alone with the French government to address governmental concerns and ensure acceptance of the SMI-Pechiney plan; and finally, all three allied players confronted Tréfimétaux management with an irresistible fait accompli. As long as Tréfimétaux managers did not take sufficient initiative to convince the relevant ministries (or allies of the parent company or even key union players) to block the deal, the game was over for them.

So another major lesson seems to be the importance of mapping and assessing the critical parties and then sequencing your negotiating efforts appropriately and retaining the initiative. And not incidental, I suppose, was the fact that an analogous approach had worked a decade before in the TLM transaction.

Third is the closely related lesson that, in multiparty negotiations, it is helpful to divide the other players into at least three groups: (1) unconditional allies, (2) those who will become allies if you can solve their problems and meet their interests, and (3) more or less unconditional opponents. Each group must be dealt with differently and often sequentially. Pechiney's senior management fell into the second category once a price was agreed on; the relevant French ministries were also in the second category but with much more complex interests to address; and Tréfimétaux management, at least during the process, was in the third.

The fourth lesson is the way you structure a deal, which, while advancing your own interests, must be as responsive as possible to other players' real interests and constituencies to maximize the chances of agreement. Deal structure can be important not merely for legal, financial, and tax purposes but, in some cases, as a powerful and positive signal to key players or audiences that their interests are being met. Further, the right deal structure enables key players to give an acceptable, even attractive, account of the deal to their constituents in a way that maximizes the chances of acceptance.

The final lesson is that once the deal is done, the negotiation does not stop. There must be an ongoing, intensive process to ensure that the original rationale for pursuing the deal remains viable and that the negotiated arrangement continues to generate value.

Your "lessons" very nicely capture our experience.

In 1988, two years after the Tréfimétaux deal, you were quoted as saying, "We succeeded in restructuring our industry with minimum cash outflow, achieving an important position in Europe, and we are now among the three global leaders. We obtained these results with the consent of other firms and the local governments involved in the deal. We can say that we are satisfied. We must now continue to focus our efforts on the managerial and industrial implementation of the plan in order to ensure the group's further development. Once we have achieved further industri-

al consolidation through new organizational initiatives and investments, we can proceed to negotiate new agreements." Where did you turn next?

The Kabelmetal AG Deal

During 1989, there were rumors in the market that Kabelmetal AG, a division of the Munich-based MAN conglomerate — which was involved in businesses ranging from the production of lorries and precision machinery to the fabrication of copper and copper alloy products — might no longer be considered a core business of the group. In our highly capital-intensive business, size offers a potentially decisive competitive advantage. Kabelmetal, our major German competitor, had a turnover of about $900 million, making it roughly comparable to our combined Italian-French operations. Through the links our parent holding company had with Allianz, a major MAN shareholder, we set up a meeting to explore MAN's interest in a possible sale. When we reached an agreement in principle on a sale, however, we stopped negotiating with MAN altogether and moved to a second phase of the acquisition.

I'm confused. Why did you stop negotiating with MAN after merely reaching an agreement in principle to sell?

There was another aspect of our provisional deal with MAN, which was that MAN would resume negotiations with us only *after* we had reached an agreement with the Vorstand members of Kabelmetal that a sale was in their interest and that they approved going forward. Then we would resume negotiations at the shareholder level. So it was a three-step process — MAN, the Kabelmetal Vorstand, then MAN — to complete the deal, within which we agreed that a *no* at any stage would terminate the negotiations.

Why did you give such veto power to the Vorstand?

Virtually everyone involved asked that question. You must realize that the Vorstand had de facto veto power anyway. The realities of German corporate governance are very different from those in France and a number of other European countries.

One element that is particularly nettlesome for would-be acquirers is the management structure of publicly held stock corporations. Each public company in Germany has a supervisory board — half elected by shareholders and half elected by employees — and a Vorstand or executive management board. Vorstand members are appointed by the supervisory board, typically for five-year terms. Realistically, if an acquisition of a German company is to succeed, it must be endorsed by the Vorstand.

Vorstand members cannot be removed from office unless a court of law proves just cause; typically, Vorstand members remain firmly entrenched for at least the duration of their five-year appointments. Furthermore, it is common for half the members of the supervisory board to be employee representatives inclined to select Vorstand members sympathetic to labor. In pursuing a merger or other combination, a buyer must work cooperatively with an entrenched management that is likely to be protective of workers' interests.

Another caveat: in Germany, a number of publicly traded companies have begun to enforce strict limits on the voting power that any one shareholder can hold. German law allows firms to add provisions to their articles of incorporation that restrict a shareholder's voting power to less than 5 percent of the total — regardless of the number of shares owned. This is essentially an antitakeover measure. Given a firm's ability to invoke such severe limits on outside control, an acquisition in Germany often makes sense only if the buyer's objectives are consistent with those of management; if there is any misunderstanding between buyer and Vorstand, the purchase is bound to be disappointing.

So if it does not sanction a deal, a German Vorstand can cause an acquirer endless problems and effectively poison a transaction. In my view, this was one key factor that doomed Pirelli's effort to acquire Continental. While Pirelli had shareholder support and ample financing, Continental management staunchly opposed the deal and ultimately thwarted it. With effort, a supervisory board could replace a recalcitrant Vorstand, but such a step would be radical in Germany and would result in grave problems.

In our case, rather than pursuing the kind of forceful power play we used with Tréfimétaux, we felt we had to persuade Vorstand members that the combination was in their interest. And, rather than let them assert their power, we preemptively acknowledged it and moved to sell the Vorstand on our vision for the combined entity in the new Europe of 1992.

"National cultural differences might have mattered a great deal, had we, as potential Italian owners, not taken pains to be very flexible."

That must have taken some effort. It seems that a German management team with an essentially passive shareholding parent would resist being acquired by a smaller Italian competitor with what promised to be a very involved owner.

Indeed, the Kabelmetal managers were skeptical and highly reluctant at the outset. They had been largely autonomous under MAN ownership. And Kabelmetal had a proud, successful history after its founding in 1860, more than twenty-five years before either SMI or Tréfimétaux. So we needed to paint a larger vision of where we could go together. We had to offer Kabelmetal a major place in this more expansive vision, a more significant role in Europe, I might add, than their current situation permitted. We pointed to our successful combination and restructuring of the Italian and French operation, which, of course, Kabelmetal management had followed closely. We assured them that, not only would we keep the present Vorstand — assuming their results continued to be positive — but, as we integrated our French, German, and Italian operations, they would have a leading role in management of the combination.

Instead of focusing on the loss of autonomy that Kabelmetal would suffer, relative to its current passive ownership, we urged the managers to consider the advantages of being a controlling shareholder that knew the business intimately and was absolutely committed to becoming one of the strongest competitors in Europe. Unspoken was the obvious threat: if they said no, we would soon be attacking them more aggressively in the marketplace. By saying yes, they would both eliminate us as a competitor and be poised to reap major competitive advantages from the scale that the combination would confer.

This was not merely a self-interested group of German managers trying to preserve their autonomy, power, and position. While the MAN group owned 77 percent of Kabelmetal AG, the minority shareholders were widely dispersed. Both legally, as fiduciaries, and personally, the Vorstand wanted to do what was best for all their shareholders and would continue to keep the interests of their minority owners in mind even if we bought MAN's holdings.

How much did national cultural differences matter?

They might have mattered a great deal, had we, as potential Italian owners, not taken pains to be very flexible. Incidentally, that was true with the Tréfimétaux acquisition as well. While there were certainly stylistic and managerial differences between us, our commitment to locally managed firms made a difference. Moreover, we were all in the same business, had been for years, and were committed to being so. Rather than speaking German, French, or Italian, we all spoke "copper transformation" as a first business language. And we all shared a strategic vision of the central importance of efficiently structured size for competitive success in our industry. As a result of this agreement with the Vorstand on the guiding principles and shared vision for a combined entity, we completed the acquisition in December 1990 for some $349 million.

What about the more detailed operating aspects?

We avoided detailed operating plans in the early stages. It would have been a major mistake to begin an itemized assessment of how we would combine our operations, who would be cut, who would take the lead on which responsibilities, and the like. That would only cause fear and potential organizational backlash. So we kept the discussions quiet, mainly at the top management level, and focused on guiding principles and shared vision. Later, when the deal was announced, we launched an implementation plan in line with agreed-on principles. Even after the deal was done, we still had to work with and persuade the Vorstand members on new initiatives rather than imperiously issue orders.

How has it worked out?

Quite well. Our management choices with Kabelmetal closely paralleled our experiences with Tréfimétaux. We started with board-level coordination and have recently moved to group-level management with the same sort of structure: a Vorstand with each board member directly responsible for management of an international division plus horizontal international staff functions (MIS, financial and administrative systems, procurement, technology development, and so on). We simply scaled up the management structure we had put in place in 1993 for the French-Italian operations.

In 1992 and 1993, the recession hit our French and Italian operations especially hard, and we needed to accelerate their restructuring. Our overall results during the first few years were boosted by strong German performance, which made it easier for Kabelmetal to become central to the group sooner. Recently, we radically simplified the legal and industrial structure of the French-Italian-German operations (including a smaller Spanish joint venture). We increased the share capital of Kabelmetal by DM 189 million (US $135 million), from a par value of DM 135 million (US $96.4 million) to a par value of DM 325 million (US $232.1 million). With respect to its 77 percent share of the capital increase, SMI contributed in kind all its copper and copper alloy fabricating subsidiaries. SMI's German partners, to account for their 23 percent share of the capital infusion, issued a stock offering, raising DM 43.5 million (US $31.1 million) in cash.

The recapitalized company, rechristened KM Europa Metal AG, became the new holding company for the group. Whereas previously Kabelmetal's minority shareholders had owned 23 percent of a single subsidiary within the group, after the recapitalization, they controlled 23 percent of the holding company that owned *all* the group's subsidiaries. Consequently, Kabelmetal was given an enhanced managerial and industrial role. (Debt remaining from the 1990 Kabelmetal acquisition continued to reside with SMI. To expedite debt repayment, SMI issued new shares of stock and undertook a systematic sale of nonessential fixed assets.)

Ironically, in terms of profit, the Italian and French entities had traded places with Kabelmetal and were now the most profitable within the group. The seven-person Vorstand of KM Europa Metal AG, incidentally, had three German members, three Italian, and one French, though selection was based on merit, not on a U.N.-like criterion of geographic balance.

Following these domestic and cross-border acquisitions, and after significant restructuring, consolidation, and debt reduction, we have become one of the most important European competitors in semifinished copper and copper alloy products. With only 2.3 times the number of employees it had in 1965, the SMI group in 1995 produced more than eleven times its 1965 tonnage in fourteen plants across Europe, with annual turnover in excess of US $3 billion, a profit upswing of about US $100 million compared to 1993, and every indication that the positive trend is continuing. The group's return on equity is now 9.2 percent. Our next challenge is to further boost profitability, which is too low. But we are now making all decisions with the consolidated balance sheet in mind.

Lessons from the Kabelmetal AG Deal

I see many of the same negotiating lessons we distilled from your Delta, TLM, and Tréfimétaux experiences, though applied here very differently.

Again, the driving logic was industrial. The time horizon was protracted, requiring discipline to adhere to a consistent, long-term strategy. You had to distinguish among the various parties on the other side and understand as thoroughly as possible each player's interests — MAN and Kabelmetal's Vorstand — from that player's perspective. Understanding their interests and the no-deal alternatives needed a detailed assessment of national political, economic, and corporate governance practices — which differ sharply between France and Germany, and between either of these countries and Italy.

With the assessment, you had to discern potential allies and blockers and develop an approach, proposals, and a sequence to meet each player's interests better than the no-deal alternatives. Then you had to persuade each party of the possible value in embracing rather than undermining a proposed combination. Once the deal was done, in order to maximize and sustain its potential value, you needed to create a structure in which the parties kept negotiating their common interests productively.

I would say that you have captured the approach exactly.

Thank you and good luck with your operating results and your next deal.

Successful Negotiating across Borders

My advice, distilled from my interviews with Ceccuzzi, builds on general principles of effective negotiations and SMI's experiences. Its applicability goes far beyond cross-border transactions.

1. Be very clear about the industrial and strategic logic behind your proposed acquisition and the genuine value it will create.

2. Take the long view. Be prepared to be patient, perhaps for years, as circumstances ripen the potential for the deal (unless your own forcing actions can hasten this result without undue risk of escalation). Then, act decisively but be careful not to stimulate an emotional counterreaction.

3. Well before any potential transactions, become familiar with the industry and establish good personal relationships; draw on these assets to develop the deal.

4. As with any deal, prepare by mapping the likely players, the interests that your approach will evoke, the players' no-deal alternatives, and their likely positions vis-à-vis your approach.

5. In creating the player map, factor in the procedures of corporate governance in the target company's country and the relevant characteristics of the political economy.[5] In particular, assess which parties are likely to be involved and which are likely to be motivated and able to block a deal or make it more costly. If you are not deeply familiar with governance and the local political economy, find advisers who are.

6. With the *individual* player map provisionally in place, assess potential alignments in the coalition, delineating:
•Those likely to favor the deal — especially the potential deal-driving coalition or the entity with the most significant stake in success — ideally cutting across organizational boundaries and perhaps including stakeholders outside either the acquiring firm or the target. Distinguish between the likely unconditional allies and those who would be allies if you address their concerns.
•Potential blocking coalitions — opponents that may individually or as a group have the power to stop the deal. Distinguish between those with objections you can meet and those who may be unconditionally opposed.
•Patterns of influence or deference among the other players, in particular, whether one group will defer to another or if one group's position will determine or influence another's.

7. Customize your approach to each group; maximize chances of success by carefully sequencing negotiations and making explicit choices about the nature of your persuasive emphasis at each point. Think carefully about when you will meet with others separately and in larger groups.

8. Decide on a strategy for dealing with potential deal blockers. Should you try to meet their interests to convert them into supporters? Should you sidestep them, play them off against each other, or simply try to overcome them directly or with the help of other parties that either are influential with would-be blockers or can override them?

9. Focus on how *they* are likely to see things, not on how *you* think they should see them. Where possible, craft your approach so it offers value and a vision in their terms, yet in a manner that accomplishes your objectives. Imagine and help to give them a story they can tell themselves, peers, families, and constituents about why they *should* favor the deal.

10. Craft a deal structure not only for legal, financial, organizational, and tax purposes, but also for key audiences and constituencies whose interests you are taking into account. Especially in politically salient deals, pay attention to the messages conveyed by your approach and the structure of the deal.

11. Retain the initiative in negotiating cross-border deals; don't be blindsided by the other party.

12. Act to ensure the sustainability of the deal, remembering that once the deal is done, negotiation does not stop.

References

This article benefited from the generous cooperation of Sergio Ceccuzzi, the research assistance of Janet Martinez and David Kotchen, and the comments of David Lax. Pietro Gennaro originally suggested this case and generously shared his previous work on the subject.

This article is based on the Harvard Business School case series Dr. Sergio Ceccuzzi and SMI: Negotiating Cross-Border Acquisitions in Europe (A) and (B), Nos. 897-084 and 897-085, by James K. Sebenius.

Copies of the teaching cases are available from Customer Service, Harvard Business School Publishing, Boston, MA 02163.

■ 1. For a discussion of the statistics in this introduction, see, for example,
European Commission Directorate General for Economic and Financial Affairs, "Mergers and Acquisitions," in *European Economy: Supplement A, Economic Trends*, Supplement A, number 3

(Brussels, Belgium: March 1995), pp. 1-9; and
J. Bleeke and D. Ernst, eds., *Collaborating to Compete: Using Strategic Alliances and Acquisitions in the Global Marketplace* (New York: Wiley, 1993).
■ 2. See, for example:
T.C. Schelling, *The Strategy of Conflict*, revised edition (Cambridge: Harvard University Press, 1980);
H. Raiffa, *The Art and Science of Negotiation* (Cambridge: Belknap Press of Harvard University Press, 1982);
D.A. Lax and J.K. Sebenius, *The Manager as Negotiator: Bargaining for Cooperation and Competitive Gain* (New York: Free Press; London: Collier Macmillan Publishers, 1986);
M.H. Bazerman and M.A. Neale, *Negotiating Rationality* (New York: Free Press, 1992); and
W. Ury, *Getting Past No* (New York: Bantam Books, 1991).
Some of this advice has been customized to financial situations in sources such as:
J.C. Freund, "Friendly Deal Requires Acquisition Mating Dance" *Legal Times*, volume 8, 14 October 1985, p. 10 ff;
G.E. MacDougal and F.V. Malek, "Master Plan for Merger Negotiations," *Harvard Business Review*, volume 48, January-February 1970, pp. 71-82;
R.F. Bruner, "Understanding Merger Negotiation: Teaching with a Merger Bargaining Exercise (Part I)," and "Understanding Merger Negotiation: Testing Rational Choice and Behaviorism in Simulated Bargaining (Part II)," *Financial Practice and Education*, volume 2, Spring/Summer 1992, pp. 7-17 and 55-65; and
S. Reed Foster and A. Reed Lajoux, *The Art of M&A: A Merger/Acquisition/Buyout Guide*, second edition (Burr Ridge, Illinois: Irwin, 1995).
■ 3. See J. Franks and C. Meyer, "Ownership, Control, and the Performance of German Corporations," (London: London Business School and University of Oxford, mimeo, 1995).
Of course, since reunification, the Treuhandanstalt has presided over a greatly increased volume of privatizations and liquidations of enterprises in former East Germany. This article focuses more on negotiations in what was the Federal Republic of Germany.
■ 4. M. Albert, *Capitalism Against Capitalism* (London: Whurr, 1993), p. 90.
For more on the AGF-AMB negotiation and associated issues, see:
R. Sally, "A French Insurance Firm and 'Fortress Germany': The Case of AGF and AMB" and associated appendix (Fontainebleau, France: INSEAD Cases 394-052-1 and 394-052-5, 1994);
H.J. Kim, "Markets, Financial Institutions, and Corporate Governance: Perspectives from Germany," in *Law and Policy in International Business*, volume 26, January 1995.
T. Baums, "Takeovers versus Institutions in Corporate Governance in Germany," in *Contemporary Issues in Corporate Governance*, D.D. Prentice and P.R.J. Holland, eds. (Oxford, England: Clarendon Press, 1993).
■ 5. See, for example:
J. Charkham, *Keeping Good Company: A Study of Corporate Governance in Five Countries* (Oxford, England: Clarendon Press, 1994).

Reprint 3923

Part V
International Joint Ventures and Strategic Alliances

[25]

THE DESIGN AND MANAGEMENT OF INTERNATIONAL JOINT VENTURES

An international joint venture is a company that is owned by two or more firms of different nationality. International joint ventures may be formed from a starting (or greenfield) basis or may be the result of several established companies deciding to merge existing divisions. However they are formed, the purpose of most international joint ventures is to allow partners to pool resources and coordinate their efforts to achieve results that neither could obtain acting alone.

International joint ventures and other forms of corporate alliances have become increasingly popular. For example, in the airline sector, virtually every major carrier has links with foreign carriers. These may be equity- or nonequity (i.e., code share, frequent flyer programs, etc.)-based and are culminating in truly global network arrangements such as Star Alliance and One World.

As Exhibit 7–1 illustrates, a broad range of strategic alliances exists. They vary widely in terms of the level of interaction and type. While many of the comments in this chapter focus on equity joint venture—the alliance form usually requiring the greatest level of interaction, cooperation, and investment—many of the issues are applicable to other forms of alliances. For example, IKEA, the giant Swedish furniture retailer, operates a series of nonequity buyer–supplier alliances around the world. IKEA provides component suppliers with product design, technical assistance, leased equipment, and even loans. IKEA's suppliers get new skills, direct access to a large and growing retailer, and steadier sales. This not only generates for IKEA low-cost and high-quality supply but a sense of partnership with, and loyalty to/from, suppliers.

Joint ventures have moved from being a way to enter foreign markets of peripheral interest to become a part of the mainstream of corporate activity. Virtually all MNEs are

---

This chapter was prepared by Paul W. Beamish.

EXHIBIT 7–1 Range of Strategic Alliances

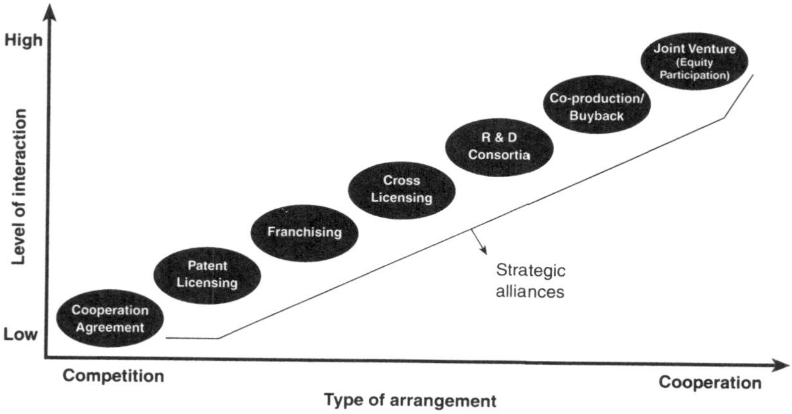

using international joint ventures, many as a key element of their corporate strategies. Merck, for example, has joint ventures with Astra (1997 JV sales of $2.3 billion), Johnson & Johnson (1997 JV sales of $.5 billion), Du Pont (1997 JV sales of $1.3 billion), Pasteur (1997 JV sales of $.6 billion), Rhône-Poulenc (1997 JV sales of $.7 billion), and so forth. Even firms that have traditionally operated independently around the world are increasingly turning to joint ventures.

The popularity and use of international joint ventures and cooperative alliances remained strong through the 1990s. The rate of joint venture use does not change much from year to year. In general, joint ventures are the mode of choice about 35 percent of the time by U.S. multinationals and in 40 to 45 percent of foreign subsidiaries formed by Japanese multinationals.

The popularity of alliances has continued despite their reputation for being difficult to manage. Failures exist and are usually widely publicized. Dow Chemical, for example, reportedly lost more than $100 million after a dispute with its Korean joint venture partners caused the firm to sell its 50 percent interest in its Korean venture at a loss, and to sell below cost its nearby wholly owned chemical plant.

While early surveys suggested that as many as half the companies with international joint ventures were dissatisfied with their ventures' performance, there is reason to believe that some of the earlier concern can now be ameliorated. This is primarily because there is far greater alliance experience and insight to draw from. There is now widespread appreciation that joint ventures are not necessarily transitional organization forms, shorter-lived, or less profitable. For many organizations they are the mode of choice.

Why do managers keep creating new joint ventures? The reasons are presented in the remainder of this chapter, as are some guidelines for international joint venture success.

Why Companies Create International Joint Ventures

International joint ventures can be used to achieve one of four basic purposes. As shown in Exhibit 7–2, these are: *to strengthen the firm's existing business, to take the firm's existing products into new markets, to obtain new products that can be sold in the firm's existing markets, and to diversify into a new business.*

Companies using joint ventures for each of these purposes will have different concerns and will be looking for partners with different characteristics. Firms wanting to strengthen their existing business, for example, will most likely be looking for partners among their current competitors, while those wanting to enter new geographic markets will be looking for overseas firms in related businesses with good local market knowledge. Although often treated as a single category of business activity, international joint ventures are remarkably diverse, as the following descriptions indicate.

Strengthening the Existing Business

International joint ventures are used in a variety of ways by firms wishing to strengthen or protect their existing businesses. Among the most important are joint ventures formed to achieve economies of scale, joint ventures that allow the firm to acquire needed technology and know-how, and ventures that reduce the financial risk of major projects. Joint ventures formed for the latter two reasons may have the added benefit of eliminating a potential competitor from a particular product or market area.

Achieving Economies of Scale. Firms often use joint ventures to attempt to match the economies of scale achieved by their larger competitors. Joint ventures have been used to give their parents economies of scale in raw material and component supply, in research and development, and in marketing and distribution. Joint ventures have also been used as a vehicle for carrying out divisional mergers, which yield economies across the full spectrum of business activity.

Very small, entrepreneurial firms are more likely to participate in a network than an equity joint venture in order to strengthen their business through economies of scale. Small firms may form a network to reduce the costs, and increase the potential, of foreign market entry, or to meet some other focused objective. Most of these networks tend to have a relatively low ease of entry and exit and a loose structure and require a limited investment (primarily time, as they might be self-financing through fees). International equity joint ventures by very small firms are unusual because such firms must typically overcome some combination of liabilities of size, newness, foreignness, and relational orientation (often they were initially successful because of their single-minded, do-it-themselves orientation).

Raw Material and Component Supply. In many industries the smaller firms create joint ventures to obtain raw materials or jointly manufacture components. Automakers, for instance, may develop a jointly owned engine plant to supply certain low-volume engines to each company. Producing engines for the parents provides economies of scale, with each company receiving engines at a lower cost than it could obtain if it were to produce them itself.

EXHIBIT 7–2 Motives for International Joint Venture Formation

New Markets	To take existing products to foreign markets	To diversify into a new business
Existing Markets	To strengthen the existing business	To bring foreign products to local markets
	Existing Products	**New Products**

The managers involved in such ventures are quick to point out that these financial savings do not come without a cost. Design changes in jointly produced engines, for example, tend to be slow because all partners have to agree on them. In fact, one joint venture that produced computer printers fell seriously behind the state of the art in printer design because the parents could not agree on the features they wanted in the jointly designed printer. Because all of the venture's output was sold to the parents, the joint venture personnel had no direct contact with end customers and could not resolve the dispute.

Transfer pricing is another headache that arises in joint ventures that supply their parents. A low transfer price on products shipped from the venture to the parents, for instance, means that whichever parent buys the most product obtains the most benefit. Many higher-volume-taking parents claim that this is fair, as it is their volume that plays an important role in making the joint venture viable. On the other hand, some parents argue for a higher transfer price, which means that the economic benefits are captured in the venture and will flow, most likely via dividends, to the parents in proportion to their share holdings in the venture. As the share holdings generally reflect the original asset contributions to the venture and not the volumes taken out every year, this means that different parents will do well under this arrangement. Clearly, the potential for transfer price disputes is significant.

Research and Development. Shared research and development efforts are increasingly common. The rationale for such programs is that participating firms can save both time and money by collaborating and may, by combining the efforts of the participating companies' scientists, come up with results that would otherwise have been impossible.

The choice facing firms wishing to carry out collaborative research is whether to simply coordinate their efforts and share costs or to actually set up a jointly owned company.

Hundreds of multicompany research programs are not joint ventures. Typically, scientists from the participating companies agree on the research objectives and the most likely avenues of exploration to achieve those objectives. If there are, say, four promising ways to attack a particular problem, each of four participating companies would be assigned one route and told to pursue it. Meetings would be held, perhaps quarterly, to share results and approaches taken and when (hopefully) one route proved to be successful, all firms would be fully informed on the new techniques and technology.

The alternative way to carry out collaborative research is to establish a jointly owned company and to provide it with staff, budget, and a physical location. In early 1999 for example, discussions were under way for a proposed, not-for-profit consortium of major drug companies that would fund work on decoding the human genome. At a cost of $75–100 million from participants, the proposed joint venture would compete directly with the small biotech companies already working on the project. The large pharmaceutical companies share an interest in having open access to a map of genetic landmarks, as they feel this will be essential to the way new drugs will be tested and developed in the future.

In the United States, a somewhat different problem arose when the president of a joint research company established by a dozen U.S. computer firms discovered that the participating companies were not sending their best people to the new company. He ended up hiring more than 200 of the firm's 330 scientists from the outside.

A sensitive issue for firms engaging in collaborative research, whether through joint ventures or not, is how far the collaboration should extend. Because the partners are usually competitors, the often expressed ideal is that the joint effort will focus only on "pre-competitive" basic research and not, for example, on product development work. This is often a difficult line to draw.

Marketing and Distribution. Many international joint ventures involve shared research, development, and production but stop short of joint marketing. The vehicles coming out of the widely publicized joint venture between Toyota and General Motors in California, for instance, are clearly branded as GM or Toyota products and are sold competitively through each parent's distribution network. Antitrust plays a role in the decision to keep marketing activities separate, but so does the partners' intrinsic desire to maintain separate brand identities and increase their own market share. These cooperating firms have not forgotten that they are competitors.

There are, nevertheless, some ventures formed for the express purpose of achieving economies in marketing and distribution. A three-way venture formed between Bacardi International of the United States, Martini and Rossi of Italy, and Bass, Britain's largest brewer, to sell a combined portfolio of the brands of all three companies in England and Wales is a typical example of what can be done. Each firm is hoping for wider market coverage at a lower cost. The trade-off is a loss of direct control over the sales force, potentially slower decision making, and a possible loss of direct contact with the customer.

Somewhat similar in intent are cooperative marketing agreements, which are not joint ventures but agreements by two firms with related product lines to sell one another's products. Here companies end up with a more complete line to sell, without the managerial complications of a joint venture. Sometimes the cooperative marketing agreement can in fact entail joint branding, as the Neilson International in Mexico case discusses.

Divisional Mergers. Multinational companies with subsidiaries that they have concluded are too small to be economic have sometimes chosen to create a joint venture by combining their "too small" operations with those of a competitor. Fiat and Peugeot, for example, merged their automobile operations in Argentina, where both companies were doing poorly. The new joint venture started life with a market share of 35 percent and a chance for greatly improved economies in design, production, and marketing. Faced with similar pressures, Ford and Volkswagen have done the same thing in Brazil, creating a jointly owned company called Auto Latina.

Similarly, Dresser Industries of Illinois and Komatsu of Japan combined existing businesses to create an equally owned joint venture to compete in the construction and mining equipment business in the Western Hemisphere. Komatsu's motivation for entering the venture was to establish a manufacturing source for its products in North America, as balance of trade pressures and currency values made sourcing from Japan ever more risky. Explaining Dresser's desire for the joint venture, a vice president stated that the equipment business was becoming ever more capital-intensive, and the only routes to success were to be a very narrow niche player or a major full-line producer. The Komatsu deal created the latter—a strong full-line company with first-year sales in excess of $1.5 billion, ranked number two in the Americas.

A divisional merger can also allow a firm a graceful exit from a business in which it is no longer interested. Honeywell gave up trying to continue alone in the computer industry when it folded its business into a venture with Machines Bull of France and NEC of Japan. Honeywell held a 40 percent stake in the resulting joint venture.

Acquiring Technology in the Core Business

Firms that have wanted to acquire technology in their core business area have traditionally done so through license agreements or by developing the technology themselves. Increasingly, however, companies are turning to joint ventures for this purpose, because developing technology in-house is seen as taking too long, and license agreements, while giving the firm access to patent rights and engineers' ideas, may not provide much in the way of shop floor know-how. The power of a joint venture is that a firm may be able to have its employees working shoulder to shoulder with those of its partner, trying to solve the same problems. For example, the General Motors joint venture with Toyota provided an opportunity for GM to obtain a source of low-cost small cars and to watch firsthand how Toyota managers, who were in operational control of the venture, were able to produce high-quality automobiles at low cost. Most observers have concluded that the opportunity for General Motors to learn new production techniques was more significant than the supply of cars coming from the venture.

Reducing Financial Risk

Some projects are too big or too risky for firms to tackle alone. This is why oil companies use joint ventures to split the costs of searching for new oil fields, and why the aircraft industry is increasingly using joint ventures and "risk-sharing subcontractors" to put up some of the funds required to develop new aircraft and engines.

Do such joint ventures make sense? For the oil companies the answer is a clear yes. In these ventures, one partner takes a lead role and manages the venture on a day-to-day basis. Management complexity, a major potential drawback of joint ventures, is kept to a minimum. If the venture finds oil, transfer prices are not a problem—the rewards of the venture are easy to divide between the partners. In situations like this, forming a joint venture is an efficient and sensible way of sharing risk.

It is not as obvious that some other industry ventures are a good idea, at least not for industry leaders. Their partners are not entering these ventures simply in the hopes of earning an attractive return on their investment. They are gearing up to produce, sooner or later, their own product. Why would a company be willing to train potential competitors? For many firms, it is the realization that their partner is going to hook up with someone anyway, so better to have a portion of a smaller future pie than none at all, even if it means you may be eventually competing against yourself.

Taking Products to Foreign Markets

Firms with domestic products that they believe will be successful in foreign markets face a choice. As discussed in Chapter 1, they can produce the product at home and export it, license the technology to local firms around the world, establish wholly owned subsidiaries in foreign countries, or form joint ventures with local partners. Many firms conclude that exporting is unlikely to lead to significant market penetration, building wholly owned subsidiaries is too slow and requires too many resources, and licensing does not offer an adequate financial return. The result is that an international joint venture, while seldom seen as an ideal choice, is often the most attractive compromise.

Moving into foreign markets entails a degree of risk, and most firms that decide to form a joint venture with a local firm are doing so to reduce the risk associated with their new market entry. Very often, they look for a partner that deals with a related product line and, thus, has a good feel for the local market. As a further risk-reducing measure, the joint venture may begin life as simply a sales and marketing operation, until the product begins to sell well and volumes rise. Then a "screwdriver" assembly plant may be set up to assemble components shipped from the foreign parent. Eventually, the venture may modify or redesign the product to better suit the local market and may establish complete local manufacturing, sourcing raw material and components locally. The objective is to withhold major investment until the market uncertainty is reduced.

Following Customers to Foreign Markets. Another way to reduce the risk of a foreign market entry is to follow firms that are already customers at home. Thus, many Japanese automobile suppliers have followed Honda, Toyota, and Nissan as they set up new plants in North America and Europe. As in the Wilmor case, very often these suppliers, uncertain of their ability to operate in a foreign environment, decide to form a joint venture with a local partner. There are, for example, a great many automobile supplier joint ventures in the United States originally formed between Japanese and American auto suppliers to supply the Japanese "transplant" automobile manufacturers. For the Americans, such ventures provide a way to learn Japanese manufacturing techniques and to tap into a growing market.

Investing in "Markets of the Future." Some of the riskiest joint ventures are those established by firms taking an early position in what they see as emerging markets. These areas offer very large untapped markets, as well as a possible source of low-cost raw materials and labor. The major problems faced by Western firms in penetrating such markets are their unfamiliarity with the local culture, establishing Western attitudes toward quality, and, in some areas, repatriating earnings in hard currency. The solution (sometimes imposed by local government) has often been the creation of joint ventures with local partners who "know the ropes" and can deal with the local bureaucracy.

Even a local partner, however, is no guarantee of success, as the rules of the game can change overnight in such regions. This can be due to a new government coming to power, a revision of existing practice in response to a financial crisis, pressure from international funding agencies, and so forth.

Bringing Foreign Products to Local Markets

For every firm that uses an international joint venture to take its product to a foreign market, a local company sees the joint venture as an attractive way to bring a foreign product to its existing market. It is, of course, this complementarity of interest that makes the joint venture possible.

Local partners enter joint ventures to get better utilization of existing plants or distribution channels, to protect themselves against threatening new technology, or simply as an impetus for new growth. Typically, the financial rewards that the local partner receives from a venture are different from those accruing to the foreign partner. For example:

- Many foreign partners make a profit shipping finished products and components to their joint ventures. These profits are particularly attractive because they are in hard currency, which may not be true of the venture's profits, and because the foreign partner captures 100 percent of them, not just a share.
- Many foreign partners receive a technology fee, which is a fixed percentage of the sales volume of the joint venture. The local partner may or may not receive a management fee of like amount.
- Foreign partners typically pay a withholding tax on dividends remitted to them from the venture. Local firms do not.

As a result of these differences, the local partner is often far more concerned with the venture's bottom line earnings and dividend payout than the foreign partner. This means the foreign partner is likely to be happier to keep the venture as simply a marketing or assembly operation, as previously described, than to develop it to the point where it buys less imported material.

Although this logic is understandable, such thinking is shortsighted. The best example of the benefits that can come back to a parent from a powerful joint venture is Fuji Xerox, a venture begun in Japan in the early 1960s between Xerox and Fuji Photo. This is among the most successful American–Japanese joint ventures in Japan.

For the first 10 years of its life, Fuji Xerox was strictly a marketing organization. It did its best to sell Xerox copiers in the Japanese market, even though it was painfully obvious that the U.S. company had done nothing to adapt the machine to the Japanese market. For example, to reach the print button on one model, Japanese secretaries had to stand on a box. After 10 years of operation, Fuji Xerox began to manufacture its own machines, and by 1975 it was redesigning U.S. equipment for the Japanese market. Soon thereafter, with the encouragement of Fuji Photo, and in spite of the resistance of Xerox engineers in the United States, the firm began to design its own copier equipment. Its goal was to design and build a copier in half the time and at half the cost of previous machines. When this was accomplished, the firm set its sights on winning the Deming award, a highly coveted Japanese prize for excellence in total quality control. Fuji Xerox won the award in 1980.

It was also in 1980 that Xerox, reeling under the impact of intense competition from Japanese copier companies, finally began to pay attention to the lessons that it could learn from Fuji Xerox. Adopting the Japanese joint venture's manufacturing techniques and quality programs, the parent company fought its way back to health in the mid-1980s. By 1991, Xerox International Partners was established as a joint venture between Fuji Xerox and Xerox Corporation to sell low-end printers in North America and Europe. In 1998, exports to the United States grew substantially with digital color copiers and OEM printer engines. Both the lessons learned from Fuji Xerox and the contributions they have made to Xerox have inevitably helped Xerox prosper as an independent company.

Using Joint Ventures for Diversification

As the previous examples illustrate, many joint ventures take products that one parent knows well into a market that the other knows well. However, some break new ground and move one or both parents into products and markets that are new to them.

Arrangements to acquire the skills necessary to compete in a new business is a long-term proposition, but one that some firms are willing to undertake. Given the fact that most acquisitions of unrelated businesses do not succeed, and that trying to enter a new business without help is extremely difficult, choosing partners who will help you learn the business may not be a bad strategy if you are already familiar with the partner. However, to enter a new market, with a new product, and a new partner—even when the probability of success for each is 80 percent—leaves one with an overall probability of success of (.8 x .8 x .8) about 50 percent!

In recent years, there has been some discussion about whether joint ventures can be viewed as vehicles for learning. Here the modes of learning go beyond knowledge transfer (i.e., existing know-how) to include transformation and harvesting. In practice, most IJV partners engage in the transfer of existing knowledge, but stop short of knowledge transformation or harvesting. Further, there is little empirical evidence that the learning activities of transfer, transformation, and harvesting relate directly to positive IJV performance.

Requirements for International Joint Venture Success

The checklist in Exhibit 7–3 presents many of the items that a manager should consider when establishing an international joint venture. Each of these is discussed in the following sections.

EXHIBIT 7–3 Joint Venture Checklist

1. Test the strategic logic.
   - Do you really need a partner? For how long? Does your partner?
   - How big is the payoff for both parties? How likely is success?
   - Is a joint venture the best option?
   - Do congruent performance measures exist?
2. Partnership and fit.
   - Does the partner share your objectives for the venture?
   - Does the partner have the necessary skills and resources? Will you get access to them?
   - Will you be compatible?
   - Can you arrange an "engagement period"?
   - Is there a comfort versus competence trade-off?
3. Shape and design.
   - Define the venture's scope of activity and its strategic freedom vis-à-vis its parents.
   - Lay out each parent's duties and payoffs to create a win-win situation. Ensure that there are comparable contributions over time.
   - Establish the managerial role of each partner.
4. Doing the deal.
   - How much paperwork is enough? Trust versus legal considerations?
   - Agree on an endgame.
5. Making the venture work.
   - Give the venture continuing top management attention.
   - Manage cultural differences.
   - Watch out for inequities.
   - Be flexible.

Testing the Strategic Logic

The decision to enter a joint venture should not be taken lightly. As mentioned earlier, joint ventures require a great deal of management attention, and, in spite of the care and attention they receive, many prove unsatisfactory to their parents.

Firms considering entering a joint venture should satisfy themselves that there is not a simpler way, such as a nonequity alliance of the type referred to in Chapter 1, to get what they need. They should also carefully consider the time period for which they are likely to need help. Joint ventures have been labeled "permanent solutions to temporary problems" by firms that entered a venture to get help on some aspect of their business; then, when they no longer needed the help, they were still stuck with the joint venture.

The same tough questions a firm may ask itself before forming a joint venture need to be asked of its partner. How long will the partner need it? Is the added potential payoff high enough to both partners to compensate for the increased coordination/communications costs which go with the formation of a joint venture?

A major issue in the discussion of strategic logic is to determine whether congruent measures of performance exist. As Exhibit 7–4 suggests, in many joint ventures, incongruity exists. In this example the foreign partner was looking for a joint venture that would generate 20

Exhibit 7–4 Measuring JV Performance: The Search for Congruity

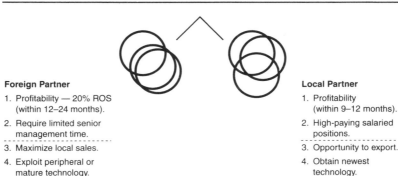

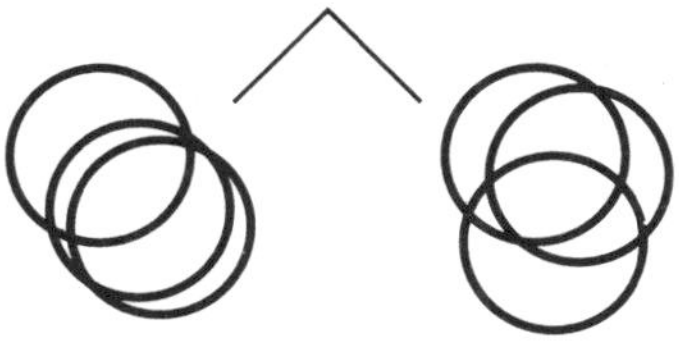

Foreign Partner

1. Profitability — 20% ROS (within 12–24 months).
2. Require limited senior management time.

- -

3. Maximize local sales.
4. Exploit peripheral or mature technology.

Local Partner

1. Profitability (within 9–12 months).
2. High-paying salaried positions.

- -

3. Opportunity to export.
4. Obtain newest technology.

percent return on sales in a 1–2 year period and require a limited amount of senior management time. The local partner in turn was seeking a JV that would be quickly profitable and be able to justify some high-paying salaried positions (for the local partner and several family members/friends). While each partner's performance objectives seem defensible, this venture would need to resolve several major problem areas in order to succeed. First, each partner did not make explicit all their primary performance objectives. Implicit measures (those below the dotted line in Exhibit 7–4), are a source of latent disagreement/misunderstanding. Second, the explicit versus implicit measures of each partner were internally inconsistent. The foreign partner wanted high profitability while using little senior management time and old technology. The local partner wanted quick profits but high-paying local salaries.

Partnership and Fit

Joint ventures are sometimes formed to satisfy complementary needs. But when one partner acquires (learns) another's capabilities, the joint venture becomes unstable. The acquisition of a partner's capabilities means that the partner is no longer needed. If capabilities are only accessed, the joint venture is more stable. It is not easy, before a venture begins, to determine many of the things a manager would most like to know about a potential partner, like the true extent of its capabilities, what its objectives are in forming the venture, and whether it will be easy to work with. A hasty answer to such questions may lead a firm into a bad relationship or cause it to pass up a good opportunity.

For these reasons, it is often best if companies begin a relationship in a small way, with a simple agreement that is important but not a matter of life and death to either parent. As confidence between the firms grows, the scope of the business activities can broaden.

A good example is provided by Corning Glass, which in 1970 made a major breakthrough in the development of optical fibers that could be used for telecommunication applications, replacing traditional copper wire or coaxial cable. The most likely customers of this fiber outside the United States were the European national telecoms, which were well known to be very nationalistic purchasers. To gain access to these customers, Corning set up development agreements in 1973 and 1974 with companies in England, France, Germany, and Italy that were already suppliers to the telecoms. These agreements called for the European firms to develop the technology necessary to combine the fibers into cables, while Corning itself continued to develop the optical fibers. Soon the partners began to import fiber from Corning and cable it locally. Then, when the partners were comfortable with each other and each market was ready, Corning and the partners set up joint ventures to produce optical fiber locally. These ventures have worked extremely well, and their continuing success became particularly important in the late 1980s, as growth in the U.S. market leveled off. Corning is widely acknowledged as one of the world's most successful users of joint ventures.

When assessing issues around partnership and fit, it is useful to consider whether the partner not only shares the same objectives for the venture but also has a similar appetite for risk. In practice this often results in joint ventures having parents of roughly comparable size. It is difficult for parent firms of very different size to establish sustainable joint ventures because of varying resource sets, payback period requirements, and corporate cultures.

Corporate culture similarity—or compatibility—can be a make-or-break issue in many joint ventures. It is not enough to find a partner with the necessary skills, you need to be able to get access to them and to be compatible. Managers are constantly told that they should choose a joint venture partner they trust. As these examples suggest, however, trust between partners is something that can only be developed over time as a result of shared experiences. You can't start with trust.

Shape and Design

In the excitement of setting up a new operation in a foreign country, or getting access to technology provided by an overseas partner, it is important not to lose sight of the basic strategic requirements that must be met if a joint venture is to be successful. The questions that must be addressed are the same when any new business is proposed: Is the market attractive? How strong is the competition? How will the new company compete? Will it have the required resources? And so on.

In addition to these concerns, three others are particularly relevant to joint venture design. One is the question of strategic freedom, which has to do with the relationship between the venture and its parents. How much freedom will the venture be given to do as it wishes with respect to choosing suppliers, a product line, and customers? In the Dow Chemical venture referred to earlier, the dispute between the partners centered on the requirement that the venture buy materials, at what the Koreans believed to be an inflated price, from Dow's new wholly owned Korean plant. Clearly the American and Korean vision of the amount of strategic freedom open to the venture was rather different.

The second issue of importance is that the joint venture be a win-win situation. This means that the payoff to each parent if the venture is successful should be a big one, because this will keep both parents working for the success of the venture when times are tough. If the strategic analysis suggests that the return to either parent over time will be marginal, the venture should be restructured or abandoned.

Finally, it is critical to decide on the management roles that each parent company will play. The venture will be easier to manage if one parent plays a dominant role and has a lot of influence over both the strategic and the day-to-day operations of the venture, or if one parent plays a lead role in the day-to-day operation of the joint venture. More difficult to manage are shared management ventures, in which both parents have a significant input into both strategic decisions and the everyday operations of the venture. A middle ground is split management decisions, where one partner has primary influence over certain functional areas, and the other partner over different functional areas. This is the most common form.

In some ventures, the partners place too much emphasis on competing with each other about which one will have management control. They lose sight of the fact that the intent of the joint venture is to capture benefits from two partners that will allow the venture (not one of the partners) to compete in the market better than would have been possible by going it alone.

The objective of most joint ventures is superior performance. Thus the fact that dominant-parent ventures are easier to manage than shared-management ventures does not mean they are the appropriate type of venture to establish. Dominant parent ventures are most likely to be effective when one partner has the knowledge and skill to make the venture a success and the other party is contributing simply money, a trademark, or perhaps a one-time transfer of technology. Such a venture, however, begs the question "What are the unique continuing contributions of the partner?" Shared-management ventures are necessary when the venture needs active consultation between members of each parent company, as when deciding how to modify a product supplied by one parent for the local market that is well known by the other, or to modify a production process designed by one parent to be suitable for a workforce and working conditions well known by the other.

A joint venture is headed for trouble when a parent tries to take a larger role in its management than makes sense. An American company with a joint venture in Japan, for instance, insisted that one of its people be the executive vice president of the venture. This was not reasonable, because the man had nothing to bring to the management of the venture. He simply served as a constant reminder to the Japanese that the American partner did not trust them. The Americans were pushing for a shared-management venture when it was more logical to allow the Japanese, who certainly had all the necessary skills, to be the dominant or at least the leading firm. The major American contribution to the venture was to allow it to use its world-famous trademarks and brand names.

A second example, also in Japan, involves the French firm referred to at the start of this chapter. This company was bringing complex technology to the venture that needed to be modified for the Japanese market. It was clear that the French firm required a significant say in the management of the venture. On the other hand, the French had no knowledge of the Japanese market and, thus, the Japanese also needed a significant role in the venture. The logical solution would have been a shared-management venture and equal influence in decisions made at the board level. Unfortunately, both companies wanted to play a dominant role, and the venture collapsed in a decision-making stalemate.

Doing the Deal

Experienced managers argue that it is the relationship between the partners that is of key importance in a joint venture, not the legal agreement that binds them together. Nevertheless, most are careful to ensure that they have a good agreement in place—one that they understand and are comfortable with.

The principal elements of a joint venture agreement are listed in Exhibit 7–5. Most of these are straightforward and relate to topics discussed in this chapter. One item on the list that has not been discussed is the termination of the venture.

Although some managers balk at discussing divorce during the prenuptial period, it is important to work out a method of terminating the venture in the event of a serious disagreement, and to do this at a time when heads are cool and goodwill abounds. The usual technique is to use a shotgun clause, which allows either party to name a price at which it will buy the other's shares in the venture. However, once this provision is activated and the first company has named a price, the second firm has the option of selling at this price or buying the first company's shares at the same price. This ensures that only fair offers are made, at least as long as both parents are large enough to be capable of buying each other out.

Making the Venture Work

Joint ventures need close and continuing attention, particularly in their early months. In addition to establishing a healthy working relationship between the parents and the venture general manager, managers should be on the lookout for the impact that cultural differences may be having on the venture and for the emergence of unforeseen inequities.

International joint ventures, like any type of international activity, require that managers of different national cultures work together. This requires the selection of capable people in key roles. Unless managers have been sensitized to the characteristics of the culture that they are dealing with, this can lead to misunderstandings and serious problems. Many Western managers, for instance, are frustrated by the slow, consensus-oriented decision-making style of the Japanese. Equally, the Japanese find American individualistic decision making to be surprising, as the decisions are made so quickly, but the implementation is often so slow. Firms that are sophisticated in the use of international joint ventures are well

EXHIBIT 7–5 Principal Elements of a Joint Venture Agreement

- Definitions
- Scope of operations
- Management:
  1. Shareholders and supervisory roles regarding board
  2. Executive board
  3. Arrangements in the event of deadlock
  4. Operating management
- Arbitration
- Representations and warranties of each partner
- Organization and capitalization
- Financial arrangements
- Contractual links with parents
- Rights and obligations and intellectual property
- Termination agreements
- Force majeure
- Covenants

Source: "Teaming Up for the Nineties—Can You Survive without a Partner?" Deloitte, Haskins & Sells International, undated.

aware of such problems and have taken action to minimize them. Ford, for example, has put more than 1,500 managers through courses to improve their ability to work with Japanese and Korean managers.

It is important to remember that cultural differences do not just arise from differences in nationality. For example:

- Small firms working with large partners are often surprised and dismayed by the fact that it can take months, rather than days, to get approval of a new project. In some cases the cultural differences appear to be greater between small and large firms of the same nationality than, say, between multinationals of different nationality, particularly if the multinationals are in the same industry.
- Firms working with two partners from the same country have been surprised to find how different the companies are in cultural habits. A Japanese automobile firm headquartered in rural Japan is a very different company from one run from Tokyo.
- Cultural differences between managers working in different functional areas may be greater than those between managers in the same function in different firms. European engineers, for example, discovered when discussing a potential joint venture with an American partner that they had more in common with the American engineers than with the marketing people in their own company.

A very common joint venture problem is that the objectives of the parents, which coincided when the venture was formed, diverge over time. Such divergences can be brought on by changes in the fortunes of the partners. This was the case in the breakup of the General Motors–Daewoo joint venture in Korea. Relations between the partners were already strained due to GM's unwillingness to put further equity into the venture, in spite of a debt to equity ratio of more than 8 to 1, when, faced with rapidly declining market share, the Korean parent decided that the venture should go for growth and maximize market share, whereas General Motors, itself in a poor financial position, insisted that the emphasis be on current profitability. When Daewoo, without telling General Motors, introduced a concessionary financing program for the joint venture's customers, the relationship was damaged, never to recover.

A final note concerns the unintended inequities that may arise during the life of a venture. Due to an unforeseen circumstance, one parent may be winning from the venture while the other is losing. A venture established in the late 1990s between Indonesian and American parents, for instance, was buying components from the American parent at prices based in dollars. As the rupiah declined in value, the Indonesian partner could afford fewer components in each shipment. The advice of many experienced venture managers is that, in such a situation, a change in the original agreement should be made, so the hardship is shared between the parents. That was done in this case, and the venture is surviving, although it is not as profitable as originally anticipated.

In reviewing any checklist of the things to be considered when forming a joint venture, it is important to recognize that such a list will vary somewhat depending on where the international joint venture is established. Exhibit 7–6 summarizes 12 characteristics of joint ventures according to whether they are established in developed versus developing countries.

EXHIBIT 7–6 Summary of Differences of Joint-Venture Characteristics

	Developed Country	Developing Country	
Characteristics	*Market Economy*	*Market Economy*	*Planned Economy (China)*
Major reason for creating venture	Skill required	Government pressure	Government pressure
Frequency of association with government partners	Low	Moderate	Very High
Overall use of JVs versus other modes of foreign involvement	Significant (20-40%)	High (but contingent on country, industry, and technology level)	Very high (regardless of country, industry, or technology level) but declining
Usual origin of foreign partner	Other developed countries	Developed countries	Ethnic Related Locales (i.e., Hong Kong, Taiwan)
Proportion of intended JVs actually implemented	High	Relatively high	Low (under 50%)
Use of JVs with a predetermined duration	Low (except in certain industries)	Low	Previously high, but declining
Most common level of ownership for foreign MNE	Equal	Minority	Minority
Number of autonomously managed ventures	Small	Negligible	Negligible
Ownership-control relationship*	Direct (dominant control with majority ownership; shared control with equal ownership)	Difficult to discern because most MNEs have a minority ownership position	Indirect
Control-performance relationship in successful JVs	Inconclusive	Shared or split	Split control
Instability rate	30%	45%	Low
MNE managerial assessment of dissatisfaction with performance	37%	61%	High

Sources: Paul W. Beamish, "The Characteristics of Joint Ventures in Developed and Developing Countries," *Columbia Journal of World Business,* Fall 1985, pp. 12-19; and Paul W. Beamish "The Characteristics of Joint Ventures in The People's Republic of China," *Journal of International Marketing,* Vol. 1 No. 2, pp. 29-48.

Most of the descriptions of the characteristics considered are self-explanatory. Yet, more fine-grained analyses are always possible. For example, the discussion in this chapter has generally assumed a traditional equity joint venture, one focused between two firms from two different countries. Yet other types of equity joint ventures exist (see Exhibit 7–7), including those between firms from two different countries that set up in a third country (i.e., trinational), those formed between subsidiaries of the same MNE (i.e., intrafirm) and those formed with companies of the same nationality but located in a different country (i.e., cross-national domestic joint ventures). Further, many joint ventures have more than two

EXHIBIT 7–7 Japanese JV Ownership Structure, Performance, and Termination Rate

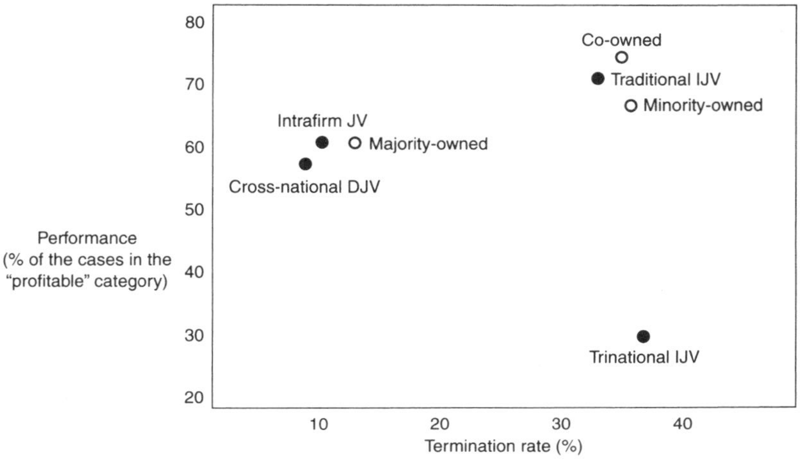

Source: Shige Makino and Paul W. Beamish, "Performance and Survival of Joint Ventures with Non-Conventional Ownerhsip Structures," *Journal of International Business Studies,* Vol. 29 (4), 1998, p. 811.

partners. Interestingly, the traditional JVs (formed by Japanese MNEs) tend to simultaneously be more profitable and to have a higher termination rate than the alternative structures available.

Summary

For the reasons outlined in this chapter, international joint ventures are an increasingly important part of the strategy of many firms. They are, however, sometime difficult to design and manage well, in part because some organizations do not treat them as "true" alliances (see Exhibit 7–8). The fact that some ventures are performing below their management's expectations should not be an excuse for firms to avoid such ventures. In many industries, the winners are going to be the companies that most quickly learn to manage international ventures effectively. The losers will be the managers who throw up their hands and say that joint ventures are too difficult, so we had better go it alone.

In the future, will we see more or fewer international joint ventures? Certainly the reduction in investment regulations in many countries, coupled with increased international

EXHIBIT 7–8 The True Alliance versus the Pseudo Alliance

	The True Alliance	The Pseudo Alliance
Planned level of parent input and involvement	Continuing	One-time
Distribution of risks/rewards	Roughly even	Uneven
Parent attitude toward the JV	A unique organization with unique needs	One more subsidiary
The formal JV agreement	Flexible guideline	Frequently referenced rulebook
Performance objectives	Clearly specified and congruent	Partially overlapping/ ambiguous

experience by many firms, suggests there may be fewer joint ventures. Yet other countervailing pressures exist. With shortening product life cycles, it is increasingly difficult to go it alone. And with the increase in the number of MNEs from emerging markets, both the supply and demand of potential partners will likely escalate.

Supplementary Reading

Beamish, Paul W., and J. Peter Killing, eds. *Cooperative Strategies: European Perspectives, Cooperative Strategies: North American Perspectives,* and *Cooperative Strategies: Asian Perspectives.* San Francisco: The New Lexington Press, 1997. (Three volumes.)

———. Special Issue on Cooperative Strategies, *Journal of International Business Studies,* Vol. 27, No.5, 1996.

Berdrow, Iris, and P. W. Beamish. "Unfolding the Myth of IJV Learning." Ivey Working Paper Series, 1999.

Datta, Deepak K. "International Joint Ventures: A Framework for Analysis." *Journal of General Management,* Vol. 14, No. 2, Winter 1988.

Doz, Yves L., and Gary Hamel. *Alliance Advantage.* Cambridge, MA: Harvard Business School Press, 1999.

Fey, Carl F. "Important Design Characteristics for Russian–Foreign Joint Ventures." *European Management Journal,* Vol. 13, 1995, pp. 405–15.

Hamel, Gary, Yves Doz, and C. K. Prahalad. "Collaborate with Your Competitors—and Win." *Harvard Business Review,* January-February 1989.

Inkpen, Andrew C., and Paul W. Beamish. "Knowledge, Bargaining Power and International Joint Venture Stability." *Academy of Management Review,* Vol. 22, No. 1, 1997.

Killing, Peter. "How to Make a Global Joint Venture Work." *Harvard Business Review,* May-June 1982, pp. 120–27.

Lane, Henry W., and Paul W. Beamish. "Cross-Cultural Cooperative Behavior in Joint Ventures in LDCs." *Management International Review,* Special Issue 1990, pp. 87–102.

Schaan, Jean-Louis. "How to Control a Joint Venture Even as a Minority Partner." *Journal of General Management* Vol. 14, No. 1, Autumn 1988.

Schaan, Jean-Louis, and Paul W. Beamish. "Joint Venture General Managers in Developing Countries." In *Cooperative Strategies in International Business.* Ed. F. Contractor and P. Lorange. Lexington, MA: Lexington Books, 1988, pp. 279–99.

[26]

International Joint Venture Instability: A Critique of Previous Research, A Reconceptualization, and Directions for Future Research

Aimin Yan*
BOSTON UNIVERSITY

Ming Zeng**
INSEAD

This paper conducts an in-depth critique of previous research on international joint venture instability by pointing out its major limitations: lack of clear conceptualizations and consistent operationalizations, lack of clarity in the relationship with performance, static focus on the eventual destination rather than developmental processes, and lack of managerial relevance. To overcome these deficiencies, we propose a significant reconceptualization in which instability is defined as a neutral, dynamic, process-based, and multifaceted phenomenon. Directions for future research are provided.

Paul Beamish and Peter Killing, the editors of the 1996 the *JIBS* Special Issue on Global Perspectives on Cooperative Strategies suggest that it is time to "consolidate the current and future thinking" on international cooperation. In this paper, we contribute to this objective by examining one of the

*Aimin Yan (Ph.D. Pennsylvania State University) is Associate Professor in the School of Management of Boston University. His research has focused on organizational theory/design issues in international strategic alliances, particularly, governance structures, formal and informal control mechanisms, performance/organizational effectiveness, and change and development in international joint ventures.

**Ming Zeng (Ph.D. University of Illinois) is Assistant Professor of Asian Business at INSEAD. His research focuses on the evolution of international joint ventures and the dynamics of foreign direct investment.

We thank Mike Peng, Jean-François Hennart, and Paul Beamish for their comments/help, and Thomas Brewer for his continuing encouragement during the preparation of this article. A previous version of the paper was presented at the 1997 Academy of Management Meeting in Boston.

most important subjects—international joint venture (IJV) instability.

This paper was intended to achieve three objectives. First, we provide a theoretical synthesis and a critical review of previous research on the subject. Over the past three decades, IJV instability has been studied from different perspectives and, as a result, inconsistent empirical findings have been generated. Integration and consolidation of previous work can offer insights for further theoretical and empirical advancement. Second, we identify the major limitations in previous research. Among other deficiencies, the current literature is dominated by a static approach that treats instability as the end status of IJVs (e.g., termination or liquidation), whereas the process aspect of the phenomenon is largely ignored. The third and the most important objective of this paper is to provide a foundation for future research to overcome the identified deficiencies in previous research. Toward this end, we offer a comprehensive reconceptualization, in which instability is defined as a neutral, dynamic, process-based and multifaceted phenomenon. We argue that instability is not necessarily a liability. Rather, long-term IJV success should be built upon adaptations and reconfigurations.

Below we first review prior research following three major threads: conceptualizations and operationalizations, major contributing factors, and the instability-performance relationship. Second, we critique the literature by pointing out the major limitations and deficiencies, including lack of theoretical work and inconsistent operationalizations, lack of clarity in the instability-performance relationship, narrow focus on the eventual destination rather than the process, and lack of managerial relevance. We argue that these limitations have hampered this domain of research from making theoretical advances and contributing to IJV practices. Third, we offer our reconceptualization of IJV instability. Finally, we conclude with directions for future research.

PREVIOUS RESEARCH ON IJV INSTABILITY

With the rapid growth of research, it is a challenging task to review the instability literature both in breadth and in depth. In our review we primarily focus on those studies that directly and empirically examined IJV instability. However, we analyze the issue of instability in the broader context of IJV development whenever possible. While trying to be inclusive, our critique is organized around three fundamental questions: What is IJV instability and how has it been operationalized? What are the key contributing factors to instability? And what are the performance implications of instability? A brief sketch of the studies included in this review is listed in Table 1.

IJV Instability: Conceptualization and Operationalization

Previous research has conceptualized and operationalized IJV instability in two ways. An outcome-oriented approach characterizes instability as termination of IJVs through various avenues or as change in the sponsors' ownership structure. A process-oriented approach, however, defines instability as major reorganizations or contractual renegotiations.

Instability as termination or changes in ownership structure. The dominant approach in literature treats instability as termination of the IJV or change in its ownership structure. This approach was originated in Franko's (1971) pioneering study of US manufacturing IJVs abroad and was later adopted by a variety of scholars (e.g., Gomes-Casseres, 1987; Lee & Beamish; Makino, 1995; Hennart & Zeng, 1997). Franko considered three categories of instability: 1) the US firm increased its ownership to more than 95%, thus converting it to a wholly-owned subsidiary; 2) the US firm increased its equity holding from a minority or 50-50 split to a majority under 95%; and 3) the IJV was sold out or liquidated by mutual consent. Franko reported an instability rate of 28.5%.

Adopting Franko's measures, Gomes-Casseres (1987) studied 5,933 US manufacturing subsidiaries abroad and reported that about a third of the IJVs went through some form of ownership changes. However, he found that liquidation and bankruptcy were not primary forms of instability, accounting for only 10 percent of the unstable cases. Outright sales occurred in 37% of the IJVs, and changes in ownership structures accounted for the remaining 52% of the unstable ventures. More recently, using similar measures, Hennart and Zeng (1997) studied Japanese IJVs in the US and observed very high ownership instability (68%). In contrast, relatively low instability rates have been reported among Japanese IJVs in Asia (Makino, 1995), Korean ventures (Lee & Beamish; 1995), and IJVs in China (Beamish, 1993).

Some scholars have defined the instability concept more narrowly, that is, instability as termination (Berg & Friedman, 1978; Harrigan, 1988; Kogut, 1989; 1991; Bleeke & Ernst, 1991; Makino, 1995; Park & Russo, 1996; Hennart, Kim, & Zeng, 1998). Berg and Friedman (1978) measured instability as termination through either sales or liquidation, and observed an instability rate of 41%. Harrigan (1988) reported that about 55% of the 895 inter-firm alliances in her study were terminated and thus unstable. More recently, Barkema and Vermeulen (1997) built a longitudinal database of foreign entries by 25 Dutch multinationals in 72 countries between 1966 and 1994. Of the 228 IJVs in the database, 49 percent were terminated before 1994.

Kogut (1989, 1991) examined IJV termination by focusing on either dissolution or acquisition. Whereas a dissolution represents a failed IJV as a result of "either a business failure or irresolvable conflict among the partners" (1989, p. 187), acquisition occurs when the venture is acquired by one of the sponsoring partners or a third party due to different valuations of the joint venture. Of the 92 IJVs in his sample, 27 were terminated through dissolutions and 37 through acquisitions. Dissolution was found to be driven by changes in competitive rivalry within the venture's industry, while acquisition was driven by changes in the option values embedded in the IJV's contractual agreement. Park and Russo (1996) found that, in a sample of 204 joint ventures in the electronics industry, 56 were terminated through liquidation and 82 through acquisition, representing an overall instability rate of 68%.

Instability as reorganizations or contractual renegotiations. Several studies have paid attention to the structural and operational aspects of IJVs. In addition to termination, Killing (1983) classifies IJVs as unstable when they experience a drastic shift in the venture's parent control structure. During the two-year observation period, 7 out of the 35 IJVs were terminated and 5 others underwent a major reconfiguration of their control structure due to poor performance. Therefore, about 35% of the IJVs in this relatively small sample were categorized as unstable. Use of major reorganization as a measure of instability was also found in several other studies (e.g., Beamish, 1984; Lee & Beamish, 1995)

In the same vein, using IJV data published in Mergers and Acquisitions between 1971 and 1981, Blodgett (1992) investigated instability by focusing on interpartner renegotiations of a prior contract. The unit of analysis of this study was the IJV contract rather than the venture itself, and incidence of contract renegotiations was used to indicate instability. The more process-oriented perspective represented by Killing(1983) and Blodgett (1992) is important because the focus has migrated from documenting the ultimate destinations/death rates of IJVs to investigating factors triggering or contributing to instability in operating IJVs.

Factors Contributing to Instability

In the majority of prior studies, instability has been treated as a dependent variable to signify the IJV's ultimate destination. Consequently, various factors contributing to instability have been identified, including conflicts in shared management, cross-cultural differences, ownership structures, characteristics of the sponsors, and external environmental forces.

Interpartner conflict in co-management. A key feature of IJVs is shared management between partners from different countries. Partners could disagree on just about every aspect of an IJV's management. Therefore, interpartner conflict in co-management is often a driving force for instability (Killing, 1983; Kogut, 1989). Harrigan (1988) found that differences between the partners in founding goals, strategic resources, and corporate cultures were responsible for shorter JV duration. On the other hand, joint ventures between direct competitors were found more likely to fail because potential interpartner competition and conflict undermined the partnerships (Park & Russo, 1996; Park & Ungson, 1997).

Cross-cultural differences. Cultural differences often influence the way in which the partners in an IJV make strategic decisions and solve problems. For example, Japanese and American managers tend to see interfirm alliances very differently: the former treat them as primarily interpersonal relationships whereas the latter see them as enduring by design, irrespective of the specific managers involved (Turner 1987). Jones and Shill (1993, p.131) point out that in IJVs in Japan, cross-cultural differences "lead to endless, energy-and-time consuming debates—futile talk that produces a lot of heat and prevents the company making the decisions it has to." The positive effect of cultural differences on IJV instability has also been evidenced in empirical studies with larger samples (Li & Guisinger, 1991; Shenkar & Zeria, 1992; Pennings, Barkema, & Douma, 1994; Hennart & Zeng 1997). However, the findings of several recent studies demonstrate that the relationship between partner cultural differences and IJV stability may be more complex than previous research has suggested. For example, Barkema and Vermeulen (1997) argue that the different dimensions of cross-cultural differences between IJV partners might have different effects on IJV instability. They found that interpartner differences in uncertainty avoidance and long-term orientation have a significant negative impact on IJV survival, while differences in power distance, individualism, and masculinity did not affect IJV survival. Similarly, Park and Ungson (1997) tested the effect of interpartner cultural differences on IJV dissolution but found no support for most of the hypothesized relationships. However, they found a significant effect of interpartner nationality on IJV termination, but in an opposite direction to previous findings: The greater the cultural distance, the less likely the venture is to dissolve.

Control/ownership structures. The structure of parent control has been found to influence IJV instability, although the direction of this effect remains ambiguous. Killing (1993) found that a dominant management structure can minimize coordination costs and hence outperform shared control IJVs. However, an unequal division of ownership may give the majority holder greater power which may be used to the detriment of the minority owner. Therefore, a balanced ownership structure in which partners' bargaining power is evenly matched is more likely to produce mutual accommodations (Harrigan, 1988). Empirically, Bleeke and Ernst (1991) found that alliances with an even split ownership had a higher success rate (60%) than ventures dominated by one company (31%). Beamish (1984) found that performance was enhanced when control was shared between the foreign and the local partner. Performance suffered, however, when the foreign partner exercised dominant control. Several recent dissertation research studies (Yan, 1993; Hebert, 1994; Yan, 1997) found that control over the IJV's daily operations exerted the strongest effect on IJV performance. Nevertheless, at a more general level, the control-performance relationship is nonlinear and more complex than previous researchers expected, and is likely to be contingent upon other organizational and interorganizational variables.

Characteristics of parents. Franko (1971) concluded that policy changes in the multinational enterprise (MNE) partner were responsible for IJV instability. When an MNE decides to tighten control over its foreign subsidiaries, it is likely to turn some IJVs into wholly-owned subsidiaries. Other partner characteristics, such as a parent firm's financial problems (Hennart, Roehl & Zietlow, 1999) and the partners' prior IJV experience (Harrigan, 1988; Park & Russo, 1996; Makino & Delios, 1996) were also found to influence IJV instability.

External environments. Changes in external environments, such as local government policies and industry structures, may also influence IJV instability. It has been widely documented that unanticipated major changes in local political environments (e.g., changes in government policies regarding foreign direct investment in general and equity IJVs in particular) affect international business operations and contribute to IJV instability (Vernon, 1977; Blodgett, 1992; Brewer, 1992; Boddewyn & Brewer, 1994). The past several decades have witnessed such drastic changes in many countries (Contractor, 1990; Vachani, 1995; Yan & Gray, 1994).

Industrial dynamics may also influence the evolution of joint ventures. For example, IJVs are found to be less stable in industries that experience intensive consolidation or volatile growth (Kogut, 1989, 1991; Hennart & Zeng, 1997).

Relationship to Performance/Success

Most previous studies have not examined instability and performance simultaneously, and are therefore unable to establish an unequivocal relationship between the two variables. As an exception, Harrigan's (1988) study included duration and sponsor-perceived success as well as stability as indicators of performance. In her sample, 66.7% of the "unstable" ventures were judged as unsuccessful by one or more sponsors, echoing a high correlation between instability and partners' assessment of performance. Killing (1983) used both IJV longevity and parent assessments of performance to indicate IJV success. The two measures were found consistent in assessing the failure cases in his sample. Similarly, Geringer and Hebert (1991) argue that longevity provides a necessary condition and a good proxy for IJV success.

Other researchers, however, have questioned the linkage between instability and performance. For example, using termination as a measure of instability, Berg and Friedman (1978) documented several cases in which a joint venture was terminated, not because of failure but as an outcome of success. They argue that a successful IJV can become critical to one of its parent's overall businesses, therefore prompting this parent to turn the venture into a wholly owned subsidiary. Gomes-Casserès (1989) also argued that IJVs may be terminated because they have successfully accomplished their initial objectives. In fact, many successful IJVs were found to undertake structural changes, but they did so as adaptive actions to changed external environments or internal strategies of their parents (Gomes-Casseres, 1989; Yan & Gray, 1994). Hennart, Kim, and Zeng's (1998) recent study reported clear differences between different types of instability (measured as termination by selloffs versus liquidation). They found that variables that have been predicted to affect IJV instability only influence the possibility of sell-off, not that of liquidation. Therefore, it would be misleading to treat instability as synonymous with failure.

To summarize, while most researchers conceptually agree that the linkage of instability to performance is more than complex, many used the former as a proxy for the latter. Little research has been done to investigate the relationship and possible interactions between the two variables.

MAJOR LIMITATIONS AND DEFICIENCIES IN INSTABILITY RESEARCH

The above review suggests that significant research has been conducted to explore the phenomenon of IJV instability. These studies have not only appropriately identified instability as a critical issue for research, but also contributed to our understanding of the fragility of international partnerships. It is arguable that the investigation of IJV instability has become one of the most active domains of scholarly work in international management (Parkhe, 1993). However, the literature is deficient and limited in some important aspects, as discussed below.

Conceptualization and Operationalization

While instability has long been a

major subject in IJV research (Parkhe, 1993), until very recently, the literature lacked a theoretical definition for the concept. Most studies do not provide a conceptualization but "define" it by operationalizing it. Given the lack of theoretical work, not surprisingly, the empirical literature features a variety of measures of instability, ranging from dissolution and reorganization, to renegotiation of contracts. Multiple ways to terminate a venture are also documented.

The use of different measures is not a problem per se. The problem rests in the fact that prior researchers have paid little attention to articulating the relationship between the specific measures they elect to use and the operational schemes adopted by others. Therefore, we know little about the relationships between the various measures of IJV instability. To make the situation worse, the choice of a particular measure is often data-driven—more for the researcher's convenience or data availability than for theoretical rigor. These problems clearly have contributed to the noncumulative nature of previous findings. Since each measure used may be aligned with a unique set of theoretical assumptions or rationales (unfortunately, in many cases these assumptions or rationales are not explicitly specified), it is likely to produce highly idiosyncratic results (Kogut, 1989; 1991). In addition, much previous work has depended solely upon static, secondhand data sources. For example, it is common that an IJV is operationally categorized as "terminated" when, for potentially numerous unknown reasons, it fails to appear in the next issue of the same report.

Scholars of IJVs today have learned, and probably have become accustomed to, being extremely cautious when reading and interpreting previous findings. To what degree are the various measures different or correlated? To what extent is a specific measure appropriate to IJVs across different populations? While some good exploratory efforts have been made (e.g., Gomes-Casseres, 1987; Geringer & Hebert, 1991; Hennart, Kim, & Zeng, 1998), the above basic questions largely remain unanswered.

Relationship to Performance/Success

In the current literature, the instability-performance relationship remains unclear. While most researchers agree that instability is not equivalent to failure, operationally, many insist that longevity is a key measure of success and that termination indicates failure. Even Inkpen and Beamish's (1997) definition, the most conceptual and comprehensive so far, treats instability as something undesirable as it stresses the "unplanned and premature" nature of instability. The lack of clarity in the relationship between instability and performance has created difficulty in understanding previous research results, has hindered communication among IJV scholars, and has undermined significantly the theoretical and practical value of prior research findings.

End Destinations as Instability

Previous work on instability (and on IJVs in general) has been dominated by a static approach (Westney, 1988; Parkhe, 1993; Doz, 1996) in which the focus is placed on the IJV's end consequence, such as sellout, acquisition, liquidation or bankruptcy. The dynamic process by which stability or instability develops has been largely ignored in previous research.

Using the end consequences of IJVs to conceptualize and operationalize IJV instability has value, if the focus is placed on tracing the contributing factors to instability rather than counting the death rates. However, this approach has significant limitations. First, it is conceptually problematic to assert that all terminated IJVs are unstable, because termination may be anticipated or "planned" by the partners at founding (Kogut, 1989; Inkpen & Beamish, 1997). It is equally problematic, on the other hand, to assume that all IJVs that have not yet been terminated are stable. Joint ventures do not change from stable to unstable the night before their termination. Second, most previous studies used ownership changes as a proxy for instability. This approach is limited because instability can be multi-dimensional, as reflected in changes in the IJV's strategy, core business processes, key products and markets, and partner contributions of critical resources. Without considering the developmental process, it is impossible to gain a rich understanding of these multiple sources of instability. The nature of instability can only be ascertained with detailed knowledge of the actual evolution of IJVs (Doz, 1996).

Practical Relevance

The commonly asked "so what" question is appropriate to pinpoint the lack of practical relevance of previous research on instability. What are the key managerial implications of the research findings produced over the past several decades? It is a challenging question for IJV scholars to answer; but a good one to reflect upon. For example, from a modal choice viewpoint, we have warned practitioners that IJVs are more unstable than wholly-owned subsidiaries, and that many IJVs eventually turn out to be corporate odd-couples. Even such general caution has not been effective, because in the past two decades a radical proliferation, rather than a decrease, of IJVs has been witnessed both in the U.S. and world-wide (Anderson, 1990; Geringer & Hebert, 1991). The real practical value of IJV research rests on providing practitioners with insights regarding how to manage the IJV's evolution, particularly, how to reconfigure its structures and take adaptive actions over time in order to strengthen performance and prevent premature death. To this end, we now propose a reconceptualization of instability.

TOWARD A RECONCEPTUALIZATION OF IJV INSTABILITY

Recent Theoretical Progress

Since the turn of this decade, several significant attempts have been made to explore the process in which IJV instability evolves. For example, the interpartner competitive learning perspective (Hamel, 1991; Lyles, 1994; Inkpen & Beamish, 1997) has provided a powerful explanation for IJV termination. This perspective argues that IJV partners are engaged in a race for learning to acquire each other's skills, resources, and competencies. Once one of the partners has successfully accomplished its learning objectives, the race is over and the IJV is terminated. This view was originally advanced by Hamel (1991) and further developed in Inkpen and Beamish (1997). Building upon the bargaining power argument (Harrigan & Newman, 1990; Yan & Gray,

1994), they argue that changes in bargaining power balance resulting from interpartner learning represents a key source of IJV instability. Conceptually, they define instability as "a major change in relationship status that was unplanned and premature from one or both partners' perspectives" (p. 182). This definition, arguably the first to be theory-based, has considered a wide range of changes in IJVs, going beyond shifts in ownership structures or termination.

Another notable contributor is Doz (1996) who provided a detailed account of the interactions between initial conditions and organizational learning and the subsequent impact on the evolution of cooperation within IJVs. The evolution of an IJV is characterized by cycles of learning, re-evaluation, and readjustment. Initial conditions may determine alliance outcomes when these conditions are highly inertial and prevent meaningful learning between partners. Most recently, Yan (1998) provides an analysis of both the driving and restraining forces for IJV instability from an organizational theory angle. Drawing upon the organization stability/change paradox (Poole & Van de Ven, 1989), it is argued that unexpected environmental and organizational contingencies, undesirable venture performance, obsolescing bargain, and interpartner competitive learning are major sources of IJV instability. On the other hand, the initial conditions of the venture, for example, the political and legal environments at the IJV's founding, its initial resource mix, the balance of partner bargaining power, and the pre-venture relationship between the partners serve as stabilizing forces for IJVs. It is argued that IJVs evolve under the effect of both sets of forces.

Reconceptualization

While development of a full theory lies beyond the scope of this paper, we want to reconceptualize instability and to pinpoint several key dimensions of the concept. We propose that instability research refocus on the process of IJV development, reveal the dynamic evolution and changes over the venture's life, offer insights on the effect of these changes on IJV performance, and provide useful, practitioner-friendly implications with respect to initiation and management of organizational changes in IJVs. Toward this objective, we provide the following redefinition:

> Instability refers to the extent to which the IJV alters its strategic directions, renegotiates its contract/agreements, reconfigures its ownership and/or management structures, or changes the relationship with its parents or the relationship between the parents that may have a significant effect on the venture's performance.

Neutralization. This redefinition consists of several characteristics. First, the concept is neutralized. Because instability and stability are each defined as the opposite of the other, a value-based judgement of either term is biased and incomplete. If stability were assumed to be the primary, fundamental organizational state, instability would be defined as aberrations from the stable state or upheavals disrupting stability. However, from an organizational change perspective, organizations are not stable—they continuously evolve and are being renewed and reproduced over time (Poole & Van de Ven, 1989). From this perspective, stability would be strange and abnormal. Perrow (1987) argues that although stability may stand for steadfastness and predictability, it can also represent stagnancy and lack of adaptiveness. Similarly, instability may signify change, adaptation and progress as well as turbulence and unpredictability. Changes in IJVs should be no surprise, as the ability to adapt has been often cited as one of the most important factors for IJV success (Killing 1983; Doz, 1996). Rather, it would be surprising if an IJV remained unchanged over a long period of time. Organizational restructuring/reengineering has become an overwhelmingly popular practice worldwide, but no one seems to be alarmed by the vast instability created by such practices. Then, why should we be impatient about similar changes in IJVs? The following quote is illustrative:

> Alliances are often criticized as unstable because many of them last only several years. But compared to what? Are partnerships less stable, in general, than organizational arrangements inside firms? In the 1980s, General Electric created roughly 100 strategic alliances; some prospered, others failed, and many needed redesign during their lives. But in the same period, General Electric reorganized itself dramatically, reduced total employment by 100,000, and bought and sold scores of business. GM and IBM both overhauled their internal operations and organization in the 1980s, and then made a multitude of corrections and refinements. During this period of organizational earthquakes and aftershocks inside GE, GM and IBM, were the core operations of the companies less turbulent than their alliances? (Badaracco, 1991; pp. 127-128)

From the static outcome to the dynamic process. Our reconceptualization of instability calls for a shift from a static, ultimate outcome-oriented approach to a dynamic, process-oriented approach. Stability, or lack thereof, describes a pattern of behavior (of a physical subject, an individual or, by extension, a social or organizational entity) or alterations of the pattern over a period of time. A key dimension embedded in the concept is that it is longitudinal. It is necessary to study instability (or stability) as a process if the way in which original behavior, status, or structure is altered over time and the causes behind the observed changes are to be revealed. While outcome-based studies contribute to an understanding of the consequences of instability, a process-based approach is essential to capture the causes and dynamic development of instability. For example, while trust between IJV partners has been proposed as a key factor in IJV success, little is known about the process and mechanisms through which interpartner trust is established and maintained over time. As Madhok (1995) argues, a shift in focus from "ownership to relational dynamics" between IJV partners is essential to our understanding of the evolution of IJVs.

Relationship to performance. The shift in focus to the dynamic process of IJVs changes instability from a dependent to an independent variable. This change is non-trivial because it opens a new ground for theoretical and empirical exploration of the relationship between instability and performance. The complex but rich dynamics in the IJV's evolution will present numerous contingencies for researchers to explore. Consequently, it may be arbitrary to claim a restructuring effort as good or bad because instability may exert positive and/or negative effects on IJVs, or, as Blodgett (1992; p. 481) speculated, have nothing to do with performance.

Similarly, the feedback effect of performance on instability also warrants attention. As previous research has revealed, superior performance is able to stabilize structural changes and reduce interpartner conflict and power struggles, as well as to change the relative bargaining power of the partners (Yan & Gray, 1994). On the contrary, poor performance often creates conflict and suspicion between partners, which in turn bring quick demise of the joint venture (Doz, 1996).

The multiple facets of instability. Instability is a multifaceted concept. First, new contingencies may be created when the IJV redirects its strategic foci, changes its key objectives, repositions in the markets, or undertakes major growth or downsizing. These changes may be necessitated or prompted by environmental, interorganizational, as well as intraorganizational factors. Second, instability occurs when the partners renegotiate contracts. The IJV contract and major agreements (e.g., on technology transfer or management licensing) define the legal and institutional frameworks in which the IJV operates. Any significant changes or attempts to change will make the venture unstable. Third, as well documented in the literature, reconfiguration of the venture's ownership/control structure represents a major source of instability, because such changes create new bargaining dynamics and/or alter strategic stakes of the partners.

A fourth facet of instability concerns the IJV's relationship with each parent and the relationship between parents. The IJV becomes unstable when changes occur in the amount of decisional autonomy rendered to the IJV management or in the IJV's role in each parent's overall business (e.g., the parent-venture quasi-internal transactions). Changes in interpartner relationship may result from major shifts in their relative bargaining power (Yan & Gray, 1994), competitive learning (Hamel, 1991; Inkpen & Beamish, 1997), emergence/resolution of disputes and conflict, or building/deconstruction of trust between them (Madhok, 1995).

In summary, our reconceptualization of IJV instability helps reconcile inconsistencies in the literature (e.g., on the instability-performance relationship), integrates research on the different facets/aspects of instability, and opens a wide range of new research opportunities. Next, we offer several directions for future research.

CONCLUSIONS AND FUTURE RESEARCH DIRECTIONS

By providing a comprehensive review and critique of the literature on IJV instability, a key purpose of this paper is to consolidate and integrate previous research. We contend that, by identifying the various conceptual and operational approaches to instability and revealing their interrelations, such an integration effort is useful for advancing IJV research. In this regard, our proposed reconceptualization of instability may serve as a fundamental first step toward future theory building. Now we offer the directions for future research.

First, a consistent conceptualization and operationalization of IJV instability is essential for cross-study comparisons and, thus, knowledge accumulation. The proposed reconceptualization provides a possible framework to integrate different dimensions of instability. While substantial progress in this direction might take a long time, at the very least, studies should be clear in defining and measuring instability, articulating relationships with prior definitions and measures, and considering the underlying theoretical and methodological problems associated with a particular choice. If research focus is placed on instability as an outcome, thus, a dependent variable, independent variables need to be clearly defined and the relationship theoretically explored. However, as we argued above, instability is better treated as a multi-faceted process variable; hence, integrative studies that examine the interactions among the multiple dimensions of instability are especially needed to advance theory building. For example, future research needs to spell out the relationships between contract renegotiations and strategic changes, and between changes in ownership structure and reconfiguration of the venture's management control structure. Second, the proposed shift to a dynamic, process-oriented approach to instability is crucial for future research. The current IJV literature has paid considerable attention to either the very beginning of the venture (in the tradition of modal choices) and the ultimate end of the venture (as reflected in the current research on stability), while the mid-life of IJVs has been left understudied at best (Doz, 1996). The complexity and richness of IJVs as a unique form of organization rests on its cross-cultural and cross-organizational interactions. While focusing on only the opening and the closing games, current research has missed the most exciting and arguably the most challenging part of the story. One of the most promising areas for future research is to reveal the process by which IJV development unfolds and thus offer insightful implications on how to initiate and manage organizational changes on an ongoing basis. While both conceptual and empirical work on the dynamic aspects of IJVs has started to accumulate (e.g., Hamel, 1991; Yan & Gray, 1994; Doz, 1996; Inkpen & Beamish, 1997; Yan, 1998), the field is in serious need of more rigorously designed, process-oriented, data-rich studies.

Third, future research has to offer convincing evidence on the instability-performance linkage. Making the concept of instability free from value judgment represents only the first step. Consistent with our reconceptualization, recent attention has been paid to the performance effect of internal and external changes in IJVs, such as contract renegotiations (Blodgett, 1992), interpartner competitive learning and knowledge transfers (Hamel, 1991; Lyles, 1994; Inkpen & Beamish, 1997), and changes in bargaining power and reconfiguration of control structures (Yan & Gray, 1994; Inkpen & Beamish, 1997). Future research should also examine the feedback effect of IJV performance on instability. Killing (1983) initially observed the phenomenon that superior performance stabilizes IJVs. Yan and Gray provided additional evidence for the performance feedback effect on changes in interpartner relative bargaining power and parent control structure (1994), and offered a conceptual framework that specifies how the levels of partner and IJV management satisfaction prompt structural modification, reconfiguration, and termination (1995).

Fourth, both conceptual and empirical research is needed to compare and contrast the unique as well as common challenges in managing WOSs, IJVs, and other types of alliance. On one hand, Gomes-Casseres (1987) argues that instability in IJVs and other organizational forms might be driven by the same set of factors. On the other hand, Inkpen and Beamish (1997) insist that the factors associated with IJV instability are not necessarily the same as those for all types of alliance, therefore, generalization of the findings should be made with caution. IJV instability can only be understood when compared with instability of other types of organizational forms (Hennart, Kim & Zeng, 1998). Future work should spell out the unique dynamics in each form, and at the same time identify the features shared by all forms. Cross-population comparisons, however, should be theoretically and methodologically rigorous and go beyond superficial contrasts of death rates.

Finally, we want to stress the issue of methodology in future research on instability. Our reconceptualization calls for a methodological readjustment. Changes in the IJV's ownership and control structures, parent strategic objectives, interpartner relationships, as well as the multiple-way interactions among these factors, and the venture's performance require in-depth, longitudinal data and repeated-measure designs (Doz, 1996). Simply relying on second-hand data and sophisticated statistical packages, as many previous studies did, is no longer adequate. In order to build rigorous IJV theories, more inductive, grounded theory building efforts are also warranted.

REFERENCES

Anderson, Erin. 1990. Two firms, one frontier: On assessing joint venture performance. *Sloan Management Review*, Winter: 19-30.

Badaracco, Joseph L. 1991. *The knowledge link*. Boston, MA: Harvard Business School Press.

Barkema, Harry & Freek Vermeulen. 1997. What differences in the cultural backgrounds of partners are detrimental for international joint ventures? *Journal of International Business Studies*; 28(4): 845-64.

Beamish, Paul W. 1984. *Joint venture performance in developing countries*. Unpublished doctoral dissertation, University of Western Ontario, London, Ontario, Canada.

________. 1993. Characteristics of joint ventures in the People's Republic of China. *Journal of International Marketing*, 1(1): 29-48.

________ & Peter Killing. 1996. Introduction: Global perspectives on cooperative strategies. *Journal of International Business Studies*, 27(5): iv-ix.

Berg, Stanford V. & Pilip Friedman. 1978. Joint ventures in American industry. *Mergers and Acquisitions*, 13(2): 28-41.

Bleeke, Joel & David Ernst. 1991. The way to win in cross-border alliances. *Harvard Business Review*, 69(6): 127-35.

Blodgett, Linda L. 1992. Factors in the instability of international joint ventures: An event history analysis. *Strategic Management Journal*, 13(6): 475-81.

Boddewyn, Jean J. & Thomas L. Brewer. 1994. International-business political behavior: New theoretical directions. *Academy of Management Review*. 19(1): 119-43.

Brewer, Thomas, L. 1992. An issue-area approach to the analysis of MNC-government relations. *Journal of International Business Studies*, 23(2): 295-309.

Contractor, Farok. 1990. Ownership patterns of U.S. joint ventures abroad and the liberalization of foreign government regulations in the 1980's: Evidence from the benchmark surveys. *Journal of International Business Studies*, 21(1): 55-73.

Doz, Yves L. 1996. The evolution of cooperation in strategic alliances: initial conditions or learning processes? *Strategic Management Journal*, 17(Summer): 55-85.

Franko, Lawrence G. 1971. *Joint venture survival in multinational corporations*. New York, NY: Praeger.

Geringer, J. Michael & Louis Hebert. 1991. Measuring performance of international joint ventures. *Journal of International Business Studies*, 22(2): 249-63.

Gomes-Casseres, Benjamin. 1987. Joint venture instability: Is a problem? *Columbia Journal of World Business*, Summer: 97-102.

Hamel, Gary. 1991. Competition for competence and inter-partner learning within international strategic alliances. *Strategic Management Journal*, 12(1): 83-103.

Harrigan, Kathryn R. 1988. Strategic alliances and partner asymmetries. In F. Contractor & P. Lorange, editors, *Cooperative strategies in international business*. Lexington, MA: Lexington Books, pp. 205-26.

________ & William H. Newman. 1990. Bases of interorganization cooperation: Propensity, power, persistence. *Journal of Management Studies*, 27(4): 417-34.

Hebert, Louis. 1994. *Division of control, relationship dynamics and joint venture performance*. Unpublished Ph.D. dissertation, The University of Western Ontario, London, Ontario, Canada.

Hennart, Jean-François, Dong-Jae Kim & Ming Zeng. 1998. The impact of joint venture status on the longevity of Japanese stakes in U.S. manufacturing affiliates. *Organization Science*, 9(3): 1-14.

Hennart, Jean-François, Thomas Roehl & Dixie S. Zietlow. 1999. "Trojan Horse" or "work horse"? The evolution of U.S.-Japanese joint ventures in the United States. *Strategic Management Journal*, 20(1): 15-29.

Hennart, Jean-Francois & Ming Zeng. 1997. *Is cross-cultural conflict driving international joint venture instability? A comparative study of Japanese-Japanese and Japanese-American IJVs in the United States*. Paper presented at 1997 Academy of Management Meeting, Boston, MA.

Inkpen, Asdrew C. & Paul Beamish W. 1997. Knowledge, bargaining power and international joint venture instability. *Academy of Management Review*, 22(1): 177-202.

Jones, Kevin & Walter Shill. 1993. The dilemma of foreign affiliated companies: Surviving middle age in Japan. In J. Bleeke and D. Ernst, editors, *Collaborating to compete*. New York, NY: John Wiley & Sons.

Killing, J. Peter. 1983. *Strategies for joint venture success*. New York, NY: Praeger.

Kogut, Bruce. 1989. The stability of joint ventures: Reciprocity and competitive rivalry. *The Journal of Industrial Economics*, 38(2): 183-98.

________. 1991. Joint ventures and the option to expand and acquire. *Management Science*, 37(1): 19-32.

Lee, Chol & Beamish, Paul W. 1995. The characteristics and performance of Korean joint ventures in LDCs. *Journal of International Business Studies*, 26(3): 637-54.

Li, Jiatao & Stephen E. Guisinger, 1991. Comparative business failures of foreign-controlled firms in the United

States. *Journal of International Business Studies,* 22 (2): 209-24.

Lyles, Marjorie A. 1994. The impact of organizational learning on joint venture formations. *International Business Review,* 3(4): 459-67.

Madhok, Anoop. 1995. Revising multinational firms' tolerance for joint ventures: A trust-based approach. *Journal of International Business Studies,* 26(1): 117-37.

Makino, Shige. 1995. *Joint venture ownership structure and performance: Japanese joint ventures in Asia.* Unpublished Ph.D. dissertation, the University of Western Ontario, London, Ontario, Canada.

__________ & Andrew Delios. 1996. Local knowledge transfer and performance: Implications for alliance formation in Asia. *Journal of International Business Studies,* 27(5): 905-27.

Park, Seung H., & Michael V. Russo. 1996. When competition eclipses cooperation: An event history analysis of joint venture failure. *Management Science,* 42(6): 875-90.

Park, Seong H. & Gerardo R. Ungson, 1997. The Effect of national culture, organizational complementarity, and economic motivation on joint venture dissolution. *Academy of Management Journal,* 40 (2): 279-308.

Parkhe, Arvind. 1993. "Messy" research, methodological predispositions, and theory development in international joint ventures. *Academy of Management Review,* 18(2): 227-68.

Pennings, Johannes M., Harry Barkema & Sytse Douma. 1994. Organization learning and diversification. *Academy of Management Journal,* 37(3): 608-40.

Perrow, Charles. 1987. *Complex organizations: A critical essay* (Third Ed.). New York, NY: McGraw-Hill, Inc.

Poole, Marshall S. & Andrew H. Van de Ven. 1989. Using paradox to build management and organization theories. *Academy of Management Review,* 14(4): 562-78.

Shenkar, Oded & Yoram Zeria. 1992. Role conflict and role ambiguity of chief executive officers in international joint ventures. *Journal of International Business Studies,* 23(1): 55-75.

Turner, Louis. 1987. *Industrial collaboration with Japan.* London: Routledge.

Vachani, Sushil. 1995. Enhancing the obsolescing bargain theory: A longitudinal study of foreign ownership of U.S. and European multinationals. *Journal of International Business Studies,* 26(1): 159-80.

Vernon, Raymond. 1977. *Storm over multinationals.* Cambridge, MA: Harvard University Press.

Westney, D. Eleanor. 1988. Domestic and foreign learning curves in managing international cooperative strategies. In F. Contractor & P. Lorange, editors, *Cooperative strategies in international business.* Lexington, MA: Lexington Books.

Yan, Aimin. 1993. *Bargaining power, management control and performance in international joint ventures: Development and test of a negotiations model.* Unpublished Ph.D. dissertation, the Pennsylvania State University, University Park, Pennsylvania.

__________. 1998. Structural instability and reconfiguration of international joint ventures. *Journal of International Business Studies,* 29(4): 773-96.

__________ & Barbara Gray. 1994. Bargaining power, management control and performance in international joint ventures: A comparative case study. *Academy of Management Journal*, 37(6): 1478-517.

________. 1995. Reconceptualizing the determinants and measurement of joint venture performance. *Advances in Global High-Technology Management*, 5: 87-113.

Yan, Yanni. 1997. *Ownership and control in international joint ventures*. Unpublished Ph.D. dissertation, University of Cambridge, Cambridge, United Kingdom.

TABLE 1. A Summary of Previous Empirical Research on IJV Instability

Study	Sample & Method	Operationalization	Key Findings
Franko (1971)	1,100 U.S.-foreign IJVs formed 1961-1968. Correlation & regression.	(1) Transformed to U.S. WOSs; (2) the U.S. firm increased equity to become a majority; and (3) sell-off/liquidation.	28.5% instability rate. Policy changes of the partners, rather than interpartner conflicts, were responsible for IJV instability.
Berg & Friedman (1978)	123 domestic JVs in chemical industry formed 1924 -1969. Tabulation.	Termination through either sell-off or liquidation.	40.7% termination rate. JVs are short-lived; but successful JVs were also found terminated.
Killing (1983)	35 IJVs in North America and Europe. Tabulation.	Major reorganization and termination.	35% instability rate. IJVs with dominant control or independent structure are more stable. Longevity is consistent with managers' perception of success.
Beamish (1984)	66 IJVs in 27 less developed countries. Non-parametric statistics.	Major reorganization, equity changes.	Overall instability 45%; with government partner, 58%; with foreign private partner, 23%. IJVs in developed countries more stable than those in developing countries.
Gomes-Casseres (1987)	5933 foreign manufacturing subsidiaries of U.S. firms between 1900 and 1975 Tabulation.	(1) Transformed to U.S. WOSs; (2) sold to a local partner or a third party, and (3) liquidation.	33% instability rate. The rate of liquidation was lower in IJVs than in WOSs. The rate of termination by selling off was almost twice as high for IJVs as for WOSs. Instability is not synonymous with failure; it is often adaptive actions to changes in its external environment.
Harrigan (1988)	895 inter-firm alliances formed between 1974 and 1985. Regression.	Termination.	54.8% termination rate. Strategic asymmetry between partners (differences in nationality, size, IJV experience, etc.) increases instability.
Kogut (1989)	92 manufacturing joint ventures. Event history analysis.	Termination through dissolution.	29% dissolution rate. Concurrent ties among the same partners enhance stability, while changes in industry concentration and growth rates increases instability.

Kogut (1991)	92 manufacturing joint ventures. Event history analysis.	Termination through acquisition.	40% acquisition rate. Unexpected growth in the market increases the option value of the joint venture and thus its instability.
Bleeke & Ernst (1991)	49 cross-border alliances. Tabulation.	Termination through either acquisition or liquidation.	40% termination rate. Flexibility and ability to evolve beyond initial expectations are critical to IJV success. An even split of ownership is more successful.
Blodgett (1992)	1339 IJV contracts. Event history analysis.	Contractual renegotiations.	IJVs are unstable when partners start out with uneven shares of equity, the contracts have been negotiated before, and they are formed in open economies.
Lee & Beamish (1995)	31 Korean manufacturing IJVs in developing countries formed 1973-1988. Descriptive statistics and regression.	Equity changes and major reorganization.	19% instability rate. Stability differs between IJVs formed with government partners and those formed with private partners.
Makino (1995)	Japanese IJVs in Asia. *Toyo Keizai* database 1992. Non-parametric statistics.	Termination rate as the ratio of IJVs terminated to total number of IJVs formed 1986-1991.	12.9% termination rate. Local ownership policy has no effect on performance but has negative effect on survival.
Park & Russo (1996)	204 IJVs in electronics industry formed 1979-1988. Event history analysis.	Termination either through liquidation or sales to a third party.	27.5% termination rate. Product stream and technology, home-industry competition, and other alliances between the same partners influence duration.
Park & Ungson (1997)	186 IJVs in electronics industry formed 1979-1988. Event history analysis.	Termination either through liquidation or sales to a third party.	No effect of cultural distance on dissolution, but U.S.-Japan IJVs lasted longer than U.S.-U.S. ventures. Partner pre-venture relationships enhance stability.
Hennart, Kim & Zeng (1998)	284 Japanese affiliates in the United States in 1980. Event history analysis.	Three types of termination: 1) selloff; 2) liquidation; and 3) exit.	26.4% termination rate. A higher rate of exit was attributable to sell-off. Factors in termination by sell-off were different from those in termination by liquidation.
Hennart, Roehl & Zietlow (1999)	57 US-Japanese manufacturing IJVs operating in the United States in 1980. Tabulation.	Cross-category changes in ownership structure.	63% instability rate. "Trojan Horse" argument is not supported. Financial problems of the partners and/or the IJV, interpartner conflict, etc. increase instability.

[27]

© Academy of Management Executive, 1999, Vol. 13, No. 1

Knowledge transfer in international joint ventures in transitional economies: The China experience

Steven X. Si and Garry D. Bruton

Executive Overview

China is one of the fastest growing economies in the world. A major factor in the country's economic development has been the large number of international joint ventures established within China in recent years. Although China is now the world's most active joint venture market, satisfaction with the performance of many international joint ventures in China is declining. This can be traced in part to the inability of many firms to properly assess their knowledge acquisition goals within the joint venture. Western partners' new information needs differ substantially from those of their Chinese counterparts. As a result, the joint venture partners may judge the success of their venture from vastly different points of reference. These differing goals do not automatically lead to joint venture dissatisfaction, nor do the differences necessarily need to be eliminated. Rather, the characteristics and needs of both the joint venture itself and of each partner should be studied in tandem to determine when a joint venture should devote consequential resources to meeting these knowledge acquisition goals, and when such allocation is likely to be unproductive. The application of such a contingency model to knowledge acquisition ultimately will help increase the satisfaction among international joint venture participants in China.

International joint ventures are key to many firms international strategy, and this is particularly so in China. The economic growth rate in China has been over 8 percent per year since 1979—one of the fastest in the world, and one that is expected to continue in the future.[1] Because China is also home to 25 percent of the world's population, many Western firms view the country as a prime target market. Although China is the world's most active joint venture market,[2] dissatisfaction with the performance of joint ventures in China is beginning to rise.

Profits are generally the focus of Western dissatisfaction with Sino-Western joint ventures, but this may be merely an associated outcome. The lack of understanding of each partner's knowledge needs may be the root cause of international joint ventures' performance problems within the country. The investigation of international joint ventures in established economies has shown that one of the motivating factors in establishing the venture, and one of the criteria by which its success is judged, is the knowledge transfer between the parties and the synergy this brings to the joint venture.[3]

Such knowledge transfer is particularly important in China as Western firms seek to learn about the Chinese market and how to compete in it, while Chinese firms desire knowledge about relevant new technologies or management skills. If the understanding of China is improved, and the parties achieve better cooperation and communication from better knowledge acquisition, then the resulting financial performance of these international joint ventures will improve as well.

But firms should not institute rigidly defined knowledge acquisition goals without first evaluating whether the benefits outweigh the costs, which can be great in both time and resources.

The Chinese Environment

Before 1979, China's economy was an orthodox Communist system with strong central control of nearly all economic decision making. Since then, the country has sought to move toward a market economy and is now frequently referred to as a socialist economy with market characteristics. This rapid transformation has helped feed Chinese firms' hunger for knowledge about new technologies and management skills, inaccessible before the economic liberalization. For Western firms, China is a far more complex environment than encountered elsewhere in the world, with a potentially confusing montage of business classes within any given industry, each regulated by different laws.

For Western firms, China is a far more complex environment than encountered elsewhere in the world, with a potentially confusing montage of business classes within any given industry, each regulated by different laws.

There are the large state businesses that most Westerners commonly associate with a Communist government. However, a segment of the economy that has greater industrial output but is not widely understood in the West comprises village and township enterprises that to a large degree are independent of the central government.[4]

Not only are there different laws for an international joint venture than for the domestic partner alone, but there may also be different laws depending on whether the Chinese partner is a state business or a village or township enterprise. Requirements governing the joint venture also vary depending on who has control and what assets are provided by whom.

China's legal system is not a consistently applied system of recognized rights and wrongs, but rather a series of broad guidelines that give an individual judge leeway to determine rights and wrongs.[5] Furthermore, a provincial government may write regulations prohibiting the sale of a product not produced in its own region. Thus, the Western joint venture partner is highly likely to place greater emphasis on knowledge acquisition in China than would be the case in other business environments.

Despite their explosive growth, knowledge about joint ventures in China remains limited.[6] The 1979 Law on Joint Ventures made such alliances the principal means for outsiders to enter the Chinese market.[7] Since 1989, the year of the Tiananmen Square incident, the number of joint ventures approved has increased by 500 percent.[8] Yet dissatisfaction with their performance is common among non-Chinese partners, regardless of the measurement criteria used.[9]

Knowledge Acquisition

The goals of joint ventures go beyond mere economic benefits. Knowledge, its management,[10] and its acquisition are critical issues facing senior managers.[11] Firms lean heavily on their past joint venture experiences and use them to direct present and future actions, building on their understanding of markets, technologies, or management styles each time they ally with another firm.

Knowledge acquisition and learning are critical to international joint ventures in China,[12] but the goals of individual parties to such ventures have not been established.[13] Nor has the assumption that the goals of the parties differ been objectively determined.[14]

Through a series of in-depth, structured interviews with five focus groups, the 10 major goals for the parties to international joint ventures in China were established. (Appendix A). The ten resulting knowledge goals are presented in Table 1 as part of three broad categories that typically summarize knowledge acquisition in mature economies: 1) knowledge of governmental issues; 2) knowledge of culture; and 3) knowledge of market characteristics.[15]

To better understand how the parties to a joint venture may rate the importance of these goals quite differently, 125 randomly chosen Sino-Western joint ventures, each with a minimum of 50 employees and each in business for over one year, were surveyed in Shanghai.[16] One Chinese and one Western manager from each joint venture were

Table 1
Rankings of Knowledge Acquisition Goals of International Joint Ventures in China

Knowledge of Governmental Issues
Understanding Government Behavior
Learning National Policies, Rules & Relevant Laws
Understanding the Partner's Economic System
Knowledge of Culture
Learning More About the Partner Firm's National Culture
Learning the Negotiation Styles of the Partner's Nation
Gaining Knowledge of New Managerial Types & Styles
Knowledge of Market
Gaining Knowledge of Partner's Market Characteristics
Gaining Understanding of Labor Resources
Gaining Understanding of Capital Resources
Learning New Technologies

invited to respond to the survey. Responses from 78 Chinese and 69 Western managers were received.[17] Fifty-two percent of these responses came from joint venture presidents and vice presidents, while the remaining 48 percent were from mid level managers.[18] The results of the survey are summarized in Appendix B.

The interviews demonstrated that the goal emphasis of the two groups was substantially different. Of the ten knowledge goals presented, the Chinese and Western partners placed significantly different priorities on nine. Chinese managers focused on those features that they have not currently mastered, such as technology, management skills and capital understanding. Western managers focused on their own radically different gaps—understanding the local market, government policy, and the political system. These results are very like those expected from mature economies.

Influences on Knowledge Goals

The presence of different classes of businesses within the same industry, a legal system radically different from those in most Western countries, and the strong influence of *guanxi* (personal relationships),[19] all influence joint ventures in China. A firm with prior experience in China may have built relationships and internal knowledge and can therefore overcome these problems without devoting new resources.

When both the Chinese and the Western partner are also from the same industry, there is greater potential and desire to obtain knowledge from each other. But the union of joint venture partners from different industries is also quite common in China. Central or provincial governments may strongly encourage a joint venture between unrelated Chinese and Western businesses. The Chinese firm may bring certain critical resources to the table, such as access to raw materials. However, in cases where there is little commonality between the partners, there is less potential for, or benefit from, expending resources to meet knowledge acquisition goals.

The technical nature of the joint venture also affects its knowledge goals. If firms employ high technology in their production processes, communication between the parties is critical to the efficient functioning of the organization. The machinery in a high-tech environment is complex, and without good communication, errors in production and maintenance can occur. The designated market for the joint venture's output is also critical. If the product is designed strictly for export, the need for meeting knowledge acquisition goals is somewhat less because the potential need for government support is limited. Such joint ventures employ Chinese citizens, typically at high wages, and do not compete with local firms. Consequently the Western firm needs to learn less from its Chinese partner about the local government, regulations, and culture.

The need for government support is greater when the output of the joint venture is sold within China. In this case, the joint venture competes with local firms and could potentially put them out of business. Thus, it is critical to interact smoothly with local regulators and government officials, whose protection from the vagaries of Chinese law and regulation is important. Reliance on the local partner becomes even more important when the venture sells its output to government entities rather than the general public. In these situations a clear understanding of the local circumstances, culture, and politics is important to success, and the role of government officials looms larger.

These contingency concepts are summarized in Figure 1. A joint venture entity needs to understand the dimensions of its own as well as its individual partners' knowledge acquisition goals. Utilizing the model, the firm can determine how much effort should be devoted to meeting these often-unaligned goals.

Three Categories of Knowledge Goals

The managers who rated the importance of the various knowledge issues were also queried about their firms' experiences in knowledge acquisition. In addition, they were asked about their satisfaction with the joint venture's performance and asked to rate it on a seven-point scale. Combining this performance information and the model discussed above, three categories of firms became evident. The first category comprises international joint ventures where the knowledge goals of both parties were considered by the joint venture but deduced to be not critical to the success of the venture—approximately 20 percent of the sample. These joint venture parties may have had knowledge desires, but devoting extensive time and resources to insure that they were met was not a priority for success. Joint Venture A is an example.

The second category consists of joint ventures where neither extensive time nor resources were expended to consider the knowledge goals of the parties when firms designed and evaluated their success strategies. However, for these ventures the knowledge goals were critical to their ultimate success, and ignoring such needs led to substandard performance. These firms represented about 50 percent of the sample. Joint Venture B is an example.

Finally, the last category consists of firms where the knowledge goals of both parties were integral

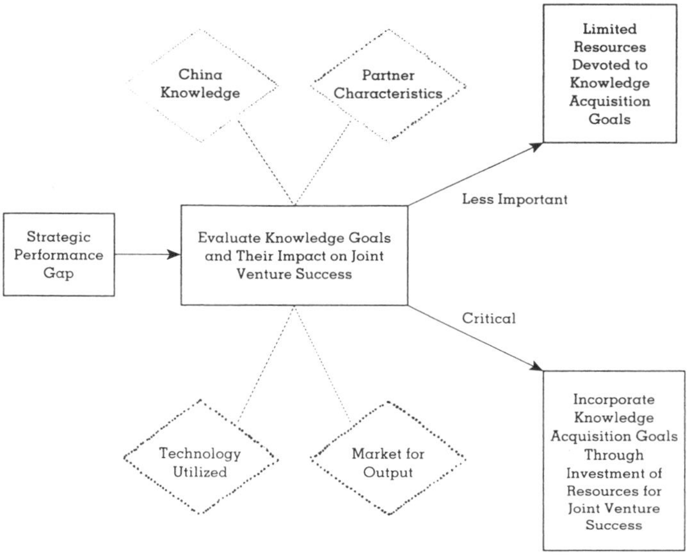

FIGURE 1
Knowledge Model to Guide International Joint Venture Evaluation

throughout the joint venture process. These joint ventures were found to have prospered, and they represent about 30 percent of this sample. Joint Venture C is an example.

Fast Food Joint Venture: Limited Emphasis On Knowledge Goals

Joint Venture A's Western partner is a U.S. fast food company that has been active in China for over five years and has locations throughout the country. This venture is in Shanghai, where 50 outlets have been in operation for over three years. The required labor skills are minimal and an abundance of qualified workers is available. The firm has made only minimal efforts to change its U.S. menu. Thus, beyond the knowledge inherited from the parent firm, there is no significant information about either the labor market or cultural issues that will enhance the U.S. firm's position.

The Chinese partner is a large state company from outside the food industry that is well connected to local government. Government access was what the Western firm most desired from its Chinese partner. The Chinese partner's being outside the food industry limits the market knowledge the U.S. firm can glean from it, as well as the extent to which the U.S. firm can provide benefit to its partner.

The food industry uses low technology, so the level of employee training and skills required is minimal. Since the firm's menu is essentially a replication of its U.S. offerings, menu planning will not substantially benefit the Chinese partner.

The firm sells its product directly to consumers, and there is no direct dealing with the government to consummate sales. The Western firm therefore has limited needs for understanding the Chinese governmental system.

That the knowledge acquisition goals of both the Chinese and the Western party are not critical to the operations of the venture is demonstrated by the U.S. company president's comment: "Our product is easily identified by the customer. Additionally, while we (both) needed to know about diverse cultures, in fact, China understood our culture well because they saw a lot of it on TV."

Manufacturing Joint Venture: Knowledge Goals Important But Not Emphasized

Joint Venture B's Western partner is a European machinery manufacturer that makes machinery for the food, rubber, and chemical industries. The joint venture is approximately three years old and is the European partner's first joint venture in China and one of its first in a transitional economy. The firm has extensive experience in international business, particularly in Europe, but lacks knowledge about Chinese governmental affairs, culture, and market. At this stage, it believes that its other international experience will overcome these shortcomings. However, the joint venture has been troubled by misunderstandings between the partners and the government regulators of the joint venture.

The Chinese joint venture partner is a large state machinery manufacturer that wants to learn about operational issues to increase its own international competitiveness. Because such market knowledge is neither publicly acknowledged nor readily available, the European firm frequently feels its Chinese joint venture partner is trying to obtain company secrets. In turn, the Chinese firm feels the European firm is not forthcoming.

The machinery manufacturing industry relies on intensive technology in its manufacturing process, as does this joint venture. In such an environment, accurate and complete communication is critical. This requires establishing a high level of trust and a good working relationship, something difficult to accomplish when the partners have unstated knowledge goals that are directing their activities. Additionally, knowledge shortcomings in areas such as governmental affairs or culture can actually impede accurate communication. These factors have contributed to the lackluster success of this joint venture.

There is a desire to sell part of the output of this machinery joint venture within China. However, most firms that would buy such machinery are large government businesses rather than individuals, and they purchase what the government encourages them to buy. An understanding of the local policies and how to encourage such purchases through governmental channels, official and unofficial, is critical. Effective relationships with the government officials who might encourage these purchases have yet to be developed.

Joint Venture B has not emphasized knowledge acquisition goals to any substantial degree either in establishing the joint venture or in evaluating its success. Instead, it has focused on the quantifiable issues of production levels and sales. The European president of the joint venture has proclaimed, "We do not have time to wait until we know such issues (knowledge goals). We came here to utilize a technological advantage." He implied that his technological advantage would be lost if the firm took the time to emphasize such knowledge goals, since they require considerable time and effort to develop. The end result has been that the joint venture's performance suffered, and the rating by the joint venture executive on the seven-point scale was at the low end.

Communications Joint Venture: Knowledge Acquisition is Recognized and Reflected In Firm Performance

Joint Venture C's Western partner is a German firm that produces communications equipment, is a very active international firm with several joint ventures across China, and has been active in the China market for over ten years. Despite this length of time, or perhaps because of it, the firm continues to place strong emphasis on governmental affairs and market knowledge. The firm feels such issues are particularly important in a transitional economy. Thus, the firm actively states its knowledge needs to its partner and enquires directly as to its partner's needs. The joint venture records these issues and they become part of the firm's performance evaluation process.

The Chinese partner is a large state firm that produces electronics. For issues such as quality control and assembly, the firm's partner operates in a closely related industry that generates the Chinese partner's own knowledge acquisition goals. The German parent does not find its partner's wishes to increase its own international competitive posture a threat; instead, this is viewed as creating a potentially stronger partner. The firm takes a long-term view of the relationship with the Chinese firm, thus it is very selective about choosing its partners. Once selected, the relationship is operated with long-term expectations. Accordingly, there is a relatively free flow of information between the partners, and the latest technology is employed in the joint venture. Consistent with this outlook, when the international joint venture holds its frequent training sessions, it invites not only the employees of the joint venture, but also employees of the Chinese parent.

Communications equipment is technology intensive, and there is a strong need for good communication and working relationships between partners because of the faster pace of change and greater complexity.[20] Partners must communicate fully and work together toward all of their goals if they are to avoid conflict. Additionally, this joint venture is aided by the continued escalation of the technological level of the operation. A local partner may leave a joint venture once it has learned all it can from the international partner, but if the technology employed is at the cutting edge, there is less incentive to leave.

This joint venture produces communication equipment for both domestic use and international export. Since the communications industry is still highly regulated in China, current and accurate knowledge about government rules, policies, and politics is critical. The Western partner actively seeks to work with its Chinese partner to both meet and work with these government entities.

Both sides of this international joint venture have supported knowledge acquisition goals throughout the process. This has helped to foster the joint venture's success. Although this success has yet to produce immediate financial returns, a platform for long-term strategic success has been established. Its German president admitted, "We have not been profitable in the past several years, but strategically we are successful as we build for the future."

Putting Knowledge Acquisition in Perspective

International joint ventures are not all the same. There are situations where the joint venture is established for no reason other than to obtain knowledge or information from the other party. However, most firms enter into a joint venture where knowledge acquisition is one part of a complex set of goals. In an international Western-Chinese joint venture, once the various goals are identified, the international firm must determine how significant those goals are to the success of the venture and must act accordingly.

If managers are not satisfied with a joint venture's performance, they can utilize the proposed model to visualize how knowledge acquisition goals may be affecting that dissatisfaction. The model aids managers by helping them to think through the unique characteristics of the international joint venture and the actions that may be critical to its success. If it is determined that the Sino-Western joint venture should devote time and resources to meeting the partners' knowledge acquisition goals, there are a variety of means to go about this. As noted in Case C, some items are as simple as clearly writing down the basic issues that the partners want to learn and incorporating them into the firm's performance evaluation. Joint Venture C employed managerial training as one key element in meeting such goals.

Organizational learning can be far more complex if the basic nature of the organization must be altered.[21] While a complete review of such organizational learning is beyond the scope of this article, executives will need to investigate this topic further if they determine the contingency variables in their given situation encourage such knowledge acquisition. The China market, as in most transitional economies, has tremendous potential for Western firms. However, the Western firms must think through their own and their Chinese partners' knowledge needs.

The China market, as in most transitional economies, has tremendous potential for Western firms. However, the Western firms must think through their own and their Chinese partners' knowledge needs.

They cannot rely simply on measurable issues such as output and sales without first determining if those variables are most appropriate for the given firm. If they do not analyze and think through these issues, the joint venture has the potential to be part of the approximately 50 percent of international joint ventures that are dissatisfied with their performance. This advice is offered specifically for managers active in China. Yet it can be translated to other transitional economies where the local understanding and knowledge of the Western partner firm needs to be improved and the special knowledge needs of the domestic partner recognized.

Appendix A

What Are the Goals in a Sino-Western Venture?

To generate a list of international joint venture goals, five focus groups were conducted with ten participants each. The participants of the focus groups each had Sino-Western international joint venture experience. The focus groups were conducted in conjunction with the Shanghai Management Training Center. A large number of the joint ventures operating in China were formed by firms in Hong Kong and Taiwan. It can be argued that these ventures represent businesses from "greater China" rather than international joint ventures, because of the language and cultural similarities. Therefore, the focus group and later survey sample included only firms from North America and Europe.

The five separate focus groups were conducted over a three-month period and produced a relatively large sample for China research—50 participants. Participants first discussed major criteria for good international joint venture knowledge transfer and acquisition. The subjects were then asked to list items and to rate them on a seven-point scale according to their importance for international joint ventures. Each session was about an hour long and the discussion among participants was audiotaped in order to obtain the full richness of the information provided through later observation and analysis.

In addition, the existing literature, not only in the West but also in China, was reviewed. Finally, a list of 27 potential goals was generated from these two distinct sets of information. That list of 27 potential goals was presented to 51 Sino-Western joint venture experts (both academicians and practitioners), 28 from China and 23 from Western nations. These experts were interviewed independently about the goals and asked to rate them from most important to least important. From these rankings, a smaller list of ten of the most important goals was generated. This list appears in Table 1. (Because of the unequal size of the Chinese and Western respondents it was decided that simply totaling the various rankings was not appropriate. Additionally, since some of the variables had overlap in potential meaning, and exploratory factor analysis was utilized. Those factors with loadings of +/− .50 or greater were employed. The names reflected in Table 1 reflect the titles given to those loadings.)

Appendix B

Importance of Knowledge Acquisition Goals

(Scale 1 to 5 with 1 for least important)

	Means of Importance	
	China n = 78	Western n = 69
Governmental		
Understanding Government Behavior	1.8	4.15*
Learning National Policies, Rules & Relevant Laws	2.09	4.07*
Understanding the Partner's Economic System	1.13	3.87*
Culture		
Learning More About the Partner Firm's National Culture	3.91	4.02
Learning the Negotiation Styles of the Partner's Nation	2.01	3.91*
Gaining Knowledge of New Managerial Types & Styles	3.95	2.72*
Market		
Gaining Knowledge of Partner's Market Characteristics	2.87	4.08*
Gaining Understanding of Labor Resources	0.85	4.16*
Gaining Understanding of Capital Resources	4.08	0.87*
Learning New Technologies	4.51	1.01*

* Statistically significant at $p < .01$

Endnotes

[1] *Institute of Economic Review*, (number 155, February 1996, pp. 56–80) The rise of China as an Economic Power.

[2] Paul Beamish writing in the *Journal of International Marketing* (1993, 1(2): 29–48) The characteristics of joint ventures in the People's Republic of China.

[3] There are many different examinations of joint ventures and their motivating rationale. For example, K. Harrigan in her 1985 book (*Strategies for Joint Ventures*, Lexington, Mass. Lexington Books) and later her writing in the *Strategic Management Journal* (1988, Joint ventures and competitive strategy. 9(2): 141–158) provides excellent insight. Similarly, Kogut's 1988 article in the *Strategic Management Journal* (Joint ventures: Theoretical and empirical perspective, 9:319–332) and F. J. Contractor and P. Lorange's article in the book they edited *Cooperative Strategy in International Business* (1988, Lexington Mass., Lexington Books) also provide useful insight. However, while these various writings use different terms they all indicate that while economic motives may still predominate there are other motives that may be as strong including knowledge acquisition.

[4] The information on industrial output was drawn from an excellent article on the Chinese economy by C. Goodhart and C. Xu in the *National*, The characteristics of joint ventures in the People's Republic of China, 1996.

[5] For an excellent review of the historical evolution of the legal system in China see the widely read Chinese history book by John King Fairbank (1992) *China: A New History*.

[6] Most of the investigations of joint ventures in China have typically examined the macro-economic variables which impact that decision of descriptive examinations of joint ventures in China. A. Yan and B. Gray in their 1994 *Academy of Management Journal* article (Bargaining power, management control, and performance in United States-China joint ventures: A comparative case study, 37:1478–1517) confirm this point of view with their good summary of the articles on joint ventures in China.

[7] An excellent book reviewing the different aspects of investing in China including joint ventures and direct investment is *Investing in China: Ten Years of the Open Door* Policy by Richard Pomfret (1991), New York: Harvester/Wheatsheaf.

[8] One of the unique characteristics of Chinese joint ventures is that far more are approved than actually reach realization. For example, in 1995 there were over 27,000 joint ventures approved by the government but only 17,000 in operation.

[9] Paul W. Beamish writing in *Journal of International Marketing* (1993, vol. 1, no. 2, pp. 29–48) The characteristics of joint ventures in the People's Republic of China.

[10] C. K. Prahalad and Gary Hamel discussed the need to cultivate a better understanding of knowledge management as part of their overview of the needs for the strategic management discipline to have an improved understanding of business (1994, Strategy as a field of study: Why search for a new paradigm? *Strategic Management Journal*, 15: 5–16).

[11] D. R. Webster writing in *Business Horizons* (1989, International joint ventures with Pacific Rim partners, 32(2): 65–71) actually argues that such knowledge may be one of the most critical items to the joint venture.

[12] Much of what has been written about joint ventures in China has sought to address the learning needs of managers. For example, articles by authors such as M. Vonglinow and M. B. Teagarden (The transfer of human resource management technology in Sino-U.S. cooperative ventures: problems and solutions, *Human Resource Management*, 1988, 27(2): 201–229) and W. H. Davidson writing in the *California Management Review* (Creating and managing joint ventures in China, 1987, 27(4): 77–94) seek to provide managers basic information about

differences in management styles and activities within Chinese joint ventures as compared to other Western firms.

[13] A. Yan and B. Gray, writing in the *Academy of Management Journal* (1994, 37: 1478–1517) Bargaining power, management, control, and performance in United States-China joint venture: A comparative study, indicate from their case studies that there are differences in motivating goals for establishing the joint ventures for the U.S. and Chinese partners. However, while some of these goals clearly involve knowledge acquisition, they do not address specifically what the knowledge acquisition goals of the two groups might be.

[14] W. H. Newman states there will be such divergence in goals writing in the *Academy of Management Executive* (Focused joint ventures in transforming economies, 6(1): 67–75) as he discusses successful joint ventures in China.

[15] The literature on organizational knowledge acquisition in joint ventures from which these three categories were distilled includes, in addition to the previously cited work on joint ventures, G. Hamel's 1991 article in the *Strategic Management Journal* (Competition for competence and interpartner learning within international strategic alliances, 12 (special issue): 83–104); and A. Parkhe's 1991 article in the *Journal of International Business Studies* (Interfirm diversity, organizational learning, and longevity in global strategic alliances, 22: 579–602).

[16] These firms represented a wide range of industries and various levels of Western ownership.

[17] Both Chinese and English versions of the surveys were sent to the firm. To ensure that the two forms of the surveys were compatible the Chinese version was translated back into English by different scholars than had conducted the original translation to check for translation inconsistencies. The English version was similarly translated into Chinese and back into English. Additionally, there is a cultural bias of East-Asian cultures to give even rather than odd number responses. Therefore, only even response numbers were used in the survey.

[18] The response rate was partially supported by the local government response to the survey. The anonymous nature of the survey was guaranteed to ensure that there was accurate response to the survey.

[19] There are a number of good articles available to readers which discuss the concept of guanxi such as E. W. K. Tsang writing in the *Academy of Management Executive* (1998, vol. 12(2): pp. 64–73) Can guanxi be a source of sustained competitive advantage for doing business in China.

[20] K. Singh writing in the *Academy of Management Journal* (1997, 40: 239–367, The impact of technological complexity and interfirm cooperation on business survival) argues that business alliances can act to mitigate the liability of newness in high technology in high complexity technology based industries.

[21] For an excellent review of the organizational learning theories as they apply to organizational change of each writer, see A. C. Edmondson, (1996) writing in *Human Relations* 49: 571–625, Three faces of Eden: The persistence of competing theories and multiple diagnoses in organizational intervention research.

About the Authors

Steven X. Si is an assistant professor of international business/management in the Department of Management, Concordia University. Professor Si received his PhD in strategic management from the Washington State University in 1996. He has published articles in peer reviewed academic journals such as *International Journal of Organizational Analysis*. He has also presented papers in national and international conferences, including Academy of Management and Academy of International Business. His research interests include international business issues, and the management of international joint ventures and alliances.

Garry D. Bruton is an assistant professor of management at the M. J. Neeley School of Business, Texas Christian University, specializing in entrepreneurship and strategic management. His research interests include high technology entrepreneurship, private equity, and international business. His research has appeared in the *Academy of Management Journal*, *Academy of Management Executive*, and the *Journal of Business Venturing*, among other publications.

[28]

© Academy of Management Executive, 1998, Vol. 12, No. 4

Learning and knowledge acquisition through international strategic alliances

Andrew C. Inkpen

Executive Overview

Global competition is forcing firms to rethink the question of how new organizational knowledge is acquired. New knowledge provides the foundation for new skills, which in turn can lead to competitive success. However, few firms systematically manage the process of knowledge acquisition. This paper explores international strategic alliances and their potential for learning and knowledge acquisition. In bringing together firms with different skills, knowledge bases, and organizational cultures, alliances create unique learning opportunities for the partner firms. Based on the assumption that organizational learning is both a function of access to new knowledge and the capabilities for using and building on such knowledge, the paper focuses on alliance knowledge accessibility and firm learning effectiveness.

Understanding Knowledge

The acquisition of new organizational knowledge is increasingly becoming a managerial priority. As the global competitive environment continues to intensify, this priority takes on new significance. New knowledge provides the basis for organizational renewal and sustainable competitive advantage. In various studies, knowledge acquisition has been linked with operational performance as well as with the performance of specific organization tasks.[1] Strategic management researchers have begun to identify knowledge as the key resource that managers need to appreciate and understand if they are to create sustainable competitive advantages.[2] Understanding knowledge means an appreciation for the complexities of acquiring, transferring, and integrating knowledge in a learning environment. In the global arena, the complexities increase in scope as multinational firms grapple with cross-border knowledge transfers and the challenge of renewing organizational skills in various diverse settings.

With a focus on the process of knowledge acquisition, this paper examines learning through strategic alliances, relatively enduring interfirm cooperative arrangements that utilizes resources and/or governance structures from autonomous organizations. Alliances are generally formed for the joint accomplishment of individual firm goals linked to the strategic mission of each partner firm.[3] Strategic alliances can have a variety of organizational arrangements, such as joint ventures (JVs), licensing agreements, distribution and supply agreements, research and development partnerships, and technical exchanges. Broadly, the governance structures of the various forms can be differentiated as either equity alliances or non-equity alliances. Equity alliances involve the transfer or creation of equity ownership either through direct investment or the creation of an equity JV. Non-equity alliances do not involve any transfer of equity nor do they usually entail the creation of a new organization.

In bringing together firms with different skills and knowledge bases, alliances create unique learning opportunities for the partner firms. By definition, alliances involve a sharing of resources. In some cases, the shared resources are strictly financial, limiting partner learning opportunities.[4] Of primary interest in this paper are alliances in which firms gain access to the skills and knowledge of their partners. This access can be a powerful source of new knowledge that, in most cases, would not have been possible without the formal structure of an alliance. Partner firms that use this access as the basis for learning have the opportunity to acquire knowledge that can be used to enhance partner strategy and operations.

Despite the logical notion that alliances create learning opportunities, and although organizations often talk in glowing terms about their alliances' learning potential, my research suggests that learning through alliances is a difficult, frustrating, and often misunderstood process.[5] More significantly, I would argue that creating a successful alliance learning environment is the exception rather than the rule. Consider the following case of a 50-50 equity JV between Hito, a Japanese firm and Alpha, an American firm.[6]

For several reasons, this alliance created a high potential learning situation. Alpha had the opportunity to acquire knowledge directly associated with Hito's technological and strategic capabilities. The venture manufacturing plant was established in vacant space in an existing Alpha plant near Alpha headquarters. Alpha managers could easily visit and interact with alliance managers. The plant was designed as closely as possible to be a replica of a Japanese plant, largely to satisfy a major Japanese customer. This provided Alpha the opportunity to gain firsthand knowledge of Japanese manufacturing processes. Hito was willing to share its technology with Alpha. Because the JV products were functionally similar to Alpha products, Alpha managers were familiar with the technology used in the JV. The JV was achieving greater productivity and lower defect rates than Alpha. By its fourth year of operation the JV had become one of its primary Japanese customer's most reliable suppliers, indicating that the venture was producing very high quality products. Finally, Alpha worked closely with the JV as an intermediate processor, allowing for interaction between parent and JV manufacturing personnel.

Alpha management indicated that a primary objective was to learn from the JV in the areas of manufacturing and customer service. Despite this initial learning intent and the high learning potential, over three years of observation, I saw little in the way of learning systems being implemented and according to senior Alpha managers, the learning experience was less than satisfactory. In fact, Alpha's manufacturing vice president dismissed the learning opportunity and commented: "What the JV does would never work in our company." Alpha management saw the JV as an autonomous subsidiary rather than a closely related division. There were few interactions between the JV and Alpha at the managerial level and top management at Alpha seemed unwilling to initiate learning efforts. For example, Hito offered to share some proprietary process technology with its American partner at no cost. The American firm was not interested, or at least made no effort to acquire the technology.

The Alpha-Hito example is not an isolated case. In many other alliances I have studied, firms have been unable to exploit alliance learning opportunities. There are various explanations for the failure to learn: the alliance knowledge was undervalued; the necessary knowledge "connections" were not put into place; the nature of the knowledge itself made learning difficult; the parent corporate culture did not support learning. The primary objective in this paper is to examine alliance learning in order to understand the conditions that support effective learning. I focus primarily on alliance forms that combine resources from more than one organization to create a new organizational entity (the "child") distinct from its parents. In the majority of cases, this form of alliance will be an equity JV. Focusing on this type of alliance allows for a clear delineation of the partner relationship and the nature of alliance knowledge. As well, research has shown that equity JVs are more effective for the acquisition of knowledge associated with partner capabilities than contract-based alliances such as licensing.[7] I also focus on international strategic alliances, defined as alliances with partners headquartered in two or more countries. Nevertheless, it should be emphasized that the findings apply to a broad range of interfirm relationships beyond equity JVs and in both a domestic and international context.

CORE THEMES

Organizations As Learning Systems

Managers are urged to improve their organizations' learning systems and to leverage new knowledge into core competencies. Some writers argue that knowledge is the primary organizational resource and that the creation and utilization of knowledge is the key to sustainable advantage.[8] All too often, however, the prescriptions are not grounded in the practical realities of management. While managers usually agree that learning in their organizations is a good thing, they are often baffled when asked to describe how their organization learns, acquires, and manages new knowledge. One of the problems is that organizational learning is a systems-level concept that can become useful only when its component parts are thoroughly understood and brought down to an operational level.

Toward that end, this paper focuses on organizational knowledge acquisition and creation as a valid foundation for understanding how knowledge travels and changes within organizations.[9] While organizations cannot create knowledge without individuals, unless individual knowledge is shared with other individuals and groups, the knowledge will have a limited impact on organizational effectiveness.[10]

While organizations cannot create knowledge without individuals, unless individual knowledge is shared with other individuals and groups, the knowledge will have a limited impact on organizational effectiveness.

Thus, organizational knowledge creation should be viewed as a process whereby the knowledge held by individuals is amplified and internalized as part of an organization's knowledge base.[11] Clearly, knowledge creation and utilization are closely linked. As individual knowledge becomes accepted by other organizational members and is utilized in organizational processes, the knowledge creation process is occurring because knowledge is moving beyond one individual's perspective.

Strategic Alliances Create Learning Opportunities

A primary objective in this paper is to move beyond abstract notions of learning to the reality faced by managers trying to build new skills and competencies. Over the past two decades there has been a substantial increase in the formation of international strategic alliances. For many firms, alliances are no longer a peripheral activity but a mainstay of competitive strategy. One of the strategic benefits of alliances is the opportunity to learn from a partner. By focusing on alliance knowledge management, this paper develops a framework of collaborative learning that should prove instructive for managers struggling to exploit alliance learning opportunities. If this is the age of "alliance capitalism,"[12] as some researchers have argued, alliances will undoubtedly become more important as a tool of competitive strategy. The framework should also be useful because it provides practical insights into knowledge creation that can be utilized beyond the alliance context. For example, managers in multinational firms seeking to combine skills and knowledge from different parts of the world must deal with knowledge management challenges similar to those faced by alliance managers.

Knowledge Acquisition and Learning Can be Managed

Knowledge acquisition, although haphazard and non-linear, is not a random process. As other researchers have found, organizations can institute policies, structures, and processes to facilitate learning and knowledge acquisition.[13] At one level, the formation of an alliance represents a strategic initiative that has the potential to create experiences, actions, and strategic choices that provide the basis for learning. However, the formation of the alliance cannot ensure that its learning potential will be realized. Managers must take explicit steps to capitalize on the alliance knowledge potential. From my research, various collaborative activities and organizational actions emerged as the basis for accessing and exploiting alliance knowledge.

The following sections discuss the key issues surrounding learning through alliances and explore the conditions that stimulate and facilitate learning. The discussion is organized around a series of questions and issues, as shown in Figure 1. The first question deals with the valuation of alliance knowledge. If alliance knowledge is viewed as valuable, the partner firm is more likely to initiate learning efforts. The next question deals with the accessibility of alliance knowledge. Depending on the type of knowledge and the partner's degree of protectiveness, some alliances will have more accessible knowledge than others. A further issue is the firm's effectiveness at learning. I discuss three factors that influence learning effectiveness in the alliance context: knowledge connections between a partner firm and its alliance, the relatedness of alliance knowledge, and cultural alignment between the partner and its alliance.

The Value of Alliance Knowledge

The formation of an alliance is an acknowledgment that an alliance partner has useful knowledge. If the knowledge were not useful, there would be no reason to form an alliance. Alliance knowledge can be viewed from three perspectives. First, there is knowledge about how to design and manage alliances.[14] Second, parent firms may seek collaborative access to other firms' knowledge but will not necessarily wish to internalize the

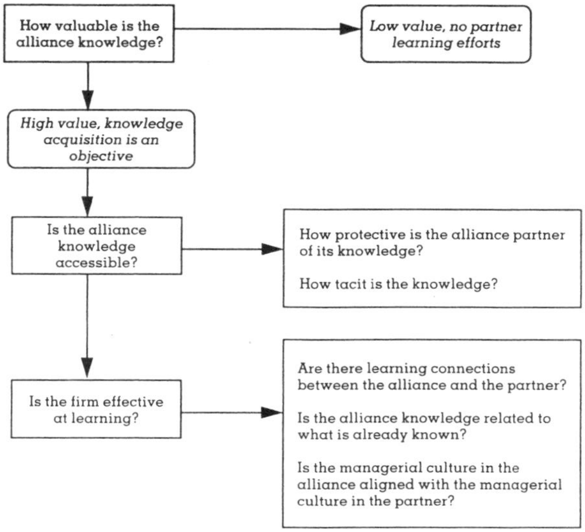

FIGURE 1
The Alliance Knowledge Acquisition Process

knowledge in their own operations. For example, a firm primarily involved in distribution activities may form an alliance with a manufacturer to ensure a stable product supply. Through the alliance, the distributor firm gains access to manufacturing skills. If the distributor has no acquisition intent associated with its partner's manufacturing skills, the manufacturing knowledge embodied in the alliance outputs has limited value to the distributor beyond the terms of the collaborative agreement.

Third, knowledge from an alliance can be used by the parent company to enhance its own strategy and operations. This type of knowledge, referred to as alliance knowledge, differs from the second type of knowledge because it has value to the parent outside the alliance agreement. In the absence of an alliance this type of knowledge remains inaccessible. The acquisition of alliance knowledge has been suggested as one of General Motors' (GM) objectives in its New United Motor Manufacturing Inc. (NUMMI) JV with Toyota.[15] In NUMMI, formed in 1984 and still operating, the manufacturing and engineering processes are controlled by Toyota. Initially, GM hoped to learn about the efficient production of small cars and transfer its knowledge to GM plants.

Alliance Knowledge: Access Versus Acquisition

Even though alliance knowledge is deemed useful, a firm will not necessarily actively seek to acquire the knowledge. Firms involved in alliances have a choice as to the resources and efforts that can be devoted to alliance knowledge acquisition. In some alliances, partners aggressively seek to acquire alliance knowledge while in others, the partners take a more passive approach to knowledge acquisition. A firm using an alliance as a substitute for knowledge it cannot create on its own may be content to remain dependent on a partner and thus, may place a relatively low value on knowledge acquisition. In this scenario, if the alliance is terminated (and most are at some point), the dependent firm may find that its knowledge base has eroded.

An alliance partner's approach to knowledge acquisition will be a function of the perceived value of alliance knowledge. Going back to the earlier example of the Alpha-Hito JV, although the knowledge was judged to be of sufficient value to warrant forming a relationship, the American partner discounted the value of the Japanese partner's knowledge, partly because of ambiguity about why the Japanese partner was successful and how

Japanese partner skills could be utilized by the American firm. With ambiguity comes misunderstanding and reluctance to dig deeper into the value of the knowledge. Clearly, if a firm wishes to imitate the strategy of a rival (or a partner) and learn from this firm, it must first understand why the firm has a competitive advantage, and then it must determine what resources are required to replicate that advantage.[16] For alliance learning strategies to be viable, firms must overcome the ambiguity associated with their partner skills.

For alliance learning strategies to be viable, firms must overcome the ambiguity associated with their partner skills.

Many American alliance parents are searching for the key to a Japanese mystique, rather than trying to develop a fundamental understanding of the link between the Japanese partner's skills and its competitive advantage.

In the Alpha-Hito JV, the key knowledge contribution to which the American partner sought access was the knowledge associated with developing and maintaining relationships with Japanese customers. As it turned out, Japanese partner knowledge about manufacturing processes and quality control became more important. Other firms are able to overcome initial skepticism about the value of their partner's knowledge and create a successful learning experience. For example, a manager described the following situation not long after forming an alliance with a Japanese partner:

> When we first went to Japan we thought our partners wanted an alliance so they could learn from us. We were shocked at what we saw on that first visit. We were amazed that they were even close to us, let alone much better.

In this particular case, the American firm was able to build a successful alliance and initiate efforts to learn from its Japanese partner. To create a successful learning environment, American firm managers had to shift their view of partner capabilities and in particular, believe that what they were seeing was both different and potentially useful.

GM initially undervalued the learning potential of its JV. Its initial learning expectations were focused on manufacturing processes, primarily for small cars in the United States context. However, NUMMI has evolved to play a key role in managerial development and training for GM, both in the United States and internationally. More importantly, the learning has gone far beyond manufacturing processes. For example, at GM Argentina's truck plant, more than 60 managers, supervisors, and team leaders have visited or will visit NUMMI. GM Argentina managers openly acknowledge NUMMI as the benchmark for lean production and continuous improvement, quality, and human resource systems. GM Argentina managers also have expectations of real change based on the NUMMI visits, as a manager explained: "all visits to NUMMI and Eisenach [Germany] will have ROI objectives; the visits must generate a positive return." When GM's Adam Opel Division decided to build a new plant in Eisenach several years ago, the objective was "to build a plant like NUMMI." The president of GM Brazil in the mid-1990s worked in NUMMI and instituted many NUMMI ideas in the Brazilian operation.

The Accessibility of Alliance Knowledge

To acquire alliance knowledge it must be accessible. Two factors limit knowledge accessibility: partner protectiveness and knowledge tacitness.

How Protective are Alliance Partners?

For competitive reasons, alliance partners may be highly protective of their knowledge resources. In a situation of high competitive overlap between the partners, one or all firms may be very reluctant to share knowledge because of the risk of knowledge spillover to a partner.[17] If alliance partner firms are competitors or potential competitors, it seems reasonable to suggest that a firm would have a limited incentive to share knowledge. In fact, a firm may have little incentive to form alliances, let alone share knowledge that could potentially lead to the creation of a competitor.

In cases of high competitive overlap, firms may work hard to prevent knowledge leakage to their alliance partners. For example, in a Japanese-American JV, the Japanese firm insisted that the JV head office be located in a separate building located a short distance from the plant. In addition, personnel working in the office, which included various American partner personnel assigned to the JV, were restricted in their access to the plant. As a final effort to prevent knowledge acquisition by the American partner, the Japanese firm insisted that the JV general manager could not be from the American partner and had to be hired from outside. The rationale for the Japanese firm's protective actions was that the Japanese partner was the plant operator and the technology involved was highly proprietary. Not surprisingly, the American partner learned little about the Japanese partner skills and the alliance was terminated after only a few years when the Japanese partner acquired the JV business.[18]

Increasing trust between alliance partners may mitigate partner protectiveness. When a new alliance is formed, there will often be a sense of hesitancy by the partners in terms of sharing knowledge, particularly if the partners have no prior collaborations. In my research, I have observed that if an alliance survives the critical honeymoon period, deeper ties between the partners becomes the norm. In many cases, ties develop between the managers involved in the alliance. Thus, after a relationship is formed and a pattern of interactions develops, partner firms may decrease their efforts to protect knowledge spillover. Specifically, as trust increases and mutual partner understanding develops, alliance knowledge should become more accessible.

The Tacitness of Alliance Knowledge

Organizational knowledge creation involves a continuous interplay between tacit and explicit knowledge. Tacit knowledge is hard to formalize and not easily visible, making it difficult to communicate or share with others. In organizations, tacit knowledge involves intangible factors embedded in personal beliefs, experiences, and values. When individuals in organizations are asked to describe how and why things are done in a certain way, they often say "I am not sure, its just the way things are done around here." An inability to articulate or describe an organizational process indicates that the knowledge supporting the process is highly tacit.

In contrast, explicit knowledge is systematic and easily communicated in the form of hard data or codified procedures. Often there will be a strong tacit dimension associated with how to use and implement explicit knowledge. For example, a manager from a European division of GM, describing an initial visit to NUMMI, said "We were amazed at what we saw." Because NUMMI's quality control was so high, there were few cars that had to be repaired after assembly was completed. The European managers did not believe the number of repair cars could be so low. Thinking that NUMMI management must have moved the repair cars to another location, the managers actually looked for additional repair cars. The number of repair cars, their location, and how they were accounted for represent explicit knowledge that can easily be communicated to an outsider. The underlying rationale for the small number of repair cars is more difficult to communicate because it involves Toyota's production system and overall approach to manufacturing, quality control, and workforce management. This knowledge has a high degree of tacitness.

The more tacit the knowledge that an alliance partner seeks to acquire, the more difficult the acquisition. As well, the more tacit the knowledge, the greater the likelihood that the knowledge is valuable. American firms in alliances with Japanese firms focus their learning efforts on explicit knowledge.[19] When the American firms formed alliances with an objective of learning from their Japanese partners, the learning expectations revolved around what the Japanese knew, rather than how and why the Japanese firms knew what they knew. The American firms expected that there would be visible differences in the alliance that could be easily identified and incorporated in the parent. The absence of highly visible changes to systems and processes was often equated with low learning potential. This is consistent with the argument that in their approach to organizational learning, Western firms tend to focus on explicit knowledge that can be created through analytical skills and concrete forms of oral and visual presentation.[20]

Other research supports the argument that tacit knowledge is difficult to acquire through an alliance. In a study of Chinese JVs, the Chinese partners encountered significant difficulty in learning complex manufacturing skills from their U.S. partners.[21] In the case of NUMMI, the learning opportunities and experiences of the partners were very different. Although GM has turned NUMMI into a positive learning experience, much has been written about how GM initially struggled to learn from NUMMI.[22] For GM to learn from Toyota and upgrade its manufacturing capability, changes in fundamental operating philosophies were required. GM's learning has been described as "a slow and painful process" because the Toyota knowledge was deeply embedded with Toyota's history and culture.[23] In particular, GM needed to learn about the Toyota production system and its emphasis on cost efficiency, quality, flexibility and innovation. To reduce its dependency on GM and successfully implement a local assembly strategy in the United States, Toyota needed to learn only how to transfer an existing management process to North America. The local knowledge that Toyota needed was more explicit than the knowledge base that GM had to build to successfully to learn from Toyota. Using NUMMI as a foothold in North America, Toyota has successfully built wholly-owned assembly plants in Kentucky and Ontario and is building a new plant in Indiana.

Learning Effectiveness

Knowledge must be accessible before it can be acquired. However, accessibility is not sufficient for effective learning. An alliance partner's effectiveness at learning and acquiring knowledge is also important. Some organizations, like individuals, may lack the capacity to learn. Effectiveness at learning is closely related to the concept of absorptive capacity. Absorptive capacity has been defined as a firm's ability to recognize the value of new knowledge and assimilate the knowledge for commercial purposes.[24] Three factors influence learning effectiveness in the alliance context: knowledge connections between a firm and its alliance, the relatedness of alliance knowledge, and the cultural alignment between parent executives and alliance managers.

The Establishment of Knowledge Connections

The creation of organizational knowledge requires the sharing and dissemination of individual experiences. Unlike most assets, organizational knowledge can actually grow when shared.[25]

Unlike most assets, organizational knowledge can actually grow when shared.

As one organizational unit shares knowledge with other units, those units are now in a position to amplify, modify, and clarify the knowledge. For knowledge in an alliance to migrate to the parent, there must be knowledge connections between the alliance and the parent. These connections create the potential for individuals exposed to alliance knowledge to share their observations and experiences. Knowledge that connects with other knowledge can be discussed, debated, and possibly discarded. The knowledge may also be further developed and move upwards in the organization. Because individual knowledge is inherently fragile, new knowledge may be ignored or viewed as irrelevant without knowledge connections. With knowledge connections in place, new knowledge has a higher probability of survival and integration into an organization's knowledge base.

Knowledge connections that are consciously managed can alleviate the distance that often exists between parent organizations and their alliances. One of the problems alliance managers encounter is that parent managers are often far removed from the realities of managing a complex international partnership. Because the parent managers are unfamiliar with the alliance and possibly inexperienced with alliance management, they often make demands that are viewed as unreasonable by the managers actually operating the alliance business.

Knowledge connections occur through both formal and informal relationships between individuals and groups. These internal managerial relationships facilitate the sharing and communicating of new knowledge and provide a basis for transforming individual knowledge to organizational knowledge. Four generic management processes create a knowledge connection between alliance and parent firms: personnel transfers between the alliance and parent; technology sharing; alliance-parent interactions, including visits and tours of alliance facilities; and linkages between parent and alliance strategies.[26]

Although personnel transfers may be associated with explicit knowledge, they will be most effective as a means of gaining access to tacit knowledge. In GM's JV agreement with Toyota, GM is allowed to assign 16 managers to NUMMI. These managers are assigned to NUMMI for two years and then rotated back to GM. Technology sharing is a mechanism that provides access primarily to explicit knowledge. Alliance-parent interactions and linkages between parent and alliance strategies create the potential for both explicit and tacit knowledge to be acquired. GM, for example, established a technical liaison office in NUMMI specifically to coordinate visits by GM personnel. This type of interaction provided GM with access to both explicit manufacturing knowledge and more tacit insights associated with human resource management and quality control. The linkage of parent and alliance strategies often occurs as an evolutionary process as initially autonomous alliances become more integrated with parent competitive strategy. Several JVs that when formed were quite independent of the American parent and relied extensively on a Japanese partner for product technology and marketing support, became less independent as ties between the JV and parents increased. In one case, plans were underway for the parent and JV to jointly explore several new international projects. Both parents realized that pooling their knowledge made sense given the ongoing consolidation in their industry.

The four processes create connections for individual managers to communicate their alliance experiences to others and form the foundation for the integration of knowledge into the parent's collective knowledge base. As individuals interact through the various connections, the interactions become larger in scale and faster in speed as more and more actors in the organization become involved. This process has been described as a spiral of organizational knowledge creation.[27] In the spiral, knowledge starts at the individual level, moves up to the group level, and then to the firm level. As the knowledge spirals upward in the organization, it may be enriched and extended as individuals interact with each other and with their organizations.

Is Alliance Knowledge Related To What Is Already Known?

Learning researchers have long recognized that what can be learned is directly related to what is already known. Prior knowledge permits the effective utilization of new knowledge. New knowledge in an area we are familiar with is generally easier to acquire than knowledge about an unfamiliar area. Unrelated knowledge will be difficult to acquire and may, in fact, have limited value because of a lack of common language for understanding the knowledge.

Two types of related knowledge are important: knowledge of the partner and knowledge about alliance management. If firms have worked together in the past, it is likely that they have developed basic understandings about each other's skills and capabilities, which should provide an impetus for further learning. Previous ties between alliance partners can generate an initial base of interpartner trust. As a result, experienced partners can forgo the relationship building processes that will be necessary for partners working together for the first time. On the other hand, inexperienced partners must go through a relationship building period that may interfere with learning.

Despite the logical notion that prior partner relationships is a factor in learning effectiveness, a counter argument must be acknowledged. When there are significant differences between the partners, the learning opportunity is enhanced because of the potential new knowledge that is outside the firm's knowledge base. Continuing this line of thinking, the greater the difference between the partner firms, the more difficult it is to create a learning relationship, and the greater the probable value of learning. The problem for the learning firm is that an enhanced learning opportunity that cannot be exploited ultimately has little value. If the knowledge is so far removed from what is known, learning may not be possible.

The second type of related knowledge is concerned with alliance management. As firms gain alliance management experience, they should become more efficient at utilizing alliances as learning opportunities because of a learning curve associated with the diffusion of learning within the firm.[28] A diverse background of alliance experience can be a robust basis for learning because of the increased probability that incoming knowledge is in a form familiar to the parent. Firms that have a base of collaborative experience should have greater knowledge of how to manage, monitor, and acquire knowledge from their alliances. Once a firm begins collaborating, it develops experience in cooperation and a reputation as a partner. Alliance-experienced firms will be more likely to appreciate the learning opportunities created by their alliances. Furthermore, as a firm develops a broad range of collaborative experience and moves up the learning curve, the skills necessary for knowledge acquisition are refined.

An obvious concern for firms involved in alliances or considering alliance involvement is the potential loss or spillover of knowledge to an alliance partner. Substantial knowledge acquisition by one partner over time can erode the value of the knowledge contributed by the other partner, breaking down the bargaining relationship between the partners. Such spillovers should be considered an inevitable result of alliance involvement. Although a firm in an alliance risks knowledge spillover, there is also the opportunity to capitalize on spillovers of the partner's knowledge. As indicated, the ability to acquire partner knowledge is partially the result of prior experience in alliance management. Alliance involvement can be viewed as a broadening experience that adds to the firm's capacity to assimilate new experiences. Increases in learning capacity are an alliance by-product. The more alliances a firm is involved in, the greater its learning capacity and the more likely partner knowledge can be acquired.

The previous discussion also suggests a possible paradox in that the more a firm learns, the less it may need to remain in an alliance. Taken to an extreme, firms that are effective at learning and eliminating partner need may find it difficult to find alliance partners. Undoubtedly, some firms may actively pursue alliance learning strategies while seeking to prevent their partners from learning. The more likely scenario is an alliance in which both partners recognize that give-and-take must be the norm for a viable alliance strategy. In the case of NUMMI, GM made no secret of its learning objectives. But since Toyota and GM are competitors, both firms will have proprietary knowledge that cannot be shared. That NUMMI has been in existence since 1984 is evidence that the partners have been able to develop a mutually beneficial learning relationship.

Cultural Alignment Between Alliance and Parent Management

The American managers in the Alpha-Hito JV were convinced that Alpha manufacturing processes could be substantially improved if an effort was made to learn from the alliance. The Japanese partner, as well, was quite willing to share its technology. At the executive level in Alpha, several levels above the alliance manager level, there was a very different perspective. The executives questioned the learning potential, given the JV's modest financial results, and the applicability of what they referred to as "Japanese" management techniques in the American plants. This case illustrates what Edgar Schein referred to as a lack of alignment between different organizational cultures.[29] In this case, the two cultural communities are the managers with direct involvement in the alliance and the American parent executives. Relative to the assumptions of the parent executives, alliance managers had very different assumptions about the alliance relationship, objectives, and performance. Because the two communities had different assumptions, when the organization attempted to learn from its alliance, the cultures collided and learning was frustrated. My discussions with GM managers who have been assigned to NUMMI illustrate a similar situation. These managers have described their frustration in trying to convince colleagues and senior managers of the relevance of their learning experience.

Key Issues to Consider

Managers must accomplish several key objectives to successfully implement an alliance learning strategy. These objectives, shown in Table 1, are incorporated with a series of questions designed to stimulate managerial thought and action.

The first objective is to evaluate partner knowledge inherent in the alliance. Partner firms must be realistic about the value of their partner's knowledge and its relevance for enhancing their firm's strategy. Firms must get beyond stereotyped views of partner capabilities and make a concerted effort to understand partner core competencies. In the knowledge evaluation stage, the structure of the alliance plays a key role. For example, if a firm insists on controlling all of the key operational tasks in the alliance, there will be few learning opportunities. If your partner does not play a major role in alliance management, learning opportunities will be limited because you cannot learn from a silent partner.

After determining the alliance knowledge value, firms are then in a position to assess knowledge accessibility and initiate learning efforts. Throughout this process it is critical that partner managers occasionally step back and ask: do we really understand what it is we are trying to learn? All too often, learning expectations are inconsistent with partner capabilities and alliance tasks.

All too often, learning expectations are inconsistent with partner capabilities and alliance tasks.

If learning efforts are initiated, firms must ensure that existing knowledge is brought to bear on the current learning opportunities. For example, research has shown that previous experience in domestic alliances can be a stepping stone to the successful launch of an international alliance.[30] If a firm has managers with experience in previous alliances or in previous relationships with the partner, these managers' experiences should be utilized. Given the complexity of alliance management in general, involving managers with relevant experiences can greatly facilitate the knowledge acquisition process.

The final objective is to ensure that the parent and alliance managerial cultures are in alignment. Parent and alliance managers must work jointly to remove the stigma of "us" versus "them." The alliance should not be viewed as a threat by parent managers, nor should it be viewed as an orphan by those managers working in the alliance. For alliance learning to occur, knowledge must move from the alliance to the parent. Knowledge transfer will only occur if there are interactions between the managers on both sides. If the managers don't trust each other or harbor suspicions of the other's motives, the spiral of organizational knowledge creation will not happen.

Successful Knowledge Management

In an increasingly competitive global environment, successful firms must be able to expand their knowledge base and develop new skills. Firms that are unable to learn risk being left behind. History shows us that the leading firms in one generation are rarely the leading firms in the

Table 1
Key Issues in Alliance Learning

Objective	Major Questions
1. Assess and value partner knowledge	• what were the strategic objectives in forming the alliance? • what are the core competencies of our alliance partner? • which partner contributes key alliance inputs? • what specific knowledge does the partner have that could enhance our competitive strategy? Is that knowledge or some of the knowledge embodied in the alliance? • what are the core partner skills relevant for our product/markets? • are we realistic about partner skills and capabilities relevant to our strategy and capabilities?
2. Determine knowledge accessibility	• have learning issues been discussed in the alliance negotiations? • how have key alliance responsibilities been allocated to the partners? which partner controls key managerial responsibilities? • do we have easy geographic access to the alliance operations? • does the alliance agreement specify restrictions on our access to the alliance operations? • has our partner taken explicit steps to restrict our access? If yes, can we eliminate these restrictions through negotiation or assignment of managers to the alliance?
3. Evaluate knowledge tacitness and ease of transfer	• is our learning objective focused on explicit operational knowledge? • where in the alliance does the knowledge reside? • is the knowledge strategic or operational? • reality check: do we understand what we are trying to learn and how we can use the knowledge?
4. Establish knowledge connections between the alliance and the partner	• do parent managers visit the alliance on a regular basis? • has a systematic plan been established for managers to rotate between the alliance and the parent? • are parent managers in regular contact with senior alliance managers? • has the alliance been incorporated into parent strategic plans and do alliance managers participate in parent strategic planning discussions? • what is the level of trust between parent and alliance managers? • do alliance financial issues dominate meetings between alliance and parent managers?
5. Draw on existing knowledge to facilitate learning	• have the partner firms worked together in the past? • in the learning process, have efforts been made to involve managers with prior experience in either/both alliance management and partner ties? • are experiences with other alliances being used as the basis for managing the current alliance? • are we realistic about our partner's learning objectives? • are we open-minded about knowledge without immediate short-term applicability?
6. Ensure that partner and alliance managerial cultures are in alignment	• is the alliance viewed as a threat or an asset by parent managers? • in the parent, is there agreement on the strategic rationale for the alliance? • in the alliance, do managers understand the importance of the parent's learning objective?

next. In many industries, firms with global reach and strengths are challenging the dominance of incumbents. Witness the decline in market share for the Big Three automotive firms in North America. Initially, a failure to recognize the differences in Japanese competitors' skills was a key element in the Big Three's inability to counter the competitive thrust of the Japanese firms. In GM's case, its JV with Toyota has been a key factor in increasing management's focus towards manufacturing quality. The JV has been a source of new knowledge that could not have been acquired without a cooperative relationship.

There can be a significant learning payoff through collaborating. As alliances increasingly become a fact of life in the business environment, exploiting the learning potential of alliances will become more important. By bringing together different firms with unique skills and capabilities, alliances can create powerful learning opportunities. However, without active management of the learning process and an understanding of the nature of alliance knowledge, many of these opportunities will remain unexploited. To successfully exploit the learning opportunities, firms must overcome several hurdles. First, before knowledge can be acquired, firms must attach a value to alliance knowledge. Clearly, a decision to initiate knowledge acquisition efforts must be balanced with the cost of doing so. Second, the knowledge must be accessible. A partner firm may take steps to explicitly prevent knowledge spillovers to other firms. Or, as tacit knowledge, alliance knowledge may not be easily acquired and transferred. Third, the firm must have the capacity to learn and have the necessary systems and processes for knowledge to be acquired. Capacity to learn is an organizational skill that can be enhanced by building a base of related knowledge, by establishing knowledge connections, and by breaking down cultural misalignments between the alliance and parent managers.

In summary, few managers would dispute that knowledge is a critical corporate asset and its creation is essential for corporate survival. However, because knowledge is invisible, its management—creation and use—is a major managerial challenge. Alliances can be a vehicle for gaining access to new knowledge outside traditional organizational boundaries. Properly managed, alliances can yield new and valuable insights that can lead to tangible performance improvements. Without active parent firm involvement in the alliance learning process, learning will not occur.

Endnotes

[1] For example, D. Epple, L. Argote, and R. Devadas, "Organizational Learning Curves: A Method for Investigating Intra-Plant Transfer of Knowledge Acquired Through Learning by Doing," *Organization Science*, 2 (1991) pp. 58–70 showed how knowledge transfer improved manufacturing productivity. Y. L. Doz, "The Evolution of Cooperation in Strategic Alliances: Initial Conditions or Learning Processes? *Strategic Management Journal*, 17 (Special Issue, Summer, 1996) pp. 55–85 found that learning cycles over time contributed to alliance efficiency and adaptability. H. Barkema, J. Bell, and J. Pennings, "Foreign Entry, Cultural, Barriers, and Learning," *Strategic Management Journal*, 17 (1996) pp. 151–166 found that learning and experience supported international expansion strategies.

[2] For example, the Winter 1996 Special Issue of the *Strategic Management Journal* is devoted to knowledge-based theories of the firm.

[3] A. Parkhe, "Interfirm Diversity, Organizational Learning, and Longevity in Global Strategic Alliances," *Journal of International Business Studies*, 22 (1991) pp. 579–601.

[4] For example, because of the enormous risks, alliances are usually formed for oil and gas exploration. In these alliances, one partner is usually the designated operator and the other partners have financial interests. The learning opportunities are limited for the non-operator partners.

[5] A. C. Inkpen, "Creating Knowledge Through Collaboration," *California Management Review*, 39 (1996), no. 1, pp. 123–140; A. C. Inkpen and M. M. Crossan, "Believing is Seeing: Joint Ventures and Organization Learning," *Journal of Management Studies*, 32 (1995) pp. 595–618.

[6] Company names are disguised.

[7] D. C. Mowery, J. E. Oxley, and B. S. Silverman, "Strategic Alliances and Interfirm Knowledge Transfer," *Strategic Management Journal*, 17 (Special issue, Winter 1996), pp. 77–92.

[8] For example, see R. M. Grant, "Toward a Knowledge-based theory of the firm," *Strategic Management Journal*, 17 (Special issue, Winter 1996), pp. 109–122.

[9] G. Hedlund and I. Nonaka, "Models of Knowledge Management in the West and Japan," In P. Lorange, B. Chakravarthy, J. Roos, and A. Van de Ven, eds., *Implementing Strategic Processes: Change, Learning and Co-operation* (Oxford: Basil Blackwell, 1993) pp. 117–144.

[10] D. H. Kim, "The Link Between Individual and Organizational Learning," *Sloan Management Review* 35 (Fall 1993), pp. 37–50.

[11] I. Nonaka has written extensively in the area of knowledge creation. See: I. Nonaka, "A Dynamic Theory of Organizational Knowledge," *Organization Science* 5, (February 1994) pp. 14–37; I. Nonaka, "The Knowledge-creating Company," *Harvard Business Review*, 69 (November/December 1991) pp. 90–104. Nonaka and H. Takeuchi have argued that one of the limitations of organizational learning theory is its failure to develop the concept of knowledge creation. See I. Nonaka and H. Takeuchi, *The Knowledge Creating Company: How Japanese Companies Create the Dynamics of Innovation* (New York: Oxford University Press, 1995).

[12] J. Dunning, Reappraising the Eclectic Paradigm in An Age of Alliance Capitalism," *Journal of International Business Studies* 26 (Third Quarter 1995) pp. 461–492.

[13] E. C. Nevis, A. DiBella, and J. M. Gould, "Understanding Organizations as Learning Systems," *Sloan Management Review* 36 (Winter 1995) pp. 73–85.

[14] M. A. Lyles, "Learning Among JV-Sophisticated Firms," In F. Contractor and P. Lorange, eds., *Cooperative Strategies in International Business* (Lexington, MA: Lexington Books, 1988) pp. 301–316.

[15] M. Keller, *Rude Awakening: The Rise, Fall, and Struggle for Recovery of General Motors* (New York: William Morrow, 1989).

[16] R. Grant, "The Resource-Based Theory of Competitive Advantage: Implications for Strategy Formulation," *California Management Review*, 34 (Spring 1991) pp. 119–135.

[17] An interesting question is why Toyota is not more protective of its technology in the NUMMI JV. Based on my interviews with NUMMI and GM managers, there are three reasons: 1) Toyota needs an amicable relationship with GM for political reasons; 2) Toyota recognizes that a deep understanding of the Toyota Production System is not possible without years of study and involvement and 3) NUMMI does not have Toyota's most advanced manufacturing technology.

[18] The JV was originally formed because the Japanese partner wanted local market support in the United States and the American partner sought access to the Japanese partner's technology.

[19] A. C. Inkpen and P. W. Beamish, "Knowledge, Bargaining Power and International Joint Venture Stability," *Academy of Management Review*, 22 (1997) pp. 177–202.

[20] Nonaka and Takeuchi, *op. cit.*, 1995.

[21] A. Yan and B. Gray, "Bargaining Power, Management Control, and Performance in United States–China Joint Ventures: A Comparative Case Study," *Academy of Management Journal* 37 (1994) pp. 1478–1517.

[22] For example, see: J. L. Badaracco, *The Knowledge Link*

(Boston: Harvard Business School Press, 1991); T. A. Mahoney and J. R. Deckop, J. R., "Y'Gotta Believe: Lessons From American- vs. Japanese-run U.S. Factories," *Organizational Dynamics*, 21 (4, 1993) pp. 27–38; and T. Sasaki, "What the Japanese Have Learned From Strategic Alliances," *Long Range Planning*, 26 (6, 1993) pp. 41–53.

[23] R. M. Grant, "Prospering in Dynamically-Competitive Environments: Organizational Capability as Knowledge Integration," *Organization Science*, 7 (1996) pp. 375–388.

[24] The term absorptive capacity was first used by W. M. Cohen and D. A. Levinthal, "Absorptive Capacity: A New Perspective on Learning and Innovation," *Administrative Science Quarterly*, 35 (1990) pp. 128–152. For a study that explores organizational determinants of absorptive capacity, see J. M. Pennings and F. Harianto, "The diffusion of technological innovation in the commercial banking sector," *Strategic Management Journal*, 13 (1992) pp. 29–46. P. J. Lane and M. Lubatkin, "Relative Absorptive Capacity and Interorganizational Learning," *Strategic Management Journal*, forthcoming, found that a firm's ability to learn from another is a function of existing knowledge bases, organization structures and compensation policies, and dominant firm logics.

[25] J. B. Quinn, P. Anderson, and S. Finkelstein, "Leveraging intellect," *Academy of Management Executive* (10, 1996, no. 3) pp. 7–27.

[26] Inkpen, *op. cit.*, 1996.

[27] Nonaka, *op. cit.*, 1994.

[28] D. E. Westney, "Domestic and Foreign Learning Curves in Managing International Cooperative Strategies," In F. Contractor and P. Lorange, eds., *Cooperative Strategies in International Business* (Lexington, MA: Lexington Books, 1988) pp. 339–346.

[29] E. H. Schein, "Three Cultures of Management: The Key to Organizational Learning," *Sloan Management Review*, 38 (Fall 1996), pp. 9–20.

[30] H. G. Barkema, O. Shenkar, F. Vermeulen, J. H. Bell, "Working Abroad, Working With Others: How Firms Learn to Operate International Joint Ventures," *Academy of Management Journal*, 40 (1997) pp. 426–442.

About the Author

Andrew C. Inkpen is an associate professor of management at Thunderbird, The American Graduate School of International Management. He received his PhD from the University of Western Ontario in 1992. His current research interests include the management of knowledge in strategic alliances, trust in joint ventures, and learning in multinational organizations. His research has been published in various journals, including the *Academy of Management Review, Organization Science, Strategic Management Journal, California Management Review, Journal of International Business Studies,* and *Journal of Management Studies.*

[29]

Building Trust in International Alliances

Arvind Parkhe

Two facts stand out unambiguously in today's global business. One, international alliances are proliferating, underscoring the strategic importance managers increasingly attach to "competition through cooperation." Two, trust is key to successful international alliances. Together, these two facts point to the need to better understand trust, a task that was attempted in an earlier article (Parkhe, 1998). Yet such understanding, while necessary, is not sufficient. This article, the second of a two-part series, shows how partners can proactively manage an alliance relationship in order to develop trust. Toward this goal, the discussion includes trust generation through process-based, characteristic-based, and institutional-based mechanisms, which are to a significant degree within alliance managers' control. Managers must also be mindful of several critical features of alliance dynamics. These are described in some detail, as is the need to appropriately "calibrate" trust level in an alliance to the lifecycle stage of the alliance. With proper management attention, too much and too little trust can be avoided.

Trust but verify.

—Russian proverb

It hurts in my heart to hear Northwest say the trust is gone.

—KLM president Pieter Bouw

In the 1960s, General Motors Corporation's annual reports often contained explicit references to *not* reaching out to other companies. GM prided itself on doing things in-house. IBM, 3M, and scores of other companies similarly were corporate loners. That was then. The differences today are striking. Companies are entering into alliances with greater frequency and urgency, and in many cases alliances touch the very core of participants' vital competitive advantages. This fundamental shift is accompanied by deep changes in corporate and industry cultures.

For example, Ford was a company that tended to be strongly top-down, with a rigid hierarchy, and that managed external relations unilaterally. A Ford decision was final and was not explained even when the other party was not satisfied. With U.S. nationals in-charge of most overseas divisions, Ford was also "culturally challenged." Today, the company is more flexible. Ford explains more and listens more (Lewis, 1990). Teamwork is easier, major foreign offices are headed by for-

Arvind Parkhe, Department of Management, Kelley School of Business, 1309 East Tenth Street, Bloomington, IN 47405-1701 <aparkhe@indiana.edu>.

eign nationals, and Ford's participation in alliances is much easier and greater than before. Importantly, these changes inside Ford and those in its external relations are not unrelated. As Dan Ciampa, CEO of the Rath and Strong consulting group put it, "Unless an organization knows how to foster collaborative relationships internally, it won't be good at making such relationships outside."

Ford is not alone; numerous other companies have also undertaken serious reforms. Xerox's Palo Alto Research Center recently developed new products jointly with Sun Microsystems Inc. The Center's head, John Seely Brown, understands how the current wave of alliances gives companies a track record of cooperation: "People who think they can screw each other because we are going to terminate six months later are missing the point, because what we're building is a web of trust and shared understandings" (Byrne, 1993). Often, relationships with inauspicious beginnings solidify into major partnerships. In 1986, Texas Instruments sued eight Japanese companies, including Hitachi, for dumping memory chips and violating intellectual property rights. TI demanded—and got—stiff royalties totaling over $315 million. But during this process, "Hitachi had to lay its cards on the table to negotiate royalty payments," says Pat Weber, president of TI's semiconductor group. The haggling gave the companies not only "a damned good understanding of each other's technology, but a good respect for each other's capability." In December 1988, TI stunned the industry by announcing a partnership with its former adversary, Hitachi.

Plainly, we are entering a new era, an era in which cooperation and competition often coexists between alliance partners. In this environment, understanding and managing the "softer" side of collaborative relationships becomes crucial. Drawing upon ideas developed in my previous article (Parkhe, 1998), this article shows how managers can purposefully cultivate trustful alliance relationships. Toward this goal, the next section discusses how trust-generation mechanisms (Zucker, 1986) that are within management's control can be effectively implemented in international alliances. The following section addresses the evolution of cooperative relationships over time. As partners deal with each other in an alliance, they learn more about each other's motives, capabilities, and attitudes toward control, conflict, cooperation, and competition. Trust may deepen as a relationship matures, but this process is hardly automatic. Trust must be nurtured continually because, like a house of cards, trust is hard to build and easy to destroy, which strongly suggests that alliance dynamics must be managed carefully. Following this discussion, I argue that alliances go through various stages of lifecycle, and at any particular stage of a relationship, the level of trust must approximately "match" the lifecycle stage.

"Production" of Trust in International Alliances

At least three bases exist for the occurrence and growth of trust in relationships (Zucker, 1986). These include process-based, characteristic-based, and institutional-based trust. Each of these trust-building factors is, to some degree, within management's control, and each factor therefore merits attention during the design and implementation stages of an alliance. Each will be discussed in turn.

Process-Based Trust Production

Consistency of past behaviors tends to generate expectations of predictability. Consistent, reliable interactions thus tend to produce an impression of trustworthiness. Such an impression is further strengthened if both parties to an alliance anticipate a mutually beneficial relationship extending well into the foreseeable future. Thus, trust can develop from the alliancing process itself, and furthermore, trust is seen to be at once forward-looking (tied to expectations of a promising future) and backward-looking (tied to a reassuring past history). As described below, backward-looking trust development can be based upon alliance partners' private history of cooperation or a company's reputation, and forward-looking trust develops from expectations of a continuing, mutually productive relationship.

Process-based Trust from Ongoing Interactions with Alliance Partner

At least initially, people are unsure of the trustworthiness of persons or companies they have never dealt with before. In alliances, therefore, managers match observed (actual) behaviors against expected (cooperative) behaviors. The better this match, the more confident one becomes in placing trust in a partner. Trust is usually slow and difficult to build up, yet it is quick and easy to tear down. Lewis (1990) described this process as follows: "People learn differently from negative and positive experiences. Just one unpleasant incident ..... imprints the event on your memory. Like touching a hot stove, you keep your distance after that. A good experience, by contrast, must be repeatedly reinforced before people accept the pattern".

Alliance managers can put knowledge of this asymmetry to good use. First, the ease of trust destruction is reminiscent of a cardinal rule taught to freshman medical students: Do no harm. It is important for a physician to contain damage before he or she can attempt healing and recovery. Likewise, managers attempting to build trust must first prevent trust erosion, particularly in youthful alliances where trust is only beginning to emerge. Trust is brittle, and once damaged, it is doubly difficult to reestablish. Knowing this should help focus attention, especially in the critical early stages of a relationship, on avoiding surprises, being trustworthy and being *known* to be trustworthy.

However, anticipating and preventing possible damage to a trustful relationship is only the first step. Next, managers must actively employ the principle of "repeated reinforcement of positive experiences" to nurture trust. Thus, in their ongoing interactions, alliance partners should install formal and informal channels of communication that improve behavior transparency. The goal is two-fold: one, to ensure that each partner knows of the other's alliance-related actions on a timely basis, so that each company may make inferences about the other side's ability and willingness to uphold the letter and spirit of the alliance; and two, to minimize surprises and to resolve behavioral discrepancies quickly and amicably. Over time, sustained attention to such measures may lead to tighter personal bonds between alliance managers, improving the "sociopsychological filter" through which information regarding an alliance and alliance partner is processed (Parkhe, 1998). Such process-based trust development often has spillover benefits well beyond the immediate alliance at hand, to the relationship as a whole. For instance, after years of successful cooperation, General Electric and Snecma (a French aero-engine manufacturer) work together almost as a single team, with substantial joint learning, mutual high regard for each other's skills, and considerable shared understandings about how each firm thinks and works (Lewis, 1990). Issues get resolved faster and easier, as there is a great deal of mutual comfort. In turn, this makes it easier to initiate and develop new programs together, as Snecma demonstrated when it chose GE over Pratt & Whitney.

One key requirement for such mutual comfort to arise is sustained involvement at all phases of an alliance by people at the operational, planning, and senior management levels. Yet this is often not done. One study of alliances found that senior management involvement declines precipitously with time. The study, conducted by Coopers & Lybrand (an accounting and consulting firm) and Yankelovich, Skelley, and White (an opinion research firm), showed that 46% of senior management time allocated to alliances goes into the conceptual phase of developing an alliance. This figure drops to 23% during development of the business plan, and shrivels to just 9% by the time a management system for a new alliance is being structured.

The consequences of senior management inattention can be disheartening, as shown by the unhappy marriage of General Motors and Isuzu. GM owns a hefty stake (37.5%) of Isuzu, yet GM was blind-sided when Isuzu posted a $381 million pretax loss on sales of $9.02 billion (Miller & Treece, 1992). GM's vice president for Asian and Pacific operations, Thomas S. McDaniel, conceded: "We found ourselves not very knowledgeable about the problems and how Isuzu got into them." Surprisingly, such senior management indifference reached all the way to the top of GM hierarchy, where officials couldn't even correctly pronounce the name of the company with whom GM had shared a 21-year alliance history. At a press conference, former GM chairman Robert C. Stempel mispronounced Isuzu as "eye-zoo-zoo," followed by vice-chairman John F. Smith Jr.'s "eh-zoo-soo." The correct pronunciation: "eee-soo-zoo." Contrast this example with the emphatic views of James R. Houghton, Corning Glass Works chairman, on the need for personal involvement by top managers:

> When we formed a joint venture with Ciba-Geigy in 1985 (Ciba Corning Diagnostics Corporation), I insisted that I go on the board along with the highest executive from Ciba-Geigy. Such visible commit-

ment ..... underlines the new company's importance. It also says to the employees of the joint venture that the two partners are regularly talking and agreeing on policy issues. If such roles are delegated, the opportunity for divisiveness is greater" (Houghton, 1987, p. 14).

In the early 1940s, James Houghton's father, who was then Corning's chairman, boarded a train four times a year to travel from upstate New York to upstate Michigan for Dow Corning board meetings. At the time, Dow Corning annual revenues were relatively small (about $200,000). But the senior Houghton's active support set a strong example for others at Corning.

Process-based Trust from Reputation Effects

The above discussion pointed to how a shared cooperative history can spark process-based trust. Often, however, a company has little direct prior experience with an alliance partner. Trust may still develop in such relationships, based not on direct interactions, but rather on a partner's reputation. A reputation represents a cumulative record of past behaviors. By extrapolating a past record into the future, third parties can make vicarious inferences about likely future behavior of an alliance partner. The better a company's past record, the stronger its reputation, and the more comfortable we feel is assuming continuing trustworthiness in the future.

Quite literally, a good reputation is becoming one of the greatest assets a company can possess. As international alliances contribute more to companies' global competitiveness, so the importance of reputation as a trustworthy alliance partner will correspondingly grow as well. Like other valuable assets, a reputation requires deliberate, upfront investments. What sorts of investments are required, and what sort of a reputation should alliance managers seek to build?

To take the second question first, two of the keys to a successful cooperative strategy are to be Nice (never being the first to cheat) and to be Provocable (always swiftly taking reprisals against partners who cheat) (Axelrod, 1984).[1] Earning a reputation for being Nice requires the "investment" of diligent work in developing mutual understanding, and of self-restraint, as a company purposely forgoes certain short-term gains that a partner may perceive to be exploitative in nature. The message is simple and powerful: Play fair with the other side before you can expect them to play fair with you. This means each partner recognizes the other's interests in entering into an alliance, and attempts to structure and run the alliance in such a way that it serves the interests of all parties involved. For example, putting your best people into an alliance tells everyone, including your partner, that the alliance is important to you (Byrne, 1993). Conversely, not offering your best and brightest sends a signal that is not conducive to building trustful relationships.

Another technique to strongly convey fair play can be called "issue spotting." Lewis (1990) suggests that rather than expecting a partner to raise all issues that affect its interests, one can take the lead. Proactively bringing issues to a partner's attention when you spot them reduces surprises, and helps build confidence that each partner is looking out for the other's interests. Executives and board members routinely do this for each other in successful alliances, including Autolatina, Ciba Corning Diagnostics, and the Ford-Mazda alliance.

Lewis (1990) takes this thought further, arguing that a winning strategy is to always be constructive. In an ideal relationship, he notes, each side behaves rationally, fully understands the other's views, communicates well, is reliable, avoids coercion, and respects the other as someone whose perceptions and interests deserve to be taken into account. Yet in reality, perceptions and interests of partners are likely to differ somewhat. To improve your ability to work together and advance your interests, it pays to be constructive, which is akin to Axelrod's strategy of being Nice.

This may be easier said than done, however. Many managers are too competitive for their own good (Axelrod, 1984), unable or unwilling to break out of an "us versus them" mindset. As Dick Dulude, a Corning group president, reported: "We have had some 'tough guys' as partners ..... If you regard another person as impossible, or expect a difficult person to change, you have little hope of building effective relations. You have to change yourself to make things work better, and they generally will" (Lewis, 1990: 241). This pattern of investing effort into learning a partner's legitimate needs, and working to fulfill them, can create a Nice reputation.

Still, no matter what the reputation, companies must run the "chemistry test" on each prospective partner. William Norris, founder of Control Data and a pioneer in using cooperative ventures internationally, was told by cynics that a proposed joint venture with the Romanian government would bleed Control Data of its computer peripherals technology, and then the Romanians would dump the venture. Norris decided to go on a fishing trip with the prospective partners on the Danube. He became convinced that these people were straightforward, and signed the agreement, which turned out to be mutually profitable (Lynch, 1989).

Process-based Trust from a Long "Shadow of the Future"

Another trust-producing mechanism that lies within management's control deals with maintaining expectations of a continuing, mutually productive relationship over the foreseeable future. Such expectations of profits in the future tend to promote cooperative behavior in the present. In other words, the future casts a shadow back upon the present, generating trustful behavior. (Conversely, cooperation and trust tend to suffer with the approach of the terminal date of an alliance.)

The shadow of the future is tied to alliance partners' time horizons, frequency of interactions, and behavior transparency. Long time horizons refer to a far-sighted outlook toward a cooperative relationship, reflecting a high value placed upon future payoffs from a partnership. Frequent interactions are achievable by slicing up large activities into smaller ones. This leads to cooperative performance reviews (matching of actual versus expected behaviors) at shorter and more regular time intervals, which in turn strengthens cooperation and increases trust. And behavior transparency refers to the speed and reliability with which alliance partners learn about each other's actions (or in chess language, "moves"). Quick and reliable information ensures high behavior transparency, which minimizes misunderstandings, reduces uncertainty, and encourages sustained cooperation. In sum, long time horizons, frequent interactions, and high behavior transparency are factors that alliance managers can influence in order to lengthen the shadow of the future and enhance process-based trust.

LSI Logic Corporation, manufacturer of custom-made microchips, discovered out of necessity how a shared and interdependent future can cast a shadow back upon the present and generate trust (see Davidow & Malone, 1992). As is often the case, rigid contractual procedures used to govern LSI's relationships with its customers. But the company realized that it could manufacture and deliver new products to customers faster than those customers could move contracts through their own legal departments. Says Wilfred Corrigan, LSI's CEO: "Our most aggressive customers said to us, 'Look, stock the product on our verbal order because we can't process the paper to you and you can't process the paper internally fast enough for the time window we have to operate in.'" So, LSI chose to forge ahead with production and let the paperwork follow weeks or months later. America's leading producer of gate arrays now enters into long-term business relationships, trusting that the other side is equally responsible and fair-minded.

Characteristic-Based Trust Production

International alliances press into contact companies that may be quite dissimilar in their background characteristics. Two of such characteristics are societal cultures of headquarters countries and corporate cultures of partner firms (Parkhe, 1991). The greater the similarity of societal and corporate cultures, the greater may be the knowledge of and familiarity with each other's modes of thinking and behaving, hence the greater the comfort level and the lower the learning cost and time. Conversely, building trust may be harder when cultures are highly dissimilar, since homogeneous expectations and shared assumptions about the alliance may not exist as readily. Harder, but not impossible. It is important to realize that with sufficient investment of time and effort, the obstacles to trust-building imposed by differences in characteristics can be effectively managed.

For example, we've all heard the stereotypes: cryptic British reserve, irreverent American informality, Italian chaos, French protocol, German rigidity, Japanese vagueness, and Latin American disregard for punctuality (Lewis, 1990). Valid or not, such stereotypes point to the need to look for and understand differences in perception and interpretation of phenomena. Trust generation is possible both where cultural similarity already exists between partners, and also where deliberate efforts are undertaken to understand and overcome differences.

Cultural differences can be subtle or obvious, trivial or fundamental. For example, communication patterns vary between low-context countries (such as the United States), where most information is contained in explicit codes, such as spoken or written words, and high-context countries (such as Saudi Arabia), where sending and receiving messages is highly dependent upon the physical context and non-verbal communication. Such differences can impact initial negotiations before alliance formation, as well as ongoing communications afterward. Effectively dealing with communication and countless other areas of potential cultural differences requires investing in intercultural awareness training programs, encouraging informal contact, and improving behavior transparency. Managers who fail to take these steps may soon join the ranks of AT&T group executive Robert Kavner, who regretted after the failed AT&T-Olivetti alliance, "I don't think we or Olivetti spent enough time understanding behavior patterns. We knew that culture was different but we never really penetrated. We would get angry and they would get upset" (Wysocki, 1990).

On the other hand, managers who represent Corning in its foreign optical fiber ventures attend, with their spouses, Berlitz classes for six to eight weeks of full-time language and cultural training. (Interestingly, this practice is used even where English is widely used, since some prior knowledge of local social norms helps managers get accepted, and allows them to pick up nuances in meetings.) At Japan's NEC, managers going abroad get elaborate training in Western customs. This includes differences between Japanese and American decision making, several periods of simulated negotiations with non-Japanese, and a course in English conversation so intense that teachers are replaced every few days. Even Western social etiquette is covered—table manners, cocktail party conversations, and English-language jokes.

The point of these programs is to move from culture shock to culture empathy, so managers understand how their views are colored by their background, how their behavior can impact cross-cultural dealings, and how to recognize cultural influences in others' conduct. Such efforts can pay off nicely in overcoming cultural differences and generating trust between partners. In an empirical study, Johnson, Cullen, Sakano, and Takenouchi (1997) found that partner cultural sensitivity is an important contributor to trust-building for both U.S. and Japanese alliance partners. Similarly, contrary to popular belief, Park and Ungson (1997) found the international alliances they studied to be more, not less, stable than domestic alliances. Why? One possible explanation is that learning between partners may offset cultural differences. In addition, these authors noted, prior relationships between partners create trust and familiarity. Trust reduces opportunistic behavior and can facilitate conflict resolution. And familiarity enhances a partner's transparency and reduces the costs of monitoring its activities.

Institutional-Based Trust Production

The above discussion suggested that process-based trust may arise from past or future interactions, and characteristic-based trust may arise from attributes of a partner, such as societal and corporate cultures. But each of these requires detailed, specific, non-transferable information regarding a partner. What about cases where such information is not available? And what about fast-changing situations where any available information is soon outdated? There is a third way. This way relies for generation of trust upon formal mechanisms, as described below.

Institutional-based Trust from Intermediary Mechanisms

The more assured a company feels that its alliance partner will follow through on its promises, the more trustworthy the partner will be, by definition. Greater assurance of cooperative behavior can be achieved by structuring an alliance relationship so that (a) the attractiveness cheating is reduced, (b) the cost of cheating is increased, and/or (c) the gains from cooperation are increased. Two types of mechanisms are available to bring about these results. The first type seeks to discourage cheating before it occurs, while the second type seeks to punish cheating after it has occurred. Either way, the purpose is to develop an alliance structure that provides built-in incentives toward cooperative, trustworthy behavior.[2] Each will be described in turn.

The first mechanism, seeking to prevent wrongdoing before its occurrence, requires a show of good faith by both sides. Each company can take actions that "lock" it into the alliance and create costly obstacles (exit barriers) to casually abandoning the relationship. For example, nonspecific assets, such as general purpose trucks and airplanes, are salvageable if an alliance breaks down; such assets therefore provide no clear cues about desire to cooperate or to cheat (Williamson, 1985). But alliance-specific assets (such as Donnelley's new plant built solely to manufacture exterior mirrors for Honda) are not easily redeployable. Companies can show good faith through a variety of such upfront commitments, including entering into reciprocal agreements (e.g., guaranteed purchase of each other's products and services at guaranteed prices) and making nonrecoverable investments. Nonrecoverable investments include specific physical assets like plant and equipment, but go further to also include site specificity, human asset specificity, and dedicated assets (Williamson, 1985). In each case, these involve alliance-specific costs (1) that are incurred in advance of alliance 0commencement and (2) whose value for alternative uses is greatly reduced, sometimes to the level of scrap value only. Put another way, these costs are largely sunk.

The second mechanism seeks to promote cooperative behavior by reducing potential gains from cheating through prospective punishments after the fact. Opportunism can be deterred through contractual safeguards, or legal stipulations in the partnership agreement, that inflict penalties for omission of cooperative behaviors or commission of violative behaviors. By anticipating at least some of the possible contingencies, and by stipulating appropriate provisions (and punishments) for each contingency beforehand, such measures attempt to produce clearer expectations and fewer surprises, and thus increase the level of confidence in each other's likely behavior. Note, however, that these provisions are primarily preventive, not punitive. Companies typically hope that these safeguards never have to be used, so their purpose is deterrence beforehand, not revenge afterward.

Institutional-based Trust by Providing Implicit "Guarantees"

Another institutional-based mechanism designed to produce trust and signal one's trustworthiness also relies on formal social structures. A five-star hotel, an R-rated movie, a CPA degree, and an MD diploma all have something in common. In each case, an independent, qualified body has attested publicly, "To Whom It May Concern," that the holder of the certificate or credential meets certain standards of competence and performance. The goal is to reveal company or individual attributes that are general (beyond particular transactions) and objective (anyone would reach the same conclusions). Such objectivity rests on membership in a professional subculture within which carefully developed behavior patterns are expected to be followed, suggesting a baseline level of trustworthiness. However, unlike the mechanisms discussed above, implicit guarantees of competence or trustworthiness are not yet available in the context of alliances. Is a "databank" or a clearing house of prospective alliance partners possible, from which one may choose companies depending upon specific alliance requirements? Important implications flow from this line of thought, as discussed in the final section of this paper.

Managing Alliance Dynamics

From the standpoint of building trust, five features of ongoing alliance management are noteworthy.

Understand the Trust Timeline and Sequence

Friendly relationships can turn hostile rather quickly, and vice versa. In 1983, Hitachi agreed to pay $300 million to settle a major lawsuit filed against it by IBM, which had accused Hitachi of stealing IBM technology. Yet soon afterward, the companies' collaboration was strong and growing. Hitachi supplied IBM with some high-end printers that IBM resold under its own label. In turn, Hitachi resold under its own name some IBM-made notebook PCs. And in a "continuation of a warming trend" in the two companies' relationship, IBM and Hitachi reached a pact in 1992 to jointly develop the "brains" and printing mechanism for a new generation of high-volume printers.

It is thus useful to diagnose the chronological sequence by which one or more of the trust-development sources discussed above are activated in building trust. Although the actual sequence may vary substantially from one relationship to the next, one hypothetical sequence might unfold as follows. Companies A and B are put in touch with each other by company C, which has positive working experiences with both A and B (trust induced by reputation effects). As alliance negotiations get under way, A and B discover common positions on corporate values and strategic tracks (characteristic-based trust). Encouraged, A and B push further into issues of structuring the deal. They come to a mutually satisfactory agreement on strengthening cooperation by adopting a reciprocal purchase agreement plan (discouraging cheating before it occurs), as well as provisions for legal sanctions (imposing punishments if cheating should occur) (intermediary mechanisms). The alliance commences operations, and A and B observe with pleasure as the other side lives up to the letter and spirit of the cooperative agreement, even in—rather, especially in—unanticipated situations (process-based trust from ongoing interactions). The alliance is successful, and A and B begin to contemplate expanding the scale and scope of the relationship (lengthening shadow of the future). By being alert to such a sequence (e.g., reputation effects → alliance structuring → growing cooperative history → shadow of the future), a manager can better understand trust-building triggers, as well as accurately reinforce a partner's perceptions.

Build Trust Slowly

Another advantage of constructing a trust timeline is that it underscores the attractiveness of starting each relationship in small, measured, specific steps, instead of huge deals. As each partner learns about the other's culture, procedures, and trustworthiness, cooperation can gradually be expanded as needed to fill strategic needs.

Texas Instruments Inc. and Hitachi Ltd. started slowly in 1988, doing joint research to develop new memory chips. By 1996, the two companies had greatly deepened their relationship, jointly funding a $500 million chip plant near Dallas. Robert England, head of TI's memory-chip operations, says much of the first year was spent "bridging the culture gap," because they soon discovered they had different decision-making processes: "In an American company, you have a meeting to discuss an issue, brainstorm, and then you decide." At Hitachi, executives usually came to a decision among themselves and then used a meeting to ratify it. Now, the two companies have learned to meet halfway.

Former Ford president, Philip Benton Jr., concurred: "It's absolutely essential to start slowly to build trust. The first time two companies work together, the chances of succeeding are very slight. But once you find ways to work together, all sorts of opportunities come up—and your likelihood of severing that relationship and starting the whole process over again becomes remote. Learning to work together is so hard, it would be foolish to throw all that away just because you see another girl across the street" (Sherman, 1992, p. 78).

In the context of speed of trust-building, it is worth noting that all industries are not equal. Different industries seem to have different concepts of time, so that clock-time comparisons between, say, the contract research industry and the auto industry would be almost meaningless. In the contract research industry, alliances tend to be very short, typically not lasting more than a few months. In contrast, time runs at a snail's pace in the auto industry. The cycle time for a platform can easily last five to seven years before major changes are made to the platform. This is also the typical length of time for a single contract for a part. The notion of time is still more sluggish in trucks. In Ford's F-series truck, one master contract between Ford and a supplier was used for thirty years (with annual revisions) before a new contract was written, when the truck platform was redesigned. In short, the time frame for building trust must be understood in relation to "industry-based" time, not clock time.

Watch for Divergence of Partners' Strategic Directions

Regardless of how long two companies may have worked together, managers should remember that the strategic fit of a once-perfect match may diminish as the partners' evolving internal capabilities, strategic choices, and market developments pull them in separate directions. Germany's Siemens AG and South Korea's Lucky-Goldstar Group set up a joint venture company, Goldstar Telecommunications, in 1970 to seek technology cooperation in telephone communications, particularly in mechanical public exchange systems. However, the tie-up began to wane in the early 1980s as Korea's telephone communications system turned from mechanical to electronic systems. In 1992, the alliance formally ended.

Siemens has also witnessed other deals dissolve with the changing strategies of its partners. Alfred Prommer, a former Siemens vice president involved in crafting alliances, describes the shock of executives in Munich when they were informed in a totally unexpected phone call that their strategic partner in computers, RCA Corp., had decided it no longer had any interest in making computers: "It was just unbelievable that they [Siemens executives] get a phone call saying, 'OK, we were just in a board meeting and we just decided to get out of computers.'" David E. Gold, managing partner of Indosuez Technology Group, a venture capital fund in Menlo Park, California, says anytime there is an alliance, such a possibility exists: "Things will always change, and they won't always change with the same velocity or in the same direction for the two companies."

Trust building is still possible when the technology underlying an alliance changes or when a relationship no longer makes strategic sense for one or both of the partners, because such situations provide opportunities to build reputation. A relationship can be severed in unseemly ways, or in constructive ways that take into account the other side's legitimate interests. Openly and constructively managing diverging partner interests reinforces trustworthiness, and such behavior may become known beyond the particular relationship to a broader audience of future potential alliance partners, creating solid reputation.

Further, in volatile industries with rapidly changing strategies, trust between alliance partners can be maintained even when specific alliances are terminated. In some high-technology industries, for example, flexibility built into the alliance structure allows partners to adjust to changes in their internal and external environments. Such flexibility can be attained by entering into a general (or blanket) cooperative agreement, such that the overall relationship outlasts individual alliances. RCA and Sharp have a long-established cooperative agreement within which they have worked on a series of specific ventures over the years. The relationship fades when an alliance ends, to be reactivated later on an as-needed basis.

Watch for Asymmetry in Value Creation or in Value Appropriation

Value creation in an alliance depends first on whether the market and competitive logic of the venture is sound, and then on the efficacy with which the partners combine their complementary skills and resources, i.e., how well they perform joint tasks. Each partner then appropriates value in the form of monetary and other benefits (Hamel, 1991).

In 1980, TRW Inc. and Fujitsu Ltd. entered into a joint venture with the idea that TRW would market Fujitsu-made point-of-sale terminals, automated teller machines, and small-business computers in the United States. Fujitsu would thereby gain access to U.S. markets, and TRW would have the products to become a player in new business markets. But by 1982, the deal collapsed and Fujitsu bought out TRW's share of the joint venture. Explained Sidney Webb, who was president of TRW-Fujitsu: "It became apparent ..... that to penetrate the U.S. market with Fujitsu products was going to take a lot longer than was originally expected. TRW came to the conclusion that, whereas in Fujitsu's case this joint venture was at the heart of their computer business and that they must do it no matter what it takes and how long it takes, in TRW's case it was very peripheral to their core businesses. So TRW concluded that it didn't make any sense to continue to do something that wasn't in the main thrust of their business" (Alster, 1986). In this failed venture, the problems of value-creation asymmetry were compounded by significant characteristic-based differences between the partners. TRW was using standard U.S. methods for computing payback periods, whereas Fujitsu was playing a game equally standard in Japan, building long-term market share. A second basic difference involved technical core versus non-core activities. If an alliance is not in the core of one partner (TRW), but at the center of another's business (Fujitsu), difficult issues of unequal commitment arise. Absent a foundation of trust, these partners were unable to cope with the challenges.

More recently, U.S. Airways entered into an alliance with British Airways in 1993, when the former was in tough economic straits. But after British Airways unveiled its link-up with American Airlines in June 1996, U.S. Airways sued the U.K. carrier. US Airways has long considered the deal one-sided in British Airways' favor, that is, highly asymmetric in value appropriation. One factor was that U.S. Airways had to give up lucrative routes to Britain from Philadelphia, Baltimore, and Charlotte, N.C. The two carriers are still embroiled in a dispute over departure times from Charlotte that has delayed U.S. Airways' plans for new service between Charlotte and London's Gatwick Airport and has also delayed British Airways' plans to begin new Denver-Gatwick flights (Goldsmith, 1998).

How then can trusting relationships be built? One key is to minimize perceptions of asymmetry in value creation or in value appropriation and, especially in a relationship of unequals,[3] to treat the weaker partner fairly (Kumar, 1996). Fairness encompasses two types of justice: distributive justice, or the perceived fairness of the outcomes received, and procedural justice, or the perceived fairness of the powerful party's process for managing the relationship.

For instance, one of the guiding principles of Marks & Spencer, the British retailer, is to work closely with suppliers in long-term partnerships in order to achieve distributive justice. This company believes that manufacturers, especially those in the Far East, are often so keen to get its business that they will accept prices that are too low to warrant the investments necessary for improving their operations and products further. Because Marks & Spencer seeks long-term relationships with suppliers, it views that situation as unacceptable—as one that hurts both sides. Thus, when a manufacturer realized in 1995 that it had miscalculated the amount of labor required to make a kitchen product (and was therefore losing money on the deal), Marks & Spencer cut its own gross margin on the product and gave that money to the manufacturer.

In building trust, both distributive and procedural justice are important. But which is more important, the perceived fairness of the outcomes received or the perceived fairness of the stronger party's process for managing a relationship? In the auto industry, manufacturers are generally in a stronger position than dealers, and in a study of 800 dealers in the United States and the Netherlands, Kumar (1996) expected distributive justice to be more important, since dealers were thought to care only about margins and outcomes. Counterintuitively, procedural justice was found to be far more important. The study revealed dealers' reasoning for this finding: Outcomes are affected by many factors (including competitive conditions), only some of which are under the control of the more powerful auto manufacturers. However, a manufacturer is always considered in control of its policies and procedures. The weaker partner (dealer), therefore, sees the manufacturer's system of procedural justice as reflecting more accurately the manufacturer's real attitudes toward the dealer.

Staffing Issues

The fifth critical element of effectively managing alliance dynamics involves attaching adequate importance to the actual management positions in the alliance membrane, and filling these positions with the "right people." The right people, according to Ellis (1996), are much like diplomats. They are able to create an environment of trust, maintain broad strategic vision, and feel empathy for others, even those who are still competitors in other areas. They act as a shuttle between the partners, creating relationships, reminding their own team to focus on the big picture, and explaining opposing viewpoints.

Asks Ellis, are these special managers born or made? A little of both. Some of their characteristics are unteachable competencies—inner traits such as optimism, cleverness, creativity, pragmatism, and vigilance. Other aspects can be taught. For example, companies can help managers develop a broad perspective by giving them assignments lasting several years at a time in different parts of the business.

One option for companies seeking good alliance managers is to gradually develop teachable skills in promising candidates. A second option is to hire a professional alliance manager. (However, such managers have no long-nurtured internal networks necessary for alliance success.) A third, and perhaps best, option is to hire a few people in every department who already have the unteachable traits described above—the traits that enable someone to adapt more quickly if promoted to alliance management (Ellis, 1996).

An important corollary of the above discussion is that turnover of alliance managers must be minimized. These managers act as boundary spanners between alliance partners, and close personal ties between such persons are key to building trust. Thus, limiting their turnover ensures continuity, preserves institutional memory, and ultimately helps generate interfirm and interpersonal trust. Conversely, companies that play the "power game" (Kumar, 1996) prefer their managers *not* to develop personal relationships with their counterparts, fearing such ties will weaken managers' resolve to push hard for the best possible deal. To prevent that from happening, Jose Ignacio Lopez, GM's former purchasing czar, reassigned buyers to suppliers with whom they had not dealt.

Still, more companies are playing the "trust game," not the power game. And in the trust game, continuity is vital. In Ciba Corning Diagnostics (CCD), both partners recognize the importance of continuity, so when key people at Ciba or Corning have changed jobs or retired, they have usually remained on the board. In contrast, the president of a large Japanese tool maker, dealing with a U.S. partner that had gone through three ownership changes over the preceding decade, complained: "We never know who we are dealing with" (Lewis, 1990).

Companies are creating new positions of responsibility that reflect the heightened importance of the trend toward alliances (with titles such as vice president-joint ventures, director of intercompany relations, and so on). Take Hewlett-Packard, a company considered very adept at working with competitors. Since 1984, H-P has sold more than 15 million laser printers that use a motor made by Canon Inc. of Japan. In ink-jet printers, meanwhile, H-P and Canon each sell models using different technologies, and "we compete like hell in the marketplace," says John Eaton, business development manager for H-P. H-P keeps its many alliances running smoothly by designating one employee as a "relationship manager." Says Mr. Eaton: "That person is supposed to say, 'Hey guys, we're in this alliance for good business reasons. Yeah, we know we compete in other places and things. But let's keep that in one place and keep this alliance in another'" (Templin, 1995).

Finally, in alliances that cut across large, multiunit firms, greater structure is required (Lewis, 1990). For example, Ford's various divisions are scattered worldwide, but Mazda's operations are relatively centralized and coordinated in Hiroshima. So as the Ford-Mazda alliance grew, coordination became an issue. In response, each firm set up a staff function as its side of a single interface (Northern Pacific Business Development at Ford, International Business Development at Mazda) where relationship issues could be discussed. Joint programs continue to be managed within relevant line structures in each firm, and program people continue to interact with each other directly. As a complement to these links, the two staff groups meet monthly, and they have become the forum for monitoring and reinforcing the alliance.

Calibrating Trust Level to Match Cooperative Relationship

As noted, there is a delicate tradeoff between reliability and flexibility (Parkhe, 1998). Flexibility is necessary for partners to have a viable relationship in the face of changing circumstances, yet unlimited flexibility affords companies the opportunity and incentive to cheat, reducing the reliance partners can place on each other. Thus, always giving the other side the benefit of the doubt (reflecting too much trust) sets oneself up for exploitation, while treating all poor outcomes as opportunistic behavior (reflecting too little trust) creates a spiral of joint retaliation (Heide & Miner, 1992). So where is the line separating too much and too little trust, and what is the "appropriate" level of trust at particular stages (Lei, Slocum, & Pitts, 1997) of a relationship?

Guarding Against Too Much Trust

Mature alliances often progress from low to high levels of trust over time, as a variety of trust-generating mechanisms (discussed above) provide opportunities for partners to assess each other's trustworthiness. Unduly hastening this process, by placing too much unwarranted trust in an untested partner, can expose a company to grave damage, including possible loss of "family jewels" such as core technologies.

In 1986, engineer-turned-entrepreneur Anthony LaPine decided to apply innovative new technology to build 3.5-inch hard disk drives. He persuaded Prudential Bache Trade Corp. to join him, and together they identified Kyocera Corp., a low-cost Japanese producer of drives, as the third member of their high-tech alliance. A factory was built, and production began in Japan with the use of LaPine technology. Just months later, Kyocera began slowing shipments of disk drives to LaPine's customers, who as a result defected in droves. Sales plummeted, prompting wholesale layoffs at LaPine. LaPine eventually filed suit in California against Kyocera, charging that Kyocera "had fraudulently induced LaPine to enter agreements in order to gain access to LaPine's technology and proprietary information." Looking back with 20/20 hindsight, LaPine probably placed too much trust too soon in Kyocera.

Likewise, Acme-Cleveland Corp. once licensed Mitsubishi Heavy Industries to manufacture and sell one of its machine tools, only to watch Mitsubishi become its rival in the U.S. market. Acme-Cleveland incorrectly assumed Mitsubishi's ambitions were limited to Asia. Now, says CEO B. Charles Ames, Acme-Cleveland is being "darn careful to make sure the company that is going to manufacture (telecommunications equipment) for us does not have any apparent interest in getting into (the U.S.) market." And, he adds, Acme-Cleveland will make sure that its licensing agreements include market restrictions.[4]

> **Moral:** *A company can trust too much too soon, without sufficient cues from a partner that the trust (and the vulnerability it creates) will not be abused.*

Although such abuse may not always occur, it is best to think ahead, to make contingency provisions (e.g., limits to information sharing, terms of a breakup), and to remember that full disclosure of all proprietary knowhow is never required, even to the most trustworthy, long-term alliance partners. As Lewis (1990) notes, even competitors can build trust if they segregate their conflict, and conflicting objectives are less of a problem than deception about them. Trust requires honesty, which in turn requires clarity about where full disclosure should not be expected. For example, Kraar (1989) reports that for all its new acceptance of interdependence with Hitachi in developing a DRAM chip, Texas Instruments "is zealously guarding its technological jewels." The agreement with Hitachi catalogues precisely the intellectual property that belongs to each company.

Several additional ways exist to guard against too much trust and to safeguard core knowhow. One way is to share only the results of applying technology. At General Electric's aircraft engine group, technological knowhow resides in the engineering skills, documents, and computer software used to design and produce the high-temperature sections of jet engines. Snecma's core strengths include its high-pressure compressor technology. Such knowhow can be used for alliances, as long as it is not disclosed.

Another way is to define an interface between two partners' separate parts while they keep their core technologies to themselves. CFM International is an alliance created by GE and Snecma in 1974 to collaborate on the development of jet engines. When CFM builds on the proprietary skills of the two parents, GE and Snecma do the relevant work in their own facilities. Each company's knowhow is safe, because it would be hard to reverse-engineer the completed engine modules they transfer to each other. Nor is it necessary for core technology to stay at home. Rockwell International safeguarded truck axle knowhow in a European joint venture with Fiat's IVECO unit by putting a Rockwell engineer in charge of the alliance's engineering records. This way, the information could be physically located in the venture, yet accessible only to Rockwell's engineers.

In short, match trust level to the stage of evolution of a cooperative relationship, keeping in mind that cooperation has limits. With progressive and reciprocal increases in trust on both sides, the scale and intensity of cooperation can gradually be increased. Such calibrated increases in cooperation provide some assurance against untimely, excessive trust levels.

Guarding Against Too Little Trust

Just as it is possible to trust too much too soon, it is possible to trust too little too late. Using undue caution, that is, unwillingness to trust despite solid cues of trustworthiness appropriate for the lifecycle stage of a partnership, is costly. Indeed, it is easy to focus on vulnerability to exploitation stemming from too much trust, while overlooking the high pricetag associated with too little trust. This pricetag includes the loss of much of what makes alliances attractive in the first place, including the cost-cutting, synergy-producing, efficiency-enhancing benefits of trust. In addition, cautions Lewis (1990), "Too little trust will backfire: It creates ill will and reduces the incentive to work harder at being reliable" (1990, p. 247).

Too little trust may be said to exist when: (1) A partner's general reputation, specific alliance history, or future strategic interests signal trustworthiness, yet these trust-producing cues are ignored; and (2) Very high safeguards are erected, safeguards that don't accurately reflect current knowledge regarding a partner. Recall that safeguards are devices that seek to reduce gains from opportunism and increase the cost of opportunism. Safeguards are not costless, and overreliance on them for alliance governance can exact a price so high that it erases any gains from cooperation.

In the biotechnology industry, for example, many recent alliances are based on the concept of "milestones." These are predetermined goals that must be achieved to trigger payments. Thus, payments by Britain's SmithKline Beecham PLC to Cephalon Inc. in West Chester, Pennsylvania, are based on milestones. Such an alliance structure involves low vulnerability and reveals correspondingly low trust. But it also disengages SmithKline and Cephalon managers from events within the alliance or in the biotechnology industry, relinquishing control of their interactions to a mechanical policy of milestones. Although such a structure may suit the limited purpose of some alliances, in many situations that require adaptation, judgment, and the building of progressively greater levels of trust, it falls short.

In sum, companies are constantly groping to find the "right" level of trust at particular stages of a partnership. In these efforts, managers must avoid committing Type I error (rejecting a true hypothesis, or not trusting a trustworthy partner) as well as Type II error (accepting a false hypothesis, or trusting an untrustworthy partner). As shown, both errors can be expensive, and in their own distinct ways, both trusting too much and trusting too little can wipe out gains from an alliance strategy.

Overview

The new global competition is far more subtle and interesting than the old global competition. Companies are increasingly pooling their costs, risks, and rewards in international alliances, which have emerged as a major competitive weapon. The relations between companies are now marked less by frontal attacks between direct competitors, and more by the potential for flank attacks, Trojan horses, and hidden agendas, in short, ties where trust will play a growingly important role as a counterweight to the potential hazards in alliancing. Consequently, understanding trust in international alliances, and using this understanding to effectively build trust, become crucial management tasks. A previous paper (Parkhe, 1998) addressed the former task; the present paper attempted to deal with key aspects of building trust in international alliances.

As a first step, managers must know the various trust-building factors that are within their control, and learn to appropriately use each factor, consistent with particular partners and partnerships. Three such trust-building factors were described: process-based, characteristic-based, and institutional based generation of trust. The key points that emerged from this discussion are that purposeful action by managers of alliance partners can lead to development and growth of trust, and such purposeful action often involves deliberate investments—of management time, funds, compatible infrastructure with partner firm, and so on.

Furthermore, building trust also requires an appreciation of five important features of alliance dynamics. The first of these is to understand the paths by which, and timing with which, trust has developed in a particular alliance. This understanding can help further cement strong points of a relationship, while redressing the weaker points. The second aspect is to build trust slowly, since needless haste can be costly and destabilizing. The third feature to focus on is each partner's strategic direction, for a divergence in directions can be addressed effectively if there is trust between partners and flexibility of alliance structure. The fourth element of alliance dynamics concerns asymmetry in alliance value creation and value appropriation. Perceptions of asymmetry can lead to trust erosion, while perceptions of fairness lead to a stronger, more robust alliance. Finally, trust building calls for close attention to staffing issues, including selecting the right type of people, putting them in appropriate positions in the alliance interface, and limiting their turnover.

Next, this paper asked the question, is it possible to trust too much or too little in an alliance? The answer in both cases is yes, which means a "calibration" of the level of trust to the stage of an alliance relationship is desirable. Ways to guard against too much or too little trust were discussed, along with relevant and timely real-life examples.

In sum, this paper took note of the strong trend toward collaboration, often between direct competitors. While such a trend is unmistakable, it is possible to overdraw conclusions from it, including some authors' premature forecast of an emerging "culture of cooperation." Effective collaboration requires a sober assessment of trust. Trust arises along certain paths in each relationship. To effectively build trust, managers must pay close attention to these paths. Where these paths are not open, other institutional-based mechanisms for deliberate production of trust may be available.

Acknowledgment: I am grateful to two anonymous *JWB* referees for their detailed and thoughtful suggestions on earlier versions of this paper. I especially appreciate constructive input from Richard N. Osborn, the Editor. This study was made possible by a research grant from the Kelley School of Business, Indiana University, Bloomington, Indiana 47405, USA.

NOTES

1. A good reputation includes two additional properties, according to this research (Axelrod, 1984). One is to be Forgiving (quickly reciprocating cooperation), and the other is to be Clear (not being too clever or difficult for a partner to understand). Together, the four elements (being Nice, Provocable, Forgiving, and Clear) add up to a surprisingly simple and effective interaction strategy known as Tit for Tat, which consists of (1) starting with cooperation and then (2) matching each move (cooperation or cheating) that a partner makes. Earning a reputation for a Tit for Tat player seems to effectively tap the benefits of cooperation without permitting a partner to take undue advantage of oneself.
2. It can be debated whether such institutional arrangements actually produce trust, or whether they are merely a functional substitute for it (see Granovetter, 1985, p. 489), and indeed, Husted (1989) recommends the term "trust-like behavior." Nonetheless, the fact remains that the mechanisms described below seek to align alliance partners' incentives in ways that promote trustworthy behavior. In Barney and Hansen's (1994) terminology, this would be classified as semi-strong form trust.
3. For instance, huge manufacturers such as Mercedes-Benz sell their products through small mom-and-pop dealers. And major retailers such as France's Carrefour, Japan's Ito-Yokado, Britain's Marks & Spencer, and America's Toys R Us buy from numerous relatively small manufacturers.
4. Interested readers may wish to read Reich and Mankin (1986) and Hamel (1991) for numerous additional examples of (a) placing too much trust in an alliance partner, and (b) viewing alliances as "races to learn."

REFERENCES

Alster, N. (1986). Dealbusters: Why partnerships fail. *Electronics Business*, April 1, 70-75.

Axelrod, R. (1984). *The evolution of cooperation*. New York: Basic Books.

Barney, J. B., & Hansen, M. H. (1994). Trustworthiness as a source of competitive advantage. *Strategic Management Journal, 15*: 175–190.

Becker, G. S. (1997). Why every married couple should sign a contract. *Business Week,* December 29, 30.

Byrne, J. A. (1993). The virtual corporation. *Business Week,* February 8, 98-103.

Davidow, W. H., & Malone, M. S. (1992). *The virtual corporation*. New York: Harper Business.

Ellis, C. (1996). Making strategic alliances succeed: The importance of trust. *Harvard Business Review,* (July-August): 7–8.

Goldsmith, C. (1998). British Airways appears eager to settle with US Airways, bring it into alliance. *Wall Street Journal,* May 15, A6.

Granovetter, M. (1985). Economic action and social structure: A theory of embeddedness. *American Journal of Sociology, 91*: 481–510.

Hamel, G. P. (1991). Competition for competence and interpartner learning within international strategic alliances. *Strategic Management Journal, 12*: 83–103.

Heide, J. B., & Miner, A. S. (1992). The shadow of the future: Effects of anticipated interaction and frequency of contact on buyer-seller cooperation. *Academy of Management Journal, 35*: 265–291.

Houghton, J. R. (1987). Joint ventures that endure. *Industry Week,* April 20, 14.

Husted, B. W. (1989). Trust in business relations: Directions for empirical research. *Business and Professional Ethics Journal, 8*: 23–40.

Johnson, J. L., Cullen, J. B., Sakano, T., & Takenouchi, H. (1997). Setting the stage for trust and strategic integration in Japanese-U.S. cooperative alliances. In P.W. Beamish & J.P. Killing (Eds.), *Cooperative strategies: North American perspectives.* San Francisco: Lexington Press.

Kraar, L. (1989). Your rivals can be your allies. *Fortune,* March 27, 66–76.

Kumar, N. (1996). The power of trust in manufacturer-retailer relationships. *Harvard Business Review,* (November-December): 92–106.

Lei, D., Slocum, J. W. Jr., & Pitts, R. A. (1997). Building cooperative advantage: Managing strategic alliances to promote organizational learning. *Journal of World Business, 32*(3): 203–223.

Lewis, J. D. (1990). *Partnerships for profit.* New York: Free Press.

Lynch, R. P. (1989). *The practical guide to joint ventures and corporate alliances.* New York: John Wiley & Sons.

Miller, K. L., & Treece, J. B. (1992). GM and Isuzu: A waste of synergy. *Business Week,* February 10, 107.

Park, S. H., & Ungson, G. R. (1997). The effect of national culture, organizational complementarity, and economic motivation on joint venture dissolution. *Academy of Management Journal, 40*: 279–307.

Parkhe, A. (1991). Interfirm diversity, organizational learning, and longevity in global strategic alliances. *Journal of International Business Studies, 22*: 579–601.

Parkhe, A. (1998). Understanding trust in international alliances. *Journal of World Business, 34* (3): 219–240.

Reich, R., & Mankin, E. (1986). Joint ventures with Japan give away our future. *Harvard Business Review, 64*(2): 78–86.

Sherman, S. (1992). Are strategic alliances working? *Fortune,* September 21, 77–78.

Templin, N. (1995). Strange bedfellows. *Wall Street Journal,* November 1, A1, A12.

Williamson, O. E. (1985). *The economic institutions of capitalism.* New York: Free Press.

Wysocki, B. (1990). Cross-border alliances become favorite way to crack new markets. *Wall Street Journal,* March 26, A1, A12.

Zucker, L. G. (1986). Production of trust. In B. Staw and L. L. Cummings (Eds.),*Research in organizational behavior,* Vol. 8 (pp. 53–111). Greenwich, CT: JAI Press.

[30]

Journal of General Management
Vol. 22 No. 4 Summer 1997

Sustaining Strategic Alliances: Options and Guidelines

by
T. K. Das and Bing-Sheng Teng

Many strategic alliances fail. A seven-stage process is proposed which may help to avoid many of the pitfalls.

Strategic alliances have become a popular competitive weapon in today's business environment. By definition, strategic alliances refer to interfirm co-operative arrangements aimed at pursuing mutual strategic goals. Examples of strategic alliances include joint ventures, joint R&D, product swap, equity investment and sharing, licensing, and others. The number of newly forged alliances has been growing at more than 25 per cent annually in recent years [1, 2]. Nevertheless, while many firms are rushing into such alliances as a quick-fix solution to their problems, the failure rate of strategic alliances has been consistently high [3]. A recent report on airline alliances found that fewer than 40 per cent of regional and fewer than 30 per cent of international alliances have been successful [4]. Many partners terminated their alliances before achieving intended objectives. It has been a busy two-way street: companies keep pulling themselves out of alliances even as more companies continue to forge new alliances. Hence, some theorists have suggested that strategic alliances may be a transitional governance mode, leading eventually to either more permanent organizational forms via mergers and acquisitions, or to dissolution. Thus, it is necessary to study alliances in some depth in order to understand the causes of alliance failures, and to provide effective guidelines for more sustainable alliances.

The Stages of Strategic Alliance Management

Interest in strategic alliances can be partly accounted for by some highly publicized success stories, such as the alliances between Intel and IBM, AT&T and TSYS, and Ford and Mazda. These developments have reinforced the legitimacy of strategic alliances, and the belief that success lies in careful planning and implementation. In that context, this paper will explore ways to make strategic alliances more sustainable and effective, with particular

---

T. K. Das is Professor of Strategic Management and Bing-Sheng Teng is a Doctoral Candidate in Baruch College, City University of New York, USA.

Journal of General Management
Vol. 22 No. 4 Summer 1997

attention to the major stages of the strategic alliance management process. We suggest that the process of alliance management can be divided into seven major stages: considering strategic alliances, selecting alliance partners, negotiating the alliance agreement, setting-up of the alliance, operating the alliance, evaluating alliance performance, and modifying the alliance.
50 There are a few key options that need consideration at each stage, and the success of the alliance would depend upon the soundness of the choices made. Thus, strategic alliance management can be viewed as a continuous decision making process, so that an alliance may potentially fail if a wrong move is made at any stage.

While the advantages of strategic alliances have been adequately spelled out in the literature [5], the pitfalls present at several stages of the alliance process have not been adequately stressed [6]. Indeed, we are yet to develop a balanced view of strategic alliances. A lack of understanding of the contingent aspects of alliances may well have contributed to many failures. It must be recognized that the advantages and disadvantages of any decision in the alliance process constitute two sides of the same coin, and they go hand in hand. Taking advantage of certain options means embracing certain pitfalls also. Therefore, the pros and cons of various options in strategic alliances must be evaluated carefully at each alliance stage. Although several studies have discussed the benefits and costs of alliance decisions, a weakness of the existing literature is that this approach has not led to any step-by-step guidelines for the different stages of strategic alliance management [7]. Few studies have taken a contingent approach in connecting the circumstances attaching alliances and the preferable options.

This paper is an attempt to fill the gap, i.e., to weigh the benefits and pitfalls of some key options at various alliance stages. Contingent guidelines will be developed with the objective of helping managers to build sustainable alliances. In the first stage, considering strategic alliances, we lay out the costs and benefits of strategic alliances vis-a-vis internalization and market transactions. In the second stage of selecting an alliance partner, the choice between having an equal or an unequal partner is examined. The third stage, negotiating the alliance agreement, is concerned with the gains and costs of pursuing either flexibility or embeddedness in the alliance. Setting up the alliances, the fourth stage of alliance management, will deal with staffing and other human resource management issues. Guidelines for operating the alliance, the fifth stage, are based on an examination of competition and co-operation. In the sixth stage, evaluating the alliance performance, two sets of criteria are considered, i.e., private benefits vs common benefits, and equity vs efficiency. Again, the objective is to select the option that would generate enough benefits to offset pitfalls. Finally, in modifying the alliance, we focus on the contrast between a short-term and a long-term orientation.

To understand better the costs and benefits of key options in strategic alliances would not only make strategists more cautious about forging alliances, but would also provide a more systematic approach to what is

Journal of General Management
Vol. 22 No. 4 Summer 1997

involved in sustaining strategic alliances. Strategic decision makers would thus be armed with substantial knowledge about the implications of available options at each stage of the alliance process.

Is Strategic Alliance the Answer?

The first stage of strategic alliance management is to evaluate alliances as a strategic option, along with other alternatives such as vertical and horizontal integration and market-based transactions. Strategic alliances are a special mode of conducting interfirm transactions, in the sense that the firms internalize some of the interfirm transactions into a somewhat formal structure, while conducting the rest of the transactions via price mechanisms. Consider the example of a joint R&D agreement, in which the investing party provides capital to its partner for specified R&D activity. In this case, the two parties exchange their resources in an internalized, participative manner, different from discrete exchanges handled through the price mechanism. At the same time, the two firms may also conduct other exchanges in the market. The point is that strategic alliances represent a hybrid organization mode between market transactions and internal transactions, so that the gains and pitfalls of alliances should be examined in conjunction with these alternatives.

As compared to market transactions, strategic alliances have the advantage of eliminating the risks and uncertainties of market transactions, which include demand uncertainty and competitive uncertainty [8]. Markets could fail because these uncertainties cost the firms extra in order to secure the deal. Dyer [9], for example, has described how Chrysler suffered from costly transactions with its suppliers. Eventually, Chrysler moved from an arms-length supplier relationship to a supplier alliance, which significantly reduced the total cost of the transactions. In the 1980s, IBM formed an alliance with Epson, in an attempt to ensure the availability of quality printers compatible with its computers. Another example is the alliance formed by IBM, Motorola, and Apple, the purpose of which was to develop and popularize the PowerPC chips by reducing competitive and demand uncertainty. It seems clear that when the uncertainties of interfirm transactions are high, it is more efficient to conduct the transactions within the organization (internalization), or through strategic alliances.

Hierarchical integration appears to be the ultimate approach in controlling uncertainties in transactions. Under certain circumstances, internalization could be the most cost-efficient approach. GM, for instance, decided that to integrate Ross Perot's Electronic Data Systems it was essential to possess every kind of technology related to carmaking. In such cases, strategic alliances may not provide enough protection or assurance for the transaction. Therefore, it should be emphasized that internalization, including mergers and acquisitions, is a viable option when significant costs can be saved from doing it in-house.

Nevertheless, internalization has its own share of problems. To completely internalize the transaction may control uncertainty, but it could

Journal of General Management
Vol. 22 No. 4 Summer 1997

52

also be more expensive than strategic alliances. An example is acquiring the suppliers of raw materials just to make sure of the availability of raw materials. In most cases, it would not be appropriate to do so, because the extra costs incurred for integrating and operating these supplier businesses can easily exceed the costs saved from eliminating market uncertainties. By comparison, strategic alliances offer an attractive option, i.e., internalizing only those transactions through which the firm can save substantially. Such partial internalization allows the firms to integrate whatever is warranted. Thus, strategic alliances are the feasible choice when both complete internalization and market transactions are too costly [10].

The foregoing discussion shows that sometimes strategic alliances could be advantageous to other strategic alternatives. However, strategists must be aware of the pitfalls of strategic alliances as well, before being convinced that strategic alliances are the solution. The biggest threat to alliances arises from the fact that they are co-operative by nature so that they inevitably generate problems in managing the interfirm relationship. Interfirm trust, managerial co-ordination, opportunistic behavior of the partners are just a few issues that complicate the management of alliances [11]. Because of these unique problems, strategic alliances are often seen as a rugged road to success. Unfortunately, these relational factors tend to be underestimated by the partner firms, since most of them are not experienced in co-operating with other firms. The point is that these issues of co-operation are critically relevant even in the stage of evaluating the feasibility of alliances. Some of these issues will be discussed in detail later in this paper. The guideline for firms in this first stage is:

Guideline 1: Strategic alliances are a viable option only when substantially beneficial in partially integrating two firms; otherwise, they should be avoided because of their managerial complexity.

Selecting Alliance Partners

The second stage of alliance management is selecting the appropriate alliance partner. The choice of an alliance partner has a profound impact on the sustainability of the alliance, just as the choice of a spouse largely determines the fate of a marriage. As suggested in the literature, an ideal partnership should involve two or more companies with complementary resources and skills, compatible objectives in the alliance, and a certain level of interfirm trust [12].

First, emphasis on the complementary resources and skills of the partners ensures that the intended synergy sought to be created by combining two firms is not an illusion. When the partners bring in their distinctive competencies to the partnership, the chances of success becomes greater than in an alliance formed by companies with similar skills. It is apparent that the benefits of alliances come mostly from pooling various resources possessed by the partners. Second, the partners must have compatible objectives in the alliance in order that the alliance is beneficial to both

Journal of General Management
Vol. 22 No. 4 Summer 1997

partners. Some firms enter into strategic alliances to capture secretly the know-how of their partner. In this case, the alliance becomes a cover for the hidden agenda and the firm has no real interest in sustaining the alliance. General Motors and Daewoo formed an alliance in 1986, which eventually failed. The failure can be attributed to their incompatible goals: while Daewoo was interested in upgrading their car models, GM was preoccupied with keeping the cost down [13]. Obviously, incompatible objectives of the partners will tend to bring the alliance down in short order. Third, a sense of interfirm trust is a vital criterion for selecting alliance partners. Strategic alliances are essentially partnerships that require the firms to integrate their private interests with the common interests of the alliance [14]. Only a sense of trust may allay the firms' suspicion of each other and postpone expected returns to a future period.

Besides these general rules in selecting partners, certain patterns of partnership seem to be more successful than others. Bleeke and Ernst [15] have drawn attention to the relationship between the market position of the partners and the possibility of alliance dissolution. It was found that the following types of alliances often fail: collusion between competitors, alliances of the weak, alliances of a weak company and a strong company. On the other hand, alliances of strong, complementary equals, such as AT&T and Philips, survive longer and have a better chance for successful performance. Some researchers (e.g., [16]) have gone further and even suggested that alliances work better when the partners are equal in size.

Seemingly plausible as it is, the foregoing argument should not be accepted without extra caution. First of all, it must be stressed that 'strong' or 'weak' are measured by the competitive position of each partner in their own industries, rather than in terms of size and financial might. A firm, such as Netscape, could be a strong player in its industry without being gigantic in size. Popular alliances in the bio-pharmaceutical field often involve one large pharmaceutical company with production and marketing capacity, and one small biotech company with R&D expertise. Many of these alliances have been successful, countering the assertion that a symmetry in size is essential for the success of an alliance.

Second, and more important, the conclusion that only strong-strong alliances produce results seems to leave no hope for those firms that are not strong players in their own industries. In the words of Bleeke and Ernst [17], 'if you can't succeed on your own, an alliance with another weak company won't make things any better'. However, it need not be so! Relatively weak companies can find a way by pooling their resources, as long as there are certain competitive advantages that can be brought to the alliance. If the prospective partners have distinctive competencies in areas that can be integrated, they could forge a successful alliance. One telling example is the success story of the alliance between Northwest and KLM airline of Holland [18]. Neither one could be labelled as a strong player in the cross-Atlantic market before they forged the alliance. In 1992, KLM took a 25 per cent stake in Northwest, and the two airlines were able to combine their respective

Journal of General Management
Vol. 22 No. 4 Summer 1997

customer groups and develop a common brand for travelers. By pooling resources, Northwest and KLM expanded their combined Altantic market share from 7 per cent to 11 per cent. Thanks to the alliance, Northwest posted an operating profit of $830 million in 1994, recovering from a $60 million loss in 1991. Therefore, it seems possible for non-market-leaders to stand together and perform. The guidelines regarding the choice of alliance partner are:

Guideline 2a: Ideal alliance partners should have complementary resources, compatible objectives, and a certain level of interfirm trust.

Guideline 2b: A relatively weak market position and small size should not prevent a firm from being part of an alliance; rather, the key is that there must be a fit between the partners.

Negotiating the Alliance Agreement

The third stage of the alliance process is to negotiate an alliance agreement with the potential partner. The important task to be accomplished at this stage is to specify the governance structure of the alliance, as well as other contractual clauses that bind the partners [19]. In this section, we first discuss the choice of the alliance structure, and then turn to other contractual clauses that are used to supplement the structural agreement.

Strategic alliances are known for the variety of their agreements relating to their governance structures. Among the common structures are joint ventures, equity investment, research consortia, joint R&D, joint marketing, licensing, product swap and others. These governance structures serve various purposes of the partners, and the partners' preferences largely depend on how they envision the alliances. Despite the variety, however, one underlying issue seems to matter considerably when it comes to structural choice, namely, how much flexibility and embeddedness the alliance should have. In other words, the trade-off between structural flexibility and structural embeddedness greatly influences the choice.

Flexibility serves as a key benefit of strategic alliances, as compared to traditional hierarchical organizations. With strategic alliances, the partners may be involved in a project partly, without contributing any or all the needed capital, technology, and human resources. Since the risks are shared by the partners, sunk costs of the project are reduced. As a result, it becomes easier for the partners to exit from the alliance, if things do not work out as expected. Several governance structures are particularly effective in giving the partners more flexibility: licensing, joint R&D, joint marketing, research consortia, and others. In such cases, the partners can relatively easily terminate the alliance, primarily because of their common attribute: an absence of shared equity ownership. These alliances are termed 'non-equity alliances'. Since there is no new equity investment or exchange, the partners keep their own companies intact. The alliance is thus more like a contract that can be vacated with relative ease. Thus, these governance structures do not embed the partners too deeply in the alliance.

Journal of General Management
Vol. 22 No. 4 Summer 1997

Embeddedness, nevertheless, is also a necessary element for sustaining alliances. First, to embed the partners in the alliance helps align the interests of the partners, as the partners realize that they are in the same boat. Second, deeply embedded partners are discouraged from behaving opportunistically. Since it is difficult for a firm to exit quickly, retaliation for opportunistic behavior is certain. Third, a sense of trust may be generated by embeddedness, as the partners become more committed to the alliance. As opposed to nonequity alliances, equity alliances (including joint ventures and equity investment) can be used to ensure embeddedness. When firms participate in joint ventures or take an equity position in other firms, their ability to pull out easily is restrained. It usually involves complicated, and costly new arrangement to free the partners from shared equity ownership. One partner, and maybe even a third party, would have to take over the entity, probably after fresh negotiations. Thus, partners of equity alliances sacrifice some degree of flexibility that is enjoyed by those in nonequity alliances.

The choice, therefore, depends on whether flexibility or embeddedness is more warranted in a particular alliance. Following the logic of our foregoing discussion, the general rule is that:

Guideline 3a: When the need for internal stability (e.g., aligned interests, interfirm trust, and satisfactory co-operation), outweighs the need for controlling uncertainties in the competitive environment, equity alliances should be preferred.

Besides the choice between equity and nonequity alliances, there are other contractual arrangements that need to be negotiated, including exit clauses, arbitration clauses, lawsuit provisions, and details of co-operation and monitoring. These arrangements affect the degree of flexibility and embeddedness as well. For example, exit clauses facilitate the process of terminating alliances, and therefore give the partners an extra degree of flexibility. By comparison, lawsuit provisions and detailed monitoring procedures attach more embeddedness to the alliance. Whether or not to provide for these contractual arrangements is contingent upon the need for flexibility and embeddedness. Strategic alliances can be viewed as a balance between flexibility and embeddedness: they are more flexible than hierarchical organizations and more embedded than arms-length contracts. Thus, to keep both elements in an alliance in a dynamic balance is important for sustaining the alliances. When equity alliances are adopted, the chances are that embeddedness rather than flexibility is emphasized. Thus, exit clauses that provide a certain degree of flexibility are warranted. On the other hand, since nonequity alliances sacrifice embeddedness for flexibility, lawsuit provisions and detailed monitoring procedures will bring some embeddedness back into the alliance. Therefore, the suggestion for the negotiation of these contractual arrangements is:

Guideline 3b: Exit clauses are needed more in equity alliances, while lawsuit provisions and detailed monitoring procedures are needed more in nonequity alliances.

Journal of General Management
Vol. 22 No. 4 Summer 1997

Setting Up the Alliance

After the structure of the alliance is agreed upon, the next stage is to set up the alliance entity. The entity could be completely separate from the parent firms, as in the case of joint ventures. It can also be part of the existing
56 organizations, such as a task force to conduct joint R&D. The staffing of the alliance and other human resource management issues can have a significant impact on the performance of the alliance.

In staffing the alliance, the critical concern lies in the control of the joint enterprise. As we discussed before, strategic alliances are characterized by uncertainties in co-operation. The partners do not necessarily subscribe to the same or even compatible objectives for the alliance. Thus, control becomes a critical means to keep the alliance on track. By assigning your own people to the key positions in the alliance, the partners exercise managerial control of the alliance. Partners often fight hard for the post of the general manager in a joint venture. Some have suggested that joint venture partners should aim at securing a majority of the venture's directors, and positions responsible for quality control and technology. In this sense, the conventional wisdom is that the more managerial control, the better. However, pursuing dominant control in an alliance is not risk-free. In fact, excessive control could adversely affect the alliance's performance. Strategic alliances are essentially hybrid organizations that merge resources and competence. Thus, letting one firm have a predominant position in the alliance could discourage the other partner, whose commitment to the alliance may ebb in consequence. A reasonable share of controlling power that encourages positive involvement is more desirable. Meanwhile, other features, such as interfirm trust and social knowledge of the partners, may well serve as a substitute for control.

Besides controlling the alliance, staffing and human resource issues also largely determine the sustainability of alliances. Firms sometimes dump their off-peak managers to the alliance, a practice that leaves the alliance with few chances for success. In fact, managing strategic alliances is an extremely demanding task, and the performance of the alliance is usually crucial to the partners. Thus, only the very best managers should be assigned to the alliance. Another issue in staffing an alliance is that oftentimes managers' tenure in the alliance is too short to link with results. Given the complexity of managing strategic alliances, a short tenure hampers learning and effective accumulation of experience. Without a certain consistency, the management of alliances could be bumpy. One factor contributing to the potential problem of short tenure is the key role of informal interpersonal relationships for success in alliances. It takes time to develop mutual understanding and psychological contracts among the managers of both sides, and frequent turnovers inevitably damage these intangible but valuable interpersonal ties.

Finally, to set up a sustainable alliance, the partners should work consciously toward blending their cultures. Cultural differences between

Journal of General Management
Vol. 22 No. 4 Summer 1997

the partners have caused the failure of many alliances, as the partners found themselves unable to compromise and assimilate enough. One such example was the alliance between Raytheon and Lexitron, a small word processing firm [20]. Since Lexitron had a difficult time coping with Raytheon's rigid rules, several of Lexitron's key personnel left the firm. The lesson is that cultural clashes can be fatal. Being aware of the potential harm, the partners should work hard to set up an alliance that harmonizes their cultures. Managers who have had experience working in or with other companies should be given priority in assignments to alliances. In addition, the rules and procedures in the alliance should be flexible enough to accommodate different cultures. To let the personnel from both companies work closely with each other can speed up the course of blending cultures as well. In sum, the guideline for setting up the alliance is: 57

Guideline 4: The partners should not pursue predominant managerial control in the alliance; rather, more attention should be given to (a) committing the best personnel, (b) keeping alliance personnel for a long term, and (c) blending their cultures.

Operating the Alliance

To operate the alliance, and carry out the project goals, is yet another stage in the alliance process. Given the acknowledged difficulties of implementation, strategic alliances seem to be particularly troublesome in execution. One major reason, as observed by many researchers, is that the partners have to strike a simultaneous balance between two seemingly contradictory themes: co-operation and competition.

On the one hand, interfirm co-operation is the hallmark of strategic alliances. What differentiates strategic alliances and single-firm strategies is the requisite attribute of collective action. The pooling of the partners and their resources is supposed to create 'collaborative advantage' [21], an advantageous competitive position no single firm can achieve. In order to capitalize on combined resources, a satisfactory level of co-operation is essential. Nevertheless, partners often have trouble in nurturing a high level of co-operation, due to either a lack of trust or the pursuit of self-interest [22]. Firms may indeed engage in opportunistic behavior to take advantage of the partners. Since the partners often fail to build on a constructive, co-operative working relationship, many alliances collapse before producing expected results. Thus, creating a high level of co-operation is the key to sustaining strategic alliances.

On the other hand, competition is an essential element in operating strategic alliances as well. Competition is the driving force of the market, and is not absent in strategic alliances. It would be terribly wrong to enter a strategic alliance just to avoid competition. As long as the partners are direct or indirect competitors, competition would always be on their minds. One reason many alliances formed by competitors fail is that the firms try to 'collude' with their competitors. The partners had better realize that an

Journal of General Management
Vol. 22 No. 4 Summer 1997

58

alliance would not make friends of competitors. In the words of a senior manager of Microsoft, 'This is business. We're not allied with Apple out of love' [23]. Thus, competition between the partners is nothing to be concerned about, and open competition that creates a certain tension between the partners could be healthy for the alliance. A sense of competition could stimulate the partners more actively to protect their firm-specific technology and other competencies. Indeed, losing one's resource carelessly to the partner is detrimental to the sustainability of the alliance, because then the gaining partner will come back and say 'now what are you going to do for us' [24].

It seems clear that both co-operation and competition are indispensable for sustaining an alliance. Nevertheless, since the two ingredients are essentially at odds with each other, a balance can be difficult to achieve and maintain. It requires the managers to separate clearly these two factors when they operate the alliance. On the one hand, in operational and functional areas, managers from both sides should be as co-operative as possible. To that end, there should be explicit clauses about the behaviour of each partner in the alliance. The managers should also make efforts, both formally and informally, to convince the partners that their firms are committed to the agreement. The purpose is to create a smooth, co-operative working relationship. On the other hand, competition should be nourished in areas related to interfirm learning. It should be stressed that strategic alliances are *de facto* learning races, so that whoever learns more would have a head start. In addition, the alliance personnel should never give more information to the partner than what is specified in the agreement. Thus, in operating the alliance:

Guideline 5: The partners should always regard co-operation and competition as dual roles in strategic alliances; co-operation should be emphasized in operational areas, while competition should mostly be capitalized through interfirm learning.

Evaluating Alliance Performance

Performance evaluation is a necessary stage related to strategy implementation, as it provides feedback on the status of the alliance. In strategic alliances, however, performance evaluation has been very controversial. It is unclear whether financial and market performance measures, such as market share and profitability, are the appropriate ones. The reason alliance performance evaluation is so difficult is because not only are the interests of the partners often divergent, but the interests of the separate entity, such as the joint venture, and the parent firms often differ as well. Whose criterion to use is a tough call. In addition, the objectives of many alliances are quite different from those of traditional firms, and they are not easily quantifiable. For instance, there are a few American-Japanese alliances related to the information superhighway [25], whose eventual purpose is to set the standard for the industry. In this case, it would not be appropriate to use current financial measures to evaluate their performance.

Journal of General Management
Vol. 22 No. 4 Summer 1997

Consequently, it has been suggested that input measures and the state of the alliances (e.g., harmony, morale, productivity, and learning) are better than financial and market indicators.

On top of the problems of improving the effectiveness and relevancy of alliance evaluation, we suggest that there are two issues that must be thought through by the partners: common vs private benefits, and efficiency vs equity. According to Khanna et al. [26], the outputs from alliances can be differentiated between common benefits and private benefits. Common benefits are those shared collectively by all participants, while private benefits accrue only to a subset of participants. Therefore, the partners should decide *ex ante* what type of benefits they wish to measure, whether only common benefits or both types of benefits. This issue could have salient implications for how the partners perceive the alliance, since the composition of private benefits and common benefits vary greatly across alliances. In some alliances, such as joint R&D and joint marketing, the partners tend to receive more private benefits than common benefits from the deal. In other types of alliances, such as joint ventures, common benefits are more prominent than private benefits. Thus, it does not make sense to rely mainly on the amount of common benefits, if the alliance is joint R&D or marketing. Likewise, in the case joint ventures the partners should assign more importance to the evaluation of common benefits. 59

A related issue that is interwoven into the evaluation of alliance performance is the priority between efficiency and equity. Traditionally, efficiency has been the yardstick of an organization's performance, and it is still the dominant criterion for single organizations. Nevertheless, the situation of strategic alliances, which involves distributing benefits among the partners, could be dramatically different. Ring and Van de Ven [27] have suggested that equity is yet another key criterion used in evaluating the performance of an alliance. Psychologically, the partners have a need for being treated fairly. Therefore, it is possible that they also rely on the criterion of equity, in addition to the criterion of efficiency. In other words, the partners could sacrifice some need for efficiency in exchange for equity. Imagine a joint venture that is producing satisfactory private benefits for each partner, but one partner perceives the distribution of returns as unfair. It is likely that that particular partner would evaluate the alliance negatively. A desire to restore the sense of equity may even motivate the partner to renegotiate the alliance. In this sense, it seems clear that the evaluation of alliance performance is informed with the values and expectations of individual partners in the alliance.

We assume that an alliance is more sustainable when the partners have a consensus about the alliance's performance. Thus, the best way to prevent divergent performance evaluation is to make the partners agree on the measures beforehand. Another remedy is to strive to make the deal appealing to both parties, given that a biased distribution of performance benefits among the partners cannot last very long. Hence:

Journal of General Management
Vol. 22 No. 4 Summer 1997

Guideline 6a: A comprehensive evaluation of an alliance's performance should include various measures as appropriate, such as market and financial indicators as well as input measures and the state of the alliance (e.g., harmony, morale, productivity, and learning).

Guideline 6b: The emphasis on either common benefits or private benefits is contingent upon the nature of the alliance, and the equity criterion should be given sufficient consideration.

Modifying the Alliance

A sustainable strategic alliance often involves appropriate modifications. According to a study by McKinsey, most successful alliances modified themselves dramatically during their first few years [28]. This is not surprising, as our previous discussion has indicated that it is very easy to make a suboptimal decision in various stages of the alliance process. Modifying the alliance along the way at least provides a means for correcting some of the inopportune decisions. Overall, the sustainability of the alliance is enhanced because of the facility to attend to problem areas, if any. However, for those alliances which are perceived as unsustainable, modification may take the form of termination. Although there are numerous ways to modify an alliance, we focus on the choice between positive modification and negative modification.

By positive modifications, we mean those that are intended to give the alliance a second chance for survival. In contrast, negative modifications refer to those that tend toward termination of the alliance. A decision may also unwittingly lead the partners to make positive modifications on a hopeless alliance, or to abandon an alliance which could be revived. The issue here is closely related to the temporal orientations of the partners [29]. The partners may have either a short-term orientation or a long-term orientation. A short-term orientation regards the alliance as transitional, so that it is expected to dissolve sooner or later. Special emphasis is on the prompt, current financial performance of the alliance. On the contrary, firms with a long-term orientation tend to view the alliance as semi-permanent, and they pay less attention to the current performance of the alliance.

Stafford [30] has suggested that the partners differ in terms of the period of time in which they expect performance results from the alliance. Many alliances dissolved because the partners took a short-term orientation, or 'expecting too much too soon' [31], so that they did not have the patience to wait for the results. In this sense, the partners preoccupied with a short-term orientation tend to make negative modifications when the actual results take longer than their own timetable. Such a mistaken conception of time orientation may have contributed to the high failure rate of strategic alliances. The partners should be apprised that in most strategic alliances a fairly long-term orientation is necessary for success. Strategic alliances are time-consuming projects from the very first stage, and the actual pooling of two or more firms together often takes longer than what is hoped for. Thus,

Journal of General Management
Vol. 22 No. 4 Summer 1997

the partners should be prepared beforehand for a fairly long haul. One approach is to study the rate of progress of similar alliances that have been forged before. By being psychologically prepared for a relatively long-term horizon may discourage unfortunate negative modifications from being entertained.

Although a short-term orientation could be negative for an alliance, a long-term orientation that ignores prompt results could bring trouble as well. Newman [32], for example, found that successful joint ventures in transitional economies focused on current, prompt results. Indeed, it would be hard for an alliance to take a very long-term orientation, because an interfirm coalition cannot after all sustain itself too long without some tangible results. As compared to hierarchical organizations, strategic alliances are less amenable to a very long temporal orientation. Given those extra uncertainties about the level of co-operation, it is inappropriate in practical terms for the partners to commit exclusively to long-term results. Certain short-term results are essential to keep the alliance going. If no results are obtained after a reasonable period, the partners should not be trapped into escalating commitment. In such a case, making positive modifications may mean ignoring the market signals and could well be wasteful. Hence:

Guideline 7: Either short-term or long-term orientation could lead to deleterious modification of the alliance; by comparison, a medium temporal orientation is a better guide in the modification process.

Concluding Remarks

This paper has attempted to lay out a step-by-step action plan for strategic alliance management. Rather than offering a list of sundry tips, we focused on a few key issues pertaining to various stages of the alliance process. These issues, such as the balance between co-operation and competition, have profound implications on making alliances more sustainable. Previous studies have not organized these key issues in a systematic manner. To fill this gap in the literature, we have located the issues in our seven-stage framework of alliance management. Furthermore, guidelines for each stage have been developed to best attend to these key issues. The central theme of this study is that strategic alliance management is a complex undertaking, and that an alliance can be sustained only if decision makers understand their options at each stage as well as the consequences of exercising each option.

Our approach to each key issue has been basically dialectical, i.e., identifying the benefits as well as the pitfalls of the options. We believe that such an approach allows a more comprehensive appreciation of each issue. This approach has helped in identifying some of the misunderstandings and over-simplifications in the existing literature. For example, in the second stage of selecting an alliance partner, we have proposed that endorsing only strong-strong alliances can be too narrow a focus. Alliances forged by relatively weak players can also produce good results. Another example can

Journal of General Management
Vol. 22 No. 4 Summer 1997

be found in the stage of operating an alliance, where we have clarified the need for a balance between co-operation and competition in alliances.

Sustaining strategic alliances is a challenge for strategists. A number of issues, many uniquely present in strategic alliances, are not conducive for survival. However, the greatest opportunity, as emphasized in this paper, is to view an alliance from a holistic perspective. By thinking ahead at each stage of the alliance process, firms can avoid many of the pitfalls on the road to sustainable alliances.

References

[1] Bleeke, J. and Ernst, D., 'Is Your Strategic Alliance Really a Sale?', *Harvard Business Review*, Vol. 73, No. 1, 1995, pp. 97-105.

[2] Yoshino, M. Y. and Rangan, U. S., *Strategic Alliances: An Entrepreneurial Approach to Globalization*, Boston, MA: Harvard Business School Press, 1995.

[3] Parkhe, A., 'Interfirm Diversity, Organizational Learning, and Longevity in Global Strategic Alliances', *Journal of International Business Studies*, Vol. 22, 1991, pp. 579-601. See also his article 'Strategic Alliance Structuring: A Game Theory and Transaction Cost Examination of Interfirm Co-operation', *Academy of Management Journal*, Vol. 36, 1993, pp. 794-829.

[4] 'Airline Alliances: Flying in Formation', *Economist*, July 22, 1995, p. 59-60.

[5] Badaracco, J. L., Jr., *The Knowledge Link: How Firms Compete Through Strategic Alliances*, Boston, MA: Harvard Business School Press, 1991. See also Hagedoorn, J., 'Understanding the Rationale of Strategic Technology Partnering: Interorganizational Modes of Co-operation and Sectoral Differences', *Strategic Management Journal*, Vol. 14, 1993, pp. 371-385; and Lewis, J. D., *The Connected Corporation: How Leading Companies Win Through Customer-Supplier Alliances*, New York: Free Press, 1995.

[6] Devlin, G. and Bleackley, M., 'Strategic Alliances - Guidelines for Success', *Long Range Planning*, Vol. 21, No. 5, 1988, pp. 18-23. Also, Lei, D. and Slocum, J. W., Jr., 'Global Strategic Alliances: Payoffs and Pitfalls', *Organizational Dynamics*, Vol. 19, No. 3, 1991, pp. 44-62; and Serapio, M. G., Jr. and Cascio, W. F., 'End-Games in International Alliances', *Academy of Management Executive*, Vol. 10, No. 1, 1996, pp. 62-73.

[7] Beamish, P. W. and Inkpen, A. C., 'Keeping International Joint Ventures Stable and Profitable', *Long Range Planning*, Vol. 28, No. 3, 1995, pp. 26-36. Also, Forrest, J. E., 'Management Aspects of Strategic Partnering', *Journal of General Management*, Vol. 17, No. 4, 1992, pp. 25-40.

[8] Burgers, W. P., Hill, C. W. and Kim, W. C., 'A Theory of Global

Journal of General Management
Vol. 22 No. 4 Summer 1997

Strategic Alliances: The Case of the Global Auto Industry', *Strategic Management Journal*, Vol. 14, 1993, pp. 419-432.
[9] Dyer, J. H., 'Improving Performance by Transforming Arms-Length Relationships to Supplier Partnership: The Chrysler Case', paper presented at the annual meeting of the Academy of Management, Vancouver, Canada, 1995.
[10] Gulati, R., 'Does Familiarity Breed Trust? The Implication of Repeated Ties for Contractual Choice in Alliances', *Academy of Management Journal*, Vol. 38, 1995, pp. 85-112.
[11] Alexander, E. R., *How Organizations Act Together: Interorganizational Coordination in Theory and Practice*, Luxembourg: Gordon and Breach, 1995. Also, Alter, C. and Hage, J., *Organizations Working Together*, Newbury Park, CA: Sage, 1993; Mohr, J. and Spekman, R., 'Characteristics of Partnership Success: Partnership Attributes, Communication Behavior, and Conflict Resolution Techniques', *Strategic Management Journal*, Vol. 15, 1994, pp. 135-152; Das, T. Das, T.K. and Teng, B., 'Risk Types and Interfirm Alliance Structures', *Journal of Management Studies*, Vol. 33, No. 6, 1996, pp. 825-841; Das, T.K. and Teng, B., 'Strategic Alliance Structuring: A Risk Perception Model', paper presented at the annual meeting of the Academy of Management, Cincinnati, OH, Auguest 1996; Das, T.K. and Teng, B, 'The Dialectics of Strategic Alliances', paper to be presented at the annual meeting of the Academy of Management, Boston, MA, August 1997; and Gulati, R., 'Social Structure and Alliance Formation Patterns: A Longitudinal Analysis', *Administrative Science Quarterly*, Vol. 40, 1995, pp. 619-652.
[12] Brouthers, K. D., Brouthers, L. E. and Wilkinson, T. J., 'Strategic Alliances: Choose Your Partners', *Long Range Planning*, Vol. 28, No. 3, 1995, pp. 18-25. For a discussion of the role of different types of resources and the preference for alliance configurations, see Das, T. K. and Teng, B., 'Resource and Risk Management in the Strategic Alliance Making Process', *Journal of Management* (forthcoming).
[13] Walters, B. A., Peters, S. and Dess, G. G., 'Strategic Alliances and Joint Ventures: Making them Work', *Business Horizons*, Vol. 37, No. 4, 1994, pp. 5-10.
[14] Khanna, T., Gulati, R. and Nohria, N., 'Competition, Co-operation and Sub-optimal Behavior in Alliances', Working paper, Harvard Business School, 1995.
[15] Bleeke and Ernst, *op. cit.*
[16] Brouthers, et al, *op. cit.*
[17] Bleeke and Ernst, p. 101, *op. cit.*
[18] Airline Alliances (see [4]), *op. cit.*
[19] Parkhe, *op. cit.*
[20] Sankar, C. S., Boulton, W. R., Davidson, N. W., Snyder, C. A. and Ussery, R. W., 'Building a World-Class Alliance: The Universal Card-TSYS Case', *Academy of Management Executive*, Vol. 9, No. 2, 1995, pp. 20-29.
[21] Kanter, R. M., 'Collaborative Advantage: The Art of Alliances',

63

Journal of General Management
Vol. 22 No. 4 Summer 1997

64

Harvard Business Review, Vol. 72, No. 4, 1994, pp. 96-108.
[22] Ring, P. S. and Van de Ven, A. H., 'Structuring Co-operative Relationship Between Organizations', *Strategic Management Journal*, Vol. 13, 1992, pp. 483-498.
[23] Sherman, S., 'Are Strategic Alliances Working?', *Fortune*, September 21, 1992, pp. 77-78.
[24] Hamel, G., 'Competition for Competence and Interpartner Learning Within International Strategic Alliances', *Strategic Management Journal*, Vol. 12, 1991, pp. 83-103.
[25] Armstrong, L. and Holyoke, L., 'Look Who's Stuck in the Slow Lane', *Business Week*, March 28, 1994, pp. 28-29.
[26] Khanna, et al, *op. cit.*
[27] Ring, P. S. and Van de Ven, A. H., 'Developmental Processes of Co-operative Interorganizational Relationships', *Academy of Management Review*, Vol. 19, 1994, pp. 90-118.
[28] Sherman, *op. cit.*
[29] Das, T. K., *The Subjective Side of Strategy Making: Future Orientations and Perceptions of Executives*, New York: Praeger, 1986. See also Das, T. K., 'Time: The Hidden Dimension in Strategic Planning', *Long Range Planning*, Vol. 24, No. 3, 1991, pp. 49-57; and Ganitsky, J. and Watzke, G. E., 'Implications of Different Time Perspectives for Human Resource Management in International Joint Ventures', *Management International Review*, Vol. 30, Special issue, 1990, pp. 37-51.
[30] Stafford, E. R., 'Using Co-operative Strategies to Make Alliances Work', *Long Range Planning*, Vol. 27, No. 3, 1994, pp. 64-74.
[31] *Ibid*, p. 72.
[32] Newman, W. H., 'Focused Joint Ventures in Transforming Economies', *Academy of Management Executive*, Vol. 6, No. 1, 1992, pp. 67-75.

Part VI
Expatriation and Repatriation: Issues of Cultural Adaptation

[31]

THE EXPATRIATE EXPERIENCE:
A CRITICAL REVIEW AND SYNTHESIS

David C. Thomas

ABSTRACT

In this paper the empirical research that defines our understanding of the experience that firms have with staffing with expatriates and the experience of these managers with an overseas assignment is critically reviewed. In attempting to generalize from the body of literature an effort was made to establish those relationships that are 'given' as a basis for a paradigm defining the expatriate experience. What was found, however, were a striking number of contradictions or paradoxes. While much is known, it is these contradictions that largely defines the present state of this body of knowledge. A framework for future research is presented and methodological limitations of the literature reviewed are discussed.

INTRODUCTION

Understanding the special circumstances of expatriate managers has sparked significant research interest for at least twenty years. Recently, some researchers have

Advances in International Comparative Management, Volume 12, pages 237-273.

ISBN: 0-7623-0174-0

suggested that expatriates are playing an increasingly important role in managing today's global organizations (Kobrin, 1988; Thomas, 1994; Torbiorn, 1994). The additional difficulty presented by overseas assignments combined with the often critically important nature of the expatriate role make the experience of these managers of special interest. In this article the empirical research that defines our understanding of the expatriate experience is critically reviewed. The term expatriate experience is used in order to encompass both the experience that firms have with staffing with expatriates and the experience of these managers with an overseas assignment. It is the practical need to understand the topic of expatriation from both the point of view of the firm and that of the expatriate manager that has dictated the topic areas that have received research attention. The review is organized according to these topic areas that have emerged in the literature. First, the reasons that expatriates are sent on assignment, their selection, and their reasons for accepting such a posting are discussed. Then, attention is turned to various definitions of successful expatriation, including turnover, task performance, and the adjustment of expatriates to their situation. As an outgrowth of the adjustment literature the relationship of adjustment to performance and stages of adjustment are reviewed. Then a number of factors related to the various dimensions of expatriate success are examined. Finally, attention is focused on the issues of repatriation, and the relationship of the expatriate assignment to the manager's career. Following the review, comments on the body of literature regarding expatriation both in terms of how it informs a paradigm of the expatriate experience and its limitations are offered. A synthesis of the body of literature is presented in a framework for future research.

The articles for this review were identified through a computer search of the international business databases and a manual search of scholarly publications. As with any review, choices had to be made with regard to which articles to include. Here, articles were screened to eliminate those that did not present original empirical work and the study is limited to articles published in English.

REVIEW OF LITERATURE

The Role of Expatriates

Almost thirty years ago Perlmutter (1969) classified the preferences of multinational firms for a particular staffing strategy as "polycentric" (local foreign managers only) "ethnocentric" (home-country managers predominate) or "geocentric" (a mix of nationalities at home and abroad). Despite the increased costs, often cited high failure rates (for an exception, see Peterson, Napier, & Won, 1995; for a critique, see Harzing, 1995), and as some suggest (Kobrin, 1988), a trend toward using local nationals, it is surprising how little research has addressed the question of why firms use expatriates. Franko (1973), based on "interview and questionnaire data from more than 25 European and U.S. firms, as well as a survey of published material covering the roughly 170 U.S. and 60 European enterprises with manufacturing enterprises in seven or more countries" (p. 32), concluded that the use of expatriates followed a cycle consistent with the stage of internationalization of the firm. That is, expatriates predominated in top managerial jobs in early stages of internationalization for both European and U.S. multinationals, with the use of third country national managers growing as the technology of the firm diffused among nations (Franko, 1973). Stage of internationalization or organizational life cycle models continue to be popular in the theoretical and prescriptive literature related to the staffing patterns of the multinational firm (e.g., Adler & Ghadar, 1990; Milliman, VonGlinow, & Nathan, 1991).

Much of the research regarding the use of expatriates has been content to describe the differences in levels of expatriates in the foreign affiliates of firms with different countries of origin. Generally, results have indicated that firm nationality is related to use of expatriates with Japanese-owned firms having more expatriates in their foreign affiliates than their American or European counterparts (e.g., Beechler, 1992; Kopp, 1994; Peterson et al., 1995; Tung, 1981). The presence of greater numbers of expatriates in Japanese-owned firms has been used as an indicator of a particular role for expatriates such as managerial control (Baliga & Jaeger, 1984; Rosenzweig & Nohria, 1994). However, this review suggests that the assumption that greater expatriate presence is indicative of a particular expatriate mission is not supported in the empirical literature.

A small number of studies have addressed the reasons for expatriate usage from other than an organizational life cycle or purely descriptive perspective. In an early examination of the use of expatriates, Edstrom and Galbraith (1977) conducted comparative case studies in four European firms. From these data they suggested that firms transferred personnel internationally for one of three reasons: to fill a technical requirement, to develop the manager, or to develop the organization. Survey research using a similar typology has found that British firms cited the need to fill a technical requirement and managerial control of the foreign operation as the major reasons for using expatriate managers (Scullion, 1991). Also, Peterson et al. (1995) found that British, German, Japanese, and U.S. firms all cited filling a technical requirement as the main reason for using expatriates. In contrast, New Zealand firms were more likely to cite the development of the organization and the development of the expatriate manager as the major reasons for using expatriates (Enderwick & Hodgson, 1993). Also, Park, Sun, and David (1993) found, in a survey of managers of U.S. firms in Korea, that the most important reason stated for staffing with a local national instead of an expatriate was the manager's lack of local knowledge.

In one of the few empirical studies to examine organizational determinants for staffing with expatriates, Boyacigiller (1990) found that in the foreign affiliates of a large multinational bank the task complexity found in the affiliate and the cultural distance of the affiliate from headquarters were positively related to the use of expatriates in the foreign affiliate. In a recent longitudinal study of the staffing patterns of 50 American affiliates of Japanese firms, Beechler and Iaquinto (1994) found, contradictory to Franko's (1973) stage model, a positive relationship between the company's international experience and the use of expatriates. Additionally, affiliate size was positively related to the use of expatriates, while both affiliate ownership and the change in affiliate capitalization were negatively related to the use of expatriates (Beechler & Iaquinto, 1994). These contradictory findings potentially result from changes over the twenty years between the studies. However, a clear articulation of specifically what changes have taken place to affect staffing patterns has not emerged.

While these studies identify some of the determinants of staffing with expatriates, such as nationality of the firm, and size and complexity of the foreign affiliate, the potentially contradictory results coupled with a range of methodological issues, discussed later, provide a very incomplete picture of what might motivate firms to fill a position with an expatriate. Therefore, our ability to relate this staffing decision to firm strategy, firm performance, and perhaps most important the expectations that the firm has of expatriates remains limited. What seems clear, however, is that the role of the expatriate, as determined by why s/he was sent overseas, is variable and can be influenced by a number of organizational level factors.

Surely, given the often critical nature of staffing the management of an overseas subsidiary, we should not be satisfied with the level of knowledge in this area. One can only assume that researchers and managers alike have been satisfied with the explanatory power of the relative molar typologies developed more than twenty years ago (e.g., Edstrom & Galbraith, 1977) and/or perhaps the organizational and environmental antecedents of the staffing decision seem so obvious that they have failed to spark research interest. It is suggested here that both the expatriate and the firm would benefit from a clearer understanding of the organizational and environmental determinates of filling an overseas post with an expatriate.

Selection of Expatriates

Related to the purpose for staffing with an expatriate are the criteria used by the firm for expatriate selection. Research in the area of the selection of expatriate managers focused initially on the development of lists of criteria thought to be important to success in foreign assignments. A number of studies which gathered self reports of selection criteria (Borrmann, 1968; Hays, 1971; Howard, 1974; Ivancevich, 1969; Miller 1975; Tung, 1981) were consistent in their conclusions that technical competence was the primary decision criteria used by firms in selecting international managers. A more recent survey of twenty-four multinational companies (Haselberger & Stroh, 1992) indicated that little has changed since these early studies, with managerial competence and technical competence leading the list of selection criteria. Miller (1975) suggested the overemphasis on these criteria was because high technical qualifications present a lower perceived risk of adverse consequences to the selecting manager. Also, firms may have placed the most emphasis on criteria that are most easily measured. Interestingly, host organizations also view technical expertise as an important selection criterion for expatriates assigned to them. Zeira and Banai (1985) found that expertise in the specific assignment was second only to host country language proficiency as a desirable selection criterion. Also, some differences in selection criteria based on the nationality of the respondent have been noted. For example, Stone (1991) found that the ability to adapt was ranked as the most important selection criterion by Australian managers and expatriates on assignment and ranked second to technical competence by Asian managers.

Decision to Accept Assignment

The selection decision is tied to the motivation of individual's to take an overseas assignment. The pool of potential applicants available to the manager making a staffing decision is limited by a number of factors including restrictions imposed by other organizational requirements, and those imposed by the individuals themselves. One of these is the willingness of applicants to accept the overseas posting. Reasons for seeking an overseas assignment range from personal development to financial gain. In an early examination of this topic, Cleveland, Mangone, and Adams (1960) found that the motives of Americans for accepting an assignment (a sense of vocation, financial rewards, and the desire to escape undesirable circumstances) were related to but not isomorphic with the motives for remaining on assignment. Similarly, Miller and Cheng (1978) found that Americans accepting their first overseas posting did so for different reasons than did those accepting an additional overseas posting. Notably, experienced expatriates were less likely to be motivated by the opportunity to advance their career than were new expatriates. Relatedly, Brett, Stroh, and Reilly (1993) found that willingness to relocate overseas was significantly related to the expatriate's focus on career advancement. The substantial literature on job choice might be drawn upon to provide additional insight into the decision to accept an overseas assignment. For example, people pursue jobs that have job characteristics that they find attractive, but their choice is also influenced by their probability of getting the job (e.g., Rynes & Lawler, 1983).

Conspicuously absent from the literature are tests of the relationship between the motivation for accepting an overseas assignment and expatriate success. Also, based on the domestic relocation literature (Brett & Werbel, 1980), a case can be made for a relationship between willingness to accept an overseas assignment and expatriate effectiveness (Feldman & Thomas, 1992). However, tests of this relationship are also absent from the literature.

It seems, therefore, that a number of opportunities exist to refine our understanding of the decision to accept an overseas assignment and the relationship of this decision to outcomes that are important both to the firm and the expatriate.

Definitions of Expatriate Success

Definitions of expatriate success or failure have varied widely in the published literature. While a consensus seems to be building for a multidimensional definition (e.g., Benson, 1978; Black, Mendenhall, & Oddou, 1991; Feldman & Thomas, 1992; Hawes & Kealey, 1979, 1981) the empirical literature has tended to focus on three outcomes of the expatriate experience. These are turnover, adjustment, and task performance.

Perhaps the most frequently used criterion of expatriate success (failure) has been turnover, or more specifically, the premature return of expatriates to their home country (Black & Gregersen, 1990). As a measure of success this construct has most often been operationalized as intent to remain the originally agreed time of the assignment (Banai & Reisel, 1993; Birdseye & Hill, 1995; Black & Gregersen, 1990; Feldman & Thomas, 1992; Gregersen & Black, 1990; Guzzo, Noonan, & Elron, 1994). However, other turnover related variables such as organizational commitment (e.g., Gregersen & Black, 1990; Guzzo et al., 1994; Naumann, 1993a) and job satisfaction (e.g., Black & Gregersen, 1990; Dunbar, 1992, 1994; Feldman & Thomas, 1992; Gomez-Mejia & Balkin, 1987; Naumann, 1993b) have also been the subject of recent inquiry.

The second major focus of expatriate success has been the ability of the expatriate to overcome culture shock (Oberg, 1960) and adjust to the new environment. A psychological definition of adjustment describes it as a condition consisting of a relationship with the environment in which needs are satisfied and the ability to meet physical and social demands exists (English, 1958). The antecedents to expatriate adjustment have been the subject of a significant amount of research. However, Church (1982), in a review of the sojourner adjustment literature, on which much of the expatriate adjustment literature is based, noted the absence of a clear definition of adjustment. Benson (1978) also noted that the expatriate adjustment construct is often ill-defined. Operationalizations of sojourner adjustment have included satisfaction (Hawes & Kealey, 1979, 1981; Kealey, 1989; Klineberg & Hull, 1979; Torbiorn, 1982), absence of stress (Hammer, 1987; Kealey, 1989), psychological mood (Golden, 1973), effective intercultural interaction (Hawes & Kealey, 1979, 1981; Hull, 1979; Ruben & Kealey, 1979), and the ability to deal with conflict, anxiety, and life style changes (Abe & Wiseman, 1983). Likewise, measurements of the adjustment of expatriate business people have been varied. In some cases the premature return from the expatriate assignment has been used as a proxy for failure to adjust (Mendenhall & Oddou, 1985).

A number of studies have relied on self reports of adjustment to various facets of the environment (e.g., Black, 1988, 1990a; Black & Gregersen, 1991a; Black & Stephens, 1989; Torbiorn, 1982). This overall adjustment has been refined in later work to include three dimensions of adjustment (Black, Gregersen, & Mendenhall, 1992; Black et al., 1991; Parker & McEvoy, 1993; Takeuchi & Hannon, 1996). These dimensions are general living adjustment, work adjustment, and interaction adjustment, and seem to be influenced by somewhat different antecedents (Black & Gregersen, 1991a; Parker & McEvoy, 1993). In support of this dimensionality, two of these constructs seem consistent with the behavioral skill/ability domains that the sojourner adjustment literature suggests as facilitating intercultural effectiveness (Hammer, 1987), and the third relates to the adjustment of job changers (e.g., Brett & Werbel, 1980). An additional method of measuring the adjustment of expatriate managers, that draws on the adjustment to job changes literature (Feldman & Brett, 1983) has been to employ multiple indices of adjustment such as general job satisfaction, facet job satisfaction, intent to remain, and psychological well-being (Feldman & Tompson, 1993). Therefore, while a consensus as to the appropriate indicators of expatriate adjustment is not evident, there would seem to be less debate on the notion that the construct is multidimensional.

Task performance is the third major indicator of expatriate success that has received research attention. Mendenhall and Oddou (1985) suggest that a distinctive feature of the expatriate role is the requirement that expatriates meet the often conflicting performance expectations of home office superiors and host nationals. Some research on the performance of expatriates has been able to gather supervisor ratings of performance (e.g., Clarke & Hammer, 1995; Stoner, Aram, & Rubin, 1972). However, because objective data on the performance of expatriate managers is often difficult to obtain, most studies of this employee group have relied on the expatriate's self report of performance (e.g., Black & Porter, 1991; Feldman & Thomas, 1992; Feldman & Tompson, 1993). Only very recently have researchers begun to examine the processes used to evaluate expatriate performance (e.g., Gregersen, Hite, & Black, 1996).

This lack of consensus on the dimensions of expatriate success suggests that any global comments about the relationship between antecedents and a general construct labeled expatriate success/effectiveness, or for that matter expatriate adjustment, must be treated with some caution. For this reason, in the remainder of this review of the relationships of variables to the expatriate experience, an attempt is made to carefully specify the appropriate dimension of the expatriate experience.

The U Curve Adjustment Hypothesis

Much of the research on the expatriate experience has been based on an assumption of a cycle of adjustment to the foreign environment which follows a U shaped pattern, first reported by Lysgaard (1955). The model is extended to a W when repatriation is considered (Gullahorn & Gullahorn, 1963). This stage model of adjustment, where sojourners progress at regular intervals through four phases of; honeymoon, culture shock, adjustment, and finally mastery, has been the subject of reviews by Church (1982) and Black and Mendenhall (1991). Church concluded that "support for the U curve hypothesis must be considered weak, inconclusive, and over generalized" (p. 542). Church also suggested that studies had failed to show support for the generality of both the phases and the time parameters of the U curve, making the description of the curve extremely variable. In their subsequent review, Black and Mendenhall (1991) found support for the U curve hypothesis in twelve of eighteen empirical studies. However, they noted a number of methodological deficiencies, including lack of statistical tests and wide variability in definitions of the adjustment construct, which make the results less than compelling. Also, Nicholson and Imaizumi (1993) found a different pattern of adjustment in the work and nonwork environments in their study of Japanese expatriates. Different adjustment patterns for expatriates and for their spouses have also been noted (Briody & Chrisman, 1991).

It was noted that none of the studies previously reviewed incorporated the type of longitudinal within subject with control design required to specify the pattern of an individual's adjustment over time. In the one study discovered that employed such a design no difference was found in the adjustment patterns of American university students overseas and at home, and the pattern of adjustment (mood changes) did not support the U curve hypothesis (Nash, 1991). It was also noted that, with one exception (Black & Mendenhall, 1991), no attempt has been made to specify a theory as to why individuals might move through the stages of adjustment specified by the U curve. The failure of the U curve hypothesis to adequately explain the patterns of adjustment observed has led some theorists to consider nonlinear models of the adjustment process (e.g., Fenwick & Haslett, 1994) and at least one author (Osland, 1994) to consider a metaphorical treatment of the expatriate experience.

It is suggested later in this article that concern for expatriate adjustment might be minimized in favor of consideration of longer term outcomes of the expatriate experience. However, the idea that expatriates might go through some systematic and discernible pattern of adjustment remains an attractive notion both from an academic and a practical perspective.

Relationship of Adjustment to Performance

Much of the literature on the expatriate experience has assumed a direct positive relationship between the adjustment and the performance of the expatriate manager (e.g., Mendenhall & Oddou, 1985). Earley (1987) provided empirical support for this relationship in a study of U.S. managers sent to Korea for a short assignment. In that study, performance was found to be negatively related to expatriates' perceptions of the intensity of their adjustment to the new culture. Nicholson and Imaizumi (1993), in a study of 91 Japanese expatriate managers, found that self-reports of performance were positively related to work adjustment, but not to general or interaction adjustment. Also, Gregersen and Black (1990) found that interaction and general adjustment were positively related to intent to stay on assignment while no relationship was found for adjustment to work. However, the empirical support for a positive relationship between adjustment and performance is even more equivocal. Some evidence (Kealey, 1989; Ruben & Kealey, 1979) has been presented that suggests that the highest performing individuals, in terms of transferring skills and knowledge to host nationals, are also the most likely to experience severe culture shock. More recently, Parker and McEvoy (1993) found that while work adjustment was positively related to performance, a significant negative relationship existed between general living adjustment and performance of expatriates, after controlling for work adjustment and interaction adjustment. Also, Clarke and Hammer (1995) found that performance and adjustment were predicted by different antecedents in a study of Japanese and American managers. This evidence, combined with such issues as the variety of measures used for adjustment, the likely multidimensional nature of the adjustment construct, the reliance on self-reports of performance, and the general lack of empirical work in this area, seems to suggest that the nature of the relationship between expatriate adjustment and performance is an open issue.

In summary, while a significant amount of research exists regarding expatriate adjustment at least four substantive issues remain. These are the clear definition of and the possible multidimensionality of the construct, the possibility that different facets of adjustment are influenced by different antecedents, the exact nature of any patterns of adjustment for the expatriate and family members, and finally, the specification of the relationship be different facets of adjustment and different facets of performance.

Factors Affecting Expatriate Success

The lack of a consistent definition of expatriate success has not prevented the development of a fairly large body of literature which purports to explain the success or failure of these international employees. The factors that have been related to one measure or another of expatriate success include individual, organizational, and environmental variables. A complete categorization of these empirical findings requires a 3 x N (measures of success) matrix, the usefulness of which is questionable. In Table 1 a map of the literature with regard to the extent to which empirical evidence was found is presented. The following paragraphs describe the key findings with regard to the effects of the three categories of antecedent variables on a set of outcomes often used to indicate expatriate success.

Individual Factors

In the search for an international type, some early research on international effectiveness focused on the personality characteristics of effective sojourners (e.g., Cleveland et al., 1960; Guthrie & Zektrick, 1967; Mottram, 1963; Sewell & Davidson, 1956; Stein, 1966). In their review of empirical studies of individual antecedents to acculturation, Mendenhall and Oddou (1985) identified three dimensions of individual characteristics (self-orientation, others orientation, per-

Table 1. Map of Empirical Evidence of Antecedents to Expatriate Effectiveness

Antecedent	Effectiveness Related Outcomes				
	Adjustment	Turnover (Intent to remain)	Satisfaction and Commitment	Task Performance	Repatriation Adjustment
Individual					
Traits	D	D	D	I	I
Skills and Abilities	S	I	S	I	I
Demographics	N	N	N	I	N
Foreign Language Fluency	S	I	D/N	I	N
Overseas Experience	N	I	D/N	I	I
Family Situation	S	S	S	I	I
Nationality	I	I	I	I	I
Gender	I	I	I	N	I
Organizational					
Job Characteristics	S	S	N	N	N
Organizational Level	N	I	N	N	I
Training	S	S	S	S	I
Support	N	I	N	I	N
Environmental					
Cultural Novelty	S	N	I	I	I
Social Support	S	I	I	I	I

Key: I = Insufficient evidence, largely uncharted territory.
N = New, small amount of relatively recent research.
S = Substantial body of evidence (some may be contradictory).
D = Small amount of research, some of it dated.

ceptual orientation) thought to be related to effectiveness. However, the failure of empirical tests to establish consistent relationships between personality characteristics and measures of sojourner success such as task performance, adjustment, and satisfaction (Stening, 1979) resulted in a shift in emphasis to the behavior of successful sojourners (Brein & David, 1971) or their social skills (Furnham & Bochner, 1986). Subsequently, several factor analytic studies (Abe & Wiseman 1983; Hammer, 1987; Hammer, Gudykunst, & Wiseman, 1978) have identified behaviors or personal abilities that sojourners, who described themselves as being satisfied with and functioning well in a foreign culture, considered important to their success. The factors derived from these studies are: (1) the ability to manage psychological stress; (2) the ability to effectively communicate; and (3) the ability to establish interpersonal relationships.

Some research explicitly directed at examining the characteristics of expatriate success has sought the opinions of these managers regarding critical success factors. Several surveys of American expatriates' perceptions of the factors related to success/failure have been conducted (Hays, 1971, 1974; Tung 1981). Consistent among the studies was that family situation (lack of spouse adjustment) was mentioned as the factor most likely to be linked to expatriate failure. In a recent similar study of expatriates of 26 different nationalities (Arthur & Bennett, 1995) five characteristics of individuals believed to be related to success were identified. In order of importance to respondents these were: (1) family situation, (2) adaptability, (3) job knowledge, (4) relational ability, and (5) openness to other cultures.

Clearly, the studies reviewed indicate a wide range of individual characteristics that potentially influence the nature of the expatriate experience. Also, the classification of these characteristics (e.g., Mendenhall & Oddou, 1985) into broad skill dimensions seems a useful way to inform practice in the absence of a more definitive definition of a prototypical expatriate.

Demographics

While the theoretical justification for the inclusion of demographic variables in studies of the expatriate experience has rarely been made, the need to examine the nature of the relationships of these factors to expatriate success remains. Demographic characteristics of expatriates such as age, tenure, educational level and marital status have all received some research attention. The age of the expatriate has been found to be positively related to organizational commitment (Banai & Reisel, 1993; Naumann, 1993a), work adjustment (Nicholson & Imaizumi, 1993; Takeuchi & Hannon, 1996), and job satisfaction (Naumann, 1993b; Stroh, Dennis, & Cramer, 1994), but negatively correlated with willingness to relocate (Brett et al., 1993), intent to leave (Birdseye & Hill, 1995), and general satisfaction (Feldman & Tompson, 1993). Tenure of expatriates has been found to be positively related to job satisfaction (Naumann, 1993a, 1993b) and negatively related to intent to leave (Birdseye & Hill, 1995). The education level of expatriates was found to be negatively related to job satisfaction and commitment to the organization by Naumann (1993a), and positively related to general adjustment and interaction adjustment, but not work adjustment, by Takeuchi and Hannon (1996). Feldman and Tompson (1993) found that married expatriates were more satisfied and were higher performers, and a number of studies have found that the adjustment of the spouse and or family is positively related to expatriate adjustment (Black, 1988, 1990b; Black & Gregersen, 1991a; Black & Stephens, 1989; Nicholson & Imaizumi, 1993; Stroh et al., 1994) and negatively related to intent to leave (Birdseye & Hill, 1995; Black & Stephens, 1989).

Like personality characteristics, the contribution of the effect of demographics alone to the development of a paradigm defining the expatriate experience is somewhat limited. However, as indicators of life stage, career stage, and family situation in combination with organizational and environmental variables they should prove more useful. For example, the results found for age may be perfectly consistent when examined in concert with other variables such as the motivation for accepting the overseas assignment. Also, these results indicate the need to control for a number of demographic elements in future empirical work.

Foreign Language Ability and Previous International Experience

Two individual level variables with established theoretical linkages to expatriate success are the ability of the expatriate to communicate in the language of the host country and his/her previous international experience. Benson (1978) cites several empirical studies in support of his argument that foreign language skill is not necessarily an effective predictor of sojourner success. However, in a review of the sojourner adjustment literature, Church (1982) indicates substantial support for a positive relationship between language fluency and degree of interaction with host nationals and to a lesser extent with satisfaction and adjustment. Brein and David (1971) have suggested that fluency allows sojourners to develop a so called conversational currency that can facilitate interactions with host nationals. Benson (1978) suggests that language fluency may be a correlate of, but not a predictor of adaptation. Significant relationships between the language fluency of expatriate managers and their success have rarely been reported. However, Naumann (1993a) found that the degree of fluency in the language of the host country was positively related to organizational commitment, and Nicholson and Imaizumi (1993) found that level of fluency in English was positively related to interaction adjustment for Japanese expatriates in Britain. Also with Japanese expatriates, Takeuchi and Hannon (1996) found language fluency to be positively related to willingness to communicate and to general, interaction, and work adjustment.

In his review of the sojourner adjustment literature, Church (1982) cites evidence in support of the argument that the quality of international experience may be as important as the amount in facilitating adjustment to another culture. While the amount of prior overseas experience seems to be measured frequently in studies of expatriate managers, reports of significant results are somewhat sparse. An early study by Miller (1975) indicated that prior work experience was related to need satisfaction for American expatriates. More recently, the amount of prior overseas experience was found to be positively related to general living adjustment in a study by Parker and McEvoy (1993), to all three facets of adjustment for Japanese managers by Takeuchi and Hannon (1996), and to job satisfaction in a study by Naumann (1993b). Also, Dunbar (1992) found that American managers with prior experience abroad were more likely to use appropriate intercultural behaviors. Interestingly, Black and Gregersen (1990) found that previous overseas experience was negatively related to the amount of role discretion reported by expatriates.

This review suggests that both language fluency and prior overseas experience may be important to expatriate success. However, the particular elements of success to which these antecedents apply and the mechanisms through which they operate have not been clearly articulated. The intuitively appealing notion that foreign language fluency and previous overseas experience are positively related to expatriate success seems, at best, to be an oversimplification of the relationship. The likelihood is that the relationship between language fluency and expatriate effectiveness is not linear. For example, anecdotal evidence suggests that the return for a small amount of foreign language knowledge (knowing a few words) is great, but that to achieve substantial additional benefit a significant degree of language fluency (the ability to develop conversational currency) is required. A similar relationship might be posited for overseas experience with the additional recognition that all overseas experiences are not identical and that the ability of individuals to learn from prior overseas experiences might be highly variable. Additionally, the effects of these two variables are likely to be influenced by the amount of intercultural interaction required by the assignment and the degree of cultural novelty in the situation.

Nationality of Expatriates

Early studies of foreign student adjustment (for a review, see Church 1982) indicated that nationality of the sojourner was an important variable. While the vast majority of research on the expatriate experience has been conducted with Americans, some evidence regarding national differences has been presented. For example, Tung (1981) reported lower failure rates (premature return) for Europeans and Japanese than for American expatriates. Similarly, Enderwick and Hodgson (1993) found that New Zealand expatriates were significantly less likely to return prematurely than were Americans. In two direct comparisons, Dunbar (1994) found that German expatriates living in Japan reported significantly greater cultural skill and knowledge, job satisfaction, and lower operational challenges than did American expatriates in Japan, and Stening and Hammer (1992) found significant differences in the self perceived effectiveness of Japanese and American expatriates in Thailand. These results suggest that the cultural background of the expatriates themselves, as well as the characteristics of the foreign culture, may influence some aspects of their effectiveness. However, theoretical development as to why these differences might exist has lagged the empirical findings. Consistent with the suggestion by Peterson et al. (1995), it is suggested here that specific analysis of the effects of the national culture of the expatriate on the expatriate experience is a requirement of future research.

Gender of Expatriates

Recently, the possible effect of the gender of the expatriate manager has become a salient issue. However, Adler (1987, p. 169) notes that "about the single most uncontroversial, incontrovertible statement to make about women in international management is that there are very few of them." Indeed, recent estimates suggest that perhaps less than 3% of expatriates are female (Adler, 1984; Brewster, 1991). However, the profile of the typical female expatriate suggests that the small number of female expatriates might be the beginning of a trend. A survey of 52 women expatriates in Asia reported: an average age of 28.8 years; 62% were single; almost all had a graduate degree; they were in very junior positions; and they spoke 2.5 languages on average. Ninety percent were the first women in the overseas position, with 22% of those being the first female manager expatriated anywhere by their firm (Adler, 1987). A very similar profile was reported in a study of 45 female expatriates in Hong Kong (Westwood & Leung, 1994). Adler (1984) surveyed international personnel managers from sixty American and Canadian companies concerning their perceptions of barriers to women expatriates. Fifty-four percent indicated that their firm would hesitate in sending a women on an expatriate assignment. In order, the personnel managers listed foreigner's prejudice against women (72.7%), dual careers (69.1%), selection bias (53.8%), women not interested (24.5%), women unqualified (18.2%), and women not effective (5.6%) as factors preventing women from becoming expatriates (Adler, 1984). These results are consistent with previous findings that top managers feel that women face significant resistance when seeking overseas assignments (Thal & Cateora, 1979). However, a survey of 1,129 graduating MBAs from the United States, Canada, and Europe indicated that male and female MBA graduates were equally interested in international careers (Adler, 1986). Also, women are more likely to find an expatriate experience in large firms and with financial institutions (Adler, 1984).

A central issue in the research on women expatriates has been the extent to which women face greater difficulty overseas than men. Surveys have generally indicated the preference of overseas business people for dealing with male executives (e.g., Izraeli, Banai, & Zeira, 1980). Stone (1991) reported differences among Asian and Australian managers with regard to their attitudes toward women expatriates. In Westwood and Leung's (1994) survey of 45 female expatriates in Hong Kong, 62% reported that sex discrimination was higher overseas than at home, and 58% reported that they had encountered some form of overt discriminatory behavior. However, some research has suggested that being female can be an advantage overseas. Adler's (1987) survey of 52 women expatriates in Asia indicated that 42% felt that being female was an advantage, 22% found it irrelevant, 16% said that being female had both positive and negative effects, and 20% found it primarily negative. Anecdotal reports suggest that advantages may accrue to women because they are small in number and are therefore highly visible, they are afforded higher status because of their uniqueness, or because they have better interpersonal skills than men (Adler, 1987; Taylor & Napier, 1996; Westwood & Leung, 1994). Female expatriates seem to have generally positive feelings about the expatriate assignment with 97% in Adler's (1987) sample saying their assignment was a success, and 86% of Westwood and Leung's (1994) respondents feeling that their overseas assignment would enhance their career.

If women managers as a whole are an under-researched group, this is particularly true of women expatriates. The small number of studies that have been conducted are largely descriptive or anecdotal in nature and have focused on the reasons why there are so few women expatriates. While a number of more recent articles on women expatriates can be found, careful examination reveals that they are largely based on empirical evidence first reported in a very few studies in the mid 1980s.

Antal and Izraeli (1993) suggest that a greater presence of women in the expatriate community in future may result from recent developments such as a shortage of qualified men, legal and social pressure for equal opportunity, the increasing familiarity with women in management positions, and the increasing ability of women to self-select for an overseas assignment because of changing company attitudes. Whether this prediction is correct or not, much more work is needed to understand the issues surrounding the placement of women in overseas positions.

Job and Organizational Factors

In addition to characteristics of individuals, several job and organizational variables have been shown to be related to expatriate success. Job-related variables have most often been operationalized in terms of role characteristics: role novelty, role ambiguity, role discretion, role conflict, and role overload. The job level of the expatriate has also received some attention. The organizational factors that have received a significant amount of attention are the degree of training provided to the expatriate and, relatedly, the amount of realism of the expatriate's prior knowledge about the assignment.

Expatriate Job Characteristics

The argument for inclusion of job characteristics in the study of expatriate success stems from the idea that an expatriate assignment involves the adjustment to a new role as well as to a new environment (Black, 1988). Consistent with the literature on domestic job changes (e.g., Feldman & Brett, 1983) and role theory (Sarbin & Allen, 1968), several role characteristics appear to have negative effects on expatriate success. Specifically, work adjustment has been found to be negatively related to role ambiguity (Black, 1988, 1990a, 1990b; Black & Gregersen, 1991a; Takeuchi & Hannon, 1996), role novelty (Black, 1990b; Nicholson & Imaizumi, 1993; Stroh et al., 1994) and to role conflict (Black, 1990b; Black & Gregersen, 1991a; Takeuchi & Hannon, 1996), and positively related to intent to remain (Black, 1990a). Role overload (Takeuchi & Hannon, 1996) has also been found to be negatively related to work adjustment. Interestingly, however, workload levels have been found to be negatively related to intent to leave (Birdseye & Hill, 1995). Naumann (1993a, 1993b) found a negative relationship between role ambiguity and job satisfaction, a negative relationship between role conflict and job satisfaction (Naumann, 1993b) and a negative relationship between organizational commitment (Naumann, 1993a) and both role ambiguity and role conflict. Also, consistent with role theory, role discretion has been found to be positively related to work adjustment (Black, 1988, 1990b; Black & Gregersen, 1991a) and negatively related to intent to leave (Black, 1990b).

In general, these results suggest that, as expected, work role characteristics have an influence on the work adjustment of expatriates. However, in some cases role characteristics have shown some spill over effect on other facets of adjustment. Specifically, a positive relationship between role discretion and general adjustment (Black, 1990a) a negative relationship between role ambiguity and both general and interaction adjustment (Black, 1990b; Takeuchi & Hannon, 1996) and a negative relationship between role conflict and all three adjustment factors (Black, 1990b) have been recorded.

Some prior research suggests that the organizational level of job changers influences the types of strategies available to them to deal with the effects of moving to a new role (Feldman & Brett, 1983) and hence on the probability of favorable outcomes. With regard to expatriates, the organizational level of the expatriate has been found to be positively related to satisfaction (Feldman & Tompson, 1993), intent to remain (Feldman & Tompson, 1993; Gregersen & Black, 1990), and self reports of performance (Feldman & Tompson, 1993), but negatively related to work adjustment (Gregersen & Black, 1990), and, for Japanese expatriates, negatively related to interaction and general adjustment (Takeuchi & Hannon, 1996). These results raise further issues regarding the multidimensional nature of the adjustment construct and the notion of variable effects of antecedents on different adjustment factors. While the role characteristics of the expatriate seem an important avenue for understanding the expatriate experience, comprehensive models that link antecedents of role characteristics through to outcomes are rare (e.g., Thomas, 1994) and have not been empirically tested.

Organizational Factors

Organizational factors that have been found to influence expatriate success include the amount of organizational support provided expatriates and their families, the extent to which the expatriate was provided with realistic information about the country and the assignment and the amount of cross-cultural training provided. Of these factors, the amount of training provided expatriates has received the most attention.

The conventional wisdom regarding cross-cultural training of expatriates seems to be that while the positive effect on sojourners is well-documented (e.g., Landis & Brislin, 1983), firms often fail to provide such training because of a belief that it is not effective (Mendenhall & Oddou, 1985). The failure of firms to provide extensive cross-cultural training has been documented in empirical studies in a number of different countries (e.g., Domsch & Lichtenberger, 1991; Enderwick & Hodgson, 1993; Tung, 1981). Regarding the effectiveness of cross-cultural training programs, Black and Mendenhall (1990), in a review of 29 empirical studies, found broad support for a positive relationship between cross-cultural training and outcomes related to expatriate effectiveness. Specifically, they found that of the studies examining the effect of training on self-oriented skills (9), adjustment (9), relationships with host nationals (19), and perceptual skills (16) all found a positive relationship. Of the 15 studies that examined the relationship between training and performance eleven found a positive relationship (Black & Mendenhall, 1990). In a meta-analysis of 21 studies, Deshpande and Viswesvaran (1992) found that cross-cultural training had a positive correlation with self-development, perceptual skills, relational skills, adjustment, and performance. Subsequent studies have been largely confirmatory of these findings (e.g., Brewster & Pickard, 1994; Naumann, 1993a, 1993b). Therefore, the empirical research generally supports the effectiveness of cross-cultural training on outcomes related to expatriate success. However, the literature reviewed tends to treat cross-cultural training as an undifferentiated entity without regard to differences in training types, such as informational training, area studies, cultural awareness training, and intercultural skills training. In a review of these four training types, Kealey and Protheroe (1996, p. 161) conclude " ... that no study of expatriates has yet been done which measures the longer term results of training for expatriates and which is designed so as to eliminate alternative explanations for performance levels overseas." Also, the possible contingent nature of different types of training is less clear. Despite the advocacy of combining cognitive and experiential approaches to cross-cultural training (Bird, Heinbuch, Dunbar, & McNulty, 1993; Earley, 1987; Harrison, 1992), theoretical models which suggest that different approaches to cross-cultural training will be effective in different circumstances (Gudykunst & Hammer, 1983; Tung, 1981), and the question of the appropriateness of predeparture versus in country training (Black & Mendenhall, 1989), little empirical research has addressed these issues.

Related to the issue of cross-cultural training is the extent to which the expatriate has an accurate or realistic conception of the situation to which s/he is moving. According to the literature on the realistic job preview (e.g., Meglino & DeNisi, 1987) one would anticipate that realistic expectations by the expatriate would be related to positive outcomes. That is, accurate information about the environment provides the opportunity for expatriates to make anticipatory adjustments (Gullahorn & Gullahorn, 1963). Feldman and Tompson (1993) found a positive relationship between the extent to which expatriates received a realistic preview and their overall satisfaction. Similarly, Stroh et al. (1994) found a positive relationship between accurate job expectations and expatriate adjustment and job satisfaction, and Black (1990b) found a positive relationship between expatriates predeparture knowledge about the host country and all the facets of expatriate adjustment. Black and Gregersen (1990) found that over met expectations about the environment were positively related to general satisfaction and over met expectations about job discretion were positively related to work satisfaction. Consistent with the findings regarding role clarity and role expectations, these results emphasize the relationship of uncertainty reduction as an important consideration in the expatriate experience.

A third organizational factor that has been found to be related to elements of expatriate success is the extent of organizational support received by expatriates. As one measure of organizational support, Black (1990b) found that the amount of contact (through visits to headquarters, letters, telexes) that expatriates had with the parent company was positively related to some facets of adjustment. DeCieri, Dowling, and Taylor (1991) found that the level of company assistance was a significant predictor of psychological adjustment in a study of Australian expatriate spouses. Stroh et al. (1994) found the level of organizational support positively related to expatriate job satisfaction. In an exploratory study of dual career expatriates, Harvey's (1997) findings confirm that organizational support is positively related to expatriate job satisfaction, but also indicate that the support requirements of dual career couples are unique. Guzzo et al. (1994) exposed the complicated nature of the relationship of the expatriate to the organization with their finding that expatriate's commitment to the organization mediated the relationship between perceived organizational support and intent to quit.

Environmental Factors

A number of factors external to the expatriate and over which he/she has little control have been shown to influence his/her success. Of these, the novelty or toughness of the new culture and the amount of social support available have received some attention in the empirical literature.

Cultural Novelty

The extent to which the host country culture is different from the expatriate's home culture has been theorized to make the adjustment process more difficult (Church 1982; Mendenhall & Oddou, 1985). Consistent with this idea, empirical studies of expatriates have found that cultural novelty is negatively related to interaction adjustment (Black & Stephens, 1989; Parker & McEvoy, 1993), general adjustment (Black & Stephens, 1989; Stroh et al., 1994), willingness to accept an assignment (Aryee, Chay, & Chew, 1996), intent to stay (Black & Stephens, 1989) and positively related to social difficulty (Ward & Kennedy, 1993). Satisfaction with the environment was also found to be negatively related to turnover tendencies (Birdseye & Hill, 1995). However, the empirical support for the negative effect of cultural novelty on outcomes is not universal. Parker and McEvoy (1993) found a positive relationship between cultural novelty and general adjustment for a sample somewhat atypical from that usually studied in that it was somewhat younger and included forty three percent women. Similarly, Black and Gregersen (1991a) found a positive relationship between cultural novelty and general adjustment but a negative relationship to interaction adjustment for American expatriates in Asia. In a study of Japanese expatriates by Takeuchi and Hannon (1996), cultural novelty was positively related to all three facets of adjustment. Similarly, Janssens (1995) found that cultural novelty was positively related to level of intercultural interaction for Europeans on assignment in Europe, North America and Asia. These contradictory findings suggest the possibility of mediating processes between cultural novelty and the outcomes specified. For example, in the Takeuchi and Hannon (1996) study, the environmental differences encountered by Japanese in the United States may have resulted in overmet expectations which influenced their perceptions of adjustment difficulties. In any case, these contradictory findings suggest the need for further exploration of the mechanisms through which cultural novelty influences the expatriate experience.

Social Support

The logic behind the effect of social support on the expatriate experience is that being able to draw on social relationships provides a mechanism for dealing with the stress associated with an overseas assignment. Social support from host nationals has been found to be positively related to interaction adjustment (Black, 1990a) and general adjustment (Black, 1990a) and, in a later study, to all three facets of adjustment (Black & Gregersen, 1991a). Social support from home country nations was positively related to work adjustment (Black & Gregersen, 1991a) and all three facets of adjustment (Black, 1990a). Thus, the empirical results generally support the direct positive effect of social support on adjustment. Also, some differences in the nature of the social support of expatriates and their spouses has been documented. For example, Briody and Chrisman (1991) found that expatriates derived their social support primarily from host country nationals while spouses interacted primarily with home country nationals.

Repatriation

The notion that reentry to one's home country after a long sojourn requires a process of adjustment similar to that of the initial transfer overseas has long been recognized (Gullahorn & Gullahorn, 1963). Additionally, some authors (Black et al., 1992; Feldman & Thomas, 1992) argue that repatriation is distinct, both in degree and kind, from other types of job-related geographic transfers. First, the degree of novelty (cultural, organizational, job, etc.) is higher for a transfer between as compared to within a country. Second, in the repatriation situation, the individual is returning to their home country after a period of absence of typically two to five years for Americans and British (Black & Gregersen, 1991b), and potentially longer for Germans or Japanese (Peterson et al., 1995). During this time both the individual and the home country have undergone changes largely independent of each other. Unlike the domestic job changer, the repatriate is likely to be confronted with these changes all at the same time. Also, for most expatriates, the repatriate experience is qualitatively different from the expatriate experience. That is, most repatriates (80% according to Black & Gregersen, 1991b) are returning home from an assignment in a country in which they had little or no prior experience. Therefore, their prior knowledge and expectations about the country they are moving to are likely to be substantially different in the case of repatriation versus expatriation.

While the practitioner literature has recognized the repatriation problem for some time (e.g., Clague & Krupp, 1978; Murray, 1978) little empirical work regarding repatriation exists. Some anecdotal evidence suggests that the adjustment during repatriation is more difficult than during expatriation and that reentry adjustment follows a somewhat different pattern than expatriate adjustment (Adler, 1981). Also, expatriates have generally reported dissatisfaction with the repatriation process (Gomez-Mejia & Balkin, 1987; Napier & Peterson, 1991).

In one of the few studies to directly examine repatriation adjustment Black and Gregersen (1991b) found that, for American expatriates, work adjustment was positively related to role discretion and role clarity, and negatively related to time overseas, social status and housing conditions; interaction adjustment was positively related to age and role discretion, and negatively related to total years overseas and housing conditions; and general adjustment was positively related to age and role discretion, and negatively related to total years overseas, social status and housing conditions. These results were largely confirmed in a replication with a sample 173 Japanese expatriates who had recently returned from a foreign assignment (Black, 1994). In summarizing results, the possibility that factors that facilitate expatriate adjustment may in turn inhibit repatriation is noted by the authors (Black, 1994; Black & Gregersen, 1991b). For example, the improved housing conditions that most expatriates experience overseas may help them cope, but the drop in housing conditions on return has a negative effect. Likewise, the longer employees are overseas the more difficult is their adjustment on return. However, other research (e.g., Black, 1988; Tung, 1988) suggests that it takes one or two years to adjust and become effective in a foreign assignment.

In a study of 174 repatriated Americans, Gregersen (1992) found that commitment to the parent organization was positively related to tenure with the firm, level of repatriation compensation, and the value that the firm placed on international experience, but negatively related to the repatriate's years of international experience. Interestingly, the number of years of international experience has previously been shown to be positively related to commitment to a local foreign operation but not related to the commitment to the parent company while on assignment (Gregersen & Black, 1990). Noted by the author is the possibility of different antecedents to commitment by expatriates from different cultures (Luthans, McCaul, & Dodd, 1985; Near, 1989).

Reports that expatriates are often neglected on their return, put in holding patterns, and that their international experience is not valued by their firms have been noted by a number of authors (e.g., Adler, 1981; Feldman & Thomas, 1992; Harvey, 1989; Tung, 1981). However, as shown here, the systematic study of the repatriation process has received very minimal attention. The empirical results that have been reported demonstrate the possibility of contradictory relationships between some antecedent factors and the expatriate versus the repatriate experience.

Expatriate Careers

As opposed to treating expatriation and repatriation as isolated incidents, some recent literature has considered the relationship of the expatriate experience to the individual's overall career path (e.g., Feldman, 1991; Feldman & Thomas, 1992; Oddou & Mendenhall, 1991; Stephens, 1994). In general, expatriate assignments do not seem to have had positive effects on managerial career development. Adler (1981) reports that four out of five expatriates leave the firm upon reentry and that graduating MBA's (Adler, 1987) perceive an international assignment as a risky career move. Oddou and Mendenhall (1991) found that, while an international assignment facilitated the individual's movement to a higher career stage (Dalton & Thompson, 1986), in general, expatriates reported that their overseas assignment has not had a positive long-term effect on their career, that their firms don't take advantage of the skills they learned overseas, and that their assignments were better for their personal development than for their professional careers. However, the extent to which the expatriate assignment fits with career plans seems to influence effectiveness while on assignment. Feldman and Thomas (1992) found that perceiving a connection between the expatriate assignment and long-term career plans was positively related to overall performance, relationships with host nationals, skill acquisition, intent to remain, job satisfaction, and mutual influence, and was negatively related to psychological stress. Similarly, the intention to remain on assignment has been found to be positively related to the extent to which the expatriate assignment fits with the individual's overall career plan (Feldman & Tompson, 1993) and the extent to which the assignment was perceived as a promotion (Birdseye & Hill, 1995). Also, the extent to which the expatriate assignment fits with career goals and the perception that the expatriate assignment would have a positive impact on career was found to be positively related to both satisfaction with the expatriate assignment and with the repatriation process in a study of 89 American expatriates (Gomez-Mejia & Balkin, 1987). With regard to the effect of spouse's career on expatriation, Stephens and Black (1991) found that expatriates whose spouse had given up a significant salary in the United States were less committed to their assignment in Japan. The organizational reason for the expatriate assignment has also been shown to be related to career outcomes. Dunbar and Ehrlich (1993) found that expatriates who were sent abroad for their own development were more career satisfied than those sent overseas for organizational change or to fill a vacant position.

As shown in this review, research that deals with the expatriate experience in terms of the individual's career is somewhat limited. Much is still to be discovered about the factors that influence the impact that expatriate assignments have on the long-term career development of managers. Additionally, the empirical results to date which relate to longer term career issues deal exclusively with American expatriates. Importantly, as found by Granrose (1994), career patterns, career goals, career tactics, and career plans may vary according to the national culture of the individual.

GENERALIZATIONS AND CONTRADICTIONS

In attempting to generalize from the body of literature it was hoped to establish those relationships that are 'given' as a basis for a paradigm defining the expatriate experience. What was found, however, was a striking number of contradictions. It is these contradictions or paradoxes that largely define the state of the literature on the expatriate experience. In the following section these contradictions are described with regard to the level of analysis (individual, organizational, environmental) to which the issue applies and are summarized in Table 2. Following these descriptions a synthesis of the literature into a framework, that incorporates these level of analysis issues is offered. Finally, a discussion of the methodological limitations of the research is presented.

Contradictions at the Individual Level

Perhaps the most pervasive contradiction discovered is what might be called the adjustment-performance paradox. The relationship between expatriate adjustment

Table 2. Summary of Contradictions or Paradoxes

Individual Level	
• A direct positive relationship exists between expatriate adjustment and effectiveness	• The same characteristics that make an expatriate effective also make it more difficult to adjust
• Married expatriates adjust better	• The main reason for expatriate failure is the failure of the spouse to adjust
• Bias against selecting women for overseas postings	• Women may be more suited and better prepared for expatriate roles
Organizational Level	
• Firms select expatriates on technical skill with little regard for the effect on their career	• Expatriates accept overseas postings primarily to advance their career
• Expatriates report significant personal development as a result of their overseas experience	• Firms rarely recognize or utilize the expatriate's newly acquired skill
• Organizational support makes expatriate adjustment easier	• Organizational support for expatriates makes repatriation more difficult
• Cross-cultural training is effective on a number of areas related to effectiveness overseas	• Firms fail to train (lack of a belief in effectiveness or the effectiveness of different training methods not known)
Environmental Level	
• Cultural difference between home and host cultures results in adjustment difficulties	• Cultural novelty may facilitate certain types of adjustment

and expatriate performance has been assumed to be a direct positive one and this assumption underlies a great deal of empirical research. However, this review of empirical research did not indicate overwhelming support for this assumption (e.g., Parker & McEvoy, 1993). In fact, it seems possible that, as first described by Ruben and Kealey (1979), the highest performing expatriates may also be those who experience the most severe culture shock and have the most difficult time adjusting. That is, the same characteristics that allow expatriates to be effective (e.g., others orientation, perceptual skills) may make it more stressful to adjust.

A second individual characteristic which seems to have a paradoxical relationship to expatriate success is the family situation of the expatriate. This review suggested that married expatriates adjust better than do single expatriates and that social support (potentially provided by the spouse in some cases) is also important to expatriate adjustment. However, substantial evidence exists to suggest that the main reason for an expatriate's premature return to their home country is the failure of their family (spouse) to adjust (Black, 1988, 1990a; Black & Gregersen, 1991a; Black & Stephens, 1989; Nicholson & Imaizumi, 1993; Stroh et al., 1994). This apparent paradox suggests that the relationship between the expatriate's family situation and their effectiveness is likely to be much more complex than has been conceptualized to date.

A third contradiction at the individual level of analysis has to do with the gender of the expatriate. Very few expatriates are women and there seems to be a bias against selecting women for overseas assignments. However, this review suggested that women expatriates are likely to be more highly educated and better prepared for expatriate assignments than their male counterparts. Additionally, women's management styles (Davidson & Cooper, 1987; Freedman & Phillips, 1988) seem to be more consistent with the relational and perceptual abilities that some authors (e.g., Mendenhall & Oddou, 1985) suggest are required for overseas effectiveness. As the presence of women in management roles in general and the expatriate role in particular increases, the need to understand the issues involved in placing women overseas will certainly increase.

A final important individual difference issue involves the national culture of the expatriate. The vast majority of expatriate studies have been limited to studying Americans abroad. However, in the few studies involving other nationalities cultural differences have had a sometimes contradictory effect on a variety of outcomes. For example, the reasons for staffing with expatriates, selection criteria for expatriates, failure rates as measured by premature return, relationship between adjustment and performance, and antecedents to organizational commitment have all been shown to vary by nationality. These results, coupled with increased globalization, dictate that the examination of the experiences of non-U.S. expatriates must be expanded.

Organizational Level Contradictions

The first contradiction related to organizational factors has to do with differences in the expectations between the firm and the expatriate. The characteristics of a firm which lead it to staff a particular sub unit with expatriates have only partly been explored (e.g., Boyacigiller, 1990) and these characteristics may vary substantially depending on the national origin of the firm. What does seem relatively clear, however, is that firms tend to select expatriates on their ability to fill a technical requirement with little regard for the effect on the expatriate's career. However, expatriates accept overseas assignments primarily to advance their career and are more effective and satisfied if they see the connection between the expatriate assignment and their career. Also, the clarity of the role expectations that the firm has for the expatriate seem to have a significant relationship to expatriate experience (e.g., Black, 1988, 1990a; Black & Gregersen, 1991a; Takeuchi & Hannon, 1996). The possible negative impact effect of the expatriate assignment on the expatriate's career leads to the next contradiction.

Expatriates report considerable individual development along a wide range of skill and knowledge dimensions as a result of their overseas assignment. However, upon return to their home country, their newly won skills are rarely utilized and the net effect of the expatriate assignment is often described as having a neutral to negative effect on their long-term career. Additionally, while it can take several years for an expatriate to become truly effective longer tenure overseas results in more difficult repatriation. These effects have been of considerable concern with regard to the value of an expatriate assignment, given a traditional view of careers. However, the changing nature of careers suggests that careers are becoming a more fragmented set of jobs held together by a subjective sense of where one is going in one's work life (Schein, 1996). This newer perspective suggests that the addition of international experience to an individual's competency profile may change the nature of the relationship between overseas experience and career. That is, individuals may be motivated to accept an overseas assignment for self development reasons with the knowledge that some short-term benefits may be sacrificed for longer term career goals.

Perhaps the most studied organizational factor related to the expatriate experience is the amount of cross-cultural training provided. That cross-cultural training is effective, but that firms fail to avail themselves of it, is almost axiomatic in the expatriate literature. While it seems clear that cross-cultural training can have very positive benefits, our review found that the examination of the effectiveness of training may have been oversimplified. That is, despite theoretical expositions that suggest that different approaches to cross-cultural training may be effective in different circumstances and questions of pre-departure versus in-country training, these issues have not been examined. Also, it would be naive to suggest that the quality of cross-cultural training was consistent across programs or that quality does not have an impact on effectiveness. Perhaps organizations aren't all that ill advised in being suspicious of cross-cultural training after all.

Contradictions at the Environmental Level

At the environmental level it is the degree of cultural difference between the home and host culture that provides interesting contradictory findings. The logic that the greater the differences between one's home and host country the greater the adjustment difficulties has been supported in a number of studies (e.g., Black & Stephens, 1989; Stroh et al., 1994). However, contradictory results exist (e.g., Black & Gregersen, 1991a; Parker & McEvoy, 1993; Takeuchi & Hannon, 1996) suggesting that cultural novelty may facilitate certain types of adjustment. The relationship of cultural novelty to the expatriate experience is clearly not as simple as it has often been portrayed. It seems possible that a number of variables, such as the expectation that expatriates have about the foreign environment, might mediate the relationship.

In summary, the review of the literature on expatriation failed to yield the law like generalizations which are necessary for the foundation of a paradigm. Instead, what was presented was a somewhat fragmented body of literature which is fraught with contradictions. This is probably the result of the somewhat atheoretical nature of the study of expatriation. Research in this area has been motivated in large measure by the desire to solve the practical problem of high expatriate failure rates with the attendant high cost. What is required is a more scientific approach to the phenomenon that is concerned with understanding the nature of the relationships among variables in the specific domain of the expatriate experience. To facilitate this development the following section presents a synthesis of the existing empirical literature in a framework on which mid-range theory and empirical investigations can be based.

SYNTHESIS

At present, despite some notable contributions (e.g., Black et al., 1991; Mendenhall & Oddou, 1985), theory remains underdeveloped and relies on the application of concepts from other areas such as organizational job change (Feldman, 1976; Nicholson & West, 1988), domestic relocation (Brett & Reilly, 1988), or sojourner adjustment (Church, 1982). While the application of theory from other domains has yielded useful insights, it is suggested that what is needed is a theoretical framework that recognizes the multiple outcomes of the expatriate experience, that considers the idea that these outcomes may have a variety of different antecedents, and that captures the longitudinal nature of the phenomenon. Figure 1 outlines a framework that is presented as the basis for this theoretical development.

As shown in Figure 1, the domain of the expatriate experience encompasses both the firm's experience with staffing with expatriates and the expatriate's experience with the overseas assignment. The research on expatriation implicitly or explicitly recognizes that both the organizational context and characteristics of the individual must be considered in order to understand behavior in an organization. An obvious addition to the framework is consideration of environmental characteristics that vary because of the international nature of the phenomenon of interest. Therefore, it is suggested that outcomes of expatriation are contingent on individual, organizational, and environmental level variables. The specific variables identified in the model are indicative and it is not suggested that they exhaust the possibilities. However, they are presented as a set of items that clearly require consideration in future empirical work.

The second stage of the model identifies the need to consider the additive or multiplicative effects of combinations of the antecedent variables. As a very salient example, a number of differences with regard to the nationality of expatriates were reported in this review. These results strongly suggest that the nationality of the expatriate may moderate the effect of several of the variables related to both the firm's use of expatriates and individual's experience with expatriation. Another example is provided with regard to the level or type of organizational support provided to expatriates. Organizational support programs can be classified

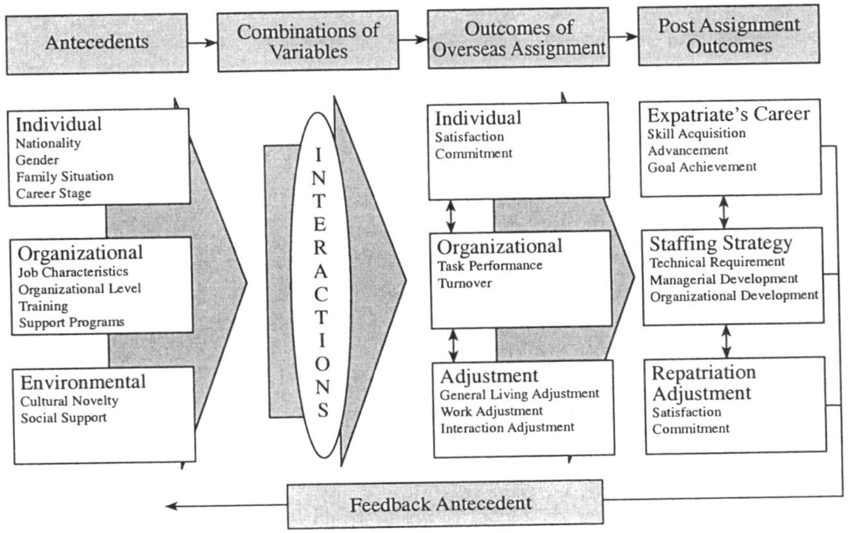

Figure 1. Conceptual Framework of the Expatriate Experience

into three categories; financial inducements, general support, and family support (Guzzo et al., 1994). However, to date no attempt has been made to consider critical individual characteristics of the expatriate that may affect the success of different programs. These two examples are suggestive of the type of interactive effects that must be considered to systematically develop a body of knowledge regarding the expatriate experience.

The third stage of the model concerns those outcomes related to the experience of the expatriate while on assignment. Of these, as shown in this review, expatriate adjustment has received the most attention. While adjustment may be a critical factor with regard to the expatriate experience, the assumption made in much of the literature, that adjustment mediates the relationship between antecedents and other first level outcomes is absent here. Instead, it is suggested that adjustment is related to both individual and organizational outcomes, but that the specific nature of that relationship must be established based on the variability of the antecedent conditions. Specifically the nature of the relationship of adjustment to task performance has been called into question in this review. Also, variables such as task performance and turnover, while obviously related to the individual expatriate are categorized as organizational outcomes in this framework. The rationale is that these types of outcomes are of primary concern from the perspective of the firm's experience in staffing with expatriates.

In keeping with the need to develop more longitudinal models of expatriation, this framework extends to a fourth stage which is concerned with second stage outcomes that occur after the expatriate returns from the overseas assignment. Both repatriation adjustment and the effect of an expatriate assignment on the manager's career have received a small amount of recent attention. However, the extent to which the expatriate's experience and the firm's experience with expatriates influence staffing strategy is uncharted territory. As was suggested earlier in this review, the factors which might motivate the firm to staff with an expatriate have only been partially explored. Also, it is this staffing decision that completes the cycle of the expatriate experience and contributes to the determination of the individual, organizational, and environmental antecedents identified as the first stage of the framework. That is, post assignment outcomes identified can just as easily be the starting point of the cycle as the end. For example, staffing strategies determine such organizational level antecedents as job characteristics and training programs and the effect of an overseas experience on an individual's repatriation and career advancement influence the composition of the pool of applicants for subsequent overseas assignments.

The purpose of the framework presented here has been to synthesize the literature on expatriation in a manner that identifies the domain of the topic and specifies the categories of variables to be considered in order to facilitate further theoretical development and provide insight into areas requiring additional investigation. The framework suggests that the expatriate experience can be conceptualized as a cycle involving three levels of variables and that these variables interact to form the network of relationships that is the expatriate experience. Appropriate research questions concern the specific relationships among the variables presented in the framework. Implicit in this framework is that both the firm and the expatriate have an interest in understanding the nature of the expatriate experience and that these perspectives, while different, are related to the extent that they can be captured under the general categories of variables presented above. The following are examples of the types of research questions that are facilitated by reference to the framework.

- *Interactions Among Antecedents.* Based on the review presented here a number of questions concerning the cross-level interaction among individual, organizational, and environmental variables can be posed.

  Example: How do individual level variables (nationality, gender, family situation, career stage) influence the effectiveness of organizational support programs on such first level outcomes as satisfaction, commitment and performance?

- *Relationship Among Antecedents, First, and Second Level Outcomes.* An assumption in much of the literature is that an effective expatriate assignment is positively related to post assignment outcome. However, contradictions in the literature reviewed here suggest that this relationship is not a given.

Example: To what extent does performance on assignment influence the expatriate's longer term career? Does this effect differ for individuals at different career stages?

- *Relationships Among Outcome Variables.* While the literature reviewed here suggests multiple outcomes of the expatriate experience, potentially influenced by different antecedents, it is also recognized that these variables are not orthogonal. It is, therefore, necessary that the relationship among outcome variables be investigated.

  Example: How is adjustment (or facets of adjustment) related to performance (or facets of performance)?

  Example: How does the experience of expatriates and the experience of the firm with expatriates affect the long-term staffing strategy of the firm?

The synthesis of the expatriate literature into the framework presented here was motivated by gaps in the existing literature and by contradictions or paradoxes in the empirical findings. It is intended as a vehicle to promote a more scientific, theory driven, inquiry into the expatriate experience. It is also possible, however, that some of the apparent contradictions in the expatriate literature are the result of methodological limitations. These limitations are discussed in the following section.

Methodological Limitations

The first methodological issue also takes the form of a contradiction. The most often cited reason for studying expatriates has been the high cost of expatriate turnover with various estimates of premature return from assignment and costs of turnover cited. Most often, however, these studies have gone on to examine the adjustment of the expatriate without measuring turnover directly and often without measuring intention to leave. That is, the empirical studies reviewed here often effectively changed the nature of the phenomenon under investigation in their operationalization of constructs. Also, the costs of turnover (e.g., Misa & Fabricatore, 1979) and rates of failure (Peterson et al., 1995) are, at best, very general estimates. In fact, under close scrutiny (Harzing, 1995), the often reported 'high' failure rate of expatriates is based on very questionable empirical evidence.

Other limitations in the extant literature on the expatriate experience are fairly apparent. With the exception of research on expatriate adjustment, the research has until now lacked a coordinating concept. The expatriate adjustment literature, itself, suffers from a failure to unambiguously define the term adjustment. Additionally, the vast majority of studies of expatriates have been limited to Americans, but often generalized to broader populations. As shown in this review, the nature of the expatriate experience may be very different depending on the nationality of the expatriate.

The majority of empirical studies have employed fairly unsophisticated research designs and methods. Those studies that are not purely descriptive or anecdotal have typically been cross-sectional pencil and paper surveys of expatriates on or recently returned from assignment, sometimes supplemented by interviews. The cross-sectional nature of the studies denies the longitudinal nature of the phenomenon being studied, as demonstrated in the model presented above. Often, these studies have had very low response rates with little effort made to deal with nonresponse bias. Also, in most cases, both the dependent and independent variables have been measured using the same method thereby potentially trivializing the results reported (Campbell & Stanley, 1963). Additionally, the reference to baseline data or control groups is extremely rare. Therefore, the attribution to the overseas experience of any of change reported relies on the ability of participants to accurately self-report on these matters (Nisbett & Wilson, 1977).

Also absent from this literature is any consideration of the conceptual or methodological considerations discussed in cross-cultural research (Brislin, Lonner, & Thorndike, 1973). Many of the methodological problems associated with cross-cultural research, such as construct relevance and equivalence, are appropriate to studies of expatriation, despite the fact that the study is conducted in the host culture. Additionally, essentially all expatriate studies have avoided the issues associated with translation by assuming English language proficiency of respondents. These issues will become more apparent as more studies consider expatriates of nationalities other than Americans.

More sophisticated longitudinal with control group research designs combined with such methods as in-depth interviews, intensive case studies, participant observation, and small group experiments can help to overcome some of the limitations noted. If ever a case can be made for the necessity of multiple methods the examination of the expatriate experience would seem to be it. Consistent with Malpass (1977), the basis of the solution to many of the methodological problems inherent in the expatriate literature may be the development of better theory. It is hoped, therefore, that the summary of the empirical literature and the framework presented here is a step in that direction.

ACKNOWLEDGMENTS

The author is grateful to the editors and two anonymous reviewers for their helpful comments and to Lee Ah Chong for assistance in researching the articles for the review. Some support for this research was provided by the International Business Department, The Chinese University of Hong Kong.

REFERENCES

Abe, H., & Wiseman, R. L. (1983). A cross-cultural confirmation of the dimensions of intercultural effectiveness. *International Journal of Intercultural Relations, 7*, 53-67.

Adler, N.J. (1981). Re-entry, managing cross-cultural transitions. *Group and Organization Studies, 6*, 341-356.

Adler, N.J. (1984). Women in international management: Where are they? *California Management Review, 26*, 78-89.

Adler, N.J. (1986). Do MBAs want international careers? *International Journal of Intercultural Relations, 10*, 277-300.

Adler, N.J. (1987). Pacific basin managers: A gaijin, not a woman. *Human Resource Management, 26*, 169-191.

Adler, N.J., & Ghadar, F. (1990). Strategic human resource management: A global perspective. In R. Pieper (Ed.), *Human resource management in international comparison* (pp. 235-260). Berlin: de Gruyter.

Antal, A.B., & Izraeli, D.N. (1993). A global comparison of women in management: Women managers in their homelands and as expatriates. In E.A. Gagenson (Ed.), *Women in management: Trends, issues, and challenges in managerial diversity* (Vol. 4, pp. 206-223). Newbury Park, CA: Sage.

Arthur, W., & Bennett, W. (1995). The international assignee: the relative importance of factors perceived to contribute to success. *Personnel Psychology, 48*, 99-114.

Aryee, S., Chay, Y.W., & Chew, J. (1996). An investigation of the willingness of managerial employees to accept an expatriate assignment. *Journal of Organizational Behavior, 17*, 267-283.

Baliga, B.R., & Jaeger, A. (1984). Multinational corporations: Control systems and delegation issues. *Journal of International Business Studies, 15*, 25-40.

Banai, M. & Reisel, W. D. 1993. Expatriate managers' loyalty to the MNC: Myth or reality? An exploratory study. *Journal of International Business Studies, 24*, 233-248.

Beechler, S. (1992, November). International management control in multinational corporations: The case of Japanese consumer electronics firms in Asia. *OECD Economic Journal*, pp. 20-31.

Beechler, S.L., & Iaquinto, A.L. (1994). *A longitudinal study of staffing patterns in U.S. affiliates of Japanese transnational corporations*. Paper presented to the International Management Division of the Academy of Management, Dallas, TX.

Benson, P.G. (1978). Measuring cross-cultural adjustment: The problem of criteria. *International Journal of Intercultural Relations, 2*(1), 21-37.

Bird, A., Heinbuch, S., Dunbar, R,. & McNulty, M. (1993). A conceptual model of the effects of area studies training programs and a preliminary investigation of the model's hypothesized relationships. *International Journal of Intercultural Relations, 17*, 415-436.

Birdseye, M., & Hill, J.S. (1995). Individual, organizational/work and environmental influences on expatriate turnover tendencies: An empirical study. *Journal of International Business Studies, 26*(4), 787-813.

Black, J.S. (1988). Work role transitions: A study of American expatriate managers in Japan. *Journal of International Business Studies, 19*, 277-294.

Black, J.S. (1990a). Locus of control, social support, stress and adjustment in international transfers. *Asia Pacific Journal of Management, 7*(1), 1-29.

Black, J.S. (1990b). Factors related to the adjustment of Japanese expatriate managers in America. *Journal of Management Studies, 28*, 417-427.

Black, J.S. 1994. O Kaerinasai: Factors related to Japanese repatriation adjustment. *Human Relations, 47*(12), 1489-1508.

Black, J.S., & Gregersen, H.B. (1990). Expectations, satisfaction and intention to leave of American expatriate managers in Japan. *International Journal of Intercultural Relations, 14*, 485-506.

Black, J. S. ,& Gregersen, H.B. (1991a). Antecedents to cross-cultural adjustment for expatriates in Pacific Rim assignments. *Human Relations*, *44*(5), 497-515.

Black, J.S., & Gregersen, H., B. (1991b). When Yankee comes home: Factors related to expatriate and spouse repatriation adjustment. *Journal of International Business Studies*, *21*(4), 671-694.

Black, J.S., Gregersen, H.B., & Mendenhall, M.E. (1992). Toward a theoretical framework of repatriation adjustment. *Journal of International Business Studies*, *22*(3), 737-760.

Black, J.S., & Mendenhall, M. (1989). A practical but theory-based framework for selecting cross-cultural training methods. *Human Resource Management*, *28*(4), 511-539.

Black, J.S., & Mendenhall, M. (1990). Cross-cultural training effectiveness: A review and a theoretical framework for future research. *Academy of Management Review*, *15*, 113-136.

Black, J.S., & Mendenhall, M. (1991). The U-curve adjustment hypothesis revisited: A review and theoretical framework. *Journal of International Business Studies*, *22*, 225-247.

Black, J.S., Mendenhall, M., & Oddou, G. (1991). Toward a comprehensive model of international adjustment: an integration of multiple theoretical perspectives. *Academy of Management Review*, *16*(2), 291-317.

Black, J.S. & Porter, L.W. (1991). Managerial behaviors and job performance: A successful manager in Los Angeles may not succeed in Hong Kong. *Journal of International Business Studies*, *22*(1), 99-114.

Black, J.S. & Stephens, G.K. (1989). The influence of the spouse on American expatriate adjustment and intent to stay in Pacific Rim overseas assignments. *Journal of Management*, *15*(4), 529-544.

Borrmann, W.A. (1968). The problem of expatriate personnel and their selection in international enterprises. *Management International Review*, *8*(4-5), 37-48.

Boyacigiller, N. (1990). The role of expatriates in the management of interdependence, complexity and risk in multinational corporations. *Journal of International Business Studies*, *21*(4), 357-381.

Brein, D., & David, K.H. (1971). Intercultural communication and the adjustment of the sojourner. *Psychological Bulletin*, *76*(3), 215-230.

Brett, J.M., & Reilly, A.H. (1988). On the road again: Predicting the job transfer decision. *Journal of Applied Psychology*, *73*, 614-620.

Brett, J.M., Stroh, L.K., & Reilly, A.H. (1993). Pulling up roots in the 1990s: Who's willing to relocate? *Journal of Organizational Behavior*, *14*, 49-60.

Brett, J.M., & Werbel, J.D. (1980). *The effect of job transfers on employees and their families: Final report*. Washington, DC: Employee Relocation Council.

Brewster, C. (1991). *The management of expatriates*. London: Kogan Page.

Brewster, C., & Pickard, J. (1994). Evaluating expatriate training. *International Studies of Management and Organization*, *24*(3), 18-35.

Briody, E.K., & Chrisman, J.B. (1991). Cultural adaptation on overseas assignments. *Human Organization*, *50*(3), 264-282.

Brislin, R.W., Lonner, W.J., & Thorndike, R.M. (1973). *Cross-cultural research methods*. New York: Wiley.

Campbell, D.T., & Stanley, J.C. (1963). *Experimental and quasi-experimental designs for research*. Chicago: Rand McNally.

Church, A.T. (1982). Sojourner adjustment. *Psychological Bulletin*, *91*(3), 540-572.

Clague, L., & Krupp, N. (1978). International personnel: the repatriation problem. *Personnel Administrator*, *23*, 29-33.

Clarke, C., & Hammer, M.R. (1995). Predictors of Japanese and American managers job success, personal adjustment, and intercultural interaction effectiveness. *Management International Review*, *35*(2), 153-170.

Cleveland, H., Mangone, G., & Adams, J.C. (1960). *The overseas Americans*. New York: McGraw-Hill.

Dalton, G.W., & Thompson, P.H. (1986). *Novations: Strategies for career management*. Glenview, IL: Scott, Foresman.

Davidson, M., & Cooper, G. (1987). Female managers in Britain: A comparative perspective. *Human Resource Management*, *26*(2), 217-242.

DeCieri, H., Dowling, P.J, & Taylor, K.F. (1991). The psychological impact of expatriate relocation on partners. *International Journal of Human Resource Management*, *2*(3), 377-414.

Deshpande, S.P., & Viswesvaran, C. (1992). Is cross-cultural training of expatriate managers effective: A meta-analysis. *International Journal of Intercultural Relations*, *16*, 295-310.

Domsch, M., & Lichtenberger, B. (1991). Managing the global manager: Predeparture training and development for German expatriates in China and Brazil. *Journal of Management Development*, *10*(7), 41-52.

Dunbar, E. (1992). Adjustment and satisfaction of expatriate U.S. personnel. *International Journal of Intercultural Relations*, *16*, 1-16.

Dunbar, E. (1994). The German executive in the U.S. work and social environment: Exploring role demands. *International Journal of Intercultural Relations*, *18*, 277-291.

Dunbar, E., & Ehrlich, M. (1993). Preparation of the international employee: Career and consultation needs. *Consulting Psychology Journal*, *45*, 18-24.

Earley, P.C. (1987). Intercultural training for managers: A comparison of documentary and interpersonal methods. *Academy of Management Journal*, *30*(4), 685-698.

Edstrom, A., & Galbraith, J.R. (1977). Transfer of managers as a coordination and control strategy in multinational organizations. *Administrative Science Quarterly*, *22*, 248-263.

Enderwick, P., & Hodgson, D. (1993). Expatriate management practices of New Zealand businesses. *International Journal of Human Resource Management*, *4*(2), 407-423.

English, H.B. (1958). *A comprehensive dictionary of psychological and psychoanalytical terms*. New York: David McKay.

Feldman, D.C. (1976). A contingency theory of socialization. *Administrative Science Quarterly*, *21*, 433-451.

Feldman, D.C. (1991). Repatriate moves as career transitions. *Human Resource Management Review*, *1*, 163-178.

Feldman, D.C., & Brett, J.M. (1983). Coping with new jobs: A comparative study of new hires and job changers. *Academy of Management Journal*, *26*, 258-272.

Feldman, D.C., & Thomas, D.C. (1992). Career management issues facing expatriates. *Journal of International Business Studies*, *23*(2), 271-293.

Feldman, D.C., & Tompson, H.B. (1993). Expatriation, repatriation, and domestic geographical relocation: An empirical investigation of adjustment to new job assignments. *Journal of International Business Studies*, *24*(2), 507-529.

Fenwick, M., & Haslett, T. (1994). *A cusp-catastrophe model of cross-cultural adjustment*. Paper presented to the annual meeting of the Academy of International Business, Boston.

Franko, L. (1973). Who manages multinational enterprises? *Columbia Journal of World Business*, *8*, 30-42.

Freedman, S., & Phillips, J. (1988). The changing nature of research on women at work. *Journal of Management*, *14*(2), 231-251.

Furnham, A., & Bochner, S. (1986). *Culture shock: psychological reactions to unfamiliar environments*. New York: Methuen.

Golden, J.S. (1973). Student adjustment abroad: A psychiatrist's view. *International Education and Cultural Exchange*, *8*, 28-36.

Gomez-Mejia, L., & Balkin, D. (1987). The determinants of managerial satisfaction with the expatriation and repatriation process. *Journal of Management Development*, *6*(1), 7-17.

Granrose, C. (1994). Careers of Japanese and Chinese expatriate managers in US multinational firms. *Journal of Asian Business*, *10*, 59-79.

Gregersen, H.B. (1992). Commitments to a parent company and a local work unit during repatriation. *Personnel Psychology, 45*, 29-54.

Gregersen, H.B., & Black, J.S. (1990). A multifaceted approach to expatriate retention in international assignments. *Group and Organization Studies, 15*(4), 461-485.

Gregersen, H.B., Hite, J.M., & Black, J.S. (1996). Expatriate performance appraisal in U.S. multinational firms. *Journal of International Business Studies, 27*(4), 711-738.

Gudykunst, W., & Hammer, M. (1983). Basic training design: Approaches to intercultural training. In D. Landis & R.W. Brislin (Eds.), *Handbook of intercultural training* (Vol. 1). Elmsford, NY: Pergamon.

Gullahorn, J.T., & Gullahorn, J.E. (1963). An extension of the U-curve hypothesis. *Journal of Social Issues, 19*, 33-47.

Guthrie, G.M., & Zektrick, I. (1967). Predicting performance in the Peace Corps. *Journal of Social Psychology, 71*, 11-21.

Guzzo, R.A., Noonan, K.A., & Elron, E. (1994). Expatriate managers and the psychological contract. *Journal of Applied Psychology, 79*(4), 617-626.

Hammer, M.R. (1987). Behavioral dimensions of intercultural effectiveness: A replication and extension. *International Journal of Intercultural Relations, 11*, 65-87.

Hammer, M.R., Gudykunst, W.B., & Wiseman, R.L. (1978). Dimensions of intercultural effectiveness: An exploratory study. *International Journal of Intercultural Relations, 8*, 1-10.

Harrison, J.K. (1992). Individual and combined effect of behavior modeling and the cultural assimilator in cross-cultural management training. *Journal of Applied Psychology, 77*(6), 952- 962.

Harvey, M.C. (1989). Repatriation of corporate executives: An empirical study. *Journal of International Business Studies, 20*, 131-144.

Harvey, M.C. (1997). Dual career expatriates: Expectations, adjustment and satisfaction with international relocation. *Journal of International Business Studies, 28*(3).

Harzing, A.K. 1995. The persistent myth of high expatriate failure rates. *The International Journal of Human Resource Management, 6*(2), 457-474.

Haselberger, A., & Stroh, L.K. (1992). Development and selection of multinational expatriates. *Human Resource Development Quarterly, 3*, 287-193.

Hawes, F., & Kealey, D.J. (1979). *Canadians in development. An empirical comparison of adaptation and effectiveness overseas*. Ottawa: CIDA Communications.

Hawes, F., & Kealey, D.J. (1981). An empirical study of Canadian technical assistance. *International Journal of Intercultural Relations, 5*, 239-258.

Hays, R.D. (1971). Ascribed behavioral determinants of success-failure among US expatriate managers. *Journal of International Business Studies, 2*(1), 25-37.

Hays, R.D. (1974). Expatriate selection: Insuring success and avoiding failure. *Journal of International Business Studies, 5*(1), 25-37.

Howard, C.G. (1974, March-April). Model for the design of a selection program for multinational executives. *Public Personnel Management*, pp. 138-145.

Hull, W.F. (1979). *Foreign students in the U.S.* New York: Praeger.

Israeli, D.N., Banai, M., & Zeira, Y. (1980). Women expatriates in subsidiaries of multinational corporations. *California Management Review, 23*(1), 53-63.

Ivancevich, J.M. (1969, March). Selection of American managers for overseas assignments. *Personnel Journal*, pp. 189-193.

Janssens, M. (1995). Intercultural interaction: A burden on international managers? *Journal of Organizational Behavior, 16*, 155-167.

Kealey, D.J. (1989). A study of cross-cultural effectiveness: Theoretical issues, practical applications. *International Journal of Intercultural Relations, 13*, 387- 428.

Kealey, D.J., & Protheroe, D.R. (1996). The effectiveness of cross-cultural training for expatriates: An assessment of the literature on the issue. *International Journal of Intercultural Relations, 20*(2), 141-165.

Klineberg, O., & Hull, W.F. (1979). *At a foreign university: An international study of adaptation and coping*. New York: Praeger.

Kobrin, S.J. (1988). Expatriate reduction and strategic control in American multinational corporations. *Human Resource Management, 27*(1), 63-75.

Kopp, R. (1994). International human resource policies and practices in Japanese, European and United States multinationals. *Human Resource Management, 33*(4), 581-599.

Landis, D., & Brislin, R.W. (Eds.). (1983). *Handbook of intercultural training*. Elmsford, NY: Pergamon.

Luthans, F., McCaul, H.S., & Dodd, N. (1985). Organizational commitment: A comparison of U.S., Japanese, and Korean employees. *Academy of Management Journal, 28*, 213-218.

Lysgaard, S. (1955). Adjustment in a foreign society: Norwegian Fulbright grantees visiting the United States. *International Social Science Bulletin, 7*, 45-51.

Malpass, R.S. (1977, December). Theory and method in cross-cultural psychology. *American Psychologist*, pp. 1069-1078.

Meglino, B.M., & DeNisi, A. (1987). Realistic job previews: Some thoughts on their more effective use in managing the flow of human resources. *Human Resource Planning, 10*, 157-167.

Mendenhall, M., & Oddou, G. (1985). The dimensions of expatriate acculturation. *Academy of Management Review, 10*, 39-47.

Miller, E.L. (1975). The job satisfaction of expatriate American managers: A function of regional location and previous work experience. *Journal of International Business Studies, 6*(2), 65-73.

Miller, E.L., & Cheng, J.L. (1978). A closer look at the decision to accept an overseas position. *Management International Review, 18*, 25-33.

Milliman, J., Von Glinow, M.A., Nathan, M. (1991). Organizational life cycles and strategic international human resource management in multinational companies: Implications for congruence theory. *Academy of Management Review, 16*(2), 318-329.

Misa, K.F., & Fabricatore, J.M. (1979, April). Return on investment of overseas personnel. *Financial Executive*, pp. 42-46.

Mottram, R. (Ed.). (1963). *The selection of personnel for international service*. New York: World Federation for Mental Health.

Murray, J.A. (1978). International personnel repatriation: Culture shock in reverse. *MSU Business Topics, 21*, 29-33.

Napier, N.K., & Peterson, R.B. (1991). Expatriate re-entry: what do repatriates have to say? *Human Resource Planning, 14*, 19-28.

Nash, D. (1991). The course of sojourner adaptation: A new test of the U-curve hypothesis. *Human Organization, 50*, 283-286.

Naumann, E. (1993a). Antecedents and consequences of satisfaction and commitment among expatriate managers. *Group and Organization Management, 18*(2), 153-187.

Naumann, E. (1993b). Organizational predictors of expatriate job satisfaction. *Journal of International Business Studies, 24*(1), 61-80.

Near, J.P. (1989). Organizational commitment among Japanese and U.S. workers. *Organization Studies, 10*, 281-300.

Nicholson, N., & Imaizumi, A. (1993). The adjustment of Japanese expatriates to living and working in Britain. *British Journal of Management, 4*, 119-134.

Nicholson, N., & West, M. (1988). Transitions, work histories, and careers. In M.B. Arthur, D.T. Hall, & B.S. Lawrence (Eds.), *Handbook of career theory* (pp. 181-201). Cambridge: Cambridge University Press.

Nisbett, R.E., & Wilson, T.D. (1977). Telling more than we can know: Verbal reports of mental processes. *Psychological Review, 84*(3), 231-259.

Oberg, K. (1960). Cultural shock: Adjustment to new cultural environments. *Practical Anthropology, 7*, 177-182.

Oddou, G.R., & Mendenhall, M. (1991). Succession planning for the 21st century: how well are we grooming our future business leaders? *Business Horizons, 34*, 26-34.

Osland, J.S. (1994). Working abroad: A hero's adventure. *Training and Development, 49*, 49-51.

Park, H., Sun, D.H., & David, J.M. (1993). Local manager selection for U.S. firms in Korea. *Multinational Business Review, 1*(2), 57-65.

Parker, B., & McEvoy, G.M. (1993). Initial examination of a model of intercultural adjustment. *International Journal of Intercultural Relations, 17*, 355-379.

Perlmutter, H. (1969). The tortuous evolution of the multinational corporation. *Columbia Journal of World Business, 4*, 39-41.

Peterson, R.B., Napier, N., & Won, S-S. (1995). *Expatriate management: The differential role on multinational corporation ownership*. Paper presented to the annual meeting of the Academy of International Business, Seoul, Korea.

Rosenzweig, P.M., & Nohria, N. (1994). Influences on human resource management practices in multinational corporations. *Journal of International Business Studies, 25*(2), 229-251.

Ruben, B.D., & Kealey, D.J. (1979). Behavioral assessment of communication competency and the prediction of cross-cultural adaptation. *International Journal of Intercultural Relations, 3*, 15-47.

Rynes, S.L., & Lawler, J. (1983). A policy capturing investigation of the role expectancies in decisions to pursue job alternatives. *Journal of Applied Psychology, 68*, 620-651.

Sarbin, T., & Allen, R. (1968). Role theory. In G. Lindzey & E. Aronson (Eds.), *The handbook of social psychology*. Reading, MA: Addison Wesley.

Schein, E. (1996). Career anchors revisited: Implications for career development in the 21st century. *Academy of Management Executive, 10*(4), 80-88.

Scullion, H. (1991, November). Why companies prefer to use expatriates. *Personnel Management*, pp. 32-35.

Sewell, W.H., & Davidson, O.M. (1956). The adjustment of Scandinavian students. *Journal of Social Issues, 12*, 9-19.

Stein, M.I. (1966). *Volunteers for peace*. New York: Wiley.

Stening, B.W. (1979). Problems in cross-cultural contact: A literature review. *International Journal of Intercultural Relations, 3*, 269-313.

Stening, B.W., & Hammer, M.R. (1992). Cultural baggage and the adaptation of expatriate Japanese managers. *Management International Review, 32*(1), 77-89.

Stephens, G.K. (1994). Crossing internal career boundaries: The state of research on subjective career transitions. *Journal of Management, 20*(2), 479-501.

Stephens, G.K., & Black, J.S. (1991). The impact of spouse's career orientation on managers during international transfers. *Journal of Management Studies, 28*(4), 417-426.

Stone, R.J. (1991). Expatriate selection and failure. *Human Resource Planning, 29*(1), 9-17.

Stoner, J.A., Aram, J.D., & Rubin, I.M. (1972). Factors associated with effective performance in overseas work assignments. *Personnel Psychology, 25*, 303-318.

Stroh, L.K., Dennis, L.E., & Cramer, T.C. (1994). Predictors of expatriate adjustment. *International Journal of Organizational Analysis, 2*, 176-192.

Takeuchi, R., & Hannon, J.M. (1996). *The antecedents of adjustment for Japanese expatriates in the United States*. Paper presented to the annual meeting of the Academy of International Business, Banff, Canada.

Taylor, S., & Napier, N. (1996). Working in Japan: Lessons from women expatriates. *Sloan Management Review, 37*, 76-84.

Thal, N.L., & Cateora, P.R. (1979). Opportunities for women in international business. *Business Horizons, 22*(6), 21-27.

Thomas, D.C. (1994). The boundary-spanning role of expatriates in the multinational corporation. *Advances in International Comparative Management, 9*, 145-170.

Torbiorn, I. (1982). *Living abroad: Personal adjustment and personnel policy in the overseas setting*. New York: Wiley.

Torbiorn, I. (1994). Operative and strategic use of expatriates in new organizations and market structures. *International Studies of Management and Organization, 24*, 5-17.

Tung, R.L. (1981). Selection and training of personnel for overseas assignments. *Columbia Journal of World Business*, 16, 68-78.

Tung, R.L. (1988). *The new expatriates: Managing human resources abroad*. Cambridge, MA: Ballinger.

Ward, C., & Kennedy, A. (1993). Where's the culture in cross-cultural transition? Comparative studies of sojourner adjustment. *Journal of Cross-Cultural Psychology, 24*(2), 221-249.

Westwood, R.I., & Leung, S.M. (1994). The female expatriate manager experience: Coping with gender and culture. *International Studies of Management and Organization, 24*, 64-85.

Zeira, Y., & Banai, M. (1985). Selection of expatriate managers in MNCs: The host environment point of view. *International Studies of Management and Organization, 15*(1), 33-51.

[32]

Serving Two Masters: Managing the Dual Allegiance of Expatriate Employees

J. Stewart Black • Hal B. Gregersen

A MANAGER WHO TAKES AN ASSIGNMENT IN A FOREIGN COUNTRY HAS THE IMMENSE TASK OF ADAPTING TO A NEW CULTURE AND NEW BUSINESS PRACTICES. The firm naturally wants to get the most out of this employee, both during the assignment and after repatriation. But the question of allegiance often gets in the way of the individual's and the firm's success. To whom is the expatriate most committed — the parent firm or the local unit? Black and Gregersen have studied and interviewed numerous expatriates. In this paper, they describe four allegiance patterns and the factors that affect them, and they suggest policies for promoting the most desired pattern: high dual allegiance.

J. Stewart Black is assistant professor of business administration, and Hal B. Gregersen is visiting professor, the Amos Tuck School of Business Administration, Dartmouth College.

Each year hundreds of thousands of expatriate managers all over the world find themselves torn between their allegiance to the parent firm and their allegiance to the local foreign operation. To understand this tension, consider the following situation. A Dutch expatriate manager in a multinational consumer products firm is faced on the one hand with a parent firm that wants a set of products introduced in the host country (a large developing nation) as part of its global brand image strategy. On the other hand, the host country government wants high technology transferred into the country, not just consumer products placed on store shelves. Market research suggests that local consumers are interested in some of the core products but not others and in products not currently part of the firm's core set. The parent firm has a philosophy encouraging participative decision making, but host national employees expect managers to make decisions without burdening them.

Faced with serving two masters, many expatriate managers end up directing their allegiance too far in one direction or the other, creating serious costs and consequences for both themselves and their organizations. For example, if individuals are too committed to the local operation relative to the parent firm, it is difficult for the home office to coordinate with them. A senior Honda executive commented to us that Honda had incurred "nontrivial" costs trying to coordinate its global strategy for the new Honda Accord because some expatriate managers were too focused on the local situation. Expatriates who are overly committed to the parent firm relative to the local operation often inappropriately implement policies or procedures from the home office. The medical equipment division of a large U.S. multinational firm recently tried to implement home office financial reporting and accounting procedures that simply did not apply to and would not work in its newly acquired French subsidiary.

Perhaps most important, the high competitive pressure, great geographical distances, and wide cultural diversity of global operations combined with ineffective management of expatriates can set off a vicious cycle that erodes or even destroys a firm's global competitive position:

1. Unbalanced allegiance can lead to a variety of failures during and after international assignments.
2. As managers hear about these failures, firms find it increasingly difficult to attract top international candidates.
3. Increasingly worse candidates are sent overseas, producing

even worse organizational results and more failed careers.
4. This further limits the pool of willing and qualified candidates.
5. Over time the firm's overseas competitive position erodes.
6. This cycle spirals downward until it becomes nearly unstoppable.

Today's multinational firms need managers who are highly committed to both the parent firm and the local operation and who can integrate the demands and objectives of both organizations. As one senior executive put it, the bottom line question is, "How can we get expatriate managers who are committed to the local overseas operation during their international assignments, but who remain loyal to the parent firm?" Unfortunately, our research suggests that expatriate managers with high dual allegiance are a rare commodity.[1]

This is not surprising in light of studies of dual commitment in domestic contexts, such as commitment to a union and an organization (e.g., United Auto Workers and General Motors) or commitment to a profession and an organization (e.g., nursing and a specific hospital). These studies have found that certain factors have different effects on the two targets of commitment and that people hold different patterns of commitment. Some individuals are unilaterally committed to one organization over the other, some have low levels of commitment to both, and others have high levels of commitment to both.[2]

In this article we present a description of the patterns, causes, and consequences of expatriate dual allegiance. In brief, expatriate managers can be grouped into one of four allegiance patterns. They can be overly committed to the parent firm or the local operation, highly committed to both organizations, or committed to neither. These four basic patterns are presented in the Figure 1 matrix. Much more important than the patterns of dual allegiance are the factors that cause them and the related organizational and individual consequences. We describe the causes and consequences associated with each pattern and illustrate them with actual cases generated through numerous interviews and surveys (most managers asked that their names and firms be disguised). We also examine what firms are doing now and what they can do in the future to more effectively manage their expatriate managers.

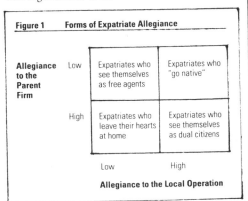

Figure 1 Forms of Expatriate Allegiance

Allegiance to the Parent Firm		Allegiance to the Local Operation: Low	Allegiance to the Local Operation: High
	Low	Expatriates who see themselves as free agents	Expatriates who "go native"
	High	Expatriates who leave their hearts at home	Expatriates who see themselves as dual citizens

Free Agents

As an undergraduate, Paul Jackson majored in Asian studies and studied for two years in Japan. At graduation, he had intermediate fluency in Chinese and near fluency in Japanese. He immediately went on to receive a master's degree from the American Graduate School of International Management in Phoenix. He was hired by a major east coast bank and two years later was sent on a three-year assignment to Hong Kong. The expatriate package Paul and his family received made life in Hong Kong enjoyable. However, Paul felt little loyalty to the parent firm back home or the Hong Kong operation. First and foremost, Paul was committed to his career. Because he was such a hard charger, the bank invested a substantial amount of time and money into him for language and technical training. He worked hard but always kept an ear out for better jobs and pay. Two years into his Hong Kong assignment, he found a better position in another firm and took it. Four years into that company and assignment, he took a job with a different U.S. bank and its Taiwan operation. Four years later, he took a job as vice-president and general manager for the Japan subsidiary of a large west coast bank.

When we interviewed Paul about his work history, he said, "I can't really relate to your question about which organization I feel allegiance to. I do my job, and I do it well. I play for whatever team needs me and wants me. I'm like a free agent in baseball or a hired gun in the old West. If the pay and job are good enough, I'm off. You might say, 'have international expertise, will travel.' "

Interestingly, Paul was actually part of a network we discovered of "hired-gun free agents" in the Pacific Rim. The network consisted of a group of about ten American managers hired as expatriates (not as local hires), who were either bi- or trilingual, and who had spent over half of their professional careers in Asia. This group of free agents passed along information to each other about various firms that were looking for experienced expatriate managers for their Asia operations.

Hired-Gun Free Agents

These expatriates have a low level of commitment to both their parent firms and their local operations. They are first and foremost committed to their own "gun-slinging" careers. When asked what long-term career implications this approach might have for them, these expatriates commonly indicated that it would be very difficult for them to ever "go back home" and move up the headquarter's hierarchy in any firm. However, most did not want to for several reasons. First, they felt the experience their children received from both an educational (schools are generally international, private, and paid for by the firm) and general life perspective was far superior to what they would receive back home. Second, the expatriates would be worse off financially if they went home and had to give up the extra benefits of their expatriate packages. Third, most were confident that they would not be given a job back home with the status, freedom, and importance of those jobs they held overseas. Consequently, most of these hired guns seemed happy with their lives and careers overseas.

Firms tend to view these expatriates with some ambivalence. On the one hand, even though these hired guns receive special benefit packages, they tend to be slightly less expensive than sending expatriates from the home country. Furthermore, these expatriates have already demonstrated their specialized skills, such as language, and their ability to succeed in international settings — qualities that are often lacking in a firm's internal managerial or executive ranks. This may be especially important to U.S. firms: on average 15 percent to 20 percent of their expatriate managers fail in their overseas assignments, at great cost to the firm, because they have serious problems adjusting to the foreign culture.

On the other hand, these free agent expatriates often leave the firm with little warning. Replacing them is usually costly and difficult and can have negative consequences for both the parent firm and the local operation. Sometimes these hired guns serve their own short-term career objectives at the expense of the firm's long-term interests. Also, as mentioned, few of these expatriates are willing to repatriate to the home office. This makes integrating their international experience or specific country or regional knowledge into the firm's global strategy formulation process next to impossible.

Plateaued-Career Free Agents

Our research uncovered another type of expatriate with low levels of commitment to both the parent firm and the local operation. This type of expatriate typically comes from the ranks of home country employees rather than of hired international experts. These expatriates are generally not committed to the parent firm before leaving for the overseas assignment in part because their careers have often plateaued. They take the international assignment because they don't see themselves going anywhere in the home operations, and they hope an international stint will change things. Or they are simply attracted by the sweet financial packages common to most overseas assignments. Unfortunately, many of the factors that led to low commitment before the international assignment result in low commitment to the local operation once the manager is overseas.

Several factors can contribute to development of this type of expatriate. First, if firms simply allow candidates for overseas assignments to self-select, they open the door for this type of expatriate. As one expatriate said, "I figured I was stalled in my job [back in North Carolina], so why not take a shot at an overseas assignment, especially given what I'd heard about the high standard of living even mid-level managers enjoyed overseas." Research has shown that certain personal characteristics correlate with successful adjustment to international assignments.[3] A self-selection process leaves personal characteristics of the expatriates to chance. Second, placing a low value on international operations can increase the probability that plateaued managers will apply for overseas assignments and decrease the probability that high-potential managers will volunteer for them. In such an environment, high-potential managers know that the place to get ahead is not overseas somewhere, out of sight and out of mind, but at home. Finally, lack of predeparture cross-cultural training can also reinforce low levels of commitment to the parent firm and the local operation. U.S. firms may be particularly vulnerable to this factor; roughly 70 percent of all U.S. expatriates receive no predeparture cross-cultural training.[4] Lack of firm-sponsored training can contribute to the view that "the company doesn't care about me, so why should I care about it?" Lack of training can also inhibit the expatriate from understanding the foreign culture and becoming committed to the local operation.

Unlike the hired guns, many of the plateaued-career free agents are not happy in their overseas assignments. Their low level of commitment often results in little effort to adjust to the local operation and culture. At worst, they fail the assignment. A failed overseas assignment not only inhibits the individual's career advancement, it can strike a severe blow to the individual's identity and self-confidence. Of course, there are also costs to the firm. Beyond the $100,000 to $250,000 it costs to bring the employee and family home and send out a replacement, the firm incurs the costs of damaged client and supplier relationships.[5] The lack of leadership during the replacement process can contribute to damaged internal and external relations. Failed assignments can also generate rumors back home that international posts are the "kiss of death" for a career, which in turn makes it more difficult to attract good candidates in the future.

Even if lack of commitment doesn't result in a failed assignment, it can still be costly to the person and the organization. Bob Brown was a typical plateaued manager for a major U.S. aircraft manufacturer who transferred to Taiwan three years before his interview with us. Bob was *not* very excited about living in Taiwan and neither was his family. His wife and daughter repeatedly asked to go back home. Bob pointed out that there was really no job for him to go back to. His daughter became so distraught

> Failed assignments can generate rumors back home that international posts are the "kiss of death" for a career.

that she began doing extremely poorly in school. This and other pressures put a severe strain on Bob's relationship with his wife. In an interview, Bob summed it up by stating that his home life was in shambles and that work was merely a paycheck, but a fat one (his compensation and benefit package was worth about $210,000 per year).

Perhaps the parent and local firm were getting their money's worth out of Bob, but it seems unlikely. Past studies have found that of those expatriates who complete their assignments, about one-third are considered ineffective.[6] Also, it is hard to imagine that a manager whose career has plateaued back home could be paid two to three times a normal compensation package and still provide a good return on that expense. If, as we suspect, such managers cannot, then this represents a serious economic loss to firms.

To summarize, low commitment to the parent firm and the local operation seems to be found in two general types of expatriate managers — hired-gun free agents and plateaued-career free agents. Although the causes and consequences of each type are different, both types represent potentially serious costs to the individual, parent firm, and local operation, since 41 percent of our sample fell into this group.

Going Native

The next allegiance pattern involves having high levels of commitment to the local operation but low levels of commitment to the parent firm. These expatriates usually form a strong identification with and attachment to the country's culture, language, values, and business practices. Consequently, these expatriates are often referred to as those who "go native."

Gary Ogden had been with a large computer company for fifteen years. He was the country manager for the firm's instrument division in France and had been in Paris for about four years, his third international assignment. Of his fifteen years with the parent firm, over half had been spent overseas, including six of the last eight years. Given that this was his third international stint, it hadn't taken long for Gary, his wife, and their three daughters (ages six, nine, and eleven) to settle in to life in France. His girls had enrolled in regular French schools when they moved to Paris and were now fluent for their ages. Gary's French was not perfect but he was comfortable in business situations. He had spent long hours trying to understand the local business situation, and he thought that corporate was constantly requesting and demanding things that either worked against objectives for the French unit or couldn't be done effectively or sometimes at all in France. Still, Gary loved it so much in France that he had already requested an extension, even though his contract only required him to stay another six months. When asked to describe his commitment to the parent firm and the local operation, he responded, "My first commitment is to the unit here. In fact, half the time I feel as if corporate is a competitor I must fight rather than a benevolent parent I can look to for support."

Our research suggests that individuals like Gary Ogden who have spent a number of years overseas, who adjust to the local culture, and who feel at odds with corporate headquarters are the most likely to go native. As managers spend more time away from the home office, their identities seem less and less tied to the parent firm. The firm becomes both literally and psychologically distant, as compared to the local operation. Additionally, the lack of formal communication with the home office through mechanisms such as sponsors (individuals assigned to keep in touch with specific expatriates) also serves to cause or reinforce this commitment pattern. Firms that are structured in international divisions and have cadres of "career internationalists" may be particularly vulnerable to this pattern.

What are the consequences of going native in terms of expatriate allegiance? Let's consider the individual's perspective. First, Gary felt that he had effectively managed the local situation. He pointed out that his knowledge of the language, culture, and union structure had enabled him to avoid an almost certain and probably very costly strike. Unfortunately, because the strike never happened, Gary felt that corporate did not recognize his achievement. Second, because Gary knew that his career depended to some extent on the evaluations made of him back at corporate, when he had to "fight" the parent firm, he had to do it subtly: "Sometimes I would simply ignore their directives if I didn't think they were appropriate or relevant to our operations. If it's really important, eventually someone from regional or corporate will hassle me, and I'll have to respond. If it isn't important or if they think I implemented what they wanted, they just leave me alone. As long as the general results are good, it doesn't seem as if there are big costs to this approach." Gary also indicated that on occasion he had to fight corporate more overtly. Although this may have cost him back at corporate, fighting these fights and especially winning them helped him gain the trust and loyalty of the local national employees. Their greater loyalty made it easier for him to be effective in the country. Interestingly, this effectiveness often later earned him points and slack back home.

Third, when Gary was repatriated after international assignments, he disliked the lack of responsibility compared to what he enjoyed overseas and the general lack of appreciation and utilization of his international knowledge. He nearly quit the firm both times he was repatriated. His low commitment to the parent firm heightened his dissatisfaction. Gary stated that both times it was receipt of another overseas assignment that kept him from leaving the firm.

From the parent firm's point of view, one of the common problems associated with expatriates who go native is the difficulty of getting corporate policies or programs implemented at the local level. Often the intense commitment to the local foreign operation leads these expatriates to implement what they think is relevant, in a way they deem appropriate, and then to ignore or fight the rest. This can be very costly, especially when the parent firm is trying to closely coordinate activities in a wide variety of countries for the good of global corporate objectives.

Also, to the extent that low commitment to the parent firm contributes to repatriation turnover, the parent firm loses the opportunity to incorporate the knowledge and experience of these expatriates into its global strategy or to incorporate some of these individuals into their succession plans. Interestingly, our research found that most expatriates, regardless of commitment pattern, do not feel that the international knowledge and experience they gained overseas is valued by their firms (91 percent of U.S. expatriates, 97 percent of Japanese expatriates, and 89 percent of Finnish expatriates). In general, firms do not seem to be utilizing these valuable resources.

Despite the negative aspects of expatriates who go native, many corporate executives recognize that these expatriates are not all bad. The high level of allegiance to the local operation generally leads these expatriates to identify with and understand the host national employees, customers, and suppliers. This understanding can translate into (1) new products and services or adapted products and services that are well targeted to the local market and (2) managerial approaches that are suited to the host national employees.

The importance of a managerial style modified to suit host national employees must not be overlooked, especially by U.S. firms. Although most U.S. firms assume that good managers in New York will do fine in Tokyo or Hong Kong and consequently select expatriates based primarily on domestic track records, evidence suggests that managerial characteristics that are related to performance in the United States are *not* related to performance in foreign countries.[7]

This potentially positive aspect of these expatriate managers may be particularly true in firms at a multidomestic stage of globalization.[8] In most multidomestic firms, each overseas unit competes in its national or regional market independent of the firm's other organizational units in other countries. The primary information flow is within the local operation, rather than between it and the parent firm. There is a premium on understanding the local market and the host national people and culture. Expatriates with relatively high allegiance to the local operation may be particularly beneficial in this situation.

In summary, managers who have spent a lot of time away from the parent firm, who can adjust to foreign cultures, and who lack formal communication ties to the parent firm are the most likely to go native; they constituted about 15 percent of our sample. There are pros and cons to this pattern for both the individual and the parent firm. Expatriates who go native often have valuable insights into the local operation, culture, and market; they can adapt procedures, products, or managerial approaches to fit the local situation. They may also be less likely to return prematurely and to invoke the serious costs associated with early returns. However, they also can frustrate global coordination efforts and may not be committed enough to the parent firm after repatriation to pass their knowledge on for country, regional, or global strategic planning.[9]

Hearts at Home

The third type of expatriate manager is highly committed to the parent firm but has little allegiance to the local foreign operation. We refer to these expatriates as those who "leave their hearts at home"; they constituted about 12 percent of our sample. These expatriate managers identify much more strongly with the parent firm than they do with the local operation and the local country's culture, language, and business practices.

Earl Markus was the managing director of the European headquarters of a large building supply firm's "do-it-yourself" retail division. This was Earl's first international assignment in his twenty-two years with the firm. He was married and had two children, both of whom were in college and therefore did not move with their parents to European headquarters in Belgium. Earl had worked his way up from a store manager to southwest regional manager and eventually to vice-president of finance over the previous twenty-two years.

The European operations were fairly new, and Earl saw his mission as expanding the number of retail outlets from the current nine in Belgium to fifty throughout western Europe. The president and CEO of the U.S. parent firm had assigned the COO, Frank Johnson, to work closely with Earl during his three-year assignment.

One year into the assignment, Earl was on schedule and had opened fifteen new outlets in three countries. But he was very frustrated. He said that he had seriously considered packing up and going home more than once during the year. He claimed Europeans were lazy and slow to respond to directives. When asked about his allegiance, he said that there was no contest. He was first and foremost committed to corporate, and when the next two years were up, he was headed back home. As an example of how things had gone, Earl described the implementation of the inventory system.

About eight months into the assignment, Frank Johnson suggested that Earl implement the new computerized inventory system that had just been phased into U.S. outlets. Frank was excited about the system's ability to reduce costs and shrinkage (i.e., theft), and he had high expectations of similar benefits for its use in Europe. For proper operation, the system required daily recording of sales and weekly random physical inventory of specific items. These reports needed to be transferred within forty-eight hours to the central office, which would generate total and store-by-store reports. The forms and procedure manuals were printed, and a two-day seminar was held for all European store managers and directors of operations and relevant staff members. Two months later, Earl inquired about how the system was operating. It wasn't. He said all he got from his managers were "lame excuses" about why the system wouldn't work, especially in Belgium.

This case illustrates some of the main causes and consequences of expatriates' allegiance being tilted strongly in favor of the parent firm. It is not surprising that our research found a significant correlation between long tenure in the parent firm and allegiance to it. These expatriates had invested time, sweat, and heartache with the parent firm, and they expected a "return" on this investment. Over time, the expatriates' identities had intertwined with the identities of the parent firm. A high level of allegiance to the parent firm was a natural consequence.

Our research found two other factors that, in combination, contributed to this allegiance pattern. The first factor was poor adjustment to the host country and culture, in part fostered by selection processes that primarily considered domestic track records. Because these expatriates could not relate to the host country's culture and people, they could not develop a strong sense of allegiance to the local operation. The second factor was having a sponsor in the home office who was formally assigned to the expatriate to maintain a formal tie. This tie focused attention and allegiance toward the parent firm and away from the local operation.

What personal and organizational consequences resulted from this allegiance pattern? Earl Markus was frustrated; he had considered leaving the overseas assignment several times. It was his fear of negative career consequences more than anything else that kept him from going. In addition to early return costs, which we discussed in the section on free agents, organizations can also incur the cost of having ineffectual managers. These managers often try to implement and enforce programs that are inappropriate for the local operation, or they implement them in ways that offend local employees, customers, or suppliers. Earl's inventory implementation effort antagonized employees and created an adversarial relationship that hampered other programs and changes he subsequently tried to initiate.

However, just as in the case of going native, not all the consequences of leaving one's heart at home are bad. Our research found that U.S. expatriates who had a high commitment to the parent firm during the international assignment were more likely to want to stay with the parent firm after their repatriation. Thus to the extent that these expatriates gain valuable experience, knowledge, and skills during their international assignments, their parent firms have greater opportunities to gain future returns from them. Unfortunately, the low commitment to the local operation reduces the knowledge these expatriates can gain. Nevertheless, expatriates who leave their hearts at home can provide another advantage. They often make it easier for the home office to coordinate activities between headquarters and the subsidiary. In Earl's case, it was very easy for the corporate purchasing agent to utilize the buying power of headquarters' centralized purchasing activities for the European operations. This coordination gave the European operations access to substantial price savings.

The ability to coordinate easily with the home office may be particularly beneficial for firms at the export stage of globalization. The primary objective of most firms at this stage is to sell in foreign markets products developed and manufactured in the home country. Information flows primarily from the parent firm to the local operation. The home office plays a key coordinating role, and good coordination with the subsidiaries is important. Expatriates with relatively high commitment to the parent firm are less likely to resist following the home office's coordination efforts than expatriates with low levels of commitment to the parent.

Dual Citizens

The final category consists of expatriate managers who are highly committed to both the parent *and* the local operation — dual citizens. We use the word "citizen" because it seems to reflect this group's behavior, attitudes, and emotions. These managers tend to see themselves as citizens of both the foreign country and their home country and as citizens of both the local operation and the parent corporation. They feel responsible for serving both organization's interests.

Joan Beckenridge was the director of a prominent U.S. consulting firm's Japan office. This was Joan's second international assignment in her thirteen years with the firm. Her first assignment was a one-year special project stint in Singapore seven years before. Joan was one of three candidates considered for the job in Japan and had been selected based not only on her past performance but also on assessments by outside consultants. Because the job required a high degree of interaction with host nationals in a novel culture, Joan was given five-months notice before departing for Japan. During this time she received about sixty hours of cross-cultural training. In addition, her spouse received about ten hours of survival briefing. Four months after arriving in Japan, Joan received another forty hours of cross-cultural training. She also took advantage of hundreds of hours of language training, paid for by the parent firm.

Perhaps most important, Joan had a clear set of objectives for her assignment. The Japan office had been established to serve the Japanese subsidiaries of the firm's U.S. clients. At this point, the office's growth was limited by the slowed pace of expansion of U.S. client firms to Japan. Joan was charged with developing Japanese clients. This would serve two objectives. First, it would increase the office's growth potential, and second, it would make it easier to secure Japanese firm's U.S. subsidiaries as clients, which would expand U.S. operations.

Most U.S. firms do not provide any cross-cultural training for international assignments.

Despite these preparations, Joan found herself frustrated in one area. Headquarters and the local operation had differing expectations regarding business and entertainment expenses. Headquarters did not realize how much time and money it took to cultivate effective relationships in Japan. Joan's Japanese business associates were fond of pointing out that their country had the highest business entertainment expenses as a percent of sales in the world. Joan felt the tension between corporate "bean counters" who worried over entertainment expenses and local staff who floated contact opportunities that Joan couldn't develop. However, unlike many expatriates in similar situations, Joan had a mechanism for working out these differences. She had a high-level sponsor at corporate who was officially assigned to help her. Through this sponsor, Joan could educate corporate and bring corporate and local expectations in synch.

It was also clear from the beginning how this assignment fit Joan's overall career path and how her repatriation would be handled. Although she was not guaranteed a specific position upon repatriation, Joan knew what her general opportunities would be if she met her objectives in Japan.

Perhaps the most important factor in Joan's effectiveness was that she had a great degree of autonomy in deciding how to achieve the assignment's objectives. She had the flexibility to deal with the inevitable conflicts and ambiguities that cropped up in the job.

When asked about her allegiance, Joan said, "I feel a strong sense of allegiance to both companies [the local operation and the parent firm]. Although they sometimes have different objectives, I try to satisfy both whenever I can." When the two organizations conflicted, Joan would work to bring them together rather than simply following one or the other.

The personal and organizational consequences of Joan's dual citizenship orientation were primarily positive.

Joan indicated that it was sometimes frustrating to be torn between parent and local needs but that the clarity of her objectives, the latitude she had to pursue them, and the relative infrequency and small magnitude of the conflicts made the work rewarding and satisfying. Joan did well in her five years in Japan and received a substantial promotion upon repatriation to a position in which her knowledge was utilized in domestic and international expansion plans. For the organization, Joan's dual-citizen orientation helped her build solid relations with Japanese clients and government officials and helped the home office establish relationships with Japanese clients' U.S. subsidiaries. Joan believed her dual focus also gave her a greater ability to recruit high-quality Japanese employees, which was difficult for competitors.

Thirty-two percent of our sample of U.S. expatriate managers fit this allegiance pattern. Although it would be inaccurate to say that these expatriates never returned home early, never left the firm after repatriation, or never had adjustment or performance problems during international assignments, this group had a higher probability than the others of completing the foreign assignment, staying with the firm upon repatriation, and adjusting well to the overseas stay. These expatriate managers were much more interested than the others in understanding the needs, objectives, constraints, and opportunities of both the local operation and the parent firm. They talked of using this understanding to benefit both organizations. They could effectively implement corporate policies in the local operation and pass information from the local operation back to corporate in order to help shape strategy and policy development.

As indicated in Joan Beckenridge's case, *role conflict* played an important part in determining commitment. When the parent and local organizations had different expectations, demands, and objectives, the managers who had to negotiate these differences suffered from role conflict. The greater the role conflict, the less managers felt responsible for the outcomes and the less they felt committed to either organization. As one expatriate put it, "It's hard to feel responsible for what happens when you're being torn in opposite directions." In contrast, the greater the consistency between the two organizations, the more expatriate managers felt responsible for what happened and the more they felt committed to both organizations.

Role ambiguity produced a similar dynamic. Whereas role conflict follows from clear expectations that conflict, role ambiguity occurs when expectations from both organizations simply are not clear. Poor coordination between the parent firm and the local operation was a common source of role ambiguity. When we asked one expatriate manager how much responsibility he felt for what happened on his job, he replied, "How can I feel responsible, when I don't even know what I'm supposed to do or what's expected of me?" In contrast, the clearer the role, the more expatriates felt responsible for what happened at work and committed to both organizations.

Another factor related to dual allegiance was *clarity of repatriation programs.* Over 60 percent of U.S. firms have no systematic or formal repatriation program.[10] Clear, systematic repatriation programs facilitate high levels of commitment to both organizations. Such programs seem to free expatriates from worrying about going home and allow them to focus on the job at hand. This facilitates allegiance to the local operation. Such programs also seem to communicate that the parent firm cares about their expatriates and has thought about reintegration. This creates a greater sense of obligation to the parent firm.

> Many of the perks — company house, car, and driver — given to expatriate executives isolate them and inhibit their adjustment to the environment.

The most powerful factor in creating dual allegiance was *role discretion.* Role discretion is the freedom to decide what needs to be done, how and when it should be done, and who should do it. The more discretion expatriate managers have, the more they feel responsible for what happens at work and committed to the local operation. Because they generally view the parent firm as responsible for the amount of freedom they enjoy, this translates into a greater sense of commitment to the parent firm as well. Part of the reason that discretion is the most powerful factor is that most expatriate managers experience some role conflict and ambiguity. Role discretion gives the manager the freedom to define expectations and resolve conflicting ones.

Although dual citizens are desirable for any firm at any globalization stage, they are most critical for firms at the coordinated multinational stage. Such firms need information to flow back and forth between the home office and foreign subsidiaries and from one foreign subsidiary to another. They need managers who identify with both the people back home and those in the local operation. They need managers who will stay in the assignment, who will try to meet the needs of both organizations, and who will stay with the firm after repatriation so that their international experience, knowledge, and skills can be utilized.

Policy Implications

Although most executives in multinational firms are aware of the issues concerning expatriate allegiance, few of the expatriates we interviewed said that their firms understood the causes and consequences of the different allegiance patterns or had systems for developing dual-citizen expatriates. However, many firms had found ways to counterbalance "lopsided" allegiance. Below we present what some of these firms are doing, and we propose steps for developing dual-citizen expatriates.

Strategy 1: Counterbalancing Going Native

Managers who have several years of international experience and who have successfully adjusted to foreign cultures in the past are most likely to go native. Although these managers tend to have a low commitment to the parent firm, they are also good candidates to send overseas because they lower the risks and associated costs of failed assignments and premature returns. What can firms do if their current policies tend to produce too many expatriate managers like Gary Ogden?

• **Limit Time away from Corporate.** Honda brings expatriates home to Japan for a few years before they go overseas again. This method reinforces the link between the manager and the parent firm. Honda believes that it is not logical to expect career internationalists who move from one foreign assignment to the next to be highly committed to the parent firm.

• **Send Managers with Strong Ties to Corporate.** Firms can send managers overseas who have longer tenure in the parent firm. The longer managers have been with the firm, the more they have invested in it, the more they identify with it, and the more they are committed to it. Also, long tenures build personal connections that keep individuals involved with corporate. However, this recommendation is problematic for firms such as General Electric (GE), General Motors (GM), and Ford, which increasingly use international assignments to develop younger, high-potential managers.

• **Establish Corporate Sponsor Programs.** GE uses sponsors to counterbalance the tendency to go native. The company assesses the expatriate's career objectives and chooses a senior manager, often in the function to which the expatriate is likely to return, who is willing to serve as sponsor. The sponsor maintains contact with the expatriate throughout the assignment, including face-to-face meetings; evaluates the expatriate's performance during the assignment; helps clarify the expatriate's career objectives and capabilities before repatriation; and provides career advice and help finding a position back at headquarters. Some divisions even commit to hiring the expatriate manager back into a specific position before the foreign assignment begins.

Executives at several firms with sponsorship programs gave us additional advice. Overall, they recommended that sponsor assignment be systematized. First, the sponsor should be senior enough relative to the expatriate to be able to provide a broad view of the organization. Second, the sponsor should receive specific guidelines about the form, content, and frequency of contacts with the expatriate. Too often the sponsor is simply assigned, and that's it. If the sponsor takes the initiative and fulfills the responsibility, things go well. Otherwise, the sponsorship is in name only. Finally, the responsibility of planning for repatriation should not rest solely with the sponsor but should be incorporated into the firm's career systems.

• **Provide Predeparture and Postarrival Cross-Cultural Training.** Most U.S. firms do not provide any cross-cultural training for international assignments. While it may seem that predeparture training would increase a tendency to identify with the host culture and thus go native, our data indicate that such training creates a sense of obligation to the parent firm stemming from the firm's demonstrated concern for the expatriate.[11] Although we only examined the impact of predeparture training because fewer than 10 percent of the expatriates received postarrival training, we suspect that a similarly positive effect could be generated by providing training after arrival if the expatriate understands that the parent firm, and not the local operation, is paying for and sponsoring the training.

Strategy 2: Counterbalancing Hearts at Home

Although many U.S. executives seem unconcerned with the tendency of expatriates to leave their hearts at home, our research suggests that the consequences of this tendency are just as serious as those for going native. The lack of organizational practices in this area forces us to rely on our research for ways that firms might counterbalance the tendency of managers like Earl Markus to leave their hearts at home.

• **Send Younger Managers.** The managers most likely to be highly committed to the parent firm and much less committed to the local operation are those with long tenures at the parent firm and little international experience. Thus firms such as GE, GM, and Ford, which are increasingly sending younger managers overseas for career development, are perhaps unintentionally counterbalancing the hearts-at-home tendency.

• **Facilitate Cross-Cultural Adjustment.** Helping the expatriate manager adjust to the nonwork environment is another powerful counterbalancing force. Ironically, many of the perks — such as company housing, car, and driver — that are given to senior expatriate executives actually isolate them and inhibit their adjustment to the environment. Family members, especially the spouse, are often more directly exposed to the foreign environment because they do not have the insulation provided by the corporate structure. Therefore, a firm's efforts to facilitate the family's adjustment can have a positive effect on the manager's adjustment.[12]

• **Provide Cross-Cultural Training for the Family.** Ford is one of the few U.S. firms that tries to consistently provide training and preparation for the families and especially spouses of its expatriates. Although Ford executives did not intend this training to counteract the hearts-at-home tendency, our research suggests that this is a likely consequence.

• **Encourage Host National Sponsorship Programs.** Interacting with host nationals outside of work can help both families and managers adjust. Host nationals, who understand their own culture, are the best sources of instruction and especially feedback in getting along on a daily basis. However, such interaction is not always easy to develop. Firms can help by asking host national employees and their families to assist specific expatriates during the first few months. Care should be taken to match the sponsoring family's characteristics (e.g., number and ages of children) with those of the expatriate family. Several Japanese auto firms actually have hired Americans who speak Japanese to help their expatriate managers and families adjust to life in the United States.

The Amos Tuck School's joint M.B.A. program with the International University of Japan has a sponsorship program. A special employee in Japan is assigned to help U.S. professors with logistical problems, such as housing and travel, during their stay. Several Tuck professors who spent a term in Japan expressed pleasant surprise at the willingness of both the special employee and other employees to go beyond logistical assistance and to help them navigate the cultural and business terrain. This assistance gave them important insights into the culture and people and helped them adjust to the new environment.

Strategy 3: Creating Dual Citizens

Although these mechanisms are useful for counterbalancing negative tendencies, the most important steps firms can take are those that create high levels of dual allegiance. Our research suggests that the primary target for fostering expatriates like Joan Beckenridge is the job.

• **Plan Overseas Jobs Strategically.** A firm that clearly defines the expatriate's job, reduces conflicts concerning job expectations, and gives the expatriate a fair amount of freedom in carrying out assigned tasks will foster a high level of dual allegiance. The idea is simple, but execution is complex.

One of the easiest but rarely utilized techniques for increasing role clarity is allowing the incumbent and the new manager an overlap period of several days or weeks. The more complex the job and the less experienced the new entrant, the longer the overlap. Several expatriates specifically mentioned this method as a relatively low-cost means of facilitating adjustment and effectiveness. Expatriates in Japan and Korea said that this overlap was necessary for properly introducing the replacement to employees, clients, and suppliers. Of course, sometimes there is no incumbent, and this option is not available.

Role clarification in and of itself does not necessarily reduce role conflict. In fact, clarification of job expectations can reveal previously hidden role conflicts, which most often stem from the differing expectations of the parent firm and the local operation. Thus firms must try to increase role clarity and decrease role conflict simultaneously. This requires understanding and integrating the perspectives of the parent firm and the local operation.

A firm's best intentions cannot entirely eliminate role ambiguity and conflict. This is probably why role discretion emerged as the single strongest factor in promoting high dual allegiance. Having a fair amount of freedom to decide what tasks to do, how and when to do them, and who should do them gives expatriates the flexibility to cope with ambiguity and conflict. However, too much discretion without clear objectives may make expatriates unintentionally work against the best interests of the parent firm, the local operation, or both. Firms need to consider all three job elements simultaneously.

We believe that role clarity, conflict, and discretion are best approached not as targets of manipulation but as outcomes of broader policy and strategic processes. If a firm wants to make significant, long-term, and effective changes in the expatriate manager's job, it should carefully assess the following issues:

1. Why is this expatriate being sent to this particular post? (Because there are no host nationals capable of filling the position? In order to provide developmental experience for the expatriate?)
2. How will job success be measured? What do you really want this particular person to do in this position?
3. Are the objectives of the parent firm and the local unit

consistent? Are they consistent between the local unit as a whole and the individual's department?

4. How much should the parent firm coordinate and control the local operation? How much freedom and autonomy should the local unit have? Is the expatriate's level of discretion consistent with these coordination needs?

Without an assessment of these strategic issues, firms may adjust expectations in ways that are dysfunctional for the firm's overall strategy. For instance, firms may provide overlap time that serves only to clarify the severe expectation conflicts between the two organizations. Or firms may give too much freedom to expatriate managers. Consequently, such ad hoc adjustments are likely to have short-term positive results at best and severe negative results at worst. In contrast, an analysis that begins with the broader context naturally leads to appropriate job adjustments and a higher probability of a high dual allegiance.

Some readers may feel that their firms have moved beyond the coordinated multinational stage. Global firms need managers who are capable not just of dual citizenship but of world citizenship. Many firms are moving in this direction, but our data suggest that most expatriate managers are still struggling to successfully reach dual allegiance. It seems to us that the first practical step toward developing global managers for global firms is to develop managers who see themselves as dual citizens. Dual-citizen expatriates are best developed through (1) careful selection processes; (2) cross-cultural training before and after arrival; (3) well-planned career systems that lead to clear, consistent job expectations and appropriate discretion levels; and (4) repatriation programs that effectively utilize expatriates' knowledge, skills, and experience. These steps will help expatriates more successfully serve two masters and help firms more effectively manage their expatriates. ◆

References

1. H.B. Gregersen and J.S. Black, "Antecedents to Dual Commitment during International Assignments," *Academy of Management Journal* 35 (1992): 65-90.

This article is based primarily on two international research projects. First, we did a questionnaire study of 321 U.S. expatriate executives and managers while they were on assignment in Europe (Belgium, England, the Netherlands, and Germany) and the Pacific Rim (Japan, Korea, Taiwan, and Hong Kong). These expatriates had worked on average more than fourteen years in their U.S. multinational firms representing a wide range of industries. We also completed in-depth interviews with more than 30 expatriates in both Pacific Rim and European countries. Second, we completed a study of expatriate commitment during repatriation for 174 Americans, 173 Japanese, and 104 Finns returning to their respective home countries after international assignments.

2. C.V. Fukami and E.W. Larson, "Commitment to the Company and Union: Parallel Models," *Journal of Applied Psychology* 69 (1984): 367-371;

M.E. Gordon and R.T. Ladd, "Dual Allegiance: Renewal, Reconsideration, and Recantation," *Personnel Psychology* 43 (1990): 37-69;

H.B. Gregersen, "Multiple Commitments at Work and Extrarole Behavior during Three Stages of Organizational Tenure," *Journal of Business Research* 25 (1992); and

N.B. Tuma and A.J. Grimes, "A Comparison of Models of Role Orientations of Professionals in a Research-Oriented University," *Administrative Science Quarterly* 26 (1981): 187-206.

3. J.S. Black, "Personal Dimensions and Work Role Transitions," *Management International Review* 30 (1990): 119-134; and

M.E. Mendenhall and G. Oddon, "The Dimensions of Expatriate Acculturation," *Academy of Management Review* 10 (1985): 39-47.

4. J.S. Black and M. Mendenhall, "Cross-Cultural Training Effectiveness: A Review and a Theoretical Framework for Future Research," *Academy of Management Review* 15 (1990): 113-136.

5. J.S. Black, "Work Role Transitions: A Study of U.S. Expatriate Managers in Japan," *Journal of International Business Studies* 19 (1988): 277-294;

J.S. Black and H.B. Gregersen, "Antecedents to Cross-Cultural Adjustment for Expatriates in Pacific Rim Assignments," *Human Relations* 44 (1990): 497-515;

L. Copeland and L. Griggs, *Going International* (New York: Random House, 1985); and

K.F. Misa and J.M. Fabricatore, "Return on Investment of Overseas Personnel," *Financial Executive* 47 (1979): 42-46.

6. See R.L. Tung, *The New Expatriates* (Lexington, Massachusetts: Lexington Books, 1988) for a review.

7. J.S. Black and L.W. Porter, "Managerial Behavior and Job Performance: A Successful Manager in Los Angeles May Not Be Successful in Hong Kong," *Journal of International Business Studies* 22 (1991): 99-114; and

E. Miller, "The International Selection Decision: A Study of Managerial Behavior in the Selection Decision Process," *Academy of Management Journal* 16 (1973): 234-252.

8. M. Porter, "Changing Patterns of International Competition," *California Management Review*, Winter 1986, pp. 9-40.

9. H.B. Gregersen, "Commitments to a Parent Company and a Local Work Unit during Repatriation," *Personnel Psychology* 45 (1992): 29-54.

10. M.G. Harvey, "Repatriation of Corporate Executives," *Journal of International Business Studies*, Spring 1989, pp. 131-144.

11. Research consistently shows that good predeparture training helps expatriate managers adjust to and perform well in their jobs overseas. See:

Black and Mendenhall (1990).

12. See also J.S. Black and G.K. Stephens, "The Influence of the Spouse on U.S. Expatriate Adjustment in Overseas Assignments," *Journal of Management* 15 (1989): 529-544.

Reprint 3346

[33]

Addressing the Dual-Career Expatriation Dilemma

Michael Harvey, Puterbaugh Chair of American Free Enterprise, University of Oklahoma

The need for qualified international managers has become a critical issue for many multinational corporations (MNCs) worldwide. The high failure rate of expatriates has been a concern of international human resource managers for a decade. The impact of the family and, in particular, the spouse of the transferred international manager has become of increased interest to international human resource managers. The dual-career family is a reality that can no longer be addressed informally or on an ad hoc basis. The United States Department of Labor had predicted that 81 percent of all marriages would be dual-career partnerships in 1995. Frequently, potential expatriates refuse to relocate internationally due to the reluctance of their spouses to give up their own careers (Reynolds & Bennett, 1991). The dual-career couple challenge is an issue the MNCs' employers can no longer ignore (Dowling, et al., 1994) and is clearly emerging as a very significant mobility issue (Lublin, 1993).

Background

United States multinational based corporations (MNCs) appear to be plagued by high failure rates of expatriate managers, i.e., leaving the company, early return to domestic organization, performance during expatriation significantly below expectations (Mendenhall, et al., 1987; Mendenhall & Oddou, 1988; Wederspahn, 1992; Dowling, et al., 1994). The turnover or early return of expatriate managers have explicit as well as implicit costs associated with the managers' return to the domestic market. The direct cost of training, relocating, and compensating expatriate managers is estimated to be three times as high as their domestic counterparts (Wederspahn, 1992; Fuchsberg, 1992). At the same time, the implicit cost of an expatriate manager's failure may be greater due to the reduced service level to customers in foreign markets, lost customers, and the disproportionate time that human resource managers must spend with "failing" expatriates.

While there have been a multitude of explanations advanced for the high failure rate of expatriates, e.g., lack of training, inadequate selection criteria, ineffective compensation programs, ineffectual leadership and the like, none may be more significant than the impact of the spouse/family on the expatriate manager (Harvey, 1985; Black & Stephens, 1989; Harris, 1989; De Cieri, Dowling & Taylor, 1991; Haveman, 1992; Dowling, et al., 1994). Many MNCs appear to not consider the spouse/family as an important consideration, in that they do not interview them during the selection process and frequently do not include them in formal training programs (Harvey, 1985, 1989; Black & Stephens, 1989; Reynolds & Bennett, 1991). The impact of the spouse/family on global assignments is projected to become an even more compelling influence due to the number of dual-career families in the United States (Adler, 1986; Munton, 1990). MNCs that ignore expatriate spouses' and their careers do so at their own peril (Pascoe, 1992).

If MNCs wish to take advantage of the career development aspects of international assignments and the benefits to the organization of the use of expatriate managers in foreign assignments, human resource managers must consider the potentially disastrous consequences of international transfers to both partners in dual-career couples (Stephens & Black, 1991). The problem issues include: (1) the expatriate manager not successfully completing the foreign assignment, therefore having a negative effect on career path; (2) the trailing spouse having to abandon his/her career due to transfer spouse's, thereby increasing discontent and stress in the family unit; (3) the dual-career couple attempting to maintain both careers by the expatriate commuting back and forth between the home and host countries (Bunker et al., 1992; Lublin, 1992; Harvey, 1995); (4) inability to replace trailing spouse's income during expatriation, increasing financial stress during the overseas assignment; and (5) potential candidates for expatriation refusing to relocate overseas due to dual-career family configuration (Pascoe, 1992; Feldman & Thompson, 1993; Noe & Barber, 1993; Harvey, 1995).

In the United States, women are going to work in increasing numbers and now constitute 45 percent of the labor force (Statistical, 1992). According to the United States Bureau of Labor, in 1993 both spouses worked in 58 percent of all married couples with children under the age of 18, compared to only 36 percent twenty years ago (Coolidge & D'Angelo, 1994). In 1988, dual-career couples accounted for 21 percent of all professional households (Household, 1989). As dual-career couples become more the norm than the exception, they are having an increased impact on the mobility of the professional labor force (Bradbury, 1994). Past research has shown that the labor force participation of wives has greatly reduced the likelihood of family migration (Parnes, et al., 1975; Lichter, 1982; Bielby & Bielby, 1992; Blair, 1993; Arkin, 1993). This reluctance to relocate should be exacerbated during international relocations. Researchers have determined that adjustment of the expatriate to the overseas assignments is strongly influenced by the spouse and children's adjustment. A large portion of expatriate failures are attributed to non-work related, family issues (Copeland & Griggs, 1985; Harvey, 1985; 1995; Fuchsberg, 1992). The resulting family stress compounds the adjustment stress associated with the expatriate's new position and organizational expectations. The family has both a direct and indirect impact on the adjustment of the expatriate when relocating overseas. The direct impact can be illustrated by the potential loss of the trailing spouse's income and potential future earnings, i.e., career disruption when returning to the domestic market. Indirectly, the spouse and children influence the level of tension, stress and satisfaction when expatriating to a foreign country by creating a dysfunctional family environment that creates stress that can spillover into the work environment (Vannoy &

Philliber, 1992; Wiggins-France & Shehan, 1994; Solomon, 1994; Frame & Shehan, 1994). Confusion about what the trailing spouse needs during an international relocation has led some companies to do an internal needs assessment. The needs assessments are used to determine the unique requirements of the trailing spouses relative to their careers. Marriott Corporation, Mobil Corporation, Square D Company and Ameritech survey their dual-career couples directly. The United States Air Force, AT&T, Ford Motor Company, and Allstate Insurance Company conduct focus groups interviews and collect feedback from ongoing management and employee groups. This information is used to customize expatriation compensation and support packages.

Presently, 90 percent of expatriates are males, 78 percent are married. It is estimated that 46 percent of the companies' spouses have careers in the United States and 88 percent of companies surveyed by the Foreign Trade Council believe that dual-career issues will become a more acute problem in international assignments (Solomon, 1994). Human resource managers estimate that by the year 2000, 20 percent of expatriates will be females, increasing the problems associated with relocation of the dual-career family (Ioannou, 1994), and over 80 percent of all marriages in the United States by 1995 will represent dual income/dual-career partnerships (Dowling, et al., 1994).

The focus of this paper is five related issues: (1) theoretical background to analyzing dual-career family units; (2) the stress associated with dual-career international relocations; (3) social support networks needed to facilitate stress management by the dual-career couple; (4) career and family life-cycles as mediating variables during international relocation of dual-career couples; (5) development of a decision model to be used by human resource managers when relocating dual-career couples internationally.

Exploring the Theory Behind the Dual-Career Family

Dual-career couples are frequently defined as both partners employed and psychologically committed to their work (Burke & Greenglass, 1987; Falkberg & Monachello, 1988) or employed in upwardly mobile jobs (Hertz, 1986); whereas, the dual income and/or earner couple has both the husband and wife who earn an income outside the household (Karambayya & Reilly, 1992). This research is concerned with the dual-career professionals who represent logical targets for expatriate assignments. Of particular interest is the "trailing spouse," i.e., the spouse of the transferred employee (Reed & Reed, 1993) and his/her impact on the family's willingness to relocate overseas. The trailing spouse's influence on the successful completion of the expatriate assignment is of primary concern. As was mentioned earlier, presently a vast majority of expatriate managers are males, therefore, the trailing spouse issue focuses on the wife's willingness to disrupt her career and relocate overseas. Married women are much less likely than married men to report being willing to move for improved job opportunities for themselves or their spouse (Markham, et al. 1983; Markham & Pleck, 1986; Bielby & Bielby, 1992). Therefore, the spouse's impact on completing an expatriate assignment could be significant.

There are three models that are frequently used to analyze family migration relative to organizational relocations: (1) neoclassical market model; (2) relative resources and couples' decision making; and (3) gender-role and provider-role ideology. Each of these theoretical approaches to family mobility will be explored prior to development of a model for managing dual-career international relocations. The neoclassical approach to migration of family centers on the spouses maximizing family well-being and, in doing so, forgoing opportunities that are optimal from a personal calculation of utility maximization (Mincer, 1978). If a spouse (wife) is faced with a net gain from relocation opportunity, but the husband's net loss is of a greater magnitude, then foregoing the relocation maximizes family utility as well as the husband's utility (Bielby & Bielby, 1992). There has been significant empirical data to support the neoclassical model which shows dual-career families migrate less than those with a single earner (Mincer, 1978), and as important to international relocation, husbands' earnings increase after migration, while wives' earnings and employment levels decline (Lichter, 1980; Spitze, 1984; Maxwell, 1988). This model does not assume that the husband's potential gains from moving are more important than the wife's in decisions regarding migration. Instead, the model assumes each spouse's potential gain or loss is weighted equally in computation of family well-being. The model is based on the generally held assumption that husbands' gains for opportunities elsewhere tend to exceed wives' losses from moving (Bielby & Bielby, 1992).

The relative resources and couples' decision-making model is founded on social exchange theory (Emerson, 1976) and yields predictions similar to the neoclassical model. The main difference is that social exchange theory involves the concept of power as the mechanism through which decisions are made (Blumstein & Schwartz, 1983; England, 1989). That is, the spouse in command of the most resources is able to impose outcomes to further his/her own goals to the detriment of the partner's. If financial resources provide leverage in bargaining between spouses, then the partner with greater earning capacity is likely to determine the outcome of a relocation decision (Hood, 1983).

The gender-role and provider-role ideology model ignores the household roles husbands and wives occupy, the gender-role beliefs they subscribe to regarding these roles, and the effect of their beliefs on both the process and the outcome of their decision making (Hood, 1983). An asymmetry is introduced in the dyad when the potential trailing spouse has the right to exercise power in a given area as well as his/her relative resources. Thus, when the provider role is defined as the husband's responsibility, the wife's net economic gain (loss) from a prospective geographic move is likely to be discounted relative to that of the husband (Bielby & Bielby, 1992).

Based on the three theoretical models presented above, Exhibit One was derived to illustrate potential problems with dual-career couples during relocation (see Exhibit One). The qualifiers, i.e., low, moderate, and high used in Exhibit One, are indicative of the level of stress, dysfunctional consequences of relocation, and in general, the difficulty associated with the international relocation of dual-career couples based upon the three theoretical models that have been presented. The theoretical bases for these predictions can vary to a degree based upon which theory base is used, but for the most part, there is a consistency of predictions among the three theoretical approaches. The degree and deviation of the impact of relocation on dual-career couples is most strongly influenced by the primary income earner's status as well as the magnitude of the relocation, i.e., domestic, international, global (Bielby & Bielby, 1992; Higgins et al., 1992; Jones & Fletcher, 1993; Frame & Shehan, 1994; Harvey, 1995). These predictions are of particular importance to international human resource managers when identifying potential candidates for foreign assignments and in constructing proactive personnel strategies directed at the dual-career expatriate family. The overriding conclusion from the past research on dual-career families is that there is a significant increase in the stress levels in the family unit. Due to role conflict and difficulty in reallocating time to accomplish normal family activities stress spillover from the work environment to the family as well as the converse. It is anticipated that stress will be elevated during an international relocation because of a lack of a infrastructure. Therefore, MNCs must be prepared to develop support mechanisms for the dual-career family or the resulting stress associated with international relocation will play a major role in the continued failure of expatriate managers (Higgins et al., 1992; Higgins & Duxbury, 1992; Karombayya & Reilly, 1992; Parasurman et al., 1992; Stephens, 1994; Harvey, 1995).

The following research propositions are presented relative to the issues associated with dual-career families and international relocation:

■ **Proposition One:** There will be a stronger positive relationship between work-conflict and family-conflict for dual-career couples than for traditional couples.

EXHIBIT I

Dual-Income/Dual-Career Couples and Relocation

	RELOCATION DESTINATION		
DUAL-INCOME	**DOMESTIC**	**INTERNATIONAL**	**GLOBAL**
Husband greater income earning capacity ...husband relocated.	L	L	L
Husband greater income earning capacity ...wife relocated.	M	M/H	M/H
Wife greater income earning capacity ... husband relocated.	M	M	M
Wife greater income earning capacity ...wife relocated.	L	M	M
DUAL-CAREER			
Husband greater income earning capacity ...husband relocated.	L	M	M/H
Husband greater income earning capacity ...wife relocated.	M	H	H
Wife greater income earning capacity ... husband relocated.	H	H	H
Wife greater income earning capacity ...wife relocated.	M	M/H	M/H

EXHIBIT 2

Stressors in Work-Family Context and Resulting Potential for Conflict

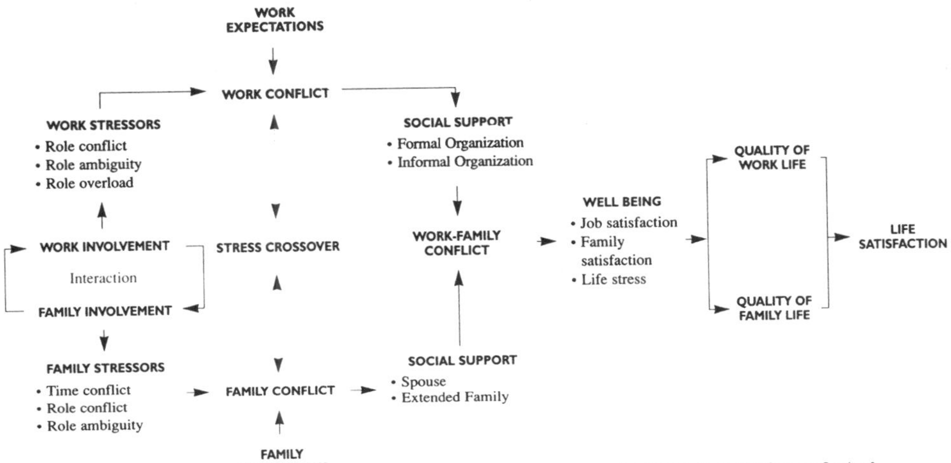

Adapted from: Kopelman et al, 1983; Parasurman, Greenhaus & Granrose, 1992; Higgins, Duxbury & Irving, 1992; Sears & Galambos, 1991

■ **Proposition Two:** The trailing spouse's career orientation, i.e., non-workplace, preparing for workplace position, dual-income, and dual-career will impact willingness to relocate, e.g., domestically, internationally, and globally.

■ **Proposition Three:** The trailing spouse in a dual-career couple may have significant influence on the potential expatriate manager's willingness to relocate if their income is greater than their partner's.

■ **Proposition Four:** An expatriate manager who has a spouse with a career is less likely to successfully complete the international assignment.

Stress in the Dual-Career Expatriate Family

Stress in the dual-career family is derived from both work and the family (see Exhibit Two). The level and duration of stress present in dual-career couple relocations makes it a pivotal issue that needs to be effectively addressed prior to as well as during the expatriation assignment. Work stressors are generally identified as role conflict, role ambiguity, and role overload. These three work related stressors have been found to be associated with several incidences of psychological strain such as tension, anxiety, and job dissatisfaction (Billings & Moos, 1982; Burke, 1988). Family stressors which are representative of pressures within the family domain include family conflict resulting from multiple role pressures and conflicts, as well as, the obligations of parenthood on the adult members of the family (Kopelman et al., 1983). Research on dual-career couples indicates stressors are more severe for two-career parents than for non-career oriented parents.

The interaction of work and family stressors creates work-family conflicts which may have a number of undesirable consequences, i.e. health risks, decreased productivity at work, marital dissatisfaction of partners, reduced life expectancy and life satisfaction (Greenhaus & Beutell, 1985; Voydanoff, 1988; Fletcher, 1988). The conflict that increases stress and has a negative impact on the transferee's health stems from time-based issues, strain-based issues and behavioral-based issues (Greenhaus & Beutell, 1985). All of these

dual-career, work-family conflict issues can be expected to occur with expatriates when they are relocated to an overseas assignment. Therefore, it would be helpful to have a theoretical basis to analyze how to effectively deal with the stressors as well as the resulting conflict that occurs during an overseas relocation.

Earlier researchers suggested that work and home events were segmented, i.e., they do not affect each other or create conflicting expectations and roles among family members similar to the relative resources and couple's decision-making model presented earlier (Jones & Fletcher, 1993). A more frequently adopted model of work and family interaction predicts "spillover" from one situation to the other. The spillover model suggests that work and non-work experiences are positively related. Thus, individuals who have varied and stimulating work experiences will have similarly varied and stimulating out of work experiences, and vice versa (Frankenhaueser et al., 1989; Lambert, 1990). A compensatory model of work and family events indicates that there will be a negative relationship between work and home, e.g., individuals may compensate for boring unstimulating work by seeking opposite experiences out of work (Karasele, 1979; Staines, 1980).

An additional model that could be helpful in understanding the stress of an international relocation for an expatriate and family is the demands, supports, and constraints model. This model considers stress to be the result of the balance of three factors: (1) job demands, (2) job supports, and (3) job constraints where:

(Demands + Constraints) – Supports = Stress Level

where:

Demands = the degree to which the environment contains stimuli which peremptorily demand the individual's attention and response.

Constraints = the degree to which the environment prevents or confines the individual from surviving or coping.

Supports = the degree to which the environment has available resources including those of an intellectual, technical, social, and financial nature (Fletcher, 1991).

The same definitions/relationships hold for stress in the family unit. When combined, the resulting imbalance in the two equations identifies the level of stress between work and family. The ability of the model to take into account a wide range of stressors makes it an appropriate framework in which to analyze the stress created by expatriate relocation to a foreign assignment.

The stressors commonly associated with international relocation for dual-career couples are: (1) an altered financial state, e.g., immediate loss of spouse's income; (2) loss of close relationships in both family and work situations; (3) problems in adopting to new culture (both organizational and external culture); (4) problems associated with establishing new residence and "settling" the family; (5) pressure to find replacement employment for the trailing spouse; and (6) pressure to succeed in the expatriate position (Ammons et al., 1982; Frame & Shehan, 1994). These outcomes have inhibited the geographic mobility of dual-career families and some studies have found that an increasing percentage of potential candidates that are from dual-career marriages are refusing to transfer (Shaklee, 1989; Crendall, 1990). This reluctance to relocate on the part of dual-career couples has led some organizations to less often consider them as potential candidates for relocation (Le Lovarn, 1987). This reluctance to relocate appears to be accentuated at different stages of the family and career life-cycles for international expatriate assignments (Reynolds & Bennett, 1991; Dowling, et al., 1994).

The following research propositions are presented relative to the issues associated with dual-career families and stress during an international relocations:

■ **Proposition Five:** Dysfunctional levels of work role stressors, family role stressors, and the resulting work-family conflict will be negatively related to job satisfaction, willingness to relocate internationally, and performance during international relocation.

■ **Proposition Six:** Dysfunctional level of work role stressors, family role stressors, and the resulting work-family conflict will be negatively related to family satisfaction.

■ **Proposition Seven:** Work role stressors, family role stressors, and work-family conflict experienced during international relocation by the trailing spouse will be negatively related to the expatriate's work performance, willingness to complete international assignment, and willingness to undertake a second international relocation.

Addressing Dual-Career Stress Issues During Expatriate Relocation

According to a corporate survey, 75 percent of corporations currently provide some type of employment assistance to the spouses of domestically relocated employees (Collie, 1989). The justification for the expense is tied to the reduced productivity of the relocated employee due to the stress on the trailing spouse (Anderson & Stark, 1988; Foxman & Polsky, 1988). Without significant corporate attention to what is referred to as the "mobility syndrome" in dual-career families, research suggests that the trailing spouse frequently exhibits depression, health problems, little community involvement, strong dependency on their spouse for emotional support, and makes poor adjustments to his/her new community (Anderson & Stark, 1988).

Recently, a survey found that without formalized organizational support for the trailing spouse, dual-career couples relocate less frequently and that programs to address the trailing spouse are decisive factors in the decision to relocate (Reed & Reed, 1993). NCR Corporation, US Sprint, Kodak, BP America and Mobil Corporation provide elaborate assistance programs to dual-career couples with the purpose of shortening adjustment time and increasing post-transfer productivity. Any model of work-family dynamics and stress needs to emphasize the role of social support in alleviating stress and strain to the individuals as well as the family unit. Of particular importance to MNCs is that social support has been identified as an important factor contributing to job satisfaction, family-work conflict reduction, worker productivity, and the well-being of individuals in dual-career work relationships (Bird & Bird, 1986; Frone & Rice, 1987; Wiley, 1987).

There are four types of social support that can be provided by the spouse and/or the organization for which he/she works: (1) emotional support – providing trust, empathy, attention and affection; (2) instrumental support-providing time, resources, or skills; (3) informational support – provision of facts, opinions, and advice; and (4) appraisal support – entails providing evaluation and feedback on performance (House, 1981; Granrose, et al., 1992). To help insure effective support for the dual-career family during an international relocation, each of the four types of social support needs to be provided. The providers of the support may be the spouse as well as the organization. It should be noted that some of the social support may be provided exclusively by the spouse or from the organization; and, at times both entities may simultaneously provide an element of social support.

Exhibit Three illustrates a model of social support for the dual-career family relocating to a foreign location (see Exhibit Three). The model is divided into two primary providers, the spouse and the organization. While there is a degree of overlap in social support, each entity can provide support that the other cannot. The "spouse" portion of the model will be discussed briefly, in that, the primary focus of this paper is to examine the support programs of MNCs for expatriate dual-career families relocating overseas.

EXHIBIT 3

Theoretical Model of Social/Psychological Support for the Expatriated Dual-Career Family

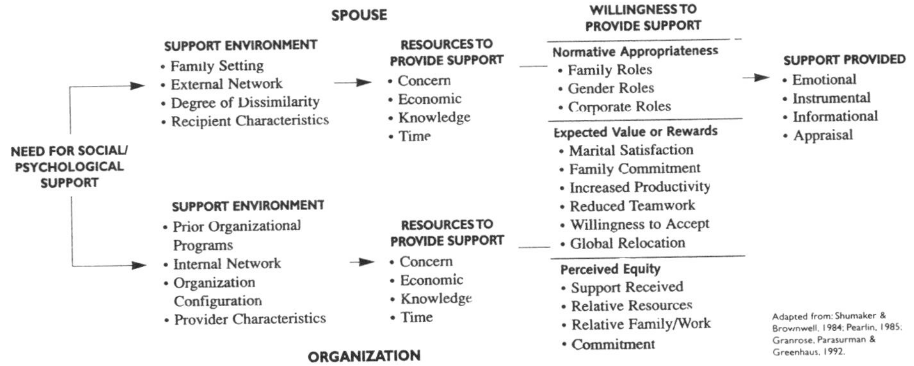

Adapted from: Shumaker & Brownwell, 1984; Pearlin, 1985; Granrose, Parasurman & Greenhaus, 1992.

The support environment (see Exhibit Three) provides a context for exchange of support within the marriage. The primary types of support from the spouse are emotional and instrumental, but the conclusiveness of the support environment may be contingent on the level of commitment to the family by both spouses, the "quality" of the marriage, i.e., cumulative interpersonal relationship history, the stage of the family life-cycle, as well as, the financial well being of the family. Within this environment, the following issues impact the level and quality of social support:

1. Family Setting - the internal family organization and existing relationships among family members, i.e., level of confrontation, affection, understanding of family members' values and the expectations of family members (Schumaker & Jackson, 1979; Schumaker & Brownwell, 1984). An additional consideration is the level of past support provided by each spouse and the level of reciprocity between the dual-career spouses concerning support (Tousig & Michello, 1988).

2. External Network - the number and quality of relationships beyond family that can/have provided social support to family members. The size (small rather than large) and the intensity (level of interaction) of the external network increases the quality/level of social support (Tousig & Michello, 1988). The importance of the external network is related to reducing the need for the spouse to provide all the social support – a consideration of significance when considering international relocation when the external network support may be disrupted.

3. Degree of Dissimilarity - the discontinuity between the domestic support system and the available support in the international environment are the issues associated with this element of social support. How disruptive is the relocation to the social support being received by the dual-career couple?

4. Recipient Characteristics - the spouse who receives the support may play an instrumental role in the support exchange by selecting coping strategies, eliciting support, or choosing the level of support he/she is willing to accept from internal and as external supporters (Granrose, et al., 1992). An additional issue is when, how, and the frequency of communication of the need for support once it is given by the spouse (Schumaker & Brownwell, 1984; Tousig & Michello, 1988) and the perceived legitimacy and reasonableness of the request by the potential support provider (Perlin, 1985).

The resources to provide support examine the basic cost and utility issues of economics, knowledge, and time. The one issue less tangible is the level of concern that the spouse feels for his/her mate. That level of concern is normally the triggering mechanism to determine the "cost" that is appropriate given the level of stress and/or dissatisfaction of the spouse. The level of resources devoted to spousal support has not been extensively examined by researchers, but the emotional aspects of the family play an important role in willingness to expend resources for support (Huber & Spitze, 1981).

Leading from the resources to provide support, is the willingness to provide support which is divided into the normative appropriateness, expected value of rewards, and perceived equity dimensions (see Exhibit Four). The issue of norms examines the traditional roles of those who have historically provided social support and how their contributions are affected by the international relocation. The expected value or reward from the social support is the benefit component of the cost/benefit exchange equation when making the decision to support or not to support the spouse. Being a support provider may involve substantial emotional and resource costs, but may also provide rewards of self-validation, efficiency, and trust (Schumaker & Brownwell, 1984).

Marital satisfaction and the level of family commitment may be quasi indicators of the spouse's willingness to support a partner during an international relocation, two factors that are very difficult to quantify (Granrose, et al., 1992). The expected values received from the organization's commitment of resources to the social support of the dual-career family are more tangible and can impact explicit returns to the MNC, such as, increased productivity, reduced turnover, and willingness to accept global relocations.

The model of social support for expatriate dual-career families provides an infrastructure to develop specific programs which address the unique aspects of dual-career, international relocations. But, to develop effective corporate programs for social support of dual-career families, additional dimensions need to be included. The stage of career life-cycle, stage of family life-cycle are not the only issues that can impact the need for support for other critical issues; such as, level of education, assignment duration, geographic location of assignment, and the level of cultural and economic dissimilarity between the domestic environment and that of the foreign assignment may also influence the need for support. Exhibit Five provides a visual representation of the variables that will impact the selection of an appropriate support strategy for MNCs relocating expatriate dual-career families.

The following research propositions are presented relative to the issues associated with social support for members of dual-career families during an international relocation.

■ **Proposition Eight:** A non-competitive and reciprocal family unit will be positively related to instrumental and emotional social support provided by members of dual-career couples.

■ **Proposition Nine:** Work support and support of the trailing spouse will be positively related to job satisfaction, performance, and successful completion of an international assignment by expatriate managers.

■ **Proposition Ten:** Work support and family support for the trailing spouse will be positively related to family satisfaction and, therefore, there will be reduced work-family conflict.

The stage of the career life-cycle has significant implications for the development of strategies to address the trailing spouse during an international relocation.

Career and Family Life-Cycle Impact on Global Relocation

Work-career models identify major periods or "stages" through which workers will normally pass during their professional life, from the time they enter the labor force until they retire (Hall & Nougaim, 1968; Hall, 1986; Veiga, 1973; 1983). Each of these stages is partly under control of the individual and partly under control of organizational "others." The concept of career life-cycles is multidimensional and complex, integrating aspects of work (Arthur, 1984), time (Lawrence, 1984), and space (Super, 1982) in both an individual and an organizational perspective (Schein, 1978; Gunz, 1989).

According to classical models of career life-cycles, individuals evolve in their careers through a series of stages: (1) trial and exploration (until about age 25); (2) growth and establishment (until the 40s); (3) then maintenance; and finally (4) decline (after the 50s). Each stage is generally closely linked to biological age and to some degree to stages in the family life-cycle (to be discussed in a later section). It is thought that each stage is characterized by a set of tasks and roles and is distinct in its associated needs, motivations, attitudes, and behaviors (Tremblay & Roger, 1993). The career stages are important factors in the gender-role and provider model presented earlier. The role delineation between expatriate and trailing spouse becomes ambiguous when both members of the dual-career couple want to continue their career during an international relocation. If not properly timed or effectively handled by the MNC's human resource personnel, the trailing spouse may have the power/influence to have the potential expatriate refuse a relocation. While at a different stage of the trailing spouse's career, he/she may support an international relocation (Greenhaus & Bastell, 1985; England, 1989; Feldman & Thomas, 1992; Higgins et al., 1992; Vannou & Philliber, 1992).

There are four distinct features in the conceptualization of career life-cycles which provide insights into problems associated with dual-career expatriates' relocation and the resulting work-family stress: (1) the career life-cycle has a long-term perspective which extends beyond the current time period and the immediate performance/satisfaction of individuals; (2) the concept focuses on objective aspects of a career (activities), as well as, on subjective aspects that accompany these activities (experiences); (3) it views career effectiveness from a variety of perspectives, as something that does not consist merely of attaining socially-sanctioned positions or ranks, but also of realizing goals that are personally important to the individual; and (4) the career life-cycle concept explicitly recognizes that career outcomes are the joint result of individual efforts and of outside and/or organizational forces over which the individual does not have complete control (Beckhard, 1987; Orpen, 1994). The term "organization career management" typically refers to various policies and practices, deliberately established by organizations, to improve the career effectiveness of their employees. Whereas, "individual career management" reports the personal efforts made by individuals to advance their own career goals which may, or may not, coincide with those of their organizations (Hall, 1986; Orpen, 1994). The stage of the career life-cycle has significant implications for the development of strategies to address the trailing spouse during an international relocation. The Foreign Trade Council recently published a survey of 120 Fortune 500 countries where 88 percent of the respondents indicated that dual-career issues will become more acute in the near future. The need for expatriate managers and the limited pool of candidates necessitates MNC addressing the dual-career issue rather than avoiding it as they have done in the past (Solomon, 1994).

The career life-cycle for the dual-career couple may serve to illustrate the potential differences between the couples' careers. Exhibit Four demonstrates the potential differences in the career cycles of the expatriated spouse and trailing spouse. There may be a delay in the start of the career life-cycle of the trailing spouse which could be attributed to a number of circumstances, e.g., helped to support spouse during their education, difficulty in finding employment in city where spouse was employed, delayed education opportunities, and the like. Just as frequently, the trailing spouse may interrupt their career due to a number of similar circumstances. The lack of parallel career paths may produce significant tension and conflict in the dual-career family unit. The lack of synchronization between the two career life-cycles could have an impact on managing an expatriate relocation to a foreign assignment. The career "demands" of each spouse may be affected by the stage of the career life-cycle they are in when the relocation opportunity presents itself.

The career life-cycle phases each have a potential impact on both members of the dual-career couple. Using the three theoretical approaches, i.e., neoclassical, relative resource and couple's decision-making, and gender-role and provider-role ideology, the following examples illustrate the inherent influence on dual-career couples who are/did relocate internationally: (1) Stage One of Career Life-Cycle: If the trailing spouse has yet to begin his/her career, there may be an opportunity to continue education, so that upon returning to the home country, the international experience differentiates him/her when looking for a domestic entry level position; (2) Stage Two of Career Life-Cycle: An international relocation during this stage of the trailing spouses career could provide an opportunity to start a family assuming the trailing spouse is the wife. The break in the career as well as the additional support staff available during international relocation may serve to encourage starting a family; (3) Stage Three of Career Life-Cycle: May be the most difficult stage in a career life-cycle for the trailing spouse to relocate. Frequently, the trailing spouse has vested, i.e., partner, tenure, senior management position in their career; therefore, a commuting relationship for the dual-career couple may be a plausible alternative during the spouse's international transfer (Bunker & Vanderslice, 1982; Bunker et al., 1992); (4) Stage Four of Career Life-Cycle: The trailing spouse may be employed by the MNC to develop relocation information and "tools" to assist future dual-career couples who are to be relocated internationally.

The family life-cycle is an additional metronome in the stages of a family that can provide valuable insights into the predisposition to and

EXHIBIT 4

Non-Parallel Spouse/Trailing Spouse Career Life-Cycles

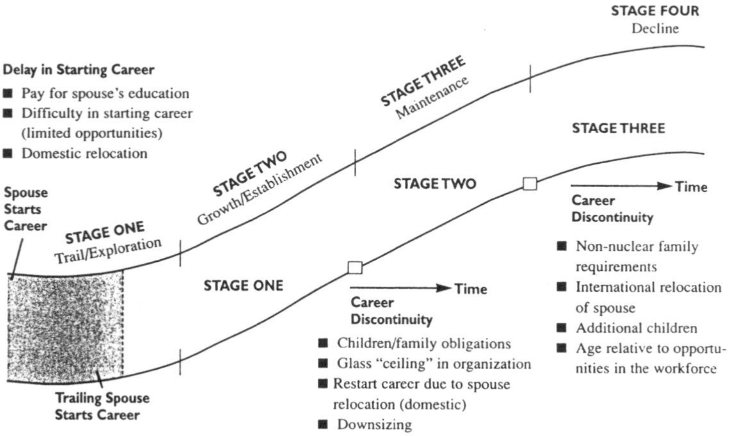

probable success of an international relocation. Just as the career life-cycle can be used to understand the professional roles, obligations and expectations of dual-career couples, the family life-cycle provides predictors of the personal needs, time constraints, and family requirements which could influence willingness to undertake an overseas relocation.

The family life-cycle is divided into various stages: (1) Bachelor Unit; (2) Newly Married Couple; (3) Full Nest I: Youngest Child Under Six; (4) Full Nest Ii: Youngest Child Over Six; (5) Full Nest Iii: Older Married Couples With Dependent Children; (6) Empty Nest I: Older Married Couples, No Children Living With The Unit; (7) Empty Nest Ii: Older Married Couple, Retired; (8) Sole Survivor, in Labor Force; and (9) Empty Nest Iii: Sole Survivor, Retired (Kotler & Armstrong, 1991). Each of these stages represents life-demands on the dual-career family members which create work-family conflict. Relocation can be influenced by what stages of the cycle the family is in and the characteristics of the relocation. One of the primary indicators of the family life-cycle in the dual-career family is that of role overload. When role overload occurs, a need to cycle roles may be prompted. Deciding when to start a family or to have additional children may be based on the influences of the family life-cycle and the career life-cycle. The family conflict created by young children heightens the stress for each member of the dual-career couple (Ventura, 1987). And, because women in dual-career families still perform most of the parenting, the decision to postpone childbearing until after significant career/job training may be especially important to them (Wiersma, 1994).

Both the career life-cycle and the family life-cycle will provide valuable insights into effectively providing for the trailing spouse during an expatriate relocation. Given the complexity of the dual-career family and the likely probability of its occurrence in expatriate relocations, specific proactive corporate strategies need to be developed for dual-career families in various stages of their career and family life-cycles.

The following research propositions are presented relative to the potential impact of career and family life-cycles on dual-career couples:

- **Proposition Eleven:** Stages of the family life-cycle can be used as indicators of willingness to relocate internationally as well as directly impact the specific characteristics of compensation/support packages for dual-career couples.
- **Proposition Twelve:** Stages of the career life-cycle for both members of dual-career couples

EXHIBIT 5

MNC Strategies to Provide Social Support to Trailing Spouse During International Relocation

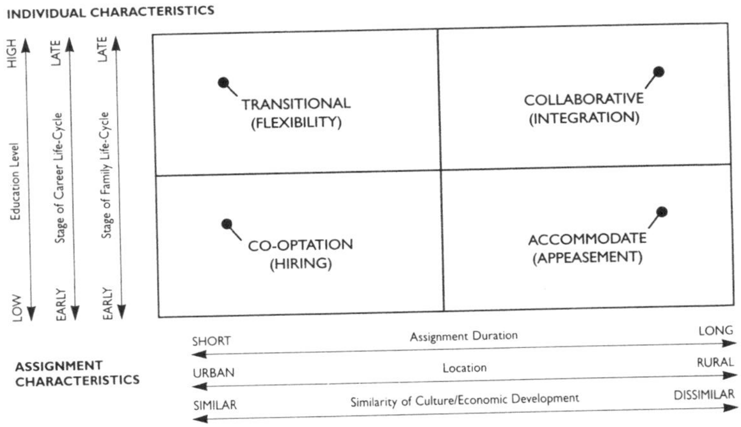

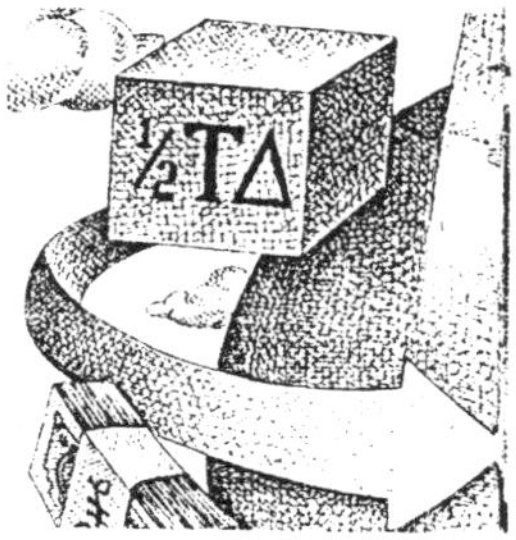

influence willingness to relocate internationally, time to adjust during foreign assignment, and probable success in completing an international assignment.

■ **Proposition Thirteen:** The selection process when dual-career couples are involved should include analysis of family support needs based upon stage of family life-cycle.

Strategic Decision Model for MNCs to Address International Dual-Career Relocations

The need for corporate support programs for internationally relocated dual-career couples has spawn new services by companies like Prudential Relocation International Services, International Organization Resources, Windham International, KPMG Peat Marwick and others who address issues associated with dual-career families' needs and, in some instances, provide support mechanisms in the host country (Solomon, 1994). The primary value of many of these program is to highlight the problems to perspective transferees, to underscore the need for social support to be provided for the dual-career couple by the MNCs and, in some cases, to actually assist the couple after relocation. Companies such as CIGNA, Eastman-Kodak, IBM, Raychem Corporation, NCR, Mobil Corporation, DuPont have instituted: (1) employment databases; (2) informal networking systems; (3) internal placement postings; (4) in-house counseling on the issues associated with international relocation; (5) development of a flexible "cafeteria" approach to support the trailing spouse's wants during the relocation.

There are a significant percentage of MNCs who do not provide assistance to the dual-career couple and do not feel that it is the corporate responsibility to treat these families differently than other expatriate families (Reynolds & Bennett, 1991; Dowling, et al., 1994). But, for those MNCs who recognize the unique family-work conflict created by dual-career families, a comprehensive assistance/support program needs to be developed.

The international relocation of dual-career families is a very complex set of interrelated challenges for international human resource managers. Development of effective strategies to address the obstacles associated with relocation of dual-career couples must incorporate characteristics of the couple/family as well as the environment to which they are being transferred. Exhibit Five portrays a set of essential individual, as well as environmental, constraints that impact any strategy to address dual-career international transfers (see Exhibit Five). By simultaneously evaluating the characteristics of the trailing spouse and the type of environment the family is going to experience during the relocation, multiple strategies can be formulated by international human resource personnel in MNCs.

The personal characteristics, e.g., educational level, stage of career, and family life-cycle have been discussed earlier. The three environmental issues also can have a significant influence on the most appropriate strategy to accommodate dual-career trailing spouses. One of the most relevant issues is the length of the assignment. The longer the duration of the relocation, the more severed the displaced, trailing spouse will feel relative to his/her career (Bielby & Bielby, 1992; Higgins & Duxbury, 1992; Sears & Galambos, 1992; Frame & Shehan, 1994). The stress associated with the relocation is strongly influenced by the duration of the spouse's assignment.

The specific geographic location may also influence the level of stress and relative dissatisfaction from being relocated overseas. As Exhibit Five depicts, the foreign location can be subdivided into urban-rural, similar-dissimilar cultures and similar-dissimilar levels of economic development. The assumption made, is that a significant portion of expatriates' relocation would be to urban areas, therefore, more rural locations would create additional hardships on the trailing spouse and his/ her career (Noe & Barber, 1993). Similarly, the greater the difference between their home culture and that of the host culture where the spouse is relocated will also create higher levels of dysfunctional stress and could exacerbate the job search in the host country. This assumption has been widely supported most noticeably by the works of Hofstede (1980) and researchers who have follow-up on Hofstede's concept of cultural distance. The same logic would hold for economies with a different level of economic development and the trailing spouse's ability to maintain his/ her career after the relocation to the foreign assignment of their spouse. The level of similarity/ dissimilarity between the home and host country reflects what researchers refer to as cultural novelty (Mendenhall & Oddou, 1985; Torbiorn, 1982; Black, 1988; Black & Gregersen, 1991). The same logic would hold for economies with a different level of economic development and the trailing spouse's ability to maintain his/her career after the relocation to the foreign assignment of their spouse.

While the individual and environmental characteristics are illustrated as dichotomous, it must be clearly understood that each construct is a continuum of different stages or phases for each element. For example, educational levels would be high school degree, some college, bachelor, masters, J.D., Ph.D., rather than no education or graduate degree. Each of the various stages may represent a need for a slightly different strategy for addressing the requirements of the trailing spouse. For simplicity, the discussion of the human resource strategies will examine only the extremes of each continuum, e.g., short-long, urban-rural, etc.

Five separate social support strategies are developed for assisting the trailing spouse during an overseas relocation. Each of these strategies will be briefly discussed:

1. Transitional Strategy:

Individual Characteristics – high education level, late stage of career life-cycle, late stage of family life-cycle.

Assignment Characteristics – short assignment duration, urban location, similarity of culture and level of economic development.

The locus of conflict for the trailing spouse in quadrant one of the matrix centers on the individual's personal attributes. The assignment is of less concern because of the consistency between the home and host culture and level of economic development. In addition, the length of the assignment for the spouse is defined and has been classified to be of short duration.

The exact stage of the career and family life-cycles can make an inordinate difference in the corporate strategy to address the dual-career relocation in quadrant one. If the children are still at home, the strategy to address international relocation will be different than for the "empty nest" couple. Assuming the couple is "empty nest," the company might want to encourage the couple to undertake a commuter relationship, i.e., trailing spouse remains in the home country while the expatriate temporarily relocates to the host country.

The popular views of the commuting lifestyle are generally pessimistic. Although, the benefits of commuting, especially with regard to work goals, have not been totally examined, the general assumption seems to be that the commuting lifestyle is one of chronic role strain and stress (Rhodes & Rhodes, 1984). The decision to commute is often a decision to give priority to work-related values (Bunker et al., 1992); an assumption that may not be too unrealistic, given the family-career phase of dual-career couples in quadrant one. If both individuals are dedicated to their careers and family obligations are reduced due to children being in college or married, undertaking a commuting strategy may be appropriate. The commuting lifestyle provides the opportunity for intense concentration and more time at work by the separation of work and non-work life (Bunker & Vanderslice, 1982), and may allow commuters to more completely fulfill work-role expectations (Gerstel & Gross, 1981). Not recognizing the concept of commuter marriages as a viable option in addressing dual-career couples ignores the concept of family and career role expectations and will compound staff immobility and turnover in the MNC (Reynolds & Bennett, 1991; Dowling, et al., 1994). As of 1985, more than a million couples were experimenting with the commuting lifestyle (Dahl, 1985), and the prevalence of this lifestyle is expected to increase as the proportion of professional women in the work force continues to increase (Johnson & Packer, 1987). A 1991 study by Runzheimer International, Ltd. of 51 United States MNCs indicated that one third of the companies allow international commuter assignments to assist working spouses of employees transferred abroad (Lublin, 1993).

Five separate social support strategies are developed for assisting the trailing spouse during an overseas relocation.

2. Co-Optation Strategy:

Individual Characteristics – Low level of education, early state of career life-cycle, early stage of family life-cycle.

Assignment Characteristics – short assignment duration, urban location, and similar cultural/economic level of development.

In quadrant two, the trailing spouse may be early enough in his/her career to forego strategic emphasis on maintaining the career. The spouse may have finished college/professional school and have started the first job, or have delayed his/her education to support the spouse. The MNC has the option of inter-company employment of the spouse in the host location (Dowling, et al., 1994). In addition, the trailing spouse may be employed as a consultant to provide valuable information in his/her area of expertise to the MNC. This approach has been used by MNCs where the trailing spouse was a lawyer, social

psychologist, MIS professional, college professor, medical professional, i.e., doctor, nurse, public health expert (Harvey, 1993). The short duration complements the early stage of the career life-cycle. The key strategic consideration is demonstration to the trailing spouse that the professional experience gained during the international assignment of his/her spouse will enhance his/her own career upon return to the home market.

To effect a smooth transition to the host country employment, the human resource manager must anticipate and develop plans to address obstacles to the acculturation of the trailing spouse. It should not be assumed that only career issues need to be addressed and that the more traditional problems associated with an international relocation do not have to be addressed by the MNC. Adjustments may encompass a wide variety of work and non-work related issues such as: different values, attitudes, beliefs toward professionals who are expatriates, and loss of cultural "signposts" in the home country, e.g., friends, family, one's professional identity (Anderson, 1994). Therefore, cross-cultural training has to be given to the trailing spouse and the issue becomes how to effectively meet the goals of cross-cultural training (Pruegger & Rogers, 1994). There is a wide variety of methods to address the cultural differences between the home and host countries such as: cognitive lecture based (Early, 1987); interpersonal (Hammer & Martin, 1992); experimental/ simulations (Bowen, 1987); and social learning theory perspective (Black & Mendenhall, 1990). A program that meets the cognitive as well as the affecting needs of the trailing spouse must be used in the co-optation strategy. One of the critical dimensions of the co-optation strategy is to empower family members to maintain a positive attitude during the expatriation experience. Means to accomplish the goal of empowerment are illustrated in Exhibit Six. These guidelines for the expatriate and the trailing spouse illustrate the means to actively influence attitude and behavior in the relocated family unit.

3. Collaboration Strategy:

Individual Characteristics – high education level, later stage of career life-cycle, later stage of family life-cycle.

Assignment Characteristics – long assignment duration, rural location, dissimilarity of culture and level of economic development.

The collaborative MNC trailing spouse strategy centers on "working together" in a joint endeavor. The trailing spouse has had an extended career and has reached a certain level of professional success that can be used to assist the MNC. There are cases where joint appointments might be appropriate given the long duration of the assignment. Ideally, couples would have complementary professional careers where the trailing spouse's experience would benefit the MNC objectives in the foreign market.

Trailing spouses may also be employed in a joint venture and/or strategic alliance by the MNC. In this situation, the conflict of dual employment in the same MNC can be avoided and, by including opportunities with affiliates, the number of employment opportunities is expanded. One successful approach has been to hire the professional trailing spouse to develop training materials for other expatriates. In addition, when the trailing spouse has specific qualifications, i.e., psychologist, social psychologist, professor etc., they can be used to assist in the actual training of new, younger expatriates. The training of expatriates and their families can be augmented by using expatriate managers and their trailing spouses who have returned home after a successful overseas assignment (Gomez-Mejía & Balkin, 1992). The cross-cultural adjustment of managers and their families who are sent overseas is contingent on modification of attitudes as well as behavior. There are three related, but separate, aspects or dimensions of cross-cultural adjustment that influence the rate of adjustment: (1) adjustment to the job; (2) adjustment to interacting with host-country nationals; and (3) adjustment to the general non-work environment (Black, Gregersen & Mendenhall, 1992). The trailing spouse could provide insights into two of the three general areas of adjustment. The family's experiences could be chronicled and developed into training materials for future expatriates and their families.

The input from these expatriates' trailing spouses could provide executives and their families valuable insights in adjusting their mental maps and attitudes prior to actually relocating overseas, thereby, reducing the level of cultural shock. Anticipatory expectations on the spouse's and family's part should help to reduce work-family conflict during the foreign assignment (Torbiorn, 1982; Black & Mendenhall, 1990; Black, et al., 1991; Black & Gregersen, 1991). If the expatriate's trailing spouse could assist others in integration or assimilation of a foreign culture, he/she could have a positive impact on acculturation of the family. Successful acculturation patterns will influence education, friendship patterns, learning

EXHIBIT 6

Empowering Family Members to Maintain a Positive Attitude Upon Expatriation

OBJECTIVE	RECOMMENDED "DO'S"	"TABOOS"	TOOLS OR SUPPORT NEEDED
Gain real expectations	■ Ask for all family members to be introduced to families who have survived similar situations and who are returning from the same location	■ Do not "glamorize" ■ Do not ignore the stress on the family unit due to relocation ■ Do not assume that the family or spouse supports the relocation	■ Pre-selection consultations with returning expatriates ■ Pre-selection visits to the target environment. Upfront information to allow candidates to assess their coping skills
Stress the importance of transferring tolerance and flexibility to one another	■ Do reset priorities ■ Look for ways to achieve your needs within the context of the new environment ■ Remember that your former ways of doing things are not necessarily the most efficient for the environment you are entering ■ Remember to recognize and appreciate what you gain as many of these good things are not transferable upon return home ■ Remember that the compromises you are making are not permanent ■ If needed, constructively share frustration with a peer of a third nationality who can offer his or her own perspective	■ Do not legitimize negativity ■ Do not condemn negativity and sadness ■ Don't concentrate on what you are giving up ■ Do not complain in front of your host country citizens ■ Look to the future rather than focusing on the past	■ Introduction to mediums available for socialization in the target locale. Example: Football is a medium to gain school unity in the Midwest. This does not mean that schools on the East Coast are not united ■ Connection to third country nationals
Display confidence in each member's ability to adapt	■ Respect your own time frame for adjustment ■ Allow each family member time to become at peace with themselves ■ Arrange periodical sessions to discuss progress ■ Show children that they can solve many problems on their own. Ask children to write down frustrations, drop them in a box, search for a solution themselves. During the next family forum, ask if your help is still requested	■ Do not express or transfer frustration within the family ■ Don't push ■ Don't transfer stress ■ Don't assume anyone is "doing fine" ■ Don't trivialize another person's concerns	■ Pre-cross-cultural training in adjustment, social support and cultural learning to accelerate acculturation
Synthesize new culture with old	■ Appreciate the differences not just the similarities ■ Use a mediating response for multicultural attitudes ■ Concentrate on forming cross-cultural friendships	■ Avoid retreating into the first culture ■ Avoiding adopting new culture at the expulsion of the first culture ■ Avoid using any one culture to perceive another or, conversely, assimilate the two into a monolithic pair	■ Training programs that simulate cross-cultural social and communication skills
Act as role models for one another and the children	■ Set boundaries for children's behavior ■ Become more active in structuring new activities for children	■ Do not feel guilty for the hardship being placed on the children	■ Inter-cultural sensitivity training
Discover target environment	■ Investigate local housing market ■ Become familiar with transportation, medical, emergency services ■ Identify community, sports, continuing education opportunities ■ Visit schools ■ Read newspapers or articles published in the target environment ■ Learn culture together and separately ■ Share discoveries with one another ■ Visit tourist offices ■ Study maps; learn the names of and routes between main streets, important institutions, schools, shops, etc. ■ Learn the hours of operation as soon as possible ■ Learn the hours when it is best not to get things done	■ Do not isolate family to "protect" from environment ■ Do not travel only in home country ■ Do not assume that there are no sites of interest in the host country ■ Do not only travel to tourist locations in the host country	■ Predeparture trip ■ Expatriate manual which is aimed to attract, motivate, and retain and which clearly articulates policies concerning relocation ■ Counselor who knows the target area & the family's priorities to help with information
Incorporate the target language into the home	■ Practice using the target currency and measurement system before you go ■ Communicate in the target language ■ Set one specific hour for English to be spoken ■ Master pleasantries and essential phrases and expressions in order to function at a survival level	■ Uphold commitments and agreed to schedules for communicating in the target language	■ Funding and encouragement for language training ■ Language tapes
Incorporate the target culture into the home; begin before you go	■ Practice using all applicable etiquette before you go ■ Read about politics, religion, art, and literature	■ Avoid comparisons between cultures and values	■ Information acquired from meetings with former expatriates and experience from trial visits ■ Cultural briefings

the language of the country, as well as the general satisfaction of the transferees (Berry et al., 1989; Ward & Kennedy, 1994). Creatively designing work environments and assignments appears to be the key consideration when developing a collaboration strategy.

4. Accommodation Strategy:

Individual Characteristics – low education level, early stage of career life-cycle, early stage of family life-cycle.

Assignment Characteristics – long assignment duration, rural, dissimilar cultures and levels of economic development.

The trailing spouse who has the individual and assignment characteristics described by quadrant four has a difficult time adjusting to an international relocation. A typical case would be a spouse who has delayed self-education to support a spouse during his/her education and also has delayed starting a family. Now that the children have arrived and the trailing spouse is starting his/her career, the family is to be relocated overseas. There will be a great deal of stress and associated family-work conflict relative to these dual-career families. The resulting conflict could have an impact on the employee's productivity during the assignment as well as on the probability of successfully lasting the term duration of the foreign relocation.

The focus of the MNC strategy of accommodation would be to reduce the "pain," dissatisfaction, isolation and relocation discomfort of the trailing spouse. Due to the long duration of the assignment, family perks are important elements in the relocation package. Extended travel for the family with additional vacation time for the relocated employee being common elements in MNC strategies which address this situation. 3M provides an "employment dislocation" allowance, like a signing bonus to professional athletes, to diminish relocation reluctance on the part of the trailing spouse (Black, et al., 1992). 3M also pays tuition in the host country to continue the spouse's education to retain professional skills and to obtain appropriate work when they return to the domestic market. Kodak are directing their efforts to finding jobs for trailing spouses during the international

EXHIBIT 7

Relative Advantages/Disadvantages of Labor Pools for Foreign Assignment

CONSIDERATION	HOME COUNTRY NATIONAL			HOST COUNTRY NATIONAL			THIRD COUNTRY NATIONAL		
	High	Moderate	Low	High	Moderate	Low	High	Moderate	Low
Relative Cost*	■					■	■		
Past Training	■					■		■	
Availability (number)		■		■					■
Loyalty		■		■					■
HQ. Confidence	■					■		■	
Complexity of Compensation Package	■					■		■	
Cultural/Political Sensitivity			■		■		■		
Corporate Culture/Communication and Understanding	■					■		■	
Family Problems/Issues	■					■		■	
Motivation to Succeed in Organization	■					■		■	
Probability of Assignment Fulfillment			■		■		■		
Target of Competitor Recruiting		■			■		■		
Willingness to Extend/Take Additional Foreign Assignment			■	■			■		

* Data and insights used to construct the generalized indicators in this Exhibit were obtained from: Baker and Ivancevich, 1971; Miller, 1972; Hays, 1974; Harris and Morgan, 1979; Tung, 1981, 1982; Mendenhall, Dunbar and Oddou, 1987; Tung, 1988; Barham and Devine, 1990; Black, Gregersen and Mendenhall, 1992; Marquardt and Engel, 1993; Dowling, Schuler and Welch, 1994.

assignment of the partner (Black, Gregersen, & Mendenhall, 1992). Equal employment opportunities for the trailing spouse, particularly if it is the wife, are difficult to find in many geographic locations; and in some, it is nearly impossible for the trailing spouse to get a work permit without waiting an extended length of time, e.g., Middle Eastern countries and many Asian countries (Ball & McCulloch, 1988; Jelinck & Adler, 1988; Dowling, et al., 1994).

An additional aspect of the strategy to accommodate the trailing spouse is to emphasize and/or promote opportunities for the spouse to "internationalize" his/her career while on the foreign assignment. The trailing spouse is in the early stages of his/her career life-cycle and could gain invaluable experience in the international dimension of the profession. This opportunity could be accomplished through educational experience and through a project/temporary assignment for the MNC. There is always a remote possibility that the trailing spouse's company could provide a position in the host country. This type of serendipitous event should not be an integral dimension of the trailing spouse strategy due the low probability of it occurring.

The trailing spouse is in the early stages of his/her career life-cycle and could gain invaluable experience in the international dimension of the profession.

The following propositions are presented relative to the issues associated with MNC training strategies developed to address the needs of dual-career families:

■ **Proposition Fourteen:** The unique work and personal needs of the dual-career family necessitates a variety of strategies to effectively provide the organizational support environment during an international relocation.

■ **Proposition Fifteen:** The earlier the stage of the career life-cycle of the trailing spouse the less impact there will be on his/her willingness to undertake an international relocation.

■ **Proposition Sixteen:** The lower the level of education of the trailing spouse the less impact a disruption in his/her career will have on an international relocation of the dual-career family.

■ **Proposition Seventeen:** The longer the duration of the international assignment the greater the level of work-family conflict that will be present in the dual-career family.

■ **Proposition Eighteen:** The greater the dissimilarity of the culture and level of economic development between the home country and that of host country, the higher the level of family stressors, work stressors, and the resulting work and family conflict that will increase dissatisfaction with international relocation.

Summary/Conclusions

A recent survey of potential expatriate managers indicated that 67 percent of the respondents felt "spouses reluctance to give up own career" was a major constraint to international assignment (Barham & Devine, 1990). Assuming that the United States Department of Labor statistics are accurate projections, 81 percent of all marriages will be dual-income/dual-career partnerships by 1995 (Reynolds & Bennett, 1991). The dual-career family has become an integral component of the decision to relocate expatriate managers overseas (Black, et al., 1992) and if not properly handled by the MNC human resource staff, the frequency of expatriate failure will continue to plague United States based MNCs (Black, 1988). The spouses' acceptance of an international relocation and their subsequent adjustment can be a contributing factor to the completion of a successful overseas assignment given that most American expatriates have spouses who accompany them overseas (Harvey, 1985; Black & Stephens, 1989; Black & Gregersen, 1991).

One question that needs to be asked is: "Why do MNCs want to continue using expatriates, given the cost and problems?" United States based MNCs, historically have had a predisposition to send expatriate managers to foreign subsidiaries and joint ventures (Mendenhall et al., 1987; Mendenhall, 1988; Gray, 1991, Black et al., 1992; Feldman & Thomas, 1992; Feldman & Thompson, 1993). The advantages of using expatriates are thought to be: (1) loyalty to the company; (2) known commodity from a technical skills standpoint; (3) familiarity with corporate culture; (4) typically have college business education; (5) carry the corporate "flag" in the foreign location; (6) add prestige to the foreign operation; and (7) a consistent work ethic with headquarters expectations. In addition, the other two potential labor pools, i.e., host and third country nationals, also have their significant limitations (see Exhibit Seven). There are some indications that United States based MNCs are reducing expatriate staff, but this may be a reoccurring phenomena (Lester, 1993; Edstrom & Galbraith, 1994; Mueller-Maerki, 1995; Selmer, 1996). In addition, international opportunities for female expatriates appear to be a new career alternative that will increase expatriation so as to increase their access to top management positions (Westwood & Leung, 1994).

A manager's decision to relocate is a complex equation of assessing favorable, career development opportunities afforded by the relocation, job tenure, career stage and family characteristics (Noe, et al., 1988). This evaluative criterion becomes more difficult to compute when the assignment under consideration is an international position and the spouse has a career. The inter-related nature of work and family in dual-career families compounds difficulties in making the choice to relocate and the conflicts once the decision has been made to take an international assignment.

In an effort to better comprehend the influence of the dual-career family on international relocation decisions, researchers must explore family theory and the stress that may be associated with the dual-career family. The decision model presented in this paper is not intended to exclude potential expatriate candidates due to their dual-career family status. But, rather, the model can be used to inform candidates of potential problems, advise them on the type of support they might need and attempt to match candidates with positions and environments that are most conducive to success. The assumption that the family is a dual-income family may inaccurately portray the relative importance of the trailing spouse's career. To underestimate the importance of the career cycle of the trailing spouse may limit the number of potential expatriates interested in an international relocation and, at the same time, reduce the probability of success of the expatriate who relocates internationally. Both the family and career life-cycles of the dual-career partners can play a pivotal role in the willingness of the couple to relocate.

To effectively address the influence of dual-career families on expatriate relocation, MNCs must develop an awareness of the significance of the issue on potential relocation candidates. Honeywell Incorporate attempts to identify potential candidates years in advance to monitor their development and to expose managers to training and relocation experiences to broaden their cultural experiences. Even smaller organizations like Armstrong World Industries, Black & Decker Corporation, and Raychem Corporation are attempting to build a global competency inventory of potential expatriate managers. The MNC or the expatriate will have to provide social support to the trailing spouse relative to family-work conflicts as well as to their careers. The level of support will be contingent upon the duration of the foreign assignment, the degree of dissimilarity of both the host culture and its level of economic development. Internally to the dual-career family, the stage of the family life-cycle and career life-cycle of the trailing spouse must be examined.

A variety of programs to address the needs of the dual-career family must be developed by human resource managers in MNCs. The resulting strategies should be attuned to the unique requirements of the various stages of the dual-career family. In today's labor market, it is impractical and irresponsible not to fully factor in the magnitude of the influence of the dual-career family on expatriate relocation.

References

Adler, N. 1986. "Do MBAs Want International Careers?," *International Journal of Intercultural Relations*, vol. 10, #3, pp. 277-300.

Allen, N. & J. Meyer. 1993. "Organizational Commitment: Evidence of Career Stage Effects?," *Journal of Business Research*, vol. 26, pp. 49-61.

Ammons, P., J. Nelson & J. Wodarski. 1982. "Surviving a Move: Sources of Stress and Adaptation Among Corporate Executive Families," *Family Relations*, vol. 31, pp. 207-212.

Anderson, C. & C. Stark. 1988. "Psychological Problems of Job Relocation: Preventive Roles in Society," *Social Work*, Jan-Feb, pp. 38-41.

Anderson, L. 1994. "A New Look At An Old Construct: Cross-Cultural Adaptation," *International Journal of Intercultural Relations*, vol. 18, #3, pp. 293-328.

Arkin, A. 1993. "Managing the Stress of Relocation," *Personnel Management*, vol. 25, #1, pp. 53-56.

Arnold, J. & N. Nicholson. 1991. "Construing of Self and Others at Work in the Early Years of Corporate Careers," *Journal of Organizational Behavior*, vol. 12, pp. 621-639.

Arthur, M. 1984. "The Career Concept: Challenge and Opportunity for its Further Application," in *Working with Careers*, Arthur, M., Bailyn, Levinson & Shepard (ed.) New York: Columbus Business School.

Aryee, S. "Antecedents and Outcomes of Work-Family Conflict Among Married Professional Women: Evidence from Singapore," *Human Relation*, vol. 45, #8, pp. 813-837.

Ball, D. & W. McCulloch. 1988. *International Business: Introduction and Essentials*, Plano, TX: Business Publications.

Barham, K. & M. Devine. 1990. *The Quest for the International Manager: A Survey of Global Human Resource Strategies*, Ashridge Management Resource Group/The Economist Intelligence Unit, Special Report #2098.

Berry, J., V. Kim, S. Power, M. Young & M. Bujaki. 1989. "Acculturation Attitudes in Plural Societies," *Applied Psychology: An International Review*, vol. 38, pp. 185-206.

Beckhard, R. 1987. "Managerial Careers in Transitions: Dilemmas and Directions," in *Organizational Careers: Some New Perspectives*, Van Maeven (ed.) New York, NY: Wiley.

Bielby, W. & D. Bielby. 1992. "I Will Follow Him: Family Ties, Gender-Role Beliefs, and Reluctance to Relocate for a Better Job," *American Journal of Sociology*, vol. 97, #5, March, pp. 1241-1267.

Billings, A. & R. Moos. 1982. "Work Stress and the Stress-Buffering Roles of Work and Family Resources," *Journal of Occupational Behavior*, vol. 3, pp. 215-232.

Bird, F.W. & G.A. Bird. 1986. "Strategies for Reducing Role Strain Among Dual-Career Couples," *International Journal of Sociology of the Family*, vol. 16, #1, pp. 83-94.

Black, S. 1988. "Workrole Transitions: A Study of American Expatriate Managers in Japan," *Journal of International Business Studies*, vol. 15, pp. 113-136.

Black, S. 1992. "Socializing American Expatriate Managers Overseas," *Group & Organizational Management*, vol. 17, #2, June, pp. 171-192.

Black, S. & G. Stephens. 1989. "The Influence of the Spouse on American Expatriate Adjustment in Overseas Assignments," *Journal of Management*, vol. 15, pp. 529-544.

Black, S. & H. Gregersen. 1991. "The Other Half of the Picture: Antecedents of Spouse Cross-Cultural Adjustment," *Journal of International Business Studies*, third quarter, pp. 461-477.

Black, S., H. Gregersen and M. Mendenhall 1992. *Global Assignments*. San Francisco, California: Jossey-Bass Publishers.

Black, S., M. Mendenhall & G. Oddou. 1991. "Toward a Comprehensive Model of International Adjustment: An Integration of Multiple Theoretical Perspectives," *Academy of Management Review*, vol. 16, #2, pp. 292-310.

Blair, S. 1993. "Employment, Family and Perceptions of Marital Quality Among Husbands and Wives," *Journal of Family Issues*, vol. 14, #2, June, pp. 189-212.

Blumstein, P. & P. Schwartz. 1983. *American Couples*. New York: Morrow.

Bowen, D. 1987. "Developing a Personal Theory of Experimental Learning: A Dispatch from the Trenches," *Simulation and Games*, vol. 18, #2, pp. 192-206.

Bradbury, S. 1994. "Dual Career Couples in R&D Labs," *Research & Technology Management*, vol. 37, #1, Jan-Feb, pp. 44-48.

Brenker, B. & V. Vanderslice. 1982. "Tradeoffs: Individual Gains and Relational Losses of Commuting Couples," American Psychology Association Convention, *Proceedings*, Washington, DC.

Briody, E. & J. Chrisman. 1991. "Cultural Adaptation on Overseas Assignments," *Human Organization*, vol. 50, #3, pp. 264-282.

Bunker, B. & V. Vanderslice. 1982. "Tradeoffs: Individual Gains and Relational Losses of Commuting Couples," American Psychological Association Convention, *Proceedings*, Washington, D.C.

Bunker, B., J. Zubek, U. Vandershice, & R. Rice. 1992. "Quality of Life in Dual Career Families: Commuting Versus Single Residence Couples," *Journal of Marriage and the Family*, May, pp. 399-407.

Buono, M. 1994. "Research and Network 1994," *Working Women*, March, pp. 70-71.

Burke, R. 1988. "Some Antecedents and Consequences of Work-Family Conflict," *Journal of Social Behavior and Personality*, vol. 34, pp. 287-302.

Burke, R.& E. Greenglass. 1987. "Work and Family" in *International Review of Industrial and Organization Psychology*, C. Cooper & L. Robertson (ed.) New York: Wiley Publishing Co.

Collie, H. 1989. "Two Salaries, One Relocation: What's a Company to Do?," *Personnel Administrator*, Sept, pp. 54-57.

Coolidge, L. & D. D'Angelo. 1994. "Family Issues to Shape the Professional's Future," *The CPA Journal*, May, pp. 16-21.

Copeland, I. & L. Griggs. 1985. Going International: *How to Make Friends and Deal Effectively in the Global Market Place*, New York: Random House.

Crendall, L., J. Dwyer, & R. Duncan. 1990. "Recruitment and Retention of Rural Physicians: Issues for the 1990's," *The Journal of Rural Health*, vol. 6, #1, pp. 19-38.

Dahl, J. 1985. "As Long Distance Marriages Rise, Some Couples Actually Prefer It," *The Wall Street Journal*, June 24, pp. 21.

De Cieri, H., P. Dowling & K. Taylor. 1991. "The Psychological Impact of Expatriate Relocation on Partners," *The International Journal of Human Resource Management*, vol. 2, #3, pp. 377-414.

Dowling, P., R. Schuler & D. Welch. 1994. *International Dimensions of Human Resource Management*, second edition. Belmont, California: Wadsworth Publishing Company.

Driessnack C. 1987. "Spouse Relocation: A Moving Experience," *Personnel Administrator*, Aug, pp. 95-102.

Early, P. 1987. "Intercultural Training for Managers: A Comparison of Documentary and Interpersonal Methods," *Academy of Management Journal*, vol. 30, pp. 685-698.

Edstrom, A. & J. Galbraith 1994. "Alternative Policies for International Transfers of Managers," *Management International Review*, vol. 34, pp. 71-82.

Emerson, R. 1976. "Social Exchange Theory," *Annual Review of Sociology*, vol. 2, pp. 335-362.

England, P. 1989. "A Feminist Critique of Rational Choice Theories: Implications for Sociology," *American Sociologist*, vol. 20, pp. 14-28.

Ettorre, B. 1993. "A Brave New World: Managing International Careers," *Management Review*, April, pp. 10-15.

Falkberg, L. & M. Monachello. 1988. "Dual Career and Dual Income Families: Do They Have Different Needs," Working paper, University of Calgary.

Fawcett, K. 1994. "Trailing Spouse Often Fend for Self," *USA Today: European International Edition*, Aug 19, A12.

Feldman, D. & D. Thomas. 1992. "Career Management Issues Facing Expatriates," *Journal of International Business Studies*, Second Quarter, pp. 271-293.

Feldman, D. & H. Thompson. 1993. Expatriation, Repatriation, and Domestic Relocation: An Empirical Investigation of Adjustment to New Job Assignments," *Journal of International Business Studies*, Third Quarter, pp. 507-529.

Fletcher, B. 1988. "Occupation, Marriage and Disease-Specific Mortality Concordance," *Social Science and Medicine*, vol. 27, pp. 615-622.

Fletcher, B. 1991. *Work, Stress, Disease and Life Expectancy*, New York: Wiley and Sons.

Foxman, L. & W. Polsky. 1988. "Spousal Employment Assistance," *Personnel Journal*, February, pp. 36-38.

Frame, M. & C. Shehan. 1994. "Work and Well-Being in The Two Person Career," *Family Relations*, vol. 43, pp. 196-205.

Frankenhaueser, M., U. Lundberg., M. Frederikson., B. Belin., M. Tuomisto. & A. Myrsten. 1989. "Stress On and Off the Job as Related to Sex and Occupational States in White Collar Workers," *Journal of Organizational Behavior*, vol. 10, pp. 321-346.

Frone, M. & R. Rice. 1987. "Work-Family Conflict: The Effect of the Job and Family Involvement," *Journal of Occupational Behavior*, vol. 8, pp. 45-53.

Fuchsberg, G. 1992. "As Cost of Overseas Assignments Climb, Firms Select Expatriates More Carefully," *Wall Street Journal*, Jan 9, B1.

Gerstel, N. & H. Gross. 1981. "A Special Case of Dual-Career Families: Couples Who Live Apart," Groves Conference on Marriage and the Family, *Proceedings*, Mount Airy, PA.

Goad, P. 1994. "Singapore Study Shows Rise in Dual-Career Families," *The Asian Wall Street Journal*, vol. 16, #21, May 23, p 6.

Gomez-Mejia, L. & D. Balkin. 1992. "The Determinants of Managerial Satisfaction with Expatriation and Repatriation Process," *Journal of Management Development*, vol. 6, #1, pp. 7-17.

Granrose, C., S. Parasuraman & J. Greenhaus. 1992. "A Proposed Model of Support Provided by Two-Career couples," *Human Relations*, vol. 45, pp. 1367-1393.

Gray, A. 1991. "Foreign Assignments: Why the High Failure Rate," *Business Horizons*, September-October, pp. 11-12.

Greenhaus, J. & N. Beutell. 1985. "Sources of Conflict Between Work and Family Roles," *Academy of Management Review*, vol. 10, pp. 76-88.

Gregersen, H & S. Black. 1990. "A Multifaceted Approach to Expatriate Retention in International Assignments," *Group & Organizational Studies*, vol. 15, #4, pp. 461-485.

Gunz, H. 1989. "The Dual Meaning of Managerial Careers: Organizational and Individual Level of Analysis," *Journal of Management Studies*, vol. 26, pp. 225-250.

Hall, D. & Nougaim. 1968. "An Examination of Maslow's Need Hierarchy in an Organizational Setting," *Organizational Behavior and Human Performance*, vol. 3, pp. 12-35.

Hall, D. 1986. "An Overview of Current Career Development Theory and Practice," in *Career Development in Organizations*, d. Hall (ed.), San Francisco, CA: Jossey-Bass.

Hammer, M. & J. Martin. 1992. "The Effects of Cross-Cultural Training on American Managers in a Japanese-American Joint Venture," *Journal of Applied Communication Research*, vol. 20, pp. 161-181.

Harris, J. 1989. "Moving Managers Internationally: The Care and Feeding of Expatriates," *Human Resource Planning*, vol. 12, #1, pp. 49-53.

Harvey, M. 1985. "The Executive Family: An Overlooked Variable in International Assignments," *The Columbia Journal of World Business*, Summer, pp. 84-93.

Harvey, M. 1989. "Repatriation of Corporate Executives: An Empirical Study," *Journal of International Business Studies*, vol. 20, #1, pp. 131-143.

Harvey, M. 1993. "Empirical Evidence of Reoccurring International Compensation Problems," *Journal of International Business Studies*, vol. 28, Winter, pp. 785-799.

Harvey, M. 1995. "The Impact of Dual-Career Families on International Relocations," *Human Resource Management Review*, vol. 5, #3, pp. 228-244.

Haveman, J. 1992. "Coping in Critical Moves: Overseas Assignments Can Lead to Severe Family Problems," *The Washington Post*, March 24, B6.

Hertz, R. 1986. *More Equal than Others: Woman and Men in Dual Career Marriages*, Berkeley, California: University of California Press.

Higgins, C & L. Duxbury. 1992. "Work-Family Conflict: A Comparison of Dual-Career and Traditional-Career Men," *Journal of Organizational Behavior*, vol. 13, pp. 339-356.

Higgins, C., L. Duxbury & R. Irving. 1992. "Work-Family Conflict in the Dual-Career Family," *Organizational Behavior and Human Decision Processes*, vol. 51, pp. 51-75.

Hill, C & K. Tillery. 1992. "What Do Male/Female Perceptions of an International Business Career Suggest about Recruiting Policies?," *SAM Advanced Management Journal*, Autumn, pp. 10-14.

Hofstede, G. 1980. *Cultural Consequences: National Differences in Thinking and Organizing*, Sage Publications, Beverly Hills, CA.

Hood, J. 1983. *Becoming a Two-Job Family*, New York: Praeger.

House, J. 1981. *Work, Stress, and Social Support*, Reading, MA: Addison-Wesley.

Household and Family Characteristics. 1989. United States Bureau of the Census, Washington DC., US. Government Printing Office.

Huber, J. & G. Spitze. 1981. "Wives' Employment, Household Behaviors and Sex Role Attitudes," *Social Theory*, vol 60, #1, pp. 150-169.

Ioannou, L. 1994. "Women's Global Career Ladder." *International Business*, Dec, pp. 57-60.

Jelinck, M. & N. Adler. 1988. "Women: World-class managers for global competition," *Academy of Management Executive*, vol. 2, #1, pp. 11-19.

Johnson, W. & Packer. A. 1987. *Work Force 2000: Work and Workers for the 21st Century*, Indianapolis, IN: Hudson Institute.

Jones, F. & B. Fletcher. 1993. "An Empirical Study of Occupational Stress Transmission in Working Couples," *Human Relations*, vol. 46, #7, pp. 881-903.

Kanchier, C. 1992. "The 7 Stages of Making a Change." *Executive Female*, Jan-Feb, pp. 31-34.

Karambayya, R. & A. Reilly. 1992. "Dual Career Couples: Attitudes and Actions in Restructuring Work for Family." *Journal of Organizational Behavior*, vol. 13, pp. 585-601.

Karasele, R. 1979. "Job Demands, Job Decision Latitude and Mental Stress: Implications for Job Design." *Administrative Science Quarterly*, vol. 24, pp. 285-308.

Kopelman, R., J. Greenhaus & T. Connolly. 1983. "A Model of Work Family and Interrole Conflict: A Construct Validation Study," *Organizational Behavior and Human Resources*, vol. 32, pp. 198-215.

Kotler, P. & G. Armstrong. 1991. *Principles of Marketing* (5th ed.), Englewood Cliffs, NJ: Prentice-Hall.

Lambert, S. 1990. "Processes Linking Work and Family: A Critical View and Research Agenda." *Human Relations*, vol. 43, pp. 239-257.

Lawrence, B. 1984 "Age Grading: The Implicit Organizational Timetable," *Journal of Occupational Behavior*, vol. 5, 23-35.

Layton, A. 1993. "Relocation Policies Must Reflect Diversity." *Personnel Journal*, August, pp. 22-23.

Le Lovarn, S. 1987. "Canadian Managers' Decision Involving Two-Career Couples." *Canadian Journal of Administrative Sciences*, vol. 4, #2, pp. 113-124.

Lewis, S. 1991. "Dual-Career Families in the U.K. An Update." *Women in Management Review*, vol. 6, #4, pp. 3-9.

Lester, T. 1993. "The Unmaking of a Myth." *International Management*, vol. 48, #10, pp. 48-49.

Lichter, D. 1980. "Household Migration and the Labor Market Position of Married Women," *Social Science Research*, vol. 9, pp. 83-97.

Lichter, D. 1982. "The Migration of Dual-Worker Families: Does the Wife's Job Matter?," *Social Science Quarterly*, vol. 63, pp. 48-57.

Louis, M. 1980. "Career Transitions: Varieties and Commonalties," *Academy of Management Review*, vol. 5, pp. 342-348.

Lublin, J. 1993. "Spouses Find Themselves Worlds Apart as Global Commuter Marriages Increase." *Wall Street Journal*, Jan 26, p B8.

Markham, W. & J. Pleck. 1986. "Sex and Willingness to Move for Occupational Advancement: Some National Sample Results," *Sociological Quarterly*, vol. 27, pp. 121-143.

Markham, W., P. Macken., C. Bonjean. & J. Corder. 1983. "A Note on Sex, Geographic Mobility, and Career Advancement," *Social Forces*, vol. 61, pp. 1138-1146.

Maxwell, N. 1988. "Economic Returns to Migration: Marital States and Gender Differences," *Social Science Quarterly*, vol. 69, pp. 109-121.

McCook, L., S. Charlesworth & J. Scholl. 1991. "Dual-careers: Du Pont's Program for Dual-Career Couples." *Training & Development*, Aug, vol. 45, #8, pp. 40-44.

Mendenhall, M & G. Oddou. 1985. "The Dimensions of Expatriate Acculturation," *Academy of Management Review*, vol. 10, pp. 39-48.

Mendenhall, M. & G. Oddou. 1988. "The Overseas Assignment: A Practical Look." *Business Horizons*, Sept-Oct, pp. 78-84.

Mendenhall, M., E. Dunbar & G. Oddou. 1987. "Expatriate Selection, Training, and Career Pathing: A Review Critique." *Human Resource Management*, vol. 26, #3, pp. 331-345.

Mincer, J. 1978. "Family Migration Decisions." *Journal of Political Economy*, vol. 86, pp. 749-775.

Mueller-Maerki, F. 1995. "Expatriates Need Not Apply." *The Wall Street Journal*, October 16, pp. A14(W), A14(E), col. 3.

Munton, A. 1990. "Job Relocation, Stress and the Family." *Journal of Organizational Behavior*, vol. 11, pp. 401-406.

Naumann, E. 1993. "Antecedents and Consequences of Satisfaction and Commitment Among Expatriate Managers." *Group & Organizational Management*, vol. 18, #2, June, pp. 153-187.

Noe, R. & A. Barber. 1993. "Willingness to Accept Mobility Opportunities: Destination Makes a Difference." *Journal of Organizational Behavior*, vol. 14, pp. 159-175.

Noe, R., B. Steffy & A. Barber. 1988. "An Investigation of the Factors Influencing Employees' Willing to Accept Mobility Opportunities," *Personnel Psychology*, vol. 41, pp. 559-580.

Orpen, C. 1994. "The Effects of Organizational and Individual Career Management on Career Success," *International Journal of Manpower*, vol. 15, #1, pp. 27-37.

Parasurman, S. J. Greenhaus & C. Granrose. 1992. "Role Stressors, Social Support, and Well Being Among Two-Career Couples," *Journal of Organizational Behavior*, vol. 13, pp. 339-356.

Parnes, H., C. Jusenius, F. Blau., G. Nestel, R. Shortidge, and S. Sanders. 1975. *A Longitudinal Analysis Of The Labor Market Experiences Of Women*, Columbus Ohio, Ohio State University, Center for Human Resource Research.

Pascoe, R. 1992. "Employers Ignore Expatriate Wives at Their Own Peril," *Wall Street Journal*, March 2, p A20(w), p A12(E), col 3.

Peak, M. 1994. "Fathers Earn the Most...When Their Wives Stay Home," *Management Review*, February, p 6.

Perlin, L. 1985. "Social Structure and Processes of Social Support," in *Social Support and Health*, S. Cohen & S. Syme (ed.), New York: Academic Press, pp. 43-60.

Perry-Jenkins, M. & K. Folk. 1994. "Class, Couples, and Conflict: Effects of the Division of Labor on Assessment of Marriage in Dual-Career Families," *Journal of Marriage and the Family*, vol. 56, February, pp. 165-180.

Pruegger, V. & T. Rogers. 1994. "Cross-Cultural Sensitivity Training: Methods and Assessment," *International Journal of Intercultural Relations*, vol. 18, #3, pp. 369-387.

Reed, C. & B. Reed. 1993. "The Impact of Dual-Career Marriage on Occupational Mobility in the Local Government Profession." *American Review of Public Administration*, vol. 23, #2, June, pp. 141-154.

Regan, M. 1994. "Beware the Work/Family Culture Shock," *Personnel Journal*, Jan, pp. 35-36.

Reynolds, C. & R. Bennett. 1991. "The Career Couple Challenge." *Personnel Journal*, March, p 48.

Rhodes, J. & E. Rhodes. 1984. "Commuter Marriage: The Toughest Alternative." *Ms*. June, pp. 44-45.

Richardson, D. & V. Rullo. 1992. "Going Global: Are You Ready for an Overseas Assignment," *Management Accounting*. June, pp. 31-39.

Schein, E. 1978. *Career Dynamics: Matching Individual and Organizational Need*. Reading, MA: Addison-Wesley.

Schneer, J. & F. Reitman. 1993. "Effects of Alternative Family Structures on Managerial Career Paths," *Academy of Management Journal*, vol. 36, #4, pp. 830-843.

Schumaker, S. & A. Brownwell. 1984. "Toward a Theory of Social Support: Closing Conceptual Gaps," *Journal of Social Issue*, vol. 4, pp. 11-36.

Schumaker, S. & J. Jackson. 1979. "The Adverse Effects of Nonreciprocated Benefits." *Social Psychology Quarterly*, vol. 42, #2, pp. 148-158.

Sears, H. & N. Galambos. 1992. "Women's Work Conditions and Marital Adjustment in Two-Earner Couples: A Structural Model." *Journal of Marriage and the Family*, vol. 54, November, pp. 789-797.

Selmer, J. 1996. "Expatriate or Local Bosses? HCN Subordinates' Preferences in Leadership Behaviour," *International Journal of Human Resource Management*, vol. 7, #1, pp. 165-178.

Smith, C. 1992. "Dual Careers, Dual Loyalties," *Asian Pacific Journal of Human Resources*, vol. 30, #4, pp. 19-30.

Solomon, C. 1994. "Success Abroad Depends on More than Job Skills." *Personnel Journal*, April, pp. 51-60.

Spitze, G. 1984. "The Effects of Family Migration on Wives' Employment: How Long Does it Last?," *Social Science Quarterly*, vol. 65, pp. 21-36.

Statistical Abstract of the United States. 1992. United States Bureau of the Census, Washington DC., US. Government Printing Office.

Staines, G. 1980. "Spillover Versus Compensation: A Review of the Literature on the Relationship Between Work and Non-Work." *Human Relations*, vol. 33, pp. 111-129.

Stephens, G. 1994. "Crossing Internal Career Boundaries: The State of Research on Subjective Career Transitions," *Journal of Management*, vol. 20, #2, pp. 479-502.

Super, D. 1982. "A Life-Span, Life-Space, Approach to Career Development," *Journal of Vocational Behavior*, vol. 6, pp. 282-298.

Torbiorn, I. 1982. *Living Abroad*, New York: Wiley.

Tousig, M. & J. Michello. 1988. "Seeking Social Support," in *Basic and Applied Social Psychology*, J. Singer (ed.), vol. 9, #1, pp. 1-12.

Tremblay, M. & A. Roger. 1993. "Individual, Family and Organizational Determinants of Career Plateau," *Group & Organizational Management*, vol. 18, #4, December, pp. 411-425.

Tung, R. 1987. "Expatriate Assignments: Enhancing Success and Minimizing Failure," *Academy of Management Executive*, vol. 1, #2, pp. 117-126.

Vannoy, D. & W. Philliber. 1992. "Wife's Employment and Quality of Marriage," *Journal of Marriage and the Family*, May, pp. 387-398

Veiga, J. 1983. "Mobility Influences During Managerial Stages," *Academy of Management Journal* vol. 26, pp. 64-85.

Ventura, J. 1987. "The Stresses of Parenthood Reexamined," *Family Relations*, vol. 36, pp. 26-29.

Voydanoff, P. 1988. "Work and Family: A Review and Expanded Conceptualization," *Journal of Social Behavior and Personality*, vol. 3, #4, pp. 1-22.

Wederspahn, G. 1992. "Costing Failures in Expatriate Human Resource Management," *Human Resource Planning*, vol. 15, #3, pp. 27-35.

Westwood, R. & S. Leung 1994. "The Female Expatriate Manager Experience: Coping with Gender and Culture," *International Studies of Management & Organization*, vol. 24, #3, pp. 64-85.

Wiersma, U. 1994. "A Taxonomy of Behavioral Strategies for Coping with Work-Home Role Conflict," *Human Relations*, vol. 47, #2, pp. 211-221.

Wiggins-Frame, M. & C. Shehan. 1994. "Work and Well Being in the Two-Person Career: Relocation Stress and Coping Among Clergy Husbands and Wives," *Family Relations*, vol. 43, pp. 196-205.

Wiley, D. 1987. "The Relationship Between Work and Non Work Role Conflict and Job Related Outcomes: Some Unanticipated Outcomes," *Journal of Management*, vol. 13, #3, pp. 467-472.

Winfield, F. 1985. *Commuter Marriage: Living Together Apart*, New York: Columbia University Press.

Biographical Sketch

Dr. Michael G. Harvey holds the Puterbaugh Chair in American Free Enterprise at the University of Oklahoma, Norman, Oklahoma (Ph.D. from the University of Arizona). He has previously published in a wide variety of academic journals, such as, *Sloan Management Review*, *Columbia Journal of World Business*, *Journal of International Business Studies*, *Journal of Business Venturing*, among others.

[34]

© Academy of Management Review, 1990, Vol. 15, No. 1, 113–136.

Cross-Cultural Training Effectiveness: A Review and a Theoretical Framework for Future Research

J. STEWART BLACK
Dartmouth College
MARK MENDENHALL
University of Tennessee, Chattanooga

Increased internationalization in the economic, political, and social arenas has led to greater interpersonal cross-cultural contact. Because much of this contact has not been successful, cross-cultural training has been proposed by many scholars as a means of facilitating more effective interaction. A review of the cross-cultural training literature is presented, and it is determined that cross-cultural training in general is effective. The article also offers a theoretical framework based on social learning theory for understanding past research and for guiding future research; this is important because in this context variables seem to operate differently in international versus domestic areas.

The field of international management has been observed to be in a nascent, preparadigm state of development (Adler, 1983; Beaty & Mendenhall, 1989; Kyi, 1988; Roberts, 1970; Roberts & Boyacigiller, 1984; Schollhammer, 1975). Kyi (1988) perhaps best summarized these findings when he stated, "The paucity of papers in the hypothetico-deductive category . . . is related to the stage of the development of the field and the nature of comparative analysis. At this stage, there are no deductively developed theories in [international] management and most so-called 'theories' are experienced-based hunches or empirical generalizations. Well-integrated deductive theories with a central core concept, such as 'market and rationality' in economic theory, have not appeared yet" (p. 209).

This preparadigm state is especially descriptive of the newer subfield of cross-cultural international human resource management (Adler, 1983; Beaty & Mendenhall, 1989). Adler (1983) found that from 1971 to 1980 only one percent of the 11,000 articles published in 24 management journals focused on cross-cultural work interaction. Of the major international business journals from 1984 to 1988, only 9 percent of the articles were devoted to international human resource management issues, and in the *Academy of Management Review*, for the same period, only one and one half percent of the articles dealt with international human resource management issues; however, none were attempts at theory building (Beaty & Mendenhall, 1989).

This is particularly unfortunate because increased internationalization in the economic, political, and social arenas has led to a greater frequency of, and depth in, cross-cultural interactions (contacts between two or more people from different cultural backgrounds). These interactions occur in a variety of work-related situations, including short-term business trips to foreign countries, long-term overseas assignments, and even work in one organization.

However, work-related cross-cultural interactions are not always successful. For example, studies have found that between 16 and 40 percent of all expatriate managers who are given foreign assignments end these assignments early because of their poor performance or their inability to adjust to the foreign environment (Baker & Ivancevich, 1971; Black, 1988; Dunbar & Ehrlich, 1986; Tung, 1981), and as high as 50 percent of those who do not return early function at a low level of effectiveness (Copeland & Griggs, 1985). Other studies have found that negotiations between businessmen of different cultures often fail because of problems related to cross-cultural differences (Adler, 1986; Black, 1987; Graham, 1985; Tung, 1984). Unsuccessful cross-cultural interactions become even more important when the costs of failure are high, and they often are. For example, studies have estimated that the cost of a failed expatriate assignment is $50,000 to $150,000 (Copeland & Griggs, 1985; Harris & Moran, 1979; Misa & Fabricatore, 1979). For a firm that has hundreds of expatriate employees worldwide, such costs can easily reach into the tens of millions of dollars. In fact, Copeland and Griggs (1985) have estimated that the direct costs to U.S. firms of failed expatriate assignments is over $2 billion a year, and this does not include unmeasured losses such as damaged corporate reputations or lost business opportunities.

Cross-cultural training (CCT) has long been advocated as a means of facilitating effective cross-cultural interactions (Brislin, 1981; Landis & Brislin, 1983; Bochner, 1982; Harris & Moran, 1979; Mendenhall & Oddou, 1986; Tung, 1981). Despite the normative arguments for the use of cross-cultural training, its use in American business organizations is not very widespread. Studies have found that only 30 percent of managers who are sent on expatriate assignments (one to five years) receive cross-cultural training before their departure (Baker & Ivancevich, 1971; Black, 1988; Runzheimer Executive Report, 1984; Tung, 1981). Various reasons have been cited by business organizations for the low use of cross-cultural training, and the most prevalent of these is that such training is not thought to be effective (Baker & Ivancevich, 1971; Mendenhall & Oddou, 1985; Schwind, 1985; Tung, 1981; Zeira, 1975); thus, top management sees no need for the training (Runzheimer Executive Report, 1984) and is unwilling to support it, financially or otherwise. Essentially, American top managers believe that a good manager in New York or Los Angeles will be effective in Hong Kong or Tokyo (Miller, 1973). This is illustrated not only in the lack of training provided but also in the use of the domestic track record as the primary criterion for selecting candidates for overseas assignments (Miller, 1973). Such a culturally insensitive perspective seems to be an important reason for many faulty international human resource practices and the high expatriate failure rates (Adler, 1986; Black, 1988; Baker & Ivancevich, 1971; Mendenhall & Oddou, 1985; Ronen, 1986; Tung, 1982). It would seem, then, that an attempt to comprehensively review the empirical literature on cross-cultural training in an effort to examine its effectiveness or ineffectiveness and an attempt to advance a theoretical grounding for valid cross-cultural training program development and evaluation is especially important.

Thus, this article has two purposes. The first is to review the extant empirical literature on the effectiveness of cross-cultural training. Three reasons indicate that this is an appropriate and timely effort: (a) the opportunities for and the necessity of engaging in cross-cultural interaction are widespread, (b) the costs of unsuccessful interactions can be substantial, and (c) many firms seem to believe that cross-cultural training is not effective and that no empirical evidence exists that supports the efficacy of cross-cultural training. The lack of a systematic review of the literature may have contributed to conflicting views by corporate leaders and academics about whether cross-cultural training facilitates more effective cross-cultural interactions. Most corporate leaders do not provide cross-cultural training for employees and cite doubt of the training's effectiveness as the reason. Academics, in contrast, who advocate the necessity of cross-cultural training tout its importance but do not offer empirical evidence to support their assertions. A comprehensive review of the literature would aid in the resolution of the debate.

The second purpose is to propose a theoretical framework for understanding the literature and guiding future research. This latter aim seems particularly important because the empirical as well as prescriptive work on cross-cultural training to date has been criticized for lacking a clear theoretical base (Adler, 1983; Brislin, 1981; Bochner, 1982; Landis, Brislin, & Hulgus, 1985).

Review of the Literature

Although no study has attempted a comprehensive review, two reviews have examined the cultural assimilator type of training and its effectiveness (Fiedler, Mitchell, & Triandis, 1971; Mitchell, Dossett, Fiedler, & Triandis, 1972), but neither examined other approaches, nor did they offer a theoretical framework. Brislin and Pedersen (1976) conducted a comprehensive review of cross-cultural training approaches, but they focused on developing a typology of training methods. Other somewhat-related reviews include the nature of cross-cultural adjustment (Church, 1982; Mendenhall & Oddou, 1985; Stening, 1979), the impact of cross-cultural assignments on expatriates' careers (Mendenhall, Dunbar, & Oddou, 1987), and the degree to which cross-cultural training is utilized (Baker & Ivancevitch, 1971; Mendenhall et al., 1987; Tung, 1981). Athough related, none directly attempts a comprehensive review of the empirical literature or offers a theoretical framework. If, as some scholars have argued (Adler, 1983; Beaty & Mendenhall, 1989; Kyi, 1988; Roberts, 1970; Roberts & Boyacigiller, 1984; Schollhammer, 1975), international management in general is in a preparadigmatic, pretheoretical stage of development, then it is not surprising that such subareas as cross-cultural training also lack theories and models.

In order to delineate the efficacy of cross-cultural training programs, a review of the extant literature was performed across a variety of disciplines in the social sciences. Much writing exists on the value of utilizing cross-cultural training programs for potential expatriates and others who work in a multicultural milieu; however, only studies that empirically evaluated the effectiveness of cross-cultural training programs were included. A computer-aided, interdisciplinary literature search was used for a number of data bases, and after eliminating nonempirical studies, 29 studies were included in the formal review process.

Because most studies used a variety of training methods and because few studies systematically tried to compare the efficacy of training methods, training will be treated herein as a generic activity, and the focus will be to ascertain its overall impact on the dependent variables used to measure its effectiveness. The relationship between training and each of the dependent variables was coded as (a) not addressed in the study (left blank), (b) positive (recorded as a +), (c) nonsignificant (recorded as 0), and (d) negative (recorded as −). A summary of the studies reviewed is given in Table 1.

From the review of the literature, three primary dependent variables were commonly used as indicators of training effectiveness (a) cross-cultural skill development, (b) adjustment, and (c) performance (see Table 1). Each of these variables and its relationship to training effectiveness is discussed next.

Cross-Cultural Skill Development

Living and working overseas or within a multicultural context in one's home country requires

Table 1
Review Summary of Cross-Cultural Training Effectiveness

Study	Subjects & Sample Size	Variables of Training Effectiveness: Cross-Cultural Skills: Self	Relationship	Perceptual	Adjustment	Performance	Misc*
Befus (1988)	Missionaries n = 64				+		F,C
Chemers (1969)	Managers, Teachers n = 48		+	+		+/0	F,T
Chemers et al. (1966)	Students n = 42		+	+		+/0	L,C,T
Dege (1981)	Teaching assistants n = 30	+	+			+	F
Earley (1987)	Managers n = 80		+	+	+	+	F,C,T,LG
Fernandez (1986)	Nurses n = 31	+					L
Gudykunst et al. (1977)	Navy personnel n = 530		+		+		F,C,T,LG
Katz (1977)	Students n = 24		+	+		+	L,C,LG
Landis et al. (1985)	Army officers n = 923			+			F,C
Landis et al. (1985)	Students n = 45		+	+			L,T,C
Landis et al. (1976)	Army officers n = 170		+	+			F,C
Lefley (1986)	Mental health agencies n = 97					+	F,LG
Lefley (1985)	Psychologists n = 122		+	+		+	F,LG
McDaniel et al. (1988)	Teachers n = 180					+	F,LG
McGroarty (1984)	Teachers of English as a second language n = 29		+	+			F
Mitchell et al. (1972)	Peace corps volunteers n = 23		+		+		F,C
Mitchell & Foa (1969)	Students n = 64		+			0	L,C
Nayar et al. (1968)	Students n = 72		+	+		+	L,T
Neimeyer et al. (1986)	Students n = 20	+					L
Newbold et al. (1982)	Medical interns n = 6		+		+		F,LG
O'Brien & Plooij (1976)	Nurses n = 74	+		+			L,C,LG
O'Brien et al. (1970)	Public health workers n = 265	+			+	+	F,T,LG
PSI (1982)	Peace corps teachers n = 79	+	+				F

Table 1—Continued
Review Summary of Cross-Cultural Training Effectiveness

		Variables of Training Effectiveness					
		Cross-Cultural Skills					
Study	Subjects & Sample Size	Self	Relationship	Perceptual	Adjustment	Performance	Misc*
Randolph et al. (1977)	Students n = 35	+	+	+		+	L,C
Salisbury (1971)	Eskimo students n = 53	+	+		+	+	F,C,LG
Steinkalk & Taft (1979)	College administrators n = 43			+	+		F,C
Vigushin (1982)	College staff n = 126			+			F
Weldon et al. (1975)	Students n = 128		+	+		0	L,C
Worchel & Mitchell (1972)	Military officers n = 110	+	+	+	+	+	F,C,T,LG

* The code for the miscellaneous column is: L = laboratory study, F = field study, C = control group was used. T = Training programs were compared for relative effectiveness. LG = longitudinal study.

an individual to use interaction skills that transcend those that are effective when dealing with others from one's immediate in-group (Adler, 1986; Mendenhall & Oddou, 1985; Torbiorn, 1982). Thus, the development of cross-cultural skills in trainees has been a major objective in the evaluation studies reviewed here. The link between possessing these skills and subsequent success in overseas assignments has been demonstrated elsewhere (for reviews see Brein & David, 1971; Church, 1982; Mendenhall & Oddou, 1985). The purpose here is to ascertain whether cross-cultural training can indeed foster the development of such skills in trainees.

The skills needed to be successful in a new culture can be subsumed under three dimensions: skills related to the maintenance of self (mental health, psychological well-being, stress reduction, feelings of self-confidence), skills related to the fostering of relationships with host nationals, and cognitive skills that promote a correct perception of the host environment and its social systems (Mendenhall & Oddou, 1985).

The self dimension. Of the 29 studies, 10 examined the relationship between cross-cultural training and the development of greater feelings of well-being and self-confidence (Dege, 1981; Fernandez, 1986; McGoarty, 1984; Neimeyer, Fukuyama, Bingham, Hall, & Mussenden, 1986; O'Brien & Plooij, 1976; O'Brien, Fiedler, & Hewett, 1970; PSI Associates, 1982; Randolph, Landis, & Tzeng, 1977; Salisbury, 1971; Worchel & Mitchell, 1972), and all 10 found a positive relationship. In examining the validity of the findings of these studies, two points should be noted. First, all 10 studies relied on self-report measures of variables related to the self dimension (e.g., O'Brien & Plooij, 1976). This approach may have inflated the relationship between training and the self dimension dependent variables because of common method variance problems. However, studies by Worchel and Mitchell (1972), Salisbury (1971), and O'Brien and Plooij (1976) included control groups and found significant differences in pre- and posttest measures of self-confidence between the experimental and control-group subjects. Second, despite the fact that studies that utilized control groups found significant relationships between training and self-confidence, it is possible that subjects assigned to the experimental groups through common method measures may have inflated the relationship because of Hawthorne effects of knowing they were in an experimental group.

The Relationship Dimension. Nineteen of the 29 studies examined the relationship between cross-cultural training and skills related to fostering relationships with host nationals (Chemers, 1969; Chemers, Lekhyananda, Fiedler, & Stoulurow, 1966; Dege, 1981; Earley, 1987; Gudykunst, Hammer, & Wiseman, 1977; Katz, 1977; Landis, Brislin, Swanner, Tseng, & Thomas, 1985; Landis, Day, McGrew, Thomas, & Miller, 1976; Lefley, 1985; McGroarty, 1984; Mitchell & Foa, 1969; Mitchell et al., 1972; Nayar, Touzard, & Summers, 1986; Newbold, Carroll, Hartman, Mitchell, & Story, 1982; PSI Associates, 1982; Randolph et al., 1977; Salisbury, 1971; Weldon, Carlston, Rissman, Slobodin, & Triandis, 1975; Worchel & Mitchell, 1972). Each of these 19 studies found a significant relationship between cross-cultural training and self-reported measures of relationship skills.

More than half of the studies that examined the effectiveness of cross-cultural training on relational skills used control groups (Chemers et al., 1966; Earley, 1987; Gudykunst et al., 1977; Landis, Brislin, Swanner et al., 1985; Landis et al., 1976; Mitchell et al., 1972; Mitchell & Foa, 1969; Randolph et al., 1977; Salisbury, 1971; Weldon et al., 1975; Worchel & Mitchell, 1972). In addition, the studies of Earley (1987), Salisbury (1971), and Worchel and Mitchell (1972) were longitudinal in nature. All of these studies found a significant relationship, and the longitudinal studies found the relationship to persist over time. However, relational skills were measured through self-reports, which opens these studies and their findings to the same limitations and issues that concerned the self dimension.

The Perception Dimension. A total of 16 of the 29 studies examined the relationship between cross-cultural training and the development of appropriate perceptions relative to members of another culture, and all 16 studies found a positive relationship (Chemers, 1969; Chemers et al., 1966; Earley, 1987; Katz, 1977; Landis, Brislin, Hulgus et al., 1985; Landis, Brislin, Swanner et al., 1985; Landis et al., 1976; Lefley, 1985; McGroarty, 1984; Nayar et al., 1968; O'Brien & Plooij, 1976; Randolph et al., 1977; Steinkalk & Taft, 1979; Vigushin, 1982; Weldon et al., 1975; Worchel & Mitchell, 1972). Again, more than half the studies examining the perception dimension used control groups (Chemers, 1969; Earley, 1987; Katz, 1977; Landis, Brislin, & Hulgus, 1985; Landis, Brislin, Swanner et al., 1985; Landis et al., 1976; O'Brien & Plooij, 1976; Steinkalk & Taft, 1979; Randolph et al., 1977; Weldon et al., 1975; Worchel & Mitchell, 1972), and Earley (1987), O'Brien and Plooij (1976), and Worchel and Mitchell (1972) were longitudinal in nature. This lends some support to the conclusion that cross-cultural training has a positive impact on individuals' correctly perceiving other cultures and members of those cultures. Additionally, Weldon et al. (1975), Landis, Brislin, & Hulgus (1985), Randolph et al. (1977), Vigushin (1982), and Worchel and Mitchell (1972) all supported this conclusion using objective measures of perception (the comparison of perception or knowledge of the subjects with that of the host national group). This independent measure of the perception dimension overcomes some of the limitations related to common method variance already discussed concerning the self-reported measures of the self and relational dimensions.

Adjustment

The main argument for using cross-cultural training is that it allows individuals to more rapidly adjust to the new culture and, therefore, to be more effective in their new roles. Adjusting to a new culture involves the gradual development of familiarity, comfort, and proficiency regarding expected behavior and the values and assumptions inherent in the new culture, all of which are different from the individual's native culture (Torbiorn, 1982). A total of 9 studies examined the relationship between cross-cultural training and adjustment (Befus, 1988; Earley, 1987; Gudykunst et al., 1977; Mitchell et al., 1972; Newbold et al., 1982; O'Brien, Fiedler, & Hewett, 1970; Salisbury, 1971; Steinkalk & Taft, 1979; Worchel & Mitchell, 1972). All 9 studies found a positive relationship between cross-cultural training and adjustment. Seven of these nine studies used control groups (Befus, 1988; Earley, 1987; Gudykunst et al., 1977; Mitchell et al., 1972; Salisbury, 1971; Steinkalk & Taft, 1979; Worchel & Mitchell, 1972), and Earley (1987), Salisbury (1971), and Worchel and Mitchell (1972) were longitudinal in nature. Earley (1987) and Mitchell et al. (1972), in addition to using control groups and longitudinal designs, also used independent measures of adjustment and found a significant relationship between cross-cultural training and adjustment; this use of independent measures of adjustment increases the confidence one can place in their findings that cross-cultural training has a positive impact on cross-cultural adjustment.

Performance

Institutions that send individuals overseas or into a multicultural work setting expect those individuals to perform, whether that involves building a dam, managing a factory, negotiating a contract, teaching children to read, or converting host-nationals to a new religion. Thus, the relationship of cross-cultural training to performance is a critical concern: Does such training aid work performance in the cross-cultural setting, or are its effects negligible? Fifteen of the 29 studies examined the relationship between cross-cultural training and performance, and 11 of the 15 studies found a significant relationship between cross-cultural training and performance (Dege, 1981; Earley, 1987; Katz, 1977; Lefley, 1985, 1986; McDaniel, McDaniel, & McDaniel, 1988; Nayar et al., 1968; O'Brien & Plooij, 1976; O'Brien et al., 1970; Salisbury, 1971; Randolph et al., 1977; Worchel & Mitchell, 1972). Three lab studies found generally nonsignificant relationships between cross-cultural training and performance (Chemers et al., 1966; Mitchell & Foa, 1969; Weldon et al., 1975). Mitchell et al. (1972), in their review of culture assimilator training, argued that in general lab studies do not allow sufficient time for the effects of cross-cultural training to be manifested in performance. However, one field study found significant and nonsignificant relationships between cross-cultural training and various measures of performance (Chemers, 1969). It should be noted that none of the studies found a significant negative relationship between cross-cultural training and performance. Studies by Earley (1987), Worchel and Mitchell (1972), Lefley (1986), and O'Brien et al. (1970) all used independent measures of performance, and all found a significant and positive relationship between training and performance.

Several concluding remarks can be made concerning the effectiveness of cross-cultural training. First, on average about one half of the studies examining each dependent variable used control groups, which allows for some confidence to be placed in the consistency of the findings. Only 6 of the 29 studies included both control groups and a longitudinal design; therefore, even though it does seem that cross-cultural training has a long-term effect on all the dependent variables examined, it is clear that more longitudinal studies are needed that include rigorous research designs, before definitive conclusions about the impact of training over time can be made. Second, many of the studies of skill-related dependent variables did not use independent measures of dependent variables and, thus, common method variance limitations must be kept in mind concerning the apparent positive relationship between training and skill development. Third, it is important to note that those studies that included rigorous research designs (e.g., control groups, longitudinal designs, independent measures), such as Earley (1987), Salisbury (1971), and Worchel and Mitchell (1972), found support for a positive relationship between cross-cultural training and the following dependent variables: cross-cultural skill development, cross-cultural adjustment, and performance in a cross-cultural setting. Thus, the empirical literature gives guarded support to the proposition that cross-cultural training has a positive impact on cross-cultural effectiveness.

Need for a Theoretical Framework

This review indicates that, in general, cross-cultural training seems to have a positive impact on skill development, adjustment, and performance; however, the lack of a theoretical framework leaves unanswered the question about why cross-cultural training is effective. Thus, in order to systematically understand the conditions that cause cross-cultural training to be effective or ineffective a theoretical framework, which encompasses cross-cultural training and its relation to cross-cultural interaction, is needed.

Any attempt to move toward a theoretical understanding of the effectiveness of cross-cultural training must begin with a basic understanding of cross-cultural interaction. Although it is beyond the scope of this article to present a comprehensive review of the theoretical literature on cross-cultural interaction, several points can be summarized based on other, more detailed reviews (Brislin, 1981; Bochner, 1982).

Most discussions of cross-cultural interaction begin with a definition of culture. In their classic review of culture, Kluckhohn and Kroeberg (1952) cited over 160 definitions of culture. Based on their exhaustive review, Kluckhohn and Kroeberg (1952) concluded that culture consists of patterns of behaviors that are acquired and transmitted by symbols over time, which become generally shared within a group and are communicated to new members of the group in order to serve as a cognitive guide or blueprint for future actions. Thus, cross-cultural interactions bring people together who have different patterns of behaving and believing and who have different cognitive blueprints for interpreting the world (Triandis, Vassiliou, Tanaka, & Shanmugam, 1972). If people who have different culturally based behaviors and beliefs must interact, difficulties arise because faulty attributions are made about the motives and meanings of the others' behaviors since the attributions are based on the attributor's own cultural norms and worldview (Bochner, 1982).

Cross-cultural training enables the individual to learn both content and skills that will facilitate effective cross-cultural interaction by reducing misunderstandings and inappropriate behaviors. If this is accepted as the major objective of cross-cultural training, it becomes necessary to understand how people learn to appropriately interact with others and how they use that knowledge for effective interactions.

In an effort to focus learning theory on the more specific issue of training, Noe (1986) proposed a model of how training facilitates performance. This suggested that two aspects of an individual's motivation had an important impact on the effectiveness of training. Noe argued that an individual's motivation to learn and his or her motivation to transfer what was learned into action were critical elements in the relationship of training and performance. However, Noe did not delineate how individuals actually learn or how they transfer that learning to behaviors. In order to understand the relationship between training and performance, these aspects of the model require additional attention.

Cognitive and behavioral theorists have long competed to explain how individuals learn and how they use this knowledge (for reviews on cognitive and behavioral learning theories and the debate between them see Bochner, 1982; Hilgard & Bower, 1975; Swenson, 1980). According to the cognitive theories of learning, learning takes place through the mental processing of information and the determination of subsequent behavior. Behavioral theories argue that learning is determined by behaviors and experienced consequences. In response to this 20-year debate Latham and Saari (1979) noted, "To show that behavior is determined only by cognitions, one would have to find a control group consisting of subjects who cannot think. Similarly, to prove empirical support for the argument that behavior is due to environmental consequences alone, one would have the impossible task of forming a control group for which there was no environment" (p. 240).

Social learning theory (SLT) has been advocated as a synthesis of the cognitive and behavioral learning theories (Bandura, 1977; Hilgard & Bower, 1975). Davis and Luthans (1980), who compared SLT with other theories of behavior, argued that it is the most useful in understanding organizational behavior. Additionally, general reviews of learning in particular have argued for the superiority of SLT (Hilgard & Bower, 1975; Swenson, 1980). For example, Swenson (1980) stated that SLT was viewed as a consensus position on most aspects of learning. SLT not only integrates cognitive and behavioral theories, it also encompasses the motivational aspects stressed by Noe (1986) within the concept of self-efficacy, and it covers the issues of how individuals both learn and utilize what they learn during a training situation, aspects that Noe did not emphasize. In addition, SLT is becoming the dominant framework in U.S. management training (Latham & Saari, 1979; Manz & Sims, 1981). These make for compelling reasons to use SLT as the theoretical framework for understanding cross-cultural learning and training. However, greater depth and breadth of novel behaviors that trainees must learn during cross-cultural training present a challenge to SLT's explanation of the success or failure of cross-cultural training. Consequently, it is important to see if the domestic and the foreign contexts can both be explained through SLT.

Social Learning Theory: An Overview

According to SLT, learning is affected by both observation and experience (Bandura, 1977). A central premise is that individuals use symbols to engage in anticipatory action, that is, they anticipate actions and their associated consequences. This enables people to determine how they will behave before an actual situation. Also, it is argued that individuals learn from experience and that the experienced consequences of their behavior shape what they learn as well as their future behavior. As described by Bandura (1977), SLT has four central elements: attention, retention, reproduction, and incentives.

Attention. Before behavior can be modeled, the subject must notice it. Several factors influence the attention process of the subject, including: (a) the status of the model, (b) the attractiveness of the model, (c) the similarity of the model, (d) the repeated availability of the model, and (e) past reinforcement for paying attention to the model (actual or vicarious).

Retention. Retention is the process by which the modeled behavior becomes encoded as a memory. Two representational systems are involved in this process. The imaginal system is utilized during exposure to the model. At this time the subject associates sequences of corresponding sensory images with the physical contiguity of the model. These images are stored as cognitive maps, which can guide the observer when he or she tries to imitate the behavior. In the second system, a verbal system, the coded information is abbreviated into verbal systems, and groups of constituent patterns of behavior are integrated into larger units. It should be noted that both the repeated modeling of a behavior and the repeated cognitive rehearsal of the modeled behavior help to secure the retention process.

Reproduction. The third major component involves the translating of the symbolic representations into actions. As individuals try to imitate the modeled behavior, they check their performance against their memory of what was modeled. Motoric reproduction of the modeled behavior can, of course, be inhibited by physical differences between the model and the person imitating the model, how well the model is observed, and how well the modeled behavior is retained.

Incentives and the Motivational Processes.

The fourth element of SLT, incentives, can come from the environment, from vicarious association, and from the individual. Each of these can affect several aspects of the learning process. For example, incentives (a) can affect which models are observed and how much attention is paid to them, (b) can influence the degree to which the modeled behavior is retained and rehearsed, and (c) can influence which learned behaviors are emitted. It is important to note that Bandura (1977) argued on the basis of empirical work that incentives play a much larger role in influencing what behavior is emitted as opposed to what behavior is learned. He concluded that individuals learn numerous behaviors that are not emitted because they are not positively rewarded. However, if the reward structure is changed, the behaviors are performed.

In relation to the motivational processes of learning, Bandura (1977) distinguished between two types of expectancies: efficacy expectations and outcome expectations. Self-efficacy is the degree to which the individual believes he or she can successfully execute a particular behavior. This expectation is similar to the effort-to-performance expectancy proposed by Vroom (1964). In his review of the literature, Bandura (1977) found that higher levels of self-efficacy led individuals to persist at imitating modeled behavior longer and to be more willing to try to imitate novel behavior. The sources for increasing self-efficacy, in order of importance, include past experience ("I've done it or something like it before"), vicarious experience ("other people have done it"), and verbal persuasion ("people say I can do it").

Outcome expectations are people's beliefs that the execution of certain behaviors will lead to desired outcomes. There is a clear similarity between this type of expectation and the expectancy-of-performance-to-outcome (instrumentality expectancies) proposed by Vroom (1964). Bandura concluded that incentives influence what people learn and that incentives, efficacy, expectations, and outcome expectancies influence what learned behaviors are acted out.

Although a number of empirical findings are reviewed by Bandura (1977), three are important to summarize because they provide insight about fundamental elements in the learning process. The first finding is that gradual modeling is more effective than one-shot modeling, especially if the modeled behaviors are novel. Gradual modeling involves providing successive approximations of the final behavior and it is more effective because (a) observers pay more attention to models and modeled behaviors that are familiar, (b) observers can more easily retain models that are similar to cognitive maps they already possess, (c) observers have higher expectations of efficacy and outcome of behaviors that are familiar, and (d) observers are more likely to be able to reproduce familiar behaviors. The second finding is that individuals can learn completely through symbolic modeling, that is, by watching actions and mentally rehearsing them. As previously mentioned, this symbolic learning process can be facilitated by other variables and by the use of multiple models. Finally, Bandura found that participative reproduction, in general, is more effective than symbolic processes. Participative reproduction simply means that the observer actually practices (compared to only cognitively rehearsing) the modeled behavior. The external, and especially the internal, feedback processes serve to refine the observer's ability to reproduce the modeled behavior at a later time.

Social Learning Theory and Cross-Cultural Training

SLT provides both a theoretical framework for understanding past research and a guide for future investigation. Because few of the past empirical studies of cross-cultural training have attempted a systematic study of training methods, this section treats cross-cultural training in a generic manner.

Social Learning Theory and Skill Development

The review of the literature on cross-cultural training and skill development found that cross-cultural training tended to increase various skills that facilitated effective cross-cultural interaction. This section examines how cross-cultural training might achieve this within the theoretical framework of social learning theory.

The Self Dimension. Cross-cultural training increased trainees' confidence in themselves and their ability to act effectively in a cross-cultural setting. According to SLT, as trainees receive either verbal or visual models of appropriate and inappropriate behaviors for the impending cross-cultural interaction, and for associations between these behaviors and expected consequences, that trainees rehearse (cognitively or behaviorally) these behaviors and consequences. Such cognitive maps will increase the individual's efficacy and outcome expectations because he or she has learned the appropriate behaviors (vicariously) and made associations about the expected outcomes. According to SLT, higher self-efficacy and outcome expectations would have a positive impact on the retention and reproduction learning processes, which, in turn, would have a positive impact on outcome variables such as adjustment and performance. This learning process would explain why individuals who received cross-cultural training reported higher levels of confidence and other self-hygiene factors than those who did not (Church, 1982; Mendenhall & Oddou, 1985). For example, as the public health workers in the O'Brien et al. (1970) study were trained through culture assimilator exercises, they were presented with verbal models of how to interpret the behavior of the people of Honduras and Guatemala and how to behave appropriately. The information gained gave the volunteers confidence that they could now function appropriately in these two countries and cultures.

The Relationship Dimension. The review of the literature indicated that cross-cultural training increased trainees' relational skills. Most cross-cultural training provides models that both describe cognitive maps of individuals from the other cultures and explain appropriate and inappropriate behaviors for interacting in these settings. Because trainees have both modeled behavior and information, upon which they can imagine models of behavior, and because they have formed expectations about the consequences of certain behaviors, when they actually are confronted with the cross-cultural situation they can recall the models and imitate them better than individuals who have not been trained. Additionally, even if the models are not perfect or not perfectly imitated, the increased self-efficacy that the trained individuals have gained would lead them to persist longer than nontrained individuals in imitating more novel behaviors in the actual cross-cultural situation. This, in turn, would generate both external and internal feedback, which would serve to refine the modeled behaviors; all of this would help to facilitate the trained individuals' skills at establishing relationships with individuals from the other culture. As an example, the workers in Earley's (1987) study were subjected to a simulation in which they were required to interact with individuals who represented South Koreans (the target culture). Through this simulation, trainees had the opportunity to see (attend) and practice (retain) interpersonal interaction skills, which they later recalled and utilized in South Korea.

The Perception Dimension. Most cross-cultural training includes information about how people of other cultures view the world as well as their cognitive tendencies (e.g., ethnocentrism), which cause problems in cross-cultural situations. This information enables the trainee to make cognitive associations between congruent behaviors and the cognitive maps of members of the other culture. Assuming the information provided to the trainee is correct, and the cognitive maps the trainee creates are accurate, when the trainee imagines models of behavior in the actual situation, these behaviors will be appropriate and will enable the individual to be effective in the cross-cultural interaction.

Training, which provides a means for modeling behaviors such as being tolerant of ambiguity or reserving judgment about the actions of those of the other culture and the consequences of such behavior, can serve as an important vicarious learning experience for the trainee and can result in cognitive behavior/consequence associations as well as efficacy and outcome expectations. The social learning process would result in the same but opposite results concerning the modeling of inappropriate behaviors such as ethnocentricity. Thus, according to SLT, cross-cultural training leads both to trainees' perceiving they have accurate perceptions of the target culture and to trainees actually having correct perceptions of the target culture. For example, some workers in Earley's (1987) study also went through an interaction simulation called *BaFa BaFa*, in which two teams tried to trade with each other without knowing the other's rules of trading. Debriefing sessions illustrated that without knowing the rules most participants made inaccurate attributions, which had a dysfunctional effect on their attempts to trade. Thus, trainees were able to make anticipatory behavioral adjustments by determining to reserve judgment about the actions of South Koreans until they had more information, which, subsequently, had a positive effect on their adjustment in South Korea.

Social Learning Theory and Adjustment

Adjustment to a cross-cultural situation generally has been viewed as the process and end state of being familiar and comfortable while interacting in the host culture. Thus, adjustment is most relevant when an individual will live in another culture for some period of time. Social learning theory also provides a framework for understanding why various skills are important for adjustment and how they facilitate this process. Simply stated, cross-cultural adjustment involves the knowledge of which behaviors to execute or suppress in given situations and the ability to effectively actualize this understanding. Cross-cultural training can provide models of appropriate and inappropriate behavior in general or specific, hypothetical or simulated situations; it can provide information from which trainees can imagine appropriate and inappropriate behavior and associated consequences; it can increase individuals' efficacy and outcome expectations; and it can facilitate symbolic and/or participative rehearsals of the modeled behaviors.

All of these results can lead to several important links between cross-cultural training and adjustment. First, by having models of appropriate and inappropriate behavior upon which to base behavior, cross-culturally trained individuals would have a greater ability to imitate the models in actual situations. Also, because cross-culturally trained individuals would have higher efficacy and outcome expectations, they would be more likely to imitate and to persist in imitating the modeled behaviors that would begin the feedback process. Additionally, such models of appropriate behavior would enable trainees to better recognize model behavior in host nationals, which would increase the trained individuals' retention of the models and their ability to reproduce the behaviors. Also, trained individuals would have higher levels of self-efficacy, which would lead them to be more persistent in attempting to execute new behaviors. This persistence would facilitate the learning process in the host culture, and it also would aid in the individual's understanding of, and ability to execute, appropriate behavior.

As an example, Navy personnel in the study by Gudykunst et al. (1977) were trained by two methods (factual briefing and integrated method) in preparation for living in Japan. The integrated, multimethod training included both symbolic and participative modeling. This symbolic modeling (e.g., lectures on Japanese culture and culture shock) enabled trainees to use their imaginal systems to create anticipatory associations between appropriate and inappropriate behaviors in the Japanese culture and to understand likely positive and negative consequences. Participative modeling (e.g., contrast American role play, BaFa BaFa simulation, and field trips) allowed trainees to utilize both verbal and imaginal systems, to have repeated exposure to the models of desirable behavior, and to practice those behaviors. Based on SLT, repeated exposure would increase attention processes, which, in turn, would have a positive effect on the retention process. Additionally, given the novelty of the Japanese culture (relative to American culture), participative modeling would increase the retention of desirable behaviors. As SLT would predict, the trainees exposed to this more comprehensive training were more adjusted to Japan than trainees who received only the factual briefing.

Social Learning Theory and Performance

The relationship between cross-cultural training and performance in the theoretical framework of SLT is based on the assumption that tasks that are performed in a cross-cultural setting have dimensions that are related to the host culture. At the least, this assumes a positive relationship between adjustment to living in a foreign culture and effectively performing organizational tasks; that is, that successful adjustment to living in a foreign culture requires an understanding of the host culture. At the most, it assumes that every task has cultural dimensions to it and that effectively performing these tasks requires an integration of appropriate behavior. Without one or both of these assumptions, it could be argued that living in a foreign culture has no influence on work performance, and that work performance has no relationship with cultural dimensions; therefore, there would be no reason for cross-cultural training to have an impact on work performance in a cross-cultural setting. Thus, if one can assume that a person's effective execution of tasks and responsibilities in a cross-cultural situation are determined by the cultural dimensions of the setting, then cross-cultural training would have an impact on performance in a number of ways.

First, based on the previous discussion, SLT provides a means of understanding why cross-cultural training has an impact on the acquisition of various skills and on adjustment to the culture, as well as how certain skills may facilitate adjustment. If adjustment is viewed as the person's ability to know and execute appropriate behaviors relative to the cross-cultural situation, then to the degree that performance is tied to culturally determined behavior, cross-cultural training would also have a positive impact on task performance. Within the SLT framework, cross-cultural training would enable individuals to determine in advance appropriate behaviors and culturally congruent ways of performing job tasks. Also, if cross-cultural training allowed for more cognitive and behavioral rehearsal, the individual would have higher efficacy and outcome expectations as well as greater proficiency regarding certain behaviors before actually entering the cross-cultural setting, all of which would facilitate the effective execution of the job tasks. Obviously, to the extent that performance is unrelated to culturally determined appropriate behaviors, then other theoretical models of performance would be more relevant and cross-cultural training would be less relevant. For example, based on empirical evidence, Porter and Lawler (1968) argued that ability, motivation, opportunity, and role perceptions are the key determinants of performance. If these factors are unrelated to the cross-cultural situation, then logically (as well as within the theoretical framework of SLT) one would not expect cross-cultural training to have an impact.

However, the studies reviewed found that cross-cultural training did lead to greater levels of performance in various groups of individuals. This suggests that in most cases performance does have culturally related components and that the processes described with the framework of SLT of how skills are acquired, how modeled behaviors are imitated, and how the adjustment process is facilitated explain why cross-cultural training facilitates performance. Figure 1 illustrates how elements of cross-cultural training and SLT would interact in affecting cross-cultural skill development, adjustment, and performance.

Theoretical Implications

The primary focus of the previous section was to examine how SLT might explain the empirical findings of the effectiveness of cross-cultural training; however, SLT also provides a means by which cross-cultural training can be systematically investigated in the future.

Attention Processes in Cross-Cultural Learning

Social learning theory suggests that similar models receive more attention than dissimilar models. In a cross-cultural training situation, the more the model or trainer seems similar to the trainees, the more the trainees relate to the trainer and the more attention they pay to the modeled behaviors. It is important to remember that the modeling can be in the form of (a) lectures, which require symbolic associations based on imagined relationships between behaviors and consequences, (b) watching films, which requires symbolic associations based on observed relationships between behaviors and consequences, and (c) role playing, which requires symbolic associations based on observed and experienced behaviors and consequences. No studies in the cross-culture training literature have examined the impact on trainee learning of having trainers who are similar to the trainees. For example, if businessmen are being trained for overseas expatriate assignments, what would be the impact of using trainers who are expatriates, trainers who are consultants (but utilize models from actual expatriates through means such as case studies), or trainers who are university professors and lack expatriate or business experience?

Proposition 1: The use of similar models results in greater attention to the modeled behavior and more effective training.

Individual differences might affect the degree to which individuals attend to the training and, therefore, the degree to which the training is effective. Locus of control might be an important individual difference in this regard. For example, because individuals with internal locus of control orientations (internals) believe that events are determined by their own actions and abilities, it could be expected that they would have higher efficacy and outcome expectations, which, in turn, might lead to more motivation to attend to the training content. Additionally, in a review of the locus of control construct, Lefcourt (1983) indicated that internals also attend more closely to new or ambiguous environments. In the context of this article, according to SLT individuals differ in their abilities to anticipate cross-cultural situations, which by their nature are new and ambiguous. Therefore, internals might pay more attention during cross-cultural training, which would have a positive impact on the learning process and the effectiveness of the training.

Additionally, Ratiu (1983) found that individuals who were rated as most internationally effective by their colleagues were more likely to alter their stereotypes of foreigners, whereas those rated as least internationally effective were more likely to maintain their stereotypes. Although this individual difference factor has not been highly researched, it may be evidence of what others (Oddou & Mendenhall, 1984) have referred to as *cognitive flexibility*. Thus, it might be that individuals who have a high level of cognitive flexibility would be more willing to accept and incorporate fundamental notions from cross-cultural training; therefore, they might benefit more from cross-cultural training than individuals who have lower levels of cognitive flexibility.

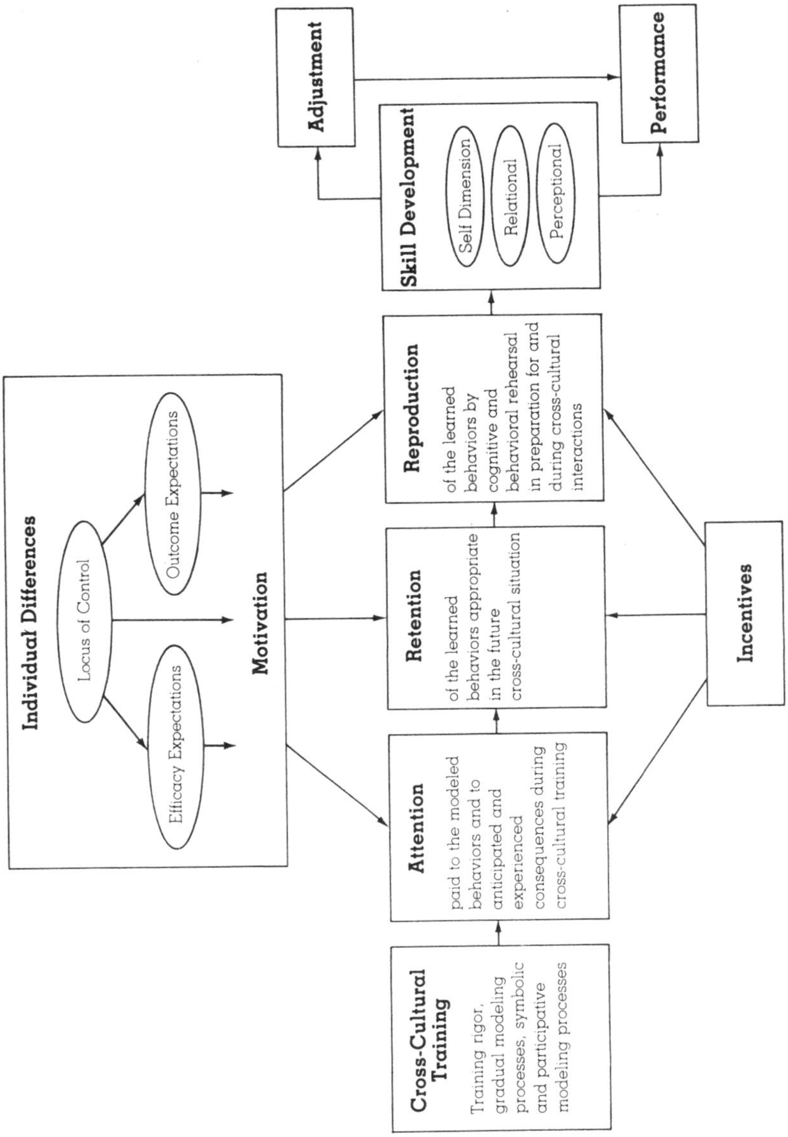

Figure 1. Model of cross-cultural training and social learning theory.

The Retention Process in Cross-Cultural Learning

Social learning theory suggests that modeled behavior that is appropriate in the cross-cultural situation and is perceived as similar to behavior the observer has already learned is easier to retain and imitate than dissimilar behavior. This means that new behavior and its consequences can be incorporated into already existing cognitive maps. Once incorporated, the new symbolic representations become part of, and are retained in, the past cognitive maps; therefore, they can be retrieved in the future. Thus, presenting new and culturally different behavior and consequences in a way that allows the learner to perceive them as similar to known behavior and associated consequences would facilitate the learners' ability to retain these new behaviors, which in turn would have a positive impact on the appropriate execution of the new behaviors in the cross-cultural situation.

Proposition 2: Presenting novel behavior in a form which allows the learner to perceive it as similar to his or her own behavior will enable the learner to more effectively retain the new behavior.

Social learning theory also suggests that novel behavior is best learned through modeling successive approximations of the final behavior. Thus, by first providing a basic model of the behavior and its consequences in a cross-cultural situation which are appropriate in the new culture, a reference or starting point can be provided for the learner. The gradual addition of successive and more complex approximations of the complete model of new and novel behavioral norms allows the trainee to build associations between each successive approximation and the previous ones. Essentially, in SLT it is argued that cross-cultural trainers should first provide the skeleton of the new behavior and then gradually add the flesh until the complete model is presented. Once the symbolic associations have been constructed, the modeled behavior can be retained more easily than by presenting the complex model of the behavior.

Proposition 3: Gradual modeling of novel behaviors that are needed for cross-cultural interactions has a greater impact on the retention processes than one-time modeling.

Social learning theory implies that cognitive and behavioral rehearsal of the modeled behaviors that are appropriate for the cross-cultural situation will facilitate retention. Once the trainee has formed the original cognitive associations between the components of the behaviors and the related consequences, both cognitive rehearsals and a combination of cognitive and behavioral rehearsals will reinforce and refine the trainee's cognitive map, which, in turn, serves to facilitate the retention of the behavior.

Proposition 4: Cognitive and behavioral rehearsal facilitate the retention of models of novel behavior.

These retention-oriented propositions evoke general questions for investigation in the area of cross-cultural training; for example, what training method or combination of methods (e.g., lecture, factual briefing, cultural assimilator, role play, field trips, etc.) is best for learning the behaviors of a different and novel culture? Gudykunst et al. (1977) found that a combination of lecture and experiential methods may be more effective than training through lecture alone. Based on SLT, very novel behaviors might be best modeled through a combination of methods. In addition, gradual modeling and participative modeling should be incorporated so that trainees can easily comprehend the novel behavior, make associations between the behavior and its consequences, and rehearse the behaviors; all of these, in turn, will enable trainees to reach a higher retention level.

The Reproduction Process in Cross-Cultural Learning

The *motoric reproduction process*, as Bandura (1977) referred to it, is the execution of the learned behaviors in actual situations. In SLT accurate and effective reproduction of learned behaviors depends on the attention and retention processes, the person's incentive to reproduce the behavior, and the person's ability to reproduce it. Because of the relationships among attention and retention processes and motoric reproduction, it follows that the more similar the modeled behavior is to what has been learned and reproduced in the past, the easier the new behavior will be to learn and reproduce. In contrast, the more novel the modeled behaviors, the more difficult they will be to learn and reproduce.

Proposition 5: The more novel the modeled behaviors relative to what has been learned and reproduced in the past, the more difficult it will be to reproduce them accurately in the future.

This proposition raises some general questions about the relationship between the novelty of the culture (and, therefore, the novelty of the behaviors necessary for effective cross-cultural interactions) and the rigor of the cross-cultural training. Past reviews on factors that affect cross-cultural adjustment have found that the more novel the new culture, or what Mendenhall and Oddou (1985) referred to as *culture toughness*, the more difficult the adjustment for the expatriate. Based on this review's findings, it seems reasonable to speculate that the more novel the culture and behaviors necessary for effective cross-cultural interactions, the greater will be the necessary rigor of the cross-cultural training. Although no clear consensus concerning the definition of training *rigor* exists, Mendenhall and Oddou (1986) provided typologies of training methods and ranked the methods in terms of rigor, where rigor is largely a function of the degree of cognitive involvement required of the learner. Although these scholars did not make specific reference to SLT, the training methods they classified as low rigor (e.g., lectures and factual briefings) involved only symbolic modeling processes, whereas those they classified as high rigor involved symbolic and participative modeling processes.

Social learning theory also suggests that, assuming a person is physically capable of reproducing a learned behavior and has an incentive for reproducing the behavior, the more novel the modeled behavior, the more important will be the attention and retention processes, relative to the accurate reproduction of the learned behavior in the cross-cultural situation. The more attention the trainee pays to the modeled behavior, the more information he or she has to form associations that will facilitate the retention of the model. Also, the greater the trainee's retention of the model, the easier it will be for the individual to recall the modeled behavior and the more useful that recollection will be in guiding the actual motoric reproduction.

Proposition 6: The more novel the modeled behaviors, the more important will be the attention and retention processes for accurate and effective motoric reproductions.

It is possible to derive a number of general questions for future cross-cultural training research from this proposition. For example, if the new culture and its attendant behavioral norms are extremely novel, what is the difference in motoric reproduction of purely symbolic versus symbolic and behavioral rehearsal during the retention process? Also, what is the trainee's affective response to different methods during the attention and retention processes?

In addition, past experiences as well as the attention and retention processes influence the individual's level of self-efficacy, which, in turn, influences several aspects of motoric reproduction. In cross-cultural training, if a person has a low level of self-efficacy, despite the training to learn the new behaviors necessary for effective cross-cultural interaction, it would be probable that the individual would not attempt to reproduce the learned behaviors during appropriate cross-cultural situations. In contrast, if the individual has a high level of self-efficacy, he or she would probably persist at that effort to reproduce the learned behavior longer than an individual who has a lower level of self-efficacy.

Proposition 7: The higher the person's self-efficacy, the more likely the person is to execute the learned behavior and to persist in executing the behavior.

This proposition in combination with others presents many questions for future study in the cross-cultural training area. For example, is a high level of self-efficacy more important for learning novel behaviors of a novel host culture than it is for learning similar behaviors in a similar host culture? In other words, is there an interaction effect between novelty of the behaviors and the degree of self-efficacy?

Motivation and Incentives in Cross-Cultural Learning

Within SLT, incentives can have an important impact on the attention, retention, and reproduction processes. Incentives can be actual or vicarious, immediate or expected; they can have an external or internal origin; and they can influence the extent to which individuals attend to the modeled behavior. Incentives can influence the extent to which modeled behavior is cognitively or behaviorally rehearsed; therefore, they can influence the extent to which the behavior is retained. Additionally, and strongly emphasized by Bandura (1977), even if behaviors are learned, incentives largely determine if the learned behaviors will be executed. For example, even if an individual learns how to effectively interact with Japanese subordinates, if there are no incentives for exhibiting those behaviors, and if the individual is instead rewarded via praise, recognition, promotions, or salary raises for behaviors that have nothing to do with interacting with Japanese subordinates (or is rewarded for actions that contradict the learned behaviors necessary for effective interactions with Japanese subordinates), it is likely that the person will not execute these behaviors.

Proposition 8: Incentives influence the trainees' attention, retention, and especially their reproduction of modeled behavior in cross-cultural training.

This proposition also generates general research questions. What will be the impact of external rewards for receiving cross-cultural training on the degree of retention and reproduction of learned behaviors? What will be the impact of vicarious rewards for receiving the training on the effectiveness of the cross-cultural training (e.g., feedback regarding how past trainees have benefited from the training)? What will be the impact of the trainee's reaction to past training situations or his or her expectations that the current training will be beneficial?

Relationship Between Adjustment and Cross-Cultural Training

Scholars have defined *adjustment* in three ways. Some scholars have defined adjustment in terms of the psychological comfort and familiarity an individual feels for the new culture (Black, 1988; Mendenhall & Oddou, 1985; Torbiorn, 1982). In contrast, culture shock has been used as a measure of adjustment and has been described as a state of not knowing how to behave appropriately in the new culture and being overwhelmed by this anxiety (Oberg, 1960). Other scholars have defined adjustment in terms of the individual's ability to get along with and effectively interact with host nationals (Brein & David, 1971; Brislin, 1981; Landis & Brislin, 1983).

Because cross-cultural training familiarizes the individual with the culture (and the new and appropriate behaviors in that culture), the individual would be expected to feel comfortable and familiar with the culture more easily and quickly. Likewise, because of the subsequent cultural familiarity and advanced cross-cultural understanding on the part of the trainee, cross-cultural training would lead to less anxiety and culture shock and thereby facilitate adjustment. In terms of adjustment (if it is defined as effective interactions with host nationals), the trainee learns through cross-cultural training the appropriate behaviors for effective interactions and increases his or her self-efficacy, both of which enable the individual to reproduce the behaviors that would lead to effective interactions more quickly than a nontrained individual.

Proposition 9: Cross-cultural training reduces the severity of normal culture shock and reduces the time necessary to reach a level of cultural proficiency.

This proposition in combination with propositions about the novelty of new behavior suggests general questions for future research. For example, would the impact that rigorous cross-cultural training has on reducing culture shock be the largest when the host culture is quite novel and the individual interacts with host nationals on a frequent and involved basis? Would rigorous cross-cultural training have a less dramatic effect on culture shock when the host culture is novel but the individual has little or no need to interact with host nationals?

The Relationship Between Performance and Cross-Cultural Training

Although no universally accepted definition of performance exists in the cross-cultural literature, at least two major operationalizations were found. First, past researchers have discussed cross-cultural performance in terms of whether the individual stayed in the new culture the expected length of time or whether the individual requested or was requested to return early (Baker & Ivancevich, 1971; Tung, 1981). Through cross-cultural training trainees should gain a realistic expectation of their jobs and lives in the foreign country and culture. Realistic job expectations in general have been associated with greater satisfaction and lower job turnover (see Steers & Mowday, 1981, or Wanous, 1980, for a review).

Cross-cultural training also would allow the trainee to make anticipatory determinations of what behaviors to act out. If those determinations were correct, the training would enable the trainee to execute appropriate behavior without having to learn by trial and error. Therefore, the person could avoid some instances of inappropriate behavior and the associated negative consequences that might be experienced by a nontrained individual. Such experience could, in turn, lead to higher levels of job satisfaction, lower intentions to return early, and less failure.

Proposition 10: Cross-cultural training would lead to more realistic expectations, greater job satisfaction, lower intentions of returning early, and lower rates of early returns from cross-cultural assignments.

However, because it is possible that an individual would not return early, yet would be ineffective, performance also was operationalized in terms of performance evaluations, usually given by the individual's supervisor (Earley, 1987; Hawes & Kealey, 1981). If the individual's job has dimensions that are related to effective cross-cultural interaction, and if cross-cultural training facilitates effective relationships with host nationals, it also should lead to high performance evaluations. Preliminary empirical evidence suggests that the hypothesized relationship between adjustment and performance is significant (Earley, 1987). Extending this logic, cross-cultural training would have the greatest impact on individuals (e.g., top executives) whose jobs require a large amount of interaction with host nationals and deep integration into the culture.

Proposition 11: Cross-cultural training leads to higher performance, especially for individuals whose jobs require a high level of interaction with host nationals.

Based on the framework presented, there is at least one more general issue to consider. Although none of the studies reviewed attempted to examine and compare the impact of training for different subjects (businesspeople, military personnel, educators, etc.) or the impact of different environmental contexts (e.g., job characteristics that require a high demand for interacting with host nationals versus a low demand for such interaction), it is possible that moderating effects exist. For example, it is possible that because many military personnel are isolated from the foreign environment through base compounds, that training may be less effective for them than for expatriates who are involved in the transfer of technology and who live and work among host nationals. However, it seems that rather than focusing on differences in subjects, that it would be more productive to examine the impact of differences in context. For example, would cross-cultural training have the same effect on a senior military officer and a senior business executive who both would need to interact frequently with host nationals in order to be effective? Tung (1982) and Mendenhall et al. (1987) argued that the degree to which cross-cultural training is needed and is effective depends upon the degree to which the individual must interact with members of other cultures. The framework of SLT complements this argument; accordingly, not only would training have the greatest impact when the new culture and context are novel compared to the individual's home culture, but also when the individual must interact frequently with individuals of the foreign culture.

Conclusion

The first purpose of this paper was to provide a comprehensive review of the extant empirical literature on cross-cultural training. This review suggests that cross-cultural training has a positive impact on the individual's development of skills, on his or her adjustment to the cross-cultural situation, and on his or her job performance in the cross-cultural situation. However, compared to the training literature in general (see Latham, 1988, for a review), the area of cross-cultural training has received little empirical attention.

Because most past empirical research on cross-cultural training has lacked theoretical grounding, this article presented SLT as a theoretical framework. In the process of examining SLT in relation to cross-cultural training, some important new insights about SLT have emerged. Although it does not seem that the context of international training compared to the context of domestic training challenges any fundamental assumptions of SLT or presents any totally new variables that should be incorporated into SLT, the international context does seem to rearrange the importance of various factors within SLT.

The first difference concerns the variable of novelty. Although novelty plays an important role in SLT within the domestic training context, it plays a critical role in the international training context. Generally, the degree of novelty of new behaviors is significantly higher in the international context. In both domestic and international contexts new work-related behaviors must be learned; however, in most cross-cultural training situations new nonwork behaviors must be learned as well. For example, an individual preparing for an assignment in Japan might need to learn new accounting procedures, how to make decisions by consensus, how to work within the rules of sempai(senior)/kohai (junior) relationships, how to give and receive gifts, and how to behave appropriately on extremely crowded trains and subways. Thus, the depth and breadth of the role of novelty in SLT seems to be much greater in international contexts.

This also raises the importance of two related aspects of SLT. First, given that in a cross-cultural training situation, in general, an individual will be required to learn behaviors of greater breadth and depth of novelty, the attention and retention aspects of the SLT become much more important in the international context. For example, in a domestic training context, it is likely that low levels of attention and retention will negatively affect the trainee's accurate reproduction of the modeled behavior, but it is also likely that the behavior could be reproduced in some form because the modeled behavior is familiar. In an international context, because of the generally higher level of behavior novelty, low levels of attention and retention may render the trainee unable to reproduce the modeled behavior in any fashion (Gudykunst et al., 1977). Thus, a higher minimum threshold of attention and retention may be necessary in international contexts.

In addition, there is reason to believe that the role and sequencing of symbolic and participative modeling processes of SLT are different in international versus domestic contexts. Because most domestic training situations involve behaviors that are familiar, the sequencing of symbolic or participative modeling processes and whether the processes are used in combination or separately seem less important in domestic versus international contexts. The results of the study by Gudykunst et al. (1977) suggest that symbolic modeling should precede participative modeling; symbolic modeling alone may not be sufficient for the training to have a positive and significant impact on outcomes, such as cross-cultural adjustment. For example, although symbolic modeling processes may be sufficient for training a person to handle a new reporting procedure or even a new set of job responsibilities in the domestic context, symbolic learning alone is not likely to be sufficient for training a person to speak a different language or for training him or her to interact effectively with people from a different culture. Thus, while the theoretical axioms of SLT do not necessarily change with respect to symbolic and participative modeling in the cross-cultural training context, the importance of participative modeling in SLT, relative to successful cross-cultural training and the sequencing of symbolic and participative modeling, does change.

In addition, if the greater depth and breadth of novelty in international contexts make the attention and retention processes more important, then the motivational factors also increase in importance. It may be that even though greater motivation to attend to and retain new behaviors has a positive impact on the learning process in the domestic context, the required minimum threshold level is lower than that required in the international context. Given that the depth and breadth of novelty in international contexts are greater than in domestic training contexts, a higher minimum level of motivation may be necessary in order for effective attention and retention processes to occur during cross-cultural training situations. Cross-cultural training effectiveness in the studies reviewed may be explained partly by almost all the trainees being volunteers for the cross-cultural work situation and, therefore, being more likely to be motivated than randomly selected individuals.

Finally, another variable of SLT that seems to operate differently in an international context is self-efficacy. In both the domestic and international contexts it seems that the greater the level of self-efficacy, the more likely the individual is to persist in trying to reproduce the modeled behaviors. However, given the greater level of novelty associated with cross-cultural training situations, it seems that there may need to be a higher minimum level of self-efficacy expectations in the international context before an individual will attempt to reproduce the modeled behavior at all, let alone persist in trying to reproduce it. There is some evidence that individuals who dropped out of cross-cultural training situations lacked the confidence that they would need to successfully execute the new behaviors (PSI, 1982).

Several conclusions are worth noting. First, based on the published empirical evidence, it seems that cross-cultural training is effective in developing important cross-cultural skills, in facilitating cross-cultural adjustment, and in enhancing job performance. Second, most past empirical research on this subject has lacked theoretical grounding. The area of cross-cultural training will be facilitated by correcting this practice, and using SLT as a heuristic framework is a first attempt to move the field in a more theoretically based direction. Finally, although SLT seems to be a robust theory that can be applied to both domestic and international training contexts, the importance of certain variables of SLT is different in cross-cultural training situations.

References

Adler, N. (1983) Cross-cultural management research: The ostrich and the trend. *Academy of Management Review*, 8, 226–232.

Adler, N. (1986) *International dimensions of organizational behavior*. Boston, MA: Kent.

Baker, J. C., & Ivancevich, J. M. (1971) The assignment of American executives abroad: Systematic, haphazard, or chaotic? *California Management Review*, 13(3), 39–44.

Bandura, A. (1977) *Social learning theory*. Englewood Cliffs, NJ: Prentice-Hall.

Beaty, D., & Mendenhall, M. (1989) *International management research: Toward an agenda*. Unpublished manuscript.

Befus, C. P. (1988) A multilevel treatment approach for culture shock experienced by sojourners. *International Journal of Intercultural Relations*, 12, 381–400.

Black, J. S. (1987) Japanese/American negotiations: The Japanese perspective. *Business and Economic Review*, 6(1), 27–30.

Black, J. S. (1988) Work role transitions: A study of American expatriate managers in Japan. *Journal of International Business Studies*, 19, 277–294.

Bochner, S. (1982) *Cultures in contact: Studies in cross-cultural interaction*. New York: Pergamon Press.

Brein, M., & David, K. H. (1971) Intercultural communication and adjustment of the sojourner. *Psychological Bulletin*, 76, 215–230.

Brislin, R. W. (1981) *Cross-cultural encounters*. New York: Pergamon Press.

Brislin, R. W., & Pedersen, P. (1976) *Cross-cultural orientation programs*. New York: Gardner Press.

Chemers, M. M. (1969) Cross-cultural training as a means of improving situational favorableness. *Human Relations*, 22, 531–546.

Chemers, M. M., Lekhyananda, D., Fiedler, F. E., & Stolurow, L. (1966) Some effects of cultural training on leadership in heterocultural task groups. *International Journal of Psychology*, 1, 301–314.

Church, A. T. (1982) Sojourner adjustment. *Psychological Bulletin*, 91, 540–571.

Copeland, L., & Griggs, L. (1985) *Going international*. New York: Random House.

Davis, T., & Luthans, F. (1980) A social learning approach to organizational behavior. *Academy of Management Review*, 5, 281–290.

Dege, D. B. (1981, May 21–25) *Format and evaluation of the cross-cultural component of a foreign teaching assistant training program*. Paper presented at the meeting of the International Communication Association, Minneapolis.

Dunbar, E., & Ehrlich, M. (1986) *International practices, selection, training, and managing the international staff: A survey report*. New York: Columbia University, Teachers College, Project on International Human Resource.

Earley, P. C. (1987) Intercultural training for managers: A comparison of documentary and interpersonal methods. *Academy of Management Journal*, 30, 685–698.

Fernandez, T. M. (1986, Oct 9–11) *Guide design: Sensitivity to black-white interactions when giving nursing care*. Paper presented at the 15th Annual Conference of the International Society for Individualized Instruction, Atlanta.

Fiedler, F., Mitchell, T., & Triandis, H. (1971) The culture assimilator: An approach to cross-cultural training. *Journal of Applied Psychology*, 55, 95–102.

Graham, J. (1985) The influence of culture on the process of business negotiations: An exploratory study. *Journal of International Business Studies*, 16(1), 81–95.

Gudykunst, W. B., Hammer, M. R., & Wiseman, R. L. (1977) An analysis of an integrated approach to cross-cultural training. *International Journal of Intercultural Relations*, 1, 99–110.

Hammer, M. R., Gudykunst, W. B., & Wiseman, R. L. (1978) Dimensions of intercultural effectiveness: An exploratory study. *International Journal of Intercultural Relations*, 2, 382–393.

Harris, P., & Moran, R. T. (1979) *Managing cultural differences*. Houston, TX: Gulf.

Hawes, F., & Kealey, D. J. (1981) An empirical study of Canadian technical assistance. *International Journal of Intercultural Relations*, 5, 239–258.

Hilgard, E. R., & Bower, G. H. (1975) *Theories of learning*. Englewood Cliffs, NJ: Prentice-Hall.

Katz, J. (1977) The effects of a systematic training program on the attitudes and behaviors of white people. *International Journal of Intercultural Relations*, 1, 77–89.

Kluckhohn, C., & Kroeberg, A. L. (1952) *Culture: A critical review of concepts and definitions*. Vintage Books.

Kyi, K. M. (1988) APJM and comparative management in Asia. *Asia Pacific Journal of Management*, 5, 207–224.

Landis, D., & Brislin, R. (1983) *Handbook on intercultural training* (Vol 1). New York: Pergamon Press.

Landis, D., Brislin, R. W., & Hulgus, J. F. (1985) Attributional training versus contact in acculturative learning: A laboratory study. *Journal of Applied Social Psychology*, 15, 466–482.

Landis, D., Brislin, R., Swanner, G., Tseng, O., & Thomas, J. (1985) Some effects of acculturative training: A field evaluation. *International Journal of Group Tensions*, 15, 68–91.

Landis, D., Day, H. R., McGrew, P. L., Thomas, J. A., & Miller, A. B. (1976) Can a black "culture assimilator" increase racial understanding? *Journal of Social Issues*, 32(2), 169–183.

Latham, G. (1988) Human resource training and development. *Annual Review of Psychology*, 39, 545–582.

Latham, G., & Saari, L. (1979) Application of social learning theory to training supervisors through behavior modification. *Journal of Applied Psychology*, 64, 239–246.

Lefcourt, H. M. (1983) *Research with the locus of control construct* (Vol. 2). New York: Academic Press.

Lefley, H. (1985) Impact of cross-cultural training on black and white mental health professionals. *International Journal of Intercultural Relations*, 9, 305–318.

Lefley, H. (1986) Evaluating the effects of cross-cultural training: Some research results. In H. Lefley & P. Pederson (Eds.), *Cross-cultural training for mental health professionals* (pp. 265–307). Springfield, IL: Thomas.

Manz, C. C., & Sims, H. P. (1981) Vicarious learning: The influence of modeling on organizational behavior. *Academy of Management Review*, 6, 105–113.

McDaniel, C. O., McDaniel, N. C., & McDaniel, A. K. (1988) Transferability of multicultural education from training to practice. *International Journal of Intercultural Relations*, 12, 19–33.

McGroarty, M. (1984, March 6–11) *Design and evaluation of cross-cultural workshops for ESL teachers and administrators*. Paper presented at the annual meeting of Teachers of English to Speakers of Other Languages, Houston.

Mendenhall, M., Dunbar, E., & Oddou, G. (1987) Expatriate selection, training, and career-pathing: A review and critique. *Human Resource Management*, 26, 331–345.

Mendenhall, M., & Oddou, G. (1985) The dimensions of expatriate acculturation. *Academy of Management Review*, 10, 39–47.

Mendenhall, M., & Oddou, G. (1986) Acculturation profiles of expatriate managers: Implications for cross-cultural training programs. *Columbia Journal of World Business*, 21(4), 73–79.

Miller, E. (1973) The international selection decision: A study of managerial behavior in the selection decision process. *Academy of Management Journal*, 16, 234–252.

Misa, K. F., & Fabricatore, J. M. (1979) Return on investment of overseas personnel. *Financial Executive*, 47(4), 42–46.

Mitchell, T. R., Dossett, D., Fiedler, F., & Triandis, H. (1972) Cultural training: Validation evidence for the cultural assimilator. *International Journal of Psychology*, 7, 97–104.

Mitchell, T. R., & Foa, U. G. (1969) Diffusion of the effect of cultural training of the leader in the structure of heterocultural task groups. *Australian Journal of Psychology*, 21, 31–43.

Nayar, E. S. K., Touzard, H., & Summers, D. A. (1968) Training, tasks and mediator orientation in heterocultural negotiations. *Human Relations*, 21, 283–310.

Neimeyer, G. J., Fukuyama, M. A., Bingham, R. P., Hall, L. E., & Mussenden, M. (1986) Training cross-cultural counselors: Comparison of the pro-counselor and anti-counselor trial models. *Journal of Counseling and Development*, 64, 437–439.

Newbold, R. C. III., Carrol, J. G., Hartman, M. E., Mitchell, H. E., & Story, M. R. (1982) A training program in medical communications for foreign native medical graduates. Project for the Educational Commission for Foreign Medical Graduates, ERIC ED 219010-HE015252.

Noe, R. A. (1986) Trainee's attributes and attitudes: Neglected influences on training effectiveness. *Academy of Management Review*, 11, 736–749.

Oberg, K. (1960) Culture shock: Adjustment to new cultural environments. *Practical Anthropologist*, 7, 177–182.

O'Brien, G. E., Fiedler, F. E., & Hewett, T. (1970) The effects of programmed culture training upon the performance of volunteer medical teams. *Human Relations*, 24, 209–231.

O'Brien, G. E., & Plooij, D. (1976) Development of cultural training manuals for medical workers with Pitjantjatjara aboriginals. In G. E. Kearney & D. W. McElwain (Eds.), *Aboriginal cognition* (pp. 383–396). New Jersey: Humantic Press.

Oddou, G., & Mendenhall, M. (1984) Person perception in cross-cultural settings: A review of cross-cultural and related literature. *International Journal of Intercultural Relations*, 8, 77–96.

Porter, L. W., & Lawler, E. E. (1968) *Managerial attitudes and performance*. Homewood, IL: Irwin.

PSI Associates, Inc. (1982) Peace corps stateside teacher training for volunteers in Liberia (Vol. 1) Evaluation report. (Contract No. 82-042-1003) Washington, DC: Peace Corps.

Randolph, G., Landis, D., & Tzeng, O. C. (1977) The effects of time and practice upon culture assimilator training. *International Journal of Intercultural Relations*, 1, 105–119.

Ratiu, I. (1983) Thinking internationally: A comparison of how international executives learn. *International Studies of Management and Organization*, 13, 139–150.

Roberts, K. H. (1970) On looking at an elephant: An evaluation of cross-cultural research related to organizations. *Psychological Bulletin*, 4(5), 327–350.

Roberts, K. H., & Boyacigiller, N. A. (1984) Cross-national organizational research: The grasp of the blind men. In

B. M. Staw & L. L. Cummings (Eds.), Research in organizational behavior (Vol. 6, pp. 17–31). Greenwich, CT.: JAI Press.

Ronen, S. (1986) *Comparative and multinational management*. New York: Wiley.

Runzheimer Executive Report (1984) Expatriation/repatriation survey. (No. 31). Rochester, WI: Runzheimer Associates, Inc.

Salisbury, L. (1971) *College orientation program for Alaskan natives: COPAN–education for survival*. University of Alaska at Fairbanks, Institute of Social, Economic, and Government Research.

Schollhammer, H. (1975) Current research in international and comparative management issues. *Management International Review*, 13, 17–31.

Schwind, H. F. (1985) The state of the art in cross-cultural management training. In R. Doktor (Ed.), *International human resource development annual* (Vol. 1, pp. 7–15). Alexandria, VA: American Society for Training and Development.

Steers, R., & Mowday, R. (1981) Employee turnover and post-decision accommodation processes. In L. L. Cummings and B. M. Staw (Eds.), Research in organizational behavior (Vol. 3, pp. 237–249). Greenwich, CT: JAI Press.

Steinkalk, E., & Taft, R. (1979) The effects of a planned intercultural experience on the attitudes and behaviors of the participants. *International Journal of Intercultural Relations*, 3, 187–197.

Stening, B. (1979) Problems in cross-cultural contact: A literature review. *International Journal of Intercultural Relations*, 3, 269–313.

Swenson, L. L. (1980) *Theories of learning*. Belmont, CA: Wadsworth.

Torbiorn, I. (1982). *Living abroad*. New York: Wiley.

Triandis, H. C., Vassiliou, V., Tanaka, Y., & Shanmugam, A. (Eds.) (1972) *The analysis of subjective culture*. New York: Wiley.

Tung, R. (1981) Selecting and training of personnel for overseas assignments. *Columbia Journal of World Business*, 16(1), 68–78.

Tung, R. (1982) Selection and training procedures of U.S., European, & Japanese multinationals. *California Management Review*, 25(1), 57–71.

Tung, R. (1984) *Key to Japan's economic strength: Human power*. Lexington, MA: Lexington Books.

Vigushin, J. (1982) Helping campus personnel help foreign students: A counseling simulation. *Humanist Educator*, 20(3), 134–142.

Vroom, V. (1964) *Work and motivation*. New York: Wiley.

Wanous, J. P. (1980) *Organizational entry*. Reading, MA: Addison-Wesley.

Weldon, D. E., Carlston, D. E., Rissman, A. K., Slobodin, L., & Triandis, H. C. (1975) A laboratory test of effects of culture assimilator training. *Journal of Personality and Social Psychology*, 32, 300–310.

Worchel, S., & Mitchell, T. R. (1972) An evaluation of the effectiveness of the culture assimilator in Thailand and Greece. *Journal of Applied Psychology*, 56, 472–479.

Zeira, Y. (1975) Overlooked personnel problems in multinational corporations. *Columbia Journal of World Business*, 10(2), 96–103.

J. Stewart Black (Ph.D., University of California, Irvine) is Assistant Professor of Business Administration in the Amos Tuck School of Business Administration at Dartmouth College. Correspondence regarding this article can be sent to him at the Tuck School of Business Administration, Dartmouth College, Hanover, NH 03755.

Mark Mendenhall (Ph.D., Brigham Young University) is the J. Burton Frierson Chair of Excellence in Business Leadership in the School of Business Administration at the University of Tennessee, Chattanooga.

The authors wish to thank Hal Gregersen for his helpful comments on an earlier version of this manuscript.

The International Journal of Human Resource Management 10:3 June 1999 459–476

The role of inpatriation in global staffing

Michael Harvey, Cheri Speier and Milorad M. Novicevic

Abstract The probability of a global organization developing a competitive advantage will be dramatically diminished without a sufficient supply of qualified managers. The expatriate manager has played a central role in the organizational evolution from an international to multinational perspective. As the era of the global organization evolves, the need for increased diversity and multiculturalism in the global workforce is heightened. This paper explores a complementary model of global staffing based upon inpatriation of host-country and third-country nationals to serve as 'linking pins' between the organization's headquarters and foreign subsidiaries. The ultimate goal and value in inpatriation lies in its ability to facilitate competitive advantage through an increased emphasis on developing multiple strategic perspectives through multiculturalism.

Keywords Inpatriation; global human resource management; multi-culturalism.

Introduction

In a recent survey of Fortune Global 500 firms, Arthur Andersen and Bennett & Associates found that 81 per cent respondents indicated that their companies intended to expand in emerging markets around the world (Expatriate, 1997). Many of these emerging markets (e.g., China, Russia, India, Indonesia, Thailand, Malaysia, Turkey, Philippines and several Eastern European countries, as identified by the World Bank) represent difficult relocation assignments for expatriate managers. The economic level of development is different, the cultural distance from Europe and the United States is significant, the risk (social, political, safety, medical) is high and there is a complexity of doing business that would be difficult to comprehend in a short three to five year expatriate assignment. Therefore, it is anticipated that the failure rate for expatriates will be higher, refusal to relocate will escalate, and the complexity of transferring expatriates from Europe and the United States will become exceedingly difficult. What will be the cost, refusal rate, failure rate of these managers? Is there a more effective way of developing global managers? These questions become inordinately important if one subscribes to the theory that there is a linkage between international human resource management and the strategic goals of the organization to develop a renewable competitive differential through its core competency (Galbraith and Kozanjian, 1986; Bartlett and Ghoshal, 1992; Schuler *et al.*, 1993; Poole and Jenkins, 1996). Answers to these questions are somewhat limited given that extensive academic research into expatriate managers has tended towards an assumption that expatriation is the dominant

Michael Harvey, Puterbaugh Chair in American Free Enterprise, Michael F. Price, College of Business Administration, University of Oklahoma, Norman, OK 73019 (e-mail: mharvey@cbafac.ou.edu). Cheri Speier, Assistant Professor in Management Information Systems, Eli Broad Graduate School of Management, Michigan State University. Milorad M. Novicevic, PhD student, Michael F. Price College of Business Administration, University of Oklahoma.

corporate international human resource strategy utilized by many MNCs (Scullion, 1991; Ali and Camp, 1995).

The shifting demand for products/services in emerging markets presents a unique set of problems for MNCs accustomed to marketing their products in developed countries, not the least of which are the human resource issues associated with providing competent manpower to compete in these emerging markets effectively. With that in mind, the objectives of this paper are five-fold:

- examination of global strategic staffing based upon competency-based theory;
- development of a model of inpatriation illustrating the shift in strategic international human resources orientation when staffing global positions;
- assessment of the issues associated with acculturating inpatriate managers into the home-country organization;
- examination of the problems of assimilating inpatriate managers into the home-country organization;
- assessment of the outcomes associated with utilizing inpatriate managers to provide the strategic 'linking pin' between organizational elements in a global organization.

A competency-based approach to global strategic staffing

As a greater number of MNCs expand abroad, competition for competent top management talent to manage overseas operations will steadily intensify. Managers who can operate across cultures effectively will be one of the key means for creating competitive success in the global marketplace (Oddou and Derr, 1993; Frey-Ridgway, 1997). To meet the challenge, MNCs must develop new ways to identify, attract, cultivate and retain international executive talent (Moynihan, 1993). This need for qualified talent will persist for the foreseeable future at all levels in the organization from top management through supervisory managers. The creativity and resourcefulness in finding an ample number of qualified managers who can manage across cultures effectively becomes the strategic challenge of international human resource managers.

One complementary source of qualified global managers is through inpatriation. Inpatriation is the process of selectively transferring host-county and/or third-country national managers into the home/domestic organization of a MNC on a semi-permanent to permanent basis (Harvey, 1993b). Inpatriate managers can be brought from foreign operations or are hired from outside the organization in the host countries where the MNC operates. It has been argued that inpatriate managers can provide a global perspective in developing strategy and in managing host-country nationals that escapes many expatriate managers (Harvey and Buckley, 1997). It is frequently stated that very few expatriate managers can cross cultural barriers and become wholly accepted by the host-country managers/employees (Beeth, 1997). Developing a multicultural, international workforce is considered to be one of the primary requisites of competing in the global marketplace effectively, particularly in emerging markets (i.e., China, Russia, India) (Kamoche, 1996).

The perceived advantages of integrating inpatriate managers into the domestic organization are: 1) they provide unique cultural/social knowledge, understanding and insights in 'doing business in' that are difficult for competitors to imitate (Dierickx and Cool, 1989; Sohn, 1994; Doz *et al.*, 1997); 2) they can provide a critical strategic communication point for host-country managers to help insure clarity of mission; 3) they can provide a diversity of perspectives when developing policies, strategies and plans for competing in developing countries effectively; 4) they can provide and maintain continual contacts with government officials and channel-of-distribution members; 5) they can develop a contextual understanding of how to globalize but yet act locally; 6) they are an alternative to high cost/failure expatriates who do not provide a cultural 'window' into doing business in the host country; and 7) they provide the diversity necessary to move from multi-domestic, to multinational, and ultimately to global organizations. As workforces become more diverse, there is an increased need for a overarching civic culture to evolve which explicitly addresses relations and interactions among home-country nationals and inpatriates. MNCs must focus on relational values such as equity and respect for differences to be truly effective in their integration of multiple perspectives in developing strategy (Chen and Eastman, 1997).

In the past, human resource managers in the home-country organization considered inpatriates and host-country nationals to be less attractive candidates for many assignments. This reluctance to use 'foreign' managers frequently stemmed from the headquarters desire to maintain control over subsidiaries and expatriate managers were thought to provide for more contextual control in the traditional headquarters perspective (Truss *et al.*, 1997). Additionally, the expatriate 'carried the corporate culture flag' into the global subsidiary organization. Many distinctions between inpatriates and expatriates can be observed (see Table 1). In addition to very different skills and motivational differences between expatriates and inpatriates (see Table 1), advances in communications and information technologies have facilitated performance-control systems increasing the attractiveness of inpatriates and host-country nationals as primary candidates for key senior management positions in the global marketplace (Coller and Morginson, 1998).

Table 1 *Expatriate/inpatriate appropriateness analysis*

	Location of assignment			
	Expatriate		*Inpatriate*	
Candidate characteristics	*Developed*	*Developing*	*Developed*	*Developing*
Organizational cultural 'fit'	H	L	H	H
Flexibility (social/cultural/family)	M	L	H	H
Difficulty in adaptation	M	H	M	L
Relative cost characteristics	H	H	L	L
Motivation to participate	M	L	H	H
Loyalty	H	L	H	H
Headquarters confidence	H	M	M	H
Level of peer acceptance	L	M	M	H
Level of stress	M	H	M	L
Formal business education	H	H	L	L
Internal political understanding	H	L	M	H
Renewable resource (willingness to extend)	L	L	H	H
Willingness to accept position	M	L	H	H

Notes
Level of appropriateness
H = High
M = Moderate
L = Low

The more traditional headquarters focus on expatriates is thought to stem from administrative heritage' or ethnocentrism in the headquarters' corporate culture (Bartlett and Ghoshal, 1989; Edström and Galbraith, 1994). This corporate culture, e.g. holistic, historically determined, tied to ritual and symbols, and difficult to change (Fenwich *et al.*, 1993), is subject to proactive intent, and can be the product of management decisions (Flamholtz, 1996). It is frequently concluded that employees who adopt appropriate behaviours as enshrined in corporate norms and values can be trusted to act in the interest of the organization (Deal and Kennedy, 1982; Welch and Welch, 1997). Corporate culturalism expects, and necessitates, employees to internalize management-driven values and to adopt and cherish them as their own (Willmott, 1993; Huault, 1996). It has been assumed in the past that expatriate managers were the most appropriate ones to institute cultural control in foreign operations. Given their ability to articulate and disseminate the company's value system through embedded individual behaviours, expatriates have been viewed as the sole option for many MNCs (Ghoshal and Bartlett, 1994, 1995, 1997). In addition, expatriates are known commodities from a skill/competence standpoint and, therefore, have been perceived as being less risky in foreign assignments (Edström and Galbraith, 1994).

A model of inpatriation

The workforce in developed economies appears to be becoming more dependent on an ever-increasing influx of educated workers from developing and transition economies (Johnston, 1991; Solomon, 1997; Seib, 1998). The use of inpatriate managers presents a unique set of problems for MNCs who are bringing these individuals to their home country. Multicultural workforces necessitate a flexible human resource system that can accommodate and exploit the different synergies presented by inpatriate managers. At the same time, these workforces provide the basis for developing a competitive advantage both globally and locally. Promoting diversity and empowerment (trust) in inpatriate managers enhances the likelihood of deriving a sustainable competitive advantage (Poole and Jenkins, 1996). To better understand the use of inpatriate managers a model of inpatriation has been developed and is presented in the remainder of this section.

The model depicted in Figure 1 proposes a proactive utilization of inpatriates to accelerate the globalization within an organization. It is anticipated that a declining number of expatriate managers should be used in the future due to the growth in market opportunities in developing countries where it is anticipated that expatriates would experience a great deal of difficulty in adjusting to both internal and external environments. This belief is based on five critical assumptions: 1) expatriates' cost/failure/ performance record is questionable; 2) expatriation will become more complex due to an increased number of dual-career couples and female expatriate candidates; 3) future emerging markets will present more difficulties in attracting expatriates (higher referral rates) and these countries will present greater adjustment problems due to cultural novelty and level of economic development (higher failure rates); 4) inpatriate managers have the cultural/economic background to address the problems in the emerging markets more effectively; and 5) global competitors have and will continue to adopt a multicultural perspective to the global operations.

In an effort to provide domestic managers an opportunity to develop international skills, expatriate managers could and should be used in developed countries. It is anticipated that the level of adjustment will be less in these countries and, therefore, the

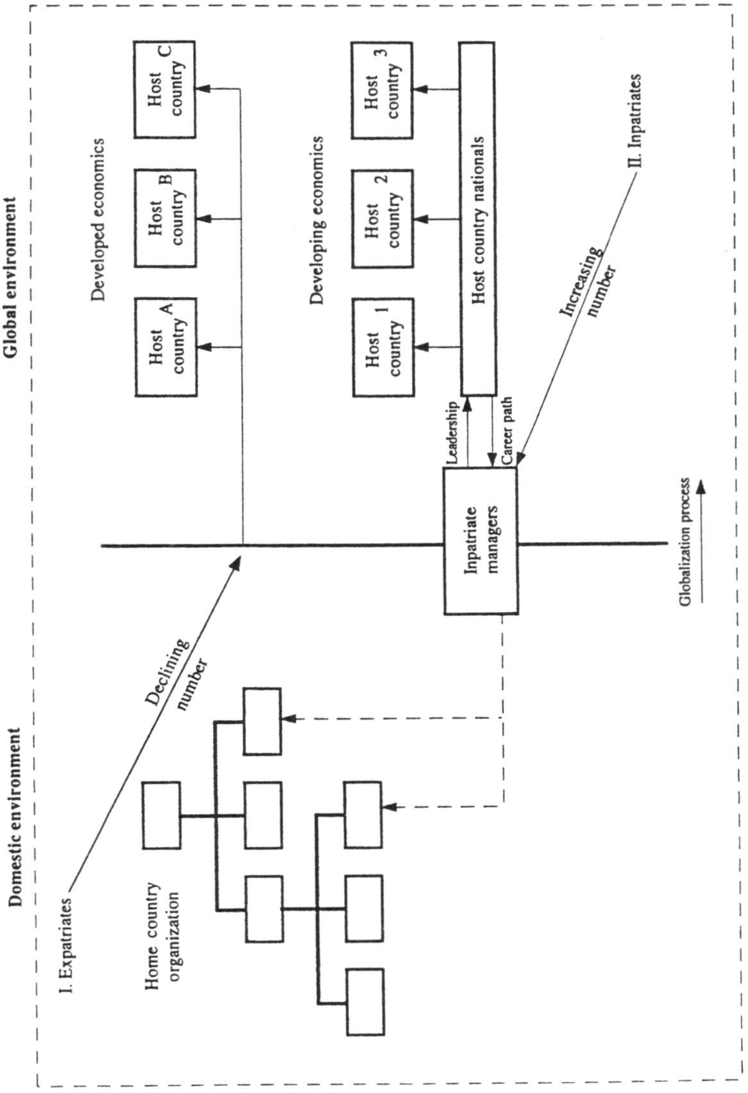

Figure 1 *Model of global management through inpatriation*

probability of attracting/retaining expatriate managers will be higher. Continuing to provide the present type of expatriate assignment also helps to ensure that the domestic managers can play a significant integrating role in the future of the organization. If managers were not expatriated, over time the organization would become control-dependent on the inpatriate managers for their knowledge of global business (Korbin, 1988). In addition, expatriates have to continue to play a central role in the strategic thrust of any global organization to effectively develop a core competency based upon differentiation or uniqueness of the organization's strategies (Goddard, 1997).

The need for a global experience base becomes more apparent when one considers the influence of top management's background and their resulting corporate strategic perspective (Murray, 1989; Michael and Hambrick, 1992; Wiersema and Bentel, 1992; Sambharya, 1996). The 'dominant logic', i.e., the attitudes, beliefs and mindsets of top management, strongly influences the strategic thrust of the organization (Prahalad and Bettis, 1986). For example, career experiences in addition to functional orientation can be expected to have a significant influence on organizational outcomes (Hambrick and Mason, 1984; Simon and Davies, 1996). If domestic managers were not allowed to expatriate, their contribution to the firm's globalization strategy would be limited. The expatriates' contribution to the multicultural management team provides the control factor that most headquarters managements require in the development of competitive strategy (Dadfer and Gustavsson, 1992; Granstrand *et al.*, 1993; Welch, 1994).

The second critical dimension of the model depicts the inpatriates' role in the globalization of the management of the organization. A group of inpatriate managers is selected and transferred to the headquarters of the global organization. The specific role they are to play necessitates becoming the 'linking pin' between the domestic headquarters and the emerging markets that the organization is attempting to penetrate. These inpatriates perform a boundary-spanning role between the headquarters and the foreign subsidiary. They occupy roles on the boundaries between operational locations and, at the same time, cultures (Thomas, 1994). The management role of the inpatriate managers should be to provide competent leadership to the expansion efforts in developing/emerging markets. The inpatriate managers would be located in the headquarters' organizational structure but would make frequent trips to the developing-country subsidiaries to provide direction regarding the globalization strategy of the organization. By locating the inpatriate managers in the home country, top management would not experience the loss of control generally felt and partially exercised when using host-country nationals located in their own country. In addition, by having the inpatriate managers domiciled in the domestic organization, the process of both multiculturalism and transculturalism can be activated in the MNC. By utilizing their subtle cultural input, the organization has undertaken the first strategic step in developing a multicultural management group and global learning organization based upon experience which is needed to compete in the global market effectively (Hofstede, 1980; McBride, 1992; Simon and Davies, 1996; Nemetz and Christensen, 1996; Aguirre, 1997; McMillen *et al.*, 1997; Reynolds, 1997).

Inpatriate managers can also provide invaluable input into human resources functions in the emerging markets. They can provide accurate advice on the adaptation of technical dimensions of the human resource process (i.e., selection criteria, compensation plans, performance evaluations and training/development for host-country nationals). They can also provide a means for transferring the appropriate dimensions of the home organizations's culture to the host-country subsidiary. The culturally sensitive 'exporting' of corporate culture to locations in the emerging markets allows the control function to be exercised in an acceptable and effective manner (Schein, 1990). Rather than enforcing an 'outside' organizational culture, the inpatriate's insights into the host-country culture allow the organizational climate in a separate subsidiary to evolve over time.

The primary means to embedding control becomes the inpatriate managers, who will more than likely be accepted by host-country nationals more readily than are expatriates. The cultural embedding mechanisms which will be most effective are: 1) what the inpatriate managers pay attention to, measure and control; 2) how the inpatriate managers react to critical differences between the two organizational cultures (domestic/host country); 3) the inpatriates providing a role model (mentoring) for other host-country nationals; 4) inpatriate managers' operationalization of rewards and status for host-county nationals; and 5) assisting with and establishing operating criteria for recruiting, selection, promotion among host-country nationals (adapted from Schein, 1983, 1990). This cultural adaptation of the home-country organizational culture to the subsidiaries is a critical factor in increasing the functional consistency or organizational fit among the various organizational units thereby helping to establish the inter-unit linkages and balancing the needs for autonomy (cultural identity), co-ordination ('fit' between organizational units) and control (home management concern) for the purpose of increased competitiveness in these emerging markets (Schuler *et al.*, 1993).

The co-ordination/integration performed by inpatriate managers is particularly important when the headquarters perceives the benefits of co-ordination as a quasi source of control in countries where local markets vary dramatically from the home country (Jackson *et al.*, 1989; Schuler *et al.*, 1993; Welch, 1994). The human resource function has often been allocated to host-country nationals to provide this inter-culturalization of hiring (Dowling and Schuler, 1990). However, this accentuated human resource managers' concerns about the loss of control in foreign operations. Therefore, the boundary-spanning function of inpatriate members becomes critical to tying the two organizational entities together effectively (Thomas, 1994). Using inpatriate managers who have high commitment to and contextual understanding of both the global and local organizations facilitates change, strategic integration and organizational learning (Doz and Prahalad, 1986; Mueller, 1996; Kamoche, 1997).

Inpatriate managers could also provide mentoring to high potential managers from host-country nations to ensure a succession plan when new inpatriate managers are moved into the core of the home-country organization. It is important for a career path to be established for inpatriate managers that allows them full opportunity to become an integral aspect of the home-country organization. In order to benefit fully from the multiculturalism created by the inpatriate managers they must be viewed as a part of the core management team and not as peripheral to the global strategic management team (Harvey, 1997; Harvey and Miceli, forthcoming). This process also opens a career path for high-potential host-country nationals to become future inpatriate managers.

Issues associated with inpatriate acculturation to the organization's home country

To inpatriate managers into the domestic organization effectively, a process of acculturating them must be developed. Acculturation (i.e., 'the process by which individuals change, both by being influenced by contact with another culture and by being participants in general acculturative changes underway in their own culture':

Berry, 1990: 235) should become a focal point of any organizational inpatriation programme. If the acculturation process is not administered effectively, there will be a great deal of conflict between the inpatriate and the organizational culture. This conflict is frequently translated into stress in the inpatriate manager and varying degrees of rejection of inpatriates by the members of the domestic organization (Harvey, 1997). A basic premise of acculturation is that the inpatriate managers will adapt to the domestic organizational culture but in time the culture will be modified by the presence of inpatriate managers from different cultures (Sayegh and Lasry, 1993).

There are four acculturation patterns that are typically available to the inpatriate and at the same time to the domestic organization inpatriating the manager. It is important to note that the inpatriate manager's perspective on being acculturated may be consistent/inconsistent with the intent of the acculturation programme established by the home-country institutional environment and organization (see Table 2). The four acculturation strategies are: 1) *integration* – reflects a desire to maintain key features of the inpatriate manager's own culture while adopting aspects of the host organizational culture; 2) *assimilation* – requires the inpatriate managers to relinquish their own cultural identity for the sake of adopting the organizational culture of the home-country organization; 3) *separation* – can be characterized by the desire of the inpatriate manager to maintain all the features of their cultural identity while rejecting relationships with members of the home-country organization; and 4) *individualism* – inpatriates who reject group ascriptions *per se* and prefer to be treated and treat others in the home-country organization as individual rather than as members of a group (the organization) (Bourhis *et al.*, 1997). As can be seen in Table 2, by combining the four potential orientations of inpatriates with the four of the home-country organization, the matrix becomes interactive. Of interest is the degree to which the home-country organization and the inpatriate managers match or mismatch (Barnett and Toyne, 1991). When analysing the conflict that arises when there is an inconsistency in acculturation strategies, the matrix model could provide valuable insights into the presence of intercultural conflict and how to resolve the conflict.

The acculturation intentions of the organization can be articulated in a formal programme that states as a goal what strategy of acculturation it is following. On the other hand, the acculturation strategy of the individual must be determined by human resource management. An immigrant acculturation scale (IAS) developed to ascertain the acculturation goals of those entering a new culture can provide such insights (Berry, 1984). When the goals of the organization and those of the inpatriate manager are consistent, acculturation will occur in a more orderly fashion and more rapidly (Alkhazraji *et al.*, 1997). The problems occur when there is not a consistent acculturation strategy between the two entities. As is illustrated in Figure 2 below, the conflict that can be created by incongruent acculturation goals can vary in intensity and the resolution of the conflict can also have a broad range of outcomes. In an effort to understand the differences in acculturation goals and to encourage congruency between the two entities, organizations should develop a well-articulated acculturation process to demonstrate what is being done in the process and what are the goals of the programme. The difficulties of inpatriates in acculturating to the home country highlight issues for these 'transplanted' managers. In addition to changes the inpatriates undertake given exposure to the home-country culture, these individuals must also be assimilated into the organization's culture. The assimilation process requires an understanding of the differences between the inpatriate work experience and the cultural context of the home-country organization.

Table 2 *Acculturating inpatriate managers to home-country organizations*

Home country orientation relative to inpatriates	*Orientation towards inpatriation acculturation*			
	Integration	*Assimilation*	*Separation*	*Individualism*
Integration	Accommodation of differences and modification of corporate culture over time (consistent expectations)	Conflict over whether inpatriate or organization accommodates to one another	Moderate conflict over organization's desire to accommodate and individiual's desire to maintain social distance	Strong conflict over organization's desire to integrate and inpatriate's desire to remain autonomous
Assimilation	Strong conflict over which changes, corporate culture or inpatriate	Modification to normative inpatriate behaviour to be accepted (consistent expectations)	Moderate conflict over organization's strategy to incorporate inpatriate . . . their desire to remain separate	Strong conflict over the long-run value of the inpatriate of 'fitting' corporate culture vs. providing unique perspective to MNC
Segregation	Conflict around lack of organizational commitment to integrate inpatriates (turnover)	Conflict over willingness to change to be accepted in organization and not being accepted	Willingness to become/ maintain social distance (consistent expectations)	Mild conflict . . . and results consistent but motivation different
Individualism	Conflict for inpatriate not having belongingness needs satisfied . . . organization's culture weakened due to dependency of inpatriates	Conflict over change in behaviour and lack of acceptance	Moderate conflict – goals accomplished for different reasons	Acceptance/definition of values as being an individual . . . quality of personal characteristics (consistent expectations)

Assimilating inpatriate managers in the home-country organization

Developing a multicultural management to compete effectively in the global marketplace ultimately becomes the economic justification for developing an inpatriation programme. The benefits derived from such an inpatriation programme are based upon the cultural diversity (social knowledge), precise understanding of the political/economic nuances of particular countries and having an understanding of the individual and group dimensions that are presented in an organization's setting in foreign countries. This multicultural insight/perspective, which includes creativity, innovation, problem solving and work-group cohesiveness, provides an MNC with a globally distinctive competency to compete with global competitors more effectively (Peng *et al.*, 1991; Wong and Birnbaum-Moore, 1994; Cox, 1991). To ensure that the benefits of cultural diversity accrue from an inpatriation programme, the inpatriate managers must be assimilated into the management core of the organization effectively.

Much of the existing research on newcomer adjustment and assimilation in the international literature has dealt with expatriates (Baker, 1992; Gregersen and Black, 1992). The primary determinant of adjustment assimilation of an inpatriate into the domestic organization's management is a recognition of cultural distance, and/or novelty, of the inpatriates from the home-country culture. There is a need to determine the cultural heterogeneity of inpatriates to the home country and the resulting impact of these differences in addressing organizational processes (Earley and Singh, 1995; Pineda and Whitehead, 1997). For example, the variations in managerial use of personal opinions from existing organizational norms could occur when inpatriate managers from different cultural systems are tied more closely to their own societal culture than that of the organization to which they were inpatriated (Hofstede *et al.*, 1990; Schneider and de Meyer, 1991). The dominant cultural force for inpatriates during the early stages of the process will remain the home culture. Therefore, developing an understanding of these cultures becomes imperative to developing inpatriate programmes effectively.

A majority of the institutional theory-based research exploring the interrelationships among societal cultures, organizational culture and the behaviour of managers (both home and host country) have used the nation-state as the unit of analysis (Peng *et al.*, 1991). The primary reason for this focus is that organizations use society-based criteria to obtain and maintain organizational legitimacy (Jorgensen *et al.*, 1986). This organizational legitimacy is confined by national, social, economic and political organizations/institutions which in turn expect a degree of consistency between the national culture and that of the organization (Kissundu *et al.*, 1983). The differences between the inpatriates' culture and the culture to which they are being inpatriated are dynamic, making the assimilation process for inpatriate managers a multifaceted, complex process that needs to be carefully conceptualized and implemented (Segall *et al.*, 1990). The assimilation process will become increasingly complex as organizations inpatriate a large number of managers from different cultures (which are culturally distant from each other, as well as from the home country of the organization) at various levels within the organization (top, middle, supervisory) and they perform different functional jobs upon inpatriation. The inpatriate manager cannot be an isolated incident, at one level in the organization, in one functional area. The multicultural global organization must assimilate inpatriates throughout the organization to induce a distinctive competency to differentiate itself from other global competitors (Schneider, 1989; Hamel and Prahalad, 1990; Bartlett and Ghoshal, 1995, 1997).

A number of human resource issues must be addressed in an effort to assimilate the inpatriate managers into the home-country organization. Assimilation (i.e., 'the process of interpenetration and fusion in which persons and groups acquire the memories, sentiments, and attitudes of other persons and groups and, by sharing their experiences and history, are incorporated with them in a common cultural life': Park and Burgess, 1921: 735) is frequently referred to as a shorthand process of assisting inpatriates in 'learning the ropes', 'fitting in', through which they become like home-country mangers (Barker, 1995; Kazal, 1995; Rumbaut, 1997). This assimilation process is thought of as being more or less an unconscious process as the inpatriates incorporate those things in societal and organizational culture that allow them to be accepted. The greater the distance between the cultural beliefs of the inpatriate and those of the organization's home country, the longer the assimilation will take and the more difficult the transformation of the inpatriate to being 'accepted' in the organization (Warner and Srole, 1945).

Just as important as cultural assimilation is the difficulty of socio-economic assimilation (i.e., achieving parity with the home-country managers in income and perks as well as social acceptance of the inpatriate managers) (Berry *et al.*, 1992). Frequently, these managers receive lower salaries and much less support than their domestic counterparts (Harvey, 1993a). Inpatriation must allow the incoming managers the same economic expectations as their national counterparts. The rate/means of 'catching up' is a significant managerial issue when addressing inpatriate human resources policies (Borjas, 1990). The question becomes: 'how does the human resource management process need to be modified to accommodate inpatriation?'

Expected outcomes from introducing inpatriation into SGHRM systems

The socially complex process of inpatriate socialization, development and integration with expatriates can be accomplished only through an effective SG (strategic global) HRM system of bundling expatriation and inpatriation practices. Such complementary practices provide synergies that may expand the repertoire of senior managements' strategic choices and create a source of sustainable competitive advantage, provided they are designed and implemented in a firm-specific way (see Figure 2). The evolving strategy of a global management staffing system incorporates the following competency-based criteria for the global pool of candidates: 1) ability to motivate and enact the process of competition among subsidiaries exploiting the imperfections in the internal labour market and fostering flexibility and responsiveness of the local workforce to headquarters initiatives; 2) ability to motivate and enact the process of co-operation and organizational learning among subsidiaries by facilitating the transfer of effective practices; 3) ability to efficiently enact consistency in the internal cultural environment of the subsidiaries; and 4) ability to develop customer loyalty in the subsidiary's external network by fostering quality and enhancing corporate global reputation (Lado and Wilson, 1994).

The more traditional bureaucratic model of management staffing in MNCs has included the principles of dependence on hierarchical authority in the parent organization and of reliance on formal rules and standard expatriate-based staffing policies of the corporate SGHRM. Its salient features are based on viewing foreign assignments as: 1) job vacancies to be filled in; 2) extension of the parent organization's hierarchical relationships; and 3) behaviour-based rewards for individuals with accountability of assignees through management development (Edström and Galbraith, 1994). However, the high rate of technological and organizational changes makes it very difficult to define a stable set of assignment tasks that an assignee will be hired to perform or will be measured against.

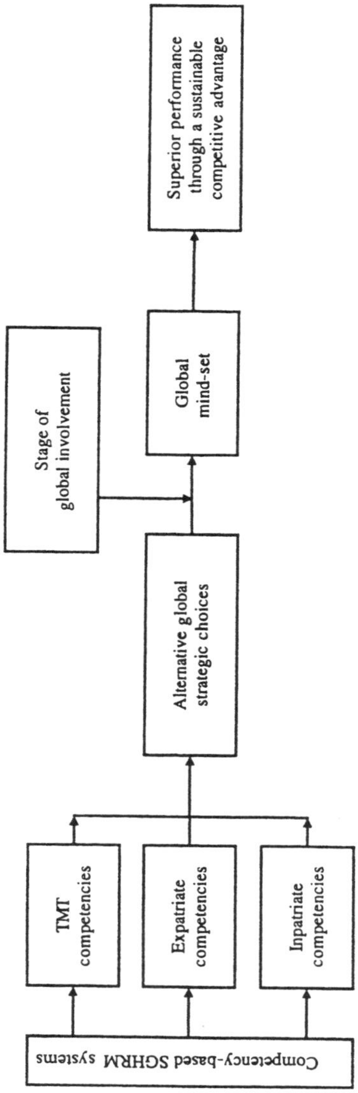

Figure 2 *Designing competency-based SGHRM systems to create a sustainable competitive advantage*

A SGHRM system fosters a competency-based approach to global staffing, emphasizing a divergence from the internal cultural 'fit' – equally emphasizing the 'fit' among the strategic choices of global business strategies, patterns of individual competencies and capabilities, and global environments. Within this framework, the ultimate goal of an SGHRM system should be to produce the necessary individual competencies and to increase the co-ordination of effort among global subsidiaries while not sacrificing local responsiveness. Focusing on the candidates' social knowledge, cross-cultural skills and functional expertise rather than on the nature of their jobs, the corporate SGHRM must ensure that the individual assignees have the ability to learn and develop the right set of competencies and the appropriate set of actionable knowledge rather than making a trade-off based on the candidates' past skills and capabilities in the parent organization.

The significance of the inpatriation process within the strategic global staffing policies and practices is positively related to the global organization's emphasis on the development of organizational capabilities: quality, speed, low-cost operations, learning, innovation and customer focus (Urlich and Lake, 1990; Lawler, 1996; Kamoche, 1997). This emerging SGHRM strategic choice-related view of individual competencies is associated with the corporate focus on high individual performance of globally assigned managers. The global staffing selection in such SGHRM systems is designed for hiring the candidates who possess more than needed competencies and the 'total global compensation system' is designed to reward the selected candidates who display the needed competencies (Milkovich and Bloom, 1998). The competency-based SGHRM system, fostering learning through inpatriate socialization and teamwork with expatriates, is different from an assignment-based system, fostering top-down management control and up-front selection of candidates securing organizational stability. In other words, the inpatriation process is activated through flexibility whereas the expatriation process is activated through the fit in SGHRM practices of staffing candidates in the network of the global organization.

SGHRM staffing systems can thus become firm-specific strategic resources influencing corporate strategic choices and leading to sustainable competitive advantage. The key reason for development of this firm-specific resource approach to global staffing is the resulting dynamic capabilities model which allows the appropriate incorporation of inpatriate candidates into the corporate staffing strategies for global integration. This resource variation produced by strategic inclusion of inpatriate managerial resources leads to the pattern of strategic choices in a global organization which may contribute to the advantageous development of the firm's transnational capability (Kamoche, 1996). The particular contribution of this paper lies in providing the theory-based guidelines for corporate SGHRM to design a competency-based fast-track programme for promising global executives.

Conclusion and implications

This paper has addressed the emerging shift from emphasis on expatriation to emphasis on inpatriation in a strategic global human resource staffing system of policies and practices. The shift represents a proactive SGHRM response to accelerated globalization of MNC strategies operationalized in a dynamic balance of multicultural and transcultural dimensions in global MNC staffing. The dynamic balance is achieved by strategic synergies of expatriation- and inpatriation-based policies and practices to match the changing environmental demands of growing emerging markets.

As market opportunities increasingly migrate into developing countries with high cultural distance from the parent company and as MNC strategies shift their focus from a multinational to a global perspective, the issues limiting expatriation-based staffing call for expansion in MNCs' inpatriation policies and practices. To capture the multidimensional impact of the emerging inpatriation trend, we have, first, examined the necessary set of competencies of global management in the face of emerging economic importance of developing economies. Second, we have analysed the issues limiting expatriation-based policies and practices in order to identify boundaries in current practices of controlling overseas operations. Third, we have examined and justified the strategic MNC need to differentiate inpatriation from expatriation in order to develop advantageously and maintain multicultural dimensions in its global staffing practices. Fourth, we have developed a model of the emerging global management staffing system based on complementarity of expatriation- and inpatriation-based staffing policies and practices. Finally, we have assessed the SGHRM planning prerequisites needed to facilitate acculturation and assimilation of inpatriates into the parent MNC organizations.

The main contribution of this paper is in providing a multifaceted strategic rationale for international human resource researchers and practitioners to differentiate the inpatriate and expatriate pools of candidates for global staffing in order to design an optimized SGHRM system. This differentiation arises from the resource-based and power dependence theoretic perspectives that view global strategic staffing management in the light of creating a sustainable competitive advantage by leveraging human resource competencies globally. This new dynamic view of global human resource competencies parallels Ghoshal and Bartlett's (1997) view of the 'individualized' transnational corporation supporting the ideal of an effective global manager who acts across functions and cultures as a 'transpatriate'.

References

Aguirre, M. (1997) 'Multiculturalism in a Labour Market with Integrated Economies', *Management Decision*, 35(7): 489–96.

Ali, A.J. and Camp, R.C. (1996) 'Global Managers: Qualities for Effective Competition', *International Journal of Manpower*, 17(6/7): 5–18.

Alkhazraji, K.M., Gardner, W., Martin, J. and Paolillo, J. (1997) 'The Acculturation of Immigrants to U.S. Organizations: The Case of Muslim Employees', *Management Communication Quarterly*, 11(2): 217–65.

Baker, H. (1992) 'Employee Socialization Strategies and the Presence of Union Representation', *Labor Studies Journal*, 17: 5–17.

Barker, E. (1995) 'Race, Religion, and Nationality in American Society: A Model of Ethnicity – from Contact to Assimilation', *Journal of American Ethnic History*, 14(2): 38–75.

Barnett, S. and Toyne, B. (1991) 'The Socialization, Acculturation, and Career Progression of Headquartered Foreign Nationals', *Advances in International Comparative Management*, 6: 3–34.

Bartlett, C. and Ghoshal, S. (1989) *Managing Across Borders: The Transnational Solution*. Boston, MA: Harvard Business School.

Bartlett, C. and Ghoshal, S. (1992) 'What is a Global Manager?', *Harvard Business Review*, 70: 124–32.

Bartlett, C. and Ghoshal, S. (1995) 'Changing the Role of Top Management: Beyond Systems to People (Part Three)', *Harvard Business Review*, May–June: 132–43.

Bartlett, C. and Ghoshal, S. (1997) *The Individualized Corporation*. New York: Harper Business.

Beeth, G. (1997) 'Multicultural Managers Wanted', *Management Review*, May: 17–21.

Berry, J. (1984) 'Cultural Relations in Plural Societies: Alternatives to Segregation and their Socio-psychological Implications'. In Miller, N. and Brewer, M. (eds) *Groups in Contact*. New York: Academic Press.

Berry, J. (1990) 'Psychology of Acculturation: Understanding Individuals Moving Between Cultures'. In Briskin, R. (ed.) *Applied Cross-Cultural Psychology*. Newberry Park, CA: Sage.

Berry, J., Poortinga, Y., Segall, M. and Daren, P. (1992) *Cross-Cultural Psychology: Research and Applications*. Cambridge: Cambridge University Press.

Borjas, G. (1990) *Friends or Strangers: The Impact of Immigrants on the U.S. Economy*. New York: Basic Books.

Bourhis, R., Möise, L., Perreault, S. and Senécal, S. (1997) 'Towards an Interactive Acculturation Model: A Social Psychological Approach', *International Journal of Psychology*, 32(6): 369–86.

Chen, C. and Eastman, W. (1997) 'Toward a Civic Culture for Multinational Organizations', *Journal of Applied Behavioral Science*, 33(4): 454–70.

Coller, X. and Morginson, P. (1998) 'Transnational Management Influence over Changing Employment Practices: A Case from the Food Industry', *Industrial Relations Journal*, 29(1): 4–17.

Cox, T. (1991) 'Multicultural Organization', *Academy of Management Executive*, May: 35–50.

Dadfer, H. and Gustavsson, P. (1992) 'Competition by Effective Management of Cultural Diversity', *International Studies of Management and Organization*, 22(4): 81–92.

Deal, T. and Kennedy, A. (1982) *Corporate Culture: The Rites and Rituals of Corporate Life*. Reading, MA: Addison-Wesley.

Dierickx, I. and Cool, K. (1989) 'Asset Stock Accumulation and Sustainability of Competitive Advantage', *Management Science*, 35(2): 1504–14.

Dowling, P. and Schuler, R. (1990) *International Dimensions of Human Resource Management*. Boston, MA: PWS-Kent.

Doz, Y. and Prahalad, C.K. (1986) 'Controlled Variety: A Challenge for Human Resource Management in the MNC', *Human Resource Management*, 24(1): 55–71.

Doz, Y., Asakawa, K., Santos, P. and Williamson, P. (1997) 'The Multinational Corporations', INSEAD working paper series, #97/60/SM.

Earley, P. and Singh, H. (1995) 'International and Intercultural Management Research: What's Next?', *Academy of Management Journal*, 38: 327–40.

Edström, A. and Galbraith, J. (1994) 'Alternative Policies for International Transfers of Managers', *Management International Review*, Special Issue(1): 71–82.

Expatriate Manager Programs: Best in Class Study (1997) Arthur Andersen & Bennett & Associates, www.arthurandersen.com.

Fenwich, M., Welch, D. and De Cieri, H. (1993) 'Organizational Control Through Staff Transfers: A Concept Revised', paper presented at the 10th European International Business Association Annual Meeting, Lisbon, Spain, 12–14 December.

Flamholtz, E. (1996) 'Effective Organizational Control: A Framework, Applications, and Implications', *European Management Journal*, 14(6): 596–611.

Frey-Ridgway, S. (1997) 'The Cultural Dimensions of International Business', *Collection Building*, 16(1): 12–23.

Galbraith, J. and Kozanjian, R. (1986) *Strategic Implementation: The Role of Structure in the Process*. St. Paul, MN: West Publishing.

Ghoshal, S. and Bartlett, C. (1994) 'Linking Organizational Control and Managerial Action: The Dimensions of Quality of Management', *Strategic Management Journal*, 15: 91–112.

Ghoshal, S. and Bartlett, C. (1995) 'Building the Entrepreneurial Corporations: New Organizational Processes, New Managerial Tasks', *European Management Journal*, 13(2): 139–55.

Ghoshal, S. and Bartlett, C. (1997) *The Individualized Corporation: A Fundamentally New Approach to Management*. New York: Harper Business.

Goddard, J. (1997) 'The Architecture of Core Competence', *Business Strategies Review*, 8(1): 43–52.

Gordon, M. (1964) *Assimilation in American Life: The Role of Race, Religion, and National Origins*. New York: Oxford University Press.
Granstrand, O., Hakanson, L. and Sjölander, S. (1993) 'Internationalization of R&D: A Survey of Some Recent Research', *Research Policy*, 22: 413–30.
Gregersen, H. and Black, S. (1992) 'Antecedents to Commitment to the Parent Company and a Foreign Operation', *Academy of Management Journal*, 35: 65–90.
Hambrick, D. and Mason, P. (1984) 'Upper Echelons: The Organization as a Reflection of its Top Managers', *Academy of Management Review*, 9(2): 193–206.
Hamel, G. and Prahalad, C. (1990) 'The Core Competency of the Corporation', *Harvard Business Review*, 68(2): 79–91.
Harvey, M. (1993a) 'Empirical Evidence of Reoccurring International Compensation Problems', *Journal of International Business Studies*, 24(4): 785–99.
Harvey, M. (1993b) 'Training Inpatriate Managers to Succeed in the Domestic Organization', Fourth Symposium on Cross-cultural Consumer and Business Studies, *Proceedings*, pp. 210–16.
Harvey, M. (1997) 'Inpatriation Training: The Next Challenge for International Human Resource Management', *International Journal of Intercultural Relations*, 21(3): 393–428.
Harvey, M. and Buckley, M. (1997) 'Managing Inpatriates: Building Global Core Competency', *Journal of World Business*, 32(1): 35–52.
Harvey, M. and Miceli, N. (forthcoming) 'Exploring Inpatriate Managers Issues: An Exploratory Empirical Study', *International Journal of Intercultural Relations*.
Hofstede, G. (1980) *Culture's Consequences: International Differences in Work-Related Values*. Beverly Hills, CA: Sage.
Hofstede, G., Neuijen, B., Ohayv, D. and Sanders, G. (1990) 'Measuring Organizational Cultures: A Qualitative/Quantitative Study across Twenty Cases', *Administrative Science Quarterly*, 35: 286–316.
Huault, I. (1996) 'French Multinational Companies' Strategies and Co-ordination Mechanisms: The Role of Human Resource Management in Europe and Nigeria', *International Journal of Resource Management*, 7(2): 572–84.
Jackson, S., Schuler, R. and Rivero, C. (1989) 'Organizational Characteristics as Predictors of Personnel Practices', *Personnel Psychology*, 42: 727–86.
Johnston, W. (1991) 'Global Workforce 2000: The New World Labor Market', *Harvard Business Review*, March–April: 115–27.
Jorgensen, J., Hafsi, T. and Kissundu, M. (1986) 'Towards a Market Imperfections Theory of Organizational Structure in Developing Countries', *Journal of Management Studies*, 23, 417–42.
Kamoche, K. (1996) 'The Integration–Differentiation Puzzle: A Resource-capability Perspective in International HRM', *International Journal of Human Resource Management*, 7(1): 230–44.
Kamoche, K. (1997) 'Knowledge Creation and Learning in International HRM', *International Journal of Human Resource Management*, 8(3): 211–25.
Kazal, R. (1995) 'Revisiting Assimilations: The Rise, Fall and Reappraisal of a Concept in American Ethnic History', *American Historical Review*, 100(2): 437–71.
Kissundu, M., Jorgensen, J. and Hafsi, T. (1983) 'Administrative Theory and Practice in Developing Countries: A Synthesis', *Administrative Science Quarterly*, 28: 66–84.
Kobrin, S. (1988) 'Expatriate Reduction and Strategic Control in American Multinational Corporations', *Human Resource Management*, 33(4): 581–99.
Lado, A.A. and Wilson, M.C. (1994) 'Human Resource Systems and Sustained Competitive Advantage: A Competency-based Perspective', *Academy of Management Review*, 19(4): 699–727.
Lawler, E.E. III (1996) *From Ground Up: Six Principles of Building the New Logic Corporation*. San Francisco: Jossey-Bass.
McBride, M. (1992) 'Management Development in the Global Village', *Journal of Management Development*, 11: 48–58.

McMillen, M., Baker, A. and White, J. (1997) 'Cultural Analysis, "Good Conversation" and the Creation of Multicultural Learning Organizations', *Management Learning*, 28(2): 197–216.

Mayrhofer, W. and Brewster, C. (1996) 'In Praise of Ethnocenticity: Expatriate Policies in European Multinationals', *The International Executive*, 38(6): 749–78.

Michael, J. and Hambrick, D. (1992) 'Diversification Posture and Top Management Team Characteristics', *Academy of Management Journal*, 35(1): 9–37.

Milkovich, J.T. and Bloom, M. (1998) 'Rethinking International Compensation', *Compensation and Benefits Review*, April: 15–23.

Moynihan, M. (1993) *The Economist Intelligence Unit Global Manager: Recruiting, Developing and Keeping World Class Executives*. New York: McGraw Hill.

Mueller, F. (1996) 'Human Resources as Strategic Assets: An Evolutionary Resource-based Theory', *Journal of Management Studies*, 33(6): 757–85.

Murray, A. (1989) 'Top Management Group Heterogeneity and Firm Performance', *Strategic Management Journal*, Summer special issue (10): 125–41.

Nemetz, P. and Christensen, S. (1996) 'The Challenge of Cultural Diversity: Harnessing a Diversity of Views to Understand Multiculturalism', *Academy of Management Review*, 21(2): 434–63.

Oddou, G. and Derr, C.B. (1993) 'European MNC Strategies for Internationalizing Managers: Current and Future Trends', *Research in Personnel and Human Resource Management*, Supplement 3: 157–70.

Park, R. and Burgess, E. (1921) *Introduction to the Science of Sociology*. Chicago: University of Chicago Press.

Peng, T., Petersen, M. and Shyi, Y. (1991) 'Quantitative Methods in Cross-national Management Research: Trends and Equivalence Issues', *Journal of Organizational Behavior*, 12: 87–107.

Peterson, R., Sargent, J., Napier, N. and Shim, W. (1996) 'Corporate Expatriate HRM Policies, Internationalization, and Performance in the World's Largest MNCs', *Management International Review*, 36(3): 215–30.

Pineda, R. and Whitehead, C. (1997) 'The Effects of Ethnic Group Culture on Managerial Task Activities', *Group & Organization Management*, 22(1): 31–52.

Poole, M. and Jenkins, G. (1996) 'Competitiveness and Human Resource Management Policies', *Journal of General Business*, 22(2): 1–19.

Prahalad, C. and Bettis, R. (1986) 'Dominant Logic: A New Linkage between Diversity and Performance', *Strategic Management Journal*, 7(6): 485–501.

Reynolds, C. (1997) 'Strategic Employment of Third Country Nationals: Keys to Sustaining the Transformation of HR Functions', *Human Resource Planning*, 20(1): 33–40.

Rumbaut, R. (1997) 'Paradoxes (and Orthodoxies) of Assimilation', *Sociological Perspectives*, 40(3): 493–511.

Sambharya, R. (1996) 'Foreign Experiences of Top Management Teams and International Diversification Strategies of U.S. Multinational Corporations', *Strategic Management Journal*, 17: 739–46.

Sayegh, L. and Lasry, L. (1993) 'Immigrants Adaptation in Canada: Assimilation, Acculturation, and Orthogonal Cultural Identification', *Canadian Psychology*, 34: 98–109.

Schein, E. (1983) 'The Role of the Founder in Creating Organizational Culture', *Organizational Dynamics*, 12: 13–28.

Schein, E. (1990) 'Organizational Culture', *American Psychologist*, 45(2): 109–19.

Schneider, S. (1989) 'Strategy Formulation: The Impact of National Culture', *Organizational Studies*, 10(2): 149–68.

Schneider, S. and de Meyer, A. (1991) 'Interpreting and Responding to Strategic Issues: the Impact of National Culture', *Strategic Management Journal*, 12: 307–20.

Schuler, R., Dowling, P. and De Cieri, H. (1993) 'An Integrative Framework of Strategic International Human Resource Management', *International Journal of Human Resource Management*, 1: 717–64.

Scullion, H. (1991) 'Why Companies Prefer to Use Expatriates', *Personnel Management*, November.

Segall, M., Dansen, P., Berry, P. and Poortinga, Y. (1990) *Human Behavior in Global Perspective: An Introduction to Cross-Cultural Psychology*. New York: Pergamon.

Seib, G. (1998) 'Immigrant Stock: A Fresh Round in a Hot Debate', *The Wall Street Journal*, 4 March: A20.

Simon, L. and Davies, G. (1996) 'A Contextual Approach to Management Learning: The Hungarian Case', *Organization Studies*, 17(2): 269–89.

Sohn, J. (1994) 'Social Knowledge as a Control System: A Proposition and Evidence from Japanese FDI Behavior', *Journal of International Business Studies*, 25(2): 295–324.

Solomon, C. (1997) 'Destination USA', *Global Workforce*, April: 18–22.

Thomas, D. (1994) 'The Boundary-spanning Role of Expatriate Managers in the Multinational Corporations', *Advances in International Comparative Management*, 9: 145–70.

Truss, C., Gratton, L., Hope-Hailey, V., McGovern, P. and Stiles, P. (1997) 'Soft and Hard Models of Human Resource Management: A Reappraisal', *Journal of Management Studies*, 34(1): 53–73.

Urlich, D.W. and Lake, D. (1990) *Organizational Capability*. New York: Wiley.

Warner, L. and Srole, L. (1945) *The Social Systems of American Ethnic Groups*. New Haven, CT: Yale University Press.

Welch, D. (1994) 'Determinants of International Human Resource Management Approaches and Activities: A Suggested Framework', *Journal of Management Studies*, 31(2): 139–64.

Welch, D. and Welch, L. (1997) 'Being Flexible and Accommodating Diversity: The Challenge for Multinational Management', *European Management Journal*, 15(6): 677–85.

Wiersema, M. and Bentel, K. (1992) 'Top Management Team Demography and Corporate Strategic Change', *Academy of Management Journal*, 35(1): 91–121.

Willmott, H. (1993) 'Strength in Ignorance; Slavery is Freedom: Managing Culture in Modern Organizations', *Journal of Management Studies*, 30(4): 515–51.

Wong, G. and Birnbaum-Moore, P. (1994) 'Culture, Context and Structure: A Test of Hong Kong Banks', *Organizational Studies*, 15: 99–123.

Wright, P., McMahan, G. and McWilliams, A. (1994) 'Human Resources and Sustained Competitive Advantage: A Resource Based Perspective', *International Journal of Human Resource Management*, 5(2): 301–26.

The International Journal of Human Resource Management 10:3 June 1999 488–500

The coffee-machine system: how international selection really works

Hilary Harris and Chris Brewster

Abstract The literature on expatriate selection tends to present lists of criteria, with the implicit assumption that the process is formal and rational. The limited empirical work there is in this area suggests that these criteria have little impact on selection in practice. This paper argues that a deeper understanding of selection systems is needed and presents research showing the outcomes of different kinds of systems, suggesting that closed, informal systems predominate and outlining the practical and research implications of such systems.

Keywords International selection; expatriate management; international manager competencies; IHRM; selection systems.

Introduction

The rapid globalization of business has led to an ever-increasing need to 'internationalize' managers within organizations. Many large organizations now see international management experience as a prerequisite for promotion to senior management positions. International assignments fulfil certain key purposes for both the organization and the individual. For the organization these include control and socialization in the prevailing culture and transfer of expertise and for the individual they are a major opportunity for personal development. These assignments do, however, present a considerable risk to the organization. In terms of cost, sending a manager on an international assignment can cost three times normal salary and on costs. Failure, defined, not just in terms of premature return home, but as under-performance, can be, in its short- and long-term effect on business in the host country, very expensive.

The extent to which selection practice matches this requirement is, however, questionable. Examination of the international manager-selection literature reveals a mismatch between theory and practice, with extensive lists of theoretical criteria relating to effective international managers, most of which resemble a cross-cultural 'wish list' in respect of the vast array of skills and abilities required. Selection processes are equally depicted as both formal and professional. How much the theory of international manager selection reflects actual practice has, however, been questioned (Brewster, 1991).

This article reports the results of a study into international manager selection which queries the assumption that selection in this area is in practice a rational, objective process; outlines the implications of actual practice for effective international selec-

Dr Hilary Harris, Cranfield School of Management, Cranfield, Bedford MK40 0AL, UK (tel: +44 (0) 1234 751122; fax: +44 (0) 1234 751806; e-mail: h.harris@cranfield.ac.uk). Professor Chris Brewster, Cranfield School of Management, Cranfield, Bedford MK40 0AL, UK (tel: +44 (0) 1234 751122; fax: +44 (0) 1234 751806; e-mail: c.j.brewster@cranfield.ac.uk).

tion; and suggests a new research agenda for exploring the process of international selection.

Selection of international managers

We have focused discussion in this section on the selection of international managers. The selection of other types of expatriates – technical specialists or short-term assignees for example – will have many aspects of the selection systems in common. However, each type will have items which are distinct – to ensure consistency we are examining just managerial appointments here; we draw conclusions about selection for other types of expatriates at the end.

Selection systems

In terms of selection systems, research evidence points to the use within companies of 'pools' of existing employees with high potential, from which future international managers are picked (BIC, 1991; Brewster, 1991). Initial assessment of 'high potential' would appear to be undertaken jointly by line managers and personnel specialists and often takes place at very early stages in an employee's career, sometimes involving selection of an élite corps straight from university or graduate business school. Sophistication of systems and definition of high-potential employees vary widely between organizations. However, Business International Corporation's (1991) report *Developing Effective Global Managers for the 1990s* observes that assessments of high potential are usually based on:

1 the firm's needs, as defined by business lines and strategic goals;
2 external market conditions; and
3 employee identification with the value system set by top management.

The report also notes that, among most MNCs surveyed, 'high potentials' are proposed by their immediate supervisors and then screened by a committee composed of senior managers from the country of operation where the person works as well as of representatives of the parent-company's personnel department. Assessment centres are commonly used to assess initial potential, followed by annual reviews. Few companies explicitly tell employees they have been designated as 'high potentials'. First international postings for people identified in high-potential pools are often not implemented until the individuals have acquired a certain level of maturity and management experience within the domestic environment; typically the age range for first postings would be late-20s to mid-30s.

Selection criteria: the theory

Research into selection criteria for international assignments shows a split between theory and practice. In surveys asking for general views on what makes effective international managers, the criteria mentioned as being critical differ from those reported as being used in practice. The literature on the criteria used for expatriate manager selection also has a tendency towards prescription and a heavy North American bias. There have been several reviews of this literature (Dowling *et al*., 1994; Mendenhall and Oddou, 1985).

Phillips (1992) suggests that there is little or no difference between the personal qualities required for success in managing domestic or international business, but successful development of international business demands a higher level of skills and qualities. This is because managers working abroad will be involved in a wider range of activities, roles and responsibilities than those required in the home market. Likewise, it has been suggested that the international manager has many characteristics of the effective manager operating in a less complex environment. The international manager, however, needs additional skills to reconcile the cultural problems created by the international environment. Possessing an awareness of the difficulties is not enough in this situation.

This confusion may in some ways be related to the fact that the majority of the studies are not specific in defining the type of expatriate to whom such criteria relate (Tung, 1982). Equally, there is little consideration as to whether criteria will vary according to country, host-country role and number of expatriates employed (Bjorkman and Gersten, 1990; Tung, 1982; Torbiorn, 1982). Forster (1996), however, notes that the many different criteria presented in the literature tend to fall into three broad categories. These are technical competence at work; personality traits/attributes; and interpersonal social skills and personal and family situations.

In his review of the literature relating to selection criteria, Brewster (1991) argues that successive authors have adapted previous categorizations of criteria, or developed new ones, so comparability between studies is limited. He notes that many of the American studies originate with the 1970 Business International list of fifteen categories of skills for the international manager:

> Experience, adaptability and flexibility, technical knowledge of the business, competence, ability and past performance, managerial talent, language skills, potential, interest in overseas work, appreciation of new management and sensitivity, proper education, initiative and creativity, independence, good ability to communicate, maturity and emotional stability.
>
> (Business International, 1970)

A number of researchers have added to the list: for example, Hays (1974) emphasized the importance of 'relational abilities' and the 'family situation'; Zeira and Banai (1985) introduced country of origin and 'appearance (dress and looks)', the latter also discussed more recently by Stone (1991) as an unwritten but critical selection factor for women expatriates.

Ashridge Management Research Centre's study of international managers (not necessarily expatriate managers) revealed clear agreement among respondents on attributes which appear desirable whatever the company's strategy. These include strategic awareness, adaptability in new situations, sensitivity to different cultures, ability to work in international teams, language skills and understanding international marketing (Barham and Devine, 1991). The list is significant in that four out of the top six characteristics identified represent more 'soft' skills, underlining the human relations aspect of international management and an ability to handle unfamiliar situations.

Several authors have attempted to produce more discrete, wider categories. Rehfuss (1982), for example, identifies five groups: 'relational' or interpersonal abilities; 'cultural empathy' (including motivation, language, maturity and an 'x' factor, operationally defined as the ability to live abroad); technical skill; domestic performance; and spouse/family. Torbiorn (1982) identifies eight criteria: adaptability; language; motivation; level of education; social manners; family adaptability; medical status; status of the job.

Mendenhall and Oddou (1985) identify three sets of individual cross-cultural skills as follows:

Self-efficacy skills – including reinforcement substitution, stress reduction and technical competence.

Relational skills – including relationship development, willingness to communicate, and language.

Perceptual skills – including understanding why host nationals behave and think in the way they do and making correct inferences as to the motives behind these behaviours.

A key observation from this literature is the emphasis on interpersonal and cross-cultural skills as determinants of success for international assignments. The stress on 'soft skills' reflects a more general departure from reliance on traditional 'hard' skills for successful management.

Coulson-Thomas (1992) asked senior managers in ninety-one organizations to identify the qualities for effective international operation that are sought in members of a senior management team. Fourteen items were revealed. In order of preference, they were listed as: strategic awareness, customer focus, individual responsibility, communication skills, creativity, perspective, team player, objectivity, self-discipline, international awareness and perspective, breadth, transnational confidence and effectiveness, European awareness and perspective, language ability. It is interesting to note that, despite the imminent upgrading of the EU, these managers were still rating language ability as the least important characteristic of effective international operation.

As a result of interviews with currently operating international managers, Barham and Wills (1992) identified a deeper, core competence, which is essentially holistic in nature, which underpins specific behaviour competencies and skills. The authors labelled this a 'being' competence and split it into three interlinking parts: cognitive complexity, emotional energy and psychological maturity. Cognitive complexity refers to the ability to perceive several dimensions in a stimulus rather than only one (differentiation), as well as being able to identify multiple relationships among the differentiated characteristics (integration). Features of cognitive complexity include cultural empathy, active listening and a sense of humility. The second 'being' competence is emotional energy, which includes emotional self-awareness, emotional resilience and risk acceptance, together with the emotional support of the family. The final 'being' competence relates to psychological maturity and represents a manager with a value system which helps them to formulate the dominant goals or themes which make their lives meaningful. Included in this competence is curiosity to learn, a 'present' orientation to time and personal morality.

More recently, Birchall *et al.* (1995) defined ten competencies related specifically to the international manager's job. These were: global awareness, international strategy, international negotiation, international marketing, international finance, cultural empathy, addressing ethical dilemmas, building international teams, working with stakeholders and foreign language skills. Birchall *et al.* asked 102 respondents to rate the competencies on a scale of 1–5, with 5 indicating that the behaviour was of vital importance to successful performance overall. The top five rated competencies as a result of this study were: international negotiation, global awareness, international strategy, international marketing and cultural empathy.

Selection criteria: the practice

Given the emphasis on interpersonal skills in management theory, it is somewhat surprising to find evidence in the research into current practices of MNCs of the continuing adoption of more traditional criteria for selection of expatriates. Brewster's 1988 survey of international personnel executives from European multinational corporations identified the following top criteria used to select expatriates: 'technical expertise; language; family support; potential; knowing company systems; experience; marital status; medical status; independence and motivation'. Likewise, in the Ashridge survey (1989–90), the top factors were identified as: 'Technical skills/expertise for the job; potential; knowledge of company systems; understanding the market and customers; language; necessary part of career path; family support; knowledge/understanding of culture good' (Barham and Devine, 1991). (It should be noted that Brewster's survey asked for unprompted criteria, while the Ashridge survey indicated a set of criteria, with space for additional criteria and ranking.)

These findings appear to correlate with Brewster's (1991) observations concerning the two main findings from research into selection practices among MNCs. The first finding is that expatriates are primarily selected on the basis of their technical competence alone (Baliga and Baker, 1985; Harvey, 1985; Mendenhall *et al.*, 1987; Miller, 1972; Tung, 1981; Zeira and Banai, 1984). The second finding is that there is an underlying assumption of the universal nature of managerial skills (Baker and Ivancevich, 1971).

The reliance on technical competence may well relate to technical expatriates rather than managerial level expatriates. However, Miller's (1972) early explanation of companies' preference for technical competence still appears to have relevance today. In his view, companies' perception of international selection as a high-risk operation leads to a tendency to place too much emphasis in recruitment on technical and managerial qualifications, to ensure that the job can be done competently. This view appears to be supported to some extent by subsequent research highlighting the lack of agreement with respect to defining successful performance for expatriate managers and evidence of the resulting general confusion relating to criteria relevant to ensuring success. Antal and Izraeli (1993) argue that, in the face of uncertainties about the role of expatriates, organizational need for certainty in this high-risk area leads managers to select others who are most similar to themselves and, consequently, presumably more likely to be seen as trustworthy and predictable.

Research into actual selection procedures again tends to support Miller's early explanation. Brewster (1991) notes widespread reliance on personal recommendation for expatriate postings from either a specialist personnel staff member or line managers. This results in more or less predetermined selection interviews which consist more of negotiating the terms of the offer than determining the suitability of the candidate. Despite differences in research findings, it would appear that the majority of organizations do not interview the spouse and/or family (Brewster, 1988; Tung, 1982; Bjorkman and Gertsen, 1990). Formal testing for potential expatriates is also limited, with restricted use of personality and psychological tests and a general suspicion of the validity of cultural awareness or adaptability tests (Brewster, 1988; Forster, 1996; Scullion, 1994; Tung, 1981, 1982; Bjorkman and Gertsen, 1990).

Typology of international manager-selection systems

We developed a typology of international manager-selection systems from the general literature on formalization of selection procedures and from the literature relating to expatriate management-selection practice, which identifies four possible variations of selection systems in the field of international management.

The first two variations relate to the nature of selection procedures. The expatriate-management literature identifies the use of both 'open' and 'closed' selection procedures in organizations. An 'open' system is one in which all vacancies are advertised and anyone with appropriate qualifications and experience may apply and candidates are interviewed with greater or lesser degrees of formalized testing. Selection decisions are taken by consensus among selectors. In contrast, a 'closed' system is one in which selectors at corporate headquarters choose, or nominate to line managers, 'suitable' candidates. In this situation, there may be only one manager involved in the selection process at head office. The candidate is informed only when agreement about acceptability has been reached between head-office personnel and the line manager. The selection interview in this process consists of a negotiation about the terms and conditions of the assignment.

The second two variations of the selection process relate to the existence of formal and informal systems operating at organizational level. As has been discussed before, substantial evidence exists of the mediating effects on the formal organizational systems of informal mechanisms, leading to unintended outcomes with respect to stated organizational policy. In this way, four distinct categories of selection processes can be derived.

A *closed/informal* system reflects a scenario in which individual preferences of selectors, which may be more or less unclear, will be allowed to determine who is seen to be acceptable due to the lack of influence of formal systems, the lack of open debate about criteria and the lack of accountability engendered by the fact that employees are unaware that the process is happening. Under this typology, it is argued, the individual preferences of selectors may be inconsistent and incoherent in relation to identifying and assessing characteristics of effective international managers.

	FORMAL	**INFORMAL**
OPEN	• Clearly defined criteria • Clearly defined measures • Training for selectors • Open advertising of vacancy (internal/external) • Panel discussions	• Less defined criteria • Less defined measures • Limited training for selectors • No panel discussions • Open advertising of vacancy • Recommendations
CLOSED	• Clearly defined criteria • Clearly defined measures • Training for selectors • Panel discussions • Nominations only (networking/reputation)	• Selectors' individual preferences determine criteria and measures • No panel discussions • Nominations only (networking/reputation)

Figure 1 *Typology of international manager-selection systems*

In an *open/informal* system, although employees have access to vacancies, decisions as to who should be selected are usually arranged between relevant managers on the basis of personal recommendation and reputation and, although candidates may be put forward for interview, the selection decision is made before any formal interview takes place. In this scenario, the tendency for managers to select 'clones' of existing managers is increased. This type of system will see formal selection criteria agreed; however, the extent to which these and the match of candidates are debated and discussed may be limited. This will lead to decreases in consistency and in coherent thinking concerning the key characteristics of effective international managers and less attention to formal criteria.

A *closed/formal* system involves selectors assessing candidates against formal criteria and discussing candidates' match with them. However, the lack of personal contact with the candidate and the fact that the field of potential applicants is determined by the selectors, with the attendant risk of omission of suitable candidates, may allow individual preferences of selectors to be reflected in the nominating process. The influence of networking and reputation is a key feature of this type of system.

Within an *open/formal* system, selectors assess candidates against formalized criteria and determine the best 'fit' through continual comparison of their own assessments against other selectors' assessments, thus constraining the use of individual preferences and ensuring a questioning of assumptions. This will be reflected in more consistency in evaluations and greater clarity in thinking in relation to the critical components of effective international management. This type of system is also likely to produce a close match between individual selectors' schemas of the ideal job-holder and formal selection criteria. The objectivity of this type of system will be enhanced by the use of psychometric and other tests.

Exploring practice

We explored the empirical behaviour in organizations selecting international managers through two separate procedures.

First, we carried out interviews with the senior international HRM specialist in nine major 'blue-chip' international firms. These were all UK-based household name organizations, with extensive experience in international operations, amounting in *all* cases to more than half their total operations, and all with relatively large numbers of expatriates. They were in the air transport, petrochemicals, telecommunications, heavy engineering, pharmaceuticals, brewing and distribution and international aid sectors. All were operating in many countries including both First and Third World states. These were detailed interviews lasting over an hour and a half in all cases, and much longer in some, where we used a few open questions to encourage the interviewee to discuss expatriate policies, actual practice in recruitment and selection, and some of the advantages and problems of their current approach. We found that, without exception, the interviewees were very ready to talk about these issues and very open in describing the 'warts and all' reality of their organizational process.

Second, we selected three of the organizations which seemed to us to stand at different points in our analytical framework for more detailed analysis. Two of the three organizations were situated at opposite ends of the *closed/open* continuum, with one representing a *closed* system and the other an *open* system. The other was positioned in the middle of the *closed/open* continuum. For the purposes of this paper, the three organizations are identified with the names Amstar (*closed system*), Cirus (*open system*) and Brymay (*hybrid system*).

The methodology employed for the second stage of the research consisted of a case-study approach. Information about international manager-selection processes was collected from two sources: the first through semi-structured interviews with HR personnel and key selectors within the individual organizations; the second via an examination of organizational literature in the form of policies and administration forms, etc. A critical part of the research was seen to be the identification of personally held beliefs about the characteristics of effective international managers. To try to ensure an unbiased summary of the characteristics of effective international managers (both on the researcher's part and that of the individual selectors), repertory grid technique was chosen as an integral part of the case-study design. This consisted of asking individual selectors to compare and contrast up to nine international managers whom they knew personally, split into categories of *highly effective*, *moderately effective* and *not effective*. As far as possible, women international managers were included in the sample.[1] The results from the repertory grid interviews yielded a set of 'constructs', or statements concerning effective/non-effective international manager behaviour which were further analysed using the grid analysis package (GAP) developed by Slater (1972). An explanation of how to interpret the results from this package is available from Smith (1986).

In this article we draw on the research data and analysis identified in the first two procedures.

Findings

Our detailed exploration of the nature of the international manager-selection process within the three organizations allowed them to be plotted onto the typology of international management selection systems. Amstar was placed in the *closed/informal* quadrant, Cirus was placed in the *open/formal* quadrant, while Brymay fell across the quadrants on the typology, with different systems being used for different appointments. The description of the system was seen to fall almost equally between the *open* and *closed* quadrant, but in terms of degree of formality it was argued that it fell more into the *informal* quadrant. This positioning was seen to indicate a very hybrid system in which there were real tensions between espoused formal policy and current organizational practice.

The degree to which differences in selection processes resulted in the posited outcomes with respect to the use of selectors' individual preferences in selection decision making was explored via the repertory grid analyses. These aimed to address the extent to which the type of selection process resulted in the posited outcomes with respect to clarity and consistency of thinking in relation to effective international managers and the degree to which the constructs derived from the repertory grid interviews with selectors matched formal company criteria.

Degree of clarity, consistency and link with formal criteria

Three key analyses were used. These were: the extent to which the grids depicted a clarity of thinking in relation to the characteristics of effective *international* managers; the degree of consistency both within and across individual selectors' grids within each organization; and the degree to which the individual grids reflected formal selection criteria within the organization.

Clarity of thinking The constructs emanating from the repertory grid analyses indicated that there was a large degree of difference in terms of sophistication of thinking about characteristics of international managers among the selectors at Amstar: the only construct which is used consistently being *mobile*. The focus of the grids with respect to determinants of effective performance appears to be based more on determinants of effective *domestic* performance. In contrast, selectors in Cirus were seen to be clearer in their thinking about the characteristics of effective international managers. In discussion with staff at head office, the constructs which were seen to be specifically related to the needs of working in an overseas environment were: *linguist*; *effective communicator with regional groupings*; *good relations between field and head office*; *good emissaries*; *understands responsibilities towards local environment and agencies*; *values different approaches to work in cross-cultural respect*; *culturally sensitive*; *strong interpersonal skills*; *secure with feedback inter-organization and more flexible/adaptable*. The analysis of clarity of thinking in relation to characteristics of effective international managers in Brymay revealed more of an emphasis on specific international skills than was the case in Amstar, but a more limited scope of constructs than with Cirus. The constructs could be grouped around the themes of: *confidence based on experience overseas*; *manages interface between centre and field*; *more internationalist* and *cultural empathy*. Most of the selectors, however, still rated effective business-management capabilities as the most important distinguishing factors between good and bad international managers.

Consistency Consistency within grids was evaluated by a qualitative examination of the number of times a particular construct was used more than once in relation to the three sorts of effectiveness of international manager. Degree of consistency of thinking across individual selectors' grids was assessed by a qualitative analysis of the constructs identified as most distinctive to the selector, to see to what extent the constructs arising were replicated across grids at an organizational level. Analyses within Amstar indicated a lack of consistency both within and across grids. There were wide variations in the constructs used to describe effective international managers by the same selector and comparisons across grids revealed no areas of commonality in terms of the constructs used to describe effective international managers. In contrast, the results from Cirus showed a high degree of consistency within grids, with the majority of selectors using a common set of criteria to describe the effective managers. The degree of consistency across grids was also seen to be quite high, with four common themes emerging: *consultative management style*; *team management skills*; *linguistic/communication skills* and *professional management skills*. In the case of Brymay, the degree of consistency of thinking within individual selectors' grids reflected a mixed picture. Two of the grids showed little or no consistency in criteria related to effective international managers, while the other four showed slightly more consistency. Consistency of thinking across grids was limited. Only two common themes were detected in more than one grid. These were *high energy* and *business sense*.

Match with formal criteria In terms of linkage with formal criteria, the results were in line with the general propositions from the typology. Amstar's *closed/informal* international management-selection system meant that it was not possible to identify formal criteria for the majority of selection cases. However, a key component of selection is the potential rating of the individual which is assessed as a result partly of the annual performance and development reviews. This is supported by the focus on determinants of effective *domestic* management behaviours revealed by the constructs elicited from selectors within Amstar. An assessment of the degree of coherence between individual selectors' constructs and formal assessment criteria contained within the annual performance and development review revealed very little correlation with the formal system in relation to competencies, but a greater degree of agreement in relation to appraisal qualities. In three out of the four grids, more than half of the formal competencies listed in the annual review of performance were not seen to be linked to the constructs relating to effective management behaviour, from either an international or a domestic perspective. More linkages could be detected between the grid constructs and the appraisal qualities, with all but one of the grids containing constructs which could be subsumed into the formal list of appraisal qualities. Three main qualities were seen to be important in all grids, these were: *achievement motivation*, *capacity to motivate* and *helicopter vision*.

Cirus demonstrated a high degree of coherence with formal selection criteria. The analysis of the link of constructs to the formal criteria included in the person specification for field director/programme manager positions showed that by far the majority of constructs fitted within the official list of selection criteria. The linkage was seen to be extremely strong in relation to *consultative, team management skills*, with less priority ascribed to the very specific international aptitudes such as awareness of the cultural, social and political environment.

An analysis of the extent to which the constructs reflected formal criteria within Brymay was difficult to assess due to the variance in usage of any formal job specifications. The emphasis on business performance could be seen to relate to the way in which performance was measured in Brymay, where performance against key result areas (KRAs) was the main method of determining good or bad performance. The grid from the head office personnel manager showed more agreement of constructs with formal criteria set out on the official interview assessment form used in country manager selection, although this is hardly surprising given that the manager was involved in the creation of the form.

Discussion

One of our key findings is that much of the literature fails to encompass the reality of expatriate selection. In many organizations the selection of the relevant expatriate falls under what we came to call the 'coffee-machine system'. It was this expression, coined by one cynical expatriate we spoke to, that we adopted to summarize what we found to be the most frequent approach to expatriate selection.

The coffee-machine system is the most common form of expatriate selection. What happens is that a senior line manager is standing by the coffee machine when he (usually a man) is joined by a colleague:

'How's it going?'
'Oh, you know, overworked and underpaid.'
'Tell me about it. As well as all the usual stuff, Jimmy in Mombai has just fallen ill and is being flown home. I've got no idea who we can get over there to pick up the pieces at such short notice. It's driving me crazy.'
'Have you met that Simon on the fifth floor? He's in the same line of work. Very bright and looks like going a long way. He was telling me that he and his wife had a great holiday in Goa a couple of years ago. He seems to like India. Could be worth a chat.'
'Hey, thanks. I'll check him out.'
'No problem. They don't seem able to improve this coffee though, do they?'

What happens next is that the organization's processes are brought in to play to legitimize the decision that has, in effect, already been taken. Personnel files will be scrutinized. Simon will probably have an informal discussion with the manager concerned and, if still interested, will be interviewed, but the interview will be more like a negotiation about the terms and conditions under which the job will be done, rather than what an external observer would recognize as a selection interview. There will not usually be any other candidates. Either just prior to the interview or once an agreement on Simon's transfer has been reached, the international human resources department will become involved, dealing with the financial aspects, the physical transfer arrangements, the family issues, the flights and so on.

Among the organizations we studied, this pattern is by far the most common form of selection. This is the reality of the 'closed/informal' cell in our model. We found a smaller number of organizations where this kind of selection occurred for some appointments whereas for others there was a more hybrid system, with an ostensibly 'open/formal' system being heavily influenced by informal practices. We have so far identified only one organization where an 'open/formal' approach was consistently followed for all international management appointments.

The implications of these forms of recruitment are very much as predicted in the model. First, the careful analysis of candidates against some list of ideal-type criteria sits rather uncomfortably with the reality of the coffee-machine system. These lists may have some theoretic value in prescribing what should be included, but they bear very little relationship to the criteria in the selectors' minds during this process. Hence, in part, the fact that repeated research shows that, despite the prevalence of these lists, the major criterion applied in the practice of expatriate selection continues to be technical ability or current job performance.

Second, the likelihood of the different selectors having quite different criteria in their minds is high. Among the three organizations where repertory grid techniques were applied to the selectors to identify the personal constructs which lay behind their selection decisions there was a clear gradation depending upon their selection system. In Amstar, where the coffee-machine system held sway, selectors evidenced not only very different assumptions about what made for a successful expatriate, but even individuals tended to have mixed and sometimes contradictory constructs. In Brymay, there was a greater coherence, but still marked differences in views. In Cirus, where all expatriate selection was undertaken in a formal and open manner, there was clear coherence and much greater consistency in thinking about the characteristics of effective international managers in relation to the specific needs of that organization.

Third, the manner in which the coffee-machine system acts to restrict the pool of potential candidates is obvious. Almost by definition, the pool is limited to those subordinates well-known to the selector and the other managers with whom they come into contact. It is likely to involve only the technical specialists in their field of work, even where that is irrelevant to the post under consideration. This is seen to be particularly problematic for women, given the fact that between 85 and 95 per cent of international managers are currently men. Within a selection context where the nature of the vacancies reflect a male-typed bias, there appears to be even more need for selection systems to ensure that potential 'prejudice' on the part of selectors is constrained by a process which forces them continually to question their assumptions about women's suitability and, critically, their acceptability in international management positions. The nature of such a system is also more likely to engender debate about the extent to which criteria for selection follow equal opportunity principles. Within such a system, individual preferences of selectors should be more consistent and coherent as a result of the constant discussion and debate in which the likelihood of equal opportunity issues being raised is increased. However, our research into selection systems for international assignments points to a preponderance of systems where primarily subjective knowledge of an individual determines who is seen to 'fit in' best with the existing organizational norms (Brewster, 1991; Scullion, 1994).

Fourth, the prescriptive advice to selectors which insists on involving the family in the selection decision is rather pre-empted by this approach. It is, of course, possible to check retrospectively, but still prior to the transfer, that the family is not going to create problems during the assignment. But this is a long way from what is generally proposed as good practice.

Fifth, the ability of the organization to take a strategic view of expatriation is severely limited. Almost inevitably, the role of the international HR department in these cases becomes one, familiar to many researchers in the area, of dealing with the financial, physical and social issues that fall out from the selection, rather than having an input into whether an expatriate assignment is required or advantageous, or what kind of assignment it could be for what kind of expatriate. The line managers involved have little overall responsibility for a strategic view of international assignments. As a result, the organization continues to take reactive decisions about expatriation.

Finally, the model as proposed here needs further testing and development. On the evidence presented here, it helps us to understand what is happening in the reality of international organizational selection. However, it does not, as presented, take into account the size or sector of organizations, their relative stages of internationalization or the proportion of their business conducted internationally. The model has been tested only against a particular group of major, experienced, British MNEs. Wider testing may enable these and similar additional criteria to be included in the model, or to be applied as relevant antecedents of explanation of the model.

Note

1 For an explanation of the method and applications of the repertory grid, see Bannister and Fransella (1986) and Stewart *et al.* (1991).

References

Ali, A.J. (1991) 'Expatriate and Saudi Managers' Perceptions of Japanese and U.S Competitiveness: A Survey', *Business Horizons*, 34(6): 35–8.

Antal, A. and Izraeli, D. (1993) 'A Global Comparison of Women in Management: Women Managers in Their Homelands and as Expatriates'. In Fagerson, E. (ed.) *Women in Management: Trends, Issues and Challenges in Managerial Diversity*. Beverly Hills, CA: Sage.

Baker, J. and Ivanevich, J. (1971) 'The Assignment of American Executives Abroad: Systematic, Haphazard or Chaotic?', *California Management Review*, 13(3).

Baliga, C. and Baker, J. (1985) 'Multinational Corporate Policies for Expatriate Managers: Selection, Training and Evaluation', *SAM Advanced Management Journal*, 50(4): 31–8.

Bannister, D and Fransella F. (1986) *Inquiring Man:The Psychology of Personal Constructs*. London: Croom Helm.

Barham, K. and Devine, M. (1991) *The Quest for the International Manager: A Survey of Global Human Resource Strategies*. London: Ashridge Management Guide/Economist Intelligence Unit.

Birchall, D., Hee, T. and Gay, K. (1996) 'Competences for International Managers', *Singapore Institute of Management*, Jan.: 1–13.

Bjorkman, I. and Gertsen, M. (1990) 'Corporate Expatriation: An Analysis of Firms and Country-specific Differences in Scandinavia', unpublished paper quoted in Brewster (1991).

Brewster, C. (1988) *The Management of Expatriates*, Human Resource Research Centre Monograph 2. Cranfield: Cranfield Institute of Technology.

Brewster, C. (1991) *The Management of Expatriates*. London: Kogan Page.
Business International Corporation (BIC) (1991) *Developing Effective Global Managers for the 1990s*. New York.
Coulson-Thomas, C. (1992) *Creating the Global Manager*. Maidenhead: McGraw Hill.
Dowling, P.J., Schuler, R.S. and Welch, D. (1994) *International Dimensions of Human Resource Management*, 2nd ed. Boston: PWS-Kent.
Forster, N. (1996) *The Management of Expatriates: A Survey of UK-Based International Organisations*. In press.
Harvey, M. (1985) 'The Expatriate Family: An Overlooked Variable in International Assignments', *Columbia Journal of World Business*, Spring: 84–92.
Hays, R. (1974) 'Expatriate Selection: Insuring Success and Avoiding Failure', *Journal of International Business Studies*, 5: 25–37.
Mendenhall, M., Dunbar, E. and Oddou, C. (1987) 'Expatriate Selection, Training and Career Pathing: A Review and Critique', *Human Resource Management*, 26(3): 331–45.
Mendenhall, M. and Oddou, G. (1995) 'The Dimensions of Expatriate Acculturation: A Review', *Academy of Management Review*, 10: 39–47.
Miller, E. (1972) 'The Selection Decision for an International Assignment: A Study of the Decision-Makers Behaviour', *Journal of International Business Studies*, 3: 49–65.
Phillips, N. (1992) *Managing International Teams*. London: Pitman.
Rehfuss, J. (1982) 'Management Development and the Selection of Overseas Executives', *Personnel Administrator*, 27(7): 35–43.
Scullion, H. (1994) 'Staffing Policies and Strategic Control in British Multinationals', *International Studies of Management and Organization*, 24(3): 86–104.
Slater, P. (1972) *Notes on Ingrid and Grid Analysis Package*. Manchester: University of Manchester Regional Computing Centre.
Smith, J.M. (1986) 'An Introduction to Repertory Grids – Part Two: Interpretation of Results', *Graduate Management Research*, Autumn.
Stewart, V., Stewart, A. and Fonda, N. (1981) *Business Applications of Repertory Grid*. Maidenhead: McGraw-Hill.
Stone, R. (1991) 'Expatriate Selection and Failure', *Human Resource Planning*, 41(1): 9–18.
Torbiorn, I. (1982) *Living Abroad: Personal Adjustment and Personnel Policy in the Overseas Setting*. New York: Wiley.
Tung, R. (1979) 'US Multinationals: A Study of their Selection and Training for Overseas Assignments', *Academy of Management Proceedings*, 39: 298–301.
Tung, R. (1981) 'Selection and Training of Personnel for Overseas Assignments', *Columbia Journal*, 23: 129–43.
Tung, R. (1982) 'Selection and Training Procedures of US, European and Japanese Multinationals', *Human Resource Management*, 23: 129–43.
Wills, S. and Barham, K. (1994) 'Being an International Manager', *European Management Journal*, 12(1): 49–58.
Zeira, Y. and Banai, M. (1984) 'Present and Desired Methods of Selecting Expatriate Managers for International Assignments', *Personnel Review*, 13(3): 29–35.
Zeira, Y. and Banai, M. (1985) 'Selection of Expatriate Managers in MNCs: The Host Environment Point of View', *International Studies of Management and Organisation*, 15(1): 33–51.

[37]

A CONTINGENCY FRAMEWORK OF SELECTION AND TRAINING OF EXPATRIATES REVISITED

Rosalie L. Tung
Simon Fraser University

In light of the major changes and developments that have taken place in the world since the publication of my 1981 *Columbia Journal of World Business,* this article contains a critical assessment of whether the contingency paradigm of selection and training identified in the 1981 article still holds. The article first identifies the seven most salient changes that have taken place since the early 1980s. Despite these changes, it appears that the contingency paradigm still holds although additional stipulations have to be included to reflect the realities of the new economic world order. The article stresses, moreover, that a piece-meal approach to international human resource management is ineffective and inappropriate. To maximize efficiency, a holistic and systematic approach has to be adopted which addresses all aspects of IHRM, including selection, training, compensation, appraisal and repatriation. The repatriation function is hypothesized to play a pivotal role in integrating all other aspects of the IHRM system.

This special issue of *Human Resource Management Review* directed at the future of international human resource management (IHRM) in the Twenty-first century provides me with a good opportunity to reflect upon the changes that have taken place in the world since the publication of my 1981 *Columbia Journal of World Business* article entitled, "Selection and training of personnel for international assignments" where I proposed a contingency framework for the selection and training of expatriates for international assignments. This article will first provide a brief overview of these changes. Then it will examine whether the contingency paradigm I proposed in 1981 is still relevant and, if so, whether modifications are necessary in light of these changes.

Direct all correspondence to: Rosalie L. Tung, The Ming & Stella Wong Professor of International Business, Simon Fraser University, Burnaby, B.C., Canada V5A 1S6. E-mail: tung@sfu.ca

Human Resource Management Review,
Volume 8, Number 1, 1998, pages 23–37

ISSN:1053–4822

CHANGES AND NEW DEVELOPMENTS SINCE THE EARLY 1980S

The changes that have taken place in the world since the early 1980s have been many and startling. I will focus on the most salient changes and developments that have an important bearing on IHRM. These are: (1) shift in the calculus of global competition; (2) formation of global strategic alliances; (3) conflicting demands on multinational corporations to maintain an appropriate balance between global integration and local responsiveness; (4) emergence of network organizations; (5) growing diversity in the workforce both at home and abroad; (6) growing convergence of core competencies for domestic and international managers; and (7) increasing use of overseas assignments for career development purposes.

1. Shift in Calculus of Global Competition

With the end of the cold war, countries around the world have focused increasingly on economic competition and cooperation. Countries, which were once ideological adversaries, now collaborate on the economic front. In some cases, the economic imperative takes precedence over ideological differences. For example, the People's Republic of China (PRC), which espouses communism and was once a close ally of North Korea, normalized diplomatic relations with South Korea in 1992. By 1996, South Korea had emerged as the fourth largest trading partner of the PRC. These political changes have facilitated the globalization of industries. One of the best definitions of globalization I have encountered to date is "deregulation on a global scale."[1] With deregulation, all countries have an equal opportunity to join in the competition.

Increasingly, competition comes not only from the industrialized west but from the newly industrialized economies and/or emerging markets. Singapore and South Korea, two newly industrialized economies, have graduated recently to the ranks of the OECD. The PRC, an emerging market, has experienced the fastest economic growth rate in the world in the past decade. Many have projected that China will be the world's largest economy by the early part of the Twenty-first century. This projection becomes more probable with its reintegration with Hong Kong in July 1997. The latter's GNP per capita exceeded that of its former colonial master, Great Britain.

In fact, the regions of the world that have experienced the fastest rates of growth, both economic- and population-wise, come from Asia. As we await the dawning of the new millenium, many have offered their projections of what the world would be like at the turn of the century. According to one estimate, if the world's population were reduced to a microcosm of 100 people, 57 of these will be Asians, 70 will be non-Caucasians and 51 will be women. Thus, the new world order will be significantly different from the one we were exposed to in the late 1970s and even early 1980s. In terms of implications for IHRM, this means that, increasingly, our competitors and collaborators in the world are going to be non-Caucasians and women. Non-Caucasians tend to possess a mindset that is significantly different from our own. This affects their attitude toward business, including competition and cooperation (Tung 1994). Even in the case of Mexico, which is geographically closer to us, there is substantial cultural difference. The basis for business transactions in Mexico is personal relations as opposed to legal contracts in both the United States and Canada, and the relationship between the superior and subordinate can be characterized as paternalistic in Mexico but bureaucratic in both U.S. and Canada (Paik & Teagarden 1995).

For many decades now, non-western countries have been trying to learn and understand about the west; however, westerners have only begun recently to learn about non-western societies. Hence, there will be a lot of catching up to do. In the decades ahead, women will outnumber men. Tannen (1990) has coined the term "genderlect" to refer to the sometimes insurmountable gap that exists between male and female in their communication patterns and styles. In light of the growing participation of women in professional and managerial ranks, IHRM (not just domestic HRM) policies and practices have to be revised to accommodate this new development.

2. Formation of Global Strategic Alliances

An emerging trend in global competition is the formation of global strategic alliances between entities from two or more nations. Global strategic alliances encompass international joint ventures, co-marketing, co-production, and joint research and development. In May 1997, for example, five airlines from three continents have formed "Star Alliance," a collaborative arrangement with an "alliance development committee" to coordinate various operations among the companies. These five airlines are Air Canada, Lufthansa, SAS, Thai Airways, and United Airlines. In October of the same year, Brazil's Varig will join the alliance (*Korea Herald,* May 17, 1997, p. 12). There is a growing recognition among international firms that, to compete effectively, they may have to collaborate with their competitors. International firms, such as IBM, Phillips, and Nippon Telegraph and Telephone, which were once averse to such collaborative efforts, have been quickly entering into such arrangements (*Business Week,* May 18, 1987).

The emergence of such alliances implies that there will be (a) a growing number of Americans working abroad; (b) a growing number of Americans working for U.S.-based subsidiaries of foreign multinational corporations; and (c) an increasing number of foreign nationals on assignment in the United States.

3. Global Integration versus Local Responsiveness

A phenomenon unique to the last decades of the twentieth century is the emergence of diametrically opposed forces which exert simultaneous demands upon global companies. On the one hand, there is the push for global integration. This arises from the need to source worldwide, capitalize on economies of scale, quantum advances in telecommunication, reduced transportation cost, emergence of global competitors and the growing homogeneity of demand by customers worldwide. On the other hand, there is the pull toward local responsiveness. This stems from regional economic integration and cultural differences (Moran & Reisenberger 1994, p. 116). To succeed, indeed to survive, global companies have to maintain a delicate balance between these two opposing forces. Expatriate managers are often called to perform this complex task of satisfying the objectives of corporate headquarters and those of its subsidiary when the objectives of the two groups may often diverge (Bartlett & Ghoshal 1989). This balancing act has been referred to as the "art of being local worldwide" (Sullivan 1996). As Moran and Reisenberger (1994, p. 120) stated, the slogan is no longer "think global, act locally," but "think globally and locally, act appropriately."

4. Emergence of Network Organizations

In response to the formation of global strategic alliances and the quest for high performance in light of the global recession of the late 1980s, many organizations have resorted to organizational restructuring, including the establishment of network organizations.

Jack Welch, chairman and CEO of General Electric, for example, has simplified the corporate organizational structure by dismantling the groups and sectors within the company and eliminating several layers of senior management. Welch has coined the term "boundarylessness" to characterize this new organizational form. The objective is to remove the real and imaginary boundaries (barriers) to communication and teamwork created by traditional vertical and hierarchical structures. The four essential boundaries to be spanned include vertical (hierarchical levels), horizontal (specialization and compartmentalization), internal/external, and geographic/cultural. With boundarylessness, the organization seeks to leverage critical firm resources through speed, flexibility, integration, and innovation (Ashkenas, Ulrich, Jick, and Kerr 1995; Tichy and Charan 1989). Network organizations represent a significant departure from the pyramidal structures with rigid compartmentalization characteristic of traditional organizational charts. In a network organization, geographic location is rendered somewhat meaningless, i.e., it does not matter as much whether a manager is physically located in Detroit, Singapore or Moscow. What matters most is whether the person can relate to his/her counterparts from other functions/disciplines, companies, and possibly industries, in other countries. Thus domestic managers (i.e., those who are not on expatriate assignments) also have to contend with many of the same challenges and dynamics which were once the exclusive domain of international managers.

5. Growing Diversity of Workforce at Home and Abroad

In the mid-1980s, the Hudson Institute coined the term "Workforce 2000" to refer to the projection that between 1985–2000, only 15 percent of first-time job entrants to the U.S. workforce will be white male. This phenomenon is not unique to the United States. In Canada, by the turn of the Twenty-first century, it is estimated that about 20 percent of the country's population will consist of ethnic minorities. Even homogeneous societies, such as South Korea, are anticipating greater diversity among its organizational ranks in the decades ahead. In the case of LG, a leading Korean conglomerate, its objective is to hire 20 percent non-ethnic Koreans among its professional and managerial ranks by the year 2005. This diversity poses tremendous challenges to organizations which policies and practices are designed for a rather homogeneous workforce, i.e., white male workforce in the case of the United States.

Thomas Kochan (1995), in his presidential address to the Tenth World Congress of the International Industrial Relations Association, called for the launching of a renaissance in industrial relations research. In his opinion, new paradigms should be developed that can account for workplace diversity in its broadest sense. Traditional paradigms in industrial relations assume that there are only two distinct interest groups: labor and management. Current workplace diversity extends beyond race and gender to encompass other forms of differences, however, such as those between full-time and part-time workers, single versus multiple job holders, and so on. With diversity, a whole range of workplace conflicts comes to the fore—discrimination/harassment on the basis of race, gender and other social affiliations; breakdowns in communication attributable to cultural differences; and work and family issues. These new types of workplace conflicts "are not easily resolved through the formal system of negotiations, grievance handling, or legal enforcement procedures that assume a clear labor-management dividing line." According to Kochan (1995), workplace diversity challenges organizations to "develop new processes and institutions for legitimating differences arising from personal diversity and resolving conflicts and solving problems" (p. 3).

6. Growing Convergence of Core Competencies required of Domestic and International Managers

In light of the formation of global strategic alliances among entities from disparate corners of the world with different mindsets, the emergence of network organizations which span huge geographical distances, and the growing diversity of the workforce at home and abroad, it has been argued that there will be a growing convergence of core competencies required of domestic and international managers (Tung 1993; Tung 1997). Domestic managers, who were once quite removed from the dynamics of interacting with nationals of other countries and companies in other industries, find that they increasingly have to contend with these forces in their day-to-day work. In a survey of executives from around the world about the requisites of the CEO for the year 2000, the proverbial future, the consensus of opinion was that the person "must have a multi-environment, multi-country, multifunctional, maybe even multi-company, multi-industry experience" (Bennett 1989, p. 1). This trend toward convergence has important implications for IHRM and HRM. Specifically, these are: (a) the distinction between HRM and IHRM is becoming blurred; thus existing paradigms, policies and practices which separate the two have to be re-examined and modified; (b) domestic managers (i.e., those whose careers will primarily be in one geographical location) can use international assignments as a means to develop the new skills and core competencies required of senior management. This latter points to the seventh and last development addressed below.

7. Increasing Use of Overseas Assignments for Career Development Purposes

As noted above, the increasingly blurred distinction between core competencies required of domestic and international managers has led many executives to realize that international assignments, where properly engineered, can have a positive impact on their overall career development. This realization, combined with the requirements of managing global strategic alliances, have meant that more and more people are undertaking overseas assignments, albeit for the primary purpose of overall career development, rather than merely filling a job requirement abroad, as was often the case until the early 1980s. In the mid-1980s, some have argued that because of the high cost of expatriation and the localization requirements of many host governments, expatriation will be on the decline. This prediction did not materialize in many organizations despite the continued high cost of expatriation and localization policy requirements of many host governments.

In fact, multinational corporations are increasingly using overseas assignments for developing their fast or elite trackers for senior management. Global companies, such as Ford Motors, have professed that they will not promote anyone to the position of CEO unless the person has served abroad. Global companies from many other countries in west Europe and Japan, have long espoused this policy (Tung 1988). New players in the global economic arena, such as the Korean conglomerates (chaebols), have placed an equal emphasis on the need to serve abroad in order to advance up the organizational hierarchy. In Tung and Arthur Andersen (1997), an overwhelming majority believed that an international assignment had a very positive impact on their overall career development (mean score of 4.2 on a 5-point scale). This perspective towards international assignments exists despite the fact that almost 60 percent of the respondents expressed concern about repatriation, such as their company not guaranteeing them a job at home upon their successful completion of their overseas assignment.

CONTINGENCY PARADIGM REVISITED

In light of the seven changes and developments which have taken place since the early 1980s, is the contingency paradigm of selection and training I developed in 1981 still relevant? The answer is a resounding "yes," although the selection criteria and training programs will have to be more complex. The dimensions/perspectives to be added to these two IHRM functions will be discussed below.

Selection

In my 1981 article, I hypothesized that different criteria should be emphasized for various categories of international assignments. For jobs in the CEO (i.e., head of an overseas operation) and functional head (i.e., those sent to establish a functional department abroad, e.g., head of marketing) categories which involve more extensive contacts with people in the host society and a longer duration of stay abroad, I noted that besides technical competence, greater emphasis should be placed on human relational skills, i.e., the ability to interact effectively with host country nationals. This is particularly crucial in assignments to countries characterized by large cultural distance from the home society. IHRM policies and practices at 80 U.S. multinationals provided empirical support that companies which adopted a contingency approach to their selection and training of expatriates experienced higher rates of success in their international assignments. This proposition essentially holds true with the following added provisions:

1. Where assignments are undertaken in the context of global strategic alliances, besides cross-national cultures, it is important to take into consideration the different corporate cultures that exist among the various companies that comprise the cooperative arrangement. Corporate culture refers to "shared beliefs top managers in a company have about how they should manage themselves and other employees, and how they should conduct their business(es)" (Lorsch 1986, p. 95). A strong corporate culture can have a homogenizing effect on cross-national culture. Thus, in the past, where expatriate assignments typically were from corporate headquarters to a wholly- or majority-owned operation abroad (i.e., same corporate culture), the expatriate is subjected to less difference because of the homogenizing effect of corporate culture. With the growing incidence of global strategic alliances, expatriates may increasingly be sent to companies where their parent company is only a partner in the foreign operation. Thus, ample consideration has to be given to the differences in corporate cultures among the partners. Furthermore, in assignments to global strategic alliances and network organizations which entail collaboration with foreign nationals in other disciplines and functions, due consideration has to be given to the significance of professional culture. Professional culture refers to the code of ethics and other commonalities shared by people who belong to a particular professional group, such as physicians and accountants. Behaviors and norms also tend to vary across industries. Similar to corporate culture, professional culture can have a homogenizing effect on cross-national culture. Thus, in the past, where expatriates were typically assigned to work with others who come from more or less similar functional backgrounds in the same industry (i.e., same professional culture), they may encounter less difference on the job. With the increased need to work with multiple industries and functions, the differences may be exacerbated. Black and Men-

denhall (1991), building on Tung (1981), offered a refined theory of training for cross-cultural encounters. The additional situational factor in their proposed model is job novelty. "Job novelty" refers to the difference between requirements of the international assignment and the person's previous position. Different corporate and professional cultures contribute to the level of job novelty encountered in an international assignment.

2. In light of the multiple environments (such as multicompany, multi-industry) indicated above, it is very important that the expatriate be flexible, resourceful, creative and possess strong negotiating skills. Flexibility is required for moving with ease from one type of environment (be it country-, industry-, company-, or function-) to another. Because of the need to balance the conflicting demands of global integration, on the one hand, and local responsiveness, on the other, the expatriate has to be flexible. Resourcefulness is also necessary because no person can be expected to perform single-handedly all of these multiple roles. Hence, the person has to be resourceful, i.e., be able to know when to call on whom on what matters. Creativity is needed because in a rapidly changing environment, the expatriate often has to venture into uncharted territories. Therefore, the person cannot rely exclusively on tried and true practices; rather, the person has to be creative and deal with new challenges as they arise. Last, but not least, the expatriate has to possess strong negotiating skills. Negotiating was ranked as the third most important skill to be possessed by CEOs in the future in the Korn/Ferry International and Columbia University Graduate School of Business study of 1,500 top executives in twenty countries (*21st Century Report* 1989). Unlike the traditional expatriate of the past, where negotiating was primarily with the host government, local nationals and corporate headquarters, the expatriate of the future has to negotiate with partners in strategic alliances and peoples in multiple functions and industries. Thus, the expatriate of the future has to possess strong negotiating skills to help him/her navigate smoothly among multiple types of cultures (cross-national, corporate and professional) and environments. In short, the expatriate of the Twenty-first century can truly be described as a "person for all seasons" (Tung 1995a).

3. In my 1981 article, I argued for the need to possess strong human relational skills to function effectively in international assignments. In Tung and Arthur Andersen (1997), I elaborated on the specific human relational skills required for effective performance abroad. These include: greater sensitivity to the needs of others (4.02), cooperative as opposed to competitive (4.02), listening rather than lecturing (4.13), espousing an inclusive leadership style (3.95), being compromising rather than domineering (3.91), engaging in rapport rather than report talk (3.81), being more compassionate and understanding (3.79), emphasizing harmony and avoiding conflict (3.38), and being more nurturing (3.33). (The figures in parentheses after each attribute are the mean scores for the respondents). It is interesting to note that these characteristics are usually

attributed to female, as opposed to male (Tannen 1990). Since it is usually more common for women to exhibit these traits, it has been hypothesized that women may be better suited for international assignments (Tung 1995b).

Training

In my 1981 article, I hypothesized and provided empirical evidence to support the assertion that for assignments to countries where the cultural distance is great and for jobs requiring extensive and intensive contacts with the host society (such as CEO and functional head), more rigorous cross-national training programs should be provided. The training programs in ascending order of rigor are: area studies programs, culture assimilator, language training, sensitivity training, and field experiences. Again, this recommendation still holds true with the following added provisions:

1. Since expatriate assignments are used increasingly for overall career development purposes and given the growing convergence of core competencies required of domestic and international managers, it is important that the development of cross-national skills (i.e., skills to enable a person to work with peoples from other cultures) take on a lifelong dimension, as opposed to a one-shot program with an area-specific focus. This, of course, implies that companies must invest more heavily in training programs.
2. With the increased incidence of international competition and/or cooperation, it is more important than ever that expatriates learn a foreign language. In a twelve-country study of almost 3,000 executives from around the world, those from Europe, Asia, and South America perceived knowledge of a foreign language as critical to a firm's competitive advantages. Only respondents from the four English-speaking countries (United States, Canada, United Kingdom and Australia) deemed such skills as unimportant. In Tung and Arthur Andersen (1997), it was found that the majority of U.S. expatriates spoke more than one language. This may have contributed to the high rate of expatriate success in this sample.
3. In the past, training programs that provided language skills typically focused on verbal communication. While the latter can provide understanding, communication competency should go beyond the mere acquisition of oral language proficiency and extend to non-verbal skills. Hall (1976) has noted, for example, that only 30 percent of communication are verbal. Thus, various cultures attribute different meanings and interpretations to nonverbal communication, that is, the silent language. Miscommunication, both verbal and nonverbal, arises when the message intended by the sender deviates from the message perceived by the receiver. This gap between intention and perception can stem from the different fields of experience of the sender and the receiver, including the meanings and interpretations assigned to specific words and the encod-

ing/decoding of messages on either side (Howell 1982; Ronen 1986). These different fields of experience are largely culture based. Peoples from high-context cultures (such as Japan, Latin and Mediterranean countries) thrive on implicit messages, whereas members from low-context societies (such as the United States and north European countries) emphasize directness. The five-stage model of communication competency developed by Howell (1982), and subsequently adapted by Ting-Toomey (1992), has been applied to the process of cross-national communication (Tung 1993). The five levels of communication competence are: unconscious incompetence, conscious incompetence, conscious competence, unconscious competence, and unconscious super-competence. An example of unconscious incompetence is referring to Korea as the "second Japan." Although the sender may think she/he is paying a compliment to the receiver, an ethnic Korean, the latter may feel insulted because of the bitter feelings that many Koreans still harbor toward the Japanese as a result of cruelty during the 40-year Japanese annexation of Korea. Thus, communication competency goes beyond mere language facility, although it is definitely associated with it. In international assignments, a desirable goal is to attain level 3 (conscious competence) and above. At levels 4 (unconscious competence) and 5 (unconscious super-competence), the person becomes truly bicultural and bilingual and moves spontaneously between members of one culture and another.

4. The goal of sensitivity training, a more rigorous program identified in Tung (1981), is to raise consciousness/awareness of cross-cultural differences. In the Twenty-first century, because of the need to work with peoples from other companies, industries and functions, this level of awareness has to be raised to accommodate other types of differences. Furthermore, programs designed to raise consciousness/awareness should help people to look beyond the differences and capitalize on the attributes that make such individuals/sub-group unique and distinct. Langer (1989) coined the term mindfulness to refer to raising consciousness/awareness so that we can free ourselves from traditional mindsets to innovate and make progress. The opposite of mindfulness is mindlessness, a pattern "determined in the past, (in which) we blot out intuition and miss much of the present world around us" (Langer 1989, p. 118). With mindfulness, we can become more innovative and flexible through "less indiscriminate discrimination" (Langer 1989, p. 168). The objective of such programs is to sensitize participants to the fact that a person's behavioral patterns, values, and attitudes are products of the unique cultural and environmental milieu in which that person was raised. To quote Allan Hall (Tung 1988, p. 30), deputy director of the Center for International Briefing at Farnham Castle (United Kingdom), "it is useless, stupid, unnecessary, and beside the point to say that (one's culture) is better than that (of the host country's); it is merely different." Thus, in the past while the goal of cross-cultural training was to manage diver-

sity/differences, the objective in the future is to value, and ultimately, celebrate this diversity.

In the past, cross-cultural training has focused on learning about the attitudes and behaviors of peoples in the host society. Therefore, an assimilation mode of acculturation was proposed. This helps avoid the "ugly American" image abroad. Berry (1997), using two dimensions (cultural preservation and attraction to other culture), identified four modes of acculturation between members of the majority and minority cultures. These are: integration (need for cultural preservation and attraction to other culture), assimilation (no need for cultural preservation and attraction to other culture), separation (need for cultural preservation and no attraction to other culture), and marginalization (no need for cultural preservation nor attraction to other culture). Research on international diversity suggests that integration is the most functional mode of acculturation between members of the minority and majority cultures. In Tung and Arthur Andersen (1997), most expatriates believed that integration and assimilation were pivotal to effective performance abroad. However, as noted earlier, given the conflicting demands of global integration, on the one hand, and local responsiveness, on the other, an expatriate which espouses an acculturation mode only may fail to satisfy corporate objectives of global integration. Worse yet, they may be chastised for having "gone native." To maintain an appropriate balance between these two conflicting demands, an integration mode is desirable. In addition, local nationals often expect that expatriates know a lot about their home countries, when such may not be the case. Consequently, expatriates should be encouraged to preserve and combine the better elements from both the host and home countries in order to perform effectively in the country of assignment as well as in their home office.

5. An important component of cross-cultural training is to provide the expatriate with a realistic preview of what is expected in the overseas position. In Tung and Arthur Andersen (1997), many expatriates felt that their respective companies failed to provide them with a realistic job preview of what was expected in their international assignment (mean score of 2.8 on a 5-point scale). Obviously, the more different the job abroad is from the previous position (i.e., high job novelty), the more realistic the job preview should be to facilitate effective performance.

DISCUSSION AND CONCLUSION

In reviewing developments over the past 15 years and in light of projected trends in the Twenty-first century, it appears that a contingency paradigm for selection and training, with the additional provisions and dimensions stipulated throughout the article can help companies steer their way smoothly into the new millenium. These additional stipulations are necessary because of the increased complexity of the world environment characterized by global cooperation and competition, yet the desire to preserve national and personal identity and distinctiveness.

However, organizations would be remiss to assume that appropriate selection criteria and adequate cross-cultural training programs alone are adequate to assure successful expatriate assignments. A very critical aspect of IHRM which is often neglected is repatriation. In Tung and Arthur Andersen (1997), the majority of expatriates expressed high overall satisfaction with their current/last international assignment (mean score of 4.1 on a 5-point scale). However, when overall satisfaction was decomposed into satisfaction with their company's expatriation and repatriation program and policies, a different picture was revealed. The mean score for "satisfaction with their company's expatriation program and policies" was 3.37 while that for their company's "repatriation program and policies" was only 2.61.

Furthermore, the majority of expatriates in Tung and Arthur Andersen (1997) expressed serious to very serious concerns about repatriation. Consequently, even if only a small percentage of repatriates actually experienced major setbacks in their career upon return, these incidences tend to be magnified a hundred-fold. These misgivings about expatriate assignments could unravel an otherwise highly effective IHRM system within the company. Given the significance of repatriation to the overall effectiveness of expatriate assignments, a holistic and systematic approach to IHRM is proposed. See Figure 1 about here. A holistic and systematic approach calls for the organization to pay attention to all aspects of IHRM. These include compensation and performance appraisal. An effective compensation program allows the organization to motivate and retain competent executives to undertake international assignments, yet minimize cost to the company. A comprehensive appraisal system entails the provision of a fair and equitable way of assessing an expatriate's performance abroad. It is obviously beyond the scope of this paper to go into these other aspects of IHRM. It is sufficient to note here that a piecemeal approach to IHRM favored by some companies, such as the mere provision of cross-cultural training programs as a quick fix to international assignments, is inadequate.

In Figure 1, the repatriation function is posited as playing a pivotal role in integrating all other components of the IHRM system. In the area of selection, this refers to the need for managers to take into consideration the overall qualification of the candidate at the time of expatriation to determine (a) how the person will fit into the overseas position; and (b) how he/she would fit back in the home office upon return. In the area of training, besides the provision of training on the outbound journey, it is imperative that the organization provides repatriation training to facilitate re-absorption upon return. In this regard, again a contingency approach is called for—the longer the time the person has been away and the more novel the job upon return, the more rigorous the repatriation training. In the area of compensation, since many expatriates experience a reduced standard of living upon return due to the cessation of various types of overseas premiums, the company should provide some assistance to alleviate this financial stress. The latter is particularly acute if the price of real estate at home has escalated substantially while the person was away. In the area of performance appraisal, those at home should have a

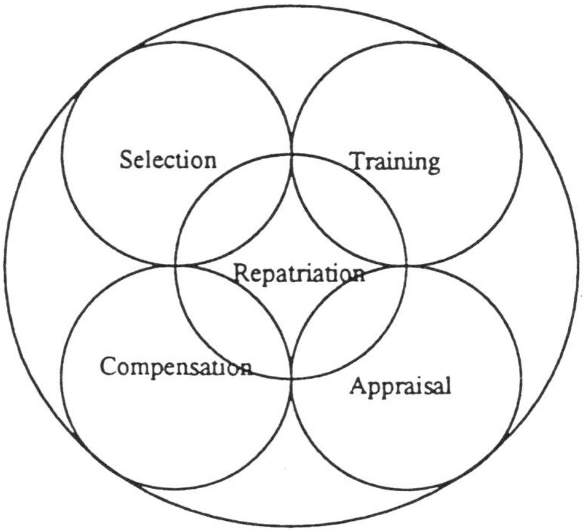

Figure 1. A Holistic Approach to IHRM

fair and accurate basis upon which to compare the expatriate's performance with those in the home operation. Furthermore, due consideration must be given to the fact that repatriates often experience a reverse culture shock upon return. Consequently, while the person is returning home, he/she is susceptible to financial stress (discussed above) and family stress (associated with the spouse's searching for new employment and children settling into new social settings) (Harvey 1989). These various forms of stress can be compounded if the new job at home is very different from the job performed abroad, i.e., high job novelty.

In summary, for an organization to benefit fully from the fruits of international assignments, it is imperative that they adopt a holistic and systematic approach which takes into consideration all aspects of IHRM because, collectively, they can help the company to attain its long-term objective of developing a truly global mindset among its executives to contend with the challenges of the Twenty-first century.

NOTE

1. Interview with Mr. Tae-won Lee, President of Hanjin Group, September 1996.

REFERENCES

Ashkenas, A., D. Ulrich, T. Jick, and S. Kerr. 1995. *The Boundaryless Organization*. San Francisco, CA: Jossey-Bass.

Bartlett, C. and S. Ghoshal. 1989. *Managing across Borders: The Transnational Solution*. Cambridge, MA: Harvard Business School Press.

Bennett, A. 1989. "The Chief Executives in Year 2000 Will Be Experienced Abroad." *Wall Street Journal* (February 27): 1.

Berry, J. W. 1997. "Individual and Group Relations in Plural Societies." Pp. 17–35 in *Cross-Cultural Work Groups,* edited by C. S. Granrose and S. Oskamp. Thousand Oaks, CA: Sage Publications.

Black, J. S. and M. Mendenhall. 1991. "A Practical But Theory-Based Framework for Selecting Cross-Cultural Training Methods." In *International Human Resource Management,* edited by M. Mendenhall and G. Oddou. Boston: PWS-Kent Publishing Co.

Hall, E. T. 1976. *Beyond Culture.* Garden City, NY: Anchor/Doubleday.

"Hands Across Europe: Joint Ventures Will Help Companies Compete against Japan and the U.S." 1987. *Business Week* May 18.

Harvey, M. C. 1989. "Repatriation of Corporate Executives: An Empirical Study." *Journal of International Business Studies* 20(1): 131–144.

Howell, W. S. 1982. *The Emphatic Communicator.* Prospect Heights, IL: Waveland.

IBM and Towers Perrin. 1992. *Priorities for Competitive Advantage.*

Kochan, T. A. 1995. *Launching a Renaissance in International Industrial Relations Research.* Paper presented as the presidential address at the meeting of the International Industrial Relations Association, May, Washington DC.

"Five Airlines Form First True Global Alliance." 1997. *Korea Herald* (May 17): 12.

Langer, E. J. 1989. *Mindfulness.* Reading MA: Addison-Wesley.

Lorsch, J. 1986. "Managing Culture: The Invisible Barrier to Strategic Change." *California Management Review* 28(2): 95–124.

Moran, R. T. and J. R. Reisenberger. 1994. *The Global Challenge.* New York: McGraw-Hill.

Paik, Y. and M. B. Teagarden. 1995. "Strategic International Human Resource Approaches in the Maquiladora Industry: A Comparison of Japanese, Korean and U.S. firms," *International Journal of Human Resource Management* 6: 568–587.

Ronen, S. 1986. *Comparative and Multinational Management.* New York: John Wiley.

Sullivan, D. 1996. "Organization Structure in Multinational Corporations." Pp. 3573–3597 in *International Encyclopedia of Business and Management,* edited by M. Warner. London, U.K.: Routledge.

Tannen, D. 1990. *You Just Don't Understand: Men and Women in Conversation.* New York: Ballantine.

Tichy, N. and R. Charan. 1989. "Speed, Simplicity, Self-Confidence: An Interview with Jack Welch," *Harvard Business Review* (September-October): 112–120.

Ting-Toomey, S. 1992. *Cross-Cultural Face Negotiation: An Analytical Overview.* Paper presented at the Pacific Region Forum Simon Fraser University, (April). Burnaby, B.C., Canada.

Tung, R. L. 1981. "Selection and Training of Personnel for Overseas Assignments." *Columbia Journal of World Business* (Spring): 68–78.

______. 1988. *The New Expatriates: Managing Human Resources Abroad.* Cambridge, MA: Ballinger.

______. 1993. "Managing Cross-National and Intra-National Diversity." *Human Resource Management* 32: 461–477.

______. 1994. "Strategic Management Thought in East Asia." *Organizational Dynamics* (Spring): 55–65.

______. 1995a. *Wanted: A Person for All Seasons: An Examination of Managerial Skills and Core Competencies for the Twenty-first Century.* Paper presented at the 55th Annual Meetings of the Academy of Management, (August 6–9) Vancouver.

______. 1995b. *Women in a Changing Global Economy.* Paper presented at the 10th Annual Conference of the Society of Industrial/Organizational Psychology (May 17–20) Orlando, Florida.

______. 1997. "International and Intranational Diversity." Pp. 163–185 in *Cross-Cultural Work Groups,* edited by C. S. Granrose and S. Oskamp. Thousand Oaks, CA: Sage Publications.

Tung and Arthur Andersen. 1997. *Exploring International Assignee's Viewpoints: A Study of the Expatriation/Repatriation Process.* Chicago, IL: Arthur Andersen.

USING INTRA-NATIONAL DIVERSITY FOR INTERNATIONAL ASSIGNMENTS: A MODEL OF BICULTURAL COMPETENCE AND EXPATRIATE ADJUSTMENT

Myrtle P. Bell
David A. Harrison
University of Texas-Arlington

Considerable international HRM literature focuses on training expatriates to increase cultural awareness and provide realistic previews of life and work in the host country, thereby increasing expatriate effectiveness and adjustment. This article emphasizes a complementary form of improving expatriate adjustment, namely, selection on individual differences resulting from the bicultural life experiences that individuals may bring with them to potential assignments. Parallel themes in literatures on biculturalism and on the knowledge, skills, abilities, and other requirements (KSAOs) for expatriate effectiveness are discussed. A model integrating these bicultural life experiences/KSAOs and effects of other constructs on expatriate adjustment is proposed. Research and managerial implications follow.

The expansion of corporations across continents and borders has also expanded the frequency, depth, and breadth of intercultural interactions—both within and across organizational boundaries. In most international operations, lower level employees tend to be host country nationals, while managers tend to be parent country expatriates whose previous intercultural experiences are limited (Hait 1992; Napier & Peterson 1992). This has introduced important human resource management (HRM) problems, perhaps requiring unique combinations of human resource strategies. This paper examines some of those international HRM problems and explores how they might be addressed by integrating research on bicultural life experiences with research on the adjustment of expatriates.

Direct all correspondence to: Myrtle P. Bell, Department of Management, P.O. Box 19467, University of Texas-Arlington, Arlington, TX 76019.

Human Resource Management Review,
Volume 6, Number 1, 1996, pages 47–74

ISSN:1053–4822

Specifically, we propose that characteristics of bicultural individuals might facilitate their effectiveness on international assignments. We begin with a summary of the literatures on biculturalism and on international HRM. We then highlight the parallels between bicultural competencies and the knowledge, skills, abilities, and other attributes (KSAOs) necessary for expatriate effectiveness. Next, we present a model of how individual differences associated with bicultural life experiences should foster better expatriate adjustment, describing and supporting propositions within the model. Finally, we discuss implications of the model for researchers studying expatriate adjustment and for practitioners selecting and training candidates for expatriate positions.

This article contributes to the international HRM literature in three ways. First, it (re-)emphasizes the importance of individual differences in the effectiveness of expatriates. Second, it focuses attention on the competencies that can arise from bicultural life experiences as an important set of those individual differences. Third, it specifically discusses and suggests ways that firms could use some of these distinct competencies in staffing for international assignments.

INTERNATIONAL HRM LITERATURE AND EXPATRIATE EFFECTIVENESS

A major theme in the international HRM literature is the inadequate match of expatriates to their overseas position, and the resulting failure and early return of assignees. Although exact figures are not generally published by firms, estimates of expatriate failure rates and associated costs are high (Tung 1988; Harris 1979). The failure rates for U.S. based multi-national corporations (MNCs) are considerably higher than those of foreign based MNCs (Naumann 1992; Tung 1988).

The indirect, non-quantifiable costs of expatriate failure are also substantial and may include loss of business opportunities, loss of good will, and loss of valuable personnel if the expatriate quits the firm (Black & Mendenhall 1989; Harvey 1983; Naumann 1992). Non-quantifiable costs to the expatriate may include career damage, family problems, and loss of self-esteem (Mendenhall & Oddou 1985).

Early emphasis on the match of expatriates to their assignments focused on the need for selecting those who are technically proficient, while it neglected relational skills (Mendenhall, et al. 1987; Mendenhall & Oddou 1985; Tung 1981). As is now commonly acknowledged in international HRM, technical proficiency is a necessary but not sufficient condition for expatriate effectiveness (Tung 1984). Therefore, as technically proficient expatriates have continued to fail, the HRM focus has expanded to include realistic job previews and cross-cultural training, with both academic and practitioner-oriented literatures now emphasizing the need for these preassignment processes. Both processes are meant to increase the awareness of what is expected on an international assignment, and to build skills for successful intercultural interaction for the expatriate and for his or her family (Black 1989; Harvey 1985; Tung 1981). Possession of these skills is assumed to lead to better adjusted expatriates, who are also assumed to be more effective performers.

The criterion of interest in this literature has primarily been expatriate adjustment and/or retention. It is important to note that expatriate adjustment and effectiveness are not identical constructs. Effectiveness is somewhat broader, yet is clearly intertwined with the adjustment and retention of expatriates. That is, adjustment could well be argued to be an intervening variable to effectiveness or a dominant dimension of effectiveness. Certainly, those who fail to adjust and return early are no longer in the job and cannot be effective. In that sense, appropriate adjustment is a necessary condition for effective performance. There is also literature that indicates some expatriates are "brown outs" who do not leave the assignment early, but who psychologically withdraw and fail to perform effectively, despite completing the assignment (Harvey 1983). Such expatriates may cause more harm by staying under those circumstances than they would by leaving early (Harvey 1983). Therefore, for ease of presentation, we will use adjustment and effectiveness more or less interchangeably, while recognizing certain distinctions between the two.

In sum, recent international HRM research has concentrated on ways to *build* or *train* the appropriate KSAOs needed for expatriate effectiveness, especially with regard to specific content knowledge about the culture to which a person is being expatriated with less emphasis on selection. On the other hand, domestic HRM research has tended to concentrate on ways to *select* employees who already hold those KSAOs necessary to "fit" a particular position, perhaps more general constructs. We emphasize those more general constructs, as they involve experience in the processes of learning about another culture that might facilitate learning of a third culture. We propose a better balance of these broad international and domestic HRM themes, suggesting that more emphasis might fruitfully be placed on the individual differences (e.g., biculturalism) that potential expatriates hold. Selection on these differences, when coupled with specific content-related cross-cultural training, could markedly increase expatriate effectiveness. We propose that bicultural life experiences are an important but ignored set of those individual differences, differences that should lead to special competencies related to expatriate adjustment.

BICULTURALISM LITERATURE

Although specific terminology varies somewhat among disciplines, a useful summary definition of biculturalism is: the state in which individuals maintain their distinctive cultures, including values, attitudes, customs, beliefs, and habits while simultaneously interacting with and learning from those of other cultures. As such, biculturalism is a broad construct, defined to have cognitive, affective, and behavioral components. However, there is limited empirical work on the combination of these components (e.g. Garza, Romero, Cox,

& Ramirez 1982). Instead, literature on biculturalism in various social science disciplines is dominated by theory (LaFromboise, Coleman, & Gerton 1993). In the earliest theoretical work, DuBois (1903) discussed *double-consciousness* as a state of being for African-Americans living in predominantly white America. Ninety years later, in their thorough work on the psychological impacts of biculturalism, LaFromboise et al. (1993) summarized the extensive and diverse body of literature on the subject. Much of that literature concerns the negative ramifications of biculturalism, including stress and role ambiguity (e.g. Fordham 1988; Sung 1985). On the other hand, some literature has proposed that there are rewards and resources uniquely available to bicultural individuals, especially when they are interpersonally competent in both of the cultures to which they belong (Bell 1990; Garza et al. 1982; Valentine 1971). Consistent with the latter literature, this article proposes that biculturalism is a potentially positive attribute in today's increasingly heterogeneous and global organizations. Specifically, because of diversity in cultural backgrounds, value systems, and expectations, and especially the developmental processes that led to their acquisition, bicultural people already *possess* cognitive, affective, and behavioral repertoires that are useful for international assignments, repertoires that cannot be learned solely through short term cross-cultural training. Unlike cross-cultural training, which may be limited to a few weeks or months, these bicultural competencies are often learned over a lifetime, and therefore may be considered individual differences of the potential expatriate.

PARALLEL ELEMENTS IN BICULTURAL COMPETENCE AND KSAOS FOR EXPATRIATE EFFECTIVENESS

LaFromboise et al. (1993) proposed that a bicultural individual's understanding and effective behavior in two different cultures, termed *bicultural competence,* better enables him or her to cope with the stress of acculturation. Dimensions of bicultural competence include: knowledge of both cultures' beliefs and values (general cultural awareness); positive attitudes toward both cultural groups (acceptance); confidence that one can live effectively within two groups without compromising one's cultural identity (bicultural self-efficacy); ability to communicate effectively with both groups (dual fluency); possession of a continuum of acceptable behaviors for both groups (broad role repertoire); and stable social networks in both cultures (groundedness). KSAOs similar to those competencies are also described in the international HRM literature as necessary for expatriate effectiveness (Black & Mendenhall 1989; Gregersen & Black 1990; Mendenhall et al. 1987). It is also believed these KSAOs can be imparted, to some extent, through cross-cultural training (Black & Mendenhall 1989). Figure 1 portrays the elements common to bicultural competence and expatriate effectiveness. Although the terminology is not identical, the parallel themes are clear. The following sections discuss the relationship of each pair of elements to bicultural individuals and to expatriates, provide a comparison of the bicultural competencies and KSAOs with the self, relation-

Bicultural Competencies		**KSAOs for Expatriate Effectiveness**
General Cultural Awareness	Cognitive Elements	Knowledge of host country's beliefs and values
Acceptance	↓	Positive (non judgmental) attitude toward host country nationals
Bicultural Efficacy	↓	Ability to interact effectively with host country nationals
Dual Fluency	↓	Host country language and non-verbal communications skills
Broad Role Repertoire	↓	Knowledge of acceptable behaviors
Groundedness	Social Behavior Elements	Frequent interaction with host country nationals

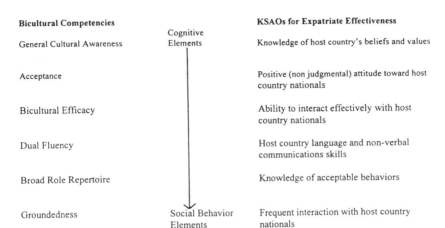

Figure 1. Parallels between Bicultural Competencies and KSAOs for Expatriate Effectiveness.

Adapted from LaFromboise et al. (1993), Black and Mendenhall (1989), Gregersen and Black (1990), and Mendenhall et al. (1987).

ship, and perceptual factors proposed by Black, Mendenhall, and Oddou (1991), and propose that bicultural competencies or expatriate KSAOs are generalizable across intercultural interactions.

General Cultural Awareness and Acceptance

For the expatriate, knowledge of a host country's beliefs and values and a non-judgmental perspective on those beliefs and values are advantageous (Shilling 1993). In various articles, open-mindedness and non-authoritarianism have been described as important expatriate characteristics (Naumann 1992, Shilling 1993). Brislin (1981, p. 55) described such persons as "tolerant of others different from themselves and . . . able to appreciate the fact that others have a legitimate point of view." In a similar way, cross-cultural training programs for expatriates are proposed to help foster knowledge of various aspects of a host country's culture (Mendenhall et al. 1987; Tung 1981). Black and Mendenhall (1989) proposed that modeling be used to provide knowledge of the host country culture's beliefs and values and to facilitate positive, non-judgmental attitudes toward those beliefs and values. Among other things, culture assimilators are designed to expose expatriates to some of the basic concepts, customs, and values of another culture (Fiedler, Mitchell, & Triandis 1971).

For bicultural individuals, general cultural awareness and acceptance are "trained" as part of their life experiences (Cox et al. 1991; Garza et al. 1982; LaFromboise et al. 1993; Valentine 1971). Further, their bicultural experiences enable them to hold accepting attitudes toward the customs, beliefs, and values of each culture to whom they belong (Garza et al. 1982). On the other hand, mono-culturalism may encourage individuals' displays of closed-mindedness and authoritarianism with respect to interactions with other cultures (Niyekawa-Howard 1970). McCaffery (1986, p. 167) has stated that it is especially difficult for expatriates to reflect on their own culture, as "most people do not have a solid, explicit sense of the meaning and practicalities of their own culture." That statement would have been especially appropriate if it had been restricted to monocultural expatriates.

Bicultural Self-Efficacy and the Generalization Effect

The ability to interact confidently and effectively with host country nationals, with its broad reaching effects, is critical to the success of expatriates (Shilling 1993). That confidence may be partly instilled in expatriates through predeparture visits, which provide first hand information about the host country and culture, thereby reducing the expatriate's uncertainty. Such predeparture visits and cross-cultural training may help the expatriate to learn some of the KSAOs needed to be effective on an assignment. Similarly, visits and training may serve to screen out those who may feel unwilling or unable to attain those KSAOs (Caudron 1991).

Bicultural self-efficacy is described as the "belief, or confidence that one can live effectively, and in a satisfying manner, within two groups" (LaFromboise et al. 1993, p. 404). As with general cultural awareness and acceptance, the process of developing bicultural self-efficacy for the bicultural individual occurs over his or her lifetime (Garza et al. 1982; LaFromboise et al. 1993; Valentine 1971). Research has found that self-efficacy develops through repeated task-related experiences and changes over time as new information and experience are acquired (Gist & Mitchell 1992). Feeling confident that one can effectively navigate two cultures is an outcome of doing and having done so.

International HRM literature discusses behaviors and attitudes that are helpful to expatriates when interacting with host country nationals. Biculturalism, bicultural competence, and similar terms encompass the behaviors and attitudes of certain individuals when interacting across cultures. Moreover, according to Niyekawa-Howard (1970, p. 3), "a bicultural person is more likely and more willing to understand a third and fourth culture than a monocultural person will be to understand a second culture." She termed this a *generalization effect,* referring to "non-culture-specific learning that results from abstracting and generalizing the knowledge one has acquired from living in a second culture" that can be used in facilitating understanding in other cultures. In other words, for bicultural individuals who are being considered for expatriate positions, it is not necessarily those competencies or knowledge of the *content* unique to being embedded in culture A and culture B that are important. What is paramount is the *process of having developed those competencies* (Sikkema & Niyekawa 1987). That process, including the acquisition of knowledge of the beliefs and values of more than one culture, the development of positive attitudes towards two cultures, the attainment of communication skills in two languages, the building of confidence that one can interact within two cultures, the learning of behaviors acceptable in two cultures, and the creation of stable social networks in those cultures is critical. Sikkema and Niyekawa (1987, p. 8) suggested that a person who has learned "how to learn" another culture would develop "an aptness for sensing or perceiving another person's feelings, views and needs, regardless of the cultural background." Similarly, we propose that bicultural individuals' experience of learning to learn another culture (through their acquisition of bicultural competencies) can be generalized to acquiring such competencies again on international assignments.

Dual Fluency

For the expatriate, intercultural verbal and non-verbal communications skills are vital (Albert 1986; McEnery & DesHarnais 1990; Shilling 1993). Having knowledge of the host country language may also be a positive signal to host country nationals that the expatriate has made the effort. However, a technical understanding without a cultural understanding of words can cause serious problems for expatriates (Caudron 1991). Beamer (1992, p. 293) aptly stated that while "fluency in another language is unarguably valuable, (it) does not always produce cultural fluency . . . (nor) automatically accompany linguistic skill." Understanding non-verbal communication in the host country can also help to avoid costly misunderstandings (Singelis 1994). Some important elements of non-verbal cross-cultural communication include facial expression, eye movement, and gestures (Furnham & Bochner 1986). Citing numerous sources, Furnham and Bochner (1986) noted that the Japanese eschew negative facial expressions, Filipinos may smile or laugh even when angry, and Arabs and Latin Americans have high levels of eye contact when compared with Europeans.

For the bicultural individual, the ability to communicate within and between two cultures, which we have termed dual fluency, involves "effectiveness in communicating ideas and feelings to members of a given culture, both verbally and nonverbally" (LaFromboise et al. 1993, p. 405). LaFromboise and colleagues (1993) found that it was important for the bicultural individual to maintain competency in both his or her native and second languages, for example, Spanish and English. It is important to note that dual fluency does not mean simple knowledge of vocabulary and grammar in two *different* languages. For example, many ethnic groups in the U.S. share a basic language, but have different meanings, connotations and understandings of the same words (Valentine 1971). Understanding of non-verbal communication patterns is important for bicultural individuals as well. For example, African-Americans, when passing another African-American who is a stranger, may communicate acknowledgment via a slight nod or smile (Cogdell & Wilson 1980).

Role Repertoire

For the expatriate, cross-cultural training often includes role playing and culture assimilators to help in forming a set of behaviors appropriate to the host country (Black & Mendenhall 1989; Tung 1984). The broader and more differentiated this set of potential behaviors, the more likely an expatriate can choose and perform those that fit different situations. In essence, such a person has greater flexibility and adaptability than one who has a limited set of behaviors from which to choose. The terms adaptability and flexibility are often noted in international HRM literature as requirements for expatriate effectiveness (e.g. Datta & Rasheed 1993; McEnery & DesHarnais 1990). In his field study of U.S. expatriates in Japan, Harrison (1992) found that expatriates trained to have a broader repertoire using behavior modeling and culture assimilators performed more effectively than did a no training control group, as the trainees gained knowledge about the culture and behaviors accepted there.

For the bicultural individual, a broad role repertoire refers to his or her knowledge of a wide range of behaviors appropriate to two cultures, and the ability to engage in those behaviors. Again, a broad role repertoire is learned throughout a bicultural individual's life experiences. For example, Polgar (1960, p. 217) noted that Native American teenagers learn a variety of behaviors through "concurrent socialization into two or more cultures." Similarly, Valentine (1971, p. 143) noted that African Americans draw upon "both a distinctive repertoire" of African American group behavior, and "simultaneously, patterns derived from the mainstream cultural system."

Groundedness

Social support networks have been posited as an important determinant of expatriate effectiveness (Black & Gregersen 1991). Some researchers have recommended that companies actively solicit help in indoctrination and social support from host country nationals as well as from those having previous expatriate experience (Albert 1986) International HRM researchers also note the importance of social integration in expatriate effectiveness (Feldman & Thomas 1992). Similarly, Black, Gregersen, and Mendenhall (1992, p. 130) found that having social support from host country nationals was helpful in expatriate spousal adjustment by providing both "emotional support and information about the culture."

Groundedness for the bicultural individuals refers to their affiliation with a well-developed social support system in both cultures (LaFromboise et al. 1993). Bicultural persons have learned to develop and maintain effective support groups in two cultures over many years (LaFromboise et al. 1993; Polgar 1960; Valentine 1971). In her work on the bicultural experiences of African-American women, Bell (1990, p. 475), noted their personal interactions and life experiences interacting with whites provides them with greater "cross-cultural expertise" than whites tend to have.

Structure of Bicultural Competencies

Bicultural competencies begin with a foundation of cognitive elements and grow to social behavior elements. General cultural awareness and acceptance are cognitive factors, reflecting the attitudes bicultural individuals hold toward those of other cultures. The development of and possession of these attitudes will facilitate bicultural self-efficacy, or the confidence that one can interact effectively within both cultures. Having bicultural efficacy will also help the expatriate in learning to communicate effectively within both cultures, which will also aid one in learning appropriate behaviors. Understanding what behaviors are appropriate will also help one in building a stable social network of persons in both cultures. Black and Gregersen (1991, p. 466) noted that having a stable social network of host country nationals "can provide feedback on the appropriateness of behaviors," information, and help in understanding host cultures, which as previously discussed, is influential in expatriate effectiveness. Similarly, Bochner (1981) noted that host country nationals may provide significant culture-learning and training to expatriate friends.

Links to Self, Others, and Perceptual Factors

Black et al. (1991) proposed that self, relationship, and perceptual dimensions are important in expatriate effectiveness. Those dimensions are included in the present model in the KSAOs for expatriate effectiveness or bicultural competence. Their self-dimension included "skills that enable the expatriate to maintain mental health, psychological well-being, self-efficacy, and effective stress management" (Black et al. 1991, p. 294), and is encompassed in our model by bicultural self-efficacy, acceptance, broad role repertoire, and groundedness (as social support increases one's psychological well being and reduces stress—see Furnham & Bochner 1986). Their relationship dimension included "the array of skills necessary for the fostering of relationships with host nationals" (Black et al. 1991, p. 294), encompassed herein through dual fluency, role repertoire, and groundedness. Black et al.'s (1991, p. 294) perceptual dimension referred to the expatriate's ability to "correctly perceive and evaluate the host environment and its actors" and is included herein as acceptance and general cultural awareness.

A CONCEPTUAL MODEL OF THE EFFECT OF BICULTURAL LIFE EXPERIENCES ON EXPATRIATE ADJUSTMENT

Figure 2 depicts a model of the proposed linkages between bicultural life experiences and expatriate adjustment. The central insight in the model comes from the strong conceptual parallels of bicultural competencies and the KSAOs that should help to facilitate expatriate adjustment. These parallels were discussed in detail in the previous section. We now turn to the set of initial independent variables involved in bicultural life experiences, explain their

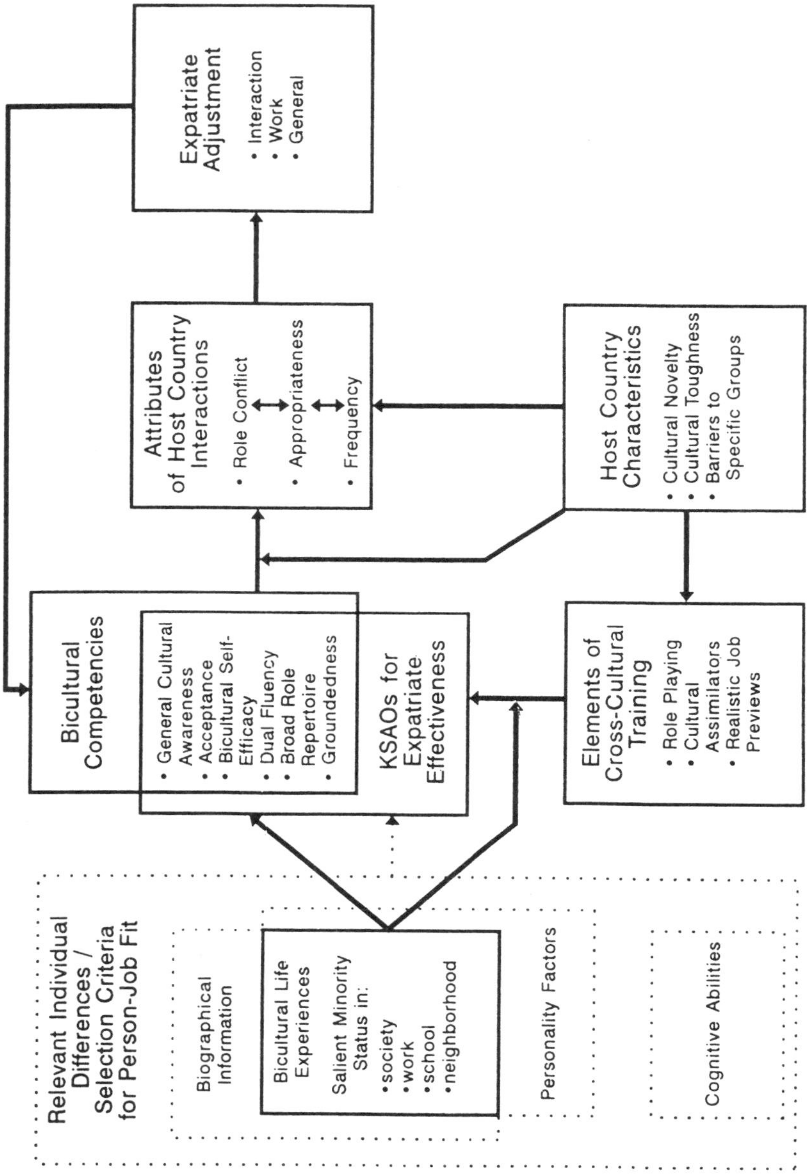

Figure 2. Effects of Bicultural Life Experiences on Expatriate Adjustment

impact on bicultural competencies or expatriate KSAOs, and propose how these latter constructs affect attributes of intercultural interactions. These qualities of interactions have a subsequent effect on expatriate adjustment. The effects of these sets of constructs on expatriate adjustment are moderated by cross-cultural training and specific characteristics of the host country to which an expatriate is assigned. Although we discuss all of the linkages in the model, we provide formal propositions only for those effects that involve the central topics of our article: bicultural experience and competencies.

Relevant Individual Differences/Selection Criteria for Person-Job Fit

As we have noted, with the exception of technical proficiency, individual differences of expatriates have been under-studied. This is ironic, as an entire stream of research and broad-based philosophy of selection on individual differences originated from the mechanisms used to choose U.S. spies for "expatriate assignments" during World War II. The Office of Strategic Services (OSS), a precursor to the CIA, conducted multiple-day, physical, emotional, personality, and cognitive ability assessments of spy candidates before selecting them for overseas duty (Cook & Herche 1992; Thornton 1992). Further, domestic HR research has emphasized selection of job candidates on broad sets of individual differences to facilitate person-job fit.

Consistent with other authors (e.g. Schmitt, Gooding, Noe, & Kirsch 1984), we propose that primary sets of these individual differences are biographical information, personality factors, and cognitive abilities. Indeed, Schmitt et al. (1984) report that the highest correlations of these sets of individual differences with turnover, (the extreme form of expatriate (mal)adjustment), involve biographical information and personality. Bicultural life experiences are a confluence of biographical and personality dimensions. When translated into a set of bicultural competencies, we propose that they are crucial individual differences that have been overlooked in selection for expatriate assignments.

Bicultural Life Experiences as Crucial Individual Differences

Although a bicultural individual may not be knowledgeable about the culture of a specific host country, he or she will have certain attributes that should be adaptable to life in yet another culture. Through his or her life's experiences, such a person will have had opportunities to develop bicultural competencies. If those competencies have been developed, that development should be transferable to an international assignment.

Bicultural life experiences often stem from an individual's salient minority status in his or her society, workplace, school, and neighborhood. For example, an ethnic minority who is working for a company large enough to have international positions is likely to be quite familiar with being the minority in many different situations. Such a person is likely to be one of few minorities in a department or work group (Cox & Nkomo 1990; Herbert 1990) and may be one of very few minorities in his or her neighborhood. He or she may have attended a university that was predominantly comprised of majority students, and taken courses as one of very few ethnic minorities (Herbert 1990). The salience of these differences facilitates the development of cultural awareness and efficacy (LaFromboise et al. 1993).

McGuire, McGuire, Child, and Fujiota (1978) noted that in integrated societies, ethnicity is more salient to minority group members than it is to majority group members. In comparison to minorities, ethnic majorities in positions to be considered for international assignments may have never experienced being the ethnic minority in any work or social gathering. For example, a supervisor at work is most likely to be white and is likely to live in a racially homogenous area, isolated from ethnic minorities (Gillmor & Doig 1992). According to Bell (1990, p. 475), ethnic majority professionals generally have had "fewer personal interactions or life experiences" with minority people and communities than minorities have had with the majority group. Similarly, Konrad, Winter, and Gutek (1992) argued that because of the greater contact that minority individuals have with majority individuals, minority individuals will have more realistic, less stereotypical attitudes toward majorities than vice versa. In general, because of the lower salience of their ethnicity and fewer personal interactions with minorities, ethnic majorities are not likely as are ethnic minorities to have developed the KSAOs/bicultural competencies important in international assignments.

The preceding discussion is not to suggest that simply because a person is a minority or encounters people in a majority culture he or she will necessarily develop bicultural competencies. There is no deterministic relationship between bicultural life experiences and bicultural competencies. Instead, it is those who are going through bicultural life experiences and actively seek to learn from them, who will become bicultural. Likewise this is not to suggest that only minorities in a particular culture can develop bicultural competencies. Members of majority cultures, if they actively pursue opportunities to interact with and learn from ethnic minorities in their own cultures, may develop bicultural competencies as well.

Still, Cox et al. (1991) noted that Americans of Hispanic, African, and Asian background are often bicultural. On the other hand, citing the 1988 Hazuda, Stern, and Haffner study done of (Anglo) white and Hispanic interaction in Texas, they noted evidence of biculturalism among Hispanics, but little among whites (Cox et al. 1991). This is particularly relevant for the expatriate area because in the few studies that have reported race or ethnicity of expatriates, it is clear that whites are overwhelmingly chosen for such assignments (e.g. Feldman & Thomas 1992). For the typical expatriate, then, an international assignment might be the first introduction into an important situation in which he or she is not part of the ethnic majority (Winsbury 1989).

In their study of individual differences and organizational attachment, Tsui, Egan, and O'Reilly (1992) found that increasing demographic diversity in organizational settings resulted in lowered attachment for whites and men, but that had no effect on attachment for non-whites and women (minority groups in the sample studied). Similarly, Wharton and Baron (1987) found that men in completely male (homogeneous) work environments were more satisfied than men who worked with females. It follows that the experience of expatriation for majority males might result in similar outcomes (dissatisfaction and turnover). These findings, as well as the earlier arguments, support our first proposition:

> **Proposition 1.** The extent of an individual's bicultural life experiences will have a positive effect on his or her development of bicultural competencies.

CROSS-CULTURAL TRAINING

Unlike past literature on expatriate adjustment, which has placed primary emphasis on cross-cultural training, our model regards it as is only one avenue toward gaining the KSAOs needed for expatriate effectiveness. The proposed impact of such training is also moderated by bicultural life experiences. Cross-cultural training for expatriates may include role plays, culture assimilators, sensitivity training, and similar tasks. Many authors have made clear that such training should be tailored to the country of expatriation in attempt to provide expatriates with realistic previews of life there (e.g. Black & Mendenhall 1989; Caudron 1991).

In a review of the literature on cross-cultural training, Black and Mendenhall (1990) found a positive relationship between cross-cultural training and self-efficacy regarding one's ability to interact across cultures, in 9 of 10 studies examined. They also found a positive relationship between cross-cultural training and intercultural relational skills in 19 of 19 studies. The intercultural relational skills are roughly equivalent to some of the KSAOs described here.

A bicultural expatriate must still receive training specific to the host country. However, this training should enhance an already positive relationship for the bicultural expatriate. Training will have a greater impact on those who have not yet developed the requisite attitudes, skills and behaviors necessary for successful intercultural interactions. Living conditions, social norms and customs, and other aspects of life in another country should be addressed to help both bicultural and monocultural expatriates formulate realistic previews as specifically relate to life in that particular country. However, it is expected that the generalization effect common to those who have bicultural life experiences will facilitate more rapid adjustment to those differences.

It is again critical to emphasize that it is not the content of knowledge of a previous culture that is most important for developing bicultural competency, rather, it is the *process* of having learned a different culture that will provide those having bicultural life experiences with an advantage as expatriates. Such individuals could capitalize on the decreasing marginal effort associated with acquiring skills in another culture (Niyekawa-Howard 1970). In other words, having already experienced and adjusted to the different social norms, customs, and behaviors of more than one culture should enable bicultural individuals to more readily adjust to yet another culture, even without training. We consider the bicultural individual to have likely already had a realistic preview of the salient aspects of being the minority and different from the majority culture, which is what most expatriates experience in the host country.

We assume in this discussion that training involves building both process-oriented (general, applicable to many situations) and content-oriented (specific, applicable to a single situation) competencies. To the extent that training focuses exclusively on *content* rather than *process,* bicultural individuals (who have already learned to learn about another culture) may be ready to utilize the information received immediately, while monocultural individuals may not find it as useful because they have fewer of the process skills to make the content knowledge effective. Therefore, training is expected to differentially affect monocultural individuals' adjustment to life in another culture relative to that of bicultural individuals. Persons having greater bicultural life experiences and the resulting KSAOs will need less process-oriented cross-cultural training to be effective as expatriates, because to some degree, they enter pre-trained. Since biculturals already have process training, content-based training will be more effective for them than it will be for monoculturals.

> **Proposition 2a.** Process-oriented cross-cultural training will have a larger effect on the attainment of the KSAOs for those who do not have extensive bicultural life experiences than for those who do.

> **Proposition 2b.** Content-oriented training will be more effective for persons who are bicultural than for persons who are monocultural.

In support of these propositions, we note that the conflicting findings on the effects of previous expatriation on future assignments (Black 1991; Black & Gregersen 1991) may be partly due to the expatriate's failure to attain and retain the necessary KSAOs in the prior assignment and to the focus on content training and less focus on process training. This will be discussed further in a later section.

INTERACTION BETWEEN BICULTURAL COMPETENCE AND HOST COUNTRY ATTRIBUTES

Our model proposes that the beliefs, attitudes, and bicultural skills composing bicultural competency improve expatriate adjustment through their mediating impact on properties of host country interactions. The key attributes of host country interactions are: role conflict experienced by the expatriate, appropriateness of the expatriate's behavior, and frequency of expatriate interactions with host country nationals. Although each is an identifiable construct, they are partially overlapping. It would be difficult to change the level of one of these constructs without somehow affecting levels of the others. Many of these constructs are also new to the expatriate literature. Therefore, we will often support their connections to other parts of the model with logical arguments rather than evidence from previous studies. The antecedents of these properties of host country interactions are some combination of the six KSAOs or bicultural competencies discussed previously.

Role Conflict

Role conflict involves the incompatibility of two sets of expectations from other persons or groups (Kahn, Wolf, Quinn, Snoek, & Rosenthal 1964). The sources of incompatibility for expatriates are their own and the host country's values, customs and beliefs with respect to specific roles they may play in a country. Brislin et al. (1986, p. 279) noted that such roles are "culture-bound and determined by the community or culture at large." The more accepting expatriates are, the more they will be able to cope with different roles and expectations in the host country. The greater the bicultural self-efficacy possessed by expatriates, the more confidence they will have that potential role conflicts can be resolved satisfactorily. Brislin (1981) also noted that expatriate's ability to shift roles increases effectiveness, particularly when close collaboration with host country nationals is necessary. The broader the expatriates' role repertoire, the easier it will be for them to engage in various behaviors to avoid role conflict (Brislin et al. 1986).

Appropriateness

Appropriateness is a property of exhibited social behavior, defined in terms of the fit of one's behavior with the social expectations of others. For the expatriate, it specifically refers to knowledge and use of behaviors acceptable in the host country. We posit that appropriateness will be a function of all of the KSAOs or bicultural competencies. Appropriateness will be facilitated by general cultural awareness, which is previous social knowledge about what behaviors are expected. Those expatriates who have knowledge of the typical or normative behavior in host country's culture will also be more likely to exhibit it (Brislin et al. 1986). Appropriateness will also be affected by acceptance in the sense that those higher in acceptance will be more willing to engage in patterns of behavior that are appropriate to the host country, even when it is at odds with their conventional behavior. That is, one who is more willing to tolerate different behaviors will also be more likely to take part in them. Dual fluency could be described as specific knowledge about appropriate verbal and nonverbal communicative behaviors in the host country (Beamer 1992; Caudron 1991; McEnery & DesHarnais 1990; Shilling 1993). Bicultural self-efficacy will provide the confidence necessary for an individual to build an effective repertoire of behaviors appropriate to a second culture (LaFromboise et al. 1993). Having a broad (flexible) role repertoire has clear implications for the appropriateness of displayed behavior. The wider the variety of behaviors from which an expatriate can choose, the more likely he or she can adapt behavior to fit situation-specific expectations. As Brislin (1981) noted, expatriates who can judge themselves from others' point of view and modify their behavior accordingly have an advantage in intercultural interactions. In addition, the broader social support system implicit in the notion of groundedness will provide biculturally competent expatriates with more feedback on expected behavior, and will help them add to and "sharpen" their role repertoire (Black & Gregersen 1991).

Frequency

Frequency of interaction refers simply to how often expatriates engage in verbal or nonverbal communication with host country nationals. This frequency will be greater for those who have general cultural awareness and bicultural self-efficacy about those interactions. In general, the more self-efficacy that individuals have about their ability to perform a behavior, the more likely they are to engage in it (Bandura 1977). Dual fluency will affect frequency in that if expatriates are able to communicate effectively in the host country, the more likely they are to interact with host country nationals. On the other hand, if expatriates do not know how to communicate with host country nationals, they will be more reticent about engaging in interactions with them. Similarly, the more behaviors expatriates have at their disposal, the more likely they are to engage in those behaviors. Finally, the more persons expatriates have in their social support system, the more communication they will have with those persons.

In sum, an expatriate's possession of the KSAOs or bicultural competencies will lead to improved levels of attributes of host country interactions. That is,

> **Proposition 3.** A higher degree of bicultural competence will be associated with lowered role conflict, increased knowledge and enactment of behaviors appropriate to the host country, and increased frequency of interactions with host country nationals.

HOST COUNTRY CHARACTERISTICS

Clearly we do not wish to imply that as long as a person has achieved some level of bicultural competency, he or she will do well in any expatriate assignment. Instead, host country characteristics also have strong implications for expatriate effectiveness. The characteristics of the host country that effect our model include: cultural novelty, cultural toughness, and barriers to specific groups. Cultural novelty refers to the degree of difference of the country of expatriation from the expatriate's home country (Hofstede 1984; Naumann 1992). In his extensive work, Hofstede (1984) examined cultural differences on scales of power distance (valuation of power, prestige, and wealth), uncertainty avoidance (mechanisms for coping with uncertainty), individualism (relationship between individuals and the society), and masculinity (socialized sex roles). By examining those four areas, the degree of cultural novelty of the target host country to another country can be determined.

Cultural toughness or rigidity refers to the variation in behaviors that a culture allows, with a more culturally rigid country being harder to adjust to (Black et al. 1992). Hofstede (1984) noted that Africa, the Middle East, and the Far East were culturally "tough" for Americans, while Australia and New Zealand were less tough. Considerations of living conditions, social and cultural factors, and legal and political factors have been included in definitions of cultural novelty and/or toughness; however, there are no prescribed or all-inclusive dimensions (Naumann 1992).

Barriers to specific groups refers to generally recognized limitations placed on the behaviors and outcomes of certain members of a culture. These barriers might include overt or legally mandated prohibitions against employment of certain groups, or restrictions on the roles or positions members of certain groups may occupy, where they may live, whom they may marry, and so on. Such barriers also include covert or unofficial restrictions on the activities of certain group members.

Host country characteristics have three effects in the model. First, they affect the cross-cultural training practices of a firm. Cross-cultural trainers develop different role plays, culture assimilators, or realistic previews, dependent upon the characteristics of the host country (Fiedler et al. 1971; Tung 1984). Recently, many corporations have begun tailoring training programs to specific countries. For example, DuPont has developed training activities specific to expatriates heading to Asia and South America (Kitsuse 1992). Similarly, SAS Corporation's Intercultural Communications Center provides training for 65 different countries (Kitsuse 1992).

The second effect of host country characteristics is moderation of the link between KSAOs or bicultural competencies and attributes of host country interactions. We believe that levels of general cultural awareness, acceptance, bicultural self-efficacy, dual fluency, broad role repertoire, and groundedness will have a stronger effect on host country interactions in some countries than in others, depending on the degree of cultural toughness,novelty, and barriers to specific groups in the host country (Black & Mendenhall 1989; Feldman & Thomas 1992; Hofstede 1984; Mendenhall et al. 1987). In countries where social norms for patterns of behavior are more rigid, KSAOs or bicultural competencies will be *more* important than in countries where norms are more flexible. That is, culturally "tougher" countries will more quickly and consistently distinguish those having the requisite skills for host country interactions from those without them. A similar argument could be made for cultural novelty, with the impact of KSAOs or bicultural competencies on host country interactions being even stronger as a host country's culture deviates more from one's home country.

> **Proposition 4a.** The effect of KSAOs or bicultural competencies will be greater the more culturally novel or tough the host country is compared with an expatriate's home country.

In a different way, laws and long-standing cultural practices in some host countries may prohibit the use of certain minorities, nationalities, or women (Furnham & Bochner 1986). For instance, although the demise of apartheid in South Africa has reduced discrimination against persons of African descent to some extent, we would expect certain implicit and explicit barriers to still be in place there. Similarly, by some accounts, Koreans, Pakistanis, and African-Americans might encounter prejudice if expatriated to Japan (Fernandez &

Barr 1993). In such countries, we would expect the effects of bicultural competencies on expatriate adjustment to be null or considerably weaker than in other countries. While we acknowledge that there are probably some barriers to certain racial or ethnic minority groups *everywhere,* we believe that in particular countries, those barriers will be so severe that they may outweigh or neutralize any benefits of bicultural competencies or KSAOs that certain expatriates may have.

> **Proposition 4b.** In certain countries, the effects of bicultural competencies/KSAOs for successful expatriate performance will be negated by long-standing barriers to certain groups.

The third effect of host country characteristics in the model is a direct effect on the attributes of host country interactions. Different countries clearly have different patterns of interaction, for example, with respect to time and bodily contact (Dodd 1977). Some countries adhere to strict regulations about time and punctuality (for example, Japan), while others are more fluid with respect to time (for example, nations in Latin America: Furnham & Bochner 1986). While some countries allow for high physical contact between acquaintances and strangers, others allow limited contact between anyone but relatives or close friends (Furnham & Bochner 1986).

EXPATRIATE ADJUSTMENT

Adjustment is defined as the degree of psychological comfort felt regarding an expatriate's host country situation (Gregersen & Black 1990). Its dimensions, described by Black et al. (1991), are interaction, work, and general adjustment. Similarly, Brislin (1981) termed the three aspects defining "success" in an international assignment as interaction effectiveness, task effectiveness, and psychological adjustment. Consistent with these authors, we represent interaction, work, and general adjustment as major dimensions. We also believe that interaction adjustment is the most fundamental dimension of the three, as both work and general adjustment are based on interactions. Black et al. (1992, p. 119) also noted that adjustment to interacting with host country nationals is "generally the most difficult of the three adjustment dimensions."

Interaction Adjustment

Interaction adjustment is the expatriate's psychological comfort regarding interactions with host country nationals (Black et al. 1992). Brislin (1981) described the interaction component as involving warm and cordial relationships with host country nationals, participation in their activities, and development of respect for those activities. In their empirical study of over three hundred expatriates assigned to eight countries, Gregersen and Black (1990) found interaction adjustment was positively related to intent to stay. We believe that interaction adjustment is almost inevitable for expatriates who experience lowered role conflict and have appropriate and frequent interactions with host country nationals.

As discussed previously, role conflict results from incompatibilities between expectations from other persons or groups (Kahn et al. 1964). Uncertainties about one's role in a new culture may lead to stress, frustration, and anxiety for the newcomer (Parrillo 1985). Conversely, certainty and appropriateness of behavior in new settings lead to comfort, lack of stress, and psychological adjustment. Frequency of interaction with host country nationals in a social setting is one of the ways that expatriate newcomers become aware of appropriate behaviors there, as host country nationals may act as sources of information and help in understanding of the host country (Black & Gregersen 1991; Bochner 1981). An expatriate who has frequent interactions, exhibits appropriate behaviors, and experiences lowered role conflict in those interactions will adjust more rapidly to them. Feldman and Thomas (1992) noted that effective expatriates frequently interacted with host country nationals.

Work Adjustment

Work adjustment refers to the expatriate's psychological comfort felt regarding the job or tasks assigned (Black et al. 1992). Because work adjustment is often supported by common or similar policies and requirements in the home and host country operations, it may be the least difficult of the three dimensions (Black et al. 1992). Despite some similarities between home and host country operations, however, the "aspects of the corporate culture of the foreign operation . . . are dramatically different" and act to impact the expatriate's effectiveness (Black et al. 1992, p. 117). Role conflict, appropriateness, and frequency all affect expatriate work adjustment. Role conflict at work is clearly related to distress or psychological discomfort in that setting (Kahn et al. 1964), thus the connection in this model between role conflict and work adjustment.

We also posit that the appropriateness of an expatriate's behavior, again defined as the fit of behavior to the expectations of others, will strongly influence work adjustment, which is a psychological reaction to one's work. Organizational socialization is the process in which a newcomer learns appropriate behaviors and attitudes necessary for effectiveness in the organization (Morrison 1993). Black (1992) has argued that the experiences of a newcomer to a domestic organization are significantly different from those of an expatriate on assignment. They therefore require different socialization tactics and result in different outcomes than would be expected from a domestic new hire. Nonetheless, expatriates undergo socialization tactics as part of the process of learning appropriate behaviors and adjustment to a new work situation. Their adjustment is affected by their success in learning appropriate on-the-job behaviors. Black et al. (1992) described a situation in which an engineer in the U.S. might, as normal practice, interview end-users of a proposed computer program regarding requirements. While that request might generate useful feedback in the U.S., in a country such as India, end-users may be unaccustomed to such inquiries. In that case, soliciting input would be inappropriate behavior on the job and might be frustrating to the engineer.

With respect to frequency, Feldman and Thomas (1992, p. 286) found it was important to "get to know the host nationals well." They also found the effective expatriates were those "more willing to get involved in activities that bring them into contact with other people" (Feldman & Thomas 1992, p. 287). We posit that the more frequent an expatriate's interaction with host country nationals at work, the more quickly and thoroughly he or she will develop an understanding of the work requirements and expected behaviors there.

General Adjustment

Black et al. (1992) described general adjustment as including an expatriate's psychological comfort with non-work factors, including food, transportation, entertainment, and health care in the host country. In an example of (dis)comfort regarding food in a host country, Black et al. (1992) described a situation in which an expatriate family in Japan chose a fresh fish dinner, but lost their appetites because of the freshness of the fish. Although its body was sliced and prepared, the fish was still alive (Black et al. 1992). Such experiences in a host country may result in psychological discomfort, frustration, and anxiety.

As for work adjustment, general adjustment is strongly influenced by the attributes of host country interactions, specifically by the frequency of those interactions and the appropriateness of behaviors an expatriate exhibits. Inappropriate behaviors in the host country are more likely to result in negative outcomes, leading the expatriate to make incorrect external attributions about the host country culture, and therefore to further withdraw from it (Brislin et al. 1986). An expatriate who has frequent interactions with host country nationals will be less surprised and frustrated by the differences in the non-work factors inside the host country. On the other hand, an expatriate who has less frequent interactions or is isolated from the host country's culture (for instance, by remaining completely in expatriate housing) might retain much of his or her conventional behavior patterns and fail to adjust to that culture. In sum, having improved levels of attributes of host country interactions will lead to greater expatriate adjustment. Specifically,

> **Proposition 5.** Experiencing lowered role conflict, using more appropriate behaviors, and having more frequent interactions with host country nationals will facilitate expatriate interaction, work, and general adjustment.

Recursive Effect of Adjustment

Black and Gregersen (1991) found no relationship between previous international experience and adjustment. Black et al. (1991, p. 294) however, noted that "previous overseas experience does seem to facilitate the adjustment process," although the exact process of facilitation has not been determined. These conflicting conclusions emphasize the importance of long-term intercultural experience, in particular, the development of bicultural competence, which may be more transferable, enduring, and generalizable to other cultures (c.f. Church 1982). In keeping with this notion and indicated by the feedback loop in Figure 2, we propose that expatriate adjustment leads to the acquisition of more of the skills required for future expatriate effectiveness, and to greater levels of bicultural competencies. Consistent with research findings on self-efficacy (c.f. Gist & Mitchell 1992), we believe that the effect of a successful expatriation is a greater sense of bicultural self-efficacy, which will increase an expatriate's confidence about future intercultural interactions and his or her general cultural awareness, acceptance, and acquisition of the other necessary skills. Likewise, an early return or poor adjustment to an assignment is likely to preclude an expatriate from taking the extra effort needed to build new KSAOs or bicultural competencies, or from accepting a future expatriate assignment.

> **Proposition 6.** Expatriate adjustment will lead to further and future development of bicultural competencies.

DISCUSSION

Implications for Research

Future research should further explore the impact of cross-cultural training on bicultural expatriates and the costs of such training. We have proposed that cross-cultural training required for persons already skilled in bicultural interactions will be less costly and lengthy than training of monocultural individuals. Without minimizing the importance of such savings in training costs, they might well be overshadowed by the savings resulting from decreased expatriate failures if biculturally competent individuals are selected for expatriation. Investigation of the utility of selecting bicultural expatriates should be of interest to both researchers and practitioners.

Provide for coherent tests of the present model and its propositions, measures for some of the constructs need to be developed and refined. A generally accepted instrument for the measurement of biculturalism is sorely needed. Measure of the depth and breadth of bicultural life experiences might include questions about: the percentage of work and social time spent interacting with persons of different races or ethnic backgrounds, the racial or ethnic composition of one's neighborhood, workplace, or school environment, the number of languages spoken, method of learning them, and frequency of speaking them, and other similar items. Measures do exist for general cultural awareness and cultural knowledge (Fiedler et al. 1971), but acceptance, bicultural self-efficacy, dual fluency, broad role repertoire, and groundedness are all constructs that need instrumentation. For the attributes of host country interactions, role conflict and frequency can be measured with relative ease. Measurement of appropriateness will be more difficult, but methods similar to those employed with culture assimilators are recommended as a starting point. Black and Gregersen (1991) have developed and refined measures of expatriate adjustment.

For the host country characteristics, Hofstede (1984) has developed measures for determining the degree of cultural novelty and toughness. Barriers to specific groups would require testing on a country-by-country basis, and should consider the legal and historical parameters of the country. It would involve a thorough examination of both official and unofficial policies regarding treatment of ethnic minorities within the culture. For example, the Japanese do not recognize those of Korean descent as potentially holding full citizenship in Japan. This would be one element that could potentially be one of several different markers of barriers to specific groups in that country. On the other hand, countries that have adopted affirmative action legislation, at least officially, are attempting to reduce barriers to specific groups.

Managerial Implications and Recommendations

Stone (1991) recommended that MNCs develop procedures specifically for international selection instead of relying on procedures developed for domestic selection. Mendenhall et al. (1987, p. 334) noted that HRM has consistently overlooked "key criteria that are predictive of overseas success in their recruiting and screening of potential overseas workers." An implication of the present model for international HRM selection is that managers should strongly consider including bicultural life experiences or more directly, *bicultural competencies,* in the selection process. Rather than targeting groups of people on the basis of ethnic background, however, managers should attempt to select individuals who have learned and can generalize from their bicultural experiences.

Just as some members of majority ethnic groups may have some bicultural life experiences, not all ethnic minority members will have extensive bicultural experiences. Those ethnic minorities who live, work, and primarily interact with similar persons will not have developed significantly greater skills in intercultural interaction than ethnic majorities who live, work, and primarily interact with similar persons will have developed. That is, bicultural competence is a multidimensional and continuous, rather than dichotomous, construct (LaFromboise et al. 1993; Yancey, Eriksen, & Juliani 1976). Different persons will possess and manifest different levels. It is therefore important that organizations assess the levels of these important latent constructs rather than focus merely on overt indicators such as race or country of origin.

Literature notes that some U.S. companies have begun hiring foreign students who have been educated in U.S. institutions for positions in their native country's operations (Tung 1984). The expatriation of bicultural individuals to the culture of their competence could be similarly beneficial, with less risk to and less investment for the corporation. For example, the expatriation of bicultural Japanese American employees to Japan may increase their success in adjustment there. Expatriation of Hispanic Americans employees to Latin American cultures could be advantageous as well. This, however, is utilization of the bicultural's culture-specific knowledge rather than his or her non-specific, generalizable bicultural competence.

Limitations

One limitation of our model is that we did not include all possible influences on expatriate adjustment. Instead, we have focused on those influences that may flow from the individual experiences that a bicultural expatriate brings to the overseas assignment. We incorporated other variables when we believed they had a mediating or moderating effect on the flow of those constructs. We do not expect that bicultural life experiences will completely determine how well an expatriate adjusts. There are other variables, including organizational variables such as social support and logistical help, job related variables such as role clarity and novelty, and so on, that are only partly subsumed by what we have discussed here (Black et al. 1991).

Our concentration on the bicultural life experiences of ethnic minorities could also be considered a limitation of this model and its exposition. As ethnic minorities have been shown to be more often biculturally competent than ethnic majority members (Cox et al. 1991), and as there is more literature on the biculturalism of ethnic minorities, this article has discussed bicultural competence primarily in reference to ethnic minority members. It is noted however, consistent with LaFromboise et al. (1993), that it is *individuals,* rather than groups, who are or may become biculturally competent. In keeping with that point, we note that some ethnic majority members may be bicultural as well. Although there is evidence that they do not typically develop bicultural competence in particular studies (c.f. Cox et al. 1991; Garza et al. 1982), it is important to note that an ethnic majority member who has lived, worked, and interacted with ethnic minorities for extended periods could be biculturally competent and could use the same bicultural competencies in international assignments as ethnic minorities would use.

Further, while many of our citations have referenced U.S. based MNCs and expatriates, our propositions are not limited to them. On the contrary, anyone who has experienced being an ethnic minority in any nation and who has developed the bicultural competencies to deal with it, could use these attributes. For example, bicultural Hispanic Americans or African-Americans could serve as expatriates from the United States. Bicultural Asians living in Canada could be expatriated from Canada, and so on. Furnham and Bochner (1986), citing Pearce and Catabiano (1982), noted that "Italio-Austrians" were bicultural, having learned communication skills of both countries, while "Anglo-Austrians", being primarily exposed to the dominant group, were monocultural, having learned only one communication code.

It is also important to note that although we have discussed bicultural life experiences primarily with respect to racial or ethnic minorities, other, *non-ethnic* minority groups may possess some of these attributes as well. Non-ethnic minority groups—such as women in some fields, or the visibly physically disabled—may have developed analogs of these bicultural competencies, assuming their differences were salient enough for them to have developed to help adjust to interactions with dissimilar others. The greater suitability of women for international assignments has been proposed by other researchers

(Adler & Izraeli 1988; Tung 1984), who cited their specific differences from the typical majority male expatriate. We reiterate that the *process* of learning to interact well and consistently with significantly different others is very important. However, the effect of learning to interact well with persons of *different cultures* is one factor that separates intercultural interactions from inter-gender or other interactions, which may involve fewer important and salient differences between persons.

Finally, this theory does not apply to expatriates who are isolated from the host country and its nationals. For example, some expatriates live and work in cloistered communities or "compounds" comprised of few, if any, host country nationals. Such a situation could be likened to an aircraft carrier stationed in a foreign country. It houses several thousand people from its country of origin and has all the necessary facilities on board. While the sailors aboard it would be technically expatriated, they would not be experiencing life in the host country or interactions with host country nationals. Therefore, the specific competencies discussed in this article would not apply.

CONCLUSION

The changing demographic composition of the United States has heightened the need to best utilize and manage diversity for maximizing employee and corporate potential. Similarly, increased globalization of corporations and subsequent requirements for intercultural interactions are compelling researchers and practitioners seek to improve the effectiveness of those interactions. Tung (1993) has suggested that many of the similarities in processes and dynamics of managing diversity in cross-national and intra-national contexts might be used to tap into the unleashed potential of employees. We have proposed that the process of having developed bicultural competencies is one such similarity that may be generalized to international intercultural interactions to improve expatriate effectiveness. Within that general proposal are the three contributions of this article to the international, HRM, and organizational behavior literatures.

The first contribution is a re-emphasis of the importance of selection mechanisms for expatriates, in addition to the current focus on training those chosen to be expatriates. We have demonstrated the need to select those who have or will develop the KSAOs needed for effectively interacting, working, and living with persons of other cultures, as well as to continue cross-cultural training of those KSAOs. This merging of domestic and international HRM literatures addresses a void in expatriate selection procedures that researchers have repeatedly suggested needs addressing (Black et al. 1991; Tung 1981, 1984). Tung (1982, p. 57) specifically stated it was "imperative that researchers and practitioners in the field of *selection and* training for expatriate assignment understand the means for reducing failure and poor performance" (emphasis added). We believe bicultural life experiences and especially bicultural competencies are relevant criteria that will reduce expatriate "failure and poor performance in overseas assignments" via the intervening mechanism of improving the qualities of interactions with host country nationals.

The second contribution is our integration of research on bicultural life experiences with research on the experiences of expatriates. General cultural awareness, acceptance, bicultural efficacy, dual fluency, broad role repertoire and groundedness are attitudes and skills of biculturally competent individuals that are also requirements for expatriate effectiveness. Recognition of these parallels provides for further exploration and integration of these concepts. To guide research on these parallels, we have also presented a conceptual model specifying the links to and from these bicultural competencies, including testable propositions about the moderating and mediating effects of cross-cultural training and host country interactions.

The third major contribution of this article is to bring an important area to the research community through which expatriate adjustment and success may be increased. Given the increasing need for international effectiveness, awareness of areas for improvement is vital. Selection of more biculturally competent people as expatriates is a clear example of how the skills of bicultural persons in operating between *intra*-national cultures might help to improve organizational success in *inter*-national intercultural relations.

ACKNOWLEDGMENTS

This article is a revised version of a paper originally presented at the 1994 National Academy of Management meetings where Zaida Martinez, Ken Marino, and Dan Ondrack provided insightful comments. The authors are especially grateful to Abdul Rasheed for stimulating initial ideas and to Kenneth Price, Margaret Shaffer, Iris Perkins, and Alison Konrad for helpful suggestions. Natalie Harris provided invaluable assistance on an earlier draft of the model.

REFERENCES

Adler, N. and D. Izareli. 1988. *Women in Management Worldwide*. Armonk, NY: M.E. Sharpe.

Albert, R. D. 1986. "Conceptual Framework for the Development and Evaluation of Cross-Cultural Orientation Programs." *International Journal of Intercultural Relations* 10: 197–213.

Bandura, A. 1977. *Social Learning Theory*. Englewood Cliffs, NJ: Prentice-Hall.

Beamer, L. 1992. "Learning Intercultural Communication Competence." *Journal of Business Communications* 29: 285–303.

Bell, E. L. 1990. "The Bicultural Life Experience of Career-Oriented Black Women." *Journal of Organizational Behavior* 11: 459–477.

Black, J. S. and H. Gregersen. 1991. "The Other Half of the Picture: Antecedents of Spouse Cross-Cultural Adjustment." *Journal of International Business Studies* 22: 461–477.

Black, J. S., H. B. Gregersen and M. E. Mendenhall. 1992. *Global Assignments*. San Francisco: Jossy-Bass.

Black, J. S. and M. Mendenhall. 1989. "A Practical But Theory-Based Framework for Selecting Cross-Cultural Training Methods." *Human Resource Management* 28: 511–539.

______. 1990. "Cross-Cultural Training Effectiveness: A Review and a Theoretical Framework for Future Research." *Academy of Management Review* 15: 113–136.

Black, J. S., M. Mendenhall and G. Oddou. 1991. "Toward a Comprehensive Model of International Adjustment: An Integration of Multiple Theoretical Perspectives." *Academy of Management Review* 16: 291–317.

Bochner, S. (ed.) 1981. *The Mediating Person: Bridges Between Cultures*. Cambridge, MA: Schenkman.

Brislin, R. W. 1981. *Cross-Cultural Encounters*. New York: Pergamon.

Brislin, R. W., K. Cushner, C. Cherrie, and M. Yong. 1986. *Intercultural Interactions*. Beverly Hills: Sage.

Caudron, S. 1991. "Training Ensures Success Overseas." *Personnel Journal* 70(12): 27–30.

Church, A. T. 1982. "Sojourner Adjustment." *Psychological Bulletin* 91: 540–572.

Cogdell, R. and S. Wilson. 1980. *Black Communication in White Society*. Saratoga, CA: Century Twenty One.

Cook, R. A. and J. Herche. 1992. "Assessment Centers: An Untapped Resource for Global Salesforce Management." *Journal of Personal Selling & Sales Management* 12(3): 31–38.

Cox, T., S. A. Lobel, and P. L. McLeod. 1991. "Effects of Ethnic Group Cultural Differences on Cooperative and Competitive Behavior on a Group Task." *Academy of Management Journal* 34: 827–847.

Cox, T. and S. Nkomo. 1990. "Invisible Men and Women: A Status Report on Race as a Variable in Organization Behavior Research." *Journal of Organizational Behavior* 11: 419–431.

Datta, D. K. and A. M. Rasheed. 1993. "Planning International Joint Ventures: The Role of Human Resource Management." In *Multinational Strategic Alliances,* edited by R. Culpan. New York: The Haworth Press.

Dodd, C. 1977. *Perspectives on Cross-Cultural Communication*. Dubuque, IA: Kendall/Hunt.

DuBois, W. E. B. 1903. *The Souls of Black Folk*. New York: The New American Library.

Fiedler, F. E., T. Mitchell, and H. Triandis. 1971. "The Culture Assimilator: An Approach to Cross-Cultural Training." *Journal of Applied Psychology* 55(2): 95–102.

Feldman, D. and D. Thomas. 1992. "Career Management Issues Facing Expatriates." *Journal of International Business Studies* 23: 271–293.

Fernandez, J. P. and M. Barr. 1993. *The Diversity Advantage*. New York: Lexington.

Fordham, S. 1988. "Racelessness as a Factor in Black Students' School Success: Pragmatic Strategy or Pyrrhic Victory." *Harvard Educational Review* 58: 54–84.

Furnham, A. and S. Bochner. 1986. *Culture Shock: Psychological Reactions to Unfamiliar Environments*. New York: Metheuen & Co.

Garza, R. T., G. J. Romero, B. G. Cox, and M. Ramirez, III. 1982. "Biculturalism, Locus of Control, and Leader Behavior in Ethnically Mixed Small Groups." *Journal of Applied Social Psychology* 12: 237–253.

Gillmor, D. and S. K. Doig. 1992. "Segregation Forever?" *American Demographics* 14: 48–51.

Gist, M. E. and T. R. Mitchell. 1992. "Self-Efficacy: A Theoretical Analysis of Its Determinants and Malleability." *Academy of Management Review* 17: 183–211.

Gregersen, H. B. and J. S. Black. 1990. "A Multi-Faceted Approach to Expatriate Retention in International Assignments." *Group and Organization Studies* 15: 461–485.

Hait, A. G. 1982. "Employee Benefits in the Global Economy." *Benefits Quarterly* 8: 21–27.

Harris, P. 1979. "The Unhappy World of the Expatriate." *International Management* (July): 49–50.

Harrison, J. K. 1992. "Individual and Combined Effects of Behavior Modeling and the Cultural Assimilator in Cross-Cultural Management Training." *Journal of Applied Psychology* 77: 952–962.

Harvey, M. G. 1983. "The Multinational Corporation's Expatriate Problem: An Application of Murphy's Law." *Business Horizons* 26: 71–78.

———. 1985. "The Executive Family: An Overlooked Variable in International Assignments." *Columbia Journal of World Business* (Spring): 84–93.

Herbert, J. I. 1990. "Integrating Race and Adult Psychosocial Development." *Journal of Organizational Behavior* 11: 433–446.

Hofstede, G. 1984. *Culture's Consequences: International Differences in Work Related Values*. Beverly Hills: Sage.

Kahn, R. L., D. M. Wolfe, R. Quinn, J. D. Snoek, and R. A. Rosenthal. 1964. *Organizational Stress*. New York: Wiley.

Kitsuse, A. 1992. "At Home Abroad." *Across the Board* 29(9): 35–38.

Konrad, A. M., S. Winter, and B. A. Gutek. 1992. "Diversity in Work Group Sex Composition: Implications for Majority and Minority Members." *Research in the Sociology of Organizations* 10: 115–140.

LaFromboise, T., H. L. K. Coleman, and J. Gerton. 1993. "Psychological Impact of Biculturalism: Evidence and Theory." *Psychological Bulletin* 114: 395–412.

McCaffery, J. A. 1986. "Independent Effectiveness: A Reconsideration of Cross-Cultural Orientation and Training." *International Journal of Intercultural Relations* 10: 159–177.

McEnery, J. and G. DesHarnais. 1990. "Culture Shock." *Training and Development Journal* 44: 43–47.

McGuire, W. J., C. V. McGuire, P. Child, and T. Fujiota. 1978. "Salience of Ethnicity in the Spontaneous Self-Concept as a Function of One's Ethnic Distinctiveness in the Social Environment." *Journal of Personality and Social Psychology* 36: 511–520.

Mendenhall, M., E. Dunbar, and G. Oddou. 1987. "Expatriate Selection, Training, and Career Pathing: A Review and Critique." *Human Resource Management* 26: 331–345.

Mendenhall, M. and G. Oddou. 1985. "The Determinants of Expatriate Acculturation." *Academy of Management Review* 10: 39–47.

Morrison, E. W. 1993. "Longitudinal Study of the Effects of Information Seeking on Newcomer Socialization." *Journal of Applied Psychology* 78(2): 173–183.

Napier, N. and R. Peterson. 1992. "Expatriate Re-Entry: What Do Repatriates Have to Say?" *Human Resource Planning* 14: 19–28.

Naumann, E. 1992. "A Conceptual Model of Expatriate Turnover." *Journal of International Business Studies* 23(3): 499–531.

Niyekawa-Howard, A. M. 1970. "Biculturality and Cognitive Growth: Theoretical Foundations for Basic and Applied Research." Paper Number 1, July, East-West Center.

Parrillo, V. N. 1985. *Strangers to These Shores: Race and Ethnic Relations in the United States*. Boston: Houghton Mifflin.

Polgar, S. 1960. "Biculturation of Mesquakie Teenage Boys." *American Anthropologist* 62: 217–235.

Ramirez, M., B. G., Cox, R. Garza, and A. Casteneda. 1977. "Dimensions of Biculturalism in Mexican-American College Students." Technical report prepared for Organizational Effectiveness Research Programs, Office of Naval Research, Arlington, VA.

Schmitt, N., R. Z. Gooding, R. A. Noe, and M. P. Kirsch. 1984. "Meta-Analyses of Validity Studies Published Between 1964 and 1982 and the Investigation of Study Characteristics." *Personnel Psychology* 37: 407–422.

Shilling, M. 1993. "Avoid Expatriate Culture Shock." *HRMagazine* 38(7): 58–63.

Sikkema, M. and A. Niyekawa. 1987. *Design for Cross-Cultural Learning*. Yarmouth, ME: Intercultural Press.

Singelis, T. 1994. "Nonverbal Communication in Intercultural Interactions." In *Improving Intercultural Interactions,* edited by R. W. Brislin and I. Yoshida. Thousand Oaks, CA: Sage.

Sung, B. L. 1985. "Bicultural Conflicts in Chinese Immigrant Children." *Journal of Comparative Family Studies* 16(2): 255–269.

Thornton, G. C. 1992. *Assessment Centers in Human Resource Management*. Reading, MA: Addison-Wesley.

Tsui, A. S., T. D. Egan, and C. A. O'Reilly, III. 1992. "Being Different: Relational Demography and Organizational Attachment." *Administrative Science Quarterly* 37: 549–579.

Tung, R. L. 1981. "Selection and Training of Personnel for Overseas Assignments." *Columbia Journal of World Business* (Spring): 68–78.

———. 1982. "Selection and Training Procedures of U.S., European, and Japanese Multinationals." *California Management Review* 25: 57–71.

———. 1984. "Strategic Management of Human Resources in the Multinational Enterprise." *Human Resource Management* 23: 129–143.

———. 1988. "Career Issues in International Assignments." *Academy of Management Executive* 11: 241–244.

———. 1993. "Managing Cross-National and Intra-National Diversity." *Human Resource Management* 32: 461–477.

Valentine, C. A. 1971. "Deficit, Difference, and Bicultural Models of Afro-American Behavior." *Harvard Educational Review* 41(2): 137–157.

Wharton, A. S. and J. N. Baron. 1987. "So Happy Together? The Impact of Gender Segregation on Men at Work." *American Sociological Review* 52: 574–587.

Winsbury, R. 1989. "Diary of an Expat." *Management Today* (December): 64–69.

Yancey, W. L., E. P. Eriksen, and R. N. Juliani. 1976. "Emergent Ethnicity: A Review and Reformation." *American Sociological Review* 41: 391–403.

Part VII
Ethics and Corporate Social Responsibility in Cross-Cultural Context

[39]

When is different just different, and when is different wrong?

Values in Tension:

by Thomas Donaldson

When we leave home and cross our nation's boundaries, moral clarity often blurs. Without a backdrop of shared attitudes, and without familiar laws and judicial procedures that define standards of ethical conduct, certainty is elusive. Should a company invest in a foreign country where civil and political rights are violated? Should a company go along with a host country's discriminatory employment practices? If companies in developed countries shift facilities to developing nations that lack strict environmental and health regulations, or if those companies choose to fill management and other top-level positions in a host nation with people from the home country, whose standards should prevail?

Even the best-informed, best-intentioned executives must rethink their assumptions about business practice in foreign settings. What works in a company's home country can fail in a country with different standards of ethical conduct. Such difficulties are unavoidable for businesspeople who live and work abroad.

But how can managers resolve the problems? What are the principles that can help them work through the maze of cultural differences and establish codes of conduct for globally ethical business practice? How can companies answer the toughest question in global business ethics: What happens when a host country's ethical standards seem lower than the home country's?

Competing Answers

One answer is as old as philosophical discourse. According to cultural relativism, no culture's ethics are better than any other's; therefore there are no international rights and wrongs. If the people of Indonesia tolerate the bribery of their public officials, so what? Their attitude is no better or worse than that of people in Denmark or Singapore who refuse to offer or accept bribes. Likewise, if Belgians fail to find insider trading morally repugnant, who cares? Not enforcing insider-trading laws is no more or less ethical than enforcing such laws.

The cultural relativist's creed – When in Rome, do as the Romans do – is tempting, especially when failing to do as the locals do means forfeiting business opportunities. The inadequacy of cultural relativism, however, becomes apparent when the practices in question are more damaging than petty bribery or insider trading.

In the late 1980s, some European tanneries and pharmaceutical companies were looking for cheap waste-dumping sites. They approached virtually every country on Africa's west coast from Morocco to the Congo. Nigeria agreed to take highly toxic polychlorinated biphenyls. Unprotected local workers, wearing thongs and shorts, unloaded barrels of PCBs and placed them near a residential area. Neither the residents nor the workers knew that the barrels contained toxic waste.

We may denounce governments that permit such abuses, but many countries are unable to police transnational corporations adequately even if they want to. And in many countries, the combination of ineffective enforcement and inadequate regulations leads to behavior by unscrupulous companies that is clearly wrong. A few years ago, for example, a group of investors became interested in restoring the SS *United States*, once a luxurious ocean liner. Before the actual restoration could begin, the ship had to be stripped of its asbestos lining. A bid from a U.S. company, based on U.S. standards for asbestos removal, priced the job

DRAWINGS BY MICHAEL REAGAN

Ethics Away from Home

at more than $100 million. A company in the Ukrainian city of Sevastopol offered to do the work for less than $2 million. In October 1993, the ship was towed to Sevastopol.

A cultural relativist would have no problem with that outcome, but I do. A country has the right to establish its own health and safety regulations, but in the case described above, the standards and the terms of the contract could not possibly have protected workers in Sevastopol from the known health risks. Even if the contract met Ukrainian standards, ethical business people must object. Cultural relativism is morally blind. There are fundamental values that cross cultures, and companies must uphold them. (For an economic argument against cultural relativism , see the insert "The Culture and Ethics of Software Piracy.")

At the other end of the spectrum from cultural relativism is ethical imperialism, which directs people to do everywhere exactly as they do at home. Again, an understandably appealing approach but one that is clearly inadequate. Consider the large U.S. computer products company that in 1993 introduced a course on sexual harassment in its Saudi Arabian facility. Under the banner of global consistency, instructors used the same approach to train Saudi Arabian managers that they had used with U.S. managers: the participants were asked to discuss a case in which a manager makes sexually explicit remarks to a new female employee over drinks in a bar. The instructors failed to consider how the exercise would work in a culture with strict conventions governing relationships between men and women. As a result, the training sessions were ludicrous. They baffled and offended the Saudi participants, and the message to avoid coercion and sexual discrimination was lost.

The theory behind ethical imperialism is absolutism, which is based on three problematic principles. Absolutists believe that there is a single list of truths, that they can be expressed only with one set of concepts, and that they call for exactly the same behavior around the world.

The first claim clashes with many people's belief that different cultural traditions must be respected. In some cultures, loyalty to a community – family, organization, or society – is the foundation of all ethical behavior. The Japanese, for example, define business ethics in terms of loyalty to their companies, their business networks, and their nation. Americans place a higher value on liberty than on loyalty; the U.S. tradition of rights emphasizes equality, fairness, and individual freedom. It is hard to conclude that truth lies on one side or the other, but an absolutist would have us select just one.

The second problem with absolutism is the presumption that people must express moral truth using only one set of concepts. For instance, some absolutists insist that the language of basic rights provide the framework for any discussion of

continued on page 52

Thomas Donaldson is a professor at the Wharton School of the University of Pennsylvania in Philadelphia, where he teaches business ethics. He wrote The Ethics of International Business *(Oxford University Press, 1989) and is the coauthor, with Thomas W. Dunfee, of* Business Ethics as Social Contracts, *to be published by the Harvard Business School Press in the fall of 1997.*

The Culture and Ethics of Software Piracy

Before jumping on the cultural relativism bandwagon, stop and consider the potential economic consequences of a when-in-Rome attitude toward business ethics. Take a look at the current statistics on software piracy: In the United States, pirated software is estimated to be 35% of the total software market, and industry losses are estimated at $2.3 billion per year. The piracy rate is 57% in Germany and 80% in Italy and Japan; the rates in most Asian countries are estimated to be nearly 100%.

There are similar laws against software piracy in those countries. What, then, accounts for the differences? Although a country's level of economic development plays a large part, culture, including ethical attitudes, may be a more crucial factor. The 1995 annual report of the Software Publishers Association connects software piracy directly to culture and attitude. It describes Italy and Hong Kong as having "'first world' per capita incomes, along with 'third world' rates of piracy." When asked whether one should use software without paying for it, most people, including people in Italy and Hong Kong, say no. But people in some countries regard the practice as *less* unethical than people in other countries do. Confucian culture, for example, stresses that individuals should share what they create with society. That may be, in part, what prompts the Chinese and other Asians to view the concept of intellectual property as a means for the West to monopolize its technological superiority.

What happens if ethical attitudes around the world permit large-scale software piracy? Software companies won't want to invest as much in developing new products, because they cannot expect any return on their investment in certain parts of the world. When ethics fail to support technological creativity, there are consequences that go beyond statistics – jobs are lost and livelihoods jeopardized.

Companies must do more than lobby foreign governments for tougher enforcement of piracy laws. They must cooperate with other companies and with local organizations to help citizens understand the consequences of piracy and to encourage the evolution of a different ethic toward the practice.

ethics. That means, though, that entire cultural traditions must be ignored. The notion of a right evolved with the rise of democracy in post-Renaissance Europe and the United States, but the term is not found in either Confucian or Buddhist traditions. We all learn ethics in the context of our particular cultures, and the power in the principles is deeply tied to the way in which they are expressed. Internationally accepted lists of moral principles, such as the United Nations' Universal Declaration of Human Rights, draw on many cultural and religious traditions. As philosopher Michael Walzer has noted, "There is no Esperanto of global ethics."

The third problem with absolutism is the belief in a global standard of ethical behavior. Context must shape ethical practice. Very low wages, for example, may be considered unethical in rich, advanced countries, but developing nations may be acting ethically if they encourage investment and improve living standards by accepting low wages. Likewise, when people are malnourished or starving, a government may be wise to use more fertilizer in order to improve crop yields, even though that means settling for relatively high levels of thermal water pollution.

When cultures have different standards of ethical behavior – and different ways of handling unethical behavior – a company that takes an absolutist approach may find itself making a disastrous mistake. When a manager at a large U.S. specialty-products company in China caught an employee stealing, she followed the company's practice and turned the employee over to the provincial authorities, who executed him. Managers cannot operate in another culture without being aware of that culture's attitudes toward ethics.

If companies can neither adopt a host country's ethics nor extend the home country's standards, what is the answer? Even the traditional litmus test – What would people think of your actions if they were written up on the front page of the newspaper? – is an unreliable guide, for there is no international consensus on standards of business conduct.

Balancing the Extremes: Three Guiding Principles

Companies must help managers distinguish between practices that are merely different and those that are wrong. For relativists, nothing is sacred and nothing is wrong. For absolutists, many things that are different are wrong. Neither extreme illuminates the real world of business decision making. The answer lies somewhere in between.

When it comes to shaping ethical behavior, companies must be guided by three principles.

- Respect for core human values, which determine the absolute moral threshold for all business activities.
- Respect for local traditions.
- The belief that context matters when deciding what is right and what is wrong.

Consider those principles in action. In Japan, people doing business together often exchange gifts – sometimes expensive ones – in keeping with long-standing Japanese tradition. When U.S. and European companies started doing a lot of business in Japan, many Western businesspeople thought that the practice of gift giving might be wrong rather than simply different. To them, accepting a gift felt like accepting a bribe. As Western companies have become more familiar with Japanese traditions, however, most have come to tolerate the practice and to set different limits on gift giving in Japan than they do elsewhere.

Respecting differences is a crucial ethical practice. Research shows that management ethics differ among cultures; respecting those differences means recognizing that some cultures have obvious weaknesses – as well as hidden strengths. Managers in Hong Kong, for example, have a higher tolerance for some forms of bribery than their Western counterparts, but they have a much lower tolerance for the failure to acknowledge a subordinate's work. In some parts of the Far East, stealing credit from a subordinate is nearly an unpardonable sin.

People often equate respect for local traditions with cultural relativism. That is incorrect. Some practices are clearly wrong. Union Carbide's tragic experience in Bhopal, India, provides one example. The company's executives seriously underestimated how much on-site management involvement was needed at the Bhopal plant to compensate for the country's poor infrastructure and regulatory capabilities. In the aftermath of the disastrous gas leak, the lesson is clear: companies using sophisticated technology in a developing country must evaluate that country's ability to oversee its safe use. Since the incident at Bhopal, Union Carbide has become a leader in advising companies on using hazardous technologies safely in developing countries.

Some activities are wrong no matter where they take place. But some practices that are unethical in one setting may be acceptable in another. For instance, the chemical EDB, a soil fungicide, is banned for use in the United States. In hot climates, however, it quickly becomes harmless through exposure to intense solar radiation and high soil temperatures. As long as the chemical is monitored, companies may be able to use EDB ethically in certain parts of the world.

What Do These Values Have in Common?

Non-Western	Western
Kyosei (Japanese): Living and working together for the common good.	Individual liberty
Dharma (Hindu): The fulfillment of inherited duty.	Egalitarianism
Santutthi (Buddhist): The importance of limited desires.	Political participation
Zakat (Muslim): The duty to give alms to the Muslim poor.	Human rights

Defining the Ethical Threshold: Core Values

Few ethical questions are easy for managers to answer. But there are some hard truths that must guide managers' actions, a set of what I call *core human values*, which define minimum ethical standards for all companies.[1] The right to good health and the right to economic advancement and an improved standard of living are two core human values. Another is what Westerners call the Golden Rule, which is recognizable in every major religious and ethical tradition around the world. In Book 15 of his *Analects*, for instance, Confucius counsels people to maintain reciprocity, or not to do to others what they do not want done to themselves.

Although no single list would satisfy every scholar, I believe it is possible to articulate three core values that incorporate the work of scores of theologians and philosophers around the world. To be broadly relevant, these values must include elements found in both Western and non-Western cultural and religious traditions. Consider the examples of values in the insert "What Do These Values Have in Common?"

At first glance, the values expressed in the two lists seem quite different. Nonetheless, in the spirit of what philosopher John Rawls calls *overlapping consensus*, one can see that the seemingly divergent values converge at key points. Despite important differences between Western and non-Western cultural and religious traditions, both express shared attitudes about what it means to be human. First, individuals must not treat others simply as tools; in other words, they must recognize a person's value as a human being. Next, individuals and communities must treat people in ways that respect people's basic rights. Finally, members of a community must work together to support and improve the institutions on which the community depends. I call those three values *respect for human dignity, respect for basic rights,* and *good citizenship.*

Those values must be the starting point for all companies as they formulate and evaluate standards of ethical conduct at home and abroad. But they are only a starting point. Companies need much more specific guidelines, and the first step to developing those is to translate the core human values into core values for business. What does it mean, for example, for a company to respect human dignity? How can a company be a good citizen?

I believe that companies can respect human dignity by creating and sustaining a corporate culture in which employees, customers, and suppliers are treated not as means to an end but as people whose intrinsic value must be acknowledged, and by producing safe products and services in a safe workplace. Companies can respect basic rights by acting in ways that support and protect the individual rights of employees, customers, and surrounding communities, and by avoiding relationships that violate human beings' rights to health, education, safety, and an adequate standard of living. And companies can be good citizens by supporting essential social institutions, such as the economic system and the education system, and by working with host governments and other organizations to protect the environment.

Many companies don't do anything with their codes of conduct; they simply paste them on the wall.

The core values establish a moral compass for business practice. They can help companies identify practices that are acceptable and those that are intolerable – even if the practices are compatible with a host country's norms and laws. Dumping pollutants near people's homes and accepting inadequate standards for handling hazardous materials are two examples of actions that violate core values.

Similarly, if employing children prevents them from receiving a basic education, the practice is intolerable. Lying about product specifications in the act of selling may not affect human lives directly, but it too is intolerable because it violates the trust that is needed to sustain a corporate culture in which customers are respected.

Sometimes it is not a company's actions but those of a supplier or customer that pose problems. Take the case of the Tan family, a large supplier for Levi Strauss. The Tans were allegedly forcing 1,200 Chinese and Filipino women to work 74 hours per week in guarded compounds on the Mariana Islands. In 1992, after repeated warnings to the Tans, Levi Strauss broke off business relations with them.

Creating an Ethical Corporate Culture

The core values for business that I have enumerated can help companies begin to exercise ethical judgment and think about how to operate ethically in foreign cultures, but they are not specific enough to guide managers through actual ethical dilemmas. Levi Strauss relied on a written code of conduct when figuring out how to deal with the Tan family. The company's Global Sourcing and Operating Guidelines, formerly called the Business Partner Terms of Engagement, state that Levi Strauss will "seek to identify and utilize business partners who aspire as individuals and in the conduct of all their businesses to a set of ethical standards not incompatible with our own." Whenever intolerable business situations arise, managers should be guided by precise statements that spell out the behavior and operating practices that the company demands.

Ninety percent of all *Fortune* 500 companies have codes of conduct, and 70% have statements of vision and values. In Europe and the Far East, the percentages are lower but are increasing rapidly. Does that mean that most companies have what they need? Hardly. Even though most large U.S. companies have both statements of values and codes of conduct, many might be better off if they didn't. Too many companies don't do anything with the documents; they simply paste them on the wall to impress employees, customers, suppliers, and the public. As a result, the senior managers who drafted the statements lose credibility by proclaiming values and not living up to them. Companies such as Johnson & Johnson, Levi Strauss, Motorola, Texas Instruments, and Lockheed Martin, however, do a great deal to make the words meaningful. Johnson & Johnson, for example, has become well known for its Credo Challenge sessions, in which managers discuss ethics in the context of their current business problems and are invited to criticize the company's credo and make suggestions for changes. The participants' ideas are passed on to the company's senior managers. Lockheed Martin has created an innovative site on the World Wide Web and on its local network that gives employees, customers, and suppliers access to the company's ethical code and the chance to voice complaints.

Codes of conduct must provide clear direction about ethical behavior when the temptation to behave unethically is strongest. The pronouncement in a code of conduct that bribery is unacceptable is useless unless accompanied by guidelines for gift giving, payments to get goods through customs, and "requests" from intermediaries who are hired to ask for bribes.

Motorola's values are stated very simply as "How we will always act: [with] constant respect for people [and] uncompromising integrity." The company's code of conduct, however, is explicit about actual business practice. With respect to bribery, for example, the code states that the "funds and assets of Motorola shall not be used, directly or indirectly, for illegal payments of any kind." It is unambiguous about what sort of payment is illegal: "the payment of a bribe to a public official or the kickback of funds to an employee of a customer...." The code goes on to prescribe specific procedures for handling commissions to intermediaries, issuing sales invoices, and disclosing confidential information in a sales transaction – all situations in which employees might have an opportunity to accept or offer bribes.

Codes of conduct must be explicit to be useful, but they must also leave room for a manager to use his or her judgment in situations requiring cultural sensitivity. Host-country employees shouldn't be forced to adopt all home-country values and renounce their own. Again, Motorola's code is exemplary. First, it gives clear direction: "Employees of Motorola will respect the laws, customs, and traditions of each country in which they operate, but will, at the same time, engage in no course of conduct which, even if legal, customary, and accepted in any such country, could be deemed to be in violation of the accepted business ethics of Motorola or the laws of the United States relating to business ethics." After laying down such absolutes, Motorola's code then makes clear when individual judgment will be necessary. For example, employees may sometimes accept certain kinds of small gifts "in rare circumstances, where the refusal to accept a gift" would injure Motorola's "legitimate business interests." Under certain circumstances, such gifts "may be accepted so long as the gift inures to the benefit of Motorola" and not "to the benefit of the Motorola employee."

Striking the appropriate balance between providing clear direction and leaving room for individual judgment makes crafting corporate values statements and ethics codes one of the hardest tasks that executives confront. The words are only a start. A company's leaders need to refer often to their organization's credo and code and must themselves be credible, committed, and consistent. If senior managers act as though ethics don't matter, the rest of the company's employees won't think they do, either.

Conflicts of Development and Conflicts of Tradition

Managers living and working abroad who are not prepared to grapple with moral ambiguity and tension should pack their bags and come home. The view that all business practices can be categorized as either ethical or unethical is too simple. As Einstein is reported to have said, "Things should be as simple as possible – but no simpler." Many business practices that are considered unethical in one setting may be ethical in another. Such activities are neither black nor white but exist in what Thomas Dunfee and I have called *moral free space*.[1] In this gray zone, there are no tight prescriptions for a company's behavior. Managers must chart their own courses – as long as they do not violate core human values.

Consider the following example. Some successful Indian companies offer employees the opportunity for one of their children to gain a job with the company once the child has completed a certain level in school. The companies honor this commitment even when other applicants are more qualified than an employee's child. The perk is extremely valuable in a country where jobs are hard to find, and it reflects the Indian culture's belief that the West has gone too far in allowing economic opportunities to break up families. Not surprisingly, the perk is among the most cherished by employees, but in most Western countries, it would be branded unacceptable nepotism. In the United States, for example, the ethical principle of equal opportunity holds that jobs should go to the applicants with the best qualifications. If a U.S. company made such promises to its em-

Many activities are neither good nor bad but exist in *moral free space.*

ployees, it would violate regulations established by the Equal Employment Opportunity Commission. Given this difference in ethical attitudes, how should U.S. managers react to Indian nepotism? Should they condemn the Indian companies, refusing to accept them as partners or suppliers until they agree to clean up their act?

Despite the obvious tension between nepotism and principles of equal opportunity, I cannot condemn the practice for Indians. In a country, such as India, that emphasizes clan and family relationships and has catastrophic levels of unemployment, the practice must be viewed in moral free space. The decision to allow a special perk for employees and their children is not necessarily wrong – at least for members of that country.

How can managers discover the limits of moral free space? That is, how can they learn to distinguish a value in tension with their own from one that is intolerable? Helping managers develop good ethical judgment requires companies to be clear about their core values and codes of conduct. But even the most explicit set of guidelines cannot always provide answers. That is especially true in the thorniest ethical dilemmas, in which the host country's ethical standards not only are different but also seem lower than the home country's. Managers must recognize that when countries have different ethical standards, there are two types of conflict that commonly arise. Each type requires its own line of reasoning.

In the first type of conflict, which I call a *conflict of relative development*, ethical standards conflict because of the countries' different levels of economic development. As mentioned before, developing countries may accept wage rates that seem inhumane to more advanced countries in order to attract investment. As economic conditions in a developing country improve, the incidence of that sort of conflict usually decreases. The second type of conflict is a *conflict of cultural tradition*. For example, Saudi Arabia, unlike most other countries, does not allow women to serve as corporate managers. Instead, women may work in only a few professions, such as education and health care. The prohibition stems from strongly held religious and cultural beliefs; any increase in the country's level of economic development, which is already quite high, is not likely to change the rules.

To resolve a conflict of relative development, a manager must ask the following question: Would the practice be acceptable at home if my country were in a similar stage of economic development? Consider the difference between wage and safety standards in the United States and in Angola, where citizens accept lower standards on both counts. If a U.S. oil company is hiring Angolans to work on an offshore Angolan oil rig, can the company pay them lower wages than it pays U.S. workers in

The Problem with Bribery

Bribery is widespread and insidious. Managers in transnational companies routinely confront bribery even though most countries have laws against it. The fact is that officials in many developing countries wink at the practice, and the salaries of local bureaucrats are so low that many consider bribes a form of remuneration. The U.S. Foreign Corrupt Practices Act defines allowable limits on petty bribery in the form of routine payments required to move goods through customs. But demands for bribes often exceed those limits, and there is seldom a good solution.

Bribery disrupts distribution channels when goods languish on docks until local handlers are paid off, and it destroys incentives to compete on quality and cost when purchasing decisions are based on who pays what under the table. Refusing to acquiesce is often tantamount to giving business to unscrupulous companies.

I believe that even routine bribery is intolerable. Bribery undermines market efficiency and predictability, thus ultimately denying people their right to a minimal standard of living. Some degree of ethical commitment – some sense that everyone will play by the rules – is necessary for a sound economy. Without an ability to predict outcomes, who would be willing to invest?

There was a U.S. company whose shipping crates were regularly pilfered by handlers on the docks of Rio de Janeiro. The handlers would take about 10% of the contents of the crates, but the company was never sure which 10% it would be. In a partial solution, the company began sending two crates – the first with 90% of the merchandise, the second with 10%. The handlers learned to take the second crate and leave the first untouched. From the company's perspective, at least knowing which goods it would lose was an improvement.

Bribery does more than destroy predictability; it undermines essential social and economic systems. That truth is not lost on businesspeople in countries where the practice is woven into the social fabric. CEOs in India admit that their companies engage constantly in bribery, and they say that they have considerable disgust for the practice. They blame government policies in part, but Indian executives also know that their country's business practices perpetuate corrupt behavior. Anyone walking the streets of Calcutta, where it is clear that even a dramatic redistribution of wealth would still leave most of India's inhabitants in dire poverty, comes face-to-face with the devastating effects of corruption.

the Gulf of Mexico? Reasonable people have to answer yes if the alternative for Angola is the loss of both the foreign investment and the jobs.

Consider, too, differences in regulatory environments. In the 1980s, the government of India fought hard to be able to import Ciba-Geigy's Entero Vioform, a drug known to be enormously effective in fighting dysentery but one that had been banned in the United States because some users experienced side effects. Although dysentery was not a big problem in the United States, in India, poor public sanitation was contributing to epidemic levels of the disease. Was it unethical to make the drug available in India after it had been banned in the United States? On the contrary, rational people should consider it unethical not to do so. Apply our test: Would the United States, at an earlier stage of development, have used this drug despite its side effects? The answer is clearly yes.

But there are many instances when the answer to similar questions is no. Sometimes a host country's standards are inadequate at any level of economic development. If a country's pollution standards are so low that working on an oil rig would considerably increase a person's risk of developing cancer, foreign oil companies must refuse to do business there. Likewise, if the dangerous side effects of a drug treatment outweigh its benefits, managers should not accept health standards that ignore the risks.

When relative economic conditions do not drive tensions, there is a more objective test for resolving ethical problems. Managers should deem a practice permissible only if they can answer no to both of the following questions: Is it possible to conduct business successfully in the host country without undertaking the practice? and Is the practice a violation of a core human value? Japanese gift giving is a perfect example of a conflict of cultural tradition. Most experienced businesspeople, Japanese and non-Japanese alike, would agree that doing business in Japan would be virtually impossible without adopting the practice. Does gift giving violate a core human value? I cannot identify one that it violates. As a result, gift giving may be permissible for foreign companies in Japan even if it conflicts with ethical attitudes at home. In fact, that conclusion is widely accepted, even by companies such as Texas Instruments and IBM, which are outspoken against bribery.

If a company declared all gift giving unethical, it wouldn't be able to do business in Japan.

Does it follow that all nonmonetary gifts are acceptable or that bribes are generally acceptable in countries where they are common? Not at all. (See the insert "The Problem with Bribery.") What makes the routine practice of gift giving acceptable in Japan are the limits in its scope and intention. When gift giving moves outside those limits, it soon collides with core human values. For example, when Carl Kotchian, president of Lockheed in the 1970s, carried suitcases full of cash to Japanese politicians, he went beyond the norms established by Japanese tradition. That incident galvanized opinion in the United States Congress and helped lead to passage of the Foreign Corrupt Practices Act. Likewise, Roh Tae Woo went beyond the norms established by Korean cultural tradition when he accepted $635.4 million in bribes as president of the Republic of Korea between 1988 and 1993.

Guidelines for Ethical Leadership

Learning to spot intolerable practices and to exercise good judgment when ethical conflicts arise requires practice. Creating a company culture that rewards ethical behavior is essential. The following guidelines for developing a global ethical perspective among managers can help.

Treat corporate values and formal standards of conduct as absolutes. Whatever ethical standards a company chooses, it cannot waver on its principles either at home or abroad. Consider what has become part of company lore at Motorola. Around 1950, a senior executive was negotiating with officials of a South American government on a $10 million sale that would have increased the company's annual net profits by nearly 25%. As the negotiations neared completion, however, the executive walked away from the deal because the officials were asking for $1 million for "fees." CEO Robert Galvin not only supported the executive's decision but also made it clear that Motorola would neither accept the sale on any terms nor do business with those government officials again. Retold over the decades, this story demonstrating Galvin's resolve has helped cement a culture of ethics for thousands of employees at Motorola.

Design and implement conditions of engagement for suppliers and customers. Will your company do business with any customer or supplier? What if a customer or supplier uses child labor? What if it has strong links with organized crime? What if it pressures your company to break a host country's laws? Such issues are best not left for spur-of-the-moment decisions. Some companies have realized that. Sears, for instance, has developed a policy of not contracting production to companies that use prison labor or infringe on workers' rights to health and safety. And BankAmerica has specified as a condition for many of its loans to developing countries that environmental standards and human rights must be observed.

Allow foreign business units to help formulate ethical standards and interpret ethical issues. The French pharmaceutical company Rhône-Poulenc Rorer has allowed foreign subsidiaries to augment lists of corporate ethical principles with their own suggestions. Texas Instruments has paid special attention to issues of international business ethics by creating the Global Business Practices Council, which is made up of managers from countries in which the company operates. With the overarching intent to create a "global ethics strategy, locally deployed," the council's mandate is to provide ethics education and create local processes that will help managers in the company's foreign business units resolve ethical conflicts.

In host countries, support efforts to decrease institutional corruption. Individual managers will not be able to wipe out corruption in a host country, no matter how many bribes they turn down. When a host country's tax system, import and export procedures, and procurement practices favor unethical players, companies must take action.

Many companies have begun to participate in reforming host-country institutions. General Electric, for example, has taken a strong stand in India, using the media to make repeated condemnations of bribery in business and government. General Electric and others have found, however, that a single company usually cannot drive out entrenched corruption. Transparency International, an organization based in Germany, has been effective in helping coalitions of companies, government officials, and others work to reform bribery-ridden bureaucracies in Russia, Bangladesh, and elsewhere.

Exercise moral imagination. Using moral imagination means resolving tensions responsibly and creatively. Coca-Cola, for instance, has consistently turned down requests for bribes from Egyptian officials but has managed to gain political support and public trust by sponsoring a project to plant fruit trees. And take the example of Levi Strauss, which discovered in the early 1990s that two of its suppliers in Bangladesh were employing children under the age of 14–a practice that violated the company's principles but was tolerated in Bangladesh. Forcing the suppliers to fire the children would not have ensured that the children received an education, and it would have caused serious hardship for the families depending on the children's wages. In a creative arrangement, the suppliers agreed to pay the children's regular wages while they attended school and to offer each child a job at age 14. Levi Strauss, in turn, agreed to pay the children's tuition and provide books and uniforms. That arrangement allowed Levi Strauss to uphold its principles and provide long-term benefits to its host country.

Many people think of values as soft; to some they are usually unspoken. A South Seas island society uses the word *mokita*, which means, "the truth that everybody knows but nobody speaks." However difficult they are to articulate, values affect how we all behave. In a global business environment, values in tension are the rule rather than the exception. Without a company's commitment, statements of values and codes of ethics end up as empty platitudes that provide managers with no foundation for behaving ethically. Employees need and deserve more, and responsible members of the global business community can set examples for others to follow. The dark consequences of incidents such as Union Carbide's disaster in Bhopal remind us how high the stakes can be.

1. In other writings, Thomas W. Dunfee and I have used the term *hypernorm* instead of *core human value*.

2. Thomas Donaldson and Thomas W. Dunfee, "Toward a Unified Conception of Business Ethics: Integrative Social Contracts Theory," *Academy of Management Review*, April 1994; and "Integrative Social Contracts Theory: A Communitarian Conception of Economic Ethics," *Economics and Philosophy*, spring 1995.

Reprint 96502

To order reprints, see the last page of this issue.

[40]

UNIVERSALIZABILITY AND RECIPROCITY IN INTERNATIONAL BUSINESS ETHICS

John Hendry

Abstract: Most writers on international business ethics adopt a universalist perspective, but the traditional expression of problems in terms of a discrepancy between (superior) home country and (inferior) host country values makes it difficult to preserve the symmetry required by a universalizability criterion. In this paper a critique of Donaldson's (1989) theory is used to illustrate some of the ways in which ethnocentric assumptions can enter into a supposedly universalist argument. A number of suggestions are then made for improving Donaldson's approach by careful attention to the requirement of universalizability, expressed in a contractarian theory in the form of agent symmetry or reciprocity.

Business has always had an international dimension. Indeed, the modern business organization can be traced in large measure to the early trading companies, whose needs for planning, coordination and financial capital led to the development of more sophisticated governance structures than were required for merely domestic concerns. With the deregulation of trade and the continued rapid development of communication and transportation technologies, however, it has now become normal for businesses to operate across countries and cultures. As a result, the pursuit of business routinely encounters problems arising from the cultural conflict of values in a way that most other practices do not. Practices such as law, medicine, and government, for example, all have an international dimension, but this does not generally intrude on their day-to-day operations in the way that it does for business. In these areas the international dimension has become the subject of separate practices, developed within supra-national institutional frameworks and impinging upon national practice in well-defined ways. In business there are no such distinctions and, as De George (1993) has pointed out, no such institutions.

This would not matter if there were a cross-cultural homogeneity of those moral values relating to business, but even if we interpret the phrase "relating to" quite tightly, there is not. There are widely recognized to be significant differences between cultures with regard to a wide range of issues perceived by one culture or another as having moral import, including the ethical aspects of employment practices, workplace behavior, financial transactions, the honoring of agreements, the social and environmental impact of business, and the relationships between business and government. In the context of these differences

©1999. *Business Ethics Quarterly,* Volume 9, Issue 3. ISSN 1052-150X. pp. 405-420

businesses have constantly to decide, explicitly or otherwise, whether to insist on the values of their home cultures, whether to adopt those of their host country cultures, or whether to accept some form of political compromise and, in the latter case, what guidance and leeway should be given to the managers charged with implementing the policy.

From a philosophical perspective, particularist approaches to ethics, such as contemporary virtue theory and communitarianism, have remarkably little to say on this issue. In one way these theories are highly sensitive to cultural context, but in focusing on the ways in which the origins and expression of values are rooted in specific cultural settings they give little attention to the problems of cross-cultural difference or, indeed, to those of cultural pluralism within individual contemporary societies.[1] From a particularist perspective the values, conceptual frameworks, and communicative practices of different societies either overlap sufficiently for a point in question to be mutually resolvable and so not at issue, or they do not. In the latter case the argument leads to an incommensurability of rival values and an effective ethical relativism that can be resolved only, if at all, by cultural evolution and convergence on an historical time scale.

Given this, it is not surprising that the philosophers who have addressed the issue have done so from an avowedly universalist perspective (e.g., Donaldson 1989; De George 1993; Elfstrom 1991; Velasquez 1995). Starting out with the assumption that cross-cultural differences should be resolvable, they at least have the motivation to find ways of resolving them. In avoiding relativism, however, it is all too easy to fall into ethnocentrism as arguments are inevitably developed from the basis of the writer's own cultural environment. This ethnocentrism may take the form of outright ethical egoism, which is certainly universalizable in principle but is, strangely enough, never advocated by the powerless or oppressed; or of allowing self-interest (in general) or the interests of a particular community to qualify the conclusions that might otherwise be reached on the basis of utilitarian or deontological arguments. It may be reflected, more subtly, in a writer's choice of universal rights or principles of conduct, or in the procedures and arguments proposed for the resolution of culturally based differences.

In this paper we illustrate some of the ways in which ethnocentric assumptions can creep into supposedly universalist arguments by looking at one particular treatment of international business ethics, that by Donaldson (1989). We then suggest ways in which these difficulties might be partially overcome by a more careful consideration of the requirements of universalizability. We begin, though, by distinguishing between three different types of cross-cultural ethical dilemma.

Cultural Variation and the Classification of Ethical Dilemmas

For the sake of clarity, it makes sense to classify culturally based ethical conflicts into three groups. First, there are those conflicts in which the ethical values characteristic of the two cultures lead to opposite conclusions: what is wrong from one perspective is right from the other. Secondly, there are conflicts in which one culture attributes moral significance to something that another does not: what is wrong from one perspective is neither right nor wrong from the other. Thirdly, there are conflicts in which contingent circumstances lead to different interpretations of what is ethically acceptable, despite agreement on the underlying values. We shall expand on these categories below, but it should be noted first that we are assuming here, for simplicity, that each culture can be represented by a characteristic set of ethical values. This assumption is implicit in most of the existing treatments of international business ethics, including that of Donaldson, and it allows us to focus attention specifically on the international, intercultural dimension of ethical conflicts. The reality is, however, much more complex as many contemporary societies are characterised by a high measure of cultural pluralism and by significant variations in ethical belief.

The first group of conflicts presents what might be thought of as the "hard" cases: those in which culturally based values lead to *opposite* conclusions, with two cultures, each considering its own values to be positively better, on moral grounds, than those of the other. This might arise, for example, in the case of employment and promotion practices, which in one culture might be based solely on technical ability, in another on seniority, and in another on gender, caste, or social status. From a North American perspective, to appoint or promote on the basis of gender, caste, seniority, or status is morally unacceptable; but from the perspective of societies in which these criteria are important, the North American practice of disregarding them in favour of skill or ability can be *equally* unacceptable.

A second and more common type of situation arises where practices that are morally unacceptable in one culture are acceptable in another, not because they are seen as morally correct there, but because they are not seen as having any significant moral import. Consider, for example, the giving of personal payments or gifts to government officials or to key people (buyers, bank managers, etc.) in companies with which one does business. In some cultures, such as that of North America, such gifts are quite simply morally unacceptable. In other cultures they are, within variously defined limits, neither morally good nor morally bad but an accepted part of business practice. In South Korea, for example, where gift giving has traditionally played an important part in the creation and maintenance of social relationships, personal gifts to company representatives are an accepted and institutionalised part of doing business. However, declining to offer such a gift (which in terms of the giver's income might well be quite substantial) would not be considered morally wrong—just socially inept and professionally incompetent.

Other examples of this second type include a variety of situations in which the economic demands of business conflict with the interests of those with whom the business has some kind of relationship, be they individuals (such as employees) or other businesses. Despite recent concerns over the effects of downsizing and the prominence of stakeholder ideas, there is a general supposition in North American culture that these interests are subsidiary to the economic welfare of the business. So long as it is based on sound business arguments the termination of relationships (the firing of loyal employees, for example, or the breach of informal understandings or agreements when these are unsupported by formal contracts) is morally acceptable. What is debatable is only what constitutes a sound business argument, and it is in economic not moral terms that the debate is ultimately framed. In other cultures, however, the moral responsibilities associated with these kinds of relationships are primary, and while economic considerations cannot be ignored the issues are debated in moral rather than economic terms.

This type of situation might also arise in connection with more general social attitudes, such as those to do with alcohol or other drugs, with sexual morality, or with decency in dress, insofar as these impinge upon the workplace. What in one culture is an issue of serious moral concern is in another a matter of personal preference or social custom.

It is important to note that in the cases we have discussed the North American or West European standards are not always the more demanding, and that even within North American and West European culture there can be significant differences. In the traditionally Protestant countries of Northern Europe, for example, the under-declaration of income to the taxation authorities, though widely practised, is generally thought to be morally wrong. In the traditionally Catholic countries of the South, however, it is largely a matter of social custom, with little or no *moral* significance; in these cultures moral weight is attached only to what are seen as more important matters.

A third and very common type of situation arises where there is *no* fundamental moral conflict between the two societies, but where differing circumstances or cultural nuances lead to dramatic differences in the societies' interpretations of what is or is not ethically acceptable practice. Examples here might include the differences between the developed and developing worlds in terms of acceptable safety standards in mining, chemical plants, or construction projects; acceptable terms and conditions of employment; or acceptable levels of pollution and environmental damage. These differences might result from a variety of factors. Most obviously, the costs and benefits of imposing high standards of safety or pollution control look very different to people who are poor and hungry, and who may die anyway if there is no employment to sustain them, than they do to people living in a wealthy society with the buffer of a highly developed welfare state. Some of the basic industries on which developing countries most depend are also some of the most polluting, and the costs of controlling this pollution can actually be higher than in developed countries. Cement, for example, is a basic need in developing countries, but without expensive pollution control equipment cement factories will pollute heavily whenever there is a break in the electricity supply—something to which most developing countries are prone; the cost of this equipment, however, would put the product out of reach of the local economy. In some cases there may be considerable ignorance in a developing country as to the real risks entailed in a process, especially where the consequences are not immediately visible. There may also be cultural or religious differences that lead to a different weighting of present against future interests, of wealth against health, or of individual lives against communal welfare. In all these cases the standards prevailing in the developed economies of North America and Europe might appear very desirable were they to be accompanied by the circumstances prevailing in those cultures, but not in the circumstances actually prevailing elsewhere.

Unintended Ethnocentrism: An Example

In what is probably the best attempt yet made to work out a comprehensive theory of international business ethics, Donaldson (1991) adopts a contractarian approach drawing on Rawls's *A Theory of Justice*. As for Rawls (1972) the contractarian approach is intended to secure the universalizability of the theory, but this turns out to be much more difficult to achieve than might be imagined, not—or not only—because of the logical difficulties involved in setting up the theory, but because of the constant intrusion of implicit and unintended ethnocentrism.[2]

Donaldson (1): The Case Against Relativism

A basic problem facing any ethical universalist is that the opposing case for ethical relativism is not merely a strong one but, *in its own terms*, unanswerable.

The relativist case begins from the observation that ethical values do vary both across cultures and across periods, and that these differences are culturally produced. From a historical perspective it is evident that both the values that have been proclaimed over time and the professedly universalist theories that have been advanced in their support (from Aristotle and Plato through St. Paul and Aquinas to Kant and the utilitarians) have, to a very large extent, been the products of particular social, political, and religious environments.[3] In our own time the differences between the ethical values of Western, Islamic, and East Asian societies, which are themselves culturally and ethically diverse, are equally apparent.

Of course, cultural relativism is not the same as ethical relativism. The fact, should we accept it, that ethical values are socially produced does *not* logically imply that they are *purely* a product of their society or culture, true only for the members of that society or culture and with no import or significance beyond it. Indeed, the ethical relativist position cannot be logically proven. But neither can it be logically refuted, for in any attempt at refutation we inevitably lay ourselves open to the argument that the very enterprise of a universalist ethics, and indeed the very concept of a moral imperative, are themselves the products of our own particular culture. On one hand, the existence of substantial and apparently irreconcilable differences in the observed ethical beliefs of different cultures in no way precludes the possibility of some universal moral truth. On the other hand the existence of a very large degree of ethical consensus across cultures in no way precludes the possibility that moral truth might be socially contingent, and that different societies in different circumstances might evolve completely different but no less valid views of morality.[4] In other words we cannot, in pursuing a universalist ethics, escape altogether the charge of possible ethnocentrism, and the degree to which we think we can is itself some measure of the degree to which that ethnocentrism has a hold over us.

Donaldson apparently thinks that we can, however, for he makes two attempts to refute the relativist position, to demonstrate that universalism is not just an assumption but a fact. In the first place he argues for its logical necessity. By pursuing the relativist position to its extremes, it is claimed, its absurdity becomes evident. Thus, if we were to believe in ethical relativism we would have to accept as valid the ethics of any society imaginable, however abhorrent these may be: a society, for example, in which murder and torture for pleasure were deemed morally good. Indeed we would, but the force of this argument is emotive, not logical. The fact that such practices are abhorrent relative to our own values does not necessarily imply that our values are anything other than socially derived. It may indicate the strength and passion with which they are held, but it says nothing about their origin.

In the second place, Donaldson argues for universalism on empirical grounds, claiming that the degree of moral common ground between cultures, and the recourse to moral language in international dispute and debate, indicate the existence of some common transcendental values. There are indeed growing signs of a convergence of ethical values internationally and Habermas (1996) has argued recently that the prospects for reaching global agreement through a process of rational discourse seem good. However, this argument ignores the fact that the language adopted in international discourses is not neutral. On the contrary, it is strongly conditioned by the political, military, and economic dominance of the particular culture from which Donaldson is writing; relativists would argue, with Foucault (1980), that it is not merely influenced but constituted by the power/knowledge relationships involved. The argument also conflates theory with practice. Despite their visible differences the cultures concerned have a lot in common. They are the products of very similar social and biological processes and it would be very surprising if these did not lead, in practice, to similar moral systems and to enough of a common moral vocabulary to make at least some moral debate between societies meaningful. This does not, however, imply the existence of any transcendental values, or provide any argument against the theory of ethical relativism.

Donaldson (2): An Algorithm for Conflict Resolution and the Categorization of Conflicts

In order to resolve international ethical dilemmas arising from the differences between a firm's home country and host country values, Donaldson proposes an algorithm in two stages. The first stage is to assign a situation to one of two categories, depending on whether or not the cultural differences are dependent on the stage of economic development (p.102):

> [In type 1 conflicts] the moral reasons underlying the host country's view that the practice is permissible refer to the host country's relative level of economic development.

> [In type 2 conflicts] the moral reasons underlying the host country's view that the practice is permissible are independent of the host country's relative level of economic development.

Taken as it is from a work that professes both a universalist approach and a general scope (the theory is not intended to be restricted to the problems faced by U.S. multinationals in developing countries), this categorization embodies some remarkable implicit assumptions. First, it is implicitly assumed that the home country has more demanding moral standards than the host country. Secondly, it is assumed that the home country is more economically developed than the host country. Thirdly, it is assumed by implication that there is a correlation between moral and economic development. Fourthly, it is assumed that the stage of economic development matters in a way in which other variations, for example in religious beliefs, cultural traditions, or governance structures, do not.

In reality, there is no known metric of overall moral development, and countries that are more demanding in some respects may be less demanding in others. The very idea of moral superiority tends to be related to an ethnocentricity, for it is usually one's own society that is deemed superior and the "other" that is inferior. Economic development is not easy to measure either, for it depends on the distribution of wealth and the development of institutional frameworks as well as on straight GDP. What is implied in the categorization is something like "the economic situation of an average US citizen," but this doesn't seem very promising as an objective benchmark and is likely to seem less so as American economic dominance is increasingly challenged by countries from East Asia. This challenge also exposes the naivete of the idea that economic development can be taken independently of wider cultural factors, and it will be surprising indeed if the idea of a correlation between moral and economic development seems quite so attractive to Americans writing in ten years time as it did to those writing ten years ago—though the argument might by then be quite appealing to the Chinese. Economic success may result in moral influence, but there is no obvious reason why this should be progressive rather than, as so often appears to be the case *within* societies, corrupting. Strangely enough it is only those who have achieved it (whether as individuals or as members of successful economies) who argue that it should provide a touchstone for morality, objectively conceived.

Donaldson's procedure for conflict resolution follows the assumptions implicit in his categorization. In the case of his type 1 conflicts, he argues (p.103) that:

> The practice is permissible if and only if the members of the home country would, under conditions of economic development [we would say, more generally, in economic and social circumstances] relevantly similar to those of the host country, regard the practice as permissible.

In the case of type 2 conflicts, he argues, the practice concerned is permissible *only* if it is impossible to conduct business successfully in the host country without undertaking the practice *and* if the practice is not a direct violation of any fundamental international right (p.10). To qualify as a fundamental international right, a prospective right must protect something of great importance that is subject to substantial and recurrent threats. It must also meet a "fairness-affordability" condition which in essence requires that the right must be strictly speaking affordable by the moral agents concerned (i.e., affordable absolutely, not merely affordable having taken account of other economically desirable ends), and that there must be some fair arrangement for sharing the cost of honouring the right between the moral agents concerned (p. 81).

The recourse to home country morals in type 1 conflicts is, of course, ethnocentric,[5] but it is a natural, and legitimate, consequence of the more insidious assumption of moral superiority. More interesting is the procedure for type 2 conflicts. Assuming that no fundamental international rights are violated (not, as we shall see, a very demanding condition), the acceptability of morally dubious practices becomes a matter of whether or not they are necessary to ensure commercial success. It is not clear whether this is an ethnocentric reflection of American liberal ideas on the moral virtues of free enterprise, or whether it is just plain wrong. There have always been many firms able to survive, let alone succeed, only by engaging in practices that their own societies have judged unethical: the illegal employment of immigrant workers, for example, the breach of health and safety requirements, or the non-declaration of cash receipts. With the stricter enforcement of domestic standards and the opening up of international trade the alternative possibility of manufacturing or subcontracting in countries where the standards appear less onerous has become increasingly attractive. Is this the stuff of which entrepreneurship is made? And who, if not the proprietor concerned, is to judge necessity or define success?

Donaldson (3): A Philosophy of Rights

Within the American liberal tradition of the philosophy of justice, Donaldson's recourse to an approach based on rights seems entirely uncontroversial. But before we discuss the individual rights proposed it is worth reflecting on how far such an approach can really claim to be universal, and untainted by American ethnocentrism. Before Locke, Western moral theory was almost entirely cast in terms of obligations rather than rights, and European philosophy has maintained that orientation. Eastern philosophies focus either on the obligations of the self or on relationships in which the rights of one party, if they are mentioned at all, are essentially derivative from the obligations or right feelings of the other. The language of rights has acquired international currency through the human rights movement, but this may well reflect a strong American influence and the need for political accommodation (rights are much easier to accept than obligations) rather than anything more fundamental.

Even within American liberalism, the focus on rights appears as a path toward obligations, rather than as an end in itself. The primary ethical question remains, as for Donaldson, the traditional one of "what should an agent do" and not "to what is a recipient entitled." From a strictly philosophical point of view, however, this poses problems, for as O'Neill (1996, pp. 128ff) has pointed out, rights and obligations are *not* equivalent starting points. In the case of universal liberty rights there is a direct connection between the specification of rights and that of resulting, negative, obligations. Any principle defining a universal liberty right also defines, by implication, some corresponding universal obligation. But Donaldson, as we shall see, does not restrict himself to liberty rights. His list of "fundamental international rights" that businesses are required to respect also includes universal welfare rights, such as the right to subsistence and to a minimal education, and such rights do not imply any universal obligations. The specification of a welfare right is in itself no more than empty rhetoric. It becomes meaningful as a basis for action *only* when it is accompanied by a specification of the particular institutional forms and the distribution of *specific* obligations through which it is to be achieved. Once the arrangements for delivery of a welfare right have been specified there will arise a secondary, and relatively non-onerous, obligation not to interfere with them, but in the absence of any such arrangements the specification of a right imposes no concomitant obligations.

If this lack of symmetry poses philosophical problems, however, it has strong political advantages: rights are more attractive than obligations. It is also peculiarly well fitted to contemporary American culture, allowing the expression of noble sentiments without imposing any unwelcome obligations. A philosophy that sought to derive welfare rights from obligations, rather than the other way around, would inevitably place very significant obligations upon the world's more affluent societies and upon the more affluent members within those societies. The former would act against America's economic interests, the latter against its liberal ideology.

Donaldson (4): A Set of International Rights

A rights-based approach also encounters the problem of what rights are to be included, and how they are to be derived. Donaldson specifies a "minimal" set of ten basic rights (including both liberty and welfare rights) to which, he suggests, all cultures could willingly subscribe (p. 81):

1. The right to freedom of physical movement
2. The right to ownership of property
3. The right to freedom from torture
4. The right to a fair trial
5. The right to non-discriminatory treatment (freedom from discrimination on the basis of such characteristics as race or sex)

6. The right to physical security

7. The right to freedom of speech and association

8. The right to minimal education

9. The right to political participation

10. The right to subsistence

The idea is that these rights should reflect cross-cultural agreement on universal moral standards. Whether they achieve this in practice, however, is at best debatable: the right to ownership of property, for example, would probably not be accepted by all societies. To the extent that they do succeed, moreover, they inevitably set the standards required rather low. Whether within or across cultures, there is ample scope for unethical actions—involving bribery and corruption, for example, or fraudulent or dishonest accounting practices—that do not violate basic human rights. There is also ample scope for disagreement on how the rights are to be interpreted. The fact that most cultures would agree to the right to non-discriminatory treatment, for example, is relatively meaningless if there are substantial differences over what constitutes discrimination. Property ownership, education, and political participation are also complex concepts that in practice acquire very different meanings in different cultural settings.

In order to become the basis of action (or, more likely, given the nature of the rights-based approach, of inaction) Donaldson's rights need to be interpreted according to a particular culture, and if his algorithm is followed this will be the culture of the home country. Even if the rights are not ethnocentric in their basic expression, they quickly become so in practice.

Universalizability and Reciprocity: An Alternative Approach

Because *any* case that we might make can itself be attributed to our own ethnocentricity, the case for ethical relativism can never be logically refuted. This need not prevent us from arguing for universalism, however. A belief in the moral nature of humanity, in the imperative force of the moral "ought," *may* be a mere illusion, but it appears to be almost universally shared and provides a reasonable starting point. The practical need, in an increasingly integrated world, to resolve the moral conflicts we encounter provides a pragmatic reinforcement for this position. In pursuing the goal of a practical universalist ethics, however, we should do what we can to observe the requirements of universalizability and avoid the traps of ethnocentric reasoning.

To do this, we first need an appropriate formulation of the universalizability requirement. In the context of a contractarian theory such as Donaldson's the essential requirement is that the agreement reached should be independent of the positions occupied by the parties to the contract, and this is typically expressed by requiring that parties drawing up the contract either do so disinterestedly or, as in Rawls's formulation (1972, pp. 136ff), without knowing what positions they will themselves occupy.

At the theoretical level, this is fine, for it effectively takes out of account the specific interests of the actors with whom we are concerned. It may also be appropriate for the practical task of developing a framework of justice, say, for a particular society, in which case it is the analyst or philosopher who has to put herself in the role of the society's members and assume on their part the Rawlsean veil of ignorance. Philosophers are, on the whole, quite good at ignorance and impartiality. In the present context, however, we are concerned with conflicts between the values and interests of two societies, and with the construction of a practical social contract for resolving those conflicts by a philosopher who is himself a member of one of those societies.

Donaldson's approach has the appearance of an analysis of what people would agree to in ignorance of their own positions, and so appears to meet the demands of universalizability, but it actually does so only to the extent that Donaldson is himself able to take an impartial and disinterested position with respect to the cultures being considered. To do this, he would have to have an understanding of the many different countries and cultures in which American firms do business equal to his understanding of the American culture of which he is a member. This is surely too much to ask. Donaldson is an American and it would be quite amazing if his analysis were not biased to some extent toward an American (as opposed to a Chinese or Iranian or Congolese or Argentinian) way of looking at things, and if that did not affect his analysis of the ethical differences between American and other cultures. In these circumstances the contractarian approach provides no guarantee of universalizability, and the practical question therefore arises: if we cannot be confident of fully satisfying the universalizability requirement, strictly applied, what can we do to ensure that we do not, at least, unwittingly flout it?

One approach, which seems particularly appropriate in our present context, may be to work from an alternative expression of the universalizability requirement in terms of a symmetric or *reciprocal* relationship between the parties involved: if the situations of any two parties to the contract are reversed this should make no difference to the conclusions reached. Since any rearrangement of actors and positions can be achieved by a series of pair-wise exchanges this formulation of the requirement as one of reciprocity is equivalent to that given above, and its practical application runs into very similar problems. However, the requirement that one place oneself in another's specific position may be much easier to act on in practice than the requirement that one ignore one's own position, especially when, as is the case here, we are concerned with situations in which there are typically just two main parties to be considered—(1) the business and (2) the members of the host country society—and especially when, as is also the case here, the position of the analyst is related through a shared culture to that of one of the parties.

In these circumstances we can adopt a simple but demanding test of universalizability. First, if the solution proposed is to be independent of the positions of the main parties involved, it must remain valid when the relative positions of those parties are reversed. Secondly, if the solution is to be independent of the position of the analyst, it must be acceptable to analysts from each of the cultures involved. (Note that these are not sufficient conditions, since they do not encompass all the potential parties to the contract, but they are necessary.)

In common with other analysts of international business ethics, Donaldson is concerned with the behavior of a business operating from a home country culture C1 within a host country culture C2, and in a situation in which he is himself positioned, as analyst, within the home country culture C1. In these circumstances our universalizability criteria would require that:

Requirement A Conclusions reached for the case of a business operating from a home country culture C1 within a host country culture C2 should remain valid for the case of a business operating from the home country culture C2 within the host country C1.

Requirement B Conclusions reached by an analyst working from within culture C1 should be such that they can also be agreed to by an analyst working from within culture C2.

Of these two requirements, the second is harder to achieve in practice than the first, and it may be that we cannot hope to develop a truly international business ethics without engaging in some kind of cross-cultural Habermasian discourse (Habermas 1990). We can, however, go part of the way toward meeting the requirement by focusing on what emerges as the key difference between cultures in Donaldson's analysis, namely the relative extent of the moral demands they impose. Thus we can require that:

Requirement B' Conclusions that hold in cases when the moral demands of the analyst's culture C1 are greater than those of another culture C2 should also hold when the demands of culture C2 are greater than those of culture C1.

With these requirements in mind, we can now suggest several modifications to Donaldson's approach.

Setting Up the Problem

The first of these concerns the way the problem is set up. At the beginning of this paper we proposed a three-way categorization of the moral issues arising in international business which was completely symmetric with regard to the cultural viewpoints involved. Either (1) the two cultures led to conflicting moral requirements; or (2) one (we did not specify which) imposed requirements that the other did not; or (3) the requirements turned out to be substantially the same, once circumstantial differences were taken into account. Because of its symmetry, this categorization allows a reversal of the positions of the parties, including the analyst, as indicated by Requirements A and B'. Donaldson's approach, however, does not. Indeed, by assuming that one, specified, culture (the culture C1 of the analyst and home country) is morally superior to all others, it rules out from the beginning any application of Requirement B'.

The asymmetry of Donaldson's asymmetric assumptions also results in a relatively narrowly drawn problem set. Although his emphasis on economic development means that the divisions are drawn somewhat differently, his type 1 and type 2 conflicts do correspond overall to our second and third categories. But he has no equivalent to our category (1). For the development of a universal ethics, however, this first category is critical. In the first place, the inherent symmetry of the situation makes it much easier to control for the specific position of the analyst: any arguments resulting from this position are likely to disrupt the symmetry in an evident manner. Secondly, it covers the "hard" cases: any procedure for solving problems within it should also lead automatically to a procedure for solving the less demanding problems within the second and third categories.

Developing an Algorithm

Our second suggestion is that, in accordance with Requirement A, any algorithm for addressing cases of moral conflict should be symmetric with respect to the two cultures involved. Of course, the two cultures typically enter the problem in different ways: one as the "home" country culture of the business concerned and the other as the "host" country culture in which it is or might be operating.[6] While this presents a practical asymmetry, however, it does not—or should not—present a moral one. Being "home" or "host" is a situation into which different actors may be placed and into which they should, if universalizability is to be upheld, be indifferently placed; it does not in itself confer any moral status.

A first step toward keeping the algorithm symmetric is to treat the moral conflict involved in a clash of cultures just like any other intracultural moral conflict. If we were to follow, for example, the well-known procedure proposed by Hare (1981), we would begin by stating the general moral principles applied by *each* culture to the problem (Donaldson, like most writers on the subject, seems remarkably unconcerned with any moral principles of the host culture) and only then concern ourselves with critical procedures for resolving the resulting conflicts.

Because, in practice, the host and home country cultures enter a business situation in different ways, there is still a danger that the procedure will be dominated by one perspective. In most of the situations discussed by international business ethics writers, for example, the balance of power and knowledge as well as the onus of the moral decision lie with the home-culture business managers. This may be unavoidable, but its effects can be mitigated by looking to our requirement A and transposing the situation from one in which the home culture characterizes the business to one in which it characterizes the host. From an American perspective, for example, we could ask how we might respond to an Islamic multinational operating in the USA and criticising our immoral lending practices, our practice of depriving men of jobs by employing women, or the social pressures to consume alcohol. If in such a case we were to argue that the Islamic multinational should accept American norms when operating in the USA, then this might suggest that on issues of these particular kinds American companies should accept Islamic norms when operating in an Islamic state.

Requirement B' suggests that in analysing cases in which the standards of one culture are morally more or less demanding than those of another, we should adopt an algorithm that encompasses the possibility, denied by Donaldson, that it is our own culture which is the less demanding. We must also be careful not to prejudge what is or is not a moral issue. It is always tempting to assume that less demanding standards than one's own have moral import while more demanding standards do not, and so to evade the possibility of our own moral inferiority. History affords enough examples, however, to demonstrate the fallacy of that assumption, and where other cultures impose stricter requirements than our own it would be prudent to assume that these might in principle have moral significance and so to put ourselves, even if only hypothetically, in a position of moral inferiority.

Even in looking at cases in which there is evidently no essential moral conflict but merely a difference in economic and social circumstances, it might be useful to apply the same type of universalizability requirements as we have proposed for the resolution of ethical differences. In particular, we should not assume either that the home country is necessarily more advanced, economically and socially, than the host country, or that the analyst's own country is so privileged. Donaldson's algorithm takes it for granted that the economic and social standards of the USA are equal to or higher than those of any other society, but this is, to say the least, highly contestable. More generally, a prescription for international business practices that is based on the economic superiority of *any* particular party (whether the host country as a category or some specific country) will always be of limited applicability.

Rights versus Obligations

Going back to the question of rights and obligations, our final suggestion is that Donaldson's list of rights should be recast, as in De George's (1993) treatment, as a list of obligations.[7] This has two potential advantages. First, since morality is primarily concerned with obligations, it is to obligations that the universality criterion should strictly be applied. Shifting the argument from obligations to rights has certain advantages but, as noted above, the two are not equivalent, and because their connection depends upon institutions, which are themselves specific to the cultures in which they are situated, the shift cannot be made without compromising the universality of the argument.

Secondly, a peculiarity of the problems encountered in international business ethics is that they are very often concerned with the relationship between businesses and individuals (citizens of the host country, employees, et cetera). While both businesses and individuals can be said to have obligations, so that their situations can in this respect be reversed in testing out the universality of a proposal, only individuals have rights of the kind cited by Donaldson.

Conclusion

The argument of this paper has been structured in the form of a critique of aspects of Donaldson's theory of international business ethics, but it could equally be applied to other treatments of the same subject and is intended to make a very general point.

A striking feature of the contemporary world is the extent to which communications technologies are breaking down culturally based value systems. Through travel, telecommunications, and especially television, people are increasingly exposed to the cultures and values of societies very different from their own. At the same time the institutional structures of family, church, and state, through which the values of individual societies have traditionally been transmitted and reinforced, are in many societies losing their authority. One consequence of this is that societies which were once characterized by a homogeneity of culture and, in particular, of ethical values are becoming increasingly pluralist. Another is that the differences between values found in different societies are increasingly being discussed and debated. Where these developments will lead is unclear. We may find ourselves, in a generation or two, in a state of near-anarchy, or we may find ourselves with a global consensus as to what is morally right and wrong. The one thing of which we can be reasonably confident is that if the latter is the case the consensus will be attributed by relativists to the power and domination of particular groups and by universalists to the effects of rational debate.

Meanwhile, however, the assumption that each national culture can be characterized by a single set of ethical values is still close enough to reality to make attempts such as Donaldson's worthwhile, and not merely for their contribution to the ethics of business. In whatever context they may arise, culturally based ethical conflicts provide the sternest test of any universalist theory of ethics. Because of the way in which international and cross-cultural differences arise routinely in the course of its day-to-day operations, without being regulated by transnational institutions, business practice is a rich source, indeed probably the main source, of such conflicts in the world today. Business ethics therefore has a potentially critical role to play in the testing and development of mainstream moral theory, well beyond its traditional remit of the mere application of ethics to the business community. If it is to play such a role, it must engage with theory, and it must do so in a rigorous fashion.

Notes

I am particularly grateful to Tom Sorell, Philip Stiles, and Pat Werhane for their comments and criticisms on an earlier draft of this paper.

[1]For a fuller discussion of this point see O'Neill (1996), especially pp. 19–20.

[2]For a critique of other aspects of Donaldson's approach see Bowie (1991).

[3]This is demonstrated most forcefully by MacIntyre (1967, 1988).

[4]This argument is not often stated, as writers on ethics tend to dismiss ethical relativism on the grounds that it cannot be proven, while omitting to mention that ethical universalism cannot be proven either: each position is, on its own terms, immune from the criticisms of the other. For a thorough analysis of the varieties of ethical relativism and their relationship to cultural relativism see Wong (1984).

[5]This ethnocentricity was pointed out by Velasquez (1995), but without any discussion of its origins.

[6]If, as seems likely, the notion of a business's "home" country becomes increasingly meaningless over the coming decades, we may have to find new ways of expressing the problems of international business ethics. For the moment, however, the expression is common to all of the main treatments of the subject.

[7]De George's approach is theoretically much less ambitious than Donaldson's, but it is also philosophically more careful.

Bibliography

Bowie, Norman. 1991. Moral decision-making and multinationals. *Business Ethics Quarterly* 1: 223–232.

De George, Richard T. 1993. *Competing with Integrity in International Business*. New York: Oxford University Press.

Donaldson, Tom. 1989. *The Ethics of International Business*. Oxford: Oxford University Press.

Elfstrom, Gerard. 1991. *Moral Issues and Multinational Corporations*. New York: St. Martin's Press.

Habermas, Jurgen. 1990. *Moral Consciousness and Communicative Action*. Cambridge, England: Polity Press.

———. 1996. On the cognitive content of morality. *Proceedings of the Aristotelian Society* 99: 335–358.

Hare, R. M. 1981. *Moral Thinking: Its Levels, Method and Point*. Oxford: Oxford University Press.

MacIntyre, Alasdair. 1967. *A Short History of Ethics*. London: Routledge.

———. 1988. *Whose Justice? Which rationality?* London: Duckworth.

O'Neill, Onora. 1996. *Towards Justice and Virtue: A Constructive Account of Practical Reasoning*. Cambridge: Cambridge University Press.

Rawls, John. 1972. *A Theory of Justice*. Oxford: Oxford University Press.

Velasquez, Manuel. 1995. International business ethics: the aluminium companies in Jamaica. *Business Ethics Quarterly* 5: 865–882.

Wong, David. 1984. *Moral Relativity*. Berkeley: University of California Press.

[41]

Toward an Understanding of Cross-Cultural Ethics: A Tentative Model

William A. Wines
Nancy K. Napier

ABSTRACT. In an increasingly global environment, managers face a dilemma when selecting and applying moral values to decisions in cross-cultural settings. While moral values may be similar across cultures (either in different countries or among people within a single country), their application (or ethics) to specific situations may vary. Ethics is the systematic application of moral principles to concrete problems.

This paper addresses the cross-cultural ethical dilemma, proposes a tentative model for conceptualizing cross-cultural ethics, and suggests some ways in which the model may be tested and operationalized.

Introduction

In a global environment, managers face a dilemma when they seek to apply moral values to business decisions in cultures outside their own. Yet, as in other topics that cut across several disciplines, ethics in cross-cultural settings may have "fallen through the cracks." Some business ethics texts do not even raise the issue (e.g., Velasquez, 1988; Shaw and Barry, 1992), while others assert that ethics in a cross-cultural context is a problem, but say little more (e.g., De George, 1986; Solomon and Hanson, 1983). Scholarly research has dealt with the role of religion (Safranski, 1986) and values in managerial behavior (e.g., England, 1975), and even ethical issues of conducting cross-cultural training (Paige and Martin, 1983), but none directly confronts the issue of ethics in a cross-cultural setting.

Several reasons explain the apparent neglect of ethics in a cross-cultural (i.e., an organization operating in two or more cultures) or multicultural context (i.e., dealing with several cultures in a single organization) (Adler, 1984). First, the individual topics (i.e., culture and ethics) themselves are difficult to study. Culture has been notoriously difficult to define, examine and understand either by itself or in its relationship to management practices (e.g., Hofstede, 1980; Kedia and Bhagat, 1988; Kroeber and Kluckholn, 1952). Likewise, the topic of ethics has stirred at least as much controversy, if not more, with regard to whether it can or should be taught (e.g., Mulligan, 1987), let alone be investigated in a scientific manner (e.g., Wines and Wilterding, 1989). Further, just as culture researchers have wrestled with definitions and measurement issues, so too must scholars seeking to examine ethics in multicultural settings. The challenge of developing operational measures for such cross-cultural concepts can be daunting (Adler, 1983; Sekaran, 1983). Thus, pursuing such a topic that combines these two concepts is, at the outset, fraught with problems.

Second, examining cross-cultural ethics presumes there may be common threads of moral values across cultures or that applying values across cultures is possible. Moral philosophers, however, differ sharply on whether universal moral values exist. While some refute the idea of universal moral truths, others argue that the notion of social progress impeaches the idea of cultural relativism: for them, the very notion of moving toward better values would be impossible if right and wrong were simply other terms for acceptable behavior or actions within a culture or society (Rachels, 1986). In other words,

William A. Wines is Professor of Legal Environment and Business Ethics in the Management Department, College of Business, Boise State University, Boise, Idaho, USA. His research interests include business ethics, employment law, and public sector collective bargaining.

Nancy K. Napier is Professor of Management and Chairman of the Management Department, College of Business, Boise State University, Boise, Idaho, USA. Her research interests include international business, mergers and acquisitions, and human resource management.

Journal of Business Ethics **11**: 831–841, 1992.

some values must be "better" than others for there to be any social progress.

Finally, in some definitions of culture, moral values appear to be an implicit component (e.g., Kroeber and Kluckhohn, 1952). For example, England's (1975) discussion of personal values suggests broad moral values (e.g., loyalty, trust) without specifying context or principles applying those values. While cross-cultural ethics may be a subset of values, recognizing differences enables us to examine them. Without a clear concept of "moral values" and their application (i.e., ethics), it is difficult to examine cross-cultural ethics. Thus, as a first step for investigating cross-cultural ethics, this paper seeks to provide a tentative model for understanding cross-cultural ethics.

Review of concepts relating to cross-cultural ethics

This section of the paper examines concepts relevant to building a model of cross-cultural ethics: (1) moral values, (2) ethics, (3) culture, (4) managerial values and (5) religion's role in international management.

Moral values and ethics

Rokeach (1968, p. 124) summarized different approaches to the term "value" in the following passage:

> The concept of *value* has at least three distinct meanings. To Thomas and Znaniecki, value is a sociological concept, a natural object that has, in fact, acquired social meaning and, consequently, "is or may be an object of activity" (1918, p. 21). To Campbell (1963), Jones and Gerard (1967), and to many others a value seems to be synonymous with an attitude because the attitude object has *valence* or cathexis. In this conception, a person has as many values as there are valenced or cathected attitude objects. To many others, including the present writer, a value is seen to be the disposition of a person just like an attitude, but more basic than an attitude, often underlying it.

Rokeach then develops his idea of what a value is in the next paragraph when he continues:

> I consider a value to be a type of belief, centrally located within one's total belief system, about how one ought or ought not to behave, or about some end-state of existence worth or not worth attaining. Values are thus abstract ideals, positive or negative, not tied to any specific attitude object or situation, representing a person's beliefs about ideal modes of conduct and ideal terminal goals. . . . Some ideal modes of conduct are to seek truth and beauty, to be clean and orderly, to behave with sincerity, justice, reason, compassion, humility, respect, honor, and loyalty. Some examples of ideal goals or end-states are security, happiness, freedom, equality, ecstacy, fame, power, and states of grace and salvation. A person's values, like all beliefs, may be consciously conceived or unconsciously held, and *must be inferred from what a person says or does*. [Emphasis added].

Others have suggested that a consensus seems to be building among some social scientists around a definition of value based largely on the work of Kluckhohn *et al.* (Connor and Becker, 1991). Such a definition is consistent with what we have cited from Rokeach: "A value is a conception, explicit or implicit . . . of the desirable which influences the selection from available modes, means, and ends of action" (Kluckholn, 1951, p. 389 as cited in Connor and Becker, 1991). Rokeach supports this in defining an attitude as "a relatively enduring organization of beliefs about an object or situation predisposing one to respond in some preferential manner" (1968, p. 134). We divide Rokeach's concept of value into two components; the precepts for action which he called "modes" we call "morals" denoting *prima facie* rules for action and Rokeach's desired end-states we shall refer to as "values." In a sense, truth can be seen as a value which is then the basis for the moral precept of "Seek ye the truth." The way in which the precept is applied when the application is unclear or in doubt is an exercise in what we call ethics. (Following Churchill, 1982).

From the smorgasbord of ethics definitions (e.g., De George, 1986; Velasquez, 1982), Churchill (1982) has offered one that differentiates ethics from moral values. Churchill's (1982) definition is appropriate and useful here because it is consistent with what we know from the social-psychology research on values and because it provides better insight into the operational aspects of ethics than others. Stated simply, for Churchill (1982), morality is the practical activity that governs human conduct in a given culture. The moral obligations function as "black letter" or clear, *prima facie* (i.e., dominant but rebuttable rather than absolute) rules of behavior (Ross, 1930). For the most part, such precepts are straightforward and are accepted by people from a given culture. Examples of accepted moral values in the United States would be sanctity of human life and individual choice (Churchill, 1982, 297).

Moral values are usually expressed as abstractions in the form of adjectives (e.g., compassionate) or nouns (e.g., beneficence). Illustrations of moral values at this level of abstraction include the Boy Scout Law which states that a boy scout is trustworthy, loyal, helpful, friendly, courteous, etc. Moral precepts are statements of ground rules for behavior. Following W. D. Ross (1930), we believe that they are *prima facie* rules of behavior. For illustration, a moral precept would be that an employee is *prima facie* loyal to her employer. A moral code is a system or collection of moral precepts – such as the Ten Commandments; although, occasionally, the term moral code is applied to a collection of abstract values – even though such a collection is not very helpful in terms of guiding behavior due to its high level of abstraction.

Ethics is the activity of applying moral precepts to concrete problems. Following Churchill (1982), we believe that ethics involves analytical, rational, and cognitive processes. In a sense, moral codes are the comprehensive, abstract principles that govern modes of conduct in a given culture.

The application of moral codes becomes complicated as individuals begin to see those values, which were perceived as "good" or "accepted" in the abstract, come to life when applied to a specific issue. For example, while it seems reasonable to expect that the two moral values mentioned above (i.e., human life sanctity and choice), could exist in many cultures, they may conflict in some cultures when a terminally ill patient seeks euthanasia from his or her physician. Thus, the *application* of principles (i.e., ethics) is expected to make the outcome complicated and may differ across cultures.

Using Churchill's (1982) broad definition, it is possible to identify moral values that are common or, at a minimum, similar across cultures. Even so, their *application* may differ from culture to culture for a number of reasons. Cultures may take the same abstract moral values and reach different practices because of (1) the place of the culture on developmental/temporal scale; (2) the weight accorded to different or competing values; and (3) the manner in which the society applies the abstract value. For example, Churchill (1982) has emphasized the need for a rational, cognitive application of moral values to problems, an approach which may be inherently more "Anglo-American" in its emphasis than that common in "Eastern" (e.g., Japan, India) cultures. This difference can be even more striking when the rational decision making process is considered on two levels. A first level of (rational) decision making involves finding the best solution for the individual decision maker; a second level of analysis involves generating a solution that is also acceptable to a larger community (Solomon and Hanson, 1983). In addition, even where cultures concur on basic values, they may apply those moral values differently. For instance, in the ancient world (circa 6th Century B.C.) Callations (an Indian people) and Greeks believed that people should respect the bodies of their ancestors; however, the Callations did so by eating the bodies, and the Greeks honored their dead with cremation (Herodotus as quoted in Rachels, 1986, p. 12).

Culture

The discussion of definitions and arguments about conflicting theories for understanding cultural differences (and similarities) among groups of people have been ongoing for at least a century. In one of the earlier discussions, Tylor (1891, p. 1, found in Sturdivant, 1985, p. 29) defined culture as ". . . that complex whole which includes knowledge, belief, art, morals, law, custom, and any other capabilities and habits acquired by man as a member of society." Later, other scholars (e.g., Mann, 1984; Kroeber and Parsons, 1958) contrasted culture and social systems as two different approaches to understand differences among groups. Although the conflict between cultural anthropologists and sociologists raged during the first half of the 20th century, Singer (1968) saw less conflict than did other sociologists. He viewed the theory of social structure as both explicitly and implicitly incorporating culture.

Somewhat similar to the social structure-culture debate was another discussion focusing on two models that differ in their emphasis on important culture dimensions (Mann, 1984, p. 75). The functionalist model suggests that a core culture is generally shared by the members of a society. Hofstede's (1980) cultural dimensions (i.e., individualism, masculinity, power distance, tolerance for ambiguity), for example, could define the "consensus culture" of a given country. This consensus core culture, distinctive to a nation state, then encompasses specialized or minority "sub cultures." A second model of culture (the conflict theory) is based upon Marxist thought, and emphasizes the similarities of groups that share some common institutional matrix or framework (Mann, 1984).

Two definitions of culture seem to have gained general acceptance – one from anthropology and one from management. Kroeber and Kluckhohn (1952), in their extensive literature review, generated over one hundred definitions of culture in an effort to develop one that would be acceptable to a range of social scientists. They defined culture as "... patterns, explicit and implicit, of and for behavior acquired and transmitted by symbols, constituting the distinctive achievement of human groups ... the essential core of culture consists of traditional (i.e., historically derived and selected) ideas and especially their attached values; culture systems may, on the one hand, be considered as products of action, on the other as conditioning elements of further action." (Kroeber and Kluckholm (1952, p. 357).

From the management perspective, Hofstede (1980) offered a definition used extensively in recent cross-cultural management research: "the collective programming of the mind which distinguishes the members of one human group from another" or alternatively "the interactive aggregate of common characteristics that influence a human group's response to its environment." (Hofstede, 1980, p. 21).

The culture literature is interesting also for what it *does not* say about values. While definitions of culture have frequently incorporated "values" or "moral values," there has been little specific explanation of what is meant by moral values or how such values translate into rules for behavior in ethical situations. To understand relationships between values and their applications in cultures, a look at "reflective equilibrium" – a concept used to develop theories of justice – may be helpful (Rawls, 1971). In developing rules which promote justice, philosophers move from values to principles which are used to decide cases the results of which are then tested against the original values.

Managerial values

Early studies on personal values of managers (e.g., England, 1967, 1975) provided a relatively thorough examination of how managers in different countries perceive their roles. England's (1967, 1975) work classified managers into four profiles (i.e., pragmatic, moralistic, affective, mixed) reflecting their perspectives on 66 concepts. Nonetheless, in a recent review of the England studies, Davis and Rasool (1988) have suggested that business managers may continue to neglect information from England's (1975) research since firms (typically American) usually reward pragmatic managers, although many operate in countries where one of the other profiles dominates.

Similar to the research on cultures, moral values seem to be part of personal value system profile. England's (1975) list of 66 values included such things as dignity, loyalty, compassion, and trust, which resonate through much of the moral philosophy literature. Unfortunately, England (1975) is unclear on whether and how these values relate to specific rules for action or behavior, and ultimately on their application to ethics issues. Clearly, loyalty may be a moral principle in many cultural contexts; the England research did not pursue in depth the translation of the general value or abstract concept to a rule of behavior.

Religion in international management

A final research area with relevance to cross-cultural ethics is the role of religion in value systems. Many studies have questioned the strength of relationships between religious affiliation and work values, at least in the U.S. (e.g., Safranski and Kwon, 1988). Even so, there may also be a nexus between religious values and management values for some countries outside the U.S. For instance, Safranski's (1986) earlier research suggests that differences in management values are related to religious philosophy; using discriminant analysis he classified members of a manager sample as either Catholic or Muslim with 70% accuracy (Safranski, 1986). Other research suggests that, while Buddhism generally appears to be a deterrent to industrialization, one of its two major sects appears to be less of a deterrent than the other sect (Kim, 1988). Thus, values reflected through religious affiliation in some cases may influence management practice.

Tentative model of cross-cultural ethics

The preceding brief review suggests several important points for building a tentative model of cross-cultural ethics. First, the culture, religion, and managerial values literature all incorporate various ideas of "values" or moral values into their discussions. While little specific research attention has been given to moral values in these areas, moral values appear to be embedded in the respective literatures nonetheless. Thus, certain moral values may exist within and across cultures.

A second point, beyond the *existence* of moral values, is that values may be held with varying degrees of intensity. Such an assumption is similar to those made in culture and values research. Rokeach (1968) in his work on values listed five (5) types of beliefs which differed in their centrality and correspondingly their resistance to change. He posited an intensity dimension in the following passage: "While it is not possible to specify in advance on conceptual grounds which beliefs within a class will be more or less intense, it is possible to order such beliefs empirically along an intensity dimension" (1968, p. 13). In culture research, Hoftstede (1980) has suggested that his four dimensions of culture are present to a greater or lesser extent across countries. Likewise, England's (1967, 1975) managerial values profile reflects different weights given to values by managers across geographic settings. The existence and likely difference in weights assigned to individual moral values, as a subset of all managerial values, should follow similar logic.

A central question in this paper is whether a framework for understanding cross-cultural ethics questions can be effectively conceptualized. An earlier model includes a simple framework for viewing moral values and ethics within a single culture (Owens, 1982). In addition, the model suggests that cultures may tend to be closed systems in which public opinion involving moral beliefs reverberate through the political and economic system to change the external environment for business decisions.

Owens's (1982) model demonstrated the relationship between moral values and managerial decisions (or ethics as the application of moral values), as moderated by political and economic contexts. In his model (Figure 1), manager decisions are the center of concentric circles. The middle layer represents the political and economic contexts, which influence decisions. The outer layer includes moral values, beliefs and public opinion, which include important cultural elements. Values and opinions influence both inner layers — the political and economic contexts as well as decisions.

Extending the Owens (1982) model to a cross-cultural perspective, it may be possible to compare two or more cultures in terms of those three dimensions. Indeed, cultures may overlap or "interface" when a firm conducts business outside its home country or when a domestic company employs

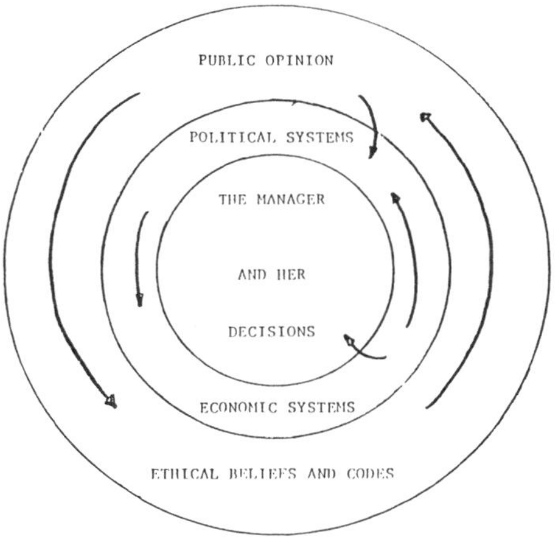

Fig. 1. Owens's (1983) Model of business ethics.

people from several cultures. The overlap may occur at several levels of Owens's model – managerial practices and decisions, context (e.g., similar economic systems) or moral values and beliefs.

The proposed conceptualization further suggests that there may be clusters of cultures with shared moral values, as Hofstede (1980) suggested with his dimensions. In such cases, cultures may be linked by "value strings" representing common moral values. Thus, there may be some moral values common to North American or European cultures and others more prevalent in East Asian cultures (Figure 2). Finally, there may be cultures that are essentially "closed," in terms of interactions with others, but which may share moral values with other cultures, such as Japan during the 250 year period from the

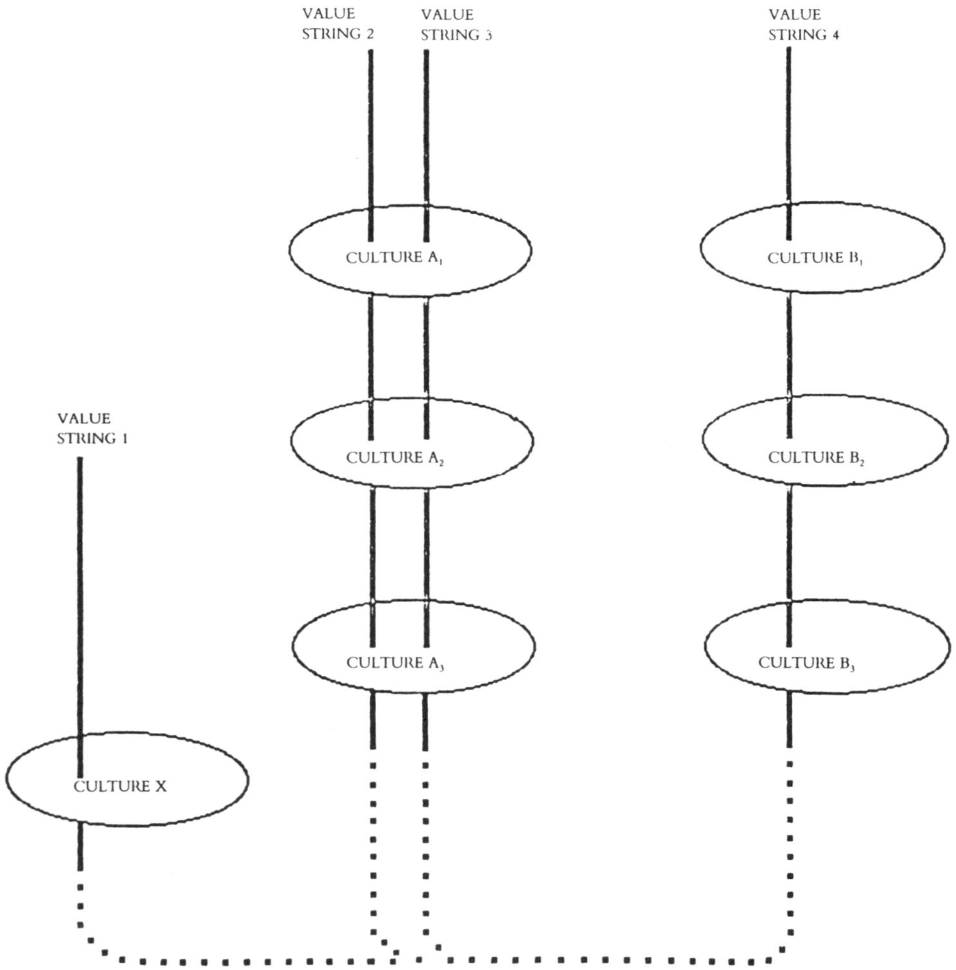

Fig. 2. A proposal model for cross-cultural ethics based on owens's (1983) model.

early 1600s to the late 1800s (Akagi, 1937; Beasley, 1951). Only those authors who confuse cultural relativism, a descriptive ethical statement, with ethical relativism seem to argue for the extreme position that societies could exist without sharing any values.

The proposed model (Figure 2) has several insights that may prove helpful in conceptualizing problems of cross-cultural ethics: (1) it allows for significant shared values to be represented as overlapping cultures; (2) it allows some nations, shown as Culture X (e.g., Japan in 17th—19th century period, Iran in the 1980s) to be represented as mostly closed cultures separate and distinct from most other cultures but which may have moral values that are similar; and (3) by incorporating Owen's (1982) model, it can demonstrate that a common value may be manifested in the economics of one culture but appear in the moral value code rather than economics of a second culture, thereby given the model additional flexibility.

Overcoming the model's limitations

The model illustrated in Figure 2, as do all models, has its limitations. It is not explicit about weighting and application variations between two cultures embracing the same abstract moral value in apparently contradictory rules or practices. Further, the model in Figure 2 suggests a static situation, when in fact the application of values may vary over time within a culture. Finally, as currently presented, it mixes macro and micro values systems, a flaw also contained in the original Owens's Schematic. A model should address the current values literature which falls into three groupings: (1) individual manager's values; (2) values within the corporate/firm culture; and (3) values in the dominant or sub cultures in a society. A useful model should address more than one level of values.

Application and weighting

An adequate model for understanding cultural variants in practices should address the application and weighting factors involved in transforming abstract values into practices. Different cultures transform an abstract moral value such as "respect for the dead" into a wide variety of practices such as burial, cremation, and eating of the dead. Even within broadly grouped practices such as cremation or burial, there are wide variations which may be primarily a function of the wealth of a society (the margin for survival) and the maturity of the civilization (Figure 3). For instance, a Viking funeral pyre in 922 A.D. included not only the Viking ship but also oxen, horses, a dog and a serving girl who was executed just before the blaze was set (Carry, 1987, pp. 25–28).

In respect to weighting of values and application, we need to be sensitive to the changes in cultures over time. As Figure 3 suggests, the application of value with regard to punishment of murder may change as a culture develops its moral sensitivity. Early punishment in a culture may be trial by ordeal, followed by execution, which over time may evolve into life sentences without parole. Similarly, application may vary between cultures in the emphasis given outcome or consequential ethics (Pastin, 1986) and the ethics of duty. This is a major division in moral philosophy. Some writers have suggested that business schools teach consequential ethical applications even as they deny moral indoctrination (Scott and Mitchell, 1986). One interesting empirical study would involve testing our hypothesis that consequential applications of moral value correlate with a society's emphasis upon commerce and modern business methods (Figure 4).

Macro-level filtering

On a societal or macro-level, we believe that moral values are filtered through application and weighting processes and then moderated by external environmental factors before being manifested in dominant cultural practices (Figure 5). The external climate, availability of natural resources, population density, available technology, and other factors included under "margin of survival" help dictate whether infanticide or adoption or abortion are practiced in cultures which all embrace nurture of children as an abstract moral value (Rachels, 1986). For example, given two cultures where the weighting of the value, "nurturing of children," is similar, one might hypothesize that environmental factors of low availability of natural and food resources, high popula-

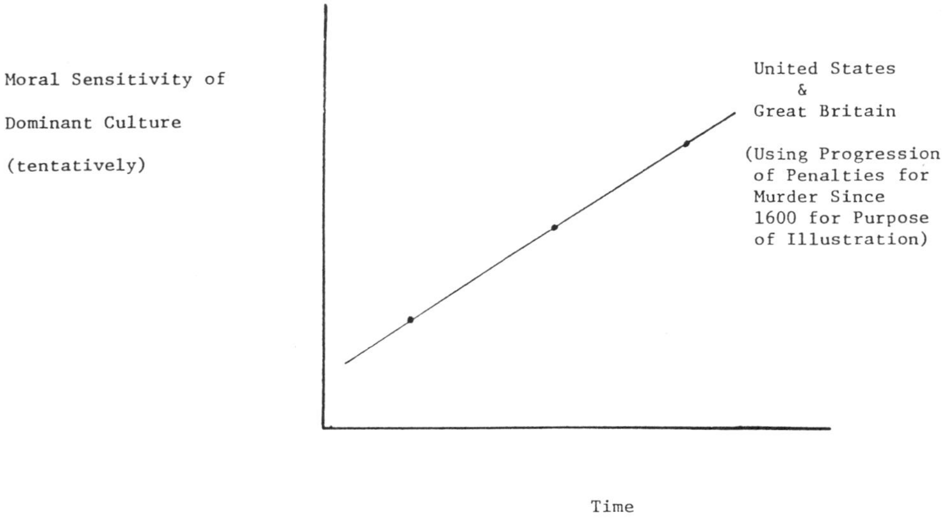

Fig. 3. Temporal changes in application of a moral value in a single culture.

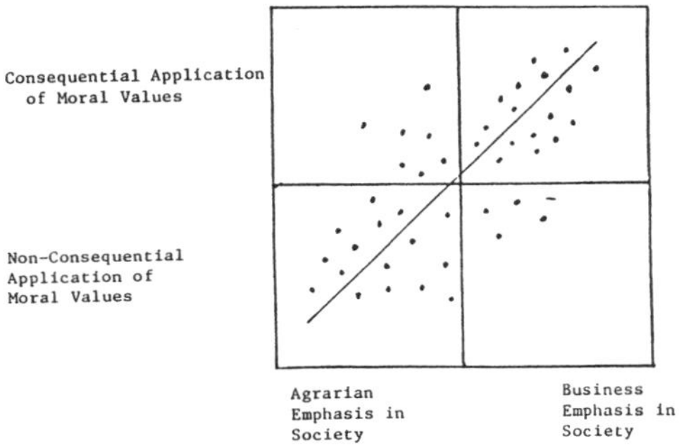

Fig. 4. Hypothesized application extension suggested for empirical testing.

tion density, low availability of technology and societal pride in being able to care for its members would lead to a predominance of infanticide or abortion, rather than adoption as a dominant cultural practice.

Micro-level filtering

At an individual micro level, the practices in the dominant and sub cultures are part of the external environment that the individual manager filters through her experience and education to arrive at her moral code (Figure 6). The way in which he or she applies a moral code is an exercise in business ethics at the micro level. For instance, a manager for Sony in Singapore must take into account the environment – the country's cultures (i.e., Malay, Chinese, Indian), the firm's strong culture, and religion (e.g., Muslim and Christianity) – and filter that through his own educational and experience background in applying his values.

This suggested conceptual framework incorporates much of what we know from the research streams studied in a comprehensive way that we believe will facilitate the next generation of research.

Summary and conclusions

This paper has suggested that there is a need for research and practice on how the application of

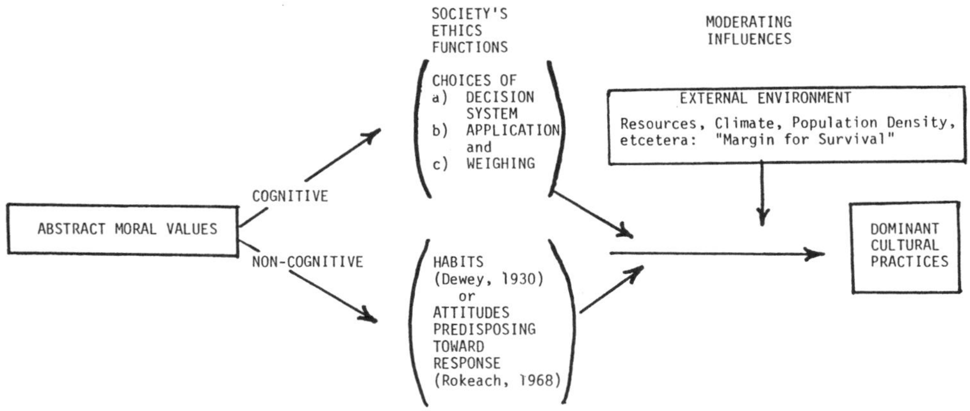

Fig. 5. Macro model of values being "filtered" and "moderated" into dominant cultural practices.

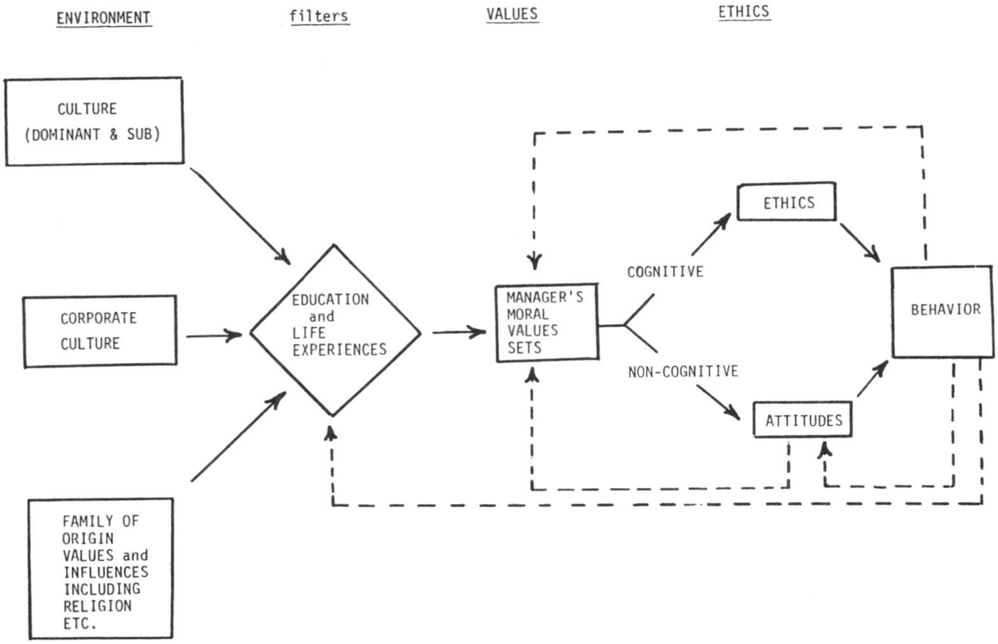

Fig. 6. Relationships among environment, values and manager's ethics (micro-level).

moral values varies across cultures. The paper briefly reviewed four streams of literature relating to cross-cultural ethics and proposed a tentative model.

The time for initiating a discussion of cross-cultural ethics seems ripe, both from a management and academic perspective. As business becomes more global, managers will be faced with translating moral values into business decisions and actions appropriate for various cultures. It is crucial that managers understand the implications of the decisions and actions they take in light of the application of moral values and codes. Further, as Nobel Laureate Kenneth Arrow (1973) has noted: ". . . a great deal of economic life depends for its viability on a certain limited degree of ethical commitment. Purely selfish behavior of individuals is really incompatible with any kind of settled economic life." (Arrow, 1973, 314).

From an academic and teaching perspective as well, the current emphasis on international and ethics issues in research and university programs raises the importance of cross-cultural ethics. The difficulties in conducting research on cross-cultural ethics have discouraged progress in this area to date. Business and academic forces are forming with the potential to overcome those obstacles to productive inquiry.

References

Adler, N.: 1983, 'Cross-Cultural Management Research: The Ostrich and the Trend', *Academy of Management Review* **8**(2), 226–232.

Adler, N. J.: 1984, *International Dimensions of Organizational Behavior* (Kent, Boston).

Akagi, R. H.: 1937, *Japan's Foreign Relations, 1542–1936: A Short History* (Hokuseido Press, Tokyo).

Arrow, K. J.: 1973, 'Social Responsibility and Economic Efficiency', *Public Policy* **21**(3), 300–317.

Beasley, W. G.: 1951, *Great Britain and the Opening of Japan: 1834–1858* (Luzac & Co., London).

Brady, F. N.: 1985, 'A Janus-Headed Model of Ethical Theory: Looking Two Ways at Business/Society Issues', *Academy of Management Review* **10**(3), 568–676.

Buller, P., J. Kohls, and K. Anderson: 1991, 'The Challenge of Global Ethics', *Journal of Business Ethics* **10**(10), 767–775.

Cadbury, A.: 1987, 'Ethical Managers Make Their Own Rules', *Harvard Business Review*, September–October, 69–73.

Carroll, A. B. (ed.): 1977, *Managing Corporate Social Responsibility* (Little, Brown, Boston).

Carry, J. (ed.): 1987, *Eyewitness to History* (Harvard University Press, Cambridge, MA).

Churchill, L. R.: 1982, 'The Teaching of Ethics and Moral Values in Teaching: Some Contemporary Confusions', *Journal of Higher Education* **53**(3), 296–306.

Connor, P. E. and B. W. Becker: 1991, 'Personal Value Systems and Managerial Decision Styles', Unpublished Paper presented at Western Academy of Management meetings, Santa Barbara, CA.

Davis, H. J. and S. A. Rasool: 1988, 'A Reconsideration of England's Values Research in Cross-Cultural Management', in R. N. Farmer and E. G. McGoun (eds.), *Advances in International Comparative Management*, Vol. **3** (JAI, Greenwich, CT), pp. 109–126.

De George, R. T.: 1986, *Business Ethics*, 2nd ed. (MacMillan, New York).

Dewey, J.: 1930, *Human Nature and Conduct: An Introduction to Social Psychology* (Random House, Modern Library Edition, New York) (Originally published in 1922).

England, G. W.: 1967, 'Personal Value Systems of American Managers', *Academy of Management Journal* (March), 53–68.

England, G. W.: 1975, *The Manager and His Values: An International Perspective* (Ballinger Publishing Co., Cambridge, MA).

Hofstede, G.: 1980, *Culture's Consequences: International Differences in Work-Related Values* (Sage Publications, Beverly Hills).

Ishida, H.: 1986, 'Transferability of Japanese Human Resource Management Abroad', *Human Resource Management* **25**(1), 103–120.

Kedia, B. L. and R. S. Bhagat: 1988, 'Cultural Constraints on Transfer of Technology Across Nations: Implications for Research in International and Comparative Management', *Academy of Management Review* **13**(4), 559–571.

Kim, K. J.: 1988, *The Effects of Buddhism on Business Practices and Behavior*. Paper presented at the Western Social Science Association meeting, April.

Kroeber, A. L. and C. Kluckhohn: 1952, *Culture: A Critical Review of Concepts and Definitions*. Vol. **47**(1) (Harvard University Press, Cambridge, MA).

Kroeber, A. L. and T. Parsons: 1958, 'The Concept of Culture and Social System', *American Sociological Review* **23**, 582–583.

Lansing, P. and T. Domeyer: 1989, 'The *Tatamae* and *Honne* of Japan's Internationalization: The Japan – South Africa – Relationship', Paper presented at the Midwest Business Administration Association meetings, April.

Magnet, M.: 1986, 'The Decline and Fall of Business Ethics', *Fortune*, December 6, 1986, 65–72.

Mann, M. (ed.): 1984, *The International Encyclopedia of Sociology* (Continuum, New York).

Mulligan, T. M.: 1987, 'The Two Cultures in Business Education', *Academy of Management Review* **12** (4), 593–599.

Napier, N. K. and G. P. Latham: 1987, *Enhancing Intercultural Communication in Foreign Subsidiaries in Hong Kong and Singapore*, Academy of International Business meetings, November 1987, Chicago, IL.

Owens, J.: 1983, 'Business Ethics in the College Classroom', *Journal of Business Education* (April), 258–262.

Paige, R. M. and J. N. Martin: 1983, 'Ethical Issues and Ethics in Cross-Cultural Training', in D. Landis and R. W. Brislin (eds.), *Handbook of Intercultural Training*, Vol. **1** (Pergamon Press, New York), 36–60.

Pascale, R. T.: 1978, 'Personnel Practices and Employee Attitude: A Study of Japanese and American Managed Firms in the United States', *Human Relations* **31** (7), 597–615.

Pastin, M.: 1986, *The Hard Problems of Management: Gaining the Ethics Edge* (Jossey-Bass Publishers, San Francisco).

Rachels, J.: 1986, *The Elements of Moral Philosophy* (Random House, New York).

Rawls, J.: 1971, *A Theory of Justice* (The Belknap Press, Cambridge, MA).

Rokeach, M.: 1968, *Beliefs, Attitudes, and Values: A Theory of Organization and Change* (Jossey-Bass Publishers, San Francisco).

Ross, W. D.: 1930, *The Right and the Good* (Oxford University Press, London).

Safranski, S. R.: 1986, 'Religion and Management', in R. N. Farmer (ed.), *Advances in International Comparative Management*, Vol. **2**, pp. 149–158.

Safranski, S. C. and I. Kwon: 1988, 'Religious Groups and Management Value Systems', in R. N. Farmer and E. G. McGoun (eds.), *Advances in International Comparative Management*, Vol. **3** (JAI, Greenwich, CT), 171–183.

Scott, W. G. and T. R. Mitchell: 1986, 'Markets and Morals in Management Education', *Selections*, Vol. **3** (2), 3–8.

Sekaran, U.: 1983, 'Methodological and Theoretical Issues and Advances in Cross-Cultural Research', *Journal of International Business Studies* **14** (2), 61–73.

Shaw, W. H. and V. Barry: 1992, *Moral Issues in Business, 5th ed* (Wadsworth Publishing Co, Belmont, CA).

Singer, M.: 1968, 'The Concept of Culture', in D. Sills (ed.), *International Encyclopedia of the Social Sciences* (Macmillan and Free Press, New York).

Solomon, R. C. and K. Hanson: 1983, *Above the Bottom Line: An Introduction to Business Ethics* (Harcourt Brace Jovanovich, Inc., New York)

Sturdivant, F. B.: 1985, *Business and Society: A Managerial Approach*, 3rd ed. (Richard D. Irwin, Inc., Homewood, IL).

Tung, R. L.: 1982, 'Selection and Training Procedures for U.S., European and Japanese Multinationals', *California Management Review* **25** (1), 57–71.

Taylor, E. B.: 1891, *Primitive Culture* (John Murray, London).

Velasquez, M. G.: 1988, *Business Ethics: Concepts and Cases*, 2nd ed. (Prentice-Hall, Englewood Cliffs, N.J.).

Wines, W. A. and J. Wilterding: 1988, 'Perspectives on Teaching Business Ethics: An Empirical Analysis of Student Attitude Changes Toward Corporate Social Responsibility Over 15 Weeks', *Midwest Law Review* **7**, 60–79.

Boise State University,
College of Business,
Department of Management,
Boise, ID, 83725,
U.S.A.

[42]

Ethics and Australian International Business Which Way to Asia?

Daniel W. Skubik

ABSTRACT. In an era of domestic and economic reform wherein deregulation/privatisation becomes a priority, short shift has too often been given to evaluative analyses of business activities. Evaluative monitoring and oversight are especially needful in highly competitive international business environments, where the temptations are very strong to adjudge individual effectiveness by the sole criterion of the bottom line. But what additional or alternative criteria should be administered, and by whom, is less clear. That any but the most vague Judeo-Christian or secular ethical standards are applicable (e.g. notions of fairness) is widely contested. The debate is significantly only widened when doing business across national borders involving peoples from different cultures and languages. This section is devoted to explicating the normative role of international codes of conduct for guiding the decision making of managers involved in multinational operations, and clarifying what ethical frameworks are available to the international manager for taking decisions which require selecting actions inconsistent with either home or host country demands.

Discussions about business ethics in the Australia-Asia context too often exhibit inclinations to gravitate towards the extremes. The result is that the recognition and resolution of ethical problems tend to be marginalised in either of two ways. On the one hand, discussions suggest that business ethics simply pose complications for business people which truly belong in the 'too-hard' or 'not my responsibility' basket (cf. Minus, 1993). On the other hand, these discussions can often translate ethical concerns as though they simply reflected cultural differences, like variations in dress and food (cf. Dunfee and Nagayasu, 1993). Consider the following examples of so-called common dilemmas in business ethics.

(1) Alford Pty Ltd, an Australian-based minerals extraction film, is invited by the junta now in power to explore for possible exploitation a site in Burma. The junta is notorious for human rights abuses, as reported by Amnesty International and other reputable humans rights groups, and has been condemned by an assortment of foreign affairs diplomats including Australia's Senator Gareth Evans. Should Alford accept the invitation to do business in Burma?

(2) Trimble Pty Ltd, a property developer in Australia, enters into a joint venture with a Japanese firm to construct a large integrated tourist resort in northern Queensland. The Japanese insisted on a contractual clause specifying the holding of a Shinto ceremony to bless the project at ground breaking – a demand which initially confused and embarrassed Trimble's negotiators, but to which they eventually agreed. Should Trimble have permitted the introduction of such religious sentiment in a secular project?

Discussions typified by the first type of case illustrated above quite quickly generate a great deal of heat, but seldom much light, on issues concerning the limits of acceptable government-business interaction. Such cases as doing business in country X are usually trotted out to demon-

Daniel W. Skubik is a lecturer in the College of Liberal Arts, Florida Atlantic University; and is also an independent consultant. He holds the PhD (philosophy), a JD (law), and an MA (Hons.).

Journal of Business Ethics **14**: 643–652, 1995.

strate either what business should never do (viz. never do business with a notorious regime), or what businesses can't be expected to decide for themselves (viz. the company's task is profit maximisation, not political reform; it is for the Australian government to pass legislation forbidding business contacts, e.g. through export restrictions, and/or diplomatically declaim the junta's activities). This understanding of business ethics comprises a useful device to justify certain anti-business demands from special interests claiming that some business just shouldn't be tolerated, or that effectively excuses business decision makers from taking responsibility for the business being done by passing off that responsibility to others. In neither way is business ethics being 'done'. That is, neither understanding of the case provides important insight into what factors are to be taken into account by business managers when taking a decision to do business overseas. It rather skirts the issues and the proper role of ethical decision making for those involved.

Discussions typified by the second case too readily and too easily conflate and confuse mores with morals, thereby ultimately trivialising the ethical decision-making process. If questioning the acceptance of the Shinto ceremony clause represents a core case of an ethical dilemma, then isn't the answer to all such questions obvious? Of course the firm should respect the religious sensibilities of the foreign party and be as accommodating as possible. The underlying query here is the practicality, not 'ethicality', of the ceremony requested. This pattern of case discussion makes it appear that business ethics just means being sensitive to cultural variations. And that sensitivity requires knowledge, but not moral judgment; experience, but not structured ethical decision making.

Such cases as these may be the meat of many ordinary discussions, but as a matter of fact they are neither truly representative nor core cases in Australian international business ethics. Rather, core questions which arise regarding the ethics of certain business practices are more properly concerned with (a) decisions within the purview of business managers, (b) stating positively what they ought to do [unlike case 1], and (c) much more than variations in non-moral cultural or religious practices [unlike case 2]. Consider the issues raised in the following two cases which better represent issues for ethical decision making in business contexts:

(3) IBM (Australia) is invited to establish a 'screwdriver' factory (i.e. a plant for assembling pre-manufactured computer components into a single, saleable unit) in Malaysia. This offshore move has the potential to generate significant cost savings for the company, not least because of the differential wage levels between Australian-based and Malaysian-based component assemblers: what IBM typically pays its workers in Wangarrata per hour will easily cover the costs of workers in Kuala Lumpur per day. What level of wages ought IBM pay its KL workers?

(4) Taiwan's electricity utility, Taipower, seeks to open negotiations with Western Australia over burial of radioactive wastes from Taiwan's unclear powered electricity generating stations. WA has the necessary and optimal open space, but no indigenous nuclear waste handling capabilities, so part of the deal would include the transfer of technology and training services to create a nuclear waste industry in Australia. To further the negotiating process, Taipower officers approach an Australian engineering and materials consultancy firm, with which it has had positive prior dealings, to request that certain supporting representations be advanced by the firm to appropriate WA and federal government officials. Of course, Taipower does not come empty handed to friends. They bring a variety of gifts to the consultancy firm's senior executives. Should the firm's executives accept the gifts and make the requested representations?

A rich categories of moral and non-moral issues are raised in these two cases, issues which cut to the core of daily business dealings, and none of which can be skirted, passed off, or put in simple cultural categories. Case 3, for example, raises the vexing issues of economic incentives and equity considerations: if IBM pays Australian level wages in Malaysia, thereby fulfilling in uncomplicated, straightforward terms the standard of equal pay for equal work, what becomes of the incentives to move offshore? If IBM pays local Malaysian subsistence wages, are economic advantages maintained through exploitation of Third World labour and at the expense of increased Australian unemployment? If IBM is to negotiate a wage level somewhere along the spectrum between these two endpoints, what are the trade-offs in general social welfare to be considered for the two communities and their workers? Case 4 likewise raises a set of significant debatable issues, including economic growth versus environmental impacts, gift giving versus bribery, and the role of business influence in formulation of public policy. These and other issues must be identified, problems addressed, and clashes or dilemmas resolved by the business managers involved.

How one might best perform those tasks is a central concern of this paper. In asking this question, we do not seek to present prescriptions, laying down simplistic do's & don't's in some checklist format. Rather, our aim is to consider ethical decision making in cultural context, and to develop fitting ethical frameworks which might be utilised as tools by relevant decision makers in the business community. Such tools can assist in identifying and resolving ethical problems when and as they arise in the daily give-ad-take of doing business overseas.[1]

What is business ethics?

Although the boundaries of our discussion have already been indicated in a general way, it may be helpful to set out in some more systematic form the scope of 'business ethics'. Mention has been made, for example, of moral and non-moral issues which can be expected to arise when doing business. A question quite naturally arising is how to distinguish one sort of issue from the other in the business context (see Hampden-Turner and Trompenaars, 1993).

As a first cut, it is important to recognise business ethics as but one branch on the tree of ethics. In a general way, ethics can be described as the investigation of right standards of behaviour between agents in a specified social environment or social setting. But of course ethics is not concerned with all possible forms of behaviour between agents; as we noted above we need to be able to distinguish say, forms of etiquette from core issues of ethics. A substantive notion of 'right' in 'right standards' then gives us a clue as to how we can proceed. So somewhat more narrowly, we can say that ethics is the investigation of those right standards of behaviour requiring constraints on the pursuit of an agent's own interests vis-a-vis another agent's interests in a specified social environment or social setting. That is, assuming we all have certain interests which we wish to pursue (e.g. acting to obtain resources such as good food and comfortable shelter), we need to investigate right standards of conduct which fairly constrain my seeking to achieve my otherwise legitimate interests when my doing so keeps you from achieving yours.

To get to business ethics, then, we might interpolate 'business' at appropriate points in our description of ethics to derive the following working definition:

> Business ethics is the investigation of those right standards of business behaviour requiring constraints on the pursuit of a business agent's interests vis-a-vis another agent's interests in a specified business environment or business setting.

Two points should immediately be noticed. First, this understanding of business ethics emphasises that the principal actor is understood to be a business agent. But the other agent affected by the potential actions of this business actor need not be another business agent; any agent who has interests which may be implicated in the business agent's activities can be a concern. This permits us to consider the affairs of a variety of agents which arise in cases such as those numbered (3) and (4), above. Not only other business people, but workers, customers, government officials and the general population touched by business activity come into focus, as well (cf. Hampden-Turner and Trompenaars, 1993).

Second, while the focus is on standards requiring 'constraints', we should not think these are confined to a list of 'what one shouldn't do' – of a rule that interferes with what I would rather do if I could 'get away with it'. That is, we need not think of constraints as rules which merely block behaviours which a business agent might otherwise perform to attain certain interests (such as profit maximisation). Sometimes the standards of business ethics will, as a matter of course, look like an patent command to refrain from certain activity (e.g. bribery is always wrong, so don't ever pay a bribe). But this is not the only, or even the most important, form a constraint can take.

Standards of behaviour which dictate realisation of interests through some constraint are more often rules adopted to facilitate cooperative behaviour between various actors. Consider the rules of the road. It doesn't matter really whether we drive on the right-or-left-hand side of the road; what matters is that we agree on a rule which we can all follow so that each of us can realise our interests in travelling safely from point to point each day. In adopting such rules constraining behaviour (I'm not after all free to drive on whatever side I might wish), we together come to have certain expectations about each other's future conduct. Thus, we can see how standards like 'honesty' and 'fair dealing' in business, which do yield rules to constrain certain behaviours of business people, are also important to the generation and maintenance of cooperative behaviour in the social or business setting in which we seek to participate. Many rules which otherwise look like merely negative commands might better be seen as a rule of coordination or cooperation. Muse once more on the rule noted above on bribery. One could look at that constraint as a simple 'don't; but it doesn't take too great imagination to see it as a rule which facilitates fair bargaining: as between two or more business agents negotiating/bidding on a project or sale with a third party, such a rule leads to an economically efficient as well as morally justifiable outcome.

One final note before we proceed. We spoke earlier of developing 'frameworks' for decision makers. Just what is meant by 'framework'? In this paper, frameworks of ethical decision making are comprised of general principles of ethical action from which standards requiring constraints on business behaviour can be derived. The derivation of any constraint comes from a certain 'calculus' of the ethical system which defines the agent's viewpoint or worldview (Skubik, 1992). That is, an ethical system is not a static view about what is good, valuable, right, etc. The system provides rules about arguments and reasons which count (and often which arguments and reasons do not count) when making a decision about how to act to reach that good, or what it means to act in the right, or to act to maintain that which is valuable, etc.

As an example, one might describe the following components of a rather common ethical framework, utilitarianism. Classical utilitarianism's central principle tells us we ought to do those acts which produce the greatest happiness for the greatest number. Assuming we are committed to that sort of ethical imperative, how do we decide what acts to do or refrain from doing? Jeremy Bentham, the 18th-century philosopher who made utilitarianism popular in the English-speaking world, developed a calculus, a means for computing the pains/costs and pleasures/benefits which flow from various possible acts. One could then determine which act did, in fact, lead to the desired outcome of the greatest happiness for the greatest number. You then were committed to perform that act rather than any other. We need not go into detail, here, about the usefulness or problems Bentham's particular calculus presents us. The point is that the principle adopted, whether utility or some other, is practically speaking rather empty without some means or measure for determining what acts follow from the principle. So besides the principles any agent might confess as central to their acting, we will need to ask about how the basic calculations are made to get from principles to acts.

To continue, assume then we have some means for calculating the desired outcome. Let us also assume we are interested in determining what stockmarket practices ought to be permitted or proscribed; specifically we want to consider whether insider trading is the sort of fair business activity which maximises utility. Upon performing the relevant calculations, let us say we discover that when compared with all possible alternative stock market rules, permitting insider trading fails to maximise utility. That is, a system permitting insider trading yields lesser benefits (or, what amounts to the same thing, greater harms) than alternative stock market systems. So we have derived a standard for stock market activity – insider trading is counterproductive and thus not to be permitted. And in this case the decision on how to act follows in straightforward fashion: don't engage in that activity if you wish to fulfill your utilitarian duty. (We can then go on to consider whether a specific, say legal, rule proscribing and punishing all insider trading likewise yields the greatest happiness for the greatest number. That is, does that enforceable constraint on business behaviour yield greater benefits than any of the alternative proscriptive-punishment rules which can be devised and considered.) Thus, the utilitarian standard properly derived from the utilitarian principle leads us to recognise the utilitarian constraint to maximise utility. Of course, one can all too easily imagine other internally coherent frameworks which might lead to different standards covering business practices, which would likely lead to conflicting constraints for business practices. What if, for example, another framework provides sound argument for permitting insider trading? When frameworks' prescriptions conflict, the agents are obviously in a difficult position.

But in addition, and perhaps more importantly in international contexts, there is the problem encountered of different framework coverage. That is, what does one do when different agents are committed to different frameworks which do not each identify the same set of practices for which standards and constraints are required? As an example, again consider the fact that while most Anglo-American frameworks consider stock market activity a focus for ethical concern and generally proscribe insider trading on ethical as well as economic grounds, other countries' stock markets are either not subject to such scrutiny or the government authorities have concluded that insider trading is not counterproductive (e.g. markets in Germany and Japan either permit or do not have meaningful resources devoted to prosecuting what would be considered clear cases of illegitimate insider activity in New York, Sydney or London).[2] What should be done when an ethical problem arising from within one framework and which requires some standard and constraint, may not even seem to be an ethical problem from within the other? Such problems of identification will be taken up in the next section as we move to cross cultural comparisons of ethical problems for business managers.

Theoretical steps

Discerning the reasons underlying business agents' actions is a difficult because relatively complex task. We can perhaps readily induce the existence of varied standards related to diverse principles within numerous frameworks – just look at the ethical diversity in business practices throughout the Asia Pacific region. But constructing these frameworks and their components, and then fairly attributing them to specific actors so as to understand business behaviours of those with whom we seek to do business, can seem a daunting task.

Using the old props of cultural stereotypes is not the way forward for modern business. Yet, one cannot simply deny or cast off cultural differences if one is to come to grips with the ways of one's potential business partner. Some middle way is needed.

This section comprises an attempt broadly to sketch that middleway, the way of employing ethical frameworks both as an aid to understand better what underlies diverse business practices and how a business person can utilise a frameworks approach to determine whether or how ethically to proceed with a possible business deal. The next and concluding subsection will outline the steps business managers can take to put this middle way into practice. But once again, note the caveat that this frameworks approach identifies a process by which ethical decision making can be facilitated; it is not a method for churning out a simplistic checklist of rights and wrongs of business practices. It assumes a general commitment to a moral point of view, and a desire to put that commitment into practice and to take responsibility for the decisions taken. It does not pass ethical responsibility to so-called experts, but entails constructing for oneself and for one's business dealings the means and limits of doing business when ethical perspectives clash (see De George, 1993).

As described above, an ethical framework comprises a coherent approach to evaluating business activity. That approach involves (a) deriving standards for constraining business activity from some basic principle or principles of the framework, and (b) identifying constraints which realise those standards. (Recall our example of classical utilitarianism, which is based upon the principle of greatest happiness for the greatest number, from which we derived the standard of fair dealing in the stock market understood in part as refusing to engage in insider trading; thus, the constraint of no insider trading was the appropriate rule to realise the standard, which was derived from the basic principle of the framework.)

To apply this framework approach (or middle way) of ethical decision making, we might best adopt a four-step process of information gathering, self-reflection and critical evaluation:

(1) gather the information necessary to construct the framework(s) used by the agent(s) with whom you are dealing (that is, identify the basic principle or principles and the calculus of that framework);
(2) engage in self-reflection so that you are consciously aware of the framework you as a business agent work within (again, that is the basic principle or principles and the calculus to which you are committed);
(3) critically evaluate the different business practices at stake according to the agents' underlying frameworks;
(4) determine which practices can be accommodated so that the business deal can go forward; which necessary practices cannot be accommodated so that the business deal might be hindered; leading to the 'on-balance' or 'all things considered' judgment as to whether or how the deal is ethically do-able.

Steps (1) and (2) require genuine reflection to gain self-knowledge, plus sensitivity to the position of others with differing backgrounds and cultural heritages as you attempt to reconstruct a framework which makes sense of the business practices at issue. Due to space constraints and the relatively straightforward nature of these steps, we shan't here discuss them in detail.[3] For now, let's turn to steps (3) and (4) to gain a greater awareness of what is at stake in this middle way.

Step (3) provides a means to facilitate cross cultural understanding. Before a business agent can judge whether or how to accommodate a different business practice, one needs to be able to discern the reasons which might be provided for linking the practice to the relevant standards, and those standards to their principles. In short, we seek to discern what can motivate or provide arguments for the diverse practices which seem to conflict and which are being followed by the different agents involved in this potential deal. We seek, in other words, on the basis of the information gathered in step (1), to reconstruct a framework from the bottom-up which can be fairly attributed to the other agent. While working from within our own framework we usually move from principle-to-standard-to-constraint and practice, we here move from practice and constraint to discern the standard and from there to the principle of the framework employed by the other. (It is frequently useful for us to reconstruct our own frameworks in this way, as well. Quite often we have good recognition of accepted business practices and know what constraints we are under, but sometimes no sure appreciation of the standards to which they are linked, or the principles which ground the standards. It is a very useful exercise to subject one's own practices to this analysis, as we shall do below.) To put some flesh to this rather abstract skeleton, let's try an example.

The practice of giving relatively expensive gifts to one's business partners, or even to those with whom one is seriously negotiating over a first deal, is common in some societies. On the other hand, it is just as common to encounter the practice of giving inexpensive gifts only, expensive gifts being generally proscribed in business dealings. How is one to understand these practices (step 3) so as to inform some judgment about how to respond when two parties holding divergent practices attempt to deal with one another (step 4)?

It is hardly sufficient to say one practice is 'Eastern' while the other is 'Western'. Even if that categorisation were in some sense accurate, it does not enhance our understanding; it merely supplies labels. And labels cannot facilitate making judgments about how to respond. More serious reflection is required here. How then might we understand these practices?

As suggested, we need to link these practices to standards prescribing such behaviour so as to discover or reasonably infer reasons for the practices' existence in the business environment. Arguments for that practice and constraint can then be constructed by linking them to a standard, which can then be linked to a grounding principle for that practice's framework. Thus, what we seek ultimately to compare are the frameworks' principles and their standards' reasons, not halting discussion at the level of noting mere differences in practices.

Now, gift giving occurs in all societies. What seems to differ is the acceptable value of the gifts and context of the giving. Higher-value gift giving in the business environment (common in East Asia) is the natural extension of gift giving from prior non-business social environments (Milner and Quilty, 1994). That is, the standard of gift giving between family members and close friends seems to have been transferred without constraint from the one social setting to the other. Gift giving in each case is thus fairly linked to the standard of how one properly treats one's friends. We can also fairly infer that the guiding principle of friendship is the same: one does business with one's friends just as one socialises with one's friends – indeed, this means the two sets of friends will inevitably and significantly overlap. Not only so, but that to occupy one set of 'being friend' is in some important sense necessary to the other. And since social friendship is (commonly) actually and logically prior to business friendship, it becomes easier to understand why each relation implies the other. In this framework, it is not gift giving that creates a friend as though friendship is purchased. Giving substantial gifts is the process of *recognising* friends for social-cum-business purposes: you are, or are becoming, my friend so I give you a real gift; not to oblige you to be a friend because I give you an expensive gift.

Conversely, nominal gift giving (more common in Anglo-American societies) indicates that different standards are operating in what are deemed to be separate contexts: one may do business with one's social friends, but such overlap is in no sense necessary. Neither is one relationship logically nor actually prior to the other. Thus, the practice of nominal gift giving must be linked to a standard not transferred from social friendship contexts; it must come from some other setting. Some exact historical account is not necessary here. Suffice to say that the standard of arms-length dealing – to be and to be seen to be impartial in one's businesslife – better captures the practice in this sort of society, rather like the standards relating to fair administration of law and not bribing officials. From within this framework, nominal gift giving is the expression of standards linked to principles like fair play: if fairness is to be maintained and is to be seen to be maintained, then any gifts of greater than nominal value implicate concerns of unfair advantage and/or untoward influence in the competitive business environment.

If these reconstructions of frameworks are reasonable ones, frameworks which account for the ethical dimensions of the conflicting practices, we have come a considerable way to understanding differing practices and what motivates them. Having achieved this level of recognition, we can move to step (4) to form judgments about what to do when business people representing these differing frameworks and practices attempt to do business with each other.

While one could surely point to the tasks in step (4) being reciprocal in nature (and thus theoretically though not practically circular), we'll assume for the purposes of our discussion here that only one business agent is going through this reflective process to determine how ethically to proceed. Should both parties be going through the process, so much the better. But that is not necessary to the task at hand (cf. De George, 1990).

Likewise, for purposes of discussion here and given the anticipated primary audience, we'll also assume that in this example the Australian business agent is the principal business agent and one committed to the nominal gift giving framework outlined. Thus, step (4) of the process leads our agent to ask the following queries: will the other party expect me to engage in their form of substantial gift giving? is such gift giving a necessary practice to doing business successfully? (cf. Donaldson, 1989, pp. 102–104) If the answer to both of these questions is 'yes', can I ethically accommodate their practice or must I refrain and thus likely lose the deal?[4]

In this case, a strong argument can be mounted that accommodation of substantial gift giving many ethically be permissible. How so? Consider the principles and reasons for deriving nominal gift giving standards and practices. Does accommodation of substantial gift giving compromise in any significant way the principles of fairness and reasons for the Australian practice? or, is the breach of the standard and its associated practice and constraint only facial? If the expectation and necessity of the other agent's substantial gift giving practice are sincere and culturally well-grounded, then there seem to be no grounds for asserting a significant breach or compromise of the Australian agent's overall framework if substantial gifts are exchanged. Fairness is still maintained and can be seen to be maintained just by accommodating the other's practice. There is no undue influence, no overbearing of independent business judgment. And on the other agent's construction of the exchange, the making of a friend. On the other hand, if the expectation that the Australian agent is to engage in the practice or the necessity of the practice does not exist, the argument for accommodation is weaker. And if neither exists or is insincerely asserted (i.e. both parties understand the gift to function as a reason to do the deal – a.k.a. a bribe per Noonan, 1984), the reasons for accommodation disappear; indeed may raise reason specially not to accommodate but to shift the burden of accommodation to the other party.

Practical steps

This four-step decision-making process, what has here been called the frameworks or middle way of ethical decision making, should be followed whenever a business agent is confronted with actual or potential clashes in business practices. The clashes may or may not be ethical in character . . . may or may not require sensitive resolution of moral disagreement. One way of determining whether and how ethical issues do require resolution is to pursue the process proposed. Below is an outline of the practical steps one can take and the associated questions one can ask to utilise this frameworks approach to best advantage. Following the flow of this chart will help channel personal reflection and corporate discussion one clashes are identified, leading to an ethically justifiable decision concerning whether and how one might proceed with a business deal in the light of initial differing practices.

Note that only one sub-branch of the flowchart clearly leads to one ethically declining to do business with the other, due to irreconciliable differences in ethical outlook. All other branches purport to provide some guidance to doing the deal in the light of justifiably different practices. For business decision makers, this augurs well: ethics need not be seen as the spoil sport of daily business life. The call to be ethical is not a call to withdrawal from the field of active international business dealings.

Indeed, with but few alterations, the chart, like the frameworks process itself, can be used to step through ethical conflicts of other types. One is not limited to clashes of international practices, alone. Thus, while specifying for example that the other agent is a stakeholder in one's own business (rather than a potential business partner) and is calling for a change in corporate practice and policy (recall the business-in-Burma case from section 1), the chart and process remain useful tools for dialogue and reflection which lead to ethically justifiable decisions.

The basic rubric is that one must be committed to ethical reflection and dialogue, to giving serious attention to one's own practices and framework, and respect to principles and

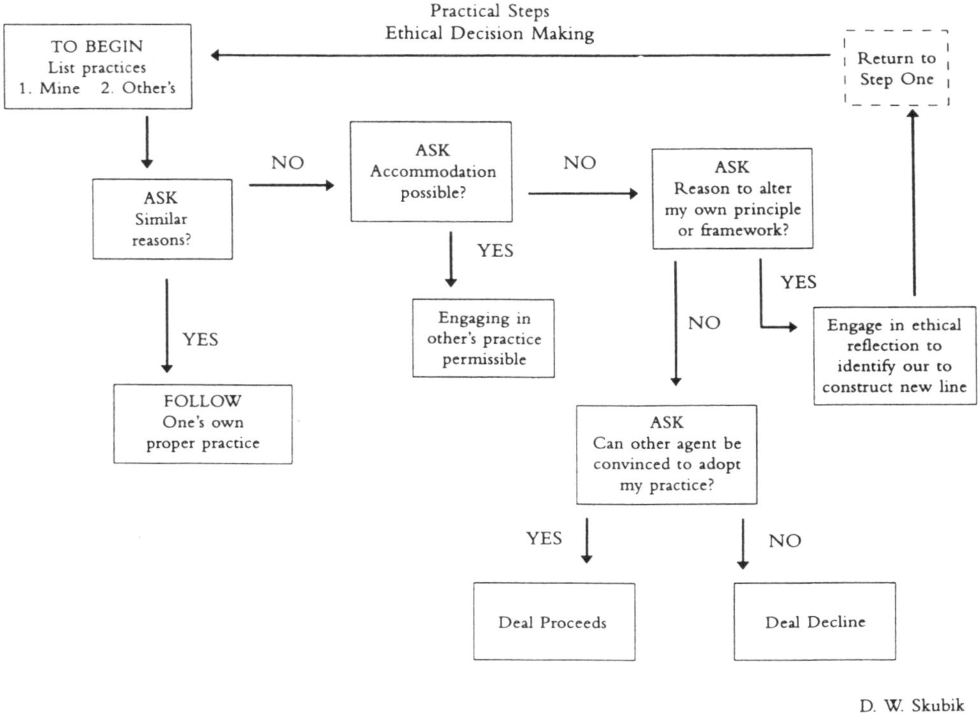

Chart.

practices not one' own. In this way, business people demonstrate confidence in themselves and respect for others. And isn't that just what is reflected in the practical wisdom of our Western Judeo-Christian ethical bottom line: love your neighbour as yourself; that is the fulfillment of your duty?

Notes

[1] While the ethical tools proffered are constructed with an eye to Australia-Asia international business affairs, it should be noted that many of the sorts of problems which can arise and require resolution in the international sphere similarly arise between parties within individual countries. To that extent, these frameworks are meant to be useful at all levels and sizes of firms in their business dealings, and thus should not be thought limited to multinational corporations doing business across country borders.

[2] For relatively recent spurs to change, see Glenn Whitney, "Europe Moves to Curb Insider Trading: Blatant Violations Bring About a Change in Attitudes", *Wall Street Journal*, Thursday, 4 Nov 1993, A11.

[3] For a slightly different formulation and further explication of these steps, see Skubik (1994), wherein comparison is also made with Thomas Donaldson's (1989) seminal work.

[4] We set aside here the complication of whether acceding to the practice would be legal. Of course, if accommodating the practice would be illegal the business agent has critical, if not decisive, reason to cease further analysis. There can be cases where illegality is not ethically decisive, but for the sake of simplicity we shall assume here that accommodation does not impinge on any legal duties of the agent.

References

De George, R. T.: 1993, *Competing with Integrity in International Business* (Oxford University Press, NY).

De George, R. T.: 1990, 'Ethics and Coherence', *APA Proceedings* **64**(3), 39–52.

Donaldson, T.: 1989, *The Ethics of International Business* (Oxford University Press, NY).

Dunfee, T. W. and Y. Nagayasu (eds.): 1993, *Business Ethics: Japan and the Global Economy* (Kluwer Academic, Boston).

Hampden-Turner, C. and A. Trompenaars: 1993, *The Seven Cultures of Capitalism* (Doubleday, NY).

Milner, A. C. and M. Quilty (eds.): 1994, forthcoming, *Australian-Asian Perceptions Project: Perceptions of Business Ethics* (Australian National University, Canberra).

Minus, Paul M. (ed.): 1993, *The Ethics of Business in a Global Economy* (Kluwer Academic, Boston).

Noonan, J. T.: 1984, *Bribes* (Macmillan, NY).

Skubik, D. W.: 1993, 'Ethics and International Business' (with teaching notes), in P. Graham (ed.), *Australian Marketing: Critical Essays, Readings and Case Studies* (Prentice Hall, Sydney), pp. 251–258.

Skubik, D. W.: 1992, 'Two Perspectives on Human Rights and the Rule of Law: Chinese East and Anglo-American West', *World Review* **31**(2), 28–45.

College of Liberal Arts,
Florida Atlantic University,
2912 College Avenue,
Davie, FL 33314,
U.S.A.

[43]

ASIA PACIFIC JOURNAL OF MANAGEMENT VOL 12, NO 2: 37-61

EXPLORING THE ETHICAL BEHAVIOR OF MANAGERS: A COMPARATIVE STUDY OF FOUR COUNTRIES

David J. Fritzsche, Y. Paul Huo, Sakae Sugai, Stephen Dun-Hou Tsai, Cheong Seok Kim and Helmut Becker*

Donaldson and Dunfee's (1994) social contracts theory of economic ethics was subjected to empirical scrutiny to determine whether it can explain differences in behavior between cultures. Data collected utilizing a series of vignettes developed by Fritzsche and Becker (1984) were examined for differences in indicated ethical behavior among American, Japanese, Korean and Taiwanese managers. Rationale for the behavior was classified according to hyper and community norms which were supported or violated. The results suggest that the three East Asian countries do not neatly cluster together in relation to the U.S. in terms of their patterns of ethical behavior. Nonetheless, when we examined the specific rationale for the decisions provided by the managers, the effects of Asian cultural characteristics became more notable. We also found that the social contracts theory provided a much needed bridge between ethical universalists and relativists. The specific reasons underlying their decisions are discussed in the light of cultural and social differences.

1. INTRODUCTION

The culture of the United States has been influenced strongly by its European heritage and Judeo-Christian philosophy. A central cultural concept is that of natural law, which transcends domains. Saint Thomas Aquinas summarized the issues in the thirteenth century in his treatise on law when he stated that "the natural law" includes the preservation of human life, the promotion of family life, an orderly social life and the quest for knowledge (Pegis, 1944). Velasquez and Rotankowski (1985) argue that under natural law, people of all nationalities are bound together by certain fundamental principles of right and wrong.

* The authors are Professor Of Management And International Business, Florida International University; Associate Professor Of Management, Washington State University and Visiting Associate Professor Of Management Of Organizations, The Hong Kong University Of Science & Technology; Professor Of Business Administration, Tokyo International University; Chairman And Professor Of Business Management, National Sun Yat-Sen University; Professor Of Industrial Engineering, Kangweon National University; and Professor Of Business Administration, University Of Portland, respectively. All correspondence should be addressed to Dr. Y. Paul Huo, Department of Management and Systems, Washington State University, Pullman, WA99164, U.S.A.

This research project was partially supported by a research grant from the School of Business and Management, The Hong Kong University of Science and Technology.

The cultures of East Asian nations have evolved along a different path, drawing inspiration from Confucian philosophy. Interestingly, Confucius spoke in terms of a moral order which is universal. He stated: "The life of the moral man is an exemplification of the universal moral order" (Sang, 1927). He goes on to say: "There are four things in the moral life of a man ..." (1) "To serve my father as I would expect my son to serve me..." (2) "To serve my sovereign as I would expect a minister under me to serve me..." (3) "To act toward my elder brother as I would expect my younger brother to act toward me..." and (4) "To be the first to behave toward friends as I would expect them to behave toward me .... The duties of universal obligation are five .... The duties are those between ruler and subject; between father and son; between husband and wife; between elder brother and younger; and those in the intercourse between friends: these are the five duties of universal obligation." There appears to be a great deal in common between Aquinas's natural law and Confucius's universal law.

Kant (1964) argued for certain universal rights in his first categorical imperative. Evans (1981) proposed ten commandments that govern the normative relationship between strategy and social responsibility. Donaldson (1989) cites the "Universal Declaration of Human Rights" supported by the United Nations and lists the following "fundamental international rights", with the proviso that the list is probably not complete:

- The right to freedom of physical movement
- The right to ownership of property
- The right to freedom from torture
- The right to a fair trial
- The right to non-discriminatory treatment
- The right to physical security
- The right to freedom of speech and association
- The right to minimal education
- The right to political participation
- The right to subsistence

However, the quest for universal rules of ethics has its dissenters. Advocates of cultural moral relativism often argue that there are no objective measures of right or wrong and all morality is relative to the customs, mores, practices or laws of a particular culture or society (Williams, 1992). According to this vein of thinking, "right" and "wrong" are simply other terms for acceptable behavior or actions within a culture or society (Rachels, 1986). Thus, the relationship between acceptable behavior and moral values is culture-dependent in itself.

A recent theoretical development may provide a bridge across this gap. Donaldson and Dunfee (1994) have developed a social contracts theory of economic ethics. They posit a series of hypernorms – global norms – which apply to all persons worldwide. Hypernorms represent the basic principles which are fundamental to human existence and are reflected in a convergence of religious, political and philosophical thought. Hypernorms include

- core human rights, including those relating to personal freedom, physical security and well-being, political participation, informed consent, and ownership of property; and
- the obligation to accord equal dignity to the humanity of each individual.

According to Donaldson and Dunfee, hypernorms are created via a macro social contract. The macro social contract is comparable to Aquinas's natural law or Confucius's universal law as it pertains to economic life. The macro social contract provides moral free space wherein local economic communities may create micro social contracts which prescribe moral norms for the community in addition to the extant hypernorms. Local economic communities may consist of corporations, industries, professions and even the economic dimensions of states and cultures. It should be noted that a norm resulting from a micro social contract may not conflict with a hypernorm. While hypernorms pertain to all people, community norms developed under a micro social contract pertain only to the people within the local community. This may explain why moral behavior may differ among cultures even though they share the same moral values (hypernorms), a phenomenon discussed by Dubinsky et al. (1991) and Wines and Napier (1992). The communities are following their own community norms which create additional moral requirements beyond hypernorms. Thus, hypernorms provide a universal dimension while community norms allow for relativism so long as it does not violate universal rules.

Empirical studies have shown some differences in ethical practices across cultures. Graduate students in a laboratory setting provided data which led Hegarty and Sims (1978) to conclude that foreign nationals tended to be less ethical. Marketing managers surveyed by Becker and Fritzsche (1987a) exhibited differences in indicated behavior across cultures, the difference being dependent upon the ethical issue addressed. Fritzsche (1985) found foreign nationals perceiving the United States as having lower ethical standards. Swinyard, Rinne and Kau (1990) examined students' attitudes towards software piracy in Singapore and the U.S. Students in the U.S. were more influenced by legality while Singapore students were more influenced by outcome. Dubinsky, et al. (1991) examined differences in perceptions among U.S., Japanese and Korean salespeople. They found differences in perceptions among managers from all three countries as to whether specific situations presented ethical questions. U.S. managers' perceptions differed from Japanese and Korean managers regarding whether their company had a policy toward such situations. There were no differences between Japanese and Korean managers' perceptions regarding company policy. However, there were differences among all three groups of managers concerning whether their company should have a policy for each situation. U.S. students were found to be more critical of ethical transgressions dealing with confidentiality, research integrity and marketing mix issues than were their United Kingdom counterparts (Whipple & Swords, 1992). Finally, White and Rhodeback (1992) surveyed Taiwanese enrolled in a management training program and U.S. graduate evening business students. The Taiwanese tended to view misrepresentation, value/goal conflicts, manipulation, technical ineptness and misuse of data scenarios as less ethical than the U.S subjects. They also viewed such situations as more likely to occur.

Exploring the Ethical Behavior of Managers

Other studies have failed to find differences across cultures. No difference was found in the ethical standards of marketing practices between British and Chinese managers doing business in Hong Kong (Lee, 1981). Australian and American managers engaged in international marketing indicated little difference in perceived ethical problems and management practices (Armstrong et al., 1990). Preble and Reichel (1988) found little difference in attitudes towards business between U.S. and Israeli students, with both groups placing considerable importance on morals in business. Danish, New Zealand and U.S. students provided similar responses to a series of ethical dilemmas (Lysonski & Gaidis, 1991). Tsalikis and Nwachukwu (1991) found that both Nigerian and American students viewed a businessman offering a bribe to a government official as unethical. They also found similar beliefs among American and Greek students regarding the ethics of specific behavioral practices of retailers (Tsalikis & Nwachukwu, 1989).

There are two reasons why ethical behavior may differ across cultures. First, some individuals may be adhering to extant hypernorms while others are not. The latter are engaged in unethical behavior. Second, the cultures may be operating under different sets of community norms. Acts which violate the norms of one group may not violate the norms of the other and, of course, do not violate hypernorms. This condition is most likely to occur between developed and underdeveloped cultures. Micro social contracts will generally contain more norms as cultures develop. Development tends to breed complexity. Complexity creates a need for rules. The resulting community norms (rules) fill the moral free space. Underdeveloped cultures tend to leave the free space much more open, possibly by default. Thus what was acceptable, not violating any hypernorm, becomes unacceptable under new community norms as a culture develops. For example, discrimination against women in the workplace used to be considered an acceptable practice in the United States, but not any more.

Many of the differences found in the above studies may be due to different community norms being adhered to. The studies which found no differences may have examined issues where hypernorms apply; or the issues may have been covered by community norms which were consistent across the cultures. More than half of the studies used student subjects. Two studies examined Asian managers – one Hong Kong and the other Taiwanese managers. One study focused on Asians and U.S. sales practitioners. No data is available for Asian managers which can be compared across Asian cultures or with U.S. managers.

The present study has two purposes. Firstly, it seeks to determine empirically whether Donaldson and Dunfee's social contracts theory can explain differences in behavior across cultures. Secondly, it will provide a first comparison of ethical behavior across Asian cultures as well as between Asian cultures and the U.S. culture. As with most other studies of ethical behavior, we will have to rely upon indicated ethical behavior as representing actual behavior.

We will examine the indicated ethical behavior of managers in four countries: the United States, Japan, South Korea and Taiwan. A comparison between managers in these countries is intriguing because three of them are located in East Asia and people in these countries have been acculturated via the Confucian philosophy. If culture does play a role in most people's ethical decisions, its effect should be reflected by some consistency across managers' community norms from these three East Asian nations. Given differences in the cultures, one would expect some significant differences in the community norms and indicated behavior of U.S. managers when compared to the behavior of the other three nations as a group. In light of the globalization trend and a growing shift in business from the Atlantic to the Pacific Basin, such East-West cultural differences are becoming increasingly important (Adler, Doktor & Redding, 1986; Buller et al., 1991; Dubinsky et al., 1991). Nonetheless, there may be a great deal of heterogeneity even within the Eastern world owing to idiosyncratic political environments and histories (e.g. Alston, 1989; Evans, 1981). As a result, we did not expect identical results for the three East Asian nations, as differing histories and social evolution in these countries very likely created differences in their value systems.

2. RESEARCH DESIGN

Data was collected for the study using a series of five vignettes. Vignettes are particularly relevant for cross-cultural research because each vignette can present a unique dilemma relating to a specific issue (e.g. conflict of interest). Compared to traditional surveys using simple questions, vignette methods offer the following advantages: (1) the ethical focus can be disguised within managerial simulations or decision-making drills so that any social desirability bias, which tends to be a function of the acceptability of specific behavioral modes, is minimized; (2) since no "right or wrong" judgment is explicitly requested, respondents are more likely to answer the questions in line with actual moral values; (3) as the estimated likelihood of taking a specific action (rather than a "yes" or "no" answer) may be requested, the acceptability of a certain type of behavior can be inferred and quantified on a continuum; (4) written comments or explanations of the response can be obtained, which may honestly reveal the rationale for a decision regardless of whether it was economically or ethically motivated. In sum, the vignette approach offers a common ground for understanding and responding to an ethical dilemma. By adding situational details, vignettes may provide standardized stimuli across respondents and improve data quality (Alexander & Becker, 1978). Becker and Fritzsche (1987a) have found that the cultural impact, if any, may vary across different ethical issues. By studying the variations in explanations for each response to the dilemma portrayed in a particular vignette, researchers can uncover the role played by culture in a given issue more easily.

The vignettes used in this study were taken from a study by Fritzsche and Becker (1984). They were based on significant ethical issues drawn from two books on business ethics (Barry, 1979; Beauchamp & Bowie, 1979), as well as from the Summer Institute on Ethical Issues in the Management of Public and Private Institutions, sponsored by the Society for Values in Higher Education (Dill, Donaldson, Goodpaster & May, 1979). The vignettes were pretested on a pilot sample, reviewed by a group of individuals working in the field of ethics, and revised accordingly (for details, see Fritzsche & Becker 1984). The vignettes were subsequently used in comparative studies of American, French and German managers and yielded satisfactory results (Becker & Fritzsche 1987a, 1987b).

The five vignettes seem to reflect critical ethical issues that deeply concern not only American managers but also managers in other countries. The issues include: (1) coercion and control; (2) conflict of interest; (3) physical environment; (4) paternalism; and (5) personal integrity. A coercion and control issue arises when some external force attempts to compel a manager to make a specific decision by using threats, extortion or other sources of power. A conflict of interest would be of concern when a manager has multiple interests that are not mutually compatible and which may cause damage to individuals or to the firm if any one of them is pursued (Beauchamp & Bowie, 1979). The physical environment dilemma is a special case of conflicting interests in which one of the affected parties is the environment. A paternalism issue concerns the balancing of respect for individual autonomy with a commitment to public welfare. Finally, personal integrity problems come into being when decisions raise issues of conscience. The vignettes were used in this study so that the data from the Asian managers could be directly compared with their American counterparts.

The English-version questionnaire was translated into Japanese, Chinese and Korean by three of the co-authors. These co-authors' first languages are Japanese, Chinese and Korean, respectively. They are all faculty members teaching in the business or industrial administration programs at their own universities in their home countries. All three of them speak fluent English and each has visited an American university for at least one year. The Asian version questionnaires were each back-translated into English by a different bilingual person who had studied in the U.S. Each person responsible for back translation also speaks English as his/her second language. The translated and back-translated versions were then compared and "decentered" (Werner & Campbell, 1970). In addition, the proper names (e.g., Ward) have been changed to local names that sound more natural in the respective countries. In the Asian versions, the hypothetical "Asian country" in Vignette 1 was also changed to "African country."

The managers surveyed in each nation were all participants of executive education programs in their respective countries. In total, 60 Japanese managers, 49 Taiwanese managers and 83 Korean managers responded to this survey. Respondents read each vignette, which portrayed an ethical dilemma, and then were asked how likely they were to take ethically ambiguous action (on a 0-10 scale), with "0" anchored as "definitely would not" and "10" anchored as "definitely would". They were then asked to write down the rationale for their choice. These open-ended responses were then independently classified by two research assistants. The partner who was responsible for data collection in that country then compared the two sets of classifications and ironed out discrepancies, if any, on the basis of his own judgment. Data gathered in these three nations were then combined with the raw data collected by Fritzsche and Becker (1984). In the following sections, we will compare the cross-national difference on a vignette-by-vignette basis.

3. FINDINGS

The demographic characteristics of the combined sample are summarized in Table 1. While a majority of the managers from all four countries hold college degrees, a higher proportion of Japanese and American managers appear to be college graduates. The Japanese managers are primarily from manufacturing firms, while approximately a third of the managers from Korea and Taiwan represent service companies. The U.S. managers are split nearly evenly between manufacturing and service firms, which is in keeping with the transition going on in the country. The U.S. managers tend to be in more senior positions than the Asian managers. However, the Japanese managers appear to be older, while the Korean and Taiwanese managers tend to be younger than their American counterparts. The Japanese managers are all male, while the managers from the other three countries are approximately 80% male. Since there are demographic differences among the managers from the four countries, we did a preliminary analysis that tested the potential effects of demographic features on the responses. No consistent effect was found for any of these demographic variables.

TABLE 1
DEMOGRAPHIC CHARACTERISTICS OF RESPONDENTS

	U.S.	Japan	Korea	Taiwan
Managers with college degrees	90%	87%	70%	73%
Type of industry:				
Manufacturing	40%	83%	69%	62%
Service	38%	17%	30%	34%
Other	22%	0%	1%	4%
Level of hierarchy:				
Senior executive	28%	8%	5%	4%
Middle management	56%	32%	29%	23%
First-line	16%	60%	66%	73%
Percentage of males	81%	100%	78%	80%
Age of respondents				
Mean	43	46	35	39
Range	28-55	31-60	23-62	24-58
Total number of respondents	124	60	83	49

VIGNETTE 1: COERCION AND CONTROL

Rollfast Bicycle Company has been barred from entering the market in a large African country through the collusive efforts of local bicycle manufacturers. Rollfast could expect to net $5 million per year from sales if it could penetrate the market. Last week, a businessman from the country contacted the management of Rollfast and stated that he could smooth the way for the company to sell in his country for a price of $500,000.

If you were responsible, what are the chances that you would pay the price?

We argue that there is a hypernorm prohibiting acts of bribery and extortion. Such acts disregard personal freedom and do not support an orderly social life. To those who answered that it is an accepted practice in many countries, we requested that they show us a country where it is practised in public without retribution. Japanese Prime Minister Kakuei Tanaka fell from power when Lockheed's payoffs came to light. Rajiv Gandhi's slide from power in India was assisted by payments made by the Swedish firm AB Bofors to Indian government officials. The norm is there even though there may be many cases where it may be disregarded. Indeed, the perpetrators do so at their own peril.

The results of our analysis of responses to the above vignette are shown in Table 2. The ANOVA analysis did not show a significant difference between any of the countries in terms of the average likelihood of taking action (paying the price). In other words, managers in these four countries indicated a similar level of receptiveness to such behavior. This fact does not imply, however, that they followed exactly the same rules in making their judgments. Our analysis of the norms used, which were suggested by the rationale provided in conjunction with their response, is shown under the "Norms" heading. Company and public policy (laws) are community norms. They may be used to support hypernorms. A violation of a norm is considered to be unethical. We were uncertain how to classify three of the rationales: 1) balance between economic and humane concerns; 2) bad return on investment; and 3) need further information to judge its worth. This uncertainty might be resolved if we could press each respondent for additional information. The response "bad return on investment" appears to be an economic filter which may have eliminated the option prior to its being evaluated on an ethical basis.

A large proportion of the Asian respondents, particularly the Japanese (36%) and Korean (53%) managers, seemed to view the payoff as some sort of "investment" and relied on the concept of return on investment (ROI) in making judgments. The economic dimension of the decision appeared to take precedence. Only a tiny proportion of Asian managers considered it a bribe or something unethical. We should be very careful, however, in interpreting such results. The tiny portion of "unethical" judgments does not necessarily reflect that most managers would be more willing to bribe a foreign businessman. It may be due to their screening business opportunities on an economic basis first. If it is rejected at that point (Japanese 22%, Koreans 25% and Taiwanese 4%), the ethical dimension of the opportunity is not considered.

It is noteworthy that, in the "other" category of explanations, many managers expressed concern over the trustworthiness of the African businessman. Many respondents suggested that a further investigation be conducted on the credibility of that individual. Some Japanese managers also pointed out the importance of a "long-term relationship" built through this channel. In their opinion, even if the money paid to the African businessman did not pay off in the short term, it could still be a good investment in the long run.

In sum, American managers seemed more likely to view this payoff scheme as illegal or unethical (following community or hypernorms), while Asian managers were less concerned about such issues in examining this case. Instead, Asian managers seemed to be

TABLE 2
COMPARISON OF AMERICAN, JAPANESE, TAIWANESE AND KOREAN RESPONSES TO VIGNETTE 1 — COERCION AND CONTROL

Source	Degree of Freedom	Sum of Squares	F	Probability
Between Groups	3	57	1.42	.236
Within Groups	304	4048		

Country	Mean
America	4.0
Japan	4.5
Korea	4.2
Taiwan	5.3

Norm[a]	Rationale for response	A	J	K	T
		(Percent of Respondents)[b]			
H	Bribe, unethical	23%	5%	4%	2%
C	Illegal	16	0	0	2
C	Against company policy	8	2	0	4
?	Balance between economic and humane concerns	0	5	0	6
U	An acceptable practice in other countries	22	0	0	27
U	Just the price paid to do business	14	14	9	4
?	Bad return on investment	0	22	25	4
U	Good return on investment	0	14	28	6
?	Need further information to judge its worth	0	21	11	26
?	Other	16	17	23	19
	Total	100%	100%	100%	100%
	Number of respondents providing rationale	107	58	53	48

[a]H = Hypernorm, C = Community norm, U = Unethical, ? = Uncertain.
[b]Percentages may not total 100 due to rounding.

Exploring the Ethical Behavior of Managers

preoccupied with returns on investment, if such a payoff can be viewed an investment, either in the short or long run. Another striking phenomenon is that a significant portion (23%) of American managers considered it an acceptable practice in other countries. This view was also quite popular among Taiwanese managers (27%) but not even mentioned by either the Japanese (0%) or Korean managers (0%). This fact suggests that, among the three East Asian countries, only Taiwanese managers have this sort of "double-standard" mentality, as do their American counterparts. In light of the U.S. Foreign Corrupt Practices Act passed in 1977, it is understandable why a large proportion of American managers view it as illegal or unethical. Asian nations do not have this type of law. Thus, this finding may be partially attributed to a difference in laws. We concur with Becker and Fritzsche's (1987a) viewpoint that, while ethics play a part in management decision making, it is easier to be ethical when the law is behind one's decision.

VIGNETTE 2: CONFLICT OF INTEREST

> *Bill Smith has recently accepted a job with a young vigorous microcomputer manufacturer. The microcomputer manufacturers are engaged in intense competition to become the first on the market with a software package which utilizes the English language and thus is easily used by the average customer. Smith's former employer is rumored to be the leader in this software development. When Smith was hired he was led to believe his selection was based on his management potential. The morning beginning the third week on the new job, Smith received the following memo from the president:*
>
> *"Please meet with me tomorrow at 8:15 for the purpose of discussing the developments your former employer has made in microcomputer software."*
>
> *If you were Smith, what are the chances you would provide your new employer with the software information?*

We believe a hypernorm prohibits Smith from providing the information. The software development was paid for by his former employer. To provide it to his new employer would be theft of personal property. That violates a core human right, is counter to Aquinas's orderly social life and contrary to Confucius's service to the sovereign (employer).

The responses to this vignette were, once again, fairly homogeneous across the four countries. There was no significant difference (per the Scheffe test) among the means of likelihood of taking action (providing the software information). However, the reasons provided by managers seemed to show some cultural differences between Japan and the other two Asian countries. Korean and Taiwanese managers were more likely than their Japanese counterparts to recognize that it was unethical for Smith to provide the confidential information and unethical for the employer to ask, while a higher portion of Japanese respondents pointed out that it was unethical for the employer to mislead Smith when he was hired (11%). In other words, the Japanese managers seemed less concerned with the ethics of providing the former employer's confidential information to the current one per se, and were more likely to condemn the current employer for misleading Smith before hiring him. This would be a violation of informed consent, a core human right and thus also a hypernorm. Interestingly, significant portions of American managers were worried about both the ethicality of information-leaking (14%) and that of misleading the newly hired (20%).

Thus, Japanese managers are relatively similar to their American counterparts when we focus on the practice of using a new job as a lure for the purpose of stealing a competitor's technical information, while Korean and Taiwanese managers resemble American managers to a greater extent where information leakage per se is concerned.

In all four nations, some managers suggested that Smith should provide some but not all information. This, of course, is a violation of the hypernorm regarding theft of property.

TABLE 3
COMPARISON OF AMERICAN, JAPANESE, TAIWANESE AND KOREAN RESPONSES TO VIGNETTE 2 — CONFLICT OF INTEREST

Source	Degree of Freedom	Sum of Squares	F	Probability
Between Groups	3	87	2.29	.079
Within Groups	305	3870		

Country	Mean
America	3.9
Japan	4.7
Korea	5.2
Taiwan	4.5

Norm[a]	Rationale for response	A	J	K	T
		(Percent of Respondents)[b]			
H	Unethical for [Smith] to provide and unethical for employer to ask	14%	5%	16%	17%
H	Unethical for employer to mislead [Smith] when he was hired	20	11	2	4
?	Protect [Smith's] reputation	7	11	0	6
U	Provide some but not all information	13	30	24	8
U	Decision based on whether security agreement is in force	15	9	0	2
U	To keep job, loyalty to new employer	23	21	36	17
?	Other	9	14	22	45
	Total	100%	100%	100%	100%
	Number of respondents providing rationale	110	57	50	48

[a]H = Hypernorm, C = Community norm, U = Unethical, ? = Uncertain.
[b]Percentages may not total 100 due to rounding.

However, this compromise solution was suggested much more frequently by Japanese (30%) and Korean managers (24%) than by their counterparts in Taiwan (8%) or the U.S. (13%). The spirit of compromise has been recognized as a major characteristic of Oriental culture. This finding, however, suggests that we have to be more careful about discerning cross-national differences within a cluster of Oriental cultures.

Another issue of interest is: Asian employees are known for showing a higher degree of loyalty than their Western counterparts, but little has been said concerning whose side they would take if there was a conflict of interest between their former and current employers. In this regard, the fairly high proportion of managers choosing "being loyal to the new employer" in all three Asian nations seems to imply that they are inclined to define loyalty in relation to the current employer. This is particularly the case for Korean managers: thirty-six percent of them suggested that Smith be loyal to the new employer. To be sure, the response "to keep job, loyalty to new employer" is not a good indicator of loyalty by itself. A large proportion of American managers (23%) also made this comment, but their rationale for doing this might be driven simply by the desire to "keep the job".

The response regarding Smith's reputation supported the hypernorm but did not seem to be based on the hypernorm or a community norm. The fact that a security agreement exists does not excuse one from violating a hypernorm. And loyalty to a new employer does not excuse theft from a former employer.

VIGNETTE 3: PHYSICAL ENVIRONMENT

Master Millers has developed a special milling process which yields a wheat flour which, when used for bread, provides a lighter, more uniform texture than conventionally milled wheat flour. Unfortunately, the process gives off more dust than the emission control equipment presently installed can handle and still maintain emission levels within legal limits. Due to lack of availability, the company is unable to install new emission control equipment for at least two years; however, if it waited that long to introduce the new process, competitors would very likely beat it to the market.

The general manager wants to use the new process during the third shift, which runs from 10pm to 6am. By using the process at that time, the new flour could be introduced and the excess pollution would not be detected due to its release in the dark. By the time demand becomes great enough to utilize a second shift, new emission control equipment should be available.

If you were responsible, what are the chances you would approve the general manager's request?

No hypernorm exists for this vignette. As long as pollution does not endanger human life, its limitations are part of a micro social contract. The emission limitation (in this case in the form of a law) is a community norm which is likely to differ from community to community. For example, California has more rigorous standards than the rest of the United States. A violation of a community norm would be considered unethical by that community but not by members of other communities which have not included the norm in their micro social contract. Of course, the vignette is posed so that the norm does apply to each of the respondent's communities.

Some differences in the propensity to take action (approving the general manager's request) seemed to exist between Japan and the other three countries. Japanese managers were least likely to adopt the new milling process. However, the foremost reason for

TABLE 4
COMPARISON OF AMERICAN, JAPANESE, TAIWANESE AND KOREAN RESPONSES TO VIGNETTE 3 — PHYSICAL ENVIRONMENT

Source	Degree of Freedom	Sum of Squares	F	Probability
Between Groups	3	388	12.82	.000
Within Groups	302	3045		

Country	Mean[a]
America	0.6
Japan	[3.3
Korea	3.5
Taiwan	3.7]

Norm[b]	Rationale for response	A	J	K	T
		(Percent of Respondents)[c]			
C	It would be illegal	24%	23%	6%	14%
C	Concern for the environment/life	16	9	20	14
C	Risk of getting caught with resulting negative consequences too great	15	32	12	16
U	The pollution would not really hurt the environment	18	0	2	5
U	Not their fault, equipment would be installed if available	8	0	2	7
U	Competitors force one to do it	3	2	10	25
U	Large potential gain with low risk	5	0	6	0
?	Other	13	35	43	20
	Total	100%	100%	100%	100%
	Number of respondents providing rationale	103	57	51	44

[a]The brackets enclose mean responses which did not differ significantly from each other per the Scheffe test.
[b]H = Hypernorm, C = Community norm, U = Unethical, ? = Uncertain.
[c]Percentages may not total 100 due to rounding.

resisting the new technology was that the risk of getting caught and the resulting negative consequences would be too great. The second most frequent explanation was "it would be illegal". We view both of these reasons as respecting the community norm. One gets caught because it is illegal. This pattern of response seems to be consistent with the relatively high conservatism and dogmatism imbedded in the Japanese culture (Evans, 1981). By contrast, Korean managers were most likely to cite their concern for the environment/life (the ethical dimension) as the major reason for not doing it. This is in the spirit of the law and is also considered a community norm. To a certain extent, Taiwanese managers also cared about the environmental damage, the legal ramifications and the negative consequences of being caught, but a relatively higher percentage of them recognized the competitive pressure and desperate need to gain profit (25%). Such a strong profit orientation may have muffled part of their concern for environmental protection. It certainly was in violation of the community norm.

The Japanese managers were, however, similar to the American managers in that a relatively large proportion of them indicated their concern for legality (political dimension) relative to their Korean and Taiwanese counterparts. This similarity may be attributed to either experience with more stringent governmental regulations on environmental protection in these two nations or the fact that managers in both countries are more dogmatic (Hofstede, 1980).

Part of the difference between Japanese managers and their counterparts in the other two East Asian countries may be attributed to the differing time frames used for managerial decision making (Webber, 1981). In the "Other" category of explanations, some Korean and Taiwanese managers argued that "the hazard of the pollution will become salient in the long-term but the threat of market competition is immediate; let's fix the immediate problem first before dealing with the long-term ones". Their preoccupation with short-term problems seems to reflect a cultural difference between these two countries and Japan. Indeed, Japanese managers have been renowned for their strong bias toward emphasizing long-term outcomes (Morita, 1992).

VIGNETTE 4: PATERNALISM

Ted Jones, senior editor of J&P Publishing Company, has just received a manuscript from one of his most successful authors. It provides the most authoritative account yet published of the history of the development of the atomic bomb. However, the final chapter contains a detailed description of how the bomb is made. Jones has tried to convince the author to omit the last chapter, stating that such information should not be made readily available to the mass market in paperback form. The author believes the chapter is critical to the success of the book and thus will not agree to its deletion.

If you were Jones, what are the chances that you would publish the book?

Jones would clearly violate a hypernorm by publishing the book with the chapter included. He would be increasing the threat to the core human right of physical security and well-being. He would be violating Aquinas's preservation of human life and Confucius's duty to family. While the information may be available, any act which would make it more easily accessible increases the threat.

TABLE 5
COMPARISON OF AMERICAN, JAPANESE, TAIWANESE AND KOREAN RESPONSES TO VIGNETTE 4 — PATERNALISM

Source	Degree of Freedom	Sum of Squares	F	Probability
Between Groups	3	89	5.82	.001
Within Groups	306	3864		

Country	Mean[a]
America	2.8 ⎤
Japan	2.8 ⎥
Korea	2.7 ⎦
Taiwan	5.1

Norm[b]	Rationale for response	A	J	K	T
		(Percent of Respondents)[c]			
H	Too dangerous to world safety	45%	30%	53%	27%
C	Concerned with legal ramifications	7	11	4	9
U	Average person could not build bomb even if given information	3	0	0	11
U	Don't see responsibility as being theirs	7	7	6	16
U	Those who want this information can get it now from other sources	23	4	6	9
C	May create image detrimental to company	5	5	8	0
H	Unethical to make it the best seller at the expense of world safety	0	5	6	2
?	Personal and societal interests must be weighed in a balanced manner	0	7	2	0
	Other	11	32	14	25
	Total	100%	100%	100%	100%
	Number of respondents providing rationale	104	57	49	44

[a]The brackets enclose mean responses which did not differ significantly from each other per the Scheffe test.
[b]H = Hypernorm, C = Community norm, U = Unethical, ? = Uncertain.
[c]Percentages may not total 100 due to rounding.

Exploring the Ethical Behavior of Managers

In responding to this vignette, both Japanese and Korean managers showed lower likelihood of publishing the last chapter than their Taiwanese counterparts. It is understandable that, given the historical trauma they experienced, Japanese managers would be highly sensitive to the threat of atomic bombs. Korean managers seemed to be as concerned as the Japanese with the threat of atomic bombs to world safety. This may be due to the fact that the history of Korea and Japan is tightly interwoven and their lands are also close to each other, so most Koreans feel the enormous threat of atomic bombs after watching what happened to Japan in 1945. By contrast, in the eyes of Taiwanese managers, the two atomic bombs dropped on Japan have helped stop the ordeals suffered by Chinese people during their eight-year war against Japan. Understandably, they would be less likely to view the consequences of spreading nuclear technology as highly threatening. The relatively high likelihood that the Taiwanese managers would publish the final chapter may also be attributed to their perception of the technical difficulty the average person would encounter in producing the bomb (11%), as well as their belief that the publisher is not responsible for such a decision (16%).

Interestingly, although Americans are generally viewed as most supportive of the freedom of publishing, in this study American managers were not much more inclined than their Asian counterparts to approve the disclosure of the technical details on how to make the atomic bomb. In fact, almost half (45%) of the American respondents said that this inclusion would be too dangerous to world safety. This is probably because, knowing the central role played by the U.S. in keeping world peace, most Americans today are seriously concerned with the atomic bomb threat posed by some autocratic regimes (e.g. Libya or Iraq). The occurrence of several international crises in the late 1970s and early 1980s have certainly deepened such a concern.

We were unsure how to classify the balancing of personal and societal interests responses. We tended to lean toward viewing this as an unethical response as we believe no personal benefits would offset the danger which would be posed to society if someone used the information to make a bomb. Legal ramifications, of course, are viewed as a community norm supporting the hypernorm as laws apply to the community.

VIGNETTE 5: PERSONAL INTEGRITY

Jack Ward is working in product development for an auto parts contractor. Ward's firm received a large contract last summer to manufacture transaxles to be used in a new line of front wheel drive cars which a major auto manufacturer plans to introduce in the near future. The contract is very important to Ward's firm, which has recently fallen on hard times. Just prior to obtaining the contract, half of the firm's employees, including Ward, had been scheduled for an indefinite layoff.

> ***Final testing of the assemblies ended last Friday and the first shipment is scheduled for three weeks from today. As Ward began examining the test reports, he discovered that the transaxle tended to fail when loaded at more than 20% over rated capacity and subjected to strong torsion forces.***
>
> *Such a condition could occur with a heavily loaded car braking hard for a curve down a mountain road. The results would be disastrous. The manufacturer's specifications call for the transaxle to carry 130% of its rated capacity without failing. Ward showed the results to his supervisor and the company president, who indicated that they were both aware of the report. Given the low likelihood of occurrence and the fact that there was no time to redesign the assembly, they had decided to ignore the report. If they did not deliver the assemblies on time, they would lose the contract. John must now decide whether to show the test results to the auto manufacturer.*
>
> *If you were Ward, what are the chances that you would notify the auto manufacturer?*

We believe Ward would violate a hypernorm by not blowing the whistle. As with the previous vignette, he would be violating the core human right of physical security. However, his actions would likely be at significant cost to him and his colleagues. Blowing the whistle is a serious matter. But then, so is loss of life.

The likelihood of reporting the design defect to the auto manufacturer was similar across the four countries, implying a more homogeneous cultural impact on the issue of personal integrity. An examination of the specific reasons provided by respondents revealed heterogeneous perceptions of the risk. Over half of the American managers (53%) believed that, even though the likelihood of occurrence for such accidents was proclaimed to be low in the case description, the chance of causing injury or death was still too great to remain silent. As we totaled the percentage of respondents providing the first two reasons, the results indicated that 64% of the American managers supported the hypernorm by considering it unethical to remain silent.

Managers in the three Asian countries seemed to weigh the economic consequences of reporting the defect relatively heavily. As with the first vignette, this may filter out the action prior to evaluating it from an ethical perspective. A fairly high proportion of the responses in all three nations can only be classified as "other". Although it is hard to sum up these miscellaneous reasons in one sentence, most of them were associated with the benefits of the employees, their family members, or the survival of the organization. For instance, one Taiwanese manager stated that "If the company lost the client due to this problem, it might lose money and a lot of employees might lose their jobs, and their family members would also suffer from the layoff". This sort of statement was fairly common in the "other" category of rationales provided by Asian managers.

Exploring the Ethical Behavior of Managers

A comparison of the comments also reveals some differences among the three Asian nations. A higher proportion of Japanese managers than their counterparts in the other two Asian countries believed that Ward had no additional responsibility and loyalty would keep him silent. This phenomenon may not only reflect the widely-known high loyalty of Japanese employees to their bosses but also suggest their inclination to clearly separate the responsibility of supervisors from that of subordinates.

In the meantime, Taiwanese managers were more likely than their Japanese and Korean counterparts to say that the company has a responsibility to the public and it is criminal and

TABLE 6
COMPARISON OF AMERICAN, JAPANESE, TAIWANESE AND KOREAN RESPONSES TO VIGNETTE 5 — PERSONAL INTEGRITY

Source	Degree of Freedom	Sum of Squares	F	Probability
Between Groups	3	89	2.38	.070
Within Groups	297	3692		

Country	Mean[a]
America	7.7
Japan	6.3
Korea	6.8
Taiwan	7.2

Norm[a]	Rationale for response	A	J	K	T
		(Percent of Respondents)[b]			
H	Chance of causing injury or death too great to remain silent	52%	37%	21%	36%
H	The company has a responsibility to the public — criminal and dishonest to remain silent	12	5	6	13
C	Risk to firm's image, profitability and long run potential too great to remain silent	13	19	17	13
U	Risk of injury or death too low to halt sale	4	0	4	0
U	Profits are what is important	0	4	6	0
U	Ward has no additional responsibility, loyalty will keep him silent	11	12	2	9
	Other	8	23	43	29
	Total	100%	100%	100%	100%
	Number of respondents providing rationale	113	57	47	45

[a]H = Hypernorm, C = Community norm, U = Unethical, ? = Uncertain.
[b]Percentages may not total 100 due to rounding.

dishonest to remain silent. This finding appears to be inconsistent with the result of Vignette 4, which indicates that Taiwanese managers were more likely to publish the threatening atomic bomb information. However, in Vignette 4 the impact of releasing the A-bomb information is highly ambiguous while the publisher has no direct responsibility to assess the risk. By contrast, Vignette 5 depicts a relatively clear danger of withholding the information and the responsibility apparently falls on the shoulders of the transaxles designer. The difference in their responses to these two scenarios is, therefore, easy to understand. Such a finding is also consistent with the increasingly strong sense of social responsibility shared by the Taiwanese in recent years.

We consider the risk to the firm argument to be a community norm, the community being the firm and its policies. The latter three response categories appear to be ducking responsibility, which clearly rests with Ward.

4. DISCUSSION AND CONCLUSION

Our data add further support to the findings of Fritzsche (1988) and Fritzsche and Becker (1983) that the likelihood of, and justification for, taking a morally ambiguous action varies across ethical issues. In addition, the data support Becker and Fritzsche's (1987a) finding that cultural impact also varies across different ethical issues.

Noticeable differences were found in the indicated behavior of the managers from the four countries for two of the vignettes. The Japanese were less likely to allow production which would pollute the environment and the Taiwanese were most likely to publish the details for making an atomic bomb.

With regard to the rationale for decisions, the bribery vignette tended to be treated by Japanese and Korean managers as a business proposition with an entry fee. Those who rejected making the payment did so mostly on economic grounds. Those who would make the payment also based their arguments primarily on economic grounds. The conflict of interest dilemma raised some interesting interpretations of loyalty. Who is one loyal to, one's previous or one's current employer? In these two vignettes, the presence of a moral issue per se was not obvious to everyone. Except for the U.S. sample, ethics appeared to be of concern to no more than 20% of the respondents in any country.

For the other three vignettes, the managers in each country seemed to be particularly concerned with a specific issue. Both American and Japanese managers appeared to be strongly influenced by the fact that polluting the environment would be illegal and highly risky. Since such concerns tend to be prevalent in industrialized nations, this phenomenon may be partially attributed to the higher degree of industrialization of these two countries. By contrast, competitive forces may have mitigated these concerns somewhat for South Korea and Taiwan. In Vignette 4, world safety appeared to dominate the reluctance of the Koreans to publish the technical information on how to make the atomic bomb but this concern played a lesser role for managers in Taiwan. As argued earlier, there are some historical reasons why this is the case, aside from cultural differences. Our findings indicate that the ethical decisions relating to paternalism are especially susceptible to the influence of people's knowledge and awareness of the focal issue. For Vignette 5, concern over ensuing injury or death in producing a defective axle was dominant in all nations but South Korea. The potential damage to the corporate image, which may hurt long-term profitability, was also a uniformly important issue.

When examining the pattern of open-ended comments, we did detect a systemic cultural difference between the U.S. and the three East Asian nations as a group. Throughout the five vignettes, it was very common to see expressions of uncertainty in the Asian managers' wording, such as "it depends", "further investigation is needed" or "many other factors also need to be considered". Few Asian respondents gave straightforward opinions. This tendency may partially reflect Asians' higher tolerance of ambiguity in written communication but, paradoxically, it also likely indicates East Asians' lower tolerance for the limited availability of information.

A spirit of compromise was also present in the responses made by managers from the three East Asian nations. Many Taiwanese respondents suggested the need to strike a balance between economic gains and humanitarianism. Japanese managers were also concerned with the compromise between corporate benefits and social benefits, although they tended to argue that "we need to care about the social benefits because they will affect the survival of our company in the long run". Such a commitment to societal interests may be attributed to Japanese *Shintoism* (Evans, 1981). Nonetheless, relatively few Korean managers made these sort of compromise statements.

In sum, the open-ended responses uncovered some critical differences in terms of decision-making rules among managers of the four countries. At least according to the present data, the Japanese managers seem to be more similar to their American counterparts in that they may be a bit more influenced by legal and economic risks than the managers from the other two Asian countries. This could be at least partially attributed to the different stages of economic development: Japan is a "developed" economy already, while Taiwan and South Korea are "newly industrialized" countries (Dubinsky, 1991; Koch, 1989). Differences also appear in the concept of loyalty, an area needing further research.

The social contracts theory appears to provide a basis for explaining most of the differences in indicated behavior and rationale provided by the managers in the four countries. Hypernorms were associated with four of the vignettes, with a community norm being associated with the fifth. There appear to be differences in the norms followed even when there may be no difference in behavior. For example, a higher percentage of Korean and Taiwanese managers provided a response supporting the hypernorm against theft, while Japanese managers cited the rationale supporting informed consent. In some cases, American and Asian managers tended to cite common norms. Approximately one quarter of the American and Taiwanese managers cited the payment in Vignette 1 as an acceptable practice in other countries (common argument in violation of the hypernorm). None of the

TABLE 7
SUMMARY OF RATIONALE FOR INDICATED BEHAVIOR[a]

	Coercion and Control	Conflict of Interest	Physical Environment	Paternalism	Personal Integrity	Mean
SUPPORTING HYPER AND COMMUNITY NORMS						
American	47	34	55	57	77	54
Japanese	7	16	64	51	61	40
Korean	4	18	38	71	44	35
Taiwanese	8	21	44	38	62	35
CONSIDERED UNETHICAL						
American	36	51	34	33	15	34
Japanese	28	60	2	11	16	23
Korean	37	60	20	12	12	28
Taiwanese	37	27	37	36	9	29
UNCERTAIN[b]						
American	16	14	13	11	8	12
Japanese	65	25	35	39	23	37
Korean	59	22	43	16	43	37
Taiwanese	55	51	20	25	29	36

[a]All numbers are percentages.
[b]Includes classifications which did not appear to directly support or violate norms as well as those listed under the heading of "other".

Japanese or Korean managers provided that response. The American and Japanese managers were more concerned with the legality of installing the new equipment in the third vignette (argument is in support of the community norm).

A summary of the classification of the open-ended comments is shown in Table 7. On average, a higher percentage of Americans provided a rationale classified as supporting a hypernorm or a community norm. However, this varied from vignette to vignette. There was little difference in the mean percentage for unethical rationales across countries. The mean percentage for uncertain classification appeared to be the mirror image of the norm supporting classification. There was considerable variation by vignette, which generally supports the above discussion.

The social contracts theory did appear to provide an explanation for most of the rationales not categorized as "other". Only four of the rationale categories defied classification as supporting hypernorms, community norms or as supporting neither and thus classified as unethical (ignoring the other category). The theory provides a richness that allows for ethical relativism via community norms, while requiring universalism via hypernorms. This makes it particularly appealing when dealing with cross-cultural applications.

Trevino (1992) suggests that external social systems may affect the development of morality through the socialization process. If this is indeed the case, future research should also probably explore the relationship between certain cultural dimensions (e.g. Hofstede's work-related values) and ethical behavior. Such an approach should help increase the generalizability of cross-national comparisons of ethical behavior. Indeed, in some definitions of culture, moral values seem to be an implicit component (e.g. Kroeber & Kluckhohn, 1952). Advocates of cultural relativism argue that words such as "right", "wrong", "justice" and "injustice" derive their meaning and truth value from the attitudes of a given culture (Donaldson, 1989). Hofstede (1980) also points out that, by definition, culture determines what is socially desirable, thereby influencing the moral values embedded in a society. Here again we see the applicability of micro social contracts and their associated community norms. Since the heterogeneity of ethical behavior can now be attributed to differences in community norms within cultures rather than nation-specific characteristics, we may easily infer how people in other nations might deal with similar ethical dilemmas on the basis of their predominant community norms.

There is a fine line between "what is legally right" vis-à-vis "what is socially tolerable", even in a given cultural context. The former can usually be inferred (albeit imperfectly) from the laws, while the latter tends to be heavily influenced by social norms and numerous other individual and organizational attributes. In practice, ethical decisions are likely to be subject to the influence of both types of factors. In light of the wide-ranging responses to the open-ended questions, however, our vignette-based study seems to have captured the social norm aspect of ethical issues beyond legal concerns.

A word of caution is in order. The current study, as with all studies using vignettes to study ethical issues, utilizes indicated behavior rather than actual behavior from which to infer the ethics of managers. Unfortunately, the extent to which indicated behavior mirrors actual behavior is not known (Arnold & Feldman, 1981; Randall & Gibson, 1990). Nevertheless, the primary purpose of the study was to compare behaviours across cultures. Even if the indicated behavior differs from the actual behavior, one would expect the gap caused by social desirability bias to be similar across cultures. Our cross-national comparison of ethical decisions is, consequently, still very revealing.

The use of vignettes in data collection has also imposed some limitations on the generalizability of our findings. Firstly, since each vignette is brief in length and does not contain all the relevant information, respondents may have to infer or postulate other aspects of the scenario (e.g. the firm's financial condition) in order to visualize the full picture. Needless to say, such inferences tend to be biased by their personal backgrounds and prior work experiences. The judgments they made could be biased accordingly. Secondly, there may be a "bystander" effect associated with the vignette method. Some respondents might be personally detached when they exercised judgment on the ethical dilemmas presented in the vignettes. The judgments could hinge on whether they imagined themselves as characters in the vignettes or simply third-party observers. Finally, each respondent's interpretation of the vignettes may be affected by the cultural, social and political environments of the country where he or she has been socialized. The differing patterns of responses in these countries might reflect a combined effect of such macro factors but it is hard to pinpoint which one (e.g. political or economic environment) has had the strongest impact.

Although Evans (1981: 210) noticed that the cultural and historical heritage of the modern world is becoming blurred and bridged, our findings seem to suggest that it may be inappropriate to treat the East Asian nations as a culturally homogeneous cluster. Heterogeneity can be seen at least in their patterns of indicated behavior in dealing with business ethics. Although such a heterogeneity does not necessarily reflect a cross-national difference in terms of fundamental moral values, it does reflect cross-cultural differences in ethics (for the distinction between moral values and ethics, see Churchill, 1982).

As such, any conclusions drawn from this study must be interpreted with caution. Even if these three Asian nations could be viewed as a cluster due to some similarities, it is still possible that they do not share identical "value strings" (cf. Wines & Napier, 1992) in the ethics perspective. Management research in the past has been overly parochial and inadequate in both breadth and depth (Boyacigiller & Adler, 1991). Undoubtedly, further cross-cultural research is needed to both empirically verify the existing models of business ethics and theoretically extend the scope of ethics studies.

REFERENCES

1. Adler, N.J., Doktor R. and Redding, S. G., 1986, From the Atlantic to the Pacific century: Cross-cultural management reviewed, *Journal of Management* 12: 295-318.
2. Alexander, C.S. and Becker, H.J., 1978, The use of vignettes in survey research, *Public Opinion Quarterly* 42: 93-104.
3. Alston, J.P., 1989, 'Wa,' 'ganxi' and 'inhwa': Managerial principles in Japan, China, and Korea, *Business Horizon* 32: 26-31.
4. Armstrong, R.W., Stening, B.W., Ryans, J.K., Marks, L. and Mayo, M., 1990, International Marketing Ethics: Problems Encountered by Australian Firms, *European Journal of Marketing* 24: 5-18.
5. Arnold, H.J. and Feldman, D.C., 1981, Social desirability response bias in self-report choice situations, *Academy of Management Journal* 24: 377-385.
6. Barry, V., 1979, *Moral issues in business*, Belmont, California: Wadsworth.
7. Becker, H and Fritzsche, D.J., 1987a, A comparison of the ethical behavior of American, French and German managers, *The Columbia Journal of World Business* 22 (4): 87-97.
8. Becker, H and Fritzsche, D.J., 1987b, Business ethics: A cross-cultural comparison of managers' attitudes, *Journal of Business Ethics* 6: 123-129.

9. Beauchamp, T.L. and Bowie, N.E., 1979, *Ethical theory and business*, Englewood Cliffs, New Jersey: Prentice-Hall.
10. Boyacigiller, N and Adler, N.J., 1991, The parochial dinosaur: Organizational science in a global context, *Academy of Management Review* 16: 262-290.
11. Buller, P.F. Kohls, J.J. and Anderson, K.S., 1991, The challenge of global ethics, *Journal of Business Ethics* 10: 767-775.
12. Churchill, L.R., 1982, The teaching of ethics and moral values in teaching: Some contemporary confusions, *Journal of Higher Education* 53(3): 296-306.
13. Dill, D.D., Donaldson, T.J., Goodpaster, K.E. and May, W. W., 1979, *Syllabi for the teaching of management ethics*, Summer Institute on Ethical Issues in the Management of Public and Private Institutions, New Haven, Connecticut.
14. Donaldson, T., 1989, *The ethics of international business*, New York: Oxford University Press.
15. Donaldson, T. and Dunfee, T.W., 1994, Toward a unified conception of business ethics: Integrative Social Contracts, *Academy of Management Review* 19: 252-284.
16. Dubinsky, A.J., Jolson, M.A., Kotabe, M. and Lim, C.U., 1991, A cross-national investigation of industrial salespeople's ethical perceptions, *Journal of International Business Studies* 22: 651-670.
17. Evans, W.A., 1981, *Management ethics: An intercultural perspective*, Boston: Martinus Hijhoff.
18. Fritzsche, D.J., 1985, Ethical Issues in Multinational Marketing, in G.R. Laczniak and P.E. Murphy (eds.), *Marketing Ethics: Guidelines for Managers*, Lexington, Massachusettes: D.C. Heath and Company, pp. 85-96.
19. Fritzsche, D.J., 1988, An examination of marketing ethics: Role of the decision maker, consequence of the decision, management position, and sex of the respondent, *Journal of Macromarketing* 8(2): 29-39.
20. Fritzsche, D.J. and Becker, H., 1983, Ethical behavior of marketing managers, *Journal of Business Ethics* 2: 291-299.
21. Fritzsche, D.J. & Becker, H., 1984, Linking management behavior to ethical philosophy — An empirical investigation, *Academy of Management Journal* 27: 166-175.
22. Hegarty, W. H. and Sims, H. P. Jr., 1978, Some Determinants of Unethical Decision Behavior: An Experiment, *Journal of Applied Psychology* 63: 451-457.
23. Hofstede, G., 1980, *Culture's consequences: International differences in work-related values*, London: Sage.
24. Lee, K.H., 1981, Ethical Beliefs in Marketing Management: A Cross-cultural Study, *European Journal of Marketing* 15 (1): 58-67.
25. Lysonski, S. and Gaidis, W., 1991, A cross-cultural comparison of the ethics of business students, *Journal of Business Ethics* 10: 141-150.
26. Kant, I., 1964, *Groundwork of the metaphysics of morals*, H. J. Paton, trans. New York: Harper & Row.

27. Koch, J V., 1989, An economic profile of the Pacific Rim, *Business Horizon* 32: 18-25.
28. Kroeber, A.L. and Kluckhohn, C., 1952, *Culture: A critical review of concepts and definitions*, Cambridge, Massachusettes: Harvard University Press.
29. Lysonski, S. and Gaidis, W., 1991, A Cross-Cultural Comparison of the Ethics of Business Students, *Journal of Business Ethics* 10: 141-150.
30. Morita, A., 1992, Why Japan must change, *Fortune*, March 9: 66-67.
31. Pegis, A.C., 1944, *Basic Writings of Saint Thomas Aquinas* vol. 2, New York: Random House.
32. Preble, J.F. and Reichel, A., 1988, Attitudes Towards Business Ethics of Future Managers in the U.S. and Israel, *Journal of Business Ethics* 7: 941-949.
33. Rachels, J., 1986, *The elements of moral philosophy*, New York: Random House.
34. Randall, D.M. and Gibson, A.M., 1990, Methodology in business ethics research: A review and critical assessment, *Journal of Business Ethics* 9: 457-472.
35. Sang, L.Y., 1927, *The Story of Confucius: His Life and Sayings*, Philadelphia, Pennsylvania: David McKay Company.
36. Swinyard, W.R., Rinne, H. and Kau, A. K., 1990, The Morality of Software Piracy: A Cross-Cultural Analysis, *Journal of Business Ethics* 9: 655-664.
37. Trevino, L.K., 1992, Moral reasoning and business ethics: Implications for research, education, and management, *Journal of Business Ethics* 11: 445-459.
38. Tsalikis, J. and Nwachukwu, O., 1989, Cross-Cultural marketing Ethics: On the Ethical Beliefs Difference of Greeks and Americans, *Journal of International Consumer Marketing* 1 (3): 45-63.
39. Tsalikis, J. and Nwachukwu, O., 1991, A Comparison of Nigerian to American Views of Bribery and Extortion in International Commerce, *Journal of Business Ethics* 10: 85-98.
40. Velasquez, M.G. and Rostankowski, C., 1985, *Ethics: Theory and Practice*, Englewood Cliffs, New Jersey: Prentice Hall, Inc.
41. Webber, R.A., 1981, *Time and management*, New York: Moffat Publishing.
42. Werner, O. and Campbell, D., 1970, Translating, working through interpreters, and the problem of decentering, in R. Naroll & R. Cohen (eds.), *A Handbook of method in cultural anthropology*, New York: National History Press, pp. 398-420.
43. Whipple, T.W. and Swords, D.F., 1992, Business Ethics Judgements: A Cross-Cultural Comparison, *Journal of Business Ethics* 11: 671-678.
44. White, L.P. and Rhodeback, M.J., 1992, Ethical dilemmas in organization development: A cross-cultural analysis, *Journal of Business Ethics* 11: 663-670.
45. Williams, G.J., 1992, *Ethics in modern management*, New York: Quorum Books.
46. Wines, W.A. and Napier, N.K., 1992, Toward an understanding of cross-cultural ethics: A tentative model, *Journal of Business Ethics* 11: 831-841.

[44]

Creating and Sustaining Ethical Capability in the Multi-National Corporation

Paul F. Buller   Glenn M. McEvoy

Multinational corporations are continually seeking sources of competitive advantage. In addition to strategic, technological, financial, and organizational capabilities as sources of competitive advantage, this paper argues that ethical capability also can be an important source of sustainable advantage. The paper presents the challenges of ethics in an international context, discusses the resource-based view of competitive advantage, and describes how a multinational company can develop and sustain ethical capability through the related processes of transformational leadership, organizational learning, and human resource management.

Multi-national corporations (MNCs) face a variety of questions regarding the appropriate business practices to use in the different countries in which they compete. MNCs face challenges in determining the right product, market, finance, and human resource management strategies across different national cultures. Increasingly, among the many questions facing MNCs are those concerning business ethics, that is, the rightness or wrongness of certain business actions across cultures. Recent writings on international business ethics suggest that the decisions regarding appropriate ethical actions are complex and multifaceted (Buller, Kohls, & Anderson, 1997; DeGeorge, 1993; Donaldson, 1989, 1996; Jackson, 1997). Further, there is little guidance in the literature about how an MNC can enhance its capability in dealing with international business ethics. This paper briefly reviews current approaches to addressing questions of ethics in a cross-cultural context. It then builds on Litz's (1996) contention that sound ethical practice is an overlooked potential source of competitive advantage to the MNC. A discussion of the resource-based perspective of competitive advantage serves as the foundation of our proposition that ethical capability is a sustainable source of competitive advantage. The paper concludes with a

Paul F. Buller, School of Business Administration, Gonzaga University, Spokane, WA 99258, USA. Glenn M. McEvoy, Department of Management & Human Resources, College of Business, Utah State University, Logan, UT 84322, USA.

description of how transformational leadership, organizational learning, and human resource management (HRM) are integral to building MNC capabilities in global ethics.

Ethical Capability

The central premise of this article is that an MNC's ethical capability may be an overlooked source of competitive advantage. Ethical capability is defined here as an organization's ability to identify and respond effectively to ethical issues in a global context. Ethical capability involves firm-specific: 1) knowledge and skills to understand ethical frameworks and respond effectively to cross-cultural ethical situations; 2) leadership, team work, and organizational culture that facilitate ongoing dialogue and learning about global ethics; and 3) human resource systems and other organizational practices that acquire, develop, and sustain these capabilities. The proposed positive relation of ethical capability to competitive advantage is built on a resource-based perspective of the firm. This perspective argues that firm-specific resources and capabilities, that are valuable, rare, and inimitable, are sustainable sources of competitive advantage. Before developing this argument further, it is important to understand the nature and challenges of global ethics.

Frameworks for Examining Cross-Cultural Ethics

Several frameworks and algorithms have been proposed to address business ethics in a global context (Buller et al., 1997; DeGeorge, 1993; Desai & Rittenburg, 1997; Donaldson, 1989, 1996; Jackson, 1997). These frameworks suggest that there is no simple answer to the question of what is right and wrong ethical behavior across different national cultures. Donaldson (1996), for example, observed that U.S. businesses have tended to adopt one of two extreme positions when faced with ethical questions across cultures: relativism or absolutism. The relativist perspective takes the familiar stance— "when in Rome, do as the Romans do." At the other extreme, the absolutist perspective argues that the home country cultural (and ethical) values must be applied everywhere as they are at home. According to Donaldson (1996):

> "Companies must help managers distinguish between practices that are merely different and those that are wrong. For relativists, nothing is sacred and nothing is wrong. For absolutists, many things that are different are wrong. Neither extreme illuminates the real world of business decision making. The answer lies somewhere in between." (1996, 52).

Donaldson (1996) proposed several core values that broadly define the moral imperatives for MNCs and provide a moral compass for global business practices: respect for human dignity, respect for basic rights, and good citizenship. He then provided a set of algorithms that guide decision making in situations where ethics collide across cultures. He proposed the concept of "moral pluralism" to show how the outcomes of these algorithms can range from the MNC insisting on its own (home country) ethical principles to the MNC accommodating the ethical values of the host country. Thus, although Donaldson concludes that there is a set of core values that can serve as a basic threshold for all MNCs, there also should be "moral free space" that allows for judgment based upon the unique circumstances involved in a given situation.

DeGeorge (1993) also has proposed several international moral norms that can be applied to MNCs. In contrast to Donaldson, he argued that the complexity of multinational situations makes the use of simple algorithms inadequate. Rather, he suggested that each situation requires judgment and moral imagination. He offered a number of guidelines, particularly for MNCs operating in less developed countries, and for dealing with issues of hazardous products or processes and corruption. In addition, DeGeorge identified three types of ethical conflicts: 1) pressures on individuals to violate personal norms, 2) inconsistent cultural norms, and 3) host country versus home country interests and values. He argued that each of these types of conflicts ultimately needs to be resolved at a higher level of influence, a concept he termed *ethical displacement*. Ethical displacement involves the development of sufficient policies, procedures, structures, rewards, and background institutions to reinforce ethical practices.

Jackson (1997) also observed that MNCs:

> "face an intricate multilayered array of cultural, ethical, and legal norms. The norms subsist at local, national, regional, international, and global levels. The presence of such normative complexity and depth signals the need for ethics programs that assimilate such characteristics." (p. 1128).

He suggested a number of pragmatic steps toward building a "cosmopolitan" culture of ethical awareness in the MNC. This cosmopolitan culture is one that is neither relativistic or absolutist, but that is sensitive to cross-cultural differences regarding ethics. Such a culture goes beyond simple rule formulations or ethical algorithms, and is characterized by a higher level of moral sensitivity based on ongoing education and collaboration among decision makers across-cultures. This notion of a cosmopolitan culture is similar to Vega's (1997) concept of "common norming" in which conflicting parties attempt to find the common moral ground through ongoing dialogue.

Buller et al. (1997) have proposed a pragmatic framework to guide managerial decision making in situations involving cross-cultural ethical conflict. Their model, based on conflict management theory, suggests that there is a continuum of at least six possible alternative strategies for responding to cross-cultural ethical conflict ranging from adaptation to the host country's ethical standards to complete insistence on the application of home country standards. They provide a decision tree to guide managers through the decision process in situations where ethics collide across cultures. The decision tree is intended to encourage contingency thinking and identify plausible courses of ethical action.

In summary, these emerging frameworks are consistent in their view that making appropriate ethical decisions in the MNC is a complex process. Although there may be situations in which the MNC can rightfully insist on universal moral principles, there may be other instances in which the MNC should adopt the local ethical norms. There are also situations in which the MNC is compelled, through collaboration and/or imagination, to develop a unique response to a cross-cultural ethical dilemma, one that attempts to find the common ground among disparate moral views. For the purposes of this paper, we propose three possible general responses of the MNC when faced with a cross-cultural ethical conflict: *relativism* (i.e., adopting the local norms), *cosmopolitanism* (i.e., identifying the common moral ground), and *universalism* (i.e., enforcing universal moral principles).

Ethical Capability as a Sustainable Source of Competitive Advantage

An organization's capability to be ethically and socially responsible across cultures may be an overlooked source of competitive advantage (Litz, 1996). This section of the paper builds on the resource-based theory of competitive advantage by proposing that ethical capability is a potential source of sustainable competitive advantage. It then describes how a firm's leadership, learning processes, and human resource management activities can be primary means through which ethical capability is created and sustained in the MNC.

Resource-Based Perspective of Competitive Advantage

A prominent emerging perspective in the strategic management literature is the resource-based view of the firm (Wenerfelt, 1984; Barney, 1991). Resource-based theory proposes that a firm is defined by the resources that it controls. Further, it assumes that all competitors are not homogeneous but, rather, they differ based on the resources that they possess. These resource-based differences explain differences in performance across firms. If a firm possesses resources that are valuable, rare, inimitable, and the firm has the organizational capability to exploit these resources, it possesses a sustainable competitive advantage (Barney, 1991). Three general types of resources can be sources of competitive advantage: physical capitol (e.g., plant, equipment, finances), organizational capitol (e.g., structure, planning, systems), and human capitol (e.g., skills, judgment, adaptability). Note that sources of advantage include both tangible and intangible resources. Barney (1991) and others (Senge, 1990; Brenneman, Keys, & Fulmer, 1998) have argued that certain firm-specific, intangible sources of advantage (such as organizational history, culture, and learning) can be particularly important to sustaining competitive advantage precisely because these resources are extremely difficult to imitate.

Litz (1996) has pointed out that the strategic management literature has overlooked social responsibility and ethical response capabilities as potential sources of competitive advantage. He argued that:

> "to the extent that the firm is able to recognize its interdependence, reflect on the ethical standards appropriate to the situation, and react in a timely and responsive manner, it possesses valuable, rare, inimitable, and non-substitutable assets, that is, it possesses strategic resources." (1996, 1360).

Litz (1996) identified three crucial resources for competitive advantage based on ethical capability: perceiving interdependence, thinking ethically, and responding effectively. Perceiving interdependence specifically acknowledges the stakeholder perspective of the firm. With respect to the MNC, important stakeholders include host country institutions as well as the MNCs foreign suppliers, customers, and employees. According to stakeholder theory, a firm that recognizes and effectively satisfies the diverse needs of its various stakeholders will be able to sustain its institutional legitimacy (Freeman, 1984). There is increasing evidence that effective management of stakeholders can improve the financial performance of the firm (Waddock & Graves, 1997). For example, effectively balancing the needs of various stakeholders can lead to enhanced corporate reputation (Royal Society for the Encouragement of the Arts, Manufacture and Society, 1996), increased solidarity, commitment, loyalty, and productivity of employees, and lower costs in maintaining complex networks of suppliers, customers, agents and geographically dispersed employees, particularly in globalization strategies (Zadek, 1998). In addition, an organization's ability to engage in ongoing, constructive dialogue with its various stakeholders can be an important source of competitive advantage (Fulmer, Gibbs, & Keys, 1998; Wheeler & Sillanpaa, 1997). As Sharma and Vredenburg (1998) found, such dialogue can lead to the development of greater capabilities for stakeholder integration, higher order learning, and continuous innovation, that in turn can contribute to competitive advantage.

Thinking ethically involves the resource of ethical awareness. In the context of the MNC, ethical awareness includes an understanding of the various ethical frameworks (e.g., utilitarianism, rights-based, justice) as well as sensitivity to the differences among ethical perspectives across cultures. As noted above, effective dialogue among stakeholders can be an important source of organizational learning. Dialogue is a process of collective thinking and exploration of underlying assumptions, beliefs and values. According to Fulmer et al. (1998):

> When organizations must "unlearn" previously unsuccessful patterns, dialogue offers a path to follow. As companies move to global operations, dialogue becomes even more important. . . . (p. 15)

The organizational learning that emerges from the dialogue among diverse stakeholders in the MNC allows for greater awareness of and sensitivity to the ethical values, beliefs and practices across cultures. This organizational learning can be a highly sustainable source of advantage (Fulmer et al., 1998; Senge, 1990).

Responding effectively involves the resource contribution of effective issues management, that is, taking the appropriate ethical action in a timely manner. As discussed earlier, discerning the appropriate ethical response in an international context is complex and the ability to apply relevant cross-cultural ethics models is critical to the decision-making process. This capability assumes that the first two capabilities—perceiving interdependence and thinking ethically—are in place. In addition, it involves the requisite structures, processes, procedures and other means of creating and sustaining ethical behavior and decision-making.

In summary, we argue that MNCs, to the extent that they can develop the capability to perceive, deliberate about, and respond effectively to ethical issues across cultures, can enhance their competitive advantage. These capabilities can be developed through effective dialogue with international stakeholders and through organizational practices designed to facilitate organizational learning and appropriate action regarding global ethics. In the next section, we argue that the MNCs human resource management systems can be a primary means for developing ethical capability.

Human Resources Management as a Key Source of Advantage

Assuming that ethical capability can be a source of sustainable competitive advantage, how can such capability be developed? There is a growing consensus that the key to developing competitive advantage in MNCs is the effectiveness of the human organization (Bartlett & Ghoshal, 1995; Pfeffer, 1994; Pucik, Tichy, & Barnett, 1992). More specifically, MNCs can enhance their competitiveness by integrating their human resource management activities with their strategic goals (Schuler, Dowling, & De Cieri, 1993; Taylor, Beechler, & Napier, 1996). These so-called strategic international human resource management (SIHRM) systems are optimally designed in accordance with the MNCs strategic challenge—achieving the appropriate balance between global integration and local responsiveness (Taylor et al., 1996). Strategic choices for the MNC include focusing primarily on multidomestic strategy (i.e., emphasis on meeting local needs), global strategy (i.e., emphasis on global efficiency), or transnational strategy (i.e., simultaneous emphasis on local responsiveness, global efficiency, and worldwide organizational learning) (Bartlett & Ghoshal, 1995). The appropriate international strategy is a largely a function of industry characteristics and firm resources.

The challenge of effective strategic human resource management in MNCs is to design human resource systems and practices that are consistent with strategy. In this regard, Taylor et al. (1996) suggested three possible MNC orientations regarding human resource management practices: adaptive (i.e., adapting to practices in the host country), exportive (i.e., imposing home country practices), or integrative (i.e., using some combination of best practices regardless of origin). In addition to strategy, an MNCs approach to SIHRM may also be determined by the relative

Table 1
Possible Configurations in the MNC

	Local Responsiveness -------------------------------		Global Consistency
STRATEGY	multidomestic	transnational	global
HRM	adaptive	integrative	exportive
ETHICS	relativist	cosmopolitan	universal

influence of home country and host country culture, values and practices.

Table 1 summarizes possible configurations of strategy, human resource management, and ethical responses for the MNC. Although the separate literatures on international strategy, human resource management, and ethics suggest that approaches should differ based on the relative importance of local versus global demands, it is not clear how strategy, human resources, and ethics are (or should be) best integrated in the MNC. For example, a company following a multidomestic strategy may well employ an adaptive approach to human resource management. It does not necessarily follow, however, that this company would also follow a relativistic approach to ethics. There may be some ethical issues (e.g., employment of child labor) that might require the MNC to follow a universal policy (e.g., a code legislating against child labor) under any circumstances, even if local customs and values allow the employment of young children. Alternatively, a global strategy may require some consistency across cultures regarding human resource and ethics practices. However, there may be instances (e.g., gift giving or nepotism) in which one could argue from an ethical perspective that local values and norms should be honored. Although beyond the scope of this paper, a fruitful avenue for future research would be to develop and test various configurations of strategic, human resource management, and ethics practices of MNCs.

Taylor et al. (1996) argued that an effective SIHRM system "should be constructed around specific organizational competencies that are critical for securing competitive advantage (p. 960)." Barney and Wright (1998) have shown how resource-based theory applies specifically to human resource management as a source of competitive advantage. They proposed that human resource practices contribute to competitive advantage only if they provide value (i.e., enhance cost leadership or differentiation), are rare, are difficult to imitate, and the organization has the systems and practices in place to derive the potential of its human resources. In particular, they contend that, to the extent that a firm can develop firm-specific skills, effective teamwork and culture among diverse employees, and human resource systems that are synergistic across the disparate organizational units, the firm can harness valuable, rare, and inimitable resources.

Extending this notion, ethical capability would include firm-specific: 1) knowledge and skills to understand ethical frameworks and respond effectively to diverse ethical perspectives across

Figure 1. Creating and Sustaining Ethical Capability

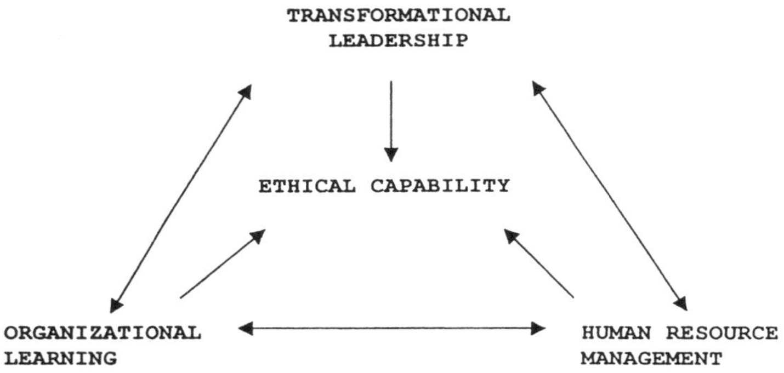

cultures; 2) leadership, team work, and organizational culture that facilitates effective ongoing dialogue on ethical differences; and 3) human resource management and other organizational practices that create and sustain these capabilities. Thus, we would argue that ethical capability in a global context is certainly one source of competitive advantage that an SIHRM system could build.

Creating and Sustaining Ethical Capability

Specific ways in which the MNCs human resource (HR) function can help to build and maintain ethical capability include three primary interrelated aspects that are shown in Figure 1: **transformational leadership, enhancing organizational learning** and **implementing specific HR practices**. Each of these elements is described next. It is important to acknowledge, however, that while we are focusing primarily on the role of the HR function, ethical capability is developed in partnership with line managers, HR professionals, ethics officers, and other employees. However, as Ulrich and Lake (1990) have shown, the HR function can play a key role as a catalyst for developing and maintaining ethical capability. We build on their work in the following discussion.

Transformational Leadership

The process for creating and sustaining ethical capability is best initiated and facilitated through transformational leadership on the part of the CEO and other key leaders, including those responsible for human resources. Transformational leaders articulate a vision that includes ethical principles, communicate the vision in a compelling way, and demonstrate consistent commitment to the vision over time (Tichy & Devanna, 1986). Tichy (1993) described transformational leadership as a complex drama played out over three stages: *Awakening*, when the need for changes is recognized; *Envisioning*, when a vision is created and employees become committed to it; and *Re-architecting*, that entails the creation of an organization to support the vision. In the awakening stage, leaders must carefully articulate why the move to ethical capability is necessary and generate broad support for change among other key leaders in the organization. Part of working through this initial stage is recognizing and addressing points of resistance to change. There are a number of reasons why managers and employees might resist adopting new skills and organizational practices necessary for creating ethical capability. The transformational leader must be sensitive to these sources of resistance while instilling a compelling motivation to change. The envisioning stage helps overcome resistance by engaging employees in a definition of what ethical capability will look like for the MNC. Collaboration among the MNCs various stakeholders is essential in developing this vision or mind set. Re-architecting involves building the requisite structures, systems, policies, and practices to support the vision of ethical capability. The reputation for strong ethical cultures in companies like Johnson & Johnson, Motorola, Royal Dutch/Shell, Texas Instruments, and others can be traced directly to transformational leaders who consistently, by their words and deeds, signaled the importance of and commitment to high moral standards (Brenneman et al., 1998; Moorthy et al., 1998).

Enhancing Organizational Learning

Ulrich and Lake (1990) state that at the heart of building organizational capability (and by extension, ethical capability) is creating "shared mindsets" among the internal and external stakeholders of the company regarding its strategic goals and the processes to reach those goals. In developing a shared mindset, it is critical that the senior HR managers, in partnership with other senior managers in the MNC and from the overseas affiliates, develop consensus on the appropriate HR agenda, including a specific attention to the challenge of cross-cultural ethics (Eisenstat, 1996). Successful MNCs have learned that they cannot simply export practices that are effective domestically to overseas operations. As Table 1 suggests, although exporting human resource management or ethics practices might be appropriate under certain conditions, other possible configurations might be required. Developing the capability to deal with this complexity demands that the organization learn from its international stakeholders.

Several conditions facilitate organizational learning. First, it is critical that top managers of the MNC provide leadership in recognizing the value of human resources and developing a broader cross-cultural understanding and sensitivity (Barney & Wright, 1998; Brenneman et al., 1998). Second, the MNC must engage its various international stakeholders, including employees from home and host countries, in a collaborative effort to find the common ground with respect to human resources and ethical practices (Donaldson, 1996). As noted earlier, cross-cultural dialogue is an important tool for developing new mindsets and creating shared meanings (Fulmer et al., 1998). For example, Snow, Davidson, Snell, and Hambrick (1996) have described how MNCs can use transnational teams to develop values, policies, and practices to achieve global efficiency, local responsiveness, and organizational learning. Through ongoing research, dialogue, and action learning, these transnational teams can create a set of human resource management practices and ethical principles that could be applied in various contexts in which the MNC operates (Fulmer et al., 1998; Luthans, Marsnick, & Luthans, 1997). The outcome of this collaborative effort would be a set of human resource practices that are adaptive, integrative, and/or exportive, and a set of moral principles that are locally responsive, cosmopolitan, and/or universal in their application across different situations (See Table 1).

The ultimate goals of this initial organizational learning process are: 1) to establish a ***corporate code of ethics*** that is globally integrative yet locally responsive, consistent with the models of global ethics described above; 2) to create mechanisms for an ***ongoing process of organizational learning and responsiveness***; and 3) to create an ***ethical culture*** across all MNC operations. Based on a clear corporate code of ethics and a continuous learning process, the MNC can develop specific management practices to shape and reinforce an ethical corporate culture. These practices are described more fully below.

Implementing Specific HRM Practices

As noted, an international code of ethics is a necessary, but not sufficient, step in building ethical capability. Codes of ethics are essential in providing clear direction about ethical behavior in various situations. However, employees must have the ability and motivation, and the organizational support, to understand and implement the code of ethics. Moreover, formal codes, rules, and legal guidelines cannot cover all possible situations and do not obviate the need for moral judgment and imagination (DeGeorge, 1993; Donaldson, 1996). So, ethical capability must be further enhanced through developing specific human-resource management practices linked to cross-cultural ethical competencies. Below we focus on the major human resource activities of selection, training and development, appraisal, compensation, and organization design and change, although other organizational activities are certainly relevant in building ethical capability. It is also important to recognize that there is not one prescribed set of human resource management practices for MNCs to follow. Rather, specific practices should vary (e.g., adaptive, integrative, exportive) depending upon the strategy of the MNC and the unique cultural characteristics of countries in which it operates (Luthans et al., 1997; Taylor et al., 1996).

Although "shared mindsets" (i.e., assumptions, values, and beliefs) are at the heart of ethical capability, these core values and beliefs must be created and reinforced by the various management practices that govern employees' behaviors in the organization. Human resource management practices that are central to shaping ethical values, beliefs, and behaviors can be organized into three general areas: generating competencies, reinforcing competencies, and sustaining competencies.

Generating Competencies

Generating competencies involves acquiring the necessary ethical values and behaviors through ***selection*** processes and/or developing values and behaviors through ***training and development***.

Selection

Top executives agree that one of the most important things they can do to influence firm performance is to hire and promote the right people. Staffing decisions in the MNC are particularly complex. For example, in many MNCs, lower level employees tend to be host country nationals, while higher level managers tend to be parent country expatriates, often without much intercultural experience (Bell & Harrison, 1996). One reason for the traditionally high failure rate among U.S. expatriates is that selection criteria for these managers historically have emphasized technical, rather than relational or cultural, skills (Mendenhall, Dunbar, & Oddou, 1987). It is now widely recognized that relational and intercultural skills also are critical to expatriate effectiveness (Tung, 1993). Intercultural competence may allow expatriate employees to be more effective, in part, because it better equips them to "cope with the stress of acculturation" (Bell & Harrison, 1996, p. 50).

Due to the challenges of global ethics, selection criteria for managers and other employees working across cultures should certainly include ethical competence (e.g., moral development), sensitivity to differences in ethics across cultures, and ability to make sound decisions in situations when home and host country ethics collide. Previous cross-cultural experience would certainly be valuable. Other useful selection criteria would include, adaptability, flexibility, and the capacity to learn in the face of changing conditions. Of course, staffing decisions should be made based on: 1) a thorough needs analysis to identify the specific jobs to be filled as well as the knowledge, skills and abilities needed for effective performance; 2) careful screening of candidates based on multiple structured interviews and other valid selection procedures; and 3) realistic job previews that communicate the kinds of situations that the new employee is likely to face. The screening of candidates should also include an assessment of ethical awareness, sensitivity, and responsiveness perhaps through the use of ethical dilemmas that are likely to confront employees in the company.

In addition, MNCs should expand their search for job candidates beyond the domestic labor pool to attract the best global talent. Leading companies such as Unilever and IBM have developed sophisticated databases that enable managers and human resource professionals to identify qualified job candidates from across their international operations (Snell, Snow, Davison, & Hambrick, 1998). Ideally, these databases would include information about employees' experience, competencies, and preferences. Such systems would be valuable in staffing management, human resources, and other relevant job positions (e.g., ethics advisors/committees) with individuals who are sensitive and responsive to the diverse moral values and issues across the MNC's operations.

Training and Development

Training and development activities also are important in building ethical capability. Resource-based theory suggests that training in firm-specific rather than general skills creates greater potential for competitive advantage because firm-specific skills are more rare, valuable, and difficult to imitate (Barney & Wright, 1998). So, to the extent possible, ethics-related training should emphasize firm-specific rather than general moral issues, principles and practices. As discussed earlier, firm-specific skills can be identified and developed through dialogue among international stakeholders across the MNCs geographical units.

Training and development activities can enhance several types of competencies. First, all employees must be trained to understand and apply the MNC's code of ethics, as well as the multitude of international laws and codes of conduct. Training in various ethical frameworks and models is also warranted. Beyond that, cross-cultural training can be effective in developing greater cultural awareness and ability to interact across cultures (Black & Mendenhall, 1990). Presumably, this kind of training also would be effective with respect to cross-cultural differences in ethics. Bell and Harrison (1996) suggested that cross-cultural training should emphasize both content (e.g., knowledge of other cultures) and process (e.g., how culture influences cognition and behavior). However, as Husted, Dozier, McMahon, and Kattan (1996) have observed, cross-cultural training may be more effective in transmitting attitudes than in transmitting moral reasoning across cultures. For this reason, some have suggested that selection of individuals with diverse cultural experience may be preferred to cross-cultural training in generating ethical competencies in the MNC (Bell & Harrison, 1996; Jackson, 1997).

An alternative approach that addresses some of the shortcomings of cross-cultural training is cross-cultural team building for transnational teams, used by such companies as Motorola, Shell, Ford, and Glaxo–Wellcome (Snell et al., 1998). This approach goes one step further than traditional cross-cultural training programs by

> "developing coherent work processes that take advantage of differences on the team by establishing ground rules and protocols that integrate members. When coupled with training in conflict resolution and negotiation skills, cross-cultural team building can substantially improve integration and efficiency." (Snell et al., 1998, 153)

Motorola's *Ethics Renewal Process* provides one example of how organizations can implement this approach (Moorthy, DeGeorge, Donaldson, Ellos,

Solomon, & Textor, 1998). With a trained core of senior executives, Motorola's Director of Global Leadership and Organizational Development facilitates ethical awareness, skill development, and team building in diverse teams of managers in the company's foreign operations. The teams identify ethical issues and collaborate on possible solutions. Particular attention is paid to dialogue on local ethical perspectives that may differ from the Motorola corporate code of ethics. Local ethics committees are formed, trained in various ethical frameworks, and authorized to develop policies and guidelines to address local ethical issues. For example, Motorola has developed specific guidelines for gift giving in Japan that differ from the company's guidelines on gift giving in other countries. The products of these local ethics committees are then shared with other similar committees around the world. To date, Motorola has formed fourteen ongoing ethics committees across its global operations. Clearly, this kind of comprehensive approach to cross-cultural ethics training and development can enhance the organizational learning process and create the firm-specific knowledge and skills that contribute to sustainable competitive advantage.

Reinforcing Competencies

Once they have been acquired or developed, cross-cultural ethical competencies must be reinforced through ***performance appraisal*** and ***compensation/rewards*** systems.

Performance Appraisal

Appraisal processes should signal clearly the MNC's standards and expectations regarding ethical behaviors. To be effective, ethical standards should include both behavioral and outcome measures. In addition, employees should receive timely and regular feedback regarding their performance. Effective performance feedback reinforces behaviors that are consistent with expectations and helps the employee make any necessary improvements. Finally, the performance appraisal process itself (i.e., appraisal interviews, goal setting, feedback, coaching) can be an effective tool for enhancing trust and communication between managers and employees. Increased trust and communication can in turn reinforce the shared mindset regarding ethics in the MNC (Barney & Wright, 1998).

Performance expectations regarding ethics should also be developed between the MNC and its suppliers and customers (Donaldson, 1996). It is incongruent when the MNC has high internal ethical standards whereas its own suppliers and customers engage in unethical behaviors. Ideally, acceptable ethical standards should be jointly developed with suppliers and customers. This process will help to clarify for managers the kinds of suppliers and customers with which the MNC can do business. And, as with internal appraisal processes, effective processes designed and implemented with suppliers and customers also can enhance trust and communication reinforcing a shared mind set regarding ethics.

Rewards and Recognition

One purpose of performance appraisal is to provide a systematic basis for allocating rewards. To be effective, compensation and recognition systems should be: 1) linked directly to ethical behaviors and outcomes; 2) timely; 3) visible; 4) durable (i.e., produce long-term motivation); and 5) contribute to a shared mindset regarding ethical values and behaviors (Ulrich & Lake, 1990). In addition, thoughtfully designed reward systems include both monetary and non-monetary rewards linked to ethical performance. Effective leaders, such as Jack Welch at General Electric, are renowned for their prompt, hand-written notes acknowledging exemplary employee performance (Byrne, 1998). This type of informal recognition can provide strong reinforcement for company values. An example provided by Donaldson (1996) emphasizes the power of recognizing and rewarding ethical behavior:

> "Around 1950, a senior (Motorola) executive was negotiating with officials of a South American government on a $10 million sale that would have increased the company's annual net profits by nearly 25%. As the negotiations neared completion, however, the executive walked away from the deal because the officials were asking for $1 million for 'fees.' CEO Robert Galvin not only supported the executive but also made it clear that Motorola would neither accept the sale on any terms nor do business with those government officials again. Retold over the decades, this story demonstrating Galvin's resolve has helped cement a culture of ethics for thousands of employees at Motorola". (p. 60).

This example also demonstrates the particular challenge of linking rewards with appropriate behaviors in instances where ethical and other outcomes (e.g., financial) may be in conflict. The MNC must be clear about its priorities and reinforce them accordingly to reduce employees' ambiguity under these circumstances.

Sustaining Competencies

Organizational mechanisms for sustaining ethical competencies over time include ***organization design*** (e.g., structure and reporting relationships), ***communication***, and ***ongoing capacity for change***.

Organization Design

The central purpose of organization design is to allocate and coordinate the key tasks that must be completed to create and sustain competitive advantage. Consequently, emphasis should be placed on organizing those tasks and resources that add value, are rare and inimitable (Barney & Wright, 1998). In building ethical capability, the HR department adds value through its selection, training, appraisal, and compensation activities that are linked to ethical behavior (Schuler et al., 1993; Taylor et al., 1996). Ideally, these activities are internally consistent and continually aligned with the organization's needs as it evolves in a changing global environment. In this respect, organization design is best viewed as a process for continually identifying key tasks and modifying the reporting relationships, responsibilities, and coordinating mechanisms to accomplish those tasks. Further, in a dynamic, global environment, organic forms such as networks, team-based organizations, and temporary structures, can enhance organizational learning, stimulate moral imagination, and allow for greater flexibility and responsiveness to changing conditions (Fulmer et al., 1998; Nonaka & Takeuchi, 1995; Snell et al., 1998).

Another aspect of organization design is creating partnerships with suppliers, customers, and other organizations that can enhance the organization's competitiveness. Effective strategic alliances can produce resources that are valuable, rare and difficult to imitate (Barney, 1991). International partners are sources of learning regarding different ethical values and practices. Through exploring different perspectives, partners may discover common ethical ground or forge a cosmopolitan ethical culture that achieves a higher level of moral development (Donaldson, 1996; Jackson, 1997).

Additionally, MNCs have a moral obligation to support their organizational units and employees by developing appropriate structures, systems, policies, procedures, and other background institutions to reinforce ethical practices (DeGeorge, 1993). In this regard, an increasing number of MNCs are establishing ethics officers, advisors, ombudsmen, and/or committees to focus more attention on ethical issues and practices (Center for Business Ethics, 1992; Ethics Officer Association, 1997). The HR function can be instrumental in facilitating the staffing of these positions with individuals of diverse cultural perspectives. Many companies have found that it is important for the ethics function to be highly visible and accessible, as well as somewhat independent, within the organization. This type of structure may provide quicker access and greater confidentiality for employees who have concerns about ethics.

Communication

Clear and consistent organizational communication is central to creating and sustaining a shared mindset of ethics in the MNC. As noted earlier, there is no question that the CEO and other top managers are critical in establishing ethical capability in the MNC. Top managers signal expectations by their words and, more importantly, by their example. Moreover, effective global companies like Royal Dutch/Shell (The Shell Report, 1998) and Motorola (Moorthy et al., 1998) have developed explicit statements of their global ethics principles and values and made them available to their employees throughout the world. The worldwide web, email, and other communication technologies have made it possible for these and other companies to solicit real time feedback and facilitate ongoing discussion regarding their ethical values and principles. In addition, many companies have established ethics hotlines via telephone or computer to provide immediate and confidential support for employees facing ethical dilemmas. In countries where the telecommunications infrastructure is less developed, "hot boxes" (manual systems) provide a means for communication. These various approaches provide an essential infrastructure for ongoing dialogue on ethical practices throughout the MNC.

Ongoing Capacity for Change

Paradoxically, a key task for transformational leaders is to instill in the organization an ongoing capacity for change (Tichy, 1993). Several activities are central in creating a capacity for continuous improvement in ethical capability: 1) conducting periodic audits of the ethical and cultural climate; 2) developing a vision and a plan for continually improving ethical capability; 3) understanding and overcoming possible points of resistance to change; and 4) identifying and implementing the right tasks, structures, processes, systems, and other resources necessary to develop and sustain ethical capability. The HR function, in partnership with key managers and ethics professionals, can be instrumental in facilitating this process of ongoing organizational change and improvement.

Summary

MNCs operate in a context of diverse, sometimes conflicting, moral values and norms. The emerging consensus is that companies must become more sensitive to cross-cultural ethical differences and more sophisticated in applying the appropriate ethics in any given situation. This global ethical capability can be a sustainable source of advantage for the multinational corporation because it involves developing resources that are valuable, rare, and inimitable. The organization can enhance its ability to exploit and sustain its ethical capability through transformational leadership, ongoing organizational learning, and the design and implementation of its human resource management practices.

Acknowledgment: The authors would like to thank two anonymous reviewers for their helpful suggestions in the preparation of this manuscript.

References

Barney, J. (1991). Firm resources and sustained competitive advantage. *Journal of Management, 17*: 99–120.

Barney, J., & Wright, P. (1998). On becoming a strategic partner: The role of human resources in gaining a competitive advantage. *Human Resource Management, 37*(1): 31–46.

Bartlett, C., & Ghoshal, S. (1989). *Managing across boarders: The transnational solution.* Boston: Harvard Business School Press.

Bartlett, C., & Ghoshal, S. (1995). Changing the role of top management: Beyond structure to purpose. *Harvard Business Review, 73*(1): 86–96.

Bell, M., & Harrison, D. (1996). Using intranational diversity for international assignments: A model of bicultural competence and expatriate adjustment. *Human Resource Management Review, 6*(1): 47–74.

Black, S., & Mendenhall, M. (1990). Cross-cultural training effectiveness: A review and a theoretical framework for future research. *Academy of Management Review, 15*: 113–136.

Brenneman, W. B., Keys, J. B., & Fulmer, R. M. (1998). Learning across a living company: The Shell companies' experience. *Organizational Dynamics*, (Autumn): 61–70.

Buller, P., Kohls, J., & Anderson, K. (1997). A model for addressing cross-cultural ethical conflicts. *Business and Society, 36*(2): 169–193.

Byrne, J. (1998). Jack: A close-up look at how America's #1 manager runs GE. *Business Week*, June, 8: 90–106.

Center for Business Ethics (1992). Instituting ethical values in large corporations. *Journal of Business Ethics, 11*: 863–867.

DeGeorge, R. (1993). *Competing with integrity in international business*. New York: Oxford University Press.

Desai, A., & Rittenburg, T. (1997). Global ethics: An integrative framework for MNEs. *Journal of Business Ethics, 16*: 791–800.

Donaldson, T. (1989). *The ethics of international business*. New York: Oxford University Press.

Donaldson, T. (1996). Values in tension: Ethics away from home. *Harvard Business Review*, (Sept-Oct): 47–62.

Eisenstat, R. (1996). What corporate human resources brings to the picnic: Four models for functional management. *Organizational Dynamics*, (Autumn): 7–22.

Freeman, R. (1984). *Strategic management: A stakeholder approach*. Boston: Pitman Publishing, Inc.

Fulmer, R. M., Gibbs, P, & Keys, J. B. (1998). The second generation learning organizations: New tools for sustaining competitive advantage. *Organizational Dynamics*, (Autumn): 7–20.

Husted, B., Dozier, J., McMahon, J. T., & Kattan, M. (1996). The impact of cross-national carriers of business ethics on attitudes about questionable practices and form of moral reasoning. *Journal of International Business Studies (Vol 2)*, : 391–411.

Jackson, K. (1997). Globalizing corporate ethics programs: Perils and prospects. *Journal of Business Ethics, 16*: 1227–1235.

Litz, R. (1996). A resource-based view of the socially responsible firm: Stakeholder interdependence, ethical awareness, and issue responsiveness as strategic assets. *Journal of Business Ethics, 15*: 1355–1363.

Luthans, F., Marsnik, P, & Luthans, K. (1997). A contingency matrix approach to IHRM. *Human Resource Management, 36*(2): 183–200.

Mendenhall, M., Dunbar, E., & Oddou, G. (1987). Expatriate selection, training, and career pathing: A review and critique. *Human Resource Management, 26*: 331–345.

Moorthy R., Donaldson, T., Ellos, W., Solomon, R., & Textor, R. (1998). *Uncompromising integrity: Motorola's global challenge: 24 global case studies with commentaries*. Shaumberg, IL: Motorola University Press.

Nonaka, I., & Takeuchi, H. (1995). *The knowledge-creating company: How Japanese companies create the dynamics of innovation*. New York: Oxford University Press.

Pfeffer, G. (1994). *Competitive advantage through people*. Boston: Harvard Business School Press.

Pucik, V., Tichy, N., & Barnett, C. (1992). *Globalizing management: Creating and leading the competitive organization*. New York: John Wiley & Sons.

Royal Society for the Arts, Manufacture & Commerce (1996). *Tomorrow's company: The role of business in a changing world*. London: RSA.

Schuler, R., Dowling, P., & De Cieri, H. (1993). An integrative framework of international human resource management. *International Journal of Human Resource Management, 1*: 717–764.

Senge, P. M. (1990). *The fifth discipline*. New York: Doubleday.

Sharma, S. & Vredenburg, H. (1998). Proactive corporate environmental strategy and the development of competitively valuable organizational capabilities. *Strategic Management Journal, 19*: 729–753.

Snell S., Snow, C., Davison, S., & Hambrick, D. (1998). Designing and supporting transnational teams: The human resource agenda. *Human Resource Management, 37*(2): 147–158.

Snow, C., Davison, S., Snell, S., & Hambrick, D. (1996). Use transnational teams to globalize your company. *Organizational Dynamics*, (Spring):50–66.

Taylor, S., Beechler, S., & Napier, N. (1996). Toward an integrative model of strategic human resource management. *Academy of Management Review, 21*: 959–985.

The Shell Report (1998). *Statement of General Business Principles*. London: Shell International, Group External Affairs.

Tichy, N., & Devanna, M. (1986). *The transformational leader*. New York: John Wiley & Sons.

Tung R. (1988). Career issues in international assignments. *Academy of Management Executive, 11*: 241–244.

Tung R. (1993). Managing cross-national and intra-national diversity. *Human Resource Management, 32*: 461–477.

Ulrich, D. & Lake, D. (1990). *Organizational capability: Competing from the inside out*. New York: John Wiley & Sons.

Vega, G. (1997). *Caveat emptor*: Ethical chauvinism in the global economy. *Journal of Business Ethics, 16*: 1353–1362.

Waddock, S. & Graves, S. (1997). The corporate social performance-financial performance link. *Strategic Management Journal*, 303–319.

Wernerfelt, B. (1984). A resource-based view of the firm. *Strategic Management Journal, 5*: 171–180.

Wheeler, D. & Sillanpaa, M. (1997). *The stakeholder corporation: A blueprint for maximizing stakeholder value*. London: Pitman Publishing.

Zadek, S. (1998). Balancing performance, ethics, and accountability. *Journal of Business Ethics, 7*: 1421–1441.

Name Index